Hitchhiker's Guide to
Visual Basic® and
SQL Server™

SIXTH EDITION

William R. Vaughn

Microsoft ®*Press*

PUBLISHED BY

Microsoft Press
A Division of Microsoft Corporation
One Microsoft Way
Redmond, Washington 98052-6399

Library of Congress Cataloging-in-Publication Data
Vaughn, William R.
   Hitchhiker's Guide to Visual Basic and SQL Server /
William R. Vaughn. -- 6th ed.
     p.   cm.
   Includes index.
   ISBN 1-57231-848-1
    1. BASIC (Computer program language) 2. Microsoft
Visual Basic for Windows. 3. SQL server. I. Title.
   QA76.73.B3V39 1998
   005.26'8--dc21   98-34434
                                        CIP

Printed and bound in the United States of America.

1 2 3 4 5 6 7 8 9 QMQM 3 2 1 0 9 8

Distributed in Canada by ITP Nelson, a division of Thomson Canada Limited.

A CIP catalogue record for this book is available from the British Library.

Microsoft Press books are available through booksellers and distributors worldwide. For
further information about international editions, contact your local Microsoft Corporation
office or contact Microsoft Press International directly at fax (425) 936-7329. Visit our
Web site at mspress.microsoft.com.

Acquisitions Editor: Eric Stroo
Project Editor: Sally Stickney
Technical Editor: Robert Lyon

I dedicate this edition to those I've left behind—those who helped make me who I am today and molded who I hope to become tomorrow.

CONTENTS AT A GLANCE

iv

CONTENTS AT A GLANCE

C O N T E N T S A T A G L A N C E

DUSTY ARCHIVES
(Chapters on the Companion CD)

TABLE OF CONTENTS

TABLE OF CONTENTS

TABLE OF CONTENTS

x

T
A
B
L
E

O
F

C
O
N
T
E
N
T
S

TABLE OF CONTENTS

xv

DUSTY ARCHIVES
(Chapters on the Companion CD)

T
A
B
L
E

O
F

C
O
N
T
E
N
T
S

ACKNOWLEDGMENTS

As the technology we're working with gets more complex, the need to draw on more and more people to make my books complete increases as well. This sixth edition of the *Hitchhiker's Guide* was by far the hardest to write of the entire series. I was overwhelmed by the number of things that changed or appeared for the first time in Visual Basic 6.0. I called on many, many people to help me sort out how the new and different would affect the tried and true. The steadfast Dave Stearns and the omnipotent David Stutz both contributed on several fronts. Sometimes they were there just as a sounding board when I griped about how something was implemented. More often than not they provided essential tutorial help and reviews. David Sceppa, Jim Lewallen, and Jim Wilson (the ADO one) all got roped into doing reviews, as did Amrish Kumar and others. Brad Hoffman, Ron Bailey, Rick Nasci, and Brad Nelson both provided a pipe into the testing labs where they worked RAID for me. Robert and Pat O'Farrell both helped work through the DOW chapter. The assistance of these people really helped keep my workload down. I would also like to thank my Microsoft Press editors, Sally Stickney and Robert Lyon, who contributed a lot of themselves to the book to organize, refine, and polish in a way that kept my voice and opinions intact.

As always, there are people whose faces I see far too infrequently. These are the people who send me mail to ask questions, to pass along an "attaboy," or just to share a joke to lighten my day. And there are those on the mailing lists where I hang out who rein in the detractors or belligerent Microsoft haters. I extend a special thanks to all of you. No doubt I've forgotten to mention a few people. And as with earlier editions, a few others are best forgotten, lest I burn any more bridges.

William R. Vaughn
Redmond, Washington
August 1998

PART I

Understanding
Data Access Interfaces

1

The Road Ahead

The Internet Craze

Evolving Standards

Where We Are Now

And Where We're Headed

seem to introduce each new edition of the *Hitchhiker's Guide* with the same observation: "Boy, a lot has changed in the last year." 1997 and 1998 were no exception. They will probably be known as the years that the press and many developers discovered the Internet and Java. Now that the initial dust has settled, it's clear that the Web is going to play a decisive role in our future (yours and mine). However, I can say that although many developers think they've discovered a new path to nirvana, others see this architecture as a boiled-over version of 3270 technology.

NOTE   Don't know what 3270 architecture is? Well, this setup puts semiconscious terminals (only a few IQ points smarter than dumb terminals) at the end of a wire that's ultimately connected to a mainframe. Actually, the terminal firmware was not unlike early browser software. It let developers build screens with edit regions and fixed-text areas.

The Internet Craze

The Internet has been around for a long time, but no one outside the government and the academic community really paid much attention to it. My brother kept referring to it (as ARPANET), but I never knew what he was talking about. (That's not so unusual, though—he's also been known to ramble on about FORTRAN-computed apogees and perigees to his UTEP classes—well beyond me.) As I see it, the Internet stopped being a wallflower when Sun, Netscape, Novell, et al. discovered that Microsoft's 32-bit platforms were gobbling up market share. To add insult to injury, much of this expansion was being accomplished on the back of a language that they had discounted as too slow, too clumsy, and not academically pure: Microsoft Visual Basic. Unfortunately, Visual Basic 5.0 left open an avenue of attack—its lack of 16-bit support. Visual Basic's detractors seemed to unify around a strategy to encourage the adoption of the Internet as a new universal standard platform with Java its only development language—a language that Sun alone controlled. This new paradigm would somehow solve all cross-platform problems and relegitimize UNIX, Macintosh, OS/2, and other operating systems as viable platforms—and wrest the control of the operating system away from Microsoft. Sure, the controversy is a lot more complex than this, but I'm welcome to my simplistic opinion. The point? Well, the Internet has opened a number of new ways for Visual Basic developers to get at and expose their data—even Microsoft SQL Server data. Many of you are considering the Internet as an alternative way to expose your company information to the planet—or just to those within your own company. Somehow, I doubt the Internet will go the way of CB radios—it has already proven to be more than just a passing fad.

TIP Want to wander out into freeway traffic right away and start working with some code? Well, charge off and check out Chapter 3—where I provide a number of examples that you can solder together—and get a feel for the interfaces.

Evolving Standards

Some of the trade press and the Microsoft bashers seem to overlook the fact that standards are what made this industry viable. Even weak standards provided the needed stimulus and structure for the PC industry to grow during its earliest days. For example, in the mid-1970s, the S-100 bus was technically laughable but made it possible for hundreds of companies to build "compatible" cards for the earliest PCs. The burned-out wrecks of companies that chose to create their own "standard" litter the roadside. Even when IBM introduced the 5130 (the first IBM PC), it too was technically bankrupt when compared to other systems on the market—but it sparked a rush to be compatible. Here again, companies large and small tried to improve upon the challenged IBM PC design. When they varied from the standard, however, they discovered that their innovations often made it impossible for customers to run pivotal applications such as Lotus 1-2-3. Ask Tandy about its (excellent) Tandy 2000, or Digital Equipment Corporation about its (innovative) Rainbow, or CPT Corporation or Texas Instruments about their (several) attempts at high-tech PCs. These systems were often faster and smarter—but generally not compatible. Compaq systems, however, bent over backward to be tightly compatible (to the point of being sued by IBM), and that company survives to this day.

When Microsoft Windows was released in 1985, its goal was to create a new kind of standard. No, at the time it wasn't an operating system. Windows 1.0 was simply a relatively crude graphical user interface and MS-DOS program launcher. However, Microsoft (and Bill) expected that once this standard was in place, software vendors could refocus their efforts on writing applications. No longer would they need to write complex device drivers for the hundreds of video, printer, and other peripherals their applications needed to be competitive. The standard platform would provide all these drivers and interfaces. And yes, this "standard" was pretty shaky when it first appeared, but after over a decade of refinement, Windows has evolved into not one but two "real" operating systems and a recognized standard worldwide. I'm convinced that without a single force driving this standard, the self-interest of the individual hardware and software companies would have diffused the focus of the industry and made the innovation and spread of this technology virtually impossible.

Today, we are witnessing a cacophony of Microsoft competitors attempting to convince the press, the courts, the government, and so-called forums that these standards are hurting competition, innovation, and consumers. Some seem to be buying the story, and others seem willing to sell their support to the highest bidder. What the Windows standard and its widespread acceptance are really hurting is the very existence of the competitors' obsolete technology. Sure, I understand their frustration. They have a duty to their stockholders. They can't just give up and depart the scene quietly—nor should they. Their continued pressure simply drives Microsoft to greater heights and into more paradigms.

Such conflict is the price of innovation. Microsoft really needs the industry and its customer base to keep it evolving toward better solutions. The pressure has always been there. Week after week, Microsoft meets legions of CIOs, managers, developers, users, educators, and architects with ideas, suggestions, and bug reports—many demanding that Microsoft implement their pet solution. And Microsoft does listen. But no, it doesn't implement every idea it hears about. In many cases, Microsoft leaves these innovations to third-party independent software vendors (ISVs) and others (even competitors) to implement. Yes, Microsoft has been known to buy or license technology from these winners and leverage the best of their ideas—especially where they fit into the growth of the overall Windows standard.

NOTE Let me make one thing perfectly clear. When I use the terms *Internet*, *Web*, or *WWW*, I mean *public* connectivity over the World Wide Web. When I use the word *intranet*, I mean *private* connectivity—what we've been using for years—over your own LAN or WAN. More and more, people (especially the press) seem to be using these terms interchangeably. All this new technology is tough enough to understand—let's not make it more difficult by confusing the basic terms we use to describe it. Sure, I see why people get mixed up—the terms are ambiguous. Some connectivity strategies work in a variety of ways—on the Internet *and* on your private LAN—the *intra*net. This flexibility is great, but sometimes it makes for vague descriptions. The newness of the technology and how well the person explaining the technology understands how these pieces fit together can also contribute to the confusion. Yep, I'm learning it too, so bear with me.

I digress, however. This book is not about the virtues or malignancies of Java and the Internet or about how Microsoft has or has not stifled innovation. It is about building successful Visual Basic applications that access SQL Server. So yes, I'll discuss where the new Internet technology makes sense and where it doesn't—but in pragmatic terms based on everyday reality. I'm afraid I've been around too long to be easily lured over to the 3270-like architecture that I (and much of the industry) abandoned in favor of the PC over 20 years ago. Nevertheless, over the last year, the technology has continued to evolve. Visual Basic 6.0 has virtually taken over Microsoft Visual InterDev's functionality, and we'll see the ultimate assimilation of this separate product in favor of a more powerful Visual Basic. Visual Basic 6.0 offers at least a half-dozen new ways to use the Web to deploy and run applications and components. We'll talk about many of these.

Where We Are Now

Before we go any further, let's stop for a minute to assess where we are now in terms of development tools and technology. Let's cruise by some of the latest tools and technology Microsoft provides for developers. These new tools include SQL Server 7.0; Visual Basic (and Microsoft Visual Studio) 6.0; ActiveX Data Objects; Component Object Model (COM); Microsoft Transaction Server; Visual Basic, Enterprise Edition; and other development platforms. In the sections that follow, I'll briefly describe the current state of each of these.

SQL Server 7.0

The most important innovation since the last edition of this book is certainly SQL Server 7.0. (Ah, this version might have slipped out a bit, so it might not be on the streets yet; but I do discuss the innovations it brings to Visual Basic developers.) Not only has SQL Server 7.0 been completely reengineered (now that the Sybase license has expired), but it has been ported to another operating system: Windows 95/98. Yes, that means SQL Server 7.0 will run on the Microsoft Windows 95 and Microsoft Windows 98 platforms. You won't have to prototype in Microsoft Access—of course, Microsoft Access 9.0 also gives you the option of using either the ISAM-based Microsoft Jet engine or SQL Server 7.0. Wherever possible, I'll explain what these new changes mean to you.

Visual Basic 6.0

As Visual Basic applications have expanded and as their roles have matured, the mechanisms for connecting Visual Basic to databases have also multiplied and evolved. Visual Basic 6.0 is no exception; it adds support for several new methodologies and a litany of new approaches to existing paradigms. Pressure exerted on Microsoft by developers has yielded much of this better performance and higher productivity, especially when it comes to accessing data. Those companies that used Visual Basic 4.0's performance as a springboard for launching competitive database interfaces or simply for performance-tuning applications have now discovered that this differentiating factor is gone—a number of those companies are gone, too.

If new data access paradigms, high productivity, and an optimizing compiler are the good news about Visual Basic 6.0, the *really* good news is that Microsoft SQL Server, Developer Edition, still ships with Visual Basic 6.0, Enterprise Edition. Yes, the initial version is SQL Server 6.5, but SQL Server 7.0 is not far off and (might) be incorporated into the product later. This inclusion of the latest products underscores how serious Microsoft is about making sure that developers have the best tools to do the job. I think you'll be pleased with the combination of tools Microsoft has bundled together with SQL Server, Developer Edition—designed with you, the client/server developer, in mind.

TIP The Developer Edition of SQL Server is just that—a hobbled version that won't support more than five connections. You won't be able to support a production environment with it. Unless, of course, your attorneys are bored and you don't mind being sued by Microsoft for license violations.

The rest of the story is sobering for some developers. Visual Basic 6.0, with all its speed and features, is still 32-bit only. Yes, that's right—32-bit only. It won't run or create a control or compile an executable that runs on any 16-bit (or 8-bit) platform. But you've figured that out by now. (If this information is a surprise, you'd better check on your stock of candles.) For those of you still stuck with 16-bit clients, you don't have to stay with Visual Basic 3.0 or 4.0 (16-bit). You can use Visual Basic 6.0 to create 32-bit components to run on a Distributed COM (DCOM) server such as Microsoft Transaction Server (MTS), a strategy many have found to be viable. These components can be accessed in a number of ways from your existing 16-bit systems—even your Macintosh. Visual Basic 6.0 also includes paradigms that generate Hypertext Markup Language (HTML) or Dynamic HTML (DHTML) to connect your browser (regardless of platform) to your Visual Basic–authored middle-tier components. Once you move to 32-bit Wintel client platforms, you gain a dizzying number of new alternatives—and I'll try to describe most of them in this book.

ActiveX Data Objects

We've also seen the birth and early growth of YADAA (yet another data access acronym): ADO, for Microsoft ActiveX Data Objects. This new object model is designed to eventually eliminate the need for the Visual Basic Library for SQL Server (VBSQL), Data Access Objects (DAO), Remote Data Objects (RDO), and ODBCDirect—once and for all. OK, well maybe not immediately, but soon. No, that does *not* mean that Microsoft is going to drop support for these data access interfaces. It does mean that you won't feel the need to use them down the road. We'll spend an entire part of this book (Part V) on ADO.

TIP Worried about migrating from RDO to ADO? Never fear, I've devoted an entire chapter (Chapter 34) to the subject. After you read this chapter, your conversion will be as simple as reading the evening paper with a cat on your lap.

The Maturation of COM

So much has changed that the job of the systems architect has grown far more complex in some respects but easier in others. This job redefinition always happens when new tools, techniques, and designs are introduced. The current era seems to parallel the early days of the electronics industry when the first integrated circuits were developed. From that point forward, hardware developers no longer had to build systems using discrete components (transistors, resistors, and capacitors). They could choose from an ever-growing number of integrated parts that combined logic gates and support circuitry mounted on a standard dual-inline-package (or DIP) that fit in a standard socket. This revolution (which doesn't seem that remarkable as we look back) introduced special-purpose integrated circuits (ICs) that could replace complex I/O controllers, timers, and bus managers. Before long, we had programmable controllers for dumb terminals, and these controllers enabled the birth of the first general-purpose programmable microprocessor.

How does this brief history of electronics parallel our current software technology? Well, consider that these ICs were built in a standard way—and because of this standardization, many (competing) vendors could build them. They all fit into standard sockets—again because of standards. In the same way that standards allowed engineers to design ICs, Visual Basic 5.0 gave you, today's front-line developer, the ability to create standard components and expect them to work anywhere they are required. Because of the standards encouraged by COM and implemented in Visual Basic, Microsoft Visual C++, and Microsoft Visual J++, you can be assured that your ActiveX custom control or dynamic-link library (DLL) will work in any of the multitude of applications and subsystems that support COM. No, I'm not turning the *Hitchhiker's Guide* into another book on COM. I am, however, going to show you how you can successfully design COM into your data access applications and make the most of its benefits.

COM was big news when Visual Basic 5.0 shipped—Microsoft (and the Visual Basic development team) finally got it to work. All editions of Visual Basic let you create, debug, and deploy COM components. Visual Basic 5.0, Professional and Enterprise Editions, even let you create native code versions of your components, which lead to faster execution and open more doors for Visual Basic component-based solutions. Do you remember when the Visual Basic 4.0 documentation described a technique for building your own remote automation component manager? This brilliant idea was like suggesting that you could build a Boeing 777 in your backyard—out of balsa. Visual Basic 5.0, Enterprise Edition, addressed this problem by including the first version of MTS. For the first time, you could build components designed to be deployed and executed remotely without having to worry about the complexities of getting this technology to work. MTS is going to be a part of Microsoft Windows NT before long (in version 5.0—it's already part of Windows NT's Option Pack) and should play a pivotal role in how distributed architecture systems are designed.

Microsoft Transaction Server

This last year or so spawned more than just the Internet craze. We also witnessed the birth of a new class of server (at least for the PC industry)—the *component* server. Although its name—Microsoft Transaction Server (MTS)—belies its true purpose, I think this new type of development engine will add an entirely new paradigm to the list of important architectures. For the first time, you'll be able to create applications that are based on sharable components without having to worry about how, where, and when those components are invoked. Too often, new systems have failed because they've tried to reinvent the vast amount of integrated technology MTS provides. Because these systems take so long to develop (often 6 to 18 months), we're just now hearing MTS success stories. In the fifth edition of the *Hitchhiker's Guide*, I didn't cover MTS—it simply wasn't ready when I wrote the book in the weeks before Christmas 1996. In the meantime, the public has shown remarkable acceptance of this technology, and in this edition of the *Hitchhiker's Guide*, I include a number of tips on how to use MTS with Visual Basic and SQL Server.

Visual Basic, Enterprise Edition

To better address the special needs of client/server developers, Microsoft bundled a number of applications, special documentation, and custom controls to create Visual Basic, Enterprise Edition. It includes the RemoteData control and supports the RDO programming interface. The RemoteData control and the RDO interface are specifically designed for connecting to remote database engines via the best available ODBC drivers. In short, the RDO model provides a thin, tightly coded object interface to the ODBC API. Visual Basic 5.0, Enterprise Edition, extended the RDO interface and included the ODBCDirect interface and a litany of new applications, designers, and add-ins to support client/server development. These include Visual Database Tools, MTS, and SQL Server itself. In addition, Visual Basic 5.0, Enterprise Edition, also included a sophisticated TSQL debugger and UserConnection designer to help work with stored procedures. (Part IV of this guide is devoted to the RDO interface and these tools.) As I mentioned earlier, Visual Basic 6.0 now supports yet another mid-level interface: ADO. This interface is provided in both the Professional and Enterprise Editions and is discussed in Part V.

Microsoft Development Tools

Microsoft is now promoting at least ten development platforms: C++ (and Visual C++), Microsoft Excel, SQL Server, Microsoft FoxPro, Microsoft Access, Microsoft Visual J++, Microsoft Outlook, Visual InterDev, and Visual Basic—and I probably left out a couple. Moreover, this tally doesn't count Visual Basic, Scripting Edition, and Microsoft Active Server Pages.

We're also witnessing the evolution of more and more wizards, designers, and other tools that make the design, development, testing, and deployment of database applications easier. Under the covers, these automated interfaces still generate RDO and ADO code. However, you must continue to be aware of what's going on behind the scenes—such knowledge is critical to the success and performance of any data access application. These innovations increase developer productivity and let you create better applications more quickly, but you still need to understand these low-level interfaces to make the most efficient applications.

While all these new and improved tools seem really cool (and they are), you can still encounter a number of dangers out there. Working with client/server and database development tools is something like leading your development team on a walking (wading?) tour of a Florida swamp. Sure, you can find plenty of safe paths through the razor grass and slimy cypress logs; but some of those mossy bumps sticking out of the muck aren't stones—they're the backs of alligators; and that attractive low-hanging vine is really a water moccasin basking in the sun. I hope to be able to point out these hazards as we go—just watch where you step.

And Where We're Headed

Before we really hit the road with our thumbs out, let's get our bearings. In this edition of the *Hitchhiker's Guide*, I cover a number of new technologies and leave some of the outdated ones behind. Here's the way I've organized this edition:

- Part I introduces data access methods and potential architectures. In Chapter 3, you'll be able to dive into the deep end right away and look at some samples on DAO, RDO, and ADO.

- Part II explains how to construct SQL Server applications. We'll cover such topics as making connections with, writing queries for, and retrieving data from SQL Server.

- Parts III and IV tell you everything you need to know about DAO and RDO.

- Part V, which is new to this edition, examines ADO and its bevy of new data access paradigms. It also introduces the OLE DB data access architecture.

- Part VI, also new to this edition, describes the new data access tools. The Visual Basic and Visual Studio teams have been busy creating a number of new tools that replace the User Connection designer and Visual Database Tools that let you manage data and datacentric applications more easily than ever.

As new paradigms are added, old ones need to move aside to make space. I've archived certain fifth edition chapters over to the CD as viewable documents so that you can still access them if you want to. Here's what you'll find in the dusty archives on the companion CD:

- **VBSQL chapters** I archived these chapters (Chapters 29–36 of the fifth edition) because SQL Server 7.0's support for DB-Library hasn't changed from version 6.5.

- **ODBC API chapters**   This paradigm (which I described in Chapters 37–38 of the fifth edition) has gone static in the last year, and you shouldn't use it for new designs. For you masochists out there, however, the CD does include the ODBC 3.5 Declare files.

So here we are again, ready to launch out on the new adventures and challenges promised by Visual Basic 6.0 and SQL Server. I hope this edition of the *Hitchhiker's Guide* will make your development chores more like fun and less like playing Doom without a mouse.

2

Data Interfaces

Accessing SQL Server from Visual Basic

Understanding the Low-Level Interfaces

Taking the Next Step

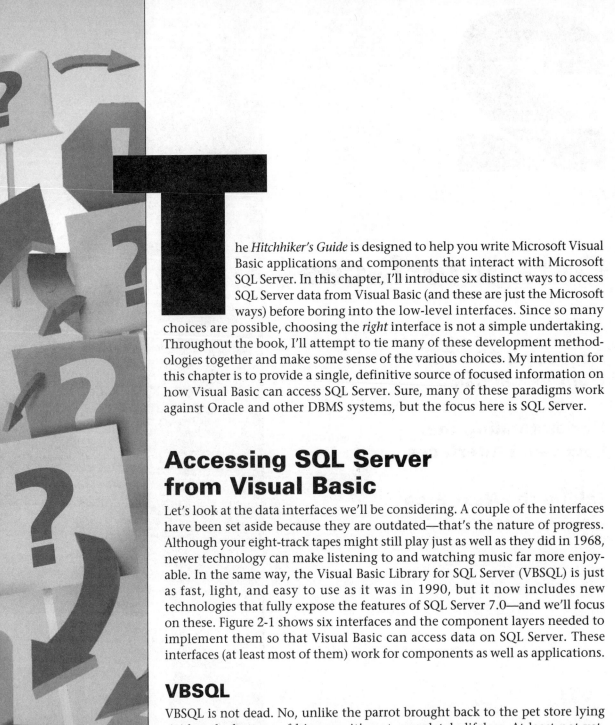

The *Hitchhiker's Guide* is designed to help you write Microsoft Visual Basic applications and components that interact with Microsoft SQL Server. In this chapter, I'll introduce six distinct ways to access SQL Server data from Visual Basic (and these are just the Microsoft ways) before boring into the low-level interfaces. Since so many choices are possible, choosing the *right* interface is not a simple undertaking. Throughout the book, I'll attempt to tie many of these development methodologies together and make some sense of the various choices. My intention for this chapter is to provide a single, definitive source of focused information on how Visual Basic can access SQL Server. Sure, many of these paradigms work against Oracle and other DBMS systems, but the focus here is SQL Server.

Accessing SQL Server from Visual Basic

Let's look at the data interfaces we'll be considering. A couple of the interfaces have been set aside because they are outdated—that's the nature of progress. Although your eight-track tapes might still play just as well as they did in 1968, newer technology can make listening to and watching music far more enjoyable. In the same way, the Visual Basic Library for SQL Server (VBSQL) is just as fast, light, and easy to use as it was in 1990, but it now includes new technologies that fully expose the features of SQL Server 7.0—and we'll focus on these. Figure 2-1 shows six interfaces and the component layers needed to implement them so that Visual Basic can access data on SQL Server. These interfaces (at least most of them) work for components as well as applications.

VBSQL

VBSQL is not dead. No, unlike the parrot brought back to the pet store lying rigid at the bottom of his cage, it's not completely lifeless. At least not yet. VBSQL, provided in both VBX and OCX forms, was the *first* native interface to SQL Server. It's obsolete (or at least terribly outdated) and has already been (partially) replaced by the ODBC API. It will eventually be replaced by ActiveX

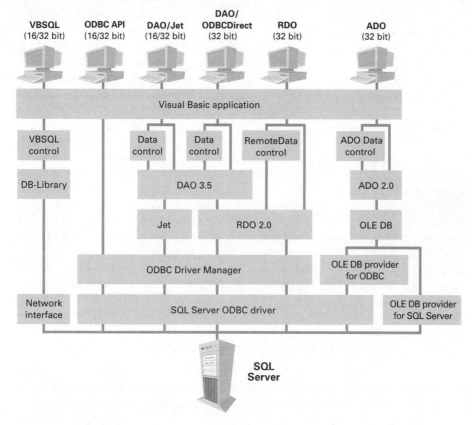

Figure 2-1 *Six interfaces to access SQL Server from Visual Basic*

Data Objects (ADO). Work stopped some time ago on DB-Library and VBSQL, but SQL Server (even 7.0) still uses Tabular Data Stream (TDS) protocol to communicate with the outside world. However, the new SQL Server 7.0 TDS has a number of extensions not supported by DB-Library. This limited support means that existing DB-Library and VBSQL applications will work against SQL Server 7.0, but many of the new features (and there are a lot of them) won't. How does this affect you? Simply, you need to stop *new* development in VBSQL and shift to ADO (if possible) or Remote Data Objects (RDO).

Let's take a short detour here and review some changes to Visual Basic that have had implications for VBSQL. Between 1993 and 1995, Microsoft completely rewrote Visual Basic, and it's no longer the mostly assembly-language monolithic application that Visual Basic 3.0 was. In most ways, Visual Basic 4.0 was an entirely new product. As such, it came to depend heavily on OLE technologies (Microsoft now calls most of these technologies ActiveX technologies), Visual Basic for Applications (VBA), and other loadable components, including the Microsoft Jet database engine and RDO. As a result of this redesign, Visual Basic 4.0 was able to create OLE DLLs and applications that act as OLE servers and clients. It was also able to support development add-ins such as Microsoft Visual SourceSafe. The later versions of Visual Basic are no different except that they can also create fully compiled ActiveX executables and DLLs.

Although Visual Basic 4.0 was provided in both 16-bit and 32-bit versions, for use on 16-bit Microsoft Windows and 32-bit Microsoft Windows 95 and Microsoft Windows NT systems, all subsequent versions of Visual Basic are 32-bit only. On close inspection, these two versions are very different in many respects. For example, the 32-bit versions of Visual Basic are designed to work with 16-bit Unicode strings. (Unicode, in case you don't know, is a 16-bit-per-character storage format used to support languages that need additional bits to represent their alphabets.) This single aspect of the 32-bit versions can have a significant impact on the conversion of 16-bit Visual Basic 3.0 applications that pass strings to DLLs; VBSQL applications are among these. In addition, since the Windows operating system itself has changed drastically, calls made from Visual Basic applications to Windows APIs must be recoded and, in some cases, completely redesigned. Because of these differences, application conversion to the Windows 9x or the Windows NT platform can be a challenge, especially with a larger application. You can make conversions easier by studying the documentation and Knowledge Base articles on the subject. In most cases, you should be able to port existing Visual Basic 3.0 applications to 16-bit Visual Basic 4.0 without (much) trouble—assuming you don't use any nasty tricks based on inside knowledge of the Visual Basic or Windows architecture. Moving from 16-bit Visual Basic 3.0 applications to 32-bit Visual Basic will be increasingly difficult as we move toward future versions of Visual Basic that are less accommodating to 16-bit nuances.

NOTE Can you say "rewrite"? VBX custom controls are supported in the 16-bit version of Visual Basic 4.0, but you must use OCX equivalents of all custom controls (now called ActiveX controls) for 32-bit programs. And guess what—not all control vendors are ready with 32-bit versions. (The slowest to convert will probably be those who have gone out of business.) Most of the applications written for Visual Basic 3.0 can be imported into the current versions of Visual Basic and recompiled, but some will require significant recoding, rethinking, and other adjustments before they'll work as before.

Although Visual Basic itself has changed radically, the methods and techniques used for developing VBSQL applications are generally unchanged. Although Visual Basic 5.0 permits implementation of user-written event handlers, you still need a custom control to implement the DB-Library error and message callback routines for both the 16-bit and the 32-bit operating systems. The Microsoft SQL Server group developed a VBSQL.OCX to support 32-bit operating systems and released it with SQL Server 6.0. It is designed to be a virtual clone of the 16-bit version. The latest version of this control is on the CD that is included with this book and ships with SQL Server Developer and Workstation editions, 6.0 and later.

NOTE I've moved the material on VBSQL from the fifth edition of *Hitchhiker's Guide* (Part V, "The Visual Basic Library for SQL Server") to the Dusty Archives area on the CD.

ODBC API

The ODBC API—that is, the application programming interface to open database connectivity—is available through the use of API Declare statements, as provided in the files ODBC16.txt and ODBC32.txt.

The ODBC API continues to be an enigma. Thanks to some unclear messages being sent out by Microsoft (myself included), many of you are confused about its role. Although ODBC is vital for Microsoft's connectivity strategy, accessing ODBC via its API is *not* an ideal programming interface for Visual Basic developers. If you think of the ODBC API as a low-level interface and not as a primary development path, you'll be a lot happier. The API becomes interesting only when the other interfaces (such as RDO) fail to meet immediate needs—then, and only then, should you consider programming to this API.

Many developers coded to the ODBC API on 16-bit platforms when they didn't have (or couldn't use) RDO or VBSQL. I can tell you that those folks are in for a fairly tough job now that it's time for them to convert to 32-bit. They'll soon discover that many of the rules have changed, as is bound to happen with any API approach. Many of the routines they coded so carefully before no longer work in the 32-bit Unicode world. Because of these and other problems, I don't currently recommend this interface for Visual Basic developers.

The Microsoft ODBC API dev types have provided very little support for Visual Basic over the years. The ODBC API Declare files that appeared in Visual Basic 5.0 were written by yours truly, and they were never completely written for Visual Basic 6.0 or ODBC 3.*x.* Frankly, you're on your own if you go down that alley.

One more thing: the ODBC API was to become the new *native* interface to SQL Server. It didn't really happen—at least not completely. OLE DB is in the wings ready to take over not long after SQL Server 7.0 arrives. For those of you still considering the ODBC API approach, however, consider that it leaves a lot to be desired when it comes time to build successful client/server applications. No, no, no, this doesn't mean that RDO and the ADO to ODBC approach is flawed. On the contrary, these indirect object-oriented interfaces are specifically implemented to abrogate the problems associated with the direct API coding associated with the ODBC API.

> **NOTE** I've moved the chapters on the ODBC API from the fifth edition of the *Hitchhiker's Guide* (Part VI, "The ODBC API") to the Dusty Archives area on the CD.

DAO/Jet

Data Access Objects (DAO) has really lost ground in the past couple of years as a chosen means for getting at SQL Server. Now that RDO and ADO have arrived, most developers find DAO far too limiting for accessing ODBC data sources. Since Microsoft Access has now switched to permit developers to use SQL Server 7.0 (or Jet), it's clear that Jet's appeal has been significantly reduced. Sure, Microsoft Access is still a viable ISAM DBMS engine, but ADO and RDO do a better job when accessing SQL Server. I include DAO (probably for the last time) in this edition of the *Hitchhiker's Guide* to help those transitioning to the newer interfaces.

Some developers inflict their DAO/Jet performance problems on themselves. Many of the same developers who are attracted to Visual Basic and Jet also belong to the Flat Earth Society, where dBASE and flat-file ISAM databases put bread on the table. When the flat-earthers incorrectly port age-old techniques and designs over to relational schemas, they often doom their systems to pitifully low performance from the start.

The Jet database engine is a body of code that is used for performing a specific set of functions. An engine can be a mathematical processor, a business rule processor, or some other set of code that can be intelligently controlled. Jet is available in several versions, which are described here. All versions are referenced through DAO with or without the Data control.

- Jet 1.1, supplied with Visual Basic 3.0 and accessed whenever you use the Data control or DAO/Jet, is now obsolete, even for 16-bit platforms.

- Jet 2.0 and Jet 2.5, available for use with Visual Basic 3.0 through "compatibility layers" and service packs for Microsoft Access, yield better efficiency from the engine, although many of Jet's features and objects aren't implemented in DAO 1.1. This method is also obsolete. (It was obsolete when it was introduced.)

- Jet 2.5 and Jet 3.0 and the new DAO, as available for use with Visual Basic 4.0, all enable new DAO features and are fully supported by Visual Basic 4.0 DAO. This method is all but obsolete, but it's useful for 16-bit platforms.

- Jet 3.5, as available with Visual Basic 5.0, enables even more DAO features—but only in a 32-bit version.

- Jet 3.51, as available with Visual Basic 6.0, adds some minor revisions to accommodate Office upgrades. We expect to see Jet 4.x in the next version of Office. What it changes is anyone's guess.

Visual Basic 6.0 exposes Jet 3.51, the newest version of the Jet database engine, first implemented in Microsoft Access 97 (which is included with Microsoft Office 97). Jet 3.5x can be used only in 32-bit operating systems such as Windows 95 and Windows NT. We were really lucky to get 16-bit support in Visual Basic 4.0—it was nearly dropped in *that* development cycle. Each of the Jet engine interfaces is implemented with a type library, which provides a means of making components available in the engine interface so that a developer can choose the most suitable object model. The various Jet object models support different sets or subsets of the Visual Basic DAO model.

Because Jet 3.51 as supplied with Visual Basic 6.0 no longer runs in 16-bit environments, your type library choices are limited. However, you can still choose the "compatibility" type library that continues to recognize your older (and generally outdated) 16-bit code. Before you start to code a new application, or once you've imported an existing Visual Basic application, you need to choose one of the three matching type libraries:

- The Microsoft DAO 3.51 Object Library is for 32-bit systems only. This type library supports all the new Recordset objects but not the outdated Dynaset, Snapshot, or Table objects, properties, and methods used with Visual Basic 3.0. This library is used to help filter out the outdated objects, and you should use it for all new Visual Basic development.

- The Microsoft DAO 2.5 Object Library is for 16-bit systems only and isn't provided in current versions of Visual Basic. It supports the Recordset objects and *most* of the outdated DAO objects, including the

Dynaset, Snapshot, and Table objects. Some objects and methods introduced with Visual Basic 2.0 aren't supported (such as the ListFields and ListIndexes methods). This is the *only* library supported in 16-bit systems.

- The Microsoft DAO 2.5/3.51 Compatibility Library supports the new Recordset objects and the same set of objects supported by the Microsoft DAO 2.5 Object Library. This library is used to provide the widest compatibility for Visual Basic application conversions.

The dialog box for choosing a library is found in the Visual Basic References dialog box (available via the Project menu) and is shown in Figure 2-2.

A database engine is like any other engine you're familiar with. As with the engine in your dad's sports car, you can run the RPM into the red and throw a rod on SQL Server if you aren't careful with the tasks you ask it to perform.

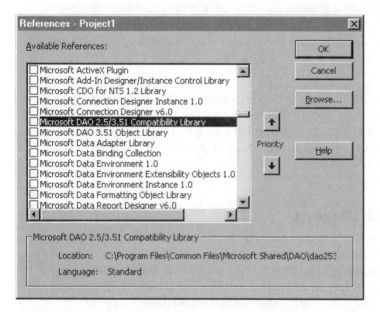

Figure 2-2 *Visual Basic References dialog box for choosing a type library*

In an attempt to improve Jet's performance against ODBC back-end servers, a number of changes were made in the Jet database engine to help it deal with external databases and their special needs. Most of the changes were made in Jet 3.0, but one important change introduced in Visual Basic 4.0 was the addition of the ODBCDirect interface, which appears officially for the first time in DAO 3.5.

The Jet 3.0 and 3.51 enhancements did make Jet faster—to an extent. In some respects, these versions are *much* faster than Jet 1.1. For one thing, the new versions delegate more query processing to the back end instead of trying to pull the data over the network to process queries locally. For another, their caching and buffering have improved. They populate Data control Resultset objects in a background task, and they support multiple result sets from stored procedures, though they do it in a somewhat strange way. The new versions of DAO/Jet trap errors and build a collection of all those encountered while running a query. They support the transaction model better by basing transaction scope on the Workspace object. They also support SQL pass-through better, even

Many of you are trying to decide whether to use the DAO partly implemented in Visual Basic 2.0, fully implemented in Visual Basic 3.0, further enhanced in Visual Basic 4.0, expanded to support RDO in Visual Basic 5.0, and replicated for ODBC back-end databases with the RDO model. A number of considerations make this decision tough, but after you've read this book, you'll have a pretty good idea of what to do. Or maybe you'll decide to go into decorative landscaping instead—it's a lot less stressful.

with attached tables, and they provide better and more intelligent connection management schemes, permitting you to override connection sharing.

Unfortunately, however, even the newest versions of DAO/Jet don't utilize all the new SQL Server features and some of the more sophisticated aspects of TransactSQL (TSQL) and stored-procedure programming. The principal reason for these omissions is the desire to have DAO/Jet act as a generic interface. Therefore, no substantive functionality can be added to support SQL Server–specific features that aren't supported elsewhere. For example, DAO/Jet doesn't support server-side cursors, and stored-procedure output parameters and return codes are still unavailable. Using DAO/Jet, there is still no way to limit the number of rows returned by a query (other than through the WHERE clause), and queries are still canceled by embedded TSQL RAISERROR statements. Queries that are executed through DAO are still run synchronously, with no way to cancel a query that has run amok, and messages and PRINT statements returned from the server are still ignored.

NOTE   One thing Jet is not is a suitable multitasking engine; that is, you shouldn't try to build a distributed component server with it. Although Jet is internally multithreaded, it isn't designed to deal with more than one operation at a time and will lock out other requests (and users) until each query is complete.

DAO/ODBCDirect

Just before the senior product manager for the DAO/Jet team left for Australia (literally), he sent out a memo announcing the introduction of another DAO programming model: ODBCDirect. This interface decouples DAO from the Jet database engine and reconnects DAO to ODBC databases (only) through RDO. The intent was to create a database-independent interface that used the familiar ISAM-oriented DAO programming model but broke its ties to the Jet engine, which is not particularly well suited to remote data access. Frankly, that was the intent in the first place—to create a programming interface that didn't lean toward one database architecture or another. Unfortunately, that's not what was originally implemented. DAO/Jet proved to be very ISAM-oriented and couldn't deal adequately with the realities of client/server design without the help of some careful coding. Sure, you could write front-end applications to SQL Server using DAO/Jet, but you had to remember to watch where you stepped.

When it came time to make DAO do what remote developers needed in Visual Basic 4.0, its ties to Jet made easy changes virtually impossible—and this is when RDO was created. ODBCDirect leverages the work done by the RDO team by cross-wiring DAO objects to the RDO ODBC interface instead of to Jet. No, ODBCDirect doesn't mean that you can run Visual Basic 4.0 (which supported the ODBCDirect beta) applications in 16-bit mode. Remember that ODBCDirect uses RDO, and RDO is strictly 32-bit. The Office 9x applications also use ODBCDirect—but not RDO unless you have a Visual Basic 5.0, Enterprise Edition, license (or one of the other RDO development platforms).

ODBCDirect also doesn't implement all the RDO interface—but nearly all. For example, it doesn't expose the event-driven operations. Should you use RDO over ODBCDirect? Let's leave that question for the sections on ODBCDirect (Chapter 17) and RDO (Part IV).

In short, ODBCDirect isn't obsolete; but it hasn't changed since Visual Basic 5.0 SP3, and you won't catch me recommending it.

RDO

The RemoteData control and RDO 2.0 merge the flexibility of RDO and ODBC with the ease of use of bound controls. This lightweight middleware 32-bit technology was introduced with Visual Basic 4.0 and has emerged as the interface of choice for most SQL Server front ends.

The RemoteData control was supposed to bring on a new acceptance of bound controls. It didn't happen. This custom control has been plagued with a number of complex issues that have made it hard to love. It was supposed to address the specific needs of remote ODBC database engines, especially SQL Server when leveraging bound controls. In Visual Basic 6.0, the RDC is pretty much as it was in Visual Basic 5.0 (SP3). It's working better now, but it still has a number of problems that keep it from being my first pick when it comes to choosing interfaces.

You can use the RemoteData control as a replacement for the standard Data control. Because the RemoteData control utilizes RDO, it can totally eliminate the need for the Jet database engine. With the RemoteData control, you can create applications that use bound controls, just as you can with the standard Data control. However, the RDO interface differs somewhat from the DAO/Jet interface. But I think you'll find that the RDO model has all the functionality you need; in fact, many of the Jet methods and properties that the RDO model lacks were in the DAO model only to support Jet's ISAM heritage.

The RDO model is designed around the ODBC API: it supports an object hierarchy parallel to that used by the API. This approach gives you more control over the user interface and the back-end interface as well as a lot more flexibility—however, it can be very dangerous. The RDO model exposes the ODBC handles you'll need to use direct ODBC calls. So if RDO doesn't support some required feature, you can attempt to use the ODBC API to implement it. However, I don't recommend that you depend on direct API calls. In most cases, you can use the built-in RDO properties and methods to get the job done.

Remote Data Objects are virtually unchanged since Visual Basic 5.0—new features were put in the ADO interface instead of in RDO. No, Microsoft hasn't abandoned RDO; it has simply shifted its attention over to RDO's (eventual) replacement: ADO.

ADO

ADO is the newest data interface to emerge from the badger works at Microsoft. This object interface to OLE DB was introduced for use with Microsoft Internet Information Server (IIS) and has been upgraded twice since then. ADO 2.0 ships with Visual Basic 6.0. Because it's simply an ActiveX object library like RDO, you can use it with any ActiveX component host. As initially implemented, ADO exposed a small subset of RDO 2.0's functionality. However, ADO 2.0 encompasses much of the functionality of RDO, DAO, and VBSQL and is destined to become the new "all-in-one" programming interface.

The ActiveX Data Control (more fondly known as the ADO Data control) is a direct replacement for both the RemoteData control and the Data control. It's designed to work with ADO instead of DAO or RDO. It binds and works pretty much like the other Data Source controls—even those you write yourself.

In a small way, I've tried to help guide the evolution of this new data access interface—but not as much as I would have liked. As I write this book, we're still months away from seeing the first ADO 2.0 application. Sure, ADO 1.0 and 1.5 made great strides toward replacing RDO functionality. However, you might find that ADO 2.0 has been implemented a bit differently than you might have been led to believe. No, there won't be any wizards to convert your code from RDO or DAO to ADO. To make such conversions easier, however, I wrote a white paper, "ADO from an RDO Developer's Point of View," in the fall of 1997. In this paper, I outline many of the ways that ADO 1.5 doesn't match up with RDO 2.0 and show that the task of converting will be somewhat daunting. You'll find the ADO 2.0 version of this paper in Chapter 34. In a nutshell, I recommend that if ADO works for your new design, use it. But don't be afraid of using RDO—it'll be around for awhile. ADO is certainly the better choice for distributed architectures and the Web because it supports disjoint result sets that can be easily passed over the wires. RDO, on the other hand, has something ADO has yet to earn: experience.

Data Interface Summary

Table 2-1 summarizes the capabilities of the six interface choices to access SQL Server from Visual Basic.

Understanding the Low-Level Interfaces

In this section, I'll explain how SQL Server uses TDS protocol to converse with the outside world. All the data access interfaces translate their API or object-based interfaces into TDS—some more efficiently than others, and some more completely than others.

DB-Library

DB-Library (DBLIB) is the set of C-language API functions that do for C developers what the VBSQL functions do for Visual Basic developers. DBLIB was the first "native" interface to SQL Server and was exposed quite nicely to Visual Basic developers by an interface that I dubbed VBSQL. (Yes, I confess, I really did coin the term VBSQL.) This interface is not obsolete (they made me say that). However, it has been replaced twice by more recent data access interfaces—first

Table 2-1
Visual Basic Data Access Interface Choices for SQL Server

Interface	Comments
VBSQL 16-bit and 32-bit support	Similar to DBLIB. High-speed, low-level API. Accesses virtually all Microsoft SQL Server 6.5 features and the core 7.0 features. Very small footprint and broad acceptance as a production-level interface. Used only with SQL Server. Uses custom Declare files to access C functions especially adapted for Visual Basic. Status: Obsolete.
ODBC API 16-bit and 32-bit support	High-speed, low-level, database-independent interface for relational data sources. Accesses virtually all SQL Server features, although fewer than VBSQL. Uses custom Declare files to access C-based functions. No specific Visual Basic support. Declare files are hard to find. Binding and 32-bit string issues make interface complex. Status: Aging. Still has widespread support, but being replaced by OLE DB.
DAO/Jet 16-bit (Visual Basic version 3.0, 4.0) and 32-bit support (Visual Basic version 4.0 and later)	Upper middleware for ISAM databases, with the ability to access ODBC data sources. Faster development, slower performance. Limited support of SQL Server features—especially stored procedures and multiple result sets. Can bind to specific Visual Basic controls. Status: Basically static. Few changes being made at this point.
DAO/ODBCDirect 32-bit support only	Object interface that remaps DAO objects to equivalent RDO objects. Same support for SQL Server as RDO. Asynchronous operations, but no events. Faster than Jet, slightly slower than API-based models. Status: No significant improvements since Visual Basic 5.0 SP3.
RDO 32-bit support only	Thin object-oriented interface for ODBC API. Same support for SQL Server as ODBC API but far easier and safer to program. Advanced batch-mode cursor library. Extensive asynchronous and event-driven support. Application can use bound controls or RDO programmatic interface. Generally faster than Jet, but somewhat slower than API-based models. Status: No significant improvements since Visual Basic 5.0 SP3.
ADO 32-bit support only	Thin object-oriented interface that maps OLE DB API. Version 2.0 provides similar (although not identical) functionality as RDO 2.0. Support for virtually all SQL Server features. Status: Up-and-coming replacement for all of the above.

by the ODBC API and more recently by OLE DB. SQL Server 7.0 and all previous versions of SQL Server support DBLIB, but it hasn't changed since the last release of SQL Server 6.5. In addition, I'm hearing more and more questions from people trying to maintain VBSQL applications after having installed Windows NT 4.0 and its numerous service packs and the latest versions of SQL Server 6.5. No, I haven't tried to replicate these errors, but I suspect that there might be some fundamental problems here as the support libraries required to run DB-Library are falling further and further behind. This fairly dismal status report should provide you with even more incentive to move off this interface and on to something more universally supported—if you can.

If you still want to use VBSQL, and you don't own a licensed copy, you can purchase it by ordering the SQL Server, Developer's Edition, which includes the SQL Server Programmer's Toolkit. It also includes the SQL Server Transact-SQL Reference. VBSQL is also included with Visual Basic 5.0 and 6.0, Enterprise Editions, on the Microsoft Developer Network (MSDN) subscription service CD, and on the CD included with this book—yes, the latest 16-bit and 32-bit versions. If you use the control on this book's companion CD, you still need to get a license for it by buying MSDN, SQL Server Developer Edition, or Visual Basic 5.0, Enterprise Edition.

The VBSQL libraries do not support all the DBLIB functions—but, fortunately, you won't need all of them. For example, C developers spend a significant amount of time dealing with fairly involved binding of SQL arguments to C data types. This binding is completely unnecessary in Visual Basic because virtually all arguments are returned in the form of variants that can be converted, as necessary, with built-in Visual Basic functions—or are converted automatically as you assign values to variables.

NOTE VBSQL is really a "VB-ized" interface to a C library, making it very different from a purely C interface as implemented by the ODBC API.

In actuality, most VBSQL functions are merely linkages to C-based DBLIB functions. You'll see, however, that a number of Visual Basic functions have no C equivalents. For example, the SQLOpenConnection function isn't supported in C; this VBSQL "utility" function is provided to perform a series of C calls that are normally sent as a set.

Two-phase commit

Another set of C functions not supported in VBSQL (or the ODBC API) is the two-phase commit protocol, which is used to keep two or more SQL Server databases in synchronization. This protocol is fairly complex, as DBLIB logic goes. It involves setting up a special dialog with each of the servers being used. To ensure completion of the transaction if something goes wrong before all the servers can finish the operation, the protocol logs the transaction with a mother server. Since the VBSQL interface doesn't support this protocol, I recommend that you write a separate C-language program (or dynamic-link library) to perform this operation with DBLIB if you must use the two-phase commit. Even C developers think long and hard before implementing two-phase commit, and once you take a close look at automatic Distributed Transaction Coordinator (DTC) features in SQL Server 6.*x* and later, you might decide that you won't miss two-phase commit at all. Better yet, consider using Microsoft Transaction Server to do the job.

ODBC

Open Database Connectivity (ODBC) is one of the most misunderstood interfaces that Microsoft supports. The term *ODBC* has been used to mean everything from a database-independent application programming interface to the data access interface used in Visual Basic 2.0. If you ask a dozen developers which interface is faster, or better or easier to use, ODBC will often come out on the bottom. Unfortunately, much of this derision is unfounded. ODBC *can* be just as fast, just as good, and just as easy as other interfaces if used correctly. But that's the rub—many developers don't use it correctly. It's kinda like using cold-drink cups to hold hot coffee. After about a minute, you learn some science about the melting point of wax. And now you either hate paper cups, coffee, the burger place, or the kid behind the counter who just started on Tuesday.

ODBC is really a (relational) database-neutral API based on the SQL Access development group's specification. No, this group is not associated with the Microsoft Access team. To be more specific, an application can write to the ODBC API and access different relational data sources simply by attaching different ODBC drivers. Theoretically, an ODBC application could connect to SQL Server via the SQL server driver, and to an Oracle database via the Oracle driver, with no need for a change in the application's executable. (And, theoretically, an application could also connect in the same way to a Jet database via the Jet ODBC driver. Yes, Microsoft did develop an ODBC driver, a limited one, that can read and write to Jet databases by using the ODBC API. It ships with Office and now with Visual Basic.) At this point, there are dozens of ODBC drivers that permit ODBC application front ends to reach virtually every kind of database; I also hear rumors about an 80-column card driver being supported by IBM.

> **NOTE** As a developer of ODBC drivers, you have a choice: Do you want your driver to expose some or all functionality of the database management system, or should your driver make the database management system look like a lowest-common-denominator generic database? The SQL Server ODBC driver can exploit much of the SQL server's functionality, and it allows an application to make the ODBC equivalents of most of the calls it normally would have made via DBLIB. Execution of stored procedures and triggers that generally aren't supported in other server-based database engines is fully supported here. If your code takes advantage of specific database engine features that aren't universally supported, you might end up where you started—with a database-specific application. This time, however, you will have written this database-specific application with a generic interface that might not be able to use all the database features you need.

The difficulty you might experience in programming to the generic ODBC interface is similar to what you'll experience when you use any other API-based interface. There are about 55 ODBC APIs; VBSQL has over 120. ODBC is as fast an interface as DBLIB or VBSQL, but ODBC is less aware of SQL Server–specific features. However, the ODBC functions are more complex than their VBSQL equivalents. Each ODBC call is designed to accept many, many more arguments— and each argument has many, many options. As a point of comparison, the *Microsoft ODBC Programmer's Reference and SDK Guide* contains over 800 pages of options, but the VBSQL programmer's reference for Visual Basic is not even half that long.

What about Visual Basic and ODBC?

The Jet database engine, which ships with Visual Basic, Microsoft Visual C++, and Office applications, connects to external non-ISAM databases via the ODBC API as do RDO, ADO, and ODBCDirect. When you use DAO/Jet to access ODBC databases, you use DAO or the Data control to write your code, not the ODBC API. Jet builds and submits queries to the external server via the ODBC API and driver manager. Without stealing the thunder from later chapters, let me just say here that the DAO implementation first introduced in Visual Basic 4.0 is a significant improvement over the DAO implementation in earlier versions. Part III of this guide details how all the DAO, Jet, and ODBCDirect pieces fit together in Visual Basic.

OLE DB

This interface is described as "A general-purpose set of interfaces designed to let developers build data access tools as components using the Component Object Model (COM). OLE DB enables applications to have uniform access to data stored in DBMS and non-DBMS information containers, while continuing to take advantage of the benefits of database technology without having to transfer data from its place of origin to a DBMS." Well, that's the definition up on the Web—it's almost enough to cross Mr. Date's eyes. What this really means is that OLE DB is Microsoft's newest low-level data access interface. As a Visual Basic developer, do you care? Sure you do, because you can use OLE DB technology to get at lots more data sources. OLE DB calls these "information containers" or "providers." Eventually, OLE DB will have providers for the vast majority of data sources, including Jet, SQL Server, and Oracle (to start with), mail, directories, and about any other source of data you can describe. And here's the really neat part: you can write your own OLE DB provider in Visual Basic 6.0. This way you can support your obscure or proprietary database with your own Visual Basic–authored data provider.

OLE DB is part of Microsoft's Universal Data Access platform. This architecture was designed to facilitate development of multitier enterprise applications that require access to diverse relational or nonrelational data sources across intranets or the Internet. Universal Data Access consists of a collection of software components that interact with each other using a common set of system-level interfaces defined by OLE DB. Universal Data Access components consist of data providers, which contain and expose data; data consumers, which use data; and service components, which process and transform data (for example, query processors and cursor engines).

OLE DB provides four discrete services that your code can leverage to build your specific data access solutions. These services in the Universal Data Access platform work with each other via the service component architecture.

- A cursor service provides an efficient, client-side cache with local scrolling, filtering, and sorting capabilities.

- A synchronization service provides batch updating and synchronizing of data cached in the client or middle tier.

- A shape service allows the construction of hierarchically organized data with dynamic behavior under updates.

- A remote data service provides efficient marshaling of data in multitier environments over connected or disconnected networking scenarios.

OLE DB defines interfaces for accessing and manipulating all types of data. These interfaces will be used not just by data-consuming applications but also by database providers. By splitting databases apart, they'll be able to use the resulting components efficiently. For example, components called service providers can be invoked to expose more sophisticated data manipulation and navigation interfaces on behalf of simple data providers.

No, you don't need to learn how to program to the OLE DB API. Actually, it would be very hard (if not impossible) to do from Visual Basic. That's where ADO comes in. ADO is the object-oriented interface to OLE DB that you *can* and should be programming to instead of VBSQL and ODBC.

Microsoft OLE DB Provider for ODBC Drivers

The Microsoft OLE DB Provider for ODBC Drivers allows ADO to connect to any ODBC data source. As you know, ODBC drivers are available for every major DBMS in use today, including SQL Server, Access (Jet database engine), and Microsoft FoxPro, as well as non-Microsoft database products such as Oracle. The OLE DB provider for ODBC is free-threaded and Unicode enabled. In addition, the provider supports transactions, although different DBMS engines offer different types of transaction support. For example, Access supports nested transactions, up to five levels deep.

The OLE DB provider for ODBC is the default for ADO, and when used with SQL Server 6.5, all provider-dependent ADO 1.5 properties and methods are supported, except as noted in the ADO language reference topics. I'll weigh the positive and negative aspects of this provider in Part V.

Taking the Next Step

From here on, I'm going to assume that your primary goal is to develop a high-performance front-end application or component that interacts with SQL Server. If your data needs are so limited that SQL Server is not really an option and won't be one in the near future, you need to consider DAO/Jet or some other development strategy. If that's your situation, take this guide back to the store and try to get your money back—or, better yet, put it on the shelf and take it back down a year from now if you discover that your design isn't giving you the performance you expected. Otherwise, let's get busy and create some samples that use DAO/Jet, DAO/ODBCDirect, RDO, and ADO.

3

Data Access: A Jump Start

Getting Ready to Create Samples

DAO/Jet Road Test

DAO/ODBCDirect Road Test

RDO Road Test

ADO Road Test

Comparing the Samples

n this chapter, I'll walk you through eight simple Microsoft Visual Basic applications that access Microsoft SQL Server. These applications use the DAO/Jet, DAO/ODBCDirect, RDO, and ADO data access interfaces introduced in Chapter 2. And you won't have to slog through twenty-plus chapters of information before getting to try out the techniques we're about to examine. Unlike earlier editions of the *Hitchhiker's Guide*, this chapter no longer includes samples from VBSQL and the ODBC API. If you still need examples of those interfaces, you should dig out an earlier edition of the *Hitchhiker's Guide*. Data source control examples are included in the DAO/Jet, DAO/ODBCDirect, RDO, and ADO sections of this chapter—but the jury is still out on this new "drag and drop" binding paradigm, so don't get your hopes up. The other interfaces (that is, other than RDO and ADO) are pretty dated at this point, so I think this lightweight approach will help you focus on the mainstream techniques.

Getting Ready to Create Samples

Each sample application performs the following three tasks:

- Opens a connection to SQL Server

- Executes a query based on a user-supplied value

- Returns values from the result set into a grid control or to a set of text boxes on a Visual Basic form

Because the sample applications aren't expected to edit the results, I haven't provided the additional code that you would need for managing updates. The applications use the *pubs* database, included with SQL Server, so you can test them with any version of SQL Server.

Even though you could develop the sample applications in different versions of Microsoft Visual Basic, for the most part, I'm assuming that you're using Visual Basic 6.0. The source code for all the samples is on this guide's companion CD as Visual Basic 6.0 projects.

Creating a Data Source Name

For the samples in this chapter and the others you'll want to execute later in the guide, you need to register a data source name (DSN). A DSN contains parameters from the connect string and other information provided by the developer when it is installed. Once registered, the DSN includes the name of the data source, the name of the server, the type of driver, and other data about the network interface and security settings. In 32-bit systems, all this information is kept in the Microsoft Windows Registry, so it can be somewhat costly to retrieve—but faster than trying to get on MSN on a rainy Saturday.

You can set up DSNs in a variety of ways, including using the ODBC control panel applet, using programmatic API calls, and simply copying files. Some connection techniques don't use DSNs at all. In fact, the ADO and OLE DB interface doesn't usually need DSNs because it uses several new connection strategies that we'll talk about in the ADO chapters (Part V). In this chapter, we'll be creating a User DSN; we'll discuss the other types of DSNs in later chapters.

> **TIP** In Appendix A, you'll find out how to set up your own test database to use in the examples in later chapters.

For the purposes of the samples in this chapter, we need to create a User DSN that points to your SQL Server's *pubs* database. To do this, open the ODBC applet in the Windows Control Panel. This starts the ODBC Data Source Administrator. On the User DSN tab, you have the options of adding, removing, or configuring an ODBC DSN. Click the Add button if you don't already have a DSN that points to the *pubs* database. If you choose to add a new DSN, select *SQL Server* as the driver name, as shown in Figure 3-1. If you don't see *SQL Server* in the list of available drivers, either you didn't check it in the Visual Basic Setup dialog boxes or it's been misplaced. Go back and reinstall it now—without this driver, you won't get anywhere.

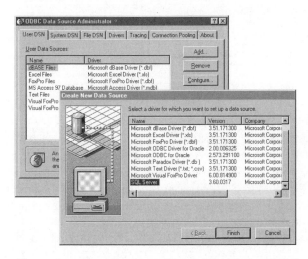

Figure 3-1 *Creating a new User DSN with the ODBC control panel applet*

NOTE The ODBC drivers that ship with Visual Basic 5.0 don't work with Sybase SQL Server. I understand that Sybase, Visigenic (now Inprise/Borland), and other ODBC driver vendors have suitable Sybase drivers.

Clicking the Finish button starts a wizard to create a SQL Server DSN, as shown in Figure 3-2. In this first screen, enter the following information:

- **The name of your data source** This doesn't have to be any particular name, but it should be something that identifies where the SQL Server data is coming from. I usually name my data sources after the database, *not* the server. (For the purposes of this sample application, use *pubs* as the new DSN.)

- **An optional description of the data source** Again, you have free rein; enter anything that helps identify this data source. This information shows up in the ODBC dialog boxes.

- **The network name of the server that is running SQL Server** Nope, don't add \\ to the name. For Microsoft Windows NT or OS/2 servers, simply give the server name. It's more complicated if the server is somewhere out on the World Wide Web, but we'll talk about that later.

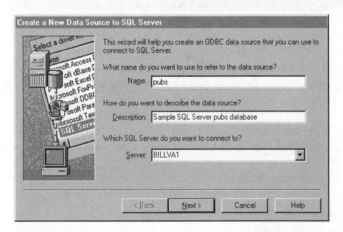

Figure 3-2 *The first screen of the data source wizard, which you use to create a new data source to SQL Server*

Click Next. This takes you to the security screen shown in Figure 3-3, in which you describe how ODBC should try to get through the network and SQL Server security. Although you might have to supply a login ID and a password at this time, these values are not stored in the DSN. If you plan to provide a SQL Server login ID and password, choose the With SQL Server Authentication... option and enter the login ID and password in the boxes provided. If you don't know your login ID and password, you need to get them from your system administrator. If you plan to pass your current Windows user ID to SQL Server and let it use Windows NT authentication, simply click Next to go to the next dialog box.

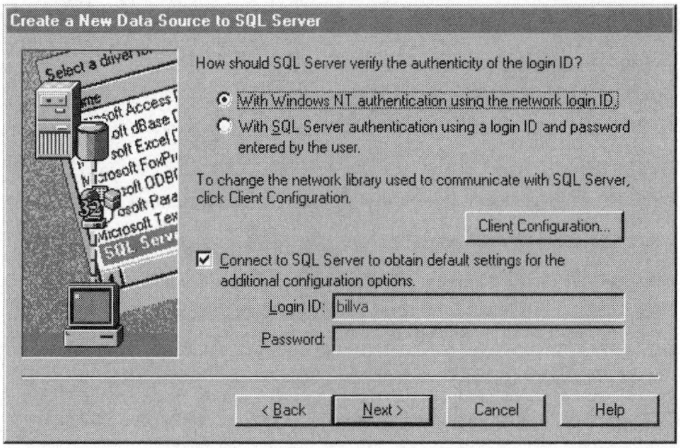

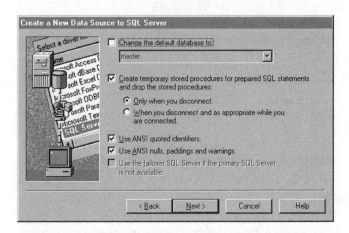

Figure 3-3 *The second screen of the data source wizard, which allows you to specify authentication and configuration information to connect to SQL Server*

NOTE Visual Basic 6.0 includes the new ODBC 3.6 ODBC Driver Manager and support code that has a (mostly) new set of interactive ODBC DSN dialog boxes. Although these might not be familiar to old ODBC hands, they are pretty intuitive and offer far more flexibility than previous versions.

When you press Next on the security dialog box, ODBC attempts to make a connection to your SQL Server. Yes, it must be running and recognize the ID and password provided. If it doesn't, you'll hang for 60 seconds or so while ODBC waits for some server somewhere to respond. If you do get in, however, you'll see the screen shown in Figure 3-4.

Figure 3-4 *The third screen of the data source wizard, which allows you to specify the name of the default SQL Server database*

You are now connected to SQL Server. To choose the default database from the list of available databases, check the Change The Default Database To checkbox and choose *pubs* from the drop-down list. Don't worry about the other options at this time—the default options are fine.

Depending on your version of ODBC, you'll typically have two more screens that you can ignore for now, so simply press Next until you get to the last screen.

When you press the Finish button on the last screen, the dialog box shown in Figure 3-5 is displayed. This dialog box lists the configuration information.

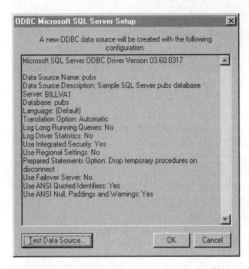

Figure 3-5 *Dialog box that shows selected data source configuration information*

Here's where you get to verify the settings you just made. Click the Test Data Source button to test the data source—if this doesn't work, go back and make whatever changes the error dialog boxes call for. When you connect successfully, press OK and your DSN will be registered for you.

Using Visual Basic 6.0

Each of the samples in this chapter is started from the Standard EXE or Data Project templates. You are presented with a choice of these templates when Visual Basic first begins. The Data Project template loads an uninitialized Data Environment and a Data Report along with the ADO Data control (Adodc) as well as other controls and references to ADO 2.0 and a number of other type libraries. We won't be using the Data Environment or Data Report, but it won't hurt to have them loaded.

To help you appreciate the tools and wizards available with Visual Basic, we're going build our sample applications the hard way first and then let Visual Basic do it for us in later chapters. This approach might seem like a pain (kind of like doing complex long division with a dull crayon), but it will demonstrate how much time you can save by letting Visual Basic do the work for you.

The Data Environment Designer

The newest member of the Visual Basic 6.0 team is the Data Environment Designer. This tool visually exposes objects in the database such as views, tables, and stored procedures and can also store and manage queries you write. All of these objects are ultimately exposed as ADO Command objects accessed by one or more ADO Connection objects. The enticing part of the Data Environment paradigm is its promise to let you drag one of these Command objects over to a form where Visual Basic installs a control and label for each column in the Recordset created by the Command. I've included an entire chapter on the Data Environment (Chapter 37), so we're going to leave any more discussion of this topic for later. For now, let's just stick with the more traditional approaches.

NOTE In Visual Basic 3.0, all language components were built in. In contrast, all versions of Visual Basic since 4.0 force you to specify the components required for an application, but only those that are really needed. This way, you need *not* include language support for DAO or other components if you don't need them. That's the good news. The bad news is that many of the default language elements built into Visual Basic 3.0 are *not* automatically included in Visual Basic projects: you must specifically *reference* them. This means that your code, which compiled just fine in Visual Basic 3.0, might not compile in later versions of Visual Basic unless you do some fancy footwork. (In some cases, there are several versions of the component to support different levels of backward compatibility—but that's another story.) In general, if you haven't referenced a library, you get an error message that complains about being unable to recognize a user-defined method or property.

Libraries and Controls Used with Samples

Each of the data interfaces used for the sample applications requires one or more supplementary data access libraries or components in order to function. These provide a programmatic or bound-control interface between Visual Basic and SQL Server. All of the components are included in Visual Basic 6.0, Enterprise Edition. Yes, you can use ADO with the Professional Edition. Table 3-1 lists the data interface libraries, and Table 3-2 lists the controls.

Table 3-1
Data Interface Libraries for the Sample Applications

Data Interface	Library
DAO/Jet	Microsoft DAO 3.51 Object Library
DAO/ODBCDirect	Microsoft DAO 3.51 Object Library
RDO	Microsoft Remote Data Object 2.0
ADO	Microsoft ActiveX Data Objects 2.0 Library

Table 3-2
Controls for the Sample Applications

Control	Name in Components Dialog Box	Toolbox Display
Data control	By default, is in Toolbox	
RemoteData control (MSRDC)	Microsoft Remote Data Control 6.0	
ADO Data control (Adodc)	Microsoft ADO Data Control 6.0	
MSFlexGrid control	Microsoft FlexGrid Control 6.0	
DataGrid control	Microsoft DataGrid Control 6.0	

Visual Basic Forms

Two types of Visual Basic forms are used in the samples. Because each data interface I describe in this chapter can be used with or without a data source control, I've created two different forms. Both forms contain a TextBox control that allows the user to enter a title to be searched in the *pubs* database. The results are displayed either in TextBox controls or in a MSFlexGrid or DataGrid control.

Form with a data source control

Figure 3-6 shows the form that uses a data source control to access SQL Server. This form contains a MSFlexGrid control, a data source control, and a TextBox control as well as Label and CommandButton controls. Depending on the sample (DAO/Jet, DAO/ODBCDirect, RDO, or ADO), the data source control will be the Data control, the RemoteData control, or the ADO Data control, respectively. (With the ADO sample, the DataGrid is used instead of MSFlexGrid.)

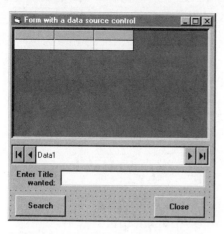

Figure 3-6   *Visual Basic form used for the DAO/Jet, DAO/ODBCDirect, RDO, and ADO samples that also use a data source control*

Form without a data source control

Figure 3-7 shows the form that doesn't use a data source control but instead uses the data interface directly to access SQL Server. This form contains one TextBox control to accept the name of the title that will be used as a search argument and three other TextBox controls (and labels) to display the resulting data. This form will be used for the DAO/Jet, DAO/ODBCDirect, RDO, and ADO samples that don't use a data source control.

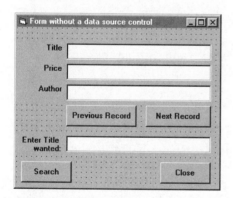

Figure 3-7   *Visual Basic form used for the DAO/Jet, DAO/ODBCDirect, RDO, and ADO samples that access the data interface directly and don't use a data source control*

DAO/Jet Road Test

In the past, when Visual Basic developers have needed to access SQL Server with a data object model, the DAO/Jet interface was their first (and sometimes only) choice. Figure 3-8 shows how SQL Server can be accessed using DAO/Jet.

Figure 3-8 *DAO/Jet interface to access SQL Server from Visual Basic*

The sample applications in this section illustrate the basic use of the DAO/Jet interface for accessing SQL Server with and without the Data control. In the "DAO/ODBCDirect Samples" section, we'll take a look at a way to bypass Jet by using the ODBCDirect.

DAO/Jet and Data Control Sample

The "default" Data control is a bound-control interface that by default connects the Jet database engine with SQL Server through the ODBC Driver Manager and the SQL Server ODBC driver. The Data control hasn't been used extensively in larger SQL Server shops up to now, but it's easy to set up and program. The Data control's real advantage is its ability to access the heterogeneous-join capability of the Jet engine and map complex page-based data (like TEXT and IMAGE columns) to picture box controls. To implement the sample application that uses the Data control, you need very little additional code. Simply set the form-control properties at design time. To set design-time properties, you'll need to add the Data control, set the Connect property, and set the DatabaseName property.

Adding the Data control

To begin, start a new Visual Basic project (Standard EXE) and add the Data control to the form. In current versions of Visual Basic, once you add the Data control to your form, the DAO object library is automatically referenced; with no additional hassle, you can now use both the Data control and DAO.

TIP When you install Visual Basic 5.0, the VB.INI file is reinstalled. The Visual Basic 5.0 version of the file doesn't include a line to activate the Data control, however, so if you expect to continue using the Data control from Visual Basic 3.0, add a line to the VB.INI file: DataAccess=1

Setting the Connect property

The Connect property is simply a string that tells the ODBC Driver Manager everything the interface needs to get you connected with your SQL Server. It includes which driver to use, the name of your server, and who is using it. It has about a dozen parameters—most of which are optional. Because most of the techniques we look at here use ODBC, we'll end up using the connect string one way or another. It turns out that ADO and OLE DB also use a similar string (called the ConnectString). To keep your life simple, these examples code the ODBC connect string with the minimum number of parameters.

Using the Properties window in Design mode (set the focus to the Data control and press F4), set the Data control's Connect property as shown below. Notice that this connect string sets the default database to *pubs*.

```
ODBC;UID=<your user ID>;PWD=<your password>;DATABASE=pubs;
```

NOTE You don't even have to include the *Database=pubs* argument if you've set the default database in the *pubs* DSN or your system administrator has set one for your login ID.

Use your own SQL Server user ID (UID) and password (PWD) in this string. (If you don't know your user ID and password, check with your SQL server administrator.) Let's say that your user ID is *Fred* and your password is *MidField*. Here's what the connect string will look like:

```
ODBC;UID=Fred;PWD=MidField;DATABASE=pubs;
```

TIP Don't try to pretty up the connect string by adding extra spaces— these are seen as part of the values, so leave them out.

If you're using Windows NT authentication (integrated security), one of the features available with SQL Server 4.2 and later versions, you won't need a user ID or password because the Windows NT environment can manage user security, in which case your Windows network domain user name and password will be used to validate your access to SQL Server. And with ODBC 3.0 and later, you'll have to add *Trusted_Connection=Yes* to your connect strings if you still expect the system to let you in. If you want to use Windows NT authentication, use the following connect string:

```
ODBC;UID=;PWD=;Trusted_Connection=Yes;
```

The ODBC layer interprets this string as a signal to attempt to use Windows NT authentication.

TIP DAO/Jet and DAO/ODBCDirect prefix their connect strings with "ODBC;". This argument should *not* be used for RDO or ADO connect strings.

Setting the DatabaseName property

Now set the Data control's DatabaseName property to the ODBC DSN that you've already established. We already set up one named *pubs*—remember?

When the time comes to communicate with the database, the connection settings are gathered from the DSN and from the Data control's ODBC connection properties. Values from the DSN provide the default values. The DSN doesn't include either the user ID or the password, however, although the values that were last used might be stored in the DSN as a default UID and PWD. Any details you don't provide at design time are gathered via ODBC-created dialog boxes at run time. To avoid these dialog boxes, be sure to provide all the required parameters to the Data control's Connect property or DSN entry. If the values you or your user supplies are wrong, these dialog boxes will *always* appear. No, DAO/Jet doesn't provide a way to turn off this behavior. We'll come back to the run-time connection dialog boxes again later when we get to the DAO/Jet chapters in Part III of this guide.

All the data interfaces except VBSQL require you to use a connect string and a DSN or its equivalent. In addition, all interfaces, including the ODBC API, support DSN-less and file-based DSN connections. Once you've created a DSN and a working connect string, you can use this information each time it's called for in the sample applications.

Don't bother with the rest of the Data control properties at this point. We're going to set them programmatically. Yes, this approach is a little tougher, but you can handle it—right?

Adding the MSFlexGrid control

To get a feel for how easy (or hard) it is to use the MSFlexGrid control, you can set up the control in Design mode, or you can simply use the sample from the companion CD. To set up the MSFlexGrid control yourself, you'll first need to select "Microsoft FlexGrid Control 6.0" in the Components dialog box, which can be accessed from the Project menu. When the MSFlexGrid control has been selected, it appears in your toolbox. Double-click its icon to add it to your form.

Setting the MSFlexGrid control properties

Once the MSFlexGrid control is added to your form, set its DataSource property to the Name property of the Data control being used. For example, for the DAO/Jet and DAO/ODBCDirect samples, set it to *Data1* or simply choose *Data1* from the drop-down list. You can't set this property in code at run time. Because we're going to execute a query that's built on the fly, you also can't use the Retrieve Fields feature of the MSFlexGrid control. Sure, you can set up a dummy query that returns the same columns that the working query returns, but we're going to let Visual Basic fill in the grid headings for us.

Next, right-click on the MSFlexGrid control, and choose Properties. On the General tab of the Property Pages window, set the Cols property to 3 and Fixed Cols to 0. We won't set the column headings because these are handled automatically when the Recordset populates the grid. If you want to, you can set AllowUserResizing to 1 - Columns to permit columns to be resized.

Adding the remaining controls

Table 3-3 lists all the controls needed for the samples that use a data source control. Add the remaining controls (TextBox, 2 CommandButtons, and Label) to the form, and set their Name properties as shown in this table.

Table 3-3
Controls for Samples That Use a Data Source Control

Control	Name
TextBox	TitleWanted
CommandButton	SearchButton
CommandButton	CloseButton
Label	(default name)
data source control (already added)	(default name)
grid control (already added)	(default name)

Once you add these controls, your form should look similar to the one shown in Figure 3-9.

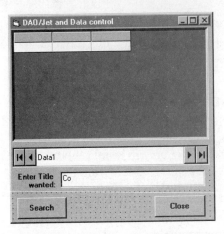

Figure 3-9 *DAO/Jet and Data control sample form with all the controls added*

Coding the SearchButton_Click event procedure

For the SearchButton_Click event procedure, we simply set the Data control's RecordSource property to the SQL query, as shown in the sample code that follows. (OK, this *is* a little complicated, but it's not unusual for a real-world application. After all, in most serious client/server applications, you don't just point to a single table and pull back all the rows; when your database tables have 100,000,000 rows, that would be a fatal mistake, not just an inconvenience. But *you* know that!) Note that the SQL query filters rows by using the value from the TitleWanted text box, concatenating the contents of the TextBox control with the SQL query and surrounding it with single quotes. When the result set is created with the Refresh method, I make sure the whole result set gets populated so that we can run another query later. To make sure you get this right, use a Debug statement to view the syntax before it is executed; leaving out the Debug statement is arrogant and angers the saints:

```
Private Sub SearchButton_Click()
Data1.RecordSource = "Select Title, Price," _
    & " Au_Fname + ' ' + Au_Lname Author" _
    & " From Titles T, TitleAuthor TA, Authors A" _
    & " Where T.Title_ID = TA.Title_ID" _
    & " And TA.Au_ID = A.AU_ID" _
    & " And Title like '%" & (TitleWanted) & "%'"
Debug.Print Data1.RecordSource
Data1.Refresh
End Sub
```

> **TIP** I only use the space underscore (_) line-continuation character here to get the long SQL statement to fit within the printed page. Visual Basic isn't very smart about dealing with continued code lines, and they tend to decrease performance. The only time you really need line-continuation characters is if the line is too long to parse. Don't use them just to make your code more readable.

The Data control's Refresh method is used to establish a connection and execute the query automatically. The Jet database engine processes the request and returns when (and only when) the first qualifying row is ready. The Data control then populates any bound controls and manages the current-row pointer.

Setting the Data control options property

If the syntax of the preceding SQL statement seems a little unusual, it's because the statement doesn't use Jet database engine SQL syntax. It was written in the Transact-SQL (TSQL) dialect, used exclusively by SQL Server. Therefore, you must tell the Jet database engine not to parse the query or check its syntax but simply to pass it through to SQL Server for processing. To do this, set the Data control's Options property to 64 (*dbSQLPassThrough*).

You can set this property at design time by setting it to 64 using the Data control's Property window, or you can do it in code:

```
Data1.Options=dbSQLPassthrough
```

TIP Don't hard-code the Options property to 64—always use the enumerated constant—*dbSQLPassThrough*. And don't use this constant when defining how a DAO query should be executed—that's *dbQSQLPassThrough*.

Because the query is using SQL PassThrough, the resulting Jet Recordset object allows only read-only access. You can set the Data control's ReadOnly property to True if you want to, but you don't really need to; it gets set automatically at run time.

Coding the CloseButton_Click event procedure

The Data control automatically manages the Data Access Object that it creates, so you don't need any special code to close databases or result sets. To end the application gracefully, however, add the following code to the CloseButton_Click event procedure:

```
Private Sub CloseButton_Click()
Unload Me
End Sub
```

Notice that I didn't just use an END statement here. That statement should be avoided like a cheap lawnmower, since it doesn't permit Visual Basic procedures to finish their applications correctly.

Evaluating the results

When you run this application, Visual Basic passes control to the unseen code managed by the Data control. Until the Data control has connected and run the initial query (if any), you won't see the initial form. This is a fundamental problem with the Data control—it makes it appear that your entire application

SQL Server 6.0 made a fairly radical change in its SQL parser. Basically, it adopted a SQL syntax virtually (but not exactly) identical to that used by the Jet database engine. This change means that the join syntax you use when working with Microsoft Access should work almost without change in TSQL queries. I've left these examples in the old format because they still work against SQL Server 6.0 and against older versions of SQL Server as well. It's tough to teach this old dog new tricks. I'll talk about the differences in syntax again later.

is terribly slow to load. You'll find out how to negate this problem (at least partially) in the DAO chapters (Part III). Once control returns to your application, Visual Basic and the Data control automatically display the rows of the Recordset object according to the latest results of the SQL query. Since we didn't fill in a value in the RecordSource property, no rows are returned, so the MSFlexGrid shouldn't be filled in.

When you perform a search by entering a title and clicking the search button, the results will be displayed in the MSFlexGrid control. In accordance with the size of the MSFlexGrid control, the first and nth rows of the Recordset object are displayed. If more than one title matches the query criteria, you can use the MSFlexGrid control's scroll bars to move either forward or backward to another row in the Recordset object. To end the application, click the Close button. This action unceremoniously unloads your form.

DAO/Jet Sample

By default, the DAO data interface connects to the Jet database engine, which interacts with SQL Server through the ODBC Driver Manager and the SQL Server ODBC driver, as was shown in Figure 3-8.This sample application illustrates the basic use of the DAO/Jet interface for accessing SQL Server without benefit of the Data control. In this case, we implement the data binding and create the data objects in code. We also include code to clean up the DAO interface when we're done. (All these ancillary operations were managed automatically by the Data control in the previous sample application.)

Creating the form

In this sample, the current row of the result set will be displayed in three text boxes instead of in the MSFlexGrid control. Sure, you could use a grid control in unbound mode, but that would be overkill for this sample application; besides, using the TextBox controls illustrates a more basic type of front end— a model that many serious front-end applications still use.

To get started, open a new Visual Basic project (Standard EXE), and set up your form with the controls listed in Table 3.4.

Table 3-4
Controls for Samples That Don't Use a Data Source Control

Control	Name
TextBox control array	DataFound(0), DataFound(1), DataFound(2)
Four CommandButton controls	PreviousButton, NextButton, SearchButton, CloseButton
TextBox	TitleWanted
Four Label controls	(default names)

Once you add these controls, your form should look similar to the one shown in Figure 3-10.

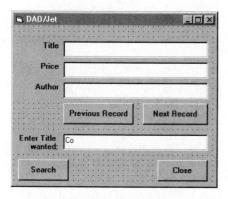

Figure 3-10   *DAO/Jet sample form with all the controls added*

The navigation buttons (Previous Record and Next Record) are used to navigate up and down the result set. When you click these buttons, your event procedure will move the current record pointer to the adjacent record. This sample application, as already mentioned, uses the DAO/Jet interface without also using the Data control. If we were using it along with the Data control, however, we would note that the Data control also has buttons that reposition the current record pointer to the first and last records of the result set. We could add first-record and last-record buttons if we wanted to; they would make the code for this sample application only a couple lines longer.

The rest of the work for this sample application is done in code. Since you won't be using bound controls, you need to code procedures that move data from the current record to the TextBox controls. You also have to code procedures to open the database, create the result set, and close the DAO objects when you're done with them. (I added code to disable the Previous Record and Next Record buttons when clicking them would have caused problems.) For the most part, you don't need to worry about data type binding—it's done for you automatically.

Setting a reference to DAO

Using the References dialog box in Visual Basic (available via the Project menu), add a reference to DAO. As we saw in Chapter 2 (Figure 2-2 on page 19), you can choose from two to a half-dozen different DAO libraries; for now, choose the Microsoft DAO 3.51 Object Library if you're working with 32-bit Visual Basic and the Microsoft DAO 2.5 Object Library if you're working with 16-bit Visual Basic (Visual Basic 4.0). If you don't set a reference to DAO, your application will fail to compile as you make your first reference to a DAO method or object. (In the previous sample application, the DAO reference was automatic when the Data control was added to the form.)

Coding the global variables

To start with, declare global variables that are used to contain the Database and Recordset objects created in other procedures:

```
Dim Db As Database
Dim Rs As Recordset
Dim SQL As String
```

Coding the Form_Load event procedure

Now we'll write code to open the database connection and instantiate the Database object. In this case, instead of just setting design-time properties, we'll use code in the Form_Load event procedure, as shown below.

The code below uses a connect string with the following format:

```
ODBC;UID=<your user ID>;PWD=<your password>;
```

Enter your SQL Server user ID and password in this string, just as you did in the previous sample application. (And if you *still* don't know your user ID and password, consider getting into a new line of work.)

The following code assumes that the workstation running the sample application has already been logged on with a valid user ID and password to a Windows NT domain and that SQL Server has been set up with Windows NT authentication:

```
Private Sub Form_Load()
On Error GoTo FLEH
Set Db = OpenDatabase("pubs", False, False, "odbc;uid=;pwd=;")
Exit Sub
FLEH:
    Debug.print "Error:"; Err, Error$
    Msgbox "Could not open connection"
        Resume Next
End Sub
```

If your error handler gets a 429 error ("ActiveX component can't create object or return reference to this object"), you didn't reference the DAO objects properly or you misspelled one of the objects. Press F1 to get more details on this error. If you get a successful open, the Database object in the *Db* variable is valid and can be used to create your record set.

In the object-oriented world, you have classes or types of objects. You also have $12 words like *instantiate*, which means "to create an instance or copy of one class of object." Thus a rabbit is a *class* of object, a specific lop-eared bunny is an *instance* of the rabbit object, and what two consenting lop-eared bunnies do in the privacy of their own hutch is a form of *instantiation*.

Coding the SearchButton_Click event procedure

In this procedure, the query is executed and the data is fetched into the Recordset object. The same SQL statement that was used in the previous DAO/Jet and Data control sample is used here.

As was done in the DAO/Jet and Data control sample, the query uses the value in the TitleWanted text box. Notice that we use the MoveLast method to fully populate the result set (and free up the connection for another operation). This SQL syntax is still not compatible with the Jet engine, however, so we use the SQL pass-through option again. In this case, it is specified in the OpenRecordset method with the value *dbSQLPassThrough*:

```
Private Sub SearchButton_Click()
SQL = "Select Title, Price," _
    & " Au_Fname + ' ' + Au_Lname Author" _
    & " From Titles T, TitleAuthor TA, Authors A" _
    & " Where T.Title_ID = TA.Title_ID" _
    & " And TA.Au_ID = A.AU_ID" _
    & " And Title like '%" & (TitleWanted) & "%'"
Debug.Print SQL
Set Rs = Db.OpenRecordset(SQL, dbOpenSnapshot, dbSQLPassThrough)
If Rs.EOF = False Then
    Rs.MoveLast     ' To fully populate the Recordset
    Rs.MoveFirst
    If Rs.RecordCount > 0 Then ShowRecord
Else
    MsgBox "No records found. Choose another title to search for."
End If
End Sub
```

Coding the ShowRecord procedure

Once the data has been fetched into the Recordset object, the next step is to move the data into the DataFound TextBox controls, where the user can see it. This procedure assumes that the Recordset object has been created. If there is no current record—as when the current record pointer is positioned beyond either end of the Recordset object, or when there are no records at all—the appropriate buttons are disabled and no attempt is made to reference the current record:

```
Sub ShowRecord()
' Fill the DataFound text boxes from the Recordset.
If Rs.BOF = False And Rs.EOF = False Then
    ' Note the three different ways to address
    ' the Recordset fields.
    DataFound(0) = Rs!Title
    DataFound(1) = Format(Rs("Price"), "$###.##")
    DataFound(2) = Rs(2)
End If
PreviousButton.Enabled = Not Rs.BOF
NextButton.Enabled = Not Rs.EOF
End Sub
```

Coding the Recordset navigation buttons

The navigation buttons can allow the user to see any additional rows of the result set. These buttons use the MoveNext and MovePrevious methods to position the pointer for the current record within the record set. Note that this code doesn't prevent movement past either end of the Recordset object; the ShowRecord procedure automatically deals with this contingency:

```
Private Sub NextButton_Click()
Rs.MoveNext
ShowRecord
End Sub

Private Sub PreviousButton_Click()
Rs.MovePrevious
ShowRecord
End Sub
```

Coding the CloseButton_Click event procedure

To make sure your application leaves no operations pending and closes the connection to SQL Server cleanly, close both the Recordset object and the Database object before quitting the application. In addition, to end the application gracefully, unload the form in the CloseButton_Click event procedure:

```
Private Sub CloseButton_Click()
Rs.Close
Db.Close
Unload Me
End Sub
```

Evaluating the results

Notice that the DAO/Jet *coded* application loads much faster than the DAO/Jet and Data control sample. It might also run faster, but because of the nature of the query we're using, you probably won't notice the difference. When you perform a search by entering a title and clicking the search button, your code executes the OpenRecordset method. When control returns to your application, your code displays the first row of the Recordset object in the TextBox controls. If more than one title matches the query criteria, you can use the navigation buttons to move to another record (either forward or backward) in the result set and display the data from the new current record. Once you position the current record pointer off either end of the result set, the controls are disabled.

This application has taken considerably more code to implement the same basic functionality as was provided by the DAO/Jet and Data control sample (46 lines vs. 8 lines). Does this mean that the Data control or other data source control applications can dramatically reduce the code required to implement data access solutions? Well, yes—but at a price. The data source control applications take a significant amount of control away from your applications. Many developers find this an unacceptable expense that their customers aren't willing to pay.

DAO/ODBCDirect Road Test

Earlier we saw how the DAO data interface connects by default to the Jet database engine, which interacts with SQL Server through the ODBC Driver Manager and the SQL Server ODBC driver. The samples in this section show how to bypass the Jet database engine completely and create a DAO interface to SQL Server via the ODBCDirect interface. DAO objects, methods, and properties created using ODBCDirect can still be used in conjunction with the Data control or by themselves. That is, once you open a connection using the Data control, the DAO objects it exposes through its properties can be used as if you had created them in code. Even though ODBCDirect uses the 32-bit RDO libraries under the hood, you can't use the objects yourself. But there's no reason why you can't create your own RDO objects—even with an application that also uses ODBCDirect. You'll need the Enterprise license, however.

Starting with Visual Basic version 5.0, you can use DAO to access SQL Server without Jet. That is, you can create an ODBCDirect Workspace object that connects with SQL Server through the ODBC Driver Manager and the SQL Server ODBC driver, as shown in Figure 3-11. However, using this technique disables any benefit DAO derived from Jet—without enabling all of the flexibility and features of RDO.

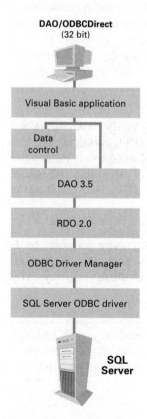

Figure 3-11 *DAO/ODBCDirect interface to access SQL Server from Visual Basic*

The following two sections describe how to use ODBCDirect with and without the Data control. In the final analysis, the RDO interface might be especially interesting for client/server developers—a lot more interesting than using DAO to access RDO.

DAO/ODBCDirect and Data Control Sample

ODBCDirect is probably not as interesting to SQL Server front-end developers as it is to Microsoft Office and other Visual Basic for Application (VBA) hosts that need to access SQL Server. Because these platforms don't include a Visual Basic Enterprise Edition or other RDO license (which is required to access RDO directly), use of the ODBCDirect interface to RDO is a viable, albeit circuitous, approach.

To implement the sample application that uses the Data control in ODBCDirect mode, you need very little additional code—simply set the form-control properties at design time. To do this, start from the DAO/Jet and Data control sample, and set the Connect, DefaultType, and DatabaseName properties as described below.

Getting started

Start from the DAO/Jet and Data control sample, and verify that you have a reference set to DAO. Even though ODBCDirect uses RDO, you don't have to add a reference to the RDO 2.0 library—unless you plan to use it elsewhere. No, you can't use the RDO objects that the Data control references—these are hidden by DAO.

Setting the Data Control Properties

To enable ODBCDirect, set the Data control's DefaultType property to *1-UseODBC*. That's it. Once you set this property, RDO is used to implement all of the Data control's functions. You need to clear the Options property—you don't have to tell DAO to bypass Jet.

Setting the Connect property

The Connect property is set just as it is for the DAO/Jet and Data control sample. Verify that the Data control's Connect property is set as follows:

```
ODBC;UID=<your user ID>;PWD=<your password>;
```

Enter your SQL Server user ID (UID) and password (PWD) into this string. Yes, you RDO types, you still need to prefix the connect string with *ODBC;*— this is still DAO. Again, you don't need to include your user ID and password if you're using Windows NT authentication.

NOTE   If you don't prefix your connect string with *ODBC;*, you might get nada, nothing, no error, zippo—including no data. With later versions of ODBC, however, an error might be returned.

Setting the DatabaseName property

As in the DAO/Jet and Data control sample, verify that the Data control's DatabaseName property is set to *pubs*, the DSN that you've already established.

Setting the MSFlexGrid properties

The MSFlexGrid control is set up in the same way it was in the DAO/Jet and Data control sample.

Coding the SearchButton_Click event procedure

Again, this routine is identical to the code we used for the DAO/Jet and Data control. That's the advantage to using this technique—you can often use your existing DAO applications and code without change.

```
Private Sub SearchButton_Click()
Data1.RecordSource = "Select Title, Price," _
    & " Au_Fname + ' ' + Au_Lname Author" _
    & " From Titles T, TitleAuthor TA, Authors A" _
    & " Where T.Title_ID = TA.Title_ID" _
    & " And TA.Au_ID = A.AU_ID" _
    & " And Title like '%" & (TitleWanted) & "%'"
Debug.Print Data1.RecordSource
Data1.Refresh
End Sub
```

You use the Data control's Refresh method to establish a connection and execute the query automatically—just as you did earlier with the DAO/Jet and Data control sample. When you execute this method, DAO processes the request via RDO and returns when (and only when) the first qualifying row is ready. The Data control then populates any bound controls and manages the current-row pointer—just as with the DAO/Jet and Data control sample.

Coding the CloseButton_Click event procedure

The Data control automatically manages the DAO object it creates, so you don't need any special code to close databases or result sets. You can use the existing code without modification.

Evaluating the results

You won't notice much difference between this sample and the DAO/Jet and Data control sample—except perhaps for the difference in speed. Just as in the earlier sample, you perform a search by entering a title and clicking the search button. Once control returns to your application, Visual Basic and the Data control automatically display the rows of the Recordset object in the MSFlexGrid control according to the latest results of the SQL query. In accordance with the size of the MSFlexGrid control, the first and nth rows of the Recordset object are displayed. If more than one title matches the query criteria, you can use the MSFlexGrid control's scroll bars to move either forward or backward to another row in the Recordset object.

DAO/ODBCDirect Sample

This sample application illustrates the basic use of the DAO/ODBCDirect interface for accessing SQL Server without benefit of the Data control. The code differs from the DAO/Jet sample in that a parameterized QueryDef object is used. We'll start from the DAO/Jet sample application and morph it to use ODBCDirect.

Coding the global variables

Declare global variables that are used to contain the Connection and Recordset objects created in other procedures. Note that we've added a Workspace to the variables being declared and substituted a Connection for the Database object:

```
Dim Db As Connection
Dim Ws As Workspace
Dim Rs As Recordset
Dim Qd As QueryDef
Dim SQL As String
```

Coding the Form_Load event procedure

Here's where the differences arise. First we need to tell DAO that we *don't* want to invoke Jet. To do this, we need to create a new Workspace object using the new Type property set to *dbUseODBC*. Without this step, Jet is loaded the first time you reference a DAO object. Next we'll write code to open the database connection and instantiate the Connection object using the DAO OpenConnection method that closely matches the equivalent RDO method—instead of using the normal DAO OpenDatabase method. Finally, we create a QueryDef to hold our parameter query.

```
Private Sub Form_Load()
Set Ws = DBEngine.CreateWorkspace("ODBCWS", "", "", dbUseODBC)
On Error GoTo FLEH
' Note that we open a "Connection" object here not
' a Database object.
Set Db = Ws.OpenConnection("pubs", False, False, "odbc;uid=;pwd=;")
SQL = "Select Title, Price," _
    & " Au_Fname + ' ' + Au_Lname Author" _
    & " From Titles T, TitleAuthor TA, Authors A" _
    & " Where T.Title_ID = TA.Title_ID" _
    & " And TA.Au_ID = A.AU_ID" _
    & " And Title like ?"
Set Qd = Db.CreateQueryDef("Sample", SQL)
ExitFL:
Exit Sub
FLEH:
    Debug.Print "Error:"; Err, Error$
    MsgBox "Could not open connection"
    Resume ExitFL
End Sub
```

Coding the SearchButton_Click event procedure

In this procedure, the query is executed and data from the first row is moved
into the TextBox controls (in your code). This code is very similar to that used
in the DAO/Jet sample except that here we're using RDO's (and ODBCDirect's)
ability to run parameter queries.

```
Private Sub SearchButton_Click()
Qd(0) = "%" & TitleWanted & "%"
Set Rs = Qd.OpenRecordset(dbOpenSnapshot)
If Rs.EOF = False Then
    ' To fully populate the Recordset
    Rs.MoveLast
    Rs.MoveFirst
    If Rs.RecordCount > 0 Then ShowRecord
Else
    MsgBox "No records found. Choose another title to search for."
End If
End Sub
```

Coding the procedures

The operational procedure code is identical to that used in the earlier DAO/Jet
code sample. That's the whole idea behind ODBCDirect. Although not all DAO
code works against ODBCDirect, most of the basic (so to speak) operations do.

Evaluating the results

This application does load faster than the DAO/Jet code version—but the
differences should be minuscule. This sample probably won't load any faster than
the RDO version, however. After the form loads, everything works as before.

I think you'll find that this technique is slightly more complicated than using DAO/Jet, but it can yield much better performance. Unfortunately, many of the techniques you used to deal with data using DAO won't work with ODBCDirect. But I'll talk about that later.

RDO Road Test

Remote Data Objects (RDO) have become the flagship data access interface since their introduction with Visual Basic 4.0. Although ADO might overtake RDO's position as the data access interface of choice, RDO is still used worldwide to provide a comprehensive, flexible, and high-speed interface to all versions of SQL Server. The RDO interface has had a significant impact on how Visual Basic developers access SQL Server. It was designed from the ground up to interface with intelligent database engines like SQL Server, so it can't help being an ideal solution for front-end developers. The RDO interface doesn't need an intermediate layer such as the Jet database engine; it relies on the intelligence of the remote SQL Server engine. The RDO data interface connects to SQL Server *directly* through the ODBC Driver Manager and the SQL Server ODBC driver, as you can see in Figure 3-12.

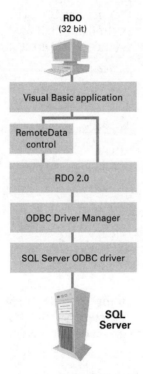

Figure 3-12 *RDO interface to access SQL Server from Visual Basic*

The RDO objects, methods, and properties can all be used in conjunction with the RemoteData control, and they can also be used by themselves. Only the Visual Basic Enterprise Edition includes RDO and the RemoteData control—

and then only with 32-bit versions of Visual Basic. The following two sample applications demonstrate features available when you use the RemoteData control and the RDO interface. Although RDO can be used via DAO/ODBCDirect, the two samples in this section show how to access RDO "directly."

RDO and RemoteData Control Sample

Like the Data control, the RemoteData control is easy to set up and program. Its primary advantage is that it is a direct interface to the ODBC Driver Manager and is designed specifically for use with ODBC data sources, especially SQL Server. Since the RDO and RemoteData control sample uses the same form layout as the DAO/Jet and Data control sample, only a few minor changes will be necessary.

Starting from the DAO/Jet and Data control sample, remove the Data control from the form and replace it with the RemoteData control. To do this, you'll need to select Microsoft RemoteData Control 6.0 in the Components dialog box, which can be accessed from the Project menu. The RemoteData control, once it is checked in the Components dialog box, appears in the Toolbox. Delete the Data control, and add the RemoteData control to your form. Change the DataSource property of the MSFlexGrid control to the name of the RemoteData control (MSRDC1); you don't need to change the other MSFlexGrid settings.

Setting the RemoteData control properties

As already mentioned, the RemoteData control shares many properties with the Data control, but these properties must be reset. Set the RemoteData control's Connect property as follows:

```
UID=<your user ID>;PWD=<your password>;
```

Notice that the connect string is not preceded by *ODBC;* as it *must* be when you code the Connect property for DAO/Jet and DAO/ODBCDirect. Enter your SQL Server user ID and password in this string, just as you did in the Data control samples. (Yes, you can set the user ID and password with the RemoteData control's UserName and Password properties, but you don't need to bother with this if they are already included in the Connect property.) Now set the DataSourceName property to *pubs*, the DSN you've already established—yes, they can use the same ODBC data source. The RemoteData control makes this easy; it has looked up all the registered DSNs and exposes them in a drop-down list.

We don't have to set the SQL property (the equivalent of the RecordSource). We'll do that in code later. If we were to set it now, it would force the RDC to run a query before we saw the form for the first time—further delaying the application load time.

Coding the procedures

The RecordSource property isn't implemented in the RemoteData control, so instead of setting this property (as we did in the sample application using the Data control), we'll set the SQL property to the same SQL query. Because it isn't necessary to bypass the Jet database engine, we don't need to set the Option property. To execute the query, use the Refresh method, as before. In this case, however, it applies to the RemoteData control (MSRDC1). As in the Data control sample applications, here too the Refresh method automatically establishes a connection (if one isn't already open) and executes the query. The RemoteData control then populates any bound controls and manages the current-row pointer, as was also the case in the Data control samples. Here is the entire code listing for the RDO and RemoteData control sample:

```
Private Sub SearchButton_Click()
MSRDC1.SQL = "Select Title, Price," _
    & " Au_Fname + ' ' + Au_Lname Author" _
    & " From Titles T, TitleAuthor TA, Authors A" _
    & " Where T.Title_ID = TA.Title_ID" _
    & " And TA.Au_ID = A.AU_ID" _
    & " And Title like '%" & (TitleWanted) & "%'"
Debug.Print MSRDC1.SQL
MSRDC1.Refresh
End Sub

Private Sub CloseButton_Click()
Unload Me
End Sub
```

Evaluating the results

When you perform a search, and once control returns to your application, Visual Basic and the RemoteData control automatically display the rows of the record set in the MSFlexGrid control. If more than one title matches the query criteria, you can use the grid scroll bars to move to another row in the result set.

You can see an important difference between this sample application and the one for the Data control if you use the SP_WHO stored procedure to determine the number of connections this sample application has opened. Even after the data has been extracted from SQL Server, the connection remains open, but it can be closed instantly, on demand. If you're running in Design mode, you might find it interesting to execute the SP_WHO stored procedure once again after the application has ended but while Visual Basic is still running in Design mode. Note that there are *no* orphaned connections.

RDO Sample

This sample application uses RDO to perform the same functions that we saw performed in the previous samples. The techniques used here are very similar to those used with the DAO interface. In both cases, your code has to work with each column's data on a row-by-row basis, and you must add code to clean up the RDO interface when you're done. This sample application uses the same form that we used in the DAO/Jet and DAO/ODBCDirect samples, so you can start from those samples. As in the DAO samples, the work involved in this sample is done in code. We won't be using bound controls, so we'll need to code procedures that move data from the current row to the TextBox controls.

Again, as in the DAO sample application, we'll need code procedures to open the connection, create the result set, and close the Remote Data Objects.

Setting a reference to RDO

To use RDO, you must set a reference to the Remote Data Objects Library. If you don't, your application will fail to compile as you make your first reference to an RDO method or object. Starting from a DAO sample, open the References dialog box from the Project menu and set a reference to "Microsoft Remote Data Object 2.0." A reference to RDO is *not* automatic when you add the RemoteData control to your form.

Coding the global variables

To start, declare global variables that you'll use to contain the rdoConnection, rdoResultset, and rdoQuery objects:

```
Dim Db As New rdoConnection
Dim Rs As rdoResultset
Dim Qy As rdoQuery
Dim SQL As String
```

In Visual Basic 3.0, and even in the 16-bit version of Visual Basic 4.0, it is *not* possible to register the Remote Data Objects. Technically, it is possible to produce 16-bit versions of the RDO interface and the RemoteData control, but they're not going to see the light of day. Microsoft stopped working on 16-bit software years ago. I suppose some third party will find the resources to build a 16-bit RDO interface if the market demands loudly enough.

Coding the Form_Load event procedure

Now we'll write code to open a connection and instantiate the rdoConnection object. In this case, instead of just setting design-time properties, code the Form_Load event procedure as shown in the sample code that follows. Notice that the code refers to the same *pubs* DSN and connect string as those used in the RDO and RemoteData control sample.

In this example, the value of the Prompt property forces the RDO interface to return a trappable error if the user ID and password are incorrect. I use this technique when I depend on Windows NT authentication to provide the login name and password.

As in the previous samples, the WHERE clause of the query is filtered by the value passed in from the TitleWanted text box. In this case, however, we take advantage of RDO's ability to execute parameter queries by creating an rdoQuery and setting its parameter to the value passed in from the TitleWanted text box. The rdoQuery is created during the Form_Load event procedure; the parameter is set in the next step:

```
Private Sub Form_Load()
On Error GoTo FLEH
With Db
    .Connect = "dsn=pubs;uid=;pwd=;"
    .EstablishConnection rdDriverNoPrompt, True
    SQL = "Select Title, Price," _
        & " Au_Fname + ' ' + Au_Lname Author" _
        & " From Titles T, TitleAuthor TA, Authors A" _
        & " Where T.Title_ID = TA.Title_ID" _
        & " And TA.Au_ID = A.AU_ID" _
```

(continued)

```
            & " And Title like ?"
        Set Qy = .CreateQuery("Sample", SQL)
End With
ExitFL:
Exit Sub
FLEH:
    Debug.Print "Error:"; Err, Error$
    MsgBox "Could not open connection"
    Resume ExitFL
End Sub
```

If your error handler gets a 429 error ("ActionX component can't create object…"), you didn't register the RDO objects properly, you're running in 16-bit mode, or you misspelled one of the objects. Press F1 to get more details on this error. If you get a successful open, the rdoConnection object referred to by the *Db* variable is valid and can be used to create your rdoResultset object.

Coding the SearchButton_Click event procedure

In this procedure, the query is executed and data from the first row is moved into the TextBox controls (in code). Another approach would be to use the Refresh method to rerun the rdoQuery query.

```
Private Sub SearchButton_Click()
Qy(0) = "%" & TitleWanted & "%"
Set Rs = Qy.OpenResultset(rdOpenStatic)
If Rs.EOF = False Then
    Rs.MoveLast
    Rs.MoveFirst
    If Rs.RowCount > 0 Then ShowRecord
Else
    MsgBox "No records found. Choose another title to search for."
End If
End Sub
```

Coding the ShowRecord procedure

Once the data has been fetched into the rdoResultset object, the next step is to move the data into the TextBox controls, where the user can see it. This procedure assumes that the rdoResultset object has been created. If there is no current record—as when the current record pointer is positioned beyond either end of the rdoResultset object or when there are no records at all—the appropriate buttons are disabled and no attempt is made to reference the current record. Notice that this code is identical to the code for the DAO ShowRecord procedure.

```
Sub ShowRecord()
' Fill the DataFound text boxes from the Resultset.
If Rs.BOF = False And Rs.EOF = False Then
    ' Note the three different ways to address the Resultset fields.
    DataFound(0) = Rs!Title
    DataFound(1) = Format(Rs("Price"), "$###.##")
    DataFound(2) = Rs(2)
```

```
End If
PreviousButton.Enabled = Not Rs.BOF
NextButton.Enabled = Not Rs.EOF
End Sub
```

Coding the Recordset navigation buttons

A user who wants to see additional rows of the result set can use the navigation buttons to view those records. The navigation buttons use the MoveNext and MovePrevious methods to position the current record pointer within the rdoResultset object. This code doesn't prevent movement past either end of the rdoResultset object, however; the ShowRecord procedure automatically deals with this contingency. Again, this code is identical to the code for the same procedure in the DAO sample application, which means that in this case the transition from DAO code to RDO code can be fairly painless.

```
Private Sub NextButton_Click()
Rs.MoveNext
ShowRecord
End Sub


Private Sub PreviousButton_Click()
Rs.MovePrevious
ShowRecord
End Sub
```

Code the CloseButton_Click event procedure

To clean up any pending operations and cleanly close the connection to SQL Server, you need to close both the Recordset object and the Database object before quitting the application. To end the application gracefully, you should also unload the form in the CloseButton_Click event procedure:

```
Private Sub CloseButton_Click()
Rs.Close
Db.Close
Unload Me
End Sub
```

Evaluating the results

This application loads as fast or faster than the DAO/Jet version because it has to open the database connection only in the Form_Load event. With RDO we can even eliminate that delay by opening the connection asynchronously. We'll learn how to do that in the RDO chapters (Part IV). When you perform a search, your code executes the OpenResultset method. Once control returns to your application, your code displays the first row of the rdoResultset object in the TextBox controls. If more than one title matches the query criteria, you can use the navigation buttons to move to another row (either forward or backward) in the result set. Once you position the current record pointer off either end of the Resultset object, the controls are disabled.

CAUTION

In Visual Basic 4.0, when a new rdoResultset object is created, any existing rdoResultset objects are maintained. They are accessible through the rdoResultsets collection. To ensure that unneeded rdoResultset objects are *not* kept, use the Close method against the rdoResultset collection before you create any new rdoResultset objects. In Visual Basic 5.0 and later, RDO automatically drops existing rdoResultset objects when you assign a value to a variable that is set to an rdoResultset.

ADO Road Test

ActiveX Data Objects (ADO) have been designed to interface to all types of information—not just relational databases. Because of this additional flexibility, ADO promises to be the interface of choice for most developers from this point forward. Although ADO doesn't have the years of development experience garnered by RDO or DAO, it leverages the years of interface development experience accumulated by earlier interfaces, so it should come up to speed quickly. The two sample applications in this section demonstrate features available with the ADO Data control and the ADO interface.

The ADO interface can connect to SQL Server *directly* through the OLE DB provider for SQL Server. ADO can also connect through the OLE DB provider for ODBC that talks to the SQL Server ODBC driver we used with DAO and RDO. ADO objects, methods, and properties can all be used in conjunction with the ADO Data control, and they can also be used by themselves. The ADO interface to SQL Server is shown in Figure 3-13.

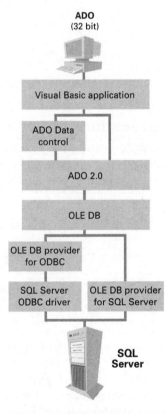

Figure 3-13 *ADO interface to access SQL Server from Visual Basic*

ADO is far easier to get a hold of than RDO. It's free, and you can download it from Microsoft's Web site (http://www.microsoft.com/data/ado/download.htm). No, you don't need Enterprise Edition or even Professional Edition to get a license to use it. Yes, it only works with 32-bit versions of Visual Basic.

ADO and ADO Data Control Sample

Like the Data control, the ADO Data control is easy to set up and program. Although the ADO Data control, the RemoteData control, and the "default" Data control all use the same form layout, there are several differences we have to deal with when we transition to ADO/OLE DB applications. First, we can't use the MSFlexGrid control. It works only with the Data control and the RemoteData control.

Starting from one of the previous DAO and Data control samples, remove the data control and the MSFlexGrid control. Open the Components dialog box from the Project menu, and select "Microsoft ADO Data Control 6.0" and "Microsoft DataGrid Control 6.0." Once checked in the Components dialog box, these controls appears in the Toolbox. Add the ADO Data control (Adodc) to your form in place of the data control you just deleted. Do the same with the DataGrid control, replacing the deleted MSFlexGrid control.

Setting the ADO Data control properties

As already mentioned, the ADO Data control shares many properties with the Data control. Set the ADO Data control's ConnectString property as follows:

```
DSN=pubs;UID=<your user ID>;PWD=<your password>;
```

You don't need to precede the connect string with *ODBC;* as you *must* do when you code the Connect property for DAO. Follow the same drill as before—enter your SQL Server user ID and password in this string, just as you did in the sample application using the Data control. No, there is no equivalent of the DataSourceName property in the ADO data control—that's why we put the DSN in the ConnectString.

Nor do we have to set the RecordSource property—we do that in code a little later. If we set that property now, it would force the ADO Data control to run a query before we see the form for the first time—further delaying the application load time.

> **NOTE** OLE DB doesn't understand the term "default database"; you'll have to set the "Default Catalog" instead—Microsoft felt the need to provide a "generic" designation for this term. But you won't need to set the default anything because we set the default database when we set up the DSN.

Setting the DataGrid control properties

You really only need to set one design-time property of the DataGrid control. Set the DataGrid control's DataSource property to the Name property of the ADO Data control, *Adodc1*. You can either type it in or choose it from the drop-down list.

Coding the procedures

To execute the query and get the DataGrid to fill, we set the RecordSource property and use the Refresh method, as before. To update the code, simply search for the current data control name and replace it with *Adodc1*. As in the sample application using the Data control, the Refresh method automatically establishes a connection (if one isn't already open) and executes the query. The ADO Data control then populates any bound controls and manages the current-row pointer, as was also the case in the Data control sample. Here is the entire code listing for the ADO and ADO Data control sample:

```
Private Sub SearchButton_Click()
Adodc1.RecordSource = "Select Title, Price," _
    & " Au_Fname + ' ' + Au_Lname Author" _
    & " From Titles T, TitleAuthor TA, Authors A" _
    & " Where T.Title_ID = TA.Title_ID" _
    & " And TA.Au_ID = A.AU_ID" _
    & " And Title like '%" & (TitleWanted) & "%'"
Debug.Print Adodc1.RecordSource
Adodc1.Refresh
End Sub

Private Sub CloseButton_Click()
Unload Me
End Sub
```

Evaluating the results

When you perform a search, and once control returns to your application, Visual Basic and the ADO Data control automatically display the rows of the record set in the DataGrid control.

Again, it's time to check out SP_WHO to see how many connections have been established by this sample application. Keep in mind that even after the data has been extracted from SQL Server, the connection remains open, but it can be closed instantly, on demand. If you're running in Design mode, you might find it interesting to execute the SP_WHO stored procedure once again after the application has ended but while Visual Basic is still running in Design mode. As with the RDO and RemoteData control sample, there are *no* orphaned connections.

ADO Sample

This sample application uses ADO to perform the same functions that we saw performed in our previous samples. The techniques used here are very similar to those used with the DAO and RDO interfaces. In both cases, your code has to work with each column's data on a row-by-row basis, and you must add code to clean up the ADO objects when you're done. This sample application uses the same form as you used in the sample application for the DAO and RDO without a data source control.

As in the sample applications for the other data interfaces, the work involved in this ADO sample is done in code. We won't be using bound controls, so we'll need to code procedures that move data from the current row to the TextBox controls. We'll need code procedures to open the connection, create the result set, and close the ADO objects you create.

Setting a reference to ADO

To use ADO, you must set a reference to the ActiveX Data Objects Library. If you don't, your application will fail to compile as you make your first reference to an ADO method or object. Starting from a DAO or RDO sample, open the References dialog box from the Project menu and set a reference to "Microsoft ActiveX Data Objects 2.0 Library." A reference to ADO is automatic when you create a Data Project or add the ADO Data control to your form.

TIP If you get a compile error when you try running this ADO sample and you have a reference set to a DAO object library, try removing the reference to the DAO object library.

Coding the global variables

To start, declare global variables that you'll use to contain the Connection, Recordset, and Command objects:

```
Dim Cn As New Connection
Dim Rs As New Recordset
Dim Cmd As New Command
```

Coding the Form_Load event procedure

Now we'll write code to open a connection and instantiate the ADO Connection object. In this case, instead of just setting design-time properties, code the Form_Load event procedure as shown in the sample code that follows. You'll notice that the code refers to the same *pubs* DSN and connect string as those used in the RDO sample applications. In ADO, we don't have to reprogram the prompt behavior because ADO defaults to "no prompts." The no-prompt behavior is preferred because we don't want to display connection dialog boxes to the user.

Again, the WHERE clause of the query is filtered by the value passed in from the TitleWanted text box. For the ADO example, we take advantage of ADO's ability to execute parameter queries by creating a Command object and setting its parameter to the value passed in from the TitleWanted text box. The Command object is created during the Form_Load event procedure; the parameter is set in the next step.

```
Private Sub Form_Load()
On Error GoTo FLEH
Cn.CursorLocation = adUseServer
Cn.Open ("dsn=pubs;uid=;pwd=;")
Cmd.CommandText = "Select Title, Price," _
    & " Au_Fname + ' ' + Au_Lname Author" _
    & " From Titles T, TitleAuthor TA, Authors A" _
    & " Where T.Title_ID = TA.Title_ID" _
    & " And TA.Au_ID = A.Au_ID" _
    & " And Title like ?"
Cmd.CommandType = adCmdText
Cmd.Name = "Sample"
Cmd.ActiveConnection = Cn
ExitFL:
Exit Sub
FLEH:
    Debug.Print "Error:"; Err, Error$
    MsgBox "Could not open connection"
    Resume ExitFL
End Sub
```

If your error handler gets a 429 error ("ActiveX component can't create object…"), you didn't register ADO properly, you're running in 16-bit mode, or you misspelled one of the objects. Press F1 to get more details on this error. If you get a successful open, the ADO Connection object referred to by the *Cn* variable is valid and can be used with your ADO Command object. You don't really need to create a stand-alone Connection object for this simple example, and I'll explain why when we get to the ADO chapters (Part V).

Coding the SearchButton_Click event procedure

In this procedure, the query is executed and data from the first row is moved into the TextBox controls (in code):

```
Private Sub SearchButton_Click()
Cmd(0) = "%" & TitleWanted & "%"
Rs.Open Cmd, , adOpenStatic
If Rs.EOF = False Then
    ShowRecord
Else
    MsgBox "No records found. Choose another title to search for."
End If
End Sub
```

Here we use the Open method on the Recordset object, passing in the Command object as an argument. This tells ADO to build the Recordset based on the Command. We set the Command parameter just before the Open. This is only one of many, many ways to execute ADO Commands.

Coding the support procedures

Once the data has been fetched into the Recordset object, the next step is to move the data into the TextBox controls, where the user can see it. You also need code to reposition the current-row pointer from row to row. This code is identical to the code for the DAO and RDO ShowRecord procedures.

Code the CloseButton_Click event procedure

To clean up any pending operations and cleanly close the connection to SQL Server, you need to close both the Recordset object and the Connection object before quitting the application. To end the application gracefully, you should also unload the form in the CloseButton_Click event procedure:

```
Private Sub CloseButton_Click()
Rs.Close
Cn.Close
Unload Me
End Sub
```

Evaluating the results

This application loads as fast or faster than the other code-based versions because it has to open the database connection only in the Form_Load event. With RDO and ADO, we can even eliminate that delay by opening the connection asynchronously. We'll learn how to do that later in Parts IV and V of this guide. When you perform a search, your code executes the Open method. Once control returns to your application, your code displays the first row of the Recordset object in the TextBox controls. If more than one title matches the query criteria, you can use the navigation buttons to move to another row (either forward or backward) in the result set. Once you position the current record pointer off either end of the Recordset object, the controls are disabled.

Comparing the Samples

I hope you learned something from this overview. Table 3-5 summarizes key points of comparison among the various applications. Can you gauge speed or overall suitability from the sample applications described in this chapter? I don't really think so. What you should be able to tell is how easy or difficult each model is to code, at least in a general sense. Real-world applications are composed of the same kinds of data access logic as those found in these sample applications: logic for opening a connection, gathering query criteria, submitting a query, and displaying the results. But so many other factors gate application speed and suitability that this sort of evaluation is by its very nature extremely complex.

Only you can decide which data interface is the right animal for you. Just be sure to stay away from the end with the teeth.

Looking Closer at the Results

Use the SP_WHO stored procedure to determine the number of connections each sample application has opened. The connection remains open even after the data has been extracted from SQL Server; it remains open until the interface deallocates the statement handle or closes the connection handle. If you're running in Design mode, you might find it interesting to reexecute the SP_WHO stored procedure after the application has ended but while Visual Basic is still running in Design mode. Look familiar? Are we establishing a pattern?

Table 3-5

Comparison of Sample Applications

	DAO/Jet and Data Control	DAO/Jet	DAO/ODBCDirect and Data Control	DAO/ODBCDirect	RDO and RemoteData Control	RDO	ADO and ADO Data Control	ADO
Data access	DAO/Jet/ODBC	DAO/Jet/ODBC	DAO/ODBCDirect/RDO/ODBC	DAO/ODBCDirect/RDO/ODBC	RDO/ODBC	RDO/ODB	ADO/OLE DB	ADO/OLE DB
Ease of coding*	1	4	2	4	1	3	1	3
Lines of code	8	46	8	51	8	52	8	49
Sample implementation	MSFlexGrid	TextBoxes	MSFlexGrid	TextBoxes	MSFlexGrid	TextBoxes	DataGrid	TextBoxes
Query type	Prepared	Prepared	Prepared	Parameterized	Prepared	Parameterized	Prepared	Parameterized
SQL Server features	Some	Some	Most	Most	Most	Most	Most	Most

* Scale is 1 = easy; 10 = hard.

To see how many connections are being used, open another window on your workstation or server and start ISQL/w or Enterprise Manager. Log on to SQL Server and, using the SP_WHO stored procedure, determine the number of connections your application has opened. One or more connections might remain open even after the data has been extracted from SQL Server, or extra connections might stay open for a time, until their result sets are fully populated.

SQL Server 6.*x* brought a number of important innovations to developers writing front-end applications. One of the most useful features is SQL Trace. This tool has been updated for SQL Server 7.0 and has been renamed the SQL Server Profiler. The SQL Server Profiler application is brutally simple to use and yields a plethora of information about what is sent to SQL Server from whatever data interface you choose. Basically, you run SQL Server Profiler on the server or on a workstation connected to the server. It establishes a connection and, using the SQL tracing hooks added to SQL 6.0, displays exactly what was sent by each connection. You can set up traces to see specific users, applications, or only certain aspects of the operation. In any case, you should take a look at the data you can capture with the SQL Server Profiler when choosing one data-retrieval strategy over another. Figure 3-14 shows an example trace for the RDO and RemoteData control sample discussed in this chapter.

CAUTION

It is not at all wise to click the square Stop button on the Visual Basic toolbar; apparently, this kills the application *and* its data interface before it has a chance to shut down its connections. What this means to you is that a number of zombied connections can be created and held as long as Visual Basic is still running. If you have a limited number of connections (as most servers do), you can cripple the server—or, worse, your workstation can run out of handles and be unable to save your application. Not good.

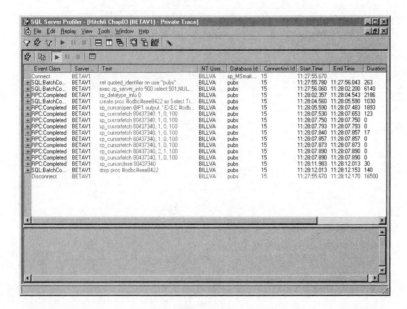

Figure 3-14 *A trace of the RDO and RemoteData control sample using the SQL Server Profiler included with SQL Server 7.0*

Notice that the trace includes the command, connection ID, and duration (in milliseconds). This kind of detail can be a telling indicator of object-level interface efficiency. That is, you're seeing what SQL Server was told to do based on the high-level command you executed in your application. Be careful though—this type of logging can also adversely affect server performance.

Choosing an Architecture

Asking the Right Questions

Dealing with the Answers

Understanding the Different Architectures

Evaluating Client/Server and Distributed Engine Architectures

can't tell you how many times I've worked on a team that didn't make the tough decisions early enough to avoid having to rework almost an entire database system after it was discovered (often the hard way) that the system had been built on a weak foundation. Left to your own devices, you might choose a database management system design that seems to meet or exceed your immediate needs. Or you might choose a design that your team is comfortable with. In either case, you're liable to discover a year from now that your choice was the wrong one. You can only hope that this design won't be so inadequate that you have to redesign or reimplement existing applications before you can find a workable long-term solution—but stranger things have happened.

I wrote this chapter so that you wouldn't have to learn all your lessons about choosing a database systems architecture at the school of hard knocks. I offer this advice because it is my wish that you'll be able to avoid the kinds of problems developers and their managers can experience if they don't ask the right questions, don't deal realistically with the answers they get, don't understand the fine print in the various choices of architectures, or don't know how to judge the different paths available and make sure they've chosen the one that best suits their particular needs.

And not all the lessons you need to learn are about the technology. For example, patience is a quality you might not even realize you need. Lately, I've heard stories of a number of companies that had spent countless hours writing, testing, and deploying code that was replaced by functionality added later by the operating system or a new server-class subsystem such as Microsoft Transaction Server (MTS) or Microsoft Index Server. Although Microsoft doesn't give everyone all the gory details of each product it's working on, it is fairly clear about which major components are under construction. Imagine trying to set up your own cellular phone company in 1970. Sure, you could have done it yourself, but the technology would have made it rough—and expensive. Frantic developers sometimes convince their managers that they should go ahead and create an application instead of waiting or using existing technology in more imaginative (and cheaper) ways. Case in point: several companies complained that they were unable to implement sophisticated distributed component designs that they had read about in the press. These projects were apparently started before MTS or a suitable third-party component server had come on line. The companies had tried to create their own object broker, memory manager, connection manager, transaction manager, and many (but usually far from all) of the other MTS features and facilities. All too often, they failed to get their homegrown system to work as well as they had envisioned. No, waiting is not always an option. But charging off and building gas stations by the highway in 1898 would have been a costly mistake.

In this chapter, I'll introduce several different approaches to database systems architecture:

- Client/server
- Distributed engine
- Distributed component
- Web-based

All but the distributed component architecture are in widespread use throughout the world, because all address specific business problems. One of these configurations—or, according to your business needs, some combination of them—might be the most suitable approach for you. After you read and digest the material in this chapter, you'll be in a much better position to choose the right architecture and configuration for your particular situation. So make yourself comfortable, and get ready to do some homework.

Asking the Right Questions

When you're developing an application to connect to Microsoft SQL Server— no matter what language you expect to use—one of the first questions you need to ask yourself is this: "What is the best database architecture for our system?" The good news is that you have many choices—and even more now that you can consider distributed component and Web-based architectures. The bad news is that because you have so many choices, this question becomes a hard one to answer. Your decision-making process gets even more complicated in systems where SQL Server is only one of several databases or database engines that are to be accessed. As you look for the best choice for your application, you'll need to put some questions to those members of your team who have the most complete understanding of the overall system design and development strategy. You should use the responses you get to the questions in the following sections to guide your decision.

Architecture

- Which type of database management system (DBMS) best matches the performance needs of our system?

- How can we avoid picking an architecture that we'll soon outgrow or that is too complex for our company's needs?

- With the number of active users we expect to support, will our proposed hardware, software, and support systems be able to handle the load?

- Is the systems architecture stable enough to support our design?

- Are we limited to (or considering) a small-footprint system?

- Is someone's cousin from Iowa helping with the design? You know, the guy who is still using that Challenge CS1000 Z80 system he bought at a flea market in Sioux City.

Development Skills

- Which strategy best matches our development skills?

- Why lead our developers into the outback of unfamiliar territory?

- Can our developers use their existing skills, or will they have to learn new techniques to be most productive?

- Do the language and its tools leverage our team's skills, or do they waste the team's time on waiting, trying to decipher complex interfaces, or figuring out what some other hot-shot developer coded two years (or two days) ago?

- How can we ensure that all the developers on our team—not just the most skilled ones—can use this strategy?

- Does our development plan account for junior-level as well as more seasoned professionals—or just hired guns brought in to clean up the mess the "kids" have made and leave?

- Have we chosen a design that a single individual is supposed to implement? If so, do we want to depend on that one person's skills, experience, and longevity?

- Is our design too complex for a single person to implement? If so, is our development team, with its share of prima donnas and lone rangers, capable of working with one another?

- Are we designing a system that our existing staff can't build? If so, what steps are we willing to take to get the system built?

Time Frame

- Does our planning cycle account for increased planning when the project is expected to consume years of resources? Sometimes complex systems do take years to implement.

- Why develop another application that takes months or years to write and even longer to modify when it needs fixing?

Performance

- How interactive do we want the application to be? How friendly, personal, or heuristic? Are our users working with green-screen systems? (If so, it won't take much to make them ecstatic.)

- How fast does the application have to be? Often speed is not a factor of the application but rather a measure of how fast the network, platform, server, or other external systems are. All programming languages wait at the same speed.

Performance History

- Has anyone successfully implemented a similar system, or are we asking our company and our developers to perch astride a cutting-edge razor?

- Does the system vendor provide independent references who will testify to the system's features and foibles in full production mode?

- Does the system suddenly die or lock up, with no rational explanation?

Existing Technology

- Does our strategy work with our existing workstation or server application mix?

- Are we required to use existing data or hardware? What about existing people and skills?

- Will this strategy mean that we have to buy and install lots of expensive equipment and retrain most of the workstation users?

- Are our workstations capable of running the applications we've designed, along with all the other applications currently running on the workstations?

- Will our new application so overload or block the system that no other work can be done while our application is running?

- Is the new application designed to run on or service a variety of systems all over the organization or to service systems on the World Wide Web?

New Technology

- Should we use unproven technology? If we're rolling out a new design instead of leveraging existing and known working code, are we willing to take the risk that the new design might never work?

- How much of the project depends on this unproven foundation?

- Will only a leading-edge implementation do the job, or will implementations already in place work almost as well?

Costs

- How much will it cost for hardware, software, licenses, and development?

- What's our budget? Even though hardware costs are dropping fast, they can be significant. (A $100 RAM upgrade spread over 50,000 systems is still more than I can afford. Software costs are far easier to justify because the solutions I suggest have very low licensing fees and don't have to be propagated nearly as far.)

- Are we measuring all the real costs: money, time lost in production, development costs, and training costs?

- Will it be expensive to replace a "lightweight" system with a "real" system when we find that the lightweight system simply isn't up to the task?

Scalability

- Does the application prototype really scale to the size we'll need in production?

- Will the n-user model that we created and tested work the way we've predicted it will when we go online with 10 or 100 or 100,000 × n users?

- Will the system—the entire system—bear up under production network traffic loads?

- Is the system woven in too tightly with a particular platform?

The Design and Reality

- Are we going to design a little-red-wagon–sized application out of Legos for hauling a box of Girl Scout cookies or tons of boulders?

- Will the system deal with the way our users really work?

- Are we honestly talking about design strategy, or are we really talking about personnel, company politics, our company's skill set, and our staff's desire or ability (or lack of it) to learn and grow technically?

Deployment and Training

- Are the users skilled enough and well enough trained not to have problems, or will their lack of skill and experience lead to more problems than our design can tolerate?

- How do we plan to get the application code to the users—and redeploy the code when it changes?

- Are we forcing a development paradigm or language on our existing staff or expecting to find a new team to develop something that the CEO read about in the paper only last week? Hiring, training, and trusting new people are tough in today's job markets. Good developers don't grow on trees—they might swing from them, but most of those guys can't document worth a damn.

The Future

- How will this strategy apply to our needs in the near future? The mid-term future? The extended future?

- If the system we've chosen will get us from here into late next year, when it will go into full production with 100 times the volume, why not build a strategy now that will work for today and tomorrow and for several quarters of tomorrows—a system that will still work when the load increases 500-fold or 1000-fold?

- Is this strategy flexible enough to work with the systems we expect to acquire in the future?

- Have we considered what approach we'll have to take if our company assimilates one of our competitors—or they assimilate us?

- Will this strategy leverage the movement of our organization into the graphical user interface (GUI) world of applications development?

- Are we concerned about reusing this application or component elsewhere?

Once you have the answers to these questions, you'll have a much better sense not only of which database architecture is best for your company but also of what is in store for you and your team as you move to that architecture.

NOTE Keep in mind that there is no single "best" solution. If you have a C-language–based development shop, for example, you'll be unlikely to accept a DBMS design decision using Visual Basic or Pascal—while Java might seem appealing (at first). And solutions at IBM are unlikely to include a top-line Compaq system running the Microsoft Windows NT operating system, regardless of how well such a configuration would match IBM's needs.

Dealing with the Answers

When it comes to selecting an architecture, each company has its own obstacles, experiences, requirements, prejudices, and politics, and in many cases these dramatically narrow the available choices. Companies tend to eat their own dog food—no matter what's in the mystery meat.

Many developers and their managers (like you) are making decisions about which language or interface to choose. Often they look for the best-performing or fastest interface. I think this focus on performance and speed is shortsighted. In my humble opinion, they should be looking at the "cheapest" (or at least the most cost-effective) techniques. That is, they should weigh the factors contributing to total cost of ownership (TCO). Performance is certainly one of these. To get the fastest-performing interface (probably one of the low-level API approaches written in assembly language), however, they sign up for a very costly development, maintenance, training, and support burden. All the TCO factors—not just a couple—should be thrown into the decision-making process.

Consider that the easiest-to-use development tools don't always yield the most scalable, efficient, or best-performing applications and components. And the tools that are hardest to use, support, and maintain don't always create the best code either. It takes more than a $4000 Shopsmith table saw to create a well-fitting cabinet—it takes a skilled carpenter (usually with the end of one digit missing). Yes, deciding which platform, paradigm, and resources to use is a complex decision. Developers, architects, and managers are all confused. To add to the confusion, if you stick just with Microsoft Visual Basic, you can choose from at least six distinct ways to access SQL Server data. I hope that the information you find in the Hitchhiker's Guide will help you make your decision.

If your company has chosen to program in C or C++, I would make sure that whoever made that decision didn't come to this dubiously correct conclusion based on earlier versions of Visual Basic. Now that Visual Basic has a full-blown native code–optimizing compiler, most of your tests should show that Visual Basic runs within a couple of percentage points as fast as C or C++ in virtually all cases—but is far easier to use to develop client/server applications. But more important, Visual Basic applications are easier to create, test, integrate, and deploy than their C or C++ (or Java) counterparts. A gentleman came up to me at SD West just last month and told me that what Visual Basic really needed was a compiler. Apparently, he was unaware that we had added one in Visual Basic 5.0.

In many, many cases, you'll make your design decisions on the basis of what your people—your corporation, developers, managers, and support staff—know best. All too often, design decisions boil down to personnel or political issues, not technical issues or the benefits of one language or technology over another. In any system, you need to factor in the ability of your developers to implement and support the design against the complexity of the application. If your staff is not skilled or confident enough to develop API-based client/server applications, you might feel that you have only one alternative: to use one of the integrated development environments, or the Data control and its snap-together data access solutions, and then live with possible performance problems and design constraints. But if you want to use SQL Server as a back-end server, you have at least six data access interface options (which were introduced in Chapter 2). And because most of the other language options (at least all the languages supported by Microsoft) support the same object interfaces, you have most of the same choices when you use C++ or other languages.

A C-based development strategy doesn't make sense if your organization has only Visual Basic developers. But if your shop is COBOL-based or FORTRAN-based, you might gain some insights into the development costs associated with one language or another, not to mention the challenging task of creating applications for Windows in COBOL or FORTRAN. This challenge is kinda like eating low-fat rice cakes with Spam. If you haven't decided between Visual Basic and C or C++, consider the development, training, and support costs involved with your choice of development strategy. You'll find that Visual Basic makes developing the interactive connection to SQL Server far easier, which results in not only faster, less trouble-prone applications but also applications that come together quicker and with fewer support headaches later on. If you aren't sure which language to use, talk with someone who has developed applications in that language. If you choose to program in C or C++, you can still use most of the strategies discussed here (but you will need a note from your mom). If you're concerned with speed of execution, I think you'll find that Visual Basic applications wait at the same speed as C or C++ programs. That is, applications developed in Visual Basic or C/C++ wait at the same speed for users, RAM access, network operations, disk drives, and video retrace—the factors that can make all applications slow to a crawl. One of your primary concerns, however, should be perceived performance of the front-end application: how fast or slow the application appears to be running to the user. The performance of different applications can be radically different; performance depends on the front-end architecture and other factors, and these factors have little to do with the language used to compile the application. In many cases, application speed has more to do with the use and number of controls in the application than with the database or how it was accessed. With Visual Basic, it's much easier to create lots of forms using lots of complex control arrangements, so a developer sitting at an 80-MB, P6/300 MHz-based machine might not realize or appreciate the frustration of a user on a more conservative system.

One more thing—don't let ignorance be an excuse for failure. Don't let anyone on your staff decide to use an architecture, language, or technique just because he or she doesn't understand the alternatives. Too often, I've seen corporate Not-Invented-Here (NIH) syndrome kill or hobble a project. I also find it frustrating to hear that a development language has been dropped, along with SQL Server, because a prototype developer couldn't get the test case to work. For example, I had a developer tell me that his tests of stored procedures proved conclusively that they took longer to execute than straight uncompiled SQL queries. Ah, no. Something was wrong with his test. Apparently, he was including the CreateQuery code in each loop. Sure, you'll spend a little more time setting up CreateQuery in the first call, but all subsequent calls should run faster—a lot faster. Throwing out both Visual Basic and SQL Server because a developer has misunderstood the implementation of a high-performance front end is like junking a Maserati because cheap tires can't hold traction when the power is applied.

Since you're thinking about using SQL Server—after all, you are reading a book on the subject—you're probably trying to decide on a design in which more than a few records will be accessed by more than a few people. In the past, if your system was expected to implement a single-user application that accessed a 5000-row table, I suggested that SQL Server would not be a cost-effective solution. Now that SQL Server is ported to Windows 95/98, however, it makes sense for far smaller sites. SQL Server can now be used anywhere, by one to virtually any number of users on platforms large and small.

The discussion in this chapter is also intended to bring up to speed those of you who have been using PC-class database systems like dBASE (and Microsoft Access) on client/server and the new alternative architectures. I'll attempt to make your decision about using one of these more sophisticated architectures somewhat easier—or at least better informed. I make a few basic assumptions

Not-Invented-Here (NIH) syndrome results from a virus that is fairly common among the more experienced and entrenched developers, here and abroad. Engineers and managers too often decide that a solution from outside can't possibly meet their special and specific needs, and they attempt a 100 percent implementation of their own before attempting to implement an 80 percent solution from someone outside. "If we didn't create it," the logic goes, "how good can it be? No one knows our business like our own people." So be careful that you don't contract this contagious disease—it can impair your (or your manager's) decision-making capabilities.

that you can either accept or reject, but they do serve to illustrate the religious differences between the architectures, all of which are gaining wider and wider acceptance. Before we examine those architectures, however, let's tour the major components of client/server architecture.

One other point before we get started. Many of you are considering whether to use a Microsoft Access database or a Visual Basic–driven DAO/Jet database to prototype a SQL Server production database. The decision to do this prototyping is often based on the premise that Microsoft Jet is a relational database engine and so is SQL Server. Well, that's true; and it's also true that both systems have tables, stored queries, referential integrity constraints, and security systems, and that they both support very similar dialects of ANSI SQL. But these features and subsystems are implemented very differently. Frankly, it would be most unwise to make design decisions based on performance, security, referential integrity management, administration, report generation, or even the way queries are executed in a Jet database. In other words, just because an optimized query seems to work in a Jet database doesn't mean that it will scale or even work at all in a SQL Server system. SQL Server database systems are more than just a set of tables and referential integrity constraints. Most production systems are simply not designed like 2-user to 22-user Jet databases. Many of these systems don't expose base tables to the developer—they expose SQL views or stored procedures or COM business objects. These systems don't depend on broad cursors (discussed in Chapter 5) to expose thousands, or even hundreds, of rows to the user—especially not the systems that support more than a few dozen users. The fundamental design philosophy of a production SQL Server database is very unlike the type of database system that you can create with the Jet engine. Can you create a viable DBMS with Jet? Sure you can. The fundamental problem is that what makes Jet databases fast and powerful often doesn't scale to SQL Server.

Too many books and articles extol the virtues of client/ server database architecture without bothering to compare the client/server model to the alternatives. This omission is a big mistake. It's not like comparing apples and oranges. It's more like comparing a quarter-ton pickup to a huge truck working at the bottom of an open-pit coal mine: delivering pizza is really tough if you can't pull into the driveway without scaring the residents, but delivering 18 cubic yards of coal can be a problem if you can't find the truck once it's loaded.

Understanding the Different Architectures

In this section, I'll introduce four different architectures:

- **Client/server architecture**   On the client side of this architecture, we find a fairly simple front-end application. On the server side, we find an intelligent engine. The server is designed to accept queries from the front-end application and return the requested information.

- **Distributed engine architecture**   This architecture places a dedicated database engine or query processor at each workstation. In this design, either a central file server or one of the workstation clients doubles as the central data repository.

- **Distributed component architecture** This architecture moves some or all of its logic to COM components managed in-process, out-of-process, or way out-of-process (out-of-system) and managed by MTS. I'll explain how to build these components in Visual Basic and how to pass the burden of their operation to MTS when we get to the ADO chapters (Part V).

- **Web-based architecture** This architecture can be implemented in a variety of ways, but I'll briefly describe how to use Visual Basic to create Web-based components and access them from Active Server Pages. Be sure to check out the ActiveX Document Migration wizard to run Visual Basic applications from Microsoft Internet Explorer.

Of course, many applications implement solutions that are a variation of these architectures. In the Hitchhiker's Guide, we focus on the client/server architecture because all four architectures just listed have client/server characteristics and because client/server is a commonly used architecture and a proven design.

Client/Server Architecture

A client/server architecture consists of an intelligent client that can request services from a networked server. On the client side of this architecture, we find a fairly simple front-end application running on a fairly simple personal computer, as shown in Figure 4-1. A sophisticated client/server application might be asked to do data validation or present lists of valid options, but most of the data integrity and business rules are enforced with the server's validation rules, defaults, triggers, and stored procedures. On the server side, we find an intelligent database server engine. The server is designed to accept SQL queries from the front-end application—usually in the form of calls to stored procedures that return clearly defined and limited-scope result sets.

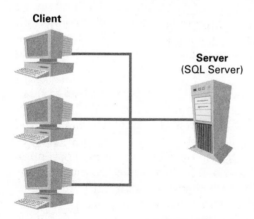

Figure 4-1 *Client/server architecture*

The client's responsibilities

Generally, the client application is responsible, at the least, for connection management, data capture, data retrieval, data presentation, and error management. Front-end applications often have responsibilities far in excess of these, but virtually all front ends must perform these fundamental tasks. Note that the term "client" in this context refers to the client application and its supporting database files, connection interfaces, and other components of the client system.

Connection management Client/server applications establish a connection with the server to submit queries (ask questions), retrieve result sets (fetch the answers), perform maintenance, or simply pass messages to the server. In this architecture, the client makes a "hard" connection with the server over a local area network (LAN) or a wide area network (WAN)—even if the connection is with a SQL Server running on the same system. This connection must be in place to perform "live" operations, but it need not stay in place after the data arrives—unless you want to change the data later. (I'll explain connection strategies in Chapter 6.) The client often disconnects from the server when the connection is no longer needed and reconnects, as required, when activity returns—such as when it's time to perform an update or requery. The client application's connection is authenticated by the LAN and SQL Server with a user-supplied or application-generated login ID and password. (This task might also mean that the first line of defense for the database security system is built into the application.) In some cases, Microsoft Windows NT provides a degree of connection security management. That is, using domain-managed security, client applications need not provide additional user names and passwords to SQL Server—once they are authenticated by Windows NT. The client must also deal with connection problems caused by trouble on the server, on the network, in the application itself, or simply by an inept user. Yes, some of the new architectures use the Distributed Component Object Model (DCOM) to assign the connection tasks to a remote server. That is, the client application uses a DCOM link to attach to a class module or a COM component running on the server (or managed by MTS). This remote object still needs to make a connection to the server. Because the object can't (or shouldn't) pass on the user ID and password (and remain reentrant), it often must use its own connection ID and password and assume security is performed through other means.

Data capture This means that the client presents forms for the user to fill in with data, or it simply gathers information from the ether. The client facilitates this process by presenting lists of valid options based on database-derived or application-derived data. For example, on the basis of validation tables in the database, a client application presents lists of valid employees or part numbers. The client also validates data values before they are sent to the database. This prevalidation often involves cross-checking form fields against other fields, either on the form or in the database. Validation can take place as fields are filled in or completed, or as the form is committed. These validation criteria are often referred to as client-side business rules. It's a good idea to keep these rules isolated in separate class modules so they can be more easily managed, deployed, and updated when they change. Another responsibility of the client is submission of prevalidated rows as updates to the database and management of exceptions when database rules, triggers, or other checks fail. This task involves getting the user to decide what to do if an update fails because of a multiuser collision or a simple validation error.

Data retrieval The client application creates data queries (questions) that are based on user or situational input. This task might mean that the application creates a SQL query on the fly, passes parameters to a local or system stored procedure, or invokes methods on business objects. The client also submits queries to the database engine for processing and retrieves the result sets, as required. This task includes processing result sets and making logical decisions based on the data returned. Another responsibility of the client is to manage data returned to the application, which might mean storing data in local arrays or passing it to subsystems that display it for the user. Depending on the way the data is fetched, the client is often responsible for consuming (fully) what it has asked for. That is, if the query or other operation asks for 50 rows, the client application must retrieve that data as quickly as possible. This responsibility should never fall on the user—users have a tendency to walk away (physically or mentally), leaving work undone. Yes, some interfaces, such as RDO and ADO cursors, fetch the data for you in background threads—but you had better know when this is happening, because if you don't, you could end up with an unscalable application.

Data presentation The client application is responsible for displaying results from queries, as needed. This task might involve filling a Grid or ListBox control or filling out a complex form containing fields that require complex conversion, as when you're working with graphics or Rich Text Format (RTF) data. For example, when a client application fetches the path of a document from the database, it might use Microsoft Word to display the document. Since many applications use a master-detail methodology, the rows from several result sets might need to be placed into two or more display areas. For example, a typical master-detail hierarchy would have zero or more order rows for each customer, and each order would have zero or more items. Finally, the client keeps data presented to the user current and valid, which usually means executing background queries on exposed data to maintain currency or executing queries to keep hidden validation rules current.

Error management The client is also responsible for trapping and dealing with the errors that can, and do, occur in the course of handling user demands and server and network vagaries. In no case should the user be presented with dialog boxes that indicate a fatal error unless all other methods of managing the error have been exhausted. Effective and comprehensive error management is the sign of a successful client application. In many cases, the client application will be forced to make a number of decisions on its own to determine the cause and scope of the error and attempt recovery. Only when it's unavoidable should the client application solicit additional information from the user, who is often the person least able to help resolve the problem. Although error management is fairly easy for the developer, the user is rarely as informed about or concerned with the intricacies of the application or the overall database system. Would you be happy with a car that demanded that you supply precise fuel-air ratios on an especially cold morning when the car's computer couldn't figure out how to get your gas-guzzler started?

The server's responsibilities

In any client/server implementation, the server is not just a data dumping ground. The server is also responsible for intelligent resource management, security management, data management, query management, database system management, and error management. The emphasis in this section is more on the client side of this architecture, but you really must understand the role the server plays before you can create an efficient, trouble-free client application. In many cases, your DBMS design will include quite a bit of development on the server. That is, you will be required not only to lay out tables but also to develop the constraints, rules, triggers, views, stored procedures, and security permissions on all of the above—not to mention the replication, backup, log-file management, and the administrative procedures to make all of this work.

You must also define the boundaries of the middle layers, the client, and the server. More and more middleware in the form of intelligent server-side (or even client-side) objects is performing logical and physical disk input/output (I/O) to the database. I expect that developers of most applications, using object-oriented techniques, will spend considerable resources developing and managing these objects. But we'll discuss the distributed component architecture a little later in this chapter.

Resource management The server is responsible for managing its own resources. These resources include RAM, connections, disk space, CPU time, threads, and a set of caches or queues. For example, the server must allocate memory to the data and procedure caches and ensure that it is used wisely. It must also divide its attention among dozens to thousands of competing users— like so many baby birds crying for fresh worms. If the server has to compete for resources with other Windows NT services, its job is made that much harder. For example, if the Windows NT server must also act as a print server or domain controller, your SQL Server operations can't help but run slower. It's kind of like asking that mommy bird to wash cars between trips to the garden.

Security management The server prevents unauthorized access to itself and your database while permitting guarded access to those with valid permission. This task involves safeguarding not only the data itself but also views, procedures, and administration of the database. Yes, some of this security is left up to the host Windows NT server and the Windows NT domain controller. SQL Server enforces the checking of data types and also enforces rules, triggers, and index structures. Incoming data must conform to a complex set of criteria that are based on permissions granted to the user or to the group to which the user belongs. Data might be accepted or rejected because of database inconsistencies, violations of rules or triggers, checks of index duplicates, or other kinds of problems. To complicate matters, SQL Server runs on Windows NT, which has its own idea about who can get access to the server. Unless your code can find its way through the Windows NT moats and minefields, it won't be able to knock on SQL Server's door to beg for a connection.

Data management The server is also responsible for the validity and integrity of the data sent to the database system from your application and every other application that has permission to access your database. This task involves writing data to database tables once it has passed the security screen and recording these changes in the transaction logs. At the lowest levels, it means allocating and initializing database pages and blocks of pages as well as managing the physical disk I/O and any indexes or temporary database objects. The server is responsible for validating data using any rules assigned to data columns and for executing any triggers assigned to those data tables that are being changed. Another task of the server is to maintain the transaction log so that the system maintains a recoverable state at all times and operations can be rolled back or committed, as necessary. The server also maintains database statistics, the error log, and other supportive structures for tracking changes in the data and the schema.

Query management The server processes SQL queries from the clients, which involves syntax and object checks and compilation of a query into a valid and efficient processing plan—even if the query is a stored procedure. The server also fetches data rows according to the plan and returns the rows to the client (often via a remote server-side object), as requested. This means establishing a two-way conversation with the application to support client management of individual result sets. The server might also keep cursor keysets locally if the query builds a server-side cursor. Managing these and all the other temporary objects can consume considerable resources on the server, so it is the client application's responsibility to ensure that these resources are managed intelligently.

Database system management In managing the database system itself, the server manages all connections to the database, using network and database security criteria to coordinate use of and access to the connections. The server also maintains tables, indexes, procedures, rules, triggers, data types, lists of valid users, and other database objects. Other tasks of database management performed by the server include allocation, initialization, and deallocation of space for all database structures; management of the procedure and data queues, the database memory, and database threads of execution; and efficient sharing of CPU time among users and internal tasks.

Error management The server must also be capable of handling a variety of errors that, in most cases, client applications (and users) never see, and never should see. When problems or conflicts arise that the server can't resolve, you can often program the server to inform the administrator (even by e-mail or a voice page) or simply to report back to the client. Again, sending error reports back to the user is counterproductive if the user can't do anything about it. For example, if the amount of space available on a device is nearly exhausted, sending a message to the user does little to solve the problem. The user can't adjust the free space or do anything but worry, ignore the error, or call the System Administrator (SA) to fix the problem. Having the system e-mail the SA when things start going wrong makes much more sense. Having a warning light go on in the client application might also be helpful—something like an "oil" light on your car's dashboard. However, any message shown to the user must provide enough information for the user to make an informed decision regarding what action to take.

The other night, I dreamed that SQL Server returned the "cost" of a query as it was being processed so I could tell the user how long it would be before results were expected. I could also cancel queries that took too long. Perhaps someday this dream will come true.

The interface

In a SQL Server client/server architecture, the interface is designed to pass queries to the server and return result sets to the client, as you see in Figure 4-2, over a network link—a LAN or WAN. The client/ server interface in a SQL Server model is somewhat complex—it uses an unpublished form of metadata called the Tabular Data Stream (TDS)—but it does not pass disk sectors or anything resembling raw disk I/O data to or from the server. This means that the interface can be simple and, because the volume of data is so low, relatively slow without severely affecting the performance of the overall system or even the performance of the client system. It can also mean that if the link is fast enough, a far greater number of users can share the server than is possible when raw I/O data is sent over the wires. Only the distributed engine architecture sends raw I/O data this way—one of the principal reasons it can't scale particularly well.

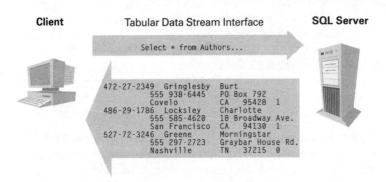

Figure 4-2 *SQL Server client/server architecture*

NOTE Even though DCOM, Remote Automation, and ActiveX technology are here, remember that the SQL server still speaks, reads, and writes in TDS. The objects that talk to the server must speak TDS to be understood—this condition hasn't changed. How the client speaks to the objects is new. All of these objects use interface layers that translate to and from TDS.

Distributed Engine Architecture

What I'm calling the distributed engine configuration places a dedicated database engine or query processor at each workstation. In this design, either a central file server or one of the workstation clients doubles as the central data repository. Figure 4-3 shows a distributed engine architecture with a centralized file server, and Figure 4-4 shows the same architecture but with a centralized database engine. The distributed engine configuration requires significantly more intelligence in the workstation front-end application than does the client/server configuration, and it needs more and faster hardware to support it. Each

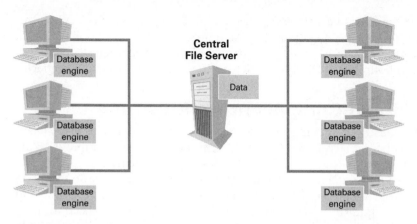

Figure 4-3 *Distributed engine architecture with a centralized file server*

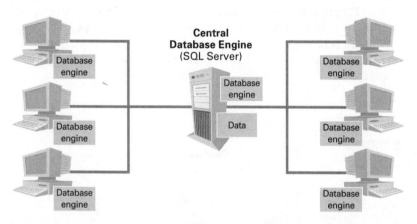

Figure 4-4 *Distributed engine architecture with centralized database engine*

workstation contains a stand-alone database engine closely coupled to a front-end application, and each workstation acts independently—ignorant, for the most part, of database activity on other workstations. Sure, the file server operating system is aware that a number of users are competing for a single file, but it has no idea what's happening at the database level—especially at the logical level, where the data is more than just clusters and sectors of a disk file. For a single-user database, this approach makes considerable sense. It also throws more CPU horsepower at the problem—which is both good and bad, as I'll explain.

The principal benefit of the distributed engine design is portability. You can set up this configuration on a laptop and take it into the field. The real problem comes up when you try to synchronize the laptop data with home-office data. A significant number of architects are configuring distributed engine systems that have to double as SQL Server front-end applications once connected to the corporate LAN. Herein lies another problem—the choice of a common interface. Many choose DAO only to discover that it doesn't address SQL Server stored procedures very well, so they choose RDO only to discover that it doesn't access Jet databases very well. SQL Server 7.0 for Windows 95/98 solves this problem by letting you run a copy of SQL Server right on your laptop in Windows 95/98. This capability means that you can program in ADO or RDO and access both local and home-office-based data using the same interface.

Distributed Component Architecture

Basically, a distributed component architecture moves logic out of the client and onto other replaceable components. This move can be as simple as taking business rules out of the body of your code and putting them into separate class DLLs or as sophisticated as running business rules or other data I/O logic on a middle-tier server. As illustrated in Figure 4-5, this architecture is based on a three-tier, or multitier, architecture that places user interface logic in the user, or client, tier; business logic in the middle tier; and data access logic in the back-end, or data source, tier. This arrangement permits you to segment your executables into functionally discrete units. It also lets you assign developers to the parts of the system that they are best able to work on. For example, you could assign C++ or Java developers (if you can find any) to work on middle-tier components, SQL Server experts to work on the data source tier, and Visual Basic developers to work on all three—but especially on the client tier.

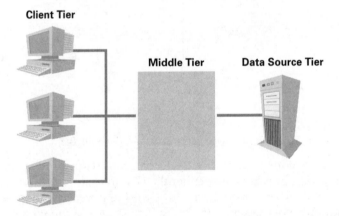

Figure 4-5   *Three-tier architecture*

NOTE   One of the tools we use to manage three-tier architectures is the Microsoft Visual Modeler. It is included in the Visual Basic, Enterprise Edition.

Moving logic out of the client has been a goal for some time now. I've been pushing developers to use stored procedures, which in many respects implement this type of architecture. Centralized logic means centralized deployment, support, and universal operation. In other words, since the root tables are usually hidden by stored procedures, the only way any application can get at the data is through these stored procedures. This centralization also means that when it comes time to change the rules of the game—the business rules—

the client applications don't need to be recompiled and redeployed to deal with these changes. This assumes, of course, that the client applications have been written to accommodate this type of change. And they should be.

When implementing a distributed component architecture with stored procedures, you are limited to the use of Transact-SQL (TSQL) logic unless you shell out to other executables or have discovered the SQL OLE interfaces. I've included some text on SQL OLE on the CD, in a document titled "A Side Trip to SQL OLE.doc." When stored procedures are used as a substitute for DLL executables, the stored procedures are really running on a "middle" tier. This constraint can be somewhat stifling because you can communicate with the stored procedures only through the proprietary TDS interface (as exposed by the data access interfaces like DAO, RDO, and ADO).

So if you've been working with SQL Server for some time now, you're probably already using this type of architecture. But you might not yet know about a relatively new way to implement distributed component architecture—with distributed Visual Basic–authored components. Because Visual Basic 5.0 and beyond can create native-code compiled components, and because Microsoft Transaction Server (MTS) is capable of managing these components, you can now move a lot more Visual Basic–authored logic to the middle tier—logic that any competent Visual Basic developer can write. Figure 4-6 shows the distributed component architecture that uses components created for MTS. Handling all this stuff without MTS would be like hitchhiking from the center line of the freeway in Montana—at night—wearing a ninja suit.

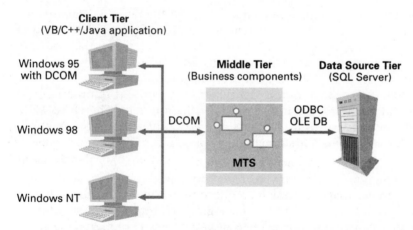

Figure 4-6 *Distributed component architecture that uses components created for MTS*

You need to keep in mind a number of issues when accessing distributed components, which is a fundamentally different process than simply accessing stored procedures. Let's take a look at some of the key issues:

- Middle-tier stored procedures are accessible from any of the data access interfaces—all of which communicate with the database via TDS protocol and a persistent database connection. You simply formulate a query that references a stored procedure (directly or indirectly) and work with the rows or OUTPUT values returned.

- Client-side (in-process or out-of-process) COM components are simply business rules or data I/O routines encapsulated into replaceable class libraries. These are referenced as any other class libraries you create and can be referenced by several applications in the same memory space. References to the properties and methods are fast and easy because the operating system isn't really involved in the intermemory operations.

- Middle-tier COM components are accessed from the client via DCOM. You just tell each client's Registry the location of the remote component, and Windows takes care of the rest. The COM components are installed on a remote server and managed there. The most significant difference here between client-side and remote COM objects is the overhead involved in referencing their properties and methods. Each time you reference a property or execute a method, the operating system has to build a set of DCOM packets and transmit them over the network. Therefore, it is more efficient to make a single method call that contains many arguments than it is to make multiple property calls that reference only a single value. No, Visual Basic and DCOM don't marshal these property references, so they can all be sent in a single packet—even when you use the With operator. This means you should redesign your applications to use method arguments instead of properties. Sure, you can still use properties, but they also imply that state is being maintained on the middle tier—another no-no. Think stateless and methods—lots of methods with lots of arguments.

Consider that you have to communicate with a remote database over DCOM—not RDO or ADO. Yes, the remote components can and do use RDO and ADO to perform the physical I/O to the database. This means that you have an entirely new set of connectivity problems, and (again) the network plays a big role in the efficiency of this interface. No, you won't be happy with just "moving" DLLs over to a middle-tier server—not without rethinking how properties and methods are marshaled over the interface. Therefore, MTS-managed components need to be less property driven and more method-argument driven, to make them more network efficient and more scalable.

IMHO

The transition from property-rich object interfaces to method-argument architecture is the most difficult task to master when moving to COM-based or MTS-based designs.

This architecture also means that you have to figure out how to build "stateless" components. When you change an object's property, you change its state. Consider that component architecture implies shared code—lots of other applications are sharing the same logic. Each time a component is invoked, MTS instantiates a copy of the code and creates a unique data segment for that specific instance of the code to use. Yes, it's up to MTS to manage each component's data and code space, loading and unloading them as needed. When you set a property on a component, that change is stored in the instance's data segment. However, if a component must maintain state between calls, MTS can't release the data segment until you tell MTS you're done making property changes. If MTS has to keep a bazillion data segments lying around, it will soon run out of resources and bog down. On the other hand, if you design your components simply to accept all needed state information as arguments to object methods, the data segments can be freed as soon as the method operation completes.

When the time comes to access SQL Server from one of these middle-tier components, you can apply most of your existing Visual Basic data access skills. You'll face some limitations, though. You won't want to use DAO/Jet, and probably not even RDO. In the first place, Jet doesn't know how to multitask very well. And RDO doesn't know how to pass back an rdoResultset to your client. ADO, however, is specifically designed for this type of implementation. But we'll get to that later, in Part V, "Using ADO and OLE DB."

Yes, you can still access stored procedures from the middle tier, and you won't have to abandon this code in lieu of the new design. Remember that in a traditional client/server system, which is two-tiered, the client manages most transaction operations. However, you will want to rethink your transaction strategies because MTS handles virtually all aspects of transaction management.

Does MTS run middle-tier components faster than if they were accessed from the same memory space as the client? Ah, no—not even close. Then why even bother? Well, the distributed component architecture offers these perks:

WARNING!
When using connection pooling, you'll discover a serious problem that the dev types haven't yet figured out. We'll talk about this problem when we get to the ADO chapters, but for now consider that the data interfaces neither monitor nor maintain state on the connection. So if you execute a SET command or simply change the default database, the next component that inherits your connection will see this change. Also, when you get a connection from the connection pool, you're not guaranteed that it is in a "virginal" state. It's kinda like ordering pizza using the party line in a college dorm. The pizza guy across town has no idea he's getting instructions from 40 different people—until the pizza is a foot high with 47 different ingredients.

- You'll be able to leverage your teams better. Many of the applications being built today are too complex to be managed and executed in conventional ways.

- Since all Windows applications are component-based, putting those components on a centrally managed server will help you stay on top of rapidly evolving business conditions (and logic).

- You can create applications that scale better because you can put more horsepower on that middle-tier server. And once MTS load balancing arrives, scaling will be even easier.

- You'll be able to manage more complex operations and transactions than can be handled safely at and by the client.

- These centrally managed components can be accessed in the same memory space (via COM), from Active Server Pages or WebClass code.

- This architecture exposes 32-bit technology to clients running other operating systems. Using Active Server Pages, you can access middle-tier components from any browser. This is a way to keep your Windows 3.x or Macintosh systems as viable platforms—all able to access SQL Server and the central database.

- You'll find it easier to manage deployment of your code. Clients won't need to be constantly installing new software. Support is cheaper and faster.

No, distributed component architectures are not a panacea. A number of trade-offs are involved, some that you might not be ready to accept. For some systems, however, they are a godsend. I'm not going to spend too much time on MTS and distributed component architectures in this edition of the Hitchhiker's Guide. But I am going to provide you with some tips and techniques you can use to help hone your Visual Basic data access skills when creating these objects (not until Part V, however).

Web-Based Architecture

And the Web. I've already expostulated on the evolution of this paradigm and where it fits (and where it gives fits). A Web-based architecture assumes very little about the users—except that they at least have a browser that can interpret Hypertext Markup Language (HTML). Most browsers can also interpret Java applets—some better or more compatibly than others—but we don't really want to tour that dark alley. You can create Web applications to query SQL Server database systems, and you can use Visual Basic to do it. Visual Basic plays lots of roles on the Web, some of which are shown in Figure 4-7 and listed here:

- Visual Basic, in the form of Visual Basic, Scripting Edition (VBScript), in Active Server Pages can be interpreted on the client or middle-tier server and can contain references to Visual Basic–authored components (or to components written in other languages).

- Visual Basic executables can be hosted in Microsoft Internet Explorer and executed on the client as Active Documents (really just repackaged Visual Basic application executables).

- Visual Basic–authored ActiveX controls can be hosted by Internet Explorer.

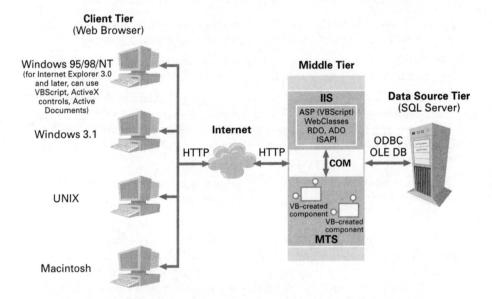

Figure 4-7 *Web-based architecture and ways that Visual Basic can be used*

Keep in mind that running from the Web implies that you don't necessarily have access to a "persistent" LAN connection. You're often restricted to accessing a component that is doing the data access chores for you on a central server. This "agent" has its own user ID and password and generates result sets (usually small) on your behalf. These are passed back to the client, where they can be displayed in HTML text boxes, or perhaps in a bound grid. This paradigm expects you to maintain state on the client since the remote components can't afford to maintain a "current" state for each and every one of hundreds of thousands of clients.

Again, if you want to use the Web architecture, you'll need to rethink your approaches to data access and many of the fundamental ways of interacting with the user. Many find the paradigm confining, and since the development tools are still evolving, they discover that they must extend their time-to-market forecasts significantly.

Active Document objects

The Active Document technology was first introduced with Visual Basic 5.0 to deploy existing Win32-based applications to the Web by converting them into a Web-friendly format for hosting within the Internet Explorer browser. Basically, this approach assumes that you'll still be able to establish a persistent connection to the SQL Server from your Web client, so it's fine for intranet deployment situations. If you can't get a hard connection back to the server, however, such as when you're connecting via the public Web through a firewall, you'll have to redesign your data access interfaces.

WebClass applications

The problem for Visual Basic developers is that Web application languages such as VBScript or Java often require programmers to work the learning curve in reverse. Developers are required to spend time familiarizing themselves with the schemata and syntax of a new, more restrictive language rather than leveraging their existing knowledge of more powerful application programming languages. Microsoft Visual Basic 6.0 WebClasses were designed to solve this problem.

Visual Basic 6.0 WebClasses offer developers the ability to create server-based applications with a browser and a platform-agnostic client—in Visual Basic, using all of the language and all of its debugging and interactive features. The WebClass-based application resides on the server, and the client can be customized to take advantage of the developer's environment, whether it's strict HTML, ActiveX support, Dynamic HTML, or XML. WebClasses are an optimal solution in heterogeneous environments where multiple versions and/or brands of browsers and operating systems are in use.

Existing Visual Basic projects can benefit from WebClass user interfaces as well. Since a WebClass is a COM-based object, it is able to talk to other COM components, such as back-end business and data access modules. Developers can add WebClasses to their existing application projects, develop the client interface using a Web development tool such as Microsoft Visual InterDev, and deploy applications for the Windows client and onto the Web—simultaneously.

Using WebClasses in Visual Basic 6.0, Visual Basic programmers have a familiar and more component-oriented starting point for building server-based Web applications. WebClasses are components created within the Visual Basic integrated development environment (IDE) that, like all other Visual Basic components, exist within an event-based programming model. The role of WebClasses in the overall Windows DNA (Distributed interNet Applications

Netscape's move to release their Navigator source to the public domain is loony tunes. Since the browser is an HTML interpreter, it's essential that it behave in a way we can (all) depend on. Now, when you write an application that depends on deterministic browser behavior, you won't know if your customer is running a version of Internet Explorer or one of the three thousand customized/hacked versions of Navigator. Letting every developer from here to Karachi hack Navigator code can only direct Netscape onto the rocks. Imagine the problems the Vikings would have had if anyone could arrange the stars as they saw fit. They would have run into the coast of South Carolina instead of Newfoundland and southerners would speak Norwegian with a southern accent. Ya shore, you betcha y'all.

Architecture) programming model is to sit on the middle tier and respond to Hypertext Transfer Protocol (HTTP) requests. Of course, within a given WebClass, the Visual Basic programmer can leverage the entire range of Visual Basic features.

The net gain of WebClass-based applications with HTML clients is to offer Visual Basic developers more choice in how they deploy their applications. Whether it's an existing project, an application already in deployment, or a completely new project, WebClasses allow developers to maximize code reuse and extend their reach to an audience they've never before been able to reach.

A litany of other variations are available when you're working with the Web, the browsers, SQL Server, and Visual Basic. I'm not going to discuss these alternatives here in the Hitchhiker's Guide, but I will include lots of pertinent (and some very impertinent) information about using Visual Basic to access SQL Server from the Web in Part V.

Evaluating Client/Server and Distributed Engine Architectures

In this next section, we'll walk through a traditional client/server configuration and a distributed engine configuration so that you can get a closer look at the specific implementations. You'll be able to see how you can assemble the theories and concepts you've been reading about into a more-or-less typical Visual Basic to SQL Server system.

A Hypothetical Client/Server Configuration

CAUTION

Don't plan to use the Windows NT Server system as a workstation and as a host for SQL Server. That's like asking someone to be a Trappist monk and an underworld attorney at the same time.

In our hypothetical client/server configuration, the centralized server is dedicated to the task of running the database engine. Too often, the database engine is forced to do at least double duty, as both a file server and a print server—and sometimes even triple duty, as a user workstation as well. Using the database engine as a file server isn't so bad, since very little counterproductive overhead might be involved. But when the database engine has to share RAM space and resources with a print spooler or other background tasks, the performance of the engine can really suffer. Consider that a print server has to contend with large, complex print images being crammed bit by bit into the slowest pile of iron connected to your computer: the printer.

In our hypothetical client/server model, front-end applications are designed to be used on fairly low-powered client PC workstations running anything from straight MS-DOS (using DB-Library from C, or VBSQL from Visual Basic for MS-DOS) to the Microsoft Windows, Windows NT, Windows 95, and Windows 98 operating systems; you'll have little need for extra CPU horsepower, local disk space, or more RAM—that is, assuming you use one of the less RAM-hungry programming interfaces.

The LAN contribution

LAN performance plays a significant role in some architectures. Ask yourself (or your system architect) if the LAN interface to your SQL Server is expected to carry any of the traffic listed on page 94.

A Quick Point About File Servers

In the general sense, I don't think you should share CPU and I/O resources by sharing files on the same server as SQL Server. However, one of the database designs that I'm finding more and more appealing is that of an image file server. IMHO, images, and large text chunks have no business being stored in the database. Sure, it's possible to store gargantuan images or files as database pages, but SQL Server isn't particularly efficient about the way these are stored, retrieved, or backed up. Yes, SQL Server 7.0 has improved how this data is stored and has even expanded the size of Varchar and VarBinary data types to 8000 bytes to accommodate small binary large objects (BLOBs). Unless you make special arrangements, however, IMAGE and TEXT data pages are stored with all of the other ordinary row-data pages and must be backed up as such. These data types gobble space on the server's devices, and since they can't be accessed separately, they can't be compressed (unless you do it in your own code) or backed up separately (at least not easily)—even though the data might never change.

There are better ways to store this type of data. In many cases, I've recommended storing page-based data in separate files on a separate file server, leaving only a pathname and offset in the database. This practice increases access performance dramatically and speeds up backup, recovery, and transaction-log handling (when the image operations are logged—which is rarely done). This approach also means that you can use a variety of compression and file media to store data. For example, you can use read-only CDs or even tape (no, not paper tape) to store the data, managing it through your own set of retrieval routines. In addition, you don't always have to transmit the page-based data over the LAN or WAN because it can be stored on a CD right on the client's system. That is, you can distribute the page-based data (especially when it doesn't change very often) on a CD deployed with the front-end application. Sure, the application might need updating, but in many, many cases, the page-based data doesn't.

Here's an additional tip: a company I worked with distributes an application that retrieves medical imagery. The company's original plan called for the database to hold complex (and rather disgusting) images of people's insides, but the final implementation simply included the data on a companion CD—the application pulls up the pictures by retrieving the path and image coordinates from the database, which are also on the CD. Likewise, if your design uses the database to retrieve large read-only data blocks, it might be a good idea to use the database to store the file's pathname instead of its contents.

- SQL queries and result sets related to database access. No, some approaches don't send either the query from the client or the result sets back to the client—they depend on DCOM or perhaps other connectivity techniques such as mail to send requests to the server.

- Print spooler traffic.

- Direct shared-disk I/O as a file server, with files simply copied or moved to and from the server.

- Traffic generated by applications using the network as the motherboard of the computer. (In this case, files shared over the network are opened by multiple users and are searched and manipulated as if they were local files on a single-user system.)

- Traffic generated by Internet or e-mail servers.

- Packet protocols that clog the network with broadcast messages (such as NetBIOS).

- Any of the new network connectivity applications—such as the ones that broadcast video or live audio over the network.

- Traffic generated by Internet access—as when using a proxy server on the network.

If more than a few of these network contributors are possible, the network could become a performance bottleneck in your design. Another factor to consider is network load as affected by external factors, time of day, increased latency, efficiency, and bandwidth. If the network is already running at capacity, it might be wise to consider faster LAN hardware or a secondary dedicated network, or perhaps an architecture that is not heavily dependent on the LAN's bandwidth. If the LAN is really a WAN and your application is expected to work across continents or oceans, bounced from satellite to satellite, you'd better be prepared for some dramatic restrictions in the type of topology and programming model you can choose.

In any case, if your LAN is expected to carry a significant load, be sure to test a sample configuration under live load conditions. Live testing is also a good idea if you want to try to connect external workstations via remote access service (RAS) or some other low-speed link. You should also ask yourself whether the LAN can take the additional load. If your LAN is already heavily burdened, it might not be such a hot idea to add another LAN-intensive application to the load. Don't expect your test with 5 users to reflect what will happen with 25 or 2500 users.

NOTE RAS uses a modem to connect external workstations to a corporate network; given the low stress placed on the network when you're using VBSQL, using a low-level data interface might be a viable alternative. Yes, you can use RDO or even ADO if you behave yourself—but stay away from cursors.

In our hypothetical client/server installation, you can use a fairly low-performance LAN or even a serial RAS link. The principal reason why you can use a relatively low-performance LAN has to do with what the LAN carries. In this hypothetical design, it carries relatively minuscule queries (of usually fewer than several dozen bytes) in one direction and retrieves only those data rows that are needed. Unless you use cursors extensively—that is, incorrectly—your LAN won't be required to carry anywhere near its capacity, multiplied by a dozen or a dozen dozen users. However, some of the object-based designs can dramatically affect the amount of LAN traffic if you aren't careful. For example, making multiple separate calls to a remote COM object can be very expensive.

This design assumes that the LAN is dedicated to your application and isn't required to support significant amounts of high-volume transaction processing. For example, if the application is going to upload complex bit-mapped graphics, a faster network would only make operations faster. But if your application makes complex queries that yield only a limited number of result rows (say, a few hundred to a few thousand), a faster network might prove unnecessary.

I got up in a SQL Server user's group meeting some time ago to address a question about performance. Others had offered advice on changes to the schema, using faster or more processors, or a different front-end programming model. I simply suggested more RAM. "A couple of gigs or more of RAM," I said, "can solve a litany of schema problems and make many poor design decisions irrelevant."

Typical client/server configurations

Table 4-1 shows three client/server configurations that will provide adequate user response. CPU type and speed are given for the low end of the number of users. If you don't have enough data cache RAM, you'll generally find that SQL Server systems are disk-bound. However, once most active data pages are in memory, you'll generally find that SQL Server systems are CPU-bound. Increasing CPU speed or moving to a Windows NT–based multiprocessor hardware platform can also improve server performance.

Table 4-1
Typical Client/Server Configurations

System Component	Typical Configuration for 1–10 Users	Typical Configuration for 10–50 Users	Typical Configuration for 40–100 Users
Server system	90-MHz (or faster) Pentium, Windows NT, 32 MB (or more) of RAM, 1.5-GB hard disk, VGA video, 16-bit network adapter	133-MHz (or faster) Pentium, Windows NT, 80 MB (or more) of RAM, 1.5-GB hard disk, VGA video, 16-bit network adapter	Multiple 133-MHz (or faster) Pentium-class processors, Windows NT, 128 MB (or more) of RAM, 2-GB hard disk, VGA video, 32-bit network adapter
Workstation	PC XT*, AT, or better (depends on operating system)	PC XT*, AT, or better (depends on operating system)	PC XT*, AT, or better (depends on operating system)

* This can be any XT-class system if you run MS-DOS, even an Osborne. For the client system's Windows operating system, a 486/50 is barely enough nowadays, especially if you're running Microsoft Office 97.

With most systems, both server and workstation will probably require at least a single-speed CD-ROM drive to load software (at least initially). Visual Basic and SQL Server are now distributed exclusively on CD. Since the whole CD isn't full, maybe the SQL Server group should have included some hit tunes by Elton John. (And maybe they did….) At least you would have something to listen to while waiting for a query to run.

Notice that the suggested server system doesn't have a particularly fast video adapter. It shouldn't need one. The server should have just enough video hardware—no more—to tell what's going on in character mode (or in low-resolution VGA mode). The hard disk is big enough to store the operating system (about 100 MB) and a small database (about 50 MB). SQL Server and its GUI-based utilities take up a lot more room than the old IBM OS/2 versions. Internet Explorer 4.01 and later also takes up a lot more room on disk and in memory. The Windows NT operating system is also much greedier than the older versions of OS/2 when it comes to hard disk space. I originally started working with a 350-MB drive on my lab server; once the Windows NT operating system and SQL Server were loaded, I had almost no room left for the rest of the ancillary utilities or for a test database of reasonable size.

There has to be sufficient allocation for swap and temporary database space, which is directly related to the number of users your system will have and to how you intend to build your cursors. And, no, the server should not be configured so that it has to swap out the server software in favor of some other program or subsystem; adding more hard disk space for a larger database or more RAM and processors for better performance is something you can expect to do as your system grows.

TIP   I'm often asked, "Is it better to buy one 4-GB disk or two 2-GB disks?" Sure, it's cheaper to buy a single large disk and certainly easier to set up, back up, and maintain. However, consider that by having each logical device on a separate drive, you end up with multiple disk I/O operations, but more importantly, multiple heads, actuator mechanisms, and logically independent disk I/O channels. Two are better than one in this case. No, SQL Server no longer assigns separate threads to each device.

As the number of users increases, the increased need for performance eventually will require you to add more RAM so that more pages are in the memory queues. With the client/server configuration, once you approach the level of 20 to 50 users, you might want to add another processor or upgrade to a more powerful CPU (or both). The Windows NT operating system needs more RAM and more disk space, so you might be tempted to use OS/2. You have this option if you stick with OS/2 1.3; more recent versions have a distinct disadvantage for SQL Server, and the most recent versions don't seem to run SQL Server at all. At some point, you'll find that the system is net-bound and that the server needs to be upgraded to 16-bit or 32-bit power on the net card. However, if your LAN is already at capacity, you'll discover that your new 100-MB net card waits at the same speed as your 10-MB net card.

The workstation system shouldn't be any more powerful than it needs to be to run the operating system, whether MS-DOS, Windows, or Windows NT. I don't recommend an XT to run the Windows operating system—unless you work for the government or are into waiting. An XT won't run Windows 95 or even Windows 3.x for that matter. If you're running an MS-DOS–based front end, an XT is fine, especially if you can add an expanded RAM card. In most cases, the operating system will take up far more resources than the SQL front-end application. CP/M will be problematic. Ah, for the simpler days….

Cost per user

Startup costs for the three configurations shown in Table 4-1 would have to include the server hardware and the license for the server engine. Add to that the cost of a single copy of the language (assuming that you choose a language, such as Visual Basic, that doesn't require multiple-use licenses) and the API interface. The disk space listed in the table is not for data in the database but for operating system overhead and user-related temporary space. The operating system, base database, temporary tables, swap file, applications, and a copy each of Doom and Age of Empires will easily take about 150–300 MB for a serious server system. Add your database disk requirements to this total—more if you plan to run Hearts or Doom over the network.

Database larger than your cache? Use your cash to add more RAM and processors: $2000 worth of server hardware upgrades can often outperform a week's worth of database tuning and is a bargain at today's fully burdened labor rates.

Figure 4-8 plots the cost of our hypothetical client/server installation, with costs shared by all users. The chart assumes a single server and one additional workstation for each additional user. Incremental costs include the workstations and their LAN hardware. This plot is fairly asymptotic, up to the point where a larger server (or maybe just more RAM) is needed to support the additional users. I put this point where the number of users exceeds 50. As you see, the initial cost of the server is quickly amortized. The model depicted in Figure 4-8 forms the foundation of many client/server cost-effectiveness studies.

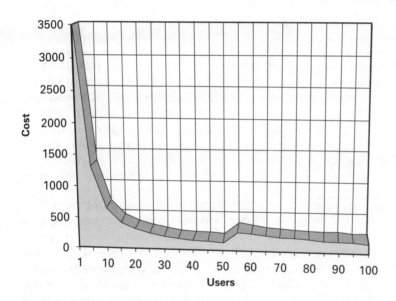

Figure 4-8 *Cost of client/server installation*

Client/server performance

Without going into a long-winded treatise on client/server performance, I'll invite you to consider this fact: some server-based client/server systems, including SQL Server, actually have higher per-user throughput as new users are added. In other words, adding more users makes processing faster for each user. The reason for this seeming paradox is commonality. Performance doesn't improve when the extra users aren't sharing the same database and shared procedures.

When they are, however, the server doesn't have to take the time to load them into memory; they're already there. When multiple users share the same stored procedure, as in SQL Server, the engine doesn't have to stop, load, and compile the procedure before executing it. Additional users might be able to use the procedure that is already sitting in RAM. This convenience means that the server can handle significantly more users and process information faster than systems that can't share work already processed for other users.

Actually, until version 7.0, SQL Server didn't really share stored procedures—they weren't reentrant. SQL Server did cache unused procedures so that they didn't have to be reloaded once a user was done with them. That is, when a stored procedure ended in earlier versions, it was marked as unused but otherwise left in memory until SQL Server needed the RAM to load another procedure. If another user who needed the procedure came along, SQL Server simply reactivated any dormant copy that happened to be in memory. The chances of a specific procedure being in RAM is a function of the following conditions:

- How much procedure cache RAM you allocate
- How many instances of the procedure fit into the cache
- How many procedures are used
- How many users access the procedures

NOTE Imagine a home in which each of 10 children and 2 parents had to eat something different at each meal. Instead of one big pot of soup on the stove at suppertime, there would be 12 tiny ones, each with a different kind of soup. In the same way, it's entirely possible to create single-server client/server systems that manage large numbers of databases, but these implementations couldn't share anything but the CPU's attention and the server's code.

SQL Server 7.0 changes the way procedures are shared among users. Now procedures—including both compiled stored procedures and compiled (and running) ad hoc queries—can be shared by any number of users. If you execute the same query more than once, SQL Server can reuse the compiled query plan and let the second and each subsequent user share the code. Since the procedure cache no longer has a preallocated area, memory needed to make this sharing work efficiently is allocated as it is needed. The result? Faster execution and better overall performance.

Figure 4-9 shows that as more users are added to this hypothetical dedicated system, performance improves. Moreover, as each user is added, the chances get better that a needed page is already in memory or that a necessary stored procedure has already been loaded. (Of course, this performance model assumes that an effective locking strategy is used.) This particular system's performance per user drops off at around 500 users; the point at which performance drops off depends on the factors listed on pages 99–100.

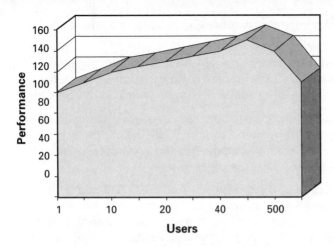

Figure 4-9 *Client/server engine performance*

- **Amount of data in the database**   Smaller databases might be more prone to throughput problems as the number of users increases, with more users fighting over fewer core pages. Here a robust locking strategy and the wise use of cursors is essential. Row locks could also either improve or degrade performance depending on how many locks SQL Server has to manage.

- **Number of data collisions**   Data collisions can occur when multiple users are accessing the same page or row. The number of collisions is inversely proportional to the size of the database core—that is, the set of data most likely to be accessed or updated. Data collisions aren't really a problem unless multiple simultaneous updates are being attempted.

- **Number of simultaneous users**   A 500-user system that has only 50 active users needs a very different resource mix than one with 500 active users. An active user is one actually running queries or making updates—not one simply logged in or who can log in but hasn't.

- **Ratio of updates and inserts to queries**   How many changes are being made at any one time and by how many users? This question is tied to the locks issue. Are updated pages/rows evenly distributed, or do most updates occur on the same shared pages or against the same few rows? This issue also applies to systems using row locks since these locks must be managed by SQL Server—imposing a significant degree of CPU overhead as the number of locks increases.

- **Broadness or specificity of update transactions**   Are update transactions broad in scope or are they focused on specific rows? For example, do update operations change a wide expanse of rows in a single operation, and must these operations be completed before other, similar transactions can proceed?

- **Efficiency of queries**   How fast do the client applications populate their result sets? Do client applications depend on users to move to the last row before cursors are closed? Are cursors being created only where required? Are cursors large enough to satisfy immediate needs, but no larger?

- **Efficiency of updates** When an application, while holding a locked page or row, takes an inordinate amount of time to complete an update, the overall performance of the database can be dramatically reduced.

- **Data distribution** How is the data spread out over the database? Are there update or query "hot spots" that increase locking problems or decrease data I/O? For example, are queries and updates focused on a relatively few number of database pages or rows?

- **Commonality of data and procedures** Can the DBMS engine share cached data pages and procedures, or are the queries so broad or so specific that they eliminate any efficiencies gained by commonality? Or when database operations access common pages, does update and access locking reduce performance? This commonality also implies that the database server is dedicated to the task at hand and doesn't have to deal with several databases at once or with ancillary processes such as acting as a print or file server or even as a workstation.

- **Number of queries per second** Is the system an online transaction processing system, or is it used for decision support?

- **Amount of data processed per query** Are some front-end applications uploading or downloading large numbers of rows—using the SQL server as an ISAM data source? Is the client application moving page-based data over the wire?

- **Production schedule** Can bulk updates or database synchronization routines be done at non-peak hours, or does the currency of the system data demand immediate across-the-board updates?

- **Number and complexity of triggers and rules** Are complex, time-consuming triggers needed to maintain complex database relationship constraints?

- **Number and usability of indexes** More indexes mean faster access for retrieval but slower updates.

- **Speed and efficiency of hardware** Hardware would include the LAN. In most cases, disk caching doesn't help here. To maintain the database's viability, the database engine needs to manage the caches. Is there enough RAM to meet the needs of the data and procedure caches and TempDB?

- **Amount of work done on the front end** Does the front-end application prequalify the updates so that all (or most) will pass centralized rule and integrity checks? Does the front-end application submit the queries as batches to increase efficiency, or are queries and updates submitted individually?

- **Replication** Is the server having to take time out to replicate or mirror some or all of the data store?

A Hypothetical Distributed Engine Configuration

Now let's turn to a hypothetical distributed engine configuration. Here we discuss the merits and pitfalls of an architecture typically implemented when you build a Microsoft Access database—with or without connecting to SQL Server. This configuration expects a copy of the Microsoft Jet Database engine to be running alongside each client application—sharing its RAM, CPU bandwidth and performing most if not all data access chores.

Running a sophisticated multiuser operating system just to get an equally sophisticated query processor to access a single-file database is like using a pile driver to install a garage sale sign. Once you add a second user, however, the configuration becomes an order of magnitude more complex. Things don't get much more complicated beyond the second user, but the system does tend to get progressively stressed and subject to failure as the shared-file database architecture gets stretched like last summer's bathing suit.

The LAN contribution

In the distributed engine configuration, the LAN hardware plays a critical (and often limiting) role. (See Figure 4-10.) Each workstation uses the network as a local disk channel. What this means is that when an application accesses a local hard disk, it accesses the operating system file I/O primitives after having passed through a number of complex logical data object layers. Once the system file I/O takes over, local hard disks are accessed via the motherboard bus, the local hard disk controller card, and the on-drive controller. Data I/O throughput is limited by the bandwidth of the motherboard bus (which generally is very fast), the power of the disk controller card, and the performance of the drive and its own controller. (The hard disk controller can include caching logic and perhaps even pre-fetch or lazy-write hardware-assisted logic that can really improve performance for this type of system. Caching controllers can help most disk operations, but in some cases they can interfere with database integrity. To deal with this contingency, the lazy-write feature is often disabled.)

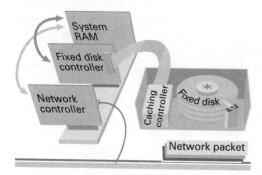

Figure 4-10 *LAN hardware in the distributed engine configuration*

What this configuration means for you is that when you execute a query, the database query processor has to read and update the indexes and any tables over the network. And this reliance on the network can mean, in a worst-case scenario, that many, many index and table blocks are passed over the network, sometimes several times in a single query.

When you access a hard disk drive over the network, you add two network controller cards, a lot of cable, and perhaps a half-dozen or more multiplexers, concentrators, and maybe even modems to the circuit. You also have to make a LAN packet of every disk I/O request. This means that for each block of data, which can range from a few hundred to several thousand bytes, a network driver has to add addressing, protocol, and checksum data to create an addressable packet of data. In some cases, the packets must be enclosed in packets that are themselves enclosed in packets as you traverse through TCP/IP, SNA, and named pipe protocol mazes. Each packet is placed on the network as space becomes available. If the LAN is busy, the driver and the net card block until they can cram another packet in edgewise. Having the LAN loaded up with mail, HTTP, other low-level file I/O, and network overhead packets doesn't make this system work any better.

At the server end, the data packet is picked off the network by the server's network controller card—when it isn't busy reading other users' packets. (Remember that you're the one who wanted this system to do double duty as a print server to save money). The packets are opened by the network driver, and the data is quickly routed to the file server's operating system as an I/O request. The file server takes the request and performs the disk I/O operation by reading or writing the requested data. The file server software then sends the requested sectors or write confirmations back—through the same gauntlet. Whew. Get the idea? A tremendous amount of processing is required to get this configuration to work. No wonder this architecture never really took off when it was first introduced in the 1980s.

Each workstation can cache parts of the database locally, in volatile RAM or temporary disk space, so if the workstation shuts down without posting "dirty" cache pages and closing the database file, the central database file can become corrupted. Because users often turn their computers on and off as if they were television sets, this form of database damage can become a way of life unless you have some heart-to-heart discussions with your users. Fortunately, most of the more recent versions of the databases designed to use distributed engine architecture limit their exposure to this kind of damage by using carefully orchestrated write operations. If one of these physical writes is interrupted, the database is marked suspect. This approach is also subject to failure modes triggered by LAN storms or disruptions—but you probably never have those. (Yeah, right.) For this design to work, the LAN must be a screamer: a device so fast that if you held it up to your ear, you could hear the bits running into each other and crying out in pain.

Because the type of network traffic is very different in this configuration, you might discover that as you add more users (though I can't tell you exactly how many more) the system gets bogged down performing even the simplest query. You'll also find that different network protocols can significantly affect scalability and throughput. For example, an Ethernet network tends to be fairly fast, and it scales nicely—up to the point where it breaks down completely. Often a significant amount of data must be sent up and down a network so that contact can be maintained with all the network nodes and resources. This overhead is a function of the network protocol in use and can account for a significant amount of the total network traffic.

When you attempt to determine whether your network can carry the load of a distributed engine design, be sure to consider the network load as it is currently implemented. In other words, how many users are already tied to the network, and what load are they putting on the existing servers and network routers? Running your tests against a dedicated LAN is a great idea for crash tests, but not for evaluating production performance.

Typical distributed engine configurations

Table 4-2 on the following page describes three typical distributed engine hardware configurations that will provide adequate user response. CPU type and speed are given for the low end of the range of users. Generally, you'll find that the system becomes net-bound or begins to be tied up because the server is waiting for disk access. Increasing the CPU speed or upgrading the server to the Windows NT operating system can improve performance. Using DoubleSpace or DriveSpace disk compression or Windows NT compressed data files has just the opposite effect: the compression/decompression activity adds to the overall load on the server. This type of system has an entirely different set of configuration constraints from those in our hypothetical client/server configuration. Here, the shared file server is not expected to do double duty as a workstation, but it still must have the horsepower to deal with any number of data-hungry workstations. Remember that each workstation is running its own database engine—the central file server is simply sharing out the database file and possibly a locking file. This configuration won't be a problem in some situations, as when a system has 40 users connected to the database but only half or fewer of them are working at any one time. Unfortunately, however, there is nothing to stop the other half from going back to work just as the first half starts a complex set of queries. As more users are added, the strain on the disk controller, the system bus, and the CPU—not to mention the load on the net card—grows more intense. In many cases, the focus of this intense activity might be data pages that all or most applications must access in common. With smaller databases, it is far more likely that a page is already being accessed (and perhaps locked) by another user.

The workstation in this configuration is expected to run not only the database engine but also a complex Windows-based front end. Each workstation will need more RAM and hard disk space—at least 4 to 6 MB—just to support the operating system. The front-end application is also more demanding of system resources and will require more RAM and more hard disk space. Note that this configuration stores working result sets (keysets) on local disk space; once that has been used up, the engine gives up trying to build result sets. To deal with this problem, the workstation must dedicate another 10 to 50 or more megabytes

Table 4-2
Typical Distributed Engine Configurations

System Component	Typical Configuration for 1–4 Users	Typical Configuration for 5–10 Users	Typical Configuration for 10–25 Users
"Server"*	Dedicated 66-MHz (or faster) 486, Windows 95/98 or Windows NT, 16MB (or more) of RAM, 400-MB hard disk, VGA video, 16-bit network adapter	Dedicated 133-MHz (or faster) Pentium-class processor, Windows 95/98 or Windows NT, 24 MB (or more) of RAM, 500-MB hard disk, VGA video, 32-bit network adapter	Dedicated 200-MHz (or faster) Pentium-class processor, Windows 95/98 or Windows NT, 24 MB (or more) of RAM, 500-MB hard disk, VGA video, 32-bit network adapter
Workstation	66-MHz (or faster) 486, Windows 95/98, 16MB (or more) of RAM, 150-MB hard disk, SVGA video, 32-bit network adapter	133-MHz (or faster) Pentium-class processor, Windows 95/98 or Windows NT, 24 MB (or more) of RAM, 500-MB hard disk, VGA video, 32-bit network adapter	200-MHz (or faster) Pentium-class processor, Windows 95/98 or Windows NT, 24 MB (or more) of RAM, 500-MB hard disk, VGA video, 32-bit network adapter

* In this case, the server can be one of the workstations, but this arrangement might not make sense if you have very many users. Remember to add more CPU and RAM capacity for a system that plays the role of both server and workstation.

of local disk space to temporary and swap space, or it must create queries that don't require as much space. The first of these options requires more hardware; the second, more programming discipline. Which do you have more of?

Cost per user

The startup cost for this hypothetical configuration must include the server hardware and the operating system. In this configuration, the workstation software must also include a license for the Windows operating system. The workstation hardware is also far more expensive, and the cost goes up as the number of users increases.

Figure 4-11 plots the cost of our hypothetical distributed engine configuration, with costs shared by each user (and remember that all the data in this and other figures is generated on the basis of particular assumptions). Incremental costs include the additional workstations and their LAN hardware. This model shows a significant difference from the slope of our hypothetical client/server system because the workstations in this configuration are more expensive and tend to cost even more as they try to compete in a more heavily populated environment. Until you have about four or five users, you don't really need a "dedicated" server.

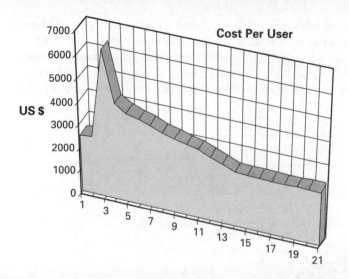

Figure 4-11 *Cost of distributed engine installation*

Distributed engine performance

Consider this fact: the distributed engine configuration can share data pages, but only if they are cached on the file server. Unfortunately, the file server can't tell the difference between a database page, a page of code, or a page from this book. The file server knows only about clusters of sectors. Heavily caching the server improves performance, since it places frequently accessed data pages in its local RAM, but you had better have the server protected with an uninterruptible power supply to prevent *n* megabytes of cache from getting cashiered into the bit bucket when the power fails. Caching systems can use lazy-write techniques to defer writing to the hard disk until a more opportune time; however, this feature must often be disabled to protect database integrity.

If the server is running on the OS/2 High Performance File System (HPFS), the Windows NT File System (NTFS), or the Windows operating system with SMARTDrive or virtual memory installed, intelligent data caching tries to keep the most frequently used data pages in RAM. However, again because the file server can't understand the structure of the database, it can't make caching anywhere close to as efficient as it could be. The remote workstation database engines exacerbate this problem, each with a mind of its own when it comes to how its own query should be dealt with. No workstation database engine knows what any other engine is doing; it might know that other users are competing for its data, but that's all. Sure, there is a shared-lock page file that all the workstation database engines can see and jointly maintain, but this file simply maps the pages of the database file and helps other workstation database engines know which data pages of the shared file are locked. If one engine locks a page, all the engines know it, but they don't know why it's locked, or who locked it, or when it will be released (if ever), and they don't know if they might be holding pages needed by other engines: the deadly embrace.

In this model, users who simply have a shared database file open will have little overall impact on the performance of the system. Nevertheless, as more active users are added to this hypothetical dedicated system, the chances increase that a needed page will be locked, and the chances of a network collision increase. Figure 4-12 shows what kind of performance you can expect in this configuration.

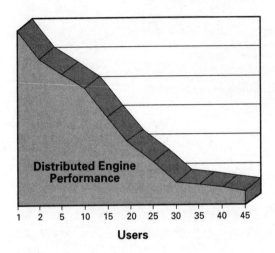

Figure 4-12 *Performance in the distributed engine configuration*

Choosing Between Client/Server and Distributed Engine Architecture

Figure 4-13 summarizes costs and performance of the two models. Let me emphasize again that these models might or might not reflect your actual situation; I'm just exposing many of the questions you should be asking as you think about choosing the most suitable back-end/front-end architecture for your specific situation.

As you can see in Figure 4-13, the efficiency of our hypothetical distributed engine architecture pretty much peaks out at around 25 users. Beyond that number, the amount of workstation, server, and network hardware you'll need to maintain performance for the active users starts to get prohibitively expensive. The following factors also can affect the system's performance and predisposition for success.

Database size

None of the figures included in this chapter puts much emphasis on the size of the database. I think we could probably come up with a factor called user rows that multiplies the total number of users by the number of the rows that need to be processed. With this product, we can create a factor that we can use to compare database load more effectively.

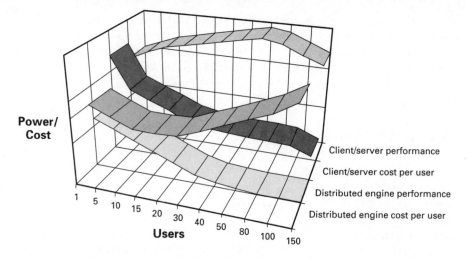

Figure 4-13 *Summary of costs and performance*

The two architectures we've been considering deal very differently with user rows. Both have to read data pages containing rows from a hard disk while searching or simply fetching the rows, but the distributed engine system has to perform this disk I/O over the network—while all the other users are doing the same thing. As the number of user rows fetched or searched increases, network activity increases, collisions increase, and the network hardware moves toward saturation. The client/server architecture also has to use the network to get the data to the users, but that's it. Except when the data is being backed up or bulk-loaded from external disk drives, the network is principally used to deliver the results of the query, not to perform the search. And since queries in a client/server model often fit into a single network packet, this side of the operation is extremely fast.

Input/output ratio

When you're measuring the performance of a database and the front-end application, be sure to design tests that accurately reflect not only the raw query speed (the time it takes to run a typical decision-support query) but also the update speed. In many configurations, the ratio of writes to reads can be very low, so a database that has unspectacular update speed might perform with total adequacy in read-only situations. When you update a database, the engine has to perform the following tasks:

- Lock one or more pages

- Allocate space for the new row

- Delete the old row

- Write the new row

- Update the index (which also involves page locking)

- Unlock the pages

Laboratory performance tests have shown that a carefully designed distributed engine system can support several hundred users. Maybe your configuration is similar to the lab's, and you can expect this level of performance. But many of the people I talk to put the practical limit much lower—around 25 active users.

When you simply execute a query, however, the engine only has to find one or more records in the database. The number of suitable indexes plays a big role here, as does the number of triggers and rules that the engine has to run on every update. More indexes will mean more work whenever the data changes, but fewer indexes will mean more scans in which all the rows in a table are read one at a time.

Data page management

In some databases, the data is stored in a physically sequential order on disk. You might be able to request this arrangement by asking for a "clustered" index. Clustering complicates updates, since multiple rows often have to be moved around on the pages, though it can mean faster retrieval—but usually only in cases where the data is accessed in sorted order. When a row is deleted from some databases, the space freed isn't released until the database is brought down and restarted in maintenance mode and empty rows are purged. This arrangement saves time during an update, but it isn't as fast as updating in place, which changes the row in situ, nor is it as efficient as dynamic page allocation and deallocation. More important, after a large update, you might discover that your database has doubled in size through the action of a single user. Be sure you know how page management methodologies will affect your design.

Index management

Make sure you also know what kinds of indexes are available to your developers. In some cases, a simple ISAM-style index with a few keys will suffice. Remember, though, that for every index you add, you gain query speed but lose update speed. Go back and rethink your write-to-read ratio. If you're doing more writes than reads in real time, then perhaps you need fewer indexes, not more. It might make sense to minimize the number of indexes you use during the bulk of the update activity and then rebuild them later in the cycle, before the bulk of the queries are made.

Lock management

Does the total number of page locks available on the file server limit the system that you're designing? Watch out for an upper limit of locks. Both data and index pages require locks. In the distributed engine model, the number of locks supported at the MS-DOS level (SHARE.EXE), not by some number you set on the server, will hold you back.

Recovery

If you're going to bet the farm (your company) on a database, is that database capable of repairing itself when the system reboots, or do you have to bring the system back up manually, restore or repair it manually, and then restart it? Watch out for systems that don't support full transaction logging. When transactions aren't logged, an unexpected interruption while the engine is writing a cached transaction to disk might result in a partial transaction and a corrupted database. And the first time you get called in over the weekend to repair a corrupted database, don't forget I told you so.

Periodic maintenance

All databases need to be serviced, and SQL Server needs to have its transaction logs backed up and cleared at least daily on most production systems. But if your workstations are spread out all over the map, how do you get the users in the next city or in another state to get off your database so you can back it up? Fortunately, SQL Server lets you back up your database with a full load and without bringing down the database. It's something like changing the tires on a race car without having the car leave the track. Make sure you can back up your database without having to get all the users off—either that or have a plan for getting them off.

Accessing a Centralized Database Engine with a Distributed Database Engine

Up to this point, we've focused on the choice between either a centralized or a distributed database engine. But what about using a distributed database engine to access data on a centralized database engine? This programming mode reflects the trend toward highly decentralized database management.

Let's say that relatively small divisions are spread out all over a company. Each subgroup has its own idea about how to prepare, manage, and store its data, and the composite data is transmitted to a central site for weekly reports. (Sound familiar?) But this company finds that weekly summaries are insufficient for timely decision making. Because many other companies have reached the same conclusion, fairly complex mechanisms have evolved for keeping departmental data synchronized with central corporate data.

A distributed engine system can manage local data effectively as long as volume and number of users are not too great. Some say that this configuration can support about 20 users; some say they can't get past 2. Centralized data can also be integrated through attachment to corporate database tables (and views) that are constantly kept up to date. And the departments, by posting changes from distributed sites to corporate tables, can also keep the central site current. At least that's how its supposed to work in theory. This strategy can be hobbled easily by slow WAN performance or sloppy application design.

Visual Basic permits implementation of any of the programming models we've examined so far. With the Jet database engine, you can easily set up a department-size database and make it available to everyone. By attaching to SQL Server tables (the Microsoft Access documentation calls this linking), you can tie corporate data to departmental data so that both the central site (and therefore other departments) and your local department can share in a common data pool. This linking is a viable way to manage data in large and small companies alike.

There are pitfalls, however. The distributed engine often expects to access data by using its own intelligence—that is, its own query engine. Because the centralized server expects to do the same thing, conflicts arise. When a workstation query processor has to perform an operation that can't be completed by remote execution of a query on the central server, the workstation's query processor must do the search itself, the hard way—by downloading data from central database tables. When it has to resort to this strategy, Jet's latest version does it in a fairly intelligent way. Instead of trying to read and join entire tables—something that, obviously, must be avoided—Jet attempts to draw a subset of the table rows to join with local data. In other cases, however, Jet simply creates a temporary stored procedure to fetch the rows and makes iterative calls to this procedure. Let's see, a 50,000-row table accessed by a stored procedure would still take 100,000 trips to the server (and back) over the LAN (or worse yet, the WAN). Ah, no, not a particularly viable solution.

Because the Jet engine can't create its native table-type Resultset object against external database tables, Visual Basic front ends are forced to build either dynaset-type or snapshot-type Recordset objects. I won't go into great detail here; I'll say only that these objects consume local resources (RAM and temporary disk space) for either keysets or data rows, which means that it's impractical to attach to tables of any size and perform simple queries without setting specific row limits in the WHERE clause of the SQL query. When the Jet engine accesses the central server, it does so via what we call a connection. The number of available connections is limited by license, by physical limitations of RAM, and by server resources. Although Visual Basic developers have more control than ever over these connections, the number of connections can easily get out of hand through injudicious use of the Data control or incorrectly managed Recordset objects. Another consideration is the accessibility of SQL Server–specific features. For example, the Jet engine can't take advantage of SQL Server server-side cursors or parameters passed from stored procedures, and it doesn't know how to access certain SQL Server data types.

What does all this mean? In general, it means that you can create completely adequate front-end programs without resorting to API-based programming models. If your applications are designed carefully and with the limitations of the architecture in mind, you'll be able to create applications that are easy to assemble and support.

PART II

Designing SQL Server Applications

5

Planning Your Design

The State Machine

A Panoramic View of Cursors and Buffers

Basic Design Decisions

Avoiding the Top 10 Design Mistakes

Creating a Virtual Application

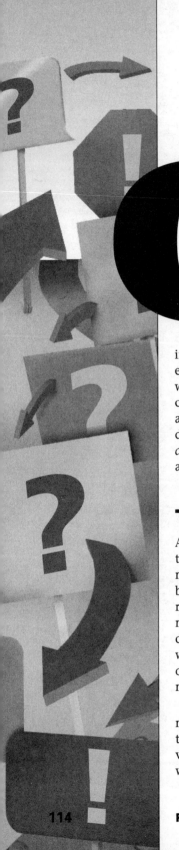

ver the past few years, many industry periodicals have caught client/server fever. Week after week, we hear about one implementation after another—some successful, some not. From case after case, a few critical design guidelines have emerged, and I mentioned a number of them in Part I.

The chapters in Part II of this guide focus more closely on the steps involved in using Microsoft Visual Basic to create successful Microsoft SQL Server front-end applications and components that avoid common pitfalls and leverage what we have learned from successful implementations. In this chapter, I'll compare the SQL Server development environment to a "state machine," offer a brief overview and review of cursors and buffers, pose some fundamental design questions, and describe how to create and use what I call a *virtual application*. I've also included a section detailing the top 10 reasons that client/server applications fail.

The State Machine

A state machine, when it's not a political organization, is a body of logic designed to deal with known responses to a known number of input requests. Most of my front-end applications are designed around the model of the state machine because each state is fairly easy to code, debug as an independent unit, and reuse from program to program. Now that the concept of multithreaded business objects has matured, knowing how and why to create objects that do or don't maintain a specific state is even more important than it used to be—but we'll consider objects in this context later in the book. For now, let's focus on how the client application must build a state machine in order to communicate with SQL Server.

The early PC game Adventure was an example of a state machine. To move from room to room in that game, you had to examine the properties of the room you were in by asking questions. Invalid questions were rejected, and valid ones returned deterministic responses. Using valid questions and action words, you could gather treasure and investigate properties or alternate paths.

Once you found an exit (there could be several), you made the transition to another room—another state. The new room had different properties, exits, and pitfalls.

In a SQL Server "adventure," any particular path you take might not provide an immediate pathway back to the previous "room," but you can continue stepping from state to state—asking questions at each level, making requests of the system, and gathering treasure in the form of returned data or metadata. Generally speaking, each data access interface we examine in this guide expects you to perform the following operations:

- Initialize the data interface, as required, which includes setting default properties, timeout values, and user names.

- Establish a connection to the SQL server, and process the errors if the connection can't be made.

- Create a query from scratch, or use one stored in a local repository, such as a Microsoft Jet MDB database, an rdoQuery, an ADO Command object, or an ODBC prepared statement.

- Execute the query on the server.

- Process the result sets (there could be several), which includes dealing with sets of rows returned in the result sets.

- Close the connection, deinitialize the interface, and terminate it, as necessary.

Basically, each of these operations is a state, and your options for proceeding from state to state are fairly limited: you can't open a connection before initializing the interface, and you can't send a query before you open a connection. Each state has its own set of messages and errors, too, which you have to deal with before you can move on. (Interstate flight to avoid handling errors is a felony, you know.)

NOTE Even when you create a remote business object, you have to consider state. You must often create the object so that it remains "stateless"—that is, it can be run without having to remember details from any previous invocations.

A Panoramic View of Cursors and Buffers

In general, and for lots of good reasons, I'm against the extensive use of cursors for retrieving data. If you haven't worked with the client/server paradigm before, you might not be entirely familiar with what cursors are or with what they do in this context. Let's stop and take a look at them here so that you'll be able to follow along in the next section of this chapter and in later chapters. Along the way, I'll tell you why I don't care much for cursors. In this section, we'll also consider some basic design decisions, and while we're at it, talk about buffers, too.

Basically, a cursor is a set of pointers to the rows returned by a query. Sure, there's more to cursors than just a set of pointers, but we'll get to that in a little while. Most cursors are like a result set except that the live data usually remains on the server—only a pointer to the base rows is maintained in the cursor. When a query is written, it describes a subset of the rows in one or more tables, and the cursor points to those rows in a result set. Cursors can be generated by SQL Server right on the server (aka server-side cursors) or by a client-side cursor library, which builds the cursor on the client. Of course, a client can also be a component, so in some cases, the cursor can be created in the middle tier. Just keep in mind that a cursor is a temporary set of pointers to live data. And yes, cursors can be built by copying the live rows to the client—leaving the live rows up on the server. But as I said, we'll spend quite a bit of time discussing the frailties and foibles of cursors.

A buffer is a client-side RAM repository where result set data is held temporarily until it can be moved to another place for storage. Buffers are usually managed by the interface layer, such as DB-Library. A buffer is very different from a cursor in that the buffer is simply a copy of the data extracted from the SQL server based on the result set; once the data is fetched into the buffer, subsequent changes made to server-side data aren't reflected. In contrast, for a cursor that points to live data, if the addressed row changes in the database, the data referenced by the cursor also reflects this change. None of the object-based interfaces expose their buffers, so we won't be talking about them much. Yes, the cursor engines used by data interfaces (such as RDO and ADO) use buffers—but we can't get at them, at least not directly.

Table 5-1 on page 123 displays the types of cursors and buffers and shows where they are (or aren't) supported in the SQL Server data interfaces we're looking at. Since you can access only one row at a time with a cursor, you must have some mechanism for positioning a current-row pointer to a selected row. Each data access interface provides a rich set of mechanisms to make it easy to point to a specific row, the next row, the previous row, the last row, the first row, or any row in between. For example, each of the data access interfaces supports the ability to use methods such as MoveFirst, MoveLast, MoveNext, MovePrevious, AbsolutePosition, PercentPosition, or Move to select the next current row. In relational databases, we don't refer to rows by number. In other words, we might fetch five rows as the result of a query, but we don't know whether these are the first five rows in a table or the last five, or whether the rows were selected at random from several tables. As we position through a cursor, we can sometimes move the current-row pointer around on a row-by-row basis—that is, move forward six rows or back two. We can even reposition the current-row pointer based on a percentage of the rows fetched. However, even if you create a cursor from an entire table (which you shouldn't), you shouldn't assume that the rows are returned in any particular order—unless you told SQL Server to do so. No, we don't design applications around table-based queries. That's because it's simply too expensive, not to mention that if you do, your application or component simply won't scale. Sure, you'll get pretty good performance for the first user—but after that forget it. This will be clearer as we get deeper into cursor handling.

The differences among the various kinds of cursors come down to these four characteristics:

- How they handle membership
- How and when they move data to the workstation
- How they scroll (or don't)
- Where the keyset is built

Understanding Cursors

The data columns from one or more rows are said to be members of the cursor if the query's WHERE clause includes them. These columns, combined into logical rows, become member rows of the result set.

For example, consider the following query:

```
SELECT Name, Type from Animals
WHERE Age > 10
```

When the query is executed, SQL Server immediately begins selecting members for the result set. In this case, the members of the result set will include all rows of the *Animals* table in which the number in the *Age* column is greater than 10.

If sorting isn't required, SQL Server passes the first rows of this result set back to the workstation as soon as they are fetched and then stops processing; further processing is delayed until the workstation retrieves the fetched rows. Generally, however, the SQL server stays 1 to 2 KB ahead of the workstation. Because of this head start, if many users are updating the database, the chances are good that another row qualifying for this result set will be added before the workstation retrieves the fetched rows. When the workstation code or data interface retrieves the result set, the added row will be included as a member as long as the SQL server hasn't already passed the point where that row would have been inserted. (This point is determined by the internal sorting order for the data.) But if the row is added after the workstation has begun processing the result set, that row is *not* included as a member. (A row accepted as a member may be deleted later by another user, but its "corpse" is still considered a member of the result set.)

The cursor's membership roll isn't complete until SQL Server has determined the last row of the result set. This process of completing the cursor's membership is called *cursor population*. Once the workstation has fetched the last row, the cursor is considered to be fully populated. Only after a cursor is fully populated can SQL Server determine how many rows are in the result set. For this reason, don't expect the RowCount or RecordCount properties or the RowsAffected value to be valid until population is complete. Also, consider that this information is not passed to the interface by the Tabular Data Stream (TDS) until the end of the result set, which means that you'll have to fetch the last row of a cursor's result set before you can expect these values to be valid.

Cursor population is not always done automatically—but it usually is. ADO and RDO (in some cases) do automatically populate cursors in the background unless you tell them to do otherwise. For example, RDO's RemoteData control and most ADO operations continue fetching rows on a background thread once you submit a query. Automatic population means that the resources locked up by the cursor population process can be freed more quickly. You should also keep in mind that server-side cursors are generated on the server *before* control is returned to your application, so they arrive fully populated.

When working with SQL Server 6.0 and later, your application can choose to build server-side cursors. In this case, the keyset (discussed later in this chapter) is built on the server itself—in the TempDB database—by SQL Server. Yes, you can also build and use these cursors in and by stored procedures. That is, stored procedures can build their own cursors (which are always built on the server) and manage them within their own logic. Do I use this technique? Nope, but I have seen it done by those who work with SQL Server for a living.

When you use server-side cursors, the entire keyset is created *before* control returns to your application, which results in considerably different behavior than when you're using client-side cursors. A *keyset* is simply the set of row pointers—one for each row in the result set. For example, if the cursor is fairly large or takes considerable time to find the rows, your client could be locked up for a significant length of time waiting for the first row. Moving to the last row of the result set, however, should be very fast—because all of the "fetching" has been done. You also must ensure that TempDB has sufficient space to accommodate the keyset multiplied by the number of users using your application. Consider that the task of managing these cursors consumes CPU horsepower on the SQL server but doesn't consume any local-area network (LAN) or client-side resources. A system might seem fast and efficient for a few users, but a production load might bring it to its knees.

In my experience, you can choose from a couple of ways to really get server-side cursors to sing. First, if you have a lot of RAM on the server, consider setting some of it aside to put TempDB in RAM. If you can keep the server-side cursors small (as you should anyway), you can gain considerable performance. Check out "When to Use TempDB in RAM" in the SQL Server 6.5 Books Online. In any case, using TempDB in RAM could be beneficial *if* all of the following conditions are true:

- You have a significant amount of available system RAM. "Significant" here means at least 64 MB, with 128 MB or more being typical for small-sized to medium-sized databases.

- Your applications have a locality of reference such that the SQL Server cache hit ratio is poor, even with a lot of available buffer cache. You can see your hit ratio by using SQL Server Performance Monitor to monitor the Cache Hit Ratio counter in the SQL Server object. For information about using SQL Server Performance Monitor, see the section in Chapter 19 titled "Monitoring Server Activity and Performance" in the SQL Server 6.5 Books Online.

- Your applications do a lot of TempDB operations. Rather than guess whether this is the case, you can use sp_lock to observe the lock activity in TempDB while queries are running. Or you can monitor TempDB space consumption by issuing this (or a similar) query interactively or from a looping batch file:

```
SELECT SUM(DPAGES) FROM TEMPDB..SYSINDEXES
```

- The TempDB operations are sized so that they will fit on the TempDB made possible by your RAM configuration.

- You are running SQL Server 6.5 or earlier. Because SQL Server 7.0 has redesigned its memory manager, any benefit of dedicating RAM to temporary stored procedures or cursors can be illusive. There's some evidence that this shortcut might be eliminated in future versions.

If you decide to use TempDB in RAM, you should verify the performance benefit you'll obtain. To do this, follow these steps:

1. Select a query or a small set of queries that typify your most frequently performed TempDB-intensive operations.

2. Run these several times, noting the execution times.

3. Reconfigure for TempDB in RAM, run the identical queries, and note the difference in execution times.

If the amount of improvement isn't significant, it's probably best to give the RAM back to the SQL cache. Because TempDB is used only for intermediate operations and is created from scratch upon each server restart, using TempDB in RAM is safe and won't harm database integrity or recoverability.

Cursorless Result Sets

All the data interfaces except DAO/Jet support at least one way of returning data—the *cursorless* result set. With a cursorless result set, the interface doesn't create a cursor at all but simply passes the data rows to your front end for processing. In all cases, this is the fastest way to get data from the server to the client or component, but it provides few of the benefits of a cursor. Although this type of result set *can* be updateable, it often isn't—you usually have to roll the update queries yourself. Because these high-speed "firehose" result sets are not scrollable (only one row is exposed, and you can move the current-row pointer forward only), they are often called *forward-only* result sets. But a forward-only result set isn't always a firehose cursorless result set. In ADO, firehose "cursorless" result sets are now built by default.

Scrolling Cursors

One of the most expensive aspects of cursor management involves supporting the ability to scroll. This capability means that once you've executed a query, a scrollable cursor permits you to position to virtually any specific row in the result set. Remember that only one row can be the "current" row, so this functionality can be very important if you need to browse through the data randomly. These repositioning methods are expensive in that they consume system resources much the way those little fishes in the Amazon River go for an explorer's toes. To increase performance, choose a cursor that has limited or no scrolling—such as the forward-only result sets described above. Gee, it looks like we're back to cursorless result sets again. Even a forward-only scrolling cursor is better than a fully scrollable cursor, but then again, a firehose cursor is even better.

TIP Not all data interfaces can create all types of cursors. Later, I provide a table (Table 5-1 on page 123) that dumps the types of cursors supported against SQL Server by VBSQL, ODBC API, DAO, RDO, and ADO.

Types of Cursors

With each of our data access interfaces, at least four major types of cursors can be used for fetching result sets from SQL Server: *forward-only* cursors, *static* cursors, *keyset* cursors, and *dynamic* cursors. Each data interface supports cursors differently, but all of them support at least two of these basic cursor types. Some data interfaces, such as RDO, support enhanced cursor management, which not only extends the concept of cursor handling but also changes the way you handle offline use of the data returned by a cursor. The process of choosing a cursor is further complicated by differences in terminology and, more significantly, by differences in implementation between ODBC drivers and the other data interfaces. I suggest you try out the various cursors before expecting one behavior or another.

As we examine cursors, consider that they are built from sets of rows from one or more tables. Cursors can also be built from the result set generated by an ordinary query, a SQL view, or a stored procedure. Not all cursors are updateable—this capacity is a function of the data interface and its ability to identify the root table and the appropriate rows to be updated. Some data interfaces, such as DAO/Jet, support complex (expensive) schemes to update the accessed rows—no matter which table contains the data. In most situations, however, you won't be able to create an updateable cursor against a stored procedure. In any case, if you have update permission for the data, you can always use your own stored procedure or update query to change the underlying data tables, as long as you can identify the set of rows to change or to delete in a WHERE clause.

> **TIP** The only way that ODBC or OLE DB can build an updateable cursor is if you have a primary key defined for the table to be updated. Before you go digging into Help because the cursor you just created won't let you change the data, go back one more time and check for the existence of the primary keys—the upsizing wizard might not have created them.

Forward-only cursors

All of the data access interfaces support "forward-only" cursors one way or another. This can be one of the lightest-weight cursors you can build. This type of cursor only permits use of methods to move "forward" in the rows returned—so you can't scroll—or even move to the last row in a single operation. If you set the size of the rowset to 1, RDO and ADO don't build cursors at all, but simply blast back the rows as fast as your application (or the data access interface) can suck them in. Many, many of my designs use forward-only, read-only cursors, with the rowset size set to 1. This is what we'll refer to later as a "firehose" cursor. Yes, even forward-only cursors can be updateable if the conditions are right.

Static cursors

A static, or snapshot, cursor also provides keyset addressability, but it moves the result set data rows to the client or component. When your code references the rows, the interface fetches against this local copy of the data. As with a keyset cursor, this cursor's membership is fixed once the result set is fully populated. Not all static cursors are read-only; some can be updated, and some support additions to their membership—again, depending on the flexibility of the interface and the drivers. The static cursor requires client or component-side storage for the keyset and for the data in each row of the result set. As a rule, when others add, change, or delete rows in the database, the changes are *not* reflected in a fully populated static cursor. Of course, when you build a static cursor, the data begins to get stale the instant it arrives. This cursor is not your best choice for data that is constantly changing. For lookup tables against values not likely to change, however, this choice makes a lot of sense.

Keyset cursors

A keyset, or dynaset, cursor stores a set of keys—basically a set of pointers—and allows a selected row to be refetched according to row-specific information stored in those keys. The keyset cursor requires separate storage for the data in each of the keys that it comprises. The remaining row data columns stay on the server where other users can access them. This access means that other users can make changes, deletions, or additions to the rows you include in your cursor. A keyset cursor's membership is fixed once the result set is fully populated. When you or other users who share the database make changes to the data, these changes are returned to your workstation when you position to a changed row. When your code adds data to the underlying database using an updateable keyset cursor, some implementations add the row to the cursor—but not all do. We'll discuss the differences when we get to the chapters on DAO, RDO, and ADO (Parts III, IV, and V). When other tasks add one or more rows to the database that would qualify for your cursor, the data is never added to your populated keyset cursor—the process of choosing rows has already been completed. If other tasks delete rows in the table your keyset points to, those rows still exist in your cursor. If, and only if, you position to one of these deleted rows, the underlying cursor logic detects that the row is no longer fetchable and trips a trappable error. None of the keyset cursor implementations automatically informs you when a row has been deleted—not until you position to the deleted row.

Dynamic cursors

Like a static or a keyset cursor, a dynamic cursor stores a block of keys. But with this type of cursor, the query that was used to generate the result set is constantly reexecuted whenever you reference the cursor. Because of this repeated activity, dynamic cursors are expensive to implement and comparatively slow, but they never limit or close out their membership: any rows that qualify for membership in a dynamic cursor are fetched whenever the cursor is positioned within a fixed range of rows that are near the subject row. You'll find, however, that most implementations don't support bookmark repositioning as commonly supported by other types of cursors. Using dynamic cursors can be like doing a paper route with an 18-wheeler.

Types of Buffers

In this section, we'll be looking at two kinds of buffers: single-row buffers and *n*-row buffers.

Single-row buffers

A single-row buffer isn't really a cursor, even though the same membership rules that apply to a forward-only keyset cursor apply here. With a single-row buffer, you can view data from only one row of the result set. Previous rows are not accessible, and the current row is not accessible once you move to the next row in the result set. Table 5-1 shows that single-row buffers are *not* supported by the DAO/Jet interface. Jet does provide a dbForwardOnly option for creating cursors, although the resource impact for single-row buffers with Jet is very different from that of single-row buffers used with the other data interfaces.

n-row buffers

An *n*-row buffer expands the scope and scrollability of the single-row buffer. In this case, a fixed number of the rows in the result set can be exposed to the workstation and the application is permitted to move freely within those rows. Although the GetRows method supported in DAO/Jet, DAO/ODBCDirect, and RDO is similar to this low-level buffering, it isn't really the same because the GetRows result set isn't scrollable until you move it to your own array.

Table 5-1
Cursors and Buffers and Their Support in Data Access Interfaces

Cursor and Buffer Types	VBSQL	ODBC API	DAO/Jet	DAO/ODBC Direct	RDO	ADO
Forward-only cursor	DB-Library default single-row buffer	Forward-only cursor option	Forward-only Recordset object	Forward-only Recordset object (RDO forward-only)	Forward-only Resultset object	Forward-only Recordset object
Static cursor	DB-Library or server-side cursor	Static cursor option	Snapshot-type Recordset object	Snapshot-type Recordset object (RDO static)	Static-type Resultset object	Static-type Recordset object
Keyset cursor	DB-Library or server-side keyset cursor	Keyset cursor option	Dynaset-type Recordset object	Keyset-type Recordset object (RDO keyset)	Keyset-type Resultset object	Keyset-type Recordset object
Dynamic cursor	DB-Library or server-side dynamic cursor	Dynamic cursor option	Not supported	Dynamic-type Recordset object (RDO dynamic)	Dynamic-type Resultset object	Dynamic-type Recordset object
Single-row buffer	Forward-only option	Default result set	Not supported	Forward-only option	Forward-only option	Forward-only option
n-row buffer	RowBuffer option	Not supported	Not supported	Not supported	Not supported	Not supported

Implementing Cursors

Visual Basic 5.0 brought another nuance to cursor management. RDO 2.0 implemented the Client Batch ODBC cursor library and made a number of other changes that affect how cursors are implemented by the data interfaces. Visual Basic 6.0 adds ADO, which takes up where RDO left off. It adds to the client library and implements an entire range of cursors using OLE DB. Let's take a closer look at how ODBC and OLE DB handle these innovations.

To understand these ODBC changes, you need to understand that the ODBC-based data interfaces all use the same ODBC Driver Manager and share the same cursor libraries listed below. Actually, the OLE DB interfaces also use the ODBC cursor libraries when you specify the OLE DB Provider for ODBC. Remember that each driver vendor is responsible for implementing this functionality, so your results will vary from driver to driver:

- **ODBC (standard) cursor library**   This is the oldest of the cursor libraries and has been characterized as a "kludge." It creates client-side cursors and little else. It's notorious for its lack of performance and its simplistic approach. Unfortunately, it's probably the most widely used library.

- **Server-side cursor library**   This was introduced with RDO 1.0 and is the first implementation of a server-side library against any back-end server—but only the SQL Server driver was provided by Visual Basic 4.0. Some people opt to use this driver, but you must disable it if you want to use this library with multiple result set queries.

- **Client Batch cursor library**   This is the newest member of the RDO cursor family. Developed by the FoxPro team at Microsoft, this library is far more efficient, sophisticated, and flexible than the ODBC client-side cursor. It supports "dissociate" result sets and optimistic batch updates. Basically, it's designed to do everything the standard ODBC client-side cursor library can do—only faster and better.

TIP   As much as I hate to admit it, you'll find that the ODBC (standard) cursor library works better in some situations (but far from all) when used instead of the Client Batch cursor library.

RDO 2.0 relaxed the Level II driver requirements because it polls the SQLGetInfo API to determine which features the driver supports. Wherever possible, RDO 2.0 attempts to circumvent the lack of support by using its own code. By using its own code, RDO 2.0 helps those drivers that lack support for full ODBC Level II conformance get by, especially when you use the new Client Batch cursor library.

NOTE   If you're working with databases other than Microsoft SQL Server or Oracle (even Sybase), you'll have to dig up your own ODBC drivers.

Basic Design Decisions

Now that we've admired the view of cursors and buffers, let's step back next to the main highway. Regardless of the data interface you choose, you'll have to make a number of design decisions before and throughout the implementation phase of development. You'll have to decide how your application or component will access data at the lowest level, no matter whether you want to add a new record to the employee table or count the number of rooms available on the fifth floor. For most problems, it won't be appropriate to use a single approach and you'll have to choose among several implementations:

- How many users are expected to run your front-end client application or component at any one time? Are there enough connections on the SQL Server to manage the load? What about space on the server—including TempDB? What other applications, databases, services, or users are accessing the server?

- Can your application or component tolerate more than one instance running on the same machine? Do the instances affect each other?

- How should server connections be made? Should a connection be established when the user first logs on, and should it be kept in place indefinitely? Will the component have to use special logon protocols?

- Will a more sophisticated connection management or sharing technique be required? Does the application or component have to share the connections being used by other code in the same memory space?

- How should security be managed? Should the application use Microsoft Windows NT domain security, SQL Server integrated security, or a custom brand? How should the application differentiate among users with different degrees of authority?

- Will the users be connecting through a LAN or WAN or over the Internet?

- Do you have a designated systems administrator to deal with all of these issues, or are you just hoping that any problems will somehow resolve themselves on their own?

- How should queries be created? Should they be created, compiled, and executed on the fly? Should you leverage stored procedures? Should you depend on parameterized queries stored in interface-declared objects or stored procedures? Should you simply build parameter queries in code?

- How should rows be fetched? Should you use a cursor, a row buffer, or a cursorless result set? Should the cursor be created on the server or on the workstation?

- Should rows be sorted, searched, and processed on the server, or should these operations be performed after the rows have been brought to the workstation?

CAUTION

When you're creating a new client/server system, plan to spend at least as much time on research and design as you do on coding. If your front-end design is flawed, the best database implementation on the planet will look like leftover pizza.

- What about bound controls? Should you depend on data-aware controls tied to the Data control, RemoteData control, ADO Data control, or to Data Environment Commands? Can you use a data-aware control without binding it to the Data control, using the control's "unbound" mode instead to add data to the control? Should you manage binding yourself?

- How should data be updated? Should you create updateable cursors, use special stored procedures, or use action queries? Does your user have permission to update base tables or only to make changes through stored procedures?

- What type of concurrency should you use? Can you afford to lock a page the whole time the cursor is open, or must you add code to deal with optimistic locking? Do you really need row-level locking?

- Will it take so much time to execute queries that asynchronous operation will be justified? Should you include code that keeps data constantly updated when it's exposed to the user? Should you inform the user of changes only when data on the screen is touched?

- Have you worked out query strategies that account for the use of server-side resources? When you sort result sets or create server-side cursors or temporary tables, are there enough resources on the server to maintain these structures? Can these structures be maintained for all active users?

- What fallback plan have you established to deal with contingencies like the main server's illness or demise? Do you have a mechanism for supporting users even when access to a remote server is unavailable? Can your front end and components be designed for tolerance of intermittent remote server access?

- What provisions have you made for many people to work on a project at the same time? Is the code broken down into pieces so as to lend itself to this type of development? Or is your front end a monolithic beast? Does it consist of one program or several?

Avoiding the Top 10 Design Mistakes

When a project is finally wrapped up and delivered, the managers gather to decide what went right, what went wrong, whom to promote, and whom to blame. All too often, it can seem that the tools and developers are assigned a significant part of the blame and the architects and systems analysts are given most of the medals. But many designs are flawed long before the first line of code is written—though the developers working in the trenches often contribute to the fallibility of the design. With apologies to David Letterman, I suggest you take note of the following top 10 reasons for systems (especially client/server systems) not meeting expectations.

10. **The design didn't deliver what the customers wanted.** In many cases, unfortunately, customers don't know what they want until you *don't* give it to them. Generally, a design that fails because it doesn't meet customer expectations is the result of an implementation without a clear (as in written) specification. When you create a specification, you have to study what needs to be done, come to an understanding about the end result, and *write it down*. This way, the designer and the customer can come to a common understanding about what the design does. You might even go so far as to use a modeling tool to help lay out your design. For example, you could use Visual Basic's Visual Modeler or the Visual Database Tools database schema designer. But then again, if you did that, you would have trouble explaining why you didn't implement what was planned—so never mind.

9. **The architect or analyst who designed the system knew how to lay bricks but not how to use a hammer—so you end up with a lot of brick outhouses.** Invariably, people build what they know how to build, using the tools they are comfortable with. If they are experts at ISAM designs, they think about ISAM solutions to the problems at hand, even if they don't always work very well. The customer has no way of knowing what the best implementation would be, and perhaps management doesn't know either. Sometimes a better understanding of the alternatives is in order before charging off to implement old or inadequate concepts. Too many times, we've seen complaints that Visual Basic or Microsoft Access or whatever was seemingly incapable of building a cursor against a giant table, when the real problem was that the complainers didn't completely understand how a multiuser client/server system is designed in the first place. For the most part, client/server applications that support dozens to dozens of dozens of users don't build SELECT * cursors on base tables—they use stored procedures, views, or server-side intelligent objects to return only the required information—not just rows.

8. **The design assumed that since the application worked for 5 users it would work for 50 or 500 or 5000.** Too often, we see designs that account for neither the volume of traffic generated by their application nor all of the applications that use the same design taken as a whole. In today's world of 500-KB e-mail messages broadcast throughout the network to announce the birth of the new group administrator's son, network bandwidth is already pretty much taxed to the limit. Scalability of any application depends on the quantity of resources consumed by each individual application. This quantity includes workstation resources but also must include network packets sent and received, round-trips to the server, and resources on the server. If a single application creates a 40-MB TempDB sorted result set, how is the system going to support 50 or 500 instances of the same application—each consuming server resources like teenagers eating M&Ms?

7. **The developer forgot the oldest maxim of all: "Stuff happens."** In a robust client/server application, much of your code should be dealing with the errors (and messages) returned from the server or the operating system running the application. Not only should the application deal with all these errors, but it also should be designed to do so from the beginning, when the developer best understands where the problems can best be trapped and addressed. All too often, a developer assumes that the network or the available resources will be just as readily available as they are when the application is written.

6. **The design called for mustard on the buns, so mustard was added to the bread recipe.** We've seen a migration away from fairly simplistic two-tier client/server applications that baked many of the business rules and field edits into the application instead of putting them on the breakfast table, where all the developers could reach them as needed. While hard-coded client-side business logic doesn't seem to have much of an impact when you write the first application, and perhaps not when you write the second, by the time you get to the fourth or the fourteenth, you can really see the problem arise. Each time you include business-rule code in an application, you risk having to go back and change each and every application when the rules change. For those shops where the business rules never change, you can disregard this problem.

5. **The design didn't account for everyone wanting to use the same clerk.** Imagine a fast-food restaurant designed to deal with dozens of customers at once but with only one cash register that all the teenagers behind the counter have to share. This same "hot spot" problem is often duplicated in client/server designs when insert/update activity is focused on the pages containing the most current rows. Unless you deal with this problem by adding a few more cash registers, your system is destined to bog down as individual applications vie for the most often used pages. Generally, for a database design (for example), the easiest way to avoid this situation is to change the data indexing scheme to make sure new rows are added to different pages in the database. That way, when the page is locked by someone down the counter ordering a full-meal-deal, another operation can complete without having to wait.

4. **The design didn't account for that cookie-hungry kid in the back room who used a pair of binoculars to watch the cook open the combination lock on the pantry.** Security is a prime concern where I work, and it should be a concern for your designer as well. Since Visual Basic and all the rest have made client/server data access so simple, even a well-meaning bungler can easily get into the corporate cookie jar and stomp all over the data—especially when the user ID and password you assign is granted permission to access

the base database tables. By building stored procedures (or server-side COM components) to gate access to the data, you prevent the kids from wandering through the pantry fingering the goodies. This design also gives you a way to implement business rules on the server and simplify application design and dissemination. Since the stored procedures can change without the applications having to be recompiled, you can make some pretty significant changes without having to change a single installed application.

3. **The design called for colorful ad copy to be delivered to the customer, and instead of including it in the Sunday paper, you baked it into each loaf of bread.** Not everyone is a fan of putting binary large objects (BLOBs) in the database. Although it is possible to do so, there aren't many cases in which this yields the best performance. Yes, there are cases in which the alternative was tried and was ultimately rejected, but in many, many cases, abysmal performance can be turned around overnight by simply leaving the photos, documents, and other BLOBs in the original source files and putting a pointer (preferably an HTTP pointer) to the file in the database.

Too many applications are being written by people who are as smart as a whip but can't tell the difference between a user and a folding chair. These techno-geeks who live and breathe their code often don't spend enough time working with the actual people who use their applications. There are places for this kind of developer—behind the scenes. But the user interface developer should be handcuffed to the user for at least a week.

2. **The design failed to account for tornadoes.** A data backup and restore regimen must be part of any workable client/server design. When it isn't, it's just a matter of time before you're faced with a mob of people angry because they can't get at their data. Few problems are more job threatening than not having a backup and restore strategy. Be sure it works, too. In many cases, you might not be able to restore a single table or even restore at all if you don't have the proper utilities and procedures in place.

1. **The design called for the bread to be rewarmed in a toaster oven (because that's what we know how to do)—even when the customer uses a microwave oven.** The NIH (Not Invented Here) problem has hamstrung companies large and small since the dawn of time. How could someone else's solution be as good as one we make right here in River City? More often than not, decisions are made based on tradition and comfort level as opposed to what works best for the situation. While trusting someone else's solution is a valid concern, it must be tempered with the realities of future viability and support. In many cases, the decision to buy or make has had more to do with people skills than technical merits; that is, if you have a shop full of APL programmers and you need to implement a PC solution, you can either retrain the staff and start from scratch, or buy an outside solution and have your staff sit on their 80-column cards—neither is particularly easy to do. Companies that don't make these tough decisions die or are absorbed sooner or later.

Creating a Virtual Application

Any database front-end application has to screen data accepted from the user. For example, when the dialog box in Figure 5-1 is presented to the user, nothing beyond the user's training and your code can guarantee the quality of what is entered and accepted into the field. If the user is totally untrained—say, a customer at a bank's ATM—the available choices must be very narrow indeed; an open field that invites any number of answers invites ambiguous responses and failed applications, too. And many fields can't be tested for validity unless values in a table are looked up or examined in relation to other values. For example, an application that captures telephone area codes might compare the user-provided value with a list of known area codes in the particular state and a list of zip code zones, and until all the validating data is complete—the state-wide area codes and the zip codes—full validation can't be had. Since most front-end applications use dozens of input fields or more, some questions arise: Where and when should field validation take place? And what about components? Obviously these can't throw up a dialog box on the server asking for additional information. Handling distributed component errors and contingencies is going to be a new and wonderfully challenging experience. I hope you don't have anything planned for your weekends until the next millennium.

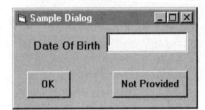

Figure 5-1 *Dialog box representing an open field*

NOTE   In the context of a form, the term *field* means a control or other element in the form for capturing or displaying data. A field is derived from one or more columns in a database row, and one or more fields can be used to determine one or more columns in the database.

There is no true consensus on the question of field validation. Most approaches taken by front-end development applications like Access or PowerSoft PowerBuilder don't leverage the extensive power that can be made available through the establishment of rules and defaults on the SQL server. These rules and defaults are the most powerful tools a database administrator has for combating violations of column integrity. When specific criteria are established for each column, the database is protected from all applications that attempt to make changes in the data.

But applications that rely completely on server-side validation are difficult to code, besides making life more difficult for data entry operators. And rules are blind: they don't know who is making a change or why, and without a lot of ugly code, it's tough to bend the rules for certain users and the inevitable special cases. Regardless of the front end or utility accessing the table, all changes must pass muster before being accepted.

The problem with the server-side validation approach is timing. Rules and defaults are applied when data is added or changed; the mechanism for invoking the rules is an INSERT or UPDATE SQL statement or a method applied to a remote object. So by the time the rules and defaults are applied, the form fields have all been completed and the user has already moved on mentally to the next form. If there are problems with the data, the user is generally forced to completely reconstruct the incorrect field, so your code has to be more complex because it has to parse the field in question from the error message before anything else can happen. And that can be difficult, since some base columns are derived from a number of form fields.

By contrast, many database front-end development applications, such as Access, permit you to create forms with built-in field validation. These edits are done independently of the remote database, so they don't reflect changes made to rules or defaults in the root tables. This type of field validation is fast, and it's fairly easy to code, but it's also application-centric: its benefits can't be shared between applications or even between forms in the same application. And when remote database defaults or rules change, the applications in question must be recoded, recompiled, and redistributed. Can you say "expensive"?

One way around this dilemma is to create to a single executable, which all users can access over the network. This solution is limited, however—it doesn't take account of changes made while an application is running or of cases in which an application is too large to download over a slow network link. This solution also requires each application to be changed when base-table field validation criteria change, which can be quite expensive if a variety of applications use the database. Some Internet applications take this approach, while others use ISAPI or DCOM interfaces in an attempt to alleviate this problem.

Another fairly common approach is to turn off all column rules so that responsibility for field validation resides solely in the front-end application. This solution is workable when only one or two applications perform data entry; any more than that, and the problem of how to validate fields gets highly complex.

Another approach to validation issues is to encapsulate data entry rules into one or more ActiveX controls. Since you can now write these in Visual Basic, this alternative makes a lot of sense. These custom controls can be as simple as a smart TextBox control with extra code behind its Click event or as sophisticated as a whole set of controls aggregated into a single ActiveX control. Either way, a control can be passed around the development team and used by everyone. If the underlying rules change, you have to rebuild the control and recompile, but that's far better and faster than ferreting out all the rules when they're hard-coded in a dozen different applications. Another approach would be to move this functionality out of process and onto the remote server, letting Microsoft Transaction Server manage the logic for you.

What I call the *virtual application* leverages server-side rules and still provides field-level validation. The virtual application automatically adapts field and form validation criteria to changes in database rules, defaults, and sometimes triggers. In the following section, we'll discuss the implementation of the virtual front end and how to make the best use of its features.

Local and Database-Driven Validation

Data entry operators often work "head down" and don't like to cursor back to correct mistakes in fields they've already entered. One school of thought says that field validation should be performed as the data is entered, or as soon as possible thereafter. This approach is hospitable to field-level validation and can be supplemented with form-level checks as a form is committed. These tests carry out cross-checks that might include several fields. One approach to field-level validation, an approach Access uses, builds edit masks and tests into the local application form and its validation code. But what this approach means, unless you're clever, is that you must design your field-level and form-level validation to match the eccentricities of the database's schema and validation changes: when the database changes, your application must change as well.

Another school of thought insists that field validation be done with the rules, triggers, and stored procedures maintained in the database. In this scenario, as the operator changes focus from one of the form's input fields to another, or at least from section to section of the form, a database query is executed that validates the data entered up to that point. One technique updates a "dataless" table that contains only a subset of the columns that are about to be updated but that are bound to the same rules as the base table. If the pseudo update or insert fails because of a rule violation, it is abundantly clear which column or columns caused the failure. This type of query is very quick and can be done in the background as the operator begins work on the next input field. When the operator commits the form, a "true" update can be executed, one that is sure to succeed—unless there are duplicate or missing records. The hitch with this approach is that it doesn't lend itself to the use of control-level validation, which can significantly reduce your code. For example, many of the checks performed by Visual Basic's masked edit control can simplify data entry and validation as data is entered—but the control is not normally cognizant of database rule changes that might affect the control's default, range, and mask property settings.

Data-Driven Validation

In a virtual application, regardless of the data interface you choose, you can create a data entry validation test by using the rules maintained in the database. While the application or form is loading, you query the SQL Server *SysComments* table, a repository of all the database's procedures, rules, defaults, and triggers, for the rules and default values that apply to specific fields in the form (if you know which rules are assigned to those fields). Each row in *SysComments* is an index with its ID object. (A listing of all SQL Server objects is kept in the *SysObjects* table.) By using a simple join or subquery between the *SysObjects* and *SysComments*

CAUTION

SQL Server's *SysComments* table is stored in open ASCII except when it's encrypted, as is possible with SQL Server 6.*x* and later. If SQL Server's *SysComments* table is encrypted, you are SOL (a technical acronym that has something to do with finding yourself up a well-known tributary without a means of propulsion).

tables and basing it on the *name* column of *SysObjects*, you can get the rule or default you want. The following sample query illustrates the subquery technique that extracts *pub_idrule* from the database:

```
Select text from syscomments where id =
(select id from sysobjects where name = 'pub_idrule')
```

> **NOTE** On some SQL servers, all objects are case-sensitive. If the SQL server in our example were set to case-sensitive mode, and if the rule were entered as *Pub_IDRule*, the sample query wouldn't work.

Here are the results of our sample query: the text of the rule as returned from the *pubs* database's *SysComments* table. This rule's job is to validate changes made to the *pub_id* field in the *Publishers* table or wherever else the *pub_id* column is used:

```
create rule Pub_IDRule as @pub_id in ("1389", "0736", "0877",
"1622", "1756") or @pub_id like "99[0-9][0-9]"
```

Making Virtual Rules

With a virtual application, validation is performed in the field's LostFocus event. To use *pub_idrule* in your form field's LostFocus event, you have to create a procedure that reads the rule from the database (as already shown), parses the arguments, and creates an array that contains valid values. The rule arguments are the operator (such as =, <, >, !=, BETWEEN, IN, or LIKE) and the value or expression being tested for.

Unless your procedure is particularly smart and you're very good at parsing non-Polish expressions, your database administrators and the developers who set the rule text will have to be aware that your application expects a fairly fixed and carefully written rule—at least one that has been written within known guidelines. For example, *pub_idrule* uses an IN clause to provide a list of valid field values. If a rule developer changed this to a set of specific tests instead, your rule parser might fail.

> **TIP** When your application depends on the syntax of a rule, it might be a good idea to tell those who are likely to change the rule. That way, your application has half a chance of working when changes are made.

Using LIKE tests in rules

The second part of *pub_idrule* uses a different approach to validate the *pub_id* field. In this case, the TSQL LIKE operator is used to accept certain characters in specified positions. Since Visual Basic now supports its own *Like* keyword, you can parse out the criteria string, convert it to Visual Basic syntax, and use it to filter the field in question. Figure 5-2 shows a sample form in which the input is validated. The code that follows shows how the form input is validated by using *Like* and the *pub_idrule*.

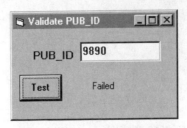

Figure 5-2 *Form in which the input is validated using a rule*

```
Dim LikeTest as String

Private Sub Form_Load()
Dim SQL$
Dim i%, Qry$
Set db = OpenDatabase _
    ("pubs", False, False, "uid=;pwd=;database=pubs;")
SQL$ = "select text from syscomments where id =" _
    & "(select id from sysobjects where name = 'pub_idrule')"
Set rs = db.OpenRecordset(SQL, dbOpenSnapshot, dbSQLPassThrough)
Qry$ = rs(0)
i% = InStr(Qry$, "like")          ' Search for "Like" value test
If i% > 0 Then
    LikeTest$ = Mid$(Qry$, i% + 6)  ' Strip off test criteria
    i = InStr(LikeTest$, Chr$(34))  ' Search for trailing quote
    LikeTest$ = Left$(LikeTest$, i - 1) ' Trim trailing quote
Debug.Print "LikeTest = "; LikeTest$
Else
    MsgBox "Could not parse rule"
End If
End Sub
```

In the Validate event—or, in this case, in the TestButton_Click event—you can now create a test that changes when the rule changes in the database:

```
Private Sub TestButton_Click()
PassFail = ""
Dim r$
If PubID Like LikeTest$ Then
    r$ = "passed"
Else
    r$ = "Failed"
    Beep
End If
PassFail = r$
End Sub
```

Converting LIKE expressions

Wouldn't it be nice if both TSQL and Visual Basic LIKE expressions used the same syntax? I guess that's too much to ask—but it's not that hard to convert. Table 5-2 shows the differences. (Notice, however, that the previous example doesn't need to be converted: the bracket [ ] syntax is roughly the same for both expressions.)

Table 5-2

Differences Between TSQL and Visual Basic LIKE Expressions

TSQL	Visual Basic	Notes
%	*	Any string of zero or more characters, as in *LIKE "do*"* returns *dog*, *doggy* and *do*.
_ (underscore)	?	Any single character, as in *"?og"* returns <u>*d*</u>*og* or <u>*b*</u>*og* but not *og* or *oggle*.
[ ]	[ ]	Any single character within the specified range (for example, *[a–f]*) or set (for example, *[abcdef]*).
[^]	[!]	Any single character not within the specified range (for example, *[!a–f]*) or set (for example, *[!abcdef]*).
[0-9]	#	Any single digit (0–9). SQL does not differentiate between the characters 0–9 and the letters, so you can specify a single digit using the bracket [ ] syntax.

Any rule expression can also contain TSQL expressions or functions, such as GETDATE() to return the current date. For example, the following rule checks whether the value being tested is within three days of the current day:

```
@value between Getdate() and dateadd (day,3,getdate())
```

If you come across a rule containing an expression, you can try substituting the Visual Basic equivalent of the statement, but this gets a little tricky since you can't create Visual Basic code on the fly and expect Visual Basic to execute it. What you can do is use a CASE statement to branch to an equivalent Visual Basic code handler and pass the parsed parameters to the statement. (You can also work out a compromise with the developer to rephrase the rule. Try a bribe—say, a case of Mountain Dew.)

Setting edit masks

What if a particular type of test would be handled better by a masked edit control? You might consider parsing the test value from the rule and creating a masked edit mask—but that seems like a lot of trouble. It might be more useful to include a mask right in the rule. Rules can have comments, so I suggest creating a mask and placing the text for the mask in a comment. For example, locating the mask would be easy if our *pub_idrule* contained the following text:

```
create rule Pub_idRule as @pub_id in ("1389", "0736", "0877",
"1622", "1756")

or @pub_id like "99[0-9][0-9]"
/* MASK={####} */
```

In this example, the mask simply permits the entry of four numbers. In more complex statements, it would be easy to specify the appropriate mask in the rule.

CAUTION

When rules are created or used, SQL Server doesn't check masks for correct syntax, since a mask is only a comment. Syntax is checked only when an application is executed and a rule is invoked, so your code has to do the error checking to ensure that your mask is right. Make sure you have a back-up mask in case the SQL administrator sets an incorrect mask value. I keep a Richard M. Nixon mask handy for just those occasions.

Virtualizing Defaults and Parsing Default Strings

Defaults, like rules, are kept in the SQL Server *SysComments* system table. Parsing default strings poses a few problems, but most of them are less complex than those you faced working with rules.

A default can contain only a constant (value) or constant expression, but this constant can be a global variable, such as *@@Connections*, or it can be a fairly complex expression; it just can't reference database tables or other columns. Many of the expressions and functions can be generated on the workstation end. For example, GETDATE() is simply the current date. You can execute DATE$ or TIME$ to get current values, unless the server is in a different time zone.

TIP If your default is simply a value, you have no worries. All you have to do is parse the value and test for it in a simple comparison statement. But if the default uses an expression that contains a global variable, you are off the road hub-deep in the muck—unless your initialization routine requeries the remote server for the current value.

The following query fetches a default value for a named column in a named table. This is probably the syntax you'll need to use, since it doesn't assume that you know the name of the default; it assumes only that there is a default on a particular table's column. In the process of developing this test code, I noticed that the default names in the *pubs* database were hardly user-friendly: most of the time, a default name ended with a fairly long number, which was probably generated by the automated routine that created the table and its components in the first place. Therefore, this technique is probably a better choice when you know the table and column names.

```
select text from syscomments where id =
(select cdefault from syscolumns
where name = "city" and id = (select id from sysobjects
where name = "Authors" and type = "U")
)
```

The return string from this query contains the syntax you need to create the default:

```
create default CityDefault as "Redmond"
```

In this case, simply parse the value between the quotes, and use it for the test value in your form field GetFocus or LostFocus validation routine. (If the default is a money value, it may be preceded with $.)

NOTE When I used the Enterprise Manager to examine and attempt to change the defaults in the *pubs* database, I noticed a number of areas where the program returned incorrect information or otherwise failed to work correctly. For example, I tried to bind a default to the *Titles* table, but it wouldn't accept the name of the default as entered. I fell back to the BINDEFAULT stored procedure, which correctly bound the new default. I used a query to verify that the default was correctly bound, but it didn't appear in the table when I examined it with Enterprise Manager. It appears that the table data is extracted from the database but not requeried when the table changes.

CAUTION
System clocks might be manually synchronized every now and then, but they are notoriously inaccurate and tend to drift. If the SQL server is in another state or country, it will also be set to a different time than your workstation. Be wary of any strategy that depends on date and time values to be completely accurate.

Administration of Virtual Applications

The kind of virtual application I've been describing can ensure that minor changes (and some that aren't so minor) made to field criteria in the database won't force you to recompile your front end. Here are a few more points to consider:

- Changes made to the database are not propagated to the front end until it requeries the SysComments table. Since your code is replicating the rule tests, no update rule violations should occur. If they do, it means that the rule has changed or that your code is bogus. Requery SysCom*ments*, rebuild your rule test, and retest the field.

- If the SQL administrator changes the rule so that your code fails to parse the new syntax, your code should quietly report the error back to the system administrator and use a fallback rule or default. Notification can take place by e-mail or with a call placed to the SQL administrator through a workstation modem playing a WAV file that contains an appropriate message.

- Your application should load default values when the form loads, and again if notified to do so. The notification mechanism is up to you. It can take the form of an e-mail message sent from the server or a time value set in a special table designed for this purpose. One thing you can do is limit the times when this type of change is permitted: choose a time when all applications are off line.

6

Making Connections to SQL Server

n Chapter 4, I said that Microsoft SQL Server is as obedient and dedicated as a Marine sergeant. Well, it turns out that this gung ho sergeant (our steadfast SQL Server) will take orders only over a network connection called, not surprisingly, a *connection*. A connection is a fairly complex set of interface, network, and SQL Server structures, agents, and protocols that temporarily link your application to a SQL server. This link can last for a few seconds or indefinitely—just how long you stay connected is up to you. However, you need to consider that connections are a server resource that shouldn't be squandered. In some cases, licensing restrictions limit the number of connections you're allowed. You might be limited to five or fewer connections, or you might have rights to an "unlimited" number. Other constraints include the amount of RAM each connection takes and the CPU time consumed to get the logical wires hooked up. You need to devise your connection strategy around judicious management of the connection resource.

Not counting Visual Basic Library for Microsoft SQL Server (VBSQL, the Visual Basic interface to DB-Library), you can set up a connection with SQL Server in two major ways: ODBC and OLE DB. In this chapter, I'm not going to get into many of the nitty-gritty details of either approach since I focus on them in later chapters, but I will introduce a number of connection strategies that apply to all the data access interfaces. OLE DB interfaces such as ADO can also connect (indirectly) through ODBC, so in some cases, you have to go through OLE DB dialog boxes just to get to the ODBC dialog boxes. (This activity ought to wear down your mouse's little ball.) Both ODBC and OLE DB collect pretty much the same basic information to get connected. Yes, the OLE DB interface does gather a lot more options, properties, and assorted widdle-waddle. The OLE DB interface needs to be a lot more flexible than ODBC because it has to connect to a cornucopia of relational and nonrelational data sources. Unfortunately, the OLE DB people aren't quite sure at this point what their final dialog boxes are going to look like or how they are going to work. Six weeks before we go to the CD burners, they're still wrangling about the terms OLE DB uses to refer to a "database" or a "server." So the documentation (both print and online) won't always match what's been (finally) implemented. I'll lead you through that swamp a little later.

Dog Paddling in the Connection Pool

Remember when we only had DAO opening connections for us and how it made us crazy that we could never seem to close a connection? (Even returning the computer to the store where I bought it didn't seem to work!) Well, this ever so special open-all-the-time behavior was the result of Microsoft Jet's "pooling" of the connections. It tried to keep connections open, assuming that you would be back sometime later and reuse the connection. By keeping the connections open, Jet could save you the time required to reopen a dormant connection. And that wasn't just a courtesy—part of Jet's problem was that it took a rather extended length of time to open a connection. You'll be interested to learn that this connection pooling technology has found a new home—in the ODBC interface. If you're using Microsoft Transaction Server (MTS) to establish your connections, the pooling option is enabled for you. Otherwise, you have to turn it on via an ODBC API. When connection pooling is enabled and you close a connection, the ODBC pool manager can leave it open; when you open another connection later on, MTS and ODBC try to reuse the already opened connection. Here we go again. I'll get into the realities of what this implementation involves later in the chapter, in the section "Permitting More Active Connections" on page 148, and later in the book. For now, just consider that you're going to have to be more careful when you connect. We are living in the 1990s, aren't we?

No matter which design or architecture you use, its database interface must be connected to the SQL server before any query operations can take place. Each data access interface manages connections differently, which can be a deciding factor in your choice of design. Connecting from components is even more challenging because you have to worry about how MTS, ODBC, or OLE DB manages pooled connections for you.

NOTE One of the most daunting tasks ahead of you is establishing your first connection to SQL Server. If you work methodically through the issues, however, you should survive to send your first query before too long. We'll go over more of the interface-specific details you'll need to be aware of in later sections of this chapter.

The checklist in Table 6-1 shows which of the data interfaces perform which connection-related operations.

Table 6-1
Connection Operation Checklist

Operation	VBSQL	ODBC API	DAO/ Jet	DAO/ ODBCDirect	RDO	ADO
Open connection via a data source control			✓	✓	✓	✓
Support "prompt" behavior modification		✓		✓	✓	✓
Open additional connections automatically to update rows			✓			
Defer releasing of connections after they have been closed	optional	✓ (3.x)	✓	optional	optional	optional
Clean up connections in Design mode		✓	✓	✓	✓	✓
Return handle to connection	✓	✓		✓	✓	

Connection Security

If the data you're accessing has any value, you must take steps to secure it. Without security systems, your data is subject to theft, damage, and accidental access. Setting up and maintaining database security is the responsibility of your SQL Server administrator, who establishes a schema of database users and data objects. Each user is granted or denied permission to access portions of the database; the portions vary from a single column in a single table to the entire database itself.

> **NOTE** Generally, your client application or component must be granted access to the database tables and columns it needs, but no more. In any case, data retrieval and updating are often performed against views or stored procedures, not on database tables themselves, a practice that filters and protects delicate referential or data integrity constraints.

Before your code can gain access to SQL Server, it must identify itself to the server. It does this by passing a login ID and password to the server. Generally, I don't associate a login ID with a person but rather with a role. SQL Server 7.0 has now adopted the term *login ID* to refer to what we used to call an *alias* in older versions of SQL Server. This approach makes the management of Windows NT user IDs and their associated SQL Server login IDs easier because a functional role is associated with an application or a component that makes the connection. In any case, before a user (or role) can access a database, the system administrator (SA) must add a specific login ID (a "user") to SQL Server and assign the user a username for that database. The SA can modify the login ID and the group or alias of a user in SQL Server. As this login ID is added, the SA also assigns a password to be used with that specific login ID. You'll have to set up these login IDs before you charge off and try to connect—unless you simply connect with the "sa" login ID and the system administrator's password. Frankly, although we're quite casual about using the "sa" login ID when demonstrating our programs at conferences, I strongly recommend that you *not* use the "sa" login ID for any applications or components—even during testing. Doing so has serious security implications and also masks other problems you'll encounter when you try to use role-based login IDs in production.

> **NOTE** To make your life interesting, each version of SQL Server uses subtly different terminology. In this edition of *Hitchhiker's Guide*, I generally follow terminology used with SQL Server 7.0. Also, I primarily use "user ID" to indicate any user defined in Windows NT and "login ID" to indicate any login defined in SQL Server.

The login ID used to establish the connection can be hard-coded in your application or component, or it can be passed along from Microsoft Windows NT, if you're using Windows NT Authentication (what we used to call "Integrated" security) or Mixed security (Windows NT Authentication and SQL Server Authentication). With Mixed security, the Windows NT domain-managed security system passes on the Windows NT user account to SQL Server—assuming, of course, that this user has been registered with the SQL Server system. An easy way to administer your database users is to set up a Windows NT group on the SQL Server system that contains all the valid SQL Server database users. Then use SQL Server Enterprise Manager (or the Security Manager in previous versions) to add the Windows NT group to the list of valid users. The login ID and password are the keys to the security system, and they should be guarded as carefully as physical access to the server.

In the latest versions of Microsoft Visual Basic, all ODBC interfaces, including RDO and ADO, support ODBC connection pooling. By default, connection management is disabled; but if it gets enabled, the ODBC Driver Manager will attempt to share your connections with other parts of your program or other components using the same transaction scope and connect string. DAO and RDO intentionally disable this feature, but it is enabled by default when you use MTS. If you decide to enable it, be especially careful because it can significantly impact how many users are permitted to gain access to your server.

Getting the Login ID and Password

If you choose to let the user enter the login ID and password (I don't), you can create a dialog box that doesn't echo the password as it is being typed. Fortunately, Visual Basic provides this feature as the PasswordChar property of its TextBox control; simply set it to an asterisk (*). You can also store the user ID and password in an INI file or in the Registry so users don't need to enter it each time. Generally, I code the application so that it logs on with its own "secret" login ID and password known only to me. I either assume that access to the system containing the application is guarded or add other user-validation code that checks for a valid user in other ways. I'm sure you can figure out these alternative approaches on your own.

Getting a Valid Server Name or Data Source Name

In the course of installing an application or a component that uses ODBC, you have the option of establishing one or more data source name (DSN) entries. These can be manually installed (registered) using the Windows Control Panel ODBC applet or the dialog boxes launched at development time from Visual Basic Data Environment dialog boxes (and elsewhere). The DSN must contain just enough information to identify the server (its Windows NT machine name) and the type of server (such as SQL Server). Other information in the DSN is optional. No, the login ID is not stored in the DSN, but it can be persisted in the Visual Basic or ODBC development interfaces to facilitate application development. You can also create a file-based DSN or use a code-based technique called a *DSN-less* connection. This DSN-less connection is the cheapest and fastest connection because it doesn't require a Registry lookup. We'll discuss these DSN-less connections at length in the RDO and ADO chapters (Parts IV and V).

When working with OLE DB, you don't use DSNs unless you're using OLE DB to connect to an ODBC data source. In this case, you build a string containing the necessary information. This string is called a *connect string*—just as it is in the ODBC world. You can also create a new ASCII file (a UDL file), called a Microsoft Data Link, to connect to OLE DB data sources. This file contains a completed OLE DB connect string. You can create a UDL file by right-clicking on the Windows desktop and choosing New/Microsoft Data Link from the pop-up menu. Once you create a UDL file, however, you have to revisit its properties: again, right-click on the desktop icon created, and choose Properties. We'll discuss how to work with UDL files when we get to the ADO chapters (Part V). Now don't get confused, like I did when I expected the Data View window (that exposes a Data Link property dialog box) in Visual Basic 6.0 to create UDL files—it doesn't. This dialog box persists its settings in the Windows Registry.

When it comes time to tell ODBC or OLE DB where to find the server, I rarely (OK, never) ask the user for the name of the SQL server, the driver, or the DSN. If you *must* ask the user to enter the resource name, however, you should present a list of valid SQL servers or DSNs instead of having the user type a name into a TextBox control. This list should be limited to just those servers that this particular user should be connecting to. To present such a list, you must poll the network for all *visible* SQL servers or use the ODBC DSN APIs and then show just those servers or DSNs the user has rights to. (The companion CD to *Hitchhiker's Guide* includes an example of using the ODBC APIs to get DSNs.)

Many versions ago, I used to recommend the Visual Basic LAN Manager custom controls for presenting the user with a list of SQL servers, but then the SQL Server development team added a new call, SqlServerEnum, to VBSQL 4.2 (created to support the Windows NT environment). This call returns a list of servers that have identified themselves as SQL servers. If you're using the Windows NT operating system (but not Microsoft Windows 95), you can use this call to search the local system or the network domain, and all the systems that have SQL Server installed appear on the list, even if the servers aren't running at the moment. (This call is understandably slow; in my tests, it took SqlServerEnum almost 25 seconds to return any results.)

NOTE I still experience problems with the visibility of SQL servers, especially from Windows 95, so don't be alarmed if your SQL server isn't on the list of valid servers presented by the SQL Server or Visual Basic 6.0 tools. Sometimes this aberration can be caused when the local area network (LAN) server is marked as not being visible. In a Windows 95 environment, the LAN APIs used to poll for SQL servers don't work as they do in Windows 3.x or Windows NT. Basically, this means that you won't be able to troll for servers in Windows 95—not until Microsoft decides to fix this visibility problem.

Avoiding the Login Dialog Boxes

In only the most unusual case should you permit your users to be confronted with the ODBC or OLE DB login dialog boxes. In the early days, this was a fairly common and unavoidable occurrence if you used DAO/Jet or didn't set the proper options when using DAO/ODBCDirect, RDO, or ADO. Let's slow down here a minute and see how this works. Whenever the ODBC Driver Manager receives a failed login attempt notification from the driver, based on the Prompt option settings, it throws up the dialog box shown in Figure 6-1. Notice that this is radically different from the dialog boxes you might have been used to seeing in the past. I triggered this dialog box because my code didn't pass a DSN, a login ID, or a password. This dialog box prompts a user to choose from the list of visible DSNs or make one up on her own by clicking New. Not good. Do you want *your* users making up their own DSNs? I wouldn't. Does this prompting behavior get better with ADO and OLE DB? Nope, it gets worse. Setting the Prompt option is further hidden beneath the valve covers—but we'll talk about that later, in the ADO chapters (Part V). When working with RDO and ADO (where you have more options), you'll find that setting up the correct prompting behavior is an important aspect of your connection strategy. In no case do you want a component running on a remote server down the hall to throw up this dialog box.

If you're using DAO and your code provides a valid DSN but the user doesn't have access, the dialog box shown in Figure 6-2 appears. This dialog box allows the user to enter a login ID and a password.

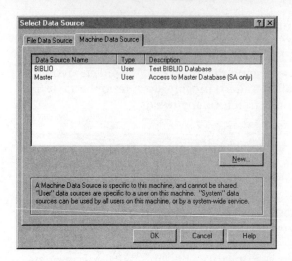

Figure 6-1 *ODBC prompts the user for the missing DSN*

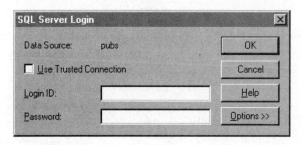

Figure 6-2 *The SQL Server Login dialog box prompting the user for a login ID and password*

Unfortunately, the SQL Server login dialog box permits the user to click the Options button, which exposes all kinds of tempting options, including the database name. (See Figure 6-3.) Swell. Even if the user did know what these options did, do you *really* want him twisting knobs and throwing switches on his own?

These lapses in security are completely preventable in all the non-DAO/Jet data interfaces. In ADO, this is the default behavior. In RDO, simply specify that the ODBC or OLE DB option must return all ODBC connection errors to the application using the Prompt property. Yes, this means that you have to code an error handler, but isn't that less hassle than having your users calling you at 7:45 p.m. during the play-offs?

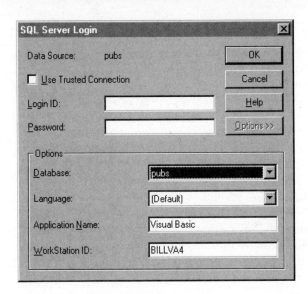

Figure 6-3 *The SQL Server Login dialog box after the Option button has been clicked*

Connection Management

When your application or component is working with SQL Server data, it's expected to communicate with the SQL server in a fairly structured way. Now that a number of alternative interfaces to SQL Server are available, some of the details of these communications might be taken care of for you, but you still must always be aware of what's happening in the background on your behalf.

As SQL Server and its interface drivers improve, fundamental aspects of front-end and component design must change to accommodate or take advantage of the improvements. For example, SQL Server 6.0 introduced server-side cursors that permit a single connection to perform more than one operation at a time. If you're writing an application that is expected to communicate with both SQL Server 4.0 and SQL Server 6.0 and later, you might consider the cost benefits of this feature.

NOTE   Does SQL Server 7.0 change the way you get or stay connected? Nope. The techniques discussed here apply to virtually all versions of SQL Server from 4.*x* to 7.0.

Permitting More Active Connections

To get the most out of a server, you might want to keep connections open only if they're going to be used immediately. This and several other techniques can permit more active connections to the server by eliminating or at least reducing idle connections—those left open between requests to the server. One technique is *opening just in time*. With the exception of the first connection, most SQL connections take only a second or less to complete when you use the VBSQL interface. The other data interfaces can take considerably longer, especially if you open a database object directly by using DAO/Jet or if you reference a registered DSN. It seems that once the connection is open, DAO, RDO, and ADO feel a need to perform several overhead exploratory queries to check out the options of the server they have just connected to. They don't cache this information, so these queries are done each and every time. The "just in time" technique slows down the workstation somewhat—how much depends on the number of connection operations—but it can be an effective way to increase the number of users who can access the SQL server at any one time.

> **NOTE** In the process of working on this edition of the *Hitchhiker's Guide*, I discovered that when connecting to SQL Server for the first time, not only did it take a long time to get connected, but the interface often timed out. However, if I tried to reconnect immediately thereafter, the connection was made instantly. I logged this as a bug, and it will probably get fixed in time for its release. If not, don't say I didn't warn you.

Another technique—*watchdog timer disconnect*—drops connections that aren't being actively used (and that don't have active queries pending). It's very much like a screen saver. This technique uses conventional logic, but it sets up a timer that watches for any activity that would reset its wait time. Once that time has expired, the timer closes the connection. The next attempt at database access is expected to fail because of a null connection or missing object, and when it does, the error handler reopens the connection and passes control back to the requesting call.

Yet another method—introduced with ODBC 3.0 (and at the beginning of this chapter)—is the ability of the ODBC interface to pool connections. When connection pooling is enabled, the ODBC interface, in conjunction with the Resource Dispenser Manager (introduced with ODBC 3.0), maintains a pool of connections from which a connection is drawn when your MTS component asks to establish a new connection. Connections are returned to the pool (but not necessarily disconnected) when you use the Close method. Because not all connections are interchangeable, connections are pooled based on their DSN, type, and transaction scope. The pool itself is sized dynamically, based on demand and idle connections. By default, if a connection is idle for more than 10 minutes (far too long in my opinion), it is "destroyed." I've heard rumors that the intelligence of this aspect is expected to increase as the use of this feature broadens. By default, ADO, RDO, and DAO/ODBCDirect *disable* this feature, but you can enable it through API calls. When you're working with MTS components, this feature is enabled by default.

Personally, I find this kind of connection management a little *too* helpful. For the most part, my applications do just fine managing their connections without having the driver maintain a pool. However, some of the Information Technology Group (ITG) applications written for internal use here at Microsoft do need connection management. The problem for these applications will be how to keep the ODBC Driver Manager's pool manager from kicking sand in their faces.

Microsoft's ITG group implements its own connection managers for several internal applications, and the concept seems to work quite well. I'm sure if you call, they will be happy to send you the source code. (In your dreams.)

NOTE If you're designing connections to the Windows NT version of SQL Server, you *should* consider leaving them open. Because the number of connections supported by the Windows NT version can be virtually unlimited, and because these servers can support gigabytes of RAM, a few dozen extra connections aren't much of a burden. The amount of overhead involved in opening a connection, closing it, and reopening it later can impose a greater burden than the extra resources the additional connections take.

A New Connection's Impact on the Server

One of the options you can provide when you connect is the application and workstation names. SQL Server Enterprise Manager shows the host (workstation) name when you view server activity. You and the system administrator will both find the host name and the application name useful in identifying your connection. That way, you (or someone else with administrator privileges) can kill your connection if you need to, or you can identify what resources or locks it is using. In the ODBC *Connect* argument and in the VBSQL functions that are used for opening connections, you can expose the parameters by using the sp_who stored procedure or a query based on this procedure. But most of the time, I use Enterprise Manager's Current Activity window to see what's going on. Figure 6-4 shows what will be returned.

Notice that the application-provided host or workstation ID (WSID) and application name (APP) values are given along with the current database and which user is connected. What would you use these parameters for? In previous versions of SQL Server, you could use SysProcedures queries to develop an application that kept a current record of who had logged on when and of what the users were doing in general at any given time. This table was dropped (or masked), however, in SQL Server 7.0. Despite this change, I'm sure there's a way to log this activity in SQL Server 7.0, but no clever developer has tipped me off on the technique yet. For an application like that, it would be especially helpful to have the name of the program spelled out. You might also want to set the Workstation Name string to reflect the current time of login or additional user-specific information.

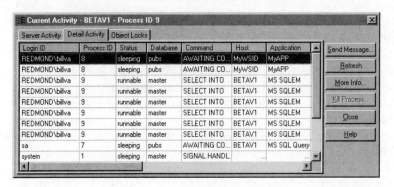

Figure 6-4 *Viewing connections in SQL Server 7.0 Enterprise Manager*

Setting the Timeout Value

The default login timeout value for establishing a connection can vary from 15 seconds to over 60 seconds; the exact value depends on the data interface you choose and the way you set timeout arguments. This means that if you pass an incorrect or misspelled server name or if the network or server is down or otherwise unavailable, you might have to wait for a full minute or longer before control is returned to your application. The problem is that your Windows operating system might be blocked and seemingly locked up for that entire time.

Most SQL servers on a local area network (LAN), as opposed to a wide area network (WAN) or remote access server (RAS), connect in a few seconds (or less). ODBC connections can take longer to complete, but the initial wait for the server to respond is usually still within 1 to 5 seconds. The *first* time a workstation opens a connection to a server, however, the time for completing the process tends to be longer by 50 percent, even if the application ends and another begins. I can only account for this extra time as LAN overhead that's not needed after the initial connection has been made and after the workstation engine components—including dynamic-link libraries (DLLs)—have been loaded and initialized. The Windows operating system holds DLLs and EXE files in memory until the space is needed, even when their reference count is reduced to 0, which might explain the shorter waiting times for subsequent connections.

NOTE I usually set the login timeout value to about 15 seconds to accommodate fully loaded networks. If you set the login timeout value any higher, users have a tendency to give your application the three-finger salute: Ctrl-Alt-Delete. Perhaps you should use an option flag for those sites that are on remote services and need more time.

Managing Connection State

If you plan to build applications or components that connect to SQL Server and enable connection pooling, read this section very, very carefully before proceeding. First consider that all database connections, regardless of how they are made, maintain state. In other words, once the connection is made, SQL Server and your application can set a number of options that apply to your (and only your) connection. For example, you can change the default database as well as various other options, such as ANSI, cursor, transaction, numeric handling, row count, and maximum rows. Some state settings are made directly, as when you specify a default database by sending a USE *database* TSQL statement. Others are set for you based on your login ID or arguments you pass in the connect string; still others are set by changing properties such as MaxRows in RDO and ADO. In addition, any temporary tables or stored procedures you create are also owned by the connection—they too are part of the connection "state." Even the temporary stored procedures created by the data access interfaces are owned by the connection and are expected to be dropped when you close the connection.

When the SQL Server connection is closed (really closed), all these settings are reset back to their initial state and the resources they consume are released. This means that the next time you connect to SQL Server, you get a connection set to a known base state, just as it was the first time—that is, *except* when you use a connection pooling mechanism. Yes, you guessed it. When you close a pooled connection, your application can no longer access the connection until you reopen it. And when you do reopen it, you get the state set and leftover from the last application or component that used it. It's like reaching for a drinking glass and noticing that not only does it have a lipstick smear on it, but it's also half-full of some brown liquid. I've been working with the developers about this problem, but I haven't seen a resolution yet—and don't really expect one to come up soon. They suggest that developers use properties whenever possible to set SQL Server connection state. This way they have half a chance to unset the operations you set. Until this problem is fully resolved, you must really be careful when assuming anything about your pooled connection. Your logic should be prepared to deal with the possibility that other users have contaminated the connection. For example, you should not build temporary tables or procedures that could get left behind because they could build up over time if the connection is never closed. You should also not change the default database or try to set MaxRows. This means that all table references should include the full three-part address *database.owner.table* unless you can be certain that no other user can change the default database. You can avoid cross-connection contamination by using a unique connect string or DSN when connecting. This way, only your component accesses the connection. But then again, more connections will be consumed.

Handling Connection Errors

The client/server interface is very much like a conversation between master and servant, with occasional moans or complaints from the kitchen. These protestations are called *error messages*. Each error message is accompanied by a number and a *details* string that describes the situation. If you develop your applications at one sitting, without errors, you may put this book down and take your place in the Museum of Living Legends. But every good front-end or component developer I know spends a great deal of time anticipating errors and the other contingencies of working with a remote server.

Because the various data interfaces handle errors differently, it's not always clear what the problem is when something goes wrong with a connection. When I'm debugging these problems, I ask my users the following set of questions before attempting to guess what went wrong:

- **Has the application ever connected? If so, what has changed since then?** The answers to these questions tell me whether I'm searching for a user-security problem or for a link problem that has affected the network. If the user has been able to get connected in the past, the likelihood of a setup, security, or network protocol problem is reduced—unless some new application or a new version of the operating system has just been installed. Upgrading drivers can impact connectability.

- **Does the application connect at some times but not at others?** I ask this question to find out whether I'm dealing with a problem related to capacity or to network traffic or availability. A "yes" response to this question could also mean that the system has been contaminated with incorrectly installed DLLs that only get invoked occasionally.

- **How many people are already connected?** When I find out, I check sp_who to see how many connections are in place. The problem might be that the connection limit is overloaded. Also, you can run SQL Server Enterprise Manager to see what's up and what's not.

- **Can you connect from other systems or applications?** If the user can connect, I know that the server is up and perhaps the problem is localized to just this workstation. If everyone is down, the problem is likely global, such as a dead server or a broken stored procedure.

- **What messages are displayed? What do the modem or network interface lights do?** The messages can lead me in the right direction, or they might only be symptoms of a problem that is masked by other configuration problems. If the modem or network lights are not showing typical traffic, a problem with the physical link is likely.

- **What were you doing when the application didn't connect?** Was the user using the program in a new way or in some unexpected manner? Is the program current and appropriate for the intended use? Was the program being pushed beyond its limits or beyond the limits of the network? Is the user connected to other network resources? Perhaps too many other applications or network resources are already being used.

- **Did the application handle the error, or did it just crash?** Knowing the answer to this question helps me identify problems that need to be addressed by better error handling on the part of the application.

- **Are the system, modem, and network plugged in?** This question seems silly, but I can't tell you how many times the simplest things have made a system malfunction.

Application-Related Problems

Once you discover that something is wrong, you can start looking at your application, if it has just been installed, or at the LAN, if everything was working up to the point when the connection failed. The workstation depends on your application and the operating system, including its LAN software component, to manage client-side resources such as RAM and device handles. If these resources are already stressed or exhausted before you attempt the connection, there is no way to predict how the operating system and your application will resolve the dogfight for the last of the resource scraps.

Problems Caused by Support Libraries

Many problems are caused because DLLs and controls are in the wrong places or weren't installed on the user's machine in the first place. If the libraries are mismatched or incorrectly installed, there is no way to tell how your application will be affected. I've seen several instances of problems that were caused by users installing a "newer" version of the ODBC drivers on top of "older" drivers. Remember that the ODBC setup dialog boxes support overriding the version checking—if you feel really brave.

The libraries are in the form of DLL, OCX, and other files that must be placed where the Windows loader can find them at run time. Most libraries are placed in the WINDOWS\SYSTEM directory by your setup program. Of course, SQL Server places its libraries in its own BINN directory to keep things interesting. In most cases, the components must also be registered in the Windows system Registry; your setup program is responsible for this as well. (Consult the Visual Basic documentation, or search online Help for more information.)

On all Windows platforms, the Windows loader behaves in the same way when it starts to look for a library. If you understand the loading sequence, you can more easily understand what's going wrong when your application fails to connect or function according to design. When your application is launched by Windows Explorer, File Manager, the Run command, or any other means, the Windows loader searches for the executable and all its components in the following places and in the following order.

- **In memory** If an existing copy of the executable or the library is in memory, all Windows has to do is create a new instance of the data segment and provide a pointer to the existing code. The library doesn't have to belong to a running application. It can be sitting in memory from a program that ended hours ago but wasn't purged because Windows didn't need the RAM. The DLL might be there because it's dead or roadkill left over from a failed program sometime in the past. You might have to reboot or at least scrape off the corpse with Pview. (See the Visual Basic 5.0 and 6.0 TOOLS directory.)

- **In the current directory** If the user is browsing a removable media drive, some networked drive, or a local hard disk, the loader searches whichever drive and directory the user is browsing. If the connection or removable media drive isn't there the next time, the loader might not find the library or might load it from some other place further down the search tree. When your application profile resets (or fails to reset) the default directory, the libraries that get loaded or don't can change sporadically.

- **In the WINDOWS, WINDOWS\SYSTEM, and WINDOWS\SYS-TEM32 directories (in that order)** Most DLLs are expected to be located in the WINDOWS\SYSTEM (or SYSTEM32) directory, but as you can see, this directory is not the first or even second place that the Windows loader searches.

- **In the directories specified by the PATH environment variable, in the order specified** A directory specified in the PATH environment variable is the usual place for applications to install their code if they haven't built proper setup programs. SQL Server seems to fall into this category because it stores its DLLs in MSQL\BINN. In some cases, they munge the PATH to put their directory high in the list, hoping that it will be searched before other locations. Unfortunately, by the time Windows gets to the PATH, it has already searched many other locations.

Windows reports that the program or library can't be found only when *all* these locations have been searched. Note that if a DLL matching the 8.3 name of the DLL being searched for happens to be in memory or in the current directory, that matching DLL is used *instead* of the version in the WINDOWS\SYS-TEM directory, which might be more (or less) current.

LAN-Related Connection Problems

A litany of network-related problems can make connecting difficult, if not impossible. To exacerbate this difficulty, network failures are often masked as other problems, since they are not always reported by specific error messages. Too often, the error reported to and by the user is a generic "could not connect" message. When we add the complication of Internet and WAN variations to these problems, it's no wonder, to me, anyway, that I've lost so much hair trying to connect to the network. To debug these situations, I start with the questions on the following page.

- **Has the user logged on to the LAN?**   This problem is especially prevalent with security systems that don't require users to log on to the network before using the workstation. If the user bypassed the network login dialog box when first booting, the only options for getting on the LAN are to log on (in Windows for Workgroups) or shut down all applications and log on as a new user in Windows 95/98 or Windows NT.

- **Are enough file or LAN connections (handles) available?**   If the user has created too many persistent connections on the workstation (the user might not be using them but hasn't closed them, either), the operating system might not be able to create any more. On some systems (especially Windows 3.*x*), the total number of LAN connections is limited. In general, with the default settings, if a user has more than four or five remote drives connected, he or she could have problems connecting to SQL Server. In some cases, you might not be able to connect without mapping to a shared drive on the SQL server.

- **Can the host server support additional users?**   It's entirely possible to exceed the limit for LAN users long before the maximum number of SQL connections has been reached. Both Windows NT and SQL Server are sold and licensed in configurations that put a cap on the total number of connections. Once this limit is reached, no additional users are permitted to log on. (As far as SQL connections are concerned, this restriction shouldn't apply to a share-level security system.)

- **Is the LAN down?**   Let's say I get a call from a user whose e-mail is down. I explain that the network is down. A few minutes later, the same user calls to report a SQL Server application that is also down for some reason, or one that is *really* slow. At that point, I'll check to see if the bridge to the SQL Server host server is down, and I'll test other shares on the network or on the host server to see if I can still access them.

- **Has an improper share been established for IPC$ (administrative share) on an OS/2 server?**   The STARTUP.CMD file on an OS/2 host server must contain a NET SHARE IPC$ statement if LAN Manager is running share-level security. With user-level security, permissions to access the IPC$ share are set on a user-by-user basis by the LAN administrator. A user who doesn't have permission to share IPC$ is out of luck.

- **Have improper permissions been assigned in user-level security, or is there an invalid LAN configuration?**   Perhaps the user doesn't have permission to access the SQL server.

- **Have you run the Client Configuration Utility to set the default device drivers and network address of the server?**   This requirement was introduced when SQL Server began supporting TCP/IP. This utility collects the parameters and addresses needed to connect the user's workstation to the specified server. This information is required when you use a TCP/IP-addressed server because the server isn't referenced by name.

One of the easiest ways to wreck a user's system is to improperly install an application. Since we have long since (OK, not that long) moved away from programs that can be installed with a single floppy by simply copying over a few files, the Setup program and regimen have grown in importance. To make it simple, just follow this advice: never, never *copy* libraries of any kind— or even applications—to the user's system. No, not *anywhere* on the user's system. Always use a program (such as Setup) that tests to see whether the libraries being overlaid are already registered or are a more recent version of the code. This is essential.

TIP Just last week a user reported that he couldn't get connected via TCP/IP, and the documentation lacked a degree of clarity on the subject. He indicated that he had discovered that the problem had to do with missing entries in the WIN.INI file. After some investigation, I discovered that SQL Server 6.0 uses the WIN.INI file in Windows 3.x to hold the needed parameters for the new TCP/IP drivers. Apparently, these WIN.INI entries are created when you use the SQL Client Configuration Utility on a 16-bit system. (Refer to SQL Server Books Online "Setting the Default Net-Library" for details.)

SQL Server–Related Connection Problems

If the LAN is functioning properly, the fault might lie with the SQL server itself. To debug these situations, I start by working through the following possible problems and solutions.

- **Did the user, application, or component enter an improper SQL login ID or password?** If the login ID and password are valid, maybe the user doesn't have permission to access this SQL server. You can watch what's going on by turning on the trace logs at the server to monitor failed login attempts.

- **Is the server running?** Did the host server include a command to launch SQL Server when the server starts? Check the services list from Control Panel or the STARTUP.CMD (OS/2 only) batch file. Use SQL Server Manager to verify.

- **Did corrupt data prevent the SQL server from starting?** If a running query that is making changes is terminated, there's a chance that the SQL server might be unable to roll back the change and so the database will be marked as suspect. Check the SQL Server error logs.

- **Has the database been improperly restored?** Occasionally, when an attempt is made to move or restore a database (or just a table), the permissions, login IDs, and passwords are not properly restored, or they end up being assigned to the wrong databases.

- **Is there too little disk or RAM space on the host server?** If it depends on local swap or temporary space, and if this space is exhausted, the SQL server might be unable to start.

- **Is the SQL server in single-user mode?** Or maybe the SQL administrator is doing maintenance work.

- **Are the user ID and password on the list for valid users?** Is the user in the group of valid users as far as Windows NT is concerned?

- **Has the server been hit by an 80-mm mortar round?** You never know.

Errors Related to Connections and Licenses

SQL Server can connect from one to several thousand users; the number depends on how many connections have been installed by the SQL administrator—and how many are licensed—as well as on system resource constraints. Each connection consumes between 10 KB and 44 KB of RAM, which can be allocated to additional procedures or data cache space. Therefore, the number of connections on any SQL server might be changed by an administrator who is trying to free additional RAM, and a common error is generated when the SQL server runs out of available connections. Because this is a common problem with limited-access SQL servers, you should always test your application to see how it behaves in these circumstances.

On SQL Server 6.0 (and later) systems, the administrator can also set the number of *licenses* that the server supports. Licenses are managed separately from connections. You can easily exhaust all the available licenses before you exhaust the number of logical connections. For example, when you set the maximum number of "connections" to 5, SQL Server 4.2 allows 15 connections before failing to permit another, which is consistent with the understanding that a single application can use several connections (and 3 connections per application should be enough, unless you use a lot of Data controls or cursors). SQL Server 6.0 is somewhat stricter with its connections. If you set a *license* limit to 5, you get 5 connections, period—regardless of the number of connections that has been set. The error returns a very informative message if you try to open a connection after the server has allocated its last one. Figure 6-5 shows a sample message returned from SQL Server 7.0.

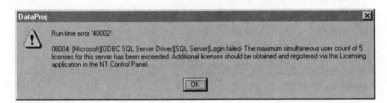

Figure 6-5 *Error message returned when the number of connections exceeds the licensing limit*

How the error is manifested will be determined by your data interface and the version of SQL Server that is running.

- In SQL Server 1.0 and 1.1 (and in some cases in current versions), a message indicating that the server has unexpectedly lost the named pipe interface is returned when there are no more connections. This message is technically correct but hardly indicative of the root cause. Apparently, the workstation opens a named pipe to the SQL server. When no more connections are available, SQL Server responds by closing the named pipe at the SQL Server end—thus the "unexpected EOF" error from the server.

- In SQL Server 4.2 (and in the Windows NT version), when the SQL server connection limit has been set to 5 but another front-end application is started, DB-Library reports a SQLEWRIT error message: "Write to SQL Server failed. This error number is unused." With VBSQL applications, DB-Library returns this SQLEWRIT error message but also sends a SQLECONN message (which would indicate some sort of LAN failure).

NOTE If you're using the SQL Server "Developer" Edition that ships with the Visual Basic and Visual Studio Enterprise editions, you'll likely run up against the connection limits because this version supports only five connections—no, not five users.

Because of this ambiguity, you should expect any one of a number of possible error messages when a connection to SQL Server fails.

Login-Related Problems

In too many cases when an error occurs during an attempted connection to SQL Server, the front-end application merely passes through the error strings returned by the SQL server or the data interface. The user is then confronted with an enlightening message like the one shown in Figure 6-6.

Figure 6-6 *Enlightening error message*

"And just what, exactly, *is* error number 40002?" your user asks you over the phone as you're trying to watch *America's Funniest Home Videos*. Passing raw error codes and error messages directly to the user generally isn't a good idea. Users already know that something has gone wrong; now they want to know what they can *do* about it. Perhaps they simply need to be patient and wait a little longer. Maybe they should send e-mail to the person in charge of the server—and maybe your application could do that automatically. In fact, the more information I give the *application* about what to do automatically when things go wrong, the fewer calls I get during my favorite TV programs. And the more information I give the *user* about corrective options or things to check for, the better. That way, the user can check his or her own system with some degree of intelligence, and the tech-support people dragged away from *their* television sets will have more of a clue about how to correct the problem. In any case, the user shouldn't be presented with a cryptic error message or an hourglass cursor that won't go away.

So, what can you do for the user when an attempted connection to SQL Server fails? You can make sure your application has a fallback plan for each of several contingencies. One of the more successful fallback plans I've used involves INI files. If the OS/2 host name is recorded in WIN.INI, a replacement server can be specified more easily (say, when the original server is being repaired, or at other times, as necessary). Sure, you might want to use the Windows Registry instead of INI files. It's a little slower, but not a lot more complex to code.

When I create a general-purpose query utility that an entire group has access to, the application often doesn't prompt for a login ID or password. With this technique, it's more important to limit access to the SQL server, physically and logically, by limiting access to the LAN and to the room where the server is maintained. I enforce this limitation through the LAN user-level or domain permissions scheme. In this case, the application uses a login name that is known only to the developer (me), the application (where it is hard-coded), and the SQL administrator. The user must gain access to the application EXE and the SQL Server IPC$ by entering a valid domain user name and password. Since the application can't be used to gain access to any but the hard-coded tables and queries specified by the application, the chances of losing data integrity are no greater than if the user had logged on with a specific SQL login ID. Nevertheless, this method does make the fact that SQL operations are taking place totally obvious to the user.

Designing and Building Queries

Types of Queries

Designing Queries
for Performance

Building Queries

Understanding Queries

Query-Related Error Messages

Debugging with Visual Basic

Addressing SQL Server Elements

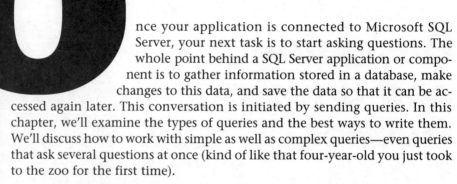

nce your application is connected to Microsoft SQL Server, your next task is to start asking questions. The whole point behind a SQL Server application or component is to gather information stored in a database, make changes to this data, and save the data so that it can be accessed again later. This conversation is initiated by sending queries. In this chapter, we'll examine the types of queries and the best ways to write them. We'll discuss how to work with simple as well as complex queries—even queries that ask several questions at once (kind of like that four-year-old you just took to the zoo for the first time).

Like a dutiful but overzealous servant, SQL Server does its best to give you whatever you ask for. If your query demands 100,000 rows, the server does what is necessary to deliver every last one of them to you. It might take hours, consume every bit of hard disk space on your client system, and bring the server and the network to their knees, but SQL Server assumes you know what you're doing. This chapter is about making sure that you do.

Types of Queries

Queries are of two types: *select* queries, which might return data rows, and *action* queries, which contain one or more Transact-SQL (TSQL) commands that update data, insert and delete data, execute data definition language (DDL) operations, or simply run maintenance operations. A select query always contains at least one SQL SELECT statement. An action query can contain any TSQL statement, including code to invoke a SQL utility such as DBCC (Database Consistency Checker). I lied. Some queries are composites of select and action operations, but these are really *batches* and must be treated differently.

In general, select queries are handled differently from action queries because the data access interface (such as DAO or RDO) is expected to manage the data rows resulting from a select query. Some data interfaces let you send either type of query almost without restriction. Others generate trappable errors if you use the wrong method or the wrong function to execute a row-returning query.

More often than not, a single query is used repeatedly throughout a program. In most cases, however, you substitute values in the query to make it applicable to the current situation. For example, you might have a query that returns the status of specific barnyard animals. The query would pass the name of the desired animal—cow, pig, or chicken—as a parameter to that query. A query might be created and stored in workstation RAM or in an MDB database. You can also define and keep queries on the SQL server as stored procedures, and it's possible to create your own repository of queries on disk, calling them up as required for execution. Stored queries can be either select or action queries, or batches of each. With the latest versions of Microsoft Visual Basic, you can create a UserConnection or Data Environment object, which can reference queries that you write or can act as an intermediary to stored procedures. We'll talk about these objects later, when we get to the DAO, RDO, and ADO chapters (Parts III, IV, and V).

A query can contain as many SQL statements as needed (up to a point), and it can combine statements that return rows with those that perform an action. Sometimes a query generates multiple sets of results—that is, a single query might return rows from several select queries, followed by the result set from one or more action queries, followed by the return rows from one or more SELECT statements, in any combination. As mentioned earlier, the TSQL documentation refers to this type of query as a *batch*. (A set of batches is called a *script*.) Batches can be difficult to manage, but they can also improve performance, and they provide a mechanism for logically binding related operations. Handling a query that generates multiple result sets is a little tricky, so each data interface takes a different approach, and we'll cover those in the relevant chapters of this guide.

TIP SQL Server 7.0 has relaxed the batch requirements, so it's easier to combine TSQL operations together in groups.

Designing Queries for Performance

The overall performance of your application or component is judged by how quickly it fetches data, and the way you phrase queries can have a significant impact on the work that the interface and the server are required to do. The harder you make the system work, the longer it takes to retrieve your data. As you design your queries, keep the following points in mind:

- **Make sure your query returns only the rows needed in the immediate situation.**   In a user-interactive front end, there is usually no need to return more than a couple dozen rows at a time. So you'll need a note from your coach to do a SELECT * query with no WHERE clause.

- **Return only the columns that are needed.**   Never use the * operator to return all columns from the tables involved in a query unless you really need *all* the columns. If you accidentally select a Text or Image column, performance can be adversely affected. The * technique also makes assumptions about the order and presence of the columns that might not be true after a table column is added or removed.

- **Update only those columns that have changed.**   Each column might have a separate rule, and update trigger processing is always complicated when you update columns unnecessarily. Each column you reference in the query means more overhead on the server, more data to transmit over the network, and more overhead on the work-station—whether or not you ever touch the data. Database normalization can assist with this situation.

- **Bring individual rows to the workstation for updating only if necessary.**   Given the power of SQL Server and TSQL logic, you now have fewer good reasons for bringing rows to the workstation to update them. With ISAM database systems, bringing each row to the workstation was considered a basic part of application design. In client/server systems, however, it's no longer necessary to bring each row to the workstation, update it, and send it back to the server. Bulk operation TSQL UPDATE statements or stored procedures can do this for you—and far faster.

- **Use stored parameter queries whenever possible.**   RDO and ADO will automatically create a stored procedure for most queries (unless you tell them not to), but this doesn't help performance if the make procedure operation is repeated every time. Both RDO and ADO provide a bevy of tools to make the process of calling parameter-based queries easy.

- **Use stored procedures whenever possible.**   Most MIS shops insist on gating access to base tables through SQL views or stored procedures that restrict access to specific operations and users. Stored procedures can also help improve performance, since they don't have to be compiled each time they are used and they often can be executed directly from the procedure cache. Any query that can be written in the form of a stored procedure should be written that way, even if it takes a number of parameters.

NOTE   Yes, SQL Server 7.0 shares compiled versions of ad hoc queries, but it still takes time to compile these queries the first time—something not required with stored procedures.

- **Avoid using cursors if possible.**   If you're convinced that you must use cursors, try read-only, forward-only, single-row *cursorless* result sets first. In any case, use the cheapest cursor possible and the smallest number of rows.

- **Don't ask for an updateable connection or result set if you don't plan to update the data.**   Don't send a ship when a rowboat will do.

- **Don't create a scrollable cursor unless you need one.**   If you don't intend to move to random rows in the result set, you don't need a scrollable cursor.

- **Limit the scope of your queries, especially update queries, when other interactive users are on line.** In my mainframe days, we never performed global database management operations during the day, when the data entry crew was using the system. We deferred all bulk processing to the swing and graveyard shifts, when the system could be dedicated to backup and bulk insert and delete operations, as well as to nightly maintenance. By shifting these tasks to nonpeak hours, the interactive users weren't affected by our heavy use of the system, and the constant changes being made by the users didn't upset our reports and audits.

- **Multiply the effect of each operation by the number of other users performing the same operation at the same time.** Each query consumes workstation and server-side RAM and disk space, including database, procedure, and data queue pages, and CPU time on both ends of the wire. Although each query carries a measurable startup overhead, the server can more easily manage queries that can be executed quickly than queries that are larger and more data-intensive.

- **Make a subset of the data to query against.** You can often improve performance dramatically by prefetching relevant rows to process. This helps SQL Server run your query faster because it doesn't have to refetch the working set each time. For example, when I need to look up valid help context IDs, I must execute a complex query that joins three tables and produces a single-row result set. Normally, this query would take about 2 seconds to execute, which wouldn't be a problem if only one query were being executed. But this query is executed by an unattended Microsoft Word macro, which performs the query for each hidden word in the document, so 2 seconds per word is a long time. To make this query faster, I create a temporary table the first time the macro is called. This table is a result set product that contains just the rows for the section I'm working on. Next, I create an index on the temporary table, using the desired help context ID column as the key. After that, each query is a simple key-based lookup, and query response time drops to .02 second or less.

- **Avoid using multiple UPDATE statements in a batch.** By combining update operations, you can improve performance, but you also complicate error recovery and database integrity—that is, unless you use the optimistic batch update feature of RDO 2.0. This interface manages the errors and collisions for you, making this type of operation less painful.

- **Consider using remote business objects.** Now that Visual Basic can create compiled Component Object Model (COM) components and Microsoft Transaction Server can be used to manage these remote server-side objects, the practicality of using Distributed Component Object Model (DCOM) to access your data is more realistic than ever.

- **Remember that data retrieved from the server begins to get stale the instant it arrives at the workstation.** This is especially true in systems where multiple users are constantly changing the data. When you execute a query, you're essentially taking a snapshot of the data at a particular point in time. Using a cursor gives you a window on the underlying data, but what the user sees and what is buffered in memory doesn't refresh itself. Unless you're using a dynamic cursor, membership of the cursor might be fixed until the cursor is rebuilt. And no, I'm not recommending dynamic cursors; they're just too expensive.

- **Never, never create a situation in which the user can open a row for editing, and then walk away from the system or otherwise hold the row for an extended period.** It's really very easy to create a situation like this when you use the pessimistic schemes that lock the data (pages or rows) the instant the Edit method is invoked and keep it locked until the data is committed with the Update method. Either use the optimistic locking option or prohibit intervention of the code between the Edit and Update methods.

Building Queries

You can find any number of ways to come up with the right SQL query to perform the task at hand. More and more graphical user interfaces (GUIs) do chores that not only make it easier for you to build SQL statements but also encourage standards and optimal techniques. This means that when you drag a couple of related tables to one of these tools' query windows, a correctly phrased JOIN statement is generated—regardless of the back end you're accessing. You'll make fewer mistakes and build better performing queries the first time. Frankly, I prefer these applications to write my joins for me. They are, at least, a good starting point. I like to take what they create and add my own subtleties to the query to get the right combination of criteria and functionality.

I used to tell everyone that I didn't like to figure out the nuances of Microsoft Jet SQL syntax, so I would use Microsoft Access to build the query for me. The problem wasn't cured by SQL Server switching to an ANSI-like syntax for TSQL because the JOIN syntax is every bit as complicated as Jet's (albeit similar). But Visual Basic now supports several ways to help you develop queries interactively. These tools were developed for use with the Microsoft Visual Studio suite, so you can expect to see them appear in more and more Microsoft languages and support applications. For the first time, Visual Basic 6.0 integrates these tools into the Visual Basic user interface. I'm not going to spend a lot of time on these tools because they're very intuitive, but I'll get you started.

Microsoft Query

The UserConnection Designer helps you build a new UserConnection object. (The designer is enabled by checking Microsoft UserConnection on the Designers tab of the Components dialog box, accessible from the Project menu. You add the Microsoft UserConnection Designer to the current project by selecting it from the Project menu.) A UserConnection object is a prestuffed class that contains all the code needed to open a connection against a back-end RDO data source and expose all or a selected set of the data source's stored procedures. You can also create your own queries using Microsoft Query by clicking the Build button in the Query Properties dialog box. I won't go into the nuances of creating a query this way because I found that the Microsoft Visual Database Tools were far more sophisticated. Not only that, but Microsoft Query is an enigma. It rarely works for me and is missing so many key elements that I find it very difficult to use in real-world situations.

Visual Database Tools

In Visual Basic 5.0, the Visual Database Tools became my favorite tools for working with SQL Server. These tools are far more than simply a set of interactive graphical query design tools. They support a wide variety of functions, from table building and alteration to database schema management. Although it is beyond the scope of this guide to get into all the features the Visual Database Tools offer, you'll find them very useful—and well documented elsewhere. Be sure to check out the ability of the Visual Database Tools to change a table's definition—yes, it can even automatically change the data type or data length of a column of an existing SQL Server table (with or without data). The only real problem with the Visual Database Tools in Visual Basic 5.0 was that they were hidden. You had to go to the Tools\DataTool directory on the Enterprise Edition CD to install them.

Visual Basic 6.0 has taken the Visual Database Tools several steps further. The Visual Database Tools are now integrated into the user interface and have become part of the new Data Environment paradigm. This integration makes the tools somewhat easier to use, despite the fact that not all of their functionality is exposed in Visual Basic 6.0—you have to install the new version of Microsoft Visual InterDev to get the rest. But that's another story.

The Visual Database Tools come in really handy when you need to develop a query against SQL Server—or against any database for that matter. The Visual Database Tools use a GUI interface to let you "draw" queries very much the way Microsoft Access does. The real (neat) difference is that you can see all four phases of the operation at once (diagram, grid, SQL statement, and results). Figure 7-1 shows a query development window in Visual Basic.

We'll get into the new database tools in Visual Basic in Part VI, but if you want to get a feel for how these work now, go ahead. I'll wait here while you make the side trip. I predict you'll want to use these tools right away.

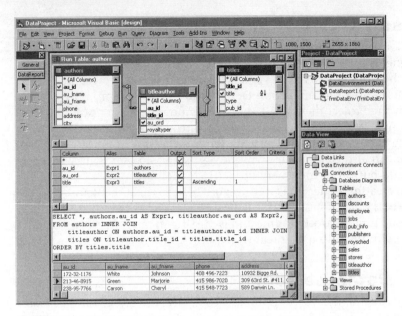

Figure 7-1 *A query development window in Visual Basic 6.0*

Doing It by Hand

If you need to tune and polish the queries you've been building, here are a few hints and techniques to make this process a more positive experience. (And no, you won't need sterile gloves.)

It's somewhat unusual to ask your server the same question over and over, but it's not unusual to ask *almost* the same question repeatedly, with subtle variations. Here's what I mean:

```
SELECT * FROM Authors WHERE City = 'Detroit'
```

and

```
SELECT * FROM Authors WHERE City = 'Redmond'
```

In general, queries are either created on the fly when SQL statements are concatenated with arguments generated by the user, or they're specially written parameter queries that depend on the interface to fill in the missing arguments.

In concatenation, which I use less and less, the program logic takes a fixed SQL statement and substitutes values in the WHERE clause to return a known set of columns. For example, if I want to query a database on farm animals to return information about all pig-type animals over the age of four, the code for performing the query will look like this:

```
SQL$ = "SELECT Name FROM Animals" _     ' This does not change
& " WHERE AnimalType = '" _             ' Nor does this
& TypeWanted & "'" _                    ' Substitute variables
& " AND Age > " & AgeWanted
```

> **TIP** Don't use the space underscore ampersand (_&) technique (as shown on the previous page) to spruce up your long query lines. It will cost you dearly at run time in lost performance. Sure, it's pretty and easy to read, but the system doesn't care what the code *looks* like. If it did, you might have to choose another font.

The *TypeWanted* and *AgeWanted* variables will be supplied by the user or the program logic—in the case of my query, *TypeWanted* = "PIG" and *AgeWanted* = 4. All of this code is executed each time the query is used. This also means that the query must be syntax-checked and compiled by SQL Server, by the Jet query processor, or by the ODBC layers each time the query is executed.

> **TIP** When building concatenated queries, be sure to separate arguments and parameters with white space. TSQL syntax ignores all white space but doesn't tolerate a query that incorrectly jams two arguments together. You must also surround dates and quoted strings with quotes—usually single quotes.

Understanding Queries

In the following sections, you'll find information about several topics and techniques that you'll need to be aware of when you're working and tinkering with your queries.

Quote Management

One of the most challenging parts of creating a concatenated query is managing quotes. Fortunately, the ODBC and OLE DB interfaces and the Visual Basic query tools know how to handle quoted parameters, so you shouldn't have a problem—at least you shouldn't have any trouble with the chore of adding framing quotes. But you still have to make sure that the strings you pass as parameters don't contain single quotes.

SQL Server 4.*x* and earlier versions expect TSQL string arguments to be surrounded with quotes, either single ('MyString') or double ("MyString"), as long as they are used in matching pairs. Not all TSQL variables require quotes, however. In TSQL queries, only dates and strings must be quote-delineated. All other kinds of numbers are simply surrounded by white space or commas.

SQL Server 6.0 and later have support for quoted identifiers. According to ANSI syntax, you need to use double quotation marks (") to delimit *keywords* (quoted identifiers) and single quotation marks (') to delimit string constants. This requirement resolves the conflict with quoted identifiers and string constants during expression evaluation at the parser level and is included to provide ANSI compatibility for delimited identifiers. Additionally, although

I don't recommend the practice, keywords specified within double quotation marks can be used as object names. If you want your object names to use keywords, reserved words, database technology terms, or names that could cause conflict with future keywords, you should first attempt to resolve possible conflicts by choosing another word for the object name. When this isn't possible, use quoted identifiers—in other words, surround the keywords in double quotes. These quoted identifiers can contain as many as 30 characters. The delimited string can contain any combination of characters represented by the current code page, except double quotation marks.

To enforce or remove quoted identifier and string constant resolution at the session level (for each connection), use the SET QUOTED_IDENTIFIER statement. This causes the current session to differentiate between single and double quotation marks when evaluating an expression. When QUOTED_IDENTIFIER is turned on, strings in double quotation marks (") won't be evaluated or checked against keywords. When you use keywords for object names or portions of object names, the QUOTED_IDENTIFIER option *must* be turned on when creating the object, as well as when accessing the object.

CAUTION
If you expect to be using connection pooling, I recommend that you do not use the SET command. We've already discussed the problems associated with connection state persistence across users sharing the same connection.

> **NOTE** If an object name or part of an object name (for example, a column) is created using a keyword when the QUOTED_IDENTIFIER option is turned on, all subsequent references to that object must be made with the QUOTED_IDENTIFIER option on. In general, it's best to avoid using keywords as object names.

When you're qualifying a column name and a table name in the same statement, be sure to use the same qualifying expressions for each; they are evaluated as strings and must match or an error is returned.

Basically, SQL Server 6.0 and later (and good programming practice) expects you to use *only* single quotes to delineate strings and dates. This guideline isn't so hard to follow until you come across a string with an embedded single quote. For example, the last name *O'Hara* poses a problem if you attempt to delineate this string in single quotes. How is the SQL parser to know where the string ends and the SQL syntax starts? It's tempting to use double quotes to delineate TSQL strings because Visual Basic prefers double quotes to delineate string expressions, and it uses single quotes to start comments.

> **NOTE** Jet SQL statements require that dates be quoted and surrounded with the pound (#) symbol: #12/31/98#. TSQL requires single quotes.

I usually write string-concatenating routines that contain a quote on either side of TSQL string and date variables, as shown in the farm-animal example. When you concatenate a string already containing an embedded quote that matches your delineator, Visual Basic dutifully passes it on to SQL Server, but when the string arrives at the server, the query fails the syntax check because of unbalanced quotes. A number of solutions have been proposed, most of them somewhat messy—but that's why developers get the big bucks:

- **Replace all embedded single quotes with two single quotes.** For example, *O'Hara* becomes *O''Hara*. This is the method I prefer and use most often. And Visual Basic 6.0 makes this even easier. All you have to do is use the new Replace function like this:

```
FixedString = Replace(QuotedString, "'", "''")
```

This new function walks the string, replacing all instances of the indicated string (a single quote in the example) with another string (two single quotes in the example).

- **Quietly replace the single quote with another character before it is sent to the server, and then resubstitute the single quote when the data is presented to the user**. The problem with this approach is that it upsets the collating sequence and makes searching more complex. More important, every program that references the data must decrypt the quote substitutes.

- **Switch to double-quote instead of single-quote delimiters.** This solution makes the Visual Basic concatenation of strings a little tougher but not impossible. It can lead to problems with strings containing double quotes, but names generally don't contain double quotes. This approach requires you to set the SQL Server Quote Identifier option to *on*. Again, this solution is not recommended.

- **Work with Text data types instead of VarChar or Char data types.** When you use Text data types, data is passed to the SQL server without the use of concatenated strings. The downside is that Text data types for small strings are expensive to store.

As a last resort, you can work through the courts to get all the O'Haras in your database to change their names, and eliminate embedded quotes that way.

NOTE When you're working with double quotes, don't forget about using CHR$(34) (or some variable set to this value) as a substitute for a double quote, or CHR$(39) (or some variable set to this value) as a substitute for a single quote. If you need to embed double quotes, simply double up the quotes:

```
"This is a double quote "" embedded in a string".
```

Parameter Queries

All the data access interfaces support at least one type of operation in which you predefine a query and then use special syntax or object properties to bind the parameters to the query at run time. Although VBSQL doesn't directly support this kind of query, there's nothing to stop you from either implementing it in code (which would take about 10 lines) or using stored procedures that can provide the same functionality. The advantage of a parameter query is that the query can be precompiled, and if it is, an execution plan is stored on the server for repeated use. For complex queries, or for those that are executed frequently, a parameter query can save a significant amount of time.

An advantage of using parameter queries with any of the ODBC or OLE DB interfaces is that string delineation is handled automatically. With ODBC and OLE DB, strings are managed by the interface, so you don't need to add additional quotes around the strings. To create my farm-animal query with the RDO interface, I simply substitute *?* in the SQL statement for each parameter to be supplied at run time and create an rdoQuery object, as follows. (Notice that I don't need to surround the *?* parameter placeholder with delineators.)

```
Dim Qy As rdoQuery
SQL$ = "SELECT * FROM Animals" _
    & " WHERE AnimalType = ? AND Age > ?"

Set Qy = cn.CreateQuery ("PickAnimal", SQL$)
Qy(0) = TypeWanted
Qy(1) = AgeWanted
```

. . .

NOTE The *Qy(0)* notation references the rdoParameters collection of the rdoQuery object.

In this case, the application can set the SQL statement once, create the rdoQuery object, and execute the query:

```
Set Rs = Qy.OpenResultset(rdOpenStatic)
```

If I need to run the query again, I simply set the rdoParameter values to the new values and use the Requery method of the rdoResultset object to automatically substitute the current parameters into the query and reexecute the code. An even easier technique would be to execute the query as a method of the Connection object. This way, you can pass in the parameters and execute the query with a single line of code and reference the rdoResultset with another line:

```
cn.PickAnimal TypeWanted, AgeWanted
Set Rs = cn.LastQueryResults
```

Does it make sense for your application to use this type of parameter query? Sure, in some cases. In most shops, however, it's far more sensible to create stored procedures on SQL Server that define all the normally executed procedures. This approach simplifies your application and improves overall system performance. Visual Basic has incorporated a number of new tools that make executing parameter-based stored procedures as easy as finding a parking place at the mall during the Superbowl.

Overlapping Queries

One of the limitations of SQL Server 4.2 was its inability to manage more than one operation on a connection. When you open a connection and submit a query for processing, you *must* process all the rows resulting from the query before you can submit another. To get around this problem, you could open an additional connection and create a separate query context that is independent of the first.

SQL Server 6.0 introduced server-side cursors, which enable you to create a cursor and immediately (well, almost) turn around and perform other operations on the same connection—once the keyset is built. This is possible because the keyset has already been populated and is being managed by SQL Server on the server, not on your workstation. SQL Server 7.0 supports this technology as well. What is really going on is a little shell game with concurrency. Basically, when you create a synchronous server-side cursor, control doesn't return to your application until the cursor is created and fully populated. For example, in RDO, if you choose asynchronous mode, you must wait until StillExecuting has changed to False or the QueryComplete event fires before proceeding. While this difference might seem subtle, it can make it far easier to use a single connection to perform multiple operations.

When you're using DAO/Jet, Jet's connection manager attempts to share the first connection as you open the second, which prevents operations on either connection until the first result set is fully populated. In this case, you *must* execute a MoveLast method or find another way to position the current-row pointer past the end of the result set. Jet 2.5 performs the MoveLast operation for you, but this "convenience" means that your workstation is locked until the last row is processed, whether you want it to be or not.

Although SQL Server 6.0 and later do permit multiple operations if you use server-side cursors, DAO/Jet doesn't attempt to use server-side cursors, and it can't share the connection with another result set. When you're using any of the other interfaces, you have to use SQL Server 6.*x* server-side cursors before attempting to share a connection, or you simply have to open another connection.

Ad Hoc Queries

An ad hoc query is like a random question—one that you hadn't anticipated ahead of time. Some situations require your code to be very flexible when it comes to meeting user needs. In some cases, users might ask a number of pertinent (or sometimes impertinent) questions about the data. No one really expects users to enter their own correctly formatted and phrased TSQL queries. So if you want to let users ask fairly unstructured or purely random questions, you have some decisions to make.

Microsoft ISQL/w (named SQL Server Query Analyzer in SQL Server 7.0) and the Query window in SQL Server Enterprise Manager permit developers to create and execute ad hoc queries—assuming they know how to use TSQL.

Allowing a text box to be exposed so that its contents can be accepted as a valid query is especially dangerous—it's what I call an *employment longevity–limiting* error. For this reason, I haven't written a single production application that permits totally ad hoc queries.

The Visual Basic data access tools and Microsoft Access also permit this type of query, and they provide a slick user interface for generating desired SQL statements. However, these tools are not available at run time for ordinary people to use. Nor would you want them to be. Many of my applications permit the user to choose from a wide selection of options that generate virtually infinite combinations of SQL statements—but the resulting SQL statements are carefully designed, and they have been screened to prevent the user from entering random UPDATE, DELETE, DROP, and other destructive SQL statements; the only available TSQL options are chosen from a menu. Yes, the user can create queries that bring the server to its knees—but this adverse effect is limited by carefully designed timeout and row-count governors.

English Queries

You now have the option of choosing yet another way to deal with ad hoc queries. A new tool, Microsoft English Query 1.0, shipped with Microsoft SQL Server 6.5, Enterprise Edition; Microsoft English Query 2.0 will ship as part of SQL Server 7.0. This new query generator lets you provide users with the capability to ask questions about your data in plain English in your existing applications. It consists of two major components:

- The English Query authoring tool, used at design time, allows you to edit English Query domains.

- The English Query engine, used at run time in your site or application, is an Automation server that you use in your Active Server Pages (ASP) scripts or other applications. It converts the user's English questions into standard SQL that retrieves information from your database. It exposes an object model that makes it easy to add natural language queries to any ASP-based Web site; any Visual Basic, Java, or C++ application; or any program that supports COM.

The English Query authoring tool allows you to edit the semantics of your domain. You tell English Query how the entities and relationships among entities map to objects (tables and fields) in your database. Entities are the nouns that you think users will want to ask about. Types of relationships include verb relationships (for example, "salespeople *sell* products"), traits (for example, "patients have *blood types*"), and adjectives (for example, "restaurants are *good*"). English Query uses this knowledge to provide true, deep natural language parsing of user-supplied questions, as opposed to keyword-based technology (which is provided by some other "English database searching" products). The result will be closer matches to users' actual queries.

Once you've completed authoring your English Query domain, the English Query engine provides a simple object model that you can use in any application that supports COM. You will supply the English Query engine with the user's English question, and the English Query engine will return one of the following responses to you:

- One or more SQL commands, which you will execute to provide the answer to the user

- An immediate answer, if the English Query engine itself can immediately determine the answer

- A request for clarification, if the English Query engine needs more information from the user to answer the question

For example, the English Query engine might convert a question such as, "What are the good restaurants in Redmond?" into this SQL statement:

```
SELECT Restaurants.Name, Restaurants.StreetAddress1,
Restaurants.Number, Restaurants.RestaurantRatingID, Restaurants.URL
FROM Neighborhoods, NeighborhoodContainment, Restaurants
WHERE Neighborhoods.Neighborhood like '%Redmond%' AND
Neighborhoods.NeighborhoodID=NeighborhoodContainment.NeighborhoodID
AND Restaurants.RestaurantRatingID>5 AND
NeighborhoodContainment.PersonPlaceID=Restaurants.RestaurantID
```

You'll then use the generated SQL statement against your database to retrieve the desired information for the user. Sample scripts are supplied to make it easy to use the English Query engine in your Microsoft Internet Information Server–based Web site, but you can use the English Query engine in any programming environment that supports COM.

Multiple Result Set Queries

Some situations call for the creation and execution of related sets of SQL statements that perform a number of steps before completion. For example, you might submit a query containing several SELECT statements and a few UPDATE and INSERT statements, which are followed by a couple of additional SELECT statements. This approach is typical of the kind of code executed by production-class stored procedures. In some cases, your code might be interested in only the final result set, but your data interface must be designed to deal with all result sets generated by a query, batch, or script. *Each* statement in a batch returns a result set, regardless of the type of statement. Only SELECT statements return rows, but each TSQL statement returns a result set that the data interface and your application *must* acknowledge. How each data interface handles multiple result sets is discussed in the chapters of this guide devoted to the respective interfaces. Keep in mind that some cursor libraries don't know how to build scrollable cursors on this type of query. SQL Server's server-side cursor library is one of these—even with version 7.0.

NOTE Although it's necessary to deal with all of the result sets generated by a query, you can disable quite a bit of background "noise" generated when you're calling stored procedures, including when trigger code is running. For a more detailed explanation of what's going on and an explanation of a problem with this, see Knowledge Base article Q113674, "INF: -T3640 Flag May Block Updates to an ODBC Application." Basically, each time a SQL Server 6.x statement in a stored procedure is completed, the server sends a DONE_IN_PROC message to the client. (These are buffered until the network packet is full.) If you have a loop in your procedure, you can guess how this can add up. The 3640 trace flag (or NOCOUNT option) turns off the generation of the message and can decrease local area network (LAN) or wide area network (WAN) traffic considerably. The 3640 trace flag sets the behavior for the whole server as a default. If you think you might run into this situation, instead of using the 3640 trace flag, use the SET NOCOUNT ON statement at the start of your stored procedure and you'll get the same effect.

Asynchronous Queries

Queries can take milliseconds to complete, or they can take hours—especially action queries or complex select queries that involve large numbers of rows. If you don't use an asynchronous option, Visual Basic will block until the query returns its first row or the result set is fully populated. Table 7-1 shows how the various data interfaces support asynchronous operations. Visual Basic 6.0 supports asynchronous operations better than ever because ADO has been added to the list of interfaces that support this feature. In addition, you don't have to poll for completion as required in Visual Basic 4.0—just catch the event that fires when the operation is complete.

You should be concerned with a basic problem here—how to prevent Visual Basic from blocking while the following operations occur:

- The connection is being opened.

- The result set is being created or re-created.

- You move to the last row to repopulate your result set with the MoveLast method.

- You subsequently move the current record pointer.

Let's take a closer look at these events.

As Table 7-1 shows, all the interfaces except DAO/Jet support some kind of mechanism for preventing lockups while the result set is being created. With Visual Basic 4.0, either your application's data interface is notified when the first row is ready or the application polls constantly to see whether the first row is ready. And therein lies one of the problems: if your application polls too

Table 7-1
Support for Asynchronous Queries in Various Data Interfaces

Data Interface	Support for Asynchronous Queries	Event Notification
VBSQL	SQLSend, SQLReady, and SQLOk functions	Only on errors and messages
ODBC	SQL_ASYNC_ENABLE as SQLSetStmtOption	None
DAO/Jet*	None; all DAO access is blocked until query is completed	None
DAO/ ODBCDirect	dbRunAsync option on Execute, OpenRecordset, and MoveLast methods	None
RDO	rdAsyncEnable option on EstablishConnection, OpenConnection, Requery, MoveLast, Execute, and OpenResultset methods	All synchronous and asynchronous operations
ADO	adRunAsync on Execute and Open methods	All synchronous and asynchronous operations

* The Jet Mdatabase engine used with the Data control supports limited background population as well as control-break termination.

frequently, the server takes longer to complete processing of the query, like a cook checking the oven every 10 seconds to see whether the TV dinner is done. (It isn't, because the oven temperature never gets above 110 degrees.) When you use an asynchronous option, control is returned to your application immediately after you request the operation—dinner isn't ready yet, but it's in the microwave and the clock is running. It's your responsibility to check for completion of the operation before using the results. Wouldn't it be nice if you got an event when the operation completed—something like the "ding" from your microwave? Well, there's good news. Visual Basic supports a robust and easily programmable event model. However, only RDO and ADO (2.0) support these events. DAO/ODBCDirect does *not* support them. This means that you don't need to (actually you really shouldn't) poll the StillExecuting or Still-Connecting properties to see whether the asynchronous operation is complete.

NOTE In a 16-bit Windows environment, there is no support for preemptive multitasking, so the entire environment is locked while a blocked component (such as Jet) waits for something to complete. In a 32-bit Windows environment, only the current application is blocked, and then only if you use the synchronous option.

What *are* you allowed to do while the query engine is running? Well, even though you can't use the connection for other data access operations, you can open additional connections and run other queries on all the interfaces except DAO/Jet. You can also complete population on other result sets from other connections—or you can launch Myst while you wait and try to figure out how to open the sea chest at the bottom of the pump-tower pit.

Counting Your Rows

I don't know how many times I've been asked, "How can I tell how many rows are going to result from the query?" Developers often ask this question because they want to build an array or initialize a grid to hold the rows or simply display a status bar to indicate the progress being made to fetch the rows. The problem is that SQL Server *doesn't know* how many rows will result from your query—it doesn't know until the result set is fully populated, *after* the query has been completed. It's like asking a farmer how many eggs he'll be collecting in the morning. He has no way of knowing until he leaves the chicken coop.

"Well," you say, "Access seems to know because it shows a progress bar that shows how far it has proceeded for any specific query." Although it is true that Access shows a status bar, it isn't true that it knows how many rows are going to result from a complex query—especially against an ODBC database. What that Access progress bar is really showing is *progress*. That's it—just that Access is still working on the query. Yes, you see a number down there, but it is an educated guess at the percentage of work done—just a guess. Ever notice what it does when it starts approaching 60 percent? It slows down. Until you get control back from testing the RowCount or RecordCount properties after having done a MoveLast in ADO, RDO, or DAO, there's no way of knowing how many rows have been found.

Setting Query Timeout

When you execute a query, it might take milliseconds or hours for the first row to be returned. Even if you're using one of the asynchronous modes, you need to set a reasonable upper limit on the time the query should be permitted to run. Using past history as a benchmark, set the query timeout to a value roughly two to three times longer than the query should take—but not much longer than that. For example, with a query that normally takes 30 seconds to run, I set the timeout at 90 seconds. I've found that some updates take considerably longer to execute than others. I speculate that if SQL Server must create another allocation unit to complete the operation, the query can take considerably longer.

Only VBSQL and RDO permit you to tell SQL Server to continue working on a query that has timed out. No, ADO doesn't let you do this. With the other interfaces, the query has been canceled by the time you get the timeout error. If you're using VBSQL or RDO (in Visual Basic 5.0), you can set the timeout value to a fairly low number—expecting a timeout error. Once the timeout event fires, you can give the user an opportunity to either cancel the operation or keep the server working on the solution.

Query-Related Error Messages

What should the user see when a query returns an error message? That's up to you and your application or component. In some rare cases, it makes sense to display the message string with a MsgBox function. In other cases, messages can be ignored. If you're writing a component, however, you sure can't expect anyone to see a message displayed on the screen in some server locked in a closet downtown. Keep in mind that a single query can return a whole laundry list of errors and messages. All of the interfaces provide a way to see all of these errors in the order in which they appear. For example, in RDO you need to check all of the rdoError objects in the rdoErrors collection. ADO supports a similar Error structure off of its Connection object. The first message you see can be a generic something-went-wrong message that isn't particularly descriptive. The real reason is buried deeper in the error-message collection.

Some errors, generally caused by the user (you did debug all your queries, didn't you?), are simply the results of incorrect query syntax. Others might signal the death of the query, the network, the connection, or the server itself. You can also expect a variety of strange messages as system, workstation, or other resources are exhausted. Your code needs to be cognizant of what was being attempted when the error occurred. An error usually means that the query is dead and can't be resurrected. But sometimes it means that the LAN or the WAN is too busy to get the job done. In other cases, you might be able to simply resubmit the query after a short time—hoping that whatever went wrong won't happen again.

I've made an interesting discovery about users' willingness to wait for a computer to complete an operation: they are generally willing to wait *as long as there is activity*. If they see the gears moving in the background, they assume that the system is doing the best it can and eventually will finish. But as the waiting period approaches 62.7 seconds, the number of users who will reboot the system approaches 98.7 percent—and not all users are this patient.

Debugging with Visual Basic

If a fairly complex application under development can't hear what the server says until run time, the task of debugging the application is significantly complicated. In fact, many problems associated with the creation of front-end applications to SQL Server are the result of the inability of the development language to *interact* adequately with SQL Server during the development cycle. SQL Server expects to be told what to do in specific terms, and it will respond in a fairly predictable way. In fact, conversing with SQL Server is like having a conversation with a blindly obedient, highly specialized, highly skilled (but anal) assistant. Transact-SQL is a truly interactive, two-way language, and Visual Basic's interactive mode is an efficient and relatively trouble-free way to develop these applications.

Visual Basic, unlike C or other edit-compile-link-debug languages, permits developers to step through the phrases of the conversation, examine the server's response, adapt the code as needed, and continue the conversation. In a radical departure from traditional C-language debugging techniques, Visual Basic developers can not only change the source code interactively but can also alter program logic and flow. For example, developers can jump over code or instruct Visual Basic to repeat code that has already been executed. This way, unanticipated responses from the server can be dealt with as they occur, and alternative code can be created or branched to while the tested logic condition still exists. Visual Basic's interactive debugging window also permits you to execute code, including all written procedures, on the fly—right in the middle of an application.

As any experienced developer will confirm, one of the toughest tasks is to set up various logic states once a problem has been found. With Visual Basic's interactive Watch window, setting a breakpoint at a particular state is now easier than ever. Once at the problem point, a developer can easily step through the code or make source changes as they are needed. More important, the developer can send SQL Server additional commands or even ask additional questions regarding its current state. Having developed applications using C, Visual Basic, and other languages, I find Visual Basic's interactive approach by far the most flexible. What used to take weeks now takes hours: Visual Basic dramatically reduces the time needed for developing interactive TSQL code. And since an optimizing compiler was introduced with Visual Basic 5.0, code execution performance is no longer an issue.

> **NOTE**   And I haven't even mentioned the TSQL debugger that carries this interactive debug paradigm right into the server. See Chapter 35, "Using the Transact-SQL Debugger," for details on TSQL debugging.

When you're working in Visual Basic's Design mode and a query's syntax fails to pass muster, you can change the query string and then reexecute the query by changing the current Visual Basic statement (what I still call the *instruction pointer*) to rerun a section of code. You can also use this feature to examine the properties of the returned data. For example, you can ask the data interface if any rows were returned (unfortunately, it won't tell you how many are in the result set), and for each of those rows, the data interface can be queried for the content and description of the columns. Select the appropriate line of code, and press Ctrl-F9 to reset the next statement to execute.

Virtually all the data access methods, properties, and API functions can be executed interactively in the Debug window. For example, you can open additional connections, submit queries, perform administrative work (like dropping tables or changing permissions), or clear result sets simply by executing the code from the Debug window. I encourage you to use this feature to work yourself out of problems at design time.

Addressing SQL Server Elements

An emerging problem in Visual Basic seems to be how SQL Server objects are referenced. So far, I've seen about four different variations implemented by the tools, wizards, data source controls, and documentation. For example, some of the tools prefix tables and stored procedure names with *dbo*, but others don't. Some put the stored procedure reference number at the end of the stored procedure, but most don't. If you don't pay attention to what's going on, you'll step on that snake over to your right. Just stand still and everything will be all right. First, understand that SQL Server 7.0 has changed the rules on object names. They can now be much longer. Let's look at the details.

According to SQL Server 7.0 Books Online, every object in a database has an identifier (name). In SQL Server, identifiers are the object names, server names, database names, and database objects such as tables, views, columns, indexes, triggers, procedures, defaults, rules, and so on. Here are some examples of when and how you can use identifiers:

- **When you or your code first creates an object** For example, when a database table is created, the table name is an identifier. You'll have to know the rules when you use the Data Environment or any of the tools to create SQL Server tables, views, columns, rules, triggers, or stored procedures.

- **When you're querying or changing data** For example, when you write a SELECT statement, any references to the database tables and columns must adhere to the identifier rules.

In SQL Server 7.0, identifiers can contain from 1 to 128 characters (only 30 characters in SQL Server 6.5), including letters, symbols (_, @, or #), and numbers. Here are the rules for using identifiers:

- The *first* character must be one of the following:

  - A letter as defined by the Unicode Standard 2.0. Unicode's definition of letters includes Latin characters *a* through *z* and *A* through *Z* in addition to letter characters from other international languages.

  - The symbol _ (underscore), @ (at sign), or # (pound sign). An identifier beginning with @ denotes a local variable or parameter. An identifier beginning with # denotes a temporary table or procedure. An identifier beginning with a double pound sign (##) denotes a global temporary object. Names for temporary objects should not exceed 29 characters, including the # or ##, because SQL Server gives them an internal numeric suffix.

NOTE The SQL Server documentation recommends that double @ symbols (@@) at the beginning of a variable name be reserved for SQL Server global variables to allow easy recognition.

- *After* the first character, identifiers can include letters, digits—a character code between 0x30 (0) and 0x39 (9)—and the @, $, #, or _ symbols.

- By default, no embedded spaces are allowed in identifiers; however, by using quoted identifiers, you can define spaces and other special identifiers.

> **NOTE** These rules apply only to nonquoted identifiers. For example, to create a database named ^mydatabase, you would use a quoted identifier. To create this database, use either SET QUOTED_IDENTIFIER ON and CREATE DATABASE "^mydatabase", or CREATE DATABASE [^mydatabase]. For more information on quoted identifiers, see Quoted Identifiers in SQL Server Books Online.

Object names don't need to be unique in a database. Column names and index names, however, must be unique within a table or view, and other object names must be unique for each owner within a database. Database names must be unique for each SQL Server. You uniquely identify a table or column by fully qualifying its name and specifying the database name, the object owner's name, and (for a column) the table or view name. Each qualifier is separated from the next by a period, as shown here:

[[*database*.]*owner*.]*table_name*

[[*database*.]*owner*.]*view_name*

Database and owner names are optional and are indicated by the square brackets ([ ]) in TSQL syntax. The default value for *owner* is the current user; the default value for *database* is the current database. For example, specifying *pubs.dbo.authors* means *pubs* is the database name, *dbo* (database owner) is the owner of the table, and *authors* is the name of the table. You can omit intermediate elements in a name and indicate their positions by using periods (a period for each element you omit) as long as you give the system enough information to identify the object:

database..table_name

database..view_name

For example, *pubs..authors* indicates the *pubs* database and the *authors* table for the current user.

> **NOTE** To eliminate possible confusion relating to the object in question, the SQL Server documentation recommends that you specify the full table or view name. In some cases, however, you might want to use an ambiguous name—such as when you want to reference the same object in more than one context (as in more than one database or for more than one owner). If you do use an ambiguous name, you have to ensure that the default database and owner are set correctly before referencing any objects.

Assume that a table and a view in the customer database both have a column named *telephone*. To refer to the telephone column in the employees table, you would specify *customer..employees.telephone*. To refer to the telephone column in the *mktg_view* view (marketing department's view), you would specify *customer..mktg_view.telephone*.

When using a distributed query, you use a four-part qualifier such as the one shown here:

linked_server_name.catalog.schema.object_name

You need to supply the following four pieces:

- The name of the linked server from which the distributed query should obtain data

- The name of the catalog or database from which the distributed query should obtain data

- The schema or owner of the table or object

- The name of the object or table

You qualify a remote stored procedure as follows:

server.database.owner.procedure

The following example shows how to identify a remote stored procedure:

remotesvr.pubs.dbo.sp_who

Specifying the server name when executing a stored procedure is important if the stored procedure will be run on a computer other than the local SQL Server computer.

Here are valid table names that use identifiers:

- thisisatesttablenameof_30_chars

- Tablenametest

- Yearly$Sales

- #T

- This_is_a_clearer_table_name

If an object is referenced without being qualified with database and owner names, SQL Server tries to find the object in the current database among the objects owned by the current user. If the current user doesn't own an object by that name, SQL Server looks for objects of that name owned by the database owner that are qualified by *database..object_name*. To reference objects in the current database, it is not necessary to specify the database name. If two or more users own objects with the same name, the name of the object owner must be specified.

Here are some guidelines for using full object qualification:

- Avoid confusion with duplicate object names. For example, if both Sue and Tom create a table named *cust_data* in the customers database and both use their first name as their login, the system administrator must specify either *sue.cust_data* or *tom.cust_data*.

- Ensure that the correct object is being referenced. For example, assume that a query specifies *pubs..authors*. Janet logs on to SQL Server using a login of janetl. Janet's login has been assigned *dbo* authority. Janet can't be sure whether she is querying the authors table that the *dbo* role created or her own (janetl) authors table.

- Any user capable of seeing all duplicate objects will want to use full object qualification.

The visibility for stored procedures that begin with *sp_* differs from the visibility for regular stored procedures. For information on the differences, see CREATE PROCEDURE in SQL Server Books Online.

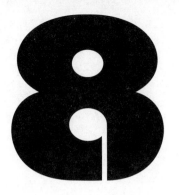

8

Retrieving Data and Working with Result Sets

The Query Process

Using Single-Row Result Sets

Using Cursors

Updating and Inserting Data

Working with Batches

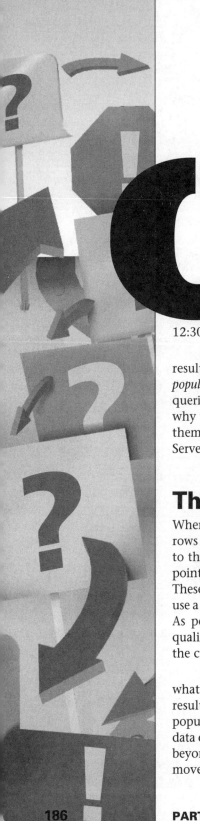

O K, you've asked your question. Now Microsoft SQL Server has returned your answer. In this chapter, you'll find out how to work with the structures and interfaces needed to decipher this answer. Don't worry, this task will be easier than getting a straight answer out of a teenager at 12:30 a.m.—but then what isn't?

In much of the early part of this chapter, I'll be referring to *populating* result sets. To be sure that you clearly understand what I mean by the term *populating*, we'll take a close look at what the word conveys in the context of queries and cursors. We talked a little about cursors in Chapter 5 (including why they're not one of my favorite things), but in this chapter, we'll discuss them in more detail. We'll also talk about making changes to the data in SQL Server and executing statements in batches.

The Query Process

When you execute a query that creates a cursor, the cursor keys (or the actual rows selected) are recorded so that the system and your application can refer to them later. The process of populating keyset cursors involves creating a pointer, or bookmark, for each row that qualifies for inclusion in the result set. These pointers are transmitted back to the client over the network unless you use a server-side cursor, in which case they are stored on the server in TempDB. As population proceeds, more rows are added to the result set until all qualifying rows have been located and added. Once this process is completed, the cursor is considered to be *fully populated*.

Let's say your query is finally ready to return the first row of data. Now what? At this point, if your query returned any rows, at least one row of the result set is ready to be processed. In some cases, the result set will be fully populated, so your application won't have to wait again while the result set data or keys are moved to the workstation. But if your result set isn't populated beyond the first row (or buffer), your application might block each time you move the row pointer to another row in the result set.

Generally, it doesn't take long to fetch a single additional row, say, when you use the MoveNext method. But if you end up having to move to the last row in the result set, or beyond the scope of the buffer (or cache), your application will block again while the data interface finishes populating the result set. This can take quite a while for a large result set. Fortunately, RDO and DAO/ODBCDirect support asynchronous operations on the MoveLast method, so your application doesn't have to wait. Well, you still have to wait, but your application is no longer blocked while the result set is being fully populated. This is another argument for smaller result sets.

NOTE Some data interfaces buffer 100 rows or so, to reduce the amount of overhead needed for repetitive fetches. Generally, the buffer size is tunable via Microsoft Windows Registry settings, object properties, or specific API options. Remember, however, that even though these buffered rows are moved to your workstation, they might not be available to you until they are accessed. And consider that buffered rows aren't refreshed when finally accessed, so they might contain stale data.

Using Single-Row Result Sets

A cursor can be overkill for many query operations, so you shouldn't use cursors unless they are necessary. Personally, I prefer the simplicity and speed of a single-row, forward-only result set because it's the fastest way to get rows back. In some cases, I don't intend to change the rows that have been fetched, and most applications for decision support and reporting are designed to extract data, not update it, so the extra overhead that the interface adds for supporting updates just goes to waste. The single-row, cursorless result set is ideal for these applications. Single-row result sets are also useful for fetching the final results from a complex query—one that might return only a single value. I expect this is the type of result set used to fetch the answer for the famous ultimate question about life, the universe, and everything—since the answer was "42."

NOTE Most of the data access interfaces support at least one type of cursorless result set that minimizes the impact on workstation RAM and disk space. Microsoft Jet supports a forward-only, read-write option but still creates a keyset or snapshot-type Recordset cursor to implement it. The default result set in VBSQL is a forward-only, single-row result set similar to the default ODBC API result set, in which only one row is available at any one time—ADO, RDO, and DAO/ODBCDirect all expose this type of result set. VBSQL provides no mechanism for directly updating its cursorless result set rows, whereas the ODBC and OLE DB interfaces support forward-only, read-write result sets, though at a slightly higher cost. But VBSQL does support Browse-mode queries that permit updates via a separate connection.

When a user working with a Windows application wants to see more than just a single row at a time, the application can fill a Grid control with the set of rows that meets the user's requirements. For example, an order-entry system might support a form containing information about a specific customer, with a detailed form underneath the first form, that contains order-item rows, as shown in Figure 8-1.

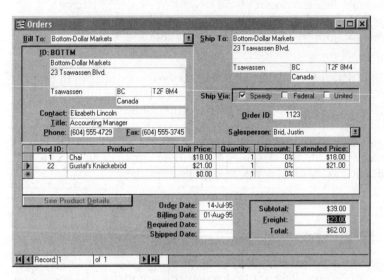

Figure 8-1 *Sample order-entry form*

In this case, using a single-row query to fetch a small buffered result set might make sense. Even if the chosen data is to be updated, a separate query using the Customer key and (possibly) a second connection can take care of the necessary changes. The details of the order information on this specific customer can be fetched with a limited-scope updateable cursor.

Remember that even though you specify a simple, cursorless result set, you can always update the underlying data—assuming you have permission to do so—by issuing an update action query. Invariably, this query requires a separate connection unless you cancel the current row-fetch operation on the first connection.

Using Cursors

A cursor is an object that contains a set of 0 to *n* pointers to the data rows resulting from your query. Cursors support a number of properties and methods used to describe and manipulate the cursor. All the object-based data interfaces support several types of cursors. (For more information on the various types of cursors, see Chapter 5.) Any cursor, regardless of its type, exposes only one row of the result set at a time. Each of the data access interfaces permits movement of the current-row pointer to other rows in the cursor, but when you're using one of the forward-only cursors, you'll be limited to the MoveNext method. You won't be able to use the MoveLast method on forward-only cursors. Why would you want to? Since you can see only the current row at any one time, moving to the last row would serve only to throw away all rows from the current row to the last—with no chance at seeing the rows in between. If this is your intent, simply use the Close method.

After a cursor has been created, you can use a variety of techniques for moving the current-row pointer to one of the other rows in the result set. All the data interfaces use somewhat different techniques, and these are discussed in the remaining parts of this guide (DAO in Part III, RDO in Part IV, and ADO in Part V). With the current-row pointer positioned to a row, you can change the data in the base table(s)—if and *only* if the cursor is updateable; not all cursors are. According to how the cursor was created, its data source, and which data interface you're using, one or more columns of the result set, or even the entire result set, might be read-only.

Remember, even if the cursor isn't updateable (and I often create read-only cursors to save time and space), you can update the data using an update action query, including those that invoke stored procedures. In many cases, you can't update tables directly anyway because they can be updated *only* via stored procedures; using update queries that call stored procedures is standard operating procedure. (SOP as we said in the army.)

CAUTION
The Microsoft Visual Basic 4.0 RDO interface's Help file is incorrect when it implies that you can use any of the cursor positioning methods against a forward-only rdoResultset object. You can use only the MoveNext method to reposition the current record pointer. This caution applies to ODBC forward-only result sets as well.

> **NOTE** RDO 2.0 lets you trap the WillUpdateRows event to change how RDO handles a pending alteration of a cursor. With this event, you can create a cursor that ordinarily wouldn't be updateable and execute appropriate code (possibly a stored procedure) when the data is to be updated. Using this event (and others), you can now use the RemoteData control against read-only data sources and still permit changes to the database. You'll discover that ADO 2.0 supports the same kind of events. We'll get to those later (in Part V).

It's entirely possible to create a cursor with no member rows or to position the current-row pointer off either end of the cursor or on an invalid row. Therefore, it's not a good idea to attempt to blindly change data. For example, if the current row of a cursor is deleted, the current row is invalid, and you must reposition to another, valid row before you can perform an update operation. This error is all too typical in a heavily used system. It's not unusual for other users to delete or change the data you're working on, forcing you to deal with the contingencies that arise. Again, error handling is going to be one of your most time-consuming (but ultimately worth the effort) tasks.

Limiting the Rows in a Cursor

You need to limit your cursor to fewer than a few dozen rows so that you can minimize the system resources required to build it. The upper limit depends on the interactive nature of the application and the density of the display mechanism—and to some extent the density of the user. Limiting the rows in a result set is easy with SQL Server. Just execute the following code, where *nnn* is the maximum number of rows:

```
SET ROWCOUNT nnn
```

Is it really *that* easy? Of course not. When you execute *SET ROWCOUNT* in SQL Server 6.*x*, you also cap the number of *updateable* rows!

Don't depend on this behavior in SQL Server 7.0, in which ROWCOUNT limits result set rows but not Insert, Update, or Delete operation rows.

TIP Wait a minute. Didn't I warn you in Chapter 7 that using SET commands was dangerous? Yup, stay away from this option when you're building components.

Consider this example:

```
SET ROWCOUNT 100
Update Animals
Set Age = Age + 1 WHERE Birthday >= GetDate()
```

In this case, only the first 100 rows of the *Animals* table meeting the WHERE clause are updated. Does any data access interface support limiting rows? Yes, ADO, RDO, and DAO/ODBCDirect all support row-count limits. These limits are implemented by sending the server a SET ROWCOUNT command. Check this out for yourself by using SQL Trace (renamed SQL Server Profiler in SQL Server 7.0). In RDO, the MaxRows property caps the number of rows returned by the query but also can affect the number of rows modified by an associated update. What about using *SET ROWCOUNT* with Jet? The code looks like this:

```
' Set maximum number of rows to be returned to 20
db.Execute "SET ROWCOUNT 20", dbSQLPassThrough
```

In this example, I use a globally declared database object, *db*, that is affected by the *SET ROWCOUNT* operation—that is, all subsequent operations on this query, regardless of type, are affected by this row limit. Of course, I'm assuming that the Execute statement doesn't have to open another connection to execute its query. For this reason, I recommend that you turn off this cap when you're done with the query:

```
' Set no maximum number of rows to be returned
db.Execute "SET ROWCOUNT 0", dbSQLPassThrough
```

TIP Some SQL Server ODBC drivers might be confused about the impact of the SQL_MAX_ROWS option (an argument of the SQLSetStmtOption function that maps to the SET ROWCOUNT statement). Some versions of the driver don't account for the fact that the ROWCOUNT setting affects UPDATE statements, too. This has changed in SQL Server 7.0—now it affects only SELECT statements.

Limiting Rows with the WHERE Clause

When you can't use *SET ROWCOUNT* or don't want to, you should cap the number of rows returned by using the SQL statement's WHERE clause. Frankly, this technique is far more reliable and more in keeping with relational database theory and practice because it simply instructs SQL Server how to limit the logical scope of the query. This technique works with all data interfaces and doesn't affect updates unless you apply the same WHERE clause to the UPDATE statement. For example, here's how to make sure the query contains enough qualifying information to limit its scope to a few dozen rows:

```
SELECT Name, AnimalType, Age, Sex
FROM Animals
WHERE ID_NO BETWEEN 1 AND 50
```

Updating and Inserting Data

Let's say the user has decided to change a data field on a form. How will the change be posted to the database? All the data interfaces have their own update methodologies, but you might feel that you *have* to use a cursor to update the row or rows involved. (You can also use bound controls to expose and update data more or less automatically.) However, you don't always need to use a cursor. As a matter of fact, as you'll recall, I don't even encourage the use of updateable cursors. I suggest a fundamental database design that doesn't support the concept of updateable cursors, but instead uses action queries that execute stored procedures.

> **NOTE** When you insert records into a database by using a cursor, the row isn't always added as a new member of the cursor. Sure, it's added to the database; it just doesn't show up in the cursor. If a row is added as a member, it often gets placed at the end, regardless of the selected order of the data. If you add data by using an action query instead of a cursor, however, the data won't appear as a member of the cursor until the cursor is refreshed or rebuilt.

If an update affects more than one table in the database, you should bind the operations into a transaction. That way, the entire transaction can be rolled back if one update or insert fails. Transaction management and error detection are mostly up to you and your code, but you can delegate this responsibility to Microsoft Transaction Server when you're working with the distributed component designs. Some operations are rolled back by SQL Server trigger code, but your code is expected to execute the rollback when an error indicates that the transaction can't be completed. Again, using a stored procedure for this type of operation makes abundant sense.

As I've said before, many MIS shops don't permit direct access to underlying tables in a database. Instead, they gate access through protected stored procedures and views. In this case, updating is easy—you simply pass parameters to the data update or insert procedure. This method used to preclude the use of bound controls, since they expected access to updateable cursors created against basic tables or views. With the current versions of Visual Basic, however, you can intercept the actual update operation by catching the right event, substituting an appropriate stored procedure call, and then simply canceling the pending update operation.

Visual Basic has also incorporated another paradigm to make displaying and manipulating data through stored procedures even easier: the Data Object Wizard. This wizard is designed to interface with the Data Environment's Command objects and build an easy-to-use object interface to this stored-procedure–based update paradigm. That is, you can define Command objects to read the data and create result sets and other Command objects to update the data. Using the Data Object Wizard, you can build a class module that acts as a data source control— a Data-control-like interface that can be bound to data-aware controls. See Chapter 38 of this guide for a more detailed discussion of the Data Object Wizard.

Unless you can gain access to an updateable view or use this event technique, you won't be able to update protected underlying tables using the Data control or the RemoteData control. Even a stored procedure might limit changes to certain users and certain times of day or might impose other restrictions that help protect database integrity (and the system administrator's job). Your application might have to connect via a special login ID and password to gain access to the update or insert procedures.

An example of this special login and password access is Microsoft's RAID front end, which is used to track applications and documentation bugs throughout the company. RAID permits anyone to access the database by using a common user ID and no password. Updates are handled strictly by the application. The application uses stored procedures that verify the user's ID, the type of change, and the validity of the data. The database itself is locked for most other access, so you can't open it with Microsoft Access and fix a few bugs by hitting the tables directly.

Working with Batches

SQL Server has always supported the ability to execute more than one statement at a time. Although you can send more than one command to SQL Server simultaneously, it executes the statements serially—one at a time in the order received. Actually, all of your SQL queries, no matter how many statements they include, are to be in the form of Transact-SQL (TSQL) command *batches*. As a refresher, let's review the rules about batches so that you won't encounter any unpleasant surprises when you send batches to SQL Server. A batch is one or more TSQL commands sent at one time. If you send an improper batch for processing to SQL Server, you'll be greeted with a TSQL syntax error, the batch will be canceled, and you'll be sent to bed without your supper.

Using Optimistic Batch Updates

When we get to the RDO and ADO chapters in this book, we'll fully examine the Client Batch cursor library. For now, let's just take a brief look at this feature. Basically, the Client Batch cursor library, with its ability to perform optimistic batch updates, is designed to let you fetch a set of rows and perform a set of operations—such as Insert, Update, and Delete—on the result set. When you open one of these result sets in batch mode, the changes are queued and *not* posted to the database as they're made. If you're using RDO and you're ready to commit the changes, you use the BatchUpdate method, which sends the entire group of operations to the server as a set. Because this type of operation is expected to be executed against an easily updated set of rows, you shouldn't get any errors. But if you do, RDO and ADO build an array containing the bookmarks of the rows that didn't get updated. This technique can improve performance and make managing form-based multirow updates far easier.

Building Batches

The optimistic batch update operation leverages SQL Server's ability to accept an entire string of statements as a single operation. For example, you can submit as many INSERT statements as you can fit into a string and submit them to SQL Server as a batch. There is an upper limit; it's around 128 KB for SQL Server 7.0 and about half that for SQL Server 6.5 and older. But the real limit is far smaller. I've found that around 50 INSERT operations are as many as I can get SQL Server to handle efficiently. Sure, you can intersperse other commands in the string as well, but not all commands can be sent together.

The following list is a brief summary of the rules and regulations that govern the creation of batches in SQL Server 6.5:

- CREATE PROCEDURE, CREATE RULE, CREATE DEFAULT, CREATE TRIGGER, and CREATE VIEW must be sent to the SQL server alone. They can't be combined with any other TSQL statements. Doing so will cause a SQL syntax error.

- CREATE DATABASE, CREATE TABLE, and CREATE INDEX can be combined with other TSQL statements in a batch.

- Rules and defaults can't be bound to columns and used during the same batch. The sp_bindrule and sp_bindefault system procedures can't be in the same batch as INSERT statements that invoke the rule or default.

- The SQL Server 6.x CHECK constraints follow the same rules as TSQL rules and defaults. A table created with CHECK constraints can't enforce those constraints in the same batch as the definition.

- When you change the default database with the SQLUse function or send the TSQL USE command in SQL Server 4.2, the change doesn't take effect until after the batch has been completed. In SQL Server 6.x, however, the batch is executed in the specified database if the TSQL USE command is contained within a batch. The database context switch is immediate.

- You can't drop an object and then reference it or reuse it in the same batch.

- You can't alter a table and then reference the new columns in the same batch.

- Any options changed with a SET statement take effect at the end of the batch. You can combine SET statements and queries in the same batch, but the SET options won't apply to the queries in that batch.

The rules and restrictions for SQL Server 7.0 have been relaxed a bit, though it's not yet clear what all of these rules will be in their final form. Consult SQL Server 7.0 Books Online for batch rules to answer any specific questions you have.

Batch Limits

A few limits also apply to batches. The SQL Server batch size of 128 KB limits the maximum number of explicit data values that can be inserted or updated in a single batch. This limit doesn't apply to page-based data, such as Text or Image, that is inserted or updated through the WRITETEXT or UPDATETEXT statement. It also doesn't apply to data inserted with the BCP command-line utility, data inserted from another table, or data passed from remote procedure calls.

Sending Multiple Batches

In ISQL, ISQL/w (renamed SQL Server Query Analyzer in SQL Server 7.0), or SQL Enterprise Manager, you seem to send several batches (scripts) to SQL Server at once. In fact, only one batch is processed at a time. The term GO is *not* a TSQL statement or operator; it is simply a batch separator for SQL Server utilities that know how to execute multiple batches. The SQL server can't execute more than one batch of commands at any one time unless you open another connection and then use the new connection to execute another batch. You must process all the results of each batch after the batch has been processed by the SQL server before you can submit another batch to process.

Working with Batch Results

When you process batches, you need to keep in mind that not every TSQL statement returns rows, but *each* statement's result set must be processed by your application. There's a one-to-one correspondence between the number of statements sent to the SQL server and the number of result sets that have to be processed. When you do a 5500-row update (which you can do with a single UPDATE statement), no rows are returned to the application; but the statement *does* generate a result set that must be processed before the next statement in the batch can be processed or before a new batch can be sent.

Fixed queries

You'll probably start a batch by sending what I call a *fixed query*. This is a hard-coded TSQL batch with just one TSQL statement. Many of my production applications have a few of these fixed batches. I use them to ask simple questions, and I expect simple, low-row-count answers. The problem with using fixed batches that send more than a few simple commands is that they tend to slow down the SQL server. They don't place much extra load on the LAN (they're typically shorter than a dozen lines), but they do consume time and CPU power on the SQL server, which has to compile these batches.

PART III

Using DAO with the
Jet Database Engine

9

The Jet Database Engine and the DAO Model

DAO/Jet and SQL Server: Some History

How Jet Accesses Remote Databases

Understanding the DAO Model

et me be the first to admit it: after five years of working with DAO, I still don't call myself an expert on the Microsoft Jet database engine. What I know of Jet is drawn from my having worked with Jet to access Microsoft SQL Server, not dBASE or even Microsoft Access databases. I'm well aware that Jet is far, far more than an easy-to-use programmatic interface to SQL Server. My opinions about how Jet is suitable for one SQL Server application or another are based on my having created applications that worked (or didn't) after I used documentation that I might have written in the first place. So I guess I have no one to blame but myself when it comes to misunderstandings about Jet.

When Microsoft Visual Basic 5.0 shipped, a very significant change was made to the Jet database engine—it was modified to break away from DAO on demand (sorta like one of those Rolls Royce turbines on a 727 when it sucks up a goose). That is, you could program DAO to load and use RDO instead of Jet as its data access interface. This is the ODBCDirect mode of DAO. From now on, we need to think about DAO and Jet separately. When I say *Jet* from here on out, I'll be describing how the Jet database engine operates on its own. When I say *DAO/Jet,* I'll be talking about how DAO behaves when it is using Jet to implement data access. When I want to refer to DAO's behavior when it's connected to RDO, I'll use the term *ODBCDirect.*

DAO/Jet and SQL Server: Some History

SQL Server developers faced a number of different hurdles when it came to developing with DAO/Jet. Because DAO/Jet had originally been designed to make SQL Server look like another ISAM back end, many of the techniques described in the Jet documentation encouraged ISAM-style development methodologies for implementing the front-end.

These techniques worked, but they often degraded system and front-end performance, and sometimes Jet simply got in the way. For example, DAO/Jet 1.1 supports a Database object that can be used interchangeably by ISAM and

SQL Server database developers. With virtually the same code as that used for ISAM databases, a developer could either open a database file or connect to SQL Server (and to any ODBC back end, for that matter). This apparently easy way to get at SQL Server led many developers to use the attachment without link (AWOL) technique to open SQL Server tables just as they opened ISAM tables.

Other ISAM optimizations tended to make Jet 1.1 merely *appear* slower than competitive front ends in connecting to SQL Server, especially when result sets contained more than a few hundred rows. For example, to remain backward-compatible with Visual Basic 2.0, DAO/Jet preloaded the result sets returned from ODBC data sources to make second-row access as fast as possible. The first row's fetch time cost a relative fortune, but all the subsequent rows were basically free. Because many SQL Server customers were working with fairly large tables or could use only stored procedures to access or update data, the basic ISAM approach led to disappointing performance and some frustration. There *were* ways to make Jet 1.1 work faster and deal with many SQL Server front-end development issues, but these techniques weren't widely known or understood—not even by yours truly.

With pressure to make the version of Jet destined to be used with Visual Basic 4.0 a more responsive, more flexible, and better performing front end to SQL Server, the Jet team redesigned the connection handler and tuned the ODBC interface and query optimizer to be more cognizant of remote database intelligence. A sophisticated buffer manager and new result set population strategy were added. The team also redesigned the query optimizer to perform many queries as interactive stored procedures on the remote server. The Jet ODBC interface was reengineered as well, to stop prepopulating ODBC result sets. Connection and query times dropped, and perceived performance significantly increased. Unfortunately, the new architecture of Visual Basic 4.0 ate up most of these speed improvements—we hadn't gained much ground.

More important, the Jet group became acutely aware of the issues that you and I face daily when we work with databases that contain millions or billions of rows and are accessed by hundreds of concurrent users. The Jet documentation team continued to work with the Visual Basic 4.0 team to create development guidelines and documentation for making any Jet-based front end as efficient as it was designed to be, emphasizing the special tuning and optimization techniques needed to make a production-quality front end.

I use it, but I don't like the term *ODBCDirect*. As far as I'm concerned, it's confusing and misleading. When in ODBCDirect mode, DAO doesn't speak "directly" to ODBC—it speaks to RDO, which speaks directly to ODBC.

The Jet 1.1 documentation didn't make it obvious, but the AWOL approach was really not the best way to connect with SQL Server. It led to long connection times and correspondingly slow queries as Jet mapped portions of the database schema each time a connection was opened or a query was made. Those were the days when you could hear developers grumbling, "I can get a date on the street faster than I can fetch a date with SQL Server!"

How Jet Accesses Remote Databases

Jet is designed to access at least three different database formats. According to how you open the Database object or attach external databases, Jet chooses the interface and drivers for accessing data in the following kinds of databases:

- **MDB (Microsoft Access–format) databases** These are a cross between true relational databases and ISAM databases. Jet databases are maintained in a single file that integrates data, indexes, reports, forms, macros, and all other support data. This is Jet's native format. It's a very common practice to attach a SQL Server table to a Jet database. This model uses a separate SYSTEM.MDW file to manage user security. (You can't create a user-security file without a utility called the Workgroup Administrator (WRKGADM.EXE) provided by Microsoft Access; the Visual Basic group chose not to include this utility.)

- **True ISAM databases such as dBASE, FoxPro, Paradox, and Btrieve** These databases are accessed via installable ISAM (IISAM) drivers. This type of database characteristically has many files, and Jet treats each one as a table. (Jet 3.5 uses an IISAM driver to access Jet 2.0 files as well.)

- **External databases accessible through an ODBC driver** Jet can access virtually any database that has an ODBC level 1–compliant driver. SQL Server is connected through this type of interface, even when you attach one or more SQL Server tables to a Jet database.

Jet manages each of these databases differently while trying to make the interface with them as seamless as possible. The objects, properties, and methods used to manipulate data are generally the same, regardless of data format. Accessing SQL Server through Jet's ODBC drivers is also generally the same except that the Jet table-type Recordset object and its associated index-based methods aren't available. Figure 9-1, which was introduced in Chapter 3, shows how Jet is used to access SQL Server.

Jet and SQL Server: Coding Queries and Creating Cursors

Let's look more closely at how Jet deals with SQL Server databases and creates cursors against SQL Server data. Jet can create a forward-only snapshot-type DAO Recordset object, which you can count as a separate type of cursor if you want to. (It's still possible to create the outdated Dynaset and Snapshot objects with Visual Basic 5.0 and 6.0, but I'm going to ignore these.) Jet can also create a dynaset-type or snapshot-type Recordset object. Altogether, then, you have three different cursors to choose from when you use Jet to access SQL Server databases. The dynaset-type Recordset object is an updateable cursor containing bookmarks for each member row. The snapshot-type Recordset object contains a static copy of the data rows. Cursors store either bookmarks or data values in workstation resources. This means that a 1000-row dynaset cursor brings 1000 times the number of bytes per bookmark into local RAM, with the data for retrieved rows overflowing to local disk space if it can't fit in RAM. (The Windows swap file is *not* involved in this type of RAM allocation.) Any of these cursors can be created with code using the DAO interface or with the Data control, which now has much broader functionality than it did in Visual Basic 3.0.

NOTE Because the ODBC API and SQL Server don't expose ISAM-level calls such as OpenTable and Seek, DAO/Jet can't create a Table object or a table-type Recordset object against ODBC data sources. This type of access is reserved for native and ISAM databases that use separately accessible indexes to walk the data rows.

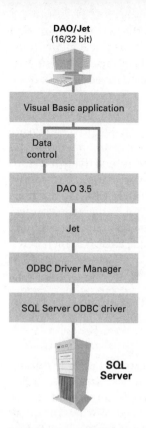

DAO/Jet
(16/32 bit)

Visual Basic application

Data
control

DAO 3.5

Jet

ODBC Driver Manager

SQL Server ODBC driver

**SQL
Server**

Figure 9-1 *DAO/Jet interface to access SQL Server from Visual Basic*

When you code a query against an ODBC data source and ask DAO/Jet to execute it, you start by executing a method that uses a SQL query as one of its arguments, or you use the Execute method of a DAO/Jet QueryDef object that contains a SQL query. Even if you simply specify the name of a SQL Server table, Jet executes a SELECT * query to fetch its data. For example, using the OpenResultset method against an attached SQL Server table in a Jet database starts a new query.

Jet's query processor then studies the SQL query. Let's assume you're using Jet's SQL syntax. (If you choose Transact-SQL instead, the Jet query processor must be bypassed.) At this point, the query processor checks the statement for correct syntax, permissions, and object references. If the query fails muster, processing goes no further and you get a trappable error.

Next, a decision is made about how to deal with the request. Jet will always send the entire SQL request to the server—unless the server can't perform the request, for one of several reasons. First, the data might come from two different sources. For example, one table could be a Jet table and the other a SQL Server table, or you could be attempting to join data from two SQL Server sources. Second, your query might have user-defined, Jet-specific, or Visual Basic–specific functions. If so, Jet evaluates and processes the functions locally. (Statistical or financial functions, for example, force local execution.) If a user-defined function (UDF) doesn't reference any data from the server, however, the UDF is evaluated first and the result is included in the SQL statement sent to the server for processing. Third, the query might be Jet-specific. Queries must be executed locally when they contain SQL commands unique to Jet (such as the TOP predicate) or when the data can't otherwise be derived from data on the server.

Regardless of how Jet decides to process the query, it executes the ODBC API SQLPrepare function, which causes the SQL Server ODBC driver to create one or more temporary stored procedures to perform the actual operation. Jet also attempts to create a parameter query that can be run interactively if it finds that at least some of the data must be drawn from the workstation. Each query is associated with a DAO Database object, which in turn is associated with a specific connection. As the query is executed against SQL Server, the connection is blocked for all other activity because SQL Server can't support multiple operations on a single connection unless it uses server-side cursors, which DAO/Jet can't use.

TIP The SQL Server ODBC driver has an option that disables the creation of stored procedures. You can set this option at data source definition time.

As Jet completes the query, it prepares a DAO Recordset object containing either the data rows stored locally on the workstation, in the case of a snapshot cursor, or pointers to the data rows back on the server, in the case of a dynaset cursor. If the query calls for the data to be sorted, as when the query contains an ORDER BY clause, SQL Server orders the rows of the result set before returning control to your application. If there's no need to perform further ordering, SQL Server returns control when the first block of rows is ready. In some cases, Jet continues working on your query in the background after the first block of data is returned to your application.

Once Jet returns control to your application and completes processing of the query, the connection is released for another operation—but not before. Again, this is because of the single-threaded nature of SQL Server connections. Unlike Visual Basic 3.0, in which any query to SQL Server locks the system until the query is complete, Jet attempts to return control to your application sooner. This isn't always possible, however, as when you ask for a sorted result set. When you're working on a 32-bit operating system such as Microsoft Windows 95 or Microsoft Windows NT, Jet's delay in returning control to your application isn't as serious a problem as it is when you're working on a nonpreemptive multitasking system that doesn't let other applications run while you wait for the results of a long query.

NOTE Need more details on the inner workings of the Jet database engine? Check out the second edition of *Microsoft Jet Database Engine Programmer's Guide* from Microsoft Press.

The Jet Query Processor

Let's take a critical look at the Jet query processor. In virtually all cases in which you're working with queries whose data is derived solely from SQL Server, you *don't* want Jet to perform the join locally. If it does, you're treating SQL Server like a file server. Who cares, if only a few rows are involved? But when you're dealing with more than a few dozen rows, local joins can slow your application to a crawl.

So that Jet can work to its full potential in a sophisticated client/server environment, you have to set a number of tuning options. Unfortunately, some of these options are difficult to reach from code because they are embedded deep in the system Registry. Visual Basic offers little support for querying or updating the Registry, so you must resort to Windows calls or to changing the Registry entries manually, which is scary.

So that Jet can process the logic involved in your query, Jet's query processor must understand how your database schema is laid out. This information must include table and column names, index names, and what features your database server supports. Jet gleans this information by executing a series of ODBC API functions against the SQL Server system tables and the special

Asynchronous Operations

A concept that confused me until one of the Jet program managers set me straight—they love to do that—is the difference between asynchronous operations in Microsoft Access and in the Visual Basic Data control background Recordset population. By default, Jet runs all its queries in asynchronous mode. This means that Jet periodically polls SQL Server for completion of the current query. While it's waiting to poll again, Jet yields to the operating system (Windows 95 or Windows NT), which can permit other Windows-based tasks to complete. Because of limitations in Visual Basic, the DAO/Jet interface is *not* capable of providing an asynchronous development environment, as supported in Microsoft Access and RDO. The Visual Basic application that has made a request (such as to open a record set) must wait until at least the first rows have returned to the workstation. Therefore, DAO/Jet programs must populate their record sets by using their own code, and they begin that work *after* the first records have been returned. The Data control *does* support asynchronous operations, however. By default, it attempts to populate a result set in the background. Just don't move to another row while this populating is going on—moving turns off the fetch.

tables installed when the ODBC drivers are set up. This process can take some time, so if you don't use an attached table, the information isn't cached and the process must be repeated many, many times—unless you're careful. I'll point out the techniques that trigger this DDL dump later on, in Chapter 12.

Another basic problem with the Jet query processor architecture is Jet's attitude toward your request. Jet assumes that you know what you're doing. (This assumption might be somewhat optimistic.) But working from this idea, the DAO/Jet interface creates the most expensive, powerful, and flexible cursor it can, unless you tell it to do otherwise. Visual Basic 3.0 gives developers few choices about the type of cursor to create, but Visual Basic 5.0 and later give you lots of choices. Versions 5.0 and later still create a read-write, full-access dynaset cursor by default, however. I suggest that you investigate forward-only scrolling snapshot-type Recordset objects, accessed via the GetRows method. This is the cheapest, fastest way to access data from SQL Server with Jet. If you don't intend to update data through this connection, set the Database object's ReadOnly property to True for even better performance.

When you're using Jet to access SQL Server, limit the scope of every operation. This means making sure that you ask for only the specific rows you need. Don't ask for columns you don't need, and that goes double for Text and Image data types. And don't fill lists with more than a few hundred rows. Users can't or won't read them, and keeping the data current will be a problem. You should also perform sorting and filtering operations via SQL queries that run on SQL Server; don't plan to filter or sort once the data is returned to the workstation.

Understanding the DAO Model

Now that you have an idea about the inner workings of the Jet engine, let's take a look at the DAO object model and how it behaves when connected to Jet. Although the same DAO programming objects are used with ODBCDirect, they might behave differently when connected to RDO.

Before Visual Basic 4.0, every object, method, property, and event (except those provided by the VBX controls) was hard-coded into the language. Unless you added a custom control, there was no way to extend the list of known Visual Basic 3.0 objects or their attributes. For components hard-wired into Visual Basic 3.0, however, such as data access, it was impossible to extend the object model. This limitation became painfully evident when Jet 2.*x* was released with Microsoft Access 2.0. Visual Basic could access the new engine indirectly through the compatibility layer, but it couldn't reach the new Recordset object or its properties and methods. Moreover, all the new security and replication features were also unavailable.

Visual Basic 4.0 departed radically from this hard-wired design when Microsoft implemented a new OLE based architecture. Each object, property, method, or event that Visual Basic recognizes in code is now defined through a type library. Basically, a type library is a dynamic description of each object, coupled with its properties and methods. This list is loaded either when the Visual Basic run-time component is created or at design time when the developer chooses a new custom control or an object library from the References dialog box. That way, new object models can be loaded as they evolve. These object models can be developed in any language, by anyone—even by other Visual Basic programs.

To deal with the various scenarios Visual Basic developers are expected to use, Visual Basic 4.0 provided three DAO type libraries: the DAO 3.0 Object Library (32-bit), the DAO 2.5/3.0 Compatibility Library (32-bit), and the DAO 2.5 Object Library (16-bit). Visual Basic 6.0 includes the DAO 3.51 Object Library (32-bit) and the DAO 2.5/3.51 Compatibility Library (32-bit).

Each of these type libraries has a specific function. The DAO 3.x libraries are designed strictly for 32-bit Visual Basic, and provide no support for the obsolete DAO features. The DAO 3.x libraries also help you identify all instances of outdated features. For 32-bit applications, you can choose the DAO 2.5/3.51 Compatibility Library, which provides backward compatibility with older versions of the DAO interface, allowing you to recompile existing Visual Basic 3.0 or Visual Basic 4.0 code (Jet 1.1 or 2.0) for 32-bit applications. For 16-bit applications, your only choice is the DAO 2.5 Object Library. In future versions of Visual Basic, however, some of these older DAO properties, methods, and objects won't be supported. To ease your move to the Jet 3.x model and ensure that your existing code will continue to run properly, you should use the Jet DAO 3.51 Object Library for new projects. This library contains only the new DAO functionality.

Yes, Visual Basic 4.0 was the last version of Visual Basic capable of making 16-bit applications. It's also the slowest and one of the buggiest versions out there. Sure, use Visual Basic 3.0. It's kinda old-fashioned, but it works.

TIP Using the DAO 3.5 Object Library ensures that your new projects will continue to function correctly in versions of Visual Basic later than Visual Basic 5.0. Therefore, you should use the DAO 3.5 Object Library in any new projects, and you should migrate any existing projects to it. Before you get started, however, be sure to read about using Remote Data Objects in Part IV of this guide, or better yet, ActiveX Data Objects (ADO) in Part V as a possible alternative to DAO.

In the Visual Basic Help, you can find the DAO/Jet object model laid out in a neat graphic. Figure 9-2 shows the DAO/Jet 2.5/3.x object model and it also includes the obsolete Recordset objects left over from Visual Basic 2.0 and Visual Basic 3.0. If you're using these objects, you should migrate your code away from them. Table 9-1 shows how to translate them to their current equivalent objects. The table also lists a number of statements that have been replaced and gives information about converting them. Several of the changes made to

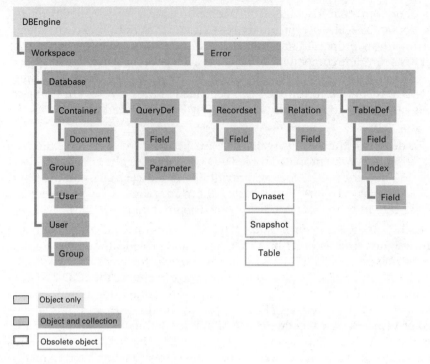

DBEngine

Workspace   Error

Database

Container   QueryDef   Recordset   Relation   TableDef

Document   Field   Field   Field   Field

Group   Parameter   Index

User   Dynaset   Field

User   Snapshot

Group   Table

☐ Object only

☐ Object and collection

☐ Obsolete object

Figure 9-2 *DAO/Jet 2.5/3.x object model and obsolete objects*

the Jet engine were done under the cowling, so your code won't appear to change. For example, when you use the BeginTrans statement in Visual Basic 3.0 code and convert to Visual Basic 4.0, this statement becomes a method of the default Workspace object. Your code doesn't change, nor does the impact of the statement.

NOTE When Microsoft shipped Access 7.0, the Access sub-version of Jet replaced the Visual Basic 4.0 version. At that point, some Jet bugs were fixed, some parts began to work better, and some new bugs were uncovered. Since Microsoft Office 97 shipped ahead of Visual Basic 5.0, this Jet version problem didn't occur. That's the nature of component architecture. It's like having a car made of parts from all over the country. Although Ford has been trying to get this kind of thing right for almost 70 years, Microsoft is really just beginning with its ActiveX-based component architecture.

Table 9-1
Conversion of Outdated DAO Code to DAO 2.5/3.*x* Code

Outdated Objects, Methods, or Statements	How to Convert to DAO 2.5/3.*x*
Dynaset object	Use dynaset-type Recordset object
CreateDynaset method	Use OpenRecordset(<sql>, dbOpenDynaset)
Snapshot object	Use snapshot-type Recordset object
CreateSnapshot method	Use OpenRecordset(<sql>, dbOpenSnapshot)
Table object	Use table-type Recordset object (not available via ODBC)
OpenTable method	Use OpenRecordset(<sql>, dbOpen-Table) (not available via ODBC)
OpenQueryDef method	Access existing QueryDef objects in the QueryDefs collection
ListIndexes method	Use TableDefs Indexes collection
ListFields method	Use TableDefs Fields collections
ListParameters method	Use QueryDefs Parameters collection
FreeLocks method	Use DBEngine.Idle method
SetDefaultWorkspace statement	Use DBEngine DefaultUser and DefaultPassword properties
SetDataAccessOption statement	Use DBEngine IniPath property
ExecuteSQL method	Use Execute method, RecordsAffected property
DeleteQueryDef method	Use QueryDefs collection Delete method

Properties and Methods

Each of the DAO classes permits your code to manipulate properties that activate options, set operational parameters, or execute methods that carry out actions (such as opening a result set or closing a database on SQL Server). Visual Basic objects are instances of class procedures that have instance variables: their *methods*. Each DAO class also supports a set of variables that affect or reflect their behavior and operation: these are called *properties*. When you want one of the objects to perform some operation or when you want to perform an operation on an object, you use one of its methods.

The DAO objects, like many in Visual Basic, are loaded dynamically when you choose them from the References dialog box available from the Project menu. When you first drag the preloaded Data control to your form, the DAO objects are referenced and loaded for you automatically so that the later versions of the Visual Basic integrated development environment (IDE) will work the way the Visual Basic 3.0 IDE does.

Several of the DAO/Jet objects aren't available to you when you're writing applications to access SQL Server. Figure 9-3 shows the same DAO Jet 2.5/3.*x* object model, but the objects that are unavailable to SQL Server are shown with dotted lines. The unavailable objects are also listed in Table 9-2. Table 9-3 lists the objects you can use and describes how they relate to SQL Server front-end development.

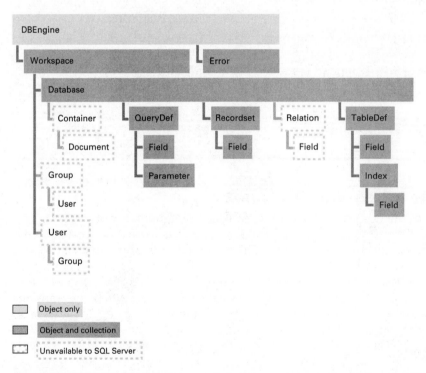

Figure 9-3 *DAO/Jet 2.5/3.x object model showing objects unavailable to SQL Server*

Table 9-2

**DAO/Jet Objects Not Available
to SQL Server Front-End Applications**

DAO/Jet Object	What It Does
Container	Holds information that describes a group of objects
Document	Includes information about one instance of a type of object (database, saved table, query, or relationship)
Relation	Manages Jet database referential integrity; can't map to attached tables or reflect SQL Server referential integrity constraints
Field	For Relation objects, the Field objects contain field definitions
Group	Maintains group-level and user-level security for Jet databases
User	Maintains group-level and user-level security for Jet databases

Table 9-3

**DAO/Jet Objects Available
to SQL Server Front-End Applications**

DAO/Jet Object	What It Does
DBEngine	Holds all other objects. Addresses overall engine options.
Error	Contains information about data access errors.
Workspace	Maintains a unique transaction scope. All transactions are Workspace-global. Holds the Databases collection. Can be set to connect to either Jet or RDO (ODBCDirect mode).
Database	Permits user to address a specific SQL Server database and holds the TableDefs collection. Database objects are used to establish a connection to SQL Server, so opening a Database object opens at least one ODBC connection.
QueryDef	A stored query maintained in a Jet database. Roughly equivalent to a simple stored procedure containing only a single SELECT statement or action query. QueryDef objects have a Parameters collection, which is used to hold query parameters.

(continued)

Table 9-3 *continued*

DAO/Jet Object	What It Does
Field	For QueryDef, TableDef, and Index objects, the Field objects contain field definitions. For Recordset objects the Field objects describe the columns of a database table and their attributes. There is one Field object for each defined column.
Parameter	Maintains the parameters passed to a specific QueryDef object when it is executed.
Recordset	A cursor. Permits sequential or random access to data rows in a result set. Contains either data rows, as in a snapshot-type Recordset object, or pointers to data rows, as in a dynaset-type Recordset object.
Connection	ODBCDirect only. Used to map to the RDO Connection object and its unique behavior.
TableDef	Describes database tables. One TableDef is created for each table in the SQL Server database. Each TableDef contains a Fields collection and an Indexes collection.
Index	Describes a table index. There is one Index object for each table index in the database. Each Index object contains a Fields collection that contains one Field object for each table field included in the index.

Collections

Collections aren't new to Visual Basic, but they now play a very important role in the development of DAO-based applications (or, for that matter, in the development of any object-based Visual Basic application). Collections are described in the Visual Basic documentation, but the focus there isn't particularly data-oriented.

A collection holds a set of related objects. It functions basically as a linked list, with behavior somewhat different from what you might be used to working with, unless you're familiar with the ListBox or ComboBox controls. Each element of a collection is called a *member*. Collection members are always added to the end of a collection, but they can be removed randomly. When a member is deleted, all the other members move up in the list—not physically, just logically. Therefore, when you use an index to reference the individual members of a collection, the index number is valid only until you delete a member. For this reason, you can delete member 0 a number of times—each time, the remaining members logically slide up to take the freed space.

Because collections are rebuilt through the Refresh method, you can't count on the order number of any one element. A TableDef object that was the fourth member a second ago might be the third, fifth, or fifty-fifth after you refresh the collection. And you do have to refresh collections on occasion, especially when you make changes that bypass Jet.

Collection members are added and removed either automatically or by using such methods as Append or Delete. As new Database or Recordset objects are created, references to the new objects are automatically placed in their associated collections.

Visual Basic 3.0 supports only a few object collections, such as the TableDefs collection of TableDef objects. Visual Basic 4.0 and later support many more, as well as the creation of user-defined collections. All the objects that are listed in Table 9-3 except the DBEngine object itself are maintained in associated collections. For example, all Database objects are maintained in the Databases collection, and all Field objects are kept in the Fields collection.

NOTE The TableDef, Recordset, Index, and QueryDef objects each have a Fields collection to manage the columns associated with each object.

To refer to collection members in code, you can use one of a half-dozen (or more) syntax forms. Let's assume that the first table in the TableDefs collection is named *Titles*. Any of the following DAO syntax variations will be supported for referring to the first table:

```
TableDefs(0)                ' By ordinal number
                            ' All collections are zero-based
TableDefs(n%)               ' Indirectly by ordinal where n% = 0
TableDefs("Titles")         ' Directly by name
MyTable$ = "Titles"
TableDefs(MyTable$)         ' Indirectly by name
TableDefs!Titles            ' Directly by name
```

Using the "bang" operator (!) is the fastest way to reference objects. If the name has embedded spaces, enclose the name in brackets or pass it in a string:

```
TableDefs![My TableName]
MyLongTableName$ = "My TableName"
TableDefs(MyLongTableName$)
```

Populating the Object Model

When your application makes a code reference to a DAO object, the DBEngine object is started automatically. A new Workspace object isn't created until you reference one of the underlying objects. If you need to use ODBCDirect, be sure to create a separate Workspace object for it—otherwise, you get a Jet Workspaces(0) object by default. When you subsequently open a Jet Workspace connection to SQL Server, as when you use the OpenDatabase method against the default Workspaces(0), Jet simply establishes a connection to SQL Server and fetches a few initialization values from a tuning configuration table. The SQL Server connection interface assigns your connection a default database, or your connect string specifies a specific SQL Server database to use. No further DAO/Jet object population takes place.

Since we're focusing on the DAO/Jet interface, let's assume that we haven't created an ODBCDirect Workspace. When you make your first reference to the TableDefs collection, DAO/Jet calls the ODBC API, which selectively populates the object model so that all relevant DAO objects reflect the current schema of your SQL Server database. Simply creating a Resultset object doesn't populate the DAO data definition language (DDL) structures. All DAO DDL information is stored in structures addressed by reference to the Database object. For example, once the DAO object model is fully populated, the TableDefs collection contains a TableDef member for each table in the SQL Server database, and each Fields collection of each TableDef object contains a description of all columns in each table—whether or not you ever reference them in code.

In most cases, you do *not* want Jet fully populating the rest of the object model to reflect the schema of your SQL Server database—trust me. One of the most expensive and time-consuming operations Jet performs is populating the Databases, TableDefs, Fields, and Indexes collections. For better performance, DAO/Jet should populate only what it needs. DAO/Jet doesn't walk the entire SQL Server database schema when you open a DAO/Jet TableDef object; it simply uses the SQLTables ODBC function to pull back selected tables' DDL information. When, and only when, you touch a Field object in code, DAO/Jet drills down using the ODBC SQLColumns function. To make matters worse, this information is cached in the Database object. Declaring this information globally doesn't pose a serious problem, however, since all procedures in the form can use it. But if it's defined in a procedure, the entire operation is repeated each time the SQL Server database is opened—not good. This warning should make it abundantly clear that Jet was designed to access ODBC data sources through *attached* tables. Jet shows its best performance (at OpenDatabase time) if the work required to map a table's schema is done once—when the ODBC data source table is attached.

TIP When changes are made in the database schema—as when tables, fields, or indexes are added or deleted—the process of fetching the DDL information *must* be repeated if you're depending on accurate mapping of the database schema. To repopulate the collections, use the Refresh method against the TableDefs, Indexes, or Databases collections. If you don't repopulate, the local copy of the DDL schema kept in the DAO interface doesn't change. That's the good news. The bad news is that when you execute a query based on a stale schema, it might fail because of an unknown object reference. Generally, a SQL Server front-end application doesn't need to query the database schema at run time—this information is useful at design time as you set up your forms and bound controls. But if your application creates new SQL Server tables using non-DAO means, as when you use SQL pass-through queries, you must refresh the TableDefs or Indexes collections.

10

Data Access Objects Up Close

Component Architecture

The DBEngine Object

Workspace Objects

Database Objects

TableDef Objects

Field Objects

Index Objects

Tables and Indexes

Creating or Adding Tables and Indexes

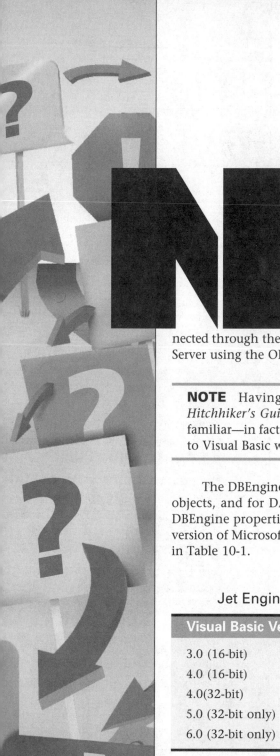

ow that you have a sense of Microsoft DAO/Jet's evolution and basic developmental approach, let's take a tour of how DAO/Jet is exposed to programmers. In this chapter, I'll describe the Data Access Objects in detail, emphasizing how they interact with Microsoft SQL Server when connected through the Jet database engine. You'll see how DAO connects to SQL Server using the ODBCDirect mode later (in Chapter 16).

NOTE Having déjà vu? Those of you who have been fans of the *Hitchhiker's Guide* from the beginning will think this chapter looks familiar—in fact, very little has changed with DAO objects as they relate to Visual Basic with the revisions of Visual Basic and SQL Server.

The DBEngine object provides top-level addressability for all local DAO objects, and for DAO/Jet it represents the Microsoft Jet database engine—DBEngine properties are applied to the Jet engine itself. Depending on the version of Microsoft Visual Basic loaded, the Jet engine is loaded as described in Table 10-1.

Table 10-1
Jet Engines Used According to Visual Basic Version

Visual Basic Version	Jet Engine Version
3.0 (16-bit)	Jet 1.0, 1.1, or 2.0
4.0 (16-bit)	Jet 2.5
4.0(32-bit)	Jet 3.0
5.0 (32-bit only)	Jet 3.5
6.0 (32-bit only)	Jet 3.51

But before we pull completely off the road, let's take a look at one of Visual Basic's most important architectural buttresses: COM.

Component Architecture

A principal difference between Visual Basic 3.0 and Visual Basic 4.0 and later is the concept of Component Object Model (COM) architecture. What COM means for you is that as newer versions of any of Visual Basic's components are developed, you can take full advantage of their bug fixes, new objects and methods, and improved performance simply by installing the new dynamic-link libraries (DLLs) and registering them with the Microsoft Windows operating system. Jet is also provided in many other Microsoft products, including Microsoft Access, Microsoft Visual C++, Microsoft Excel, and Microsoft Office applications, so when one of these applications is installed on your system, it can bring a newer version of Jet or other Visual Basic 4.0 (and later) components (such as Visual Basic for Applications) with it. The bottom line? Well, the functionality of your application could very well change as these components evolve within versions. You won't need the compatibility layer or anything else to access these changes, even if they are significant, because of the way components like Jet are plugged into Visual Basic through COM architectures. You should be aware, though, that these components might be installed whenever you add any application that updates one of Visual Basic's components. Be especially wary of any third-party application that has its own setup routine, which might overlay an older DLL on the current version of a component.

The DBEngine Object

In Visual Basic version 5.0 and later, starting a DAO application no longer automatically initializes the Jet database engine because the engine might never be invoked if the application chooses to use ODBCDirect. When the first reference to a DAO/Jet Workspace is made, the Jet engine is loaded, initialized, and started. At this point, Jet takes a look at the Windows Registry for initialization option settings. You must restart the DBEngine in order for any changes to its options to take effect. How does this affect other applications that share the engine? Each time an application that uses the Jet engine is launched, it gets its own instance data segment, which permits independent configuration and operation.

NOTE All applications using the same version share the same *code* segments, but each is allocated its own *data* segment. The Jet engine is *not* shared if you run a Visual Basic 3.0 DAO application or some other Jet 1.*x* application on the same system as a Visual Basic 4.0 or later application. They do compete for the same resources, however.

All 32-bit DBEngine (Jet 3.*x*) settings are made by way of the Windows system Registry. The 16-bit version of the engine (Jet 2.*x*) uses INI files to maintain the initialization settings. For virtually all production applications, you should set up an application-centric INI file or Windows Registry location and point to this location by using the DBEngine.INIPath property. The INIPath property doesn't contain a value unless you set it because there is no default path—the underlying code uses the current file directory or the Windows Registry entries.

To restart the Jet engine, you must first stop it. Try setting the DBEngine object to Nothing:

```
Set DBEngine = Nothing
```

Using this technique does have a drawback: all the DBEngine objects' open Database and Resultset objects are closed, somewhat rudely. It might be a good idea to close these ancillary objects before using this technique. To restart Jet, simply reference one of its objects, which brings it back on line.

Workspace Objects

One of the objects added to Visual Basic 4.0 was the Workspace object. In Visual Basic 5.0 and later, this object is used to choose how DAO is implemented—whether through the Jet engine or RDO. If you choose to use ODBCDirect to connect your DAO objects to their equivalent RDO objects, you have to set up a new Workspace—the default Workspace automatically connects DAO to the Jet database engine. Yes, you can do both—that is, you can have both a DAO/Jet Workspace *and* a DAO/RDO (ODBCDirect) Workspace at the same time.

To activate an ODBCDirect Workspace, simply create your own Workspace like this:

```
Dim Ws as Workspace
Set Ws = DBEngine.CreateWorkspace ("MyODBCDWs", "", "", dbUseODBC)
```

CAUTION

Don't expect the DAO/Jet objects you create to work the same way when you switch over to ODBCDirect. You'll find lots of subtle and not so subtle differences between these two interfaces—and no, the documentation does *not* detail what ODBCDirect does *not* do in relation to DAO/Jet. ODBCDirect objects don't even do what straight RDO objects do.

In a general sense, the Workspace object provides a transaction scope and manages security for Jet databases that have security enabled. But I'm not going to drive into that quicksand for you; if you feel the need to implement a secured Jet database, I highly recommend taking along someone with a strong back and a long rope. Note, however, that when you set up a new DAO/Jet Workspace object, you must provide a user ID and password to gate access to secure Jet databases. Once you set the Workspace object user ID and password, Jet also uses these values when attempting to open connections to remote ODBC databases such as SQL Server. But if these values don't match those intended for the SQL server, you trip a trappable error. To turn off this automatic authentication, simply change the Registry entry JetTryAuth to 0, or include a user ID and password in the connect string.

When you're writing DAO/Jet-based front-end applications, the Workspace object gives you a significant level of control over transaction scope that simply isn't available in Visual Basic 3.0. You can create a separate Workspace object for databases that need to participate in a transaction, and you can exclude those that shouldn't.

When you start the Jet database engine without indicating that the Workspace should use RDO, Jet automatically creates the default workspace, DBEngine.Workspaces(0), which is used if you don't specifically reference a

Workspace object in using the OpenDatabase method. When you use transactions, all databases in the specified DAO/Jet Workspace are affected, even if multiple Database objects are opened in the Workspace. For example, if you use a BeginTrans method, update several records in a database, and then delete records in another database, both the update and delete operations are rolled back when you use the Rollback method. Now you understand why it's important to be able to create additional Workspace objects to manage transactions independently across Database objects. Generally, all transaction operations are passed on to SQL Server for processing—Jet doesn't buffer or manage ODBC transaction operations.

New Workspace objects are created with the CreateWorkspace method of the DBEngine object. If newly created Workspace objects must be referred to after creation, you must manually append them to the Workspaces collection. You can, however, use newly created Workspace objects without appending them to the Workspaces collection. You can refer to any other Workspace object that you create and append to the collection by its Name property setting or by its ordinal number.

Using the IsolateODBCTrans Property

In some situations, when you need to have multiple simultaneous transactions pending on the same ODBC database, you open a separate Workspace object for each transaction. Although each Workspace object can have its own ODBC connection to the database, this isolation slows the system's performance. Because transaction isolation normally isn't required, ODBC connections from multiple Workspace objects opened by the same user are shared, by default. The IsolateODBCTrans property returns or sets a Boolean value that indicates whether multiple transactions that involve the same ODBC database are to be isolated. The default value is False—don't isolate transactions involving the same ODBC database.

SQL Server doesn't allow simultaneous transactions on a single connection, so if you need to have more than one transaction at a time pending against such a database, set the IsolateODBCTrans property to True on each Workspace object as soon as you open it. This forces a separate ODBC connection for each Workspace object.

Workspace Methods

The Workspace object also has a number of methods that are detailed in the Visual Basic Help file. You can execute the transaction methods against either a specific Database object (but *only* in Jet 2.5) or a chosen Workspace object. I would recommend, however, that you *not* use the Database method. Instead, use the Workspace method, for forward compatibility. If you reference neither a Database object nor a Workspace object when you're using the transaction methods, the default Workspaces(0) object is used. The Workspace object also enables the OpenDatabase method, which is used to establish a SQL Server connection.

Database Objects

The Database object provides addressability to the connection established by the OpenDatabase method. The Visual Basic 5.0 (and later) Database object, unlike that of Visual Basic 2.0, doesn't provide a transaction scope. Sure, when you execute a transaction method against one of the tables in the database, all pending transactions on this database (connection) are affected, but so are all pending transactions on all other Database objects in its Workspace—which isn't usually what you have in mind. Remember, the Workspace object is what provides top-level transaction scope; the Database object maintains information about the connection and a TableDefs collection.

NOTE A DAO/Jet Database Object is *not* the same as an ODBCDirect Connection object, although it serves basically the same function—it establishes a connection to the remote server. But the ODBCDirect Connection object can create temporary QueryDef objects whereas the DAO/Jet Database object can't—not while it is connected to Jet.

You manipulate an open database and the connection associated with it by using a Database object and its methods and properties. You can examine the collections in a Database object to map the tables, views, and stored procedures of the underlying SQL Server database and the QueryDef objects in a local Jet database. None of the forms, reports, or macros associated with a Jet database are accessible from Visual Basic. You can also use the Database object collections to modify or create SQL Server tables and indexes and Jet database queries and relationships. The Database object is also the basis for creating cursors against SQL Server data. For example, you can perform the following operations:

- Use the OpenRecordset method to create a new Recordset object directly from the Database object

- Use the Execute method to run a query against SQL Server that doesn't return rows

- Use the OpenRecordset method to execute a SQL pass-through query, with or without use of a QueryDef object, so that you can bypass the Jet query processor

- Use the Close method to close an open database and return the connection to the connection pool

The Workspace object's CreateDatabase method can't be used to create a new SQL Server database. But once you create a new SQL Server device and database, using the tools provided with SQL Server, you can create new tables and indexes with Visual Basic DAO methods. Why you would want to do this when the tools provided with SQL Server are available is beyond me, but you can use the CreateTableDef and CreateIndex methods if you really want to. Frankly, I prefer the newly integrated Visual Database Tools in Visual Basic, or

CAUTION

There is no such thing as a "default" database in the Visual Basic DAO/Jet interface. Despite what the Visual Basic or Access documentation says (or at least used to say), the CurrentDB method has no meaning and doesn't compile. It does have a use in Access Basic applications, however, since it refers to the Jet database currently opened by the user. When you see references to this object, simply substitute Workspaces(0).Databases(0) if you've already opened a database. If you haven't opened a database, the reference to Database(0) is bogus.

SQL Enterprise Manager, Transact-SQL (TSQL) statements, or, better yet, SQL OLE for creating my tables—even from inside Visual Basic applications. You can't use any of the Jet relationship methods to create or manipulate SQL Server inter-table constraint relationships. None of the Jet Relation object properties or methods maps to SQL Server relations (not even to a distant cousin); they are strictly for Jet databases. To open an existing SQL Server database, use the Workspace object's OpenDatabase method, which automatically appends it to the Databases collection.

When you use one of the three transaction methods (BeginTrans, CommitTrans, or Rollback) on the Database object, the transaction applies to all databases opened on the Workspace object from which the Database object was opened. If you want to use an independent transaction, you must open an additional Workspace object and then use it to open another Database object. Here's how to create two independent Database objects:

```
Dim Db1 As Database, Db2 As Database, Ws As Workspace, _
    Ws2 As Workspace
Dim MyUserName As String
Set Ws = Workspaces(0)                      ' Use the default Workspace
Set Db1 = Ws.OpenDatabase("DSN1", 0, 0, _
    "ODBC;UID=;PWD=;Database=Pubs")
Set Ws2 = DBEngine.CreateWorkspace _
    ("Special", MyUserName, "SpecialPW")  ' Create new Workspace
Ws2.ODBCIsolateTrans = True
Set Db2 = Ws.OpenDatabase _
    ("DSN1", 0, 0, "ODBC;UID=;PWD=;Database=Pubs")
```

It isn't necessary to specify the DBEngine object when you use the OpenDatabase method. You need to do that only when you open a Database object in a transaction context in which a specific Workspace object needs to be referenced.

You can also open a Jet database that contains *attached* tables—links to SQL Server tables—instead of opening a remote SQL Server database directly. Opening a Jet database that has attached tables doesn't automatically establish links to the specified external ODBC databases until the table's TableDef or Field objects are referenced in code or until a Recordset object is opened against the Database object. If links to these tables can't be established, a trappable error occurs. You might also need permission to access the database, or the database might already be open for someone else's exclusive use. In these cases, a trappable error also occurs.

After you open an external database, you can examine the Connect property of the Database object to determine the parameters used to access the database. When an external ODBC database is opened directly, you can't use a table-type Recordset object, nor can you use one to access any ODBC-accessed table. Each time you open an external ODBC database directly, you establish a connection to the external database server. Because the Jet engine executes additional queries on the database to determine the structure of accessed tables, don't open external databases directly. (The ability to do so is provided only for the sake of backward compatibility.)

Attached Tables vs. Direct Links

As already mentioned, there are two fundamental ways to gain access to SQL Server data via DAO/Jet. You can open a Database object against a SQL Server data source directly or against a Jet MDB database containing attached SQL Server tables, as illustrated in Figure 10-1.

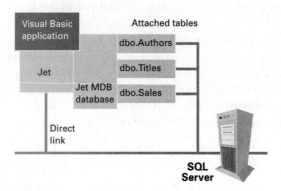

Figure 10-1 *Accessing SQL Server data with attached tables*

Each technique has advantages and disadvantages. If you choose to open the SQL Server database directly, you can execute either Jet queries or Transact-SQL (TSQL) queries to create Recordset objects or execute action queries that change data or perform administrative functions. The downside to this approach is the expense incurred when the Database object is first opened—the data definition language (DDL) queries can take considerable time to perform. And this isn't a one-time penalty, either: additional DDL queries are required when the Recordset object is created against nonattached tables. The Database penalty *is* a one-time cost, however, if you open a Database object and its associated connection and leave it open for the duration of your operation. But this strategy assumes that the connection, which is tied up for the duration of the operation, isn't a system resource that needs to be conserved.

One technique that can reduce the time needed to open a connection involves preconnecting to the SQL server during form load. You pay a price as the program loads, but all subsequent OpenDatabase operations are *very* fast. If you leave this connection open, Jet can use it as required, and since the DDL operations have already been done, it also keeps Jet aware of the available tables on your SQL Server database. This technique ties up a connection for an indefinite period of time, however.

When you need to access SQL Server data with attached tables (or *linked* tables, as the Access documentation says), you simply open a Jet database that contains linkage information about chosen SQL Server tables. The data in the tables remains in the tables. It isn't downloaded into the Jet database and is really manipulated only when you create a cursor or execute an action query that references it. When you query these attached tables or use them in a join, Jet opens a connection (or shares one that is already open) and performs whatever input/output is necessary to access the data.

Just before Visual Basic 4.0 shipped, the Jet team added a feature that permits you to create TSQL query–based Resultset objects on MDB databases. To perform a SQL pass-through query on a table attached to your MDB file, you can first set the Connect property of the attached table's Database object to a valid ODBC connect string. This Jet feature removed one of the serious impediments to using attached tables; but you still must create a Jet database and attach SQL Server tables to it, or attach your SQL Server tables to an existing Jet database. Yes, this database can be shared, and other people can use the attached tables. You can create it on the fly, too, in code.

You use the Close method to remove a Database object from the Databases collection and release the connection back to the pool. (The Databases collection should really be called the OpenDatabases collection—it doesn't actually hold databases, but rather holds Database structures that describe open database connections.) Any open Recordset objects in the database are closed automatically when the Database object is closed.

CAUTION

You can write code in a Visual Basic application to attach tables on the fly. But if you repeat this process every time the application runs, you negate most of the advantages you gained when you avoided opening the Database object directly.

TIP   To ensure that *all* of the resources allocated to an open Database object are released, set the Database object to Nothing.

When a procedure that declares a Database object is finished, the local Database objects are closed along with any open Recordset objects unless their Recordset variables are declared globally. Any pending updates are lost, and any pending transactions are rolled back without warning or error messages. Both Jet and Visual Basic manage the status and instance count of the Recordset and Database objects, so if you have Recordset objects open in other contexts, these remain open. The instance count is decremented, however, and the Database is closed and cleaned up once the instance count reaches 0.

The first database that is opened is assigned to Databases(0). The Name property setting of a database is a string that specifies the ODBC data source name or the pathname if you open a Jet database. The Connect property specifies the database type and other parameters used to connect to SQL Server external databases. For example, if you don't provide enough parameters in the *Connect* argument of the OpenDatabase method or if some of the parameters are incorrect, the user is prompted for correct information. Whatever is provided by the user and passed back from the ODBC driver is reapplied to the Connect property.

CAUTION

You should explicitly complete any pending transactions or edits and close Recordset objects and Database objects before you exit procedures that declare these object variables locally.

Examining the Connect property after the Database is open can be quite informative, and you can also do this in subsequent OpenDatabase operations. When you're opening SQL Server databases directly, the *Exclusive* argument is basically ignored. You can't gain exclusive access to a SQL server without logging in as server administrator and setting administrative options. The *ReadOnly* argument is observed, however, and you can use it to indicate your intention not to update any cursor that has been created. But this option doesn't prevent you from executing action queries that update rows independently of the read-only cursors that Jet creates.

The RecordsAffected property was introduced in Visual Basic 4.0. It contains the number of rows deleted, updated, or inserted in the running of an action query. When you use the Execute method to run a QueryDef, the RecordsAffected property setting is the number of records affected. The RecordsAffected property setting is the same as the value returned by the (obsolete) ExecuteSQL method.

Database Properties

Table 10-2 shows a list of database properties and describes what they do.

Table 10-2
Database Properties

Property	What It Does
Updatable	Indicates whether the database is read-only or read-write. Reflects the *ReadOnly* argument of the OpenDatabase method.
QueryTimeout	Determines the number of seconds that the underlying interface (in this case, ODBC) will wait for the current query to complete.
Connect	This connect string is built up on the basis of the parameters passed in the OpenDatabase method.
Transactions	This Boolean value indicates True if a database supports the transaction model (always True for SQL Server).
RecordsAffected	Shows how many rows were affected by the latest action query.

Database Methods

The Database object has a number of methods that are used to control the functionality of the queries to its tables. The CreateDynaset, CreateSnapshot, and ExecuteSQL methods are all outdated, which means that they aren't likely to be supported for much longer. (They are visible only if you use the "Compatibility" libraries.) Their functionality has been replaced with the OpenRecordset and Execute methods.

The CreateTableDef method can be used to create either Jet or SQL Server tables and is instrumental in creating attached SQL Server tables. Table 10-3 summarizes the current methods that apply to SQL Server. Table 10-4 lists obsolete methods that were supported in earlier versions of Jet, including Jet 2.5, but that are no longer supported in Jet 3.*x* and should be avoided.

NOTE In Jet 2.5, you can't close a database if transactions begun with BeginTrans are still pending. Use the CommitTrans or Rollback methods before trying to use the Close method. In Jet 3.*x*, however, using the Close method *forces* a close and a transaction rollback.

Table 10-3
Current DAO/Jet Methods Applicable to SQL Server

Method	What It Does
Close	Closes the database. Releases the connection to the pool.
CreateQueryDef	Creates a Jet QueryDef object in a Jet database. Can refer to SQL Server data by using TSQL queries.
CreateTableDef	Creates a new table definition, in either a Jet or a SQL Server database.
Execute	Runs a SQL action query.
OpenRecordset	Creates a cursor against Jet or SQL Server data.

Table 10-4
Obsolete DAO/Jet Database Methods

Method	What It Does
BeginTrans	Begins a new transaction. Basically equivalent to the TSQL command of the same name. Works only if the Transactions property is True. Convert to Workspace method.
CommitTrans	Equivalent to the TSQL Commit Transaction command. Convert to Workspace method.
Rollback	Equivalent to the TSQL Rollback command. Convert to Workspace method.
CreateDynaset	Creates a Dynaset object from a specified table or SQL query. Convert to OpenRecordset method.
CreateSnapshot	Creates a Snapshot object from a specified table or SQL query. Convert to OpenRecordset method.
ExecuteSQL	Executes a SQL query that doesn't return rows. Use Execute method.

TableDef Objects

TableDef objects hold descriptions of tables and their associated indexes. When you open a Database object directly, the TableDef object is populated as soon as it is referenced. When you open an attached table, the TableDef object is already populated. (This object is populated when the SQL Server table is first attached.)

Each Database object has only one TableDefs collection, which contains a TableDef object for each base table and view in the database. It can also include system tables. In turn, each TableDef object contains two collections: Fields and Indexes. You don't need to define the database before you open it; these structures will be filled in for you.

You can access (point to) individual TableDef objects either by using the name of the table or by using the TableDefs collection ordinal number. No matter how you open the database, the access syntax is the same:

```
Set MyDB = OpenDataBase("Work", False, False, Connect)
TableName$ = MyDb.TableDefs("Pigs").Name
TableName$ = MyDb.TableDefs(1).Name
TableName$ = MyDb.TableDefs!Pigs.Name
TableName$ = MyDb.TableDefs(1)
```

All of these address the same TableDef property (*Name*). The number of tables—TableDef objects defined for a particular database—can be returned through use of the Count property. As in all Visual Basic collections, the ordinal numbers range from 0 through Count -1.

TableDef Attributes

The TableDef object's Attribute property specifies characteristics of the table represented by the TableDef object and can be a sum of the Long constants shown in Table 10-5. Generally, you just examine these bits to see whether a particular option is enabled, since we rarely create SQL Server tables using this set of attributes. When you're creating attached tables, however, you can set the *dbAttachSavePWD* option to tell Jet that the password and login ID are to be saved in the linkage information.

Table 10-5
DAO/Jet TableDef Object Attribute Properties
Applicable to ODBC Data Sources

Constant	What It Does
dbAttachExclusive	For databases that use the Jet database engine, indicates that the table is an attached table opened for exclusive use
dbAttachSavePWD	For databases that use the Jet database engine, indicates that the user ID and password for the attached table are to be saved with the connection information
dbSystemObject	Indicates that the table is a system table provided by the Jet engine (read-only)
dbHiddenObject	Indicates that the table is a hidden table provided by the Jet engine (for temporary use; read-only)
dbAttachedTable	Indicates that the table is an attached table from a non-ODBC database, such as a Jet or Paradox database
dbAttachedODBC	Indicates that the table is an attached table from an ODBC database, such as SQL Server

TableDef Data Types

When Jet populates the TableDefs collection, it maps the SQL Server data types to equivalent DAO/Jet types—or tries to. Not all these assignments make sense, but remember that Jet isn't communicating with SQL Server directly; it gets everything through the ODBC driver, which has its own ideas about data type mapping. I'm not going to describe how to create a new table by using the DAO/Jet interface, where you must perform this mapping in reverse; you're better off using Visual Database Tools or SQL Enterprise Manager for this chore, and the Visual Basic documentation includes a short treatise on the subject.

When you describe a new table or access an existing table with the DAO/Jet TableDef object, you'll need to define (or at least understand) the data type and size for each type of data to be accessed. A big change from earlier versions of Visual Basic is the lack of CONSTANT.TXT files. Since Visual Basic now uses type libraries to manage all constants, you no longer need to manually import constant files. That's the good news. The bad news is that you must now conform to the defined constants when you create your code.

Table 10-6 shows how the Visual Basic Field object Type property maps to SQL Server data types. I thought it would also be interesting and useful to have a map showing how SQL Server data types would be represented in a Visual Basic TableDef and which SQL Server data types would be used for each of the defined FT_data types. To find out how existing SQL Server tables are mapped, I wrote

Table 10-6
Field Object Type Property Settings

Value	Setting	Description	SQL Server Data Type
1	dbBoolean	True/False	Bit
2	dbByte	Byte	TinyInt
3	dbInteger	Integer	SmallInt
4	dbLong	Long	Int
5	dbCurrency	Currency	SmallMoney, Decimal,[1] Numeric
6	dbSingle	Single	Real[2]
7	dbDouble	Double	Real
8[3]	dbDate	Date/Time	DateTime
10	dbText	0–255 string bytes	Char
11	dbLongBinary	Long binary	(OLE Image object) 0–2 GB binary
12	dbMemo	0–2 GB strings	Text, VarBinary, TimeStamp[4]

1. The dbCurrency type can map to any of these currency-type SQL Server data types.
2. The dbSingle type did not get mapped by any SQL Server data type but would be recognized as a Real SQL Server data type.
3. Value 9 is currently undefined by Visual Basic.
4. The dbMemo type is used when any of these three types is referenced.

a small application that dumped the mapping for each of the defined SQL Server 4.2 and 6.x data types. (Most of the applications I used to create the *Hitchhiker's Guide* are on the companion CD, and most of them are very simple, but they do show how I arrived at my conclusions.) There were no great differences between the two in most cases, but there were some subtle ones that you should be aware of. (See Table 10-7.) Notice that reported size doesn't always reflect the amount of space used to store the data. Because all columns were defined with their default lengths, the size does reflect how much space is reserved for the data type—or, in some cases, the maximum space that can be allocated.

Table 10-7
SQL Server Data Types Mapped to DAO/Jet Data Types

SQL Server 6.0 Data Type	Value	Reported Size	Visual Basic Data Type
Binary	11	255	Long Binary (OLE Object)
Bit	1	1	Yes/No
Char	10	255	Text (string)
DateTime	8	16	Date/Time
Float	7	8	Double
Image	11	2147483647	Long Binary (OLE Object)
Int	4	4	Long
Money	5	21	Currency
Real	$7/6^1$	8/4	Double/Single
SmallDateTime	8	16	Date/Time
SmallInt	3	2	Integer
SmallMoney	5	$21/12^2$	Currency
Sysname	10	30	Text (string)
Text	12	2147483647	Memo
TimeStamp	12	8	Long Binary (OLE Object)
TinyInt	2	1	Byte
Varbinary	12	255	Memo
VarChar	10	255	Text (string)
Decimal[3]	5	20	Currency
Numeric	5	18	Currency
Identity	4	4	Long

1. The Real SQL Server data type is reported as type "7" (double) when a SQL Server 6.0 database is read but as type "6" (single) when a SQL Server 4.2 database is read.
2. The size reported by Visual Basic is 21 for SQL Server 6.0 but only 12 when a SQL Server 4.2 database is being mapped.
3. The Decimal, Numeric, and Identity columns were all new for SQL Server 6.0. The Identity column isn't a specific data type, but I thought it would be interesting to show how it is mapped.

Table 10-8 shows data type mapping with the Visual Basic DAO/Jet interface to create a new SQL Server table on SQL Server 4.2 and 6.0. The table contains each of the Visual Basic 4.0 data types. Notice that the only difference between the two versions involves the dbCurrency and dbSingle data types. This mapping should be the same when Access is used to create a SQL Server table.

Table 10-8
Visual Basic DAO/Jet Data Types Mapped to SQL Server

Visual Basic Data Type	SQL Server 6.0 Data Type Created	SQL Server 4.2 Data Type Created
dbDate	DateTime	DateTime
dbText	VarChar (255)	VarChar (255)
dbMemo	Text	Text
dbBoolean	Bit	Bit
dbInteger	SmallInt	SmallInt
dbLong	Int	Int
dbCurrency	Decimal (18, 0)	Money
dbSingle	Real	Float
dbDouble	Float	Float
dbByte	TinyInt	TinyInt
dbLongBinary	Image	Image

The results haven't changed much from those for Visual Basic 3.0. Because SQL Server 4.2 supports 17 data types and SQL Server 6.0 supports 20 data types, not all of them can be created by Visual Basic, which supports only 11. All three integer types are supported now that the dbByte data type is fully supported. Both types of floating-point numbers are supported as well. Binary, VarBinary, SmallMoney, SmallDateTime, and TimeStamp columns could *not* be created, however. Most of these are of relatively minor importance in the bigger picture, since they are represented by similar data types that can easily be substituted. But the inability to create TimeStamp columns is a real problem if you use Jet to create your SQL Server tables.

NOTE Yep, you guessed it. I haven't spent a lot of time updating the DAO chapters for SQL Server 7.0. Since DAO hasn't changed much for SQL Server 7.0, I expect that these tables will sync up pretty closely to the SQL Server 6.5 settings. The routines are on the CD, so if you feel a pressing need to remap these settings, go for it.

Field Objects

Field objects are used in a variety of ways to define or declare the columns defined in tables, indexes, and Jet queries and relations. Row data can be reached (if the Field object is part of a Recordset object) through the Value property. Each Field object is maintained in a Fields collection associated with the TableDef, Index, QueryDef, or Relation object. The properties of a Field object that are available in accessing SQL Server data are shown in Table 10-9.

Table 10-9
DAO/Jet Field Object Properties

Property	What It Does
Name	Indicates name of the SQL Server table column.
Size	Indicates size of the field. This is a Long value. Size is determined by the Type property. It bears no relationship to the size of the data held in this field.
Type	Indicates data type of the field.
Value	Holds the data for this element, if this Field object belongs to a Recordset object.
AllowZeroLength	Indicates whether a zero-length string (" ") is a valid setting for the Value property of a Field object with a Text or Memo data type.
Attributes	Indicates one or more characteristics of a Field object.
DataUpdatable	Indicates whether the data in the field represented by a Field object is updateable.
Required	Indicates whether a Field or Index object requires a non-Null value. This maps to the NULL or NOT NULL declaration.
SourceField	Indicates the name of the field that is the original source of the data for a Field object. Used for attached tables.
SourceTable	Indicates the name of the table that is the original source of the data for a Field object. Used for attached tables.

TIP One Field object attribute that (still) didn't make it to online Help is dbRandomIncrField, which indicates a counter-type field that is generated randomly. By setting this attribute bit (64), you can create new tables, including Identity columns, using the DAO/Jet interface.

There are a number of ways—I count at least eight—of referring to the data Value property of the current row's Field object. The Value property of the current Fields collection can be addressed by ordinal number, directly:

```
Ms$ = Rs.Fields(1)
```

Or it can be addressed by ordinal number, indirectly:

```
N% = 1
Ms$ = Rs.Fields(n%)
```

It can also be addressed by column name, directly:

```
Ms$ = Rs.Fields("FootSize")
```

And it can be addressed by column name, indirectly:

```
N$ = "FootSize"
Ms$ = Rs.Fields(N$)
```

You can use the Recordset object's default collection and property (Fields.Value), so you don't really need to reference the Field object directly at all:

```
Ms$ = Rs(1)
Ms$ = Rs(N%)
Ms$ = Rs(N$)
```

Using the "bang" (!) syntax is the fastest way:

```
Ms$ = Rs!FootSize
```

Clear? Many of the examples in the documentation use the Visual Basic feature of not having to include the default property that's being referenced. For example, it's no longer necessary to code *Text1.Text = "SomeString"* because *Text1 = "SomeString"* does the same thing.

TIP What's the fastest way to address Field objects? Well, consider that all "late"-bound methods must perform additional lookup work at run time—each time the field is referenced. A late-bound Field object is one in which you use a variable to reference a column. I expect that you'll find using the ordinal number is the fastest.

NOTE The OrdinalPosition property for fields in a Recordset object will differ according to whether the dbSQLPassThrough option is used. Jet can't control the order in which columns are maintained in ODBC tables.

Index Objects

The DAO/Jet Index object defines an index for a table. These objects are kept in the Indexes collection. An Index object contains a Fields collection, which in turn contains one or more Field objects designating the columns that define the index keys. A table can have several indexes, but at least one must be defined as unique in order to satisfy Jet. When you're creating new indexes in code, you can examine or change Index object properties up to the point where they are appended to the Indexes collection. After that, they are read-only. The properties of the Index object that are of interest to SQL Server front-end developers are shown in Table 10-10. (Other index properties don't apply to SQL Server front-end applications.)

Table 10-10
DAO/Jet Index Object Properties

Property	What It Does
Name	Names the index.
Fields	Contains a string holding one or more field names that refer to the keys for a table. Multiple fields are separated by a semicolon (;).
Clustered	Doesn't apply to ODBC indexes, just to Paradox.
IgnoreNulls	Doesn't apply to ODBC indexes.
Primary	Indicates whether an Index object represents a primary index for a table. At least one Index object must have Primary = True to support updatability.
Required	Indicates whether an Index object requires a non-Null value. Because indexes in SQL Server require non-Null values, this should always be True.
Unique	Indicates whether this index is to be unique. (At least one of the indexes must be unique.)

Tables and Indexes

One of the most common questions that Visual Basic developers ask when they're using DAO objects is, "Why can't I change the data in the tables?" The principal reason you can't is the lack of unique indexes, or the lack of a designated set of fields uniquely identifying each row. If SQL Server data is to be modified by DAO objects, the table or tables used to create the Recordset object must have unique indexes. Because SQL Server doesn't require indexes of any kind, it's entirely possible to have tables containing duplicate rows; but you don't need SQL Server indexes to update tables with Jet—only a field or combination of fields that uniquely identifies the rows.

TIP It seems that rebuilding databases doesn't always restore the primary key index—at least not to ODBC's satisfaction. Before you send embarrassing mail, be sure that a primary key is established for the table that you're trying to update via ODBC.

A powerful aspect of DAO/Jet's index implementation is how it deals with external indexes. For example, you can designate a field in an attached table or view as the "unique" identifier. On the basis of this designated field, Jet then assumes that SQL Server will maintain the unique characteristics of the row, or of a combination of several fields, *and* allow you to update the data.

Despite this flexibility on the part of SQL Server, in order to use Visual Basic's DAO objects to do any data modifications, you'll have to establish unique indexes on the SQL Server tables that are to be accessed. This might mean a general redesign of one or more tables and their ability to accept duplicate rows—or at least rows with duplicate primary keys.

Creating or Adding Tables and Indexes

If you want to use Visual Basic DAO objects to create new tables and indexes, there is a set of objects and methods for doing so. But unless you're really bored and need something to occupy your time, there are better and easier ways to perform DDL housekeeping—such as using Visual Database Tools or SQL Enterprise Manager. You'll also encounter a number of limitations if you try to create a table using Visual Basic's DAO objects. For example, you'll be able to create only 11 of the 20 supported SQL Server data types. You won't be able to create TimeStamp columns or use any of the SQL Server 6.*x* constraint types. You won't be able to set up any SQL Server 6.*x* relationships, replication, or any of the other features not directly exposed by Jet. All the indexes created are established as nonclustered, so setting up a specific data ordering sequence isn't an option. Of course, there's nothing to stop you from sending TSQL queries or SQL statements via the Execute method to create the tables.

The following SQL query could define DAO code for creating a table. Note that we are able to establish a TimeStamp column and to make sure that the Text data type and Age columns are defined as permitting nulls:

```
CREATE TABLE Implements
(Name char(30) NOT NULL,
 Type char(5) NOT NULL,
 Age SmallInt NULL,
 Location char(30) NOT NULL,
 Condition Text NULL,
 Working bit NOT NULL,
 TIMESTAMP timestamp NULL)
```

Now for the DAO code. Keep in mind that there is no way to set the null characteristics of the fields. The Required property has no effect, and we can't create the TimeStamp column. The syntax is tighter than in the DAO 1.1 interface, but it still falls short of being able to create SQL Server tables, as shown on the following page.

```
Private Sub MakeNewTable_click()
Dim db As Database
Set db = OpenDatabase _
    ("biblio", 0, 0, "odbc;uid=;pwd=;database=biblio")
Dim tb As TableDef
Dim fd As Field
Dim ix As Index
db.TableDefs.Refresh
Set tb = db.CreateTableDef(Name:="DAOExample")
Tb.Fields.Append tb.CreateField _
    (Name:="Name", Type:=dbText, Size:=30)
Tb.Fields.Append tb.CreateField _
    (Name:="Type", Type:=dbText, Size:=5)
Tb.Fields.Append tb.CreateField(Name:="Age", Type:=dbInteger)
Tb.Fields.Append tb.CreateField _
    (Name:="Location", Type:=dbText, Size:=30)
Tb.Fields.Append tb.CreateField(Name:="Condition", Type:=dbMemo)
Tb.Fields.Append tb.CreateField(Name:="Working", Type:=dbBoolean)
db.TableDefs.Append tb
db.Close
End Sub
```

NOTE Many of the samples in this book use databases that are on the companion CD. See Appendix A for information on how to set up the database samples.

Configuring and Tuning the Jet Engine

The Windows Registry Database

Understanding
Jet Engine Options

Before we plunge directly into the whole topic of configuring and tuning the Microsoft Jet database engine, let's go over some basics about how the Microsoft Windows Registry works. Armed with a rudimentary understanding of how the Registry works, you'll find it easier to tell what's what when it comes time to make a few changes in the Registry.

The Windows Registry Database

One of the highlights of the Microsoft Windows 95/98 adventure is the Windows Registry database. The Registry is used to keep the thousands of settings for every imaginable option in the operating system and for every 32-bit application that runs under its control. Your 16-bit or 32-bit applications can still use INI file settings for whatever purposes you choose, but the Data Access Objects (DAO) and the ODBC drivers now depend heavily on the Registry in all 32-bit systems.

TIP For Jet 2.5 in 16-bit applications, initialization settings are saved in the VB.INI (or <APPNAME>.INI) file. Before these option settings can take effect, you must ensure that your application creates an application-specific INI file containing them and that it uses the DBEngine.INIPath property to point to the file. Going to the trouble of creating an INI file won't do much good if you don't tell Jet where to find it.

Registry Scope

Let's assume you're going to work with a 32-bit application that needs to initialize some Jet engine options. If so, your settings can be applied on either of two levels. First, they can be applied *systemwide*. Changes will affect all instances of your application, as well as each instance of the Jet engine used by applications running on the machine. If you choose this option, you need to modify the HKEY_LOCAL_MACHINE tree, especially if only one Jet-based application is running on a workstation and all the applications on that workstation can run properly using the same HKEY_LOCAL_MACHINE tree values. I don't recommend that you use systemwide settings, however, since these settings will be used as the defaults unless an application specifically overrides them with its own settings. Be careful what you change here, unless you enjoy getting calls in the middle of the night from irate users. Second, your settings can be applied so that they affect only the *currently logged-on user*. In this case, you need to reference the HKEY_CURRENT_USER folder, especially if you expect to be running more than one Jet-based application on your workstation. Generally, each Microsoft Visual Basic application should use settings in a tree that it provides for itself. If you already have such a tree for your application, you should add a Jet section to it—something like this:

The Jet database engine, not unlike the Microsoft SQL Server engine, has a small myriad of options that permit you to configure it for different application requirements. Ignoring these settings is like building a race car from components bought at Kmart: the car will work, but it won't be particularly competitive outside the parking lot.

HKEY_CURRENT_USER\Software\Visual Basic\5.0*appname*\Jet\3.5\...

You can also have settings that apply just to *one application* but that are *unique for every user*. For this option, you use your own application-specific path, but use HKEY_LOCAL_MACHINE in place of HKEY_CURRENT_USER. Every logged-on user will get his or her own set of keys for this application.

Remember that the Jet engine is shared by other applications—not just Visual Basic, but also by the entire Microsoft Office suite of tools, Microsoft Visual C++, and third-party applications. Most, if not all, applications will have access to DAO objects and the Jet engine. Therefore, any changes you make to global engine settings might very easily disturb other applications, just as their settings might disturb yours.

Once your application starts, you have an instance of the DAO/Jet DBEngine object assigned to your application. Basically, separate code segments are created for you, and all your specific parameters are maintained there. As a result, what other applications do has no immediate effect on your running application once it begins. If you change the initialization settings used by some other application, however, or if some other application changes your settings, the results can be unpredictable. How do you solve this problem? As a general rule, you never change the global Jet engine initialization settings; you create separate settings for your application. And if you have several related applications that run on the same machine, you can share initialization settings.

Creating and Using New Registry Keys

To establish a place in the Registry database where your settings can be saved, you must open the Windows Registry by using the REGEDIT application and then add the required folders and individual key entries. Although Visual Basic supplies a few intrinsic functions for altering the Registry, you can't use them to change numeric values; you can change only string settings. This means that you must work through the Windows APIs to make the changes, make the changes manually, or find a third-party source for a control or dynamic-link library (DLL) that makes these changes.

When you're working in Visual Basic Design mode, the Jet engine searches the Registry for ODBC initialization settings in the following location:

HKEY_LOCAL_MACHINE\SOFTWARE\Microsoft\Jet\3.5\Engines\ODBC

No, that location hasn't changed with Visual Basic 6.0. The contents of that location are shown in Figure 11-1.

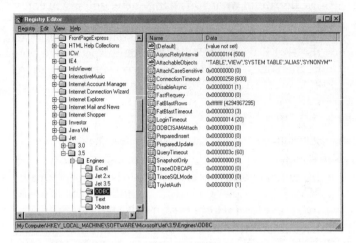

Figure 11-1 *ODBC initialization settings in the Windows Registry*

Because Jet uses HKEY_LOCAL_MACHINE as a default, you must change the Registry path by using the DBEngine object's INIPath property to point to your application's private Registry or INI file. Once you get your application working, you need to create an application key that can be installed in the Windows Registry on any system where the application is expected to run—that is, on the *target system*. For example, you can create a key for an application named SQLFrontEnd in the following Registry location:

HKEY_CURRENT_USER\SOFTWARE\SQLFrontEnd\Jet\3.5\Engines\ODBC

When you're working with Jet-based ODBC applications, you need to make your ODBC settings in a newly created ODBC section of the Jet\3.5\Engines Registry folder. As we already know, making changes to the Registry can be dangerous, especially changes to the HKEY_LOCAL_MACHINE Registry: other applications are going to be depending on these settings, and if you mess up the Registry, your system is toast. But since it's a good idea to create the default-override Registry entries in a separate Registry key, you must discipline yourself to set the INIPath property each time you start a Jet application. Locate your new key under the HKEY_CURRENT_USER Registry, and set the DBEngine.INIPath property to this location. It's also good programming practice to establish this key on your development machine. Then, each time you start a new DAO/Jet application, you can make sure you reference an application-specific Registry location as the first line of code in the Form_Load event procedure.

Once you establish another key location, be sure to keep the last three keys the same. For example, if your application is named SQLApp, you can create a new entry as follows:

HKEY_LOCAL_MACHINE\SOFTWARE\MyApps\SQLApp\Jet\3.5\

If you use a generally accepted technique when you create Registry keys, what you create might not clash with another application that your user happens to be running on your system. But anytime you blindly create a Registry entry, you might inadvertently overlay settings established by another application—perhaps even one of your own.

To use this new key, set your INIPath property before any other DAO/Jet references in your application. Keep in mind that you can't set up the Data control to start automatically, because it starts the Jet engine before your first chance to set the INIPath in the Form_Load event procedure. To set the INIPath property to the new location in code, use the following syntax:

```
DBEngine.INIPath = _
    "HKEY_LOCAL_MACHINE\SOFTWARE\MyApps\SQLApp\Jet\3.5"
```

To create an ODBC key and establish a few values, take the following steps. (If you plan to make changes or additions to the non-ODBC key settings, simply add the setting key values to the Engines key; this key is where Jet looks for non-ISAM and non-ODBC settings.)

1. Run the Windows application REGEDIT. Once the application starts, and before you do anything else, you should back up the current Registry by choosing Export Registry File from the Registry menu. This backup file might be helpful when it comes to repairing any inadvertent damage. But if *you* never make mistakes, move on to the next step. Just don't call me at 4:00 a.m. to complain that your system is dripping solder.

2. When you've backed up the Registry, examine the initial REGEDIT window, which displays the top-level Registry keys, as shown here:

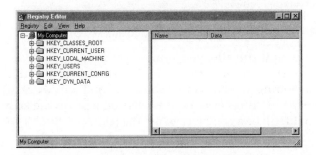

3. Click the plus sign (+) to the left of the HKEY_LOCAL_MACHINE icon. This action exposes the next level of keys.

4. Click the plus signs for SOFTWARE, for Microsoft, for Jet, for 3.5, and finally for Engines. This exposes the list of Jet engine options that you chose when Visual Basic was installed. See whether the ODBC key is already installed. If it is, you need to decide how you want to proceed. Do you want to change the existing settings or create new ones of your own? If you decide to change them, skip down to Step 6. If you want

to create your own key, go up to the HKEY_CURRENT_USER key and create the following set of keys by choosing New Key from the Edit menu. Be sure to substitute the name of your application EXE for *AppName*:

SOFTWARE\MyApps*AppName*\Jet\3.5\Engines

5. Now create a new key under the Engines key. Enter *ODBC* for the name. You now have an ODBC key.

6. Select the ODBC key under Engines, and choose New DWORD Value from the Edit menu. Name the new value *QueryTimeout*. You now have an ODBC key value entry.

Double-click on the new ODBC QueryTimeout entry. The Edit DWORD Value dialog box appears. Use this dialog box to set the new QueryTimeout value to 60 (hex 3C).

Perform Steps 5 and 6 for each default override setting you need to create. When your work on the Registry is complete, it's a good idea to back up again. You can choose to back up either the whole Registry or just the part you changed. For now, export just the part you changed—the ODBC key.

The easy way out

Now that you've waded through the preceding steps, grab a towel and take a look at the exported file you just created. The one I created in preparing this guide looks like this:

```
REGEDIT4
[HKEY_LOCAL_MACHINE\SOFTWARE\Microsoft\Jet\3.5\Engines\ODBC]
"QueryTimeout"=dword:0000003c
"LoginTimeout"=dword:00000020
"ConnectionTimeout"=dword:00000258
"AttachableObjects"=
    "'TABLE','VIEW','SYSTEM TABLE','ALIAS','SYNONYM'"
```

Since you can also edit this file, you could create your own REGEDIT import file and use it to set up the Registry when you install an application on the target machine (assuming, of course, that the keys don't already exist). If you install these keys over existing keys, your new version replaces the existing set. All that said, it would still be a good idea to use the HKEY_CURRENT_USER key instead.

Be sure to follow the format shown here, including the use of hexadecimal values. Need to convert them? Use the Windows Calculator. It has a built-in hex option. (Unless you own an old Pentium, it ought to get most of the math right.)

Testing a new key

To make sure your new Registry key works, try a few lines of code. The following Visual Basic procedure sets the location for a new Registry entry in HKEY_CURRENT_USER and tests for a correct QueryTimeout value:

```
Private Sub Command1_Click()
DBEngine.IniPath = _
    "HKEY_CURRENT_USER\SOFTWARE\MyApps\SQLApp\Jet\3.5"
Dim db As Database
Set db = OpenDatabase _
    ("biblio", 0, 0,"odbc;uid=;pwd=;database=biblio")
Debug.Print db.QueryTimeout
End Sub
```

I checked this out, and the INI file settings, which were taken from the Registry, were preempted for the new value set in the Registry, despite what the Help topic says for the QueryTimeout property of the Database object. I did note that neither the INI file settings nor the Registry settings had any effect on the default QueryTimeout value when a 16-bit Visual Basic application was running.

The Registry: A Quick Review

Here are the highlights of the material we've covered on the Registry:

- You must back up the Registry before you make any changes. You might even print out a copy of the backup file and keep it handy for reference or emergency repairs.

- If you need to make changes to the global Jet ODBC Registry entries so that you *don't* have to set the DBEngine.INIPath property, make your Registry changes in HKEY_LOCAL_MACHINE\SOFTWARE\Microsoft\Jet\3.5\Engines\ODBC.

- You should establish a new set of keys for each application you create under HKEY_CURRENT_USER\SOFTWARE\...\...\Jet\3.5\Engines\ODBC.

- Set your DBEngine.INIPath property before using any Jet objects. Be sure to set it to the ...\Jet\3.5 key, not to the ...\Jet\3.5\Engines\ODBC key.

- Once the DBEngine object is started by your application, subsequent changes to the Registry have no effect on your application. In Design mode, the DBEngine object is restarted each time your application starts, so changes you make to the Registry between runs take effect the next time you click the Start button.

- Jet functionality and registration methods are different in 16-bit and 32-bit platforms, although the settings themselves are equivalent (for ODBC, anyway).

Understanding Jet Engine Options

The following sections describe initialization and ISAM format settings for both 16-bit (Jet 2.5) and 32-bit (Jet 3.x) Microsoft ODBC drivers.

Microsoft ODBC Driver Initialization Settings

When the Jet database engine is first initialized, it reads the ODBC initialization settings shown in Table 11-1. Changing the settings has no effect on the engine once it's started. These settings are the same for both Jet 2.5 and Jet 3.x, but the Jet 2.5 settings are located in an appropriate INI file, and the Jet 3.x settings are located in an appropriate Registry key. When stored in the Registry, all these settings are described as DWORD values, with the exception of the AttachableObjects and Win32 settings, which are strings.

Table 11-1
ODBC Initialization Settings

Setting	Description
AsyncRetryInterval	The number of milliseconds between polls to determine whether the server is done processing a query. This entry is used for asynchronous processing only. The default is 500.
AttachableObjects	A list of server object types to which attaching will be allowed. The default is 'TABLE', 'VIEW', 'SYSTEM TABLE', 'ALIAS', 'SYNONYM'.
AttachCaseSensitive	An indicator of whether to match table names exactly when attaching. Values are 0 (attach the first table matching the specified name, regardless of case) and 1 (attach a table only if the name matches exactly). The default is 0.
ConnectionTimeout	The number of seconds a cached connection can remain idle before timing out. The default is 600 (10 minutes).
DisableAsync	An indicator of whether to force synchronous query execution. Values are 0 (use asynchronous query execution if possible) and 1 (force synchronous query execution). The default is 0.
FatBlastRows	(Introduced in Jet 3.5) Number of rows to "FatBlast." 0 = don't FatBlast, < 0 = (default) handle automatically, > 0 = number of rows. Determines how Jet caches "fat" cursors.
FatBlastTimeout	(Introduced in Jet 3.5) If main query takes longer than this setting (in seconds), don't use FatBlast. Determines how Jet caches "fat" cursors.
FastRequery	An indicator of whether to use a prepared SELECT statement for parameterized queries. Values are 0 (no) and 1 (yes). The default is 0.

Setting	Description
LoginTimeout	The number of seconds a login attempt can continue before timing out. The default is 20.
ODBCISAMAttach	(Introduced in Jet 3.5) Used to gate access to "Simba" and "Pecos" drivers. (These were predecessors to the Jet ODBC "Brazos" drivers.) If set to 0, these drivers aren't supported except from Microsoft Excel and Text IISAMs.
PreparedInsert	An indicator of whether to use a prepared INSERT statement that inserts data in all columns. Values are 0 (use a custom INSERT statement that inserts only non-Null values) and 1 (use a prepared INSERT statement). The default is 0. Using prepared INSERT statements can cause Null values to overwrite server defaults and can cause triggers to execute on columns that weren't explicitly inserted.
PreparedUpdate	An indicator of whether to use a prepared UPDATE statement that updates data in all columns. Values are 0 (use a custom UPDATE statement that sets only columns that have changed) and 1 (use a prepared UPDATE statement). The default is 0. Using prepared UPDATE statements can cause triggers to execute on unchanged columns.
QueryTimeout	The number of seconds Jet (ODBC) waits for a query to return the first row of the result set. The default is 60.
SnapshotOnly	An indicator of whether Recordset objects are forced to be of the snapshot type. Values are 0 (allow dynasets) and 1 (force snapshots only). The default is 0.
TraceODBCAPI	An indicator of whether to trace ODBC API calls in ODBCAPI.TXT. Values are 0 (no) and 1 (yes). The default is 1.
TraceSQLMode	An indicator of whether the Jet database engine will trace SQL statements sent to an ODBC data source in SQLOUT.TXT. Values are 0 (no) and 1 (yes). The default is 0. This entry is interchangeable with SQLTraceMode.
TryJetAuth/JetTryAuth	An indicator of whether to try using the Microsoft Access username and password to log in to SQL Server before prompting. Values are 0 (no) and 1 (yes). At one time, this was "JetTryAuth" (and it is still so in the Jet Database Engine Programmer's Guide). The default is 1.
Win32	The location of ODBC32.DLL. The full pathname is determined at the time of installation.

The Details

In the following sections, I'll try to shed some additional light on several of the more important Jet engine options, with special attention to their use with ODBC connections and queries.

AsyncRetryInterval, DisableAsync

The Visual Basic 4.0 DAO/Jet interface doesn't support asynchronous operations, so these options are of no consequence except when you're using the Data control—which supports some asynchronous operations, right? Nope. Jet *does* support asynchronous operations behind the scenes, when it sends queries to the ODBC Driver Manager. It polls for completion on the basis of the AsyncRetryInterval setting. Too-frequent polling slows the workstation down, but not polling frequently enough can also slow the response to completed queries.

AttachableObjects

You shouldn't touch this option unless you need to limit the types of SQL Server objects available to your application.

AttachCaseSensitive

When working with case-sensitive SQL servers, you might consider setting this option to prevent any case shifting during name mungeing.

ConnectionTimeout

This is a must-set option: the default of 10 minutes is far too long. Jet is now better about closing unneeded connections than it was in Visual Basic 3.0. Until the timeout period expires, however, Jet doesn't drop idle SQL Server connections—even after you close your Database object. Not only that, but the engine must remain idle long enough for the connection handler to get a chance to time out. That's why you need to set the timeout value to 1 and then use the DBEngine.Idle method to give Jet a chance to catch up and drop idle connections. I like to set the ConnectionTimeout option as high as 1 to 2 minutes and as low as 1 to 10 seconds; the setting depends on how many users are fighting for connections and on how often I open and close my Database objects. Setting the ConnectionTimeout option to 0 disables the timeout, so connections never close—been there, seen that; no, thanks.

FastRequery

Apparently, whenever the ODBC driver submits a query, this option tells the driver to build one or more temporary stored procedures. The use of temporary stored procedures does make subsequent execution of a parameter query faster—assuming that the query lends itself to this form of automation. But the problem with this option is that your application might need to submit some parameter queries that lend themselves to the creation of ODBC prepared statements, as well as some queries that do not. Because this is a DBEngine option, not an option on the OpenRecordset or CreateQueryDef methods, you have to decide before your application starts whether all parameter queries are to be converted to SQL Server temporary stored procedures. The ODBC 2.5 drivers and SQL Server 6.x support temporary stored procedures as part of the overall server design. Stored procedures, instead of being placed in the working database, are all placed in TempDB space. That's the good news. The bad news is that your TempDB space, which also stores server-side cursors, hasn't grown since you started using the new drivers, and it now needs to be larger— a whole lot larger. In SQL Server 7.0, these TempDB stored procedures aren't created at all—they're not needed.

PreparedInsert, PreparedUpdate

These options are very important to SQL Server front-end applications that don't use dbSQLPassThrough to send INSERT or UPDATE statements to SQL Server. I rarely allow Jet to update tables directly, and most of my database changes are done via SQL Server–based stored procedures, so this option doesn't make me lose any sleep.

QueryTimeout

This option can be set through the Database object's QueryTimeout property. In 32-bit Visual Basic, the default value can be set in the Registry. In 16-bit Visual Basic, the Registry and INI file settings have no effect on the 60-second timeout; you can change the value only by specifically setting the property after each Database object is opened. The ODBCTimeout property is used for executing QueryDef objects. Like the QueryTimeout property, it determines how long Jet waits for an ODBC query to return its first row. It defaults to 60 seconds or to the value assigned to the QueryTimeout property.

SnapshotOnly

Since you get to choose what kind of Recordset object is created through the dbOpenxxx options in the OpenRecordset method, the need for this option is unclear. If anyone finds a good reason for it, let me know.

TraceODBCAPI

This option lets you review the lowest-level interface to the ODBC driver. The data file created is named SQLOUT.TXT, and its location is hard-coded to be saved in the current directory. In Design mode, this is generally where the VB.EXE is loaded. This option can be very handy when it comes to investigating how Jet has parsed out a chosen query. Basically, it lets you eavesdrop on the conversation from SQL Server to ODBC to Jet.

The TraceODBCAPI option produces exactly the same output as the ODBC DSN option introduced in Visual Basic 5.0, which can be enabled through Control Panel's 32-bit ODBC icon. This Control Panel application enables you to specify how the ODBC Driver Manager will trace calls to ODBC functions and where the file will be located, so you don't have to go looking for it. On Windows 3.*x* and the Windows on Windows subsystem of Microsoft Windows NT, the ODBC Driver Manager traces calls on an all-or-nothing basis—it either traces the calls made by all applications or doesn't trace calls made by any. On Windows NT, the ODBC Driver Manager traces calls on an application-by-application basis. This Control Panel option can be enabled quite easily and doesn't affect the Registry. It also has an auto-shutoff feature. When an application terminates ODBC, the Driver Manager checks whether tracing has been selected. If so, the Driver Manager stops tracing calls to ODBC functions and clears the Trace ODBC Calls check box. To start tracing again, you must reselect the Trace ODBC Calls check box and restart your application.

TraceSQLMode or SQLTraceMode

This option is a summary of the SQL queries submitted to the ODBC driver. It indicates the ODBC API call used and the SQL syntax, as shown in the following example. I created this trace by executing the OpenRecordset method with *"SELECT * from Phones ORDER BY Email."* The first query extracts configuration information; the second performs the data retrieval.

```
SQLExecDirect: SELECT Config, nValue FROM MSysConf
SQLExecDirect: SELECT "First_Name" ,"Last_Name" ,
    "Section" ,"Email" ,"Company" ,"Site" ,"Location" ,
    "Area_Code" ,"Phone" ,"Changed"  FROM "dbo"."Phones"
    ORDER BY "Email"
```

TryJetAuth

When you set up a new Workspace object, you must provide a user ID and password to gate access to secure Jet databases. Once you set the Workspace object user ID and password, however, Jet also uses these values when it attempts to open connections to remote ODBC databases such as SQL Server. If these values don't match those intended for SQL Server, you trip a trappable error. To turn off this automatic authentication, simply set the TryJetAuth option to 0, or always provide a user ID and password in your connect strings.

Tuning *MSysConf*

MSysConf is a Jet-specific, server-based configuration table with the structure shown in Table 11-2. This table's existence is purely optional. Immediately after connecting to a server, Jet executes a query to read its contents. If any errors occur, Jet ignores them and assumes that *MSysConf* doesn't exist. And it won't, unless you add it to each database to be accessed by Jet, either directly or via attached tables.

Table 11-2
The *MSysConf* Server Table

Column Name	Data Type	Description
Config	SmallInt	The number of the configuration option
chValue	VarChar(255)	The text value of the configuration option
nValue	Integer	The integer value of the configuration option
Comments	VarChar(255)	A description of the configuration option

The Visual Basic 4.0 documentation mentions only one Config value, but there are actually several, as shown in Table 11-3. (Online Help does list all the values.) The background population options (Config value 102 and Config value 103) allow an administrator to control how fast Jet fetches rows of a query during idle time. When the fetch delay is high, network traffic is reduced but read locks are left on pages longer. With the delay set lower, locking is reduced and the move to the last record in a result set is speeded up, but network traffic increases. The chunk size option provides an ever finer level of control. These options are different from the engine Registry entries because they can be set database by database, whereas the Registry entries apply to all operations after the engine starts.

Table 11-3
Config and nValue Settings in the *MSysConf* Table

Config	nValue	Meaning
101	0	Doesn't allow storing of user ID and password in attachments.
101	1	Allows storing of user ID and password in attachments (the default).
102	D	Jet delays D seconds between background chunk fetches (default=10).
103	N	Jet fetches N rows on each background chunk fetch (default=100).

Config = 101

This value permits embedded passwords in attached tables. If the corresponding nValue isn't 0, it's ignored. But if the nValue is 0, Jet will never store user ID and password information in tables attached from this database. If you set the dbAttachSavePWD attribute when you attach a table, or if you choose to save the login ID and password locally when you attach a SQL Server table with Microsoft Access, and if the nValue is True (not 0), the attribute is ignored, as are any embedded user ID and password values. In this case, the user is forced to include a user ID and password when using the attached table for the first time or complying with integrated security restrictions. Jet caches the user ID and password for subsequent access. This option was created to permit database administrators who are concerned about security to eliminate the possibility of unauthorized users gaining access to data by using another person's computer. The query Jet uses to read this table contains the following syntax:

```
SELECT ... FROM MSysConf ...
```

The table must be publicly accessible via this exact syntax, if the table exists at all. (On a server that supports multiple databases, *MSysConf* might or might not exist in a given database.)

Config = 102

This value sets the delay between fetches of background chunks. With this option set, Jet delays nValue seconds between background chunk fetches (default = 10) when asynchronous processing is enabled. The Visual Basic Data control uses this option when populating record sets in the background.

Config = 103

This value sets fetch size for chunk data. When this option is set, Jet fetches nValue rows on each background chunk fetch. This option is coupled with Config value 102 and asynchronous operations.

NOTE For more information on Jet database programming, see the *Microsoft Jet Database Engine Programmer's Guide, Second Edition*, from Microsoft Press.

12

Using DAO/Jet to Get Connected

f you've been paying attention, you'll know by now that every front-end application needs to establish one or more connections to Microsoft SQL Server to gain access to data. But getting connected isn't as simple as it might seem on first inspection. Some SQL Server development shops spend considerable time and effort developing fairly sophisticated connection managers so that their applications won't have to be bothered with making, releasing, and sharing connections. No matter what type of data access interface you choose, however, connecting is a task that either your code or Microsoft Jet has to manage successfully. Jet 3.0 added considerable logic to its connection management code, making it consume far less connection resources and making it smarter about SQL Server connection issues. For example, this addition allowed the Jet connection manager to support domain-managed integrated security—if you set the right switches. Unfortunately, it doesn't deal with any of the state issues we talked about in Chapter 6.

To make your life easier, keep these points in mind when you establish connections with Jet:

- Unless you want the ODBC Driver Manager to take over the connection process and capture missing parameters from the user, you must ensure that all connection arguments are complete before you attempt to open a connection. If you don't, the dialog boxes *will* appear, and there's nothing you can do to prevent it—not in DAO/Jet.

- SQL Server connections that are used to populate cursors can't be reused until the population is complete. Jet has no choice in these cases but to open additional connections and then to create additional cursors or perform update operations.

- Reducing the number of rows fetched in creating a cursor to 100 or fewer permits Jet to prefetch all cursor key values and immediately free the connection. If a new record set contains more than 100 rows, Jet might have to open another shareable connection to manage data retrieval, leaving the first cursor open to manage the keyset.

- Jet automatically opens and closes additional connections to perform data fetching and updates or to populate cursors on an as-needed basis.

- Jet holds at least one connection open until the ConnectionTimeout period expires, even after all Database objects are closed, to expedite subsequent use by your application. This "courtesy" is especially troubling because the default timeout is 10 minutes.

- Jet will attempt to share connections whenever the same data source name (DSN) is referenced, even when user IDs and passwords are different.

One more point before we get into the windy passages of connection management: to make your application more responsive, you can choose to preconnect to SQL Server in the Form_Load event and leave the connection open for the duration of your application. Although this practice consumes a connection on SQL Server, it does perform the needed data definition language (DDL) queries. The DAO/Jet Database object opened with this technique can be closed, but Jet doesn't terminate the connection until it hasn't been used for the entire ConnectionTimeout period, which, as just mentioned, defaults to 10 minutes. Another way to get disconnected is to stop Jet with the following code:

```
Set DBEngine = Nothing
```

TIP When you disconnect with the Close method, you must *still* give Jet a chance to clean up using the DBEngine.Idle method after the timeout period has expired.

Jet's Connection Management Scheme

Jet devotes quite a bit of code to connection management. Its goals are to reduce the number of connections used at any one time and to hide the connection management details from developers. Jet and Microsoft Visual Basic 4.0 and later offer several advanced data access features, many of which require a multiple-connection model:

- Simultaneous browsing of multiple tables and queries, including limited background query execution

- Direct updating of tables and queries during browsing

- Data-aware (bound) controls (list boxes, DBGrid, and so on) that can be based on tables and queries

Because of the way SQL Server implements cursors, your Jet-based application might require multiple connections to implement such features, unless you use server-side cursors. Unfortunately, however, Jet doesn't support server-side cursors. Two server and driver attributes determine when more connections are called for: active statements and cursor commit/rollback behavior.

Active Statements

When all the rows you want have been fetched from the server, the result set is what I call *fully populated*. An active statement is a query whose results haven't been completely fetched from the server—the result set isn't fully populated. If there is an active statement on a connection, SQL Server doesn't allow any other statements to be executed on that connection. Jet might use multiple connections in the case of an active statement—for example, when updating a record before the entire result set is fetched. The alternatives—discarding unfetched results or forcing completion of the active statement before allowing updates—are too disruptive to users. And SQL Server does support multiple connections against a database, so Jet can support the creation of updateable Recordset objects—as long as a unique value can be used in building the bookmarks. This unique value can be a SQL Server index, or it can be one or more designated fields that indicate the unique characteristics of the row.

Cursor Commit/Rollback Behavior

Jet maintains several internal cursors in support of updateable record set operations. For efficiency, these cursors are kept in a prepared state. Servers and drivers differ when it comes to how transactions affect all the prepared or active cursors on a connection. Because Jet wraps data modifications in transactions, Jet takes steps to insulate itself from these effects. Jet identifies which cursor behavior to use by analyzing the most limiting behavior of two ODBC information values obtained via SQLGetInfo: SQL_ACTIVE_STATEMENTS and SQL_CURSOR_COMMIT_BEHAVIOR. The contents of these ODBC driver settings are determined when the connection handle is first established. (This doesn't require a connection or query against the server.) SQL Server supports only one active statement per connection, so Jet requires two connections when performing dynaset operations against SQL Server data.

An optimization introduced in Jet 2.0, carried forward into Jet 3.0 and later, allows updateable Resultset objects with fewer than 100 rows to be processed by means of a single connection. Jet accomplishes this by quickly fetching the first 100 rows before control returns to your application. If this action fully populates the result set, an additional connection isn't needed to support dynaset operations.

Connection Sharing

Jet shares ODBC connections internally whenever possible. After accounting for transaction effects and the limitations of active statements, Jet shares connections on the basis of connect strings. Two connect strings are considered equal only if *both* of the following criteria are met: the DSN values in both connect strings match, and either the Database values in both connect strings match or neither connect string has a Database value. The user ID isn't even considered. Therefore, if you attempt to use two different user IDs but the same DSN, Jet tries to share one connection between the two operations. To ensure that you can open an additional connection with a different user ID, create a separate DSN entry for each user ID.

How many connections might be required for a given query? Well, if you use the DAO/Jet interface to open two large SQL Server result sets—greater than 100 rows—a total of three connections is required. The first fetches keys from the first result set. The second fetches keys from the second result set. The third does all the updating and fetching of chunk data from both result sets. As soon as all the keys from either result set are fetched, or as soon as one of the result sets is fully populated, the corresponding connection is released. As long as the cursor is open, at least one connection remains operational. If you open a smaller result set, Jet caches the rows and quickly closes any unneeded connections.

Another interesting scenario involves Jet's ability to perform updates on joined tables. Suppose you have a fairly complex query that joins data from three tables. Because Jet can identify the index or value that makes each table unique, it can perform an update on any of the three tables by means of a single connection.

Connection Caching and Aging

To avoid constant disconnection and reconnection (since it takes so long to reconnect, given the extra overhead that is often needed), Jet maintains connections in a connection pool even when the connections aren't explicitly in use. This feature is invisible to the user but not to the system as a whole.

During idle time, cached connections are aged and eventually closed down, even if record set variables are still using the connections. When a connection is needed again, reconnection is supposed to be silent and automatic. Unfortunately, that's not always the case. Sometimes Jet can't get everything reconnected, requeried, and repositioned after an automatic shutdown. Anyway, all connections are closed down when your application exits. Two conditions prevent a connection from being timed out: an uncommitted transaction on the connection, and a query with unfetched results on the connection.

If you have objects stored in the SQL Server TempDB database, such as temporary tables or procedures or sorted results, these are lost when the connection drops. SQL Server 6.x makes extensive use of TempDB-based procedures, so this feature can be traumatic for your application. This is still a problem with SQL Server 7.0—except for the temporary stored procedures created when running queries. To avoid the loss of objects, take the following actions:

1. Set the ConnectionTimeout engine to 0, to disable the automatic disconnect.

2. Set ConnectionTimeout to a value higher than the number of seconds you intend to keep the TempDB objects open.

3. Keep pumping up the connection; keep activity on the connection with background processing of some kind, and Jet will postpone the automatic closing of connections.

Managing Connections on Your Own

Jet's connection management machine might not really suit your application's needs. If it doesn't, you can do a couple of things to disconnect much of Jet's micromanagement. In some cases, these techniques might be necessary before you can submit action queries against unpopulated result sets:

- Use a clone DSN—that is, a DSN identical to another except for its name. When a clone DSN is opened, the Jet connection manager thinks it's a separate server and that it can't be shared.

- Set the ConnectionTimeout option to 1, and use the DBEngine.Idle method to get the connection to time out as soon as possible after you close your connection. Be sure to set the DBEngine.INIPath to point to your application's Registry entry property before depending on any Jet initialization option settings.

NOTE When you use an attached table without a stored user ID and password, or if the stored user ID and password are no longer valid, Jet will attempt to log on with the user ID and password that were used to log on to the local Jet database. (This behavior can be disabled by a Registry entry.) This feature can be convenient if local and remote user IDs and passwords are kept consistent. If this login attempt fails, the user is prompted for a user ID and password by the ODBC driver's login dialog box, which can't change any other dialog fields. Once the user has logged on to a remote server, however, Jet remembers the user ID and password until the application exits, so the user isn't prompted again every time reconnection is necessary. But if the user connects to another server or database or to a different DSN, he or she will be prompted for the user ID and password that apply there.

There are basically three ways to tell the Jet engine what kind of connection you need:

- Use the OpenDatabase method to open an ODBC data source directly.

- Use the OpenDatabase method to open a Jet MDB database that contains attached SQL Server tables.

- Use the Data control to establish a connection based on its properties.

The Jet team hates it when I write about using the OpenDatabase method against a SQL Server database. They hate it because a frequent side effect of using this technique is the perception that Jet performs poorly. It's all my fault.

If the first argument of the OpenDatabase method is the pathname of an MDB file, and if the *Connect* argument doesn't begin with *ODBC*, Jet assumes that you're trying to open an MDB database (or another ISAM database format). Whether or not the Jet database contains attached tables won't be discovered until the engine inspects the individual tables. In fact, Jet won't even try to establish a connection until the attached tables are referenced. If they're never referenced, no connection is ever made.

If Jet decides that you're trying to open an ODBC data source, and if the DSN isn't already open, Jet passes a subset of the arguments that you included in the OpenDatabase method to the SQLDirectConnect ODBC API function. The connect string is really all you need to open an ODBC data source, since it can contain the DSN, the user ID and password, and optional parameters. If the arguments you include in the OpenDatabase method are insufficient to identify a DSN or to get the connection established, the ODBC Driver Manager exposes one or more dialog boxes to collect the missing pieces—and there's no way to disable this behavior.

The OpenDatabase Connect argument is used to carry most or all of the parameters to the ODBC Driver Manager. The *DatabaseName* argument can contain the DSN, but it isn't required. The *Connect* argument consists of the keyword *ODBC* followed by a semicolon (;) and all the other arguments. After the keyword, all the other arguments are optional and can be supplied in any order. The connect string is driver-dependent. For SQL Server, it needs a selected subset of the arguments listed in Table 12-1. Some outdated Microsoft documentation shows that a DBQ argument is also an option. You can try it; it's the same as the DATABASE argument. Unfortunately, however, it's not supported and might not work in your driver.

A completed OpenDatabase function can be coded this way:

```
Dim Db As Database, Connect As String
Connect$ = "ODBC;DSN=Farm;UID=bill;PWD=yup;DATABASE=Farm;"
Set Db = OpenDatabase("", 0, 0, Connect$)
```

Table 12-1
Connect String Arguments for SQL Server

Argument	Description	Example
DSN	Specifies the data source name (simply a named entry that contains the driver and server names and additional information)	DSN=MyDSN;
UID	User ID corresponding to a SQL Server login ID	UID=bill;
PWD	Password; matching password for login ID	PWD=yup;
DATABASE	Overrides SQL Server default database	DATABASE=Farm;
SERVER	Identifies the server name	SERVER=BETAV1
APP	Name of the application calling; by default, set to the name of the current form (optional)	APP=MyAPP
WSID	Workstation ID; by default, set to the workstation computer network name (optional)	WSID=MyComputer
LANGUAGE	National language to be used by SQL Server (optional)	LANGUAGE=English
TRUSTED_CONNECTION	New for ODBC 3.0; helps support integrated security	TRUSTED_CONNECTION=YES

Remember to code the connect string exactly as shown—don't add extra spaces before or after the =. If you choose to use integrated security, set the *UID* and *PWD* parameters to null:

```
Connect$ = "ODBC;DSN=Farm;UID=;PWD=;DATABASE=Farm;"
```

This tells the ODBC Driver Manager that you didn't forget the user ID and password, so it shouldn't prompt for them. This works only against SQL Server systems that support integrated security and on servers where you have rights. When your SQL Server login account is established, the system administrator sets up a default database for your account. If you provide the name of an override default database, the SQL Server choice switches to the new default database once the connection is established. If you don't have rights to this database, the switch is reversed. If you don't have rights to any databases on the server, the connection is denied and shut down from the SQL Server end.

If you provide no database name argument in the OpenDatabase method or the Data control DatabaseName property, but only the keyword *ODBC* in the connect string, the ODBC Driver Manager prompts for the correct DSN by permitting a selection from a list of all known (registered) DSNs. Once a DSN is selected, a dialog box for the user ID and password collects valid parameters. When all the parameters have been collected, one way or another, a connection attempt is made. If it's successful, the connection is completed and control returns to Jet and to the application. If the connection doesn't go through, a dialog box explaining the error is exposed. Once the connection is canceled, the user is prompted again for the correct user ID and password. If this dialog box is canceled, a trappable error is returned to the application.

With this scenario, as you can see, the user has the ability to choose from any live DSN and to provide a choice of user ID and password until he or she either gives up or finds a valid pair and gets connected. Once connected, the user has the full rights of the selected login. You should also consider how Jet shares connections made to the same database and DSN but perhaps not with the same user ID. With connection sharing, the wrong user might get connected to the right server through no fault of yours. If the user plans to connect more than once, especially with different user IDs, a different DSN should be used. This forces Jet to create and manage the second and subsequent connections as separate objects.

One of the neater ways to open an ODBC connection is to avoid using the DSN entry in the Microsoft Windows Registry. It turns out that you can supply *all* the parameters that are needed to identify the SQL Server and the type of driver to use simply by including them in the connect string. Unfortunately, however, "limitations" in some earlier versions of Jet might prevent it from opening a DSN-less connection. If you get a General Protection Fault (GPF), that's a pretty good indication that you don't have the right version of Jet. But just stick this connect string into the OpenDatabase or Connect property of the Data control, and you won't need a DSN at all:

```
Cnct$ = "ODBC;UID=;PWD=;SERVER=BETAV1;DRIVER=" & _
    "{SQL SERVER};DATABASE=pubs;"
```

Opening Attached Tables

When you attach SQL Server tables or views to a Jet database, Jet places connection and DDL information into the Jet database. This means that when you actually access an attached table, the Jet engine doesn't have to refetch anything—it just has to connect. The user ID and password can also be stored in the linkage information, so anyone with access to the Jet database can gain access to the SQL Server data. No, attached tables don't contain any data—just DDL and linkage information.

By default, attached tables are named after the SQL Server database table owner and table name. For example, if you use Access to attach to the *Pubs.dbo.authors* table, Access names this table *dbo_authors*. This naming convention can take some getting used to, so expect it when you write your Jet queries that reference these tables. You can rename the tables after Access attaches them, or you can attach them yourself in code—yes, I also said you can attach SQL Server views, just like other tables. In addition, you can create "fake" Jet indexes on these attached views, so they can be updated just like any other tables. (You can also attach temporary tables, but that's a bit trickier because when the connection gets dropped, so does the temporary table—not good.)

Opening an attached table is no different from opening any other Jet table. You just can't use the Jet table-type Recordset object to do it. Let's say you've attached the *Pubs* database tables to a Jet database named *JetPubs.MDB*. To create a cursor on a subset of the *Titles* table attached via the local *dbo_titles* table, you could code as shown on the following page.

A Testimonial for Using Attached Tables

In the summer of 1994, I attended a conference with Drew Fletcher, a program manager in the Microsoft Visual Basic group. One of the vendors at the conference was demonstrating an application that hooked up the ODBC or DB-Library interface so that developers could monitor and compare interface performance. As we watched, the vendor demonstrated a Jet-based SQL Server application that was running especially slow. After a few minutes, I discovered that he was using the attachment without link (AWOL) technique to open a large SQL Server table. With some encouragement from Drew, he changed his demo to use attached tables, which I set up for him. Suddenly the test application just zipped along, and the amount of interface traffic dropped significantly. The vendor said he hadn't known that using attached tables for connecting to SQL Server was even possible. Apparently I didn't stress this capability enough in the documentation—assuming he read it.

```
Dim Db as Database, SQL as String, Rs as Recordset
Set Db = OpenDatabase("JetPubs.MDB")
SQL$ = "SELECT DISTINCTROW dbo_titles.*, dbo_titles.title" _
    & " FROM dbo_titles WHERE ((dbo_titles.title like 'c*'));"
Set Rs = Db.OpenRecordset(SQL$,dbOpenSnapshot)
```

See any sign of a connect string? It's there, hidden in the TableDef object that describes the *dbo_titles* table.

What happens if the permissions change for the user ID embedded in the TableDef object? Well, either you need to drop and reattach the table with corrected information or you have to go into the TableDef object and change the connect string. If the structure of the underlying table changes, you can use the RefreshLink method against the TableDef object to refresh the linkage information. In any case, you need to use the Refresh method against the TableDefs collection to refresh its structure, too, if the structure changes.

Doesn't this seem like a lot of trouble? I think it does. That's why I always keep Access handy to create the Jet database, attach the tables, and create any queries I need. Believe me, it's far, far easier to get Access to do all this setup work and debug the Jet SQL than to try doing it yourself. Notice that the example above uses Jet syntax to perform the query. Check out the *like* and the table name syntax.

Creating an Attached Table with DAO/Jet Methods

Need to create an attached table on the fly? You must execute a few DAO/Jet methods to add the new table to an existing MDB database. If you need help creating the new table, check out the CreateDatabase method, or use the following example, which creates a Jet 3.0 database that uses typical (English-language) defaults:

```
Dim Ws As Workspace
Dim NewDb As Database
Set Ws = DBEngine.Workspaces(0)
' Create new, unencrypted database
Set NewDB = Ws.CreateDatabase _
    ("NEWDB.MDB", dbLangGeneral, dbVersion30)
```

Another approach would be to use the CompactDatabase method, which simply makes a compressed copy of an existing Jet database that can then be modified independently of the original.

Once the Jet database is created, you must attach the SQL Server tables and views to it. You can also create Jet QueryDef objects that refer to the SQL Server tables and views and to any Jet tables that you care to add. The Jet database can contain reports, forms, and macros, but these can't be seen or manipulated from Visual Basic. You can use Visual Basic to create and manage referential integrity or security constraints, but these can't involve ODBC

I'm not suggesting that your application attach to an ODBC table each time it fires up. That's silliness.

SQL Server tables. Remember that attached tables contain *no* data, just DDL information about the SQL Server database tables.

Here is a series of steps used to create a couple of attached tables that link the Jet database to a SQL Server table and view:

1. Create variables for the Database and TableDef objects you're going to modify.

2. Use the OpenDatabase method to open the existing Jet database.

3. Use the CreateTableDef method to create a TableDef object for the external table.

4. Set the TableDef object properties to refer to the attached table.

5. Append the new TableDef object to the TableDefs collection by using the Append method. This is the step that actually creates the linkage object in the Jet database file.

The following code creates a new database and attaches a couple of SQL Server tables:

```
Dim tdf As TableDef, db As Database, ws As Workspace
Set ws = DBEngine.Workspaces(0)
' Create new, unencrypted database.
Set db = ws.CreateDatabase _
    ("NEWDB.MDB", dbLangGeneral, dbVersion30)
Set tdf = db.CreateTableDef("Titles")
tdf.Connect = "ODBC;DSN=SSRVR1;UID=Fred;PWD=RHS;DATABASE=Pubs;"
tdf.SourceTableName = "Titles"
db.TableDefs.Append tdf
Set tdf = db.CreateTableDef("TitleView")
tdf.Connect = "ODBC;DSN=SSRVR1;UID=Fred;PWD=RHS;DATABASE=Pubs;"
tdf.SourceTableName = "TitleView"
db.TableDefs.Append tdf
```

Notice that the TableDef object is reused. If you don't want to embed the password in the table definition this way, you don't have to, but the Jet connection manager and the ODBC driver do have to get the password from somewhere. Also notice that you *don't* set the attribute property to dbAttachSavePWD. Jet sets this property when the table is created. When you're using integrated security, the UID or PWD *values* aren't required—just the *keywords*.

```
tdf.Connect = "ODBC;DSN=SSRVR1;UID=;PWD=;DATABASE=Pubs;"
```

Connecting: Common Pitfalls

A number of things can go wrong when you attempt to make a connection. Connections are simpler with Microsoft Windows NT domain-managed security, but connecting can still be tough, for lots of reasons. And the problems are often the same, no matter what data access interface you choose.

- **The DSN doesn't exist.** You didn't create one ahead of time, it has been removed, or you spelled it incorrectly.

- **Jet thinks the "DSN Name" is really an MDB.** For example, if you put "Biblio" in the DSN name thinking Jet will look for a DSN named "Biblio," you're right—sort of. Jet will first check to see whether there's a BIBLIO.MDB before checking to see whether there's a DSN with that name.

- **The DSN exists, but it's for 16-bit Visual Basic and you're using 32-bit Visual Basic.** Be sure to install the 32-bit ODBC drivers and convert any existing 16-bit DSNs.

- **The DSN exists, but it refers to a missing SQL Server.** When SQL Server is down, or if someone stole it in the night and pawned it to feed a Twinkies habit, the ODBC Driver Manager might have some difficulty trying to find the DSN on the network. The ODBC driver Help file DRVSSRVR.HLP includes instructions on how to use an ODBC "ping" program that can isolate connection problems. I've seen incorrectly installed SQL Servers refuse to respond to the network, even though they worked locally.

- **The user ID and password aren't valid.** You might have to add the user as a member of a Windows NT group *and* as a valid SQL Server login.

- **The user doesn't have rights to the default database.** You need to make sure that the user has permission to access the default (or chosen) database.

NOTE When I had to change my domain password at the office, the task proved increasingly painful as the day wore on. Each Windows NT server I connected to wanted to know my new password. I also discovered that I couldn't log on to SQL Server unless I created a new login ID. I experimented for some time and ended up using the fallback technique of establishing a file share to the server in question. Once I was connected, the Windows NT system running SQL Server asked for a password. When I provided my Windows NT domain password, SQL Server decided I wasn't an interloper after all and granted me access once again.

When you connect to SQL Server, you have to go through several very picky layers of protocol. But keep one thing in mind: what works all over the world in other people's systems should work in yours, too.

If you still can't get connected, try to set up a simple file share on SQL Server. Can you connect to this share? If so, try the connection again. For some reason, I can't always connect to a 4.2 OS/2 server until I establish a connection to a share via the Net Use command. This operation asks for a password, and once I'm connected, the system lets me access the IPC$ share needed to do all named pipe work. You can also install ISQL or ISQLW and see whether they can connect. Neither of these programs uses ODBC, so they can be used to eliminate ODBC DSN, network, and rights problems. If these don't work, you probably need to log on to the workstation, or maybe some other basic network layer isn't working. Can you see anything on the network when you use Net View from an MS-DOS prompt? Or check out SQL Server Books Online for a DB-Library "ping" program to test the LAN layers. If you find that you're not being helped by any of these suggestions, fall to your knees and pray—and while you're down there, see if the network cable is plugged in.

TIP If you just can't get connected to SQL Server, remember that you're going through Jet, the ODBC Driver Manager, the SQL Server ODBC driver, a named-pipe network interface (or its equivalent), a matching network interface on the server, the server's operating system, and a connection manager run by SQL Server itself. When you're debugging this rig, try to bypass one or more layers to eliminate their role in the problem. And make sure the drivers in use are current as well as matched with the other drivers being used.

Getting Connected with Jet: Key Points

Here are the important points to remember about connecting to SQL Server with Jet:

- The Jet connection manager keeps a number of connections open long after you close the Database object that opened them. To force termination of the connection, be sure to set the appropriate Registry (or INI) entries and use the DBEngine.Idle method, or shut down Jet by setting the DBEngine value to 0.

- If you use the direct connect (AWOL) technique, every aspect of the Jet-to-SQL Server interface is bogged down with extra DDL queries. In the past, this was the only way to execute Transact-SQL queries using SQL pass-through queries. Now, however, you can create a SQL pass-through QueryDef object in a Jet database or set the Connect property of the Database object and use the dbSQLPassThrough option.

- If you use attached tables, you have to create or gain read-write (structure) access to a Jet database and attach the SQL Server tables and views.

- Attached table structure remains static, so if the SQL Server table structure changes, you must reattach or use the RefreshLink method to reset the linkage information.

13

Using DAO/Jet to Access Data

Understanding DAO/Jet Cursors

Creating DAO/Jet Cursors

Choosing an Index

Using the ODBC Cache

GetRows and Variant Arrays

Relocating the Current-Row Pointer

Updating DAO/Jet Data Sources

Handling DAO/Jet Errors

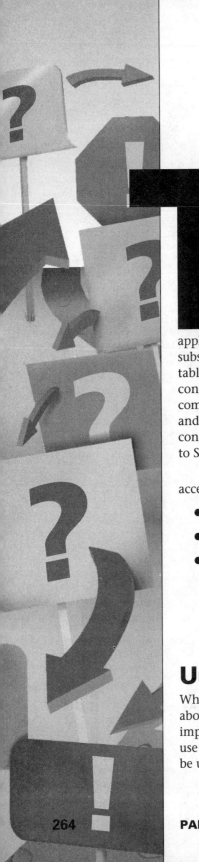

The foundation of any front-end application written in Microsoft Visual Basic is how the application accesses and manipulates data. In most Microsoft SQL Server shops, data is rarely accessed by SELECT * queries against base tables; rarely is a user even permitted read-write access to the tables. In most cases, writing an application that just uses the Data control or the RemoteData control without substantive code is usually something that can't be done because access to base tables via simple cursors simply isn't permitted. SQL Server shops that are concerned with data integrity and security usually limit access by creating comprehensive sets of stored procedures and views that gate access to vital data and manage changes to the data. As a result, many ISAM-based programming concepts you might have grown used to in the past can't be carried forward to SQL Server front-end applications.

In this chapter, we'll focus on the following areas, which form the data access component of any front-end application written in Visual Basic:

- Manipulating data (retrieving, adding, changing, and deleting server data)

- Accessing specific SQL Server features and functions

- Performing administrative operations, such as adding and deleting tables, managing security, and performing database consistency checker (DBCC) operations (which are used to manage the system and user databases and which let you scan the database structure for trouble and take corrective action)

Understanding DAO/Jet Cursors

When you use DAO/Jet to access SQL Server data, you have very little choice about how the data is accessed—you *must* use a cursor of some kind. Jet 1.1 implements the dynaset and Snapshot objects for this purpose; Jet 2.5 and 3.*x* use the Recordset object. Of the three types of Recordset objects, only two can be used to access SQL Server data.

- **Dynaset-type Recordset object** This cursor is created when a book-mark is fetched for each row in the query result set. (A bookmark is a variant value that contains enough information for the row to be located if it's ever referenced again.)

- **Snapshot-type Recordset object** This cursor is created when all the selected data values are fetched for each row in the query result set.

NOTE You can't use the DAO/Jet table-type Recordset object to access SQL Server data because it's designed to work with ISAM data, in which the index row ID values are directly accessible. Because SQL Server row ID values aren't accessible, there's no easy way to implement table-type Recordset objects.

Let's look a lot more closely at how dynaset-type and snapshot-type Recordset objects are created. Generally, you're not thinking about creating a cursor when you use the Recordset object. You're thinking about executing a query and working with the resulting rows. How you phrase the query plays a significant role in how the result set can be used, its updatability, and the type of cursor created for you. Query phrasing also plays a significant role in query performance. You create a Jet cursor using one of the following techniques, each of which generates a query:

- A table name, which is converted to a SELECT * query

- The name of a DAO/Jet QueryDef object, which contains a stored Jet SQL or Transact-SQL (TSQL) query

- A Jet-syntax SQL query

- A TSQL query, which might simply contain the name of a SQL Server stored procedure, which in turn contains a TSQL query or operation or both

Jet can deal with both Transact-SQL queries and Jet-syntax queries. If you don't specifically indicate otherwise, Jet always assumes Jet query syntax. But don't Jet and SQL Server both use ANSI syntax? Yes—but they both use supersets of the ANSI syntax, and their statements don't always cross-pollinate. For example, a SELECT * FROM AUTHORS statement works on both the Jet and the SQL Server query processor. Nevertheless, consider this common TSQL join:

```
SELECT Title, TNum, Language
FROM Topics T, Languages L
WHERE T.Lang = L.Lang
```

This join is somewhat different in Jet syntax:

```
SELECT DISTINCTROW Topics.Title, Topics.TNum, Languages.Language
FROM dbo_Topics
INNER JOIN dbo_Languages
ON Topics.Lang = Languages.Lang;
```

In the TSQL query, I used table aliasing to refer to the table names in the join, but nothing is really out of the ordinary in the syntax. In the equivalent Jet query, generated for me by Microsoft Access or by Microsoft Database Tools, the Jet join syntax is different from the syntax in the simpler TSQL form. You can use the TSQL form, but if you do, the Jet query optimizer might not recognize it as a join and might perform a rather clumsy operation to fetch the data. In the past, I invariably used Access to create these queries, and I unabashedly avoided trying to make my syntax conform to the Jet syntax. Notice, too, that the Jet query ends with a semicolon. I've found that the semicolon generally isn't required because Visual Basic apparently adds it for you if you need it.

With SQL Server 6.0, the rules changed again. SQL Server now supports the ANSI join syntax in much the same way (but not exactly) as Jet does. This means that in most cases you can simply use Jet SQL syntax for common join operations. No, Jet's ability to pass along functions in the queries is not supported—at all. Personally, I would prefer to use the old TSQL syntax or simply to let Visual Data Tools come up with the right query.

While we're on the subject of Jet syntax, SQL Server table names have the prefix *dbo_* or the table owner's name when Access first attaches the tables to an MDB database. When Jet queries the table names from the server, such as when the Data control is used, it also adds the *dbo_* prefix to the table name. This means that when you set up the DataField property of bound controls, you must also follow this convention. Otherwise, you have to go into the MDB database and rename the tables. Do this from Access—it's far easier, and Access caused the problem in the first place. And now that Visual Basic 6.0 has a number of new tools that can modify tables, you don't even need Access to perform this type of database polishing.

What happens to the query before it gets to SQL Server, since the SQL Server query processor might have problems with Jet syntax? Remember that the ODBC driver manager and the SQL Server driver are also in the execution path. When Jet creates its own syntax (when you use the Data control, or when you supply Jet syntax in a query or a QueryDef), the Jet query processor is forced to convert the query to generic ODBC syntax. The ODBC SQL Server driver then converts *that* syntax to TSQL syntax. Fortunately, ODBC syntax is very similar to the Jet style—another ANSI variation. It's not a cosmic leap, and it doesn't take a lot of CPU cycles, but it does put a pothole in the road now and then.

Jet, working with the ODBC API, makes every attempt to create its own temporary stored procedures, especially when it works with parameter queries, to speed up the process of getting the query result sets. This means that your system might end up with quite a few orphaned procedures if your application doesn't give Jet and ODBC a chance to clean them up while working with an application under development. (This is no longer a problem with SQL Server 7.0) The problem manifests itself as a raft of procedures whose names begin with *ODBC* in your *SysObjects* table. In SQL Server 4.*x*, these procedures are added to your working database. In SQL Server 6.0, they are saved in TempDB. This approach means that when your connection gets closed, any orphaned procedures are dropped along with all other instance-owned objects. Swell. The downside of using TempDB is that *everyone* uses it, regardless of the database.

SQL Server 6.0 also uses TempDB space for server-side cursors and all instance-owned temporary objects. Can you see where this is going? Obviously, TempDB space needs to be *much* larger than it was in SQL Server 4.2 installations—especially in 7 × 24 systems.

In SQL Server 7.0, TempDB is also used for cursors, sort work space, temporary tables, and the like, but not to store temporary stored procedures. Because of the way SQL Server 7.0 manages queries, it's no longer necessary to create these procedures in TempDB.

How do you get rid of the procedures in a SQL Server 4.2 system? You just go into Enterprise Manager, select the procedures, and drop them. Or you can try the following procedure, which we use here at Microsoft to clean up these ODBC droppings:

```
select "drop procedure " + b.name + "."+ a.name + char(13) + 'go'
from sysobjects a, sysusers b
where a.uid = b.uid
    and a.name like "odbc#%"
    and type = "P"
```

Run this script with ISQL (or ISQL/w), using the server administrator's account. Redirect the output to a file, and use the file as another ISQL script—again using the server administrator's account:

```
ISQL /Usa /S /Pmysapw /iCleanUp.SQL > ODBCList.SQL
ISQL /Usa /S /Pmysapw /iODBCList.SQL
```

You don't need this for SQL Server 6.0 or later. These newer versions clean up after errant users or don't create the mess in the first place, the way a good housekeeper picks up the residents' dirty socks.

> **NOTE** Opening an MDB database that contains one or more attached tables doesn't generate any ODBC activity. When you access the individual tables or run a DAO/Jet QueryDef, Jet executes a number of ODBC functions to retrieve the data. Remember that all of the table's data definition language (DDL) information is stored in the TableDef objects in the Jet database.

Once the query arrives at the SQL server, it's executed and the first rows are sent back, right? Hardly. Let's take a closer look at the traffic passed between Jet, the ODBC driver, and SQL Server. This should give you some idea of the network traffic involved and the amount of processing that must be done by the drivers and by Jet itself. What follows is a condensed version of the ODBC log dump that is generated when I execute the preceding query with attached tables.

First, you set up the environment. The ODBC API functions shown below establish ODBC environment and connection handles and set up the connect options to be used. (In this case, connect option 103 is logon timeout, set to 20 seconds; 14 is the equivalent hex value.)

```
SQLAllocEnv(phenv436F0000);
SQLAllocConnect(henv436F0000, phdbc4E770000);
SQLSetConnectOption(hdbc4E770000, 103, 00000014);
```

Next, you connect to SQL Server with the connect string embedded in the TableDef for the attached table in question. The code to perform this operation is shown below. Note that the user ID and password are embedded here. Note also that anyone can turn on the SQL Trace log and see this information. The SQLGetInfo function returns information about the driver itself. Since a Jet database can be transported to anyone's system, Jet must determine how to approach access problems by polling the driver for its current configuration. All these function calls are made against the ODBC connection handle. This means that the information is probably in the driver and no query against the server is needed.

```
SQLDriverConnect(hdbc4E770000, hwnd0578, "DSN=Workdb16;UID=;
    PWD=;APP=Microsoft Access;WSID=BETAVP5;DATABASE=workdb",
    72, szConnStrOut, 0, pcbConnStrOut, 0);
SQLGetInfo(hdbc4E770000, 9, rgbInfoValue, 2, pcbInfoValue);
SQLGetInfo(hdbc4E770000, 6, rgbInfoValue, 100, pcbInfoValue);
⋮
SQLSetConnectOption(hdbc4E770000, 101, 00000001);
```

Once the connection has been completed, a statement handle is allocated and its options are retrieved and reset, as shown below. These two options set the query timeout to 60 (0x3C) seconds and enable asynchronous operations. (Yes, Jet uses asynchronous operations by default—and no, you can't use any asynchronous features programmatically.) Again, these are driver settings, and we still haven't done anything with the server except open a connection.

```
SQLAllocStmt(hdbc4E770000, phstmt5F870000);
SQLGetStmtOption(hstmt5F870000, 0, pvParam);
SQLSetStmtOption(hstmt5F870000, 0, 0000003C);
SQLGetStmtOption(hstmt5F870000, 4, pvParam);
SQLSetStmtOption(hstmt5F870000, 4, 00000001);
```

We're finally ready to send the query, right? Guess again. The following internal ODBC queries pull down options from the *MSysConf* table. Notice that each of the first two lines appears in the log twice. I'm told that since Jet uses the asynchronous mode, these multiple entries are the by-product of Jet polling while the StillExecuting bit is True. Notice that SQLError is invoked twice. This is probably because I don't have an *MSysConf* table in my tiny test database. Once this query is complete, Jet drops the statement handle:

```
SQLExecDirect(hstmt5F870000,
    "SELECT Config, nValue FROM MSysConf", -3);
SQLExecDirect(hstmt5F870000,
    "SELECT Config, nValue FROM MSysConf", -3);
SQLError(henv436F0000, hdbc4E770000, hstmt5F870000,
    szSQLState, pfNativeError, szErrorMsg, 8192, pcbErrorMsg);
SQLError(henv436F0000, hdbc4E770000, hstmt5F870000,
    szSQLState, pfNativeError, szErrorMsg, 8102, pcbErrorMsg);
SQLFreeStmt(hstmt5F870000, 1);
```

Are we ready now to execute our query? Just about. But first, Jet must set up the same statement handle options that it dropped only microseconds ago. Jet now sets the asynchronous mode and query timeout value again, as shown below. These don't take long; they're just driver options.

```
SQLAllocStmt(hdbc4E770000, phstmt5F870000);
SQLGetStmtOption(hstmt5F870000, 0, pvParam);
SQLSetStmtOption(hstmt5F870000, 0, 0000003C);
SQLGetStmtOption(hstmt5F870000, 4, pvParam);
SQLSetStmtOption(hstmt5F870000, 4, 00000001);
```

Now we're finally ready to execute the query. By using SQLExecDirect, Jet bypasses creation of a stored procedure to run the query. Notice that Jet has to poll twice before StillExecuting returns False:

```
SQLExecDirect(hstmt5F870000, _
    "SELECT "dbo"."Topics"."TNum" ,"dbo"."Topics"."Title" ,"
    dbo"."Languages"."Language"  FROM"
    dbo"."Topics","dbo"."Languages" WHERE ("
    dbo"."Topics"."Lang" = "dbo"."Languages"."Lang" ) ", -3);

SQLExecDirect(hstmt5F870000, _
    "SELECT "dbo"."Topics"."TNum" ,"dbo"."Topics"."Title" ,"
    dbo"."Languages"."Language"  FROM "dbo"."Topics","
    dbo"."Languages" WHERE ("
    dbo"."Topics"."Lang" = "dbo"."Languages"."Lang" ) ", -3);
```

Once the query is passed to SQL Server and ODBC indicates that the first result set row is available, all that remains is the process of retrieving the data. In this case, Jet executes two ODBC functions: SQLFetch, to get the next row of data; and SQLGetData, for each individual column. This sequence is repeated for each row visited, one row at a time. Only SQLFetch generates network traffic, but plenty of such statements are executed—and this is where Jet's performance really falls down. When we talked about tuning Jet, we touched on setting the cache size. This permits Jet to make a more intelligent, 100-row fetch in a single operation. You can see below how it makes sense to limit both the number of rows and the number of columns returned in a result set. This sequence is repeated for each row and each column in the result set.

```
SQLFetch(hstmt5F870000);
SQLGetData(hstmt5F870000, 1, 4, rgbValue, 256, pcbValue);
SQLGetData(hstmt5F870000, 2, 1, rgbValue, 256, pcbValue);
SQLGetData(hstmt5F870000, 3, 1, rgbValue, 256, pcbValue);
SQLFetch(hstmt5F870000);
SQLGetData(hstmt5F870000, 1, 4, rgbValue, 256, pcbValue);
SQLGetData(hstmt5F870000, 2, 1, rgbValue, 256, pcbValue);
SQLGetData(hstmt5F870000, 3, 1, rgbValue, 256, pcbValue);
SQLFetch(hstmt5F870000);
⋮
```

Now, why did I bore you with all this detail? Because when it comes to figuring out how to tune a Jet application or any ODBC application, including those that use the RDO interface, knowing how to examine SQL trace logs is a must. When you're reporting bugs against ODBC drivers or any of the middleware, it's also a good idea to dump the log as the problem is occurring. This helps both you and the debugging crew.

How do you turn on the log? It's easy:

1. Open the Windows Control Panel, and click on either the 16-bit or the 32-bit ODBC setup icon. These are used to manage data source names (DSNs) and can optionally set or disable the trace log.

2. Click the Tracing tab. This displays the Data Source Administrator Window.

3. Click the Start Tracing Now button. Be sure to return to this dialog box and disable tracing when you're finished testing.

4. In the Log file Path area, set the name of the file to receive the trace log in a place where you can find it. Be sure to specify a path, since this file will be tough to find if you let the Windows operating system choose the default path.

5. In the Custom Trace DLL area, set any Custom Trace DLL you want to use.

6. Click OK to close the Data Source Administrator Window. From this point on, all ODBC operations will write to this log. Note that you can (and should) set up separate 16-bit and 32-bit logs.

Another option is to use SQL Trace in SQL Server 6.5 or SQL Server Profiler in SQL Server 7.0. These utilities are provided with SQL Server and can help clear up what Jet or ODBC or any interface is *really* doing. SQL Trace is fairly simple to use; you just start it and create a "base" filter. What you see is each operation sent to SQL Server. This differs from ODBC logs, which show what APIs are being executed. SQL Trace shows what commands are being executed by the ODBC driver itself. You saw one of these SQL Trace logs back in Chapter 3. SQL Server Profiler is an order of magnitude harder to use and understand because it goes far, far deeper into the bowels of the Tabular Data Stream. Once you figure it out, it can be extremely useful when you're debugging tough problems.

Creating DAO/Jet Cursors

Now let's look at cursors from the developer's viewpoint. There are two types of DAO/Jet cursors available to the developer accessing ODBC-connected data sources: dynaset-type and snapshot-type Recordset objects. (These are different from the obsolete Dynaset and Snapshot objects supported in Visual Basic 3.0. When I refer to a dynaset or a snapshot in this chapter, I am referring to a type of Recordset object.) When you use the DAO/Jet OpenRecordset method or the Data control, Jet creates a cursor as close as possible to what you specify, although it doesn't always comply exactly with your request. For example, if you request a dynaset-type Recordset object and the underlying table isn't updateable, Jet creates a snapshot-type Recordset object instead.

A dynaset-type Recordset object is a live, updateable view of the data in the underlying tables. Changes to the data in the underlying tables are reflected in the dynaset, and changes to the dynaset data are immediately reflected in the underlying tables. A snapshot-type Recordset object is a read-only, unchanging view of the data in the underlying tables. Dynaset-type Recordset objects are populated differently from snapshot-type Recordset objects.

Coding the OpenRecordset Method

The OpenRecordset method is one of the most frequently used methods, no matter what kind of table or database you are using with Jet. As we saw earlier, the new Jet 2.*x*/3.*x* engine combines several obsolete DAO/Jet methods into one comprehensive method. Specifically, the OpenTable, CreateSnapshot, and CreateDynaset methods and statements are all replaced by OpenRecordset.

When you use the DAO/Jet OpenRecordset method against a SQL Server database, you should use it off the Database object, since creating result sets on result sets is particularly inefficient. I leave the syntax to online help, but I do go over the arguments with special attention to SQL Server access needs. Most of the options shown in Table 13-1 don't apply to DAO/Jet Recordset objects created against ODBC tables, only to Jet-based tables. For example, Recordset parameters in your application can't restrict other SQL Server users' access to base SQL Server tables. The options shown in the table are set when a combination (or none) of the *Integer* constants specifies characteristics of the new Recordset object, such as restrictions on other users' ability to edit and view it.

Result Set Population

Result set population is a dynamic process that begins when the query is first executed and ends when the last qualifying row is added to the workstation-side result set. Generally, Jet cursor membership isn't closed until population is complete. Membership in the cursor is determined by the query. For example, consider the following query:

```
Select Count(*) from Chickens where eggs > 5
```

This query asks how many chickens laid more than five eggs this week. If the query engine were to freeze the entire *Chickens* table, and if the farmer could make sure that no eggs were laid while this query was being executed, you could be sure of an accurate count at any one moment. But the mechanics of the query (and chicken biology) don't work that way. Basically, the query processor begins at the first row of the *Chickens* table and tests the criterion established by the WHERE clause. If the row qualifies, it's added to the membership. But if a chicken laid only four eggs this week, its row isn't included in the total. What if the farmer's wife is in the barn choosing chickens for dinner while the query is being populated? If she chooses a chicken that was already counted, or one that would have qualified as a layer of five eggs, the count won't reflect an accurate picture of current egg production. Unless you can ensure that the dynamics of the database remain static, you can't be assured of an accurate count. This principle applies to debits and credits as well as to chickens. Just don't count your eggs (or rows) before they are laid.

Table 13-1
Recordset Option Property Settings

Option	Specification
dbDenyWrite	Other users can't modify or add records. Applies only to Jet database cursors.
dbDenyRead	Other users can't view records (table-type Recordset only). Applies only to Jet database cursors.
dbReadOnly	You can only view records; other users can modify them. Opening a Recordset as read-only can significantly improve performance.
dbAppendOnly	You can only append new records (dynaset-type Recordset only). Opening an updateable Recordset as append-only can significantly improve performance.
dbInconsistent	Inconsistent updates are allowed (dynaset-type Recordset only). Applies only to cursors.
dbConsistentOnly	Only consistent updates are allowed (dynaset-type Recordset only). Applies only to heterogeneous cursors.
dbForwardOnly	The Recordset is a forward-only scrolling snapshot. Recordset objects created with this option can't be cloned and support only the MoveNext method for moving through the records.
dbSQLPassThrough	The Microsoft Jet database engine query processor is bypassed. The query specified in the OpenRecordset source argument is passed to an ODBC back-end server for processing.
dbSeeChanges	Generates a run-time error if another user is changing data that you are editing. This option is required if your query includes a table with an Identity-type column. For queries that need to access SQL Server 6.0 Identity columns, you must also set the dbSeeChanges option when you use the OpenRecordset method to perform updates.

Another factor is involved here, too. If a query is so broad that the SQL Server query processor escalates from page locking to table locking, no updates will be possible anywhere in the table until the Recordset object is fully populated. Some chickens might be deleted before or after the count is complete, but none of these changes is reflected in the database until the cursor is fully populated.

The SQL Server query processor approaches this problem by determining which rows are members before it extracts the data—by establishing a share lock on each affected page that contains an affected row. If necessary, it escalates the page locks to one or more table locks. SQL Server then performs the query. All updates to the table pages in use are blocked until the row has been visited as you populate the cursor. That way, an update can take place on any member row, but only after it has been counted or included in the membership. Yes, SQL Server 7.0 knows how to lock down to the row, and it does so intelligently to minimize the effect on other users.

NOTE All SELECT * FROM *table* queries against ODBC data sources are escalated to table locks, as are queries that simply reference the table by name.

As you can see, it's imperative that you fully populate *all* cursors as quickly as possible. Under no circumstances should you give a user the opportunity to browse through a Recordset object that hasn't been populated in the background or before access to the data has been granted. The problem with prepopulation, however, is that it can take a very long time for large Recordset objects. Again, this means that the Recordset object's size must be limited, especially on multiuser systems with large tables. The point at which SQL Server escalates to table locking from page locking is a fixed point determined by the server administrator, so databases with large tables are more likely to cause table-lock escalation than databases with small tables. Again, the way SQL Server 7.0 manages locking and lock escalation has been redesigned and refined for better overall performance and increased scalability.

When the DAO/Jet OpenResultset method is executed, Jet automatically cancels a long-running query after a configurable amount of time. (The default is 60 seconds.) If this happens, it doesn't necessarily mean that the server didn't respond during that time or that you have been disconnected. It simply means that the query didn't return the first row of results in the time allotted.

TIP If you know that a certain query will take a very long time to execute, increase the QueryTimeout setting. Note that subsequent operations against the Recordset object, such as the MoveLast or Find methods, do *not* time out; they can run virtually indefinitely—certainly longer than your user can wait. And once they are started, no mechanism is exposed in Visual Basic for canceling these operations. You can unplug the system, disconnect the network, or give the application the three-finger salute: Ctrl-Alt-Delete.

A snapshot-type Recordset object is populated via a query that pulls back selected row data that meets the query's criteria. A dynaset, in contrast, is populated by a query that selects only the bookmark (primary key) columns of each qualifying row. In both cases, the result sets are stored in memory (they overflow to disk if they are very large), which allows you to scroll around arbitrarily. Jet doesn't use the Windows swap file; it overflows to the location specified by the TEMP environment variable.

Access is optimized to return answers and populate the Recordset object as quickly as possible. As soon as the first screen (about 25 rows) of result data is available, Access paints it. Jet doesn't do this automatically. Access uses Jet's and ODBC's ability to run the population process asynchronously. Visual Basic doesn't offer this luxury with the DAO/Jet interface. The Data control, however, does support asynchronous operations, but only on the DAO/Jet Recordset objects it creates, not on Recordset objects created in code. It also has a somewhat unfortunate problem: when you first refresh the Data control, it begins to populate the Recordset object on its own (so far, so good), but as soon as you click a button on the Data control to move to the next row, the application freezes while the Data control moves to the last row and fully populates the Recordset object. I suppose this problem will be fixed in the future.

In Visual Basic, Jet caches about 50 rows (a *cluster*) at a time, as you can see if you execute a query and examine the Recordset.RecordCount property. I executed the following query:

```
Select * from Animals
```

I discovered that the RecordCount property began at 1 as control returned to my application. When I moved to the second record, it bumped up to 51. It remained at 51 until I reached the 52nd record, where it moved to 101. Apparently, Jet does perform some background processing, even for DAO operations.

When the Jet query processor fully populates a snapshot cursor, it does no further data fetching. Once a dynaset cursor is fully populated, the query processor does no more key fetching, but it continues to fetch clusters of rows on the basis of the bookmarks if you scroll around. If a connection is needed solely for this key-fetching query, it's closed unless either of the following conditions exists:

- It's parameterized. (The connection is maintained to allow fast requerying for parameter queries.)

- Closing it will counteract connection caching.

When rows of data are needed, snapshot data is available locally. A dynaset, however, has only keys and must use a separate query to ask the server for the data corresponding to the current row's bookmark. To reduce the querying traffic, Jet asks the server for clusters of rows specified by their bookmarks rather than for rows one at a time. This reduces the currency of data because the data within the cluster tends to get stale as time goes by. But it greatly speeds movement within a small area.

Snapshot-type and dynaset-type Recordset objects differ in several performance characteristics because of their different methods of retrieving and caching data. Several points are worth noting:

- If your result set is small and you don't need to update data or see changes made by other users, use a snapshot. It's faster to open and scroll through than a dynaset.

- For a larger result set, a dynaset is faster and more efficient. Moving to the end of a snapshot requires that the entire result set (including the data) be downloaded to the client, but a dynaset downloads only the bookmark columns and then fetches the last cluster of data corresponding to those keys when it moves to the last row.

- Dynaset open time and scrolling speed are affected most negatively by the number of columns you select and the number of the query's tables that are output. Select only the columns you need. Requesting all of the columns by using *Table.** is more convenient, but it's slower. Sometimes joins are used simply as restrictions and don't need to be output at all.

- As a rule of thumb, it isn't a good idea to include OLE, Text, and Image (binary large object, or BLOB) data type columns in your multicolumn snapshot queries. Use a separate query that specifies a single row to fetch these columns when the BLOB data is requested. For dynaset-type Recordset queries, Jet fetches BLOB columns only as they are referenced in code. If there is no reference, the data isn't downloaded.

Choosing an Index

To update a dynaset-type result set, Jet must be able to locate a unique index on the table. If it can't find such an index, Jet creates a *snapshot,* which isn't updateable. The key values of a row are also called the row's *bookmark* because they uniquely identify and allow direct access to the row. Remember that SQL Server supports tables that contain duplicate rows—but you can't create a dynaset on this type of table. You can create a snapshot on this type of table or on a query that includes this type of table.

Jet is capable of creating cursors that are based on the result set of either a simple or a fairly complex join. One of Jet's most powerful features is its ability to update this result set. To do so, it requires that a unique index be available for each component table. If one or more unique indexes aren't available, the result set won't be updateable.

The Recordset object's Bookmark property contains the bookmark for the current row. Changing the Bookmark to a valid bookmark value resets the current-row pointer to the row with the associated key.

NOTE One of the most common errors is the "Invalid method for this object" error, which simply means that the Update method is invalid against a Recordset object whose Updatable property is False. If Jet can't find a unique key or if the dynaset isn't updateable for any of a litany of other valid (and some not so valid) reasons, you can't execute the Update method on the Recordset object.

When you attach an ODBC table or when Jet opens a table on an ODBC database, Jet chooses the first unique index returned by the ODBC SQLStatistics function as the *primary index*; its key columns will compose the bookmark. SQLStatistics returns clustered, hashed, and other indexes, in that order, alphabetically within each group. Jet can thus be forced to elect a particular unique index as primary if you rename the index so that it appears first alphabetically. Jet doesn't call SQLSpecialColumns(SQL_BEST_ROWID), and it makes no attempt to use a server's native record identifier in lieu of a unique index.

The longevity of such identifiers varies among servers, and after you insert a new record, there's no efficient, unambiguous way for Jet to receive the new record identifier.

You can attach a SQL server view, but it will be treated exactly as an attached table with no indexes is treated. Thus an attached view, and any query based on one, is a read-only snapshot. You can't attach server-based stored procedures because they don't resemble tables and views closely enough. But if you know that certain columns uniquely identify rows in the view (perhaps they comprise a unique index in the underlying table), you can create a "fake" unique index on the attachment itself by using a Jet DDL query such as this one:

```
db.Execute "CREATE UNIQUE INDEX Index1 " _
    & "ON AttachedTable (Column1, Column2)"
```

Don't make this query a SQL pass-through query, since it doesn't create an index on the server's table or view. SQL Server won't let you create an index on a view, but this action query tells Jet which table fields uniquely identify the table's rows, and it allows dynaset functionality, including updating. Note that this "index" isn't really an index at all. It's simply a set of parameters that lets Jet know the columns used for the unique key.

As mentioned above, you can't attach server-based stored procedures because they don't resemble tables and views closely enough. You can, however, attach temporary tables (#TEMP) and create SQL Server indexes on these tables. You can also create Jet QueryDef objects that execute stored procedures and treat them as local read-only tables.

Servers vary in precision when they handle floating-point data, so some precision might be lost. (*Floating-point data,* of course, is numeric data with digits to the right of the decimal point.) Very large or very small floating-point values might lose accuracy when they are transferred to Jet from some servers. The actual difference is slight enough to be inconsequential, but if the data forms part of a table's bookmark, Jet might think that the row has been deleted when Jet asks the server for the row by its key values and no exact match is found. Jet can't distinguish this situation from that of a genuine record deletion by another user. If this occurs and another unique index on the table doesn't involve floating-point data, you should reattach the table and force Jet to choose the other unique index as primary, by renaming it.

Using the ODBC Cache

To improve Jet's performance against ODBC databases, the Jet team added a set of RAM cache management methods that let you set the number of rows to be prefetched when you populate or browse cursors. These methods aren't as easy to use as opening a Recordset object and executing a MoveNext method, but they do improve performance dramatically.

Basically, a cache is space in local memory that holds the data most recently fetched from the server, on the assumption that the data will probably be requested again while the application is running. Caching improves the performance of any application that retrieves or fetches data from a remote server—assuming, of course, that you have the local memory to devote to caching. If you don't, Windows swaps out lower-priority pages in favor of the cache pages, which can really slow down the whole operation.

When data is requested, Jet first checks the cache for the data instead of fetching it from the server, which would take more time. Instead of waiting for the cache to be filled with records as they are fetched, you can explicitly fill the cache at any time, using the FillCache method. This is faster because FillCache fetches several records at once instead of only one at a time. For example, while each screenful of records is being displayed, you can have your application use FillCache to fetch the next screenful of records. Data that doesn't come from an ODBC data source isn't saved in the cache. BLOB data values aren't cached, and a column containing page-based data isn't fetched until its Field is referenced. Jet requests records within the cache range from the cache, and it requests records outside the cache range from the server; you decide on the size of the cache and the starting point.

Any ODBC database accessed with DAO/Jet Recordset objects can have a local cache. To create the cache, open a Recordset object from the remote data source, set the CacheSize and CacheStart properties of the Recordset object, and then use the FillCache method or step through the records using the Move methods. The CacheSize property setting is usually based on the number of records your application can work with at one time. For example, if you're using a Recordset object as the source of the data to be displayed on the screen, you can set its CacheSize property to 20 to display a screenful of records at one time.

The CacheStart property setting is the bookmark of the first record in the Recordset object to be cached; you can use the bookmark of any record. To set the CacheStart to the current record, just set CacheStart to the Recordset object's Bookmark property.

If you set the FillCache properties to a location in the result set that is partly or wholly outside the range of records specified by the CacheSize and the CacheStart properties, the portion of the record set outside of this range is ignored and isn't loaded into the cache. If FillCache requests more records than the number remaining in the remote data source, only the remaining records are fetched and no error occurs.

As always, records fetched from the cache don't reflect changes made concurrently to the source data by other users, so it's up to you to ensure that the cache is updated as necessary. FillCache fetches only those records that aren't already cached. To force an update of all the cached data, take the following steps:

1. Set CacheSize to 0.

2. Set CacheSize to the size of the cache you originally requested.

3. Use FillCache to refresh the cache.

GetRows and Variant Arrays

Another enhancement intended to improve Jet's performance is the GetRows method. GetRows might also be a viable alternative when you can afford to fetch a block of rows at a time. In general, using GetRows is much like using the ODBC cache except that the cached rows are maintained in a Variant array.

A Variant is a Visual Basic data type that basically morphs to the data passed to it. It can hold strings, binary data, Boolean values, or any other type of data except fixed-length strings and user-defined types. If you don't provide a data type when you declare a variable, it's declared a Variant, and the Variant data type has no type-declaration character. You can determine how the data in a Variant is treated by using the VarType or TypeName function.

You can use the Variant data type in place of any other data type to work with data in a more flexible way. If the contents of a Variant are digits, they can be either the string representation of the digits or their actual value, depending on the context. Consider this example:

```
Dim MyVar As Variant
MyVar = 98052
```

Here, *MyVar* contains a numeric representation: the actual value 98052. Arithmetic operators work as expected on Variant variables that contain numeric values or string data that can be interpreted as numbers. If you use the + operator to add *MyVar* to another Variant containing a number or to a variable of a numeric data type, the result is an arithmetic sum. If you use the & operator, a Variant variable can be concatenated to another string.

The value Empty denotes a Variant variable that hasn't been initialized (that is, one that hasn't been assigned an initial value). A Variant containing the value Empty is represented as 0 if it's used in a numeric context and as a zero-length string ("") if it's used in a string context. Don't confuse Empty with Null, which indicates that the Variant variable does not contain valid data.

Variants do simplify your code, but at the price of speed. It can take somewhat longer to manipulate Variant values than it takes to manipulate fixed-length or variable-length string variables and integer variables. Variants are a must, however, because they understand how to deal with Null values. Remember that a SQL Server Null value is *not* the same as an empty string.

When you access a field that can contain Null values, either you have to check for the existence of Nulls before you assign the value to an ordinary variable or you have to concatenate an empty string to the Null to convert it to an empty string. For example, suppose your query returns a personnel record that contains the value DateMarried. For many people, this is set to Null. Here's how you can move this value from a Recordset field to a variable:

```
DateMarried.Text = "" & rs!DateMarried
```

The GetRows method basically takes the rows from a Recordset object and places them into a Variant array, one block at a time. That way, Jet can reduce network overhead and improve query fetch performance. Once the data is read into the array, you can examine it there instead of in the Recordset object.

Let's look at a code sample. First you need to declare the array:

```
Dim DataCache As Variant
```

You do *not* have to size the array; the GetRows method does that for you dynamically. If you try to fill the array with more rows than there is memory (RAM) to hold them, however, the Windows swapper kicks in and performance plummets.

The next block of code uses the GetRows method to read data from an existing Recordset (named *rsj* in this example). *CacheSizeSetting* is set independently of this procedure; it's simply an integer value. Each time you execute the GetRows method, the current-row pointer moves forward in the Recordset object as if you had performed the MoveNext method the number of times indicated in *CacheSizeSetting*:

```
DataCache = rsj.GetRows(CacheSizeSetting)
```

If you run out of Recordset rows while executing the GetRows method, only the available rows are transferred, GetRows stops, and Jet sets the Recordset object's EOF property to True.

Once *n* rows have been read into *DataCache*, you can use the UBound function to determine how many rows were actually read. In the following example, I loop through all the rows that have been read and simply touch the values.

```
For row = 0 To UBound(DataCache, 2)
    For i = 0 To rsj.Fields.Count - 1
        A = DataCache(i, row)
    Next i
Next row
```

Note that the Variant array is referenced on a *column, row* basis, with 0 as the first column and row. You can assign the contents of the array elements to any variable, not just to another Variant. Visual Basic does the conversion for you. You can also pass the Variant array to another procedure.

One problem you might encounter with this technique is that the number of rows requested might not be the same as the number returned. If an error occurs, you have to retrieve the fields individually before you can determine the cause of the error.

Graphics: Picture and Image Controls

A basic problem in handling graphics is the conversion of raw binary data to a displayable form. Essentially, you can do this in two ways using the Picture and Image controls: you can use the LoadPicture method, which accepts data from a file; or you can bind the Picture or Image control to a Data control. Using a Data control is far easier than managing images yourself with code, especially since the only way to get a Picture or Image control to display a picture is via an external file and the LoadPicture method.

In essence, to add a new picture to the database, you must first save the picture into a file by using one of the graphics formats recognized by Visual Basic. These include bitmap (BMP) files, icon (ICO) files, run-length encoded (RLE) files, and metafile (WMF) files. (For some reason, PCX files are no longer recognized.

Unless you convert with a graphics conversion routine—several are supported by Windows 95—you'll have to store your bitmap images in one of these other formats.)

Once the data is in a file, use the AppendChunk method to save the data to the database, chunk by chunk. To display the data, reverse the process: first use the GetChunk method to read the data back into a file, and then use LoadPicture to reformat the file data for the Picture or Image control. You can use the FieldSize method to determine the number of bytes in the specific chunk column.

The AppendChunk and GetChunk methods are also used to store text data. Instead of using a common TextBox control, use a Rich Text Format (RTF) custom control to manage the data. The RichTextBox control provides a number of properties that you can use to apply formatting to any portion of text within the control. To change the formatting of the text, you first must select it; only selected text can be assigned character and paragraph formatting. Using these properties, you can make text bold or italic, change the color, and create superscripts and subscripts. You can adjust paragraph formatting as well, by setting left and right indents and hanging indents.

The RichTextBox control also opens and can save files in either RTF or regular ASCII text format. You can use the LoadFile and SaveFile methods to read and write files directly, or you can use the SelRTF and TextRTF properties in conjunction with Visual Basic's file input/output statements. You can load the contents of an RTF file into the RichTextBox control simply by dragging the file (from Windows Explorer, for example) or a highlighted portion of a file used in another application (such as Microsoft Word) and dropping the contents directly into the control. You can also set the FileName property to load the contents of an RTF or text file to the control. You can print all or part of the text in a RichTextBox control using the SelPrint method.

Because RichTextBox is a data-bound control, you can use a Data control to bind it to a Memo field in a Jet database or to a similar large-capacity text field in another database (for example, a Text data type field in SQL Server). The RichTextBox control supports almost all of the properties, events, and methods used with the standard TextBox control, many of which were introduced in Visual Basic 4.0 (including Locked, MaxLength, MultiLine, ScrollBars, SelLength, SelStart, and SelText). Applications that already use TextBox controls can easily be adapted to make use of RichTextBox controls. And the RichTextBox control isn't limited by the 64-KB character capacity of the conventional TextBox control; its capacity is basically unlimited.

Relocating the Current-Row Pointer

If the query result set contains any rows, the first row is exposed in the Recordset object. As you know, the one and only row that is visible in the cursor is referred to as the *current row,* where all operations on the underlying data are performed. To extract cursor data or choose a record to be updated or deleted, you must move the current-row pointer from row to row in the Recordset object. As you also know, any rows added to the cursor are appended to the Recordset object, where they remain until the query is reexecuted, at which time they resume their correct positions (if they still qualify).

DAO/Jet 3.*x* provides a number of methods for repositioning the current record pointer, which are listed below. Many of them are especially helpful to ISAM-oriented developers because they permit manipulation of the current-row pointer on the basis of row number and allow repositioning of the current-row pointer to specific or relative locations in the result set. Most of these methods also return information about the relative or specific location of the current row.

- The Move method relocates the current-row pointer ahead or back in the record set to a specific row, relative to the current row or a specific bookmark location. You can specify the number of rows to move the pointer. By default, the current-row pointer is relocated relative to the current row, but you can specify a valid bookmark location as a starting point.

- The PercentPosition method relocates the current-row pointer ahead or back in the record set on the basis of a percentage of rows already populated. It also returns the percentage-based location of the current-row pointer in the Recordset object. The percentage derived from the number of rows processed by Jet includes rows already cached.

- The AbsolutePosition method relocates the current-row pointer ahead or back in the record set to an absolute row. You can position the current-row pointer to any row in the Recordset object that has been populated or read into the cache.

- The Bookmark method relocates the current-row pointer ahead or back in the record set to a recognized key location. This method returns the current row's key value, which can be saved to reposition the current row later.

- The LastModified method returns the bookmark of the last modified record set row.

- The MoveNext and MovePrevious methods move the current-row pointer to the adjacent row, either ahead or back in the record set.

- The MoveLast and MoveFirst methods move the current-row pointer to the end or beginning of the record set.

When you use a method that repositions the current-row pointer beyond the set of the currently populated rows, Jet fetches additional keys or data rows from the SQL server to continue populating the cursor. For example, using the MoveLast method positions the current-row pointer to the last row in the record set, forcing Jet to populate it fully.

> **NOTE** Relational theory denies the existence of row pointers outside the scope of the database engine itself, and it discourages the use of row pointers for locating or manipulating result set rows. But this aspect of programming is involved in virtually all the changes to Jet 3.0 and Visual Basic that have to do with relocating the current-row pointer.

Validity of the Current-Row Pointer

At either end of the Recordset object, there is a wall you can cross—but if you do, the current record pointer becomes invalid. If you execute the MovePrevious method and the Beginning of File (BOF) property changes to True, your current record is still valid but you touch the wall. If you execute the MovePrevious method *after* the BOF property has changed to True, you go over the wall, and the current record pointer becomes invalid.

The End of File (EOF) property works in the same way. When you use the MoveNext or the MoveLast method to move to the end of the Recordset object, the EOF property remains False until you arrive at the last row. The current-row pointer remains valid, but there are no more rows in the Recordset, so you're right up against the wall. Once the EOF property changes to True, you can execute the MoveNext method again, but you'll go over the wall and the current-row pointer becomes invalid. In other cases, you get a trappable error if you attempt to move farther past either end or use the invalid current-row pointer. Yes, both RDO and ADO work the same way.

Another Data control feature that greatly simplifies record set handling is the EOFAction property. When it is set to option 2-AddNew, the Data control automatically switches into AddNew mode when the EOF wall is scaled; that is, once the user executes a MoveNext method on the Data control after the EOF property has changed to True, the control automatically starts a new, empty record. This option is also triggered when the Data control is opened on an empty Recordset object.

If you perform any operation that makes the current-row pointer invalid, you can't perform any data access operation that depends on data in the current row. This means that you can't execute the Edit method or access any of the Field properties. You *can* execute the AddNew method to add another row to the dynaset, or you can use one of the repositioning methods to relocate the current-row pointer to a valid row of the record set—if one exists. But if you delete all the rows of the record set, the BOF and EOF property settings change to True and the current-row pointer becomes invalid.

CAUTION

If you choose a forward-only snapshot-type cursor, only the MoveNext method can be used to move the current-row pointer. If you try to use the MoveLast method against an ODBC snapshot-type cursor, an error 3219 ("Invalid operation") will result. This also holds true for RDO or ODBC forward-only record sets.

NOTE A data row that has been added to a record set might not qualify for membership if a query is reexecuted, if the Requery method is used, or if the Recordset object is rebuilt. Records added by other users aren't visible to a record set once its membership is frozen, but changes made by anyone to a member row are visible after the current-row pointer has been repositioned to that row. If any change to a row disqualifies it for membership in the record set, that row remains a member of any Recordset objects that exist at the time of the change but it isn't included in any rebuilds of current Recordset objects or in any newly created Recordset objects.

Locating a Specific Row

If you need to have Jet locate a specific row in an existing Recordset object, you can use a number of techniques, including the Find methods. Frankly, I prefer requerying the database to find a specific row, but the Find methods are popular with ISAM developers and work pretty well if there aren't too many rows.

The Find methods

The FindFirst method is executed against an existing Recordset object and uses a criterion as a search argument. If a match is found, the current-row pointer is relocated to the first matching row. If no match is found, the NoMatch property is set to True; otherwise, it's set to False. When you use the FindLast method, Jet fully populates your record set before beginning the search, if it isn't populated already. Each Find method begins its search from the location and in the direction shown in Table 13-2.

Table 13-2
The Find Methods of Relocation

Find Method	Starting Point	Direction of Search
FindFirst	Beginning of record set	Toward end of record set
FindLast	End of record set	Toward beginning of record set
FindNext	Current record	Toward end of record set
FindPrevious	Current record	Toward beginning of record set

TIP Using one of the Find methods isn't the same as using a Move method, which simply makes the first or next record current without specifying a condition. You can follow a Find operation with a Move operation.

When you use one of the Find methods with a SQL Server data source, the method is implemented as either optimized or unoptimized. The optimized version is used only when the table or query is a dynaset-type record set, not a snapshot, and when the column is indexed. The Find restriction must be as follows:

```
column = value
```

or

```
column LIKE value
```

And the *like* string must be as follows:

```
smith
```

or

```
smith*
```

The optimized Find algorithm first executes a query that takes this form:

```
SELECT bookmark-columns
FROM table
WHERE find-restriction
```

Once this query completes, Jet searches the current Recordset object for a match against the new list of bookmarks. When it finds a match in a row, it repositions the current-row pointer to that row. If it doesn't find a match, it sets the NoMatch property to True. (This is a significant improvement over the unoptimized Jet 1.1 version of the Find method, which executed a SQL Server query against each individual row in the Recordset object—a *very* slow process for Recordset objects larger than a few dozen rows.)

The Seek method

One of the fastest operations Jet performs is locating records with the Seek method. Ordinarily, the Seek method isn't available to SQL Server users, but I've discovered a way to get around this limitation:

1. Execute a MakeTable query that creates a "permanent" Jet table instead of a cursor. This query can even use a SQL pass-through query and a TSQL query or stored procedure.

2. Create a new index on the new Jet table, using an action query.

3. Use the Seek method to access the data.

This technique takes slightly longer, but once you've set it up, using the Seek method is at least six times faster than creating a snapshot-type Recordset object and using the Find method—even *with* its enhancements. If you create lookup snapshots from SQL Server data and need to reference them more than a few times, this technique can really pay off. The "permanent" table you create can also be bound with the Data control, which supports table-type Recordset objects.

Updating DAO/Jet Data Sources

You can use two basic strategies to update SQL Server data with DAO/Jet. You can create an updateable cursor, or you can execute a SQL-based action query that updates rows independently of a cursor. The first strategy is popular with some developers, but the second is often dictated by the design of the database. For example, if the only available way to update your data is via one or more stored procedures, there might be no way to create an updateable cursor, so you must use one of the SQL-based techniques.

> **NOTE** If you have access only to SQL Server views, remember that you can attach a SQL Server view to an MDB database and create one or more Jet indexes on the view using Jet action queries. This makes the view updateable, at least one table at a time; you can't perform an update that affects more than one table.

Using DAO/Jet Cursors

If you have access to an updateable table or Recordset object, Jet can perform row updates on your data, using the Delete method to drop rows, the Edit method to change existing rows, or the AddNew method to add new rows. When you add a row by using a cursor, the row immediately becomes part of both the cursor and the database. If you use the SQL techniques, the new row or rows don't appear in your open Recordset object and they won't appear until it's rebuilt. Remember that adding, deleting, or modifying rows won't change the membership of existing Recordset objects that have been created by other users, but the changes will appear in these existing dynasets as the current row is positioned over the changed row. And when a database table row changes, it might affect a dynaset that is composed of only part of the changed row (that is, a subset of the columns of the table). A cursor might also be composed of a set of columns drawn from a set of tables. Therefore, a single repositioning or updating operation might require several rows of data to be fetched from several tables before the current row can be rebuilt on the basis of its component parts.

In all cases, Jet can modify the data in cursors or attached server tables that have unique primary keys (bookmarks). When a row is updated or deleted, Jet sends an Update or Delete action query to the server, qualified by a WHERE clause specifying the key values for that row (the bookmark). This query controls exactly which row is changed or dropped and protects against inadvertent multirow changes—assuming that the primary key can identify a specific row.

> **TIP** You can tell whether a result set is updateable by examining the Updatable property. If it's False, you can't use the Update method. If you try anyway, you get a trappable error that complains about an invalid method. There are many reasons why a result set might not be updateable. Often you can get around the restrictions imposed by Jet if you execute an action query that contains an UPDATE SQL statement or the right stored procedure.

Generally, inserting new rows also requires the existence of a bookmark. The dynaset must keep track of newly added records because they become indistinguishable from existing records. And if the query doesn't return all the columns constituting the bookmark, the insertion of new records isn't allowed. Exceptions to the rule exist, however; Append and MakeTable action queries don't require a unique key on the remote table. (An append query is simply a SQL query that contains an INSERT statement; a MakeTable query uses INSERT INTO syntax.)

INSERT and UPDATE statements

When an insert or update is performed, Jet no longer supplies values for every updateable field in the cursor, whether or not the field was explicitly changed or set. The new default behavior sets only those columns touched by the update operation. You can turn this behavior on and off by changing the Prepared-Insert and PreparedUpdate Registry settings. The PreparedInsert Registry setting indicates whether to use a prepared INSERT statement that inserts data in all the columns. The values are 0 (use a custom INSERT statement that inserts only non-Null values) and 1 (use a prepared INSERT statement). The default is 0. Using prepared INSERT statements can cause Nulls to overwrite server defaults and can cause triggers to execute on columns that weren't inserted explicitly.

The PreparedUpdate Registry setting indicates whether to use a prepared UPDATE statement that updates data in all the columns. The values are 0 (use a custom UPDATE statement that sets only the columns that have changed) and 1 (use a prepared UPDATE statement). The default is 0. Using prepared UPDATE statements can cause triggers to execute on unchanged columns.

This flexibility allows Jet to use a single INSERT/UPDATE statement for all inserts and updates instead of constructing a new statement every time. If you set either of the Prepared settings to 1, however, any of three side effects can occur unexpectedly:

- A trigger that fires when a column is changed might be activated, even if the column is being "changed" to its current value. (You can alter the trigger to do nothing if the old and new values match.)

- Inserts will fail if columns that don't allow null strings aren't included in your query. If you don't supply values for the columns, the Null value that Jet supplies will cause an error.

- Server defaults might be overridden at insertion time by the explicit Null value supplied by Jet.

You can force an updateable query output column to be nonupdateable (and exclude it from INSERT and UPDATE statements) by wrapping it in an expression such as one of these:

```
IntegerCol + 0
StringCol & ''
```

If a table has a TimeStamp column, Jet prevents you from updating it manually because SQL Server maintains its value.

CAUTION

If another user changes a bookmark column of a row, Jet loses its handle to the record and considers it deleted. Reexecuting the query remedies this situation if the record still meets the query's criteria. Therefore, if a trigger on the server changes the key values at the time of an update or insert, Jet might fail to update or insert the row. If Jet successfully updates or inserts the row, Visual Basic might indicate on the next reference that the row has been deleted.

Security

Jet neither enforces nor overrides server-based security. You can set up additional client-side security on attached tables and their queries, but Jet remains ignorant of server security beyond the initial connection-time logon. Security violations caused by Jet queries executed in support of dynaset operations can cause ODBC to bring up dialog boxes with server-specific error messages.

Locking, concurrency, and transactions

When SQL Server is accessed via the ODBC interface, data page locking is the responsibility of the remote database engine. Jet simply acts as a front end to the database servers; it doesn't control data sharing on back-end database engines. (In some cases, however, you can control how the remote server locks data by using back-end–specific SQL statements or administrative options.) When Jet defers to back-end schemes for page locking, there are a few implications:

- Setting the LockEdits property of the Recordset object has no effect.

- The exclusive parameter of the OpenDatabase method is illegal or ignored; you can't open a SQL server exclusively. (You can set the system to run in single-user mode, but only if you are the server administrator.)

- All updates are done with optimistic concurrency. Rows aren't locked during editing; they are checked for conflict at update time, when the bookmark-qualified UPDATE statement is further restricted. If a TimeStamp column exists in the table, as reported by SQLSpecial-Columns(SQL_ROWVER), it's qualified with its current value. If not, all columns, excluding the Memo and OLE Object columns, are tested against their former values. (The former method is preferable, especially given the precision-loss problems described earlier in connection with floating-point data.)

- Attempts to lock the entire table or database by using TSQL syntax can bring the SQL server to its knees, especially in a high-volume transaction environment.

- For maximum throughput and to provide the only reliable way of letting the back-end database engine operate its native locking scheme, you should incorporate sophisticated error handling to react correctly when locking contention occurs.

Jet wraps most data-modifying operations in short transactions, but longer transactions can sometimes occur. (In the case of a large action query, Jet wraps the entire bulk operation within a single transaction.) You are responsible for the length and breadth of your transactions, which can be arbitrarily long and broad. Bear in mind the following caveats:

- Long-running transactions over large amounts of data can lock out or block other users as SQL Server escalates from page locking to table locking. Try to avoid these transactions when users are connected. Schedule them for hours when their impact won't be felt.

- Automatic idle-time population doesn't apply to Snapshot and Dynaset objects as it does in Access, unless they are created by the Data control. If you stop moving through the result set and sit on a row for a long time, the server might hold a lock on that row or page. Because of Jet's buffering schemes, this is no longer a concern once you reach the end of the result set or when you're dealing with smaller result sets. List boxes and combo boxes, when they are bound to large server-based result sets, also don't enjoy background population.

- When performing ORDER BY operations, some servers lock all the data pages or tables involved until the sorting is finished and the results are returned. This behavior is beyond Jet's control.

Some of these caveats are relevant to any client-server environment, regardless of the front-end application. To be a good citizen in such an environment, you should make judicious use of transactions and cursors on result sets of reasonable size and you should be familiar with your server's default locking behavior.

Updating with SQL-Based Action Queries

When you need to update a SQL Server table value, an entire row, or a set of rows, the preferred method involves the use of an action query. You simply send an UPDATE statement with a WHERE clause that reflects the keys of the rows to be changed:

```
db.Execute "UPDATE Animals SET Status = 'Fried' " _
    & " WHERE Animal_ID = 17"
```

This might not be an option, however, since update operations are permitted only through the execution of stored procedures. That doesn't really change this strategy, though; you can still use an action query to perform the update. You just have to submit a different type of query. Whenever you have to execute a stored procedure by using Jet, you must use the dbSQLPassThrough option in the OpenRecordset or Execute methods:

```
db.Execute "ChangeStatus 'Fried', 17", dbSQLPassThrough
```

When you create an UPDATE statement on the fly, you have several design decisions to make. You need to consider how the rules and triggers are going to interact with the process, so you must decide whether the statement will include all the columns or only the ones that are affected. Your code must also be prepared to trap the errors that might be generated by Jet, SQL Server, and the rules and triggers. (See the "Handling DAO/Jet Errors" section on page 291.)

You also have to decide how to handle transactions, since several rows might be affected—in a single table or in tables spread all over the database. But if you're using Jet to perform heterogeneous joins, your options are very limited: you must let Jet do the update.

Jet's transaction model is built around the Workspace object, and all databases opened under a single Workspace object are in the same transaction

CAUTION

SQL Server has no mechanism for updating non–SQL Server tables, but you can control your own transactions by submitting SQL pass-through queries containing TSQL transaction statements. Watch out for Jet's connection management, though. If you use this technique, Jet won't know that you're working with transactions, so it might disconnect in the middle of a transaction, causing an immediate rollback. You should consider using Jet's Workspace transaction model instead.

scope. If you begin a transaction on two Database objects and subsequently roll back a transaction on either of the two, the rollback applies to both, as far as Jet is concerned, and Jet submits a rollback statement to both. If you need to perform independent transaction operations, create another Workspace object and open the second Database object against the new Workspace, as shown here:

```
Dim MyWorkspace As Workspace
' Create new Workspace.
Set MyWorkspace = DBEngine.CreateWorkspace("Special", MyUserName, _
    "SpecialPW")
```

> **NOTE**   ODBC doesn't support the nesting of transactions to SQL Server, no matter what interface you use, so once you execute the Jet BeginTrans method, subsequent calls are ignored until a matching CommitTrans method or Rollback method is executed.

The Jet 1.1 requirements for the sequence of operations were lifted in Jet 3.0 and later. Jet's remote transaction management allows for seamless use of server transactions in Basic code. BeginTrans now "carries into" opening a dynaset on server data, even if a connection to the server didn't exist before the dynaset was opened. The code on the next page works as expected.

ExecuteSQL? Just Say No

You could use the ExecuteSQL method instead of the Execute method to run action queries because ExecuteSQL returns the number of rows affected by the operation—but so does the RecordsAffected property of the Database object. Besides, using the ExecuteSQL method also has several unfortunate side effects:

- ExecuteSQL doesn't use Jet connection management, so the number of connections might increase.

- It forces complete population of the result set before returning control to the user, which encourages the perception of lower performance.

- It uses direct connections to the SQL server, which means that users incur added DDL overhead for no reason, since information is pulled down about the database schema but isn't used.

- The SQL Trace facility doesn't log its operations.

```
BeginTrans
Set ds = d.CreateDynaset(...)
data modifications using ds
ds.Close
CommitTrans/Rollback
```

It's no longer necessary to structure your code as follows (although this code still works):

```
Set ds = d.CreateDynaset(...)
BeginTrans
data modifications using ds
CommitTrans/Rollback
ds.Close
```

If you use the following sequence on remote data, a Rollback isn't sent to the server, as it was in Jet 1.1, and the server transaction remains open until you explicitly commit it or roll it back or until the application terminates (at which time it is rolled back):

```
Set ds = d.CreateDynaset(...)
BeginTrans
data modifications using ds
ds.Close
```

These transaction semantics also apply to SQL pass-through queries that modify server data. Explicit transactions within the pass-through queries not only are unnecessary but can also cause problems.

It's now possible to nest several bulk operations in a transaction, as in the following credit/debit–style operation:

```
BeginTrans
d.Execute("UPDATE SavingsAccount
          SET Balance = Balance - 100")
d.Execute("UPDATE CheckingAccount
          SET Balance = Balance + 100")
CommitTrans/Rollback
```

Given the keyset-driven model used by Jet, it's important to note how bulk operations (action queries such as Insert, Update, Delete, and MakeTable) are performed. For example, Jet performs a bulk operation if you use a SELECT statement to drive an INSERT statement or execute an UPDATE statement that uses a WHERE clause referencing more than one row. First the keyset for the affected records is built. Then the appropriate operation is performed for each record in the keyset, one record at a time. This is slower than performing a single qualified bulk operation on the server, but it allows for partially successful bulk queries as well as bulk queries that can't be executed by the server. When this extra functionality isn't required, it's often faster to use a SQL pass-through query and your own schemes for error management.

A new option has been added for the OpenRecordset method and the Execute method: dbFailOnError. This option permits you to execute bulk operations but still determine whether one of them has failed. For example, if you execute a Jet Update action query that affects a dozen rows, Jet executes each of the 12 operations individually but control normally won't be returned to your application until the operation completes. If any of the 12 individual update operations fails and you haven't set the dbFailOnError option, the process will be stopped but you won't receive any indication that an operation has failed. But if you *do* set the dbFailOnError option, a trappable error is fired if any of the 12 operations fails. (You have no way to tell which of the rows have been updated and which haven't—that's what transaction processing is for.)

Handling DAO/Jet Errors

SQL Server is an interactive engine that returns a litany of error messages, all of them important to varying degrees. The Jet, ODBC, and network layers also chime in once in a while. Often when a low-importance message arrives, your application doesn't need to be interrupted. But when something significant comes up, your application *will* be interrupted.

Whether the errors are trappable generally depends on your use of the Data control as well as on the operations executed at design time or before the Form_Load event is complete. For all your applications, you must establish an On Error GoTo trap to prevent an unexpected timeout from causing the application to crash. And in the case of a general ODBC error, you must be prepared to examine the Errors collection, which maintains an Error object for each error that occurs.

The Error objects were an addition to Visual Basic 4.0. They are especially helpful with ODBC applications, since the error objects give you access to the native error number returned by SQL Server. When you work with SQL Server and the ODBC drivers, errors are reported in layers. When a low-level operation fails, it reports back to its parent layer, and that layer does the same, all the way up the line. Thus a single error can create three or four Error objects, with the lowest-level error being the most significant. For that reason, the Error(0) object in the Errors collection contains the most valuable information about the root cause of the failure. (The remaining objects rarely contain anything of interest—just the driver name, the server type, and so forth.) Table 13-3 on the following page shows the Visual Basic Error object properties and describes their uses with SQL Server.

The Description property is particularly ugly if it's not reformatted. For example, the following description is returned when you don't provide the right password for the SP_PASSWORD stored procedure: *[Microsoft][ODBC SQL Server Driver][SQL Server] Old (current) password incorrect for use -- password not changed.* One way to reformat the message is to strip off the preamble. Since you know that your application always accesses SQL Server, you can keep everything after the string *[SQL Server]*:

```
E$ = Errors(0).Description
RealError$ = Mid(E$, instr(E$, "[SQL Server]") + 12)
```

CAUTION

Because of the way Jet handles errors for all ODBC clients, any error over a certain level of severity is considered fatal. Unfortunately, a RAISERROR statement is considered indicative of a fatal error, so any stored procedures you execute that use a RAISERROR statement to provide a warning message will cause Jet to terminate the operation as if a fatal error had occurred.

Table 13-3
Visual Basic Error Object Properties

Property	What It Does
Count	Gives number of Error objects in the Errors collection (0-based).
Description	Gives a short description of the error; alerts you to an error that you can't or don't want to handle.
HelpContext	Returns a context ID as a string variable for a topic in a Windows Help file.
HelpFile	Returns a fully qualified path to the help file.
Number	Names the error that occurred. (This is the *native* SQL Server error number for ODBC errors.)
Source	Represents, by means of a string expression (usually the object's class name or programmatic ID), the object that originally generated the error.

Executing Transact-SQL Queries

Using SQL Pass-Through Queries

Working with Stored Procedures

Handling SQL Server Messages

O ne aspect of working with a generic interface such as ODBC is maximizing the target systems' features. Microsoft Jet's SQL dialect is similar to the one the ODBC Driver Manager uses, but it's less comprehensive than Transact-SQL (TSQL), the dialect Microsoft SQL Server uses—even though they have evolved toward each other. As you know, TSQL is used to fetch result set rows and to perform all kinds of database management system (DBMS) maintenance. In this chapter, we'll cover various techniques for executing TSQL queries to get this work done.

Using SQL Pass-Through Queries

SQL pass-through queries can improve performance if you can do without what you lose when you bypass Jet's query processor. Many DAO/Jet applications rely completely on SQL pass-through to perform SQL Server operations. In any case, SQL pass-through should play a major role in any SQL Server front-end application that requires Jet. Figure 14-1 depicts the path of a SQL pass-through query.

The real problem with using TSQL is the Jet query processor/optimizer, in which the syntax provided in the OpenRecordset, Execute, or QueryDef objects is parsed and prepared for execution. For the most part, this rather complex (read convoluted) piece of code just gets in the way and makes your applications run more slowly than they would if you talked more or less directly to SQL Server. To use any but the simplest TSQL queries, you *must* bypass this portion of Jet (or not use Jet at all—but that's another story). The dbSQLPass-Through option does just this, and it's available on both the OpenRecordset and Execute methods. (You can also use the outdated ExecuteSQL method, which supports *only* ODBC SQL pass-through operations, but the 32-bit version of Jet doesn't support ExecuteSQL.) One of the most flexible enhancements to Jet is that it lets you create a SQL pass-through QueryDef object that contains a reference to a stored procedure. You can reference the stored procedure result set as a read-only table.

PART III USING DAO WITH THE JET DATABASE ENGINE

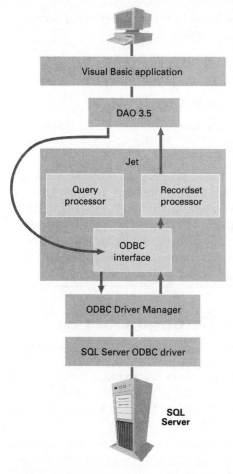

Figure 14-1 *The path of a SQL pass-through query*

NOTE SQL pass-through with attached tables was prohibited in Visual Basic 3.0 but is supported in later versions of Visual Basic. This innovation in Jet 3.0 improved ODBC data source handling.

Typical Applications

Generally, you can use SQL pass-through to perform any of the following operations (each of which requires you to provide a TSQL string and enable the SQL pass-through option):

- Execute a stored procedure and return one or more sets of results and even return values and output parameters

- Run a SQL query using TSQL syntax or return one or more sets of results

- Create a new device, database, table, or index on an external server using TSQL data definition language (DDL) statements

- Create or manage SQL Server triggers, defaults, rules, or stored procedures

- Maintain user accounts or perform other system administrator tasks

- Run maintenance operations, such as SQL Server's DBCC

- Execute multiple INSERT or UPDATE statements in a single batch

- Manage transactions independently of Jet

NOTE You can use SQL pass-through to pass single or multiple TSQL commands, stored procedures, or other TSQL statements (such as those involved in administrative functions) to the SQL server for execution. Whenever you specify a SQL pass-through query, the Jet database query processor is bypassed but the Jet *record set* processor is still used to create and manage the result sets that might be generated by your query.

Implementing SQL Pass-Through Queries

The neatest way to execute a SQL pass-through query is to have a DAO/Jet QueryDef object store the query. That way, you take advantage of the efficiency of attached tables. Nevertheless, you must create and manage a separate Jet database to hold the QueryDef object unless you create the database and QueryDef object each time you run the application. I've seen applications that did stranger things.

Although the technique we're about to look at uses the DAO/Jet QueryDef object to store and execute a foreign-language SQL query, you can't set parameters for the query by using the Parameters collection of the QueryDef object. To build SQL queries that are created in code or that require parameters, you need to construct or modify the query in code.

The result set created from a SQL pass-through query is always placed in a snapshot-type Recordset. If multiple result sets are generated by your SQL pass-through query, however, Jet can create a separate table-type Recordset object for each set of results by using a SELECT INTO query. Jet 2.5 and Jet 3.0 support the use of SQL pass-through by permitting your code to set the SQL property of the QueryDef object to contain non–Jet engine SQL syntax. (You can still place foreign SQL syntax in the SQL argument of the CreateDynaset, CreateSnapshot, or ExecuteSQL methods and use the dbSQLPassThrough option, but this outdated technique isn't recommended.)

TIP If you're *really* considering use of DAO/Jet to execute and manage the result sets from complex multiple result set queries, you should sit down and carefully reconsider. Of course, if you're still coding 16-bit applications, this might be your only viable choice, but Remote Data Objects (RDO) and even ODBCDirect manage this type of query far more easily.

Creating a SQL Pass-Through QueryDef Object

To create a SQL pass-through QueryDef object, take the following steps:

> **TIP** Folks, don't get ahead of me and try this with ODBCDirect. It doesn't work the same way. It doesn't even work here if you don't take each step in turn.

1. Use the CreateQueryDef method to create a DAO/Jet QueryDef object, using only a *Name* argument. Don't get too anxious and try to short-circuit this process. If you specify a SQL argument in the CreateQuery-Def step, you can't use foreign SQL syntax, since the query must comply with Jet engine SQL syntax. To create a temporary QueryDef object that isn't automatically saved in the database, use the CreateQueryDef method without the *Name* argument.

2. Set the Connect property of the QueryDef object to a valid connect string, which informs the Jet engine that this is a SQL pass-through query. From this point on, the Jet engine won't attempt to parse the SQL property.

3. Set the SQL property of the QueryDef object to the TSQL statement to be executed. Be sure to use correct TSQL syntax; the syntax isn't checked until the statement is executed by the SQL server for the first time.

4. If you expect your query to return one or more sets of records (rows), set the ReturnsRecords property of the QueryDef object to True, which informs the Jet engine to expect records (rows) back from the query. (Otherwise, Jet will think that this is an action query.) Any query that contains a SELECT statement has the potential to return rows. When ReturnsRecords is True, the Jet engine creates a snapshot-type Recordset object for the first set of results. Subsequent result sets are placed in "permanent" tables. If you don't set the ReturnsRecords property to True for a query that returns records, a trappable error results.

CAUTION
Careful, now. If you try to shortcut this technique, it won't work. You can't supply the SQL until the Connect property has been set.

Look at the following code, which creates a SQL pass-through QueryDef object that executes a stored procedure. The stored procedure, in turn, returns multiple result sets. In this case, we execute the sp_help *tablename* system stored procedure, which returns several result sets.

```
Private Sub Command1_Click()
Set db = OpenDatabase("C:\attach.mdb")
db.QueryDefs.Delete "MySPHelp"
Set qd = db.CreateQueryDef("MySPHelp")
qd.Connect = "ODBC;dsn=biblio;uid=;=pwd=;database=biblio;"
qd.SQL = "SP_Help " & (TableDesired)
qd.ReturnsRecords = True
```

NOTE Many of the samples used in this book use databases that are on the companion CD. See Appendix A for information on how to set up the database samples.

To execute the SQL pass-through QueryDef, use the OpenRecordset method and execute the stored QueryDef so that the first (and only the first) set of results is available:

```
Set rs = qd.OpenRecordset
```

To process any additional result sets of a SQL pass-through QueryDef, you first create and execute a temporary QueryDef object that executes a Jet SQL MakeTable query, using SELECT INTO syntax. The Jet engine creates one new (permanent) Jet table for each set of results and stores them in your database. (The table need not exist beforehand.) If more than one user of a shared database executes this code at the same time, the multiple applications might generate table-name collisions. The SELECT INTO query doesn't return records, but it builds one or more Jet tables to store the results from the QueryDef. Since a name isn't provided for the CreateQueryDef method, the Jet engine doesn't store a new QueryDef in the database, as you can see in this code:

```
Set qd = db.CreateQueryDef("")
qd.SQL = "Select [MySPHelp].* Into Result From [MySPHelp];"
qd.Execute
```

Remember, MySPHelp is the query that executes the sp_help stored procedure. Next, create and process each of the resulting tables (which contain the results of the QueryDef) by using the OpenRecordset method. Repeat this process for each result set. Unless you know how many result set tables were created, you must query the TableDefs collection. Note that the Jet engine numbers the tables sequentially: the table named *Result* contains the first set of results, *Result1* contains the second set, and so on. To deal with this a little more gracefully, we'll add some code to walk the TableDefs collection, looking for our *Resultn* tables. Remember that these are permanent tables and that *everyone* using this database can see them. It also means that you must destroy them yourself in code—as quickly as possible.

```
' Process the results of the query...
For Each tb In db.TableDefs
    If Left(tb.Name, 6) = "Result" Then
        Set rs = tb.OpenRecordset
        ShowFields rs
        rs.Close
    End If
Next tb
hits = True
Do While hits
    hits = False
    For Each tb In db.TableDefs
```

```
        If Left(tb.Name, 6) = "Result" Then
            db.TableDefs.Delete tb.Name
            hits = True
        End If
    Next tb
Loop
End Sub
```

Notice the somewhat convoluted way that we deleted the members of the TableDefs collection. Once you delete a member, all the other members iterate up, so it takes several passes to get them all. However, if you don't remove these result set tables (*Result* through *Resultn*), you can't run the query again—and neither can anyone else.

Using SQL Pass-Through Queries with Attached Tables

You can also use SQL pass-through queries with attached tables. Remember that attached tables are simply linkage entries in a Jet database that point to and describe SQL Server tables. By setting the Connect property of a Database object (after the Jet database is open), you tell Jet that the attached tables should be populated by SQL pass-through queries.

Let's look at some concrete examples of the methods we've already examined. The following sample program, SQL PassThrough Test (which is on this book's companion CD), performs the same query in a number of ways. Included in this sample is a piece of RDO code to serve as a benchmark—a sanity check, as it were. The first section sets up the global variables, as usual; there is nothing of global importance here.

```
Option Explicit
Dim db As Database
Dim rs As Recordset
Dim rd As rdoResultset
Dim JetQuery As String
Dim TSQLQuery As String
Dim qd As QueryDef
Dim er As Error
```

In the Form_Load procedure, we'll open a Jet database that serves four purposes:

- It contains a number of attached ODBC tables. These are used in the queries in a variety of ways.

- It contains a DAO/Jet QueryDef object named JetQuery, which uses the attached tables. (This object was created using Microsoft Access.)

- It serves as a place to build and store the permanent QueryDef object that we're about to create on the fly. (We can't create a temporary QueryDef object for this application.)

- It serves as a conduit for the underlying ODBC database associated with the attached tables.

The next section of code opens the Jet database. (You have to change the code to point to it, or perhaps create it yourself, if you want to run this test.) We'll then initialize two strings that contain the Jet syntax query and the TSQL query to be run later. Notice anything strange about the table names? That's right—they don't have the *dbo_* prefix. That's because I went in and removed all those prefixes after building the database.

```
Private Sub Form_Load()
Set DBEngine = Nothing
Set db = OpenDatabase("C:\Attach.mdb")
Open "Jettest.txt" For Output As #1
JetQuery = "SELECT DISTINCTROW Authors.Author," _
    & " Title_Author.ISBN," _
    & " Titles.Title, Publishers.Company_Name" _
    & " FROM ((Authors INNER JOIN Title_Author " _
    & " ON Authors.Au_ID = Title_Author.Au_ID) " _
    & " INNER JOIN Titles ON Title_Author.ISBN = Titles.ISBN) " _
    & " INNER JOIN Publishers " _
    & " ON Titles.PubID = Publishers.PubID " _
    & " WHERE (((titles.Title) Like '*Hitch*'));"
TSQLQuery = "Select Distinct Author, T.ISBN, Title, Company_Name" _
    & " From Authors A, Title_Author TA, Titles T, " _
    & " Publishers P " _
    & " Where A.Au_ID = TA.Au_ID and " _
    & " TA.ISBN = T.ISBN and P.PubID = T.PubID and " _
    & " T.Title like '%Hitch%' "
End Sub
```

The next seven sections of code are started from command buttons on Form1. These launch the individual tests. The first test is also a benchmark of sorts. It is an example of what *not* to do. It opens the database directly and simply executes *JetQuery* (DAO/Jet QueryDef). Notice the ShowJetResults procedure call near the end. This simply displays the rows of the result set. This application is also designed to create a log of the output and error messages, for debugging purposes.

```
Private Sub JetBaseTest_Click()
Dim db2 As Database
Print #1, "-----------> Starting Plain direct open Jet Test"
Set db2 = OpenDatabase("Biblio", 0, 0, _
    "ODBC;uid=;pwd=;database=Biblio;")
Set rs = db2.OpenRecordset(JetQuery, dbOpenSnapshot)
Print #1, rs.RecordCount
ShowJetResults
rs.Close
End Sub
```

The next test is the RDO benchmark to verify that things are working correctly:

```
Private Sub RDOTest_Click()
Print #1, "-----------------> Starting RDO Test"
Dim cn As New rdoConnection
```

```
With cn
    cn.Connect = "dsn=biblio;uid=;pwd=;database=biblio;"
    cn.EstablishConnection rdDriverNoPrompt, True
    Set rd = .OpenResultset(TSQLQuery, rdOpenStatic, _
    rdConcurReadOnly, rdExecDirect)
End With
ShowRDOResults
End Sub
```

Next comes the first of the Jet tests. The strategy here is to run a query through the Jet query processor that uses the attached tables. The test simply executes the DAO/Jet query against the Jet database object and creates a snapshot with the resulting rows. The advantage of this approach is that it's easy to code, but it requires a Jet database—one that already has the attached tables. This database isn't hard to create, however, even in code:

```
Private Sub JetTest1_Click()
On Error GoTo T1Eh
Print #1, "-----> Starting Jet query against attached tables Test"
' Approach 1 -- Open a Jet query against attached tables.
Set rs = db.OpenRecordset(JetQuery, dbOpenSnapshot)
ShowJetResults
rs.Close
ExitT1:
Exit Sub
T1Eh:
    ShowDAOErrors
    Resume ExitT1
End Sub
```

The next test is slightly more difficult to set up and run because it requires a predefined query stored in the Jet database. Once again, we use Access, Visual Database Tools, or the Data Environment Designer to create, tune, and save the query. The test executes a permanent DAO/Jet query that contains the same query that we executed in the first test:

```
Private Sub JetTest2_Click()
' Approach 2 -- Open Jet query against stored QueryDef object that
' accesses attached tables.
Print #1, "--------> Starting Jet query against Jet QueryDef Test"
Set rs = db.OpenRecordset("JetQuery", dbOpenSnapshot)
ShowJetResults
rs.Close
End Sub
```

Now we start to push the envelope for the Jet/ODBC interface by sending a TSQL query and *bypassing* the Jet query processor. Notice that the database that is referenced is a Jet database, not an ODBC database opened directly against the SQL server. By setting the Database object's Connect property after it's opened, we can tell Jet to perform SQL pass-through operations by establishing a connection that uses the given connect string, as shown on the following page.

```
Private Sub TSQLTest1_Click()
Print #1, "----------------> Starting TSQL query" _
    & " against attached tables DB Test"
' Approach 3 -- Execute TSQL query against attached tables.
db.Connect = "ODBC;uid=;pwd=;database=biblio;dsn=biblio;"
Set rs = db.OpenRecordset _
    (TSQLQuery, dbOpenSnapshot, dbSQLPassThrough)
Print #1, rs.RecordCount
ShowJetResults
rs.Close
End Sub
```

The following test shows an even more advanced concept. Here, we create a DAO/Jet QueryDef object in code, set the Connect property, and then set the SQL property. Notice that the SQL property is set using TSQL syntax, *not* Jet SQL syntax. This technique creates a true SQL pass-through QueryDef object—a feature introduced in Jet 2.5 and retained in Jet 3.*x*. We then create a Recordset object against this newly created QueryDef object. Notice that you don't have to set the SQL pass-through bit; that is done for you. This query can also be executed by Access or by anyone else who shares this Jet database. You can treat this QueryDef object the way you treat any Jet table. The fact that it gets its information straight from SQL Server and bypasses Jet's query processor is a powerful feature.

```
Private Sub TSQLTest2_Click()
Print #1, "-------> Starting TSQL query against SPT QueryDef Test"
On Error GoTo TSQLEH1
db.QueryDefs.Delete "TSQLT2"
On Error GoTo 0
Set qd = db.CreateQueryDef(Name:="TSQLT2")
qd.Connect = "ODBC;uid=;pwd=;database=biblio;dsn=biblio;"
qd.SQL = TSQLQuery
Set rs = qd.OpenRecordset(dbOpenSnapshot)
ShowJetResults
rs.Close
db.QueryDefs.Delete "TSQLT2"
Exit Sub
TSQLEH1:
    If Err = 3265 Then Resume Next
    Stop
End Sub
```

The next procedure is similar to the preceding ones, but it creates only a temporary DAO/Jet QueryDef object. This technique does eliminate the ability to share the QueryDef object between applications, but it also eliminates the need to delete the QueryDef object each time you run the procedure during development. Notice that we set the ReturnsRecords property to tell Jet that this isn't an action query. Does this mean that you can use SQL pass-through QueryDef objects to execute action queries? It sure does.

```
Private Sub TSQLTest3_Click()
Print #1, "--> Starting TSQL query against SPT Temp QueryDef Test"
On Error GoTo SPT3Eh
Set qd = db.CreateQueryDef("")
qd.Connect = "ODBC;uid=;pwd=;database=biblio;dsn=biblio;"
qd.SQL = TSQLQuery
qd.ReturnsRecords = True
Set rs = qd.OpenRecordset(dbOpenSnapshot)
ShowJetResults
SPT3Exit:
rs.Close
Exit Sub
SPT3Eh:
    For Each er In Errors
        Debug.Print er.Description
    Next
    Resume SPT3Exit
End Sub
```

The following two routines simply dump the result sets to a file and trap any errors that are encountered. The first procedure, ShowRDOResults, is for the RDO query. The second, ShowJetResults, is for the Jet queries.

```
Sub ShowRDOResults()
Dim errdo As rdoError
Dim cl As rdoColumn
On Error GoTo SPTEH:
Print #1, rd.RowCount
Do Until rd.EOF
    For Each cl In rd.rdoColumns
        Print #1, cl,
        Debug.Print cl,
    Next
    Print #1,
    Debug.Print
    rd.MoveNext
Loop
Print #1, rd.RowCount; "  done"
Debug.Print rd.RowCount; "  done"
quit:
Exit Sub
SPTEH:
    Print #1, Error$, Err
    Debug.Print Error$, Err
    For Each errdo In rdoErrors
        Print #1, errdo
        Debug.Print errdo
    Next
    If Err = 3146 Then Resume quit
    Resume Next
End Sub
```

(continued)

```
Sub ShowJetResults()
On Error GoTo SPTEH:
Dim fd As Field
Print #1, rs.RecordCount
Do Until rs.EOF
    For Each fd In rs.Fields
        Print #1, fd,
        Debug.Print fd,
    Next
        Print #1,
        Debug.Print
    rs.MoveNext
Loop
Print #1, rs.RecordCount; "  done"
Debug.Print rs.RecordCount; "  done"
quit:
Exit Sub
SPTEH:
    If Err = 3265 Then Resume Next
    Print #1, Error$, Err
    Debug.Print Error$, Err
    ShowDAOErrors
    If Err = 3146 Then Resume quit
    Resume Next
End Sub

Sub ShowDAOErrors()
    Debug.Print Error$, Err
    For Each er In Errors
        Print #1, er
        Debug.Print er
    Next
End Sub
```

Summary of the Query Techniques

We've just seen a number of techniques for executing what is basically the same query against SQL Server. Here is a summary of the techniques:

- **Open the SQL Server database directly, and use SQL pass-through to create a DAO/Jet Resultset object using a TSQL query string** You probably used this technique in Visual Basic 3.0. It's no longer necessary, nor is it particularly efficient.

- **Execute a string containing a DAO/Jet query against an open Jet database containing attached tables** The Jet query refers to the attached tables. This technique uses the Jet query processor to execute the query. In this case, SQL pass-through isn't used.

- **Execute a permanent DAO/Jet QueryDef object containing the same Jet SQL query as in the first example** Again, SQL pass-through isn't used.

- **Execute a string containing a TSQL query, but bypass the Jet query processor** This technique uses a DAO/Jet Database object whose Connect property has been set to connect to the SQL Server database when SQL pass-through is requested, as is done in the Open-Recordset method.

- **Create a permanent DAO/Jet QueryDef object in code to make Jet use SQL pass-through to execute it** The QueryDef object's SQL property contains a TSQL query. This technique also uses a Jet database to store the shareable SQL pass-through QueryDef object.

- **Create and execute a temporary SQL pass-through DAO/ QueryDef object that contains a TSQL query and whose Connect property points to the SQL Server** This technique is a little convoluted, but it often yields the best performance. It most closely approximates what you'll want to do later in ADO.

TIP A SQL pass-through query is always created as a snapshot-type Recordset object, so when it fetches row data it also fetches page-based data (Text and Image data types), even if that data is never accessed. This can take a long time. But a SQL pass-through query doesn't fetch the page-based data if you don't include page-based columns in the query. If you need to access page-based data, use Jet dynasets against attached tables, since dynasets fetch page-based columns only when they are accessed. Remember, too, that there is no background population of a Recordset object unless you use the Data control. In code, rows are fetched only when you request them (for example, by using the MoveNext method).

Working with Stored Procedures

It's possible to use DAO/Jet to execute stored procedures from Visual Basic. However, it's not possible to retrieve, return, or output parameters directly without writing specific support queries. These queries should retrieve the results and convert them to ordinary row values. That is, you have to write ordinary TSQL queries that return both the return and output parameter values.

Return Parameters

Besides the result set, the most common parameter returned from a stored procedure is the return status. All stored procedures return it. This integer value can indicate that a procedure has been successfully completed, or it can indicate the degree of success or the reason for failure. SQL Server has a defined set of return values, and you can define your own set. For example, one stored procedure that returns a status is sp_password, which adds or changes a password for a SQL Server login ID. If the procedure successfully changes the password, it returns 0; otherwise, it returns 1 to indicate failure for some reason. (It also provides a descriptive error message.) To execute this procedure and retrieve the return status, you need a TSQL query like this one:

```
declare @rv int
execute @rv = sp_password <old password>, <new password>,
<login ID>
select "Return status"= @rv
```

Notice that you must first declare a TSQL variable, to hold the return status, and you must use a separate SELECT statement to return the value to your application in the form of a column in a single-row result set. This query has two result sets: one for the EXECUTE statement and one for the SELECT statement. It turns out that Jet simply ignores the first result set (because it returns no rows), so coding this query is fairly simple.

To execute this query with DAO/Jet, first set up the global variables. To save time, we open an MDB database in the Form_Load event. (Remember to close it when you're done with the application.) This database is simply a place-holder Jet database—hence the use of the same name, "Attach.MDB," that we used previously. (The code that follows is also on the companion CD as "Return Status Stored Procedure.")

```
Option Explicit
Dim SQL As String
Dim db As Database
Dim qd As QueryDef
Dim rs As Recordset
Private Sub Form_Load()
Set db = OpenDatabase("c:\Attach.MDB")
End Sub
```

Next, the ChangePassword procedure sets up a query against our *Attach* database. Since there is no way to dynamically insert parameters into this query, we have to concatenate them by using the & operator. Note that an error handler is installed to deal with anticipated ODBC errors and other, unanticipated errors:

```
Private Sub ChangePassword_Click()
On Error GoTo CpEH
ReturnStatus = vbGrayed
SQL$ = "declare @rv int " _
    & " execute @rv = sp_password " & OldPassword & "," _
    & NewPassword
If Len(UserID) > 0 Then SQL$ = SQL$ & "," & UserID
SQL$ = SQL$ & " select 'Return status' = @rv"
```

Next we create a temporary QueryDef object. This technique uses the DAO/Jet Database object but doesn't save anything there. (Remember that you can use a Jet database that contains no tables.) To establish a SQL pass-through QueryDef object, set the Connect property first and the SQL property second. (If you set the SQL property first, Jet thinks that the query syntax should be correct for Jet.) Then set the ReturnsRecords property to indicate that the query returns rows—it isn't an action query.

Now we set the Database object's Connect property to contain a connect string pointing to the SQL server. This permits Jet to locate the SQL server when we create the SQL PassThrough result set, in the step that follows this one.

```
Set qd = db.CreateQueryDef("")
qd.Connect = "odbc;dsn=biblio;uid=;pwd=;database=biblio;"
qd.SQL = SQL$
qd.ReturnsRecords = True
```

And now we're ready to execute the query. The OpenRecordset method is used against the temporary QueryDef object. That's where the SQL and connect string information comes from. To execute this query, Jet establishes a connection to the SQL server specified in the QueryDef Connect property, and then Jet passes the query through to the SQL server query processor:

```
Set rs = qd.OpenRecordset(dbOpenSnapshot)
```

NOTE Incidentally, up to this point most of this code has been imported from the Visual Basic version 4.0 CD without modification. Yes, I tuned it up to take advantage of the new 32-bit Visual Basic features in some cases, and changed the DSN references, but the rest seemed to convert nicely.

Once the query is executed, the return status from the stored procedure is retrieved when the first member of the Fields collection of the first member of the Recordsets collection is examined. If 0 is returned, it means that the query worked and the password was changed. Otherwise, the query failed and somewhere along the line we got an ODBC error. Since we're done with the Recordset and QueryDef objects, we can toss them out.

An alternative strategy is to place the CreateQueryDef object in the Form_Load event and simply change the SQL property each time the QueryDef object is executed:

```
If rs(0) Then ReturnStatus = 0 Else ReturnStatus = 1
rs.Close
QuitSub:
qd.Close
Exit Sub
```

When an error occurs, the error handler tests to see whether it is one of the anticipated ODBC errors. Since most ODBC errors return with a value of 3146, we filter out those errors and simply parse the Description property of the Errors collection. This returns a somewhat ugly string full of superfluous information, but the last part of it is usable. If the error is an unanticipated Visual Basic or Jet error, the second part of the handler displays an error message drawn from the Error string returned by Visual Basic. The error handler, shown on the next page, is fairly simple. It probably should be more sophisticated, but it does the job.

```
CpEH:
    Select Case Err
        Case 3146
            MsgBox Errors(0).Description
            Resume QuitSub
        Case Else
            MsgBox Error$
        End Select
End Sub
```

When the application ends or the user chooses Exit from the File menu, the form is unloaded. This approach does a good job of cleaning up the connections and the other Jet objects.

```
Private Sub Form_Unload(Cancel As Integer)
db.Close
End Sub

Private Sub MenuFileExit_Click()
Unload Form1
End Sub
```

Output Parameters

Many shops use output parameters for returning nonrow data from stored procedures. Getting at these parameters with Jet is a challenge, but it can be done. A stored procedure that returns output parameters specifically marks one or more arguments with the *OUTPUT* keyword. For example, the following TSQL stored procedure has two input arguments and passes back a return status and two output values:

```
CREATE PROCEDURE TestOutputRS
    @LikeTitle  Varchar(128) = '%',
    @LangWanted  Int = 1,
    @MaxTnum  int OUTPUT,
    @MinTnum  int OUTPUT
AS
Select @MaxTnum = max(P.Tnum), @MinTnum = min(P.Tnum)
From Topics T, Tprops P
Where P.Tnum = T.Tnum
and Title like @LikeTitle
and Lang = @LangWanted

if @MaxTnum = NULL Return 0
Return @MaxTnum-@MinTnum
```

To execute this procedure, you need to send a TSQL SQL pass-through query like this one:

```
declare @m1 int
declare @m2 int
declare @rv int
execute @rv = testoutputrs '%r%', 1,@m1 OUT, @m2 OUT
Select 'Return Value' = @rv, 'Max Tnum' = @m1, 'Min Tnum' = @m2
```

But let's say that you used named arguments in the query to refer to the first argument of the EXECUTE statement—something like this:

```
execute @rv = testoutputrs @liketitle = 'rd', @m1, @m2
```

This isn't an option, because TSQL syntax insists that *all* the arguments be either named arguments or positional arguments; no mixture is possible. You must also supply all the output and input arguments if you use the positional syntax. I got an error:

```
Msg 201, Level 16, State 2
Procedure TestOutputRS expects parameter @MinTnum, which was
not supplied.
```

The error occurred when I failed to include the second input argument, for which I wanted the default value. The error message refers to *@MinTnum*—irrelevant in this case.

To execute this query with Jet, use the same method as the one used in the example for the return status. Apparently, Jet simply discards the rowless result set generated by the TSQL EXECUTE statement.

Handling SQL Server Messages

When you submit a query that violates a rule, the violation triggers an error message, which in turn triggers the ODBC error handler. The error message indicates which rule was violated and how the violation occurred. Likewise, if you perform an operation that causes a trigger to fire, the trigger code can execute a PRINT statement that returns a message or a RAISERROR statement that returns a number and an error message. But unless you tell Jet to expect messages, it simply tosses them away. To make matters worse, Jet interprets a RAISERROR statement as indicating a fatal error and stops processing the query that's in progress.

CAUTION

If a Null computed value is passed to a RETURN statement, the SQL server resets it to 0 and generates an error message. A TSQL EXECUTE statement doesn't return any values that can be seen by either ODBC or DBLIB; you must include the SELECT statement to expose these values in the form of a result set row. Be sure to include the keyword *OUT* in the final SELECT statement, which extracts the output values; otherwise, the value assigned to these variables will be set to Null.

> **TIP** I once executed a query that returned about a dozen rows followed by a RAISERROR statement. Jet processed the query and began populating the Recordset object. But after Jet processed the last record, ODBC returned an "ODBC call failed" message and continued to return it as long as I tried to execute a MoveNext or MoveLast against the Recordset object. I turned on LogMessages and set up an error handler that dumped the Errors collection, but I still saw no sign of the RAISERROR message or its error number. If any of your procedures uses the RAISERROR statement as a warning mechanism, you must rewrite it to take into account this peculiarity of Jet.

So how do you tell Jet to expect messages? You add a property to a DAO/Jet QueryDef object (and here is one more good reason for creating a "permanent" QueryDef object designed solely as an agent for executing stored procedures). By appending the LogMessages property, as shown in the code below, and working with the permanent Jet tables that are created, you can manage returned messages fairly well. At this point, I wouldn't recommend sharing the Jet database used to hold the QueryDef object (and perhaps some attached SQL Server tables or views); adding multiuser functionality to this interface would be pretty hairy.

To turn on SQL Server message handling, you need to follow the steps described here. (The help documentation doesn't list all of them.) Start by setting up the global variables. Note that the Database and Recordset objects are declared globally, so they must be closed manually:

```
Option Explicit
Dim SQL As String
Dim db As Database
Dim qd As QueryDef
Dim LmProp As Property
Dim Em As Error
Dim rs As Recordset
Dim tb As TableDef
Dim MsgTable As String
```

Next, open the Attach.MDB database. (This is the same database we used in a previous example, so you should probably make sure that no vestiges of that example are lying around.)

```
Private Sub Form_Load()
Set db = OpenDatabase("Attach.MDB")
End Sub
```

In the next step, the ShowMessages_Click event has the bulk of the code. First, set up the QueryDef object. (It has to be a "permanent" QueryDef object this time because we will be giving it a new property.) In this case, the SQL query to be executed is shown on the form in a text box to make testing easier. Note that I turn on an error handler to trap the various errors that we're bound to get:

```
Private Sub ShowMessages_Click()
On Error GoTo CpEH
Set qd = db.CreateQueryDef("LmQd")
qd.Connect = "odbc;dsn=biblio;uid=;pwd=;database=biblio;"
qd.SQL = Query
qd.ReturnsRecords = True
```

Now we're ready to install the new property on the QueryDef object. When we install the LogMessages property, we'll set its (Boolean) value to True to indicate that any messages that this QueryDef object creates should be saved. Note that we use the named-argument Visual Basic syntax to code this function, but you can use the old style or even the Visual Basic 4.0 With syntax. Once the Property object is created, you have to manually append it to the QueryDef properties collection. Use the Refresh method to confirm that the property has been added.

```
Set LmProp = qd.CreateProperty(Name:="LogMessages", _
    Type:=dbBoolean, Value:=True, DDL:=False)
qd.Properties.Append LmProp
qd.Properties.Refresh
```

Now that our QueryDef object is ready, we can execute it and create a snapshot-type Recordset object. After the Recordset object is built, clear out the Messages control and print the resulting rows from the first part of the query. Note that we haven't seen any sign of the print messages at this point—and we won't until we close the Recordset object. For some reason, the Jet table used to store the messages was created in Exclusive mode and can't be accessed until the Recordset object that created it is closed:

```
Set rs = qd.OpenRecordset(dbOpenSnapshot)
messages.Cls
Do Until rs.EOF
    messages.Print rs(0), rs(1)
    rs.MoveNext
Loop
```

Once we finish with the Recordset object and close it, we can see whether any messages were generated in the course of the query's execution. It's like waiting until we've torn down the barn before checking to see if the horses are inside—but that's the way it works. The following routine walks through the TableDefs collection looking for the last (highest) table starting with the name *Admin - *. Each time Jet executes this procedure, it does the same thing and creates another table, using the next name in the sequence. The name used is derived from the user ID. By default, this is *Admin*, and so *Admin - 00* is the first name generated, *Admin - 01* is next, and so forth.

```
rs.Close             ' to free Exclusive lock on Admin - xx table
MsgTable = ""
For Each tb In db.TableDefs      ' find last Admin - xx table
    If tb.Name Like "Admin -*" Then MsgTable = tb.Name
Next tb
```

If we find a table, this routine creates a record set on that table. It contains *all* the print messages generated by the earlier query. Each message occupies one row. Once all the messages are printed, we're ready to clean up the last Recordset object:

```
If MsgTable <> "" Then
Set rs = db.OpenRecordset(MsgTable, dbOpenTable, dbReadOnly)
Do Until rs.EOF
    Debug.Print rs(0)
    messages.Print Right(rs(0), 30)
    rs.MoveNext
Loop
rs.Close
End If
```

To make sure that we can execute this sample again, we toss out the QueryDef object. This isn't really necessary, since we can use the QueryDef object again later simply by changing the SQL property. We'll toss the *Admin - xx* table, too, so we don't have to find out what happens when we get to *Admin - 99*. We'll also refresh the TableDefs collection, just to make sure that Jet knows we deleted some tables:

```
QuitSub:
    db.QueryDefs.Delete "LmQd"
    qd.Close
    db.TableDefs.Delete MsgTable
    db.TableDefs.Refresh
Exit Sub
```

The error handler for this procedure is similar to the one in the earlier sample, but in this case we'll also add code to deal with early-exit problems that can leave an orphaned QueryDef object:

```
CpEH:
    Select Case Err
        Case 3146
            For Each Em In Errors
                MsgBox Em.Description
            Next
            Resume Next
        Case 3012
                db.QueryDefs.Delete Name:="LmQd"
                Resume
        Case Else
            MsgBox Error$
        End Select
        Resume Next
        Resume QuitSub
End Sub
```

And that's SQL Server message handling, Jet-style. It ain't pretty, but it's better than nothing...sort of.

15

Using the Data Control

Applying the Data Control

Using the Data Control with SQL Server

Setting Properties

Checking the Properties

Using Bound Controls

ow that Microsoft Visual Basic 6.0 has shipped, there are at least four major types of data source controls: the DAO version, the RDO RemoteData control, the ADO Data control, and the Data Environment–created ADO Command objects that can double as data source controls. All of these controls permit you to use a GUI interface to connect form-based data-aware controls such as the TextBox control and the Grid control to data sources such as Microsoft SQL Server result sets. The first control we'll discuss is the oldest—the Data control as implemented by DAO and built into Visual Basic from version 3.0 on. To keep things simple in this chapter, we'll just call it the Data control. No, not all of the data source controls can be lumped together. How they are implemented is very different, as we'll discuss in later chapters.

Should you use the Data control when you access SQL Server? My usual advice is, "Just say no." Sometimes, though, that Data control can be tempting when it appears on a lonely highway to pick you up. But once you realize that it loves to strand inexperienced hitchhikers on dead-end streets of frustration, you'll put your thumb back out and wait for a more suitable ride. If you're determined to ride with it anyway, be sure to study the documentation on the Data control and its basic use before you continue reading this chapter.

The problem with the Data control in previous versions of Visual Basic wasn't performance—not really. You could manage and tune its performance. And the problem wasn't really the connections. You could control the number of connections if you were careful—very careful. The problem was that the Data control requires the use of a cursor.

Sometimes you can create cursors against SQL Server base tables. But when it comes time to update a table row, you might not have the luxury of a read-write cursor. Your MIS department might limit SQL Server access to a few choice stored procedures or restricted-access views, so not only can't you update data directly, you also might not even be able to extract it outside the scope of a stored procedure. This situation made the Data control basically useless unless you had access (at least read-only access) to a base table or a view. You could create a Recordset object against a stored procedure's read-only result set, but you couldn't use the Data control to update this data. Besides, Jet always creates a snapshot-type Recordset object against stored-procedure data: neither Jet nor the other programming interfaces can create a keyset-driven cursor against the stored-procedure rows because they know not from whence the data has come.

With Visual Basic 5.0, the Data control received a lot of attention—especially since you could theoretically create your own bound controls. You actually couldn't create your own bound controls in version 5.0, but with Visual Basic 6.0, you really can. But unless you use the ADO Data control (the ADODC) or the RemoteData control, you can't get the neatest feature of all—the ability to trap the WillUpdateRows event, which lets you fire off an appropriate stored procedure instead of depending on an updateable cursor. Has Visual Basic 6.0 changed the way the Data control works? Not much—other than some bug fixing. But it has let developers do all of their own binding.

Since Visual Basic 5.0, the Data control is better able to deal with common data content scenarios and is a better ODBC citizen. Simply by pressing Control-Break, you can tell it to cancel the creation of a running query—or you can try to. And yes, you can set up the Data control to run via ODBCDirect, but no, it still doesn't fire the events you see from straight RDO.

Applying the Data Control

Let's assume that you have access to an updateable view or to SQL Server base tables or that you can use the read-only rows from stored procedures and use another update mechanism. The Data control does quite a bit of work for you if you can apply it to your needs, especially if you have to display and update graphics stored in the SQL Server database, since the Data control permits virtually code-free implementation. In general, you can consider the Data control for the following functions:

- Managing graphics in bound Picture and Image controls.

- Managing pick lists that show valid foreign-key selections. (One common implementation of the Data control fills a bound control from a filtered list of valid part numbers, valid state codes, or valid ship-to addresses.)

- Managing simple or complex Jet-based Recordset objects using simple table-only queries or queries that join, filter, and sort data from a variety of heterogeneous sources.

- Displaying formatted result set data in a multirow array, as with the DBGrid control.

Like Microsoft Access, the Data control can theoretically populate result sets in the background during idle time. When I execute a query that calls for more than a few hundred rows, however, the Data control's background population doesn't seem to work as expected. For example, I set up a test query that pulled back several hundred (OK, 25,000) rows using a Jet query in the RecordSource property. I know, this isn't typical of any production application, but we're just trying stuff out here, so bear with me. I also set up a Timer control to monitor the current value of the RecordCount property, which indicates how many rows have been populated.

At first, everything went fine. The Data control opened the Recordset object quickly and showed me the first row. The RecordCount property started out at 1, as I expected. After a few seconds, the timer routine detected that the RecordCount property was inching up 100 rows at a time, which was also what I expected. Jet was quietly populating the cursor in the background. The first row was visible in the three bound controls set up to display the current record, so I clicked the Next Row button on the Data control. That's when things fell apart—the whole application went dead and stayed that way until the Recordset object was fully populated. The timer control received no further events (the Microsoft Windows message loop wasn't getting any cycles), but Jet seemed to be busy populating the result set. I could tell it was busy; the Windows System Monitor said that the CPU was running at 100 percent, and my hard disk light was steadily flashing. *Something* was happening. Visual Basic was locked out the whole time, too, because the form wasn't repainted when it was supposed to be. When the query was finally finished, the Recordset object was fully populated, as evidenced by the RecordCount property jumping up to the total number of rows in the Recordset object—not good. This isn't what I call background population. I call this the same old "lock up while we do a MoveLast" strategy. So much for background population with the Data control. Perhaps this will be fixed in a later release. As it is, it's another nail in the Data control's tire.

NOTE I thought that this basic problem would be fixed in Visual Basic 5.0 or at least in Visual Basic 6.0—but it isn't. It still works in exactly the same way that it did in Visual Basic 4.0. Sigh. See the test application "Data Control BG Population" on this book's companion CD if you want to try this yourself. I guess they didn't put much work into the older technology this time.

Using the Data Control with SQL Server

To use the Data control with any data source, you have several design choices. You can set the Data control properties at design time and have the control create a cursor on its own. This technique creates one of two types of DAO/Jet Recordset objects (dynaset or snapshot) against the default Workspaces(0) object. Another approach is to create a Recordset object using the Open-Recordset method and then set the Data control's Recordset property to this new result set. This technique is useful for working with independent Recordset objects or with result sets created using parameter queries or QueryDef objects. A third approach is to create a Database object using the OpenDatabase method and then set the Data control's Database property to the new Database object.

This technique can be especially useful for working with secondary Workspace objects, since the Data control always assumes that it should use the Workspaces(0) object.

NOTE The Data control doesn't know how to deal with Table objects. Even if it did, you still wouldn't be able to use table objects against SQL Server.

When you work with SQL Server, you still have all three of these basic choices. The only real question is who will create the Recordset object. The Data control can't directly execute QueryDef objects that require parameters, and it always uses the default Workspace object. If you need to execute parameter queries or have special transaction scope requirements, create an independent Recordset object and pass it into the Data control.

Setting Properties

The Data control properties that you need to set for accessing SQL Server are shown in Table 15-1 on the following page. You have several choices when it comes to setting the RecordSource property, and these choices play a big part in the viability of using the Data control with SQL Server. We'll talk about using the ODBCDirect version of the Data control a little later.

CAUTION

Think of Data control properties as items on the menu at a truck stop outside Killeen, Texas. What you order might not be what the waitress finally shoves across the counter. When you set Data control properties, you also might not get exactly what you asked for, but Jet does its best to give you something "edible"—and you don't even have to tip when your order takes too long.

Your first choice is to set up a valid data source name (DSN) and a connect string and just use the drop-down list of table names. This list is generated by the Data control and Jet when you connect to SQL Server. The Data control and Jet execute an ODBC function that returns the names of selected tables. The list includes views but not stored procedures or system tables. Each table name has the *dbo* prefix; that's the way DAO/Jet passes table names back from ODBC.

When you set the RecordSource property by just picking one of the tables, the Data control internally substitutes a SELECT * FROM *table* query. This option brings back *all* the columns from *all* the rows in the table (dumb). Rows and columns are returned in the order in which SQL Server returns them. If you open such a query against a large table, be ready to wait—for a very long time. I recommend writing a carefully worded query that limits the result set to between a few dozen and a few hundred rows and selects only the columns you really need. If SQL Server uses a clustered index on the table, the rows are usually returned in an order that is based on the index (physical) order.

The second approach is to code a full-blown Jet SQL query in the RecordSource property using a WHERE clause that limits the number of rows returned. This query can access a single table, returning only the columns you need or returning a complex multitable or heterogeneous join that includes both Jet-fetched and SQL Server tables. You can also include an ORDER BY clause to sort the rows before they are returned. Remember, though, that every column you bring back costs time and resources. A variation on this technique is to reference a Jet QueryDef object. This query can return rows from a stored procedure or any other Jet query.

CAUTION

Picking a table name from a drop-down list is really easy—and really dangerous. This feature is designed to be used with relatively small ISAM or Jet tables, not with the gargantuan tables often used by SQL Server.

Table 15-1
Data Control Properties for Accessing SQL Server

Property	Purpose
Connect	Specifies the connect string. It is coded exactly like the OpenDatabase *Connect* argument. It always begins with *ODBC*, and it can contain a user ID, password, and default SQL Server database name. It can also contain the DSN if you don't specify it in the DatabaseName property. After the Data control opens the connection, it contains the connect string that is actually used.
DatabaseName	Specifies the DSN unless it is specified in the Connect property (which takes precedence).
RecordSource	Specifies the name of a table (not a good idea) or of a Jet SQL query. (You can use TSQL, but you have to set the SQL pass-through bit in the Options property.)
Options	Specifies any needed options. You can set the dbReadOnly (4), dbAppendOnly (8), dbSQLPassThrough (64), or dbSeeChanges (512) options. You can't set dbForwardOnly because it returns an "invalid operation" error with no further indication of what is wrong because dbForwardOnly isn't supported for the Data control.
EOFAction	If this property is set to 2, Jet and the Data control handle the empty-result-set case for you by automatically switching to the AddNew mode. I always set this property to 2.
ReadOnly	Specifies a read-only cursor. This can improve performance because Jet won't have to worry about updating the data.
RecordsetType	Tells Jet which kind of cursor to create: type 1 (dynaset) or type 2 (snapshot). After the Data control opens the result set, the Data control shows which type was actually created.
DefaultCursorType	(ODBCDirect) Specifies the type of RDO cursor operation (not used for DAO/Jet implementations).
DefaultType	Specifies whether the Data control should use Jet (dbUseJet[2]—the default) or ODBCDirect (dbUseODBC[1]).

A third viable choice is to code a TSQL query or stored procedure. If you decide to use TSQL syntax instead of Jet syntax, you should set the Options property to include the dbSQLPassThrough bit. In this case, the result set is always read-only, so you should set the RecordsetType property to dbOpenSnapshot.

Checking the Properties

Once the Data control creates a DAO/Jet Recordset object, the Data control properties reflect what has actually been created. (See Table 15-2.) You can use the Database and Recordset objects created by the Data control just as you would if you had created them in DAO code. They support the same methods and properties and manage the same types of result sets.

Table 15-2
Values of Data Control Properties After a Connection Is Opened

Property	Description
Connect	Contains the string used to establish the connection. Any missing arguments are filled in.
DatabaseName	This property doesn't change, even if you specify a different DSN in the Connect property.
Database	Set to the new Database object that is created when the connection is opened.
Recordset	Set with the new Recordset object.
ReadOnly	If the data isn't updateable, this property is set to True.
RecordCount	Set to 1 if any rows have resulted from the query. If no rows have resulted, it's set to 0. If DAO/Jet can't figure out how many rows returned (yet), it returns –1.
Updatable	Set to True if the underlying data is updateable and if Jet has identified a unique index for the keyset.
RecordsetType	Specifies what kind of cursor was created.

When you use DAO methods to reposition the current-row pointer (such as when you use the MoveNext method), the bound controls are automatically kept in sync with the current row of the result set.

As with the DAO interface, you can improve performance against ODBC data sources if you use the following:

- Attached tables.

- Forward-only snapshots. (Too bad you can't use this option with the Data control; just using a snapshot can help if there aren't too many rows.)

- The read-only option. (When the read-only option bit is set, Jet doesn't concern itself with additional overhead to update the result set.)

- The append-only option. (When the append-only option bit is set, Jet can optimize the operation because it is concerned only with adding rows, not updating existing rows.)

- Limited-scope queries that return only the columns and rows needed.

Using Bound Controls

There's nothing special about setting up bound controls against ODBC data sources. You simply set the DataSource property to a chosen Data control, and you set the DataField property to one of the columns returned by the result set. If you do this at design time, the Jet engine populates the TableDefs and Fields collections with the names and descriptions of all possible columns.

TIP If a MaskedEdit control is bound to a Data control, you might get an "Invalid property value" error message when you use the AddNew method, which doesn't work if you have specified a mask in any of the bound MaskedEdit fields. To solve this problem, clear the mask, execute the AddNew method, and then reinstate the mask. A similar problem can occur when you set the MaxLength property of the TextBox control so that the text entered (either read from the database or pasted in) is too long.

Data Control Design Issues: A Few Hints

Here are a few tips to remember about using the Data control:

- When you create an application that uses the Data control against an ODBC data source, the first Data control can potentially use two connections. Each additional Data control uses an additional connection, even if it's using the same data source name as the first. All of these connections remain open until their result sets are fully populated, when all the connections are released—except the two used to fetch fresh data from a dynaset-type Recordset object and to update rows, as necessary. Two connections remain, even if you created only a snapshot-type Recordset object.

- The limit on the number of Data controls loaded in your application is limited by the number of connections it can use, how long it takes to populate the Data controls' Recordset objects, how much memory you have for storing the keyset or snapshot cursors, and how much patience your user has.

- You can avoid a connection feeding frenzy by not completing all of the properties of your Data controls at design time. Instead, you can complete the properties at run time, one at a time, and use the Refresh method to open each control. This won't help much if you don't fully populate the result sets, however. And be aware that this serial process can make your application take far longer to load.

- Experts tell me they never permit records to be saved unless the code is bound into some pretty sophisticated error handlers—ones that can verify that the data is correct before, during, and after an update.

- A "Type mismatch" error is generated when a control is bound to a field with an incompatible type, but the Error object isn't populated when it is examined in the Data control Error event. This is a limitation of the Data control in Visual Basic 4.0 because when Jet generates an error, the Error object is cleared. It's still a problem in the current version.

16

Understanding the Jet Query Processor

Constructs That Jet Must Evaluate Locally

Restriction Splitting

Evaluation of Outputs

Removal of Execution of Crosstab Queries

Outer Joins

Generating SQL to Send to a Server

Wildcards for the LIKE Operator

Owner and Table Prefixing

Identifier Quoting

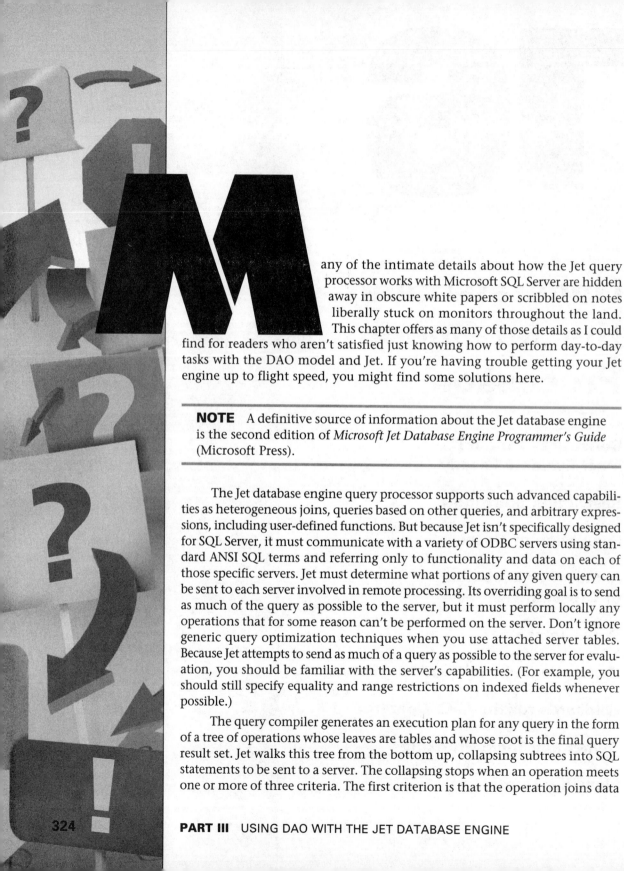

Many of the intimate details about how the Jet query processor works with Microsoft SQL Server are hidden away in obscure white papers or scribbled on notes liberally stuck on monitors throughout the land. This chapter offers as many of those details as I could find for readers who aren't satisfied just knowing how to perform day-to-day tasks with the DAO model and Jet. If you're having trouble getting your Jet engine up to flight speed, you might find some solutions here.

> **NOTE** A definitive source of information about the Jet database engine is the second edition of *Microsoft Jet Database Engine Programmer's Guide* (Microsoft Press).

The Jet database engine query processor supports such advanced capabilities as heterogeneous joins, queries based on other queries, and arbitrary expressions, including user-defined functions. But because Jet isn't specifically designed for SQL Server, it must communicate with a variety of ODBC servers using standard ANSI SQL terms and referring only to functionality and data on each of those specific servers. Jet must determine what portions of any given query can be sent to each server involved in remote processing. Its overriding goal is to send as much of the query as possible to the server, but it must perform locally any operations that for some reason can't be performed on the server. Don't ignore generic query optimization techniques when you use attached server tables. Because Jet attempts to send as much of a query as possible to the server for evaluation, you should be familiar with the server's capabilities. (For example, you should still specify equality and range restrictions on indexed fields whenever possible.)

The query compiler generates an execution plan for any query in the form of a tree of operations whose leaves are tables and whose root is the final query result set. Jet walks this tree from the bottom up, collapsing subtrees into SQL statements to be sent to a server. The collapsing stops when an operation meets one or more of three criteria. The first criterion is that the operation joins data from multiple data sources. The key to query performance on attached server tables is to ensure that little or no data filtering is done on the client machine. Client-side data processing increases network traffic and prevents you from leveraging advanced server hardware; it effectively reduces the client/server system to a file server system. You can optimize performance by being aware of what query operations Jet must evaluate on the client. All joins that span multiple data sources must be performed locally. Some servers, such as a SQL server, support multiple databases on a single machine. But because each server is a distinct ODBC data source, Jet doesn't ask the SQL server or other similar servers to do cross-database joins, only joins within a given database.

The second criterion for Jet's not collapsing subtrees into SQL statements is that the operation would not be expressible in a single SQL statement. Since Jet queries can be based on other Jet queries, several kinds of operations are allowed. These include a Group By over a Group By operation or Distinct operation, a join over one or more Group By or Distinct operations, and complex combinations of inner and outer joins. Jet sends the server as many of these operations as can be expressed in a single standard SQL statement, but it performs the remaining higher-level operations locally.

The third criterion for stopping the collapse of subtrees into SQL statements is that the particular operation is not supported on the server. Generally, the SELECT clause of a query has no effect on how much of the query Jet sends the server and how much is processed locally. Jet selects the needed columns from the server and, on that basis, locally evaluates any output expressions. For example, if an output expression (such as string concatenation) can be evaluated on the server, it's sent to the server for processing.

Constructs That Jet Must Evaluate Locally

Query clauses other than the SELECT clause (WHERE, ORDER BY, and so on) have a more important effect: the expressions in these clauses determine whether Jet must execute them locally. When expressions are executed locally, Jet must query or download all relevant rows from all data sources involved and do the work on the client machine.

Unsupported Visual Basic Operators and Functions

Visual Basic intrinsically supports many numeric, string, aggregate, and date/time functions, as well as many statistical and financial functions. Some have server-side equivalents, and some don't. Jet must locally evaluate any function that has no server-side correspondent. Jet does this by using SQLGetInfo to ask the ODBC driver which operators or functions are supported on the server. If these operators and intrinsic functions are supported by the server and driver, Jet sends them to the server for evaluation. Table 16-1 shows these operators and functions.

Table 16-1
Visual Basic Operators and Functions

General Operators		Numeric Functions	String Functions	Aggregate Functions	Date/Time Functions
AND	&	ABS	LCASE	MIN	SECOND
NOT	+	ATN	LEFT	MAX	MINUTE
IN	-	COS	LEN	AVG	HOUR
=	*	EXP	INSTR	COUNT	WEEKDAY
< >	/	INT	LTRIM	SUM	DAY
<	IDIV	LOG	MID		MONTH
< =	MOD	MOD	RIGHT		YEAR
>		RND	RTRIM		DATEPART
=		SGN	SPACE		
BETWEEN		SIN	STRING		
IS [NOT]		SQR	TRIM		
NULL		TAN	UCASE		
OR					
LIKE					

User-Defined Functions

You can define your own functions in Visual Basic. These never have server-side equivalents, so they are always evaluated locally unless they don't reference any server data. In that case, the function is evaluated and the result is sent to the server. Question: Should you? Ah, no. These won't migrate to more sophisticated applications when you want to get away from DAO/Jet—and you will.

Miscellaneous Unsupported Functionality

Jet uses SQLGetInfo and SQLGetTypeInfo to ask the ODBC driver whether a particular server supports, among other things, the following functions:

- Outer joins (which are supported by SQL Server)
- Expressions in the ORDER BY clause (which are not supported by SQL Server)
- The LIKE operator in Text and Memo columns (which is supported by SQL Server)

Miscellaneous Unsupported and Questionable Expressions

These locally evaluated constructs include the following operators and functions:

- Operations involving incompatible types, such as LIKE b + c (which are not supported by SQL Server)

- Nonstandard LIKE wildcards, such as the Microsoft Access–specific [and # (which are supported by SQL Server)

- Intrinsic functions, if arguments have incorrect types

- Explicit type-conversion functions, such as CInt and Cdbl (which are supported by SQL Server)

- Nonlogical operators where logical operators should be, such as (a > b) AND (c + d), in which the right side is arithmetic

- Logical operators where nonlogical operators should be, such as a + (b AND c) * d, which attempt to use a result from a logical operation in an addition

Restriction Splitting

When deciding whether a WHERE or HAVING clause can be sent to the server, Jet dissects the restriction expression into its component conjuncts, separated by ANDs, and locally evaluates only those components that can't be sent. Therefore, if you use restrictions that can't be processed by the server, you should add restrictions to them that *can* be processed by the server. For example, suppose you write a Basic function called SomeCalculation. The following query causes Jet to return the entire table and evaluate *SomeCalculation(column1) = 17* locally:

```
SELECT *
FROM huge_table
WHERE SomeCalculation(column1) = 17
```

Note the following query, however:

```
SELECT *
FROM huge_table
WHERE SomeCalculation(column1) = 17 AND
    last_name BETWEEN 'g' AND 'h'
```

The preceding query causes Jet to send the following query to the server, returning only those rows that match the restriction:

```
SELECT *
FROM huge_table
WHERE last_name BETWEEN 'g' AND 'h'
```

Jet then locally evaluates the restriction on only those rows, as shown here:

```
SomeCalculation(column1) = 17
```

Evaluation of Outputs

Although SELECT clause elements are usually evaluated by the server, this rule has two exceptions:

- **Queries with the DISTINCT keyword** If all SELECT clause expressions can be evaluated by the server, Jet sends the DISTINCT keyword as well. If a SELECT clause expression must be evaluated locally, so must the DISTINCT keyword operation.

- **Queries with aggregation** Jet attempts to do aggregation on the server, since this often drastically reduces the number of rows returned to the client. For example, the query

```
SELECT Sum(column1) FROM huge_table
```

is sent entirely to the server; a single row is returned over the network. But the query

```
SELECT StdDev(column1) FROM huge_table
```

causes Jet to send *SELECT column1 FROM huge_table* to the server, retrieve every row in the table, and perform the aggregation locally. It does this because StdDev isn't a standard SQL aggregate function.

Removal of Execution of Crosstab Queries

Jet sends some crosstab queries to the server for evaluation, which can mean that far fewer rows are transferred over the network. Jet sends a simpler GROUP BY form of the crosstab and transforms the result set into a true crosstab. This transformation doesn't apply to complex crosstab tables, however. To send the optimal crosstab query to the server, the following criteria must be met. (These apply only to Jet SQL queries, not to TSQL SQL pass-through queries.)

- Row and column headers can't contain aggregates.

- The value must contain only one aggregate.

- There can be no user-defined ORDER BY clause.

  All the other reasons for forcing local processing also apply.

Outer Joins

In determining where to perform joins, Jet separates outer joins from inner joins because of ambiguities inherent in mixing the two types. Therefore, any query that Jet sends through the ODBC interface will have a FROM clause containing one of the following:

- Any number of tables, all inner-joined

- Any number of inner joins and one outer join

This means that some complex queries involving inner and outer joins cannot be sent in their entirety to the server, so Jet might perform some of the higher-level joins locally. Another condition that can cause Jet to perform an outer join locally occurs when the join restriction is anything other than an outer join on one column:

```
left_table.column = right_table.column
```

Generating SQL to Send to a Server

Jet sends SQL statements to the SQL Server ODBC driver. These SQL statements are generated using the SQL grammar defined by ODBC. For the most part, this is standard SQL, but it might contain ODBC-defined canonical escape sequences. The SQL Server ODBC driver is responsible for replacing these escape sequences with SQL Server–specific syntax before passing the SQL along to the server; Jet never uses back-end–specific syntax. For example, most servers support outer joins, but servers differ widely in their outer-join syntax. Jet uses only the ODBC-defined outer-join syntax:

```
SELECT Table1.Col1, Table2.Col1
FROM {oj Table1 LEFT OUTER JOIN Table2 ON
    Table1.Col1 = Table2.Col1}
```

Jet relies on the ODBC driver to translate this to the server-specific outer-join syntax. In the case of SQL Server, the syntax is as follows:

```
SELECT Table1.Col1, Table2.Col1
FROM Table1, Table2
WHERE Table1.Col1 *= Table2.Col1
```

Wildcards for the LIKE Operator

When you use the LIKE operator, you should use the Jet wildcards (? for single-character matching and * for multiple-character matching), not the SQL Server–specific %. Jet translates these wildcards into _ and % before sending the expression to the server. The only exception involves query parameter values: because Jet forwards your parameter values to the server, they must use _ and %.

Owner and Table Prefixing

When generating queries that involve more than a single table, Jet prefixes column names with a table name. In a self-join, Jet generates a correlation name to use as a table name prefix. Jet also supplies an owner name prefix if an owner is associated with the attached table. This owner name (if it exists) is returned by the ODBC driver's SQLTables function at attach time.

Identifier Quoting

Jet calls SQLGetInfo(SQL_IDENTIFIER_QUOTE_CHAR) to determine which identifier-quoting character is supported by the server and driver. If such a character exists, Jet wraps all owner, table, and column names into this character, even if that isn't always strictly necessary. Without knowing the keywords and special characters for a particular server, Jet can't know whether identifier quoting is necessary in any given case.

Using ODBCDirect

n the late fall of 1995, the data access team at Microsoft was staring at the performance numbers and evaluating the flexibility of the new Remote Database Objects (RDO) ODBC interface. They liked what they saw, but Jet couldn't use any of this technology and neither could DAO because it was heavily intertwined with Jet. While you couldn't say that DAO was married to Jet, you could fairly say that they were living in sin. The team had to separate the two pieces. By January 1996, they had done this, and DAO 3.1 was sent out as a "free" Beta. Using the feedback from this Beta, the data access team finalized the changes incorporated into Microsoft Office 97 and later into Visual Basic 5.0 and Microsoft Visual C++. "ODBCDirect" was born.

ODBCDirect isn't really DAO, nor is it RDO or even ODBC, although it shares many of the aspects and object names of each. Figure 17-1 shows the DAO/Jet and DAO/ODBCDirect interface. The Office folks need ODBCDirect as an alternative to the ODBC API and DAO/Jet programming for reaching back-end ODBC data sources. But to the Visual Basic client/server developer who wants to access SQL Server, the merits of ODBCDirect are less obvious. Look at it this way: if you're a DAO developer, you're working with ISAM, native Jet, or ODBC data sources. If you're an Office or a Visual Basic developer, you're bound to use designs and implementation technology that leverage Jet's exceptional power to deal with this type of database. This means that you use the Table object with the Seek method, permanent QueryDef objects, and Jet SQL. You don't care about stored procedures, multiple result sets, or remote business classes, and your designs reflect these realities. You never write triggers, and you've learned to do without asynchronous operations.

But if you're a DAO developer who works with SQL Server, you've already had to lay off the Table object and the Seek method and you probably don't use the Data control that much. You execute stored procedures, but you jump through hoops trying to get them to return multiple result sets—or you rewrite your stored procedures to send back singleton queries. You make heavy use of SQL pass-through, and you might even have figured out how to get Jet QueryDef objects to work with TSQL queries inside. In other words, you've adapted your programming style to deal with the features, power, and limitations of DAO/Jet.

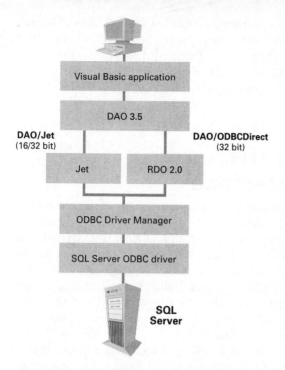

Figure 17-1 *The DAO/Jet and DAO/ODBCDirect interface to access SQL Server from Visual Basic*

ODBCDirect can't magically make your DAO code work faster and better: only in the simplest cases does switching to ODBCDirect work without your needing to redesign at least some of your code. Although ODBCDirect can make some operations work better, it requires you to recode some parts that no longer work or work differently than they did when you coded to ISAM databases or even ODBC data sources. ODBCDirect doesn't support the concept of permanent QueryDef objects, so many of the strategies we considered in the Jet chapters simply don't map to ODBCDirect. But if you decide to try out ODBCDirect, this chapter can help make the process of migrating an existing DAO/Jet application over to ODBCDirect—or perhaps straight to RDO—a reasonably straightforward task.

Before you launch yourself on this journey, however, you need to ask yourself this question: "Does my current application give me the performance I need?" If it does, don't try to fix it. If your application doesn't perform well, you should consider what you're willing to pay to make it faster or easier to code or to make it work better with SQL Server. The cost of converting to *anything*—ODBCDirect, RDO, VBSQL, or something else—might be high. Will converting to ODBCDirect be any cheaper because you're starting from DAO? Perhaps, but then again, it depends on which of the techniques we examined earlier you use and how many of them you'll have to reengineer to work with ODBCDirect. If you're starting from scratch, I don't think there's a question here—simply use RDO.

Wait! Are we missing a big advantage with ODBCDirect? Doesn't it work with 16-bit Visual Basic like DAO does? Nope, sorry, it doesn't. ODBCDirect directly links to RDO, which is 32-bit only. ODBCDirect *does* offer a big advantage, but it's for Office 97 users (more 32-bit clients). They can access most of the power and speed of RDO without having to buy a copy of Visual Basic 5.0, Enterprise Edition.

Understanding the ODBCDirect Interface

ODBCDirect is the second path that DAO 3.5 provides for accessing remote data—the first is through the Microsoft Jet database engine. In previous versions of DAO, if you wanted to access data through ODBC, DAO passed your calls to Jet, which took the query and passed it to its query optimizer, which called ODBC, as needed, to fetch the data. The result sets returned from ODBC were passed back to Jet's cursor builder, which built Resultset objects to pass back to the application. This path, though it got the job done, wasn't always the most efficient way to deal with intelligent remote database engines such as SQL Server. Developers found two disadvantages to using this path. First, it required loading Jet, even though the actual database being accessed wasn't a Jet database. Second, it could be slower due to the extra functionality Jet provided and the footprint it required. Yes, applications built this way were far easier to code, but at a price. Even with all of the optimizations turned on, DAO/Jet applications were slower than those that accessed the ODBC APIs more directly. Now, with ODBCDirect, developers have a fairly direct path to ODBC and their data—that is, ODBCDirect provides a direct path to the ODBC API by way of RDO.

ODBCDirect takes far less RAM than DAO/Jet but more than RDO. How much more? Well, someone on the data access team gave me a breakdown. Opening a server-side result set against SQL Server and doing a MoveLast cost the following amount of RAM. (I don't know how many rows were involved, nor do I know what else the Jet engine had to do up to that point. I do know that DAO/Jet is modularized so that it loads portions of its functionality only as needed—so your mileage may vary.)

- RDO 2.0: 241,664 KB

- ODBCDirect: 512,000 KB

- DAO/Jet: 643,072 KB

Most client/server developers simply want to read data in, change it, and write it back to the back end, and they want to do it fast. ODBCDirect can help you do all that. Most client/server developers also want to be able to get at powerful features supplied by remote data servers. For this, I don't think anyone will suggest that you use ODBCDirect if you haven't already been using DAO—unless you don't have a choice (such as when you work from Office).

What about RDO, which first shipped with Visual Basic 4.0, Enterprise Edition? Doesn't RDO do all this? Why not use it? There are reasons for using both RDO and DAO with ODBCDirect. But before we get into a tug-of-war between ODBCDirect and RDO, let me make this clear: these two object models are *not* in competition. They are designed for different uses and have different heritages that color their approaches to implementing client/server applications. ODBCDirect's roots are in DAO, and it is meant to be useful to existing DAO customers who want a better DAO-like interface to ODBC data sources. RDO is an entirely new interface—born late in 1995 outside of the normal DAO development teams to address some of the same client/server issues but with a different approach that doesn't pay (much) attention to DAO. Some of the objects have similar names, but in many cases they work very differently.

The basic differences between RDO and ODBCDirect are summarized in Table 17-1 on the following page. You can review these differences to figure out the costs of each approach and make an informed decision about which to use. In brief, RDO is more specialized and provides more sophisticated functionality than DAO, but RDO requires a license for, and only ships with, Visual Basic, Enterprise Edition 5.0, and later. DAO is more flexible and portable than RDO, at the cost of some advanced functionality.

NOTE   Table 17-1 is excerpted from a white paper by Emily Kruglick, Fox Data Access Program Manager, and Peter Tucker, DAO Test Lead, at Microsoft. I have edited it quite a bit, so don't blame them for this content.

ODBCDirect vs. Jet

When you choose ODBCDirect over Jet, you give up some of the most powerful aspects of the Jet engine. One thing you lose is the ability to join data in tables stored in different back ends—for instance, Oracle and SQL Server data or SQL Server and native Jet. (You must use Jet in this case because it provides heterogeneous joins.) You must also go through Jet if you're planning to use a lot of DDL (data definition language), because ODBCDirect doesn't provide table definitions or the ability to create tables using DAO's object model. You can still create tables using ODBCDirect, by executing SQL statements, but it might seem more convenient to use the DAO/Jet TableDef object. OK, that's stretching it a bit, but you get the idea: giving up Jet isn't free.

Table 17-1
RDO vs. DAO/ODBCDirect

RDO	DAO/ODBCDirect
Available in Visual Basic 5.0 (and later), Enterprise Edition, Visual C++, and Visual J++. Can be used in other tools if you have a license for Enterprise Development Tools.	Available in Visual Basic 5.0 (and later), Enterprise and Professional editions, Office 97 (and later) applications including Microsoft Excel, Microsoft Access, and in Visual C++ 5.0 (and later).
Applications can be redistributed by licensed users of the development tools listed above.	Applications can be redistributed by users of Visual Basic Enterprise and Professional editions, Office (to other Office desktops), and Visual C++.
Provides fast programmatic access to ODBC data, asynchronous processing, and support for events, which eliminates the need to poll for the completion of asynchronous operations. Also supports direct access to underlying ODBC handles for low-level API work, creatable objects for easier coding and more flexibility in object management, and queries as methods.	Provides fast programmatic access to ODBC data and asynchronous processing. Doesn't support events, creatable objects, or queries as methods. Provides no "official" support for underlying ODBC handles—they are there, just hidden.
Supports UserConnection Designer to store permanent queries in the application as UserConnection objects.	Supports the creation of temporary QueryDef objects in code.
Designed for advanced remote database functionality using sophisticated event and offline result set management.	Designed for advanced remote database functionality as well as local database functionality. Applications can be easily modified to switch between local and remote data, thus enabling upsizing to client/server or downsizing for traveling or disconnected scenarios. For more information, see "Tips for Converting Your Application to ODBCDirect" later in this chapter.
Entire object model and most property arguments are enumerated in the typelib, so they show up in IntelliSense coding.	Constants are enumerated, but properties are not.
Object model is similar to DAO, but distinct.	Object model is part of DAO. Well, a super-subset of DAO 3.0. Well, actually, it's mapped against RDO.

NOTE An existing DAO application can never be instantly ported to ODBCDirect or even RDO. Although the spelling of the DAO objects is similar for DAO, ODBCDirect, and RDO, the way they are implemented by the underlying layers plays a significant role in how they are used and applied by developers. DAO applications, just like VBSQL applications, have a characteristic design modality. You often must reengineer this fundamental design to effectively use the interface. You *can* create a single application to interface both to Jet and ODBC databases using DAO/Jet and ODBCDirect, but you have to be careful. Figure 17-2 shows the degree of their overlap.

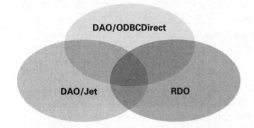

Figure 17-2 *DAO/Jet, DAO/ODBCDirect, and RDO functionality overlap*

Activating ODBCDirect

All DAO objects are referenced from the base DBEngine object. Once DAO is loaded, your code determines which underlying interface will be used to implement the DAO objects—Jet or RDO. Basically, you can create a DAO Workspace to access either interface, but it defaults to DAO/Jet. You can override this default by using the DefaultType property of the DBEngine object. You can have both at the same time by creating additional Workspace objects. This allows you to begin coding an application against a Jet database using a DAO/Jet Workspace and then later convert it to access a remote SQL Server database through ODBCDirect by simply opening a new ODBCDirect Workspace. Once you create a Workspace, you can't change its spots (er, type).

For the conversion of a DAO/Jet to an ODBCDirect application to go smoothly, however, you must keep in mind what functionality is supported in both Workspaces. We'll look at the specific differences later, and a later section in this chapter will show you how to convert a DAO application to ODBCDirect. We're back in the "code for both interfaces" business again. That is, you have to write your code so that the objects work pretty much the same no matter which interface you're connected to. Of course, if you don't plan to create an application that must work against both types of Workspaces, this isn't a problem.

After you decide to create an ODBCDirect Workspace, you have a couple of choices about how to do it. The most direct way is to use the DBEngine object's CreateWorkspace method. You can't declare a "New" Workspace object the way you can declare objects in RDO. DAO 3.5 implements a new fourth parameter, *Type*, that allows you to specify which type of Workspace to create. You can use either *dbUseJet* for a Jet Workspace or *dbUseODBC* for an ODBC-Direct Workspace, as shown here:

```
Dim wksODBC as Workspace
Dim wksJet as Workspace

Set wksODBC = DBEngine.CreateWorkspace( _
    "HelloODBCWS", "sa", "", dbUseODBC)
Set wksJet = DBEngine.CreateWorkspace( _
    "HelloJetWS", "admin", "")
```

Another, less obvious, way to create a Workspace is to let DAO do it for you. You simply set the DefaultType property (or not), and the first reference to the Workspace (even indirectly) forces DAO to load either RDO (for ODBC-Direct) or the Jet database engine, as follows:

```
Dim wksDefault as Workspace

DBEngine.DefaultType = dbUseODBC
' Since the default type is dbUseODBC, the default
' Workspace will be an ODBCDirect Workspace.
Set wksDefault = DBEngine.Workspaces(0)
```

Connecting to Databases

As you'll see when we get to Part IV of this book, RDO doesn't use a Database object to establish a connection—it uses its own unique rdoConnection object. ODBCDirect also uses its own Connection object. For the most part, ODBC-Direct's Connection object is similar to DAO's Database object, although they differ in several functional aspects. We'll touch on those differences in a moment.

ODBCDirect and RDO approach the problem of choosing the cursor type a little differently. RDO supports a global rdoDefaultCursorDriver property on the rdoEngine object. This defines the application-wide default for all rdo-Environment objects that you create. ODBCDirect has a global default that can't be changed—dbUseDefaultCursor, which is equivalent to RDO's rdUse-IfNeeded. You can override both options by changing the DBEngine object's DefaultCursorDriver property, changing the rdoEngine object's rdoDefault-CursorDriver property, or by changing the rdoEnvironment object's Cursor-Driver property. By setting these options before you establish a connection, you can completely disable cursors or choose ODBC client-side, SQL Server server-side, or the new Client Batch cursor libraries. Each has its advantages and disadvantages—as you'll see in later chapters.

IMHO

To tell the truth, the Connection object and the Database object are identical under the covers. However, some of the new ODBCDirect features are exposed on the Connection object but not on the Database object because the DAO people want you to migrate away from the Database object to the Connection object for future compatibility.

NOTE Remember that in many ways ODBCDirect is simply a frontal interface (OK, a mask) for RDO. Virtually everything that ODBCDirect does, it does by calling RDO.

Because ODBCDirect's default is set to dbUseDefaultCursor, the RDO (or the ODBC driver manager) decides which cursor to use. It selects SQL Server server-side cursors if they are available. In most cases, if the server doesn't support cursors, local cursors are used. Actually, RDO won't let you select a cursor or cursor driver that's incapable of doing what you ask. The underlying ODBC technology tries to gracefully choose the most appropriate cursor based on the properties and options specified. If the driver can't work under the given parameters, it quietly (or sometimes not so quietly) returns a "Driver not capable" error message and reverts to an operational mode that it can handle, if one is available.

ODBCDirect supports RDO's concept of "No Cursor." You specify this by setting the DefaultCursorDriver property to dbUseNoCursor. This sets up a forward-only, read-only Recordset that fetches one record at a time from the server. This Recordset requires the least overhead. It's also the least functional, but it's usually the fastest way to dump data back to the client.

Comparing Database Objects and Connection Objects

Once you've chosen your default cursor, it's time to establish a connection with your data. Remember, once the connection is established, you can't change cursor drivers. With DAO/Jet, you had no choice—you simply called Open-Database and Jet built a connection for you and managed it for all subclients in your application. ODBCDirect, like RDO, has no connection manager. To maintain DAO code compatibility, ODBCDirect allows you two similar paths to your database, the Database object and the Connection object.

What do you gain by using the Connection object instead of the Database object? Well, the Connection object has the ability to run asynchronous operations and create temporary QueryDef objects (prepared statements, for those of you more familiar with RDO 1.0 or ODBC), whereas the Database object is more compatible with the Jet path. For example, you can't create QueryDef objects from a Database object unless you're working with a Jet database. This flies in the face of several of the SQL pass-through techniques I talked about in earlier chapters. This means that you must convert your code to the Connection object to maintain this type of functionality against SQL Server. But wait, before you go off and start ripping up the old roadbed, let's see what other little surprises lie around the bend.

Why use the Database object? If you're writing code that you want to be able to switch easily from one type of Workspace to another because you're planning to change the database back ends (that is, from Jet to SQL Server), using the Database object makes plenty of sense, especially since the Connection object is supported as a property of the Database object. But if your code needs to use QueryDef objects against remote databases or is going to run asynchronous queries, you should use a Connection object—or at least the Connection property of the Database object. When you open a Connection object or a Database object and you need the functionality provided by the other object, each has an associated property for this purpose. That is, the Database object has a Connection property and the Connection object has a Database property. This can come in handy if some shared code that uses both types of objects. For instance, you might want to write all your code so that it can run through either Jet or ODBCDirect, but then, much later in the code, you might want to run a specific query asynchronously if it is available. By connecting to the database using OpenDatabase, you can use the same code whether or not you're using ODBCDirect. Then, later in the code, you can check to see whether you're in ODBCDirect, and if you are, you can jump on over to the Connection object and execute the statement asynchronously. (See Example 1 later in this chapter, on page 352.)

Here is sample code that opens both the Connection object and the Database object:

```
Dim dbs As Database
Dim cnn As Connection

Set dbs = OpenDatabase("", _
    dbDriverRequired, False, _
    "ODBC;dsn=DBSer;database=pubs;uid=sa;pwd=pass;")
DefaultType = dbUseODBC
Set cnn = OpenConnection("", _
    dbDriverNoPrompt, False, _
    "ODBC;dsn=DBSer;database=pubs;uid=sa;pwd=pass;")
```

rdoConnection Objects vs. ODBCDirect Connection Objects

Let's put the rdoConnection object and the ODBCDirect Connection object side by side. This comparison, shown in Table 17-2, reveals lots of interesting differences that highlight the different levels of implementation. For the sake of brevity, I've removed all of the entries in which both objects provide the same functionality.

You can see from Table 17-2 that a few RDO features aren't supported by ODBCDirect or are handled in the following ways:

- You have to create a new Workspace object if you need a different cursor driver for a specific connection.

Table 17-2
rdoConnection Objects vs. ODBCDirect Connection Objects

RDO rdoConnection Object Properties and Methods	DAO/ODBCDirect Connection Object Properties and Methods	Description
AsyncCheckInterval	Not available	Can't change polling interval.
CursorDriver on rdoEnvironment, rdoEngine, Default-CursorDriver	DBEngine object's DefaultCursorDriver	Each Workspace can be assigned its own cursor driver just as each rdoConnection can be assigned its own, but assignments are made via this DBEngine property.
Begin/Commit/Rollback-Trans	Only on Workspace	Manage transactions. No Connection-based transaction management.
CreateQuery	CreateQueryDef	Create new temporary client query.
EstablishConnection	Not available	Used with stand-alone rdoConnection objects.
hDbc	Hidden and not supported	Exposes underlying ODBC handle.
LastQueryResults	Not available	Used for UserConnection objects.
LoginTimeout	Only on Workspace	Used with creatable Connection objects.
LogMessages	Not available	Points to ODBC trace log.
OpenResultset	OpenRecordset	Create result sets.
rdoQueries	QueryDefs	Contain temporary (local) client-side procedures.
rdoResultsets	Recordsets	Contain open result sets.
rdoTables	Not supported	Exposes base tables.
RowsAffected	RecordsAffected	Record affected by Update/Insert/Delete.
StillConnecting	StillExecuting	Poll for asynchronous connection completion.
Version	Database.Version	
(No equivalent)	Database	Cross-references Database object.

- The low-level handles that you need to execute your own ODBC API functions are hidden and not supported. They're there, but they won't show up in the object browser and won't be supported by Microsoft.

- Transactions are managed on the Workspace level, not on the Connection or Database levels. This is in line with DAO's approach to transactions. You can build parameter-based queries only against Connection objects, not against Database objects. (Although this is the same as in RDO, it took me a while to catch this when writing some samples.)

- ODBCDirect supports asynchronous operations, but you have to poll for completion of the operations and you can't change RDO's polling interval.

- ODBCDirect doesn't support stand-alone objects, but you still can set the Recordset Connection property to Nothing and reset it later to reconnect—just as you can using RDO (well, almost). The real difference is that you can create, connect, and disconnect an rdoConnection object without dropping the object. This is not possible in DAO.

- Notice that the ODBCDirect connect string still requires the ODBC; prefix. This isn't required by RDO or the ODBC API.

Executing SQL Queries

Once the Connection (or Database) object has established a connection, you can submit queries using the chosen cursor driver (as determined by the DBEngine DefaultCursorDriver property). If you want to use another cursor driver, just change the DBEngine DefaultCursorDriver property. The next Connection (or Database) object that is built will use this new driver. In ODBCDirect, you work with QueryDef objects—but only temporary QueryDefs. If you need to pass parameters to the QueryDef object, you have to use the CreateQueryDef method against the Connection object. The ODBCDirect Database object doesn't support QueryDef objects. Once the QueryDef is created, you can set its parameters, execute it, reset its parameters, and reexecute it to your heart's content.

rdoResultset Objects vs. Recordset Objects

Before we look at how to build cursors and other result sets, let's take a closer look at a couple of objects. We'll start by comparing the RDO rdoResultset implementation to the ODBCDirect Recordset object. You can see from Table 17-3 that a few RDO features aren't supported by ODBCDirect or are handled in the following ways:

- The CacheSize and CacheStart options are no longer supported on the ODBCDirect Recordset object. They are implemented using the Query.RowsetSize property.

- A consequence of not providing the ClipString method is that you can't pass the data from a result set to a clip-aware control. Since the (old-fashioned) Grid and the new MSFlexGrid are so equipped, this means more coding when you use ODBCDirect.

- Again, the internal ODBC handles are hidden and not supported by ODBCDirect.

- The UpdateCriteria and UpdateOperation properties are combined into the UpdateOptions property bits and in additional arguments on the Update method. It's clear that migrating from RDO to ODBCDirect or back won't be easy if you use client batch techniques.

- The Resync method is also not among the supported RDO subtleties.

Table 17-3
rdoResultset Objects vs. ODBCDirect Recordset Objects

RDO rdoResultset Object Properties and Methods	DAO/ODBCDirect Recordset Object Properties and Methods	Description
ActiveConnection	Connection	Indicates current connection. Used to work with dissociate Client Batch cursors.
BatchUpdate	Update with option	Used to submit batch operations to server.
BatchCollisionRows	BatchCollisions	Contains an array of bookmarks to rows causing update collisions.
Query.RowsetSize	CacheSize	Implemented on the Query object.
Not applicable	CacheStart	Not supported in ODBCDirect.
CancelBatch	CancelUpdate with option	Used to drop changes in update cache.
GetClipString	Not provided	Used to dump result set contents to "clip-aware" controls such as the Grid or MSFlexGrid.
hStmt	Hidden and not supported	Used to gain access to underlying ODBC API.
MoreResults	NextRecordset	Used to move to next result set in a multiple result set query.
Resync	Not supported	Used with Client Batch cursors to refetch original values.
rdoColumns	Fields	Contains data columns.
RowCount	RecordCount	Indicates number of rows in populated result set.
Status	RecordStatus	Indicates success or failure of a client batch operation.
UpdateCriteria	UpdateOptions	Used in client batch updates to build WHERE clause.
UpdateOperation	UpdateOptions	Indicates how client batches should be updated.

Understanding QueryDef Objects

QueryDef objects created from a Connection object are temporary objects; they aren't saved (permanently) to the data source—unlike the DAO equivalent, which can be stored in a Jet database. QueryDef objects are powerful because they're prepared and optimized statements that can be called again and again. However, their expense doesn't outweigh the benefits if you don't use them more than once—using the Requery method. Basically, ODBCDirect (and RDO) creates a temporary stored procedure that is kept on the server in TempDB. This means a hit on TempDB, but it can also save time—if you use the QueryDef more than a couple of times to amortize the startup expense.

When you touch a QueryDef object's Parameters collection or execute a QueryDef, an instruction is sent to the server to prepare the statement. (ODBC SQLPrepare is executed.) At this time, the temporary stored procedure is created. Then, when you execute the QueryDef or open a Recordset from the QueryDef, the prepared temporary stored procedure is used by the server. Generally, this temporary procedure remains in place until you close the connection or destroy the QueryDef object. Keep this in mind as you watch TempDB grow.

QueryDef objects, like Connection objects, support asynchronous execution using both the Execute and OpenRecordset methods. (See the "Running Asynchronous Operations" section later in this chapter.) This represents a major difference from QueryDef objects created for Jet databases, which are typically saved in the database and can only be executed synchronously.

You can also use the QueryDef object to set up properties of the resulting Recordset, such as the number of records to be cached locally. In ODBC-Direct, the CacheStart property and the FillCache method of the Recordset aren't supported; instead, ODBCDirect favors using the CacheSize method of a QueryDef. (See the "Handling Recordset Objects" section later in this chapter.) The Recordset property CacheSize is still supported but is read-only and contains the number of records DAO will cache. Here is an example of how to tell DAO to use a different CacheSize than the default, which is 100 records for ODBCDirect:

```
Dim qdf as QueryDef
Dim rst as Recordset

Set qdf = cnn.CreateQueryDef("tempqd")
qdf.SQL = "Select au_fname from authors"
' The local cache for the Recordset is 200 records.
qdf.CacheSize = 200
Set rst = qdf.OpenRecordset()
Debug.Print rst.CacheSize
```

You can also use ODBCDirect QueryDef objects to execute your stored procedures. They are designed to work well with input and output parameters as well as return values. To work with stored procedures, you simply create a QueryDef object whose definition looks very much like an ODBC call to the stored procedure.

```
' Create a simple stored proc.
strSQL$ = "CREATE PROC myproc AS SELECT Title FROM Titles;"
cnn.Execute strSQL$

Set qdf = cnn.CreateQueryDef("q1", "{call myproc()}")
Set rst = qdf.OpenRecordset()
```

Note that you have to code the QueryDef SQL to include the ODBC Call syntax. RDO has moved away from this requirement. You can now create User Connection objects that expose queries and stored procedures as methods; the somewhat arcane ODBC API Call syntax is no longer required. This also means that I haven't given you anywhere near all of the syntax options required to build these call statements. I will talk about them, however, in the next several chapters.

Once you create your QueryDef object, its parameters are managed with the same Parameters collection that you're probably familiar with in DAO 3.0. When you work with older versions of SQL Server, you also have to set the Direction property that tells the driver whether the parameter is return status or an input, output, or both. But this isn't required for SQL Server 6.x and later. Here's an example of creating a stored procedure with parameters and calling it. Note that this is a *permanent* stored procedure.

```
' Create a simple stored proc
' with a return value.
strSQL$ = "CREATE PROC myproc " & _
    "(@invar int) AS " & _
    "RETURN @invar;"
cnn.Execute strSQL$

' Set up a QueryDef to talk with the
' stored procedure.
Set qdf = cnn.CreateQueryDef("q1", "{? = call myproc(?)}")

' Handle the parameters.
qdf.Parameters(0).Direction = dbParamReturnValue
qdf.Parameters(1) = 10
qdf.Execute

' Read return value.
var = qdf.Parameters(0).Value
```

rdoQuery Objects vs. QueryDef Objects

Now let's compare the RDO rdoQuery implementation to the ODBCDirect QueryDef object. Table 17-4 shows a few more RDO features that aren't supported by ODBCDirect or that are handled in the following ways:

- When you use OpenResultset in RDO, it's easy to tell the cursor type and concurrency technique by examining the rdoResultset properties. When you use ODBCDirect, it's not clear how you can tell what kind of cursor or concurrency was used to build a cursor after having executed OpenRecordset.

- The BindThreshold property gives an RDO developer a modicum of additional flexibility when it comes to handling BLOBs.

Table 17-4
rdoQuery Objects vs. ODBCDirect QueryDef Objects

RDO rdoQuery Object Properties and Methods	DAO ODBCDirect QueryDef Object Properties and Methods	Description
ActiveConnection	Database.Connection, Workspaces.Connections collection	Indicates current connection. Used to work with dissociated Client Batch cursors.
BindThreshold	(Not implemented)	Indicates how large a BLOB should be before the GetChunk method is required.
CursorType	Type	Indicates type of cursor, such as Keyset, Static, Dynamic, and so on, to be created. Used in stand-alone rdoQuery objects.
HStmt	Neither exposed nor supported	ODBC API pointer to statement.
KeysetSize	(Not implemented)	Sets keyset size parameter for certain types of ODBC cursors.
LockType	*LockEdits* argument of OpenRecordset and Lock-Edits property	Indicates concurrency type of cursor—pessimistic, optimistic, and subtypes thereof—for stand-alone rdoQuery objects.
MaxRows	MaxRecords	Indicates upper cap on number of rows to process—return or update.
Prepared	Prepare	Indicates whether a temporary stored procedure should be created for this query.
QueryTimeout	ODBCTimeout	Indicates how long to wait before giving up the query.
RowsetSize	CacheSize	Indicates how many cursor rows are fetched on each operation.

- The Keyset size property is a seldom-used property that few cursor drivers implement—so it's no great loss.

- Again, the internal ODBC handles are hidden and not supported by ODBCDirect.

Handling Recordset Objects

Probably the hardest thing to grasp when you're dealing with ODBCDirect is the variety of cursors it exposes. When you open an ODBCDirect Recordset, you can specify what type of cursor to open and what type of locking the cursor should use, as you can see in Table 17-5. (Don't get the cursor type and locking confused with the cursor driver you must choose before creating the Connection object.) These distinctions lead to many different possibilities, so let's start as simply as possible. There are four different types of Recordset objects (or cursors) that you can open. In addition, you might have already opted for the "cursorless" approach when you selected your cursor driver because not every query result set needs to be returned as a cursor.

Table 17-5
ODBCDirect Concurrency Types

Cursor Type	Description
dbOpenDynamic	Dynamic cursor
dbOpenDynaset	Keyset cursor
dbOpenSnapshot	Static cursor
dbOpenForwardOnly	Forward-only scrolling cursor
dbOpenTable	Isn't supported for ODBCDirect

You can also choose from five types of locking:

Locking Type	Description
dbOptimistic	Concur row version
dbPessimistic	Concur lock
dbOptimisticValue	Concur values
dbOptimisticBatch	Optimistic batch cursor
dbReadOnly	Read-only

Once you start combining these, you'll find that some combinations won't work together, but this situation is entirely dependent on the ODBC driver and remote database server. For instance, against the SQL Server 6.0 server-side cursor driver, dbOpenSnapshot supports only dbReadOnly.

The cursor driver you use also influences what cursors and lock types are supported. DAO ODBCDirect passes the cursor settings to RDO, which passes them directly to ODBC. This means that the driver controls the world. If it can handle the type of Recordset you're asking for, no problem; if not, it will either fall back to another type of Recordset or return an error. If an error occurs, DAO places the error information in the Errors collection. The following code shows some ways to open Recordset objects:

```
Dim rst as Recordset
Set rst = dbs.OpenRecordset("select author from authors")
Set rst = dbs.OpenRecordset("select title from titles", _
    dbOpenDynaset, 0, dbPessimistic)
Set rst = cnn.OpenRecordset("authors", _
    dbOpenDynamic, 0, dbOptimistic)
```

The first OpenRecordset brings up an interesting question. What are the defaults? In a Jet Workspace, the most functional (and often most expensive) Recordset is always opened. In an ODBCDirect Workspace, the default is the (nearly) fastest (and cheapest) Recordset, dbOpenForwardOnly and dbReadOnly. So if you want to edit your data, you need to supply a lock type other than dbReadOnly, and if you want to be able to scroll around your Recordset, you need to supply a Recordset type other than dbOpenForwardOnly. If you want even better performance, set the cursor's rowset size to 1 (via the CacheSize property) or use the dbUseNoCursor as the DefaultCursorDriver property.

Except for the different types of Recordset objects and record locking, ODBCDirect Recordset objects function roughly the same way that they do in DAO 3.0. Just keep in mind that Jet is nowhere to be seen and that the way Jet manages cursors can be really different from the way those created by the simpler (far simpler) ODBC layers are managed. You also can't update nearly as many cursors as you can with Jet because ODBC spends quite a bit of time keeping track of the base tables and update paths for complex joins. More often than not, complex joins aren't updateable with ODBCDirect or RDO cursors. This means that you'll probably have to fall back on performing updates using action queries.

Later in this chapter, I'll talk about a few more advanced areas, such as running asynchronous queries, working with multiple Recordset objects, and optimistic batch cursors. Besides those, the only change worth mentioning in ODBCDirect versus Jet is that Recordset functionality has been slimmed down. For instance, ODBCDirect doesn't support most of the ISAM functionality provided by Jet. The Table object and the ability to select indexes to use on the table-type Recordset object and in the Seek function have both been eliminated. The Find methods FindFirst, FindNext, FindPrevious, and FindLast also aren't supported by RDO—thus ODBCDirect can't perform these operations either. But you know (by now) that to get decent performance against a remote database, users should allow the back end to navigate the records rather than grab them all and navigate through the records on the client as the Find methods do.

One last change we should talk about is how record caching is handled. The default cache size in Jet is one record. The default in ODBCDirect is 100 records. Because Jet caches only one record at a time, DAO/Jet provides the FillCache method and the CacheStart and CacheSize properties. These work together so that the user can define what data to cache and then cache it. In ODBCDirect, users can use the 100-record default CacheSize or they can change it by creating a QueryDef and then altering the CacheSize property to dictate how many records should be cached.

Controlling Multiple Recordset Objects

One of the new advanced features that ODBCDirect provides is the ability to handle the return of multiple Recordset objects from one SQL call. Note that when you use multiple Recordset objects, you can't plan on updating data using the cursors. You can choose between two ways of returning multiple Recordset objects, and neither allows updating. The first way is to use local (client-side) cursors; they execute multiple selects and return the data no matter what type of Recordset you request. The second way is to use server-side cursors, although you actually use no cursor at all—you just do simple data fetches under the hood. You do this by setting up a QueryDef with a CacheSize of 1, thus telling the server to give you only one record at a time. Then you open a Recordset as dbOpenForwardOnly and dbReadOnly from the QueryDef. You can also use the dbUseNoCursor option on the Workspace's DefaultCursorDriver property, before opening the connection, to achieve this forward-only, read-only, CacheSize 1 cursor. This tells the server not to bother with cursors, just to return one row at a time. In this mode (no cursor mode), SQL Server can open multiple Recordset objects. Without these steps, SQL Server simply returns an error when you try to open a multiple Recordset query.

Once you have multiple Recordset objects being returned, you can use DAO to access each Recordset. You do this using the new NextRecordset method. It throws away the current Recordset and replaces it with the next Recordset. Then you can navigate through it as you would any Recordset. When Next-Recordset returns False, you have no further result sets to process—and yes, you have to process them all before beginning another operation or closing the Recordset. (See Example 2 later in this chapter.)

Running Asynchronous Operations

ODBCDirect also exposes the ability to open connections and run queries—both row-returning (select queries) and non-row-returning (action queries)—asynchronously. This means that control returns to your application immediately—before the connection has opened or the query has been processed by SQL Server—so you can continue with other operations. Both modes work by passing dbRunAsync to the appropriate methods. Because ODBCDirect doesn't support the RDO event model, you have to poll the StillConnecting or StillExecuting property to check whether the operation is done. As long as these properties return True, the asynchronous operation isn't finished. If you want to abort the operation, simply use the new Cancel method. Note, however, that canceling in the middle of a bulk operation isn't always wise. The operation won't roll back; it will simply stop updating in the middle. If you think you might cancel a bulk operation, you should wrap it in a transaction so that you can roll back if it isn't completed. (See Examples 3 and 4 later in this chapter.)

Optimistic Batch Updating

ODBCDirect also supports optimistic batch updating. Optimistic batch updating means that the data for a given Recordset is cached locally. All changes that you make to the Recordset are also cached locally until you specifically tell DAO to flush all changes to the server. Batch updating can really speed things up because it cuts down on the network traffic between client and server.

You accomplish optimistic batch updates by creating an ODBCDirect Workspace using the Client Batch cursor library. (Set DefaultCursorDriver to dbUseClientBatchCursor.) This is the only cursor library that supports batch updating. After opening your connection, open a Recordset with a LockType of dbOptimisticBatch, which tells the library that you plan to do batch updates.

At this point, you can use the Recordset as you normally would, reading and updating its data, but the data isn't sent to the server—not yet. The changes are cached on the workstation until you're ready to post the changes to the SQL server. After you update all the data you plan to work with, call the Update method on the Recordset by using the dbUpdateBatch option. At this point, all changes are flushed to the server and the updates are made.

How does DAO know which record in the Recordset relates to a particular record in the source? You specify it by using the UpdateOptions property of the Recordset. The default for this is the primary key. But you can override the default to use all columns or the time stamp. In addition, you can specify how record updates are executed, either by updating the record in place or by deleting it and adding a new record.

But what happens if a collision occurs (for example, if the update tries to change a record that was changed by another source after the process first looked at the records)? In that case, you can use the BatchCollisionCount property to find out how many updates failed and you can use the BatchCollisions property. The BatchCollisions property is an array of bookmarks to your Recordset that points to records that failed. Finally, you can use the VisibleValue and OriginalValue properties of the Field object in conjunction with the Value property to determine how to reconcile the failed updates.

Viewing Errors

The last thing I want to talk about is how to view errors using DAO ODBC-Direct. This topic isn't exactly new, but it's important in ODBCDirect, and it isn't all that well understood. DAO places all incoming messages and errors in its Errors collection as they arrive. Suppose you simply want to check on the status of an operation. Because a single operation can result in many errors (and messages), you want to be sure to check them all if something goes wrong. If something does go wrong, DAO ODBCDirect won't volunteer much information. You usually just get a trappable generic "3146: ODBC--call failed." This can be rather annoying. By looking in the Errors collection, you just might find more useful information. The lowest index error is usually the most detailed. Here's some sample code that you can use to print out all the errors from the collection and see exactly what we're talking about:

```
Dim e as Error
Debug.Print Err & ":  " & Error$
For Each e In DBEngine.Errors
    Debug.Print e.Number & ":  " & e.Description
Next e
```

If you tried to open a database to tell the driver not to prompt but you failed to supply the DSN in the connection string, you get "ODBC--call failed" in *Error$*. If you then look in the Errors collection, you'll find that two errors were actually returned and that Errors(0) has much more detailed information in it. These are the errors returned:

```
Errors(0).Description =
IM002: [Microsoft][ODBC Driver Manager] Data source name not found
and no default driver specified

Errors(1).Description =
3146:  ODBC--call failed.
```

ODBCDirect Examples

To make ODBCDirect a little easier to use, let's look at a few code examples that walk you through typical operations that illustrate ODBCDirect's flexibility.

Example 1: Determining Which Workspace Your Database Is Open In

The following routine demonstrates how to tell whether your database is open in an ODBCDirect Workspace or a Jet Workspace. It also shows how to grab the Connection object from a Database object and use it to perform an asynchronous SQL operation.

```
Sub DeleteRecords()
    Dim dbs As Database
    Dim cnn As Connection

    ' This will open a database in the default
    ' Workspace, no matter what type of Workspace it
    ' actually is (ODBCDirect or Microsoft Jet).
    Set dbs = OpenDatabase("", False, False, _
        "ODBC;dsn=pubs;database=pubs;uid=sa;pwd=;")

    ' Check to see whether it is ODBCDirect.
    fNoError = True
    On Error GoTo ErrorTrap
        Set cnn = dbs.Connection
    On Error GoTo 0

    ' If there was no error, it is ODBCDirect.
    If fNoError Then
        cnn.Execute "delete from authors", dbRunAsync
        cnn.Close
    Else
        dbs.Execute "delete from authors"
        dbs.Close
    End If
Exit Sub

ErrorTrap:
    fNoError = False
    Resume Next
End Sub
```

Example 2: Getting Multiple Recordset Objects from the Server

This routine demonstrates how to get multiple Recordset objects from the server and how to walk through them. It has two parts: the first demonstrates how to force local cursors to be used to get multiple Recordset objects, and the second demonstrates how to move through multiple Recordset objects in DAO.

```
Sub GetMultipleResults()
    Dim rst As Recordset
    Dim cnn As Connection

    ' Use Local Cursors.
    DefaultType = dbUseODBC
    DBEngine.Workspaces(0).DefaultCursorDriver = _
        dbUseODBCCursor
    ' Now open the connection to the database.
    Set cnn = OpenConnection("", _
        dbDriverNoPrompt, false, _
        "ODBC;dsn=DBServer;database=pubs;uid=sa;pwd=")

    strCmd$ = "select * from authors; " & _
        "select * from titles;"

    ' Execute the SQL statement.
    Set rst = cnn.OpenRecordset(strCmd$)
    ViewResults rst
    cnn.Close
End Sub

Sub ViewResults(rst As Recordset)
    Do
        While Not rst.EOF
            ' Loop through each record.
            For Each fld In rst.Fields
                ' Print each field.
                Debug.Print fld.Name & ":  " & fld.Value
            Next
            rst.MoveNext
        Wend
    ' Get the next Recordset and stop if we are done.
    Loop Until (rst.NextRecordset() = False)
End Sub
```

Example 3: Canceling a Bulk Operation

The following example illustrates how to cancel a bulk operation. When you do this, you should always wrap the code in a transaction because canceling the operation can leave data in an unknown state.

```
Sub CancelExecute()
    Dim cnn As Connection
```

```
' By setting this before touching
' the default Workspace, the default
' Workspace will be created as an
' ODBCDirect Workspace.
DefaultType = dbUseODBC

' Open a connection instead of
' a database because databases
' don't support dbRunAsync.
Set cnn = OpenConnection("", _
    dbDriverNoPrompt, false, _
    "ODBC;dsn=DBServer;database=pubs;uid=sa;pwd=")

' Start a transaction to be able
' to roll back if you cancel the
' operation.
BeginTrans

' Execute your SQL using dbRunAsync.
cnn.Execute "delete from mytable", dbRunAsync

' You should always check that the
' query is still running before canceling.
If cnn.StillExecuting Then
    cnn.Cancel
    ' If you have canceled, roll back
    ' any records that were changed.
    Rollback
Else
    ' If completed, go
    ' ahead and commit the changes.
    CommitTrans
End If

' Close the connection to the database.
cnn.Close
End Sub
```

Example 4: Using dbRunAsync to Open a Recordset

The following routine demonstrates how to use dbRunAsync to open a Recordset. Note that this can be performed from either a Database object or a Connection object, unlike when you use dbRunAsync with Execute, which can be performed only from a Connection object.

```
Sub CancelRecordset()
    Dim wks as Workspace
    Dim dbs As Database
    Dim rst As Recordset

    ' Example of how to open a Workspace
```

(continued)

```
        set wks = CreateWorkspace("Space1", "sa", _
            "", dbUseODBC)
        ' Open a database to show you can
        ' use dbRunAsync to OpenRecordset from
        ' the Database object.
        Set dbs = wks.OpenDatabase("", _
            dbDriverNoPrompt, False, _
            "ODBC;dsn=DBServer;database=pubs;uid=sa;pwd=")

        Set rst = dbs.OpenRecordset( _
            "select * from authors", _
            dbOpenDynaset, dbRunAsync)

        ' You should always check that the
        ' query is still running before canceling.
        If rst.StillExecuting Then
            rst.Cancel
        Else
            rst.Close
        End If

        ' Close the database.
        dbs.Close
        wks.close
End Sub
```

Example 5: Working with QueryDef Objects

This routine demonstrates how to work with QueryDef objects. It shows the use of stored procedures and parameters.

```
Sub WorkWithQueryDefs()
    Dim cnn As Connection
    Dim qdf As QueryDef
    Dim rst As Recordset

    ' By setting this before touching
    ' the default Workspace, the default
    ' Workspace will be created as an
    ' ODBCDirect Workspace.
    DefaultType = dbUseODBC

    ' Open a connection instead of
    ' a database because we need
    ' QueryDef support.
    Set cnn = OpenConnection("", _
        dbDriverNoPrompt, false, _
        "ODBC;dsn=DBServer;database=pubs;uid=sa;pwd=")

    ' Create the stored procedure.
    ' This will usually be done outside the program
    ' but is done here for clarity's sake.
```

```
strCmd$ = "Create proc GetDataFrom" & _
    " (@state char(2))" & _
    " as select * from authors" & _
    " where state = @state"
cnn.Execute strCmd$

' Create a QueryDef with one parameter.
' When the SQL is set, the stored procedure
' is called.
Set qdf = cnn.CreateQueryDef("myquery", "{call GetDataFrom (?)}")
qdf.Parameters(0) = "CA"
qdf.Parameters(0).Direction = dbParamInput

' Get the data.
Set rst = qdf.OpenRecordset()

' Print out the data.
While Not rst.EOF
    Debug.Print rst!au_id
    rst.MoveNext
Wend
rst.Close
qdf.Close

' Close the connection to the database.
cnn.Close
End Sub
```

Tips for Converting Your Application to ODBCDirect

The following are hints for converting existing DAO applications running against DAO/Jet and Jet databases so that they hit ODBC data sources instead. I'll assume that the database is already on the server and that you want to use only ODBCDirect to communicate with your data on a server.

- **Change the type of Workspaces you're using.** If you don't create any Workspaces, you still need to tell DAO that the default Workspace should be an ODBCDirect Workspace. You do this by setting the Default-Type property of DBEngine to dbUseODBC before executing any operations that will need the default Workspace. Once a Workspace is created, you can't change its type. If you're explicitly creating Workspaces in your application and you have set DefaultType to dbUse-ODBC, all Workspaces created while DefaultType has this setting will be ODBCDirect Workspaces. But if you want your code to be self-documenting or if you'll be using both Jet and ODBCDirect Workspaces, you can pass a fourth parameter to each CreateWorkspace, telling it what type of Workspace to create.

- **Change the database you open.** You must change the arguments passed to OpenDatabase to represent the new database you're opening. Instead of passing a database name for the first parameter, pass a connection string for the fourth parameter. Note that all connection strings start with the *ODBC;* prefix. If you also decide to open connections instead of databases, you need to change all your OpenDatabase calls to OpenConnection. Both functions take similar arguments, so this change won't take much work.

- **Choose a way to handle DDL.** ODBCDirect functionality doesn't support the TableDefs collection or Indexes collection. This means that if your application creates new TableDef objects or looks up indexes in the index collection from a TableDef, it will no longer work. If this is a problem, you have two possible ways to change your code. You can create a Jet Workspace and open a second database to the data source, doing all DDL work within it, or you can execute SQL calls to create and find objects. SQL calls are the way to go if you want to keep from loading Jet. But if you want to limit the amount of code that changes, the Jet path works very well.

- **Change the way you create and use QueryDef objects.** In ODBC-Direct Workspaces, the Database object doesn't support the CreateQuery-Def method. This method is handled by the Connection object. In your code, you must change all CreateQueryDef calls so that they are executed on the Connection property of the Database rather than the Database object itself. If you've changed all OpenDatabase calls to OpenConnection calls, you don't have to worry about this. QueryDef objects created in ODBCDirect aren't stored in the database and are lost when the object is closed or goes out of scope.

- **Change the way you open Recordset objects.** ODBCDirect Recordset objects default to the fastest Recordset type rather than to the most functional, as in Jet. Typically, this is a Recordset that can't scroll backward and is read-only. If you need more functionality in the Recordset you use, you must specify that. If you need to scroll backward or if you need bookmarks, choose a different Recordset type, such as dbOpen-Dynaset. If you need to update the Recordset, select a locking type, such as dbOptimistic. You can't open a Recordset in a Jet Workspace by providing only the Name argument, and then expect to edit data in ODBCDirect. You must also change the OpenRecordset method to supply both a Recordset type and a locking constant that will allow updating.

- **You can't use parameterized queries.** ODBCDirect doesn't support named parameters. The syntax for a parameter in an SQL statement is a question mark (?) rather than a name (as in Jet). For example, the Jet SQL SELECT * FROM Employees WHERE LastName = txtName creates a parameter txtName. In ODBCDirect, the SQL is SELECT * FROM Employees WHERE LastName = ?, whereas in the Parameters collection, the name of the parameter is Parameter1. Also note that Jet lets you write Parameters iAuthId Integer; SELECT * from authors where au_id = iAuthId. Since ODBCDirect doesn't have named parameters, you can't use the Parameters ...; part of the previous example.

These tips will get you running quickly with ODBCDirect. But for best performance, you should always go back over the program and look for optimizations. ODBCDirect offers new and different ways to improve performance, but by simply getting your program running in an ODBCDirect Workspace, you might be able to take advantage of all the power available to you.

Working with the Data Control

It turns out that most, if not all, of the functionality that I've described is also exposed by the Data control. It, too, has the properties required to create ODBCDirect Workspace objects and route its operations through RDO. Check out the Visual Basic 5.0 Data control—even in the Professional Edition—to discover the new DefaultType and DefaultCursorType properties. Once you set the DefaultType to *1 - UseODBC*, the Data control is switched over to ODBCDirect mode. You can then select a default cursor driver by setting the DefaultCursorType property, and everything else will work pretty much as I've described. Sure, lots of things won't work as they did in DAO/Jet, but that's the price of this new technology. I think you'll find, however, that you might also want to check out the RemoteData control, which has even more RDO-specific property exposures.

18

Jet: A Traveler's Diary

**Allocating
Database File Space**

**Transaction Loss
and Damage Repair**

Backing Up Access Databases

Updating Records

Tidbits

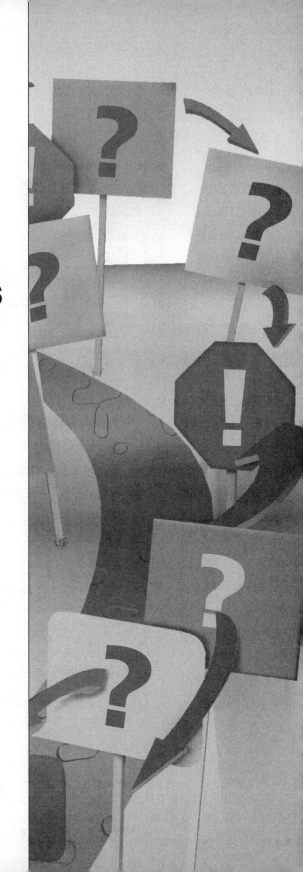

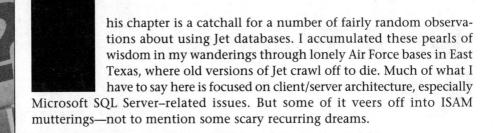

This chapter is a catchall for a number of fairly random observations about using Jet databases. I accumulated these pearls of wisdom in my wanderings through lonely Air Force bases in East Texas, where old versions of Jet crawl off to die. Much of what I have to say here is focused on client/server architecture, especially Microsoft SQL Server–related issues. But some of it veers off into ISAM mutterings—not to mention some scary recurring dreams.

Allocating Database File Space

MDB database file space is allocated through MS-DOS—not the Microsoft Windows 95/98 and Microsoft Windows NT operating systems. No space is preallocated, which is why you face the very real threat that other workstation (or file server) file allocations will rob the database of needed space. This is especially true of locally allocated sort, recordset, keyset, and snapshot row-storage space saved on disk in the TEMP directory. Running another application on the workstation that's acting as the database file server will also significantly affect the performance of the database.

Jet doesn't actively remove the space that was occupied by records deleted from MDB databases, but it reuses that space if possible. In the course of normal operations, some situations can lead to a great deal of unused overhead space being left behind, so you have to compact the MDB file periodically. Compacting is an offline process: the entire database is simply copied to another location, an operation that leaves the dead space behind. You can write an application to compact your database; see the Micorosft Visual Basic documentation on the CompactDatabase statement. But no matter how you do compacting, everyone—even that guy from Cleveland who's always logged on—has to log off.

Transaction Loss and Damage Repair

If your system loses power, you should use the RepairDatabase method against your MDB database because cached writes might not have completed and the database might have been damaged. If you find errors, you *might* be able to repair them using the RepairDatabase method. In many cases, you can recover all the data. In other cases, your database might be hopelessly trashed.

When you can't recover the database, you must rely on your last backup because there's no transaction log for restoring lost transactions. That's why you should back up mission-critical data by exporting it to other offline or external media. Everyone must be off the database before you can back it up, and finding out who is still on can be problematic. See the RepairDatabase method in online help for more information.

Losing the Jet database isn't a problem if the only items saved there are attached tables or QueryDef objects, as is commonly the case with front-end applications that use Jet to access SQL Server. If you also store data in your MDB database, however, you do need to be careful about shutting down and you must be sensitive to the possibility of lost or incomplete transactions.

Backing Up Access Databases

On the surface, what could be simpler? You just make a copy of the MDB file and the SYSTEM.MDW (formerly SYSTEM.MDA) files. But there's a problem: this strategy won't back up any data at all if the database contains only attached tables (as is typically the case when you use SQL Server). So you still need to back up the SQL server, which isn't a problem, because the SQL server doesn't have to be brought down to be backed up. But a Jet database does. Before you can copy the file as a whole, you need to get at least read-only access to it. But when another user has any object open in the database, the entire database file is locked and can't be read by a file-copy program. Can't you just get everyone else off and back it up? The trouble is, there's no way to tell who is connected, short of using the Windows for Workgroups Net Watch program; there is no sp_who in Microsoft Access or in Visual Basic. Your Jet-format database might also contain links to other attached databases—non–SQL Server databases that might not be rigorously backed up.

Does the toolkit for Visual Basic or for Access include a backup utility? The one for Access does, if you count the Import/Export File feature. By using this feature or by writing a program in Visual Basic that dumps to external media, you can back up the data. This doesn't copy the structure, permissions, referential integrity, forms, reports, or any other Access structures built into the database; the data is safe, although it is somewhat difficult to restore without a database to write to. For this reason, I recommend that you back up the database again whenever you make any structural changes so that you can restore the data painlessly.

Updating Records

Jet uses a keyset-driven cursor to update rows in SQL Server tables. If for some reason the key values change or can't be determined when it comes time to update a row, Jet reports that the row has been deleted or can't be found. This message might be caused by a trigger in the SQL Server table that assigns the primary key for the new record. If so, Jet loses track of the record, since it isn't aware of the primary-key change made by the trigger and it shows the record as deleted. A problem can also occur when fixed-length string fields are in the database and you update values without properly padding them. Try adding a TimeStamp column to the SQL Server table. This seems to help Jet locate records and columns that have changed.

Tidbits

Here are a few tips to remember during your DAO/Jet travels:

- Apparently, Jet 3.5 supports SQL Server 6.5 Null-permitted indexes. These weren't supported in Jet 3.0.

- See Q148410 "Microsoft Jet Database Engine 3.0 Reserved Errors List" in the Access Knowledge Base for a list of the Jet 3.0 reserved errors.

- To append a table to a Jet database, open a Jet MDB database and submit the following:

```
Set td = db.CreateTableDef("AttachedAuthors")
td.Connect = "ODBC;uid=;pwd=;Database=Pubs;DSN=pubs;"
td.SourceTableName = "authors"
db.TableDefs.Append td
```

- Consider using the SQL Server variable *@@Identity* to determine the last-used identity value when you add new rows. This value can be returned from a stored procedure when you use it to insert a new row.

- In DAO 2.5, if you don't close your application (Visual Basic or the EXE) or shut down the Jet engine using *Set DBEngine = Nothing*, the database object never goes out of scope, so its connection is never closed—as in never in a thousand years. Jet 3.0 and 3.5 don't work this way (thank goodness).

- The RecordsAffected property returns either 0 or –1 after issuing a SQLPassThrough Execute method. In other words, when Jet uses SQL pass-through, it doesn't return the number of rows affected by the last query. You can get this information by opening the DAO/Jet Database object directly.

PART IV

Using Remote Data Objects

19

Understanding Remote Data Objects

Understanding RDO

Design Features

Comparing RDO and DAO

Where RDO Falls Short

Getting the Latest Information on RDO

Licensing RDO

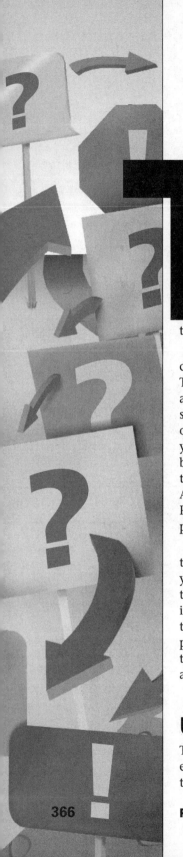

This part of the book hasn't changed much since the fifth edition of the *Hitchhiker's Guide*, where I introduced RDO for the first time. I've reviewed the chapters to make sure the information is current, updating material here and there to reflect changes that have occurred since the last edition. The most notable remarks relate to those things that the new ODBC 3.*x* drivers have bent or broken.

Even though ActiveX Data Objects (ADO) is the current golden child of data access interfaces, Remote Data Objects (RDO) is not by any means dead. Too many of you out there still find it the "just right" solution for your data access needs—especially with Microsoft SQL Server. Sure, ADO is newer and shinier, but I expect its luster to tarnish when it gets into the trenches and sits out in the rain for a night or two. But RDO won't be upgraded again, so what you see today in Microsoft Visual Basic 6.0 is just about it. Actually, RDO hasn't been upgraded since Visual Basic 5.0—unless you count the three service packs that addressed a number of RDO issues and the fixes applied for Visual Basic 6.0. And RDO does have some disadvantages, as you'll see in the section "Where RDO Falls Short" later in this chapter. If you want the new features being exposed by the developers here at Microsoft, you'll have to move to ADO.

As far as I'm concerned, however, RDO is still the bread and butter tool to get at SQL Server. This chapter and the rest of the chapters in this part walk you through the well-paved and patched streets of RDO, which are kind of like the street going up Education Hill in Redmond toward my house. It's torn up in places where they put down the new waterline, but it's easy to navigate and the traffic lights all work—when it's not raining. As many developers have pointed out to me, RDO still has some problems, but lots of you have been able to make good use of its performance and features. If I were you, I would spend a lot of time on foot examining every interesting side street in this chapter.

Understanding RDO

The Visual Basic 4.0 team (including myself) first came up with the ideas that evolved into Remote Data Objects. In effect, we created a new genre, an entirely new way to access data from Visual Basic. Since then, the new way has

PART IV   USING REMOTE DATA OBJECTS

become wildly popular. How did RDO move to the head of the class? The team created a body of code that met real developers' needs—that is, it solved real problems—without creating more problems than it fixed. For the most part, RDO 1.0 made working around problems easier than did other more complex interfaces that weren't specifically designed for client/server work. RDO 2.0 took that foundation and created the first fully event-driven data access interface in the industry.

Just for the sake of nostalgia, let's take a look at how we got to where we are with RDO. Suppose you were on the development team for Visual Basic 4.0 and you had to make the new product faster, smaller, backward-compatible with Visual Basic 3.0, and usable with the new version of SQL Server. What would you need to do?

The Visual Basic 4.0 team knew that we needed to create a clone of the DAO interface and a Data control that didn't need Jet. Our clone had to be faster and smaller, and it had to work with the existing bound controls. Most important of all, it had to leverage all the then new SQL Server 6.0 features and still work with other intelligent ODBC-based back ends. It had to be a clone of the DAO interface (or pretty nearly so) to make it easier to transition developers and documentation from DAO to RDO to DAO. We thought developers might need to take existing RDO code and move it back to DAO, but more likely they would need to move existing DAO code to RDO.

The problem was that no one had ever used the new OLE OCX technology to create such a beast. Besides, the current Data control was already an integral part of Visual Basic 4.0 and had never really been cloned. Sure, cloning it was theoretically possible, but so many complex questions remained that we weren't sure it could work.

And then a Microsoft program manager (PM) was approached at a conference by a man from New York who said he wanted some help with a new ODBC-based Data control he had written. Our PM looked at this New Yorker as if the man's coat were lined with hot watches for sale.

"Right," the PM said, "an ODBC Data control. Sure."

But gradually the PM realized that this guy held the missing pieces of the puzzle we were trying to assemble. He and his team had indeed created a rudimentary ODBC Data control. They had already solved many of the most complex problems, using nothing but a shaky beta copy of Visual Basic 4.0. (For all I knew, they had bought it from a curbside vendor on Forty-second Street.) And so far, they had done all this work with no help from Redmond.

Over the next six months, this rudimentary product was hammered and polished into a full-blown clone of the Data control and the Data Access Objects. This clone became the RemoteData control and RDO.

Now our team had a plan and a program. After working through hundreds of development glitches in RDO and the RemoteData control, we started to find bugs in the Visual Basic OCX interface, in bound controls, and in the ODBC drivers—bugs we never would have found without our friend from New York. By the time the code was committed to the golden master CDs, RDO and the RemoteData control had become the cornerstone of the new Enterprise edition of Visual Basic 4.0.

RDO is being pushed along into something altogether different from its original self. It now forms the nucleus of ADO, a class of objects that will continue to take over for RDO, DAO, and VBSQL in the years (or months) to come. "Classic" RDO and DAO aren't going away. But as new technologies (new solutions) are developed, the older solutions, no less viable, become less attractive.

Just how fast is ADO taking over the world? I expect we'll see it mature in 1998 now that it's sewn so tightly into the fabric of Visual Basic 6.0. I hope you like purple thread.

RDO 2.0 is faster, cleaner, and smarter than RDO 1.0—and not much bigger. We didn't want to create another Jet database engine. (Although that wouldn't be so bad if it addressed real client/server needs.) The team poured over SQL trace logs and performance comparisons to find where RDO was unnecessarily slowing things down or filling things up. The team made a few changes to the basic architectural assumptions—especially where prepared statements were concerned. Our team also added a significant amount of integration with Visual Basic itself, and this yielded the UserConnection Designer and the ability to express queries and stored procedures as methods. RDO 2.0 also includes one of the most powerful programming paradigms since the invention of floating-point math—*event driven* data access programming.

The version of RDO shipping in Visual Basic 6.0 is a further refinement of the code that shipped with Visual Basic 5.0, but little work has been done to expand its feature set. More emphasis was placed on ensuring that existing code continued to work and that changes made to Visual Basic 6.0 didn't substantially change its behavior. Keep in mind, however, that RDO is simply a façade on ODBC, so when ODBC 3.0 arrived, a number of changes that affect existing RDO code arrived as well. We'll look at these changes as the need arises.

Actually, RDO evolved at least twice in 1996 as Microsoft *quietly* released Visual Basic 4.0a (which included RDO 1.0a) in the first quarter and RDO 1.0b in the second quarter. It continued to be refined as versions of Visual Basic 5.0 emerged. The RDO provided in Visual Basic 5 Service Pack 3 is much more stable than its original bits.

Design Features

In case you hadn't noticed, the RemoteData control and RDO are members of the family of client/server data interfaces—a tribe that hasn't stopped growing since RDO was first built. The RDO interface is implemented via a thin layer of code over the ODBC API and Driver Manager and a specific ODBC driver. Figure 19-1, which was introduced in Chapter 3, shows the RDO interface to SQL Server.

The ODBC Driver Manager is what establishes connections, creates result sets and cursors, and executes complex procedures while using minimal workstation resources. RDO 2.0 includes a fairly sophisticated Client Batch cursor library, so we'll spend some time talking about building updateable batch cursors—something unheard of in RDO 1.0. But RDO doesn't include a cursor engine or query processor to rival those in ADO or Jet, or even a complex connection manager. This point is important to keep in mind when you're trying to diagnose some obscure problem. In most cases, the problem can be narrowed down to how the ODBC API and its drivers are implemented. We've seen most of the problems associated with RDO turn out to be "problems" with the ODBC drivers themselves or with how they were used. Even though RDO remains

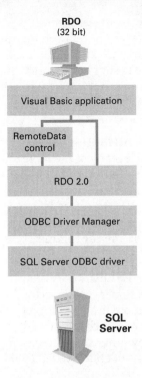

Figure 19-1 *RDO interface to access SQL Server from Visual Basic*

relatively unchanged, the ODBC drivers have changed about four times as new versions of Microsoft Internet Information Server, ADO, Visual InterDev, SQL Server, Microsoft Access, and other ODBC hosts evolve. Personally, I don't expect this difficulty to ease much.

When the time comes to implement any SQL Server front-end application, you want an easy-to-use data interface that doesn't compromise performance or make excessive demands on system resources. The ideal interface wouldn't be significantly larger than C-based DB-Library, and it would be every bit as fast for sending queries and processing simple result sets. It should be just as easy for you to build a cursorless result set or a complex updateable cursor as it is for you to execute a stored procedure with multiple result sets, with or without output parameters and return values. You should even be able to use SQL Server–side cursors as easily as you can use local client cursors. It should also be possible to limit the number of rows returned or updated, and without compromising the query being executed, you should be able to monitor all the messages and errors generated by the remote data source. This ideal interface should also permit synchronous as well as asynchronous operations, so your application won't be blocked while lengthy queries are being executed. And the asynchronous operations should be manageable via a broad swath of events that let you trap every conceivable aspect of the operations.

Is that too much to ask? Not anymore. For the most part, RDO gives you this ideal interface. It was built with SQL Server (and Oracle) in mind, especially the features available with SQL Server 6.0. It implements a set of objects

for dealing with the special requirements of accessing *remote* data, and it was designed from the outset as an alternative for developers who don't need many of Jet's features and who don't find it productive to program at the API level. In many respects, RDO can be seen as representing the best of both worlds: it comes close to or exceeds the performance of the API tools, but it isn't significantly larger, and you don't lose the flexibility of the API approach. RDO supports the following features:

- **Direct access to SQL Server stored procedures, including parameters, return status, and output values** Because many of the more sophisticated data processing shops expose *only* stored procedures or views, the data access interface must permit intimate control of access to this query-style data interface paradigm. The RDO interface is designed with MIS-class security in mind. It supports access to parameters for stored procedures and to query parameters via the rdoParameter object.

- **Complete integration with Visual Basic, Enterprise Edition** Visual Basic 5.0 and 6.0 include the UserConnection Designer, which helps build RDO-based UserConnection objects that expose user-developed queries and stored procedures as methods. Once created, the User-Connection objects can be passed around like any other shared component. They also dramatically reduce the amount of code needed to perform common RDO operations.

- **Complete interpretation of the Visual Database Tools with RDO** These tools are implemented with and for RDO 2.0 as well as for ADO. With them, you can develop and share database schemas and an interactive query development tool, and you can even tune Web-based designs.

- **Integration of the Transact-SQL (TSQL) Debugger with the IDE** This integration means that you can test and walk through TSQL stored procedures and triggers right from Visual Basic's design environment. For example, when you use the Update method and SQL Server fires a trigger because of the query, the TSQL Debugger fires up and lets you step through the procedure.

- **Sophisticated client-side cursor library** The Client Batch cursor library developed by the FoxPro team exposes optimistic batch updates and a faster, more intelligent local cursor library—head and shoulders above the ODBC client-side library. This cursor library also supports dissociate rdoQuery and rdoConnection objects.

- **Complete asynchronous event-driven support** Whereas RDO supported limited asynchronous operations, RDO 2.0 expands that support to virtually every aspect of the data access paradigm and adds the power of events that fire when the asynchronous operations complete. This means no more indeterminate blockages while the server processes long queries.

- **Events tailored to support read-only result set updatability via stored procedures** You can build cursor (or even noncursor) "non-updateable" result sets for which you can update database rows by trapping the WillUpdateRows event and executing an independent action query to perform the update.

- **Relaxed ODBC Level II compliance requirements** One of the problems RDO 1.0 developers faced was its fairly rigid compliancy requirements. This rigidity often made using RDO on subcompliant drivers difficult or at least limiting. RDO 2.0 added additional support to take up the slack where suboptimal drivers are used.

- **Redesigned prepared statement methodology** Another problem faced by RDO 1.0 developers was RDO's overenthusiastic use of prepared statements. This feature often meant slower performance for some situations and residual stored procedures loitering in TempDB. The RDO 2.0 release changed the defaults and provides a higher degree of control over the creation and execution of queries. The result is even better performance in some fairly common cases and less stored procedure trash being left on the battlefield.

- **Straight-line access to batched queries** Many MIS procedures and applications depend on the flexibility of batched queries or complex stored procedures that return one or more result sets. In many cases, batched queries neither return nor affect many rows, but they can dramatically improve performance by lowering the overhead on query submissions.

- **Full TSQL support** It's vital that the data interface to SQL Server fully support all aspects of TSQL to permit the broadest possible support for SQL Server functionality. This includes RAISERROR and DBCC support. RDO doesn't parse your SQL code the way DAO/Jet does—every operation is a pass-through query.

- **High-performance data access against remote ODBC data sources, especially SQL Server** The ability to quickly retrieve results from complex queries is a goal of every data access application. The RDO interface provides a consistent level of performance rivaled only by the ODBC API and VBSQL API interfaces. By leveraging the remote data engine, the RDO interface greatly improves response time and user productivity. Because of its size, the RDO interface also loads faster, which in turn improves overall application load time.

- **Management of return codes, input parameters, and output parameters from stored procedures** Output parameters are used heavily for singleton queries and many administrative functions. In many cases, you can't determine whether a stored procedure has been completed successfully unless you can access the procedure's return value.

When shops convert from VBSQL or DB-Library, all their code is in TSQL. At best, converting that code into generic SQLSpeak should be unnecessary when you're using RDO. At worst, it should be automatic and painless.

- **Management of multiple result sets**   You can make more efficient use of the query processor and system resources if you use a single query that returns several sets of related results. You can also improve performance by running a single query to gather data for filling multiple data-driven list boxes and menus. In addition, by combining a row-count query with a SELECT query, you can accurately set up scroll bars and status bars.

- **Limitation of the number of rows returned**   In situations where a user might select more rows than would be practical to handle, the RDO interface taps the SQL Server query governor that limits the number of rows returned from the server. That way, you can predict query response time and more easily manage the workstation or server resources required to maintain cursor keysets. This feature is implemented against any back end that supports it.

- **Utilization of server-side cursors**   SQL Server 6.*x* supports cursor keysets that are stored on the server rather than on the workstation. Under the right conditions, this type of cursor management can significantly improve system performance and reduce the resource needs of the workstation.

- **Exposure of underlying ODBC handles**   When you need more flexibility or control than is available in the object model, you should have a way of directly accessing the ODBC Driver Manager and the SQL Server driver itself. The RDO interface provides access to the ODBC environment, connection, and statement handles, so you can set options at the level of the driver and the Driver Manager.

NOTE   When you migrate to ADO, you lose low-level access to the ODBC API and the ability to run ODBC API functions using the hEnv and hStmt pointers. Frankly, there are precious few legitimate situations that really require access to these APIs. ADO should be able to pick up the slack where this functionality is no longer available.

- **Reduction of memory footprint to support "thinner" clients**   In many cases, the workstation has limited RAM and disk capacity. Therefore, the applications designed for this type of system need to economize on their use of RAM and other resources. The RDO memory footprint is dramatically smaller than Jet's, and the RDO model doesn't require local memory or disk space for its lowest-level cursors. When compared to ADO, RDO is about the same—unless you start counting the rather large Jet-like (OK, written-by-the-old-Jet-team) ADO data components—then we're back to Sasquatch-like footprints.

Comparing RDO and DAO

In many respects, the RDO and DAO/Jet data interfaces are very similar, especially at the lowest layers. You use RDO objects pretty much the way you use the Jet DAO objects: you submit a query, create a result set or cursor, and process the results from the query, using database-independent, object-oriented code. Both interfaces let you create cursors against SQL Server data tables, views, or result sets from stored procedures. Both also let you connect to SQL Server and manage transactions. But how these tasks are accomplished is very different for each interface.

With the addition of ODBCDirect to DAO, the decision whether or not to use DAO became more convoluted. Where with DAO/Jet there was little to gain by using DAO, ODBCDirect exposes enough RDO functionality to force many to reconsider this decision.

Table 19-1 on the next page lists the RDO objects and their DAO/Jet and DAO/ODBCDirect equivalents. Objects labeled *Not implemented* in the RDO column are included in the DAO/Jet interface to support ISAM implementations or methodologies that simply aren't needed in a relational model (and require the Jet database engine to implement). Generally, though, most of the DAO methods and properties that you're familiar with are supported by the RDO equivalents. For example, the Move, MoveNext, MoveFirst, MovePrevious, and MoveLast methods are all supported on keyset-type, static-type, and dynamic-type cursors. The PercentPosition, AbsolutePosition, and LastModified properties are also supported. The ISAM-oriented Find and Seek methods are *not* supported by RDO, however, nor are they ever likely to be. As many of you have already discovered, these methods, used to position the current-row pointer to a specific row in the result set, can be brutally slow. Therefore, developers who work with SQL Server databases have changed strategies and now use targeted queries to address their requirements for row searching. This targeting means that conversion of DAO code to RDO code can be fairly painless, for the most part. It's like putting on a new brand of jeans: you might discover a few more pockets, but the zipper is still in the same place. The RDO column of the table shows a couple of objects—for example, the forward-only rdoResultset object—used for fetching results on a row-by-row basis. Forward-only rdoResultset objects are simple to create, so they yield the highest possible performance when you're pulling back query results. The rdoQuery object maps directly to the ODBC SQLPrepare function, supports the creation of parameter queries, and exposes many of the more sophisticated features of the RDO data interface.

Let me put in my two cents worth here: ODBCDirect is a partial solution. Not only does it not support all of RDO's functionality, but it doesn't support many of its most powerful paradigms—as you'll see by reading this chapter. I even placed the ODBCDirect chapter (Chapter 17) first so that this distinction would be clearer. ADO, on the other hand, takes a much more rational (and less relational) approach—but we'll get to that later.

> **NOTE** Where the DAO interface refers to *records* and *fields*, the RDO interface refers, respectively, to *rows* and *columns*. This difference reflects the lineage of the data interfaces; DAO is an ISAM model, whereas RDO is a relational model.

Table 19-1
RDO, DAO/Jet, and DAO/ODBCDirect Equivalents

RDO	DAO/Jet	DAO/ODBCDirect
rdoEngine	DBEngine	DBEngine
rdoError	Error	Error
rdoEnvironment	Workspace	Workspace
rdoConnection	Database	Database/Connection
rdoQuery	QueryDef	QueryDef
rdoColumn	Field	Field
rdoParameter	Parameter	Parameter
rdoResultset	Recordset	Recordset
Not implemented	Table-type	Not implemented
Keyset-type	Dynaset-type	Dynaset-type
Static-type	Snapshot-type	Snapshot-type
Dynamic-type	None	Dynamic-type
Forward-only–type	Forward-only–type (same as a forward-only snapshot)	Forward-only–type (same as a forward-only snapshot)
rdoTable	TableDef	Not implemented
Not implemented	Index	Not implemented
Not implemented	Container	Not implemented
Not implemented	Document	Not implemented
Not implemented	Relation	Not implemented
Not implemented	User, Group	Not implemented

IMHO

Think of the RDO interface as a six-speed synchromesh transmission in a Formula One race car: you wouldn't think of going out on the track without it. Jet is more like an automatic transmission that does all the shifting for you, but it doesn't give you the flexibility you need in the S-turns. ODBCDirect is very much like a four-speed manual transmission that gives you some of the feel, but not nearly all of the flexibility of the six-speed—so you have a tendency to smoke the clutch more often. ADO is like a steering wheel that fits on a whole lot of vehicles—all with code-definable pedals.

The RDO data interface is generally simpler than the DAO/Jet one, so it should be fairly easy to implement. The real differences between the two interfaces have to do with how they expose specific SQL Server features and interfaces. Jet supports the creation and modification of the database schema through DAO methods and properties. The RDO and DAO/ODBCDirect interfaces don't support any type of schema modification because this is fully supported in the tools and utilities provided with SQL Server. Of course, you can still run MakeTable queries and use TSQL statements to execute action queries that create, modify, or delete databases and tables. You can also execute complex stored procedures that manage the database schema, and you can perform maintenance operations that are either very difficult or impossible with the DAO/Jet interface.

Where RDO Falls Short

No, RDO is not the ideal universal solution we've been waiting for—not that I'm a fan of one-size-fits-all solutions anyway. Frankly, I think universal data access solutions are like universal swimming suits. A well-fitting suit for Sam might be somewhat skimpy for Sue. RDO's architecture depends on a dedicated connection (at least a short-term connection) and the ability to have that connection present when you want to create a result set. If you want to save the contents of that result set to a file, you can, but you have to do all the work yourself—too bad you can't create a replacement result set when you want to reconstitute the data later. RDO isn't really suited for client-side Web work either. It can be used effectively on server-side or middle-tier components, but not on the client—how do you make a connection from 100,000 Web pages and expect it to work? Sure, you can use ActiveX Documents and embed RDO code and host them in a Web page, but don't expect to have the application work outside of the visibility of SQL Server.

RDO also carries with it a burden of its heritage. When RDO was first conceived, it was politically necessary for it to be patterned after the DAO object model. This model was burdened with the hierarchical Microsoft Excel–like object model. So RDO was created in DAO's image. This was a mistake. RDO's complex hierarchy of collections and interrelated objects made it tough for the team to manage scope and persistence of objects. For example, the rdoConnection and rdoResultset objects coexisted in a collection of similar objects, which had to be managed by RDO behind the scenes. This detracted from RDO's performance. RDO was also designed to be as friendly as DAO when it came to handling parameters passed to procedures. As a result of this "friendliness," RDO always called the server to find out what your query looked like. This activity not only slowed things down but also made it tough to access other ODBC data sources that didn't support the extra ODBC calls needed to support this. Sure, RDO 2.0 relaxed that requirement, but it did so by adding more code that didn't always help performance.

RDO really needed the ability to create "persisted" result sets. This functionality was in the original spec, but when it came time to get it working or ship the product, the feature was pulled. Because ADO was going to (and has) picked up this functionality, it was never added into RDO. Without the ability to save and reconstitute rdoResultset objects from files, the ability to easily deal with the disconnected user never materialized.

RDO also left a lot of developers in a quandary (that's like a swamp managed by that old Dallas Cowboys football coach in the fedora). They wanted to create applications to run on their 16-bit Windows 3.x platforms but couldn't use RDO because it was 32-bit only. It seems that very few at Microsoft expected the 16-bit to 32-bit conversion to take so long. OK, I did, but I am but a single voice. We probably couldn't have created a 16-bit version of RDO anyway— not with the staff we had and not in time. Too bad no third party took up the challenge to do it.

CAUTION

The RDO interface doesn't coddle you as much as the DAO/Jet interface does. It protects you from the complexities of the Visual Basic–to–ODBC API interface, at virtually no cost to the interface's flexibility, but it gives you responsibility for your own destiny: because the ODBC internal handles are exposed, you can scramble ODBC's synapses with the greatest of ease, if that's what you care to do.

For years, I lobbied for a data interface like RDO. It's not everything I would have liked, but it's pretty darn close—and RDO 2.0 is even closer to an ideal interface. ADO, the new (yet to be proven in battle) lieutenant, has lots of potential to come even closer yet.

For any number of reasons, RDO has also fallen short as a viable front-end to Oracle databases. Granted, many of these problems can be traced right back to the Oracle-provided ODBC drivers. It wasn't until fall 1997 that Microsoft got serious about building its own set of Oracle ODBC drivers. By then, much of the damage had already been done. These new drivers have evolved over the last year and have improved RDO's ability to address cross-platform and pure Oracle design issues.

Visual Basic 6.0 ships with a new set of Oracle drivers. Question: Are these drivers any good? BHOM (Beats the Hell Out of Me). I never tried them. I don't plan to. I do understand that these drivers were developed and tested specifically by Microsoft and have been much more thoroughly tested than the ones previously passed down by Oracle for Visual Basic 5.0.

Granted, ADO doesn't have the experience behind it, but it promises to take up where RDO leaves off. Too bad it leaves behind some of the low-level operations that some depend on. It also seems to have left off much of RDO's performance. But it's early yet.

Using ODBC Drivers for Jet

As I've said many times so far, RDO is designed with SQL Server and Oracle in mind. Because of this, a number of things were done to make it work effectively with the types of databases managed by these intelligent, remote database management systems. In addition, since RDO first came out, a number of people have tried to use RDO with other ODBC drivers—many with a great deal of success. But one group seems to be quite frustrated in its attempts to get RDO to work. These are the developers who tried to use the "Brazos" ODBC drivers for Jet. These drivers are designed for Microsoft Office applications—*not* for those mainstream applications that need access to Jet and SQL Server databases at the same time. These drivers aren't equipped to deal with a variety of ODBC Level II compliance issues, nor will they ever be. Most developers don't realize that these drivers simply load Jet and use it as the interface to the native Jet database being accessed. I can't recommend using RDO with these or any ISAM drivers. It's like mounting racing slicks to drive in the snow. There are better tools for the job. Keep in mind that ODBC is a *relational* database interface and isn't equipped to deal with "seeks" or raw table I/O like its ISAM cousins. That's why Jet is needed to access this type of data source. ADO would be a better choice in these situations because it has both SQL Server and Jet service providers. Of course, now that SQL Server for Windows 95/98 has arrived, having to use ODBC drivers for Jet might not be necessary.

Getting the Latest Information on RDO

When we shipped Visual Basic 4.0, the Internet had hardly come to life for Microsoft. Now it forms the core of many of Microsoft's strategies and support services. If you need more information on RDO or any of the topics discussed here, check out the Web Pages directory on the CD that comes with this book. I have downloaded all of the RDO Knowledge Base articles and saved them there on disk. To get more of the same, see *http://www.microsoft.com/vstudio/*.

Licensing RDO

RDO is licensed to the Visual Studio suite (Visual Basic 5.0 and 6.0, Enterprise editions; Visual InterDev, Visual J++, and Visual C++ Enterprise). Using it in design mode (which Visual Basic for Applications in any Office application is always in) requires that you have purchased and installed Visual Basic 6.0, Enterprise Edition, or one of the other host development platforms on the machine. Of course, the Registry keys aren't hard to find and copy, but *legally* you must have purchased a licensed copy of Visual Basic 6.0, Enterprise Edition, for any machine that is going to use RDO from design mode. Licensed controls (OCX/ActiveX) work in this same way, but Microsoft never before had any controls that it decided to restrict to only the Enterprise Edition.

Fortunately, a nice clean solution to these licensing requirements exists. Your customers should embrace the services model. Instead of doing all their data access code right in the Microsoft Excel workbook or Microsoft Word document, you should build Visual Basic ActiveX component servers that do the data access and return data to the calling application. The dynamic-link library (DLL) exposes an interface that encapsulates a bunch of functionality (like gathering all information about sales of a given product from possibly many sources) and is easy to work with at a high level. That DLL can be built in Visual Basic 6.0, Enterprise Edition, and then reused by any Office application or any other automation controller.

Reuse is obviously beneficial, and over time, you'll save your customers the trouble of having to maintain code in lots of workbooks. Also, that same ActiveX component can be used by your customers' other Visual Basic front ends, and therefore all the clients use the same set of business rules regardless of what tool the client was created in. Because the DLL is compiled (and not in design mode), RDO doesn't check for the existence of a license key in the Registry and you can freely redistribute it to any client machine.

20

Remote Data Objects Up Close

et's pull off the main highway and take a long, scenic, informative tour of Remote Data Objects (RDO). This is a good starting point for those of you who are new to RDO 2.0, because much has changed since RDO was first introduced. Once we've crossed this terrain together, I hope you'll be able to find your way through it on your own next time.

Understanding the RDO Model

RDO and the RDO collections provide a framework for using code to create and manipulate the components of a remote ODBC database system such as Microsoft SQL Server. Don't get me wrong, though: while the RDO interface was tuned for SQL Server and Oracle, it works with any ODBC back end. And RDO 2.0 is designed to be more tolerant of subcompliant drivers than RDO 1.0 was; the requirement to use an ODBC Level II–compliant driver has been dropped. Objects and collections have properties that describe the characteristics of database components, as well as methods that you use to manipulate them. Figure 20-1 shows the RDO model.

RDO objects are like any other Microsoft Visual Basic objects. In many respects, they behave like Visual Basic controls that have defined properties and methods but no visible representation, such as the Timer control or the VBSQL control. In other words, the RDO objects are used simply to map to one or more ODBC API functions, which in turn permit access to specific back-end result sets or options. A single RDO method or property might be executed as a single ODBC function or as a whole series of functions. Each of the RDO objects, with the exception of the rdoEngine object, is maintained in an associated collection. This means you can examine the properties and execute methods against any created object simply by wading into the right collection.

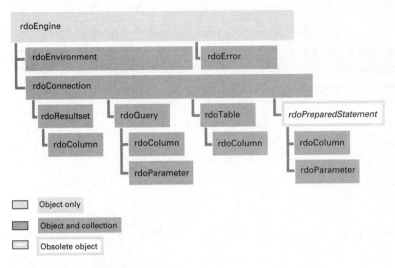

Figure 20-1   *The RDO model*

Unfortunately, this adds to RDO's overhead and complicates the creation and (intentional) destruction of objects. Keep in mind that RDO often has to maintain collection references long after the object loses scope but remains referenced elsewhere in your code. This means that "orphaned" objects are not uncommon—which also means memory leaks. RDO 2.0 introduced the concept of *stand-alone* objects. These objects are created with the *New* keyword, and they might not be assigned to an associated collection. Nor are these stand-alone objects referenced in their associated collection.

Using RDO to access Jet databases is only for those who enjoy pain and frustration. Sure, it's possible, but it's dumb. The Jet ODBC drivers are "challenged" at best and don't expose nearly all the functionality that DAO lets you use.

NOTE   If you import existing 32-bit Visual Basic 4.0 RDO 1.0 applications into the current version of Visual Basic, your code is automatically upgraded to RDO 2.0, including any references to the RemoteData control, which uses RDO.

The rdoEngine Object

When the RDO interface is initialized on first access, an instance of the rdoEngine object is automatically created. The rdoEngine object is used to set RDO-wide parameters and options. Unlike applications that use the DAO/Jet DBEngine object, each application that uses RDO gets its own rdoEngine object. When you create new rdoEnvironment, rdoConnection, or rdoResultset objects, the characteristics of the new objects are determined by the default values of the rdoEngine properties unless you override these values with arguments in the rdoCreateEnvironment or OpenResultset methods. This means that the rdoEngine object, once it has been created, is referenced only when you address the rdoEnvironments collection. The default values for rdoEngine object properties are shown in Table 20-1.

Table 20-1
Default Values for rdoEngine Object Properties

Property	What It Specifies	Default Value
rdoDefaultCursorDriver	Cursor driver type (ODBC or server-side)	rdUseIfNeeded
rdoDefaultUser	SQL Server logon ID	" " (empty string)
rdoDefaultPassword	Corresponding SQL Server password	" " (empty string)
rdoDefaultErrorThreshold	Level of severity above which errors are fatal	–1 (disabled)
rdoLocaleID	Determines which error messages language is used for RDO	rdLocaleEnglish
rdoVersion	Returns version of RDO engine DLL	6.00.xxxx
rdoDefaultLoginTimeout	Time to wait before abandonment of connection attempt	15 seconds

CAUTION

To use RDO, you *must* set a reference to the Microsoft Remote Data Object 2.0 object library in the Visual Basic References dialog box, which you reach via the Projects menu. If you don't do this, you'll trip a compile error that says your user-defined object is not recognized (or something to that effect). Fortunately, the UserConnection designer sets this reference for you.

The rdoEngine object is predefined, so you can't create additional rdoEngine objects—nor do you need to. All properties and methods executed against the rdoEngine object simply poll the ODBC Driver Manager for information. Since no specific ODBC driver has been selected (this must be done using an object such as rdoConnection), no driver-specific information can be obtained, but internal ODBC handles are automatically allocated to deal with impending connections. These settings determine how subsequent data-related operations are managed—or at least they establish the default values used when rdoEnvironment objects are created.

rdoEngine Properties, Events, and Methods

For the most part, you employ the rdoEngine to set parameters for building the rdoEnvironment objects beneath it. However, Visual Basic 5.0 introduced an important addition—events. The rdoEngine object exposes the first of these events. In the following list, I describe how to use the various properties, events, and methods exposed by the rdoEngine object:

- **Creating a new rdoEnvironment object using the rdoCreate-Environment method**   The rdoEnvironment object is used to map alternative users or separate transaction scopes. (You'll read more about managing transactions with the rdoEnvironment object in the "Transaction Management" section on page 387.) You don't have to create an rdoEnvironment to get started; the rdoEngine creates a default object for you—rdoEnvironments(0). And if you don't use separate RDO-managed transaction scopes? You don't have to reference the rdoEnvironments collection at all—the rdoEnvironments(0) is assumed.

- **Using the rdoDefaultCursorDriver property to set or examine the default cursor type** In some cases, the default (server-side cursors) can't implement some of the cursor features you need, so you must override the default and use one of the other cursor libraries. You must do this if you're trying to submit stored procedures that return anything except a simple SELECT result set.

- **Using the rdoErrors collection to get details on errors once a connection has been attempted or a cursor has been created** The rdoErrors collection is used to manage errors generated by the ODBC layers, not by Visual Basic.

- **Using the rdoDefaultLoginTimeout property to set or examine the ODBC logon default timeout value** You should set this to about 5 seconds instead of the default setting of 15 seconds.

- **Using the rdoDefaultUser and rdoDefaultPassword properties to set the user name and password for opening connections** You perform this operation if no specific values have been supplied. Generally, however, I use domain-managed security, so I leave these values alone. But the new ODBC 3.x drivers make this a little harder. You have to include Trusted_Connection=Yes in your connect string to get this to work.

- **Using the rdoDefaultErrorThreshold property to set or examine the level of severity above which errors are fatal** A fatal error is one that terminates a query and triggers a trappable Visual Basic error. No, this never worked very well, so forget trying to use it.

But the rdoDefaultError-Threshold property *still* isn't working as first intended, so I would just steer clear of it.

- **Using the rdoRegisterDataSource method to create a new DSN entry in the Microsoft Windows Registry** I never use this method, and you'll understand why after you read Chapter 21, which is about using RDO to connect to SQL Server.

- **Using the InfoMessage event to fire each time an informational message is returned to any open RDO connection** For those of you familiar with VBSQL, this event is virtually identical to the DBLIB message handler. Basically, RDO places any SQL_SUCCESS_WITH_INFO messages into the rdoErrors collection and fires the InfoMessage event to tell you that a message (not necessarily an error) has arrived. At this point, you must scan the rdoErrors collection for the details. This event also exposes the PRINT and RAISERROR TSQL statements that you execute in stored procedures or triggers.

You can change any of the default values shown in Table 20-1 before you create new rdoEnvironment, rdoConnection, or rdoResultset objects. Note, however, that rdoEnvironments(0) is created with the default values shown because it's created automatically on first reference to RDO or the RemoteData control. Therefore, by the time you get a chance to change any of the defaults, the rdoEngine has already started and the default rdoEnvironment has been created. If the default values aren't appropriate to your application, you can change the properties of rdoEnvironments(0) or the rdoEngine before opening a connection or creating a new rdoEnvironment object. You'll learn more about the rdoEnvironments object in the next section.

If this sounds like a lot of trouble and you'd just as soon not worry about it, check out the UserConnection designer—it can manage all these details for you.

NOTE Be sure to take advantage of Visual Basic's Explorer-like object browser. It makes locating the right object, method, property, or event easy—and help on the selected topic is just an F1 keystroke away. Figure 20-2 shows an example of the object browser window for the rdoEngine object. Notice how the events, properties, methods, and collections all have different icons. Visual Basic's IntelliSense also kicks in here to expose the available objects, methods, properties, and events as you type, so you don't have to look them up.

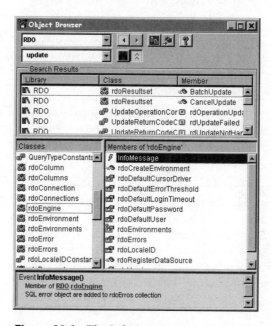

Figure 20-2 *The InfoMessage event of the rdoEngine object as exposed by the Visual Basic 6.0 object browser*

The rdoEnvironment Object

After the RDO interface instantiates the rdoEngine object, it automatically creates the default rdoEnvironment object in rdoEnvironments(0). This default rdoEnvironment object corresponds to the ODBC hEnv handle returned by the SQLAllocEnv function. The underlying ODBC environment is used to determine ODBC driver settings. For example, you can set the type of default cursor using the rdoDefaultCursorDriver property. You can do the same thing using the rdoEngine object's hEnv property and the ODBC SQLSetConnectOption function, but why bother? The object property is far easier to use, and you don't have to remember the *SQL_CUR* constants. The point is, you have the option of doing it either through the RDO interface or directly through the ODBC API. Don't get too used to this feature, however. It doesn't migrate to ADO. Most of the time it really doesn't matter—except to the poor soul who has to figure out how to debug your code after you've taken off for Tahiti. (I guess she could just call you up and ask—or better yet, fly out there and ask in person.)

RDO 2.0 adds another wrinkle here. Since you can now create a stand-alone rdoConnection object and set its properties before actually connecting, the need for the rdoEnvironment object has been reduced considerably. Sure, you still need it to build independent transaction scopes, but for the most part, you can do without it. It's still useful when you need to trap transaction events, however.

> Now that we're beginning to use Microsoft Transaction Server to manage our transactions for us, the need for client-managed transactions might be a thing of the past—like rotary dials on phones and buttonhooks.

rdoEnvironment Properties, Events, and Methods

Using the rdoEnvironment object, you can set a number of property options and initiate a number of methods. RDO also fires three events to reflect operations on any rdoConnections established under a specific rdoEnvironment. (As mentioned earlier, any property options that you set on the rdoEnvironment object will override values set on the rdoEngine object.) Here are some of the operations you can perform:

- **Using the rdoEnvironment object's LoginTimeout property to determine the number of seconds that the ODBC Driver Manager waits for a successful logon operation to complete** The default value of 15 seconds is usually fine for most local network operations, but it's not nearly enough for some busy networks or RAS connections. Actually, 5 seconds is usually enough—most servers can hook up that fast.

- **Using the rdoEnvironment object's default UserName and Password properties to open connections** These default values are both "" but you can override them using arguments to the OpenConnection method. Again, I don't use these default values for domain-managed security applications. But you still need to watch out for the need to add *Trusted_ connection=Yes* to your connect string, as previously mentioned.

- **Opening one or more connections**   You use the OpenConnection method to perform this operation. Unlike DAO or ADO, the RDO model provides no automatic connection or disconnection. When you close a connection, it closes—immediately. Actually, now that RDO 2.0 supports the EstablishConnection method on the rdoConnection object, I think the OpenConnection method will be abandoned. Sure, you can get Microsoft Transaction Server (MTS) to handle connections for you, but that's featured on another tour.

- **Managing batched transaction processing**   You can use the BeginTrans, CommitTrans, and RollbackTrans methods and the associated events to manage this kind of transaction processing across one or more rdoEnvironment connections. RDO fires events when each of these methods is executed so that you can add additional contingency handling to transaction operations. You can't use these events to derail the transaction; to complete or undo a transaction, you'll have to use the CommitTrans or RollbackTrans method.

- **Conducting multiple, simultaneous, independent, and overlapping transactions**   You can use several rdoEnvironment objects to perform these operations. Remember that client-managed transaction scope is based on the rdoEnvironment object. We're also migrating to middle-tier transaction management, so these client-side operations are often not a good idea.

- **Terminating an environment and the connection and removing them from their respective collections**   This releases the underlying ODBC hEnv and hDbc handles. Use the Close method to do this.

NOTE   ODBC 3.0 has installed a connection pooling mechanism not unlike that used by Jet to help manage limited connection resources. By default, this feature is disabled in RDO because it's really intended for use in Web servers or Microsoft Transaction Server, or by remote server-side Microsoft ActiveX components to handle hundreds (or thousands) of incoming connection requests—not the few dozen to few hundred requests received by a conventional LAN server.

If you're ever inclined to refer to an rdoEnvironment object by name, use the rdoEnvironment object's Name property or, easier yet, use its ordinal number. The default rdoEnvironments(0) object is named Default_Environment— but why you'd want to use this instead of the ordinal number 0 is beyond me. The Name property of rdoEnvironment objects is originally set from the *Name* argument passed to the rdoEngine's rdoCreateEnvironment method (except, of course, the rdoEnvironments(0) object—it's created by default and doesn't require you to call rdoCreateEnvironment). You can also refer to an rdoEnvironment object by its ordinal position in the rdoEnvironments collection, using this syntax (where *n* is the *n*th member of the zero-based rdoEnvironments collection):

```
rdoEngine.rdoEnvironments(n)
```

Or you can do it this way:

```
rdoEnvironments(n)
```

You can't create a stand-alone rdoEnvironment object using the *New* keyword—you must use rdoCreateEnvironment. (You shouldn't need to anyway). But how can you tell which objects can generally be declared as *New*? Well, Visual Basic's IntelliSense tells you. Look at what happened when I typed the declare statement in the example shown in Figure 20-3. IntelliSense couldn't find rdoEnvironment as a valid object to be used with the *New* keyword—Visual Basic won't let you make a mistake—unless you force it to.

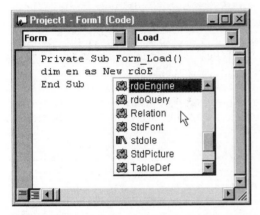

Figure 20-3 *Using Visual Basic 6.0's IntelliSense to make RDO coding easier*

Transaction Management

If you expect your application to support more than one transaction scope or to separate user name and password contexts, you should first consider using MTS to handle these operations for you. If using MTS isn't an option and you have the time and resources to reinvent this functionality yourself, consider using the rdoEngine's rdoCreateEnvironment method to create a new rdoEnvironment object with specific user ID and password values. This method accepts a unique name for the new object, a user ID, and a password. If the name you specify for the new object matches an existing member of the rdoEnvironments collection, a trappable error results. If the rdoCreateEnvironment call succeeds, a newly created rdoEnvironment object is automatically appended to the rdoEnvironments collection. To create an rdoEnvironment object that is *not* appended to the rdoEnvironments collection, simply provide an empty string for the name. To remove an rdoEnvironment object, use the Close method against it.

CAUTION

Implementation of the ODBC driver's transaction management is strictly one level deep. If you execute an RDO BeginTrans method, the ODBC layer simply sets the hDbc connection handle's option for automatic commitment to *off*. But when the CommitTrans is executed, the bit is turned back on, even if it was turned off a dozen times, and the ODBC driver issues the SQLTransact function. This makes it clear to me that you shouldn't try to do any nesting with the transaction methods—at least not by using the rdoEnvironment object.

You can use additional rdoEnvironment objects to manage independent transaction scopes. In this sense, they are very much like the Workspace object in the DAO model. For example, when you use the BeginTrans method against an rdoEnvironment object, all data-altering operations on *all* rdoConnection objects in that environment are considered to be in the same transaction scope. If you roll back a transaction on any of the common rdoConnection objects, the RDO interface walks through *all* of the rdoConnection objects opened on that rdoEnvironment and issues a rollback command. This doesn't mean that the RDO interface and the ODBC Driver Manager support two-phase commit; they don't. Each operation is atomic—it can succeed or fail on its own. If one of these subtransactions fails, its failure has no effect on previously committed operations.

To establish separate transaction scopes, you open additional rdoEnvironment objects. For those of you who fell off the truck when I mentioned two-phase commit a moment ago, this is the mechanism that SQL Server used before there was a Distributed Transaction Coordinator (DTC) to handle cross-server synchronization. Two-phase commit has never been supported from Visual Basic—not directly. You get this feature only when you let the DTC or MTS handle transactions for you.

> **NOTE** Still don't have a clue what two-phase commit is? Well, for years, SQL Server used it to manage cross-database operations. It uses a central (mother) server to keep track of transactions that involve more than one database—usually on more than one server. Behind the scenes, if all servers participating in the cross-database transaction (and there can be several) report back to the "mother" that they can commit the transaction, the mother server tells all of them to do so. If something goes wrong, the mother server tells all participating servers to roll back the transaction. This is all handled under the covers, so you needn't sweat the details.

> **TIP** The RDO interface supports fully nested transaction management using TSQL transaction statements initiated with the Execute method. For example, on a single connection, you can execute a BEGIN TRANS SQL statement, several UPDATE statements, and another BEGIN TRANS statement. Any operations executed after the second BEGIN TRANS statement can be rolled back independently of the statements executed after the first BEGIN TRANS. To commit the first set of UPDATE statements, you must execute a COMMIT TRANS statement or a ROLLBACK TRANS statement for each BEGIN TRANS executed. You can also use the BEGIN TRANS *name*, SAVETRANS *name*, and ROLLBACK *name* TSQL statements to roll back to specific points in the transaction sequence.

An Alternative Transaction Manager

Microsoft Transaction Server is one of the servers that was added to the suite of tools available for RDO developers. Although it is well beyond the scope of this guide to describe in detail how to set up and use MTS, it should be one of the first things you consider as you move your architecture toward implementation of remote business objects, especially when transactions are part of the design.

NOTE I'll offer more Microsoft Transaction Server tips and techniques in Part V.

When your design starts to span multiple servers, you often have to expand three-tier design concepts to additional levels. This is where MTS plays a critical support role—performing many complex operations that are, in many cases, simply impossible to perform without its help. MTS takes up where SQL Server's Distributed Transaction Coordinator (DTC) leaves off. It not only deals with transaction issues between servers but also manages thread pooling, object brokering, and a dozen other complex functions that you had to code yourself with earlier versions of Visual Basic.

MTS is a key element of Microsoft's Internet and intranet application strategy. The technology is based on proven transaction processing methods, but its importance transcends the domain of transaction processing monitors. It defines a general-purpose programming model for distributed component-based server applications. MTS is specifically designed to allow server applications to scale over a wide range of users, from small single-user systems to high-volume Internet servers. It provides the robustness and integrity traditionally associated only with high-end transaction processing systems. In Part V, you'll learn more about how MTS can relieve much of the responsibility of managing the logical business objects we use to build *n*-tiered applications.

Selecting a Cursor Driver

An rdoEnvironment object isn't only for setting transaction scope. It also determines, among other things, the type of cursor driver used in building cursors. I often reset the default driver type and use the Client Batch cursor driver (rdUseClientBatch), since it supports multiple result sets, which aren't easily supported by server-side cursors. You can choose the default cursor driver by setting the rdoDefaultCursorDriver property of the rdoEngine or the CursorDriver property of the rdoEnvironment object to one of five constants: *rdUseIfNeeded* (the default), *rdUseOdbc, rdUseClientBatch, rdUseServer,* or *rdUseNone.*

If you choose the default *rdUseIfNeeded*, the ODBC Driver Manager chooses the cursor driver on its own. It uses a server-side cursor, which is the default setting, whenever it can (such as when it connects to SQL Server 6.0 and later).

TIP To execute queries that return multiple result sets against a server-side cursor, set the read-only and forward-only options and set the rowset size to 1 or set the cursor driver to rdUseNone.

But unfortunately, the RDO interface has no way of knowing whether you're about to send a multiple result set or logic-constrained query, which might not be supported by a server-side cursor. SQL Server 7.0 can't handle these any better. You'll still have to use client-side cursor libraries for multiple-resultset stored procedures.

If you choose *rdUseOdbc*, it specifies that the ODBC cursor driver is to be used. In this case, cursors are built on the client. This driver supports multiple result sets and a variety of other options. But the ODBC cursor driver also consumes workstation resources in order to store the keysets or data rows, as dictated by the type of cursor you specify. I rarely, if ever, recommend this driver. It has never been tuned or polished as the Client Batch driver has, and though it is somewhat smaller, it isn't as fast or nearly as flexible.

If you choose *rdUseClientBatch*, it specifies that the FoxPro Client Batch cursor library is to be used. In this case, cursor keysets are also built on the client. This driver also supports multiple result sets and a variety of other options, including optimistic batch updates and dissociate Connection objects. Like the ODBC cursor library, the Client Batch library also consumes workstation resources to store the keysets or data rows, as dictated by the type of cursor you specify.

If you choose *rdUseServer*, you force the use of server-side cursors (where they are available). This is an option if you are connected to SQL Server 6.0 or later. In this case, the keysets or data rows are maintained in TempDB space on the SQL server. If the driver reports back that server-side cursors aren't available (such as when your application is connected to SQL Server 4.*x*), the ODBC driver simply switches back to the ODBC cursor driver and posts an informational message in the rdoErrors collection. This doesn't trip a trappable error or even give you an InfoMessage event, but it can result in dramatically different performance and operational characteristics. For example, the client will need resources to store the keyset and the network will need to handle the increased load of the returning keys. Not only that, control will be returned to the application *before* the keyset is populated.

We haven't talked much about *rdUseNone*. This option tells RDO to forgo creation of a cursor when you build rdoResultset objects. It is fast, lightweight, less demanding, and supports all stored procedures. If you create anything but a simple SELECT stored procedure, only the "cursorless" or client-side cursors can access it. In RDO 1.0, you had to build an rdoPreparedStatement, set its RowsetSize to 1, and build an rdoResultset with the read-only, forward-only options set. With RDO 2.0, this is no longer necessary when you set the *rdUseNone* option. Frankly, this is the "cursor" of choice for me because most of my applications fetch few rows and don't need to scroll around in stale data anyway.

TIP If you specify a client-side cursor, ODBC stores the temporary keysets that you build in RAM and sends the overflow to disk, storing the keys in the TEMP area on disk. You set the location of this area by changing the TEMP environment variable, which you set in AUTOEXEC.BAT or by using the System Control Panel. If the drive containing the TEMP space fills up, you are done fetching keys.

Understanding Server-Side Cursors

Server-side cursors are generally misunderstood, so we need to spend a little more time on them here. This type of cursor, first implemented on SQL Server (and not implemented on many other systems), saves space on the client system because the cursor keyset is built right on the server. That's the good news *and* the bad news. If the cursor contains too many rows, the server's resources get used up instead of the client's. In addition, the cursor is fully populated *before* control returns to your application, unless it exceeds the cursor threshold (which defaults to 100 rows). This means that the RowCount property of the rdoResultset object is accurate and that you can use the same connection again immediately without having to close the cursor. RDO handles fetching the next rowset of data from the server-side cursor as you move down in the keyset. However, RDO keeps only the *current* rowset of rows on the client. (This number is determined by the setting of the RowsetSize property of the rdoQuery object, which defaults to 100.) Whenever you step off this rowset (either forward or backward), RDO calls the ODBC API SQLExtendedFetch call to get the next/previous rowset.

Server-side cursors work well only in specific scenarios, provided that you have a fast server and the cursor is fairly small (less than 200 rows). They are best when you simply can't afford the additional network load imposed by moving a keyset back to the client. But I've seen server-side cursors perform very badly on servers with limited RAM or slower CPUs or hard drives. Also, you should make sure that TempDB is big enough, since server-side cursor data is stored there. Remember to allocate enough space in TempDB for *each* application to store its cursor keyset(s). If you have 500 applications and they each create a 100-row cursor in TempDB, that means you need room to store 500 × 100 (50,000) keyset rows. SQL Server Books Online has a treatise on server-side cursors that is worth reading. In any case, if you have enough RAM (more then 64 MB), you should consider putting TempDB in RAM—this will make server-side cursors really fly. Of course, you have to realize that server-side cursors result in more network round-trips to the server (which you can offset by using a bigger rowset size), so the speed of the link between the client and the server also comes into play.

You can use the sp_configure stored procedure to set the cursor threshold option in SQL Server, which enables SQL Server to build server-side cursors asynchronously of the client. This means you can return to your application while the server continues to populate the cursor in TempDB. This can really help appearances, and you don't have to wait for the whole cursor to populate before returning control to the client. The option is a threshold setting in which you say, "If the cursor is more than *n* number of rows, populate it asynchronously." You should keep *n* set fairly high because populating a small cursor synchronously is faster than doing it asynchronously.

NOTE Whenever you set an option or a property that the ODBC driver can't implement, it reverts to a supported option and creates an entry in the rdoErrors collection—but that usually doesn't cause a trappable error.

The rdoConnection Object

The rdoConnection object is used to manage a connection with a single SQL Server database. When you coded with RDO 1.0, once you had the rdoEnvironment object set up with the right cursor driver, you could use it to open connections to remote ODBC data sources and create rdoConnection objects with either the RemoteData control or the OpenConnection method of an rdoEnvironment object. With RDO 2.0, you can connect using another method that is easier to code. First you can declare rdoConnection objects without using the OpenConnection method—you can use the *New* keyword as follows:

```
Dim Cn as New rdoConnection
```

This instantiates a stand-alone connection object. It's not a member of the rdoConnections collection—not yet. To point to a specific SQL server or a different cursor driver, you must set the rdoConnection properties. I like to use the *With* keyword to do this; it saves time and makes the code far easier to read:

```
With Cn
    .Connect = "Uid=;Pwd=;Database=Biblio;" _
        "DSN=Biblio;Trusted_Connection=Yes"
    .CursorDriver = rdUseNone    'To set cursor library
    .LoginTimeout = 10           'To set login timeout
End With
```

It's become clear to me that the UserConnection designer's convenience and shareable aspects make even the reduced code shown here unnecessary. Be sure to spend time checking out this feature in Visual Basic 6.0. It eliminates much of this drudgery with a simple design-time process.

NOTE   Many of the samples used in this book use databases that are on the companion CD. See Appendix A for information on how to set up the database samples.

Notice that we can now reference properties on the rdoConnection object that weren't exposed in RDO 1.0. A number of "parent" properties were added to RDO 2.0 objects to support stand-alone objects. Basically, you can preset these "parent" properties by setting rdoEngine or rdoEnvironment properties, but it's awfully easy to do it here—where we can clearly see what is being done.

We're now ready to make the connection. (We'll look at the details of opening a connection in the next chapter.)

Specifying a Default Database

All of your queries depend on a specific default database—unless you use absolute addressing everywhere you call out a database table. In most cases, therefore, you need to set a default database. You can choose from several ways of determining which database to connect to:

- You can explicitly reference a SQL Server database using the Connect argument when the rdoConnection object is opened with the OpenConnection method of the rdoEnvironment object. For example, if you set the Connect argument to Database=Pubs, the connection sets the default database to Pubs.

- In a similar manner, you can specify a connect string when you use a stand-alone rdoConnection object, as shown in the preceding code.

- The SQL Server system administrator can assign the default database when the logon ID is established. This is not always a good idea, though, since the system administrator (SA) might assign this database incorrectly or the ID might get changed inadvertently. This setting is the default if you don't specify a Database value in the connect string. Remember that by default a login ID is assigned to the Master database, which is a less-than-useful choice when you're building front ends against your own database.

- You can use the TSQL Use database statement to change the currently assigned default database. This works only if you can connect in the first place. If you can't connect because you haven't specified a permissible database for the logon ID you specified, you're stuck.

NOTE If your user ID doesn't have permission to use the selected database, a trappable ODBC error will be triggered and a proposed change won't be made. This error usually prevents a connection if you use the Database option in the connect string. Or the connection might be made, but to the wrong database.

No, RDO doesn't know what the default database is, nor does it care—no matter what technique you use to set or change it. On the other hand, if you make another connection and expect the default database to be set to something other than what the SA assigned, you'd better be prepared to set it yourself.

Using the rdoConnection Object

When the rdoConnection object is successfully opened using the OpenConnection or EstablishConnection methods, it's automatically appended to the rdoConnections collection. Once a connection is established, you can manipulate a database associated with an rdoConnection object by using the object's methods and properties. The SQL server itself isn't accessed until a connection is established, and once it is, you can use one or more of the following rdoConnection methods:

- The Execute method, to run an action query or pass an ODBC SQL or TSQL statement to the SQL server for execution. This technique is useful for UPDATE, INSERT, and DELETE statements or for complex transaction management. You can also use it for DBCC operations or for executing stored procedures (action queries). You can execute a multiple result set query using the Execute method—even if some of the queries return rows. Unlike RDO 1.0, RDO 2.0 doesn't trap action queries that contain SELECT clauses—it assumes that you know what you're doing.

- The OpenResultset method, to create a new rdoResultset cursor object. And you know, of course, that cursors return a subset of the database information. They can be read-only or updateable and use a variety of fetch options. We'll look at the rdoResultset object in Chapter 24, and the rdoQuery object in Chapter 26.

- The CreateQuery method, to create a new rdoQuery object. This method creates a temporary stored procedure that can take and return parameters and result sets from and to the database.

NOTE The rdoConnection object also supports the now-obsolete Create-PreparedStatement method (it's hidden, but it's still there), but you should convert to the CreateQuery method to enable all of the new features.

- The BeginTrans, CommitTrans, and RollbackTrans methods, to manage transactions.

- The Close method, to close a connection, deallocate the connection handle, and terminate the connection. As I said before, the RDO interface doesn't cache connections. When you use the Close method, the connection closes.

NOTE When you're done with a connection, you should close it. The RDO interface won't do it for you—remember, there's no connection manager. When you close an rdoConnection object, any open rdoResultset, rdoTable, or rdoQuery objects are automatically closed as well. If the rdoConnection object simply loses scope, however, any open rdoResultset, rdoTable, or rdoQuery objects remain open until the other objects are explicitly closed.

You can use the rdoConnection object properties to help manage the result sets you create on the connection. Here are some of the operations you can perform:

- Use the StillConnecting property to see whether your asynchronous connection has been made yet. This really isn't necessary if you set up a Connect event handler. StillConnecting returns False and the Connect event fires when the connection attempt has completed.

- Use the Connect property to examine the rdoConnection object's connect string. This can be useful when you're cloning the connection. The Connect property is reconstituted after opening to reflect the connect string generated by RDO using your input and the default values provided by RDO—the values you didn't override.

- Note that the rdoConnection also exposes the CursorDriver, Login-Timeout, and QueryTimeout properties, which make building stand-alone connections easier.

- Use the LastQueryResults property to return the last rdoResultset created against the rdoConnection object. When we get to Chapter 22 on the UserConnection designer, you'll see that this is an invaluable property.

- Use the AsyncCheckInterval property to determine how often RDO polls the interface to see whether your asynchronous operation has completed. In this case, less might be more—less polling might make the interface less "distracted."

- Use the RowsAffected property to determine how many rows were affected by the last Execute action query operation. There is also a RowsAffected property on the rdoPreparedStatement and rdoQuery objects that is unaffected by Execute method operations.

- Use the QueryTimeout property to specify how long the ODBC Driver Manager should wait before abandoning a query. This property defaults to 0, which indicates that the driver doesn't time out. This isn't a good choice, because you will want to regain control over the application if the query hangs for some reason. Set this value to the time you expect your query to take times two.

- Use the ODBC API with the hDbc property to determine or set ODBC API connection options—carefully. Note that this functionality is not carried forward into ADO, so any code that depends on it cannot be converted—at least not easily.

- Use the Name property setting of an rdoConnection object to refer to that object. The Name property setting specifies the DSNAME (DSN) parameter used to open the connection. You can refer to the rdoConnection object by using the rdoConnections("name") syntax. You can also refer to the object by its ordinal number, using the rdoConnections(0) syntax, which refers to the first member of the rdoConnections collection (and is faster).

CAUTION
The ODBC hDbc, hEnv, and hStmt handles are like the unlabeled switches on your computer's motherboard. If you know how to set and use them, you can do some neat things. If you don't, you can kiss your system good-bye.

RDO 2.0 introduced an important change in the handling of object instantiation. In RDO 1.0, if you executed the OpenConnection method against a variable that already contained an open rdoConnection object, the existing object was left open and another object was created and added to the rdoConnections collection. Unless you specifically closed the connection, it remained open—even if you assigned another connection to the variable. But in RDO 2.0, if you use the OpenConnection method against a variable that contains an existing rdoConnection, the current rdoConnection object is dropped and removed from the rdoConnections collection; the new rdoConnection object is added to the rdoConnections collection. When we examine the rdoResultset object in Chapter 24, you'll discover that it now works in the same way. Basically, this change means that if you depended on the persistence of these rdoConnection objects after using the same variable to create new rdoConnection objects, you must now use a different variable when executing the OpenConnection method.

21

Getting
Connected
with RDO

**Locating and
Naming the SQL Server**

Establishing a Connection

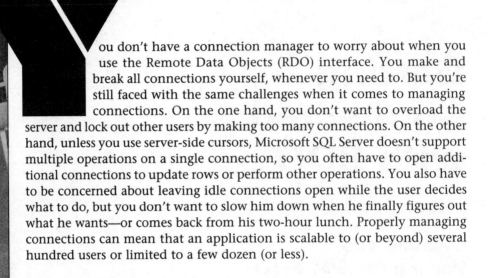

You don't have a connection manager to worry about when you use the Remote Data Objects (RDO) interface. You make and break all connections yourself, whenever you need to. But you're still faced with the same challenges when it comes to managing connections. On the one hand, you don't want to overload the server and lock out other users by making too many connections. On the other hand, unless you use server-side cursors, Microsoft SQL Server doesn't support multiple operations on a single connection, so you often have to open additional connections to update rows or perform other operations. You also have to be concerned about leaving idle connections open while the user decides what to do, but you don't want to slow him down when he finally figures out what he wants—or comes back from his two-hour lunch. Properly managing connections can mean that an application is scalable to (or beyond) several hundred users or limited to a few dozen (or less).

Locating and Naming the SQL Server

Like other ODBC-based interfaces, RDO connects to your SQL server using the information kept in the ODBC data source name (DSN) or a file-based DSN or using the information you provide in the connect string. Personally, I'm not always in favor of establishing a permanent DSN, since it can be a source of trouble when your application is installed and run in the field. To work around this problem, you can take one of several approaches:

- **Use the ODBC registry functions to determine whether a suitable DSN already exists** This technique is really a lot of trouble, as far as I'm concerned, so I rarely use it. You can use the ODBC API SQL-DataSources method to list registered DSN entries.

- **Use the rdoRegisterDataSource function to create a new DSN entry** This technique is also troublesome, but it's not as bad as using the ODBC registry functions.

- **Use an already established DSN**   Most people who use this approach install the DSN themselves or have the user install it when the application is installed. This approach can be risky, though, and it can lead users to phone you in the middle of the night.

- **Launch the ODBC Control Panel applet directly from your application, and tell the user how to set up a DSN**   Yeah, right. Unless your users are a bit more comfortable than mine are with this sort of thing, this isn't a viable option. Letting some users take this route is like turning a four-year-old loose with a 17-blade Swiss Army knife.

- **Create a file-based DSN**   This relatively new approach is virtually identical to the DSN-less connection technique explained below, except that it requires a file to store the connection information instead of requiring that you provide the information in the connect string itself. When you point to this DSN at run time, ODBC fills in the blanks just as it would with a DSN-less connection. To use the DSN, you can use the ODBC connection management dialog boxes (launched by the ODBCControl Panel applet). The file-based DSN should work fine until the connection file is lost, or not installed with the application. File-based DSNs can also lead to security problems because it is fairly easy to view or tinker with the file's ASCII contents. This is the technique of choice when you work with middle-tier components in which registered DSNs are not always available. Note that only "system" DSNs are suitable for use with some Microsoft Active Server Pages–based connections.

- **Don't use a DSN entry at all, but include all the driver information in the Connect argument of the OpenConnection method**   This approach is far less risky. All it assumes is that the name of the SQL server doesn't change, since you've hard-coded it into the application. The drawback to this technique is that it requires you to take all of the default DSN settings (we'll look at these a little later), but it's the fastest way because it doesn't require a Registry hit. It also assumes that the name of the server is cast in stone. Since I'm still connecting to servers that were set up eight years ago, this might not be a problem.

- **Put the name of the SQL server in a Registry entry (my preference) or in an INI file, and fetch the name when the application is run the first time or when the SQL server can't be located**   When an OpenConnection method fails, the message returned often says that the SQL server couldn't be found—which can mean any of a dozen things. Generally, the name of the server doesn't change after installation, but if the same application is used to access more than one SQL server, permitting the user to select from a list of valid servers is an alternative.

- **Create a UserConnection object to manage the connection**
  Actually, since the UserConnection designer was introduced in Microsoft Visual Basic 5.0, getting connected to SQL Server couldn't be made much easier. We devote a chapter to the UserConnection designer a little later, but in essence, this designer captures all of the connection parameters at design-time and automatically builds the correct Connect string for you at runtime. It supports all types of connections discussed so far including DSN-less connections.

Establishing a Connection

Once you know which SQL server to connect to, you have a couple of options for establishing the actual connection. In RDO 1.0, you can use the OpenConnection method to create an rdoConnection object, which establishes a physical link to the data source. While you can still use this technique in RDO 2.0, you can also declare a stand-alone rdoConnection object and use the EstablishConnection method to hook it to a selected SQL server. This is what the UserConnection designer does for you—except without you having to build the Connect string in code. Let's look at these two techniques a little more closely.

To establish a connection, you must somehow identify the network location of the data source, as well as the driver type. Your code also provides a number of parameters for logging the user on to the database. By choosing an appropriate *Prompt* argument, you can program the ODBC Driver Manager to prompt the user for missing arguments and thereby prevent the use of alternate arguments. However, as I've said repeatedly in my lectures, I feel extremely uncomfortable exposing these dialog boxes. On occasion, the previous login ID is shown, and the next user only has to supply the password. For some unusual applications, this might be just fine. For others, even login names are secure. For these reasons, I *always* set the *rdDriverNoPrompt* option to prevent any dialog boxes from appearing. I then must add code to trap the situations in which the user doesn't get logged on. No, this option isn't available in DAO, but it is supported in ADO—well, sort of. ADO's support of ODBC's prompt behavior is generally lacking—especially when you use the Data Environment designer—but we'll talk about that in Chapter 37.

The OpenConnection method accepts the following arguments. They can be supplied by name, supplied with Visual Basic named argument syntax, or supplied positionally.

- **The dsName argument** This argument indicates the name of the registered data source. It points to a valid, registered DSN entry (which can include the new file-based DSN). If you supply all the DSN-related parameters in the connect string, you *must* pass an empty string as the *dsName* argument. If you supply the *dsName* argument value, you can use it to identify the connection. Since you might connect to the same

DSN more than once, however, or simply pass an empty string, you can't really depend on the name to index the rdoConnections collection. You can always use the rdoConnection object's ordinal position in the rdoConnections collection to choose an open rdoConnection object.

- **The Prompt argument** This argument indicates whether the user is permitted to supply arguments to ODBC connection dialog boxes. If you don't want the user to supply a different DSN, user name, password, or default database, use the rdDriverNoPrompt constant as the Prompt argument. But if the Connect and dsName arguments don't lead to a connection (which you have to deal with in code), a trappable error results and the user doesn't see any ODBC-generated dialog boxes to assist with the connection. This feature is unique to RDO, ADO, and ODBCDirect because the DAO/Jet interface is stuck with *Prompt if required*, which displays the dialog boxes whenever there's a problem with the login information or with establishing the connection.

- **The ReadOnly argument** This is set to False if the user expects to update data through the connection. Setting it to True can improve performance because the ODBC drivers can skip code needed to support updatability.

- **The Connect argument** This argument gives the ODBC Driver Manager either the entire set of ODBC connection parameters or just the parameters that are not already supplied by the DSN entry. These parameters can include username, password, default database, DSN (which overrides the value provided in the *dsName* argument), and others. The list of arguments has been expanded for ODBC 3.*x*. These arguments are described in Table 21-1.

NOTE The arguments supported in Table 21-1 are (only) those supported by the SQL Server ODBC driver. Each ODBC driver supports its own set of arguments. You can find documentation for these arguments in the Help files included with the driver. Over the years, this list has grown and older terms have gradually been replaced, but for the most part, are still supported.

The ODBC Driver Manager uses these Connect string arguments to establish the connection. If you don't provide enough of these arguments, ODBC can't figure out how to connect and it might expose dialog boxes to capture these missing parameters. The ODBC prompt behavior determines whether or not these dialog boxes are shown. In some instances, you might get away with just providing the DSN itself because it can encapsulate enough information to get connected. If you leave out the DSN, you must provide a lot more of the arguments.

Table 21-1
Valid Connect Arguments

Argument	Description
DSN	The name of the data source, as returned by the ODBC API SQLDataSources call. If *DRIVER* is used, the *DSN* keyword isn't used but must be passed as "". When you create a data source, this is the name you provide (not the description). It can be the path and filename of a file-based DSN.
DRIVER	The name of the driver, as returned by the ODBC API SQLDrivers call. The *DRIVER* keyword isn't needed if *DSN* is used. The SQL Server driver name is *{SQL Server}*. Note the use of curly braces—needed to deal with a multiword driver name.
SERVER	The name of the Microsoft Windows NT server or Windows 95/98 system on the network on which the data source resides. "*(local)*" can be entered as the server, in which case the SQL Server running on the client system is used, even when the server isn't a networked version. Note that when the 16-bit SQL Server driver uses "*(local)*" without benefit of a network, the Microsoft Loopback Adapter must be installed.
UID	The user's login ID or an empty string to activate domain-managed security: *UID=;*. In any case, this or the workstation login name must exist on the SQL server as a valid login ID.
PWD	The user-specified password, or an empty string to activate domain-managed security: *PWD=;*.
Trusted_Connection	New in ODBC 3.0. You have to set this argument to *=Yes* if you expect ODBC to use domain-managed security—such as when you don't provide a UID and PWD.
FILEDSN	New in ODBC 3.0. The name of a DSN file from which a connection string will be built for the data source. These data sources are called file data sources. (See the following text for more details.)
SAVEFILE	New in ODBC 3.0. The name of a DSN file in which the attribute values of keywords used in making the current, successful connection should be saved. (See the following text for more information.)
StatsLog_On	New in ODBC 3.0. You must set this argument to *=Yes* if you want ODBC to log statistics for your connection.

Argument	Description
StatsLog_On	New in ODBC 3.0. You must set this argument to =*Yes* if you want ODBC to log statistics for your connection.
QueryLog_On	New in ODBC 3.0. You must set this argument to =*Yes* if you want ODBC to log the query statements for your connection. Both of these log options can really chew up processing time.
Description	The text description of the DSN.
APP	The name of your application.
WSID	The workstation ID. Typically, this is the network name of the computer on which the application resides.
DATABASE	The name of the "default" SQL Server database. This tells ODBC to switch to this database as the default before passing control to the client.
LANGUAGE	The national language to be used by SQL Server.

File Data Sources

If the connection string contains the *FILEDSN* keyword and this keyword is not superseded by either the *DSN* or the *DRIVER* keyword, the ODBC Driver Manager creates a connection string using the information in the DSN file and the Connect string. The keywords specified in a DSN file are used to create a connection string. The *UID* keyword is optional; a DSN file can be created with only the *DRIVER* keyword. The *PWD* keyword is not stored in a DSN file (or in registered DSNs). The default directory for saving and loading a DSN file is a combination of the path specified by CommonFilesDir in the Registry entry HKEY_LOCAL_MACHINE\SOFTWARE\Microsoft\Windows\CurrentVersion and in ODBC\DataSources. For example, if CommonFilesDir is C:\Program Files\Common Files, the default directory is C:\Program Files\Common Files\ODBC\Data Sources.

The ODBC Driver Manager processes the filename and its contents as follows:

1. It checks whether the name of the DSN file is valid. If not, it returns a trappable error (SQLSTATE IM014—Invalid name of file DSN). If the filename is an empty string ("") and rdDriverNoPrompt is not specified, the File-Open dialog box is displayed. If the filename contains a valid path but no filename or an invalid filename and rdDriverNoPrompt is not specified, the File-Open dialog box is displayed with the current directory set to the one specified in the filename. If the filename is an empty string or it contains a valid path but no filename or an invalid filename and rdDriverNoPrompt is specified, a trappable error is fired with SQLSTATE IM014 (Invalid name of file DSN).

2. It reads all of the keywords in the [ODBC] section of the DSN file. If the *DRIVER* keyword is not present, it trips a trappable error with SQLSTATE IM012 (Driver keyword syntax error), except if the DSN file is unshareable and therefore contains only the *DSN* keyword. If the file data source is unshareable, the Driver Manager reads the value of the *DSN* keyword and connects as necessary to the user or system data source pointed to by the unshareable file data source. Steps 3 through 5 are not performed.

3. It constructs a connection string for the driver. The driver connection string is the union of the keywords specified in the DSN file and those specified in your application's connection string. The rules for constructing the driver connection string in which keywords overlap are as follows:

   - If the DRIVER keyword exists in your application's connection string and the drivers specified by the *DRIVER* keywords are not the same in the DSN file and the application connection string, the driver information in the DSN file is ignored and the driver information in the application connection string is used. If, however, the drivers specified by the *DRIVER* keyword are the same in both places, if all keywords overlap, those specified in the application connection string take precedence over those specified in the DSN file.

   - In the new connection string, the FILEDSN keyword is eliminated.

4. It loads the driver by looking in the Registry entry HKEY_LOCAL_MACHINE\SOFTWARE\ODBC\ODBCINST.INI\<Driver Name>\Driver, where <Driver Name> is specified by the DRIVER keyword.

5. It passes the driver the new connect string.

The *FILEDSN* and *DSN* keywords are mutually exclusive: whichever keyword appears first is used, and the one that appears second is ignored. The *FILEDSN* and *DRIVER* keywords, on the other hand, are not mutually exclusive. If any keyword appears in a connection string with *FILEDSN*, the attribute value of the keyword in the connection string is used rather than the attribute value of the same keyword in the DSN file.

The *SAVEFILE* Keyword

If the *SAVEFILE* keyword is used, the attribute values of keywords used in making the current, successful connection are saved as a DSN file with the name of the attribute value of the *SAVEFILE* keyword. The *SAVEFILE* keyword must be used in conjunction with the *DRIVER* keyword, the *FILEDSN* keyword, or both, or a trappable error will result that returns SQLSTATE 01S09 (Invalid keyword). The *SAVEFILE* keyword must appear before the *DRIVER* keyword in the connection string, or the results will be undefined. The ODBC Driver Manager processes the *SaveFile* keyword as follows:

1. It checks whether the name of the DSN file included as the attribute value of the *SAVEFILE* keyword is valid. If not, it trips a trappable error with SQLSTATE IM014 (Invalid name of file DSN). The validity of the filename is determined by standard system naming rules. If the filename is an empty string and the DriverCompletion argument is not rdDriverNoPrompt, the filename is valid. If the filename already exists and you've set rdDriverNoPrompt, the file is overwritten. If DriverCompletion is rdDriverPrompt, rdDriverComplete, or rdDriver-CompleteRequired, a dialog box is displayed prompting the user to specify whether the file should be overwritten. If the user selects No, the File-Save dialog box is displayed.

2. If the ODBC driver returns SQL_SUCCESS and the filename is not an empty string, the Driver Manager writes the connection information returned in the ConnectString argument to the specified file using the format specified in the ConnectString.

3. If the driver opens the connection and the filename is an empty string, the Driver Manager displays the File-Save common dialog box with the hWnd specified. It then writes the connection information returned in OutConnectionString to the file specified in the File-Save common dialog box using the format specified in the ConnectStrings.

4. If the driver fails to open the connection, the Driver Manager returns the SQLSTATE to the application.

All of this might look kind of complicated, but it really isn't. Let's look at the contents of a typical file-based DSN.

```
[ODBC]
DRIVER=SQL Server
UID=billva
Trusted_Connection=Yes
DATABASE=Biblio
WSID=BETAV3
APP=Microsoft® Windows® Operating System
SERVER=betav1
```

You could simply use all of these file-based DSN arguments in a hard-coded connect string like this:

```
MyCS = "DRIVER={SQL Server};UID=billva;Trusted_Connection=Yes;" _
    & "DATABASE=Biblio;WSID=BETAV3;APP=MyApp;SERVER=betav1
```

An important thing to remember about the list of ODBC arguments is what's *missing*. The ODBC DSN maintenance dialog boxes collect several other important values that *can't* be set using these parameters. Among those are the ones you see in Table 21-2. This means that if you want to use DSN-less or file-based connections, you must accept these default settings—or create and register a DSN to get connected.

Table 21-2
DSN-Based Connection Parameters

Parameter	Description
Network Address	Network IP address of the SQL Server database management system (DBMS) from which the driver retrieves data. For SQL Server, you can usually leave this value set to *(Default)*. This is required for TCP/IP setups.
Network Library	Name of the SQL Server Net-Library DLL the SQL Server driver uses to communicate with the network software. If the value of this option is *(Default)*, the SQL Server driver uses the client computer's default Net-Library, which is specified in the Default Network box on the Net-Library tab of the SQL Server Client Configuration Utility. If you create a data source using a Network Library other than *(Default)* and optionally a Network Address, ODBC SQL Server Setup creates a server name entry that you can see on the Advanced tab in the SQL Server Client Configuration Utility. These server name entries can also be used by DB-Library applications.
Convert OEM to ANSI Characters	If the SQL Server client computer and SQL Server are using the same non-ANSI character set, select this option. For example, if SQL Server uses code page 850 and this client computer uses code page 850 for the OEM code page, selecting this option ensures that extended characters stored in the database are properly converted to ANSI for use by Windows-based applications. When this option is deselected and the SQL Server client machine and SQL Server are using different character sets, you must specify a character set translator (as explained in the Translation entry below).
Generate Stored Procedures for Prepared Statements	Stored procedures are created for prepared statements when this option (the default) is selected. The SQL Server driver prepares a statement by placing it in a procedure and compiling that procedure. When this option is deselected, the creation of stored procedures for prepared statements is disabled. In this case, a prepared statement is stored and executed at execution time.
Translation	Description of the current translator. To select a different translator, choose the Select button and select from the list in the Select Translator dialog box.

You can use the code in the following example to establish a connection to a SQL Server database with an existing DSN of MyRemote:

```
Dim Cn As rdoConnection, En As rdoEnvironment, Conn As String
Set En = rdoEnvironments(0)
Conn = "DSN=MyRemote;UID=Rose;PWD=Bud;DATABASE=MyDb;"
Set Cn = En.OpenConnection("", rdDriverPrompt, False, Conn)
```

The *dsName* argument of the OpenConnection method can be passed as an empty string. In this case, the DSN is taken from the *Connect* argument (unless you have included the *Driver* and *Server* arguments in an attempt to make a DSN-less connection). Each of the RDO methods supports named arguments, so you can specify each argument by using the *argument:=* syntax. For example, this OpenConnection method can also be coded as follows:

```
Set Cn = En.OpenConnection(prompt:=rdDriverPrompt, _
    readonly:=False,Connect:=Conn)
```

If you choose domain-managed security, you should use empty arguments for the *UID* and *PWD* parameters of the *Connect* argument and add the *Trusted_Connection=Yes* argument. This type of security passes your Windows NT login ID and password to the data source. If your database administrator has implemented integrated or mixed security, this technique should permit you to log on to the data source—assuming that you have permission to do so. Taking the preceding example once again, note that a domain-managed security *Connect* argument is coded as follows:

```
Conn = "DSN=MyRemote;UID=;PWD=;Trusted_Connection=Yes;" _
    & "DATABASE=MyDb;"
```

CAUTION
In many cases, improper Windows NT permissions or group membership configurations prevent users from connecting. Be sure that your Windows NT system administrator and SQL Server system administrator get these set up correctly. (I know I mess it up more often than not.)

TIP You can use the ODBCPING.EXE program installed with SQL Server to test the installation of the ODBC drivers and the link to a specific SQL server. Just type "odbcping [-S *server* | -D *DSN*] [-U *loginID*] [-P *password*]".

Opening Connections Asynchronously

RDO 2.0 has expanded the support for asynchronous operations to include the OpenConnection and EstablishConnection methods. You can start opening a connection and continue with other work while ODBC and SQL Server set up the connection. It's easy to request an asynchronous connection: all you do is use the *rdAsyncEnable* option as the last argument of the aforementioned methods. When you do, control returns immediately to your application and you can proceed to other tasks. Your connection won't be usable, but you can load forms or perform other operations that don't require use of the connection. To determine when the connection attempt is done, you can poll the rdoConnection object's StillConnecting property or simply wait for the Connect event. Actually, I prefer the latter approach because it doesn't waste cycles polling.

Coding the rdoConnection event handlers

The rdoConnection object exposes several events that help manage both synchronous and asynchronous operations on the connection. These events can be used in lieu of polling the StillConnecting property and to provide a higher degree of control over the connection process. Suppose you want to trap all opening connections on the SQL server so that you can initialize global variables or perform some server-side procedure. It's easy now, because if you declare the rdoConnection object WithEvents, you can code the event handlers to do anything you need to do in the BeforeConnect and Connect event handlers. Remember that simply declaring the rdoConnection object using the WithEvents option isn't enough to create the rdoConnection object event handlers. You still have to use a Set command to get the instance of the rdoConnection object built—with the prototype event handlers. These new connection-related events are described in Table 21-3.

Table 21-3
rdoConnection Connection-Related Event Handlers

Event	When It Fires
BeforeConnect	Before RDO calls the ODBC API SQLDriverConnect so that you can do your own prompting
Connect	After a connection operation completes—successfully or not
Disconnect	After a connection has been closed

The Connect event handler is passed a Boolean value (*ErrorOccurred*) that indicates whether the attempt to establish the connection succeeded. You can expect the Connect event to fire whether the connection was successfully established, failed to connect, or simply timed out. Whenever an error occurs, the rdoErrors collection is filled in with the details of what went wrong. Remember that the rdoEngine object's InfoMessage event also fires if an informational message is generated by the connection operation. This is fairly common because SQL Server sends back several messages informing the client of the assigned default database and the language chosen.

Working with Stand-Alone rdoConnection Objects

As I mentioned earlier, another connection method is available with RDO 2.0—stand-alone rdoConnection objects. This is where the new EstablishConnection method comes in. This method takes a couple of arguments that are identical to those passed to OpenConnection. But consider that EstablishConnection works against a dormant or stand-alone rdoConnection object—one that has never been opened, or one that was opened, dissociated (disconnected), and is ready to be reopened.

This method also works against the new UserConnection object in much the same way. I talk about this in Chapter 22. Once the connection operation is complete, control returns to your application. But has the connection been made or not? Well, if you trapped the error you'll know, but if you coded the Connect event handler, you can simply examine the ErrorOccurred Boolean argument passed back from RDO.

I put together a little sample to illustrate the use of stand-alone rdoConnection objects and coding event handlers:

```
Public WithEvents Eng As rdoEngine
Public WithEvents Cn As rdoConnection

Private Sub Form_Load()
Set Eng = New rdoEngine
Set Cn = New rdoConnection
' This sets up the event handlers
With Cn
    .Connect = "Uid=;pwd=;database=pubs;dsn=pubs;" _
        & "trusted_connection=yes"
    .LoginTimeout = 5
    .EstablishConnection rdDriverNoPrompt, True, rdAsyncEnable
End With
End Sub
```

The Form_Load procedure sets up the rdoEngine and rdoConnection objects. Notice that the rdoConnection object is "stand-alone," so we can address it to assign initial properties. Next come the rdoConnection event procedures. We use the asynchronous option here so that code passes quickly out of the Form_Load event. That gets the form loaded quickly but also gives us a chance to show off our event handler. The next stop is the BeforeConnect event:

```
Private Sub Cn_BeforeConnect(ConnectString As String, _
    Prompt As Variant)
MsgBox "About to open a connection using " & vbCrLf _
    & ConnectString, vbOKOnly, "Before Connect Event"
End Sub
```

This procedure is fired *before* the connection is established. At this point, you can't cancel the connection operation without ending the whole program—you have no "cancel" option. You can change the connect string and *Prompt* arguments, though, and this might prevent the application from connecting to somewhere that it shouldn't.

```
Private Sub Cn_Connect(ByVal ErrorOccurred As Boolean)
Dim M As String
If ErrorOccurred Then
    For Each er In rdoErrors
        M = M & er & vbCrLf
    Next
    MsgBox "Connection failed. " & vbCrLf & M
```

(continued)

```
Else
    MsgBox "Connection open..."
    Cn.Execute "use pubs"    ' To test the connection
End If
End Sub
```

This is the post-connect event handler, which is fired after RDO completes its attempt to connect. If the connection is established, ErrorOccurred is set to False. But if something went wrong, ErrorOccurred is set to True and you have to check the rdoErrors collection to see what went wrong:

```
Private Sub Eng_InfoMessage()
For Each er In rdoErrors
    Debug.Print er
Next
rdoErrors.Clear
End Sub
```

The last event handler is for the rdoEngine object's InfoMessage event. As I said earlier, this event is fired when informational messages are returned from SQL Server via ODBC. We generally throw these out as they occur because they're of little consequence. But if you have queries or stored procedures that use the TSQL PRINT statement, these messages cause this event to fire. Yes, all of these messages are appended to the rdoErrors collection whether or not you set up an event handler to fire as they arrive. Notice that the rdoErrors collection has a Clear method, which is ideal for discarding this type of message.

NOTE If you're still using Visual Basic 5.0, the code examples that shipped with that version were written in the summer of 1996, long before the code was finalized. Because of a number of important innovations added to RDO event handling, these examples no longer compile. I've included corrected examples on this book's companion CD and here in these pages. The code sample shown above is saved as Connect Event on the CD.

RDO 2.0 Collection Management

In RDO 1.0, when you execute the following code, you end up with two separate rdoConnection objects in the rdoConnections collection:

```
Dim cn as rdoConnection
Dim en as rdoEnvironment
Set en = rdoEngine.rdoEnvironments(0)
Set cn = en.OpenConnection("MyDSN",rdDriverNoPrompt, _
    False, "UID=;PWD=;Database=Pubs;trusted_connection=yes")
Set cn = en.OpenConnection("MyDSN",rdDriverNoPrompt, _
    False, "UID=;PWD=;Database=Biblio;trusted_connection=yes")
```

One of these connections is established and points to the *Pubs* database, while the other is established to the *Biblio* database. The *cn* variable addresses the second rdoConnection object.

RDO 2.0 changes the way that collections are managed. If you execute the example shown on the previous page in RDO 2.0, you end up with only *one* rdoConnection object in the rdoConnections collection—but the variable *cn* still points to the second rdoConnection. While this new technique for handling rdoConnections (and rdoResultsets) is different, it should result in fewer memory leaks. If you don't want to lose an existing rdoConnection as assigned to a variable, you must use the OpenConnection method against a separate variable.

CAUTION
RDO connections are never closed unless you explicitly close them—even, as in some cases, when the variable used to hold the rdoConnection object goes out of scope. So remember to close the rdoConnection object when you're done with it.

Other Connection Parameters

The length of time in seconds that the ODBC Driver Manager waits for the SQL server to begin responding to a request for a connection is determined by the DBEngine object's rdoDefaultLoginTimeout property or by the rdoEnvironment object's LoginTimeout property. RDO 2.0 also includes a LoginTimeout property on stand-alone rdoConnection objects that you can set before you use the EstablishConnection method. Unless you change it, rdoDefaultLogin-Timeout defaults to 15 seconds—which might not be enough for some long-distance or slow-speed connections or when the SQL server is busy. But since most local network connections begin in under 3 seconds, 15 seconds is a good default. As long as SQL Server *begins* to respond in this length of time, the connection process shouldn't time out.

Connection Problems

You might be unable to establish a connection for a variety of reasons, including lack of permission for the data source, improper network connection or permissions, or a missing or disabled data source. With SQL Server or other data sources, the number of simultaneous connections permitted might be limited by license agreements, resource constraints, or database settings. The same problems involved in attempting to connect to SQL Server via Jet also apply to connection attempts made with the RDO interface. Both interfaces use the same ODBC Driver Manager and SQL Server drivers to establish the connection. Check with your system administrator if you suspect that all available connections are allocated or that your login ID does not have permission to access the server.

22

Using the RDO UserConnection Designer

Understanding Custom UserConnection Objects

Building Custom UserConnection Objects

Executing Queries and Stored Procedures as Methods

Setting UserConnection Properties at Run Time

Using the UserConnection Object's Events

One of the challenges you have to face as a client/server developer is how to leverage the suite of queries built up over the lifetime of your application. Because this code can be deeply buried in an application, it's especially difficult to maintain and keep current. You also have queries, stored procedures, or business objects on the server that must be referenced and maintained. In RDO 1.0, accessing these stored procedures was easier than ever, but the procedures still required that each application include fairly complex ODBC call syntax used with balky rdoPreparedStatement objects—hand-coded for each application. To get it all working, you had to build a correct SQL property, make sure that all of the rdoParameter objects had the right Direction property setting, and hope that the Type property was set correctly because you couldn't change it if ODBC guessed incorrectly. On top of that, your RDO 1.0 application was responsible for providing all of the parameters to establish the connection. This meant building a correct connect string as well as setting another half-dozen parameters so that you could consistently get connected. Now that event-driven programming has arrived, connecting is a little easier, but it still involves writing and maintaining event procedures to handle the contingencies. And you must repeat all of this for every application you write. Sure, you can use class modules to help perform these operations, but this too can be a challenge because you have to define your own standards for this approach.

With RDO 2.0, setting up connections, stored procedures, and parameter collections is no longer a problem. The UserConnection designer (UCD) makes it easier to build rdoQueries than it was with RDO 1.0 and also makes the process smarter. For one thing, the UCD isolates all of the logic needed to expose these objects in one design-time graphical interface. You can create a custom UserConnection object once and include it in every application your company creates. It can be managed by a central team, and you can incorporate any changes by recompiling the application. But even recompiling shouldn't be required if the query code is kept on the server in stored procedures. Using the UCD also dramatically reduces the number of lines of code you have to write, test, debug, and maintain. Although the UCD isn't perfect, it goes a long way toward simplifying team development of applications.

NOTE No, the UCD doesn't support ADO—it is an RDO-only interface. And no, it wasn't substantially "improved" for Visual Basic 6.0. And no, the UCD isn't "replaced" by the Data Environment designer.

WARNING!
Don't expect Visual Basic 5.0's RDO's UCD to work after you install Visual Basic 6.0. Apparently, Setup overlays the Visual Basic 5.0 version of the RDO typelib when installing the Visual Basic 6.0 version. Although this might be fixed in a future service pack, it means that you won't get dual functionality (both Visual Basic 5.0 and Visual Basic 6.0 on the same machine) until they fix it. If you simply want to use the Visual Basic 6.0 UCD in Visual Basic 5.0, overlay the MSCONDES.DLL in \Program Files\Common Files\Designer and MSCDRUN.DLL in \Windows\System with the Visual Basic 6.0 versions. You'll also need to register these with REGSVR32. If you don't know what that means, don't attempt the patch.

Microsoft Visual Basic 6.0 adds another tool to make your development tasks easier—the Data Environment designer. Based on the success of the UCD, the Data Environment designer is designed to eventually replace the need for the UCD. Because of the new emphasis on ADO, this new tool generates code designed to connect to OLE DB data providers. So far, it's more flexible than the UCD, which can only use RDO to connect to ODBC data sources. We'll discuss the Data Environment designer in detail in Chapter 37.

Understanding Custom UserConnection Objects

Before we start building our own sample UserConnection object using the UCD, let's take a brief look at what's going on under the hood. The user interface of the UCD accepts a number of parameters through its dialog boxes. These feed a little run-time dynamic-link library (DLL) that performs the following chores:

- Creates an rdoConnection object and exposes all of its events as a UserConnection object

- Creates a set of rdoQuery objects—one for each query or stored procedure that you specify—and exposes them as methods of the UserConnection object

- Exposes the rdoQuery object's rdoParameters collection members as arguments of each method

All of these objects are hidden from view, but you can access them freely by referencing them off of the exposed UserConnection object. The dialog boxes facilitate the gathering of these parameters, but they don't make any decisions about the suitability of the options when they are used together. It's just as easy (OK, easier) to make a mistake when you choose these options as it was when you had to write code for them. However, it's also far easier to correct mistakes later—even *much* later, when the developer has been promoted to management (or marketing) to get him or her out of the trenches.

Creating a custom UserConnection object is simple. All you have to do is follow these steps:

1. Install and start the UCD, which is built into Visual Basic, Enterprise Edition. No, it's not in the Professional Edition, like the Data Environment is—which is another reason the UCD might lose some friends.

2. Fill in the GUI form to provide connection information. This points to your server and a specific database.

3. Choose one or more stored procedures or provide SQL to one or more queries. These can be action queries, SELECT statements, or any other TSQL statement.

4. Tune the arguments used to create the connection and the result sets.

5. Provide the syntax for one or more queries. Yes, you can press the Build button to create a query. Please don't. It launches Microsoft Query (even in Visual Basic 6.0), which (IMHO) is a crippled piece of code that should have been dropped long ago. And no, it's not documented here because it's broken in too many ways to discuss. It's really easier to paste in queries built with Microsoft Visual Database Tools or other query generators.

6. Verify or tune the parameters for the queries and stored procedures as required. Notice what's missing. No, you can't specify the size or precision of numeric parameters. Nor can you specify an initial value for the parameters. Later on you'll notice that the Data Environment designer does let you supply these settings.

That's it. To use your new custom UserConnection object, you do the following:

1. Write one line of code to instantiate it.

2. Write a single line of code to establish the connection.

3. Write a single line of code to invoke a chosen query by calling it as a method against the UserConnection object. The query parameters are simply passed as arguments to the method.

4. Write a single line of code to extract the rdoResultset from the LastQueryResults property.

Each query you add to the control is invoked as a method; this applies to arguments and all—input, output, and return values. It couldn't be simpler if I sent one of the Visual Basic developers to your office to do it for you.

TIP When the UCD first builds its list of stored procedures, that's it. It won't find more or even look for more stored procedures until the project is reloaded. Yep, it's a bug, and it wasn't fixed in Visual Basic 6.0. Add your stored procedures first, and then use the UCD to access them. It's also dangerous to change the stored procedures after the UCD has built rdoQuery objects from the metadata. If you change your stored procedures on the server, you'll have to rebuild the UCD procedures as well.

Building Custom UserConnection Objects

In this section, I'll describe step by step how to build a typical UserConnection object. I'll use the sample Microsoft SQL Server *Biblio* database for this example, so you might want to check out Appendix A for instructions on how to install it. You can also run the example against your own database if installing *Biblio* seems like too much trouble or if you don't have the space to devote to another test database.

1. Start with a new project. For this example, I chose Standard EXE as the template.

2. Choose Components from the Projects menu. In the Components dialog box, click the Designers tab and select Microsoft UserConnection. Close the tab, and wait a moment while the UCD is installed. You won't have to do this again because from this point on, the designer will be initialized whenever you start Visual Basic.

TIP For whatever reason, some of the add-ins seem to "step on" the UCD add-in code. The menu choices that are used to activate the designer don't seem to work, or they simply disappear. To repair the damage, go to the Visual Basic Add-Ins menu and deactivate all of the add-ins. After restarting Visual Basic, return to the Projects Components Designers tab and reactivate the UCD.

---

3. From the Projects menu, click Add Microsoft UserConnection. At this point, a Designers entry should be added to your project tree and the UserConnection1 designer window should be open. On top of the window, the designer automatically displays a dialog box to help you choose your data source.

4. At this point, you need to either create a new data source name (DSN) or use an existing one. My system has a DSN named BIBLIO that is set up to point to the *Biblio* test database. Later, you can try to set up DSN-less or file-based connections, but for now just use a "user" DSN.

5. While you're still on the Connection tab, be sure to fill in the "Other ODBC Attributes" dialog. If you're using domain-managed security enter "Trusted_Connection=Yes". If your DSN does not include a default database setting, then enter "Database=<your database name>".

6. Click the Authentication tab, and fill in a valid User Name and Password. I don't fill these in because I use domain-managed security—you might have to provide a valid SQL Server login ID and password to connect. Next, set the ODBC Prompt Behavior to *Never* so that we can trap all of the errors instead of letting our users see the ODBC login dialog boxes. During development, I like to check the two boxes to save the connection authentication property settings—you should, too.

7. Click the Miscellaneous tab and select Use Client Batch Cursors. You can play with the Login Timeout and Query Timeout settings later if you want to. Leave them alone for now. They should be long enough for most simple tests.

8. Click OK at the bottom of the dialog box. At this point, you should see the basic UserConnection window (shown in Figure 22-1), which is ready to accept new queries.

Figure 22-1   *The UserConnection window*

9. Click the second toolbar button (Insert Multiple Queries) in the UserConnection1 window. At this point, RDO establishes a connection to SQL Server based on the parameters you provided earlier, executes the ODBC API SQLProcedures function that returns all of the stored procedures in the selected database, and populates the list box as shown in Figure 22-2. If you don't get a list of stored procedures that looks something like the one shown in the figure, either you don't have a valid DSN set up, your login ID doesn't have permission to see the stored procedures, or the database doesn't have any stored procedures in the first place. If any of these conditions are the case, switch over to SQL Enterprise Manager and turn on the correct permissions. If you don't have access to the server to do this, ask your SA to grant the appropriate permissions. You should fix this situation before you go on. You should now see something that looks like Figure 22-2. (Actually, at this point, I've already selected my TitlesByAuthor stored procedure.)

10. Sure, the names of your stored procedures might be different than what is shown in the figure, but the dialog box should be the same. Choose one of these queries to test and click on the right arrow. We will use one of these and write our own query as an example. At this point, the designer queries the database for details about the chosen query. In my case, I chose the TitlesByAuthor example.

11. We're now ready to explore a little further and check out the query parameters so that we know what to expect. Click OK in the Insert Stored Procedures dialog box. Now, I happen to know what this query looks like on the server (because I wrote it).

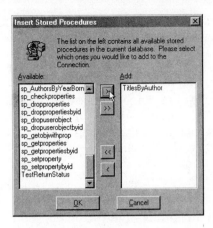

Figure 22-2 *The UCD Insert Stored Procedures dialog box*

```
CREATE PROCEDURE TitlesByAuthor @AuthorWanted VARChar(30)
AS  Select Title, Author
From Titles T, Title_Author TA, Authors A
Where T.ISBN = TA.ISBN and
TA.Au_ID = A.Au_ID and
Author like @AuthorWanted
Return @@ROWCOUNT
```

12. Because the query expects one input argument (the Author's name) and returns a return status (the number of rows found), we should expect to see these parameters exposed by the UCD. The designer now exposes the properties for our TitlesByAuthor query. Figure 22-3 shows the data that appears after clicking the Parameters tab. We can select any of the parameters to garner additional details.

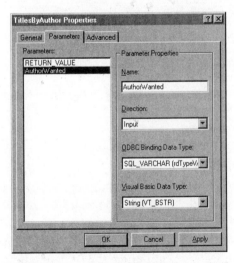

Figure 22-3 *The Parameters tab of the query Properties dialog box*

Notice that both the *RETURN_VALUE* and the *AuthorWanted* parameters are automatically recognized—by name, direction, ODBC binding data type, and Visual Basic data type. You didn't have to do anything (this time). This information was gathered at design time by an extra call (or six) to ODBC and the SQL server. But if the query is a little more complex, you might have to go in and twiddle the data type. For example, if instead of a LIKE expression in the query I used a CHARINDEX expression, the designer might think that the parameter is an integer. That's why you have to double-check to ensure that the right data type is chosen.

13. Next we visit the Advanced tab, as you see in Figure 22-4. This tab lets us set parameters for each query we define. In this case, I know that I don't want to see more than 20 hits from the query, so I set Max Rows to 20. The database is fairly large, but 30 seconds should be plenty of time to get the job done. I don't care about the Bind Threshold because I'm not working with BLOBs in this query. I set the Rowset size to 20 because I know I won't need to scroll around in the keyset. We don't use keyset size (neither does ODBC, for the most part). I also deselected Prepare Query Before Execution because this is a stored procedure and it's already "prepared." This option sets the Prepared property on the rdoQuery object that we're creating.

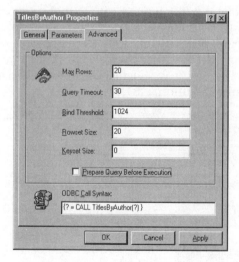

Figure 22-4 *The Advanced tab of the query Properties dialog box*

14. Click OK to close the TitlesByAuthor Properties dialog box. Notice that the query has been added to the designer's window so that we can examine the properties again later if we need to.

We're finished with the UCD for now, so we can close the UCD window. Notice that we now have a UserConnection1 class under the Designers heading in the Project window. You might also discover that the project now includes a reference to RDO 2.0—the designer added this automatically. It builds code

Security Considerations

To alleviate concern about security and password protection, you can choose from two levels of persistence for the UserConnection object's UserID and Password properties. By default, both levels are turned off so that no caching or persistence of these properties occurs and so no one can dump your code and see these sensitive parameters.

If Save Connection Information For New Run-Mode Class is checked, the user name and password properties are stored in the properties of the actual class and are persistent in the built executable or DLL.

If Save Connection Information For Design Time is checked, the user name and password properties persist only during design time and aren't written into the built EXE or DLL file. This might be safer in situations in which you're collecting user ID and password strings from the user.

to handle all of the properties and events associated with the object in RDO. Yes, even the event prototypes are ready to go—all you have to do is supply the code. That's next on the tour.

NOTE When you build a new table or stored procedure, don't forget to grant permissions for them so that the intended user can access or execute them. Although your program might work if you log in as SA, it won't if you log in as a "normal" user. Of course, even the stored procedures that you don't have permission to access are listed by the UserConnection designer—it's like looking through Tiffany's window at the tiaras.

Executing Queries and Stored Procedures as Methods

Now that we've created the UserConnection object, we're ready to take it out for a spin. The first thing we need to do is add some code to instantiate the object from its base class. Using the *New* keyword, we'll create a stand-alone instance of the UserConnection object we just built. We also need an rdoResultset object to hold the result set we're about to fetch, unless we use a control that can take an rdoResultset as an argument. I've included such a control on the companion CD—my own version of the Grid control, which I customized to accept an rdoResultset or an ADO Recordset.

```
Dim ucTest As New UserConnection1
Dim rs As rdoResultset
```

Next we need to open the connection. We can do this anywhere, but in this case it's a one-time operation, so we'll put the code in the Form_Load event procedure:

```
Private Sub Form_Load()
ucTest.EstablishConnection
End Sub
```

NOTE If you *don't* want a forward-only, read-only cursor, now, before the connection is open, is the time to reset rdoQueries(*n*).CursorType to some other type of cursor. In addition, you'll need to set rdoQueries(*n*).LockType to some other type of concurrency—unless you want rdConcurReadOnly. Once the query is executed, it's too late to change it. You can refer to your stored procedures or queries by name if you want to—it's probably safer, but slightly slower.

At this point, the connection is open—if all is going as planned—and we're ready to try executing the query. Because all of the stored procedures we added with the designer are now exposed as methods on the UserConnection object that we created, they're really easy to code. After we declare the return value variable, start typing the *next* line of code, as shown below:

```
Dim lrc As Long
lrc = ucTest.T
```

You should see something like Figure 22-5.

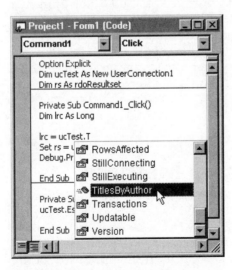

Figure 22-5 *IntelliSense enumerates properties, methods, and events*

The stored procedure we chose is now in the enumerated list of methods. Now choose the TitlesByAuthor method (just press the space bar), type the opening parenthesis, and see what happens next. Visual Basic IntelliSense knows that this method takes a single input argument (a String) and returns an integer (Long). Because of this, Visual Basic can help you write the code for the method by exposing this method, as you can see in Figure 22-6.

```
lrc = ucTest.TitlesByAuthor (|
Set rs = ucTest.LastQueryRes| TitlesByAuthor(AuthorWanted As String) As Long |
```

Figure 22-6 *IntelliSense exposes method arguments*

We'll complete the line by filling in the argument to pass to our TitlesBy-Author query. For this example, I'm simply hard-coding the parameter. You'll probably pass in a parameter via a TextBox or other control.

```
lrc = ucTest.TitlesByAuthor("%Vaughn%")
```

When this line executes, it runs the query and, if the query is available, returns the return status value and result set rows as described in the UserConnection properties. A word of caution: I have seen a number of strange instances where I trip an Invalid Use Of NULL error when using the syntax shown above. Apparently, many of the cursor drivers don't provide the return status value until the query is fully populated—they return NULL until that value is available. Well, you have a number of ways to get around this. Here are two:

- You can code the call without this return value:

```
ucTest.TitlesByAuthor "%Vaughn%"
```

You can fetch it later when the rdoResultset is at EOF. Notice that the syntax reverts back to "subroutine" mode so you can't use parentheses around the argument as required when the "function" returns a value. At this point, the rdoQuery object under the UserConnection object contains the return status value:

```
lrc = ucTest.rdoQueries(0).rdoParameters(0)
```

- You can also capture the return value as shown below but declare the variable to capture the value as a Variant. In this case, you must test for NULL in case the stored procedure doesn't return the status value until later.

```
Dim vRetVal As Variant
vRetVal = ucTest.TitlesByAuthor("%Vaughn%")
```

Referencing the New rdoResultset

To access the result set, you *must* address the rdoResultset object that was just created, which is passed in the LastQueryResults property as shown—

Stop right there. Don't move a muscle. There's something nasty in that bush over to your right. If you know it's there and know what to do, you'll be fine—just don't make any sudden movements. I was recently mauled by this creature and spent about 10 hours trying to figure out why. After the developers and I had a weeklong e-mail conversation, we concluded that this "feature" is a necessary evil with some very unusual characteristics. This beast calls itself

LastQueryResults. At first, the LastQueryResults property might *look* like an rdoResultset—but it's not. It's unusually shy: if you touch it or even look at it, it disappears. Sure, you get to look at it once—but once you reference the LastQueryResults property, no matter how you do it, it's gone.

Let's look at the implications of this paradox. Assume that you've created and executed a UserConnection object (*ucTest*) and you're ready to fetch the results of the query. That's where we were in our walk-through anyway. Before you simply set a variable declared as rdoResultset to LastQueryResults, consider this: if you have a valid rdoResultset addressed by the variable (*rs* in our example), you might not have addressability after the assignment—if the LastQueryResults returns NULL. So it's a good idea to first assign LastQuery-Results to a temporary variable. Then you can test the temporary variable and be assured of using the result set if it's available. No, you *can't* combine this into a single step like this:

```
If ucTest.LastQueryResults is Nothing Then
Else
Set rs = ucTest.LastQueryResults
```

If you try, the phantom LastQueryResults object will be gone by the time you try to assign it to *rs*. You *can* do this:

```
Set tRs = ucTest.LastQueryResults
If tRs is Nothing Then Else Set rs = tRs
```

Once the rdoResultset addressed by LastQueryResults is captured into another variable, it's safe. At that point, Visual Basic and RDO add it to the list of "referenced" objects and it starts to behave like other RDO objects. Here are a few other tips that you need to keep in mind when you're working with this property:

- Don't set a watchpoint to LastQueryResults. If you do, the watchpoint will work the first time but the underlying result set will be lost from that point on.

- Don't use a Debug reference or any other break-mode references— except to capture the rdoResultset into another variable.

- Don't use the Locals window to examine the LastQueryResults property. It isn't clear that simply having the Locals window open will touch the property and destroy it without you having to do this yourself.

- Don't let the cursor accidentally stray over the LastQueryResults property when you are in Break mode at run time. If you do, Visual Basic fetches the contents of the property and destroys it in the process.

- Don't expect to be able to use any of the LastQueryResults methods or properties more than once. Yes, LastQueryResults exposes all of the underlying rdoResultset properties and methods—but again, once they are touched, the object is history and returns Nothing.

Once you assign the LastQueryResults property to a variable declared as rdoResultset or pass it on to another control, you can treat it just like any other rdoResultset object, just as if you had created it with an OpenResultset. All of the same rules and techniques apply. The result set might not be fully populated, so you should do a MoveLast on it as soon as possible—but remember that RDO and the Client Batch cursor library might do this for you in the background. You can't use the MoveLast method or the UserConnection again without first dealing with the result set you just created. This means that you have to use the Close method on the rdoResultset. You can't use the Close method on the LastQueryResults property—it's gone. To see what ReturnStatus was sent back, we can examine the variable we used when executing the method (*lrc*). Notice that the RowCount property returns a –1 because it is not (yet) available:

```
Debug.Print rs.RowCount, lrc
```

> **NOTE** In some cases, the return status isn't available when the cursor is first opened and isn't available until you fetch the last row. It works this way in VBSQL and in the ODBC API as well, so you might already understand this limitation. In these cases, you have to wait until after the result set is populated to be able to access the value. If you try to fetch it too early, you get an Invalid Use Of NULL error as RDO attempts to pass the NULL return status to your Long variable. You can simply declare the Long variable as a variant to accommodate this reality, if you have a mind to, but you still need to check for NULL.

Wait a minute! Something's missing here. When I create a result set, I like to choose the *type* of cursor. For some situations, I use cursorless result sets, but at other times I need a keyset, static, forward-only cursor. Or if I've gone completely bonkers, I use a dynamic cursor. (Actually, that's a lie. I've never been crazy enough to use a dynamic cursor.) You can set the type of cursor that the UserConnection method will create by changing the CursorType property of the rdoQuery that the UserConnection object creates for the chosen stored procedure. RDO and Visual Basic will help you choose one because Visual Basic enumerates your choices when you address this property, as you can see in Figure 22-7.

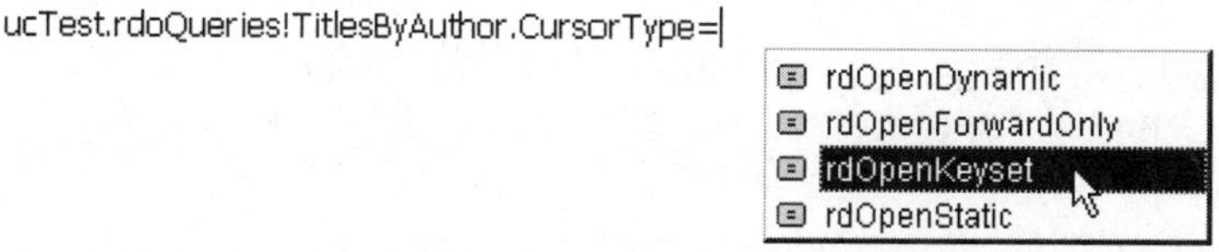

```
ucTest.rdoQueries!TitlesByAuthor.CursorType=|
```

```
    rdOpenDynamic
    rdOpenForwardOnly
    rdOpenKeyset
    rdOpenStatic
```

Figure 22-7 *DataTips expose enumerated* CursorType *constants*

> **NOTE** I discovered a bug when using this feature. It seems that each time this feature is invoked, the enumerated list box appeared a little more to the right. Apparently, by choosing a proportional font in the Visual Basic Options, I confused the code that positions the dialog boxes. This bug wasn't fixed in Visual Basic 5.0, but it has been corrected in version 6.0.

This isn't as easy as clicking a tab and selecting a cursor type from the UserConnection designer dialog boxes, but it isn't that hard to do in code. Notice that I addressed the rdoQuery object using the bang (!) syntax. I don't want to reference this member by its ordinal number because the code will break if I add another stored procedure or query ahead of it.

> **NOTE** I've provided a couple of examples for the UserConnection designer on the companion CD in the Chap22 directory.

Building Your Own Queries

OK, I lied. Since the Microsoft Query interface never really worked right, I never used it to create queries—I always used Visual Database Tools. This problem has been eliminated in Visual Basic 6.0; Visual Basic 6.0 depends on the Visual Database Tools for all query generation.

Generally, I recommend that any queries your two-tiered application executes should be in the form of stored procedures. When this isn't possible, you can take advantage of the UCD's ability to manage queries that *you* provide in the form of TSQL queries. Because Microsoft Query is cross-connected to the UCD, you can use it to build your custom queries interactively through a graphical interface—that is if you have lost your senses. I would highly recommend using Microsoft Visual Database Tools right in Visual Basic to build your queries.

> **NOTE** You'll learn how to create and execute RDO parameter queries in Chapter 25.

Getting to the Microsoft Query window is fairly straightforward. Let's go through the steps so that you're ready to use this interface when it comes time to build a complex query. (Incidentally, after you develop and test your query, it's a good idea to move it over to SQL Server as a stored procedure.) We'll create a variation on our previous query that uses the *Publishers* table. Because we already have a UserConnection object, we can go right to the UserConnection designer's main form.

1. Click the first toolbar button (Insert Query) to build a new query. Again, a connection to SQL Server is established to populate the list of stored procedures—which we won't be using this time.

2. Type the name of the new query. Call it *TitlesPubsByAuthor*. This is a Visual Basic method name, so it can't have embedded spaces. You should then see something like Figure 22-8.

3. Wait! Don't just click the Build button. This launches Microsoft Query, but we aren't ready to do that just yet. For some reason, Microsoft Query expects something to be entered into the Text box at the bottom of the dialog box. If you don't enter anything, it returns an Unable To Start error. Select Based on User-Defined SQL. For now, just enter *Select * From Authors* so we can get into Microsoft Query.

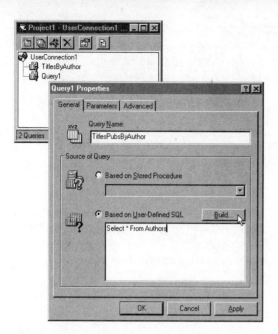

Figure 22-8 *Defining your own SQL for a user-defined UserConnection object*

4. Now click the Build button. The designer launches Microsoft Query and also executes the query right away, so we've just locked up the entire *Authors* table. Not good. We must either get out of this immediately or populate the result set to free locks on the table. By default, there's no upper limit on the number of rows that Microsoft Query pulls down, but you can set a limit by going into Microsoft Query's Options dialog box (on the Edit menu) and setting the number of rows to 10 or so. Do this now so that we don't have to worry about this again. What Microsoft Query lacks in features it makes up for in lack of client/server awareness—but I digress. Let's move on.

5. Use the interactive dialog boxes to add the *Titles*, *Publishers*, and *Title_Author* tables to the *Authors* table. (You can use the Add Tables command on the Tables menu or click the Add Table toolbar button.) Unfortunately, as you add the tables, Microsoft Query merrily tries to join them all—whether or not they're related. This gets silly after a while as Microsoft Query constantly complains that all of the rows can't be shown. It's probably better if you add the tables in order. First add *Title_Author* because it has a link to the *Authors* table. Next add *Titles* and then *Publishers* so that Microsoft Query can attempt to figure out the relationships more easily. Once you finish adding tables, your screen should look like that shown in Figure 22-9. (I rearranged the table dialog boxes so that you can see their relationship lines.)

6. We're now ready to select the columns to appear in our query, but first go to the Records menu and deselect the Automatic Query option. This prevents Microsoft Query from attempting to execute the

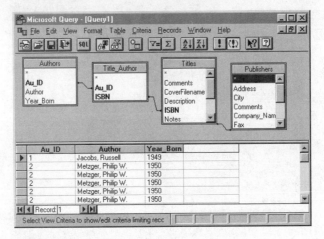

Figure 22-9 *Selecting the tables in Microsoft Query*

query as we build it. It almost seems as if the people developing this application weren't aware that these tables could be used in production and that doing random queries isn't such a good idea.

7. Delete the existing Au_ID Year_Born columns at the bottom of the query window. Using the drag-and-drop techniques you learned when using Microsoft Access, drag the ISBN, Title, and Company_Name columns to the columns area at the bottom of the query window—where you now see the Author column. At this point, your screen should look something like Figure 22-10.

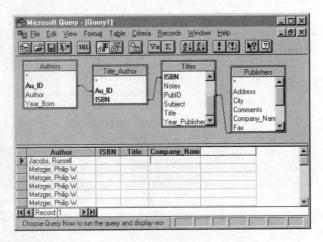

Figure 22-10 *Choosing the columns in Microsoft Query*

8. You could add sort criteria, change the way the joins work, or preview the SQL, but for now let's keep it simple and exit back to Visual Basic and the UserConnection designer. Before you leave you can test the query by clicking the ! button. I did, and the query ran, but it returned another Can't Show All Records error for some reason. Let's just click the little door icon (Return Data) and get back to Visual Basic.

9. When we return to Visual Basic, we see that Microsoft Query has passed back the SQL needed to execute our query. (See Figure 22-11.) There's no vertical scroll bar, so you just have to walk the cursor down with the arrow keys to see the bottom of the query.

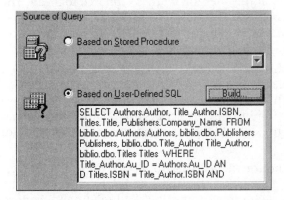

Figure 22-11 *A user-defined SQL query built by Microsoft Query*

10. Microsoft Query doesn't seem to have a way to add parameters to our user-written queries, but we can add them fairly easily by editing the SQL that Microsoft Query generated. As with RDO 1.0, we can insert a question mark (*?*) where we want RDO and ODBC to insert and manage a query parameter for us. These parameters can be only input type; return value, output, or input/output parameters aren't supported.

Let's try to add a parameter and see what happens. Edit the SQL shown in Figure 22-11, adding *AND Author LIKE ?* to the end. Click the Parameters tab when you finish editing the SQL. You should now see something like Figure 22-12.

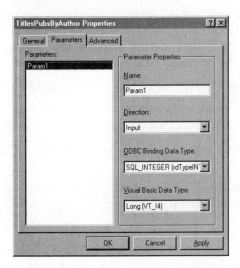

Figure 22-12 *Tuning query parameters using the UserConnection designer*

Now follow these steps to tell RDO and ODBC how to manage the added query parameter:

11. Notice that this Parameters dialog box isn't filled in nearly as intelligently as the one we saw earlier. That's because the designer and RDO have no way to tell what the question mark is supposed to mean. The designer simply guessed that the question mark was meant to represent an integer. However, in our case, we'll be providing a string, so we have to go in and change the settings.

12. Change the Name to *AuthorWanted*. This value will show up when we code the method. Change the ODBC Binding Data Type to *SQL_VARCHAR*. Change the Visual Basic Data Type to *String*. We don't have to change the Direction; it's already set at Input. Once these values are set, we can save the query. It won't be saved until we click OK or Apply. Click OK.

13. Click the View Code button in the UCD. Notice that the event handlers are already filled in. Remember that these handlers apply to all the queries that you define on this connection. You might also want to visit the Advanced tab to set some of the other properties. I didn't bother this time because we won't test this new query.

You know that SELECT queries aren't the only kind of queries in use today—far from it. Although fetching rows is important, many of our client/ server front-end operations use action queries, too. I don't think that the interactive query development strategy used in Microsoft Query is much good for this type of work. However, nothing will stop you from creating your own action queries and adding them to your user connection. Visual Database Tools or Visual InterDev might also be helpful here.

Tips on Using Your Own SQL and Parameters

You can include your own queries instead of pointing to a stored procedure. You can even code queries that contain parameters. I often take this back-road approach when I'm developing a new application—before I commit the query to a stored procedure. You need to watch out for a few chuckholes, however:

- To create a parameter query, simply insert a ? where the parameters go. For example, you can do this:

```
Select * From Authors Where Name Like ?
```

- The UCD detects this parameter marker and lets you choose a data type and direction for it.

- If you write your own procedure, you can mark the parameters only as Input. Return value, input/output, and output parameters are accessible only on stored procedure queries.

- If you access a procedure that includes an OUTPUT parameter, be sure to mark it as such. ODBC marks all of these as "input/output."

- Be sure to recheck these settings if you tune the SQL query because the UCD overrides your changes whenever the SQL is altered.

- To insert a carriage return into your query, press Ctrl-Return. Remember to include space between operators—especially on new lines. Actually, SQL Server doesn't care what your queries "look" like as long as the syntax is correct.

- Make sure you know what you're asking for when you make a parameter a CHAR as opposed to a VARCHAR. Remember that CHAR expressions are of fixed length and VARCHAR is of variable length. This means if the length of the parameter you are passing changes, you should use a VARCHAR.

Setting UserConnection Properties at Run Time

OK, sometimes the values set at design time aren't right. It's easy to code alternative arguments for the EstablishConnection method because these are exposed on the method call, but you might have to change the query's RowsetSize, CursorType, or other properties manually before the resultset is built. This is also fairly easy if you consider that the UserConnection object is simply fronting ordinary rdoConnection and rdoQuery objects. Although you can't make changes to the already-connected rdoConnection object, you can still pull out the rdoConnection object and at least examine its properties. However, you won't need to do this because all of the rdoConnection properties, methods, and events are exposed on the UserConnection object. For example, the UserConnection object's Connect property exposes the connect string—just like on the rdoConnection object. You can make changes to both the underlying rdoConnection and rdoQuery object properties before they are opened—using the same rules we discussed earlier. However, when you need to get at the rdoQuery object's properties at run time, you have to write some code to get or set the properties, as explained here:

- To change a property of one of the underlying rdoQuery objects, you have to code something like this:

  ```
  Uc.rdoQueries!MyQuery.SQL = "SELECT..."
  ```

- To manipulate the cursor type, reference this:

  ```
  Uc.rdoQueries!MyQuery.CursorType
  ```

- To access the underlying rdoConnection object, reference this:

  ```
  Uc.rdoQueries!MyQuery.ActiveConnection
  ```

Using the UserConnection Object's Events

The UserConnection object exposes an entire set of events that can help you fine-tune your custom UserConnection object for special circumstances. The events exposed are the same as for the rdoConnection object plus the Terminate event, which is always associated with user-created objects.

At a minimum, I'd also add an error handling routine (shown below) to deal with the stuff that happens when we work with SQL Server. Because the UserConnection object exposes all of the rdoConnection events, you can simply add some code to the QueryComplete event handler. Remember that this error handler becomes part of the UserConnection object and is carried around in the DSR file. This means that other developers can use your custom UserConnection object and get all of the error handling code as well.

```
Private Sub UserConnection_QueryComplete _
    (ByVal Query As RDO.rdoQuery, _
    ByVal ErrorOccurred As Boolean)
Dim er As rdoError
Dim m As String
If ErrorOccurred Then
    For Each er In rdoErrors
        m = m & er & vbCrLf
    Next er
    MsgBox "Something went wrong with the query" & vbCrLf & m
End If
End Sub
```

23

Building Result Sets with RDO

Choosing a Cursor—or Not

Support for rdoResultset Cursors

Page Locking

Specifying the Source of the Result Set

Managing Asynchronous Operations

Performance Tuning for rdoResultset Operations

The rdoResultset Object

The rdoColumn Object

So far, we've been touring the outskirts of the RDO interface, and we haven't seen any real signs of how data is retrieved. But now that you know how to use RDO to connect to SQL Server and how to create UserConnection objects, you're ready to take a leisurely ride through the streets and alleys of the model's data-fetching aspects. After this part of the tour, you'll know how, when, and why to build an RDO cursor—and when not to.

RDO cursors are created either by the cursor driver included with the ODBC Driver Manager or by SQL Server itself, which is capable of creating and managing server-side cursors on SQL Server 6.0 and later versions. (This means that if you access SQL Server 4.x, you can't use server-side cursors.) In RDO 2.0, the Client Batch cursor library replaces, or at least supplements, the ODBC cursor library. You can choose from the following four basic types of cursors that the OpenResultset method can create and manage using the rdoResultset object—or you can use "cursorless" result sets, a technique we'll go over in a moment.

- Forward-only result sets
- Static cursors
- Keyset cursors
- Dynamic cursors

If you need to review the basic construction of these cursor types, see Chapter 5. If you decide that you need the functionality provided by a cursor, you can select a specific type of rdoResultset cursor by setting the RemoteData control's ResultsetType property or the Type argument of the OpenResultset method to one of the constants shown in Table 23-1.

Table 23-1
RDO Cursor Types

Cursor Type	Constant
Forward-only	rdOpenForwardOnly
Static	rdOpenStatic
Keyset	rdOpenKeyset (default)
Dynamic	rdOpenDynamic

NOTE Be sure you understand that the forward-only, read-only, single-row (*RowsetSize=1*) result set isn't really a cursor at all. (I guess you could call it an *uncursor* or a "cursorless" result set.) All of the drivers support this form of data retrieval because it's the simplest of the four for RDO to implement, but it's read-only when the ODBC driver library creates it. Moreover, you can't move backward through the result set or even jump to the end using this form of data retrieval. This unique type of result set is created when you specify rdUseNone as the cursor type.

Each of these cursor types is implemented by the chosen cursor driver (or as it's sometimes called, the chosen cursor library). Not every cursor type can be created by every cursor library. (Table 23-4 on pages 445–447 is a capabilities chart that shows the options—basically, which type works with which driver.) Here are the RDO CursorDriver options:

- **rdUseODBC** Forces the use of the ODBC cursor library, which works with any version of SQL Server, including versions 6.*x* and 7.0. It is by far the dumbest (OK, most "operationally challenged") of all the libraries. You should avoid it like last season's fruitcake.

- **rdUseServer** Forces the use of the SQL Server cursor driver, the only driver that supports server-side cursors. If you try to use this against a pre-6.0 SQL Server, the system returns a trappable error.

- **rdUseClientBatch** Uses the Client Batch client-side cursor library. For the most part, this library is intended to replace the ODBC cursor library and should be used in its place wherever possible.

- **rdUseIfNeeded** Lets RDO choose the type of cursor library. RDO always chooses server-side cursors if they are available. In most cases, this is the default type.

- **rdUseNone** Sets up a "cursorless" result set. This forces forward-only, read-only, RowsetSize=1 for all result sets.

CAUTION
Remember that we're talking about SQL Server here. Yes, some ODBC drivers can connect to other back-end systems—even to Jet. But do they work the same way as the SQL Server drivers? Nope. Are they similar? Yep. But don't take any cosmic leaps (based on your experience connecting to SQL Server) by trying to perform the same operations on every ODBC driver.

You choose the cursor driver by setting up the rdoEnvironment object *before* the rdoConnection object is created or RDO defaults to a chosen type—such as when you create a stand-alone rdoConnection object. All operations under a single connection use the selected cursor driver. But as I've said on any number of occasions, *don't use a cursor unless you need its features*. If you simply want to fetch the data as quickly as possible, use something cheaper—and faster. To help you out, RDO 2.0 includes the rdUseNone option when creating rdoConnection objects. This is what I use most of the time—especially when I'm working with stored procedures.

> **NOTE** In RDO 2.0, the rdoPreparedStatement object has been replaced by the rdoQuery object. The old rdoPreparedStatement is still there (although hidden) so that your old code works, but you should convert to the rdoQuery object.

You can choose from several Remote Data Objects to retrieve data from SQL Server base tables:

- **The rdoResultset object** This is RDO's basic cursor object. Like the Data Access Object (DAO) Recordset object, the rdoResultset object can be used to manage any of the cursors or cursorless result sets. You create the rdoResultset object by using the OpenResultset method against the rdoConnection object or the rdoQuery object or by using a procedure method of the rdoConnection object. Executing a procedure method against the UserConnection object also exposes the LastQueryResults property, which points to an rdoResultset object. You can still use the rdoPreparedStatement statement in RDO 2.0, but it's now obsolete.

- **The rdoQuery object** This is a query definition similar to a DAO QueryDef. This object doesn't persist after your application ends, however. You create the rdoQuery object by using the CreateQuery method against the rdoConnection object; you can also create it indirectly by creating a UserConnection object. The rdoQuery object maps directly to the ODBC API SQLPrepare function.

- **The UserConnection object** This is a new object for RDO 2.0, which creates an rdoConnection object and one or more rdoQuery objects to expose stored procedures or user-written queries. We discussed this in Chapter 22.

- **The rdoTable object** This object, an addition to the RDO model, lets you expose all the rows of a chosen SQL Server table. The rdoTable object is simply a member of the rdoTables collection created to maintain compatibility with DAO. You can create an rdoResultset object against the rdoTable object, but I don't recommend it. Its real use is to expose the table's structure—not its data. No, this object is *not* equivalent to the DAO Table object—this isn't supported in RDO or ADO.

CAUTION
If you use the RemoteData control and don't specify a type of result set, the RemoteData control creates a keyset-type rdoResultset object. With the OpenResultset method, the default type is a forward-only result set.

The first three objects are fairly easy to understand and deal with. When you're working with data, the fourth object is about as useful as a set of snow skis on a beach in the Bahamas, but it's as vital as a good sunblock on the same beach when you're trying to map a table's schema. All of these objects are used, directly or indirectly, to access result set data. (The Value property of the Column object in the rdoColumns collection of the rdoResultset object contains the data from the SQL table in the query.) Since most of these properties are set to their default value, you can easily reference the data once you build an rdoResultset object.

TIP You should decide whether your query will be executed once and then forgotten or whether it will be executed several times. If you plan to execute your query repeatedly, you need to use one of the techniques that uses stored procedures or at least rdoQuery objects to execute the code. This saves you from having to recompile the code each time the query is run. As I've said before, you can execute stored procedures using either temporary or permanent stored procedures. Since the rdExecDirect option on the OpenResultset and Execute methods is now "on" by default, you don't need to specify it in code. The Prepared property also exposes this functionality when you define an rdoQuery object. These options tell RDO to create a temporary stored procedure to execute your query. This option isn't necessary if you're executing a stored procedure in the first place.

Choosing a Cursor—or Not

The choice of cursor for your application can significantly affect performance, scalability, and resource management. All four RDO cursor types are implemented by the ODBC Driver Manager and the selected driver. There is nothing extra in the RDO interface (unless you count the new Client Batch cursor library as being part of RDO) that creates or manages these cursors; the interface simply calls ODBC functions to set options and request result sets according to the methods you execute and the properties you set or examine. Unlike the Microsoft Jet database engine, which has its own cursor processor on top of the selected ODBC cursor library, the RDO interface and the ODBC cursor library don't always support updateable joins—especially for complex SQL products—so you can't always expect to be able to update a cursor generated from a join or against a result set returned by a stored procedure that includes a join. Stored procedures that don't join two or more tables can be updateable, however. In general, only single-table queries are updateable, so you should plan to open an additional connection to execute update statements or custom stored procedures to change the data. By using the Execute method right off the existing connection, the RDO interface handles all this for you—but only if your result set is fully populated. The rows you add to the database won't always appear in your cursor's membership, even if you do create an updateable cursor; that's the nature of some ODBC cursors.

CAUTION
Some RDO cursors are populated automatically, so be careful how you describe result sets and which cursor you choose for which job.

That said, a number of factors should play a role in your choice of cursor. To start with, ask yourself the following questions about the design of your application and your intended use of cursors:

- How many rows do you intend to access? Do you need all the rows of a table, or just a selected few? If you expect to scale your application, it had better be the latter.

- Can you afford to wait until the cursor is built, or will the user object to staring at an hourglass pointer?

- Do you have the necessary client or server resources to store the cursor you're specifying? Remember to multiply the number of resources used by this cursor by the number of active users. If your application holds "state" for extended lengths of time, this resource problem will be exacerbated because the connection, memory, and thread resources required to service the cursor are not freed as quickly.

- How do you expect to navigate through the result set? Do you need to move the current-row pointer randomly from point to point in the cursor, or do you need to move just once down through the rows?

- How should cursor membership be determined? Are you concerned with the changes that you and others will make to the rows included in the cursor?

- Will you want to make changes "off line" and post the updates later? In this case, only the ClientBatch cursor library will do. Be sure to check out the concurrency options designed especially for this configuration.

- How do you intend to update the data? Do you need to update the data at all? Do you intend to update via the cursor, the Execute method, or a stored procedure?

- How should the cursor be populated? Will you need access to the rows before they are all populated?

The rdOpenForwardOnly-Type Resultset Object

A forward-only cursor fetches one or more rows of data—not just the keys, as a keyset or a dynamic cursor does. It supports no scrolling so that the data can be fetched more quickly. Like all the other cursors, only one row is exposed at a time from the RowsetSize set of rows. These rows are stored on the client or, if you opt for a server-side cursor, on the server. In addition, only the Move-Next method is supported; executing a MoveLast would simply flush the cursor, so it makes no sense. In most cases, you can't use the RowCount property until you reach the last row in the result set. Until then, it returns –1. Once the last row is reached, there's no "going back." You can, however, use the GetRows or GetClipString methods to stream data from rdoResultset objects—as long as you do it before reaching EOF. Both of these methods can dramatically improve

CAUTION

Even when you use a forward-only, read-only result set, the rdoConnection object and some locks are held open until the last row of data is accessed. This type of cursor can provide better performance than other cursors, but it can also tie up connection resources and page or row locks—especially if your cursor spans too many rows.

result-set fetch performance because they eliminate any looping code required to fetch the rows one by one.

TIP When you reference the RowCount property, RDO executes an ODBC MoveLast command, so be prepared to wait for the result. Yep, RDO knows that the RowCount won't be available until the last row has been populated.

As you ought to know by now, I'm not a cursor man. I like to feel the wind in my face and see the data streaming by at the speed of light. With a read-only, forward-only, single-row result set, no cursor keyset is created and data values aren't updated as they change on the SQL server. The forward-only result set is so efficient that it's often faster to rebuild it than to create and maintain a keyset-type rdoResultset object. This type of "firehose" cursor is built when you choose rdUseNone as the cursor driver.

Can you update a cursor created with the rdOpenForwardOnly option? Sure, as long as the cursor library supports it and ODBC can identify individual rows. Remember that the most common reason for lack of updatability is the lack of a primary key. You don't have to tell ODBC about this index, you simply have to create it. This mistake is especially common with converted Jet databases because the upsizing wizard moves the data but does not reconfigure the primary keys. This feature differentiates RDO's forward-only cursor from DAO's snapshot.

The rdOpenStatic-Type rdoResultset Object

Like a forward-only cursor, a static cursor contains the chosen data rows—not just the keys, as in a keyset or dynamic cursor. Unlike the forward-only cursor, however, a static cursor is fully scrollable. The rows are stored either on the client or, if you choose server-side cursors, on the server. The static-type rdoResultset object is similar to the Jet snapshot-type Recordset object, although a static cursor isn't necessarily read-only like a DAO/Jet snapshot. A static cursor's order and membership are frozen once it's populated, so the static cursor might not *appear* to change as rows are added. Even if a static result set seems not to be changing, it can actually move farther and farther away from reality as time goes on, as the underlying data is changed.

NOTE Remember that "populating" simply means that RDO has moved all of the keys or rows to the target (the client or server cursor). It also means that the SQL Server is "done" processing your request and the server-side resources held during the query are released. Once a cursor is fully populated, the OUTPUT and Return Status are made available and the connection can be reused to execute another query. Note that server-side cursors don't return control to the application until they're fully populated. In some cases, RDO populates cursors for you in the background to free resources more quickly.

Data downloaded to the workstation is like raw chicken that's been sitting out for a while on a warm kitchen counter—it's hardly worth cooking. In a multiuser database management system, static cursors are for static data: information that can sit out overnight without losing any accuracy.

Wait a minute. Why all these ambiguities? Why is cursor selection not more definitive? Well, it turns out that the way each cursor driver is implemented significantly impacts the membership and data validity properties. For example, the ODBC cursor library doesn't support updateable static cursors at all, but the Client Batch cursor library not only supports them, it keeps track of changes to membership made by the application. So depending on the cursor driver you choose, you might have to dramatically change the techniques you use when working with a cursor.

However, as a rule of thumb, don't use a static cursor for dynamic data. A list of valid state codes or other relatively unchanging foreign-key lookup values would be ideal for this type of cursor. (I usually populate a small ListBox control or a local array with values such as these, so I generally use a forward-only result set for such values.)

The rdOpenKeyset-Type rdoResultset Object

The keyset cursor doesn't build a set of data rows; it builds a fully scrollable set of pointers to the member rows. The keyset-type rdoResultset object is similar to the Jet dynaset-type Recordset object. A key is built and saved for each row in the result set and is stored either on the client workstation or on the server machine. As you access each row, the saved key is used to fetch the current data values from SQL Server data tables. In a keyset-driven cursor, membership is frozen once the keyset is fully populated. Therefore, additions or updates that affect membership might not be made part of the cursor until it's rebuilt.

With some cursor drivers, modifications or additions made directly to keyset cursors with the AddNew and Edit methods are included in the result set, but additions or modifications made with the Execute method don't affect the cursor. Consult your server manual for details. If you want to see the results of your changes in the cursor, you might have to use the Refresh method or force ODBC to refetch the rows manually. We'll discuss this in detail later. To build a keyset-driven cursor, you must provide enough resources on the client or the server to hold the keys and a block of buffered data rows.

The rdOpenDynamic-Type rdoResultset Object

A dynamic-type rdoResultset object is identical to a keyset-driven cursor except that its membership, by definition, is not frozen. Because the RDO interface checks constantly to see that all qualified rows are included in the cursor's membership, this type of cursor carries the largest overhead. A dynamic cursor might be faster to initiate than a keyset cursor, however, because the keyset cursor carries the overhead of building the initial keyset. After that, the dynamic cursor is likely to be the slowest to fetch and update data and will place the greatest load on the client, network, and server. I never use this type of cursor because of its expense and overhead, although I'm sure it has its uses. It should definitely not be your default cursor; use it only in an emergency. That's why it's kept in that glass box with the little hammer nearby.

Building Cursorless Result Sets

When you specify the rdUseNone option as the cursor driver, RDO permits you to specify only a firehose cursor. You can also specify this type of rdoResultset by setting the read-only, forward-only properties to True and setting the RowsetSize property to 1. The *Programming ODBC for SQL Server* manual in SQL Server Books Online calls these cursors *Type A cursors* and calls server-side cursors *Type B cursors*. Kyle Geiger's book *Inside ODBC* calls them *firehose cursors* and *badminton cursors*. Whatever name you use, the effect is the same—high-speed, nonscrolling, read-only result sets. To get a firehose cursor in RDO, you have to use the rdoQuery object for your query and set the RowsetSize property to 1 before calling OpenResultset, or you can simply use the rdUseNone option for your CursorDriver. My tests have found that by changing a program to use firehose cursors instead of ODBC cursor library cursors (both flavors of client-side cursors), you can fetch 500-row result sets approximately 2.5 times faster.

A couple more tidbits that can help you make the right cursor decision: for a singleton select from a stored procedure, it is even more efficient to use output parameters for the result column values than to open a firehose cursor and fetch a single-row result set. I've found output parameters to be about 30 percent faster for a singleton select. (I'm not sure why this is so—it might be RDO, the ODBC driver, or the network efficiencies helping out, or all of these.) In addition, I've found that setting the MaxRows property of the rdoQuery object to 0 prior to calling OpenResultset saves an additional round-trip SET ROWCOUNT command from being sent to the server. If you choose to ignore my advice and work with BLOB (Binary Large Object) data, you should use a firehose cursor to return it. Just don't say I didn't warn you.

Deciding Between Client-Side and Server-Side Cursors

An important aspect of keyset or dynamic cursors involves *where* the keyset is created. If you're connecting to SQL Server 6.*x* or later, you can specify that the cursor keyset be created and maintained on the server. If you use client-side cursors, which are supported on all versions of SQL Server, cursor keysets are downloaded to the workstation and stored in local memory. Server-side cursors expose a number of interesting benefits:

- **They support multiple active result sets on a single connection.** Client cursors can have only one active (unfetched) result set on a SQL Server connection. Server-side cursors get away with this by fully populating the cursor before returning to the client so it can reuse the connection for singleton updates or more queries.

- **They support more efficient updatability than do client-side cursors.** This is because the server knows which tables and primary keys are involved, while a client cursor must figure out which tables and primary keys are involved in order to formulate SQL update statements. Both types still require another round-trip to perform the update.

Cursors are basically evil. It's that simple. Large cursors and especially read/write, fully scrollable cursors are especially evil, and dynamic cursors are the worst of all. However, you can purify almost any cursor and make it see the light by writing a good WHERE clause that limits it to a dozen or fewer rows.

- **They don't hold locks at the server on large unfetched result sets.** Client cursors hold share locks at the server until the result set is either fetched to the end or canceled. Server-side cursors avoid this by fully populating immediately. This problem is especially serious if the application waits for user input before it finishes fetching—Microsoft Query does this. The user might go to lunch, holding the share locks for a long time and thereby preventing other users from updating their data. Some client-side cursor implementations avoid this by fetching data automatically on a background thread, spooling the result set off into local memory or onto disk. This is OK as far as the server is concerned, but it can be a waste if you decide that you don't really want all the millions of rows you asked for. RDO does no automatic background fetching—that's all up to your code.

In exchange for these benefits, server-side cursors incur some cost and have some limitations:

- **Opening a server-side cursor is expensive.** Compared to simply streaming a result set back to the client, server-side cursors take longer to parse, compile, and execute, and they use more server-side CPU, disk, and TempDB resources. In addition, your query appears to run to completion and the cursor appears fully populated before control is returned to your application. Keep this in mind when you do performance tests against unpopulated cursors, which amortize the population costs as the rows are fetched. The additional cost of a server-side cursor varies by query (that is, a single table query versus a join) and type of cursor (as with a forward-only/dynamic cursor versus a keyset cursor or a static cursor).

- **Fetching from a server-side cursor requires one round-trip from client to server to open the cursor and one round-trip per RowsetSize row.** (In ODBC terms, this is one round-trip per call to SQLExtendedFetch.) On the other hand, fetching data from a client-side cursor simply moves rows from the local network buffers into local program memory. Requesting and receiving the result set is one round-trip to the server.

- **Server-side cursors can't be opened on most SQL batches or complicated stored procedures, such as those that return multiple result sets or involve conditional logic—not unless you disable the cursor by using a forward-only, read-only, single-row cursor.** How do you know whether you'll need the benefits of server-side cursors for a given result set? If you don't know how big the result set will be and aren't inclined to fetch the whole cursor (using a query tool such as Microsoft Query or Visual Database Tools), use a server-side cursor—but only if you know that the cursor's size won't bring the server to its knees. If you know in advance that the result set will be small, use a firehose cursor and fetch all the result rows immediately into client-side program variables. You'll often know in advance that the result set will be exactly one row. In this case, you should definitely use a firehose cursor and fetch the result rows immediately.

NOTE   Yep, I tried to run a multiple result set query against SQL Server 7.0, and you still can't run these with server-side cursors. Sigh.

As you can see, in some cases using server-side cursors can improve performance—if you hold your mouth right. Consider, however, that the server must have enough resources to store the cursor keyset. For example, if you build a cursor keyset that has 20 bytes per row and includes 200 rows, it requires about 4 KB of data space—only two data pages (or just half a page on SQL Server 7.0). This is not too bad, even if you have to multiply that figure by 100 users, which makes the data load 400 KB. This is a manageable number as far as data space is concerned, although it might take up most of the data cache on a small system. But what if your typical 100-user cursor is 2000 rows? You'll have 4 MB of space dedicated to the cursor keysets. That can exhaust your data cache completely unless you toss another 32 MB of RAM into the box.

What about CPU load? If you're using a P5 or P6 processor clocked at 300 MHz, you should have enough spare CPU ticks to handle the extra load, but you won't have enough if you're running a low-powered server. I've done many of my tests on my "po' folks" server, which has 16 MB of RAM but is dedicated to SQL Server (and has no UI). All of these tests have shown that server-side cursors are slower than workstation-based cursors—although not dramatically so. My 60-MHz P5 with 48 MB of RAM seems to manage the keysets faster than the 486SX server. I've also run similar tests on podium systems and found dramatically different results. Some of these systems, which are used for demos at VBits and the like, are 300-MHz P6 systems with 64 MB of RAM and a 16-MB RAM TempDB, so you can see why the results can vary.

TIP   Folks, keep in mind that the Z80, the fastest Intel chip, and the most expensive mainframe computer all *wait* at the same speed. None of these processors can make video refresh or an external database query run a microsecond faster. Unless your system is processor bound (and some are), upgrading processors won't help your server or your workstation.

So why bother with server-side cursors at all? Well, in a normal installation, the P5 is the dedicated server and the 486SX (or less) is the workstation. The workstation often doesn't have the resources to build a local cursor. Server-side cursors let you choose where the keyset gets built. I'm still convinced that it's usually possible to create systems in which server-side cursors can have a very positive impact on overall performance.

Tuning the Cursor Rowset Size

The RowsetSize property determines how big a bite the cursor driver takes out of the data when it fetches rows. Instead of making a round-trip for a single row, the cursor library fetches RowsetSize rows and works on these rows in memory. This continues until your code steps outside of that subset by changing the position of the current-row pointer—such as when you use the Move-Next, MoveLast, or AbsolutePosition properties. At that point, the ODBC driver goes out and fetches the next, previous, or selected RowsetSize rows. You can change the responsiveness of queries by bumping up the RowsetSize property, but remember that data kept on the workstation gets stale pretty quickly.

TIP If RowsetSize is set to 1, you'll find it far easier to update records in the cursor without imposing exclusive locks on other pages. The default RowsetSize is 100 rows, which tends to span several (if not dozens of) pages.

You've also seen that by changing the RowsetSize to 1, you can *partially* disable the cursor processor. But if you don't set the forward-only and read-only options as well, you can create a fairly inefficient cursor—one that fetches a single row each time you position to a new row. You might need this strategy for some pessimistic locking situations, however.

The default RowsetSize in RDO is 100 when you use the server-side CursorDriver options; this always results in a Type B cursor. If you use the ODBC driver, the default RowsetSize in the ODBC driver is 1. As you can see, setting the rowset size has a dramatic effect on the behavior of the cursor you get back, but it was done that way for backward compatibility reasons back in the SQL Server 6.0 days and because the ODBC standard doesn't have an official way to distinguish between firehose and server-side cursors.

CAUTION

As you can see in the following three tables, the RDO cursor types aren't all implemented in the same way. Different aspects of the cursors are enabled depending on the driver chosen. For example, static cursors are updateable against the SQL Server 4.2 ODBC driver but not against the server-side cursor driver. If you choose a cursor type that the driver can't support, you get a trappable run-time error: 40002, Driver Not Capable.

Support for rdoResultset Cursors

Table 23-2 shows the features of the four types of rdoResultset cursors. In addition to the restrictions shown in the table, you should note that not all SQL Server data sources support every type of cursor. In some cases, you must use the ODBC cursor library, rdUseODBC, instead of a server-side cursor, rdUse-Server. This limits the types of cursors supported by SQL Server data sources. Table 23-3 shows the types of cursors that are supported by several typical data sources and by the RemoteData control. Table 23-4 shows the capabilities of the cursor types based on the drivers and options you use.

Table 23-2
Attributes of RDO Cursors

Attribute	Forward-Only	Static	Keyset	Dynamic
Updatable	Yes (SS)[1] No (CL)[2]	No (SS) Yes (CL)	Yes	Yes
Membership	Fixed	Fixed	Fixed	Dynamic
Visibility	One row	Cursor	Cursor	Cursor
Movement of current row	Via MoveNext method only	Anywhere	Anywhere	Anywhere

1. *SS* indicates support by the SQL Server 6.*x* and 7.0 server-side library.
2. *CL* indicates support by the ODBC cursor library.

Table 23-3
Support for RDO Cursors by Typical Data Sources

Data Source	Forward-Only	Static	Keyset	Dynamic
SQL Server 4.2	Yes	Yes (CL)[1]	No	No
SQL Server 6.*x* and 7.0	Yes	Yes	Yes	Yes
RemoteData control	No	Yes	Yes	No

1. *CL* indicates support by the ODBC cursor library.

Table 23-4
Cursor Capability by Driver and Option

Driver	Cursor Type	Concurrency	Status	Updatable/ Populated?	
rdUseServer * (5)					
rdUseODBC	rdOpenForwardOnly	rdConcurReadOnly	OK	False	No
		rdConcurLock	* (3)		
		rdConcurRowver	* (3)		
		rdConcurValues	* (3)		
		rdConcurBatch	* (1)		
	rdOpenKeyset	rdConcurReadOnly	OK	False	Yes
		rdConcurLock	* (3)		
		rdConcurRowver	OK	True	Yes
		rdConcurValues	OK	True	Yes
		rdConcurBatch	* (1)		

(continued)

Table 23-4 *continued*

Driver	Cursor Type	Concurrency	Status	Updatable/ Populated?	
rdOpenDynamic	rdConcurReadOnly	OK	False	Yes	
		rdConcurLock	* (3)		
		rdConcurRowver	OK	True	Yes
		rdConcurValues	OK	True	Yes
		rdConcurBatch	* (1)		
	rdOpenStatic	rdConcurReadOnly	OK	False	Yes
		rdConcurLock	* (3)		
		rdConcurRowver	OK	True	Yes
		rdConcurValues	OK	True	Yes
		rdConcurBatch	* (1)		
rdUseServer * (5)	rdOpenForwardOnly	rdConcurReadOnly	OK	False	No
		rdConcurLock	OK	True	No
		rdConcurRowver	OK	True	No
		rdConcurValues	OK	True	No
		rdConcurBatch	* (1)		
	rdOpenKeyset	rdConcurReadOnly	OK	False	Yes
		rdConcurLock	OK	True	Yes
		rdConcurRowver	OK	True	Yes
		rdConcurValues	OK	True	Yes
		rdConcurBatch	* (1)		
	rdOpenDynamic	rdConcurReadOnly	OK	False	No
		rdConcurLock	OK	True	No
		rdConcurRowver	OK	True	No
		rdConcurValues	OK	True	No
		rdConcurBatch	* (1)		
	rdOpenStatic	rdConcurReadOnly	OK	False	Yes
		rdConcurLock	* (2)		
		rdConcurRowver	* (2)		
		rdConcurValues	* (2)		
		rdConcurBatch	* (1)		
	rdOpenForwardOnly	rdConcurReadOnly	OK	False	No
		rdConcurLock	OK	True	No
		rdConcurRowver	OK	True	No
		rdConcurValues	OK	True	No
		rdConcurBatch	OK	True	No

Driver	Cursor Type	Concurrency	Status	Updatable/ Populated?	
	rdOpenKeyset	rdConcurReadOnly	OK	False	Yes
		rdConcurLock	OK	True	Yes
		rdConcurRowver	OK	True	Yes
		rdConcurValues	OK	True	Yes
		rdConcurBatch	OK	True	Yes
	rdOpenDynamic	rdConcurReadOnly	OK	False	Yes
		rdConcurLock	OK	True	Yes
		rdConcurRowver	OK	True	Yes
		rdConcurValues	OK	True	Yes
		rdConcurBatch	OK	True	Yes
	rdOpenStatic	rdConcurReadOnly	OK	False	Yes
		rdConcurLock	OK	True	Yes
		rdConcurRowver	OK	True	Yes
		rdConcurValues	OK	True	Yes
		rdConcurBatch	OK	True	Yes
rdUseNone * (4)	rdOpenForwardOnly	rdConcurReadOnly	OK	False	No

* (1)—Supported only by the rdUseClientBatch cursor driver.
* (2)—Driver not capable.
* (3)—Cursor library not capable.
* (4)—Cursor type should be rdOpenForwardOnly, rdConcurReadOnly, *RowsetSize=1*. This library doesn't permit any modes other than the one shown.
* (5)—rdUseIfNeeded always chooses rdUseServer, so their settings are the same.

Where Populated is Yes, the RowCount property returns the number of rows in the result set. Where Populated is No, the RowCount property returns –1 to indicate that the number of result set rows isn't (yet) available.

To make things even more difficult, not all of the four cursors support all types of concurrency. Static server-side cursors with rdConcurLock aren't supported, for example, but forward-only server side cursors with rdConcurLock are. Confused? Me, too. And when you consider that driver types, cursor types, and locking options changed as the technology improved with RDO 2.0 and that they might be different if connections are made to a non-Microsoft SQL server (such as a Sybase SQL server), you have a right to be confused. To generate Table 23-4, I wrote a program that uses each type of cursor driver, cursor, and concurrency mechanism. The program is included as a sample (Cursor Map) on this guide's companion CD; I encourage you to try it yourself. I created the table against SQL Server 6.5. The query I used was a simple one-table fetch that returned about 585 rows from a table with a unique index. The cursor capabilities should map out the same for SQL Server 7.0, but I encourage you to try them yourself.

CAUTION
Server-side cursors don't currently support multiple result sets—even on SQL Server 7.0, so you can't submit any query that the RDO interface even thinks will generate multiple result sets (unless you set the rdOpenForwardOnly and rdConcurReadOnly options and set the RowsetSize property to 1).

Page Locking

Before we dive into the details of page locking, I want to alert you to an interesting "upgrade" in SQL Server 7.0: it has implemented intelligent row-level locking—and not just for inserts. Does it make sense to use this high-granularity locking style? Well, not in all cases. In the past, SQL Server didn't use this type of locking because it was too expensive in terms of CPU time and system resources. In other words, it was faster simply to lock the surrounding rows on a page basis instead of locking down individual rows. Sure, some situations really require row-level locking, and you can use this option in those situations. But like all things that sound too good to be true, this option has some costs associated with it. Fortunately, with SQL Server 7.0 you can still decide how to lock by exposing TSQL "lock hints" that force it to use more conservative page locking when it makes sense—to you.

RDO doesn't make any explicit locking or unlocking calls—all locking is handled by the ODBC driver and the SQL server. Unless you're using SQL Server 7.0 in row-lock mode, make sure you don't use "pessimistic" rdConcurLock for your concurrency type. This tells the driver that you want it to lock *all* the rows in the current rowset (based on the current RowsetSize property setting). Even in SQL Server 7.0, this can have a stifling effect on scalability if the keysets are not closed quickly to release the locks. You'll rarely want to do this anyway. If you don't plan to update the data, use rdConcurReadOnly for the locking type; if you want to edit the data, use something like rdConcurValues to do optimistic updates using old values of the columns. If you want some scrolling ability (MovePrevious), use a static cursor type (rdOpenStatic).

If you have SQL Server configured to use page locking (or you're accessing SQL Sever version 6.5 or earlier), when you open an RDO cursor, SQL Server applies a share lock to all pages in the data set that contain rows of the result set. If too many rows are locked, SQL Server escalates to table locks, and it can lock any number of tables if a query is complex enough. Only after the SQL server is convinced that the rows are no longer needed does it release the pages to other users. Regardless of the type of cursor you choose to open, you need to consider its impact on the SQL server and on other users who are sharing the data. Other users can read the rows while pages are locked, but they can't make changes on these shared pages. It's important to practice safe sharing: move to the end of your cursor as quickly as possible. Either do it in the background, as the user peruses the first 20 rows or so, or execute a MoveLast method (if you can) before the user gets any rows at all. I prefer the latter technique. It can be slow, but it's fairly simple to implement and it's generally foolproof.

If you choose a server-side cursor, the strategy is somewhat different. In this case, the type of lock chosen is held for the duration of the cursor. Fortunately, when you use SQL Server 6.x and later, you can specify a number of locking strategies right in the SELECT statement. That way, you can request dirty reads (except in some states in the South) in which no locks of any kind are placed on the rows.

In any case, having to fall back on a MoveLast method is an expensive proposition if the cursor is too large. But you know better than to create a cursor with more than a couple of hundred rows—don't you?

By setting one of the four types of concurrency control options as the LockType argument of the OpenResultset method, you can specify how and when SQL Server pages are locked as the rows in the rdoResultset object are edited and updated. If you don't specify a lock type, rdConcurReadOnly is assumed; use one of the Integer constants shown in Table 23-5 to define the lock type of the new rdoResultset object.

Table 23-5
Integer Constants for Setting the LockType Argument

Lock Type	Concurrency Option
rdConcurBatch	Optimistic concurrency with Client Batch cursors
rdConcurReadOnly	Read-only (default)
rdConcurLock	Pessimistic concurrency
rdConcurRowver	Optimistic concurrency based on a TimeStamp column
rdConcurValues	Optimistic concurrency based on row values

The RDO interface uses the ODBC API function SQLSetScrollOptions function to set values for the various types of concurrency management, but these are *not* the same strategies that you might have seen in DAO/Jet and other relational systems. They are, however, identical to the locking strategies used in other ODBC API implementations. Note that DAO/Jet does *not* support pessimistic concurrency because it's so different from the DAO/Jet pessimistic approach.

In RDO (and ODBC API) pessimistic locking, the pages containing the rows in the rowset are locked exclusively and are unavailable to other users once you create the cursor. These locks aren't imposed when the Edit or Add-New method is used, to be released when the Update method is executed—instead, they're imposed when the cursor is first opened and remain in place as long as the cursor is open. This is very different from the way that Jet/DAO manages pessimistic locking: as you reposition the current row to various points within the result set, the locks propagate with the rowset window. (Remember that the RowsetSize property determines the size of the rowset.) Pessimistic locking is the easier type to code but can be more demanding of system resources because it's capable of locking down one or more pages for considerable (infinite) lengths of time. If you must use pessimistic locking, be sure to reduce the RowsetSize property to lock only a single page. This might mean 5, 25, or 250 rows, depending on how many rows fit on a data page.

CAUTION
Remember that users are the slowest component of the system. Never, ever depend on users to move quickly through the data on their own. That's like depending on the cable TV guy to arrive and finish his work before you have to leave the house and pick up the kids from school.

> **NOTE** Since SQL Server 7.0 supports row-level locking, we have to re-evaluate many of the locking strategies and application and component designs that we depended on in the past. No, I don't think you should rush off and simply turn on row-level locking—not without verifying that it really does make things faster, better, or cheaper.

In optimistic locking, the page containing the row being edited is also locked exclusively but is unavailable to other users *only* while the Update method is being executed. This is very similar to the DAO/Jet approach. Optimistic locking assumes that other users aren't likely to be editing the row being updated. It also requires more complex error management, since your code must be prepared for update failures caused by changes made to the record after the Edit mode is entered.

The ODBC driver detects changes on the basis of either a TimeStamp column or a comparison between the actual data values on the old row before editing and the existing SQL Server row. Your error-recovery routine must decide what to do with the three different rows—the unedited version and the two changed versions (the client or component version and the server version).

Dissociating rdoResultset Objects

When stand-alone objects were added to RDO 2.0, so was another unique RDO feature: the ability to "dissociate" the rdoConnection object from an rdoResultset object—as long as it was created with the Client Batch cursor library. This means that you can do the following:

1. Open a connection to SQL Server using a stand-alone rdoConnection object, the UserConnection object, or the OpenConnection method. (Just remember to use the rdUseClientBatch cursor library.)

2. Create a static updateable rdoResultset using the OpenResultset method with the rdConcurBatch option.

3. Set the rdoResultset object's ActiveConnection to Nothing. This dissociates the rdoResultset from the connection used to create it, but unlike the Close method, it doesn't destroy the object.

4. At this point, you can continue to extract data from the rdoResultset and even make changes—adding, deleting, or changing existing rows. The Client Batch cursor library maintains the current state in local RAM (and disk) and records all of the changes in its own log.

5. When you're ready, you can associate the rdoResultset to a valid rdoConnection object and use the BatchUpdate method to post the changes made to the rdoResultset to the database. If a collision occurs, RDO and the Client Batch cursor library create an array of bookmarks pointing to the rows in the rdoResultset that didn't update for whatever reason.

One of the first questions you might want to ask is, "Can I just create a stand-alone rdoResultset and associate it with an rdoConnection later?" Nope, sorry, this feature isn't implemented. It was considered, but it didn't make the final cut. It is, however, implemented in ActiveX Data Objects (ADO).

Specifying the Source of the Result Set

Every rdoResultset object you create must have a SQL statement behind it somewhere. This SQL statement is written either in TSQL or in ODBC SQL. Basically, it tells the SQL server which rows from which tables should be included in the result set. You pass this SQL statement either in the Source argument of the OpenResultset method or in the SQL property of the rdoQuery from which the rdoResultset is created. This SQL statement can reference a stored procedure, but only if it remembers to use the "call" syntax we'll be discussing a little later. Referencing views is just as easy as making direct references to tables—SQL Server does all of the cross referencing for you behind the scenes.

Using an ODBC-syntax SQL statement is the easiest approach. RDO expects to see an ODBC-syntax SQL statement anyway, so you don't really need to set any other options in this case.

Using a TSQL-syntax SQL statement is also fairly easy, but you have to make sure that the ODBC driver doesn't choke on the statement when it creates a temporary stored procedure to execute the query. To make sure, set the SQLExecDirect option or the Prepared property. These options tell the ODBC driver to forgo creating a temporary stored procedure. While this is a NO-OP whenever SQL Server discovers that you're simply executing a stored procedure, in many situations you don't want the extra overhead of creating a stored procedure to perform a one-of-a-kind operation. Consider, however, that if you're rolling your own queries for repetitive operations, it's often much more efficient to create a parameter query with an associated temporary stored procedure to do the job. And RDO can do virtually all of the work for you if you give it half a chance.

Using the name of a stored procedure that returns rows is also fairly easy. If the RDO interface can't figure out that the Source argument is one of the other options, it assumes that it's a stored procedure. In RDO 1.0, when you executed a stored procedure, you used the ODBC Call syntax because it helped the RDO interface and the ODBC driver execute the stored procedure more efficiently. But in RDO 2.0, you should use the UserConnection object to expose your stored procedures as methods. Sure, you can still use the Call syntax, but you'd have to have rocks in your head or being paid by the hour to do so. I talked about the UserConnection designer, which is used to build custom UserConnection objects, in Chapter 22, in case you missed it. You can still use the ODBC call syntax if you want to, but it's like using that old dirt road to cross the backcountry when a new freeway can get you there four hours sooner—and the scenery isn't even that great. I'll also talk about building parameter queries a little later.

Referencing the rdoQuery object by its name is a technique I don't usually go for, since I use the OpenResultset method off of the rdoQuery when I want to reference an rdoQuery object. But this technique is also cool, and it does the same thing. In this case, the SQL statement is a property of the rdo-Query object. But as I said earlier, this is old technology and should be replaced with the UserConnection object. But you can also use the name of your query off of the rdoConnection object. That is, when you create a query using the CreateQuery method (let's call it "MyQuery"), this query is now exposed as a method off of the rdoConnection object. In code, it works like this:

```
cn.Connect = "dsn=biblio"
cn.CursorDriver = rdUseNone
cn.EstablishConnection
SQL = "{? = call AuthorsByYearBorn (?,?)}"
Set qy = cn.CreateQuery("MyQuery", SQL)
cn.MyQuery 1947, 1948          ' Invoke the query as a method
Set rs = cn.LastQueryResults    ' Get the results
```

> **NOTE** If you're building your stored procedures in another application, such as Microsoft Visual InterDev or Visual Database Tools, and you're halfway through executing the application, don't be surprised if Microsoft Visual Basic doesn't recognize your stored procedure. It asks SQL Server to look up the stored procedure when the rdoQuery is first created. If it isn't there at that time, adding it later won't help.

Using the name of a SQL Server table is a little tricky—and mostly pointless. Keep in mind that if you're manipulating tables directly, you might be building in limits to scalability, security, portability, and job security. Apparently, the RDO interface knows nothing about the schema of your database and will figure that this string (which you know is a table name) is the name of a stored procedure. To get the RDO interface to recognize your table names, you must first populate the rdoTables collection. To do this, simply execute an rdoTables.Refresh method or reference one of its members by its ordinal number. For example, referencing rdoTables(0) populates the entire collection. Of course, this means an overhead hit while the RDO interface queries the SQL server for the names of the tables and so forth. And since you've gone to the trouble of getting *all* the database table names through a separate query, your only option is to get *all* the rows—not so clever, if there are more than a few. You might as well just code *Select * from <table>*.

Managing Asynchronous Operations

Among the more powerful features of the RDO programming model is its ability to open connections and execute, populate, and rebuild queries asynchronously. Asynchronous operations, you'll recall, let you start an RDO operation without having to pass control to the RDO interface while you wait for the operation to complete. Instead, you can pass control back to your application, to the line of code directly after the asynchronous operation. In the case of the

OpenResultset method, asynchronously means that the rdoResultset object isn't all there yet. As a matter of fact, the only things working are the Still-Executing property and the Close and Cancel methods. The StillExecuting property remains True until the first row of data has returned. Once StillExecuting changes to False, the rest of the rdoResultset properties and methods are activated. If you decide to give up waiting, you can simply use the Close or Cancel methods to stop the operation.

To turn on asynchronous operations, set the rdAsyncEnable option when you use the OpenResultset method. If you use the StillExecuting property to wait for an asynchronous operation to complete, you must periodically poll the StillExecuting or StillConnecting property and then execute DoEvents to pass control back to Microsoft Windows and Visual Basic to permit other portions of your application to execute. For example, the following code creates an rdoResultset asynchronously and polls until it is open:

```
Set rs = CnMyConnection.OpenResultset ( _
    name:= "Select * From Authors Where Year_Born = 1947", _
    options:= rdAsyncEnable)
While rs.StillExecuting
    DoEvents
Wend
```

Actually, polling this often won't make things run any faster because the real polling is done by the ODBC driver. You can adjust the frequency of ODBC's polling by changing the AsyncCheckInterval property of the rdoConnection object. Polling too frequently hurts system performance and too infrequently results in your application not being notified immediately that the query has completed.

If you decide to stop waiting for an asynchronous operation to complete, you can execute the Cancel or Close methods, but this isn't such a great idea if you're in the middle of an Update or other data modification operation. (With RDO 2.0, you don't have to poll at all—you can use RDO events to determine when your asynchronous operations are complete.)

RDO 2.0 Asynchronous Enhancements

RDO 2.0 brings a new depth and dimension to asynchronous operations. First of all, asynchronous operations have been expanded to include the following methods:

- **OpenConnection and EstablishConnection** You can use these to deal with more complex connections that don't open immediately or when you want to overlap processing with the connection operation. For example, you can finish painting the initial forms while the connection is opening.

- **OpenResultset** As I've mentioned before, you can use this method to start the creation of an rdoResultset while you continue other work— perhaps to prepare the form to display the pending contents.

- **Requery**   When you reexecute a query, you're essentially repeating the process used to build it in the first place.

- **MoveLast**   To fully populate a result set, this method can also take quite a bit of time to execute. Using the asynchronous option, you can continue other work while the rows are fetched.

- **Execute**   Because many of the queries that we execute are action queries, including Update and Delete operations that can span many rows, using the asynchronous option means that users are no longer blocked while the operation progresses.

These additions mean that virtually all aspects of result set management can be executed asynchronously. The MoveNext, MovePrevious, and MoveFirst methods still don't support asynchronous operations, and, yes, these can take quite a bit of time to execute for complex result sets.

RDO 2.0 Events

RDO 2.0 also implements event-driven programming, which means that you can manage both asynchronous and synchronous (nonasynchronous) operations using a bevy of events. You can still use the StillConnecting and StillExecuting properties, but if you code an event handler for the Connected and QueryComplete events, you don't need them. The real benefit here is that you don't have to use the DoEvents operator.

Using events to handle asynchronous operations makes a lot more sense. These are listed in Table 23-6. Let's take a closer look at the events associated with creating result sets. Some of the most important events are on the rdoResultset object's parent rdoConnection object, because these events fire for *all* result sets created on the connection.

CAUTION

Every time the use of DoEvents is mentioned in front of a member of the Visual Basic development team, a strange look comes over his face—as if he had just bitten into a lemon. Apparently, DoEvents exposes your application and Visual Basic to a number of potential problems having to do with race conditions and reentrancy. These are issues that C developers have learned to live with over the years. Want to know more? Dig into the copious books on handling the Windows message loop in those books on writing applications the hard way—with C++.

Table 23-6
The rdoConnection Object's Asynchronous Query Events

Event	When It Fires
QueryComplete	After a query completes—successfully or not.
QueryTimeout	When the QueryTimeout time has elapsed and the query hasn't yet completed.
WillExecute	Before the query is run. This allows the developer to prohibit the query from running or to make last-minute adjustments to the SQL.

A number of events fire against specific rdoConnection objects as well. (See Table 23-7.) These are used to track when the rdoResultset is associated or dissociated from its parent rdoConnection and as your code traverses from one result set to another or from one row to another.

Table 23-7
The rdoResultset Object's Asynchronous Events

Event	When It Fires
Associate	After a new connection is associated with the object.
Dissociate	After the connection is set to Nothing.
ResultsChange	After current rowset is changed (multiple result sets).
RowCurrencyChange	After the current-row pointer has changed. This tracks the AbsolutePosition property. This can fire on an insert, delete, or update as the current row gets changed.
RowStatusChange	After the state of the current row has changed from unmodified to modified or to deleted (due to an edit, delete, or insert). Basically, this event tracks the rdoColumn Status property.
WillAssociate	Before a new connection is associated with the object. This allows the developer to override or cancel the operation before a new connection is made.
WillDissociate	Before the connection is set to Nothing. This allows the developer to override or cancel the operation before the connection is set to Nothing.
WillUpdateRows	Before an update to the server occurs. This allows the developer to override or cancel the operation before the server is updated.

CAUTION
Don't be surprised if the QueryComplete or Will-Execute events seem to fire a few more times than required. I found that this is especially true when working with asynchronous operations. No, they aren't going to fix it for Visual Basic 6.0.

In the "Dissociating rdoResultset Objects" section earlier in the chapter, you learned how to temporarily disconnect (or dissociate) an rdoResultset from its connection. This doesn't destroy the rdoResultset if the rdoResultset was created using the Client Batch cursor library. You can create a cursor, dissociate it from its connection, perform operations on it, associate it with an active rdoConnection object, and execute a BatchUpdate operation on it. Four separate events relate to this technique, as shown in the Table 23-7.

A couple of events can also be exposed on selected rdoColumn objects, as you can see in Table 23-8. These fire both before and after the column's data has changed. To verify the column's data, you can examine the current state of the rdoColumn object's data by examining the Value property. While you can change the Value property in the WillChangeData event procedure or even cancel the pending operation, the data is committed once the DataChanged event has fired.

Table 23-8
The rdoColumn Object's Asynchronous Events

Event	When It Fires
DataChanged	When the value of the column has changed.
WillChangeData	Before data is changed in the column. This allows the developer to cancel.

Performance Tuning for rdoResultset Operations

The following sections offer performance tips and techniques from developers at Microsoft and in the field.

Managing Temporary Stored Procedures

RDO 2.0 includes a rather significant change in the way that the rdExecDirect option is used. For one thing, it's now "on" by default. If you've never heard of this option, don't feel bad. It didn't make it into the printed documentation. Basically, you use the rdExecDirect option bit to tell RDO whether it should have ODBC create a temporary stored procedure to execute your query or, if the option is set, to execute the statement directly. Before the ODBC driver sends out a SQL statement to be executed, RDO checks this option (and the Prepared property) to determine whether it should have ODBC create one or more temporary stored procedures on the SQL server—unless you're executing a stored procedure in the first place, in which case it simply executes the procedure. These temporary procedures contain the SQL statement specified in the rdoQuery object or in the OpenResultset method and are designed to accept any parameters that might be specified for the statement.

This means that if you have code that won't work with the rdExecDirect option, you must take steps to turn it off. When you execute the OpenResultset or Execute methods or set the Option property of the RemoteData control, these are the rules used internally by RDO to enable or disable the rdExecDirect option:

- If your code supplies an option value (as either an integer or a long), RDO accepts this as a mask for the option bits. That is, if the bit is set, the selected option is enabled.

- If your code does not supply an option value, rdExecDirect is assumed to be enabled by default.

- If your code supplies a bogus value, rdExecDirect is assumed to be enabled by default—no error is generated.

SQL Server 7.0 has changed all of the rules about how temporary stored procedures are created and managed. Because it lets you share running ad hoc queries, you no longer have to worry as much about "preparing" your queries. When you "prepare" a query, SQL Server makes note of the fact that you expect to run this query again—usually with parameters. Then it tries to execute subsequent executions of the query using the same query plan. This means that additional instances of your application can share the in-memory plans as well as other applications that happen to be doing the same (or just similar) operations.

However, the rdExecDirect option is *not* set by default on the rdoQuery object, and the Prepared property *does* default to True. So unless you specify otherwise, RDO creates a stored procedure to execute your query. When your code can't run with the rdExecDirect option, you have to turn it off by passing 0 as the option or choose one of the other options.

In SQL Server 6.*x*, these procedures are created in TempDB space. In SQL Server 4.*x*, they are created in the current database. In SQL Server 7.0, they aren't created at all—they aren't needed. In some cases, several stored procedures can be created for a single statement. Generally, these procedures aren't released until you close the connection or end the application. Ending the application in Design mode doesn't necessarily clear these statements; only ending Visual Basic or your compiled EXE flushes the temporary procedures. If the ODBC driver doesn't get a chance to clear these out, they're orphaned—forever. On SQL Server 4.*x* systems, they can be quite a nuisance. On SQL Server 6.*x* systems, they're dropped as soon as the hStmt that created them is closed. To avoid the creation of these procedures in the first place, specify the rdExecDirect option when you use the OpenResultset or Execute method, as shown here:

```
Set rs = cn.OpenResultset("Select * from Authors", _
    rdOpenStatic, rdConcurValues, rdExecDirect)
```

TIP When you use the rdExecDirect option, the ODBC interface doesn't create a temporary procedure that is then used to run the SQL statement. This can save some time—but only if the statement is used infrequently. For example, if the rdExecDirect option is used with a query that's executed only once, your application's performance can be improved. If your queries can be worded to accept parameters, however, it's better to let temporary stored procedures take up some of the preprocessing that must be done whenever a new query is executed.

In RDO 2.0, the default for OpenResultset is rdExecDirect, but you can also set the Prepared property on an rdoQuery or UserConnection object. This indicates that the query is to be prepared before execution.

TIP When you set up a data source name with the new ODBC 3.*x* wizards, you'll see a new dialog box that helps ODBC (and your application) deal with these temporary stored procedures. You can tell the ODBC Driver Manager to drop these when the connection drops (the default behavior) or whenever it sees fit. With older (pre–SQL Server 7.0) servers, this might help prevent some of the orphaned stored procedures from wandering around looking for their mommies.

Using the OpenResultset Options

The OpenResultset method was originally created with only a single option, rdAsyncEnable. Hours before RDO 1.0 shipped, the team discovered that without the rdExecDirect option, users would be stuck with a lot of needlessly prepared SQL statements, so they added the rdExecDirect option. A couple of last-minute enhancements have apparently been added to RDO 2.0 as well—one of which forces the rdExecDirect option *on* by default. Table 23-9 shows each of the Options arguments. Note that these are binary values, so you can use them in any combination (that makes sense) by adding/ANDing their values together.

Table 23-9
OpenResultset Options

Option	Value	Use
rdAsyncEnable	32 (&H20)	Enables asynchronous operations.
rdExecDirect	64 (&H40)	Bypasses creation of a stored procedure to execute the query by using SQLExecDirect instead of SQLPrepare and SQLExecute. See the Prepared property, which provides similar functionality. This option is on by default, so you must specifically disable it. Pass 0 for *Options* if you want to prepare the query (disable rdExecDirect).
rdFetchLongColumns	128 (&H80)	When this option is set, the Client Batch cursor library fetches BLOB data along with the other columns instead of deferring this operation until the BLOB column is referenced. This might be needed if you can't scroll back to the row later to get the data—as in a forward-only cursor or after the connection has been dissociated.
rdBackgroundFetch	256 (&H100)	Creates a separate thread to complete result set population for Client Batch cursor library result sets. This can help alleviate nagging locking problems on larger result sets.

Let's look a little more closely at the two newest options because they didn't make it into the documentation. Both these options enable features on the new Client Batch cursor library—and don't apply to the other libraries.

rdFetchLongColumns

If rdFetchLongColumns is specified, the RDO client cursor fetches BLOB data, together with fixed-length data, as part of the initial population of static cursors. The BLOB data is the ODBC data types LONGVARCHAR and LONGVARBINARY, which, for Client Batch cursors, are temporarily stored in a separate file. The advantage to you is that you download all the data that you decide you need up front. In addition, you don't have to update properties on the cursor. The drawbacks are that your fetch time is longer and you might fill your disk with data you'll never use.

By default, Client Batch cursors don't fetch BLOB data until they're specifically referenced. In order to fetch BLOB values as needed, the cursor needs a primary key and the SourceTable and SourceColumn properties must be filled in for the BLOB field. The fetch requires one trip to the server for each BLOB value. For SQL Server, this can be performed only after the cursor has been fully populated because of the limitation of a single pending result set per connection.

rdBackgroundFetch

If rdBackgroundFetch is specified, the Client Batch cursor library uses a second (background) thread to fetch the data. The advantage of this option is that all data is eventually fetched, regardless of the actual use of the client cursor. Because client cursors use ODBC firehose cursors to fetch data, this background fetch option guarantees for SQL Server that all of the data will eventually be fetched and no locks will be held on the server. The disadvantage of background fetching, as opposed to the default "fetch as needed" option, is that you lose control over the fetch process and the fetched data might unnecessarily fill all available disk space. The Cancel and Move methods are synchronized with the background fetch, as expected.

The rdoResultset Object

The rdoResultset object is RDO's one and only interface for the result sets you create—whether they're cursors of some type or simply cursorless sets of rows. You can create rdoResultset objects in a number of ways, including those listed on the following page.

- Use the OpenResultset method off of the rdoConnection object. You use this technique to pass hard-coded SQL statements to the server for execution—especially those that you don't intend to execute more than once or those that don't have parameters. This method forces the RowsetSize to 100 and doesn't process parameter markers (?) in the SQL statement.

- Use the OpenResultset method off of the rdoQuery object. You use this technique to execute parameter queries or stored procedures—especially when you need to specify additional limitations on the operation.

- Use methods of UserConnection objects that expose queries as methods. The UserConnection object returns a LastQueryResults property that points to an rdoResultset object. You use this technique to construct prefabricated queries that can be exposed and executed using far less code and that can be maintained independently of other code.

The following sections examine the inner workings of the rdoResultset object and explain how to work with its properties, methods, and events.

RDO 2.0 Collection Management

RDO 2.0 fundamentally changes the way that the rdoResultsets and rdoConnections collections are managed. In RDO 1.0, when you executed the following code, you ended up with two separate rdoResultset objects in the rdoResultsets collection:

```
Dim cn as rdoConnection
Dim en as rdoEnvironment
Dim rs as rdoResultset
Set en = rdoEngine.rdoEnvironments(0)
Set cn = en.OpenConnection("MyDSN", rdDriverNoPrompt, _
    False, "UID=;PWD=;Database=Pubs")
Set rs = cn.OpenResultset("Select * from Authors")
Set rs = cn.OpenResultset("Select * from Titles")
```

One of these rdoResultset objects was established against the *Authors* table, while the other was established against the *Titles* table. The *rs* variable addressed the second rdoResultset object.

When you execute this code in RDO 2.0, only one rdoResultset object remains in the rdoResultsets collection—but the variable *cn* points to the *Titles* rdoResultset, the last result set created against the variable. While this technique for handling rdoResultset (and rdoConnection) objects and collections is new, it conforms to the way that collections are managed in DAO and should result in fewer memory leaks. If you don't want to lose an existing rdoResultset assigned to a variable, you need to use the OpenResultset method against a separate variable.

NOTE If you create an rdoResultset object and then use it to set the RemoteData control's Resultset property, the ResultsetType property of the RemoteData control is set to the Type property of the new rdoResultset object.

CAUTION
On SQL Server 6.x and later systems, the ODBC driver creates an hStmt when an rdoResultset object is created. If the client application's system is then hit by a beer truck, which breaks your connection and kills your application, any remaining temporary procedures stored in TempDB space are also dropped.

Exploring rdoResultset Methods and Properties

You can use the methods and properties of the rdoResultset object to manipulate data and navigate the rows of a result set. For example, you can perform the following actions:

- Use the ActiveConnection property to determine the rdoConnection used to build, refresh, or update the result set. You can set this property to Nothing to dissociate the rdoResultset object from its connection and set it back to a valid rdoConnection object as needed to requery, refresh, or execute additional queries.

- Use the Status property to determine whether the current row has been changed since the result set was first built. This property is also set when RDO performs an update on the row using either the Update or BatchUpdate method.

- Use the BatchCollisionRows and BatchCollisionCount properties to help manage collisions that occur when you use the BatchUpdate method.

- Use the UpdateCriteria and UpdateOperation properties to determine how the BatchUpdate method builds its update statements.

- Use the BatchSize property and the BatchUpdate and Resync methods with batch mode operations. All of these batch properties and methods are reviewed in Chapter 24.

- Use the RowCount property to determine how many rows were returned by the query. This property isn't valid until the result set has been fully populated, so behind the scenes, RDO executes a MoveLast for you when RowCount is referenced—at least on those rdoResultset objects that support it. If you create a forward-only result set, this is a NO-OP, so RowCount isn't valid (and returns a –1) until you reach EOF.

- Use the GetClipString property to fetch n rows of an rdoResultset into a delimited string. This can make filling a grid control a snap. Actually, any control that accepts a delimited string or supports the Clip method can accept the string generated by this method.

- Use the Type property to indicate the type of rdoResultset object created. For an rdoTable object, the Type property indicates the type of SQL Server table.

- Use the Updatable property to see whether you can change the rdo-Resultset rows. There are reasons why the Updatable property is set to True when the rdoResultset object is not updateable—but those are ODBC shortcomings. For example, when you create an rdoResultset object from a SQL join, the result might not be updateable. And while you used to be able to update similar queries with DAO/Jet, you might not be able to do it with RDO. You can always resort to a SQL UPDATE statement, but that might require another connection.

- Use the EditMode property to determine whether the AddNew or Edit methods have been invoked against this rdoResultset object.

- Use the BOF and EOF properties to see whether the current-row pointer is positioned beyond either end of the rdoResultset object. When you move through the rows in the result set one by one, you can safely loop until EOF changes to True, but once either BOF or EOF is true, there is no current row, so you must reposition the current-row pointer to a valid row.

- Use the Move, MoveNext, MovePrevious, MoveFirst, and MoveLast methods to reposition the current row. These repositioning methods work in all but forward-only rdoResultset objects, in which only the MoveNext method can be used.

- Use the PercentPosition property to indicate or change the approximate position of the current row in an rdoResultset object. If you use the PercentPosition property before fully populating the rdoResultset object, the amount of movement is relative to the number of rows accessed, as indicated by the RowCount property. This property can be handy when you're working with scroll bars on result set windows. Again, this property works only against scrollable result sets.

- Use the AbsolutePosition property to position the current-row pointer to a specific row based on the row's ordinal position in a keyset, dynamic, or static-type rdoResultset object. You can also determine the current row number by checking the AbsolutePosition property setting. Note that this property might not be particularly accurate. For example, with one row in the result set, repositioning the current-row pointer can make the AbsolutePosition property return a value of 2. The Absolute-Position property isn't available on forward-only–type rdoResultset objects. You can also use the AbsolutePosition property to position deleted rows in the result set. Unlike the MoveNext or other Move methods, it doesn't step over deleted rows. This property works only against scrollable result sets.

- Use the Bookmark property, which contains a pointer to the current row and can be set to the bookmark of any other row in the rdoResultset object. This action immediately moves the current record pointer to that row. Again, this property works only against scrollable result sets.

CAUTION

I don't recommend using the PercentPosition property to move the current row to a specific row in an rdoResultset object. The Bookmark property or AbsolutePosition property is better suited to this task.

- Use the Bookmarkable and Transactions properties to determine whether the rdoResultset object supports bookmarks or transactions.

- Avoid the Restartable property; it's really a degenerate vestige of its DAO/Jet cousin. As such, you shouldn't depend on it to determine the restartability of any query.

- Use the LastModified property to return the bookmark for the last row changed for some of the cursors—those that add new rows to the keyset. Let's look at the individual cursor types one by one:

  - Keyset server-side cursors add the new row to the cursor membership, so you should be able to use LastModified to arrive at the position of that row.

  - Static cursors on ODBC client cursors don't add the row to the membership; thus the value is undefined if this is the first edit, or it should be the bookmark for the last updated row if updates were made before the AddNew method. Server-side static cursors are read-only, so this property doesn't apply.

  - Dynamic and forward-only cursors never support bookmarks (Bookmarkable returns False), so the value of LastModified is irrelevant.

  - For Client Batch static cursors, newly added rows are added to the membership, so the LastModified property should contain a bookmark to that newly added row.

- Use the LockEdits property to check the type of locking used for updating the rdoResultset. This property checks the ODBC SQLSetScrollOptions function to determine how concurrency control is carried out.

- Use the AddNew, Edit, Update, and Delete methods to add new rows or otherwise modify updateable rdoResultset objects. (To cancel a pending edit, you can use the CancelUpdate method.) These methods work pretty much the way the corresponding DAO methods do.

- Use the Requery method to restart the query used to create an rdoResultset object. You can also use this method to reexecute an rdoQuery query.

- Use the MoreResults method to complete processing of the current rdoResultset object and begin processing the next result set generated from a query.

- Use the Cancel or Close method to terminate processing of an rdoResultset object query.

CAUTION

The AbsolutePosition property isn't meant to be used as a surrogate row number, and there's no guarantee that a row will have the same absolute position when the rdoResultset is re-created. That's guaranteed only when the rdoResultset is created with a SQL statement using an ORDER BY clause—and even then, if a member is added or removed, the ordinal numbers are completely different. Bookmarks are still the best way to retain and return to a given position.

Managing rdoResultset Events

RDO 2.0 exposes a comprehensive set of events to help manage rdoResultset objects. These events fire for both asynchronous and synchronous operations and for a number of other operations, including many batch mode tasks, as listed on the following page.

- The WillDissociate and Dissociate events fire when the ActiveConnection property is dissociated with its connection.

- The WillAssociate and Associate events fire when you reassociate the ActiveConnection property with a connection.

- The RowStatusChange event fires when the Status property changes. Examples of such changes are when you use the Edit or AddNew method followed by the Update method or the Delete method.

- The RowCurrencyChange event fires when the current-row pointer is moved. This can be caused by an AddNew method or any other move method that changes the current-row pointer.

Only the WillAssociate and WillDissociate events support the Cancel argument, which can be set to True to derail the operation in progress. I'll talk about all of the batch events in Chapter 24.

Some of the events that you might expect to be exposed on the rdoResultset aren't. For example, I expected the QueryComplete and QueryTimeout events to be handled via rdoResultset, but they're not. They are exposed off of the rdoConnection object. The rdoConnection object's event handler is passed a pointer to the rdoQuery that caused the event along with an *ErrorOccurred* Boolean value.

Handling Query-Related rdoConnection Events

The rdoConnection object is also the sync point for any queries executed against it. These events aren't exposed on the individual rdoQuery objects or even on the rdoResultset object cursors, where you might expect them. Here's a brief description of these events:

- **QueryComplete**   This event occurs after the query of an rdoResultset returns the first result set, so you can use this event as a notification that the result set is ready for processing or that an error occurred while processing the query. You should use the QueryComplete event instead of polling the StillExecuting property to test for completion of OpenResultset or Execute method queries. This event returns an ErrorOccurred flag that indicates whether an error occurred while the query was executing. If this flag is True, you should check the rdoErrors collection for more information.

- **QueryTimeout**   This event occurs when the query execution time has exceeded the value set in the QueryTimeout property—in other words, when the query has taken longer to execute than expected. Unlike other interfaces (except VBSQL), RDO can continue processing the query if you set the Cancel argument to False. In this case, the query continues for another *n* seconds as determined by the QueryTimeout property. You can't change the timeout value after the query starts. If left alone or set to True, the Cancel argument tells RDO to give up waiting for the query to complete. You can use this event to display a message box to users, asking them if they want to cancel their query or continue to wait another *n* seconds.

- **WillExecute** This event is fired before the execution of any query. You can trap this event to disallow the execution of certain queries or to make last-minute adjustments to the rdoQuery object's SQL string. The Cancel argument lets you disallow the query—you simply set it to True and RDO will generate a trappable error indicating that the query was canceled. For example, you can prescreen the query to make sure that the WHERE clause doesn't contain a prohibited operation. Thus, by setting the Cancel argument to True, you can prohibit users from executing damaging data manipulation language (DML) or data definition language (DDL) queries.

These events are fired for *all* queries executed on each rdoConnection— that is, any rdoConnection declared using the WithEvents syntax. This includes both asynchronous and synchronous queries, queries executed via the Open-Resultset or Execute methods, and queries executed from an associated rdo-Query object. The Query argument is an object reference that indicates which query was executed and caused the event. Using this argument, you can write a single event handler for all queries on the connection but still customize the handler for specific queries. When executing queries against the rdoConnection object itself, RDO creates an rdoQuery object internally, and a reference to this internal rdoQuery is passed as the Query argument.

Managing rdoResultsets

When you create an rdoResultset object, the current-row pointer is initially positioned to the first row (if there are any rows) of the result set. The Row-Count property isn't applicable to dynamic cursors, in which the number of rows can change, or to forward-only result sets that expose only one row—at least not until the last row is fetched. If there are no rows, the RowCount property returns 0, and the BOF and EOF property settings are both True. If there are rows, the BOF and EOF settings are both False and the RowCount property setting returns a nonzero value. If the number of member rows has already been determined, the RowCount property is set to that number; otherwise, it is updated as cursor rows are populated. If the cursor can't determine the row count, RDO returns –1.

Even if you request an updateable rdoResultset object, the result set might not be updateable for any of a litany of reasons:

- No primary keys are specified for the tables in the query. This is by far the most common reason for read-only result sets based on simple queries.

- The underlying database, table, or column isn't updateable based on server-side database settings.

- The cursor doesn't support updatability on the selected cursor.

CAUTION

When you use forward-only sorts of rdoResultset objects, you can't use the MovePrevious, MoveFirst, or Move methods with a negative argument. You can use only the MoveNext method. The ODBC driver doesn't support anything else.

- You opened the rdoConnection or rdoResultset object as read-only.

- Your user doesn't have update permission on the table or columns selected.

- The join is too complex for ODBC to figure out the SourceTable and SourceColumn.

In any case, you can examine the Updatable property of the rdoConnection, rdoResultset, and rdoColumn objects to determine whether your code can change the rows. But even when this property is True, you might still have problems updating the result set rows without using an update query.

Sequencing operations

If an unpopulated rdoResultset object is pending on a SQL Server data source, you can't create additional rdoQuery or rdoResultset objects, nor can you use the Refresh method on the rdoTable object until the rdoResultset object is flushed, closed, or fully populated. When you work with server-side cursors, however, you can execute additional commands against the connection before the last row is fetched because the RDO interface, independent of any needed update operations, references the cursor that is on the server. You have to fetch all of the result sets generated by a query before you can execute another query against the connection. Therefore, you must poll the MoreResults property until it returns False or until you simply close the rdoResultset.

Positioning the current-row pointer

At any one time, only one row in an rdoResultset object is exposed for data retrieval or modification: the row addressed by the current-row pointer. Remember that forward-only or cursorless result sets are *not* scrollable—their current-row pointer can be repositioned forward only one row at a time using the MoveNext method. You can reposition the current-row pointer of a scrollable cursor by using any of the Move methods or the AbsolutePosition and PercentPosition properties; they work the same way that the DAO methods do. The rdoResultset object supports bookmarks, which you can use to save the current location in a *Variant* variable. You can subsequently move back to a saved location in the rdoResultset object by setting the Bookmark property with a valid bookmark. If you modify data in the rdoResultset object and want to reposition to the last row that was changed, set the Bookmark property to the bookmark returned in the LastModified property. In most cases, RDO skips over rows that were deleted since the rdoResultset was created—with the exception of rows retrieved with a bookmark or the AbsolutePosition property. In this case, you might position to a deleted row, in which case a trappable error is triggered.

TIP When you position the current-row pointer, you can position it past either end of the result set or to a row that's been deleted. The RDO interface can also leave the current-row pointer positioned over an invalid row, such as when a row is deleted. Be sure to check the EOF and BOF properties to determine whether the current row is positioned beyond the end or the beginning of the result set. If you're using the Bookmark property to reposition the current row, you can reposition it to a row that has been deleted by another user. If so, a trappable error results.

Using GetRows

Remember what I said about the GetRows method in Chapter 13? Or did you skip Chapter 13 to get here? If so, I recommend that you go back and take a look. The GetRows method is also implemented by the RDO interface and can greatly increase the performance of this interface, just as it helps Jet. In a nutshell, GetRows lets you set up a Variant array and fetch data into it right off the wire. Once the data is in the array, you can move to any row or column and extract data as needed.

When you work with RDO in an ActiveX control running on a remote system (perhaps managed by Microsoft Transaction Server), consider using GetRows and a Variant array to return the results from your result set. You can't simply pass back an rdoResultset; RDO cannot deal with it once it arrives from a remote component. But you can move the Variant array into a display control.

Creating a Variant array is easy enough, but getting the data out can be expensive because you still have to loop through the structure. Of course, in Visual Basic 6.0 you can convert a Variant array to a delimited string with a single statement. And once it's dumped into the array, you lose all of the other Field properties and rdoResultset properties—and more importantly, the methods. I think that all of this is simply a waste of time. This is further incentive to consider ADO. ADO can pass back a Recordset object to a client.

The rdoColumn Object

The rdoColumn object is roughly equivalent to the DAO or ADO Field object. Its Value property contains the column data returned from the query. It also provides a way to read and set values in the rdoResultset object's current row.

The rdoColumns collection of an rdoResultset object contains all of the rdoColumn objects of an rdoResultset, an rdoQuery, or an rdoTable object—one for each column of the result set. An rdoColumn object's name is set from the table's column name or from the name assigned to the object in the SQL query that was used to create the rdoResultset. For example, the following query returns two columns, one named *Pigs* and the other *PigAge*:

```
Select Pigs, Avg(Age) PigAge from Animals
```

Whenever you execute a query that includes an aggregate or computed column, you should provide an alias name for the column, as shown in the preceding code. If you don't, the rdoColumn object's Name property is set to a null string—which can't be used to reference the rdoColumn object in code.

rdoColumn Properties

The rdoColumn object supports a variety of properties that can fully describe the characteristics of a result set column. Generally, you'll find that these properties are designed to be as close as possible to their DAO counterparts. You can extract information about the rdoColumn in the following ways:

- Use the Attributes property to determine many of the base characteristics of a column by using the bit flags shown in Table 23-10.

Table 23-10
Bit Flags for Determining Base Characteristics of Columns

Constant	Value	Description
rdFixedColumn	1	The column size is fixed (the default for numeric columns).
rdVariableColumn	2	The column size is variable (text columns only).
rdAutoIncrColumn	16	The column value for new rows is automatically incremented to a unique Long integer that can't be changed.
rdUpdatableColumn	32	The column value can be changed.
rdTimeStampColumn	64	The column is designated as a server-managed TimeStamp for Client Batch cursors.

- Use the SourceColumn and SourceTable property settings to locate the original source of the data. For example, you can use these properties to determine the table and column name of a query column whose name is unrelated to either the name of the column in the underlying table or the names of columns and tables used to define the query. Unless these properties are filled in, the BatchUpdate method can't execute and returns a trappable error, so in some cases you might have to supply these values using your own code.

- Use the Type property settings to get the column data type. (See online help for valid data types.) Generally, valid RDO data types map one to one to the ODBC data types.

- Use the Size property to determine the length of the data if it's an rdTypeChar. For chunk data types, use the ColumnSize method.

- Use the OriginalValue property to return a Variant containing the value of the column as it was first fetched from the database. When working with optimistic batch update operations, you might need to resolve update conflicts by comparing the column values as originally returned by RDO with the value as supplied by the user. The OriginalValue property provides this value as it was first fetched from the database.

- Use the Status property to determine whether and how a column has been changed.

- Use the BatchConflictValue property to determine the value of the column as currently stored in the database. During an optimistic batch update, a collision might occur in which a second client modifies the same column and row between the time the first client fetches the data and the update attempt. When this happens, the value set by the second client is accessible through the BatchConflictValue property.

- Use the OrdinalPosition property to get the presentation order of the rdoColumn objects in an rdoColumns collection.

- Use the AllowZeroLength property setting to get the zero-length string-handling setting. If AllowZeroLength is False for a column, you must use Null to represent "unknown" states; you can't use empty strings.

- Use the Required property settings to determine whether Nulls are permitted in the column. You can use the Required property, along with the AllowZeroLength property, to determine the validity of the Value property setting for any rdoColumn object. If the Required property is set to False, the column can contain Null values as well as values that meet the conditions specified by the AllowZeroLength property setting.

- Use the BindThreshold property to set the maximum number of bytes that RDO will bind to. When RDO peruses the rdoResultset object's rdoColumn objects, it binds to each column whose type it recognizes. Ordinarily, RDO won't bind to BLOB columns, but RDO 2.0 lets you decide. If the size of the column is below the BindThreshold value, RDO treats the column just like any other character or binary value.

- Use the ChunkRequired property to determine whether you need to use the Chunk methods to fetch the column. This property is gated by the BindThreshold property. Columns whose data size exceeds the rdoQuery object's BindThreshold value set the ChunkRequired property to True.

- Use the AppendChunk, GetChunk, and ColumnSize methods to manipulate BLOB columns if the ChunkRequired property is True.

- Use the Updatable property to see whether a column can be changed. SQL Server can restrict permissions right down to the column level, so if your user has permission for the table but not for the column, the Updatable property is set to False. Check the rdoResultset property to see why a column's Updatable property is False.

Addressing Column Data

The Value property is the property you might reference the most but never actually use in code. If you use the default collection and property settings, it's very easy to get at the data from an rdoResultset column. Remember that Visual

Writing your own applications to munge SQL Server structure is best done with SQL DMO, not RDO. If you're writing utilities, be sure to check out the competition—the boatload of tools, wizards, and utilities that come with SQL Server and with Visual Basic, Visual Studio, and Visual InterDev. Why invent something that's already in place and ready to use? Of course, if you're charging by the hour, then never mind.

Basic has already done all the needed data type binding, so when you have to convert incoming data, simply assign the data from the Value property to the program variable of your choice. For example, let's extract data from a simple rdoResultset in a variety of equivalent ways:

```
Dim rs As rdoResultsets
Set rs = cn.OpenResultset _
    ("Select PigName from Pigs", rdOpenStatic)
print rs(0)          ' This returns data from the
                     ' first column "PigName"
print rs!PigName     ' So does this
print rs("PigName")  ' So does this
A$ = "PigName"
print rs(A$)         ' And so does this
```

Mapping Database Schema

Only the rdoTable object's rdoColumns collection contains specifications for the data columns of a database table. If you need to examine a table's schema, use the rdoColumn object in an rdoTable to map a base table's column structure.

The RDO interface, unlike the DAO model, doesn't include built-in mechanisms for changing the database schema, but nothing will stop you from using TSQL statements and the Execute method to make whatever changes you want. Once you make these changes, however, you have to refresh the rdoTables collection if you expect it to contain valid schema information. I think you'll find few mapping requirements that can't be solved by directly addressing SQL Server's *sysobjects* table. But accessing system tables is dangerous and not really supported because they're likely to change from version to version.

24

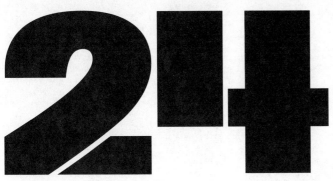

Optimistic Batch Updates

**An Overview of
Optimistic Batch Updates**

**Using RDO to Perform
Optimistic Batch Updates**

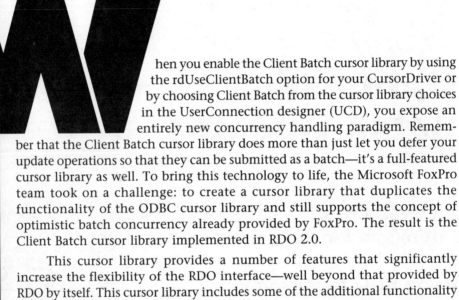

hen you enable the Client Batch cursor library by using the rdUseClientBatch option for your CursorDriver or by choosing Client Batch from the cursor library choices in the UserConnection designer (UCD), you expose an entirely new concurrency handling paradigm. Remember that the Client Batch cursor library does more than just let you defer your update operations so that they can be submitted as a batch—it's a full-featured cursor library as well. To bring this technology to life, the Microsoft FoxPro team took on a challenge: to create a cursor library that duplicates the functionality of the ODBC cursor library and still supports the concept of optimistic batch concurrency already provided by FoxPro. The result is the Client Batch cursor library implemented in RDO 2.0.

This cursor library provides a number of features that significantly increase the flexibility of the RDO interface—well beyond that provided by RDO by itself. This cursor library includes some of the additional functionality left behind when you choose not to use DAO/Jet, although it takes up more RAM than the ODBC cursor library. The Client Batch cursor library makes up for these extra resource demands with better performance than the ODBC cursor library, which it's intended to replace. It is also very closely integrated with Microsoft Visual Basic because it was originally developed specifically for Visual Basic. Let's go over the features of this technology one by one to understand how best to implement them.

NOTE The optimistic batch updates feature is also accessible from ODBCDirect. The event side of the technology isn't implemented, but you should be able to use most, if not all, of the other methods and properties. You still can't build stand-alone Connection objects in ODBCDirect, but you can dissociate and reassociate them once they are created.

An Overview of Optimistic Batch Updates

In many situations, your client application must deal with sets of rows that can (or should) be updated as a set or whose changes can (or should) be deferred until later. Consider a situation in which you have a set of rows that can be fetched, operated on, and returned later without much chance of other applications attempting to perform the same task. For example, the Lake Washington Youth Soccer Association can use a method like this to manage team rosters. The coaches can query their teams' member records from the database—often from home and over a RAS connection. The records can be updated off line and later posted back to the database as a batch. Since no other team in the league has access to the individuals on any particular coach's team, there's little chance of a conflict over access. If a conflict were to brew, the coach would certainly want to know about it.

CAUTION
Users shouldn't be forced to make decisions about data access rights. Not only does it exacerbate the problem, it can also be a pathway to corrupted data.

Unfortunately, the concept of optimistic batch updates doesn't work well when the data being worked on is under constant assault from various clients. The Client Batch library can deal with "collisions," in which changes made to one or more of the rows in the batch conflict with changes already made by other users. But these situations make the operation fairly complex as you (or your user) try to decide which update to accept—the current operation or the one already made.

Consider the case in which a user is forced to choose between three conflicting values:

- The data as first fetched and as returned in rdoResultset.rdoColumns(*n*).OriginalValue.

- The data as modified via the Update statement, as in rdoResultset.rdoColumns(*n*).Value.

- The data as modified via another user's changes, as returned in rdoResultset.rdoColumns(*n*).BatchConflictValue.

By the time the user makes a decision, another few changes might have been made, making the user's decision moot. Even if a user responds within a few seconds or your code does the job, the complexity of the code to support this decision-making process can be both overwhelming and tough to support.

The concept of optimistic batch updates is not designed nor recommended for situations in which data is constantly changing. That's not to say that there aren't plenty of applications that call for optimistic batch updates, but you have to be careful when choosing these situations and avoid those that require too much collision handling.

Using RDO to Perform Optimistic Batch Updates

The steps involved in setting up an optimistic batch update are fairly simple when taken individually, but the whole series of steps gives you plenty of room to stray. Let's walk through the steps—we have to cross over that rope bridge up ahead, so don't look down.

Establishing a Connection

The first step is to set up your connection. This is the interface to the selected server. (You can use DCOM for this operation, but we won't talk about that here.) You can use the UCD to build a UserConnection object that includes specifications for your connection. But be sure to perform these tasks:

- Specify the Client Batch cursor library for the connection (rdUseClient-Batch). You must do this *before* you establish the connection—after that, it's too late to specify which library you want.

- Grant access to the underlying table or stored procedures for the specified user.

You can roll your own connection object using stand-alone connections, or you can even use the OpenConnection method against the rdoEnvironment object, but the same caveats apply. These older techniques don't really buy you anything, but they're a little faster to work with because you don't have to wander around in the UCD to set properties—it's simply done in code. On the other hand, connection objects that are created in this way are harder to maintain, and it's tougher to share the code later.

Creating an rdoQuery Object

This step isn't absolutely necessary, but it can make handling the query parameters and other properties a lot easier—a whole lot easier. In some cases, some of the properties you need are exposed only on the rdoQuery object. In this case, you must make a decision that seriously affects how your code will approach the update process. RDO must identify the source table and column for each column in the result set. Depending on how you build your query, this information can be determined automatically by ODBC. If ODBC doesn't provide this information, you must provide it in code.

NOTE I'm not thrilled about providing this information in code. I'd prefer a way to get this metadata from the server. Executing a stored procedure loses quite a bit of its luster if you have to hard-code SourceTable or SourceColumn information.

Consider the scenario in the following list.

- If you build a query that references a stored procedure or a business object and you plan to use the BatchUpdate method, you probably have to fill in the SourceTable and SourceColumn properties for each rdoColumn object in the rdoResultset object. Basically, it works like this: when you execute a stored procedure, RDO retrieves the rows but doesn't ask where they came from. In other words, RDO can access the data and even build a WHERE clause to update the rows later, but it doesn't know where the individual columns came from. This metadata *can* be fetched using a number of techniques, but the code is expensive to run and for most cases it isn't needed. The bottom line? If you decide to fetch data using a stored procedure, plan to fill in the SourceColumn for each column in the result set you intend to update—*if* you want to use the BatchUpdate method.

- If you build a query based on hard-coded SQL and use the BatchUpdate method, ODBC should be able to determine the SourceColumn rows— at least if the query isn't too complicated. In some cases, however, you still might have to provide this information.

- If you don't plan to use the BatchUpdate method, you needn't worry about the SourceTable and SourceColumn properties. No matter how the rows are fetched, you can perform the update using other means while still using most of the optimistic batch update technology. You can plan to use the WillUpdateRows event or scan the rdoResultset object's Status property for rows that need updating and roll your own updates using stored procedures or your own update queries—even those defined by the UCD.

In any case, you have to decide whether to use stored procedures or hard-coded queries. No matter which technique you use, the resulting rdoResultset still might not be updateable—either because it's too complex or because it's simply not permitted. This all-too-common scenario means that your update strategy will have to be adapted somewhat. We'll get to the update strategy options in a minute.

NOTE You should make every attempt to use the UCD to build this connection/query interface object before you try to do this in code. The ability to use the query-as-methods feature should make it worthwhile and a lot easier to share with your development team.

Choosing the Right CursorType Option

Once the connection is open but before you attempt to execute the query, you must specify the cursor type—unless you can use rdForwardOnly, the read-only cursor built by the UCD by default. If you are rolling your own connection and query, you still must set the OpenResultset options to match your approach to updatability. Depending on how you intend to manage the result set when it arrives, you might not need anything other than a forward-only, read-only result set. You might want to settle for a nonscrolling read-only cursor if you have to update using a stored procedure, but remember that only a scrollable cursor permits you to peruse the rdoResultset Status property that indicates when individual rows and columns need updating.

Choosing the Right Concurrency Option

Before you build the result set, you need to specify rdConcurBatch as the LockType concurrency option. This is set against the UserConnection object's rdoQuery object, or it's set when you execute the OpenResultset method against your rdoConnection object. Once you enable this option, RDO and the Client Batch cursor library know that you intend to defer updates until the BatchUpdate method is executed. Sure, you can override this decision, but I'll get to that later. You want to populate your result set as soon as possible, so you might consider using the rdBackgroundFetch option when you're creating the rdoResultset.

Depending on how you plan to deal with BLOB columns, you might consider setting the rdFetchLongColumns property to ensure that the BLOB columns are fetched along with the other data. This is a requirement if you plan to dissociate the connection or use a forward-only cursor.

Executing the Row-Retrieval Query

Once the connection is open, your CursorDriver choice is cast in stone. You have to tear down your rdoConnection or UserConnection object to change this option. You *can* change the CursorType and LockType as required—whenever you rebuild the cursor. So once the cursor type and concurrency options are set, you're finally ready to open (or establish) the connection and fetch the rows. This query can be in the form of a SQL statement passed to the OpenRecordset object or built into an rdoQuery or UserConnection object. It can be a stored procedure or a hard-coded SQL statement—I prefer the former, but if you use stored procedures, your ability to use the BatchUpdate statement will be limited unless you provide the SourceTable and SourceColumn properties later on. If you plan to use the BatchUpdate method, you can create a simple but updateable rdoResultset. If you don't plan to use the BatchUpdate method, you might still want to create a scrollable result set because you'll want to make a pass over the rows to check the Status property for rows that need updating when the time comes. Remember that if you code this correctly, you have to follow the preceding setup steps only once. After that, you can reexecute the query with different parameters as many times as you need to.

Retrieving the Rows

If your query returns rows, you can display them in a grid or simply maintain the rdoResultset in local memory. Consider using the GetClipString method to fill the grid. You can choose from a number of important rdoResultset and rdoColumn properties that can be used to manage the data and facilitate the update process. Let's look at the most important and newest of these.

rdoResultset properties

AbsolutePosition You need this property to step through your rdoResultset when it comes time to check the Status property for changes—if you don't intend to use the BatchUpdate method to make the changes yourself. Remember that AbsolutePosition does not step over deleted rows, so be prepared for the errors that result. Errors indicate that the underlying row was deleted since the rdoResultset was built.

ActiveConnection This property points to the rdoConnection object used to build the rdoResultset object. Once the result set has been populated, you can set this property to Nothing to dissociate from the connection and set this property to an active rdoConnection object to reassociate it with a remote server.

BatchCollisionCount This contains the number of rows that failed to update for some reason. It's set by the BatchUpdate method. You can check this property to see whether any rows have been affected by the updates or have caused collisions.

BatchCollisionRows This is a collection of bookmarks—one for each row in the rdoResultset that failed to update when you executed the BatchUpdate method. If you create a scrollable result set, you can use this set of bookmarks to reposition to each row that failed to update. At that point, you can check the rdoColumn status property to see which column caused the failure.

BatchSize RDO and the Client Batch cursor library do not try to update the whole result set at once—they use the BatchSize property to set how many update statements are batched up in the command buffer. The default is 15 statements. You can set BatchSize to 1 when you want to update on a row-by-row basis.

Status This property serves double duty; it indicates whether the row has been "touched" by an edit, update, or delete operation or whether the BatchUpdate operation accepted this row. Its setting also indicates whether and how this row will (or should) be involved in the next optimistic batch update. You can set the status property of individual rows (or columns) in code, or you can expect the status to be changed for you when you use the Edit, Delete, or Update methods against the rows. (See Table 24-1.)

For example, suppose you're working with an unbound Grid control filled with rows from a query. The user selects one of the rows, and you detect that a change has been made in the row. At this point, you can mark the row for updating by setting the Status property of the associated rdoResultset to rdRowModified. Similarly, if a row is added or deleted, you can use the appropriate Status property setting to indicate this change. When you use the BatchUpdate method, RDO submits an appropriate operation to the remote server for each row, based on its Status property. You can also use the Edit, AddNew, and Delete methods followed by the Update method against your result set to set the Status flags for you.

Table 24-1
Status Property Values

Constant	Value	Prepared Property Setting
rdRowUnmodified	0	(Default) The row hasn't been modified or has been updated successfully.
rdRowModified	1	The row has been modified and hasn't been updated in the database—usually because you haven't executed BatchUpdate yet.
rdRowNew	2	The row has been inserted with the AddNew method but hasn't been inserted in the database.
rdRowDeleted	3	The row has been deleted but hasn't been deleted in the database.
rdRowDBDeleted	4	The row has been deleted locally and in the database.

Once the BatchUpdate operation is complete, you can examine the Status property of each row to determine whether the update is successful because RDO and the Client Batch cursor library post the success or failure of each update to this property. If the Status property value doesn't return rdRowUnmodified after the BatchUpdate, the operation to update the row couldn't be completed. In this case, you should check the rdoErrors collection and the BatchCollisionRows property for bookmarks that point to the rows that failed to update. Better yet, you should check the BatchCollisionCount property to see how many collisions occurred, and then visit each row affected using the bookmarks in the BatchCollisionRows array.

The Status property can play an important role in building a DML update query to post changes made to the batch—especially if you have to call a stored procedure for each change. For example, if you can't use the BatchUpdate method to perform the update, you can still scan the result set yourself and perform the updates for each row that has the status set to a value other than rdRowUnmodified. One approach is to code a Case statement that executes a different stored procedure or SQL query for each type of change—adds, deletes, and updates. To implement this, you loop through the modified rdoResultset and where the Status property of a selected row is *not* the value rdRowUnmodified, you can walk the rdoColumns collection to see which columns have been changed—again checking the rdoColumn object's Status property. Your code then builds an UPDATE statement or an appropriate stored procedure to perform the needed update, insert, or delete operations.

UpdateCriteria When a batch mode operation is executed, RDO and the Client Batch cursor library create a series of DELETE, UPDATE, or INSERT statements to make the needed changes. A SQL WHERE clause is created for each update to isolate the rows that are marked as changed (by the Status property). Because some remote servers use triggers or other ways to enforce referential integrity, it's often important to limit the columns being updated to just those affected by the change. This way, only the absolute minimum amount of trigger code is executed. As a result, the update operation is executed more quickly and with fewer potential errors. You should set the UpdateCriteria property to rdCriteriaKey when BLOB columns are included in the result set. Setting this property to a value other than the ones listed here results in a run-time error. The UpdateCriteria property has the settings shown in Table 24-2.

Table 24-2
UpdateCriteria Property Values

Constant	Value	rdoResultset Type
rdCriteriaKey	0	(Default) Uses only the key column(s) in the WHERE clause
rdCriteriaAllCols	1	Uses the key column(s) and all updated columns in the WHERE clause
rdCriteriaUpdCols	2	Uses the key column(s) and all the columns in the WHERE clause
rdCriteriaTimeStamp	3	Uses only the TimeStamp column if it's available (and generates a run-time error if no TimeStamp column is in the result set)

UpdateOperation This property determines whether the optimistic batch update cursor library uses an UPDATE statement or a pair of DELETE and INSERT statements when sending modifications back to the database server. In the latter case, two separate operations are required to update the row. In some cases, especially where the remote system implements delete, insert, and update triggers, choosing the correct UpdateOperation property can significantly impact performance. Newly added rows always generate INSERT statements and deleted rows always generate DELETE statements, so this property applies only to how the cursor library updates modified rows. (See Table 24-3.)

Table 24-3
UpdateOperation Types

Constant	Value	UpdateOperation Type
rdUpdate	0	(Default) Executes an Update statement for each modified row
rdInsertDelete	1	Executes a pair of Delete and Insert statements for each modified row

TIP Be sure to check out the GetClipString method against the rdoResultset object to extract the result set rows into a delimited string. It can make putting rows in a grid control a simple process. I use it in my version of the RDOADOGrid control, which is on the companion CD.

rdoColumn object properties

BatchConflictValue If a collision occurs during an optimistic batch update, this property contains the value retrieved from the database for the chosen column. That is, it's the value (just fetched from the database) that another user saved there since the last time you fetched this column. You can use this value to decide which column value to accept—your new value, the value someone else wrote to the database, or the original value. You probably won't find a BLOB-type column value here.

OriginalValue This is the value of the column when it was first fetched from the database when you created the rdoResultset. If you change the Value property, you can revert back to the original value by accessing this property. You can also use it to help decide which of the three values to accept. I don't expect the BLOB database columns to be maintained here either.

SourceColumn and SourceTable This pair of properties points back to the original source of the data. That is, when you perform a SELECT query or a join to build the result set, these columns must point back to the table and column from which the chosen column draws its data. This information isn't filled in if you are using stored procedures because the ODBC layers can't be expected to parse the SQL query to figure it out. So in many cases, you have to provide it in code—especially if you expect the BatchUpdate method to work.

Status The Status property of the rdoColumn object reflects pretty much the same information as the Status property on the rdoResultset object. In this case, however, the Status property shows, on a column-by-column basis, whether or not the column has been changed or needs to be. You can check this property when you build up your own SQL DML query to update the database. It works in pretty much the same way and with the same values we saw earlier in the section titled "rdoResultset Properties."

TIP In many cases, it's not a good idea to simply send all columns to the database when you update a row. This can cause unnecessary trigger firing and overhead that can complicate a simple operation. If you consider that some columns being updated might not be in the same tables, you can see how this practice can greatly increase DBMS thrashing.

Dissociating from the Connection

When your result set is fully populated, you can choose to disconnect from the server. This might not be such a bad idea if your user plans to stare at the rows for any length of time. But if your query contains BLOB data and you decide not to pull down these columns (the default), you can't reference these columns after you disconnect. You can scroll through the result set (assuming that you've populated it) and make as many changes as you care to using the Edit, AddNew, Delete, and Update methods. To drop the connection but keep the rdoResultset object, set the ActiveConnection property to Nothing. This fires the WillDissociate event (before the operation is complete), and if you set the

Cancel argument to True, you can stop the disconnect from taking place. Sure, you can stay connected if you want to—but keep scalability in mind if you choose to stay connected.

What happens if the application ends or you close the rdoResultset before you post the changes? Any changes you've made will be lost. This leads to the obvious question: "Can I save the rows in the rdoResultset, rebuild an rdoResultset later, and associate it with a connection to post the changes?" Nope. This isn't implemented in RDO—it *is* implemented in ADO.

Making the Changes

Once you build your rdoResultset, making the changes is easy. You can use the Edit, AddNew, Delete, and Update methods as you normally do, constrained by all of the same rules—except one. When the Update method is executed, the local copy of the rdoResultset data being managed by the Client Batch cursor library is changed and the Status property is modified to indicate that the row has been altered.

Reassociating with a Connection

When you're ready to post the changes, you must reconnect (reassociate) to an active rdoConnection object. You can use any one of these strategies:

- Create a new object using the OpenConnection method
- Use the *Dim cn As New rdoConnection* technique and the Establish-Connection method
- Use an existing UserConnection object's rdoConnection object
- Reference an existing rdoConnection object

No matter where the rdoConnection object comes from, you reconnect to it by setting the ActiveConnection property to this rdoConnection object. Does the connection have to point to the same SQL server that was used to fetch the rows? No, it can point to any SQL server as long as the same tables, permissions, and schema (for the most part) exist there too. This opens up some interesting possibilities. Don't expect the update to work if the user ID and password you provide for the connection don't have permission to make changes to the database.

Performing the Update

By this time, you have chosen one of the update strategies and are ready to update the database with the changes made to your rdoResultset. As you've seen already, you can choose from a number of strategies to work with the Client Batch cursor library and optimistic batch updates. The best choice hinges on whether you intend to use business objects, stored procedures, or user-written queries. If your system design uses stored procedures, you'll find it difficult, if not impossible, to execute a BatchUpdate—unless the SourceTable and SourceColumn properties are filled in first. So let's look at your choices.

Using the BatchUpdate method

If you can, use the BatchUpdate method to post the changes to the database. Since it performs so many functions behind the scenes, it's a shame if you can't take advantage of this technology. When BatchUpdate executes, it performs the following operations:

- Scans the provided rdoResultset, checking the Status property for any rows not marked with rdRowUnmodified.

- For each of these "modified" rows, builds an INSERT, DELETE, or UPDATE statement based on the UpdateCriteria and UpdateOperation properties.

- Groups these statements together in batches based on the BatchSize property and submits them to the connection indicated by the AssociatedConnection property.

- Fires the WillUpdateRows event for each event handler registered for the rdoResultset. (There might be several.)

- Manages any update collisions generated by the server or by the WillUpdateRows event by capturing the error row's bookmark in the BatchCollisionRows array, and tallies the number of collisions in the BatchCollisionRows property.

- Sets each rdoResultset row Status property to indicate either the reason for the collision or the success of the update, which is indicated by the rdRowUnmodified setting.

- Sets each rdoColumn object's Status property to indicate the reason for a collision and records server-side column data in the BatchConflictValue property.

- Repeats the operation for every row in the batch.

- Returns a trappable error to the method in case of errors generated by the WillUpdateRows event.

Unless you want to duplicate some or all of this code, using the BatchUpdate method can be the easiest way to get your changes posted to the server—if you can get it to work. One of the reasons it might not work could be that although you can access rows from the database by whatever means, you must use a stored procedure to update the rows. All is not lost even in this case, however, because you can use the WillUpdateRows event to trap the update operation and substitute stored procedures or your own update code.

Using the WillUpdateRows event

Let's take a closer look at this event handler. The WillUpdateRows event is raised *before* updated, new, and deleted rows are committed to the server—that is, before the chosen cursor library sends the appropriate UPDATE, INSERT, or DELETE statements to the server. This event fires even if you aren't using the Client Batch cursor library. The most important feature of this event is its ability to override the cursor library's update behavior. In other words, you can tell the cursor library that the event handler performed the update and how it was done—even if it didn't do anything. You can do this by coding an event handler, performing your own updates using stored procedures (or any other mechanism you choose), and passing back a ReturnCode argument that indicates how your code handled the operation.

If the result set uses optimistic batch concurrency, this event is raised *only* when the BatchUpdate method is called—not when the Update method is fired. In this case, the entire set of changes is about to be transmitted to the server, so your code is responsible for dealing with all rows in the rdoResultset that need updating. If the result set isn't in a batch mode, the WillUpdateRows event is raised for each call to the Update method because the changes for that row are immediately sent to the server.

The event procedure should deal with *every* row in the rdoResultset that needs updating. This means that you have to scan the rdoResultset, checking the Status property for rows that require updates. Once you find a row that needs to be updated, you must take whatever steps are necessary to update the row. One approach is to execute singleton queries that perform the operations one at a time. Although this makes error handling easier, it takes longer than an approach that batches up the operations.

TIP Another approach you can take is to create your own array of bookmarks for rows that require changes. You can do this by installing a handler for the RowStatusChange event. Each time this event fires, the Status property of the current row indicates what change must be made to the row. If you record the bookmark in your own collection or array, your array can be used later to determine which rows need to be posted to the server and what operation needs to occur.

After you deal with all of the rows in the rdoResultset that need updating, you must set the event handler's ReturnCode argument to tell the Client Batch cursor library what you did. Let's look at the options:

- **rdUpdateSuccessful** RDO assumes that your code successfully handled the update. It won't send this event to any additional clients (if there is more than one handler of this event), and the status for the rows and their columns is set to rdRowUnmodified and rdColUnmodified, respectively.

- **rdUpdateWithCollisions** RDO assumes that you've successfully handled the update but that some rows caused collisions. Your code is responsible for setting the column status flags during the handling of this event. The option rdUpdateWithCollisions is used only if you're using optimistic batch concurrency and you want to check for and handle collisions in code.

- **rdUpdateFailed** RDO assumes that your code attempted to handle the update but encountered an error while doing so. It generates a trappable run-time error to the specific Update or BatchUpdate method that is causing the WillUpdateRows event to fire.

- **rdUpdateNotHandled**   RDO assumes that your code didn't handle the update, and it will continue to raise this event to all remaining clients (if there was more than one handler of this event). If all clients return rdUpdateNotHandled, RDO performs the update itself, according to the normal rules.

The default value for the ReturnCode parameter is rdUpdateNotHandled, so if no client sinks the event or changes the value of ReturnCode, RDO performs the update.

Checking for Errors and Resolving Collisions

If something goes wrong during the BatchUpdate, the rdoErrors collection is posted with ODBC errors and a trappable error occurs on the BatchUpdate method that started the operation. The Client Batch cursor library doesn't know how to resolve collision problems such as those you might face if the reality of others using the same data you're using squashed your optimistic approach to the data. Maybe someone was trying to steal one of your key players. In any case, you have to resubmit the BatchUpdate command after setting the Force option to force the changes through, or you must simply skip the row in question.

Using the CancelBatch method

You can also use the rdoResultset object's CancelBatch method to cancel an asynchronous batch operation. This method cancels all uncommitted changes in the local cursor (used in batch mode) and returns the data to the state it was in when originally fetched from the database. This method doesn't refresh the data by requerying the server as the Refresh method does—instead, it discards changes made in the local cursor that haven't already been sent in a batch update operation. When you use the CancelUpdate method, only the current row's changes are rolled back to the state it was in before execution of the last Update method.

Using the Resync method

When a collision occurs or you simply want to avoid collisions because you haven't recently fetched data from the server, consider using the Resync method to capture the current state of the cursor's data. Resync resynchronizes the columns in the current row in the cursor library with the current data on the server (visible to your transaction). If you haven't modified the row, this method changes the Value and OriginalValue properties to match what is currently on the server. If you've modified the row, this method adjusts only the OriginalValue property in order not to lose your edits. This second case is useful when you want to avoid an optimistic concurrency conflict.

In addition, you might want to use this method when you're dealing with a row that you attempted to update using BatchUpdate but a conflict occurred because the concurrency check failed. In this case, the method adjusts the BatchConflictValue to reflect the most recent version of the column on the server. The Resync method is valid only when you're using Client Batch cursors.

25

Taking RDO Off Road

The rdoQuery Object

Working with Parameter Queries

Executing Stored Procedures

Managing Multiple Result Sets

Working with Page-Based
Data Types

Face to Face with the
rdoTable Object

e've already been down the main highways of Remote Data Objects (RDO), so now it's time to hit a few of the less traveled back roads. I hope you've packed your wet-weather gear and a pair of hip boots—in this neck of the woods, we might have to abandon the vehicle and tangle with some of the wilder, hairier aspects of the RDO interface. Get out your binoculars, too, so you can spy on such flora and fauna as the rdoQuery object, the rdoParameters collection, multiple result sets, and page-based data types. You can also expect to meet up with a rare and endangered species: the rdoTable object.

The rdoQuery Object

The rdoQuery object should be fairly familiar to you by now, because we've looked at it in passing when talking about the UserConnection designer (UCD) and when working with the rdoResultset objects created against it. Unlike the (obsolete) RDO 1.0 rdoPreparedStatement object, which maps directly to the ODBC SQLPrepare function, the rdoQuery object does not, by default, create a SQL Server temporary stored procedure to execute its queries. Although this strategy makes sense for many application situations, such as when you're executing repeated queries or parameter queries (including parameter-based SQL Server stored procedures), creating temporary stored procedures isn't always the best approach. So the rdoQuery object now defaults to the rdExecDirect mode. But if you want RDO to build a temporary stored procedure for you, you can simply set the Prepared property to True on the rdoQuery object or when you're building your UserConnection object.

In Microsoft SQL Server 7.0, the engine handles ODBC (and ADO) requests to create connection-scoped temporary stored procedures in a dramatically different way. For the first time, SQL Server creates *globally shareable* query plans, which means that RDO no longer has to create temporary stored procedures in TempDB (or anywhere else) to be executed by individual clients. When ODBC creates a semipermanent query, SQL Server simply stores it away in the global procedure cache. When the client tries to run the same (or a similar enough) query, it passes control to this preloaded query plan. This new technology revolutionizes the way temporary queries are managed. The result is faster performance and the elimination of the problems associated with residual procedures lying around.

TIP Temporary stored procedures for executing queries are stored in TempDB space on SQL Server 6.*x* systems or in your current database on SQL Server 4.2 systems—but not on SQL Server 7.0. If you're still using the older versions, be sure to make room for these stored procedures in your design.

When prebuilding temporary stored procedures is necessary, using the ODBC API SQLPrepare function behind the scenes saves the RDO interface (and you) time by precompiling SQL queries and storing them in anticipation of their execution. (Note that SQL Server 7.0 doesn't create temporary stored procedures when this call is made.) This same strategy is often used in developing SQL Server applications when queries are created off line and left in SQL Server as stored procedures, to be used by the entire team. In SQL 6.*x*, your rdoQuery stored queries can't be shared, but they can call shared stored procedures. In SQL Server 7.0, even rdoQuery-generated queries are shared.

Another important benefit of using the rdoQuery to execute stored procedures is that the RDO interface can directly manage the stored procedure return status and output parameters. But as I've said before, you should use this technology as it was intended. I've seen too many cases in which the process of creating the rdoQuery objects was put in a loop to test RDO's performance. The CreateQuery method shouldn't be executed more than once in your application—at least not more than once for **each** different query. After the rdoQuery object is created, you can use it to execute its query as many times as needed using the Requery method—even *with* parameters. And each rdoQuery object is exposed as a named method on the rdoConnection object—it's sort of like the poor man's UserConnection object.

One of the easiest ways to use the rdoQuery object is to use the UCD to capture all of the connection and query setup code at design time and generate an rdoQuery object for you. These objects are exposed on the UserConnection object, which is virtually identical to the rdoConnection object—event handlers and all. Chapter 22 is devoted to this topic.

Creating an rdoQuery Object

You can create the rdoQuery object in one of three ways, so you have more flexibility than ever when instantiating these objects:

- Use the rdoConnection object's CreateQuery method.

- Use the statement Dim qy As New rdo*Query. Yes*, you can create the rdoQuery object as a stand-alone object.

- Use the UserConnection designer (my favorite technique).

When you create an rdoQuery object using any of these techniques, the SQL server is referenced as soon as the rdoParameters collection is referenced—but not before. The RDO and the ODBC layers must then query the SQL Server to determine the number and characteristics of the parameters used in the query. In the case of hard-coded SQL, ODBC can figure this out on its own. But when you execute a stored procedure, it must ask the remote server to decode it and describe the parameters. As a result, you must be able to connect to the server so that a valid connection is available to perform this query.

Many problems, in addition to connection difficulties, can surface at this point. That's why the UCD is so helpful. All of these difficulties are resolved at design time—not at run time, when it's harder to do anything about it. On the other hand, if you use the UCD, you still need error-handling code to deal with inevitable errors such as missing servers, dead networks, or administrative problems. For example, if the SQL syntax is incorrect or if your user doesn't have sufficient permission to access the procedure or the objects it references, RDO won't be able to instantiate the rdoParameters collection. The error that results from this failure indicates an inability to reference this nonexistent object. ADO is more efficient in this area because of the ODBC API functions that can be executed to capture the stored procedure parameters. RDO doesn't permit you to define the rdoParameters collection in code—you have to let RDO build it for you. Once it does that, you can change the properties, but not before. ADO, on the other hand, lets you create your own Parameters collection or use the same RDO technique and have ODBC (or the OLE DB interface) build the structure for you.

If you use the stand-alone creation technique to create your rdoQuery object (*Dim Qy as New rdoQuery*), it isn't appended to the rdoQueries collection. (In all other cases, this is done automatically.) If a temporary stored procedure is needed, it's created only when the query is first executed. At this point, the hStmt is created to address the underlying ODBC "statement"—your rdoResultset.

The rdoQuery object's Name property is set when you create the object using the CreateQuery method, but since other techniques are at work, name collisions can occur. If you want to add the rdoQuery to the rdoQueries collection, you can't append rdoQuery objects that have duplicate names without running the risk of getting an error message such as "This environment name already exists in the collection." If you need to create another version of an existing object, you have a couple of choices:

- Drop the existing rdoQuery object by using the Close method against it.

- Change the properties of the existing rdoQuery object to match your new requirements.

The rdoQuery object can execute simple parameterless queries, but it's really designed to create queries that require one or more parameters. It can also run multiple result set queries—such as those that update a whole series of tables with a single Transact-SQL (TSQL) command. If you don't use the UCD, creating a new rdoQuery object that contains a parameter query can be challenging at first—especially if you're calling a stored procedure. This is because RDO and ODBC require you to use ODBC SQL syntax to identify the *gazintas* and the *gazoutas* (the arguments going *into* the query and those coming *from* the query). You can still use rdoQuery objects to build parameterless queries, which makes sense if you plan to execute the same query more than a couple of times over the course of your application. In this case, it's perfectly acceptable to use TSQL syntax in your queries.

OK, let's take a look at some of this theory implemented in code. First we need to set up some objects. We'll start with an rdoConnection, an rdoQuery, an rdoResultset, and a string to hold the SQL. Notice that both the rdoConnection and the rdoQuery are created as stand-alone objects. Also notice that the archaic rdoEnvironment object is nowhere to be found.

```
Dim cn As New rdoConnection
Dim qy As New rdoQuery
Dim rs As rdoResultset
Dim SQL As String
```

Notice that I didn't bother to set up these objects with event handlers. Unless you declare these objects to be instantiated WithEvents, no event handlers are exposed. And no, you can't use the New operator if you want to create event handlers. (We'll discuss this later.)

Next we'll set up these stand-alone objects in the Form_Load event so that we can use them elsewhere in the application:

```
Private Sub Form_Load()
With cn
    .Connect = "uid=;pwd=;dsn=biblio"
    .EstablishConnection rdDriverNoPrompt, True
End With
```

The rdoConnection is now open against our *Biblio* data source name (DSN) and the *Biblio* test database.

NOTE The code samples related to this chapter are on the book's companion CD in the Chap25 directory.

Now let's examine how to work with a stand-alone rdoQuery object. We'll set each property step by step, starting with the SQL property:

```
Qy.SQL = "select * from authors where author like ?"
```

Next we'll point to the rdoConnection object we just opened and set the one parameter—marked in the SQL query with a question mark (?). (When we get to the "Creating Parameter Queries" section later in the chapter, I'll show you a number of ways to pass parameters in code.)

```
Set Qy.ActiveConnection = cn
Qy.rdoParameters(0) = "%Vaughn%"
```

Next we'll set the cursor's rowset size to 1 to disable the cursor (to create a firehose cursor) and execute the query. The cursor defaults to rdOpenForwardOnly and rdConcurReadOnly:

```
Qy.RowsetSize = 1
Set rs = Qy.OpenResultset()
```

As a final step, we'll simply loop through the rows and dump the first and second columns sent back from the rdoResultset. Because this is a forward-only rdoResultset, we can use only the MoveNext method to step through the rows:

```
Do Until rs.EOF
    Debug.Print rs(0), rs(1)
    rs.MoveNext
Loop
```

NOTE   This whole exercise is for those of you who feel the need to code all of this by hand—despite the fact that the UserConnection designer does most, if not all, of it for you.

Now that the stage is set, let's look at a few typical queries and how they're coded. We'll submit a very simple query using the OpenResultset method off the rdoConnection we created earlier:

```
Set rs = cn.OpenResultset("Select Title from Titles")
```

This query is unremarkable, but it returns too many rows, so we need to add a WHERE clause that filters out all but the rows we need. Let's recode this to make it more efficient—after all, over 20,000 titles are in the database and we don't need to see nearly all of them.

```
Set rs = cn.OpenResultset("Select Title from Titles" _
    & " Where Charindex('Hitch', Title) > 0")
```

This is fine as far as it goes—it narrows down our search to just book titles that have the string *Hitch* in them, but it doesn't deal with our need to set the Title filter in our application. We also have to deal with cases that involve titles other than our own. This time, let's create an rdoQuery to manage a parameter query. The next lines of code set up a new rdoQuery object that can be used as many times as needed throughout the application. (In this example, I placed this code in the Form_Load event.) The code creates a query that returns from the *Titles* table all titles that contain the string *Hitch*—just like the earlier example.

```
SQL = "Select Title from Titles " _
    & " Where Charindex(?, Title) > 0"
Set qy = cn.CreateQuery("Qy1", SQL)
qy(0).Type = rdTypeVARCHAR
```

Now when the user fills in the TextBox control with the title string we want, we can execute this query with only the following two lines of code. RDO does the rest.

```
qy(0) = SearchForString.Text
Set rs = qy.OpenResultset
```

It's that easy. Notice how we set the first parameter (actually the *only* parameter) to the value in the *SearchForString* TextBox and ran the query. If you need to change the parameter to another value, simply use the Requery method, like this:

```
ps.rdoParameters(0) = SearchForString
rs.Requery
```

But that's not as easy as it gets. We can also code the same query as a method off of the rdoConnection object:

```
Set rs = cn.Qy1(SearchForString)
```

This syntax takes the value provided by the TextBox and executes the query. If you look at SQL Trace (or SQL Server Profiler in SQL Server 7.0), you'll see that RDO simply executes the temporary stored procedure passing in the parameter. I don't think we can pare this down any more—not until we get into ADO.

TIP   When you write your queries, be sure to enclose your literals in single quotes ('test'). If you enclose them in double quotes ("test"), SQL Server will think that you're referring to a column name.

Working with query results

When you work with result sets generated from rdoQuery objects, you use the Requery method to ensure that an rdoResultset object contains the most recent data. When you use Requery, all changes made by you and other users to the data in the underlying table are returned in the rdoResultset object, and the first row in the rdoResultset object becomes the current row. If the rdoParameter objects or the arguments passed to the query method have changed, their new values are used in the query to generate the new rdoResultset object.

NOTE   Once the Requery method has been executed, all previously stored rdoResultset bookmarks become invalid. You can't use the Requery method on rdoResultset objects whose Restartable property is set to False—you have to completely rebuild the result set.

TSQL CHARINDEX Function vs. the LIKE Operator

I prefer the TSQL CHARINDEX function to the LIKE operator because it's easier to code and more tolerant of my mistakes. But when I use CHARINDEX with a parameter, the ODBC functions used to determine the parameter data types don't always figure out that while the CHARINDEX function does indeed *return* an Integer, I'm passing in a *VarChar* string as a parameter. As a result, I have to force the parameter data type to return *rdTypeVARCHAR*, as shown in the example above. This is a new RDO 2.0 feature that makes executing complex ODBC queries far easier.

Exploring rdoQuery Properties

Once the rdoQuery object has been created (by whatever means), you can manipulate its properties to determine how the ODBC Driver Manager controls the query and to set limits on the size and complexity of the rdoResultset. Since you can create the rdoQuery object as a stand-alone object, RDO 2.0 has added a number of properties that were previously available only on the rdoQuery object's parent rdoConnection object. Here is some of what you can do:

- Use the ActiveConnection property just as you did with the rdoResultset object to set the current rdoConnection object. The events supported on the rdoResultset to watch the associations aren't exposed here. If you create a stand-alone rdoConnection object, be sure to set the ActiveConnection to a valid rdoConnection—you won't go far without one.

- Use the CursorType property just as you would on the rdoResultset object to determine the type of cursor the rdoResultset objects built from this rdoQuery. The cursor driver you use is still set on the parent rdoConnection object.

- Use the LockType property to set the concurrency option used by the rdoResultset objects built from this rdoQuery. This can be overridden by the OpenResultset method LockType option, but if you set the LockType property, you don't have to specify it on the OpenResultset later.

- Use the Prepared property to determine whether the ODBC layers use SQLPrepare or simply SQLExecute for the queries being executed. This defaults to True. If you set it to False, some of the parameter queries you might have been able to execute won't work anymore. That's because if you need to execute parameter queries, you must use ODBC call syntax or otherwise prepare the statement for execution, unless you substitute the values into the query yourself. This property has new meaning for SQL Server 7.0 developers: we no longer have to worry about "preparing" queries. All query plans are now reentrant and shareable across the server.

- Use the StillExecuting property to determine whether the query is still running—if you're using asynchronous operations. This works just as it does on the rdoResultset object. But it's better to use the QueryComplete event from the rdoConnection object.

- Use the RowsetSize property to determine how many rows are buffered internally when you build a cursor. Tuning this property can affect performance and the amount of memory required to maintain the keyset buffer. Larger rowsets store more rows and reduce concurrency; smaller rowsets reduce performance because of increased LAN traffic and server thrashing. You must set this property *before* an rdoResultset object is created. The size of the rowset is determined by the SQL Server ODBC driver—but just between you and me, its size is virtually unlimited. (The lower limit for this value is 1 and the default value is 100, but the practical limit is a function of how much memory is available.) This limit is set internally, when the RDO interface calls the ODBC SQLSetStmtOption function. Remember that when you want to set up a firehose cursor, set RowsetSize to 1 (and set the cursor to be forward only, read-only).

- Use the QueryTimeout property to indicate how long the driver manager should wait before abandoning a query. This value defaults to 0 (no timeout), but it must be set even if you don't expect the query to take a long time. When the time expires, the rdoConnection object's QueryTimeout event fires. If you don't set up an event handler (you really should), you get a trappable error.

- Use the BindThreshold property to indicate the largest column to be bound automatically. This property is important when you're working with chunk data because it sets the size of the largest chunk to be handled automatically. This value has upper limits, but it's not clear how high it can go.

- Use the MaxRows property to indicate the maximum number of rows to be processed by a query. In earlier versions of RDO and the ODBC drivers, this property affected not only the rows returned from a query but also the number of rows affected by a data modification operation such as a DELETE or UPDATE. In the current versions, only row-returning queries are affected. You can check this out (as I did) by turning on SQL Trace. Be careful—other row-returning queries can be affected by this setting.

NOTE SQL Trace has been replaced with the new SQL Server Profiler in version 7.0. This new tool does what SQL Trace did, but far, far more. That's the good news and the bad news. The problem with SQL Server Profiler, is that it's tougher to use. It has lots more features and options, and setting up a simple trace seems like a lot more trouble. That notwithstanding, it does return far more detailed information on what's going on with your queries and how the server is handling them. Yes, it's a neat tool.

- Use the RowsAffected property to indicate how many rows will be affected by an action query. SQL Server, right after it executes an UPDATE statement, returns a Rows Affected value. This property exposes that value. The RowsAffected property also appears on the rdoConnection object, which is unaffected by rdoQuery operations. If you execute a multiple result set query that contains embedded action queries, these execute normally, but the RowsAffected property remains unaffected. Note that this property isn't exposed until all the rows of a result set are processed, so you might have to loop through all of the rows to get this filled in by ODBC. It isn't exposed at all on row-returning queries or stored procedures. If you need to see the RowsAffected value, you have to issue a batch instead of a stored procedure.

- Use the Updatable property to see whether the result set generated by an rdoQuery can be updated. Ah, if only checking updatability were that easy. This property sometimes tells if the rdoQuery is updateable—but not always.

- Use the LogMessages property to activate ODBC tracing. Basically, this property points to a file used by the ODBC driver to record ODBC traffic for debugging purposes. This is not the same as the LogMessages property in the DAO model. In the RDO interface, all SQL Server messages are delivered to the Errors collection, but not every message trips a trappable error. You must check for a message every time you expect one. If a message arrives asynchronously, it might be dropped when the next set of errors arrives. This is one of those features that isn't exposed in ODBCDirect. No, the InfoMessage event doesn't fire whenever an error occurs.

- Use the hStmt property to access ODBC API functions that control the aspects of this statement. This is a "use at your own risk" property.

TIP You use the Close method to terminate an rdoQuery query and release its resources. This also removes it from the rdoQueries collection. Use the Execute method to run an action query with SQL and other rdoQuery properties. These properties include any values specified in the rdoParameters collection.

NOTE Remember that the rdoQuery object is also built when you create a UserConnection object with the UserConnection designer. You can manipulate this rdoQuery object's properties just as you can any other rdoQuery object. You simply address the object relative to its parent UserConnection object.

Working with Parameter Queries

Do you ever need to send the same query more than once? Most of my applications do. If yours do too, you might be able to use a parameter query to send it. Parameter queries generally save processing time on the workstation and on SQL Server. In front-end applications, many situations call for parameter queries—especially when the user provides a value for your application to locate or you have to perform other repetitive operations.

Every query you execute, whether or not it's a parameter query, goes through a compilation step. This takes time and server resources. In earlier versions of

SQL Server, queries that you generated on the fly in code—even parameter queries—couldn't be shared by other applications. Only stored procedures could be shared—but even then SQL Server loaded multiple copies of the same query because the code was not reentrant. At any one time, hundreds of copies of the same procedure could be left in memory—some running and some waiting to be run. Added to this load was the "ad hoc" queries that were generated by hard-coded TSQL or simply rdoQuery objects compiled into temporary stored procedures.

As I mentioned earlier, SQL Server 7.0 has reengineered this part of the engine. Compiled queries are now reentrant—they can be shared by multiple connections as long as the query is close enough to the originally compiled plan. Compiled queries are all managed in the common procedure cache—visible to all users of the server. So parameter queries are especially easy for SQL Server 7.0 to execute because it can often share the compiled code from application to application.

Earlier, we discussed how to create rdoQuery objects and use the UCD. All of these queries can be executed as methods off of the rdoConnection or UserConnection objects. When it comes time to execute a parameter query, the rdoQuery object is your most important tool.

When you provide parameters in "roll-your-own" queries by concatenating parameters to the SQL query string and call OpenResultset directly on the connection, RDO can't treat the operation as a parameterized query—it can treat them only as raw SQL. However, SQL Server 7.0 can also figure out how to make even ad hoc queries into parameter queries. For example, you can execute the following code:

```
SELECT * FROM Authors WHERE AU_ID = 5
```

The SQL Server 7.0 compiler can treat this as a parameter query. It really is a parameter query if you consider that it could have been coded with a parameter marker for the literal (5). This means that when you (or another application) execute the following code, it knows that the query plan used to execute this query is the same as the earlier query so it can reuse the already compiled code. This saves considerable time and resources.

```
SELECT * FROM Authors WHERE AU_ID = 55
```

To save yourself a lot of bother, you should build a UserConnection object to avoid having to create ODBC canonical call syntax for your query. This syntax is the source of many problems—get it wrong and you won't know about it until run time. If you insist on coding this yourself, be sure to read this entire section carefully and don't venture off into those fields on the right—they're mined.

For best performance and resource use, your application needs to reexecute the stored procedures you reference rather than drop the rdoQuery and create a new one for each iteration. In earlier versions of SQL Server, when you created an rdoQuery object, it created a temporary stored procedure to execute. When you use the Requery method, this query is referenced again and again to eliminate the need to recompile the procedure. To reexecute a query that doesn't return a result set, you simply call Execute on the rdoQuery object or use it as a method of the rdoConnection or UserConnection object. To reexecute a row-returning query, you first call OpenResultset on the rdoQuery object and then use the Requery method against the rdoResultset object you just created. If you invoke the query as a method, you must reference the rdoConnection or UserConnection object's LastQueryResults property. In any case, you can reset parameter values before each execution.

NOTE If you want RDO to manage your query's parameters, you must tell it to prepare the query. You can't use the rdExecDirect option or set the Prepared property to False. By default, an rdoQuery object is set up to prepare all queries that it runs. In contrast, the OpenResultset and Execute methods are set up to bypass the ODBC preparation steps by default. This also means that if you roll your own queries, you can't expect RDO to manage any output parameters for you.

If you don't use the Requery method on an existing rdoResultset, you burden the server with heavy TempDB activity caused by creating and dropping stored procedures for each iteration (except in SQL Server 7.0, where this problem has been eliminated). This rates very poorly with a lot of clients. You must develop a strategy that leverages the Requery method to simply change the parameters of an existing query and resubmit it if you expect to gain anything out of this technology.

Creating Parameter Queries

Because the queries you send to the server must adapt to the client's immediate needs and situation, it is essential that you build and submit queries that include replaceable arguments in any client/server application. Parameter queries form the backbone of many two-tiered and three-tiered applications. Unfortunately, coding parameter queries has always been one the toughest parts of working with RDO and is a source of many support calls. Nevertheless, building parameter queries is only slightly different from building other queries, except that you must tell RDO where the parameters should be placed in the query.

The rules about what a parameter can and can't replace are defined by SQL Server in its rules for building and coding stored procedures and TSQL statements. When you code the queries yourself, you must use the ODBC Call syntax, which lays out the parameters using a carefully orchestrated regimen— that is, if you want RDO to manage the queries and their parameters (both input and output) for you. RDO gives you a lot of rules to follow. Although breaking or simply bending the rules doesn't always result in immediate failure of the query, it can lead to inconsistent results, to say the least. On the other hand, if you create a UserConnection object with the UCD, you are notified at once that something is amiss, often while you're still in the designer. This immediate notification makes it much easier to figure out what went wrong and to develop work-the-first-time queries.

NOTE Once the rdoParameters collection has been built, it contains an rdoParameter object for each parameter marker in the SQL statement passed to the rdoQuery. These parameter markers are simply question marks—one for each parameter. You can't append objects to or delete objects from the rdoParameters collection; the collection is managed automatically by the RDO interface. But if something goes wrong as ODBC and SQL Server parse your query, this collection isn't built and RDO quietly fails.

Providing parameters

You can provide your query's parameters using a variety of techniques, each of which has advantages and drawbacks that affect your ability to leverage procedures and scale your applications. You can pass your parameters in these ways:

- **As hard-coded arguments in a SQL query string** In this case, RDO can't really help manage the parameters for you—and other people can't use the query either, even if they're performing the same search. The real disadvantage here is that to change the query, you have to recode, recompile, retest, and redeploy your application. Here's an example:

```
" Select Publisher from Publishers Where State = 'CA' "
```

- **As concatenated text or numeric values extracted from Text-Box, Label, or other controls** This is another example of a roll-your-own query. This approach is popular because it lets the user choose the parameters. It's easy to code, and you can use it to build fairly complex queries. It causes problems, though, because it doesn't deal with embedded quotes or invalid arguments. Unfortunately, RDO still can't help manage the parameters, nor can you share the query—and you still have to deal with embedded quotes in the query and any needed framing quotes. Here's an example:

```
" Select Publisher from Publishers Where State =  '" _
    & StateWanted.Text & "'"
```

- **Using an ODBC question mark (?) parameter placeholder in an SQL statement** In this case, you tap RDO's ability to manage the parameters for you. Simply setting an rdoQuery object's SQL property to this string gives RDO enough information to build a parameters collection. However, you can't really leverage this query yet—no one else can share it. But your code doesn't have to deal with embedded quotes in the parameters passed or any framing quotes because RDO and ODBC handle these for you. An example is shown here:

```
" Select Publisher from Publishers Where State =  ?"
```

- **As the question mark (?) parameter placeholders in a stored procedure call that accepts input, output, or return status arguments** We've reached the next (but not the highest) level of sophistication when building parameter queries. When you execute a stored procedure, you must use this ODBC Call syntax so RDO can manage the query and its parameters for you. Because we're executing a server-side procedure, your team members can address it, but they can't easily share the code you wrote to access it. Because ODBC handles the parameters for you, you don't have to worry about embedded or framing quotes. Here's an example:

```
"{Call GetPublisherByState (?)}"
```

> **NOTE** Stored procedure invocations that use the Call syntax (as shown above) are executed in their "native" format, so they don't require parsing and data conversion by the ODBC Driver Manager. Because of this, the Call syntax can be executed somewhat faster than other syntaxes.

- **As the question mark (?) parameter placeholders in a User-Connection object** You can also build parameter queries using the UCD. The UCD performs most of the complex tasks that you'd have to duplicate in code and provides a shareable way to build the fairly complex SQL statements required by parameter queries. That is, once you create a UserConnection object that references a stored procedure (or other query), you can share it with other developers on your team who also need access to this query.

The ODBC Call Syntax: A Summary

This table summarizes the ODBC Call syntax that you must include in your queries unless you use the UCD, which creates this syntax for you.

Query Parameter Configuration	ODBC Call Syntax
No parameters	{Call My_sp}
All parameters marked—input, output, both	{Call My_sp (?, ?)}
Some parameters marked	{Call My_sp (?, 'Y')}
With just a return status argument	{? = Call My_sp}
With the works	{? = Call My_sp (?, ?, 'Y')}

When to mark parameters

The only time you *must* use parameter markers is when you execute stored procedures that require output or return status arguments. If the stored procedure requires only input arguments, you can provide these in line as embedded values concatenated into the query (as shown in the next section). You *can* use parameter markers for any parameter query when you want RDO to manage the parameters for you.

When the rdoParameters collection is first referenced (but not before), RDO and the ODBC interface preprocess the query, create an rdoParameter object for each marked parameter, and add it to the rdoParameters collection. You can also create queries with multiple parameters, and in this case you can mark some parameters and provide the others by hard-coding or concatenation—in any combination. But all marked parameters must appear to the left of all other parameters. If they don't, a trappable error occurs, indicating "Wrong number of parameters."

How to mark parameters

Each query parameter that you want RDO to manage must be indicated by a question mark (?) in the text of the SQL statement and must correspond to an rdoParameter object referenced either by its ordinal number (counting from zero—left to right) or by its name. To execute a query that takes a single input parameter, your SQL statement should look something like this:

```
" Select Publisher from Publishers Where State =  ? "
```

Multiple parameters can be salted throughout the query, as required. You must follow a few rules, though, and we'll get to those in a minute. But you can pass parameters into each of several SELECT statements at once when you build multiple result set queries. For example, you can provide the following SQL statement to an rdoQuery for execution and expect it to manage all three parameters:

```
"Select Title from Titles " _
    & " Where Description between ? and ? " _
    & "Select Author from Authors where Author Like ? "
```

The ODBC syntax for the parameter query uses question marks as placeholders for both the input and output parameters. ODBC syntax requires Call rather than the commonly used SQL Server EXECUTE keyword. Stored procedure calls should be surrounded by braces ({}), as shown in the code fragment in the next section. Failure to use correct syntax might not prevent the procedure from being executed, but the ODBC driver might not be able to identify the parameter positions or markers. Some early versions of the ODBC driver also give you a general protection fault (GPF) when the syntax isn't to their liking.

Acceptable parameters

Not all types of data are acceptable as parameters. For example, you can't always use a TEXT or IMAGE data type as an output parameter—although the newer drivers are more tolerant of this option. In addition, if your query doesn't require parameters or has no parameters in a specific invocation of the query, you can't use parentheses in the query. For example, for a stored procedure that doesn't require parameters, you can code in this way:

```
"{ ? = Call MySP }"
```

In this case, we're still building the rdoParameters collection but using it to capture the return value parameter.

Here are the rules I mentioned earlier on what, when, and where you can use parameters:

- When you submit queries that return output parameters, these parameters must appear at the end of the list of your query's parameters.

- Although you can provide both marked and unmarked (inline) parameters, your output parameters must still appear at the end of the list of parameters. This means that your stored procedure must be coded to place all output parameters at the end of the parameter list.

- ODBC still doesn't support named parameters for stored procedures—so RDO doesn't either. You can use named parameters when calling stored procedures, but RDO can't manage them for you.

- All inline parameters must be placed to the right of marked parameters. If they aren't, RDO returns an error indicating "Wrong number of parameters." An inline parameter is one that you hard-code or provide yourself and you use instead of a parameter marker.

- RDO 2.0 supports BLOB data types as parameters. You also can use the AppendChunk method against the rdoParameter object to pass TEXT or IMAGE data types as parameters into a procedure.

Identifying the parameter's data type

When your parameter query is processed by ODBC, it attempts to identify the data type of each parameter by executing ODBC functions that ask the remote server for specific information about the query. In some cases, the data type can't be correctly determined. In these cases, use the Type property to force the correct data type or create a custom query using the UCD.

Handling output and return status arguments

In some cases, a stored procedure returns an output or return status argument instead of or in addition to any rows returned by a SELECT statement. To capture these values, you must mark each of these parameters in the SQL statement with a question mark. You might also have to set the Direction property—at least for some SQL servers. Using this technique, you can mark the position of (almost) any number of parameters in your SQL query, including input, output, or input/output parameters.

When your query returns output or return status arguments, you must use the ODBC Call syntax when setting the SQL property of the rdoQuery object. In this case, a typical stored procedure call looks like this:

```
Dim qd as rdoQuery, rd as rdoResultset, SQL as String
SQL = "{ ? = Call master..sp_password (?, ?) }"
Set qd = db.CreateQuery ("SetPassword", SQL)
qd.rdoParameters(0).Direction = rdParamReturnValue
qd(1) = "Fred"          ' The old password
qd(2) = "George"        ' The new password
set rd = qd.Execute
if qd(0) <> 0 then MsgBox "Operation failed"
```

When control returns to your application after the procedure is executed, the rdoParameter objects designated as rdParamReturnValue, rdParamOutput, or rdParamInputOutput contain the returned argument values. In the code example above, you can see the return status by examining *qd(0)* after the query is executed.

Before we move on, let's examine a slightly larger example and take a closer look at capturing parameters that are returned to our application. As I've said before, many stored procedures return nonrowset information in the form of output argument values. The following example executes a stored procedure that expects two input parameters and returns two output parameters along with a return status argument:

```
Dim SQL As String, MyOutputVal1 As Variant
Dim MyOutputVal2 As Variant, MyRetVal As Variant
Dim Cn As New rdoConnection, rs As rdoResultset
Dim Qy As New rdoQuery
Cn.CursorDriver = rdUseOdbc
Cn.Connect = "UID=;PWD=;DSN=BIBLIO"
Cn.EstablishConnection rdDriverNoPrompt
Set Qy.ActiveConnection = Cn
' Use ODBC parameter argument syntax.
Qy.SQL = "{ ? = call MyProcName (?, ?, ?, ?) }"
' Set Parameter "direction" types for each parameter,
' both input and output.
' No, this isn't necessary. It's for illustration only.
Qy(0).Direction = rdParamReturnValue
Qy(1).Direction = rdParamInput
Qy(2).Direction = rdParamInput
Qy(3).Direction = rdParamOutput
Qy(4).Direction = rdParamOutput

' Set the input argument values. Yes, this is necessary.
' Note that we are addressing the
' default rdoParameters collection.
Qy(1) = "Test"
Qy(2) = 1

' Create the result set and populate the Qy values.
Set rs = Qy.OpenResultset()
MyRetVal = Qy(0)        ' Contains the return value argument
MyOutputVal1 = Qy(3)    ' Contains the first output parameter
MyOutputVal2 = Qy(4)    ' Contains the second output parameter
```

NOTE Keep in mind that I used the example above as the "long" way to create and execute parameter queries in one of my recent lectures. The short way uses the UCD, which reduces this code to four lines. The rest of the logic is generated automatically after you run the design-time UCD.

Executing parameter queries

You have a number of choices for executing parameter queries—depending on whether your query returns rows and whether you want to retrieve them:

- If your query doesn't return rows or parameters or if you simply don't want to retrieve them (ever), use the Execute method against the rdoQuery object.

- To fetch the rows from your query, use the OpenRecordset method.

- If you created a UserConnection object, simply execute the query as a method against the UserConnection object.

- When you want to change parameters and run the query again, use the Requery method against the rdoResultset.

How to pass parameters for the *n*th time

It doesn't do any good simply to execute a parameter query once—especially if you go to the trouble of having RDO and ODBC construct elaborate mechanisms to handle the parameters. When it's time to execute your parameter for the second through the *n*th time, you simply place the new input (or input/output) parameters in the rdoParameters collection—wherever it might be—and use the Requery method. Let's look at some common scenarios. First, when you create the rdoQuery object in code:

```
rs.rdoParameters(1) = "New parameter of some kind"
rs.(2) = 14  ' Another value passed to 3rd member of rdoParameters
rs!Parameter3 = 23  ' Addressing by name
rs("Parameter4") = "Also addressing by name"  ' "Late" binding
```

Or when you need to access the parameters of a UserConnection object's query:

```
MyUc.rdoQueries(0).rdoParameters(1) = "New Param"
```

Or:

```
Dim Parm as rdoQuery    ' Declare a holder object
Set Parm = UserConnction1.rdoQueries("MyQuery")
Parm.rdoParameters(n) = "the nth parameter"
```

Once the parameters are set, you can use the Requery method to reexecute the query using the newly set parameters. As a result, the rdoResultset object is rebuilt from the beginning using the new data:

```
rs.Requery
```

The Requery method also supports the rdAsyncEnable option, so you don't have to block when ODBC is away building your result set.

You also have another option—you can simply reexecute the rdoQuery as a UserConnection object method with the new parameters. If you take this course, RDO and ODBC reuse the rdoQuery object's temporary stored procedure and pass in the new parameters. This option is slightly slower because the rdoResultset object is torn down and reinstantiated instead of being reused.

Using other rdoParameter object properties

Using the properties of an rdoParameter object, you can set a query parameter that can be changed before the query is run. You have these choices:

- Use the Name property to identify the individual query parameters. The names are built automatically and are set to Parameter*n*, where *n* is the ordinal number plus one. You can assign your own names with the UCD or by setting the Name property of the rdoParameter object before the query is executed. RDO and ODBC don't support named parameters passed to queries.

- Use the Direction property to set the parameter's function: input, output, input/output, or a return value. In RDO 2.0, the Direction property is usually set automatically, so you don't have to set this value. It's also unnecessary to set it for an input parameter—which is the default value.

- Use the Type property to determine the data type of the rdoParameter. Data types are identical to those specified by the rdoColumn.Type property. In some cases, ODBC might not be able to determine the correct parameter data type. You can force a specific data type by setting the Type property. Be careful when you set the data type—the wrong one can keep you up nights finding strange problems. Don't choose CHAR when you really mean VARCHAR.

- Use the Value property (the default property of an rdoParameter) to pass values to the SQL queries containing parameter markers used in the rdoQuery.Execute or rdoQuery.OpenResultset methods.

NOTE RDO 1.0 required that your ODBC driver support a number of Level II–compliant options and the SQLNumParams, SQLProcedure-Columns, and SQLDescribeParam ODBC API functions in order to create the rdoParameters collection and parse parameter markers in SQL statements. While you could use some drivers to create and execute queries, if your driver didn't support creation of the rdoParameters collection, RDO failed quietly and simply didn't create the collection. As a result, any reference to the collection resulted in a trappable error. RDO 2.0, on the other hand, is far more tolerant of noncompliant drivers. When you use the Client Batch cursor library, RDO 2.0 can often make up for the shortcomings of lightweight ODBC drivers.

Addressing the parameters

By default, members of the rdoParameters collection are named Parameter*n*, where *n* is the rdoParameter object's ordinal number plus one. For example, if an rdoParameters collection has two members, they are named Parameter1 and Parameter2.

But if you use the UCD, you can specify names for specific parameters. Because the rdoParameters collection is the default collection for the rdoQuery object, addressing parameters is easy. If you've created an rdoQuery object referenced by *rdoQo*, you can refer to the Value property of its rdoParameter objects by using one of these strategies:

- Reference the Name property setting using this syntax:

```
' Refers to PubDate parameter
rdoQo("PubDate")
```

Or this:

```
' Refers to PubDate parameter
rdoQo!PubDate
```

- Reference its ordinal position in the rdoParameters collection using this syntax:

```
' Refers to the first parameter marker
rdoQo(0)
```

A common mistake here is to refer to the right parameter with the wrong ordinal. I know, because I do it all the time. Remember that the return value is always the first member of the rdoParameters collection (*rdoQo(0)*)—if it's requested. If you don't put the *? =* at the front of your Call statement, it won't be extracted. In this case, the first parameter encountered after the parenthesis in the Call statement is the first parameter in the collection—addressed as *rdoQo(0)*.

> **NOTE** When your query specifies a return value parameter, you might not be able to reference it until *after* the entire result set has been populated—that is, until you reach the last row. This isn't RDO's fault—it's just that SQL Server doesn't return a value for this parameter until the procedure ends. So depending on an *@@ROWCOUNT* value placed in the return status in order to see how many rows qualified for the result set isn't a reasonable strategy.

The rdoParameters collection

Basically, you use the rdoParameters collection to expose the parameters marked in the SQL property of the parent rdoQuery object. In RDO 1.0, you had to tell RDO the direction for each parameter—return status, input, output, or both input and output. This is generally unnecessary with SQL Server because its driver can report the configuration of each query parameter. But some other database drivers might need a little help, so you have to set the Direction property of each rdoParameter object before the rdoQuery is executed. The Direction property can be set to any of the values shown in Table 25-1.

CAUTION
Watch out for the automatic naming of the parameters. RDO automatically assigns a name to each rdoParameter object in the rdoParameters collection, but it starts naming at 1, not 0 as you would expect. This means that the first (ordinal 0) rdoParameter object is named Parameter1, not Parameter0. Also, the names assigned to the members of the rdoParameters collection are not Param1, Param2, and so on. The documentation is wrong!

Table 25-1
Values for Setting the Direction Property

Constant	Value	Description
rdParamInput	0	(Default) The parameter is used to pass information to the procedure.
rdParamInputOutput	1	The parameter is used to pass information both to and from the procedure.
rdParamOutput	2	The parameter is used to return information from the procedure, as in a SQL output parameter.
rdParamReturnValue	3	The parameter is used to fetch the return status from a SQL procedure.

For most situations, you don't need to set the rdoParameter object's Type property before the query is sent, but I've already shown you a case or two in which it *is* necessary to manually set the parameter data type. Remember when we tried to pass a parameter to the first argument of the TSQL CHARINDEX function? You *do* need to set the Value property (the default property) to the value to be passed for each SQL parameter. Once the parent rdoQuery has been executed, the rdoParameter object can be examined for the input or the returned parameter values and the data type of the returned value. The data types are identical to those specified by the rdoColumn object's Type property.

When you successfully define an rdoQuery in code, then, and only then, is an rdoParameters collection created. If the syntax used in the SQL property is incorrect as far as the parameters are concerned, the ODBC Driver Manager doesn't permit the RDO interface to create the rdoParameters collection. Since no error is generated when this process fails, the first indication that something has gone wrong is error 40002, which complains about the syntax or permissions associated with the collection. The parameter syntax isn't especially picky, but I've encountered a number of errors while experimenting and doing things that I thought were fairly intuitive.

Working with ODBC Query Syntax

In some cases, you must use special ODBC query syntax to get the job done. ODBC defines extensions to the ANSI SQL syntax when you're dealing with any of the following:

- Date, time, and TimeStamp column data
- Scalar functions, such as numeric, string, and data type conversion functions
- LIKE predicate escape characters
- Outer joins
- Procedures

NOTE You don't usually have to use special ODBC query syntax if you don't care about application portability. All of the standard TSQL functions and operators work as they always have. You need these functions only in special cases when you want the ODBC driver to help pass parameters or assist in some other obscure applications.

Let's look at some practical examples of using this special ODBC query syntax. We've already examined one case in which it's used: executing a stored procedure that needs one or more parameters. Remember the '?' placeholder?

It's part of the ODBC SQL syntax extensions. The formal syntax for these extensions looks like this:

```
{[?=] call procedure-name [([parameter][,[parameter]]...)]}
```

When you apply it to one of the queries passed to an rdoQuery object, it looks like this:

```
SQL$ = {?= call MarryPig ('Miss Piggy', ?)}
```

In this example, the *MarryPig* (or is it *MerryPig*?) procedure is designed to pass back a return status and accept two parameters. We supply one of those in the code and expect another to be passed as a parameter at run time.

Executing Queries Through Stored Procedures

In SQL 6.5, when the ODBC interface executes a SQL statement, it creates one or more temporary stored procedures on the server. No, as I said before, SQL Server 7.0 no longer uses this technique. So if you're still using 6.5, these procedures contain the SQL statement specified in the rdoQuery object or in the OpenResultset method and are designed to accept any parameters that might be specified for the statement. The procedures are created either in the current database or in the SQL Server TempDB database; it depends on which version of the server you're using. In some cases, several stored procedures can be created for a single statement. Generally, these procedures aren't released until you close the hStmt (rdoResultset), the hDbc (rdoConnection), or the hEnv (rdoEnvironment), or until you close the application. Closing the application in Design mode doesn't always clear these statements; so in some cases, closing Microsoft Visual Basic is the only way to clear out these temporary procedures. To avoid creating these procedures in the first place, specify the rdExecDirect option when you use the OpenResultset method, as shown here:

```
Set rs = cn.OpenResultset("Select * from Authors", _
    rdOpenStatic, rdConcurValues, rdExecDirect)
```

When you specify the rdExecDirect option, the ODBC interface doesn't create a procedure that is then used to run the SQL statement. Having the ODBC interface create such a procedure and run the statement can be faster, but only if the statement is used infrequently.

SQL syntax extensions with date values

When you work with date, time, and TimeStamp column data, you must enclose the values in curly braces, like this:

```
UPDATE Pigs
Set DateOfBirth = {d '1995-01-31'}
```

The three date values are coded as follows:

```
{d 'date value'}
{t 'time value'}
{ts 'timestamp value'}
```

SQL syntax extensions with scalar functions

You use the scalar functions to manage string length, absolute value, or current date values. You can use them on columns of a result set and on columns that restrict rows of a result set. The syntax is fairly simple. For example, here's how we return the uppercase value of a column:

```
SELECT {fn UCASE(NAME)} FROM Pigs
```

NOTE If this stored procedure isn't in the local database, you must fully qualify its name like this: *mydb..myproc*.

Executing Stored Procedures

Stored procedures are only slightly more difficult to access than parameter queries, and I've set out most of these details already. But in this section, I'll offer a few tips that can make accessing stored procedures easier.

Stored procedures aren't always located in the default database, and while SQL Server can locate them, you might not be able to execute the procedure you want unless you're logged in to a specific database. You can execute the TSQL Use statement to switch to another database—it's fast and painless. But the statement can't always be concatenated to the front of your SQL statement. You also don't need to prepare a stored procedure invocation; you don't need to create a temporary stored procedure to execute a stored procedure. RDO and the ODBC layers should prevent this from happening anyway.

Be sure to grant permission to your intended users to access the stored procedures you create. If they don't have permission to execute the procedures, they won't get much out of them. You can prohibit access to the underlying tables and still grant access to stored procedures that reference the protected tables. Consider that stored procedures live in a world of their own. The temporary objects that they create belong to them and disappear when they end. This is the reason that when you execute a SELECT INTO statement as you execute a stored procedure, users can't see the table when the stored procedure ends. However, they can see tables if you use SELECT INTO on a permanent table (where you need to have the SELECT INTO BULK COPY mode turned on) or on a semipermanent ##Temp table. You can't open a server-side cursor on the contents of a temporary table unless that table is created *outside* a stored procedure. When a temporary table is created inside a stored procedure, the table is automatically dropped by SQL Server when the procedure ends. Thus, if you select data from the temporary table at the end of your procedure, the server tries to create a server-side cursor on the table. But as soon as the procedure exits, the base table is gone, making the cursor unable to function.

If you use the OpenResultset method to execute action queries to do such things as CREATE TABLE and INSERT INTO, you're asking SQL Server to create a server-side cursor based on the results of these statements (of which there aren't any). When running procedures like these, which don't return rows, you simply use the Execute method instead of the OpenResultset method. Using OpenResultset inappropriately causes SQL Server to do a boatload of extra and meaningless work.

Although you might not explicitly call a stored procedure, when you ask the SQL Server 6.5 driver to prepare a statement, it creates a temporary stored procedure on the server, and when it executes that statement it executes the temporary procedure. Thus, when you execute a prepared statement you execute a stored procedure, and the situation described above happens. So don't open a server-side cursor on a table that will be dropped. You can use the ODBC cursor library, since it simply streams the data down from the server and builds a static cursor on the client side. The ODBC cursor library couldn't care less whether the temp table was dropped, but if it's dropped, you obviously can't perform updates against it.

Managing Multiple Result Sets

Many of the production programs I've written use TSQL queries or stored procedures that return several distinct but related sets of result data. Some of these result sets contain rows, but not all of them do. Only queries containing the SELECT statement return zero or more rows. An UPDATE or other data modification query returns a result set but no row sets. Any SQL statement can include multiple SELECT statements or invoke stored procedures that execute one or more SELECT statements. Since stored procedures can execute other procedures, it's not always easy to tell how many sets of results a particular query will return. Each SELECT statement generates a result set that must be processed by your code or discarded before the RDO resources are released and the next result set is made available. How do you manage these multiple sets of results with the RDO interface? It turns out that the RDO interface and the ODBC API are designed to deal (at least to some extent) with this contingency by implementing the rdoResultset object's MoreResults method.

NOTE The server-side cursor driver will balk if you try to send it a query that it even *thinks* has more than one SELECT statement (or is otherwise too complex). There are two ways around this. If you must create multiple scrollable result sets, you must use one of the other cursor libraries. But you can use a server-side cursor library if you disable the cursor.

Action queries also generate rowless result sets, which must also be processed, but the ODBC drivers and the RDO interface basically ignore embedded action queries included in SELECT statements. For example, if you submit a query that includes four SELECT queries for populating four local ListBox controls and a stored procedure that updates a table, your code must deal with only four result sets. But you might not know how many result sets can be generated by a stored procedure, so your code must be prepared to process *n* sets of results.

For example, some system-stored procedures generate a result set for each column in a table or each table in a database—you generally don't know ahead of time how many to expect. You execute queries that return multiple result sets no differently from the way you execute other queries. If you use the rdoQuery object, however, you can't depend on the RowsAffected property to determine the number of rows affected by action queries since embedded action queries are ignored and don't set the RowsAffected property. You can execute a multiple result set query by using the Execute method, but you can't retrieve the affected rows from individual statements, and a trappable error results if any of the queries returns rows.

CAUTION
You can't include every combination of TSQL statements in a batch. If you don't know what constitutes a correct batch, consult the TSQL documentation.

The following steps lead you through the process of creating and managing the results of a multiple result set TSQL procedure:

1. Set up an rdoResultset object, using whatever means you choose. You might create an rdoQuery object or simply execute an OpenResultset with a TSQL query. The SQL query itself contains more than one statement—a batch. Although you can include an action query in a SELECT statement, you can't examine the RowsAffected property of the action query: its result set is basically ignored by the RDO interface. To retrieve RowsAffected from an action query, execute the action queries singly, in rdoQuery objects, or with Execute statements. You can also pass back the *@@ROWCOUNT* value from the stored procedure as a return status or additional output parameter. The rdoQuery object's RowsAffected property is used in the first case; in the second case, the rdoConnection object's RowsAffected property is used.

2. Use whatever means you want to move through the rdoResultset rows. The first result set containing a SELECT statement is made available as soon as the rdoResultset returns control to your application, as soon as StillExecuting returns False when running with the rdAsyncEnable option, or as soon as the QueryComplete event fires—and before the QueryTimeout event fires.

3. When you are through with the first result set, even if you haven't moved to the last row, you can use the MoreResults method to flush the first result set and move on to the next. MoreResults returns True if there are more result sets to process. Once you execute MoreResults, the previous result set is no longer available.

4. Once you execute MoreResults, the next row-returning result set is available. You can't tell how many result sets an arbitrary query can produce unless you write it yourself.

> **NOTE** A row-returning result set is generated by the SELECT statement. Not all SELECT statements return rows; some simply return values. But RDO treats these like rowsets.

5. If you decide to abandon the entire batch, execute the rdoResultset object's Cancel method or simply close the rdoResultset object using the Close method.

> **TIP** If you use a forward-only cursor to move through the rows of the result set, you can't examine the RowCount property to see whether the query returned any rows—not, at least, until the result set is fully populated. You can also check the EOF (end of file) property instead. If it's True, the query didn't return rows.

Here's how to execute a multiple result set query using the rdoQuery object:

1. Create your SQL statement and place it in a string variable—for instance, *MySQL*. For SQL Server, multiple statements must be separated by semicolons.

```
MySQL = "Select Author from Authors; " _
    & " Select City from Publishers; " _
    & " Update MyTable Set Age = 18 " _
    & " Where Name = 'Fred' "
```

2. Use an existing rdoQuery object from the rdoQueries collection or create a new rdoQuery object, and set a variable declared as *rdoQuery* and multiple result sets to this object (in this case, *MyQy*). This example assumes that an rdoConnection object (*Cn*) already exists. You can pass the SQL statement to the CreateQuery method, but the example sets the SQL property after creating an instance of the object. You can also use this technique if the rdoQuery object has already been created and is referenced by its name or ordinal number in the rdoQueries collection.

```
Dim MyQy As New rdoQuery      ' Create a stand-alone rdoQuery
MyQy.ActiveConnection = Cn    ' rdoConnection created earlier
MyQy.SQL = MySQL
```

3. Execute the query by using the OpenResultset method against the rdoQuery object. If you don't need the extra properties or the ability to pass parameters to the query, use the OpenResultset method directly against the rdoConnection object. The arguments you use here affect all result sets fetched from this query. For example, if you need to use a cursor on the second result set, you must specify a cursor type (such as rdOpenKeyset) when the first result set is opened, as here:

```
Dim MyRs As rdoResultset
Set MyRs = MyPs.OpenResultset _
    (rdOpenForwardOnly, rdConcurReadOnly)
```

4. You're now ready to process the first result set. Note that the Options argument rdAsyncEnable wasn't set, and so control is *not* returned to the application until the first row of the first result set is ready for processing. Even if the current rdoResultset contains rows, the RowCount property is set to –1 because the forward-only snapshot doesn't update the RowCount until after the rdoResultset is fully populated. If there are no rows, the EOF property returns True. If you use any other type of cursor, the RowCount property returns 1, indicating that the first row has been populated (there are rows to process), or 0, indicating that no rows were returned by the rdoResultset.

The following example fills a ListBox control named *NameList1* with the results of the query:

```
Do Until MyRs.EOF            ' Loop through all rows
    NameList1.AddItem = MyRs(0)  ' Use the first column
    MyRs.MoveNext                ' Position to the next row
                                 ' in the result set

Loop
```

5. The first result set is now at the EOF position. At this point, you can use either the MoreResults method to activate the next result set or the Cancel method to abandon processing of the rdoResultset—even if it's running in Asynchronous mode. Once you execute MoreResults, the previous set of rows is no longer available, even if you used one of the cursor options to create it.

```
' Activate the next set of results.
If (MyRs.MoreResults) Then...
```

6. Now you're ready to process the second result set. This example uses only the first few names and discards the remaining rows:

```
' Loop through some rows
Do While Not MyRs.EOF and MyRs(0) < "B"
    ' Use the first column
    NameList1.AddItem = MyRs(0)
    MyRs.MoveNext
Loop
' Activate the next set of results and discard remaining rows
If (MyRs.MoreResults) Then...
```

7. Now you can process the last set of results. Because this is an UPDATE statement, there are no rows to be returned and the RDO interface ignores the result set that is generated. The action query was executed, but you have no way of knowing whether it returned rows. The MoreResults method is used for the last time to release all resources connected with this query:

```
' Activate the next set of results.
If (MyRs.MoreResults) Then...
```

8. When you use the MoreResults method against the last result set, it should return False, and other resources required to process the query should be released. At this point, the rdoQuery object can be reused. If you use the Close method against the rdoPreparedStatement, the rdoQuery is removed from the rdoQueries collection. If you intend to reuse it later by passing it different parameters or simply by changing its SQL property, you can leave the rdoQuery open.

CAUTION
You get a trappable error if you try to use the MoveLast method on an rdoResultset that has no rows or can't be scrolled. Check the EOF property first.

Working with Page-Based Data Types

Before we venture into the next town, I need to get something off my chest. In my opinion (which is certainly not shared by everyone), before you commit to putting TEXT and IMAGE (BLOB) columns in your database, you need to take a *big* step back and think again. I haven't heard of very many implementations (OK, I've heard of *one*) in which putting BLOBs in the database ended up making sense. I came to this conclusion over the years by listening to countless cries for help from developers and their managers who had waded off into the BLOB swamp and needed rescuing. In virtually all cases, we were able to find faster, easier, and more supportable ways to access BLOB data—and none of them involved using the Chunk methods or storing the BLOB data in the database. Sure, you can put BLOBs in your database, and you can also deliver pizza with a pregnant camel, but it's not something I would wish on most people.

Why not save BLOBs in the database? Let's look at the facts. The TEXT and IMAGE SQL Server data types are stored on a linked set of 2-KB data pages in SQL Server 6.5. Therefore, they're called *page-based data types*. The Visual Basic documentation also refers to them as *binary large object* (BLOB) or *chunk* data. These types are used to store extremely large columns, such as graphics or "memo"-type data. It's entirely possible to use the Chunk methods to work with page-based OLE objects and graphics, but I think you might find it far easier to use the RemoteData control for this purpose.

NOTE In SQL Server 7.0, the page size has increased to 8 KB and that, coupled with the fact that BLOBs are handled more efficiently, means that BLOBs *might* make more sense in SQL Server 7.0. SQL Server 7.0 also supports longer VarChar and VarBinary types and lets you use string search functions on BLOBs, which might eliminate the need to store BLOBs in the database.

Basically, the RDO interface works the same way that Jet does in this respect—only faster. If and when you store a byte in a BLOB column, SQL Server allocates a 2-KB page to store it on. It keeps using this page until you get up to a little less than 2 KB of data, at which point it allocates another page. It continues to do this as the data is uploaded to the server. Compared to saving a file to disk, this process is extremely inefficient and can take a lot of system resources to process. When it comes time to back up the database (as you do once a week or so), these BLOB pages get saved just like any other page—even though they haven't changed since you put them on the system last spring. This means more tape, longer backup cycles, and sometimes fewer backups. It also means larger transaction logs because the operations used to upload the data from ODBC are logged. In some cases, this means disrupting the normal transaction log cycles to accommodate the BLOB transfers.

When it comes time to fetch the data, you can locate it only by using some fairly crude techniques because you can't simply write code that says *select * From Authors Where MyBlob like '%some string%'*. You can do this with Microsoft Word documents but not with SQL Server BLOB types—at least not without a text-search package. Sure, SQL Server 7.0 provides some search capabilities never offered before. And look at the hoops you have to jump through to deal with the BLOB data types. The Chunk methods are some of the least understood and most finicky around. They're no joy to use, and if you don't play your cards right, they don't return what you expect—at least not quickly. And what about displaying, editing, or manipulating this data? In most cases, the data stored isn't ASCII text at all but complex ActiveX objects or graphics structures that can be viewed only with a control designed specifically for the data type. And how do those controls take the data? Well, if you don't use the RemoteData control, you have to save the data to a file and use a LoadPicture method against the Picture control or save the data to a file and set up an ActiveX link to Microsoft Word or Microsoft Excel (or whatever was used to create the file) and pass the file reference to the link.

So what's the solution? It's become pretty clear to me that BLOB data belongs in files, such as Word DOC files, Microsoft Excel XLS files, or other native format files used to hold the data—not in databases. This means that picture data lives in BMP, GIF, or PCS files in their native formats. But how do you locate and retrieve the data? That's easy—that's what the database is for. When you record the row that would contain the BLOB column, store a pointer to the file instead. You can also store the owner, check-out status, date created, size, type, and anything else that makes sense in the database, where this type of data belongs. You can go so far as to store a set of keywords that *can* be searched with a SELECT statement. Since BLOB data is often read-only, you can store the data anywhere—even on the client's system. Make your clients take out that Doom CD and put in your data CD containing the current edition of your files and images. The database can then fetch pathnames relative to the location of the CD. And what if the files change suddenly? You can load the database with a URL pointing to the new file or image out on the Web. If the files change all the time, simply use the network to download the data. It's not as fast as local disk or CD access, but it's far faster and easier on the network than using the Chunk methods.

When it's time to display the data, you might still have to launch an ActiveX-driven version of Word or another custom application to display the text (unless you can use RTF, in which case the RichText control will do the trick). If you only need to load pictures, simply point to the file with the Picture or Image control (or your favorite alternative) and use the LoadPicture method. My tests show that this technique yields performance at least six times better than when you use BLOB methods. This also means that not all clients need to be connected by means of a LAN to get the retrieval performance they need because the data can be stored locally and retrieved locally on demand. Some very experienced people have commented that "real" BLOB management solutions cache the data using one mechanism or another to improve performance. I suspect that this is true. But this solution seems to add even more complexity and system resource expense to the design.

And now for an opposing point of view. When I expressed my opinions over e-mail, I received a dozen or so replies supporting my position. But one experienced voice said that my approach didn't lead to a bed of roses. To summarize, he said that maintenance, security, error handling, and referential integrity are nightmares when you use the file-based approach—at least for his application. In addition, overall features don't work well because of the synchronization required. When this person's team designed a new system to store its BLOB in the database, all the previous problems were handled. But a few more problems surfaced. In this person's opinion (and I share some but not all of his views), the BLOB-in-the-database approach has the following advantages:

- It's easier to keep data in sync (referential integrity) when you store the BLOB data in the database.

- Error handling and resource management (space) are better with a database than with a database and a file system.

- Database dumps, maintenance of the application data (including BLOB), reporting, and moving data from one source to another are easier from an infrastructure point of view when the BLOB is stored in the image data of the database.

- You don't have overall maintenance requirements for a second storage system (file system), which is big.

- Security, implementation, and maintenance are much better when the BLOB data is stored in the database.

My e-mail correspondent conceded the following points as arguments against storing BLOBs in the database:

- Database size is much bigger with BLOB data stored in the database. Database DBCC, dumps, and other maintenance tasks take more time and effort.

- ODBC doesn't work well, so his team used DBLIB. They gained additional speed by using a bigger packet size (4 KB to 8 KB). The default packet size is 512 bytes.

- Coding in DBLIB is more complex than in DAO.

For performance reasons, his team placed the BLOB (image data) in its own table so that queries searching for information wouldn't be involved in reading or dealing in some other way with the BLOB data. This can also help the backup situation because you can engineer a selective table backup. Only when you want to read, update, or delete the BLOB data do you have to reference the table.

I think that the arguments against my file system are valid for the most part. Although I don't agree with all of them, they do show the complexity of the solutions. For that team's situation, storing BLOBs in the database was more attractive because of the large number and relatively small size of that application's data chunks. The data chunks were usually under 50 KB (but grew to over 20 MB) and averaged 5 KB—and there were bazillions of rows. That application also had no static data.

OK, I'm done. For those of you determined to use the Chunk methods, the following section offers some sample code that should make this daunting task a little easier. But I feel like I'm throwing a can of soda to someone stuck in quicksand.

Using the Chunk Methods to Fetch Page-Based Data

The ColumnSize property of the rdoColumn object returns the actual length of the data in a BLOB column. When you use the ODBC cursor library, this value is always –1, which indicates that the data length isn't available. When you use server-side cursors or the Client Batch cursor library, the ColumnSize property always returns the actual data length of a BLOB column.

To retrieve the data from a BLOB column by using the Chunk methods, you have to use the GetChunk method, specifically, which takes as an argument the number of bytes to retrieve. That way, you can decide how many bytes to buffer per fetch. When you use server-side cursors, you can pass the value of the ColumnSize property as the number of bytes to retrieve to get all the data at once. Since the ColumnSize property isn't available when you use the ODBC cursor library, you should call GetChunk repeatedly until no more data is returned. The following code shows how to do this. First, you create an rdoResultset that contains the primary key and the BLOB column:

```
Dim s As String
Dim sTemp As String
Dim lColSize As Long
lColSize = MyResultset!MyBLOBColumn.ColumnSize
If lColSize = -1 Then
    ' Column size is not available.
    ' Loop getting chunks until no more data.
    sTemp = MyResultset!MyBLOBColumn.GetChunk(50)
    Do
        s = s & sTemp
        sTemp = MyResultset!MyBLOBColumn.GetChunk(50)
    Loop While Len(sTemp) > 0
Else
```

```
    ' Get all of it.
    If lColSize > 0 Then
        s = MyResultset!MyBLOBColumn.GetChunk(lColSize)
    End If
End If
```

When you use the ODBC cursor library and the BLOB data types, you must also select at least one non-BLOB column in the result set so that the RDO interface can use SQLExtendedFetch to retrieve the data. This is what usually happens anyway, since you need to include a key field in the result set if you want to update the data.

Tips and Techniques for Accessing BLOBs

It's tough to fetch BLOB data using a stored procedure because the ODBC cursor library doesn't bind to the BLOB columns and must know a source table name in order to go back and retrieve the image data when it's requested. Since the source of the query was just a stored procedure call, it has no way of knowing how to do this. You can use the Client Batch cursor library instead—but be sure that the SourceTable is filled in.

One problem remains: when you try the GetChunk method, you might get an "Invalid Cursor Position" error from the ODBC SQL Server driver. This happens because RDO attempts to call SQLSetPos to position to the current row so that the subsequent SQLGetData call will begin reading data from the beginning of the column. (This is in case you called Move 0 and then did a GetChunk loop again, expecting to reset the reading position to the beginning of the column.) Technically, this isn't allowed in ODBC, and the SQL Server driver returns an error. The good news is that this error is totally harmless, and you can ignore it. Since it's just the SQLSetPos call that generated the error, the SQLGetData calls (produced by the GetChunk method) work just fine. All you need to do is trap the error in an On Error trap and call Resume to ignore the error. The error happens only on the first GetChunk call for a row, so it falls into the error trap only once.

If you examine the data buffer returned from GetChunk, Visual Basic attempts to convert it to a string and display it in the debug window or watch window. The result is binary trash. The good news is that you can tell Visual Basic to print that data buffer in hexadecimal instead of as a string so that you can validate that the correct data is coming back—assuming that you know what you're looking for.

The GetChunk and AppendChunk methods work with the LongVarChar and LongVarBinary column types, also known as TEXT and IMAGE columns, in SQL Server. To identify these column types in RDO, use the rdoColumn object's Type property, which returns the constants *rdLongVarChar* or *rdLongVarBinary*, or use the rdoColumn object's ChunkRequired property to determine whether you need to use the Get/AppendChunk methods to access the column.

Random BLOB Musings

I extracted the following items from a popular Web page on handling BLOBs and brought them up to date—code and all.

- When you select a result set containing BLOB columns, you should place the BLOB columns at the end of the select list. If you usually use the Select * from table syntax, you should change this to Select char1, *text1, image1 from table to explicitly reference* each column and place the BLOB columns at the end.

- When you edit a BLOB column using the AppendChunk method, you should select at least one other editable non-BLOB column in your result set and edit the non-BLOB column as well as the BLOB column. If you don't edit the non-BLOB column, RDO won't raise an error but the data might not be saved back to the base table.

- In RDO 1.0, you couldn't bind a BLOB value to a parameter marker because the AppendChunk method wasn't available on the rdoParameter object. If you wanted to pass a BLOB as an input parameter to a stored procedure, you had to use the ODBC handle from RDO to process this through ODBC API calls. In RDO 2.0, AppendChunk is implemented on the rdoColumn and rdoParameter objects.

- If you're trying to display a bitmap image in a Picture control that's stored in a LongVarBinary column, the Picture control in Visual Basic can't accept a stream of bits via Visual Basic code. The only way to place a picture into or get the bits back out of a Picture control through code is by using a disk file. You can also use the RDC and bind the Picture box to the BLOB column. This works well for reads (displaying the Picture), but updates are unstable in Visual Basic 4.0 because of problems in Visual Basic's binding manager. To perform updates, you should use code rather than the Visual Basic 4.0 RemoteData control. The jury is still out on the Visual Basic RemoteData control—it didn't change much for 6.0, and it won't be changed again.

- With the ODBC cursor library, you can't use the GetChunk or AppendChunk methods on a result set returned by a stored procedure because the BLOB data doesn't come across the pipe with the rest of the result set. RDO has to go back and use the SQLGetData or SQLPutData ODBC API functions on the column when you request it with the RDO GetChunk or AppendChunk methods. SQLGetData and SQLPutData both require a reference to a SourceTable. Without a back reference to the original table, refetching data isn't possible.

- If you're using server-side cursors, you can get at your BLOB data. The server-side cursor knows the content of the stored procedure and can thus get at the base table. One limitation is that you can't create a server-side cursor based on a stored procedure that has more than one single SELECT statement in it (a SQL Server restriction), so you probably can't use this as your primary technique.

- If users want to update their BLOB column, they must expose their base tables and create the cursor by using a standard SELECT statement from that base table. This is true even if you're coding directly to ODBC (not an RDO thing) or to DBLIB. If you use Jet, you can't update cursors based on stored procedures because they're always read-only.

A BLOB Example

The following code is divided into three separate procedures: Command1_Click, ColumnToFile, and FileToColumn. The latter two are self-contained procedures that you should be able to paste directly into your code if you're moving BLOB data back and forth from your table to files on disk. Each procedure accepts parameters that can be provided by your application. Form_Load contains the code that makes the connection to your database and creates the table *chunktable* if it doesn't exist; FetchButton_Click calls the ColumnToFile and FileToColumn procedures with the proper parameters.

```
Option Explicit
Dim cn As New rdoConnection
Dim rs As rdoResultset, TempRs As rdoResultset
Dim SQL As String
Dim CurRec As Integer

Private Sub Form_Load()
    cn.Connect = "Driver={SQL Server}; " _
        & " Server=Betav1;Database=pubs;" _
        & " Uid=;Pwd="
    SQL = "Select int1, char1, text1, image1 from chunktable"
    cn.CursorDriver = rdUseServer
    cn.EstablishConnection rdDriverNoPrompt
    On Error Resume Next
    If cn.rdoTables("chunktable").Updatable Then Else
    If Err > 0 Then
        On Error GoTo 0
        Debug.Print "Creating new table..."
        cn.Execute "Create table chunktable " & _
            "(int1 int identity, " & _
            "char1 char(30), text1 text, image1 image)"
        cn.Execute "create unique index int1index on " _
            & " chunktable(int1)"
    End If
End Sub

Private Sub BuildAndSave_Click()
BuildAndSave.Enabled = False
MousePointer = vbHourglass
On Error GoTo 0
Set rs = cn.OpenResultset(Name:=SQL, _
```

(continued)

```
            Type:=rdOpenDynamic, _
            LockType:=rdConcurRowVer)
    If rs.EOF Then
        rs.AddNew
        rs("char1") = Now
        rs.Update
        rs.Requery
    End If
    CurRec = rs("int1")
    rs.Edit
    FileToColumn rs.rdoColumns("text1"), _
        App.Path & "\README.TXT", 102400
    FileToColumn rs.rdoColumns("image1"), _
        App.Path & "\SETUP.BMP", 102400
    rs("char1") = Now
        ' Need to update at least one non-BLOB column
        rs.Update
        FetchButton.Enabled = True
        MousePointer = vbNormal
    End Sub

    Sub FetchButton_Click()
        ' This code gets the column size of each column.
        Dim text1_len As Long, image1_len As Long
        Set rs = cn.OpenResultset(Name:=SQL, _
            Type:=rdOpenDynamic, _
            LockType:=rdConcurRowVer)
        If rs("text1").ColumnSize = -1 Then
            ' The function Datalength is SQL Server-specific,
            ' so you might have to change this for your database.
            SQL = "Select Datalength(text1) As text1_len, " _
                & "Datalength(image1) As image1_len from chunktable " _
                & "Where int1=" & CurRec
            Set TempRs = cn.OpenResultset(Name:=SQL, _
                Type:=rdOpenStatic, _
                LockType:=rdConcurReadOnly)
            text1_len = TempRs("text1_len")
            image1_len = TempRs("image1_len")
            TempRs.Close
        Else
            text1_len = rs("text1").ColumnSize
            image1_len = rs("image1").ColumnSize
        End If
        ColumnToFile rs.rdoColumns("text1"),  _
            & App.Path & "\text1.txt", _
            102400, text1_len
        ColumnToFile rs.rdoColumns("image1"), _
            & App.Path & "\image1.bmp", _
            102400, image1_len
        Set Image1 = LoadPicture(App.Path & "\image1.bmp")
        RichTextBox1.filename = App.Path & "\text1.txt"
        MousePointer = vbNormal
    End Sub

    Sub ColumnToFile(Col As rdoColumn, ByVal DiskFile As String, _
        BlockSize As Long, ColSize As Long)
```

```
        Dim NumBlocks As Integer
        Dim LeftOver As Long
        Dim byteData() As Byte    ' Byte array for LongVarBinary
        Dim strData As String     ' String for LongVarChar
        Dim DestFileNum As Integer, i As Integer
        ' Remove any existing destination file.
        If Len(Dir$(DiskFile)) > 0 Then
            Kill DiskFile
        End If
        DestFileNum = FreeFile
        Open DiskFile For Binary As DestFileNum
        NumBlocks = ColSize \ BlockSize
        LeftOver = ColSize Mod BlockSize
        Select Case Col.Type
        Case rdTypeLONGVARBINARY
            byteData() = Col.GetChunk(LeftOver)
            Put DestFileNum, , byteData()
            For i = 1 To NumBlocks
                byteData() = Col.GetChunk(BlockSize)
                Put DestFileNum, , byteData()
            Next i
        Case rdTypeLONGVARCHAR
            For i = 1 To NumBlocks
                strData = String(BlockSize, 32)
                strData = Col.GetChunk(BlockSize)
                Put DestFileNum, , strData
            Next i
            strData = String(LeftOver, 32)
            strData = Col.GetChunk(LeftOver)
            Put DestFileNum, , strData
        Case Else
            MsgBox "Not a ChunkRequired column."
        End Select
        Close DestFileNum
    End Sub

    Sub FileToColumn(Col As rdoColumn, _
        DiskFile As String, BlockSize As Long)
        ' Moves a disk file to a ChunkRequired column in the table.
        ' A Byte array is used to avoid a Unicode string.
        Dim byteData() As Byte    ' Byte array for LongVarBinary
        Dim strData As String     ' String for LongVarChar
        Dim NumBlocks As Integer
        Dim filelength As Long
        Dim LeftOver As Long
        Dim SourceFile As Integer
        Dim i As Integer
        SourceFile = FreeFile
        Open DiskFile For Binary Access Read As SourceFile
        filelength = LOF(SourceFile) ' Get the length of the file
        If filelength = 0 Then
            Close SourceFile
            MsgBox DiskFile & " empty or not found."
        Else
```

(continued)

```
' Calculate number of blocks to read and leftover bytes.
NumBlocks = filelength \ BlockSize
LeftOver = filelength Mod BlockSize
Col.AppendChunk Null

Select Case Col.Type
Case rdTypeLONGVARCHAR
    ' Read the 'leftover' amount of LONGVARCHAR data.
    strData = String(LeftOver, " ")
    Get SourceFile, , strData
    Col.AppendChunk strData
    strData = String(BlockSize, " ")
    For i = 1 To NumBlocks
        Get SourceFile, , strData
        Col.AppendChunk strData
    Next i
    Close SourceFile
Case rdTypeLONGVARBINARY
    ' Read the leftover amount of LONGVARBINARY data.
    ReDim byteData(LeftOver)
    Get SourceFile, , byteData()
    Col.AppendChunk byteData()
    ReDim byteData(BlockSize)
    For i = 1 To NumBlocks
        Get SourceFile, , byteData()
        Col.AppendChunk byteData()
    Next i
    Close SourceFile
Case Else
    MsgBox "Not a ChunkRequired column."
End Select
    End If
End Sub
```

You must change the Server, Database, UID, and PWD values in the connect string in order to connect to your database.

The code in the FetchButton_Click event expects to find two files, README.TXT and SETUP.BMP, in the current directory. These files are usually in the Windows directory. You can either move these files to your current directory or change the path to match another bitmap and text file on your hard drive.

Face to Face with the rdoTable Object

OK, I promised, and here we are—staring down that rare and endangered wild thing known as the rdoTable object. To turn on this object, you simply access it in code:

```
Dim tb As rdoTable
For Each tb In rdoTables
    ListOfTables.AddItem tb.Name
Next
```

The rdoTables collection isn't automatically populated because doing so is very expensive, especially since this functionality is almost never used. Therefore, until you reference the rdoTables collection and the rdoTable object, they are not populated. Indirect or internal references can't succeed until the rdoTables collection is populated.

> **NOTE** Few of my production programs examine the schema of a working database, but when I do need to take a drive through the schema, I used to just run SQL Enterprise Manager from my workstation. Now I can simply use the DataView Window and the integrated Visual Database Tools in Visual Basic. Unless you choose one of these tools, you must resort to TSQL statements, executed with the Execute method. I think I would rather hit myself in the head with a board.

Once the rdoTables collection is populated with all the tables in the current SQL Server database, you can examine the column properties of any table. (But you can't change any of these properties—they're all read-only.)

Here's how to get acquainted with this exotic beast:

1. Use the OpenResultset method to create an rdoResultset object based on all the rows of the base table. When you do this, you essentially execute a SELECT FROM *table* query. (If the table has more than a few hundred rows, this is a great way to bring your workstation to its knees.)

2. Use the Name property to determine the name of the table or view.

3. Use the Type property to determine the type of table. The ODBC data source driver determines the supported table type as a string. With SQL Server, the possible settings for the rdoTable Type property are Table, View, System Table, Global Temporary, Local Temporary, Alias, and Synonym. Somewhere along the line, however, it seems that the SQL Server system tables were ignored—they don't appear in the list of known tables. All I've seen are Table-type and View-type tables.

> **NOTE** The documentation says to use the RowCount property to determine the number of rows in a table or view. It also says that for base tables the RowCount property contains the number of rows in the specified database table. That's true for Jet tables, but you can't determine the number of rows in a SQL Server table unless you run an all-inclusive query against it. Therefore, RowCount for an rdoTable object is 0 until you create an rdoResultset against the rdoTable object. What else does the documentation say? It says that you can use the Updatable property to determine whether a table supports changes to its data. Wrong again: this is an rdoTable object, so the Updatable property is always False.

I wrote a little program to verify these factoids. Let's take a ride through the code and pick up the nuances along the way. I use a common grid to show the column properties, so I set up the following code in Form_Load.

```
Option Explicit
Dim en As rdoEnvironment, cn As rdoConnection
Dim cl As rdoColumn, tb As rdoTable
Dim i As Integer

Private Sub Form_Load()
Grid1.Row = 0
For i = 0 To 8
    Grid1.Cols = i + 1
    Grid1.Col = i
    Grid1.ColWidth(i) = TextWidth("MMMMMMyy")
    Grid1 = Choose(i + 1, "Type", "Size", "AllowZeroLength", _
        "Attributes", "ChunkRequired", "OrdinalPosition", _
        "Required", "SourceColumn", "SourceTable")
Next i
End Sub
```

Now we're ready to open up the connection to our test database. It has about a dozen tables, so I can show plenty of examples. I populate a list box with all the table names, as shown below. (Note that the system tables aren't included.)

```
Private Sub Populate_Click()
Set en = rdoEngine.rdoEnvironments(0)
Set cn = en.OpenConnection(dsname:="BIBLIO", Connect:="uid=;pwd=")
For Each tb In cn.rdoTables
    TableList.AddItem tb.Name
Next
TableList.ListIndex = 0
End Sub
```

To discover the details about a particular table, we'll grab the table by name. You must dereference the TableList object to get its Text property. Next, we'll create a list of columns for the table:

```
Private Sub TableList_Click()
ColumnList.Clear
Set tb = cn.rdoTables((TableList))
Rows = tb.RowCount
Updatable = tb.Updatable
TType = tb.Type
For Each cl In tb.rdoColumns
    ColumnList.AddItem cl.Name
Next
ColumnList.ListIndex = 0
End Sub
```

Once we select a column, we can simply enumerate all the properties and dump the value returned into the DBGrid. Notice the dereferencing when we choose a column name on the basis of the chosen ColumnList value:

```
Private Sub ColumnList_Click()
Grid1.Row = 1
Set cl = tb.rdoColumns((ColumnList))
For i = 0 To Grid1.Cols - 1
    Grid1.Row = 1
```

```
    Grid1.Col = i
    Select Case i
        Case 0: Grid1 = cl.Type
        Case 1: Grid1 = cl.Size
        Case 2: Grid1 = cl.AllowZeroLength
        Case 3: Grid1 = cl.Attributes
        Case 4: Grid1 = cl.ChunkRequired
        Case 5: Grid1 = cl.OrdinalPosition
        Case 6: Grid1 = cl.Required
        Case 7: Grid1 = cl.SourceColumn
        Case 8: Grid1 = cl.SourceTable
    End Select
Next
End Sub
```

Assigning Column Data to Visual Basic Controls

In Visual Basic 3.0, taking data from Recordset fields was fairly straightforward. In later versions, the task became somewhat more difficult because there are so many more field types to deal with. Here are a few suggestions that might save you some time late at night:

- When you're working with TextBox controls, simply assign the value returned from the rdoResultset to the Text property. This is the default property of the control.

- When you work with the Microsoft Rich TextBox control, you can do the same thing, but in this case the default property is the RTFText property, which is very different from the Text property. Be sure to choose the right property when you want to assign and extract data from the control.

- When you work with a control that is associated with a special-format column, be aware of the format as you attempt to update. If there's a problem with the data content of the control, the Update method fails—usually with Error 40060.

- You handle Picture and Image controls with the RDO interface in virtually the same way that you handle them with the Jet/DAO method. Basically, the controls' data must be loaded by means of the LoadPicture method.

- Remember to concatenate an empty string to a column that might contain a Null value, like this:

```
A = "" & MyRS(0)
```

26

Maintaining Data with the RDO Interface

Options for Modifying Data

Adding Data

Updating Data

Deleting Data

When Things Go Wrong

From time to time, almost any database system has to have rows added, updated, or deleted—that is, the database needs to be maintained. You already know, after reading the previous chapters in Part IV, how to retrieve data. This chapter is about using the Remote Data Objects (RDO) interface to maintain data.

Options for Modifying Data

When you use the RDO interface (as when you use the Microsoft Jet database engine), you have basically three choices for modifying the database:

- You can use a read-write cursor (if you want to modify base tables directly).

- You can use the Execute method to run an INSERT, DELETE, or UPDATE query.

- You can execute a procedure using an rdoQuery or a UserConnection object.

The problem with cursors is that they are inherently evil—especially for developers who are trying to create scalable applications. Unless you're very clever, you can't use persistent cursors for server-side components because they require your remote component to maintain a state that can lock out other users. You can use cursors for client-side data access because it's fairly easy to maintain state, but they still lock out other users who want to share the database. Sure, you can create cursors that don't lock down lots of rows or pages, and this is what you have to do if you take this approach. But it's easy to get carried away and create broad-scope cursors that lock entire regions of the database—for indeterminate lengths of time. Stateless update strategies are the most scalable. That is, the update operation doesn't depend on the row being locked while the application decides what to do, and it doesn't have to "remember" which rows were being worked on. That's where the Execute method, the rdoQuery, or the UserConnection designer–generated rdoQuery comes in handy.

As we migrate to server-side components, we'll eventually move to state-less techniques that depend not on cursors but on strategies that depend on more robust contingency handlers, which deal with the realities of heavily contested database resources. ActiveX Data Objects (ADO) takes us closer toward that reality because it implements increasingly sophisticated server-side functionality to make this type of architecture easier to implement and more efficient.

NOTE The RDO interface supports only three basic methods for modifying data in the database, but you should consider several others as well. For example, when data must be imported into or exported from the database, consider using the SQL Transfer Manager or BCP. And don't forget about the RemoteData control (the topic of the next chapter).

Read-Write Cursors

Let's assume that you're working with a more traditional two-tiered client application. If you decide on an RDO cursor, you must choose a cursor driver, a cursor type, and a locking mechanism that can yield a read-write rdoResultset cursor against a single table. This cursor must also still meet your requirements for performance and the user interface. Remember that the RDO interface (ODBC) can't update result sets generated from joined tables, views, or stored procedures. Therefore, you often have to execute several update operations if more than one table is involved in the change.

NOTE As Microsoft Visual Basic matures, it seems to be gaining power and features exponentially. Many of the more mature techniques described here are for two-tiered applications. While this is a viable architecture, the techniques don't always play well in three-tiered distributed component architectures.

Once your rdoResultset cursor is open, you can use the AddNew method against it. At this point, you shouldn't expect an error unless you forgot to check the Updatable property: if it returns False, go back and try again; you probably did something wrong. Most likely you forgot to add a primary key to the underlying table. The rdoResultset object's AddNew method does two things:

- It saves the current-row pointer so that RDO can reposition to the current row's bookmark.

- It creates a new, empty row and provides addressability to it through your rdoResultset object.

After you execute the AddNew method, all you have to do is assign new values to each of the columns in the row. At a minimum, you must provide data for all columns that can't accept Null values and have no defaults. Unless you're adding rows to a table that uses the new Identity column, you must provide a unique key value for the index columns. If the size of the column is beyond the BindThreshold value, you must use the AppendChunk method to add data to binary large object (BLOB) data columns.

> **NOTE** The RDO interface doesn't automatically fill in default values the way Jet does. Microsoft SQL Server can do this for you if your database system is set up to include defaults.

When the row is ready to save, use the rdoResultset object's Update method to save the row in the database. Errors can and do occur at this point. (See the "When Things Go Wrong" section on page 536.) So be careful. After the insertion, don't expect the new row to suddenly become a member of your rdoResultset object. Some ODBC cursors support this feature, but most don't. If you need to ensure that the new row is a member of the rdoResultset, use the Refresh method to repopulate the result set. Of course, since your result set contains less than a dozen rows, this isn't a real problem. But if you ignored my advice and created a humongous cursor, you now have to sit in your own cold bathwater.

The Execute Method

Almost every RDO-based application will end up using a UserConnection object or an Execute method for most, if not all, operations that involve data modification. Adding records with this technique is fairly simple. Basically, you create a TSQL INSERT statement containing the data for the new row, place it in a string, and execute it with the Execute method. Easier yet, since rdoQuery objects are exposed as methods on the rdoConnection object, you can simply execute the query by name. If you use either method against an rdoQuery, you can examine the RowsAffected property after the insertion to verify that the operation has taken place. You can use this technique to add more than one row at a time, and it can affect several tables in a single operation. You can also include TSQL transaction processing around the multiple-statement operation to maintain referential integrity. The operation might include DELETE or UPDATE statements as well, all bound together with BEGIN TRANSACTION and COMMIT TRANSACTION TSQL statements. You can write a stored procedure to do all of this and simply pass the new columns as parameters. You can also use the UserConnection object to create an "UpdateMyRow" method, which is fairly easy to implement. In any case, you must be prepared to roll back partially completed operations—especially when more than one table is involved. Of course, that's where Microsoft Transaction Server (MTS) comes in handy. It can handle all of these operations for you—automatically.

> **TIP** No, I don't recommend embedding transaction logic in your code. You should relegate this logic to stored procedures or, better yet, to MTS components.

Adding Data

When you want to add data to the database, keep these questions in mind:

CAUTION
When you assign new values to columns after using the AddNew method, watch out for formatting errors, such as improper date formatting and string handling.

- **Are you adding a row that other users might also be trying to add?** Be prepared for unique key violations as other users add rows to the same tables. To avoid this, have SQL Server build an Identity column for you.

- **Do you have read-write access to the base table(s)?** You need permission on at least one SQL Server database, not to mention permission to log on to the server itself. For example, your system administrator or database owner (DBO) must grant you or your logon group Execute permission on any stored procedures or updateable views or on the underlying tables.

- **Do you have to use a stored procedure to make the changes?** If so, do you have permission to use this procedure? It's entirely possible to have access to stored procedures but not to the underlying tables.

- **Are you prepared for errors, including those that might be generated by SQL Server rules and triggers?** When you add records, a variety of things can go wrong. Your code had best be ready.

- **Does the new record meet all the criteria set up for referential integrity, business rules, and validation of data columns?** Have you already edited the data? Preediting the data reduces (but doesn't eliminate) the chance that one or more fields will fail column or row validation.

- **Are you prepared for duplicate-row errors?** Most relational tables require unique row identifiers, and these are often enforced by SQL Server–unique indexes. Are you generating the primary key or are you using an automated mechanism that eliminates this collision problem?

Updating Data

For update operations, you should ask yourself the same questions as for adding data. You update existing data in much the same way that you add data, with a number of additional considerations.

TIP Don't update the primary key. This is not an "update," it's a "delete-insert." If you've built an updateable cursor, ODBC will get thoroughly confused if you try to change the pointer that it's using to reference the row.

Updating is a challenge in itself. When you add rows, you aren't nearly as concerned with having to block other users as you are when you're making changes to data that others are working with. You might already have a copy of the row to be changed on your workstation, or you could be making a blind update. If you have a copy of the row, it's probably been sitting on the screen for some time, so the data is probably growing stale. As other users modify the rows in the database, it's likely that some other user will change or delete the row you're working on. And don't forget about the possibility that a row or page you're using is in contention. In any case, you need to have error handlers in place that are prepared for more problems than you'll have when you're adding rows.

Any update operation has to deal with three versions of the row:

- The row as read from the database, before the user changed it

- The row as modified by the user (what you tried to send as the new row)

- The row as modified by some other user whose changes were completed first

Each version of the row plays a part in the locking mechanism you choose and in the decision you make when you discover that an update has failed. As you saw in Chapter 23, the RDO interface supports two types of optimistic locking (rdConcurValues and rdConcurRowver) as well as one type of pessimistic locking (rdConcurLock), with rdConcurReadOnly as the default. But in most cases, pessimistic locking is neither practical nor prudent.

The first question you have to ask is, "What should I do with the changes my user has made?" If you think your user will have to choose among the three versions of the row, you must program a mechanism for reviewing changes made (or proposed) by other users. And while the user ponders this decision, other changes to version 3 of the row might be under way, which compounds the problem. One approach might be to change locking schemes. You have basically the same choices when you're updating existing data that you do when you're adding data: using a read-write cursor, an rdoQuery object method, or the Execute method. That is, unless you decide to use server-side components such as stored procedures or distributed components to perform the operations. For systems that have to scale beyond a few dozen users, this choice seems to be the most reasonable.

Positioning the Current-Row Pointer Post Update

Keep in mind that after you call the Update method on an updateable cursor, RDO—and Data Access Objects (DAO), which works in the same way—repositions to the row you were on before the AddNew method was called. RDO does this mostly because this is how DAO handles it, and the RDO team wanted to follow the lead of DAO. It also makes sense, when you think about it—newly added records are appended to the result set, and it would be disconcerting to lose the user's current position in the result set and just leave him hanging out at the end. To provide an easy way to jump back to the newly added row, both DAO and RDO have the LastModified property, which is a bookmark. You can use it to jump back to the last modified row in the result set.

Updating with a Read-Only Cursor

You can choose from a number of ways to update database rows with RDO 2.0. It's nice if you know the key of the row to update, although in many cases you don't have access to the tables at all, so you can't depend on updateable cursors or even UPDATE TSQL statements. You *should* have access to stored procedures or remote business objects that not only know how to perform the updates but also have permission to do so. RDO 2.0 makes this easier than ever because it implements the WillUpdateRows event. This event fires whenever the Update method is executed, which gives you the opportunity to trap the operation and issue your own update operations. At this point, you can execute one or more stored procedures, call a business object or two, or do anything else that the situation demands.

This is even easier in Visual Basic 6.0 now that the Data Object Wizard helps you create procedure-based query/update classes.

You can still update rows directly using RDO. If you choose an rdoResultset to locate the row you want to change, follow these steps:

1. Use the rdoResultset method to position the current-row pointer to the row to be changed. This becomes version 1 of the row.

2. Execute the Edit method. If you're using optimistic locking, don't expect an error at this point. If you're using pessimistic locking, you might be denied exclusive access to the page containing the target row. If so, you must trap the resulting error and try again later.

3. When the Edit method succeeds, post your changes to the affected columns. This becomes version 2 of the row. Be sure to follow the formatting rules. If you change the primary key, you might set off a variety of conditions, including the same kinds of errors that can be generated when you add a new row.

4. When the changes are complete, use the Update method. This submits version 2 to the server. If you selected optimistic locking, you'll now discover whether version 2 of the row matches version 1. If this test fails, you must decide how to deal with the updated version 3 as read back from the server. If you selected pessimistic locking, your update should succeed without problems—but you'll rarely use pessimistic locking.

CAUTION

Never permit your user to provide data at this stage: every instant of waiting, from the time version 1 of the row is read to the time the update is completed, increases the chances of an error.

When the Update succeeds, the page containing the row is unlocked and released to all the other users who are attempting to read or write to rows on the page. If you move your cursor's current-row pointer to another row before using the Update method, any changes are lost. You can also abandon an edit and refresh the current row by using the Move method with a 0 argument or by using the CancelUpdate method. After a successful edit, the current-row pointer is positioned to the row that was modified—and that could be at the end of the rdoResultset cursor. To revisit the row that was just changed, use the bookmark provided in the LastModified property. If you use the BeginTrans method before beginning your data alterations, any changes are deferred until you use the CommitTrans method to save the changes or the RollbackTrans method to discard them.

Updating with the Execute Method

Another approach is to create an UPDATE statement in TSQL and use the Execute method. As when you add rows, you can perform several related operations at once.

TIP As a general rule, don't update columns that haven't changed because this can set off triggers that don't need to be executed.

The Microsoft Consulting Services developers who created the RDO interface have suggested a technique for making update or insert operations more efficient: using an rdoQuery object to perform repeated updates. You set up a TSQL update statement only once, passing the column data and WHERE clause qualifier in as parameters. You can then use the rdoQuery repeatedly and gain significant performance benefits. For this chapter, I wrote sample code that uses this technique in two ways. The first is the old way, in which we create an rdoQuery object against the rdoConnection object. The second is the new way, in which I simply put the SQL UPDATE statement in a UserConnection object and execute the query as a method—passing the parameters as arguments to the method.

The following first section of code sets up both techniques. We instantiate the UserConnection object and the rdoQuery and rdoConnection objects. Notice that the rdoQuery object is set up to contain a hard-coded query. Consider what would have to be done to this code if the database schema changes.

```
Dim Uc As New UserConnection1
Dim Qy As New rdoQuery
Dim Cn As New rdoConnection

Private Sub Form_Load()
Uc.EstablishConnection
Cn.Connect = "uid=;pwd=;dsn=biblio;database=biblio"
Cn.EstablishConnection rdDriverNoPrompt
Qy.Name = "UpdateTitles"
Set Qy.ActiveConnection = Cn
Qy.SQL = "Update Titles Set " _
    & " PubID = ? ," _
    & " Description = ?, " _
    & " Year_Published = ?," _
    & " Notes = ?" _
    & " Where ISBN = ? "
Qy.rdoParameters(0).Name = "PubID"
End Sub
```

Now we're ready to try the old way. We have to set up each of the rdoParameter objects to pass in the query parameters one by one and then execute the query. Of course, you'd probably pass in the parameters from user-filled-in controls instead of hard-coding the parameters. Notice that we can reference the first parameter by name because we named it when we built the query.

```
Private Sub UpdateTitlesButton_Click()
With Cn.rdoQueries!UpdateTitles
    .rdoParameters!PubID = 264        ' PubID
    .rdoParameters(1) = "Description"
    .rdoParameters(2) = 1997
    .rdoParameters(3) = "Some notes"
    .rdoParameters(4) = "1-55615-906-4" ' ISBN
    .Execute
End With
End Sub
```

Compare the old way I just showed you with the following code. We can replace eight lines of code with one line that performs the same ODBC and SQL Server operations:

```
Private Sub Query1Button_Click()
Uc.Query1 264, "Description", 1997, "Some notes", "1-55615-906-4"
End Sub
```

> **NOTE** This sample code is on the book's companion CD as "Update Test."

You can use these same strategies to execute stored procedures that do the updating for you. In many cases, it's the only way you can update data in a secure database. It's also an easy way to set up an update or insert operation that affects more than one table.

If you use the UserConnection designer, the technique is similar. However, the code needed to set up the connection and the query are handled for you at design time.

Deleting Data

Deleting rows isn't nearly as difficult as adding or updating them: either a delete operation completes or it doesn't. It's still possible to time out while you're trying to delete a row on a locked page, but you shouldn't have much trouble setting up an error handler to deal with the contingencies.

As before, you have the same choices: a read-only cursor or the Execute method. A cursor can delete only the current row in the rdoResultset, but the Execute method can execute a SQL query to delete one row or a whole set of rows. It can also simply truncate the entire table, stripping out all the data rows—or just drop the table. There are only a few real concerns:

- **The delete operation might be blocked by someone changing one of the rows on the target row's page.** All you can do is wait and retry—or get out your wire cutters.

- **The delete operation might drop the last row in the rdoResultset.** If this is possible, check for a RowCount of 0 after the Delete method. (I would say check for BOF equal to True and EOF equal to True, but these won't change state until you try to cross the "wall" at the end of the rdoResultset.) Since your deletions affect other users who are sharing these rows, their rdoResultset objects might also turn up empty or they just might not be able to access populated rows.

- **If you attempt an rdoResultset operation after the Delete, first make sure that there is a current row.** Otherwise, you might trip a trappable error.

- **Be prepared for trigger violations.** For example, you might violate one or more referential integrity constraints if you delete a foreign-key row. If this happens, you have to make a decision: Should the rows using foreign keys be updated? Deleted? Or should you just ignore the problem? (If you do, there goes your database's referential integrity.) Actually, SQL Server won't let you "ignore" this problem—it won't let you break established referential integrity criteria. In these cases SQL Server rolls back the operation and plops an error in your lap.

When Things Go Wrong

As errors are generated, they're placed in the rdoErrors collection. You can examine the individual members of the rdoErrors collection for details on what caused an error. Visual Basic also produces a trappable error whenever an error occurs. In your On Error handler, you can examine the rdoErrors collection and determine what action to take. I'd tell you to change the threshold of severity for tripping a fatal error—by setting the rdoDefaultErrorThreshold or the ErrorThreshold properties—but this has never worked right.

NOTE Informational messages returned from the data source don't trigger trappable errors, but these messages still appear in the rdoErrors collection. (You can use the Clear method to clear the rdoErrors collection manually.) They do trigger the InfoMessage event, though.

At any rate, your code is bound to encounter problems from time to time. For example, you should expect problems if you execute the Update method after using the Edit or AddNew methods. You can also get an error when the

ODBC Driver Manager is used to carry out an RDO request. Make sure you're prepared for the laundry list of errors that can occur in the following situations:

- **An added or updated row violates one of the database's validation rules.** You didn't follow the formatting requirements closely enough, or they changed since you last compiled your program. The error message that SQL Server generates is clear about which rule and column are affected. And note that the error generated might not be in the rdoErrors(0) collection; it might be in rdoErrors(1) or higher. (See the "Creating a Virtual Application" section on page 130 in Chapter 5.)

- **An added or updated row violates the unique key established for the row.** This problem can crop up when another user adds a row that matches your self-generated key and that user's row arrives before your record is added. When you generate your own keys, you must include transaction processing that prevents this type of failure.

- **The table's Insert trigger finds an error and rolls back the transaction.** Such an error might involve referential integrity or business rules, among other things. The Insert trigger might also have issued a RAISERROR message, which should show up in the rdoErrors collection.

- **One or more database rows or pages are locked.** When this happens, your operation hangs until the QueryTimeout period elapses. Your only recourse is to retry or abandon the operation. Consider that the operation locking the row and preventing the update might be your own code.

- **The SQL server times out.** This can happen because your QueryTimeout value isn't high enough to account for network traffic, periodic maintenance, or other conditions that slow the server down. The server might also be broken or up to its armpits in somebody else's tough query. Just retry your operation and hope for the best—or find the guy with the tough query and cut his LAN cable.

TIP If you let your SQL Server hard disks power down after a while, your connections or queries might time out from time to time. It can take 15 seconds or longer to get the hard disks back up to speed.

- **The SQL server enfolds your operation in a deadly embrace.** In these gruesome circumstances, you must reevaluate your sequence of operations to avoid this in the future. (See the "Distributed engine performance" section on page 105 in Chapter 4 if you're lucky enough not to know what a deadly embrace is.)

- **A connection error or other modal error brings the interface down.** Or maybe this time you're the one whose LAN cable got cut.

NOTE Any application that expects to be taken seriously should include handlers for a variety of errors as well as contingency plans for dealing with them. And try not to show the user raw error messages generated from the server or ODBC drivers; the user shouldn't be bothered with the gritty details. Your application should simply decide what it needs to do and then do it—quickly, quietly, and efficiently.

27

Using the RemoteData Control

What's Different About the RemoteData Control?

RemoteData Control Properties

RemoteData Control Methods and Events

Setting Up Bound Controls

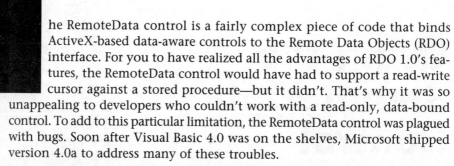

he RemoteData control is a fairly complex piece of code that binds ActiveX-based data-aware controls to the Remote Data Objects (RDO) interface. For you to have realized all the advantages of RDO 1.0's features, the RemoteData control would have had to support a read-write cursor against a stored procedure—but it didn't. That's why it was so unappealing to developers who couldn't work with a read-only, data-bound control. To add to this particular limitation, the RemoteData control was plagued with bugs. Soon after Visual Basic 4.0 was on the shelves, Microsoft shipped version 4.0a to address many of these troubles.

Microsoft Visual Basic 5.0 and RDO 2.0 brought new versions of the RemoteData control, but possibly more important, the Data control can use both Jet and ODBCDirect. More important still, ActiveX Data Objects (ADO) and the new ADO Data control in Visual Basic 6.0 promise a much more reasonable way to access data from remote data components. When you consider that bound controls have become considerably more sophisticated, the ADO Data control and ADO seem even more attractive. Visual Basic 5.0 supported the DataBindings collection, which let you choose not one but several columns of an rdoResultset to bind to. If you add to that the ability to roll your own bound controls or make your own ActiveX controls data aware, the rationale behind using a "Data Access" control becomes clearer.

Visual Basic 6.0 hasn't changed or improved the RDO RemoteData control. Except for some bug fixes, very little work has been done on this control. However, it now places a lot of emphasis on creating your own data source controls either in code or using a number of wizards and designers. We'll discuss binding later in the book and spend a lot of time on the support tools that leverage binding in a whole new way.

Don't get me wrong: some applications can gain from the quick development paradigm offered by the RemoteData control. For example, if you have to work with graphics or ActiveX objects, the RemoteData control solves a few complex problems that really didn't have other solutions—until Visual Basic 6.0.

Let's look at some potential uses for this control, with SQL Server systems in mind—that is, SQL Server systems that restrict access to data through stored procedures for queries and updates. Here is some of what you can do with the RemoteData control:

- **Fill a DBList control with all valid state codes**   The user can choose from this list instead of entering an incorrect code. The list of valid states hasn't changed since 1959—it's pretty well set. Anyway, you don't need more than about three lines of code to fill the DBList control, so the RemoteData control is overkill for a static list.

- **Fill a DBCombo control with a selected set of suppliers on the basis of a limited-scope query**   Users choose from this list when they want vendors of particular parts. But why use the RemoteData control? You don't need to update the list, and even if you did, you'd do it on a form that exposes the whole row and perhaps more. Again, the updating features of the RemoteData control aren't needed.

- **Bind a set of TextBox controls to the columns in a limited-scope result set**   This seems like a reasonable thing to do. However, you still have to validate the data being sent from the control to the database, and you don't save much with a read-only result set. The RemoteData control does fill the bound controls for you, but you still have to use your custom stored procedure to update the data. If you were to use a custom stored procedure to save these rows in a read-write temporary table uploaded to the main database, this mechanism might have some possibilities. This is where the ADO-based Data Object Wizard comes in handy; it was designed specifically for this paradigm. (See Chapter 38 for more on the Data Object Wizard.)

- **Display the picture of a selected employee on the basis of a one-row query**   This is more like it. If you don't change the picture too often, the RemoteData control can make this kind of display easy. Generally, I don't recommend putting binary large object (BLOB) data into the database. In this case, you don't need the RemoteData control to fetch or update the data.

The ODBCDirect interface or the ADO Data control might be a better alternative for developers who require access to data-aware bound controls. The RemoteData control is still totally unproven as far as I'm concerned. Until it has shown a lot more reliability than in the past, I can't, in all good conscience, endorse it.

As you can see, not many problems cry out for the RemoteData control (or the Data control either, for that matter). But let's take a closer look at this control and how it's implemented. Who knows, you might find a use for it after all.

What's Different About the RemoteData Control?

The absence of the Microsoft Jet database engine is the biggest difference between the RemoteData control and the Data control. (However, now that the Data control can use ODBCDirect and a whole new data source control and data binding paradigm in Visual Basic 6.0, the RemoteData control's singular mission is really clouded with competition.) The RemoteData control exposes a number of familiar properties as well as some properties that are unique when compared to the Data control when used with Jet. In virtually all cases, these properties work differently from the corresponding Data control properties, so you have to pay attention to how you implement the RemoteData control. The Data control, when used with ODBCDirect, does incorporate many of the same interfaces (although not nearly all), which makes it easier to use with RDO.

> **NOTE** With the RemoteData control, you can open a cursor against a stored procedure but you can't do an update. It's a stretch to think of how read-only data-bound controls can help in many SQL Server situations that depend on stored procedures. If your system administrator allows direct access to base tables, you can make better use of the RemoteData control. But it would be a shame to create applications that are dependent on this functionality only to have to dump it when a new system administrator restricts access.

Table 27-1 shows the data-related properties for the RemoteData control and the Data control, when used with ODBCDirect and Jet. Those that are virtually identical in purpose and functionality are marked with an asterisk in the column labeled "Notes." Most of the data access properties of the RemoteData control simply expose arguments of the underlying RDO methods and object properties. By the way, activating the ODBCDirect capabilities of the Data control is easy—you simply set the DefaultType property to 1-Use ODBC.

Table 27-1
The RemoteData Control and Data Control Properties

RemoteData Control	Data Control with ODBCDirect	Data Control with Jet	Notes
BOFAction	BOFAction	BOFAction	*
Connection	Database	Database	Both identify the connection.
Connect	Connect	Connect	Connect string. RDO has no *ODBC;* prefix.
CursorDriver	DefaultCursorType	N/A	Jet offers no choice of cursor driver.
DataSourceName	DatabaseName	DatabaseName	Both determine the DSN.
EditMode	EditMode	EditMode	*
Environment	N/A	N/A	Exposes the ODBC hEnv.
EOFAction	EOFAction	EOFAction	Supposed to work the same.
ErrorThreshold	N/A	N/A	No Jet equivalent.
N/A	N/A	Exclusive	Can't open SQL Server in exclusive mode.

RemoteData Control	Data Control with ODBCDirect	Data Control with Jet	Notes
KeysetSize	N/A	N/A	No Jet equivalent.
LoginTimeout	N/A	N/A	Set with Jet DBEngine property.
LogMessages	N/A	N/A	Points to ODBC log file.
MaxRows	N/A	N/A	No Jet equivalent.
Options	Options	Options	Different constants, different options.
Password	N/A	N/A	Set with Jet connect string or Workspace options.
Prompt	N/A	N/A	No Jet equivalent.
QueryTimeout	N/A	N/A	Set with Database option.
ReadOnly	ReadOnly	ReadOnly	*
Resultset	Recordset	Recordset	Different result set objects.
ResultsetType	RecordsetType	RecordsetType	Different cursor types.
RowsetSize	N/A	N/A	No Jet equivalent.
SQL	RecordSource	RecordSource	Very similar.
StillExecuting	N/A	N/A	No Jet equivalent.
Transactions	N/A	N/A	Supports transactions in Jet Recordset Transactions property.
UserName	N/A	N/A	Set with Jet connect string or Workspace options.
Version	N/A	N/A	Returns Jet DBEngine version or RDO database driver version.

RemoteData Control Properties

In the following sections, we'll go over some of the RemoteData control properties listed in Table 27-1 and discuss how to set them.

rdoEnvironment Properties

The Environment property exposes the current rdoEnvironment object. The following rdoEnvironment properties determine how the default rdoEnvironment properties are set:

- The CursorDriver property lets you select the type of cursor driver to use—server-side or ODBC cursor library. This is an rdoEnvironment property.

- The LogMessages property lets you enable ODBC tracing and is ordinarily an rdoQuery property.

- The Version property lets you see the rdoEngine version number. This maps to the rdoEngine Version property.

rdoConnection Properties

The Connection property exposes a new rdoConnection object. The following rdoConnection properties determine how this object is created:

- The Connect property specifies the ODBC connect string. This is an OpenConnection argument.

- The DataSourceName property specifies the name of an ODBC DSN if you're using one. This is the same as the OpenConnection argument.

- The LoginTimeout property specifies the length of time that elapses before the user's logon attempt times out.

- The UserName and Password properties specify the SQL Server logon ID and password, unless they're already in the connect string.

- The Prompt property specifies how the ODBC Driver Manager should prompt you at logon time. This is the same as the OpenConnection argument.

- The ReadOnly property tells the ODBC driver that this is a read-only connection. This is also an OpenConnection argument.

rdoResultset Properties

The Resultset property exposes a new rdoResultset object. Most of the remaining properties determine how the new rdoResultset object is created or managed:

- The BOFAction property determines how the RemoteData control behaves when the BOF property returns True.

    - rdMoveFirst (default): This keeps the first row as the current row.

    - rdBOF: Moving past the beginning of an rdoResultset object triggers the RemoteData control's Validate event on the first row, followed by a Reposition event on the invalid (BOF) row. At this point, the Move Previous button on the RemoteData control is disabled.

- The EditMode property indicates whether the AddNew or Edit methods are active, just as with the Data control.

- The EOFAction property is supposed to help when you're working with empty rdoResultset objects or are near the end of the result set, by automatically switching to AddNew mode when the result set is empty.

    - rdMoveLast (default): This keeps the last row as the current row.

    - rdEOF: Moving past the end of an rdoResultset object triggers the RemoteData control's Validation event on the last row, followed by a Reposition event on the invalid (EOF) row. At this point, the Move Next button on the RemoteData control is disabled.

- rdAddNew: Moving past the last row triggers the RemoteData control's Validation event on the current row, followed by an automatic AddNew, followed by a Reposition event on the new row.

- The MaxRows property maps to the rdoQuery MaxRows property and can set an upper limit on the number of rows retrieved, inserted, deleted, or updated when you're using the control.

- The Options property maps to the OpenResultset options, rdAsyncEnable and rdExecDirect. This means that you can create an rdoResultset object asynchronously. If the rdAsyncEnable bit is on, the RemoteData control creates the rdoResultset object in the background and trips the QueryCompleted event when it's done.

- The QueryTimeout property maps to the rdoQuery QueryTimeout property.

- The ResultsetType property exposes the type of rdoResultset object that is to be created or that has been created. You can open only two of the four types of cursors with the RemoteData control: rdOpenStatic opens a static-type rdoResultset object, and rdOpenKeyset opens a keyset-type rdoResultset object. This property maps to the OpenResultset method's Type argument.

- The RowsetSize property maps to the same property of the rdoQuery object.

- The SQL property maps to the same property of the rdoQuery object. It's used in much the same way as the RecordSource property of the Data control; just don't plan on sticking a table name here unless you are prepared for the consequences.

- The StillExecuting property maps to the same property of the rdoResultset object. It indicates whether the asynchronous query is done.

- The Transactions property has the same function as the Jet Recordset object Transactions property. It simply says that the server supports transactions. In the case of SQL Server, this is always True

RemoteData Control Methods and Events

In addition to the methods exposed by the underlying Connection (rdoConnection), Environment (rdoEnvironment), and Resultset (rdoResultset) objects, the RemoteData control supports a number of methods on its own. These are shown in Table 27-2.

Table 27-2
RemoteData Control Methods

Method	Description
BeginTrans, CommitTrans, RollbackTrans	These transaction methods map to the rdoConnection object.
Cancel	This method stops an asynchronous query.
Refresh	This method rebuilds the rdoResultset object on the basis of current properties.
UpdateControls	This method gets the current row from a RemoteData control's rdoResultset object and displays the data in the bound controls.
UpdateRow	This method saves the current values of bound controls to the database.

The RemoteData control has only three data-oriented events, which are shown in Table 27-3. In general, these events are used to keep invalid data from reaching the SQL Server rules.

Table 27-3
RemoteData Control Events

Events	Notes
QueryCompleted	The asynchronous query has completed. Note that this event is different from the QueryComplete event fired by the rdoConnection.
Reposition	When a RemoteData control is loaded, the first row in the rdoResultset object becomes the current row, causing the Reposition event. Whenever a user clicks any button on the RemoteData control (moving from row to row or using one of the Move methods, such as MoveNext, or any other property or method that changes the current row), the Reposition event occurs after each row becomes current.
Validate	The Validate event occurs *before* the move to a different row. You can use this event to perform calculations based on data in the current row or to change the form in response to data in the current row.

The Validate event is fairly powerful. It can undo what the user has done, preventing data from reaching the SQL server. It occurs before a different row becomes the current row but also before the Update method (except when data is saved with the UpdateRow method) and before a Delete, Unload, or Close operation. In the Validate event procedure, you get a chance to take an action on the basis of whatever criterion you choose. You can execute another query (on another connection) to check out the data, or you can simply perform a reality check on the data.

You have two arguments at your disposal when the Validate event occurs. The first is the Action argument, an integer or constant that initially indicates the operation that is causing the Validate event to occur. For example, if the Action argument is rdActionMoveLast, the operation that tried to move the current-row pointer is the MoveLast method. Once you know what has caused the reposition, you can do something about it; all you have to do before exiting the Validate event procedure is set the Action argument to some other value. For instance, you can change the operation from a MoveNext (rdActionMoveNext) to an AddNew (rdActionAddNew). You can also change the various Move methods and the AddNew method, which can be freely exchanged (any Move into AddNew, AddNew into any Move, and any Move into any other Move). An attempt to change AddNew or one of the Move methods into any others besides these either is ignored or produces a trappable error. You can stop any action by setting the Action argument to rdActionCancel. In this case, no further action takes place, and the current-row pointer remains where it was before the operation that tried to reposition it. You can't use any methods (such as MoveNext) on the underlying rdoResultset object during the Validate event.

The second argument at your disposal in the Validate event procedure is the Save argument. This argument greatly simplifies your validation routine. It's a Boolean expression that specifies whether bound data has changed. Save is True if the bound data has changed since the current row was last repositioned. Save is False if the data has not changed. Although the Save argument initially indicates whether bound data has changed, the argument can be False even if data in the copy buffer actually has changed. If Save is True when the Validate event procedure exits, the Edit and UpdateRow methods are invoked. If you set the Save argument to False, the data isn't written to the SQL server.

Table 27-4 shows the Action arguments to the Validate event. It also shows that for some reason the argument names have changed. I don't know why, but they've been shortened somewhat, so you have to recode. Don't pay any attention to the help topic that lists these—it doesn't match the object description library (ODL), so it's wrong.

CAUTION
The Validate event action constants given in the documentation are *still* wrong. Refer to Table 27-4 or the object browser for the correct values.

Table 27-4
Action Arguments to the Validate Event

RDO 1.0 Constants	New RDO 2.0 Constants	Value	Description
rdDataActionCancel	rdActionCancel	0	Cancels operation when subroutine exits
rdDataActionMoveFirst	rdActionMoveFirst	1	MoveFirst method
rdDataActionMovePrevious	rdActionMovePrevious	2	MovePrevious method
rdDataActionMoveNext	rdActionMoveNext	3	MoveNext method
rdDataActionMoveLast	rdActionMoveLast	4	MoveLast method
rdDataActionAddNew	rdActionAddNew	5	AddNew method
rdDataActionUpdate	rdActionUpdate	6	Update operation (not UpdateRow)
rdDataActionDelete	rdActionDelete	7	Delete method
rdDataActionFind	rdActionFind	8	Not used, but reserved
rdDataActionBookmark	rdActionBookmark	9	Bookmark property set
rdDataActionClose	rdActionClose	10	Close method
rdDataActionUnload	rdActionUnload	11	Form being unloaded
	rdActionUpdateAddNew	12	Update for AddNew
	rdActionUpdateModified	13	Update operation for Edit
	rdActionRefresh	14	Refresh method
	rdActionCancelUpdate	15	CancelUpdate method
	rdActionBeginTransact	16	BeginTrans method
	rdActionCommitTransact	17	CommitTrans method
	rdActionRollbackTransact	18	RollbackTrans method
	rdActionNewParameters	19	New parameters
	rdActionNewSQL	20	New SQL statement

TIP When you need to find out how Visual Basic *really* works, consult the object browser. It's directly connected to the object library's ODL that's used in the development process—so it *has* to be right.

The Validate event occurs even if no changes have been made to data in bound controls and even if no bound controls exist. You can use this event to change values and update data. You can also save data, or you can stop whatever action is causing the Validate event and substitute a different action.

In your code for this event, you can check the data in each bound control where *DataChanged* is True. You can then set *DataChanged* to False to avoid saving that data in the database.

Setting Up Bound Controls

To establish a connection to the SQL server and set up one or more bound controls, follow these steps:

1. Set the Connect property with a valid connect string. If you're used to working with the Data control, be aware that the connect string doesn't have an *ODBC;* prefix and that it doesn't support the Login-Timeout as an argument. If you put the data source name (DSN) here, it doesn't need to go in the DataSourceName property. You can also include the UID (UserName) and PWD (Password) arguments here instead of in their properties. You can still use UID=;PWD=; for Microsoft Windows NT domain security.

2. Set the DataSourceName property (if you didn't include it in the connect string).

3. Set the UserName and Password properties (if they aren't in the connect string).

4. Set the SQL property. This is coded in the same way as the rdoQuery object's SQL property. Generally, this is a SELECT statement that returns the desired columns exposed by the bound controls. Be sure to limit the scope of the result set with a WHERE clause or set the MaxRows property to 100 or so.

The RemoteData control is ready to go. You might want to set some additional properties: CursorDriver or ResultsetType, for example, to return a more suitable cursor, or the Options property, to run in asynchronous mode.

You're now ready to add one or more bound controls to your form. Choose controls that match the data type of the column being queried. For example, choose the RichText control for BLOB text or the TextBox control for Char or VarChar columns. You can also use the MaskedEdit control for numeric types, but the TextBox or Label controls also work for these. If you don't want the user to change the data, simply choose a Label control or set the Locked property on the control to True. Once you choose your control and placed it on the form, follow these two steps to bind it to the RemoteData control:

1. Set the bound control's DataSource property to point to MSRDC1 or to the name of your RemoteData control. Repeat this step for each control bound to the RemoteData control.

2. Set the bound control's DataField property to the name of the rdoResultset column that will be exposed and managed.

That's it. You can select both the DataSource and DataField property values from drop-down lists generated from all available data-like controls and from the rdoColumns collection of the rdoResultset that is created. You do this on the basis of the RemoteData control properties you set.

When the program starts, the RemoteData control and the RDO interface populate the bound controls with column data from the first row (if there are any rows) of the rdoResultset object. The RemoteData control doesn't automatically populate the rdoResultset object unless you set the rdAsyncEnable option bit in the Options property. After the rdoResultset object is fully populated, the QueryCompleted event is fired.

TIP To avoid setting focus to the bound controls if there's no current row, put all bound controls on a frame and disable the frame until the Resultset.RowCount property is greater than 0. If you delete a row, check for no rows and again disable the frame.

CAUTION

The RemoteData control performs all operations on the current row—assuming that there is one. If there are no rows in the result set, there's no current row, so the RemoteData control binds your controls to a non-current row. If you then set focus to one of these bound controls, you get a No Current Row error. (Isn't *that* special!)

Without a RemoteData control, a Data control, or their equivalent, data-aware (bound) controls on a form can't automatically access data. You can put data in bound controls manually and independently of the RemoteData control. You can also perform most remote data access operations with the RemoteData control and not write any code at all. Data-aware controls bound to a RemoteData control automatically display data from one or more columns for the current row—or, in some cases, for a set of rows on either side of the current row.

If the RemoteData control is instructed to move to a different row, all bound controls automatically pass any changes to the RemoteData control so they can be saved to the SQL server. The RemoteData control then moves to the requested row and passes back data from the current row to the bound controls, where it's displayed.

NOTE You can use the mouse to manipulate the RemoteData control, moving from row to row of the result set or to the beginning or end. But you can't use the mouse to move off either end of the rdoResultset object or to set the focus to the RemoteData control.

The RemoteData control automatically handles a number of contingencies, including empty result sets (at least it's *supposed* to do that), adding new rows, editing and updating existing rows, and dealing with some types of errors. In more sophisticated applications, however, you need to trap some error conditions that the RemoteData control can't handle. For example, if the remote server has a problem accessing the data source, if the user doesn't have permission, or if the query can't be executed as coded, a trappable error results. If the error occurs before your application starts or as a result of some internal error, the Error event is triggered.

If you alter the RemoteData control properties after the result set has been created, use the Refresh method to rebuild the underlying rdoResultset object based on the new property settings. You can also use the objects created by the RemoteData control to create additional rdoConnection, rdoResultset, or rdoQuery objects. In addition, you can set the RemoteData control Resultset property to an rdoResultset object created independently of the control. If you do this, the RemoteData control properties are reset based on the new rdoResultset and rdoConnection objects.

The Validate event is triggered before each reposition of the current-row pointer. You can accept the changes made to bound controls, or you can cancel the operation by using the Validate event's Action argument. These work like the Jet Data control's Validate event and Action arguments.

After the RemoteData control starts, the Connect property contains a fully populated connect string. The Resultset property contains the rdoResultset object that has been created, and the ResultsetType property indicates its type. You can also use any of the rdoResultset methods against the RemoteData control's Resultset property, as if it were an rdoResultset object. For example, the MoveNext method of an rdoResultset object moves you from the current row to the next row in the rdoResultset object. To invoke this method with an rdoResultset object created by a RemoteData control, you can use the following code:

```
RemoteData1.Resultset.MoveNext
```

NOTE To execute a parameter query with the RemoteData control, you must create an independent rdoResultset object with an rdoQuery query. Or you can concatenate the query parameters yourself, place the resulting query in the SQL property, and use the Refresh method.

PART V

Using ADO and OLE DB

28

Understanding ADO and OLE DB

Your First Peek at OLE DB

Your First Peek at ADO

O ver the last six years or so, Microsoft has been driven by customer demand to release an ever-expanding series of data access interfaces for Microsoft Visual Basic. Beginning with the Visual Basic Library for Microsoft SQL Server (VBSQL) and ending with the most recent interface to OLE DB, ActiveX Data Objects (ADO), a new data access interface seems to evolve every couple of years. As you've seen in earlier chapters of this guide, each of these interfaces addresses broadening customer requirements to access an ever-increasing number of data sources. As Visual Basic applications have grown more sophisticated and data-centric, so have the data access interfaces. But now, we're faced with a dizzying variety of data sources. Choosing the right one is harder than picking out just the right gift after having overlooked your thirtieth wedding anniversary. Been there, done that. No thanks.

Your First Peek at OLE DB

It's not unusual these days to find businesses that want to access databases, mail, directory, telephony, exotic, legacy data, or Internet content—all from the same application or system. The problem is that each of these data sources has its own proprietary or merely different data access interface—if an interface exists at all. Some require API access, others can be accessed by using one of the more familiar data access paradigms. This cornucopia of data sources means that the skills you've learned to access one type of data don't always apply to other types. It also means that once the data arrives it must be morphed into some common format, or your applications have to adapt themselves to the different structures and data access interface requirements. Figure 28-1 shows an application that needs to draw from a wide variety of data sources—no two of which use the same data access interface.

In this figure, notice that the application uses at least five separate APIs to access the different types of data. Some of the interfaces are Component Object Model (COM) interfaces, and some are not; some expose Automation

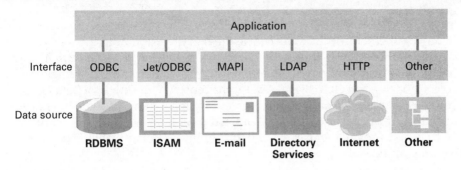

Figure 28-1 *An application drawing from diverse data sources*

(formerly known as OLE Automation), interfaces; and some are procedural. In addition, transactional control doesn't exist, so I can't safely make any changes to all the information within one transaction.

What all of this means is that the developers who write the application will have to become experts in a multitude of data access methods. Is there a better way? Well, one solution is to put all the different types of data into a single relational data store. That is, take the relational data, the ISAM data, e-mail data, directory data, and any other information, including that from the Internet, and move it into a single relational database. This approach solves the problem of having a single API or interface that also gives you transactional control, but it has a number of problems.

First, this all-in-one approach requires moving huge amounts of data out of the original source(s). Second, you typically don't own much of the data you need, such as the wealth of information on the Internet or the data from that rogue accounting department upstairs. Sure, you could get a copy of it today—but that information would soon be stale and have to be refreshed, and you would have to repeat the download or at least keep a replication engine running full time. The third problem with moving the data into a single data store is that tools today don't look for or store data into a single relational data store. E-mail applications, word processors, project management tools, spreadsheets, Web sites, and other tools expect to access their own data stores for their data. You would have to rewrite your tools to access the data in the single data store or duplicate the data to the single data store from where it naturally lives— then you still run into problems with synchronizing the data. A fourth problem is that one size does not fit all. The way that relational databases deal with data is not the best way to deal with *all* types of data. Data (structured, semi-structured, and unstructured) is stored in different containers based on how the data is used, viewed, managed, and accessed. It's like trying to store earth, wind, fire, and love in plastic buckets. Finally, the performance and query requirements are going to differ by data type, depending on what it is you're trying to do. Ah, no. This approach is not your best solution. Go back three squares, and start over. Of course, those of you out there who have tried this approach (at least to some extent) know what I'm talking about.

The "Universal" Solution

In fall 1996, Microsoft introduced the inaugural version of its answer to this complex problem. The strategy has since been dubbed *Universal Data Access*. In theory, this strategy provides access to all types of data through a single data access model—with OLE DB and ADO at the center. With Universal Data Access, you can access data in different data stores through a common set of interfaces, regardless of where the data resides or what form it takes. No, at this point, an OLE DB data provider for earth, wind, fire, or love is not available—but they're working on it.

Implementing this architecture, your Universal Data Access application speaks to a common set of interfaces that generalize the concept of data. Microsoft examined the common characteristics of all types of data, such as how you navigate, represent, bind, use, filter, sort, and share that data with other components. The result is a set of interfaces that developers can use to represent data kept in relational databases, word processors, spreadsheets, and applications of all kinds, and in project and document containers, ISAM, e-mail, and file systems—virtually all forms of information. The data stores simply expose common interfaces—a common data access model—to the data. With this Universal Data Access strategy in place, our application now looks like the model shown in Figure 28-2.

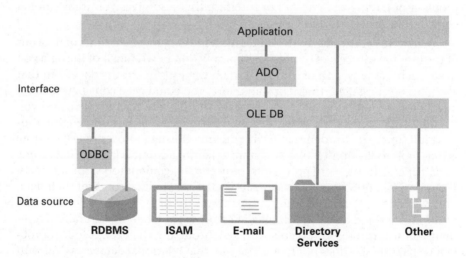

Figure 28-2 *An application using Universal Data Access*

If you want to find out more about the Universal Data Access paradigm, see *http://www.microsoft.com/data/*.

OLE DB as Seen from 10,000 Feet

ADO is the newest data access interface—it is the "Automation server," or object-level interface, to OLE DB, which is a new low-level object-based interface. OLE DB is included in the new bundle of tools dubbed the Microsoft Data

Access Components (MDAC) data access paradigm. Sound familiar? Yes, these are almost the same terms that were used to describe Microsoft's Open Database Connectivity (ODBC) some years back. However, OLE DB's architecture is not restricted to ISAM, Microsoft Jet, or even relational data sources, but is designed to interface with virtually *any* type of data—information—regardless of its format or storage method. OLE DB doesn't really do anything—it defines what its service components and data providers must do and provides standard ways to expose that functionality to developers.

OLE DB also means something else. I grasped the impact of this "something else" only when I tripped over a Web site listing all the new OLE DB service components provided by companies other than Microsoft. This third-party support means that developers will be able to choose from a wide variety of independently created OLE DB service components, ranging from hierarchical data and heterogeneous join engines to interfaces against exotic data sources.

The bad news is that you can't access OLE DB directly from Visual Basic 6.0 because of OLE DB's complex interfaces. The good news is that ADO exposes virtually all of OLE DB's functionality—so Visual Basic developers don't really need to be concerned about that limitation. But the rest of the bad news is that ADO imposes another layer that C++ applications don't require. OLE DB provides data integration over an enterprise's network—from mainframe to desktop—regardless of the data structures involved. Microsoft's ODBC, the reigning industry-standard data access interface, continues to provide a unified way to access *relational* data as part of the OLE DB specification. Over time, OLE DB is expected to replace ODBC as the standard low-level interface to data. Figure 28-3 shows you what the OLE DB architecture looks like.

As you can see in Figure 28-3, OLE DB is no more complex (on the surface) than ODBC. It uses replaceable *service components* and *data providers* to permit access to a variety of data sources through a common API. The service components munge data in a variety of ways. For example, the service components layer is where the various cursor, hierarchy, and heterogeneous join engines run. You can load whatever services you need and leave the rest out of memory until they are needed. The service components also fill in where data providers don't or can't provide needed functionality. You choose the features you need. The data providers know how to access a chosen data source. Data providers can even access ODBC data source drivers. In short, OLE DB's architecture provides a flexible and efficient database interface that offers applications, compilers, and other database providers efficient access to Microsoft and third-party data stores.

NOTE   After I'd finished writing the ADO chapters, the product managers at Microsoft informed me that they had decided to change the name of OLE DB service "providers" to OLE DB service "components." This terminology was changed to reduce the confusion between "data" providers (basically the database interfaces) and the data munging engines such as cursors, filters, and sorters.

I came back to this chapter after having spent about three weeks straight working on OLE DB and ADO code when it suddenly struck me that the specifications were somewhat odd. I got the distinct impression that they were written from the point of view of someone *writing* a service component or data provider—not based on what you, the Visual Basic developer, would want to see when *using* ADO. Over and over, I saw the sentence, "This functionality might not be implemented by your service provider." The spec included numerous references to things the provider "should" implement—leaving lots of flexibility open for interpretation and innovation. That's not all that bad. However, this approach means that developers trying to use, support, or deploy ADO are going to find it far more difficult to gain this "universal" level of compatibility among data sources (er, service components) than ever before. This kind of flexibility breeds incompatibility. In response to this problem, the Microsoft Data Access team is setting up a program to certify OLE DB service components and data providers. Will that make it easier for ADO and Visual Basic developers? We'll see.

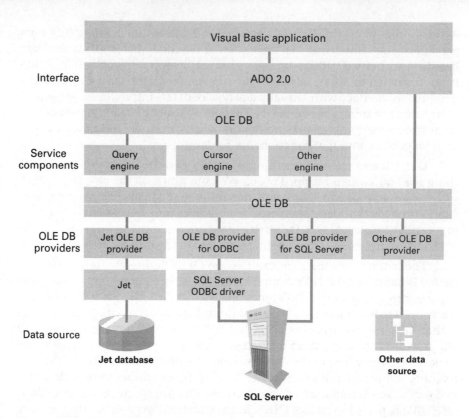

Figure 28-3 *The OLE DB architecture when using Visual Basic*

OLE DB is a freely published specification designed with industry-wide participation through Microsoft's Open Process. OLE DB should provide consistency and interoperability in an enterprise's network, from the mainframe to the desktop and across the Internet. OLE DB is the fundamental COM building block for storing and retrieving data and unifies Microsoft's strategy for information access. It will be used throughout Microsoft's line of applications and data stores. Although OLE DB has been accepted by a large number of third-party ISVs, its overall acceptance in the industry remains to be realized.

OLE DB and ODBC Data Sources

As I said before, OLE DB has been designed to eventually provide superset functionality over ODBC. Will it replace ODBC anytime soon? I doubt it—it's too busy catching up. In addition, there is simply too much Data Access Objects (DAO) and Remote Data Objects (RDO) code interwoven into the fabric of today's data access applications for this shift to happen overnight. ODBC will continue to provide a unified way to access relational data—even as part of the OLE DB specification. OLE DB is currently able to leverage existing ODBC drivers because there is an OLE DB provider for ODBC, which eliminates the need for the intermediary ODBC Driver Manager.

What does OLE DB do that ODBC doesn't? If you're accessing a wide variety of data from a COM environment, OLE DB (via ADO) is your best choice because it goes beyond relational data access methods. And because OLE DB

Unfortunately, the OLE DB provider for ODBC, referred to as "Kagera," makes a number of rather rude assumptions about how one should behave when opening or closing an ADO Recordset. This and other problems make me think that when building ADO applications, developers should probably hasten their migration to "native" OLE DB components rather than depend on ODBC to do the job. We'll discuss these bizarre connection issues later in this section.

uses COM and can be used with Remote Data Services (RDS), OLE DB is better suited for the Internet and can take advantage of features in COM such as cross-process notifications. In addition, OLE DB lowers the barriers for data access more than ODBC does. An ODBC data source must provide functionality equivalent to a SQL query in order to expose its data. In OLE DB, it is possible for simple, non-SQL data sources to expose their data very efficiently without the need for a complex SQL processor.

> **NOTE** OLE DB will be able to use Distributed COM (DCOM) in SQL Server 7.0 to communicate with off-system components and data sources.

Is ODBC 3.0 required for compatibility with OLE DB? Nope. Microsoft supports existing ODBC drivers. However, I've seen some mail that indicates there are compatibility problems with ADO 1.5 and certain ODBC drivers—but I expect this problem is transitory. You'll have a heck of a time keeping ODBC 3.*x* off your systems though. Microsoft Internet Explorer 4.01, Microsoft Office, Visual Basic, and every application from here to Detroit installs it nowadays.

OLE DB and SQL Server

SQL Server 7.0 is adding considerable functionality based on the OLE DB specification, and it is doing so in two ways. First, SQL Server 7.0 exposes a native OLE DB provider for SQL Server (SQLOLEDB.DLL) in addition to its existing ODBC and DB-Library interfaces. Second, SQL Server acts as an OLE DB "consumer" when it needs to get data from other data sources. Why does this make sense, you ask? Well, the SQL Server team wants to provide standard, COM-based access to SQL Server data as well as enable access to more kinds of heterogeneous, possibly distributed, data sources from within the SQL Server query processor. SQL Server will be able to do heterogeneous joins and perform far more complex operations on far more types of data—besides its own native formats. Have you ever wanted to do a join from a Microsoft Access or DB2 table with your SQL Server database and do it on SQL Server? Now you can. Now SQL Server is not only a data provider, but a consumer as well.

Swell, we have yet another "native" interface. Actually, SQL 7.0 no longer considers DB-Library a fully supported native interface. It's supported, just not completely, because it wasn't updated from its SQL 6.5 version.

Architectures That Use OLE DB

One of the nuances that might have escaped the casual reader is the fact that OLE DB and ADO have introduced a number of new architectures. Although these architectures have been evolving over the last year or so, they are new to many of us. In this section, I'm going map these out so that we can see where OLE DB and ADO fit into the bigger picture.

I see the architectures that use OLE DB broken down into several different—but interrelated—approaches to data access. Some architectures involve the Internet, many don't. Some involve "permanent" connections, others connect only as needed. Most involve some amount of server-side code, but not all involve client-side code.

One of the problems we're having to address with diverse systems is called *reach*. A program with reach is designed to run on (or at least be able to send data to) a wide set of platforms. More and more, we're encountering a cacophony of terminals, PCs, browsers, and bottom feeders that are our target client systems. Even when we create an application for a small business, the chances of all the systems being the same are probably 80/20. Pretty good odds. As the business grows, however, the odds of a uniform solution evaporate as other, incompatible clients are brought in. Although Microsoft Windows clients constitute 90-some percent of the clients out there, not all of them are running 32-bit Windows or Microsoft Windows NT—and only about half of them are running Internet Explorer. If you have a completely uniform set of target client systems, count yourself lucky. Take a week off and go to Vegas to cash in on your good fortune. By the time you return, your management will have purchased another company with 50 Atari 800 systems that have to be accessed by your new application. Some companies feel blessed simply if all their client systems run on electricity. Welcome to life in the fast lane.

OK, now that we know why these architectures need to exist, let's see how ADO and OLE DB address the various platforms. To do so, we need to consider what the environments look like. For the purposes of this discussion, I must narrow the focus to architectures that access SQL Server—otherwise, you'd still be reading this chapter when you were supposed to be out Christmas shopping for that perfect end-of-the-millennium gift.

Traditional client/server architecture

We start with our traditional client/server rig, as illustrated in Figure 28-4. We've gone over this setup before in the early chapters, so this review will be brief. In a traditional client/server system, we have a 32-bit Windows client running a Visual Basic application using RDO or ADO. These applications depend on a constantly available "persistent" local area network (LAN) or at least a dial-up Remote Access Service (RAS) connection. We use server-side stored procedures, and we can migrate some of the business logic off of the client and on to the server using rules and triggers.

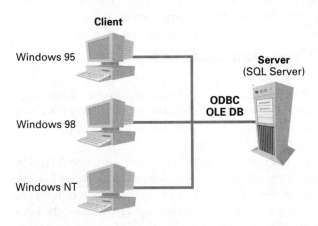

Figure 28-4 *Client/server architecture that uses OLE DB*

OK, what if your customer also has some 16-bit Windows clients? This scenario isn't that atypical, so we need to consider it for this configuration. In this case, you would have to use Visual Basic 3.0 or 4.0 (16 bit) and DAO or VBSQL on the clients. Such a motley system would be possible to implement, but messy and expensive to deploy and support.

Web-based architecture

At this point, you might have considered using Remote Automation for your 16-bit clients and calling remote COM components on a 32-bit server running Microsoft Transaction Server (MTS). But that seems like an awful lot of trouble. So what are your alternatives *now*?

As it turns out, while you went out for lunch this afternoon, your company bought a competitor who didn't make the same design choices you did. This now-defunct company chose to use Netscape for its 16-bit Windows clients and brought over a handful of old Macintosh systems as well. It used to have some Sun boxes, but those were left behind to use as doorstops. So you consider the next alternative: Web-based architecture.

HTML implementation Well, you certainly should entertain a pure HTML solution. This design generates HTML on the host and lets the client choose from static pages, or it supports the generation of dynamic pages based on options or arguments provided by the client. Does choosing an HTML solution mean you have to give up ADO? Hardly. By using ASP pages on IIS, you can still use a pure HTML interface with your clients and keep your ADO code—or at least parts of it.

ASP implementation You can use Microsoft Internet Information Server (IIS) to run ADO code embedded in Visual Basic, Scripting Edition (VBScript) on an Active Server Pages (ASP) page. ASP pages are managed by IIS, which opens the selected page and runs it like an interpreted program—kinda like running Quick Basic by remote control. (You probably run into ASP pages all the time without knowing it. Just look for the ASP extension the next time you use your browser.) If IIS finds embedded VBScript code in the ASP page, it invokes the VBScript interpreter to run it. Depending on your browser's capability, this code can have VBScript and ADO logic that can query a database and generate a Recordset to return to the browser—or it might just return pure HTML. Figure 28-5 shows a sample of this architecture.

RDS implementation ADO really outshines the other alternatives when it comes to working with the Web. The reason ADO is such a brilliant Web interface is that it's capable of generating and managing disconnected (remote) Recordset objects using RDS. RDS is already built into Internet Explorer 4, which makes it fairly easy to use (no need to download more code). Sure, Netscape supports HTML generated by VBScript on ASP pages, but it has none of the client-side RDS functionality. RDS applications embed VBScript code into selected Web pages and draw on considerable client-side functionality to extract data from a remote server.

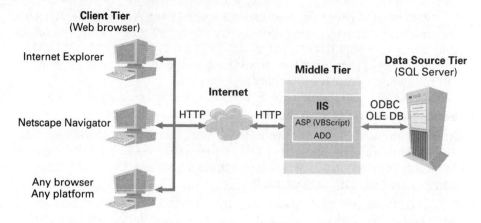

Figure 28-5 *Web-based architecture that uses ASP and OLE DB*

NOTE RDS has now been integrated with ADO to provide data remoting within the same model as ADO. This integration makes it easier to design, code, and deploy both Web-based and LAN-based applications. RDS goes beyond the current generation of Web data access tools by allowing clients to manipulate the data they see.

RDS technology uses both client-side and server-side RDS components to permit your application to run a query on a remote server. You can submit a request, and the client-side RDS components will send the query. The server-side RDS components will request the data from the data source via ADO and OLE DB and return the results to the client. The result set is returned to bound controls (like a grid). You can change the data in (some of) these bound controls, and you can submit updates, which posts changes back to the database. Figure 28-6 shows this process in which the client-side RDS components act like a Web-page-based Data control to connect an OLE DB data source to the client. It does this by sending and receiving HTTP requests and responses over the wire. Internet Explorer 3.0 or 4.0 is required to support RDS. Nope, it's not likely that Netscape will support the RDS technology—unless some government edict makes them. Stranger things have happened.

NOTE Yep, Microsoft renamed Advanced Data Connector (ADC) to Remote Data Services (RDS). Why? BHOM.

WebClass implementation The newest member of the Visual Basic data access team is a technology that permits you to create Visual Basic components that run on the middle tier. These components, called WebClasses, can be debugged interactively, and they can output HTML. This innovation is called *WebClass application* development. As you can see in Figure 28-7, creating a typical WebClass application follows the traditional form-based development paradigm you're used to.

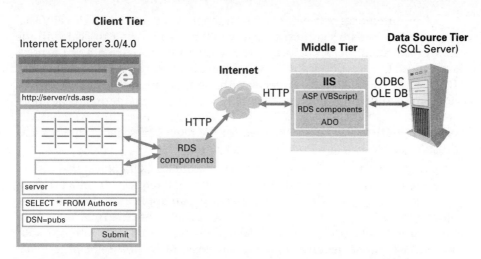

Figure 28-6 *Web-based architecture that uses RDS and OLE DB*

With Visual Basic WebClasses, the code you write runs on the server—either interpreted or in binary form. The ease and simplicity of this model have been extended to server-executed applications that deliver an HTML interface to the client. In the WebClass application model, a Web page is first created using an editor such as Microsoft FrontPage 98 or Microsoft Visual InterDev 6.0 and then loaded into the designer. This means that the presentation and user interface experts on your team will decide on the visual aspects of the program. Then it's your turn. At this point, you write code to respond to an event, typically the clicking of a Submit button. Finally, just as in a traditional Visual Basic application, you can execute the application at design time, interactively debug the code, and then deploy it. Well, the deployment part is different. You simply point to an ASP page that launches the WebClass application components.

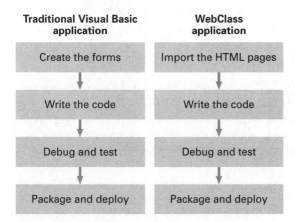

Figure 28-7 *Steps for creating a traditional application and a WebClass application using Visual Basic*

The differences between a WebClass application and a traditional Visual Basic application are significant. First, you'll need a browser to deal with the HTML (or Dynamic HTML). No, you don't create any binaries to run on the user's system—not unless you want to. So your application can be executed by *any* HTML browser. Second, users interact with the application by clicking on a link or typing a URL into the browser. Finally, and most important, all the application logic can exist in server-side code, which simply returns HTML, XML, or other MIME types that are tailored for the requesting client. Thus a client doesn't need to install a WebClass application.

At its core, a WebClass application is a standard COM object that resides on a Web server and responds to incoming HTTP requests from a browser. Architecturally, a WebClass is a container for an application's subroutines, functions, methods, and events that communicate over the Internet. At run time, an ASP page hosts the WebClass, allowing the IIS application to take advantage of the same functionality available within scripted ASP pages, such as built-in session management and request-response objects. You can create a WebClass application by starting an IIS Application project, or you can add a WebClass as a module to existing DLL projects. Figure 28-8 shows an architecture that uses WebClasses.

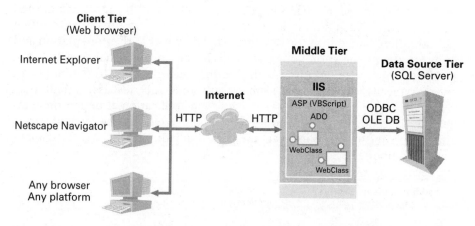

Figure 28-8 *Web-based architecture that uses WebClasses and OLE DB*

All these Web-centric architectures support ADO for data access—and we didn't even get into the DCOM architectures. ADO also lends itself very nicely to Visual Basic components run by MTS. The point of this little side trip? Well, in part, I thought you should see how flexible ADO has become. It has matured well beyond the experimental interface that first appeared in IIS in the winter of 1996–1997.

Your First Peek at ADO

In this section, we're going to drill down into the stuff that ADO is made of. As you should know by now (unless you came in late), ActiveX Data Objects (ADO) is the object-based interface to OLE DB. By using this new data access interface, which in some ways resembles DAO and RDO, developers can now access an even broader variety of data sources—using both OLE DB data providers and existing ODBC data sources through its OLE DB to ODBC bridge.

Introducing ADO 2.0

ADO 1.0 first appeared in the winter of 1996 with the introduction of Microsoft Transaction Server 1.0 and IIS 3.0. It was updated in the fall of 1997 with version 1.5, which dramatically expanded its functionality—bringing it almost up to a par with RDO 1.0. ADO 2.0 ships with Visual Studio 6.0 and Visual Basic 6.0 (and elsewhere). ADO can also be downloaded from Microsoft's Web site *http://www.microsoft.com/data/ado/download.htm*.

ADO is designed to enable your client application or component to access and manipulate data in a database server and other data stores through any OLE DB provider. Because there is an OLE DB provider for ODBC, ADO is also capable of accessing any ODBC data source—including those data sources designed for SQL Server. Included with ADO 2.0 are a native OLE DB provider for SQL Server (and Oracle) as well as one for the Jet database engine. You'll have even *more* choices when it comes time to connect up to SQL Server. (Oh joy—I think that makes nine so far.) The ADO interface to access SQL Server from Visual Basic, which was introduced in Chapter 3, is shown in Figure 28-9.

In ADO, the object hierarchy is deemphasized—most ADO objects can be created independently. This allows you to create and track only the objects you need. This model also results in fewer ADO objects and thus a smaller working set. It also means that you can approach data access problems from different angles—with new tools and techniques never before possible.

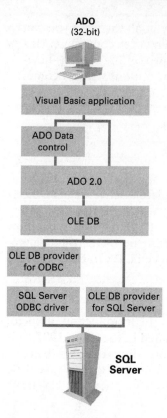

Figure 28-9 *ADO interface to access SQL Server from Visual Basic*

ADO supports key features for building client/server and Web-based applications. Basically, ADO started where RDO left off and adapted its functionality to OLE DB. No, ADO 1.0 didn't cover all this ground, but ADO 2.0 does—at least for the most part.

The following list describes some of the features supported by ADO 2.0:

- **Independently created objects** Unlike with DAO or RDO, you no longer have to navigate through a hierarchy to create objects because most ADO objects can be created independently. For example, you don't have to open a Connection object before creating a Recordset object—you simply have to declare it. This freedom allows you to create and track only the objects you need and results in fewer ADO objects, a smaller working set, easier tear-down, and fewer memory leaks caused by orphaned objects. This technology also enables an entirely new data access paradigm—that of dissociate result sets managed independently of connections and specific data sources.

- **Batch updating** This feature will help improve performance by locally caching changes to data, then writing them all to the server in a single update. Batch updating was initially implemented just as it was in RDO 2.0, using much of the same code and techniques. ADO takes it several steps further, however, as you'll see in subsequent chapters.

- **Direct access to SQL Server stored procedures (and those of other engines)** ADO 2.0 has support for stored procedures with in/out parameters, return values, and multiple result sets. Because most serious production systems are based on stored procedures, ADO includes a number of accommodations for remote procedure applications. Many of the more sophisticated data processing shops expose *only* stored procedures or views, so having a data interface that permits intimate control of stored procedures is important. Access to parameters, return status, and output parameters is also an essential part of the implementation, especially when accessing many of today's more sophisticated multi-tiered designs.

- **Different cursor types** ADO 2.0 allows several different types of cursors, including the potential for support of back-end–specific cursors. Although cursors are inherently evil, they can be useful if used judiciously. ADO 2.0 added client-side cursors and the ability to see what kind of support your data provider exposes. For example, by using the Supports method, you can determine which cursor features (such as updatability, the ability to support the Move methods, and so on) your cursor supports.

- **Limitation of the number of rows returned** In situations where a user might select more rows than would be practical to handle, the ADO interface taps the query engine's query governor, which limits the number of rows returned from the server. That way, you can predict query response time and more easily manage the workstation or server resources required to maintain cursor keysets.

- **Automatic or manual parameters management** This feature provides better performance and more control over parameters. RDO always polled the server to determine how procedure parameters should be constructed. Although this approach made programming easy, these extra calls to the server are expensive and problematic if the ODBC driver doesn't support this functionality (and it often doesn't). ADO can still populate the Parameters collection on demand, but it also lets you describe the parameters in code, which eliminates the need for these additional calls, thus improving query setup performance. Describing parameters in code can make your application more complex, however, and can also make it harder to change the underlying stored procedures without changing the code that invokes them. Now that's expensive.

- **Free-threaded objects for efficient Web server applications** When working with MTS and ASP pages, it's important that the component code knows how to behave when multiple instances are invoked. ADO supports a free-threaded model to make MTS thread management work more efficiently.

- **Complete integration with Visual Basic, Enterprise Edition** Visual Basic 6.0 adds the Data Environment and the Data Object Wizard, which can expose SQL statements or stored procedures as methods on the DataEnvironment object created. (See Chapters 37 and 38 for more information on these new tools.) ADO 2.0 is the default data access interface in most of the tools in Visual Basic (and Visual Studio).

- **Complete integration with Visual Database Tools and Visual InterDev** These tools have been designed for both ADO and RDO. You'll be able to develop and share database schemas and an interactive query development tool and even to tune Web-based designs.

- **Integration of the Transact-SQL (TSQL) Debugger with the IDE** You'll be able to test and walk through TSQL stored procedures and triggers right from Visual Basic's design environment. For example, when you use the Update method and SQL Server fires a trigger because of the query, the TSQL Debugger fires up and lets you step through the procedure.

- **Sophisticated client-side cursor library** The Client Batch cursor library developed by the Microsoft FoxPro team especially for ADO and RDO exposes optimistic batch updates and a faster, more intelligent local cursor library—head and shoulders above the ODBC client-side library. This cursor library also supports dissociate ADO and RDO objects, sorting, filtering, hierarchies, and persistence (saving and loading Recordset objects to and from a file). This functionality is exposed to all data providers.

- **Complete asynchronous event-driven support** Unlike ADO 1.5, ADO 2.0 supports events and asynchronous operations in virtually every aspect of the data access paradigm and adds the power of events that fire when the asynchronous operations complete. You won't be faced with any more indeterminate blockages while the server processes long queries.

- **Events tailored to support read-only result set updatability via stored procedures** Just as in RDO, ADO 2.0 lets you build cursor (or even noncursor) "nonupdateable" result sets for which you can update database rows by trapping the WillUpdateRecord event and executing an independent action query to perform the update. In addition, Visual Basic also includes the Data Object Wizard designed specifically to help setup complex multi-procedure fetch, update, delete, insert classes to deal with read-only result sets.

- **Expanded OLE DB data providers** Shipping with ADO 2.0 are "native" data providers for SQL Server, Jet, and Oracle (among others) that will help you get at more mainstream data. Visual Basic also lets you build your own data provider in case there's no existing way to get at your custom data.

- **Straight-line access to batched queries**   Many MIS procedures and applications depend on the flexibility of batched queries or complex stored procedures that return one or more result sets. In many cases, batched queries neither return nor affect many rows, but they can dramatically improve performance by lowering the overhead on query submissions.

- **Full TSQL support**   It's vital that the data interface to SQL Server fully supports all aspects of TSQL to permit the broadest possible support for SQL Server functionality. This includes RAISERROR and DBCC support. ADO doesn't parse your SQL code the way DAO/Jet does—every operation is a pass-through query—very much like RDO.

- **High-performance data access against remote OLE DB data sources**   Every data access application strives to retrieve results quickly—regardless of the query complexity. ADO 2.0 promises a consistent level of performance (including ODBC and especially SQL Server) rivaled only by the ODBC API and VBSQL API data interfaces. The jury is out on whether or not it will meet these goals. By more efficiently leveraging the remote data engine, the ADO interface greatly improves response time and user productivity. ADO also permits you to choose which services are loaded so you can further reduce memory footprint. The ADO team is still working on reducing load time and removing unneeded user interface DLLs from the run-time memory map. I expect we'll see steady improvements in performance as ADO matures.

- **Reduction of memory footprint to support "thinner" clients**   In many cases, the workstation has limited RAM and disk capacity. Therefore, applications designed for this type of system must economize on their use of RAM and other resources. The ADO 2.0 memory footprint is dramatically smaller than Jet's, and the model doesn't require local memory or disk space for its lowest-level cursors. ADO 2.0 is also supported by VBScript, so it is ideally suited for use on Web applications.

- **Management of return codes, input parameters, and output parameters from stored procedures**   Output parameters are used heavily for singleton queries and many administrative functions. In many cases, you can't determine whether a stored procedure has been completed successfully unless you can access the procedure's return value.

- **Management of multiple result sets**   You can make more efficient use of the query processor and system resources if you use a single query that returns several sets of related results. You can also improve performance by running a single query to gather data for filling multiple data-driven list boxes and menus. In addition, by combining a row-count query with a SELECT query, you can accurately set up scroll bars and status bars.

- **Utilization of server-side cursors** SQL Server 6.*x* and 7.0 support cursors built and maintained on the server rather than on the workstation. Under the right conditions, this type of cursor management can significantly improve system performance and reduce the resource needs of the workstation. Under the wrong conditions, server-side cursors can exhaust TempDB and bring your server to its knees.

- **Sort, Filter, and Find** ADO's client-side cursor library supports the ability to manipulate result sets once they arrive at the client (or component). This support gives your code the capability to order rows outside the scope of the original sequence, select a subset of your data based on a filter, or locate a specific subset of rows. These features use code in a rather complex client-side cursor engine that is approaching the power afforded by Jet. However, the question remains, do these client-side techniques add or subtract from overall application performance or developer productivity? The beauty of this approach is that the OLE DB providers you write in Visual Basic also get this functionality—for free.

- **Creatable Recordset objects (using client cursors)** In cases where you need to create a client-side or component Recordset from your own data without benefit of an OLE DB data provider, this is the ticket. Developers have requested this powerful feature for some time. In many cases, we could collect data from nondatabase sources but could do little to manage it until it was persisted (saved) into a database somewhere. Now we can create Recordset objects and add, change, and delete rows at will using ADO 2.0.

- **Recordset persistence (using client cursors)** Recordset persistence provides the ability to save the Recordset information (data, metadata, and properties) in a user-specified location using one of the allowed formats and the ability to recreate a Recordset from its persisted storage. Currently, the only format allowed is Advanced Data Tablegram (ADTG), the binary format used by RDS to pass remote result sets. In the future, we might see an XML representation of the underlying result set—an ASCII standard to be published as Microsoft's XML schema for OLE DB rowsets.

- **Integration with enterprise debugging** ADO 2.0 will fire both stock and custom events to Vista 6.0 to provide the client with performance and debugging information about the ADO layer. All outbound debugger events are fired at the top-level interface so that developers get as accurate a picture as possible regarding time spent in ADO versus in the OLE DB component. This means that you'll be able to walk into MTS to debug Visual Basic–authored components.

- **Support for hierarchical Recordset objects using the DataShape Component object** ADO 2.0's Microsoft Client Cursor Engine now includes functionality to shape data and create hierarchical Recordset objects. Hierarchical Recordset objects are exposed in many products:

xBase products with the SET RELATION command, Microsoft Access using Segmented Virtual Tables, and elsewhere. Hierarchies give the developer the ability to build one-to-many Recordset objects, define groupings, and specify aggregate calculations over child Recordset objects. For example, the set of orders for each customer would be a hierarchical result set. Although the developer often implements similar functionality in code, this ADO 2.0 feature eliminates much of this grunt work. The Visual Basic Data Environment also helps make declaring hierarchical relationships easy by providing a GUI tool.

The new DataShape object is used to organize one or more ADO Recordset objects into a new "shape" of data. This functionality is exposed through a rich object model with properties, events, methods, and collections. The DataShape object provides additional functionality to deal with more complex Recordset objects. The Visualizer controls visually display the run-time data produced by the DataShape object and the underlying ADO Recordset objects. This display of information can be presented in a wide variety of styles, depending on the Visualizer used. Make sure you check out the Hierarchical FlexGrid that knows how to display this object.

Although ADO supports these features, the underlying OLE DB components and drivers called by ADO might not. Check the documentation for the underlying components and drivers to determine what functionality they support. Unless otherwise noted, all the ADO objects, methods, and properties described in this guide are available when used with the OLE DB provider for ODBC and SQL Server 6.5 (or later). In other words, your mileage may vary.

At this point, ADO's most serious shortcoming is its lack of field experience. ADO 2.0 was exposed for the first time with Visual Basic 6.0. Its earlier version (ADO 1.5) has about a year under its belt. RDO, which has already proven itself in the trenches, seems simpler because it has fewer properties and options. It also has a couple of years on ADO—and you know how many times RDO has been "tuned" over the last several years. But RDO's greatest strength is also its greatest weakness: it was designed with relational databases such as SQL Server in mind. RDO doesn't work well for data sources such as Jet, mail, or postage meters.

TIP Confused about the naming convention used with ADO DLLs? It seems the developers chose to keep "15" in the name to better support older ADO code. That's why you install MSADO15.DLL instead of something with "20" in the name.

The ADO Object Model

ADO "flattens" the rather complex RDO (or DAO) object model, making ADO easier to use and understand. Figure 28-10 shows the ADO object model.

Figure 28-11 shows how ADO objects are created and their hierarchical relationships. Generally, an ADO object can be created in two ways:

- **Implicitly** An implicit ADO object is created when you refer to an ADO object that implies that you need its parent. For example, an implicit ADO Connection object is created when you open a Recordset without a direct reference to a Connection object. Similarly, an implicit ADO Parameter object is created when you use the Refresh method on the Parameters collection.

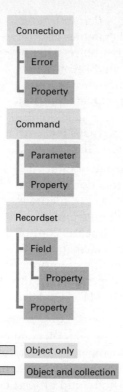

- Connection
  - Error
  - Property
- Command
  - Parameter
  - Property
- Recordset
  - Field
    - Property
  - Property

☐ Object only

☐ Object and collection

Figure 28-10   *ADO 2.0 object model*

- **Explicitly**   An explicit ADO object is created when you specifically dimension a new object or use one of the create methods. For example, when you use the ADO CreateParameter method or Dim Fld as New Field, you create an explicit object.

In some cases, ADO can use either technique to create the object. Figure 28-11 illustrates which objects can be created using each technique.

If we include the Properties collection, the ADO object model has only seven objects. Consider, however, that the ADO object model is extensible. In cases where special services or data structures have to be accessed, it is possible (and likely) that the model will be expanded to include this custom functionality. In some ways, the ADO objects are similar to RDO objects, but they often combine functionality into fewer objects with more properties and methods. Don't let the similarities lure you into thinking that you can substitute one object or property for another willy-nilly. We'll spend quite a bit of time in the following chapters getting comfortable with the ADO objects, especially as they relate to the RDO model that you're probably more familiar with.

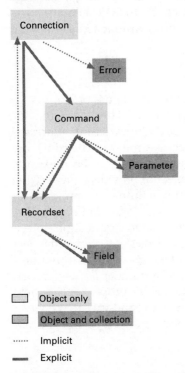

ADO 2.0

Connection

Error

Command

Parameter

Recordset

Field

☐ Object only

▦ Object and collection

...... Implicit

—— Explicit

Figure 28-11 *The ADO object model showing how ADO objects can be created implicitly and explicitly*

The ADO Objects

Let's look at each of the ADO objects in a little more depth. As we examine these objects, keep in mind that although ADO objects might resemble RDO objects, they are really very different. (Yes, I've already mentioned this point a couple of times, but if you don't remember it you'll wish you had paid attention.) In addition, these objects are not defined to map relational data tables but to expose information from *any* data source.

Connection object

The Connection object maintains connection interface information about the data provider and manages transaction scope and the errors associated with the connection. This object is similar to the rdoConnection object in many respects. Think of the Connection object as the link to where the data is stored. It acts as a gateway—a pointer—to the database, the mail server, the directory server, or the paper tape reader across the hall. The Connection object maintains properties to describe the user and to indicate the cursor "location" (the CursorType in RDO), connect string, query (command) timeout, connection timeout, and other ADO-specific properties such as Default Database and Isolation level (and more). This object, like all of the base ADO objects, can be created without actually connecting to anything. That is, you can create a Connection object without establishing a connection to SQL Server and use it to create other related objects (such as Commands) without actually having access to a data source.

Command object

The Command object maintains information about the query or command, such as a query string, parameter definitions, and so on. The Command object contains the question you want to ask about the information addressed by the Connection object. The Command object is similar to the rdoQuery object in RDO, but it supports more options and flexibility. You can execute a command string (a query) on a Connection object or provide a query string as part of opening a Recordset object without first defining a Command object. Each of these two techniques creates an implicit Command object. Yes, you can create a Command object without an associated Connection object. You can also change the current connection as needed. The Command object is useful when you need to define query parameters or execute a stored procedure that returns output parameters. It supports a number of new properties used to describe the type and purpose of the query—properties that help ADO optimize the operation being performed and save round-trips to the server to clarify the command. The Command object also exposes a number of new methods and events that we'll get into later.

Parameter object

The Parameter object is a single parameter for a parameterized Command. The Command object exposes a Parameters collection to contain all of its Parameter objects. The Parameter object provides a place to insert specifics into your queries and to fetch output parameters. That is, it lets you create a general question with spaces left open—to be filled in later with criteria that make your question apply to the current situation. This object is equivalent to the rdoParameter object in RDO, but again, it provides more detail than the RDO object. Like RDO's rdoParameters collection, ADO's Parameter object can be created automatically by sending queries to the database management system. However, you can also build this collection yourself to improve performance at run time—something RDO doesn't support. The downside to this approach is that your code gets more complex. It's another one of those tradeoffs I referred to earlier.

Recordset object

The Recordset object is a set of records (rows) returned from a query and a cursor into those records. The Recordset object returns the answer to your SQL question. It can contain no or any number of data rows. It can also be returned in several hierarchical formats, such as a set of customers and each of their orders. You can open a Recordset object (that is, execute a query) without explicitly opening a Connection object. Opening a stand-alone Recordset object can implicitly create and open a Connection object. If you create a Connection object first, however, you can open multiple Recordset objects on the same connection. Generally, the ADO Recordset object is equivalent to RDO's rdoResultset. Again, the ADO object supports a number of new (or changed) properties and methods. Another neat feature of ADO lets you create a Recordset object without benefit of a Connection object. This means you can simply create and fill in an empty Recordset object by concatenating Field objects that you define in code. You can also reconstitute a Recordset object that was persisted to a file.

Field object

The Field object contains information about a single column of data within a Recordset object. The Field object is the holder for each individual piece of data. It can store anything from a null to a single bit to a giant document or image. The Recordset object features a Fields collection to contain all of its Field objects. This object is equivalent to the rdoColumn object in RDO, but it includes far more information about the field than the RDO object, such as precision and numeric scale. Richer data type support is also available in ADO.

Property object

The Property object is a built-in or component-defined characteristic of an ADO object. There is no RDO equivalent to this object. DAO has a Property object, but it's not really the same. The Property object implements one of ADO's coolest features. It lets the developer of the ADO data provider expand ADO to address special interfaces that only this driver supports. I can't overemphasize the importance of the Properties collections on each of the ADO objects. These collections define additional attributes that only the provider supplies. It is through these collections that ADO expands its functionality based on the capabilities of the provider chosen. ADO objects have two types of properties: built-in and dynamic.

Built-in properties These properties are implemented in ADO and immediately available to any new object, using the familiar MyObject.Property syntax. Built-in properties don't appear as Property objects in an object's Properties collection, so although you can change their values, you can't modify their characteristics or delete them.

Dynamic properties These properties are defined by the underlying data provider, and they appear in the Properties collection for the appropriate ADO object. For example, a property specific to the provider might indicate whether a Recordset object supports transactions or updating. These additional properties appear as Property objects in the Recordset object's Properties collection. Dynamic properties can be referenced only through the collection, using the MyObject.Properties(0) or MyObject.Properties("Name") syntax. You'll find that each data provider (might) implement one or more special properties to deal with special provider-specific operations. Actually, I found over 280 properties associated with the Connection, Command, Resultset, and four Field objects of a simple query. We unravel what these properties mean in Chapter 29.

Error object

The Error object contains extended error information about an error condition raised by the provider. Because a single statement can generate two or more errors, the Errors collection can contain more than one Error object at a time, all of which result from the same incident. Again, the Error object is virtually identical to RDO's rdoError object and its associated rdoErrors collection.

The ADO Object Model from an RDO Perspective

Because the ADO model is considerably simpler (and flatter) than that of RDO, don't expect a 1:1 correspondence with ADO objects, properties, and methods. Lots of documentation and helpful hints on how to map the DAO and RDO model to ADO will be provided in Chapter 34. Nope, there won't be a wizard (at least not right away) that will convert code from one model to the other. We thought about that but it was simply too complex a task. Especially for a C++ developer. Figure 28-12 shows the RDO object model and compares it to that of ADO.

It seems that the Data Access Group is backing off its commitment to make ADO 2.0 functionally equivalent to RDO 2.0. As it looks now, ADO 2.1 might be closer. Question: When will ADO 2.1 ship? Well, it won't arrive with Visual Basic 6.0. Perhaps when Office 2000 or SQL Server 7.0 ships.

As mentioned earlier, the ADO object model is flatter (has fewer objects and parent-child relationship requirements) but has more properties (lots more properties), methods, and method arguments than the RDO or DAO object models. For example, ADO doesn't have equivalent objects to the rdoEngine or rdoEnvironment objects, which expose the ODBC Driver Manager and hEnv interfaces. These interfaces aren't exposed at all in ADO. However, the InfoMessage event and some (but not all) of the other properties exposed on the rdoEngine object are supported in ADO 2.0 on the Connection object. We leave behind a number of "default" properties. As we work through the rest of the ADO interface, we'll find other dissimilarities—many more subtle than this. Some of these differences are covered by new approaches to the problem (and are addressed), some are omitted for one good reason or another, and some have yet to be implemented.

One important difference between RDO and ADO is the ability in ADO to set properties of a stand-alone object before "opening" the object. This capability means you don't have to have access to the database or run the query before telling ADO how you want it built.

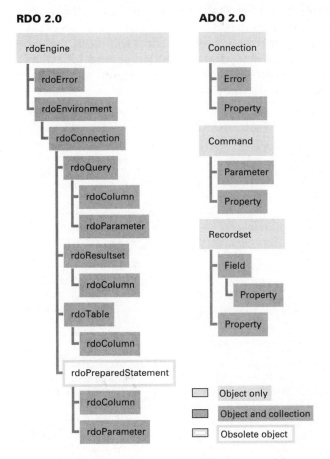

Figure 28-12   *RDO 2.0 and ADO 2.0 object models*

NOTE   Did you notice that the ADO model is missing one key aspect of the hierarchy? You can't really tell from the RDO diagram in Figure 28-12, but all its base objects—such as the rdoEnvironment, rdoConnection, rdoResultset, and rdoQuery objects—are mirrored in *collections*. This arrangement gives you a way to manage multiple connections and multiple rdoResultset objects as you see fit. Unfortunately, this feature is very expensive to implement and has lots of implications as far as unwanted object persistence. ADO doesn't implement these collections—though there's nothing to stop you from implementing your own if you're of a mind to. ADO does support a collection of Errors, Properties, Fields (columns), and Parameters—but that's it.

Let me backtrack a little for you RDO fans out there. The developers tell me that ADO 2.0 is supposed to implement a superset of both RDO and DAO. My early tests indicate that this is mostly true—as long as you don't simply match up RDO and ADO property-for-property and method-to-method. By comparing the object models, we can see how well the object models map one to the other. The only problem with laying out these interfaces side by side is that it's like comparing a custom-tuned racing engine (RDO) with an equally powerful (but experimental) "universal" power plant (ADO) designed to be used anywhere. They both make noise and have shafts that go round-and-round, but that's where the similarity ends. You'll find more information about converting RDO applications to ADO in Chapter 34.

29

ActiveX
Data Objects
Up Close

**Understanding the
ADO Object Model**

ADO Connection Object

ADO Command Object

ADO Recordset Object

ADO Field Object

ADO Parameter Object

ADO Property Object

ADO Error Object

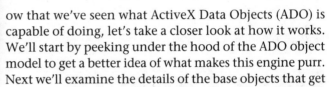

ow that we've seen what ActiveX Data Objects (ADO) is capable of doing, let's take a closer look at how it works. We'll start by peeking under the hood of the ADO object model to get a better idea of what makes this engine purr. Next we'll examine the details of the base objects that get you connected and let you submit queries and process results. What I'm really providing you with in this chapter is a mini programmer's reference that organizes the objects, methods, properties, and events into a logical sequence. I think you'll find the information here indispensable as you start test driving this new data access interface.

Understanding the ADO Object Model

First let's take a look at a diagram of the ADO object model. Figure 29-1 shows the ADO 2.0 object model introduced in Chapter 28.

The ADO object model is very different from the object/collection models used by Data Access Objects (DAO) and Remote Data Objects (RDO). For example, ADO doesn't use collections to group or manage its base objects. Yes, ADO still has collections, but not nearly as many, and they're managed differently. Dave Stearns, a senior Program Manager and database architect at Microsoft, explained to me a couple of the reasons for these differences:

- In most cases, collections aren't needed and can cause problems. DAO should never have had most of the collections it did in the first place. Sure, some of them made sense—like the QueryDefs collection of stored queries. But many of them were just snake pits waiting for unsuspecting tourists.

- RDO copied DAO's model (on purpose) and thus inherited the collections and all the problems that went along with them. We started to get away from collections in RDO 2.0 by having stand-alone rdoQuery objects.

PART V USING ADO AND OLE DB

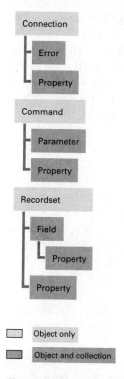

Object only

Object and collection

Figure 29-1 *The ADO 2.0 object model*

The "object" programming model was first pioneered by Microsoft Excel. For example, you would create a Worksheet object that was a part of the Workbook object. You would ask the workbook to create a new worksheet, and the worksheet's lifetime was entirely controlled by its parent (the workbook). It made no sense to create a worksheet that wasn't part of a workbook (though I'd argue that this capability would have been cool). The objects simply exposed their internal data structures as a tree of instances. This resulted in a large tree of state values that the programmer could manipulate. This arrangement was more or less appropriate for Excel, but for the most part, the objects *really* did not do things (like execute commands).

The DAO team looked at the Excel model and figured that's how object models should be done. Even though the DAO model has to do things (such as execute commands), the DAO team used the same tree of instances model for their regular data access code as well. To be fair, DAO does have to expose some document-like data. For example, each Jet database has a set of persisted queries, tables, forms, and reports that developers need to modify (just like modifying the formatting on a range in a spreadsheet). And that's how the DAO object model got started.

RDO just copied the relevant portions of the DAO model so that developers would find RDO familiar and easy to pick up and use. This "borrowing" was one of the trade-offs we had to make when begging for permission even to start building RDO. It had to be "DAO-like" even if making it that way didn't always make sense—and it didn't (at least not always). In a way, that mandate was a good thing because it made RDO more familiar to DAO developers—but the collections of objects caused a huge amount of problems in RDO 1.0 (as you may well remember). If you created an rdoPreparedStatement object, it would stay in the rdoConnections collection until the connection was closed. Developers used to think we were leaking memory since they saw some memory allocated every time they did a query; and it wasn't freed until the connection went away. And in a way it was leaking—well, it was being used and not released—I guess that's more like hoarding than leaking.

So in RDO 2.0, Microsoft made two major changes. They first made the contents of the collections transient, meaning that the collection didn't hold a reference on the contained object. If the developer didn't hold onto the rdoQuery object with a variable, it disappeared from the collection. They then made the rdoQuery object creatable on its own and made the rdoResultset object dissociable from its parent connection. Now those objects could live on their own and didn't have to be contained within a connection. Once you had a disconnected Recordset in the client cursor engine, the rdoResultsets collection didn't make sense anymore. And remember the "touch-me-once-before-I'm-gone" LastQueryResults property? That design was due to this same desire to eliminate "ghost" objects from persisting when they shouldn't. This eliminated creation of the itinerant and zombied objects that just lay around sipping CPU cycles in the back corner of your system's memory.

ADO and other data access interfaces are engines—they are about doing things, not about manipulating documents. Connections don't inherently have commands that are forever attached to or associated with them. Stored procedures are dealt with like commands, so the query as a method makes abundant sense in this case. On the other hand, code-defined commands are not like that. They exist in their own right and can be executed on any particular connection—at least where it makes sense.

In ADO, most of the collections have been ditched and all the objects are creatable on their own. The developer sets the ActiveConnection property or the Source property to a Command object or a Connection object when needed. Objects can be related for a time and then separated again. Furthermore, you don't have to use a parent object to create a child object. It's all much simpler—simpler to code, simpler to manage, and less consumptive of system resources.

NOTE The design of a tree of instances isn't really appropriate for a data access library anyway. It's much better to use Visual Basic for Applications (VBA) Collection objects if you want to hold onto a number of objects and iterate over them in a group. The Collection object can hold any kind of object, so you can stuff a bunch of Recordsets or a bunch of Commands in there and keep track of them in one place if you so desire.

OK, so now you understand why we won't be talking as much about collections of ADO objects as we do with RDO. You should think of ADO as a number of basically independent companies who don't always need a parent company to exist or get their jobs done. Of course, if you want to, you can create your own Collection objects and store the ADO objects therein. Creating your own Collection objects might make sense if you're charging by the hour or feel the need to create additional object management infrastructure.

ADO Collections

ADO does expose object collections—just not as many. With the exception of the Errors collection, you can build and manage these collections yourself in code. Unlike RDO, you can build your own Parameter objects and describe a parameter query using the Parameters collection. You manipulate all of these collections in code just as you did in RDO and DAO—remember that ADO is still a Component Object Model (COM) architecture. You can still reference members by name, by ordinal number, or by default. Table 29-1 lists the ADO collections.

> **TIP** Dave Stutz, Visual Basic architect and self-proclaimed "wonk," tells me that it's not a good idea to use the default object references. He wants you to spell out your references. That means you code "A = Text1.Text" instead of "A = Text1". I respect his opinion, but I'm already hooked on the default object shortcuts. Just don't let Dave see any of your code, and you'll be fine.

Table 29-1
ADO Collections

Collection	Type of Objects in Collection	Purpose
Parameters	Parameter	A parameter for a command
Fields	Field	A column that is part of a Recordset
Properties	Property	A provider-defined collection of read-only settings
Errors	Error	Information about errors resulting from provider operations

Each ADO collection supports the same two properties used to navigate the collection and some of the same methods described in Table 29-2 and Table 29-3.

Table 29-2
ADO Collection Properties

Property	Applies to	Purpose
Count	All	Tracks how many elements are in the collection
Item	All	Default; contains collection elements

Table 29-3
ADO Collection Methods

Method	Applies to	Purpose
Append	Fields, Parameters	Adds an additional element to the collection (See the "Append method" section below.)
Delete	Fields, Parameters	Removes a member from the collection
Clear	Errors	Removes all elements from the collection
Refresh	Errors, Fields, Parameters, Properties	Updates collection to reflect current changes

Append method

The Append method is used to create and append new Field objects to the Fields collection of a Recordset object and Parameter objects to the Parameters collection of a Command object. After appending the field to the collection, you can set other properties on the Field object. The normally read-only properties on the Field object will become read-only once the Recordset has been opened.

If you want to append new Field objects onto a Recordset, you have to do so before you set the ActiveConnection property or use any type of open. In addition, you must set the CursorLocation property to adUseClient.

You set the parameters for the Append method as follows:

- The required Name parameter must be a valid string identifier. To avoid confusion, you have to provide a unique name for each field being appended.

- The Type parameter indicates the new data type for the field. The default for this parameter is the constant adEmpty, and if you don't specify a data type, the new field will be set to adEmpty but a run-time error will be tripped.

- The optional DefinedSize parameter indicates the defined size for the new field. If you don't specify this value, the column contains an appropriate default based on the data type specified in the Type parameter.

- The optional Attrib parameter is used to specify attributes for the new field. The default for this parameter is adFldUnspecified.

Once a Recordset is open, you can't use the Append method to add additional fields to the Recordset. Attempting to do so trips a run-time error.

ADO Connection Object

An ADO Connection object identifies a specific data source. By setting the properties of this object, you identify the location and characteristics of this data source as well as your own qualifications to access it. That is, you provide your username and password, workstation name, application name, and other parameters so that the data source knows who you are and how to treat you as a subscriber to its data. In Microsoft SQL Server terms, a Connection object is just that—one of a finite number of network connections to the server. Once the Connection object has established a connection to SQL Server, no other user can use that connection until your code dies or you close it.

Managing Connection State

Connections in SQL Server maintain a *state* for each client that connects to them. For example, after you establish a connection, SQL Server sets the default database to the database the system administrator (SA) assigned to your login as your default database. As ADO (or RDO or any other data access interface) sends commands to SQL Server, some of these operations change the default properties associated with the connection—thus changing the state. Besides the default database, the RowCount, transaction scope, "Select into," and other "settable" options can change. These changes are usually (but not always) managed (scoped) on the connection, but in some cases they can impact all connected users. Some of these settings are reserved for those logging on with SA privileges, so an ordinary user login can't use them.

All of this means that you can't just arbitrarily run a command against a connection and expect it to behave as it would have if it had the same state. For example, if you opened two connections and executed a Use Pubs command against one connection, you wouldn't necessarily expect the other connection to be set to use the *pubs* database. This is a common mistake the DAO/Jet interface made. It assumed it could just open a connection whenever it needed to, and send a command, run a query, or anything it thought was necessary. Jet was oblivious of the fact that you had manually set a different default database or executed one of the Set options. Unfortunately, ADO and the OLE DB provider for ODBC do the same thing—and there's nothing we can do about it, except use the native OLE DB provider for SQL Server.

In Chapter 30, we'll discuss how to create an ADO Connection object and establish a connection to SQL Server. For now, let's take a close drive by the Connection object's collections, properties, and methods.

Connection Object Collections

The Connection object maintains two collections to handle errors and properties. The Errors collection is the one you're going to use most often, but you'll need the Properties collection to set the login prompt behavior and several other interesting properties.

Errors collection

The Errors collection is the repository for all errors associated with operations on this connection. Here is where you'll find what has gone wrong with each Recordset, action query, or other connection-related operation. Because a single SQL Server operation can result in a flood of errors and warnings, be sure to examine all the members of the Errors collection before sending me mail about some mysterious problem.

The Errors collection can hold many Error objects, and the collection supports the Count and Item properties as well as the For Each syntax for iterating over the elements of the collection. You can clear this collection by calling the Clear method on the Errors collection. By convention, the most descriptive or useful error is placed in the first position in the collection. The contents of this most useful error can also be raised as an OLE exception to the calling application. Only errors that come from the data source are appended into the Errors collection, and internal errors that occur in the provider's client library itself should be returned only via standard OLE exception handling, and not put into this collection. The Errors collection's purpose is to hold onto multiple errors returned by the data source during the course of one method invocation.

Properties collection

Each OLE DB provider exposes a number of properties that it alone documents. I spent quite a bit of time locating the documentation for these properties— at least the OLE DB provider for SQL Server properties. These can be extracted with a quick loop through the provider's Properties collection.

The Properties collection of the Connection object is read-only; that is, the membership of properties in the collection is fixed once loaded. The values of the Property objects themselves might be read-only, depending on the property and the provider.

Connection Object Methods

The Connection object exposes a number of methods used to manage the connection. (See Table 29-4.) In addition, ADO exposes each Command object as a method on the Connection object. This functionality is similar to that exposed in RDO.

Table 29-4
Connection Object Methods

Method	Purpose
Cancel	Cancels an execution of the command in progress (See the "Cancel method" section below.)
Open	Opens the connection (See the "Open method" section on page 590.)
Close	Closes an active connection and releases its resources (See the "Close method" section on page 590.)
BeginTrans	Starts a new transaction on the connection (See the "BeginTrans, CommitTrans, and RollbackTrans methods" section on page 591.)
CommitTrans	Commits the current transaction on the connection (See the "BeginTrans, CommitTrans, and Rollback-Trans methods" section on page 591.)
RollbackTrans	Rolls back the current transaction on the connection (See the "BeginTrans, CommitTrans, and Rollback-Trans methods" section on page 591.)
Execute	Executes a command against the connection that isn't expected to return rows (See the "Execute method" section on page 592.)
OpenSchema	Gets schema information and returns it in a Recordset (See the "OpenSchema method" section on page 594.)

Cancel method

The Cancel method is used to stop the execution of an asynchronous Connection.Open or Connection.Execute method call, causing the operation to return a trappable error and trip the appropriate event handler. If the Connection method call has already completed when Cancel is executed, no error is generated. If no command is currently executing on the connection, ADO ignores the call and doesn't return an error. This method can also cancel a synchronous command executing on another thread, assuming that the provider is free-threaded.

Open method

You use the Open method to establish a connection to SQL Server or any other OLE DB (or ODBC via OLE DB) provider. The Open method does *not* create a new Connection object. That job is left up to your code and Microsoft Visual Basic. That is, you have to declare the Connection object with the New option or use the Set statement to assign a valid Connection object to a declared variable. After the Open method successfully completes, the connection is live. At this point, your code can issue commands against it and process results.

The ConnectionString parameter can contain either an entire connection string or just the name of a particular data source. The provider differentiates between the two by searching for the "=" sign, which signals a pair of option-value pairs. If you supply the entire connection string, the provider sets this value into the ConnectionString property and opens the connection. If you pass only a data source name, it should be combined with the UserID and Password parameter values to form a complete connection string before setting the property and opening the connection. If both a full connection string and a user ID and password are supplied, the UserID and Password parameters are ignored.

If you want to open the connection asynchronously, set the adAsync-Connect option. If you choose this option, the connection won't be available until the State property no longer shows adStateConnecting. We'll discuss the intimate details of the ConnectionString and Open methods in Chapter 30.

Close method

The Close method tells ADO to disconnect from the remote server. Depending on how ADO, ODBC 3.*x*, and Microsoft Transaction Server are managing connections, the SQL Server connection might stick around for awhile in anticipation of being used again. Keep in mind that using the Close method doesn't destroy the Connection object. Other objects can still reference it, and you can use the Open method or reference any of its properties as needed. Set the Connection object to Nothing to release its resources (but not necessarily the SQL Server connection if you're using connection pooling).

Using the Close method to close a Connection object also closes any active Recordset objects associated with the connection. A Command object associated with the Connection object you're closing will still be there, but it will no longer be associated with a Connection object; that is, its ActiveConnection property will be set to Nothing. Also, the Command object's Parameters collection will be cleared of any provider-defined parameters.

When you're ready to reestablish the connection to the same or another data source, you can call the Open method. While the Connection object is closed, calling any methods that require an open connection to the data source generates an error.

Closing a Connection object while there are open Recordset objects on the connection rolls back any pending changes in all the Recordset objects. Explicitly closing a Connection object (calling the Close method) while a transaction is in progress generates an error. If a Connection object falls out of scope while a transaction is in progress, ADO automatically rolls back the transaction.

BeginTrans, CommitTrans, and RollbackTrans methods

Transactions, even nested ones, are managed on the Connection object scoped by the BeginTrans, CommitTrans, and RollbackTrans methods. If you want to have ADO and SQL Server delay committing changes until you give the word, you'll need to use these transaction methods. Basically, this means that any and all changes you make to the database after having begun a transaction with BeginTrans can and will be rolled back (undone) if you never execute the CommitTrans method or if you *do* execute the RollbackTrans method. The transaction methods manage transaction processing within a Connection object as follows:

- BeginTrans begins a new transaction.

- CommitTrans saves any changes and ends the current transaction. It can also start a new transaction.

- RollbackTrans cancels any changes made during the current transaction and ends the transaction. It can also start a new transaction.

Unlike DAO or RDO, ADO can support nested transactions—if the provider supports them—which is (sort of) the case for SQL Server. When you use the BeginTrans method, ADO returns a Long value to a "level" variable indicating the number of levels of nesting. For example, if BeginTrans has been executed twice before the current call, the level variable will return "3" as the current nesting level. The CommitTrans and RollbackTrans methods do not return a value.

> **NOTE** Although the first call to BeginTrans returns a value, subsequent calls seem to fail, generating the error, "Only one transaction can be active on this session." This might be an unresolved bug, or it might be that the SQL Server drivers don't support nested transactions. I'm leaning toward the latter—at least with SQL Server versions 6.5 and earlier.

Use these methods with a Connection object when you want to save or cancel a series of changes made to the source data as a single unit. For example, to transfer money between accounts, you subtract an amount from one and add the same amount to the other. If either update fails, the accounts no longer balance. Making these changes within an open transaction ensures that either all or none of the changes go through. Once you call the BeginTrans method, the provider will no longer automatically commit any changes you make until you call CommitTrans or RollbackTrans to end the transaction.

Theoretically, when using the SQL Server providers, calling the Begin-Trans method within an open transaction starts a new, nested transaction. However, our tests return errors when we try to do so. If this feature was working, the return value would indicate the level of nesting: a return value of "1" indicates that you've opened a top-level transaction (that is, the transaction isn't nested within another transaction), "2" indicates that you've opened a second-level transaction (a transaction nested within a top-level transaction), and so forth. Calling CommitTrans or RollbackTrans affects only the most recently opened transaction; you must close or roll back the current transaction before you can resolve any higher level transactions—that is, if nested transactions were working.

Closing a Connection object while there are open Recordset objects on the connection rolls back any pending changes in all the Recordset objects. Explicitly closing a Connection object (calling the Close method) while a transaction is in progress generates an error. If a Connection object falls out of scope while a transaction is in progress, ADO automatically rolls back the transaction.

Calling the CommitTrans method saves changes made within an open transaction on the connection and ends the transaction. Calling the Rollback-Trans method reverses any changes made within an open transaction and ends the transaction. Calling either method when there is no open transaction generates an error.

Depending on the Connection object's Attributes property, calling either the CommitTrans or RollbackTrans method can automatically start a new transaction. If the Attributes property is set to adXactCommitRetaining, ADO automatically starts a new transaction after a CommitTrans call. If the Attributes property is set to adXactAbortRetaining, ADO automatically starts a new transaction after a RollbackTrans call.

Execute method

When working with the Connection object, the ADO Execute method has two modes. The first mode works pretty much as it did in DAO and RDO—it executes the specified query, SQL statement, stored procedure, or provider-specific text. Typically, this kind of query doesn't return rows (as an action query does). However, in DAO and RDO, the Execute method can be executed like a function (as opposed to a subroutine) when it returns the number of rows affected as a return argument, as shown here:

```
RecordsAffected = Cn.Execute(...
```

In contrast, the ADO Execute method returns the rows affected count in a gazouta (a returned argument). That is, the number of rows affected by the operation is returned into a variable you pass *to* the method. This is more characteristic of C applications, in which variables passed to called functions serve as pointers to where the code is supposed to return values. This observation isn't a slam; it simply means that you now have to pay more attention to the variables you use to pass arguments to and *from* your methods. Yes, this argument is optional, so you don't have to pass in this variable. The Execute method can also return a Recordset using this syntax, so you need to pay attention to the variable types being passed in. So, for a *non-row-returning* command string, use the following syntax:

```
connection.Execute CommandText, RecordsAffected, Options
```

Here's an example:

```
MyCn.Execute "Use Pubs"
Dim Rows as Long
MyCn.Execute "Update Cats Set Status = 'D' Where Age = 50", Rows
```

The second, new mode for ADO (at least when compared to RDO and DAO) is the ability to create a Recordset with the Execute statement. In this case, you simply use:

```
Set recordset = MyCn.Execute (CommandText, RecordsAffected, Options)
```

You can also execute a Command procedure as a Connection method to return a Recordset. This variation is handy when you have to pass in arguments to the procedure being executed. It assumes the Command has already been set up with the correct options. No, executing Command objects as Connection object methods isn't documented very well (except here in the *Hitchhiker's Guide*). The following shows the syntax for executing a Command as a Connection method:

```
connection.Command param1, param2, Recordset
```

For example, the following statement executes the Command *GetAuthors*:

```
cn.GetAuthors rs
```

If you need to pass parameters to the Command, you place them ahead of the Recordset variable, like this:

```
cn.FindAuthors "Fred", 16, rs
```

The Recordset variable is always coded last.

The CommandText argument passed to the Execute statement is a mystery to ADO when it arrives. Unless you take some steps to prevent it, ADO will try to figure out what you're trying to do with this command to get SQL Server to execute it most efficiently. That's where the Options argument comes in—it tells the data provider how to evaluate the CommandText. Skip down to the "ADO Command Object" section later in this chapter for details on how the Options argument works. We'll also discuss the Options argument again when we talk about creating Recordset objects in Chapter 31.

The RecordsAffected parameter is used to supply a variable in which to place the number of records affected by the command—assuming it's an action query. For example, an UPDATE statement would return a value, but a SELECT statement would not. This parameter is optional, and if you don't pass a variable for this parameter (just pass a literal value) or don't supply any value at all, ADO doesn't return this information.

I'll describe the Options argument in more detail in the Command object's "Execute method" section on pages 606–608—all the information there applies here as well. For example, if you want your query to run asynchronously (and you do), add the adAsyncExecute option to your previously selected option. That is, you need to add (+), or logically AND (not concatenate), the options together.

An ExecuteComplete event is issued when the command concludes— whether or not you're running in asynchronous mode. This event fires whether or not the command returned any rows or even succeeded in running. Asynchronous operations should be a part of most of your designs—especially when the query (or operation) is expected to take more than a few seconds.

Using the Execute method on a Connection object executes whatever query you pass to the method in the CommandText argument on the specified connection. If the CommandText argument specifies a row-returning query, any results the execution generates are stored in a new Recordset object unless the adExecuteNoRecords constant is used in the Options parameter. This option seems to speed action queries up a tad. If the command isn't a row-returning query, the provider returns a closed Recordset object. In both cases, the Execute statement creates a new Recordset object—so be prepared to close it or set it to nothing once you're done with it.

TIP   To see whether an ADO Recordset is closed, check the bitmask State property for adStateClosed. This property is also used in some states when the government runs out of money. If the State property's adStateOpen bit is set, you know ADO was able to create a Recordset from your query. Watch out for other bits in the State property. The object could be more than just open.

The default Recordset object is always a read-only, forward-only cursor. If you need a Recordset object with more functionality, first create a Recordset object with the desired property settings and then use the Recordset object's Open method to execute the query and return the desired cursor type.

The contents of the CommandText argument are specific to the provider and can be standard SQL syntax or any special command format that the provider supports. If the provider (SQL Server in our case) doesn't recognize the command, you'll receive a trappable error.

OpenSchema method

One of the legacies (OK, curses) from DAO and RDO is the requirement to pull down table data definition language (DDL) from the database. I know that very few people use this option, so I won't spend much time dealing with it here.

Frankly, if you need to manipulate tables, you should use one of the dozen utilities that ship with Visual Studio or the half-dozen that ship with Visual Basic that are made expressly for this purpose. Consider that you can always use Transact-SQL (TSQL) statements to perform DDL operations. However, the OpenSchema method returns a lot more than just tables.

Connection Object Properties

The Connection object supports a number of properties that make ADO and your code more efficient. (See Table 29-5.) Let's take a quick look at these. I've included more details on most of these properties and information on how to use them in code in Chapter 30.

NOTE It looks like we lost the ability to restart a timed-out query. We had that in VBSQL and for a time with RDO, but it seems to have been left out of ADO—at least for now.

Table 29-5
Connection Object Properties

Property	Purpose
Attributes	Manages how transactions should be retained or started. (See the "Connection Object Methods" section on page 589.)
CommandTimeout	Indicates, in seconds, how long to wait for a command to execute. Default is 30 seconds. Once a query times out, it's done. ADO doesn't provide a way to restart it where it left off.
DefaultDatabase	Lets you choose (in yet another way) the default database. (See the "DefaultDatabase property" section on page 596.) Once set, the default database can't be changed using this property. OLE DB (and ADO) have stopped calling this the *Default Database*—it's now called the *Initial Catalog*.
ConnectionString	Specifies a data source by passing a detailed connection string containing a series of argument = value statements separated by semicolons. (See the "ConnectionString property" section on page 597 and Chapter 30.)
ConnectionTimeout	Indicates, in seconds, how long to wait for the connection to open. Default is 15 seconds.

(continued)

Table 29-5 *continued*

Property	Purpose
Provider	Indicates the name of the data provider for a Connection object. We'll be using *SQLOLEDB*—the SQL Server OLE DB provider (no, not the default MSDASQL *ODBC* OLE DB provider). (See the "Provider property" section on page 597.)
CursorLocation	Decides where ADO builds your cursors. (See the "CursorLocation property" section on page 597.)
IsolationLevel	Determines how ADO and SQL Server handle transactions. (See the "IsolationLevel property" section on page 598.)
Mode	Indicates the available permissions for accessing data in a Connection. For example, you can set read/write or deny read/write permissions on the Connection Recordset objects. An error is returned if you try to retrieve the Mode value before setting the Mode property. An error is also returned if you try to retrieve the Mode value before connecting to a provider. (See the "Mode property" section on page 599 and Chapter 30.)
State	Indicates whether the Connection is open or busy connecting. This property is read-only. (See the "State property" section on page 599.)
Version	Returns the version number of the ADO implementation.

Additional details for some of the Connection object properties listed in Table 29-5 are given in the following subsections.

DefaultDatabase property

The DefaultDatabase property sets the default database for the current connection. If the default database is set, your SQL queries can use unqualified syntax to access objects in that database. If the default database value has been cleared, your clients must qualify the object name with the database name. Upon connection, the provider fills in the default database information. As mentioned in Table 29-5, OLE DB (and ADO) have stopped referring to the Default Database—it's been renamed the Initial Catalog. Confused? Don't be—your code stays the same; the user interfaces have changed, so the dialog boxes used to set up the ConnectionString are being changed.

TIP To keep things interesting, there's still a Current Catalog property in the Properties collection; but there's also an Initial Catalog property, which is the one you should use in the ConnectionString.

The Connection object has both Mode and DefaultDatabase properties as well as being available in the Properties collection. ADO defines its own property names instead of using the description specified in OLE DB to guarantee that property names are the same across providers. User-defined properties will *not* have this guarantee.

ConnectionString property

This string holds the parameters needed to tell the provider everything it needs to know about opening the connection. If you want to use the OLE DB provider for SQL Server (and you do), you need to provide at least the name of the SQL Server OLE DB provider and the name of the server, as shown here:

```
Dim Cn as New Connection
Cn.Open "provider=SQLOLEDB;Server=Betav1;"
```

Sure, you can add the database= argument or the user ID and password in the ConnectionString if that makes sense. However, you had better start using Initial Catalog= to point OLE DB to your default database.

TIP   If you don't provide the right server name, your application will lock up for at least a few seconds—even if you set the ConnectionTimeout to a different value. It seems that ADO (and ODBC) waits a fixed length of time for the network to resolve the network address. Therefore, even if you've set the ConnectionTimeout to 1, you'll still get a delay. You don't have to be blocked during this wait if you use the adAsyncConnect.

Provider property

The Provider property can be set directly or set by the contents of the ConnectionString property or the ConnectionString argument of the Open method; however, specifying a provider in more than one place while calling the Open method can cause unpredictable results. If no provider is specified, the property will default to MSDASQL (Microsoft OLE DB Provider for ODBC). When the SQL Server OLE DB provider arrives, we'll be using this property more frequently. The Provider property is read/write when the connection is closed and read-only when it's open. The setting doesn't take effect until you either open the Connection object or access the Properties collection of the Connection object. If the setting is invalid, a trappable error is fired. In ADO 2.0, it is assumed that the provider string is a prog id. From the prog id, we get the clsid and instantiate the provider. If this fails, ADO falls back onto the enumerator.

CursorLocation property

The CursorLocation property let's you choose where the cursors you create (if you create any) will be built. The CursorLocation property can be set using one of the constants listed in Table 29-6.

Table 29-6
CursorLocationEnum Constants

Constant	Purpose
adUseClient	Uses client-side cursors supplied by a local cursor library. You'll need this option to enable batch-mode cursors. But most of the interesting cursors are supported only on server-side cursors. We'll get to the details about this in a moment.
adUseServer	Uses server-side or driver-supplied cursors. These cursors are sometimes very flexible and allow for some additional sensitivity to reflecting changes that others make to the actual data source. However, some features (such as dissociable Recordset objects) can't be simulated with server-side cursors, and these features will then become unavailable with this setting.
adUseNone	This is *not* an option. Although this constant looks remarkably like RDO's rdUseNone option, it doesn't do the same thing in ADO. Actually, it disables the cursor and "cursorless" operation of the provider. You shouldn't use it, and it's hidden in Visual Basic 6.0.
adUseClientBatch	Same as adUseClient—left in for compatibility with RDO.

The CursorLocation property affects connections established only *after* the property has been set—changing the property has no effect on existing connections. This property is read/write on a Connection or a closed Recordset, and read-only on an open Recordset. Recordset objects associated with connections having the CursorLocation property set will automatically pick up this setting. They can override before opening the Recordset.

IsolationLevel property

The IsolationLevel property sets or returns the isolation level, which can be set using one of the constants listed in Table 29-7.

Table 29-7
IsolationLevelEnum Constants

Constant	Purpose
adXactBrowse	Indicates that from one transaction you can view uncommitted changes in other transactions
adXactChaos	Indicates that you can't overwrite pending changes from more highly isolated transactions (No, I didn't make this one up.)

Constant	Purpose
adXactCursorStability	Default; indicates that from one transaction you can view changes in other transactions only after they've been committed
adXactIsolated	Indicates that transactions are conducted in isolation of other transactions
adXactReadCommitted	Default; same as adXactCursorStability
adXactReadUncommitted	Same as adXactBrowse
adXactRepeatableRead	Indicates that from one transaction you can't see changes made in other transactions, but that requerying can bring new Recordset objects
adXactSerializable	Same as adXactIsolated
adXactUnspecified	Indicates that the provider is using a different IsolationLevel than specified but that the level can't be determined

Mode property

The Mode property sets the access permissions for the current connection. You can set this property using the constants listed in Table 29-8 only when the Connection object is closed.

Table 29-8
ConnectModeEnum Constants

Constant	Purpose
adModeRead	Indicates read-only permissions
adModeReadWrite	Indicates read/write permissions
adModeShareDenyNone	Prevents others from opening a connection with any permissions
adModeShareDenyRead	Prevents others from opening a connection with read permissions
adModeShareDenyWrite	Prevents others from opening a connection with write permissions
adModeShareExclusive	Prevents others from opening a connection
adModeUnknown	Default; indicates that the permissions haven't yet been set or can't be determined
adModeWrite	Indicates write-only permissions

State property

The State property is a bitmask used to describe the current state of the object. This property indicates whether the object has been opened and whether it's currently busy connecting, fetching, or executing. The property is read-only and should be valid at any time. Because the State property is a bitmask, you should avoid testing it with an "=" expression. Use the AND operator instead. Actually, you should consider the valid combinations of the State property described in Table 29-9. As you can see, there aren't that many valid combinations, so you might get away with using equality expressions in your code—only to fail when they add another bit to the mask. Notice that adStateExecuting doesn't return 4, but 5—indicating that the query is open and executing. I doubt if you would (should) find a query executing against a "closed" Recordset. The same is true for the adStateFetching bit flag.

Table 29-9
ObjectStateEnum Constants

Constant	Decimal	"True" Binary	Purpose
adStateClosed	0	0000	The object is closed.
adStateOpen	1	0001	The object is open.
adStateConnecting	2	0010	The Connection object is in the process of opening.
adStateExecuting	4	0101	A query operation is still in progress (and the object is open).
adStateFetching	8	1001	The object is currently executing or opening (so the object isn't usable).

When you call any of the Execute or Open methods with the adRunAsync option, you can test the State property to determine what's currently going on (or not) or whether a Recordset was created. If the statement is still executing, the State property bits will be adStateExecuting. If waiting on a connection, the State property will have a value of adStateExecuting. When an error occurs on an asynchronously executing command, there will be no way for ADO to notify the user that an error occurs. In this case, the first time that the State property is tested after the error, a run-time error is generated. This means that the loop you used for RDO:

```
Do While rs.StillExecuting
     DoEvents
Loop
```

now becomes:

```
Do While cnn.State And adStateExecuting
     DoEvents
Loop
```

Of course, you should also consider using the object's events to determine when the operation is complete—I think it's easier.

Connection Object Events

ADO 2.0 supports events, which are notifications that certain operations are about to occur or have occurred. Events are processed by event handler routines that are called before certain operations start or after such operations conclude. Events called before an operation starts have names of the form *Will*Event (Will events), and events called after an operation concludes have names of the form Event*Complete* (Complete events).

The event handlers are controlled by the *status* parameter. Additional information is provided by the *error* and *object* parameters. In some cases, if you enable events, the error handler is not called, but the event handler is. For example, when making an asynchronous open, if you use the WithEvents syntax and assign the Connection object correctly, the event handlers fire when the connection is complete or fails to open. No trappable error occurs if it fails to open.

Typically, Will events are paired with Complete events. After the first notification, however, you can request that an event handler not receive any more notifications. Therefore, you can choose to receive only Will events or Complete events.

Connection events are issued when a transaction on a connection begins, is committed, or is rolled back; when a Command object executes; and when a Connection object opens or closes. Table 29-10 lists the Connection object events. Notice that ADO exposes RDO events such as InfoMessage here.

Table 29-10
Connection Object Events

Event	Purpose
BeginTransComplete, CommitTransComplete, RollbackTransComplete	Transaction management—Notification that the current transaction on the connection has started, committed, or rolled back
WillConnect, ConnectComplete, Disconnect	Connection management—Notification that the current connection will start, or has started or ended
WillExecute, ExecuteComplete	Command execution management—Notification that the execution of the current command on the connection will start or has ended
InfoMessage	Fires when any informational messages, including PRINT and RAISERROR messages, are sent from the server

NOTE For a detailed explanation of ADO events and how they work and interact, see Chapter 32.

Connection Transaction Management

ADO has taken transaction processing to the next level of sophistication. Instead of simply passing through transaction commands to the server, ADO takes on two-phase commit. That is, ADO and OLE DB now know how to deal with transaction operations that span servers or data sources. SQL Server 7.0 is also ready to take on part of this processing and transaction management load. You'll be able to build a transaction that involves any of the ADO providers. Such a transaction is often referred to as a *distributed* transaction. Starting a separate transaction on each Connection object accessing a data source can simulate a distributed transaction. This arrangement works well if all the modifications over each connection succeed and the associated transactions are all committed. When modifications on some connections succeed whereas others fail, however, you need to implement complex error-handling logic. The problem only becomes more cumbersome if your application is later enhanced to add additional connections to other data sources.

You can also set the isolation level of a Connection object using the read/write IsolationLevel property. The setting doesn't take effect until the next time you call the BeginTrans method. If the level of isolation you request is unavailable, the provider might return the next greater level of isolation. You set the level of isolation by changing the IsolationLevel property of the Connection object. This property sets or returns one of the IsolationLevelEnum values listed in Table 29-7.

ADO Command Object

A Command object is basically a definition of a specific command that you intend to execute against a data source. The ADO Command object plays a pivotal role in the ADO architecture. It resembles the RDO rdoQuery object in many ways, but it isn't necessarily associated with a specific connection or data source. In RDO, you create stand-alone rdoQuery objects; you can also build the ADO Command object in this way—in code using Visual Basic. You can also use the Data Environment to build ADO Command objects. (See Chapter 37 for more on the Data Environment.) Typically, you use a Command object to query a database and return records in a Recordset object, to execute a bulk operation (but not bulk copy—at least not yet), or to manipulate the structure of a database.

NOTE One of the benefits of OLE DB is its extensibility. It won't be long before we see an OLE DB provider—one that you can run from Visual Basic—that runs BCP for us. You could probably write one yourself in a couple of days. Let me know when you're done, and we can all share it!

The Command object gives you an opportunity to define a command destined to be sent to SQL Server for execution. The RDO interface spent quite a bit of time (and usually sent a sheaf of queries to the data source) to "automatically" prepare your command. Yes, this meant that you didn't *have* to tell RDO what it was executing. However, this was one of the places where RDO fell behind ODBC API applications in performance. ADO can run in automatic mode too—it does so by default. Nevertheless, you might find that a few extra statements can make your code run faster because ADO won't have to make additional round-trips to the server for clarification on how to run the command. On the other hand, those extra statements could also mean that you won't be able to change the data types or number of parameters in your commands if they are hard-coded in your applications and components. Nothing is free nowadays.

One interesting ADO technique lets you pass a Command object to the Source property of a Recordset to build a result set based on the Command query. The real advantage of Command objects is persistence. You can execute a query without using a Command object by passing a query string to the Execute method of a Connection object or to the Open method of a Recordset object. However, you eliminate any economies of scale when you do so. All the work of setting up the query and compiling it for execution is lost. Using a Command object does saves the command text in the form of a reusable procedure, however, and lets you reexecute it as many times as needed, using new parameters each time. Keep in mind that in SQL Server prior to version 7.0, these temporary queries used up space in TempDB—albeit not much.

To create a Command object independently of a previously defined Connection object, set the Command object's ActiveConnection property to a valid connection string. ADO still creates a Connection object, but it doesn't assign that object to an object variable. If you're associating multiple Command objects with the same connection, you can explicitly create and open a Connection object; this assigns the Connection object to an object variable. If you don't set the Command object's ActiveConnection property to this object variable, ADO creates a new Connection object for each Command object, even if you use the same connection string. Why? Well, the connection state problem mentioned earlier crops up again. ADO can't guarantee that the connection is in the same state after you execute your command.

To execute a Command, simply call it by its Name property on the associated Connection object or use the Execute method. Remember that before you can execute it, the Command must have its ActiveConnection property set to the Connection object. If the Command has parameters, pass values for them as arguments to the method or set them ahead of time using the Parameters collection. You'll find plenty of examples of using parameters in Chapter 31.

Command Object Collections

The Command object exposes the Parameters and Properties collections.

Parameters collection

The Parameters collection contains a set of Parameter objects used to manage the arguments to be automatically inserted into your query before it is executed. This collection lets you change the scope of your query to match the immediate needs of your application—especially in cases where you run a query more than once. No, it still doesn't make sense to build a complex parameter query if you execute it only once. Generally, we use the Parameters collection to formally define parameterized queries or stored-procedure arguments.

Using the Refresh method on a Command object's Parameters collection sends a series of queries to SQL Server to retrieve parameter information for the stored procedure or parameterized query specified in the Command object. If you haven't defined your own Parameter objects and you access the Parameters collection before calling the Refresh method, ADO automatically calls the method and builds and populates the Parameters collection for you.

If the Parameters collection of the Command object contains parameters supplied by the provider, the collection is cleared if you set the ActiveConnection property to Nothing or to another Connection object. If you manually create Parameter objects and use them to fill the Parameters collection of the Command object, setting the ActiveConnection property to Nothing or to another Connection object leaves the Parameters collection intact.

Properties collection

The Properties collection exposes provider properties, which we discussed earlier in the chapter. Just be aware that a significant amount of functionality is exposed on these Properties collections.

Command Object Methods

The Command object exposes the three methods listed in Table 29-11.

Table 29-11
Command Object Methods

Method	Purpose
Cancel	Cancels a pending asynchronous operation (See the "Cancel method" section below.)
CreateParameter	Prebuilds parameters passed to your query (See the "CreateParameter method" section on page 605.)
Execute	Executes the specified query (See the "Execute method" section on page 606.)

Cancel method

The Cancel method will cancel an asynchronously opening connection or an asynchronous Execute statement. This method can also refer to a synchronous open or execute if the cancel is executed on a second thread. The Cancel method takes no parameters and returns no values. If there are no asynchronous operations occurring, the Cancel method will have no effect (that is, it is ignored).

CreateParameter method

The CreateParameter method is used to prebuild parameters passed to your queries. You can minimize calls to SQL Server to improve performance if you know the properties of the parameters associated with the stored procedure or parameterized query you want to call. Use the CreateParameter method to create Parameter objects with the appropriate property settings, and use the Append method to add them to the Parameters collection. By using these methods, you can set and return parameter values without having to call the provider for the parameter information. Use the Delete method to remove Parameter objects from the Parameters collection if necessary. ADO uses the Parameters collection's set of Parameter objects to pass to your query unless you override the parameters when you execute the query. The CreateParameter method accepts the Parameter properties in Table 29-12 as arguments. (No, not all the properties are exposed.)

Table 29-12
Command Object CreateParameter Method Parameters

Parameter	Purpose
Name	Name of the parameter that is created. Default is "". If you don't specify a name, you can't expect to refer to the parameters by name.
Type	Data type classification of the parameter. Default is adEmpty.
Direction	Direction of the parameter. Default is adParamInput. Be sure to set this manually for OUTPUT parameters or if you have problems with ADO figuring out which direction is correct.
Size	Data size of the parameter. Default is 0. This parameter isn't needed except for variable-width columns such as Char and Varchar.
Value	Value of the parameter to be used. This parameter is the default value supplied or the actual value passed when the query is run. It can be overridden by run-time arguments passed to the Command object.

The CreateParameter method essentially creates a parameter and sets the Name, Type, Direction, and Value properties. In short, it replaces the lines

```
set p = new parameter
p.Name = "MyParm"
p.Type = adVarChar
p.Direction = adParamInput
p.Size = 42
p.Value = "MyVal"
```

with the line

```
set p = MyCommand.CreateParameter("MyParm", adVarChar, _
    adParamInput, 42, "MyVal")
```

Calling CreateParameter does *not* automatically append the parameter to the Parameters collection when called because you might want to set additional properties (precision, scale, and so on) *before* appending—since appending performs a validation.

Execute method

The Execute method is used to run the constructed query based on the properties and parameters provided in the Command object. We discussed this method earlier in the chapter, but keep in mind that the syntax is different for the Command object–based Execute method when compared to the Connection object–based Execute method. When working with the Command object, the Execute method doesn't accept a CommandText argument—it uses the string from the Command object, as shown here:

```
cmd.Execute([RecordsAffected As Long], [ParamValues As Array], _
    [Options As Long]) As Recordset
```

Using the Execute method against the Connection object executes the query specified in the object's CommandText property, just as it does when you're using it on a Command object. If the CommandText property specifies a row-returning query, and if any results are generated, ADO manufactures a new Recordset object to hold them. If the command is *not* a row-returning query, the provider returns a closed Recordset object—which you can ignore if you want to. The Execute method parameters are described in the following list:

- The RecordsAffected parameter is used to supply a variable in which to place the number of records affected by the command. This parameter is optional. If you don't pass a variable for this parameter (if you just pass a literal value) or don't supply any value at all, ADO doesn't return this information. This parameter is designed for action queries. It doesn't return the number of rows in the Recordset generated by the Execute method.

- The ParamValues parameter is an optional variant array of parameter values that the SQL Server provider uses for just *this* execution of the command. The parameter can contain an array of values. The provider uses these values to fill parameters left to right. If more values are passed in than there are parameters, the extra values are ignored.

  Parameter values passed in the ParamValues parameter array are used only for *this* execution and don't affect the underlying Parameter object's Value property. The Parameter's Value property is used when no value is passed in the ParamValues parameter array. As you can see, values passed into the ParamValues parameter array override values.

- The Option argument is a bitmask used to select the synchronous/ asynchronous options. The Option argument can be any of the ExecuteOptionEnum values listed in Table 29-13.

Table 29-13
ExecuteOptionEnum Constants

Constant	Purpose
adAsyncExecute	Runs the command asynchronously from the calling thread. RecordsAffected will always return –1 since the provider would have no way of knowing how many rows will be affected. Creates a second thread and begins execution of the command on that thread. When the provider returns from executing the command, ADO notifies your code using the ExecuteComplete event.
adAsyncFetch	Fetches results on a second thread when using CursorLocation=adUseClient. Tells ADO to begin fetching in the background after the execution of the command completes. If the user asks for a row not yet fetched, your code is blocked until that row is fetched or until no more data is available. A notification of FetchComplete occurs when the entire result set is fetched.
adAsyncFetchNonBlocking	Fetches results on a second thread without blocking when using CursorLocation=adUseClient. Tells ADO to fetch in the background, but to never block. If the user attempts to move to a row not yet fetched, ADO moves to EOF. The user can try again, however, and the next set of fetched rows will be made available. A notification of FetchComplete will occur once the entire result set has been fetched.
adExecuteNoRecords	A command that doesn't return result sets. This constant is a modifier of the adCmdText and adCmdStoredProc command types. That is, you have to use this option in combination with the others.

If the user doesn't specify any options or at least not the adAsyncExecute, the Execute method executes the command synchronously to the calling thread and returns when the command completes or when the CommandTimeout period elapses, whichever comes first.

If the query has parameters, the current values for the Command object's parameters are inserted into the query unless you override these with parameter values passed with the Execute call. You can override a subset of the parameters by omitting new values for some of the parameters when calling the Execute method. The order in which you specify the parameters is the same order in which the method passes them. For example, if there were four (or more) parameters and you wanted to pass new values for only the first and fourth parameters, you would pass Array(var1,,,var4) as the Parameters argument.

When we get to Chapter 31, we'll go over some examples and get into more detail on the Execute method.

TIP It makes more sense to create a set of Commands early in your application—or better yet, use the UserConnection or Data Environment designers to build permanent parameter queries rather than code lots of hard-coded queries. These designers leverage the ability of ADO and RDO to expose stored procedures (or any procedure) as methods on a custom UserConnection object.

Command Object Properties

The Command property is driven by its properties. It is in the Command property that you describe the command in exacting detail. We've already discussed the CommandText property, and some of the other properties will be discussed in later chapters. Table 29-14 lists the properties of the Command object.

Table 29-14
Command Object Properties

Property	Purpose
ActiveConnection	Defines the current connection string or a Connection object. Default is a Null object reference. (See the "ActiveConnection property" section on page 609.)
CommandText	Defines the executable text of the command (for example, a SQL statement, a table name, or a stored procedure name). Defaults to an empty string.
CommandTimeout	Indicates the number of seconds ADO waits before assuming that the query can't complete and returns a trappable error (and fires the ExecuteComplete event). Defaults to 30 seconds.
CommandType	Tells ADO how to process this command. (See the "CommandType property" section on page 609 and Chapter 31.)
Name	Assigns a name to or retrieves the name of a Command object. This property exposes the query as a method on the Connection object—parameters and all. This makes it easy to execute a parameterized query in code—just like in RDO 2.0.
Prepared	Indicates whether or not to save a compiled version of a command before execution. Default is False. (See the "Prepared property" section on page 610.)
State	Tells you if the Command is adStateClosed or adStateExecuting. Default is adStateClosed.

We need to talk about some of these properties in a little more detail before we go on.

ActiveConnection property

The ActiveConnection property tells ADO where the server is located—or how to get to it. This property defaults to Nothing and can be set to any valid Connection object. To dissociate the connection from the command and release the server-side resources, simply set the ActiveConnection property to Nothing. This basically closes the connection, but it also clears the Parameters collection—though only if you had set the ActiveConnection property to a connect *string* and not a Connection object. The same thing happens if you use the Close method. If you attempt to call the Execute method on a Command object before setting this property to an open Connection object or valid connection string, an error occurs—(well, duh).

TIP More and more, it seems that we have to set an object to Nothing to get it to release its death grip on client or server resources. Although I don't like this trend, this extra task is better than the "leaky" alternative of having memory tied up all over the application.

If the Parameters collection of the Command object contains parameters supplied by the provider, the collection is cleared if you set the ActiveConnection property to Nothing or to another Connection object. If you manually create Parameter objects and use them to fill the Parameters collection of the Command object, setting the ActiveConnection property to Nothing or to another Connection object leaves the Parameters collection intact.

If you close a Connection object associated with a Command object, the ActiveConnection property is set to Nothing. Setting this property to a closed Connection object generates an error. This means that ADO expects the ActiveConnection property to be active. Folks, this isn't that hard to figure out.

CommandType property

The CommandType property tells ADO what's in the CommandText string. The CommandType property setting keeps ADO from having to poll SQL Server to see what you're talking about. If you don't tell ADO what to expect, it submits one or more queries to SQL Server to test the syntax and learn what it can from the server before trying to execute the string. If the CommandType property doesn't match the type of command in the CommandText property, however, an error occurs when you call the Execute method. What did you expect?

You can specify the command type using the CommandTypeEnum constants listed in Table 29-15.

Table 29-15
CommandTypeEnum Constants

Constant	Purpose
adCmdText	Indicates that the provider should evaluate CommandText as a textual definition of a command. In other words, this is a TSQL statement that should be taken as is. TSQL statements are compiled into temporary stored procedures before execution.
adCmdTable	Indicates that the provider should evaluate CommandText as a base table name. This evaluates to "Select * from <table>", which is something you should avoid for any tables over a few hundred rows.
adCmdTableDirect	Indicates that the provider should evaluate CommandText as a base table name and forces ADO to use the OLE DB IOpenRowset interface instead of executing an ICommand. This option is important for providers that support commands but get better performance opening the table directly (like Jet).
adCmdStoredProc	Indicates that the provider should evaluate CommandText as a stored procedure. This option means that this command will *not* be compiled into a stored procedure before execution.
adCmdUnknown	Indicates that you don't know the type of command in the CommandText argument or you want ADO to figure out how to execute the statement. This constant is the default.

Prepared property

The Prepared property tells ADO to have the provider save a prepared (or compiled) version of the query specified in the CommandText property before a Command object's first execution. The default is False. In other words, if Prepared is True, ADO tells SQL Server to create a temporary stored procedure to execute the query. Creating a temporary stored procedure will slow a command's first execution, but once SQL Server compiles a command, ADO and SQL Server will use the compiled version of the command for any subsequent executions. Setting Prepared to True can result in improved performance, assuming that you execute the command two or more times—less than that and it's a wash or a waste of resources. When you upgrade to SQL Server 7.0, you won't need to create temporary stored procedures to streamline the execution of queries, but using the Prepared property will help SQL Server 7.0

know how to treat this command on a long-term basis. Of course, if you're executing a stored procedure in the first place, it's not necessary to set Prepared to True.

ADO Recordset Object

The ADO Recordset object is the pathway to the data returned by SQL Server. It contains the "answer" to your query. It consists of zero or more rowsets and result sets that contain metadata about the data returned, including row counts, column (field) descriptions, and the data values. Although you can bind the Recordset to a grid or a list to display the entire set of rows, only one row of the Recordset is accessible at any one time. That is, other rows might be addressable in the Recordset, but there is never more than one "current" row. This also means that a Recordset might contain no rows, or your current-row pointer isn't pointing to a valid row. In this case, there is no current row available. Many of the properties used in both DAO and RDO result sets also apply in ADO—at least to an extent. There are EOF (end of file) and BOF (beginning of file) properties as well as a RecordCount property and other old favorites to make using ADO Recordsets a familiar task. The Recordset methods are also similar. All of the DAO and RDO Move methods are supported as well as several that only DAO/Jet support, such as Find and Sort. And, of course, there are a bevy of new properties, methods, and events to learn. What *fun*!

The ADO Recordset is different in an exciting new way. It can be created from the ozone. That is, you can simply declare the object and start appending Field objects to its Fields collection. No, you don't create stand-alone Field objects; but the Append has enough arguments to create a basic Field object and add it to the collection in a single operation. You can't take an existing Recordset object and add, change, or remove Fields—not yet. You can clone an existing Recordset with or without data for whatever purpose suits your fancy. This feature also enables you to save Recordset data and metadata as a file. Later, the persisted file can be used to re-create the Recordset object. The persisted file can exist on a local drive, a network server, or as a URL on a Web site. We talk about how to save a Recordset to a file in Chapter 31.

In addition, the new GetString method explicitly converts a Recordset object to a string where the columns and rows are delimited with characters you specify. As with the rdoResultset GetClipString method in RDO, you can assign the string created by GetString to the Clip property of a clip-aware control (such as the Microsoft FlexGrid control) to populate it. No, this isn't your ordinary Recordset object.

Recordset Object Collections

The Recordset object supports two collections, which are listed in Table 29-16. No, there's no collection of Recordsets in ADO—but there's little to stop you from creating and managing your own.

Table 29-16
Recordset Collections

Collection	Purpose
Fields	The set of Field objects—one for each column in the Recordset (See the "ADO Field Object" section on page 650 for more details about Field objects.)
Properties	OLE DB provider–defined properties for the Field object

Recordset Object Methods

The Recordset supports a comprehensive set of methods that can be grouped into four types, as listed in Table 29-17. We'll briefly discuss these methods in these related groups to better illustrate how the methods work together and how they work with the other properties. We drive by the Recordset object again in subsequent chapters.

Table 29-17
Recordset Method Types

Method Type	Methods
Creation and state manipulation	Open, Close, Requery, Cancel, CancelBatch, CancelUpdate, CompareBookmarks, NextRecordset, Resync, Supports, Save
Population	Clone, GetRows, GetString
Navigation	Move, MoveFirst, MoveLast, MoveNext, MovePrevious, Find
Maintenance	AddNew, Update, UpdateBatch, Delete

Recordset creation and state manipulation methods

Table 29-18 summarizes the Recordset creation and state manipulation methods.

Table 29-18
Recordset Creation and State Manipulation Methods

Methods	Purpose
Open	Builds the Recordset. (See the "Open method" section on page 613.)
Close	Releases the Recordset's resources. (See the "Close method" section on page 618.)
Requery	Reexecutes the query based on current parameters. (See the "Requery method" section on page 619.)
Cancel	Terminates an asynchronous operation. (See the "Cancel method" section on page 619.)

Methods	Purpose
CancelBatch	Cancels pending updates in a Recordset in batch update mode. (See the "CancelBatch and CancelUpdate methods" section on page 619.)
CancelUpdate	Discards all the pending changes associated with the specified Recordset object, thus restoring the values for the row as of the last data retrieval method call. (See the "CancelBatch and CancelUpdate methods" section on page 619.)
CompareBookmarks	Compares two bookmarks. (See the "CompareBookmarks method" section on page 620.)
NextRecordset	Clears the current Recordset object and returns the next Recordset in the set when you execute a query that returns more than one result set. This method can also return the RecordsAffected from each result set. (See the "NextRecordset method" section on page 620.)
Resync	Refreshes the data in the current Recordset object from the underlying database. (See the "Resync method" section on page 622.)
Supports	Checks whether the Recordset supports some specific functionality. (See the "Supports method" section on page 622.)
Save	Records a Recordset structure and data to a disk file. (See the "Save method" section on page 623.)

Open method

The Open method is the bread and butter method used to execute a query and (potentially) create a result set. No, result sets don't have to include rowsets. And no, rowsets don't have to be exposed as a cursor. As a matter of fact, lots of applications work just fine and never use cursors. We'll see that, by default, ADO creates a very lightweight "cursorless" result set.

To create an empty Recordset, declare a New Recordset object, and before you set the ActiveConnection property, use the Append method to add Field objects to the Recordset Fields collection. When you're ready, use the Open method with no operands to instantiate the new Recordset. You can then use the AddNew, Insert, Delete, and Update methods on the Recordset to add rows. I've included a couple of examples of using the Open method in this context in Chapter 31.

You can also create a Recordset from a saved file by using the adCmdFile option and pointing to the file path in the Source argument. Chapter 31 has an example of creating and saving a Recordset using files.

The Open method is deceptively flexible. The Source argument can contain a Command object, which implies that the predefined Command should be executed—using the parameters it has been assigned. The Source argument can also be a SQL statement or simply the name of a table or a stored procedure.

Because you can build Recordset objects from files, this argument might also point to a file containing a persisted Recordset. ADO spends considerable CPU time figuring out what you're sending, so this flexibility might be somewhat expensive.

You don't have to have an open connection before using the Recordset object, but I expect that it would be easier to debug if you did. You tell the Open method where to get the data through the ActiveConnection argument, which can be a Connection object or a string containing connection string parameters. If you pass a connection string for this argument, ADO opens a new SQL Server connection using the specified parameters. You can change the value of this property after opening the Recordset to send updates to another provider. Or you can set this property to Nothing to disconnect the Recordset from any provider.

The Open method takes a number of arguments, which are listed in Table 29-19. These arguments tell ADO how to build the query and how to construct the cursor (if any). The following code shows the syntax for the Open method:

```
recordset.Open Source, ActiveConnection, CursorType, LockType, _
    Options
```

Table 29-19
Recordset Object Open Method Arguments

Argument	Purpose
Source	Specifies a Command object variable name, a SQL statement, a table name, a stored procedure call, or the file name of a persisted Recordset.
ActiveConnection	Provides the current connection string or a Connection object—just as on the Command object. Default is a Null object reference.
CursorType	Selects one of the valid cursor types and defaults to adOpenForwardOnly. You can also choose adOpenStatic, adOpenDynamic, or adOpenKeyset. (See the "ADO cursor types" section on page 615 for more details—but consider that these cursors are pretty standard.)
LockType	Selects one of the concurrency options and defaults to adLockReadOnly. You can also choose one of the other three options: adLockPessimistic, adLockOptimistic, and adLockBatchOptimistic. (See the "ADO LockType setting" section on page 616 for more details.)
Options	Specifies options that tell ADO that you want to re-create the Recordset from a saved file or run the query asynchronously. The options map to the CommandType property. (See the "Open method Options argument" section on page 618 for more information.)

TIP Don't set the ActiveConnection property when the Source property is set to a Command object because the connection is derived from the Command object's ActiveConnection property. (For details, see the "ADO Command Object" section on page 602.)

ADO cursor types

ADO is capable of creating and managing a wide variety of cursors, including all four standard types that we have grown to know, use, and hate: forward-only, static, keyset, and dynamic. ADO is pretty smart about handling its cursors; it populates them automatically, without your code having to do anything. But there's nothing in ADO (except the row limits) that keeps you from being dumb about cursors. It's still possible to create an impossibly large cursor that brings your client, your network, and your server to its knees. As you see in Table 29-20, there are no surprises here. I discuss cursor operations elsewhere, so let this brief summary suffice for now. Consider that the CursorType argument to the Open method sets the Recordset object's CursorType property.

NOTE The ADO team went to a lot of trouble to create the most efficient cursor possible. So ADO creates a "firehose" cursor by default. This cursor is a forward-only, read-only, single-row cursorless result set—the same one we try to build in RDO whenever possible.

Table 29-20
CursorTypeEnum Constants

Constant	Purpose
adOpenForwardOnly	Forward-only cursor. Default for server-side connections. Identical to a static cursor except that you can only scroll forward through records. This improves performance in situations when you need to make only a single pass through a Recordset. This is my favorite "noncursor." When you choose a forward-only, read-only, single-row cursor, you get the fastest way possible to retrieve data. This cursor type is available only on server-side cursors.
adOpenStatic	Static cursor. A static copy of a set of records that you can use to find data or generate reports. Additions, changes, or deletions by other users are not visible. Like the forward-only cursor, this cursor is popular for many applications. It's nearly as inexpensive as the forward-only cursor—and it can be updateable. This cursor type is the only option for client-side connections.

(continued)

Table 29-20 *continued*

Constant	Purpose
adOpenKeyset	Keyset cursor. Like a dynamic cursor, except that you can't see records that other users add; records that other users delete are inaccessible from your Recordset. Data changes by other users are still visible. This is the basic read-write, fully scrollable cursor. It is expensive, but not as lavish as the dynamic cursor. This cursor type is available only on server-side cursors.
adOpenDynamic	Dynamic cursor. Additions, changes, and deletions by other users are visible, and all types of movement through the Recordset are allowed, except for bookmarks if the provider doesn't support them. This is the most expensive cursor, meaning that it's the slowest and most consumptive of all kinds of system resources. This cursor type is available only on server-side cursors.

TIP   Remember that each feature you ask for in a cursor costs you—in CPU time, LAN bandwidth, RAM and disk space, and other system resources. Updateable, scrollable cursors make coding easier, but they are often more expensive than they need to be. In any case, keep the number of rows fetched to a bare minimum. This minimizes the impact of the cursor on your system.

Consider that when you choose client-side cursors, only static cursors are created—no matter what kind you ask for. If you want one of the other types, you must use the server-side library. Remember that a "firehose" cursor isn't really a cursor at all, but a "cursorless" result set.

ADO LockType setting

The LockType setting tells ADO how to manage concurrency—that is, how to prevent other users from changing rows you're working on or are simply trying to update. Table 29-21 lists the available lock type constants. Of course, you use this setting only if you want ADO to manage your updates for you. In more and more cases, we use stored procedures to do our updates, so we open our Recordsets using read-only cursors (if we use cursors at all). Frankly, if you use adLockPessimistic, you have rocks in your head. Using this cursor makes sense in so few cases that they ought to make you get a note from your mom before using it.

TO WHOM IT MAY CONCERN:

MY SON JUSTIN TELLS ME HE NEEDS PERMISSION TO USE WHAT HE CALLS PESSIMISTIC LOCKING. I THINK THIS IS A LITTLE STRANGE, BUT I GUESS IT IS ALL RIGHT—AS LONG AS HE GETS HOME FROM SCHOOL ON TIME AND DOESN'T TALK TO STRANGERS—ESPECIALLY BILL.

Table 29-21
LockTypeEnum Constants

Constant	Purpose
adLockReadOnly	Default. Read-only—you can't alter the data. This lock type produces the lowest-impact result sets and is easiest to scale.
adLockPessimistic	Pessimistic locking, record by record—the provider does what is necessary to ensure successful editing of the records, usually by locking records at the data source immediately upon editing. This lock type is the most difficult to scale because it locks rows or pages immediately upon open—and those locks remain in place as long as the cursor is open. This lock type is available only for server-side cursors.
adLockOptimistic	Optimistic locking, record by record—the provider uses optimistic locking, locking records only when you call the Update method. This is the lowest-impact locking strategy; however, it requires the most error-handling code.
adLockBatchOptimistic	Optimistic batch updates—required for batch update mode as opposed to immediate update mode. This lock type can be used only with static cursors built with the client-side libraries.

You have to set the LockType property before opening a Recordset to specify what type of locking SQL Server should use when opening it. Read the property to return the type of locking in use on an open Recordset object. The LockType property is read/write when the Recordset is closed and read-only when it is open.

CAUTION
Not all of the cursors support all of the LockType options. Check out the cursor tables in Chapter 31 (pages 722–723) for more details.

Open method Options argument

The options flags map to the CommandType property, tell ADO that you want to re-create the Recordset from a saved file, or run the query asynchronously. When you run the query using the adAsyncExecute option, control returns to your code immediately—the Recordset won't be ready for use until the FetchComplete event fires or the State property returns adStateOpen.

You use one or more of the constants listed in Table 29-22 with the Options argument. (See Table 29-15 for a more detailed explanation of these constants.)

Table 29-22
CommandTypeEnum Constants

Constant	Purpose
adCmdText	Indicates that the provider should evaluate Source as a textual definition of a command.
adCmdTable	Indicates that the provider should evaluate Source as a table name.
adCmdTableDirect	Forces ADO to use the OLE DB IopenRowset interface instead of executing an ICommand. This option is important for providers that support commands but get better performance opening the table directly (like Jet).
adCmdStoredProc	Indicates that the provider should evaluate Source as a stored procedure.
adCmdUnknown	Indicates that the type of command in the Source argument isn't known.
adCmdFile	Indicates that the persisted (saved) Recordset should be restored from the file named in Source.
adRunAsync	Indicates that the Source should be executed asynchronously.

Close method

When applied to the Recordset method, the Close method releases the associated data and any exclusive access you might have had to the data through this particular Recordset object. In other words, your page and row locks are released. And no, you haven't lost the Recordset object—it's still there. You'll have to set the object to Nothing to release the client-side object. The Close method clears out the cache but leaves the object behind.

You can later call the Open method to reopen the Recordset with the same or modified attributes. While the Recordset object is closed, calling any methods that require a live cursor generates an error. If you have an edit in progress, calling the Close method trips an error. You can either ignore the error, finish the edit by calling the Update method, or try the CancelUpdate method first. If you close the Recordset object during batch updating, all changes since the last UpdateBatch call are lost. If you use the Clone method to create copies of an open Recordset object, closing the original or a clone doesn't affect any of the other copies.

Requery method

The requery method reruns the Recordset query using the current set of parameters in the Parameters collection. In SQL Server 6.5 and earlier, this method reuses the temporary stored procedure created when the Recordset was first created. In SQL Server 7.0, the interface tries to leverage the cache-resident procedure it just ran. If the Source property is a string and you aren't pointing to a Command object, not using the Requery method forces ADO to re-create another temporary stored procedure instead of leveraging the work already done. If you're editing the current record or adding a new record, an error occurs. You can choose to rerun the query in asynchronous mode by adding the adRunAsync option. When the Requery method completes, the RecordsetChangeComplete event will fire.

> **NOTE** While the Recordset object is open, the properties that define the nature of the cursor (CursorType, LockType, MaxRecords, and so forth) are read-only. Thus, the Requery method can refresh only the current cursor. To change any of the cursor properties and view the results, you must use the Close method so that the properties become read/write again. You can then change the property settings and call the Open method to reopen the cursor.

Cancel method

The Cancel method stops an asynchronously opening connection or an asynchronous Execute statement. The Cancel method takes no parameters and returns no values. If there are no asynchronous operations occurring, the Cancel method has no effect—it's ignored.

CancelBatch and CancelUpdate methods

These methods are used to discard the changes made to your Recordset. When you use the AddNew method or address the Fields collection Value property and make changes, these changes are cached until you execute the Update method. You can undo these changes right up to the point of using Update by executing the CancelUpdate or CancelBatch method. (The CancelBatch method is used in batch update mode.) You can't undo changes to the current record or to a new record after you call the Update method—unless the changes are either part of a transaction that you can roll back with the RollbackTrans method or part of a batch update that you can cancel with the CancelBatch method. Once you use the Delete method, the row is deleted—again, unless it is part of a transaction. If you haven't changed the current record or added a new record, calling the CancelUpdate method generates an error.

If you're adding a new record when you call the CancelUpdate method, the record that was current prior to the AddNew call becomes the current record again.

CompareBookmarks method

This new ADO method is used to determine whether two bookmarks taken from within a single Recordset are equivalent. The CompareBookmarks method calls directly into the OLE DB IRowsetLocate::Compare method, and specific details about compare can be retrieved there—assuming you have access to the OLE DB docs.

Here are some special notes about bookmarks you should keep in mind:

- Bookmarks are comparable across sorts and filters, meaning that you should be able to take a bookmark, change the sort or the filter, and then use that bookmark in a comparison later.

- Bookmarks are comparable only within a chapter, which means that comparing bookmarks from two different children in a hierarchy is unsupported. The reason such a comparison is not supported is that the OLE DB interface being called has only a single hChapter argument.

- Bookmarks will not "legally" be comparable across Open/Close or Requery. Once the Recordset has been closed, the bookmark is no longer valid.

- Bookmarks should be comparable between two clones since they're based on the same IRowset.

Table 29-23 lists the values returned from performing a bookmark comparison.

Table 29-23
CompareEnum Constants

Constant	Purpose
adCompareEqual	The two bookmarks refer to the same row.
adCompareGreaterThan	The first bookmark follows the second bookmark in the Recordset.
adCompareLessThan	The first bookmark precedes the second bookmark in the Recordset.
adCompareNotComparable	The bookmarks could not be compared. Their structure or definition doesn't permit a comparison.
adCompareNotEqual	The bookmarks are not equal and their order isn't determined.

NextRecordset method

The NextRecordset method returns the next Recordset in a command sequence. Use the following syntax:

```
Set recordset2 = recordset1.NextRecordset( RecordsAffected )
```

In other words, if you execute a query that returns more than one result set, the NextRecordset method discards the current Recordset and returns the next Recordset in the command batch. Recordset1 and Recordset2 can be the same Recordset object, or you can use separate objects. If you provide a Long variable, ADO returns the number of records that the current operation affected.

If you open a Recordset object based on a compound command statement (for example, "SELECT * FROM table1;SELECT * FROM table2") using the Execute method on a Command or the Open method on a Recordset, ADO (and SQL Server) executes only the first command and returns the results to the Recordset. To access the results of subsequent commands in the statement, call the NextRecordset method.

As long as there are additional results, the NextRecordset method continues to return Recordset objects. If a row-returning command returns no records, the returned Recordset object will be empty; test for this case by verifying that the BOF and EOF properties are both True. You can also check the State property; if it returns adStateClosed, there are no more Recordset objects. You'll also get an InfoMessage event "No more Results" when the last Recordset has been fetched.

Don't be confused with result sets that return no rows, non-row-returning result sets, and void (set to Nothing) Recordset objects. If a non-row-returning command executes successfully, the returned Recordset object will be closed, which you can verify by testing the State property on the Recordset.

NOTE The NextRecordset method in ADO is different from the RDO MoreResults method in that MoreResults simply activates the next rdoResultset against the current variable and returns False if there are no more results. ADO was implemented differently in case a data provider could keep the individual Recordset objects alive. It seems that the SQL Server providers don't or can't. That makes sense because SQL Server never has supported this type of functionality. However, when you use client-side cursors, ADO's client cursor engine provides this functionality for you.

If an edit is in progress while in immediate update mode, calling the NextRecordset method generates an error; call the Update or CancelUpdate method first.

Suppose you need to pass parameters for more than one command in the compound statement. You do this by filling the Parameters collection or by passing an array with the original Open or Execute call. However, the parameters must be in the same order in the collection or array as their respective commands in the command series.

The ADO spec tells us that to extract output parameters from a query, we first have to fetch all the results. This is nothing new—it's how SQL Server has always worked: the OUTPUT and Return Status (Return) parameters are always sent last in the Tabular Data Stream—after the rows. I haven't found this to be the case, however. It seems that the OUTPUT parameters are available immediately after executing the query.

Resync method

The Resync method refreshes the data in the current Recordset object from the underlying database using the following syntax:

```
recordset.Resync AffectRecords, ResyncValues
```

Use the Resync method to resynchronize the current, selected, or all records in the current Recordset with data from the underlying database. This method is useful if you're using either a static or a forward-only cursor but you want to see any changes in the underlying database. When you use the Resync method, ADO doesn't rerun the query but instead returns to the server to refetch selected rows whose data values have changed since the last fetch. You won't see any new members added to your cursor. You tell ADO which rows to resynchronize using the AffectRecords parameter. The AffectRecords parameter can be one of the values listed in Table 29-24.

Table 29-24
AffectEnum Constants

Constant	Purpose
adAffectCurrent	Refreshes only the current record.
adAffectGroup	Refreshes the records that satisfy the current Filter property setting. To use, you must set the Filter property to one of the valid predefined constants.
adAffectAllChapters	Default. Refreshes all the records in the Recordset object, including any hidden by the current Filter property setting.

Calling the Resync method cancels any pending batch updates if you use the default value for the ResyncValues parameter (adResyncAllValues). Using adResyncUnderlyingValues retrieves the latest and greatest data and places that data in the Fields' UnderlyingValue property. Using the Resync method in this fashion can help you determine why your UpdateBatch call failed and allow you to handle this conflict elegantly.

If the resynchronize fails because of a conflict with the underlying data (for example, another user has deleted a record), the ADO returns warnings to the Errors collection. These warnings don't halt your program execution or fire a trappable error, though. A trappable run-time error occurs only if there are conflicts on all of the requested records. Use the Filter property (adFilterAffectedRecords) and the Status property to locate records with conflicts. The ADO team might add a trappable error to tell you when one of these errors occurs—let's see what happens.

Supports method

You would normally use the Supports method to see whether the Recordset supports some specific functionality. For example, if you wanted to know if bookmarks are supported, you would test Supports for the adBookmark bits. Yes, this is another bitmask property, so you can't really depend on code that uses an = (equals sign) to test for a value. You'll have to AND off the bits you need. Be aware that this property lets you know that ADO supports the operation indicated—not that the provider necessarily does. Comforting? This ambiguity is because what the provider might actually return is indeterminable by ADO. For example, the query could be a three-table join masquerading as a view, with one column updateable but others not. This method is available only after execution. The available values for the CursorOptions parameter of the Supports method are listed in Table 29-25.

NOTE   The Supports method applies only to the well-known options, not to all potential options. For full option capabilities, use the Properties collection.

Table 29-25
CursorOptionEnum Constants

Constant	Value
adAddNew	16778240
adApproxPosition	16384
adBookmark	8192
adDelete	16779264
adFind	524288
adHoldRecords	256
adMovePrevious	512
adNotify	262144
adResync	131072
adUpdate	16809984
adUpdateBatch	65536

Save method

The Save method is an important new ADO 2.0 method used to record a Recordset structure and data to a disk file. Recall from earlier in the chapter that Save permits you to permanently "persist" an ADO Recordset. It can then be recalled at any time in the future by referencing the file with the Open method. The data is stored in a binary format that you choose with the method, but only one format is supported at this point. More formats are on the way and should appear as ADO evolves. Once the Recordset is reopened, you can update it and add and delete rows as required. When it comes time to post these changes to the database, you need to assign a valid Connection to the ActiveConnection property and use the BatchUpdate method. ADO takes care of the rest. When you're ready to save your Recordset, use the following syntax:

```
recordset.Save FileName, PersistFormat
```

Table 29-26 lists the arguments of the Save method.

Table 29-26
Recordset Object Save Method Arguments

Argument	Purpose
FileName	Completes the pathname of the file where the Recordset is to be saved.
PersistFormat	Sets the format of the file. Currently, adPersistADTG is the only supported format.

You can use the Save method only on an open Recordset. Use the Open method to retrieve the Recordset from a named file. The Filter and Sort properties apply when ADO saves the Recordset. You can save just added, updated, deleted, or otherwise selected records. You can continue to work on the Recordset after saving it. Invoking the Save method doesn't close the Recordset. See Chapter 30 for an example using the Save method.

Recordset population methods

Once you create an ADO Recordset, you have a number of ways to extract the rows from the Field.Value property for each column and from every row. Looping through the Recordset row-by-row should be your option of last resort. Because ADO and Visual Basic provide so many automated ways to retrieve data, only rarely should you need to retrieve it manually. Let's look at your options:

If you're editing each row in a Recordset and then performing a row-by-row Update, you've missed the point of SQL Server. Very few situations require this type of client-side data processing. Most can be handled by a smart stored procedure.

- Use the ADO binding interface with the new Bindings collection to map existing rows to a Visual Basic bound control such as one of the data-aware Grid, List, or Combo controls. This technique exposes all the Recordset rows to the user with very little code on your part. You can also use this technique with stored procedures to do both the fetching and updating. Visual Basic can make it easy to set up these controls—especially if you use the Data Environment to do so.

- Use Remote Data Services (RDS) or the ADO Data control to bind a Recordset directly to bound controls. This requires virtually no code and can be a viable way to display and manage Recordsets.

- Use the GetRows method to suck down the rows into a variant array. You don't need to know how many rows are in the Recordset to do this—ADO handles all the underlying details for you. This method is extremely fast to execute, but you still have to walk the variant array row-by-row and column-by-column to move the data to a useful (or visible) location. No, you don't have to pass an impossibly large number to GetRows to get it to pull down all the rows in a result set. Simply use the adGetRowsRest to extract all remaining records from the current record forward (inclusive). Alternatively, you can leave off the argument completely, which has the same effect. We'll go over the merits and problems of GetRows in Chapter 31.

- Use the GetString method to extract the rows into a delimited string. This string is applied to the Clip property of clip-aware controls (such as the MSFlex Grid). This technique is also very fast and provides an easy way to expose the data in a visible control. You'll find out more about the advantages and disadvantages of using GetString in Chapter 31.

- Reference the individual rows by addressing the current row's Field.Value property. This requires a row-by-row, column-by-column (Field-by-Field) addressing technique, which can be very expensive. You should avoid this option.

Let's take a closer look at the Recordset object's population methods, which are listed in Table 29-27.

Table 29-27
Recordset Population Methods

Method	Purpose
Clone	Builds a temporary copy of a Recordset (See the "Clone method" section below.)
GetRows	Extracts rows of a Recordset into a Variant array (See the "GetRows method" section below.)
GetString	Extracts rows of a Recordset into a delimited string (See the "GetString method" section on page 627.)

Clone method

If you want to make a temporary copy of a Recordset, you can use the Clone method with the following syntax:

```
Set rstDuplicate = rstOriginal.Clone ()
```

Once you have a copy of your Recordset, you can make changes to it or to the original Recordset and save these changes as needed. Using the Clone method is more efficient than creating and opening a new Recordset object with the same definition as the original. The current record of a newly created clone is set to the first record.

Changes you make to one Recordset object are visible in all of its clones, regardless of cursor type. Once you execute Requery on the original Recordset, however, the clones will no longer be synchronized to the original.

Closing the original Recordset doesn't close its copies; closing a copy doesn't close the original or any of the other copies.

You can only clone a Recordset object that supports bookmarks. Bookmark values are interchangeable; that is, a bookmark reference from one Recordset object refers to the same record in any of its clones.

GetRows method

The GetRows method is used to extract the rows from a Recordset into a Variant array. First declare the Variant array variable as an open-ended array. Next use

GetRows to retrieve multiple records of a Recordset into the array. The following code shows the syntax:

```
Dim MyVariantData() as Variant
MyVariantData = recordset.GetRows( Rows, Start, Fields )
```

You don't have to worry about sizing the array because ADO sizes it for you. You *do* have to worry about exhausting all available RAM on your system if there are too many rows to deal with, but you won't let that happen, will you? You can specify a limit to the number of rows to fetch using the Rows argument and a starting point to begin the fetch with the Start argument—which you specify as a bookmark. This technique can be useful for large Recordset objects. Using adGetRowsRest as the Rows argument tells ADO to fetch all remaining rows. You can also use one of the BookmarkEnum values listed in Table 29-28.

Table 29-28
BookmarkEnum Constants

Constant	Purpose
adBookmarkCurrent	Tells ADO to start at the current record
adBookmarkFirst	Tells ADO to start at the first record
adBookmarkLast	Tells ADO to start at the last record

You can also tell ADO to extract only specified columns by setting the Fields argument. This Variant contains a single field name, an ordinal position, or an array of field names or ordinal position numbers. ADO returns only the data in these fields.

Once GetRows completes, you can use the UBound to find out how many rows and columns were read. For example, if your Recordset returns 10 rows with 4 columns each,

```
UBound (MyVariantData,1)
```

returns 4 and

```
UBound (MyVariantData,2)
```

returns 10.

Use the GetRows method to copy records from a Recordset into a two-dimensional array. The first subscript identifies the field, and the second identifies the record number. The array variable is automatically dimensioned to the correct size when the GetRows method returns the data.

TIP If GetRows is used against an adOpenForwardOnly type Recordset, the Recordset data can't be reaccessed once GetRows is executed.

If you don't specify a value for the Rows argument, the GetRows method automatically retrieves *all* the records in the Recordset object. If you request more records than are available, GetRows returns only the number of available records.

If the Recordset object supports bookmarks, you can specify at which record the GetRows method should begin retrieving data by passing the value of that record's Bookmark property.

After you call GetRows, the next unread record becomes the current record, or the EOF property is set to True if there are no more records.

GetString method

The GetString method returns the Recordset as a string. ADO 2.0 supports only a single delimited text format for the output string. You can set the delimiters yourself to describe your own string format. Use the following syntax to invoke GetString:

```
Set MyString = recordset.GetString(StringFormat, NumRows, _
    ColumnDelimiter, RowDelimiter, NullExpr)
```

The GetString method arguments are described in Table 29-29.

Table 29-29
Recordset Object GetString Method Arguments

Argument	Purpose
StringFormat	Optional. The format the Recordset should be converted to. The only option is adClipString, which indicates that columns are delimited with ColumnDelimiter, rows are delimited with RowDelimiter, and null values are indicated with NullExpr.
NumRows	Optional. The number of rows in the Recordset to convert. If NumRows isn't specified or if it is greater than the total number of rows in the Recordset, all the rows in the Recordset are converted. This is different than the NumRows argument in the RDO GetClipString method, which forces you to provide some number of rows.
ColumnDelimiter	Optional—and only with adClipString. Delimiter used between columns, otherwise defaults to TAB.
RowDelimiter	Optional—and only with adClipString. Delimiter used between rows, otherwise defaults to CARRIAGE RETURN.
NullExpr	Optional—and only with adClipString. Expression used in place of a NULL value, otherwise defaults to an empty string ("").

The string that GetString returns contains only the row data, not the schema, so a Recordset can't be reopened using this string. This method is more or less equivalent to the RDO GetClipString method.

Recordset navigation methods

The Recordset navigation methods let you reposition the current-row pointer in your result set. A number of Recordset properties also reposition the current-row pointer. We'll discuss the navigation properties in the following section. All of these navigation methods are really leftovers from the ISAM and dBase days when developers worked exclusively with cursors. Of course, you know that cursors are *evil* and that you should avoid them. However, if you have to use cursors, you have to use the navigation methods to move around in them.

The newest member of this group of methods and properties is the Find method. Like its DAO cousin, this method lets you filter the Recordset to contain a specific subset of the rows. In ADO, however, the Find operation is carried out by the local cursor engine. That's one reason it isn't supported on server-side cursors. We'll discuss the Find method in more detail in Chapter 31.

If rows are returned by your query, and once the Recordset is open, ADO positions the current-row pointer at the first row of the result set. Depending on the type of cursor you selected, you're then free to move the current-row pointer anywhere in the result set. Of course, with a forward-only cursor, you can only use the MoveNext method. If no rows are returned by your query, Recordset.EOF is True, and the navigation methods won't work.

When using the Move methods, if you position the current-row pointer off the end of the Recordset, its EOF or BOF property is set to True. We've discussed these properties and methods before, but ADO behaves somewhat differently than DAO and RDO. Because ADO gives you more control of the cache, you can also reposition within the cache with far more flexibility. Table 29-30 summarizes the Recordset navigation methods.

Table 29-30
Recordset Navigation Methods

Method	Purpose
Move	Repositions to the *n*th row. Locates the specific row in the cache or result set, fetches it, and makes it current. (See the "Move method" section on page 629.)
MoveFirst	Repositions to the first row. Fetches the first row from the cache or server.
MoveLast	Repositions to the last row. This fully populates the Recordset and can be run asynchronously. ADO then returns the last row from the Recordset.
MoveNext	Repositions to the next row. Fetches the next row from the cache or server.
MovePrevious	Repositions to the previous row. Fetches the previous row in the cache or from the server.
Find	Positions the current-row pointer to a row matching the specified criteria or to the end of the Recordset if no match is found. (See the "Find method" section on page 631.)

Move method

The Move method is similar to the RDO method by the same name. However, the ADO version takes a second argument that designates the starting point of the move. The new syntax looks like this:

```
recordset.Move NumRecords, Start
```

The NumRecords argument is a signed Long value specifying the number of records to move—or at least attempt to move—forward or backward. The optional Start argument is a bookmark or one of the BookmarkEnum values listed in Table 29-31.

Table 29-31
BookmarkEnum Constants

Constant	Purpose
adBookmarkCurrent	Default. Start at the current record.
adBookmarkFirst	Start at the first record.
adBookmarkLast	Start at the last record.

If the NumRecords argument is greater than zero, the current-record position moves forward (toward the end of the Recordset). If NumRecords is less than zero, the current-record position moves backward (toward the beginning of the Recordset). If NumRecords is zero, the record is refreshed.

If you attempt to move the current-record position to a point before the first record or after the last record, ADO sets the current-record pointer beyond the end of the result set and sets either BOF or EOF to True. An attempt to move forward when the EOF property is True or to move backward when BOF is True generates an error—just as in DAO and RDO.

This means that not all of the Move methods are permitted if the EOF and BOF states are not correct. Table 29-32 on the following page summarizes which Move methods are allowed with different combinations of the BOF and EOF properties.

Calling the Move method from an empty Recordset object generates an error. Allowing a Move method doesn't guarantee that the method will successfully locate a record; it only means that calling the specified Move method won't generate an error.

Table 29-32
Move Methods Allowed Based on BOF and EOF Property Values

BOF	EOF	Move 0	MoveFirst, MoveLast	MoveNext, Move > 0	MovePrevious, Move < 0
True	False	Error	Allowed	Allowed	Error
False	True	Error	Allowed	Error	Allowed
True	True	Error	Error	Error	Error
False	False	Allowed	Allowed	Allowed	Allowed

Table 29-33 shows what happens to the BOF and EOF property settings when you call various Move methods but are unable to successfully locate a record.

Table 29-33
BOF and EOF Changes Based on Move Method Calls

Method	BOF	EOF
Move 0	No change	No change
MoveFirst, MoveLast	Set to True	Set to True
MoveNext, Move > 0	No change	Set to True
MovePrevious, Move < 0	Set to True	No change

If you pass the Start argument, the move is relative to the record with this bookmark, assuming that the Recordset object and cursor support bookmarks. If not specified, the move is relative to the current record.

If you're using the CacheSize property to locally cache records from the provider, passing a NumRecords that moves the current-record position outside the current group of cached records forces ADO to retrieve a new group of records starting from the destination record. The CacheSize property determines the size of the newly retrieved group, and the destination record is the first record retrieved.

NOTE ADO behaves differently than RDO in that if the Recordset object is forward-only, a user can still pass a NumRecords less than zero as long as the destination is within the current set of cached records. If the Move call would move the current-record position to a record before the first cached record, an error will occur. Thus you can use a record cache that supports full scrolling over a provider or a cursor that supports only forward scrolling.

Because cached records are loaded into memory, you should avoid caching more records than is necessary. Even if a forward-only Recordset object supports backward moves in this way, calling the MovePrevious method on any forward-only Recordset object still generates an error.

Find method

The Find method is new for ADO and replicates functionality first implemented in DAO. Yep, this means that the ADO cursor engine has picked up considerable code from the Jet DBMS engine. The syntax for Find in ADO is considerably different than in DAO. In the first place, all the DAO Find methods have been combined into a single ADO method. In ADO, you provide the search direction and start location. This gives you more flexibility and should improve performance. The Find method uses the following syntax:

```
Find (Criteria, SkipRecords, SearchDirection, Start) as Boolean
```

The Find arguments are summarized in Table 29-34.

Table 29-34
Recordset Object Find Method Arguments

Argument	Purpose
Criteria	A String that specifies the column name, comparison operator, and value to use in the search.
SkipRecords	An optional Long value. If 0, the current row is used in the search. Otherwise, ADO skips down this number of rows before starting the search. This argument is useful when you want to find the next match in the result set. To skip the current row, simply set skipRecords to 1. You can also skip backward by using a negative number. This was a Boolean in ADO 1.5.
SearchDirection	adSearchForward (default) or adSearchBackward to indicate the direction the search should take in the result set. The search stops at the start or end of the Recordset, depending on the value of searchDirection.
Start	An optional Variant Bookmark to use as the starting position for the search.

The Find method Returns a Boolean value of True if a row satisfying the condition specified in criteria is found, or False otherwise.

The comparison operator in criteria can be > (greater than), < (less than), = (equal), or LIKE (pattern matching).

The value in criteria can be a string, a floating-point number, or a date. String values are delimited with single quotes (for example, "state = 'WA'"). Date values are delimited with # (number sign) marks (for example, "start_date > #7/22/97#").

If the comparison operator is LIKE, the string value can contain * (one or more occurrences of any character) or _ (one occurrence of any character). For example, "state LIKE M_*", matches Maine and Massachusetts. See, I told you the Jet people wrote this.

CAUTION

ADO is somewhat anal about LIKE expressions. You can use a Find with "A*" or "*A*" but not with "*A" because OLE DB has no way to search for something that begins with something. Strange but true.

TIP Watch out for the LIKE operator. The ADO Find method uses * instead of the % used in SQL Server and uses # to delineate dates whereas SQL Server uses quotes.

Recordset navigation properties

A couple of ADO properties reposition or set the current-row pointer. These navigation properties are summarized in Table 29-35.

Table 29-35
Recordset Navigation Properties

Property	Purpose
AbsolutePosition	Specifies the ordinal position of a Recordset object's current record. In other words, sets or returns the row number of the current record.
AbsolutePage	Identifies the current row's page number based on the PageSize and PageCount property settings. Set this property to move to the first row of a particular page. This is a "1-based" property.

AbsolutePosition property

The AbsolutePosition property sets or returns a Long value from 1 to the number of records in the Recordset object (RecordCount), or returns one of the constants listed in Table 29-36.

Table 29-36
PositionEnum Constants

Constant	Purpose
adPosUnknown	The Recordset is empty, or the current position is unknown.
adPosBOF	The current record pointer is at the beginning of the file.
adPosEOF	The current record pointer is at the end of the file.

Use the AbsolutePosition property to reposition the current-row pointer to a specific row based on its ordinal position in the Recordset object or to determine the ordinal position of the current record.

The AbsolutePosition property is 1-based and equals 1 when the current record is the first record in the Recordset. You might be able to obtain the total number of records in the Recordset object from the RecordCount property—if the cursor supports it and you've moved to the last row of the Recordset.

When you set the AbsolutePosition property—even if it is to a record in the current cache—ADO reloads the cache with a new group of records starting with the record you specified. The CacheSize property determines the size of this Recordset.

AbsolutePage property

This new ADO property leverages the PageSize property by logically dividing the Recordset object into a series of pages. Each of these pages contains a fixed number of rows based on the PageSize property (except for the last page, which can have fewer records). This property is very handy when you work with buffers or pages of *n* rows and you want to deal with only one buffer at a time. Using this property, you can easily position the current row to one of *n* buffers or pages.

Like the AbsolutePosition property, AbsolutePage is 1-based and equals 1 when the current-row pointer is positioned to the first row. You obtain the total number of pages in the Recordset by using the PageCount property. The AbsolutePage property sets or returns a Long value from 1 to the number of pages in the Recordset object (PageCount) or returns one of the constants listed in Table 29-36.

Recordset maintenance methods

The Recordset methods listed in Table 29-37 on the following page are used to change the contents of the result set. Once these changes are made, ADO can post the changes in the database for you, or you can intercept the Recordset events to make the changes yourself. This is how you can use stored procedures to read and write the rows.

These methods might look very similar to those found in DAO or RDO, but notice the absence of the Edit method and the incorporation of a number of new arguments for some of the methods. The ADO troops decided the Edit method was unnecessary because the code automatically enters edit mode when you address the Recordset Value property. Sure, the EditMode property still reflects the current edit state.

Table 29-37
Recordset Maintenance Methods

Method	Purpose
AddNew	Adds a new row to an updateable Recordset. (See the "AddNew method" section below.)
Update	In immediate mode (set when you open the Recordset), tells ADO to post the changes to the database for the current row. In batch mode, Update simply records the changes made to the cached Recordset. (See the "Update method" section on page 635.)
UpdateBatch	When in batch mode (set when you open the Recordset), tells ADO to post all changes to the database for the entire Recordset. (See the "UpdateBatch method" section on page 636.)
Delete	Tells ADO to drop the current row or a group of rows from the Recordset and the database. (See the "Delete method" section on page 637.)

AddNew method

The AddNew method implements new syntax that DAO and RDO developers need to learn:

```
recordset.AddNew Fields, Values
```

The Fields argument is optional. It's used to describe the new record by passing a single name or an array of names or ordinal positions of the fields in the new record. This way, you can create new rows from the ether—not necessarily based on an existing Recordset Fields collection. If you specify an array here, you have to provide an array of values as well—one for each field.

The Values argument is also optional. It provides a single value or an array of values for the fields in the new record. If Fields is an array, Values must also be an array with the same number of members; otherwise, an error occurs. The order of field names must match the order of field values in each array.

TIP Use the Supports method with adAddNew to verify whether you can add records to the current Recordset object. Not all cursors are updateable. You also can't update a cursor if ADO can't find a way to identify uniquely individual rows. This usually means you have to specify a primary key.

After you call the AddNew method, the new record becomes the current record and remains current after you call the Update method. If the Recordset object's cursor doesn't support bookmarks, you might not be able to access the new record once you move to another record. Depending on your cursor type, you might need to call the Requery method or completely rebuild the cursor to make the new record accessible.

If you call AddNew while editing the current record or while adding a new record, ADO calls the Update method to save any changes and then creates the new record. This approach is new for ADO—RDO used to toss the changes in progress when you called AddNew.

Your Recordset can be set to either immediate or batch mode based on the LockType specified when you opened the Recordset. In *immediate* update mode (the provider writes changes to the underlying data source once you call the Update method), calling the AddNew method without arguments sets the EditMode property to adEditAdd. The provider caches any field value changes locally. Calling the Update method immediately posts the new record to the database and resets the EditMode property to adEditNone. If you pass the Fields and Values arguments, however, ADO immediately posts the new record to the database. (No Update call is necessary.) The EditMode property value doesn't change (adEditNone).

In *batch* update mode (the provider caches multiple changes and writes them to the underlying data source only when you call the UpdateBatch method), calling the AddNew method without arguments sets the EditMode property to adEditAdd. The provider caches any field value changes locally. Calling the Update method adds the new record to the current Recordset and resets the EditMode property to adEditNone, but the provider doesn't post the changes to the underlying database until you call the UpdateBatch method. If you pass the Fields and Values arguments, ADO sends the new record to the provider for storage in a cache; you need to call the UpdateBatch method to post the new record to the underlying database.

Update method

The Update method posts any changes you make to the current record of a Recordset object to the database. Like the AddNew method, the Update method also supports ADO's new syntax that lets you specify specific fields and values:

```
recordset.Update Fields, Values
```

The Fields argument is optional. It provides a single name or a Variant array representing names or ordinal positions of the field or fields you want to modify.

The Values argument is also optional. It provides a single value or a Variant array representing values for the field or fields in the new record.

Use the Update method to save any changes you make to the current record of a Recordset object. These changes include calling the AddNew method or changing any field values in an existing record. You don't have to use the Edit method in ADO to start making changes to your Recordset. Of course, if you've created a read-only Recordset or ended up with one for one reason or another, you can't use the Update method without tripping an error. We'll look at how to update rows in later chapters.

If you want to use the Fields and Values options, you need to choose one of the options in the list on the following page.

- Assign values to a Field object's Value property and call the Update method.

- Pass a field name and a value as arguments with the Update call.

- Pass an array of field names and an array of values with the Update call.

Just as in the AddNew method, when you use arrays of fields and values, you must have an equal number of elements in both arrays and the order must match.

If the Recordset object is opened in batch mode, you can cache multiple changes to one or more records locally by using the Update method until you call the UpdateBatch method.

The current record remains current after you call the Update method.

NOTE If you're editing the current record or adding a new record when you reposition away from the current record or call the UpdateBatch method, ADO automatically calls the Update method. This saves any pending changes to the current record before transmitting the batched changes to the database. You must call the CancelUpdate method if you want to cancel any changes made to the current record or to discard a newly added record.

UpdateBatch method

The UpdateBatch method writes all pending batch updates to disk using the following syntax:

```
recordset.UpdateBatch AffectRecords
```

You can determine how ADO handles collisions by using the AffectRecords argument. The available constants for AffectRecords are listed in Table 29-38.

Table 29-38
AffectEnum Constants

Constant	Purpose
adAffectCurrent	Writes pending changes only for the current record.
adAffectGroup	Writes pending changes for the records that satisfy the current Filter property setting. To use this option, you must preset the Filter property to one of the valid predefined constants.
adAffectAllChapters	Default. Writes pending changes for all the records in the Recordset object, including any hidden by the current Filter property setting.

After having opened the Recordset using the adLockBatchOptimistic LockType, each time you use the Update method, changes to the Recordset are posted to the cache, not to the database. When you're ready to post these changes to the database, use the UpdateBatch method. Yes, this method works very much like the way optimistic batch updates work in RDO, but there are differences. For example, the UpdateCriteria are now stored as properties on the Recordset.

NOTE You can use batch updating only with a client-side cursor—and those are only static-type cursors.

If the attempt to transmit changes fails because of a conflict with the underlying data (for example, another user has already deleted a record), the provider returns warnings to the Errors collection but doesn't halt program execution. A run-time error occurs only if there are conflicts on all the requested records. Use the Filter property (adFilterAffectedRecords) and the Status property to locate records with conflicts.

Delete method

The Delete method drops the current record or a group of records based on the Filter property. Its syntax is slightly different from the Delete method in RDO. The new ADO syntax makes it simple to delete logical sets of rows based on the Filter property:

```
recordset.Delete AffectRecords
```

Use the AffectRecords argument if you want to delete more than one record from the Recordset. This argument provides a value that determines how many records the Delete method will affect. The available constants for AffectRecords are listed in Table 29-39.

Table 29-39
AffectEnum Constants

Constant	Purpose
adAffectCurrent	Default. Deletes only the current record.
adAffectGroup	Deletes the records that satisfy the current Filter property setting. To use this option, you must set the Filter property to one of the valid predefined constants. (See the "Filter property" section on page 643 for more information.)

Using the Delete method *marks* the current record or a group of records in a Recordset object for deletion. If the Recordset object doesn't allow record deletion (as when it's not updateable), an error occurs. If you're in immediate update mode, deletions occur in the database immediately. Otherwise, the records are marked for deletion from the cache and the actual deletion happens when you call the UpdateBatch method. You *can* use the Filter property to view the deleted records, and yes, you can see rows marked for deletion. In RDO, these rows were unavailable and you couldn't set the current-row pointer to a deleted record. There is no "Undelete" method to toggle the row status, but if you nest deletions in a transaction, you can recover deleted records with the RollbackTrans method. If you're in batch update mode, you can cancel a pending deletion or a group of pending deletions with the CancelBatch method.

Attempting to retrieve field values from the deleted record generates an error. After deleting the current record, the deleted record remains current until you move to a different record. Once you move away from the deleted record, it is no longer accessible—that is, unless you set the Filter property to permit reference to it.

If the attempt to delete records fails because of a conflict with the underlying data (for example, another user has already deleted a record), the provider returns warnings to the Errors collection but doesn't halt program execution. A run-time error occurs only if there are conflicts on all the requested records.

Recordset Object Properties

We've already touched on a number of the Recordset properties. As you've seen, they play a critical role in how many of the methods function. In this section, we'll take a brief look at each of the Recordset object properties and make an extended visit to some of them that won't be passed by again later in the guide. The first group of properties, which are listed in Table 29-40, apply to the currently addressed record.

Table 29-40
Recordset Object Properties That Apply to the Current Record

Property	Purpose
AbsolutePage	Specifies the ordinal position of a Recordset object's current record. In other words, sets or returns the row number of the current record. (This property is also described in the "AbsolutePage property" section earlier in the chapter, on page 633.)
AbsolutePosition	Identifies the current row's page number based on the PageSize and PageCount property setting. Set this property to move to the first row of a particular page This is a 1-based property. (This property is also described in the "AbsolutePosition property" section earlier in the chapter, on page 632.)
BOF	A Boolean value to indicate that the current-row pointer is positioned beyond the beginning of the result set. When BOF is True, the current-row pointer isn't pointing to a valid row. (See the "BOF and EOF properties" section on page 641.)
Bookmark	Returns or sets the current-row pointer based on a variant pointer. (See the "Bookmark property" section on page 642.)

Property	Purpose
EditMode	Indicates the editing status of the current record. This property, like its RDO cousin, can have one of three states: adEditNone (no edit is in progress); adEditInProgress (data has changed but hasn't been saved); and adEditAdd (a new row has been added but not saved). (See the "AddNew method" section on page 634.)
EOF	A Boolean value to indicate that the current-row pointer is positioned beyond the end of the result set. When EOF is True, the current-row pointer isn't pointing to a valid row. This property is typically used to see whether the query returned any rows. (See the "BOF and EOF properties" section on page 641.)
Status	Indicates the status of the current record with respect to batch updates or other bulk operations. (See the "Status property" section on page 648).

The Recordset properties that apply to the Recordset as a whole are listed in Table 29-41.

Table 29-41
Recordset Object Properties That
Apply to the Recordset as a Whole

Property	Purpose
ActiveCommand	Contains a reference to the Command object that was originally used to create the Recordset. The ActiveCommand on any Recordset object in the hierarchy will always point to the same command object. MyRs.ActiveCommand.CommandText, for example, returns the SQL statement used to create the Recordset.
ActiveConnection	Defines the connection or contains a Connection object. Default is a Null object reference. (See the "ActiveConnection property" section on page 641.)
CacheSize	Sets or returns the number of rows of the Recordset to cache in local memory. (See the "CacheSize property" section on page 642.)
CursorLocation	Same as the Connection property of the same name. This property is initially set from the Connection object and can be changed on a closed Recordset.
CursorType	Indicates the type of cursor used in a Recordset object.

(continued)

Table 29-41 *continued*

Property	Purpose
DataMember	Points to member of the selected DataSource. Defines the Rowset within the DataSource to wrap with a Recordset. (See the "DataMember property" section on page 642.)
DataSource	Indicates the source of data for data binding. Defines the object implementing IdataSource, which contains the Rowset to be wrapped with a Recordset. (See the "DataSource property" section on page 643.)
Filter	Indicates a filter for data in a Recordset. Once set, builds a new cursor containing just rows that pass the filter. (See the "Filter property" section on page 643.)
LockType	Indicates how ADO is to handle concurrency. This property is set when the Recordset is opened through the LockType argument to the Open method but can be set before the Recordset is open or if the Recordset is closed. (See the Recordset "Open method" section on page 613.)
MarshalOptions	Indicates which records are to be sent back to the server when updating—either all rows or only modified rows. (See the "MarshalOptions property" section on page 646.)
MaxRecords	Sets a limit on the number of rows processed by a query. Default is 0 (no limit). (See the "MaxRecords property" section on page 646.)
PageCount	Indicates how many pages of data are in the Recordset. Pages are groups of records based on the PageSize property. (See the "AbsolutePage property" section on page 633 for more information.)
PageSize	Sets or returns the number of rows ADO is supposed to keep on a logical page. (See the "AbsolutePage property" section on page 633 for more information.)
RecordCount	Returns the number of rows in the Recordset—if known. (See the "RecordCount property" section on page 646.)
Sort	Specifies one or more field names the Recordset is sorted on and whether each field is sorted in ascending or descending order. (See the "Sort property" section on page 647.)
Source	Indicates where the data in a Recordset comes from. (See the "Source property" section on page 647.)
State	This read-only property indicates whether the Recordset is open (adStateOpen) or closed (adStateClosed). (See the "State property" section on page 599.)

Property	Purpose
StayInSync	Indicates whether the Recordset will be updated with new rows when receiving a ChapterChanged notification from the underlying Irowset. (See the "StayInSync property" section on page 649.)

ActiveConnection property

The ActiveConnection property sets or returns a String containing the definition for a connection or a Connection object. Basically, this property tells you or ADO which connection is to be used (or was used) to address the server that will execute (or did execute) the Recordset object's query. Default is a Null object reference.

You can change the ActiveConnection property until you open the Recordset or set the Source property to a valid command object. After that, the property is read-only, and it reflects a reference to the Connection object used to.access the server.

Typically, you set the ActiveConnection property to a valid Connection object. You can also use a valid connection string. If you use a valid connection string, ADO creates a new Connection object using this definition and opens the connection. Additionally, once the connection is open, ADO sets this property to the new Connection object to give you a way to access extended error information or to execute other commands.

If you use the ActiveConnection argument of the Open method to open a Recordset object, or you set the Source property of the Recordset object to a valid Command object variable, the ActiveConnection property inherits the value of the argument.

BOF and EOF properties

These properties determine whether a Recordset object contains records or whether you've gone beyond the limits of a Recordset object when you move from row to row in the result set. Yes, these properties are identical to their twins in DAO and RDO.

If either the BOF or EOF property is True, there is no current record—the current-row pointer isn't positioned over a valid row. If you open a Recordset object containing no records, the BOF and EOF properties are set to True, and the Recordset object's RecordCount property setting is zero. When you open a Recordset object that contains at least one record, the first record is the current record and the BOF and EOF properties are False. If you delete the last remaining record in the Recordset object, the BOF and EOF properties might remain False until you attempt to reposition the current record.

The RecordCount property doesn't necessarily tell you whether there are rows. If it contains anything, you're lucky—it usually doesn't tell you much.

See the "Recordset navigation methods" section on page 628 for information on the role that BOF and EOF play in the Move methods.

Bookmark property

The Bookmark property can be used to save a current-row pointer and return to that row in the Recordset—assuming that the Recordset supports Bookmarks.

When you open a Recordset object that supports Bookmarks, each of its records has a unique pointer that can be used to return to the row. To save the bookmark for the current record, assign the value of the Bookmark property to a variable. To return to that record at any time, set the Recordset object's Bookmark property to that variable.

You might not be able to view the value of the bookmark. And don't expect bookmarks to be directly comparable—two bookmarks that refer to the same record might have different values. If you use the Clone method to create a copy of a Recordset object, the Bookmark property settings for the original and the duplicate Recordset objects are identical and you can use them interchangeably. However, you can't use bookmarks from different Recordset objects interchangeably, even if they are created from the same source or command.

CacheSize property

The CacheSize property is used to tell ADO how many rows to cache in local memory. The amount of memory allocated for this cache is set from this property, so it is wise to ensure that your cache is no larger than necessary. Again, remember that cursors are *evil* (is this message sinking in yet?), and large cursors are straight from the nether regions. This value must be 1 or larger—a CacheSize setting of zero isn't allowed and returns an error.

ADO uses the CacheSize property to control how many records the provider keeps in its buffer and how many to retrieve at one time into local memory. For example, if the CacheSize is 10, after first opening the Recordset object, the provider retrieves the first 10 records into local memory. As you move through the Recordset object, the provider returns the data from the local memory buffer. As soon as you move past the last record in the cache, the provider retrieves the next 10 records from the data source into the cache. This process is repeated on a background thread until the Recordset is fully populated. If there are fewer records to retrieve than CacheSize specifies, the provider returns the remaining records; no error occurs.

You can adjust the value of this property during the life of the Recordset object, but changing this value affects only the number of records in the cache after subsequent retrievals from the data source. Changing the property value alone won't change the current contents of the cache.

Records retrieved from the cache don't reflect concurrent changes that other users made to the source data. To force an update of all the cached data, use the Resync method.

DataMember property

The DataMember property contains the name of the data member to retrieve from the object referenced by the DataSource property. For the operation to work, the two properties must be used with each other. The DataMember property is used to control which of the Rowsets in the DataSource will be wrapped with the Recordset. This feature is used most often by developers writing data-bound controls.

If the DataMember property is set to the name of a rowset that isn't recognized by the object referenced in DataSource at the time the DataSource property is set, a run-time error will be generated. The DataMember property isn't case-sensitive. The DataMember property can be set only on a Recordset that isn't opened.

DataSource property

The DataSource property is used to reference an object that implements the IDataSource interface (a data source control like the ADO Data control) and contains an IRowset that is to be wrapped with an ADO Recordset. The IRowset to be wrapped is defined by the DataMember property on the Recordset and must be set before setting the DataSource Property. Here are some points to keep in mind when working with the DataSource property:

- If the string defining the data member doesn't refer to an actual valid rowset, setting the DataSource property will cause an error. You have to set DataMember before DataSource or you'll get an error.

- Once everything is properly set, ActiveCommand, ActiveConnection, and Source will all be empty on the resulting Recordset.

- Using Close with a Recordset created this way will succeed (release the IRowset reference); however, Open will then fail. Requery will close the Rowset and then error when it tries to reopen.

Settings on the Recordset are largely ignored because the IRowset already exists and already has all of its properties set before being wrapped with the Recordset.

Filter property

The Filter property indicates a filter for data in a Recordset. This is an important new property for ADO Recordsets, and it has no DAO or RDO equivalents. The Filter property is used in a variety of ways to select records to process in bulk for a number of situations. This property can contain any of the following:

- **Criteria string**   A string made up of one or more individual clauses concatenated with AND or OR operators

- **Array of bookmarks**   An array of unique bookmark values that point to records in the Recordset object

- **FilterGroupEnum values**   Any of the FilterGroupEnum constants listed in Table 29-42

Table 29-42
FilterGroupEnum Constants

Constant	Purpose
adFilterNone	Default. Removes the current filter and restores all records to view. Setting the Filter property to a zero-length string ("") has the same effect as using the adFilterNone constant.
adFilterPendingRecords	Allows you to view only records that have changed but have not yet been committed to the server; applicable only for batch update mode.
adFilterAffectedRecords	Allows you to view only records affected by the last Delete, Resync, UpdateBatch, or CancelBatch call; the only way you can view deleted rows.
adFilterConflictingRecords	Allows you to view the records that failed the last batch update attempt.
adFilterFetchedRecords	Allows you to view records in the current cache, that is, the results of the last call to retrieve records from the database.

The Filter property is used to selectively screen-out sets of records in a Recordset object. Setting the Filter property doesn't cause ADO to rebuild the cursor—just to refilter the rows; so no trip back to the server is needed. Therefore, changing the Filter property affects other properties such as AbsolutePosition, AbsolutePage, RecordCount, and PageCount that return values based on the current cursor. Setting the Filter property to a specific value will reposition the current record pointer to the first row in the new cursor built from records that qualify based on the filter. When the Filter property is cleared, the current-record position moves to the first record in the original (unfiltered) Recordset. Changes made to the filtered Recordset are applied to the original Recordset and the database, depending on the way you use Update and UpdateBatch.

The criteria string is made up of clauses in the form FieldName-Operator-Value (for example, "LastName = 'Smith'"). You can create compound clauses by concatenating individual clauses with AND (for example, "LastName = 'Smith' AND FirstName = 'John'") or OR (for example, "LastName = 'Smith' OR LastName = 'Jones'"). Use the following guidelines for criteria strings:

- FieldName must be a valid field name from the Recordset. If the field name contains spaces, you must enclose the name in square brackets.

- Operator must be one of the following: <, >, <=, >=, <>, =, or LIKE.

- Value is the value with which you'll compare the field values (for example, 'Smith', #8/24/95#, 12.345, or $50.00). Use single quotes with strings, and pound signs (#) with dates. For numbers, you can use decimal points, dollar signs, and scientific notation.

- If the operator is LIKE, Value can use wildcards. Only the asterisk (*) and percent sign (%) wildcards are allowed, but they can appear anywhere in the string and can appear multiple times. For example, %Apple% finds any string with the word *Apple* imbedded therein. Value can't be Null.

NOTE Keep in mind that your Find criteria must match the capabilities of the *provider* when it comes to case-sensitive searches. The providers don't ask the server to perform these filters—they are all done locally.

- There is no precedence between AND and OR. Clauses can be grouped within parentheses. However, you can't group clauses joined by an OR and then join the group to another clause with an AND, like this: (LastName = 'Smith' OR LastName = 'Jones') AND FirstName = 'John'. Instead, you would construct this filter as (LastName = 'Smith' AND FirstName = 'John') OR (LastName = 'Jones' AND FirstName = 'John').

- In a LIKE clause, you can use a wildcard ("*") at the beginning and end of the pattern (for example, LastName LIKE '*mit*') or only at the end of the pattern (for example, LastName LIKE 'Smit*'). I assume that you can also use the percent sign ("%") as a valid wildcard.

Expression parsing occurs in the ADO interface and acts on the names exposed in that interface. That means that the names of the fields used in the expression are the names of the field objects.

The formal syntax for the Filter expression is as follows:

```
<filter_exp> ::= (<filter_exp>)
<filter_exp> :: = <simple_exp> <boolean_operator> <simple_exp>
<simple_exp> ::= <field_name> <comparison_operator> <literal value>
<field_name> ::= the name of the field object to be filtered on
<comparison_operator> ::= ">", "<", "=", "<>", "LIKE"
<literal_value> ::= <date>,  <string>, <number>
<date> ::= VBA Date syntax
<string> ::= 'string'
<number> ::= floating point number
<boolean_operator> = AND, OR
```

The filter constants make it easier to resolve individual record conflicts during batch update mode by allowing you to view, for example, only those records affected during the last UpdateBatch method call.

Just setting the Filter property might fail because of a conflict with the underlying data (for example, another user has already deleted a record). In this case, the provider returns warnings to the Errors collection but doesn't halt program execution. A run-time error occurs only if there are conflicts on all the requested records. Use the Status property to locate records with conflicts.

See the "Bookmark property" section on page 642 for an explanation of bookmark values from which you can build an array to use with the Filter property.

MarshalOptions property

The MarshalOptions property specifies what rows are sent back to the server—all rows or only the modified rows. In other words, this property guides ADO and its providers when it decides how to update database rows when the time comes. In some cases, you must update all rows at once—whether or not they all changed. In other cases, it's more efficient to update only those rows that have changed. MarshalOptions can be one of the constants listed in Table 29-43.

Table 29-43
MarshalOptionsEnum Constants

Constant	Purpose
adMarshalAll	ADO marshals all rows.
adMarshalModifiedOnly	ADO marshals only the modified rows.

MaxRecords property

The MaxRecords property tells ADO to concatenate a SET ROWCOUNT *xx* to the next SQL statement associated with the Recordset. With ODBC providers and SQL Server, this property can limit the number of rows *updated* as well as returned by a query. This is a handy way to limit the number of rows your cursor builds, but since it also affects *all* queries on this connection, you might have unintended results if you aren't careful. ADO also sends a SET ROWCOUNT 0 to the server when the Recordset is closed to prevent unwanted side effects. However, if you use the Execute statement that uses the same connection, its operations will also be affected by the current ROWCOUNT state.

RecordCount property

The RecordCount property (sometimes) returns the number of records in a Recordset. This property is handled somewhat differently in ADO, but it still can't return information that isn't available. Although the ADO documentation says that the property can return a valid count before population is complete, this can't be accurate. SQL Server doesn't know how many rows will qualify for the result set until all of the rows are located. With server-side cursors, this value is determined before sending the first row to the client, so the RecordCount might be available when the first row arrives. However, with client-side cursors, ADO can't report anything but –1 (value unavailable) until the last row is populated. This means you probably can't get a valid count until EOF is true—or at least until ADO populates the cursor for you in the background.

If the Recordset object supports approximate positioning or bookmarks—that is, Supports (adApproxPosition) or Supports (adBookmark), respectively, returns True—this value should (might) return the exact number of records in the Recordset regardless of whether it has been fully populated. If the Recordset object doesn't support approximate positioning, this property can be a significant drain on resources because all records have to be retrieved and counted to return an accurate RecordCount value. The RecordCount property isn't supported on all cursors or with all providers, and there are many open issues regarding this value. Just remember that RecordCount isn't supported on ForwardOnly cursor types (the default with server-side cursors)—only keyset and static cursors support this property, and then only if an index is available on the base table. It also seems to be failing when calling stored procedures. When it isn't available it returns adBHOM* (-1).

NOTE In other words, simply referencing the RecordCount forces ADO to do a MoveLast (synchronously), which blocks your application until the count is available. Again, this shouldn't be a problem with small cursors.

Sort property

The Sort property specifies how to order the rows in the Recordset. This property is a string of comma-delimited Field names separated by an optional space and ASCENDING or DESCENDING. Actually, ADO seems to prefer DESC and ASC, but this might be a bug. Try the short version if the long version doesn't work. For example, you could sort the fields of the Pubs Titles table using the following Sort property string:

```
Rs.Sort = "title DESC, pub_ID"
```

The data isn't physically rearranged, but simply accessed in the sorted order.

By default, fields are sorted in ascending sequence. ADO builds a temporary index for each field specified in the Sort property if the CursorLocation property is set to adUseClient and an index doesn't already exist. Setting the Sort property to an empty string will reset the rows to their original order and delete temporary indexes. Existing indexes are not deleted.

Source property

The Source property indicates where the data in a Recordset comes from. Use the Source property to specify a data source for a Recordset object using one of the following: a Command object variable, a SQL statement, a stored procedure, or a table name. The Source property is read/write for closed Recordset objects and read-only for open Recordset objects.

If you set the Source property to a Command object, the ActiveConnection property of the Recordset object will inherit the value of the ActiveConnection property from the specified Command object. Reading the Source property does not return a Command object, however; instead, it returns the CommandText property of the Command object to which you set the Source property.

If the Source property is a SQL statement, a stored procedure, or a table name, you can optimize performance by passing the appropriate Options argument with the Open method call.

---

* adBHOM is my constant, not ADO's. It is used where the interface has no clue. (BHOM = Beats the Hell Out of Me.)

Status property

The Status property is a bitmask that indicates the status of the current record with respect to batch updates or other bulk operations. This property is a catch-all for a variety of operation status indicators. It is automatically maintained by ADO. To determine whether one of these flags is set, you'll have to AND in one of the constants listed in Table 29-44.

Table 29-44
RecordStatusEnum Constants

Constant	Purpose
adRecCanceled	The record was not saved because the operation was canceled.
adRecCantRelease	The new record was not saved because of existing record locks.
adRecConcurrencyViolation	The record was not saved because optimistic concurrency was in use.
adRecDBDeleted	The record has already been deleted from the data source.
adRecDeleted	The record was deleted.
adRecIntegrityViolation	The record was not saved because the user violated integrity constraints.
adRecInvalid	The record was not saved because its bookmark is invalid.
adRecMaxChangesExceeded	The record was not saved because there were too many pending changes.
adRecModified	The record was modified.
adRecMultipleChanges	The record was not saved because it would have affected multiple records.
adRecNew	The record is new.
adRecObjectOpen	The record was not saved because of a conflict with an open storage object.
adRecOK	The record was successfully updated.
adRecOutOfMemory	The record was not saved because the computer has run out of memory.
adRecPendingChanges	The record was not saved because it refers to a pending insert.
adRecPermissionDenied	The record was not saved because the user has insufficient permissions.
adRecSchemaViolation	The record was not saved because it violates the structure of the underlying database.
adRecUnmodified	The record was not modified.

You can use the Status property to see what changes are pending for records modified during batch updating. You can also use the Status property to view the status of records that fail during bulk operations (for example, when you call the Resync, UpdateBatch, or CancelBatch method on a Recordset object, or set the Filter property on a Recordset object to an array of bookmarks). With this property, you can determine how a given record failed and resolve it accordingly. The Status property can be one of the values listed in Table 29-44.

StayInSync property

The StayInSync property is new for ADO 2.0. It is used to determine whether the Recordset sinks ChapterChanged notifications from the underlying rowset. If set to False, the Recordset doesn't sink the notification and will not be updated with the rows from the new chapter. If set to True, the Recordset does sync the notification and will be updated with the rows from the new chapter. This property of the Recordset object is set to True by default. Setting this property on the parent Recordset to False prior to referencing the child Recordset prevents the child Recordset from changing when navigating through the parent Recordset. Setting this property on the parent Recordset will not affect the behavior of previously referenced child Recordset objects. This effect can be seen when using a hierarchical Recordset, such as that provided by the MSDataShape provider.

TIP   So what the heck is a "chapter"—besides a section of a book? Well, consider that ADO now supports "parent-child" or "item-detail" or "hierarchical" result sets. That is, ADO lets you define relationships between result sets so that they can be managed intelligently. A chapter in this context is a subset of the data that applies to a particular row. It would be the set of detail rows for an individual item in an item-detail hierarchy. It's all handled behind the scenes in ADO, so you shouldn't have to worry about it.

Synchronizing hierarchical Recordsets

A hierarchical Recordset object can make developing a one-to-many form amazingly simple. The DataEnvironment makes creating the Recordset almost foolproof. You can drag single fields from the parent Recordset onto the form as text boxes. You can drag the child Recordset onto the form as a DataGrid. As you walk through the parent Recordset, you'll see that the grid automatically references the child Recordset for the current parent record. The only code you would need to write would be to navigate through the parent Recordset.

But what if you don't want this default behavior? What if you want to reference a particular child Recordset, regardless of the current position in the parent Recordset? Well, you can use either the StayInSync property as we just discussed or the Clone method to return a separate copy of the Recordset object. These alternatives could come in handy if you want to keep your current child Recordset synchronized in its hierarchy but maintain a separate reference to it. Between these two options, you should be able to control the synchronization of your hierarchical Recordset however you see fit.

Recordset Object Events

For the first time, ADO supports events. As in RDO 2.0, these events expose another important dimension of control over what is happening, what is about to happen, or what has happened to your data—right down to the field. Even RDO doesn't give you this level of granularity. I devote an entire chapter to event handling (Chapter 32)—so stay tuned. Table 29-45 summarizes the Recordset object events.

Table 29-45
Recordset Object Events

Events	Purpose
FetchProgress, FetchComplete	Retrieval status—Notification of the progress of a data retrieval operation, or that the retrieval operation has completed.
WillChangeField, FieldChangeComplete	Field change management—Notification that the value of the current field will change or has already changed.
WillMove, MoveComplete, EndOfRecordset	Navigation management—Notification that the current-row position in a Recordset will change, has changed, or has reached the end of the Recordset.
WillChangeRecord, RecordChangeComplete	Row change management—Notification that something in the current row of the Recordset will change or has already changed.
WillChangeRecordset, RecordsetChangeComplete	Recordset change management—Notification that something in the current Recordset will change or has already changed.

ADO Field Object

The whole purpose of retrieving a Recordset is to get at the data. Here's where it's kept—in the ADO Field object. Once it arrives, this object describes the data to ADO and to you, the developer. Typically, one Field object is defined for each column in the database. No, don't get me started about "fields" and "columns" or "records" and "rows." The Field properties are used to describe the column as to data type, value, and all of the other attributes. The Field object is also used to describe the parameters passed to a query.

A Recordset object has a Fields collection made up of Field objects. Each Field object corresponds to a column in the Recordset. You use the Value property of Field objects to set or return data for the current record. Depending on the functionality the provider exposes, some collections, methods, or properties of a Field object might not be available.

NOTE One of the most significant things missing from the Field object is the OrdinalPosition property. I often used this property to map columns returning from a result set to a display control. That is, the *n*th column from the rdoColumns collection (based on the OrdinalPosition) could be mapped to the *n*th column of a grid control or the *n*th member of a control array.

The Field object has the standard Properties collection and only two methods. Table 29-46 lists the Field object methods.

Table 29-46
Field Object Methods

Method	Purpose
GetChunk	Reads page-based data from the database (See the "GetChunk method" section below.)
AppendChunk	Writes page-based data to the database (See the "AppendChunk method" section on page 652.)

GetChunk method

The GetChunk method is used to extract all or a specified number of bytes of data from a TEXT or IMAGE column. This is *not* my favorite technique for handling binary large objects (BLOBs) or character large objects (CLOBs) data. (See Chapter 25 for a blow-by-blow discussion of the merits of saving BLOBs in the database.) Basically, you have to query the database to return the BLOB (or CLOB) column—and that can be hard enough since there are lots of restrictions when doing so. Once you have the row, you can use this syntax to extract the data from the column:

```
variable = field.GetChunk( Size )
```

GetChunk returns a variant based on the Size argument. However, since you probably don't want to fill up the client system's memory with the data, you usually work with the data in reasonably sized "chunks." Because you usually have to save the data to a file anyway, 16 KB or so should be fine. You execute GetChunk in a loop, getting successive chunks of the BLOB—saving the data to a file. When there is less than Size bytes left in the column, ADO returns the remaining bytes and pads the variable with spaces. This means that you have a screwed-up binary image. You now have to make sure not to get more data than is actually there. Fortunately, you can use the Field object's ActualSize property to fetch exactly the right number of bytes.

NOTE GetChunk was modified in ADO 1.5 to take the number of characters rather than the number of bytes. This was a bug in ADO 1.0 because ADO was breaking multibyte characters in the middle of a string.

If the Field object's Attributes property is set to adFldLong, you need to use the chunk methods to retrieve the data from the field. If this Attribute property bit isn't set, simply reference as you would any other binary or character field. This Attribute property bit is equivalent to RDO's ChunkRequired property. It lets you use common (nonchunk) methods to work with smaller BLOB column values.

Each subsequent GetChunk call retrieves data starting from where the previous GetChunk call left off. If you're retrieving data from one field and then you set or read the value of another field in the current record, however, ADO assumes you're done retrieving data from the first field. If you call the GetChunk method on the first field again, ADO interprets the call as a new GetChunk operation and starts reading from the beginning of the data. Accessing fields in other Recordset objects (that are not clones of the first Recordset object) will not disrupt GetChunk operations. No, you don't have to fetch all of the data from individual BLOB or CLOB columns.

AppendChunk method

The AppendChunk method is used to save all or a specified number of bytes of data of a TEXT or IMAGE column to the database. Once you have the row, you can use this syntax to extract the data from the column:

```
field.AppendChunk Data
```

The first AppendChunk call on a Field object writes data to the field, overwriting any existing data. This process also causes SQL Server to allocate the first 2-KB (or 8-KB) page to your column—regardless of the number of bytes in the Variant Data variable. Subsequent AppendChunk calls add to the existing data page(s). New database pages are added modulo 2 KB (SQL Server versions prior to 7.0) and 8 KB (versions 7.0 and later). That is, a data chunk of 2 KB and 1 byte (or so) allocates two 2-KB data pages.

If you're appending data to one field and then you set or read the value of another field in the current record, ADO assumes that you're done appending data to the first field. If you call the AppendChunk method on the first field again, ADO interprets the call as a new AppendChunk operation and overwrites the existing data. Accessing fields in other Recordset objects (that are not clones of the first Recordset object) will not disrupt AppendChunk operations.

Field Object Properties

As we discussed earlier, the Field properties play a vital role in ADO. These properties describe your data in far more detail than DAO or RDO ever exposed. Table 29-47 summarizes the Field object properties.

All of the metadata properties (Name, Type, DefinedSize, Precision, and NumericScale) are available *before* opening the Field object's Recordset. Setting them at that time is useful for dynamically constructing forms.

Table 29-47
Field Object Properties

Property	Purpose
ActualSize	Indicates the size of the data in the column. This property should return the size of BLOB or CLOB columns. If ADO can't tell how large the field is, it returns –1. (There doesn't seem to be a constant for this value, and no, I don't think adBHOM will work.) (See the "ActualSize property" section on page 654.)
Attributes	Indicates specific characteristics of a field. (See the "Attributes property" section on page 654.)
DataFormat	Allows the developer to control the output format of data returned from the field. The DataFormat property requires the user to have the DataFormat Automation object installed. This is a new property for ADO 2.0.
DefinedSize	Returns the size assigned to the field when it was defined. This property indicates the maximum capacity of the field. This property is equivalent to the Size property in RDO.
Name	Indicates the name of the field. This name can be used to address the field using Rs("Name") syntax.
NumericScale	Returns the scale of numeric values in the field. In other words, this property indicates how many digits to the right of the decimal point are to be used to represent floating-point values. Defaults to 0.
OriginalValue	Returns the contents of the Field object's Value property before any changes were made. (See the "OriginalValue property" section on page 655.)
Precision	Returns the maximum number of digits used to represent values. NumericScale and Precision are set automatically based on the Type property when the Field is first defined. Defaults to 0.
Type	Returns the data type of the Field object. Type is also used to set NumericScale, Precision, and DefinedSize. This property is set when Field is initially defined. (See the "Type property" section on page 655.)
UnderlyingValue	Indicates a Field object's current value in the database. (See the "UnderlyingValue property" section on page 657.)
Value	Sets or returns the data associated with the Field object.

ActualSize property

The ActualSize property returns the size of the data in this field in bytes. This is important to know when working with double-byte character set (DBCS) (16-bit character) data, where each character is 16 bits. Don't confuse the ActualSize property with the DefinedSize property, which returns the *declared* size of the field. For example, a field can be declared of type text with a maximum length of 50 characters. DefinedSize will return 50 when working with single-byte character set (SBCS) data. ActualSize will return the length of the string for the particular record currently being accessed. If the provider can't determine the actual size of the data in the field, the provider returns -1. The provider can also allow this property to be set in order to reserve space for the BLOB data in the data source. However, it isn't required that the provider support the setting of this property—some data sources can't accomplish this.

TIP If you have problems getting the size of a BLOB, add the TSQL DATALENGTH(MyBlob) statement to your query to return the length—just be sure to return the BLOB as the final column in the query.

Attributes property

For a Field object, the Attributes property is read-only, and its value can be the sum of any one or more of the values listed in Table 29-48.

Table 29-48
FieldAttributeEnum Constants

Constant	Purpose
adFldMayDefer	Indicates that the field is deferred (that is, the field values are not retrieved from the data source with the whole record), but only when you explicitly access them. BLOB and CLOB columns are usually deferred.
adFldCacheDeferred	Set if the field value is cached after the first time it is read from the data source and that subsequent reads will fetch the data from that cache.
adFldUpdatable	Indicates that you can write to the field. Although a Recordset or row might be updateable, SQL Server can prevent individual rows from being changed. Test this bit to verify this fact.
adFldUnknownUpdatable	Indicates that the provider can't determine if you can write to the field. Use in conjunction with adFldUpdatable.

Constant	Purpose
adFldFixed	Indicates that the field contains fixed-length data or whether it's an IUNKNOWN or IDISPATCH type.
adFldIsNullable	Indicates that the field accepts Null values (or its nullable state is unknown).
adFldMayBeNull	Set if the field can contain nulls (not necessarily to store them though).
adFldLong	Indicates that the field is a long binary field (like a BLOB or CLOB). Also indicates that you can use the AppendChunk and GetChunk methods.
adFldRowID	Indicates that the field contains some kind of record ID (record number, unique identifier, identity, and so forth).
adFldKeyColumn	Indicates that the field is a member of a key.
adFldNegativeScale	Indicates that the scale is negative.
adFldRowVersion	Indicates that the field contains some kind of time or date stamp used to track updates—such as a TIMESTAMP. Set if the field contains a timestamp or other row versioning field that is read-only and is automatically updated by the data source each time the field is updated.

OriginalValue property

The OriginalValue property is used to return the contents of the Value property before any changes were made. In immediate update mode (the provider writes changes to the underlying data source once you call the Update method), the OriginalValue property returns the field value that existed prior to any changes (that is, since the last Update method call). This is the same value that the CancelUpdate method uses to replace the Value property.

In batch update mode (the provider caches multiple changes and writes them to the underlying data source only when you call the UpdateBatch method), the OriginalValue property returns the field value that existed prior to any changes (that is, since the last UpdateBatch method call). This is the same value that the CancelBatch method uses to replace the Value property. When you use this property with the UnderlyingValue property, you can resolve conflicts that arise from batch updates.

Type property

The Type property is used to indicate the type of data stored in the Field. For more information on OLE DB data types, see Chapter 10 and Appendix A of the Microsoft OLE DB 1.1 Programmer's Reference and Software Development Kit. The Type property can be one (or more) of the values listed in Table 29-49.

Table 29-49
DataTypeEnum Constants

Constant	Purpose
adBigInt	An 8-byte signed integer
adBinary	A binary value
adBoolean	A Boolean value
adBSTR	A null-terminated character string (Unicode)
adChapter	A chapter
adChar	A string value
adCurrency	A currency value. Currency is a fixed-point number with four digits to the right of the decimal point. It is stored in an 8-byte signed integer scaled by 10,000.
adDate	A date value. A date is stored as a Double, the whole part of which is the number of days since December 30, 1899, and the fractional part of which is the fraction of a day.
adDBDate	A date value (yyyymmdd)
adDBFileTime	(Not in spec)
adDBTime	A time value (hhmmss)
adDBTimeStamp	A date-time stamp (yyyymmddhhmmss plus a fraction in billionths)
adDecimal	An exact numeric value with a fixed precision and scale
adDouble	A double-precision floating-point value
adEmpty	No value was specified
adError	A 32-bit error code
adFileTime	(Not in spec)
adGUID	A globally unique identifier (GUID)
adIDispatch	A pointer to an IDispatch interface on an OLE object
adInteger	A 4-byte signed integer
adIUnknown	A pointer to an IUnknown interface on an OLE object
adLongVarBinary	Long variable-length binary data (Parameter object only)
adLongVarChar	Long variable-length character string (Parameter object only)
adLongVarWChar	Long, Unicode, variable-length character string (Parameter object only)
adNumeric	An exact numeric value with a fixed precision and scale

Constant	Purpose
adPropVariant	(Not in spec)
adSingle	A single-precision floating-point value
adSmallInt	A 2-byte signed integer
adTinyInt	A 1-byte signed integer
adUnsignedBigInt	An 8-byte unsigned integer
adUnsignedInt	A 4-byte unsigned integer
adUnsignedSmallInt	A 2-byte unsigned integer
adUnsignedTinyInt	A 1-byte unsigned integer
adUserDefined	A user-defined variable
adVarBinary	Variable-length binary data (Parameter object only)
adVarChar	Variable-length character string (Parameter object only)
adVariant	An Automation Variant
adVarNumeric	An variable-length exact numeric value with a fixed precision and scale
adVarWChar	Unicode variable-length character (Parameter object only)
adWChar	A null-terminated Unicode character string (Parameter object only)
adArray*	OR'd together with another type to indicate that the data is a safe-array of that type (Not in the enumeration)
adByRef*	OR'd together with another type to indicate that the data is a pointer to data of the other type (Not in the enumeration)
adVector*	OR'd together with another type to indicate that the data is a DBVECTOR structure, as defined by OLE DB, that contains a count of elements and a pointer to data of the other type (Not in the enumeration)

* These last three constants and several listed above as not being in the ADO spec are either not implemented by any providers (yet) or not in place for other unimplemented features.

UnderlyingValue property

The UnderlyingValue property returns a Field object's current value in the database. The field value in the UnderlyingValue property is the value that is visible to your transaction and might be the result of a recent update by another transaction. This might differ from the OriginalValue property, which reflects the value that was originally returned to the Recordset. This property is similar to using the Resync method, but the UnderlyingValue property returns only the value for a specific field from the current record. This is the same value that the Resync method uses to replace the Value property.

ADO Parameter Object

A Parameter object represents a parameter or an argument associated with a Command object based on a parameterized query or a stored procedure. In other words, the Parameter object is where you put the values to be passed to parameterized queries or stored procedures. Many providers support parameterized commands—SQL Server is no exception. Parameter queries are commands in which the desired operation is defined once, but variables (or parameters) are used to alter some details of the command. Sure, either an ADO parameter query can return zero or more result sets, or perform some other type of action, or both—in any combination. For example, a SQL SELECT statement could use a parameter to define the matching criteria of a WHERE clause and another to define the column name for a SORT BY clause.

CAUTION

The numbering scheme used to reference items in the Parameters collection via code is 0-based, but the references made in the Immediate window are 1-based. That is, the ReturnValue (which is always assigned the first slot in the Parameters collection) is ordinal 0 in code (...Parameters(0)), but 1 in the Immediate window.

Parameter objects represent parameters associated with parameterized queries, or the input, output, or input/output arguments and the return values of stored procedures. If you know the names and properties of the parameters associated with the stored procedure or parameterized query you want to call, you can use the CreateParameter method to create Parameter objects with the appropriate property settings and use the Append method to add them to the Parameters collection. This lets you set and return parameter values without having to call the Refresh method on the Parameters collection to retrieve the parameter information from the provider, a potentially resource-intensive operation. Easier yet, you can use the Data Environment to create custom objects to make access to parameter queries quite easy—and virtually codeless.

Parameter Object Methods

The Parameter object has but one method—AppendChunk—that lets you pass BLOB or CLOB data as a parameter to your procedure. See the Field object's "AppendChunk method" section on page 652 for more details.

Another important method also plays a vital role here—the Refresh method, when applied to the Parameters *collection*. You can use the Refresh method to instruct ADO to automatically fetch and populate the parameter binding information in the Parameters collection. You should use this method instead of manually building parameter objects and appending them to the collection. We'll discuss this method in more detail in Chapter 31. ADO and the provider refers to the contents of the CommandText property to determine the current parameters and their binding information.

The provider doesn't restrict you or your code from further appending new parameters or deleting others after you call the Refresh method, however. Some data sources, such as SQL Server, have the ability to use default values for parameters when the parameter isn't actually used at execution.

The Refresh method is a helper method designed to quickly and easily populate the Parameters collection. Additionally, if you don't set a value for a particular parameter object, the provider should assume that the parameter should not be supplied. In other words, providers should send values for parameters only where you explicitly set a value in code. Because SQL Server requires a connection to the data source in order to populate the Parameters collection, you must set the Command's ActiveConnection property to a valid and open connection before this method is called.

If you access the Parameters collection before appending any Parameter object or calling the Refresh method, the provider automatically does the Refresh operation and populates the Parameters collection for you. This approach allows you to avoid the overhead of automatically building Parameter objects by manually appending Parameter objects, but it also supplies the new user with default behavior that performs the desired action.

Parameter Object Properties

The Parameter object properties are used to describe the parameter to be inserted into your query or stored procedure. ADO provides a great deal of flexibility here to make it easy to specify exactly what the target procedure expects to see. Table 29-50 summarizes the Parameter object properties.

Table 29-50
DataTypeEnum Constants

Property	Purpose
Attributes	Indicates what kind of values are acceptable for the Parameter object. (See the "Attributes property" section on page 660.)
Direction	Indicates whether the Parameter represents an input parameter, an output parameter, or both or whether the parameter is the return status value from a stored procedure. (See the "Direction property" section on page 660.)
Name	Indicates the name of the Parameter, which can be used to reference the Parameter. For Parameter objects not yet appended to the Parameters collection, the Name property is read/write.
NumericScale	Returns the scale of numeric values in the Parameter. In other words, this property indicates how many digits to the right of the decimal point are to be used to represent floating-point values.
Precision	Returns the maximum number of digits used to represent values. NumericScale and Precision are set automatically based on the Type property when the Parameter is first defined.
Size	Sets or returns a Long value that indicates the maximum size in bytes or characters of a value in a Parameter object. (See the "Size property" section on page 660.)
Type	Returns the data type of the Parameter. Type is also used to set the NumericScale, Precision, DefinedSize, and much more. This property is set when Parameter is initially defined. (See Field object's "Type property" section on page 655 and the "Type property section" on page 661.)
Value	Sets or returns the data value of the Parameter.

Attributes property

The Attributes property determines what kind of values the Parameter will accept. Its value can be the sum of any one or more of the values listed in Table 29-51.

Table 29-51
ParameterAttributesEnum Constants

Constant	Purpose
adParamSigned	Default; indicates that the parameter accepts signed values
adParamNullable	Indicates that the parameter accepts Null values
adParamLong	Indicates that the parameter accepts long binary data

Direction property

The Direction property indicates whether the Parameter represents an input parameter, an output parameter, or both or whether the parameter is the return value from a stored procedure. Use the Direction property to specify how a parameter is passed to or from a procedure. The Direction property is read/write; this allows you to work with providers that don't return this information or to set this information when you don't want ADO to make an extra call to the provider to retrieve parameter information. The Direction property can be one of the values listed in Table 29-52.

Table 29-52
ParameterDirectionEnum Constants

Constant	Purpose
adParamInput	Default; indicates an input parameter
adParamOutput	Indicates an output parameter
adParamInputOutput	Indicates that the parameter is both input and output
adParamReturnValue	Indicates that the parameter is a return value
adParamUnknown	Indicates that the parameter direction is unknown

Size property

The Size property is used to determine the maximum size for values written to or read from the Value property of a Parameter object. The Size property is read/write.

If you specify a variable-length data type for a Parameter object, you must set the object's Size property before appending it to the Parameters collection; otherwise, an error occurs. If you've already appended the Parameter object to the Parameters collection of a Command object and you change its type to a variable-length data type, you must set the Parameter object's Size property before executing the Command object; otherwise, an error occurs.

If you use the Refresh method to obtain parameter information from the provider and it returns one or more variable-length data type Parameter objects, ADO might allocate memory for the parameters based on their maximum potential size, which could cause an error during execution. To prevent an error, you should explicitly set the Size property for these parameters before executing the command.

Type property

The Type property can have several additional settings when applied to the Parameter object. This property can be one of the values listed in Table 29-53.

Table 29-53
Type Property Constants

Constant	Purpose
adLongVarBinary	A long binary value (Parameter object only)
adLongVarChar	A long String value (Parameter object only)
adLongVarWChar	A long null-terminated string value (Parameter object only)
adVarBinary	A binary value (Parameter object only)
adVarChar	A String value (Parameter object only)
adVarWChar	A null-terminated Unicode character string (Parameter object only)

ADO Property Object

A Property object represents a dynamic characteristic of an ADO object that is defined by the provider. ADO objects have two types of properties: built-in and dynamic. Built-in properties are those properties implemented in ADO and immediately available to any new object, using the familiar MyObject.Property syntax.

- **Built-in properties** These properties do not appear as Property objects in an object's Properties collection, so although you can change their values, you can't modify their characteristics or delete them.

- **Dynamic properties** These properties are defined by the underlying data provider, and they appear in the Properties collection for the appropriate ADO object. For example, a property specific to the provider might indicate whether a Recordset object supports transactions or updating. These additional properties will appear as Property objects in that Recordset object's Properties collection. Dynamic properties can be referenced only through the collection, using the MyObject.Properties(0) or MyObject.Properties("Name") syntax.

Property Object Properties

Each Property object has its own properties used to describe it and return or set its state. There are literally hundreds of these properties. I wrote a simple application that dumps these properties for the ADO object tree. It is named "Dump ADO Properties," and you can find it on the companion CD for this guide. Let's take a closer look at the dynamic Property object properties listed in Table 29-54—are we getting recursive here?

Table 29-54
Property Object Properties

Property	Purpose
Attributes	Bit flags that indicate whether a Property object is supported, required, optional, read-only, or read/write. (See the "Attributes property" section below.)
Name	Returns the name used to locate the Property object in the Properties collection. Note that the documentation adds "DBPROP_" and underscore characters that have to be removed to match the name used by the provider.
Type	Indicates the data type of the Property object. (See the Field object's "Type property" section on page 655.)
Value	Indicates the data value of the Property object.

Attributes property

The Attributes property can be the sum of any one or more of the values listed in Table 29-55.

Table 29-55
PropertyAttributesEnum Constants

Constant	Purpose
adPropNotSupported	Indicates that the property isn't supported by the provider
adPropRequired	Indicates that the user must specify a value for this property before the data source is initialized
adPropOptional	Indicates that the user doesn't need to specify a value for this property before the data source is initialized
adPropRead	Indicates that the user can read the property
adPropWrite	Indicates that the user can set the property

Setting a property is fairly easy—it's knowing what to set or what property name to use that's the problem. For example, in RDO, we could set the connection prompting behavior by setting the Prompt property. In ADO, this property is missing—well, sort of. It is exposed, but as one of the Properties collection objects. You can set it to one of its valid values, but the documentation doesn't make this easy to discover. With a bit of digging, I discovered the valid values for the Prompt property, which are listed in Table 29-56.

Table 29-56
ConnectPromptEnum Constants

Constant	Purpose
adPromptAlways	Always prompts for connection information
adPromptComplete	Prompts only if connection information is needed
adPromptCompleteRequired	Prompts only if connection information is needed and do not allow optional information to be entered
adPromptNever	Default; never prompts for connection information; trips trappable error if information is incorrect

These options correspond to RDO's Prompt property values. To choose one of these options, you can set the Prompt "property" to one of these strings like this:

```
Cn.Properties("Prompt") = adPromptAlways
```

ADO Error Object

An Error object contains details about data access errors pertaining to a single operation. Any number of Error objects can be generated from a single data access operation so ADO stores each Error object in the Errors collection. When another ADO operation generates an error, the Errors collection is cleared, and the new set of Error objects is placed in the Errors collection. To obtain this rich error information in an error handler, use the appropriate error-trapping features of the language or environment you're working with, and then use nested loops to enumerate the properties of each Error object in the Errors collection. In some cases, trappable errors are not fired if you enable event handling.

NOTE   Each Error object represents a specific provider error, not an ADO error. ADO errors are exposed to the run-time exception handling mechanism. For example, in Visual Basic, the occurrence of an ADO-specific error will trigger an On Error event and appear in the Error object. For a complete list of ADO errors, see the ADO Error Codes topic in online Help.

Error Object Properties

The user is the person least likely to be able to fix a problem but in the best position to do so in many cases. Presenting the user with cryptic error messages isn't the best way to get the problem solved. It is an excellent way to get called at 4:00 a.m. by a user trying to figure out one of these messages.

You'll need to examine the properties of the Error object to see what went wrong. In most cases, you'll be interested in the Number and Description properties. You might (just might) want to show the user the Description to give him or her a hint on how to fix the error. Just as providers do, ADO clears the OLE Error Info object before making a call that could potentially generate a new provider error. However, the Errors collection on the Connection object is cleared and populated only when the provider generates a new error or when the Clear method is called.

Some properties and methods return warnings that appear as Error objects in the Errors collection but do not halt a program's execution. Before you call the Resync, UpdateBatch, or CancelBatch methods on a Recordset object, or before you set the Filter property on a Recordset object, call the Clear method on the Errors collection so that you can read the Count property of the Errors collection to test for returned warnings.

Table 29-57 summarizes the Error object properties.

Table 29-57
Error Object Properties

Property	Purpose
Description	Contains the text of the error.
HelpContext	Returns a pointer into the Help file—pointing to a specific Help topic.
HelpFile	Points to a Help file that has information on the error—if available.
NativeError	Returns the SQL Server error number.
Number	Returns the error number.
Source	Identifies the source of the error.
SQLState	Provides the SQLState information passed down from SQL Server. When working with an RDBMS, a SQLState can be returned, which reflects the type of error that occurred as defined in the ODBC 3.0 specification.

30

Getting Connected with ADO

Establishing a Client/Server Connection

Connecting Using a Code-Based Approach

Connecting from a Component

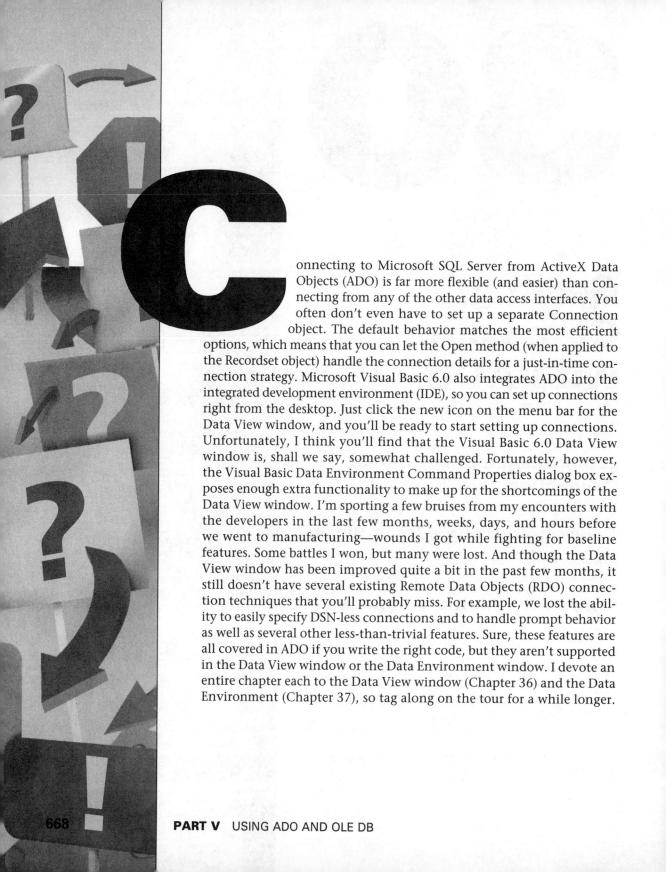

Connecting to Microsoft SQL Server from ActiveX Data Objects (ADO) is far more flexible (and easier) than connecting from any of the other data access interfaces. You often don't even have to set up a separate Connection object. The default behavior matches the most efficient options, which means that you can let the Open method (when applied to the Recordset object) handle the connection details for a just-in-time connection strategy. Microsoft Visual Basic 6.0 also integrates ADO into the integrated development environment (IDE), so you can set up connections right from the desktop. Just click the new icon on the menu bar for the Data View window, and you'll be ready to start setting up connections. Unfortunately, I think you'll find that the Visual Basic 6.0 Data View window is, shall we say, somewhat challenged. Fortunately, however, the Visual Basic Data Environment Command Properties dialog box exposes enough extra functionality to make up for the shortcomings of the Data View window. I'm sporting a few bruises from my encounters with the developers in the last few months, weeks, days, and hours before we went to manufacturing—wounds I got while fighting for baseline features. Some battles I won, but many were lost. And though the Data View window has been improved quite a bit in the past few months, it still doesn't have several existing Remote Data Objects (RDO) connection techniques that you'll probably miss. For example, we lost the ability to easily specify DSN-less connections and to handle prompt behavior as well as several other less-than-trivial features. Sure, these features are all covered in ADO if you write the right code, but they aren't supported in the Data View window or the Data Environment window. I devote an entire chapter each to the Data View window (Chapter 36) and the Data Environment (Chapter 37), so tag along on the tour for a while longer.

Establishing a Client/Server Connection

If you understand how to work with Data Access Objects (DAO) or RDO connections (or VBSQL for that matter), you have a basic understanding of how to work with ADO connections—at least as far as applications are concerned. Connecting from components is another matter. At the end of this chapter, we'll be discussing a number of connection issues that come up when you're building distributed components. When connecting, the big difference with ADO is that you can use either ODBC or OLE DB to interface to SQL Server. Most (if not all) of the things that can go wrong when making a DAO or RDO connection can go wrong when using ADO—and ADO has a few new potholes you need to watch out for. ADO still can't read your mind when it comes to figuring out your user ID or password, but it does understand how to use domain-managed security—which is almost as good. Connections can still time out, be unable to find the server, be denied because of permission violations, and just fail to connect because of the phase of the moon—just like in the past.

TIP When you're ready to make your connection, stop. You might not need to create a Connection object or even establish a connection at all. Consider that you don't need a connection to build a Command, Recordset, or Field object. These objects are all stand-alone, and you can create them without benefit of a connection.

ADO Connection Options

OK, you've decided that you need to establish an ADO connection from a typical client/server application. Before we get started, make sure you make plans to visit Chapter 37, which discusses the Data Environment. The Data Environment designer can build a Connection for you at design time and can reduce or entirely eliminate the need to write code to get connected. No, don't try to create a connection solely on the basis of a Data Link (as exposed in the Data View window)—these connections are not ready for the rigors of production applications. If you decide to try the code approach, you have lots of options. Some involve quite a bit more code than others, but most of them use the same basic ingredients to get the job done. Basically, your options for establishing a connection include the following:

- Use the Data View window and the Data Link Properties dialog box to create Data Links. This window and dialog box, shown in Figure 30-1, are essentially the ADO equivalent of the data source name (DSN) entries that ODBC developers are familiar with. The Data Link entries are persisted from application to application in the Windows Registry and are exposed in the Data View window each time you start Visual Basic. The Data Links do not set a few properties correctly, however, so you'll need to make some changes before using them in an application. (We'll talk about these tweaks you'll need to make in a moment.)

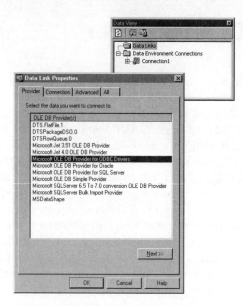

Figure 30-1 *The Data Link Properties dialog box and the Data View window*

- Use the Data Environment designer to create a DataEnvironment object containing all required connection parameters at design time. The Data Environment designer, shown in Figure 30-2, creates sharable Data-Environment objects that, like RDO UserConnection objects, can visually expose connections, tables, views, SQL queries, or stored procedures.

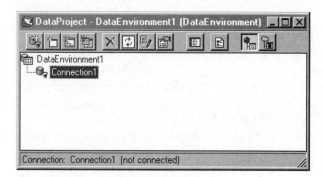

Figure 30-2 *The Data Environment designer*

- Use the Open method of an ADO Connection object with a valid ConnectionString. Again, you have several options here, as we'll soon discuss. Once the Connection object is open, you can use it wherever a method calls for an ActiveConnection argument.

- Use a valid ConnectionString as the ActiveConnection property on an ADO Command object. This approach builds a Connection object and opens it as the Command object is referenced.

- Use the Open method of the Recordset object—providing the Connection-String or an ActiveConnection as arguments. In this case, a Connection object is created for you.

- Use the Execute method of a stand-alone Connection object—specifying the ConnectionString as an argument.

- Use the ADO Data control and a valid ConnectionString to manage your connections for you.

- Use the Remote Data Services (RDS) Data control and a valid Connection-String to manage your connections for you.

All these options require a ConnectionString—one way or another. Yup, this looks very much like our old friend the RDO Connect string. We'll spend quite a bit of time talking about building and managing connect strings later in this chapter.

Before you get started, you need to think about conservation of resources. No, this doesn't mean that we're (just) worried about logging old-growth timber or saving fresh water; it means we're (also) worried about using up all the connections available on SQL Server. Unfortunately, many developers squander SQL Server resources by opening connections and then leaving them open like free sodas at the local movie theater. (OK, that's a null set nowadays, but you get the idea.)

NOTE Those of you who have discovered that Microsoft Visual Studio and the Visual Basic Enterprise editions come with the Developer Edition of SQL Server might have also discovered that you can open only five connections on this version of SQL Server. If you aren't careful, you can use up these connections quite quickly. It's good discipline, however, to work with a server that has limited resources. It improves your error handling code, and it prepares you for the real world, where connections are often as scarce as tickets to a new Broadway show.

You also need to think about security. We covered the use of proprietary user IDs and passwords for your applications (and components) primarily in Chapter 6 of this guide—so you might want to go back there for a refresher. SQL Server won't let you in if it doesn't know you by name. Even then, you might be limited to the places inside its palace that you can visit.

Building a ConnectionString

All the techniques used to establish an ADO connection include or create a valid ConnectionString. This string holds at least the basic parameters needed to get connected and contains all those parameters (basic and advanced) ADO needs to get connected after the connection is established. Once created, the ConnectionString can be passed on to other objects to reestablish a dormant connection, to establish a new one, or simply to run a one-time query. It's important that you know how to build one of these strings and how to pass it to the various methods, controls, and designers used to establish a SQL Server connection.

No, I don't know why they made the name of the ConnectionString string so long, but this is really your old friend the DAO/RDO "Connect" string in a cute disguise.

Should you use the OLE DB provider for ODBC when opening a connection to SQL Server or the native OLE DB provider for SQL Server? At one time, it was clear that the OLE DB native provider was the better choice. Because of a number of late-breaking (so to speak) issues, this decision is more convoluted. I'm afraid you'll have to make this decision on your own. If you find a problem with your driver se-lection (especially with the Data Environment), try the other provider—it might fix the problem.

The ConnectionString property specifies a data source and all of the other information you need to provide by passing a series of arguments to ADO. Each ConnectionString argument is provided in the usual ODBC *argument=value* format separated by semicolons. Notice that there are no spaces between the argument, the equal sign (=), and the value. This same format is used for OLE DB connect strings. Remember that a connect string tells ADO where to get the data. You must also specify whether to use the OLE DB provider for ODBC, which is then connected to a SQL Server ODBC driver, or to use the native OLE DB provider for SQL Server. If you choose the ODBC driver route, you'll find a plethora of arguments that you can provide to an ODBC data source, and we've gone over these in earlier chapters. All of these arguments can be used here—the string is simply going to be passed to the ODBC interface so it can connect to SQL Server. If you choose the OLE DB provider for SQL Server, many of the same connect string arguments can be used. We'll examine these arguments in detail in a minute.

ADO officially supports seven arguments for the ConnectionString property. A number of other arguments are supported but not documented. Any other arguments you provide pass directly to SQL Server or the ODBC layers without any processing by ADO—if ADO doesn't recognize the argument, it simply passes it on.

The arguments that ADO supports are as shown in Table 30-1 on page 674, outlining the Connection object's Open method. But before you wade into that creek barefooted, let's think about what we need to tell ADO so we can get connected.

- **The type of server** We need to tell ADO we want to connect to a SQL server. Remember, ADO is capable of connecting to a bazillion providers—SQL Server is only one of these. To let ADO know what type of server we want, we use the Provider argument and/or property to pass on the provider DLL name, which implies the type of server. By specifying the SQLOLEDB provider, we also tell ADO the interface we want to use. If you want to, you can also use the Driver={SQL Server} if you're connecting to the ODBC provider. ADO defaults to the ODBC provider—in case you forget to mention one.

- **The name of the server** OK, you said SQL Server, but which one? We use the ConnectionString Data Source= (or Server= if you're using the ODBC driver) argument to tell ADO the name of our server so the provider can ask Microsoft Windows NT to locate it for us on the network. If you're using the ODBC provider, you can embed this information into a DSN. OLE DB uses UDL files that serve the same purpose, and we'll talk about those in a bit. The server name is still the name of the Windows NT system the server is running on.

- **Your name and password** Now that ADO can find the provider and the server, it can't let you connect unless the server thinks you have the proper credentials and, once recognized, the appropriate per-missions. To make sure ADO knows who you are (so it can tell SQL Server), use the User ID= (or UID= if you're using the ODBC driver) argument in the ConnectionString, the UserID argument in the Open method, or the UserID property in your data source control. The same goes for your password, except this time you need to use the Password (or PWD= if you're using the ODBC driver) ConnectionString argument, the Password argument in the Open method, or the Password property in the data source control.

If you're using Windows NT domain-managed security and have SQL Server set up for Integrated or Mixed security, you won't have to provide either your name or your password because SQL Server, ADO, and Windows NT will figure all of this out for you—assuming SQL Server knows your client by its Windows client username. If you're working with a component that doesn't really know its own user ID, you need to come up with a scheme that assigns user IDs and passwords specifically for component use.

- **The name of the default database**   Once you are connected, it's better to perform operations on the right database. If your system administrator (SA) hasn't set a default database for you (or even if the SA has), you should set the default database using the ConnectionString Initial Catalog= (Database= if you're using the ODBC driver) or the DSN= argument. Actually, ADO has just implemented yet another term to refer to the default database. Now it's called the Initial Catalog. Yes, you can put this name in the ConnectionString or specify it as one of the properties in one of the connection string builders.

- **Other stuff that might help use the connection later**   You can also specify lots of other options in the OLE DB ConnectionString. Look over these options and decide if they make sense. These options include the ConnectionTimeout, Locale ID, prompt-level, and much, much more.

TIP   If your application or component goes to sleep and doesn't perform any operations against SQL Server, the remote engine will break the connection. The documentation says this time limit applies only to server-to-server connections, but I've seen some anecdotal evidence that suggests it also applies to server-to-client connections. In any case, this value is set by adjusting the *remote conn timeout* value with sp_configure. The default in SQL Server 6.5 is 10 minutes.

The ConnectionString arguments

OK, we're ready to take a closer look at the ConnectionString arguments. We can provide most of the information we want to tell ADO and the provider with these arguments. You'll notice that a few of the keywords recognized by ADO seem to have crossed over from ODBC. That is, in most cases, you can use the ODBC keywords you're used to using in DAO or RDO in the ADO OLE DB ConnectionString as well. Table 30-1 lists the ADO ConnectionString arguments.

Table 30-1
ConnectionString Arguments

Argument	Purpose
Application Name	A name you choose to identify your application to the server.
Auto Translate	A True/False value indicating whether the interface should translate.
Connect Timeout	Indicates how long ADO waits for SQL Server to start connecting.
Current Language	Language name setting passed to SQL Server.
Data Source	The name of the SQL Server you want to connect to. You can still use "DSN=" instead of this argument to point to a registered ODBC DSN. A DSN can contain a default database setting.
DSN	The name of a registered ODBC data source name.
Extended Properties	Properties not recognized by OLE DB.
File Name	Specifies the name of a provider-specific file (for example, a persisted data source object) containing preset connection information. This is the pathname to a "file-based" DSN and can also be an OLE DB UDL file.
Initial Catalog	New name for the default database.
Initial File Name	
Integrated Security	True/False. Indicates whether you expect the Windows NT domain and SQL Server to authenticate the user ID and password.
Locale Identifier or LocaleID	Specifies which international locale setting to use.
Network Address	Indicates connectivity other than named-pipes connectivity.
Network Library	Indicates connectivity other than named-pipes connectivity.
Mode	The data sharing attributes. Maps to the Connection object's Mode property.
Packet Size	Defaults to 4096. Set (at your own risk) to tune network performance.
Password	Specifies the password to use when opening the connection.
Persist Security Info	Indicates whether ADO stores user ID and password. Not encrypted.
Prompt	Indicates how ADO deals with user ID and password issues. Defaults to adPromptNever.

Argument	Purpose
Provider	Specifies the name of a provider to use for the connection. We'll use the native provider for SQL Server, SQLOLEDB.
Use Procedure for Prepare	Indicates whether ADO creates stored procedures by default. For some reason, this argument seems to default to 1. We've done a little testing with this, and it looks like SQLOLEDB is using the same constants as the SQL Server ODBC driver for this property (No = 0; Yes = 1; Yes, but drop when appropriate = 2)
User ID	The username to use when opening the connection.
Windows Handle	Permits other dialog boxes to correctly manage the window.
Workstation ID	Further identifies the application or component

Where did I get these? Well, when you use the Data Environment, it lets you examine the properties of the Connection objects you create. If you choose the OLE DB provider for SQL Server in the Data Link Properties dialog box and choose the All tab, you get a dialog box that looks like the one shown in Figure 30-3.

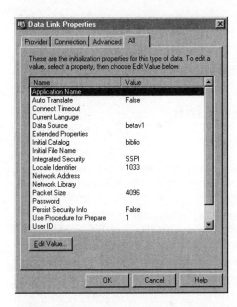

Figure 30-3 *The All tab of the Data Link Properties dialog box when the OLE DB provider for SQL Server is selected*

From the All tab of the Data Link Properties dialog box you can check and change these arguments. Also, OLE DB and ADO expose each ConnectionString argument as a Property in the Connection object's Properties collection. When connecting to SQL Server using the OLE DB provider for ODBC, all you have to do is pass in the same connect string you've been using for years—just like the RDO or ODBC API Connect property string:

```
"uid=sa;pwd=;database=pubs;dsn=MyServerDSN"
```

I set the minimum options in the Data Environment for an ADO Connection, and it generated the ConnectionString below. Ah, well, at least it's complete. No, you don't need all of this stuff. For some reason, the Data Environment seems to want to create a string with all the default values included. Recall that ODBC did about the same thing. After you opened a connection, the Connect property was updated to fill in many of the system-provided values. But this is a bit much—and I suspect not even correct. (It was created by a late Beta version of Visual Basic 6.0.)

```
Provider=MSDASQL.1;User ID=sa;Data Source=betav1;
Connect Timeout=15;
Extended Properties="Use Procedure for Prepare=1;
Auto Translate=False; Packet Size=4096;Workstation ID=BILLVA1";
Locale Identifier=1033;Initial Catalog=biblio
```

You can get away with a lot less if you write the ConnectionString yourself:

```
Provider=MSDASQL.1;User ID=sa;Data Source=betav1;
Initial Catalog=biblio
```

TIP To use a DSN-less connection and still get SQL Server to avoid creating temporary stored procedures, add "UseProcForPrepare=No" to your ConnectionString.

Building an OLE DB Data Link

As I began work on this chapter around Christmas of 1997, I noticed that something seemed to be missing in this new ADO technology puzzle—a way to create and manage the ConnectionString and other parameters. We needed a tool similar to the ODBC applet exposed in the Windows Control Panel. It seems that the OLE DB people thought so too, and, after several renditions (one of which I fully documented and had to discard), we've arrived at the latest version of the Data View window, which creates the Data Links referred to at the beginning of the chapter. These are saved in the Windows Registry (by Visual Basic) and in files (not unlike the old 16-bit INI files) with a UDL extension. Yes, I expect that the user interface is bound to evolve as users start to comment on how well (or how poorly) it works—so just stay flexible. The Data View window is built into the Visual Basic IDE, and you can open it at any time to view all registered (well, saved) Data Links. I devote a whole chapter to the Data View window and Data Links later on (Chapter 36). Upon closer inspection, you'll find that the Data View window is the new home of the Visual Database Tools. With these tools, you can create and modify tables, views, stored procedures, database schema diagrams, and queries. As I've said in earlier chapters, the Visual Database Tools are very useful tools that you'll want to have in your trunk in case your ADO application gets a flat tire.

The Data Link provides a standard means for finding, persisting, managing, and loading connections to ADO OLE DB data sources (including those using the OLE DB provider for ODBC). Rather than having each application implement a different way to accomplish these tasks, Microsoft's Data Access Group (DAG) created this functionality as a core component of OLE DB—much as the ODBC Driver Manager and Data Administrator are for ODBC. You'll see the Data Link Properties dialog box in a number of places. If you use a variety of OLE DB providers, you'll notice that the dialog box morphs itself based on the provider chosen. The Data Link Properties dialog box collects just the properties it needs for each provider.

The real promise of Data Links is the ability to install them as easily as you copy a file. They don't have to be registered—just located somewhere that your application or component can find them.

How the Data Link Properties Dialog Box Ticks

Let's assume that you want to use the Data Link Properties dialog box to set up an easy way to connect to ADO data sources—both ODBC and OLE DB. On the surface, this task seems pretty easy. But keep in mind that you won't want to use the Connection object created by the Data Link—not without tuning a few of its properties first.

Creating Data Links for OLE DB providers for ODBC

To begin the process of creating a Data Link in Visual Basic 6.0, follow these steps:

1. Click the Data View Window icon on the menu bar.

2. In the Data View Window, click the Add A New Data Link icon, which displays the Data Link Properties dialog box. All of the available OLE DB providers are listed. The highlighted provider (Microsoft OLE DB Provider for ODBC Drivers) is the default. We'll start by choosing this provider—not that this is the best choice, but we need to tour this ghetto first.

Once you click the Next >> button or the Connection tab, you're permitted to select a few connect options, as shown in Figure 30-4. Here's where it gets interesting. If you're used to RDO, you'll have to make some adjustments because you'll find that a few things simply aren't exposed—at least not on the surface. If you're new to all of this, hang on and take notes.

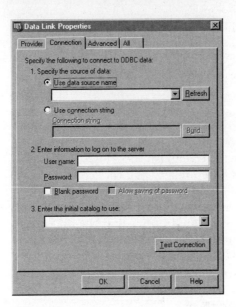

Figure 30-4 *The Connection tab of the Data Link Properties dialog box when the OLE DB provider for ODBC is selected*

Let's stop here for a few minutes and go over the Data Link Properties Connection tab bolt by bolt. You probably won't want to use the OLE DB provider for ODBC once we finish this discussion, but if you can't figure out how to get the lid off, it won't do you much good.

First you have to tell the dialog box how to get connected. The Connection tab of the Data Link Properties dialog box collects all the required information. Remember, ADO is very flexible, so you have a lot of options for how to specify these essentials.

In Figure 30-4 (under the number 1 heading), you have your first decision: use either a DSN (an ODBC-registered DSN) or a ConnectionString. If you don't have a DSN, you have to launch the ODBC control panel applet and create one and then choose it from the drop-down list, or choose the *Use connection string* option and click the Build button (unless you want to use a DSN-less connection). Either of these approaches will launch the ODBC control panel applet to let you build a new DSN, if you need to. So far, this is all fairly intuitive. In many situations, however, you'll need to build DSN-less connections. In this case, you're basically SOL*, because this dialog box has no clue how to help you. You might end up longing for the days of the RDO UserConnection designer, in which it was easy to specify the needed parameters. They were all exposed in drop-down lists. You'll need to tell ADO about the following connection string arguments:

- The server name: Server=MyServer.

- The driver name:{SQL Server}. (Notice the surrounding curly braces.)

---

* An old Army term that translates to something to the effect of being out of luck. See also "Up the creek without a paddle."

- The default database: Database=MyDB unless you know that your login ID sets this correctly for you.

- The domain-managed/integrated security option: Trusted_Connection=Yes if you want Windows to pass your Windows NT domain login ID to SQL Server.

- Anything else that would ordinarily go in your ConnectionString, such as UID, PWD, and other options.

- The fact that you know there is no DSN: DSN="". This argument should be last.

Well, you still have the ability to "build" a ConnectionString. If you want to build a DSN-less connection, you simply have to type in the connection string. Here's an example.

```
UID=;PWD=;Driver={SQL Server};Server=betav1;database=pubs;
trusted_connection=yes;DSN=""
```

TIP If you don't have a live SQL Server to access, the Data View Properties dialog box won't work. This dialog box constantly opens connections to pull down the list of valid databases, tables, and so on.

You can get a running start on the ConnectString by choosing the Use Connection String option and pressing the Build button. The first dialog box prompts you for a DSN (or lets you build one). When you've done that, you can edit the generated ConnectionString. (Yes, you have to edit in that tiny Connection string text box. No, I don't know why they didn't use a multiline text box.)

Once you set the connection properties and the connection test succeeds, you still have a couple of tabs to access—assuming you need to set some of the other options. The Advanced tab exposes only a couple of options:

- **Connection timeout** This setting defaults to 15 seconds, which is fine for most situations.

- **Access permissions** Here you get to choose how this connection should be shared with other users. You can also tell ADO that the connection should support read/write or just read-only result sets. Unfortunately, not all combinations seem to work, and some seem to be overridden by other options.

The remaining options are exposed in the catch-all All tab. No, you won't find all the property settings in the Properties collection here—not by a long shot. But you can set the remaining ConnectionString arguments on this tab. The other ODBC API options are neither exposed nor accessible. Remember that we don't have access to the ODBC hStmt handle, which is why we can't get at the Prompt argument (passed to the ODBC API when the connection is opened). Perhaps the ADO developers will see the light and fix this limitation before long.

Most of the additional properties on the All tab of the Data Link Properties dialog box are intuitive, and you don't need me to turn a spotlight on them. (They don't like that anyway.) But for some of the newer or more obscure characters, here are a few words of description:

- **Extended properties**   The developer-authored connect string

- **Initial Catalog**   Same as the Database= or default database setting

- **Locale Identifier**   Used when you need to specify an ODBC localization type

- **Location**   The path to a file-based DSN

- **Mode**   Where the Advanced tab sets its data access "mode" settings such as read-only or share-lock

- **Persist security info**   Where you can tell ADO to save the password in the Data Link

Changing one of these exposed properties is simple—just click the Edit Value button after clicking on the name of the option to edit. Of course, it's easier to change some of these by filling in the blanks in earlier dialog boxes—for example, Connect Timeout, Data Source, Mode, and others. You can alter all of these properties and more in code because they're exposed in the Properties collection by name. However, you can't alter many of these properties once the connection is open—and many more aren't exposed *until* the connection is open. There are ways to change these and all of the other ADO properties and settings in code—assuming, of course, that you get the opportunity. If you're using the Data Environment with bound controls, you have no choice—if you don't change the properties before the form containing the bound controls is loaded, you've missed your chance. You'll have to hold off loading forms containing bound controls so that you'll have a chance to make needed changes before the load or show operation takes off.

Here's a question for all you RDO experts: Notice anything missing in the Data Link Properties dialog box? As I said before, you'll discover that several options are missing. Of course, not all of the problems these options address apply to OLE DB native SQL Server connections. (We'll talk about using the OLE DB provider for SQL Server in the next section.) But here are some options that you won't find:

- **Cursor Library selection**   Nope, it's not exposed. You have to use client-side cursors with this approach. I expected it to default to server-side, but it didn't.

- **ODBC prompt behavior**   Nope, it's not exposed either. Unless you do something about it, you'll have to take the ADO default of 2. (This default is adPromptComplete, which behaves like rdDriverComplete). Theoretically, this default prompt behavior means that if the DSN keyword is provided, no ODBC prompt dialog box will appear. Swell. But what if something changes, such as a user is no longer authorized, you're out of connections, permissions change on an underlying database, or the database is simply not available for one of a million reasons? Then the ODBC interface throws up a dialog box to prompt the user for missing or incorrect information. Not good—especially if you're creating a component or working with a user that doesn't like to see these dialog boxes—or worse yet, a malevolent user who might try other user IDs or passwords when the ODBC dialog boxes appear.

At this point, I can see that ADO 2.0 can't be considered "equivalent" to RDO 2.0. I think it has fallen short in a few important—nay, critical, ways. Sure, it's more flexible, but I think that can be a disadvantage. All too often, the one-size-fits-all approach means that you end up with a Swiss army knife at a bayonet fight. Ever wonder why they say "Fix bayonets!" and not "Fix corkscrews!"?

Creating Data Links for the native OLE DB provider for SQL Server

Since the OLE DB provider for ODBC interface is kinda lame, I guess we're going to have to depend on the native OLE DB data provider for SQL Server—at least when we're working with the Data Environment, and especially when we're working with bound controls. Let's see if the Data Link Properties dialog box for the native OLE DB provider for SQL Server is any better.

Everything starts out in pretty much the same way. You can create a new Data Link using the Data View window in Visual Basic. However, instead of taking the default, you need to choose Microsoft OLE DB Provider for SQL Server. Once you do, the Connection tab exposes a whole new set of options, as shown in Figure 30-5.

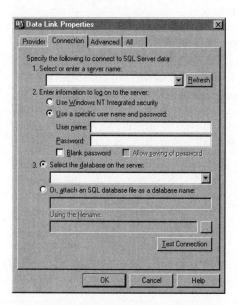

Figure 30-5 *The Connection tab of the Data Link Properties dialog box when the OLE DB provider for SQL Server is selected*

Let's slow down and take a close look at the remaining tabs:

- First you get to select the name of a server. If you're running Microsoft Windows 95/98, don't bother to press the Refresh button if the drop-down list of servers isn't populated. No, it never did work. In any case, you can fill in the name of your SQL Server.

- Next you choose the type of security you want to use. Yes, they seem to want you to verify whether your password is blank. I guess they figure that you've made a mistake if the password is really blank, and not just blank because you're using integrated security.

- Then you select the name of the default database on the server. This ends up being the Initial Catalog in the All tab properties list. You can also attach to a file-based SQL Server database. This is a new feature of SQL Server 7.0 that you might find useful.

Once you make these selections, click the Test Connection button. Actually, when you used the drop-down list to select the database, your connection was already tested. Again, if you don't have access to the target SQL Server you're SOL.

The Advanced tab is identical to that used when the OLE DB provider for ODBC is selected, but the All tab lists the properties associated with the OLE DB provider for SQL Server—a much longer list. The All tab exposes some (not all) of the OLE DB and ADO properties we've been setting through the dialog boxes and a few that are visible only through this dialog box or in the ConnectionString. I suggested they rename this tab to Some Properties, but they didn't go for it. In any case, I generally leave these alone because the basic four properties usually do the job for me.

Uh, excuse me? There doesn't seem to be a Prompt property here either. Why? BHOM—probably because of another oversight, but the default behavior for ADO OLE DB interfaces is supposed to be *no prompt*, so the applications and (more importantly) components you create *should* work. But for some reason, the OLE DB provider for SQL Server *also* defaults to adPromptComplete. No, you still can't set the Cursor Library, and it still defaults to client-side cursors. Sigh. It seems that both providers have the same problems, which IMHO, hobbles them for serious work—unless we do something about it in code.

TIP Want to see what the property settings are for each provider? It's easy—simply dump the properties in code:

```
Dim pr As Property
For Each pr In DataEnvironment1.Connection1.Properties
    Debug.Print pr.Name, pr.Value
Next pr
```

Creating Data Links from the desktop

Didn't I say that the Data Links were exposed as a sharable interface? Well, there is a way to create them without using Visual Basic. It's a little obscure, but you can also create a Microsoft Data Link with the Windows Explorer—simply right-click on the desktop or in a directory and choose New/Microsoft Data Link. The same Data Link Properties dialog box will appear. When you close the dialog box, the UDL file created contains the ConnectionString value you need to open the connection. You can reference this file when using the Open method or as an argument in the ConnectionString property.

Patching Up Data View/Environment Connections

As I promised, there is a way around these washed-out paths caused by the Data View Properties dialog box. It's not obvious, but once Ivo showed me the work-around, I took back many of the ugly things I said about the Data Environment. OK, here's the detour: consider that you never really *directly* use a Data Link to open a connection because Data Links are used *indirectly* to build Data Environment Connection and Command objects. Once you've created a Data Environment Connection object (in whatever way), Visual Basic exposes another way to change its properties—at design time. Click on a newly created Data Environment Connection object, and look at the lower right-hand portion of your Visual Basic 6.0 development environment. Yep, it was there the whole time—the Properties window for the DEConnection object, as shown in Figure 30-6. Here we find a whole new set of properties that reflect the properties of the underlying ADO Connection object—yes, this is a *DEConnection*, not really an ADO Connection at all. The DEConnection properties are described in Table 30-2.

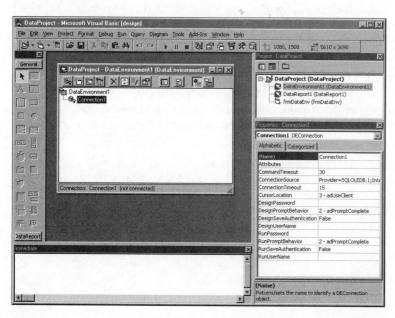

Figure 30-6 *The Visual Basic 6.0 IDE showing the DEConnection properties in the Properties window*

Table 30-2
DEConnection Properties

Property	Purpose
Attributes	Additional ConnectionString attributes
CommandTimeout	Defaults to 30 seconds
ConnectionSource	ConnectionString
ConnectionTimeout	Defaults to 15 seconds
CursorLocation	Defaults to 3 – adUseClient
DesignPassword	Design-time password
DesignPromptBehavior	Design-time prompt. Defaults to 2 – adPromptComplete.
DesignSaveAuthentication	Specifies whether authentication information is to be saved with a design-time project. Defaults to False.
DesignUserName	Design-time user ID
RunPassword	Run-time password
RunPromptBehavior	Design-time prompt. Defaults to 2 – adPromptComplete.
RunSaveAuthentication	Specifies whether authentication information is to be saved with a run-time project. Defaults to False.
RunUserName	Run-time user ID

Now that you have a way to set up the Connection correctly, you need to make at least one change—to the Prompt behavior. This property really should be changed to 4 – adPromptNever. You might want to change the CursorLocation to 3 – Use server-side cursors, but only if you aren't using the hierarchical resultsets or techniques that require the client-batch cursor library.

If you want to take a code-only approach, you can try to override these options before they do any damage. You'll have to add the following code to your application after you instantiate the DataEnvironment object and before you open it (or it gets opened).

```
Dim de As New DataEnvironment1
de.Connection1.Properties("Prompt") = adPromptNever
de.Connection1.CursorLocation = adUseServer
de.Connection1.Open
```

OK, let's move on out of this morass and onto drier ground.

Connecting Using a Code-Based Approach

In this section, I'll be showing you the ropes for taking a code-based approach. Yes, it takes more code, but you gain far more control over your applications and components.

Connecting with the ADO Connection Open Method

Now that we know how to create a ConnectionString and how to get the Data View Properties dialog box to create one for you, let's take a closer look at how to set up and code the first of our options—using the Open method on the ADO Connection object. The Open method will take our ConnectionString and pass it on to the OLE DB provider (for ODBC or for SQL Server) and get us hooked up.

The first thing you (might) need to do is declare the Connection object. I say "might" because some situations don't require a Connection object. Remember that the Recordset object can be created and filled with data without a Connection object or a Command object anywhere to be seen. Yes, ADO does create one for you, but you never see it. Generally, I declare the Connection object in a Global scope so the entire application, subsystem, or component can see it.

```
Dim Cn as New Connection    ' NO Events
```

If you want to expose events on your Connection object (and you do), you need to declare the Connection variable using the WithEvents syntax—and no, you can't use the "as New" syntax. You don't need to do both—choose one technique or the other:

```
Dim WithEvents Cn as Connection    ' With Events
```

If you've used this code in other programs, you know that it doesn't make the ADO Connection object ready to use—it just provides a template (a class), so you still need to instantiate a Connection object from this class. When building a Connection object that supports events, you have to take an additional step, which assigns (Sets) this *Cn* variable to address a New ADO Connection object:

```
Set Cn = New Connection
```

TIP To get ADO to open the connection asynchronously, you have to declare the Connection object using the WithEvents syntax and change the code to build the new Connection object. It turns out that ADO will fire the ConnectComplete event even if you don't opt to open the connection asynchronously. We'll discuss asynchronous operations a little later.

Now you have a Connection object, and you can use its methods as needed. No, there is no Connections collection to worry about. If you want to, you can create one and manage it yourself. I'd rather hit myself in the head with a board while doing Gregorian chants. Let's turn away from that painful image and peruse the Connection object properties to see which make sense for SQL Server and how to code them.

We need to code a ConnectionString in code, as mentioned earlier. You can create a stand-alone string variable to hold it, or you can pass it as a quoted literal argument in code wherever the ConnectionString or ActiveConnection argument is called for. You can also skip all of this bother and create a Data Environment or simply a Data Link. Remember that our first scenario uses the Open method against the Connection object, which is most familiar to DAO and RDO programmers and is fairly intuitive to code.

```
Cn.Open "UID=sa;pwd=;dsn=pubs;"
```

Or simply use the following code, which assumes that integrated security will help you get through the security screen:

```
Cn.Open "dsn=pubs"
```

This example uses the default OLE DB provider for ODBC and a common ODBC connect string to open the connection. A better approach uses the OLE DB provider for SQL Server:

```
CString = "Provider=MSDASQL.1;Location=Betav1;Data Source=Pubs"
Cn.Open CString
```

A third approach leverages the new OLE DB Data Link "file-based" data source. In this case, the ConnectionString is embedded in a file using standard OLE DB notation:

```
Cn.Open "File Name=c:\mydsns\BetavPubs.UDL"
```

Once you start the process of opening your data source, your application or component is blocked—and the line of code following the Open method won't run until the connection times out or succeeds. That's because you didn't use the asynchronous option. If you want to do other processing while the connection is opening, such as finish the Form_Load procedure and paint the form, you can turn on the asynchronous option adAsyncConnect:

```
Cn.Open "File Name=c:\Betav1.UDL", options:=adAsyncConnect
```

While you're waiting, you can do just about anything you want to— except try to run a query against the connection. Test the Cn.State property until it no longer returns adStateConnecting, or wait for the ConnectComplete event. This event fires either when the connection operation times out (based on the number of seconds in the ConnectionTimeout property) or when the connection is established. Check the pError value when the event fires. If the property is Nothing, nothing (terrible) happened and you should have a working connection.

Connecting with the
ADO Recordset Open Method

Our next scenario leverages ADO's Recordset Open method. In this case, ADO and Visual Basic make it easy to execute a query. Using this technique, however, you don't get to set up anything other than a firehose cursor—you have to take all the defaults. (We'll talk about these default behaviors in the next section.)

Coding the Recordset object's Open method is fairly straightforward. Visual Basic prompts you for all the needed arguments at design time, which include the Source (your SQL statement) and the ActiveConnection, which can take a valid ConnectionString as a suitable substitute. ADO will take this string and establish a connection for you along with a Connection object.

```
Dim rs as New Recordset
Dim CString as String
Dim MySQL as String
MySQL = "Select pub_name From Publishers Where State = 'CA'"
CString = "File Name=C:\MyDSN\Pubs.UDL"

rs.Open MySQL, Cstring
```

When ADO returns your Recordset, you'll have an open connection and a new Connection object to reference through the Recordset object's ActiveConnection property. Sure, you can still use the asynchronous option here too. Just add the adAsyncExecute option:

```
rs.Open source:=MySQL, ActiveConnection:=CString, _
    Options:=adAsyncExecute
```

Another variation is also possible. It seems that ADO's Open method can also be coded to pass an ODBC DSN (or ConnectionString), user ID, and password directly as arguments:

```
cn.Open "Pubs", "sa", "pwd"
```

Dealing with the Defaults

But wait a minute, do these "easy" solutions really mean trouble for your program later? Let's take a look at the defaults and find out what ADO is building for us. In the first example, the Connection object's Open method simply opens a synchronous ODBC connection with no additional parameters. (Keep your seat belt on—we'll get to activating asynchronous operations in a minute.) The Recordset object's Open method makes it very clear which options are being defaulted—its right there in the statement completion window that pops up at design time, as shown in Figure 30-7.

Take a look at the pop-up statement completion window. Notice that the CursorType defaults to adOpenUnspecified, the lock mode to adLockUnspecified, and the Options to -1. Well, that's not much help unless you know that ADO defaults its CursorType to adOpenForwardOnly and its LockType as adLockReadOnly. Now we're getting somewhere. This means we're really close

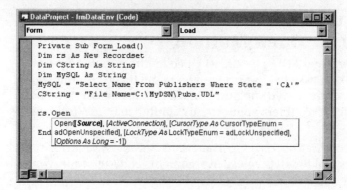

Figure 30-7 *A pop-up statement completion for the Recordset object's Open method*

to a forward-only, read-only firehose cursor—all we need to do is set the CacheSize to 1. Ah, but ADO knows about this too and defaults to a single row, thus enabling our high-speed cursorless Recordset. So by default, ADO creates a firehose cursor for us.

ADO lets you choose between two cursor locations: client-side or server-side. The default CursorLocation is adUseServer—server-side cursors. Sigh—so close. Although server-side cursors are cool for some applications, they are a PIA* for many situations—especially stored procedures. And many of the features we need day-to-day (like keyset cursors) are supported only on client-side cursors. So we can't use this lightweight code technique to get the most efficient or client-side cursors. You'll also have to settle for the Connection property defaults listed in Table 30-3.

Table 30-3
Connection Property Defaults

Property	Default
ConnectionTimeout	15 seconds
CommandTimeout	30 seconds
IsolationLevel	adXactReadCommitted
Mode	adModeUnknown
Prompt	No prompt
Provider	MSDASQL

These are all pretty reasonable—your customer won't go into delay shock if the connection times out in 15 seconds, and most common queries can be done in 30 seconds. Notice that there is no property on the ADO Connection object to set the prompting level, as there was in RDO. Fortunately, ADO defaults

---

* Another old Army term. A pain in the..., right.

to *no prompts*—I'll tell you how to change this behavior in a moment. That means that if the user enters an invalid user ID/password combination, your code will have to deal with a trappable error. Actually, that's good news. You don't want the user to have an opportunity to keep trying passwords until guessing the right one.

To set up a few more options and to get the most efficiency out of ADO, your code to open an ODBC OLE DB connection might typically look more like the sample below. OK, I would rarely use anything but adPromptNever when working with code, but the default of adPromptComplete when working with the Data Environment is not a good choice. This example shows how to change a Connection Property value:

```
Dim WithEvents cn As Connection

Private Sub Form_Load()
    Set cn = New Connection
    cn.CursorLocation = adUseClient
    cn.ConnectionTimeout = 30    ' We are using RAS
    cn.Properties("Prompt") = adPromptComplete
    cn.Open "dsn=pubs"
End Sub
```

The other prompt enumerations are listed in Table 30-4.

Table 30-4
ConnectPromptEnum Constants

Constant	Purpose
adPromptAlways	Yes, give users the ODBC prompt and lets them guess user IDs and passwords until they get it right or give up.
adPromptComplete	Same deal as above.
adPromptCompleteRequired	Same deal as above.
adPromptNever	No, don't prompt users. Return an error if the user ID or password fail.
adPromptOnlyOnTuesday	No, I was just trying to see if you were still awake.

We went over these prompting behaviors earlier in this chapter. The *real* reasons are more complicated than the brief descriptions in Table 30-4. If you must know the details of these prompt enumerations, here they are:

- **adPromptAlways** If the connection string doesn't contain the DRIVER, DSN, or FILEDSN keyword, the ODBC Driver Manager displays the Data Sources dialog box. It constructs a connection string from the DSN returned by the dialog box and from any other keywords the application passed to it. If the DSN returned by the dialog box is empty, the Driver Manager specifies the keyword-value pair DSN=Default. (This dialog box won't display a data source with the name "Default.")

- **adPromptComplete or adPromptCompleteRequired**   If the connection string specified by the application includes the DSN keyword, the ODBC Driver Manager copies the connection string specified by the application. Otherwise, it takes the same actions as it does when Prompt is adPromptComplete.

- **adPromptNever**   The ODBC Driver Manager copies the connection string specified by the application. If the attempt to connect to the database fails, no dialog box appears and an error occurs. This is definitely the option you want to use when you're building components that will run on a remote server.

More Sophisticated Connections

Using the Open method on a Connection object establishes the physical connection to a data source. After this method successfully completes, the connection is live and you can issue commands against it and process results. Of course, that assumes a great deal. Remember that when you're trying to link up with SQL Server (or any data source for that matter), you have to line up an awful lot of ducks. (Review the information about making connections to SQL Server in Chapter 6 if you need more details.) ADO doesn't really pose any new issues in client/server mode. When you try to connect through Microsoft Transaction Server (MTS) or from Visual Basic, Scripting Edition (VBScript), however, you'll encounter lots of new issues.

Once the connection is open, the ConnectionString property automatically inherits the value used for the ConnectionString argument. Well, sort of. If you examine the post-open ConnectionString, you'll notice a number of additions and alterations. Therefore, you can either set the ConnectionString property of the Connection object before opening it or use the ConnectionString argument to set or override the current connection parameters during the Open method call.

If you pass user and password information in both the ConnectionString argument and the optional UserID and Password arguments, the results can be unpredictable; you should pass such information only in either the ConnectionString argument or the UserID and Password arguments.

TIP   Frankly, I don't pass UID or passwords through the connect string. I usually depend on Windows NT domain-managed security to do the job.

Once you decide that you don't need your connection any longer, use the Close method to release the *server-side* resources it is holding. Remember that at least 56 KB of space is reserved for each connection on the server and that other clients are trying to get in. Prudent connection management is key to building a scalable application. But closing a Connection doesn't free the client-side resources—those resources are freed only when the object is no longer in scope or when you set the Connection object variable to Nothing.

Here are some additional examples of establishing a connection:

```
Dim cnn1 As Connection
Dim cnn2 As Connection
Dim cnn3 As Connection

' Open a connection using an ODBC driver without using a DSN.
Set cnn1 = New Connection
cnn1.ConnectionString = "driver={SQL Server};server=bigsmile;" & _
    "uid=sa;pwd=pwd;database=pubs; Trusted_Connection=Yes;"
cnn1.Open

' Open a connection using a DSN and ODBC tags.
Set cnn2 = New Connection
cnn2.Open "DSN=Pubs;UID=sa;PWD=pwd;"

' Open a connection using a DSN and OLE DB tags.
Set cnn3 = New Connection
cnn3.ConnectionString = "Data Source=Pubs;User ID=sa;Password=pwd;"
cnn3.Open
```

ADO Connection Tips

The following list summarizes some tips you should find helpful when you're opening ADO connections:

- After you set the ConnectionString property and open the Connection object, the provider can alter the contents of the property, for example, by mapping the ADO-defined argument names to their provider equivalents.

- Because the File Name argument causes ADO to load the associated provider, you can't pass both the Provider and File Name arguments.

- The ConnectionString property is read/write when the connection is closed and read-only when it is open.

- When used on a client-side RDS Connection object, the ConnectionString property can include only the Remote Provider and Remote Server parameters.

Using the collections, methods, and properties of a Connection object, you can do the following:

- Configure the connection before opening it with the ConnectionString, ConnectionTimeout, and Mode properties.

- Set the CursorLocation property to invoke the Client Cursor Provider, which supports batch updates.

- Set the default database for the connection with the DefaultDatabase property.

- Set the level of isolation for the transactions opened on the connection with the IsolationLevel property.

- Specify an OLE DB provider with the Provider property.

- Establish, and later break, the physical connection to the data source with the Open and Close methods.

- Execute a command on the connection with the Execute method and configure the execution with the CommandTimeout property.

- Manage transactions on the open connection, including nested transactions if the provider supports them, with the BeginTrans, CommitTrans, and RollbackTrans methods and the Attributes property.

- Examine errors returned from the data source with the Errors collection.

- Read the version from the ADO implementation in use with the Version property.

- Obtain schema information about your database with the OpenSchema method.

NOTE To execute a query without using a Command object, pass a query string to the Execute method of a Connection object. A Command object is required, however, when you want to persist the command text and reexecute it or use query parameters.

Connecting from a Component

Although most of you out there are still working with client/server systems, some of you are implementing more sophisticated *n*-tiered designs. When you need to connect from a component that runs on another system, your connectivity issues can become complicated. For starters, any number of clients are undoubtedly accessing the component at the "same" time. I won't even begin to suggest that you write your own pool manager, memory manager, thread manager, and all of the other managers you need to implement this sort of architecture. There is no need to go to all that effort. That's what MTS is for. Sure, it's possible to create all these managers on your own. But it's also possible to write your own SQL Server (even in Visual Basic) if you've a mind to—and if you do, you need to have your head examined.

Let's examine some of the issues involved in connecting from components. First, let's assume that we haven't gone squirrelly and we have decided to let MTS handle the Distributed Component Object Model (DCOM) interface and the other remote component issues for us. This makes writing and implementing these components doable—most of the hard work is already done. You do need to install your component so MTS and your client application can find it and establish DCOM (or HTTP) connectivity to it. But I'll leave that up to the MTS documentation and tools to describe. Just keep the following concepts in mind as you build your components.

- Maintaining a "stateless" connection can be important—especially when it is invoked from a component that expects to share a pooled connection. Anything you do to change the connection state, including use the SET statement, create temporary tables (#temp…), create temporary stored procedures, or change the default database, can adversely affect other components—even your own that share your contaminated connection.

- When connecting from components, consider that if you use ODBC connectivity, MTS works with ODBC to handle the connection for ADO. That is, MTS and ODBC are designed to pool or share connections for you—but only if the ConnectionString is the same. Pooled connections hang around for 30 seconds after they are closed in anticipation of other components wanting to use the same connection again. You can change this setting by using the Data Link Properties dialog box we discussed earlier in this chapter. Connections that have pending results can't be shared until all of their result sets are populated or purged. These shared connections are visible only within a single process. And no, OLE DB connections are not pooled—not yet at least. OLE DB connection pooling should arrive in future versions.

Using ODBCPING.EXE to Verify a Connection

It is extremely frustrating to debug a piece of code when you aren't sure whether or not the underlying network interfaces are working. If you find yourself in such a jam, the ODBCPING utility comes in very handy. You can use it to check whether ODBC is properly installed by connecting to a server using the SQL Server ODBC driver. This utility is a 32-bit application that is installed in the \MSSQL\BINN directory. To verify ODBC connectivity, simply provide your own server, DSN, login ID, and password to the utility.

```
odbcping [-S server | -D DSN] [-U loginID] [-P password]
```

The resulting message tells you whether or not you got connected.

- Cross-process sharing is not possible. To deal with this requirement, be sure to compile your executable into a Component Object Model (COM) component. Once you assign MTS the task of handling the object, it will pool your ODBC connections for you—as well as handling a multitude of other details.

- In Microsoft Internet Information Server (IIS) 4.0, DLLs (including Active Server Pages) and ISAPIs are always loaded in the IIS process, unless you configure them otherwise. This means that you'll normally have access to the ODBC connection pool. If you run your applications out of process, all the DLLs you use share connections among themselves but not with other applications on your system. Out-of-process components will always have their own pool.

- ADO doesn't perform connection pooling—the provider does. This distinction is subtle, but you must not forget it. ODBC connection pooling is enable per-provider, so no matter where you use it, the ODBC Driver Manager can automatically manage the connection pool. No, not all ADO data providers manage a connection pool.

- As of this writing, OLE DB doesn't (yet) support connection pooling. ODBC 3.x and its providers currently implement this feature. However, this is expected to be in place for OLE DB 2.0, which ships with Visual Basic 6.0—if not then, we'll see it in the next version of ADO.

- Consider that the component doesn't belong to your client—the client is merely borrowing it for a moment to perform a task or two. Therefore, the component must be able to access the server somehow, so you'll have to figure out a permissions scheme to grant it access to the needed stored procedures or (heaven forbid) the underlying tables. Generally, I create a special login ID and password for these components that have carefully gated access to just the stored procedures they need. The component should not just log in as SA with the SA password embedded in the control.

- The error handling techniques you used with a traditional client will seem to work, right up to the point where you post a modal dialog box where you ask the user what to do. Since there is no "user" there to see the message, the dialog box will go unanswered and MTS will flush the component. Not good. This means that you're expected to code error handlers that return error results back to the calling client, not expose dialog boxes to the local server. Of course, Visual Basic can help prevent you from making this mistake by warning you of dialog boxes like this and even by generating error message strings to return to the calling software.

- As discussed in Chapter 4, you should use "stateless" techniques to build components for multitiered designs. Sure, the component can record activity about a specific client and tell MTS to maintain its state between invocations, but this is expensive and dramatically reduces scalability. Components that maintain state can't be released back into the pool of usable components until they report they are complete. This means you should (by all means) create components that don't know if they've ever been called before and don't care. It means that you'll be invoking more methods and fewer property references over the wire—and those methods are likely to have lots of parameters.

- When you build stateless components, there is no concept of "coming back for more." You have to send all of the rows requested back to the client. In other words, when a component is requested to return a set of rows, it has to return all of those rows as a completed result set. We also know that larger result sets aren't a good idea. To address these design boundaries, you often have to build selection criteria into your components that subset the result set into segments and permit selection of specific segments on demand. This way, you can fetch what you need as you need it—and no more.

- You might need to use an alternative protocol when connecting from components, but it might be easier to get named-pipe connectivity from a remote component than from a Web-based client (where it's darn near impossible).

As you can see, very little magic is required to connect from a component—just the usual amount of hard work. We'll cover additional MTS connection issues later, so stay tuned.

31

Building ADO Recordsets

Building ADO Recordset Objects

ADO Queries

ADO Cursors

Managing Concurrency with ADO

Fetching ADO Recordset Data

Filtering, Finding, and Sorting ADO Recordset Data

ctiveX Data Objects (ADO) has taken some very aggressive steps in Microsoft Visual Basic 6.0. It has leveraged the years of work done on the Microsoft Jet, Microsoft FoxPro, and Microsoft SQL Server database engines and the Data Access Objects (DAO), Remote Data Objects (RDO), and OLE DB data access interfaces. You'll soon discover (if you haven't already) that ADO Recordsets are also far more flexible than their DAO and RDO cousins. Any number of reasons account for this flexibility, but these are especially relevant:

- ADO knows how to deal with Recordset objects independently of any connection to a database management system (DBMS). This means that you can build a Recordset in one component and pass it to another application or component and expect the client to be able to see the data and make changes as required. Plus, ADO will know what to do when you need to update one of these disjoint Recordset objects.

- You can pass Recordset objects to Web-based clients using HTML, and ADO will be able to connect these disjoint Recordset objects to bound controls. On the client side, you can use the new lightweight ActiveX Data Objects Recordset (ADOR) library to manage these objects in Microsoft Visual Basic, Scripting Edition (VBScript). The ADOR functionality is included with the client-side Remote Data Services (RDS) components.

- You can sort and seek rows in ADO Recordset objects—something you could do in DAO but not in RDO. You can also filter out only desired rows in ADO, something you couldn't do in either DAO or RDO.

- You can create your own OLE DB data providers in Visual Basic (but that's a tour for another book).

NOTE Visual Basic 6.0 supports a number of new datacentric developer tools, wizards, and designers—all of which are based on ADO. This means you'll have more help creating your code than you've ever had before.

In this chapter, we'll look at how to build ADO Recordsets. Actually, there's more to this topic than meets the eye. Sure, you can run queries in ADO, just as you can in DAO and RDO, that create sets of rows that are managed by a Recordset object. You can also have ADO build cursors or cursorless result sets, and you can create disjoint cursors—just as you can in RDO. However, ADO has at least one important new feature that neither DAO nor RDO has—it can build Recordset objects from thin air. Here's what I mean by that:

The ability to create Recordset objects from code is truly a remarkable feature. Since these ADO Recordset object rows can be searched, sorted, filtered, modified, deleted, or added to, you the developer have a new lightweight means to persist simple Recordset objects on the client. Way cool.

- You can create your own Recordset objects to manage and persist data on the client without benefit of a connection. To do this, you define the fields and the data yourself in code. You use the Recordset object's Append method to create new Field objects and set the Field object's properties if you want to set more properties than the Append arguments support.

- You can use the Open method against a Recordset object once you have appended fields to a New Recordset object. To get this to work, you must call the Open method before you set the ActiveConnection property, and you must call it without any parameters.

- You can bind code-created Recordset objects (or even Recordset objects ADO creates using a Connection object) to data-aware controls without benefit of a data source control (such as the RemoteData or ADO Data control).

- You can build Recordset objects from "persisted" files created by the Save method. Later in the chapter, we'll talk about how to save and reconstitute Recordsets using files.

I think a very common scenario for a disconnected user will be building a Recordset from a persisted file or simply from code to record and manage data until it can reconnect at a later time.

A disconnected user isn't one of those people who hangs around the bus station downtown, but rather a user who isn't currently connected to the network (or the Web). Disconnected users include legal, sales, insurance, and aluminum-siding representatives and others who often have to use their systems off line. Microsoft has worked hard to provide a number of alternatives for these disconnected users. In addition to the innovations added to ADO, SQL Server now supports a "Personal" version of SQL Server that is designed to run on Microsoft Windows 95/98. This feature alone should revolutionize the way databases are prototyped and implemented: imagine having a "take it with you" database that is automatically replicated when you re-doc back at the office.

In this chapter, we'll also discuss how to perform the more mundane tasks of creating cursors and cursorless result sets. You'll learn how to create these with the least amount of code—and in certain cases with more code, which can sometimes make your programs run faster. We also look at how to choose a cursor, and how to get the data out of a Recordset once you've opened it.

Building ADO Recordset Objects

In this section, we'll go over three different ways of building ADO Recordset objects: building stand-alone Recordset objects, building Recordset objects from files, and building Recordset objects from a remote database. Because the ability to create stand-alone Recordset objects is a new feature for Visual Basic 6.0, we need to talk about it first.

Stand-Alone ADO Recordset Objects

Suppose you have a data source that's not a database. It could be a seismic recorder, a telephone switch, a weather station, or the global positioning system strapped to the handle of your bicycle. It could also be a source of data in some proprietary file format or accessible through a nonstandard interface. When you're working with disjoint or nontraditional data sources like these, in most cases you can't (easily) make a connection to SQL Server and create a cursor. ADO and Visual Basic 6.0 have changed all this. Now you can create your own Data class and define all the needed ADO entry points to make ADO think you have an OLE DB data source.

You don't need to go that far to create your own Recordset in ADO, however. All you have to do is declare a Recordset in code and use the Fields.Append method to tack on the columns you want to define. Once you've defined the Recordset, you can use the Open method to tell ADO to build the Recordset for you. Nope, you don't need a Connection object. Remember how you used to have to build result sets in RDO? You had to establish a connection to a server and at least submit a null SELECT—one that didn't return any rows but had the right structure. You can use the same technique in ADO. However, you can also create a Recordset from scratch, by using the Append method to add new columns (Field objects) to the Recordset in code. The code for building a Recordset from the ground up looks something like this:

```
Dim rs As New Recordset

rs.Fields.Append "ID", adInteger, 4, adFldIsNullable
rs.Fields.Append "Name", adChar, 20, adFldIsNullable
rs.Fields.Append "Address", adVarChar, 40, adFldIsNullable
rs.Fields.Append "City", adVarChar, 40, adFldIsNullable
rs.Fields.Append "State", adChar, 2, adFldIsNullable
rs.Fields.Append "Zip", adChar, 10, adFldIsNullable

rs.Open
```

TIP   Keep in mind that you can't add Field objects to an open Recordset.

The Binding object and the BindingCollection object

Once you create a Recordset, you can bind its Field objects to individual bound controls. At this point, you need to use the Microsoft Data Binding Collection (MSBind library) to bind the Recordset to your data-aware controls. In the next code example, we use two TextBox controls to manage two columns of the Recordset. First we'll set the DataSource property of the BindingCollection object to the Recordset. Next we'll use the Add method to add two Binding objects to the collection. This binds the two TextBox controls to specific fields of the Recordset. Binding tells ADO to reflect any changes in the Recordset in the controls and to post any changes to the controls to the Recordset—all without (much) code.

> **NOTE** Don't get confused by the fact that there is a virtually identical DataBinding object and DataBindings collection in the VBRUN library. These have been in place since Visual Basic 5.0 to support multiple bound fields on a control—namely, a UserControl. Intrinsic controls typically have one bound property (that is, Text on a TextBox control). A UserControl can have one or more bound properties set up via the DataBindings collection and Data Bindings dialog box. If you select Procedure Attributes from the Tools menu and set the property as data bound and as shown in the DataBindings collection at design time, when you place the control on a form, the DataBindings collection is exposed as a property with an ellipses (…) in the Properties window. Under the covers, Visual Basic is managing the DataBindings collection for you.

So far, we haven't talked about the Binding object or the BindingCollection. No, these don't have anything to do with nineteenth-century ladies' garments—they're a lot easier to use and don't have the same tendency to make you light-headed when you get a little excited. Let's take a minute and focus on these two new members of the Visual Basic language.

The Binding object relates a specific data consumer property (such as a data-aware control's Text property) to a data field of a data source. Binding objects are managed in the BindingCollection and are created with the BindingCollection.Add method at run time. The BindingCollection is used to manage the Binding objects. Because neither a Class configured as a data source nor an ADO Recordset object can be bound at design time, you must use the BindingCollection to bind a Class or an ADO Recordset object to a data consumer at run time.

Let's step off the road and take a look at the Add method mentioned above. (It's not that complicated, so this won't take long.) The Add method creates a new Binding object and appends it to the BindingCollection. Its syntax works like this:

```
BindingCollection.Add(Object, PropertyName, DataField, _
    DataFormat, Key)
```

The arguments for the Add method are described in Table 31-1.

All of this manual binding seems like an awful lot of trouble when you have the Data Environment and Data Object Wizard to draw on. These tools virtually eliminate the need to manage data binding in code. I have better things to do with my Saturdays.

Argument	Purpose
Object	Required. The control or other data consumer that will be bound. This is the name of the TextBox or other data-aware control or consumer.
PropertyName	Required. The property of the data consumer to bind to. For example, the Text property of a TextBox or the Caption property of a Label control.
DataField	Required. The column of the data source that will be bound to the property specified in the PropertyName argument. This is the name of the Recordset. If you create a Recordset named MyRs, MyRs goes here.
DataFormat	Optional. A DataFormat object or a reference to a DataFormat variable that will be used to format the bound property.
Key	Optional. A unique string that identifies the member of the collection. Use this argument to refer to the Binding object in the collection by name.

OK, we're ready to look at some code to bind up those bleeding Recordsets so you can see the data in a few Visual Basic controls.

```
Option Explicit
Private colBnd As New BindingCollection
Private rs As New Recordset

  ...

' Set the DataSource of the Binding collection to the recordset.
Set colBnd.DataSource = rs

' Add to the Binding collection.
With colBnd
    .Add Text1, "Text", "Name"
    .Add Text2, "Text", "City"
End With
```

In this case, Text1 and Text2 are TextBox controls, and we set up binding between their Text properties and the Recordset Name and City columns (Field objects). Pretty easy, right?

TIP Code samples for this chapter are on the *Hitchhiker's Guide* companion CD in the Chap31 directory. Many of the samples use the *Biblio* database, which is also on the companion CD. See Appendix A for information on how to set up this database.

File-Based ADO Recordset Objects

Suppose you're working with a laptop in central Italy in a sleepy little town like Venice—well OK, maybe not sleepy, but based on my most recent visit, I've decided that Venice's phone system must have been designed by the first doge. It works fine until the strings get wet—and in Venice.... Anyway, you want to get to your home office database but can't get the connection to lock on long enough. Perhaps it's the hotel desk clerk who keeps checking to see whether you're done with the hotel's only telephone line. (This happened to me in Boston not long ago.) Wouldn't it be nice to work in a stand-alone mode? Well, in ADO you can. Using the Save method with the Recordset, you can save a file-based representation of your Recordset. Later, you can open this file-based Recordset and use it like the results of a database query. I wrote a sample application to illustrate this feature. Let's walk through the code looking for surprises—I discovered several.

I wrote this little sample to demonstrate how to perform the basic steps of saving and reconstructing file-based Recordsets. The code is shown below. Let's go over just a few notes first:

- I didn't have to create a separate Connection object. The Open statement created one for me in each case. I thought I might need a Connection object to specify a special provider, but I didn't. The options on the Save and Open methods seemed to deal with this for me.

- I reused the Recordset object for building both the server-based and file-based Recordset. I thought I might need a different Recordset—one that wasn't contaminated with ODBC or SQL Server OLE DB provider litter—but I didn't.

- If you don't use the Option:=adCmdFile option on the open, ADO thinks you're working with an ODBC data source. If you make this mistake, the OLE DB provider for ODBC (the default) gets confused with the filename.

- I used my magic grid to display the rows. As usual, this code and control are on the companion CD.

The following code saves the Recordset out to a formatted file. Nope, the Advanced Data TableGram (ADTG) format isn't an ASCII format, so you can't just create the file yourself and edit it. We might see the Extensible Markup Language (XML) format come on line before too long, and that *is* an HTML-like format that you might care to edit. If the file exists, you have to trap the error and use the Kill command to remove it.

TIP I had to add code to intercept errors caused by existing files.

```
Option Explicit
Dim rs As New Recordset
```

(continued)

```
Private Sub SaveTofileButton_Click()
On Error GoTo eh
CmnDialog1.ShowSave
rs.Save CmnDialog1.FileName, adPersistADTG
Exit Sub
eh:
    Debug.Print Err.Description, Err
    If Err = 58 Then Kill CmnDialog1.FileName: Resume
End Sub
```

The following code collects a filename from the common dialog box and uses the Recordset.Open method to read the file and populate the Recordset object. No, you don't have to set the PersistFormat property before reading the file—ADO knows how to figure this out on its own.

```
Private Sub GetDataFromFile_Click()
On Error GoTo eh
If rs.State = adStateOpen Then rs.Close
CmnDialog1.ShowOpen
rs.Open CmnDialog1.FileName,Options:=adCmdFile
RAutoGrid1.ShowADOData rs     ' display data
Exit Sub
eh:
    Debug.Print Err.Description, Err
    If Err = 58 Then Kill CmnDialog1.FileName: Resume
End Sub
```

TIP If you include DAO code in your project, you'll want to precede all your ADO references with ADODB, as in

```
Dim rs As New ADODB.Recordset
```

ADO Recordset Objects from a Remote Database

OK, so you want to get some data out of a remote SQL Server database—one that's on your own system or across the planet—perhaps even in Cleveland. That's the whole idea, right? Well, you might also want to run a query that updates the data or simply deletes it all (if you're having a *very* bad day). In this section, we cover all these issues—how to run a query that returns rows or simply run an action query that doesn't. In Chapter 32, we discuss more complex queries, such as those that return multiple result sets. But for now, we'll stick to the basics of using ADO to run more traditional client/server queries.

TIP By default, the ADO cursor type is read-only and forward-only with a cache size of 1. If you want to read the data only once and not scroll back to fetched rows, you don't have to change any of the default options.

When it comes time to build a Recordset from a query, you have a litany of options:

- **Recordset.Open method** The Source argument tells ADO what query to run. The Source argument can be a SQL statement, the name of a stored procedure, a Command object, or simply the name of a table (no, just a table name isn't a good idea). Ordinarily you provide the Open method with an active ADO Connection object, but you don't have to. You don't need a Connection object if you specify a valid ConnectionString or a registered data source name (DSN). However, you *do* need to make sure the Recordset object has been declared with the *As New* syntax or has been instantiated before you try to use the Open method, as shown here:

```
Dim rs As New Recordset
cn.Open "dsn=biblio"
rs.Open Source:= _
    "Select Author from Authors where Author like 'Vau%'", _
    ActiveConnection:=cn
```

TIP Sure, you can use the "named argument :=" syntax to refer to arguments of ADO methods. All the ADO methods support this syntax. I find it easier than remembering how many commas to use when specifying arguments by position.

- **Open method to execute a parameter query against a pre-defined Command object** In this case, you apply the parameters to the Command object's Parameters collection and then use the Command object in the Source argument:

```
cmd.CommandText = "Au42"
cmd.CommandType = adCmdStoredProc
Set prm = cmd.CreateParameter("Yearlow", adInteger, _
    adParamInput, 4, 1947)
cmd.Parameters.Append prm
Set prm = cmd.CreateParameter("yearhigh", adInteger, _
    adParamInput, 4, 1948)
cmd.Parameters.Append prm
cn.Open "dsn=biblio"
Set cmd.ActiveConnection = cn
rs.Open cmd
```

- **Execute method against a Command object or a Connection object** Assuming you run the same setup code, the following code illustrates using the Execute method to do something kinda dumb—access all the rows from the Authors table.

```
cmd.CommandText = "authors"
cmd.CommandType = adCmdTable
cmd.Name = "Authors"
Set cmd.ActiveConnection = cn
Set rs = cmd.Execute
```

- **One of the Command objects you created as a method on the Connection object** The following line of code executes the Command object using this syntax:

```
cn.Authors rs
```

If you need to pass parameters to the Command object, place them ahead of the Recordset variable, like this:

```
cn.AuthorByNameAndYear "%V%", 1947, rs
```

You always code the Recordset variable last. No, this syntax isn't documented, but it works. However, the ADO gurus tell me that this syntax might be more expensive because of late binding.

- **Data Environment designer** You can use the Data Environment designer to build Connection and Command objects and execute code based on these objects, or you can simply let Visual Basic build bound controls based on the commands. When you use the Data Environment designer to build your Command objects, the Recordset is returned as a new object whose name is based on the name of the query. For example, if you create a Data Environment Command object named dbo_Au42, Visual Basic and the Data Environment create a new Recordset named rsdbo_Au42. In addition, Visual Basic exposes the command with all of its properties with statement completion to make using this technique even easier, as shown in Figure 31-1.

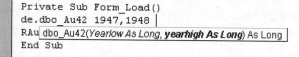

```
Private Sub Form_Load()
de.dbo_Au42 1947,1948 |
RAu dbo_Au42(Yearlow As Long, yearhigh As Long) As Long
End Sub
```

Figure 31-1 *Statement completion displayed for a Data Environment command*

On the surface, using the Data Environment seems like the best approach. The code is extremely tight and runs quickly as well. I understand that ADO 3.0 will reduce these two lines to just one—and subsequent versions will simply read your mind. So your mother-in-law was right: soon there won't be any need for programmers at all.

Examples of each technique are provided later in the chapter and on this guide's companion CD. Which technique or combination of techniques should you use? Well, as usual, it depends; but here are the basic rules:

- Use the Recordset.Open method whenever you're opening a Recordset that's going to return rows and you want scrolling or updating.

- Use the Execute method as a shortcut for opening default Recordsets. This creates a forward-only, read-only, CacheSize = 1 result set—our firehose cursor. The method itself returns this lightweight firehose Recordset.

After having used the Data Environment designer for several months now as it was being created, I can't say that I'll depend on it as heavily as I originally thought I would. While it's an ambitious undertaking, it seems to have a number of issues when working with more complex parameter-based stored procedures—especially when you try to use drag-and-drop binding. These and other problems will have to be resolved before I can wholeheartedly recommend this tool to you developers. I devote an entire chapter to the Data Environment designer (Chapter 37), so stay on the trail for more details.

- Use the query-as-a-Connection-method technique to pass in parameters to a more complex query. In this case, you can describe the Command object in great detail, including all gazintas and gazoutas. The return status and other arguments are returned in the Parameters collection of the Command object. The Recordset is returned into the last variable provided, as shown in the example below. This syntax is very unusual for Visual Basic in that it expects you to pass a structured variable—in this case, a variable addressing an instantiated Recordset object *to* the method call. ADO fills in this structure with the returning rows. If you don't declare this Recordset *As New*, you'll get error 3001, a trappable run-time error.

```
Dim rs As New Recordset
cn.MyQuery "My string argument", 5, rs
```

TIP This particularly useful syntax variation isn't documented (at least I couldn't find it), but it is fully supported and is described in the spec. One of the problems, however, is that it doesn't integrate with the statement completion option. Because of this, you aren't prompted for the method arguments as you type. I'm also afraid that the Products Support Services folks didn't like it very well because it might be slightly slower (it's late bound) and could be harder to support because it's somewhat obscure. Just don't give them a hard time when you call.

- Use Execute whenever you're executing action queries that don't return rows—such as UPDATE, INSERT, or DELETE statements—or utility procedures such as DBCC.

You should generally use Recordset.Open whenever you're creating something other than a firehose Recordset. You probably use firehose Recordsets most of the time anyway, but if you're going to use the client cursor engine and do scrolling, updating, sorting, filtering, or saving, you should use Recordset.Open. You also need to use Recordset.Open when setting pre-open properties such as MaxRecords.

TIP Dave Stearns dubbed the read-only, forward-only, RowsetSize=1 RDO result set the "firehose" cursor when he discovered how much faster it returned data. This cursorless result set is the new default for ADO. When creating Recordset objects from a component, many pundits recommend creating a firehose cursor to read the rows and executing SQL statements for the changes.

The Execute method can return a Recordset, but it doesn't give you the opportunity to set cursor type or lock type. This is done by design—the ADO team wants to encourage developers to use Recordset.Open because that sets them up for the newer design paradigms listed on the next page.

- You'll find it natural when ADO 2.0 enables you to create new Recordsets from the ether (that is, to add your own fields and fill them with your own data).

- You'll be set up for using *specialized* Recordsets when this feature is enabled in the future. A specialized Recordset is one that you can define with whatever additions you care to define—properties, methods, or events.

One of the main reasons the ADO team designed this flexibility into ADO objects was so that they could keep the Recordset object's properties where they belong—on the Recordset. In DAO and RDO, the DAO and RDO developers sprinkled Recordset properties on the Connection and Query objects that had to be set before the objects were opened, and then echoed them on the Recordset. These parallel properties made it confusing to understand which property affected which object. For example, if you change MaxRows on rdoQuery, does it affect Resultsets already created? No, but that's not totally obvious from the design of the programming model. In ADO, these properties are all kept on the Recordset, so there's no confusion about which objects are affected by property changes.

The Command object's role

The ADO Command object is an important tool in the RDO developer's toolbox. As we saw in Chapter 30, the Command object represents a specific command that you intend to execute against the data source—usually more than once. In many ways, the Command object is very similar to the rdoQuery object in RDO 2.0 (or the rdoPreparedStatement object in RDO 1.0). You can also use the Execute method against the Command object or the Connection object to create a Recordset, but this is simply a shortcut for executing one-time commands that don't require output parameters or preparation.

In any case, you use the Command object either to create Recordset objects or simply to execute an action (non-row-returning) query. Another important technique, first exposed in RDO, is the ability to execute procedures as methods of the Connection object. In ADO, *all* the Command objects you define appear as methods on the Connection object. In addition, ADO even attempts to run commands you don't formally define as Command objects. I'll show you how these techniques work in Chapter 33.

ADO Queries

In this section, I cover some information on how to best run your ADO queries. I also discuss how to "prepare" your queries. Why bother? Well, one of the problems we've had in the past with DAO and RDO was their propensity to "mother" the query. That is, they figured out (or tried to) what was best for the operation. And like a well-meaning mom, sometimes they didn't make the right choices. Remember that time when she sent you to school bundled up like Nanook of the North when the other kids wore shorts? ADO, on the other hand, is more flexible—it lets you make your own decisions about how to compose and run your query—right or wrong.

Telling ADO How to (Best) Run Your Query

ADO lets you inform it ahead of time which type of query you intend to execute and what the parameters look like. This capability can make your code run faster because ADO doesn't have to query SQL Server (as RDO and DAO do) to retrieve procedure parameters. If you don't tell ADO what kind of query you plan to run, or if you set the CommandType to adCmdUnknown, ADO tries the command three different ways:

- Is it a query? <CommandText>

- Is it a table? SELECT * FROM <CommandText>

- Is it a stored procedure? {call <CommandText>}

ADO tries to figure out what you're doing by sending "test" compile-only commands to the server to see what comes back. As soon as one of the attempts succeeds, ADO assumes that the command is correct and proceeds to execute the command using the technique it discovered by trial and error. This try-it-and-see approach can be expensive if your ADO query code is run repeatedly in your production application or component. Yes, you should take steps to minimize this behavior.

You can also provide additional code that tells ADO how to execute the command string supplied. Because ADO has to run the client-side parameter-configuration code anyway, this extra code in your application can only help make your application or component run more quickly. The ability to tell ADO what you're trying to do and how you plan to do it is one of the big differences between RDO (and DAO) and ADO. If you, as a developer, know what's being sent as a query, there is no reason that your application should make one or more round-trips to the server to verify that you're sending a common SELECT statement or a complex stored procedure. ODBC API developers can create faster applications by providing more explicit instructions—especially when compared to RDO applications that perform the same queries. Of course, these applications are more expensive to code, and far more expensive to support. But when you're being paid by the hour, who (besides your boss) is counting?

While being explicit about what you want ADO to do can make your query run faster, the real downside to this approach is the extra code—code you have to write, debug, test, and support five years from now. No, I'm not a fan of writing forty lines of code where one or two will do. Yes, you might pay a minor performance penalty, but if you play your cards right, this is a one-time hit. And if you use the Data Environment to create your Command objects, this penalty is paid at design time—so your user won't notice anything amiss. You also need to consider that being explicit means that your application or component isn't as flexible as it could be. That is, when an underlying assumption changes (as when the database schema changes), your code won't morph to the new realities—it will crash or simply misbehave over in the corner under the dining room table. No, more isn't necessarily better when it comes to code—even if it seems faster. Making these decisions is about as easy as choosing a spouse.

So, how do you tell ADO and the OLE DB provider what's going on and what's about to happen? Well for starters, you can use the ADO Command object's CommandType property to tell ADO what's in that little string package you're about to submit as a query. (We go over the CommandType property in detail, in Chapter 29.) Remember, you can tell ADO that you're about to submit one of the following options:

- A file containing Recordset data (adCmdFile) saved with the ADO Recordset Save method.

- A stored procedure (adCmdStoredProc). When you tell ADO that you're working with a stored procedure, it skips the "prepare" step and executes the stored procedure as is—why create a stored procedure that just calls another stored procedure?

- A command that doesn't return result set rows (adExecuteNoRecords). This is a modifier of the adCmdText and adCmdStoredProc command types—that is, you have to use this option in combination with the others.

- A base table reference (adCmdTable).

- A reference to a base table to be fetched through IOpenRowset (adCmdTableDirect). You use this option to force ADO to use the OLE DB IOpenRowset interface instead of executing an ICommand. This is important for providers who support commands but get better performance opening the table directly.

- A query that needs to be parsed and compiled before execution (adCmdText).

- An unknown string (the default) (adCmdUnknown).

The adCmdFile, adCmdTableDirect, and adExecuteNoRecords options are all new for ADO 2.0. For these options to work, you must also have the client cursor provider (RDS) installed. Anything you can tell ADO about the query and how you want it to be executed helps ADO make smarter decisions on your behalf when it comes time to run the query.

Running Parameter Queries at Redline

Whenever ADO (DAO or RDO) has to execute a parameter query, it has to tell the interface how to bind the query parameters to the variables used to fill in the parameter values. In other words, to give you a way to connect the parameters passed to the query to the Parameters collection, you have to tell ODBC (or whatever data provider you're using) how to address these parameters. Before ADO, you used special ODBC API calls that map the parameters to the Parameters collection. ODBC API programmers hand-coded the metrics for each parameter before running the query. RDO 1.0 eliminated this requirement but forced you to use ODBC Level II drivers that returned these metrics from the server. Under the hood, RDO made calls to the server to return the input and output parameters for each parameter query before it was executed. Once RDO determined (guessed) the metrics, it called the ODBC API to set up the bindings for each parameter. This approach often caused problems because not everyone had a Level II driver—and even those who did discovered that ODBC didn't always get the bindings right. RDO 2.0 took on much of this burden itself; because it exposed the DataType and size of the Parameter object, you could set these properties yourself. But you had to pay attention.

ADO 2.0 has implemented the same level of functionality as RDO, but it has taken the technology a step further. ADO now exposes the entire Parameter object, so you can fully define *each* query parameter (or just redefine each one) as you see fit and in far more detail. This is another way you can help speed things up—by describing each query parameter that will be sent to the server. By taking the time (and code) to build your own ADO Parameters collection, you can eliminate a number of needless round-trips. However, this approach requires somewhat more code than simply telling ADO what kind of query you're executing. Of course, you don't need to include this code at all if you use the Data Environment designer to build your Command objects. We'll get to that later, in Chapter 37.

NOTE In some cases, as when you have to pass TEXT or other complex data types to a stored procedure, you *must* set up the ADO Parameters collection in code to initialize these parameters properly.

The Parameters collection

The Parameters collection is used to manage your query parameters—one Parameter object for each parameter in your query. This collection is read/write, meaning that you can add, change, and remove Parameter objects from it at run time. This capability is a radical departure from previous versions of DAO and RDO, in which the Parameters collection was always populated automatically, and you couldn't adjust the contents at all. In ADO, you can choose to have the Parameters collection populated automatically (as in RDO) through the use of the Refresh method or you can populate it yourself—and save the round-trip(s) to the server.

The Parameters collection is a standard collection, and along with the methods listed below, it supports the standard "For Each" Visual Basic syntax. The default member for the interface is the Item method, which allows you to omit this method name in your code, making the collection lookup seem very much like an array lookup.

Calling a simple stored procedure

The following example calls a simple stored procedure. Before we use the Execute method to run the query, however, we set up the Parameters collection to avoid the round-trip required to get ADO ready to run the query. The stored procedure syntax is:

```
CREATE PROC myADOParaProc
@type char(12)
AS                    .
SELECT Title FROM titles WHERE type = @type
```

The myADOParaProc stored procedure takes one @type input parameter and returns data that matches the specified title type. The data type for the @type parameter is character, and the size is 12.

The following Visual Basic code is used to set up the Parameters collection and run the query:

```
Dim cmd As New Command
Dim rs As New Recordset
Dim prm As  Parameter

' Define a Command object for a stored procedure.
cmd.ActiveConnection = "DSN=pubs;"
cmd.CommandText = "myADOParaProc"
cmd.CommandType = adCmdStoredProc
' Set up a new parameter for the stored procedure.
Set prm = Cmd.CreateParameter("BType", adChar, adParamInput, _
    12, "Business")
Cmd.Parameters.Append prm
' Create a record set by executing the command.
Set rs = Cmd.Execute
While (Not rs.EOF)
    Debug.Print rs(0)
    rs.MoveNext
Wend
```

TIP You can combine the Append and CreateParameter methods into a single statement, as shown here, but it might be somewhat harder to support. It's your call.

```
Cmd.Parameters.Append Cmd.CreateParameter("BType", _
    adChar, adParamInput, 12, "Business")
```

Sure, you can create a new Parameter object, set each of its properties individually, and append it to the Parameters collection, but the Create-Parameter method really makes all of that work unnecessary. Notice that we didn't use a "call" statement in the CommandText statement—we simply gave it the name of the stored procedure. Yes, we could have used the db.owner.spname notation as well if the permission scheme had required it.

TIP Did you know that a VarChar can't contain a zero-length string? SQL Server converts it to a single-byte space when you do an INSERT or an UPDATE.

Table 31-2 details the ADO data types you should use for each of the SQL Server data types.

Table 31-2

SQL Server Data Types and Corresponding ADO Data Types

SQL Server Data Type	ADO Data Type
Binary	adBinary (128)
Varbinary	adVarBinary (204)
Char	adChar (129)
Varchar	adVarChar (200)
Datetime	adDBTimeStamp (135)
Smalldatetime	adDBTimeStamp (135)
Decimal	adNumeric (131) (See the "Handling decimal problems" section below for more information.)
numeric	adNumeric (131)
float	adDouble (5)
real	adSingle (4)
int	adInteger (3)
smallint	adSmallInt (2)
tinyint	adUnsignedTinyInt (17)
money	adNumeric (131)
smallmoney	adNumeric (131)
bit	adBoolean (11)
timestamp	adBinary (128)
text	adLongVarChar (201)
image	adLongVarBinary (205)

Handling Decimal Problems

If your stored procedure uses a parameter typed as *decimal*, you might find that ADO doesn't correctly detect this fact. For example, you might get the following error: "At least one parameter contained a type that was not supported." In this case, you need to force the data type to *adNumeric* in code to get the stored procedure to run.

OK, let's say you want ADO to figure out the Parameters collection for you. Maybe you don't know what the parameters are or look like, you're in a hurry, or you don't want to support the extra lines of code to define the collection yourself. Well, ADO exposes the Refresh method on the Parameters collection just for this purpose. The next example shows how this works.

This code snippet demonstrates how you can have ADO build Parameter objects for a given stored procedure to avoid the unnecessary trips to the data source. Notice that we can still use the ODBC "call" syntax—even if we are using a native OLE DB provider for SQL Server. In this case, we're passing in parameters and expecting some back. You can also use the new Data Environment designer to eliminate the need for this code. (See Chapter 37.)

TIP Having ADO build Parameter objects for you is the *hardest* way of all to pass parameters to ADO stored procedures. I've included this example mostly to show you what *not* to do—unless you're charging by the line.

```
' Assuming we have an ODBC connection called "MyConnection" open

Dim cmd As New Command
Dim param As New Parameter

' using the ODBC call syntax for SQL Server
cmd.CommandText = "{? = call MyProcedure (?,?)}"
cmd.CommandType = adCmdStoredProc
cmd.Name = "MyProc"

' create the parameters, adjust the binding properties, and append
Set param = New Parameter
param.Type = adInteger
param.Direction = adParamReturnValue
cmd.Parameters.Append param

Set param = New Parameter
param.Type = adInteger
param.Value = 5
cmd.Parameters.Append param

Set param = New Parameter
param.Type = adString
param.Direction = adParamOutput
cmd.Parameters.Append param

Set cmd.ActiveConnection = MyConnection
```

TIP If you get the "call" syntax wrong, misspell the stored procedure, or add an extra parenthesis, ADO won't complain until you try to reference or refresh the Parameters collection. You'll get errors that complain about semiobscure things like Recordsets being at EOF and somesuch. Just remember that I told you this was the hard way.

Now we're ready to execute the query. First, however, we have to fill in the parameters. You have several choices here (natch):

- Address each Parameter object of the Command object individually in code—one at a time. If the Command object returns a Recordset, you can pass it back as an argument. You have to address any stored procedure Return value or output parameters independently.

```
' Now execute the command
cmd(1) = 17                ' The first parameter
cmd(2) = "Fred" ' The second parameter
Set rs = cmd.Execute
```

- Use the Command-as-method technique. This option lets you provide the parameters as arguments to the Command object. You can also address the Recordset on the same line of code—though you still have to address the OUTPUT parameters separately.

```
MyConnection.MyProc 17, "Fred", rs
```

TIP You also have another alternative: use the Data Environment to manage the whole magilla. In this case, you use the Command object as a named method of the Data Environment and address the Recordset as a named property of the Data Environment—named after the Command object with an *rs* prefix. For example, a Command object GetAuthors would have a Data Environment property named rsGetAuthors, to address the Recordset after execution.

The following example shows how you can use the Refresh method to populate the Parameters collection *automatically* based on the stored procedure's definition on the server. This option might be desirable when access to the database catalog is fast, when you're debugging, or when you're in rapid development mode.

```
' Assuming we have an open connection called "MyConnection"

Dim cmd As New Command

' using the ODBC call syntax for SQL Server
cmd.CommandText = "{? = call MyProcedure (?,?)}"
Set cmd.ActiveConnection = MyConnection

' Use the Refresh method to autopopulate the collection.
' This can be very expensive on some data sources.
' You can omit this call to Refresh and the
' provider will automatically populate the collection
' on first access.
cmd.Parameters.Refresh

' Most or all binding information should be set after calling the
' Refresh method, but some data sources won't be
' able to determine all things (like direction),
```

(continued)

```
' so you might need to set additional properties
' after the Refresh method.

' Set the input parameter to whatever it needs to be
cmd(1) = 5

' and execute the command.
Set rs = cmd.Execute
```

I have a whole section in Chapter 36 on creating parameter queries and how to pass in and get back the parameter values.

Using Prepared Statements

The Prepared property of the Command object allows you to specify whether or not you want a query to be "prepared." Queries can be *prepared* before they are executed, or they can be executed directly. If the Prepared property is set to True, a query string is parsed and optimized at the first execution. In SQL Server 6.5 and earlier, you "prepare" a query by creating a temporary stored procedure (in TempDB) to run the query. SQL Server 7.0 and later simply share compiled procedures, so it's not necessary to create a temporary stored procedure. Any subsequent execution of the query string uses this compiled stored procedure. When your query is prepared before it is executed, processing takes longer, but performance improves for subsequent executions because the query string has already been parsed and optimized when it was first run. However, if you're executing the query string only once, you should execute the query string directly instead of preparing it.

You can also use the Prepared property for executing multiple parameter sets. An application can execute a parameterized query string more than once by supplying a different parameter set at each execution instead of reconstructing the query string whenever the parameter set is different. Again, if you're executing a parameterized query string only once, it isn't necessary to prepare the query string.

The documentation says that SQL Server doesn't *directly* support ODBC's Prepare/Execute technology. However, the workaround seems to work pretty well. When a statement is prepared, the SQL server ODBC driver (pre–SQL Server 7.0) creates a temporary stored procedure for the statement. This temporary stored procedure is built in TempDB and isn't dropped until the Recordset or Connection object is closed. If the application (or test case) dies unexpectedly, ODBC can (and does) orphan stored procedures in TempDB. These go away when (if) you reboot, but you might have to clean them out regularly to prevent TempDB from filling up. Remember that TempDB isn't backed up and is completely rebuilt when the system is booted—and of course, this flushes all of the stored procedure residue. These problems with TempDB are no longer an issue with SQL Server 7.0.

You can disable the Prepare option through the SQL Server ODBC Data Source Setup dialog box if you use an ODBC data source to connect to SQL Server. If the option is disabled, the SQL statement is stored and then sent to the server each time it is executed, where it is (re)compiled and executed.

The following example uses a prepared statement for updating a query and dynamically constructing the query with a different set of parameters at execution time:

```
Dim Cn As New Connection
Dim Cmd As New Command
Dim prm1 As New Parameter
Dim prm2 As New Parameter

Cn.Open "DSN=pubs"
Set Cmd.ActiveConnection = Cn
Cmd.CommandText = "UPDATE titles SET type=? WHERE title_id=?"
Cmd.CommandType = adCmdText
Cmd.Prepared = True
Set prm1 = Cmd.CreateParameter("type", adChar, adParamInput, _
    12, "New Bus")
Cmd.Parameters.Append prm1
Set prm2 = Cmd.CreateParameter("title_id", adChar, adParamInput, _
    6, "BU7832")
Cmd.Parameters.Append prm2
Cmd.Execute
Cmd("type") = "New Cook"
Cmd("title_id") = "TC7777"
Cmd.Execute
Cn.Close
```

This example updates data in the *titles* table by using different parameter values. The query string is prepared so that different sets of parameters can be supplied. Two parameters are required for the update operation: *type* and *title_id*. They are created by the CreateParameter method and appended to the Parameters collection with the Append method.

The first set of parameters has the values of *New Bus* and *BU7832*. You can supply different values of the parameters before the Execute method without reconstructing the query string because the Prepared property is set to True.

Nope, I don't know why some collections use Add methods and others use Append methods. It's one of the great mysteries of life.

ADO Cursors

Those of you who have heard me speak at VBits or TechEd must have heard me say (in my best church-lady voice) "Cursors are *evil*." Well, like all generalizations, this one is only partly true. In this section, you'll find out why I think that many cursors need a degree of exorcism or at least a good scrubbing with lye soap.

Cursors are very much like ice cream. Both are easy to consume, and since most of us can't limit our consumption to a single bite (so to speak), both tend to add fat and sloth to our applications and our belt lines. Like anything attractive and easy to acquire, cursors are very alluring. To make matters worse, by default, Jet and DAO build the highest-fat and most expensive cursors. It takes self-restraint to turn off fatty features such as read-write, fully scrollable, and dynamic membership. For example, if you use the Data control in Visual Basic, you get to choose among a variety of Jet cursors—but the default properties build a read-write, nonexclusive, fully scrollable, table-based Dynaset. ADO goes (almost) full tilt in the other direction—it creates read-only, forward-only, single-row result sets by default. Yes, this is our friend the "cursorless" firehose Recordset. Once you finish this section, you'll know how to choose the cursor options you need and how to build result sets without cursors.

> **TIP**   This section is designed for those of you working with ADO (or DAO and RDO) in code—not for those who have discovered the wonders of the Data Environment designer. This new technology makes the selection of cursor libraries and options far easier and far more efficient—but that's a story I'll save for Chapter 37.

What Are ADO Cursors and Why Are They Evil?

Before we get up to our elbows in axle grease, let's make sure we all understand some basic terms. When you want to extract data from a database, you use code (or manipulate controls) to specify a query that is ultimately executed by the database engine (such as Jet or SQL Server) to build a result set. Therefore, a result set is simply information from the database that can contain zero to n rows that meet the criteria you provide in your query. ADO and DAO refer to these as *Recordset* objects, and RDO refers to them as *rdoResultset* objects. As I've said many times, a cursor is simply a mechanism used to address the individual rows of the result set. That is, a cursor lets you move from row to row and maintain the contents of the rows as they change. On the surface, a cursor seems to be merely a set of pointers to the actual data. However, it is that plus a current position pointer and a set of properties to describe the data.

So what is inherently evil about cursors? Well, cursors use resources—lots of resources—such as RAM, disk space, network bandwidth, database locks, and CPU time—not to mention one of the most precious resources you have to worry about: user patience. It's very easy to create cursors that can consume every bit of available CPU time and disk space on the client (or the server), bring the network to its knees, and make you wish you had a bigger, faster server. Consider that the "evilness" of cursors usually comes to the surface as you try to build multiuser databases based on fat, poorly engineered cursors. Later in this chapter, we'll take a look at some common cursor-generating code that illustrates the impact cursors have on your systems—both the client and the server. Sure, these might be the same system (that is, your client and server might be one and the same), but typically, larger multiuser systems are impacted more heavily by depraved cursors.

Applications intended to scale beyond a few users are most prone to the insatiable appetites of evil cursors. Consider that you have to multiply most resources a single cursor consumes by the number of active users. Five users demand five times more resources than a single user. Fifty users can easily cripple a system by overwhelming the client, the database engine, the network, and the server with conflicting demands for their resources.

What Good Are ADO Cursors?

Cursors are designed to handle many of the mundane data retrieval operations we encounter when accessing databases of all kinds. In situations where you should use cursors, you can use them to manage many of the operations you would have to code yourself. In a nutshell, cursors give developers the ability to have the following chores carried out automatically:

- Provide the option of a scrollable and updateable view of the results of your query—instead of simply a forward-only, read-only set of rows

- Fetch data from a database based on a SQL query or a stored procedure

- Populate data-aware controls to display the data rows to users

- Handle the code required to add, change, and delete the data as needed

- Handle movement of the current-row pointer to various locations in the result set

Cursors are designed to help work with database tables and other row sources. Many developers find they are most useful in situations where code is transitioning from ISAM-class databases, in which direct table manipulation is an integral part of the development paradigm. Direct table access might be a problem when you're working with most sophisticated (read secure) database systems, however, because smart database administrators rarely expose root tables. More often than not, only stored procedures (and views) are visible to developers, so any cursors you build have to deal with updates without the use of cursors. Because updates are also handled exclusively through stored procedures, one would be led to believe that cursors are of limited use in larger, scalable client/server installations. However, RDO and ADO have thought of this architectural constraint. If you need to update via a custom stored procedure (or several), check out the WillUpdateRows event in RDO or the WillChangeRecordset event in ADO.

How Do ADO Cursors Work?

Let's take a closer look at how cursors are built. When using DAO's default cursor properties, it's especially easy to create an especially evil cursor. Using ADO, however, you have to bend over backward to do so. For example, the following DAO code is the simplest way to open a cursor against a database table. It uses all the DAO defaults.

```
Set rs = db.OpenRecordset("SSAN_Recipients")
```

> **NOTE** Nope, this isn't a Jet-bashing session. Jet and DAO are designed for a different set of circumstances than RDO and ADO. We're talking about cursors here, and it is possible to create these evil cursors in ADO too. However, you have to break all seven seals to do so.

This code tells Jet to create a DAO Recordset object addressing all 180 million social security recipients cataloged in the table. The SQL query built by DAO and passed to the server is simply "SELECT * FROM SSAN_Recipients". Sure, you can use similar syntax in ADO, but a firehose cursorless result set is created. The Jet database engine begins executing the query by opening the SSAN_Recipients table. It then starts to create a bookmark pointer to each row in the table that qualifies (based on the query). In this case, there is no WHERE clause, so all rows qualify. These bookmarks are returned to the client as the Recordset—all 180 million of them. No, this time the data rows are not copied to the client's data space, but the bookmarks are. Depending on how the cursor is built, your client application might not regain control until after the query has been fully built. I suspect that the query would not be complete before the client's disk space is exhausted or before the year 2010 (which depending on the systems' BIOS, might never come).

When you're working with Jet and SQL Server and you ask the engine to create a result set, the query processor locks some or all of the table's data pages based on the scope of the query. This locking is necessary to building a cohesive set of information. Once the cursor build process is begun, the entire table is locked with "share" locks until the cursor is fully populated and all the bookmarks are copied to the client. Because the client software—your code—determines whether and when that locking occurs, it's too easy to inadvertently lock out changes for large parts of the database.

Cursors expose only one row of data at a time—no matter what kind of provider or cursor you use. Although you can bind a result set to a data-aware bound control that can display several rows at once, only one of these rows can be "current" at any particular time. *Scrollable* cursors let you move forward and back to any desired row, but this feature isn't inexpensive to implement. If you don't need to scroll, don't ask for this feature. In many cases, I build a cursorless result set, populate a grid with the results, and do my own "scrolling" through the result sets. When it comes time to update the data, I build up an UPDATE, INSERT, or DELETE SQL statement and execute that directly. It's faster and cheaper than building a cursor—and it imposes far fewer locks on other pages of the database.

The following samples show how to limit the number and amount of resources the selected cursor consumes. Yes, there are ways to return information to your client application with very little resource consumption, and no, these techniques are not complex. For example, the following DAO code shows how to build a Recordset using very few system resources:

```
Set rs = db.OpenRecordset("Select Name from SSAN_Recipients " _
    & "Where SSAN='225-40-9999'", _
    dbOpenForwardOnly, dbReadOnly)
```

The following code shows this technique using ADO:

```
rs.Open ("Select Name from SSAN_Recipients " _
    & "Where SSAN='225-40-9999'"
```

In each sample, a cursor is created that includes only a single row where only one row or page share is locked and the impact on the network, server, and client is minimal. Can you conserve resources when using the Visual Basic

Data control? Sure. Just set the Options property to 12 (dbOpenForwardOnly=8, dbReadOnly=4) and the RecordSource property to the fully qualified SELECT statement shown in the previous ADO code.

What Are the Different Types of ADO Cursor?

ADO, just as the other data access interfaces, has several fundamental types of cursors that are categorized by how the database engine, data provider, and cursor driver manages the result set.

Membership

Membership refers to how and when the database engine, provider, or cursor library decides which rows qualify for inclusion in the result set. The SQL query's WHERE clause initially determines membership. However, rows are not made members of the cursor until the server's query processor finds them and adds them to the result set to be returned to the data provider. Depending on the database engine and cursor driver, the process of building the membership proceeds in different ways. Generally, membership isn't frozen until the last row of the result set has been found. This last row isn't located and added to the result set until your code (or the database engine) moves the current-row pointer to the last row of the Recordset or rdoResultset object. To make sure this happens as soon as possible, ADO starts a background operation to append eligible rows as quickly as possible. In most cases, share locks are kept in place until the membership is completed—when the result set is fully populated.

Some cursors (such as dynamic cursors) never close their membership. That is, they constantly ask the provider to requery the database to make sure that rows added or deleted (or updated) are included as current members of the result set. These cursors are especially expensive to implement, and some data providers aren't powerful enough to build them. ADO does fully support this type of cursor for those with the (very) special requirements that can justify their expense.

Some cursors permit changes to their membership after the result set is built and populated; others do not. Of course, those that don't permit changes are less expensive to build than those that permit additions and deletions to the membership.

Scrolling

Scrolling refers to the methods the database engine and cursor driver make available to move to specific rows of the result set. Some cursors maintain bookmarks or other mechanisms that permit you to move to selected rows in the result set. Scrolling cursors are fairly expensive to implement, so non-scrolling cursors are faster and more widely used in scalable applications. All cursors let you move forward to the next row until you reach the end of the result set. Even cursorless result sets support this technique. Note that if you choose a forward-only cursor, ADO won't return the RecordCount property.

Updatability

Updatability refers to the methods the database engine and cursor driver make available to permit changes in membership or data values. When your code changes or deletes an existing row, or adds a new row, the cursor driver and database engine work together to make the changes requested. To support updatability, the individual rows of the table must be individually addressable. To make them so, you must have a primary key identified for the table you want to change. Again, updateable cursors are expensive to implement.

Data movement

Data movement means whether or not the data rows are copied to the client or simply referenced indirectly through bookmarks. Some cursors are implemented by simply copying bookmarks to the client—one for each row in the result set. Others copy actual data rows to the client; this type of cursor is often called a *snapshot*. Although the bookmark technique is fairly fast, it requires the application to refetch the data from the database each time the row is referenced. On the other hand, snapshot cursors require more space on the client and move data over the network that the user might never reference. SQL Server can also create cursors that are built on the server instead of on the client. These server-side cursors seem to be a good way to handle lightweight clients that would be incapable of handling the cursor in other ways. However, this approach limits scalability by placing exhaustive loads on the server as the number of clients increases.

The DAO, RDO, and ADO data access interfaces support a variety of cursors, including some "uncursors" that are called for when you need to access data as fast as possible. Tables 31-3, 31-4, and 31-5 summarize the cursor types and cursor characteristics available with the DAO, RDO, and ADO interfaces.

Table 31-3
DAO Cursors

DAO	Membership	Updateable	Scrolling	Data Movement
Forward-only	Manual	Not	Forward only	Data copied
Snapshot	Automatic	Not	Fully scrollable	Data copied
Dynaset	Automatic	Can be	Fully scrollable	Via bookmarks

Table 31-4
RDO and ADO Cursors

RDO/DAO	Membership	Updateable	Scrolling	Data Movement
Forward-only	Manual	Can be	Forward only	Data copied
Static	Manual	Can be	Fully scrollable	Data copied
Dynamic	Variable	Can be	Fully scrollable	Via bookmarks
Keyset	Manual	Can be	Fully scrollable	Via bookmarks

Table 31-5
ADO Cursor Client-Side and Server-Side Support

ADO Cursor	Server-Side	Client-Side
Firehose	Supported (default)	Not supported (upgraded to static)
Forward-only	Supported	Not supported (upgraded to static)
Static	Supported	Supported (default)
Keyset	Supported	Not supported (reverts to static)
Dynamic	Supported	Not supported (reverts to static)

When *Should* I Use Cursors?

Yes, sometimes it makes sense to use cursors. And no, you don't need a note from your mom—one from your spouse will do. Here are some situations in which using cursors is (probably) a good idea:

- When you're working directly with tables. Keep in mind, however, that if you plan to prototype for SQL Server or another highly scalable database server, you probably won't want to permit direct table access.

- When you're working with stored procedures and are prepared to handle the updates separately.

- When you want to use bound controls. Now that Visual Basic supports the ability to create your own bound controls—or at least controls that automatically handle data display and navigation chores for you— you're no longer limited to the standard array of bound controls.

- When you want to pass an updateable Recordset from a component to a client application.

If you expect to build a scalable application, however, you need to take a number of precautions to make sure that as more users are added, performance doesn't go over the cliff:

- **Fetch fewer rows** This approach might seem simplistic—and it's easier said than done—but it can yield many benefits. For example, if you fetch fewer rows than will fit on a data page, you'll find that you can minimize the locking impact of additional users. However, you also need to consider that in many cases a lot of activity might be concentrated in relatively few data pages—where the current flights or today's results are stored.

- **Fetch smarter** Whenever possible, use the indexes in the WHERE clause. Never select all the rows and columns from a table unless you know that there are less than a few hundred rows (like when you need to populate a pick list) and you plan to move to the last row immediately. Be selective (so to speak) about the rows you choose. Even Einstein couldn't deal with more than a few dozen rows at a time. Yes, it's more complicated to build a fetch window and fetch only enough rows to populate the next display page or two. As the user pages down, keep ahead with another query that fetches the next range in asynchronous mode. This is easier with ADO's Page-mode data access features. Again, don't fetch more columns than you absolutely need. If you find that you have columns that aren't being fetched, consider putting them in another table—proper normalization or denormalization can also improve performance, but this process requires addition intelligence when you add new rows or update the data.

- **Populate immediately**   Be sure to move to the last row of a cursor (not a forward-only cursor) to fully populate it. This frees the share locks put in place when the cursor was built. Fortunately, ADO populates cursors in the background for you.

- **Avoid using a cursor unless you really need one**   Consider moving data rows directly into a grid and managing the grid yourself. For example, the control I use in many of my talks takes advantage of the RDO 2.0 GetClipString method on the rdoResultset. ADO supports several similar methods, including the GetString method. I use it to fill in the grid from any result set. This code needs more error handling, but it shows how to use the MSFlex grid as a substitute for a bound grid.

ADO CursorLocation Choices

To indicate where the cursor's result set is created, you can choose to use client-side cursors or you can defer to the default, which causes ADO to build server-side cursors. Actually, the default is no cursors at all—but that's not the same as adUseNone. Confused? Read on.

- **adUseNone**   This is not really an option. Although this looks remarkably like the rdUseNone option, it does not do the same thing in ADO. This option disables the cursor and cursorless operation of the provider. You shouldn't use it; in fact, it's hidden in Visual Basic 6.0.

- **adUseClient**   This option uses client-side cursors supplied by a local cursor library. For backward compatibility, the synonym adUseClient-Batch is also supported. By default, ADO client-side libraries create only static cursors—regardless of what type of cursor you choose.

- **adUseServer**   This option is the default. It uses data provider or driver-supplied cursors built on the server. In the case of SQL Server, these cursors are built by and on SQL Server and in TempDB. These cursors are sometimes very flexible and allow for some additional sensitivity to reflecting changes that others make to the data source. However, some features of the Microsoft Client Cursor Provider (such as dis-associated Recordsets) can't be simulated with server-side cursors, and these features become unavailable with this setting. By default, server-side libraries create forward-only cursors. And no, you still can't execute queries or stored procedures that return more than one result set with server-side cursors if you use anything other than a firehose cursor.

Many considerations are involved in choosing the cursor type and in deciding whether to use client-side or server-side cursors. You usually have to figure out exactly what functionality you need and then weigh the trade-offs in scalability and performance you'll have to live with in the cursor model you've chosen.

Client-Side ADO Cursors

Consider that the ADO client-side cursor doesn't support anything except a static cursor. The reason the client-side cursor engine doesn't allow dynamic or keyset cursors is that the ADO team thinks they are too expensive to implement on the client. Essentially, the server would have to tell the client-side cursor when rows were changed, added, or deleted in real time (or something close to it). That's expensive for both the client and the server. In addition, you can't use pessimistic locking with client-side cursors. Pessimistic locking is available only with server-side cursors.

Client-side cursors offer rich functionality at the client. This functionality includes batch operations, disconnected operation, high performance when data is bound to complex controls (such as grids), and the capability for features such as sorting and filtering at the client without reexecuting the query on the server. In addition, no *state* is maintained on the server, which will help the server to scale to a larger number of users. The price you pay with client-side cursors is that the client needs to maintain the cursor using its resources. In addition, the results are completely fetched to the client for processing—even if only a few of the rows are actually used—and the data quickly becomes "stale." This means that you can't see changes made to the data on the server after you've executed the query.

No, the ADO team doesn't plan to add functionality to the client-side cursor library. Not at this time at least. It also doesn't make a lot of sense to do so because of the overhead involved in creating the exotic cursor types on the client. Before you decide to use client-side cursors, however, you should be aware that server-side cursors do have several advantages.

Server-Side ADO Cursors

SQL Server provides a set of server-side cursor types for applications to use. Server-side cursors have several advantages as listed here:

- **Performance** If you're going to access a small fraction of the data in the cursor (typical of many browsing applications), using server-side cursors gives you a big performance boost. This enhanced performance is possible because only the required data (and not the entire result set) is sent over the network.

- **Additional cursor types** Keyset and dynamic cursor types are available only if you use server-side cursors. In addition, the client-side cursor library only supports static cursors with read-only and optimistic concurrency. With server-side cursors, you can use the full range of concurrency values with the different cursor types.

- **Cleaner semantics** The cursor library simulates cursor updates by generating a SQL update statement. This system-generated SQL statement can sometimes lead to unintended updates, however, especially if you're not using a primary key—go back ten spaces.

- **Memory usage** When using server-side cursors, the client doesn't need to cache large amounts of data or maintain information about the cursor position; the server provides that functionality.

- **Multiple open cursors** When using server-side cursors, the connection between the client and server doesn't remain busy between cursor operations. This allows you to have multiple cursors active at the same time.

By default, an ADO application uses server-side cursors that are forward-only and read-only when using either the OLE DB provider for ODBC or the OLE DB provider for SQL Server. The CursorLocation property is set to adUseServer, but the default property settings actually tell the provider not to build a cursor at all—the read-only, forward-only single rowset configuration doesn't need it. In other words, you have to twist ADO's arm (albeit not very much) to get it to build a cursor.

Server-side cursors can be especially useful when updating, inserting, or deleting records—when no cursor is needed. Server-side cursors also allow you to have multiple active statements on the same connection—well, sort of. By design, SQL Server doesn't allow multiple *active* statements per connection unless server-side cursors are used. An active statement means that some results in the statement handle are pending. No, pending results don't necessarily mean there are rows waiting to be sent. However, it could mean that multiple result sets are pending. If server-side cursors are not used and the application attempts to start more than one active statement, your application trips the "Connection Busy with Another Active Statement" error message. Actually, when server-side cursors are used, SQL Server doesn't return control to the connection until the cursor is fully populated, so it doesn't have a problem with concurrency. You might have trouble with blocking problems, however, if your cursors are too large.

Server-side cursors can be problematic for your system in a number of ways. For example, even though the cursor keyset is built on the server, this does not relieve your designers from the responsibility of creating small resultsets—as a matter of fact, this responsibility becomes even more important. If you insist on creating row-returning result sets on the server, you must add enough space in TempDB to handle these keysets and enough CPU horsepower to deal with the extra load. Server-side cursors do not transmit the keyset over to the client, so individual rows can be fetched in blocks by key—but the load on the network isn't any less. Server-side cursors are not "fat" cursors, which means that each row is fetched individually via a round-trip over the wire. Yes, this type of cursor seems attractive on first blush, but when you roll over in the morning, you're often sorry you didn't leave the bar a little earlier.

When you're (really) ready to activate server-side cursors, you can do any one (or more) of the following:

- Set the cursor type of the Recordset.Open method to anything other than the default value. The default cursor type is adOpenForwardOnly, and changing it to adOpenKeyset, adOpenDynamic, or adOpenStatic forces the use of a server-side cursor. A static cursor is the best general-purpose choice—especially for accessing stored procedures.

- Set the LockType of the Recordset.Open method to anything other than the default value. The default LockType is adLockReadOnly, and changing it to adLockPessimistic, adLockOptimistic, or adLockBatchOptimistic forces the use of a server-side cursor.

- Set the CacheSize property to anything other than the default value (1).

  Here are a few more notes on server-side cursors:

- Server-side cursors are created only for statements that begin with a SELECT, EXEC[ute] procedure_name or {call procedures_name}. Even if an application explicitly requests a server-side cursor, a cursor isn't created for statements such as INSERT—it's not needed.

- Server-side cursors can't be used with statements that generate more than one result set. If you use a server-side cursor with any statement that generates multiple record sets, your application could receive one of these errors:

  - "Cannot open a cursor on a stored procedure that has anything other than a single select statement in it."

  - "sp_cursoropen. The statement parameter can only be a single select or a single stored procedure."

The following example shows how to open a keyset server-side cursor:

```
rs.Open "SELECT * FROM titles", "DSN=pubs;", adOpenKeyset
```

Updateable ADO Cursors

A week doesn't pass that I don't get a message on creating updateable cursors. Of course, I troll several of the external (to Microsoft) list services looking for ideas to write about, so I do get (and browse) a flood of messages. Well, anyway, many folks want to know the secret formula for creating Recordset (or rdoResultset) objects that can be updated. Well, creating updateable cursors in ADO is no harder than creating them anywhere else, and the reason you can't update a result set might have more to do with the server and how the database is configured than with your code. You *should* be able to update your ADO Recordset if you just heed the advice in the following tips:

- Did you pick an updateable lock type? If so, you'll need to use adLockOptimistic, adLockBatchOptimistic, or adLockPessimistic. (Ah, I changed my mind. No, don't use adLockPessimistic.) The default is adLockReadOnly. This lock type can work with any of the cursor types—even static. Keep in mind that if you use the Execute method, the resultant Recordset is read-only, no matter what you set it to beforehand.

- Did you give ADO's data provider a way to uniquely identify the row(s) to update? To do this, you have to specify a primary key for the table and referential integrity constraints for the other tables in question. That is, you need to establish a primary-key-to-primary-key or a primary-key-to-foreign-key relationship.

- Do you have permission to update the table? This issue also relates to server-side configuration. Does your user have permission to update the table? Often you might have read, but not update, permission. You might have to use a stored procedure to do the update. See the WillChangeRecord event.

- Is the query so complex that the provider (or Hammurabi) couldn't figure out how to parse it? The data provider has to do some heavy thinking to figure out the source table and source column for each updated column. Check the SourceTable and SourceColumn properties to see whether they are exposed. You might be able to set these yourself to give ADO a hint. Frankly, this concern is usually caused by depending on ADO and its data providers to do the work for you. What you should be doing is calling a stored procedure to do the updates in the first place.

NOTE When ADO creates a client-side updateable cursor against SQL Server, it uses the FOR BROWSE TSQL extension. This extension precludes the use of the DISTINCT keyword. Still need to use DISTINCT? Use server-side cursors.

Managing Concurrency with ADO

Creating scalable applications is all about managing concurrency and resources. ADO gives you a multitude of options to permit smarter sharing of your data pages. Yes, SQL Sever 7.0 supports row-level locking, but this doesn't magically solve your concurrency problems. ADO is also smarter about populating cursors—however, automatically managing and populating cursors (especially large ones) still consumes time and system resources. In many cases, expanded concurrency (and scalability) is hobbled by the number of outstanding locks. These locks can be on rows, data pages, or index pages (and elsewhere) to prevent SQL Server from passing partially complete information to your client or to prevent referential integrity or recovery problems.

Row locking doesn't magically cure all of your scalability problems. Keep in mind that SQL Server has been winning reviews by managing fewer locks (because it uses page locks) than the competition that manages row locks.

When discussing the LockType property in Chapter 29, we talked about the mechanics of setting the ADO cursor concurrency options. Remember that you have to set the LockType property *before* you open a Recordset (at least in the Open method) to specify what type of locking SQL Server should use when opening it. Examine the LockType property to return the type of locking in use on an open Recordset object. The LockType property is read/write when the Recordset is closed and read-only once it's open.

Fetching ADO Recordset Data

Once you've opened a Recordset, you can make it available to the user (if that's necessary) in a number of ways—of course, if ADO is nothing else, it's flexible. Here are some options for presenting Recordset data to the user:

- Visit each row and assign individual field objects to display controls—such as TextBox and ListBox controls.

- Bind the Recordset to a data source control bound to a number of data-aware controls. You can do this manually, or you can use the Data Environment designer and have it done for you.

- Bind the Recordset to data-aware controls in code—yes, that's without the ADO Data control. (We already visited this binding scenario earlier in the chapter, on page 701.)

- Use the GetRows method to fill a Variant array with data to be passed elsewhere to be manipulated or displayed.

- Use the GetString method to build a delimited string representation of the data to be passed to a control with a Clip property.

- Use the GetChunk method to fetch binary large object (BLOB) or character large object (CLOB) data pages (TEXT and IMAGE types).

TIP   If you need to read SQL Server Timestamp values (which are different than the DateTime or SmallDateTime types), use the adDBTimeStamp data type.

Let's look a little closer at each of these techniques to see whether there are any ADO minefields that we need to be aware of.

Addressing Single Rows and Columns

Moving data from a Recordset object's Value property in ADO is no different than doing the same thing in DAO or RDO—simply address the Recordset variable using any of the traditional addressing techniques. Keep in mind that this method is the slowest—and ADO doesn't make it easy. The following code shows how to access the columns for a row in the Recordset:

```
Dim rs As New Recordset
Dim CString As String, SQL As String, Col As String
CString = "File Name=Pubs.UDL"
SQL = "Select * From Publishers"
rs.Open SQL, CString
Text1 = rs(1)              ' Addresses the second column
Text2 = rs("pub_name")     ' Addresses the named column
Text3 = rs!pub_name        ' The same thing ...
Col = "City"
Text4 = rs(Col)            ' Addresses the column named in Col
```

In some of my examples, I walk a small Recordset to dump all the columns for each row—including the headings. This code leverages Visual Basic's ability to walk a collection using the For Each syntax, as shown in the code below. You can use this same technique in a variety of ways to fill individual controls or simple list boxes. However, I wouldn't go further than that. There are better and faster ways to fill more complex multiline controls.

```
Dim fld as Field
For Each fld In rs.Fields
    Debug.Print fld.Name,
Next fld
Debug.Print
Do Until rs.EOF
    For Each fld In rs.Fields
        Debug.Print fld.Value,
    Next fld
    Debug.Print
    rs.MoveNext
Loop
```

Binding with a Data Source Control

Just as DAO and RDO do, ADO supplies a client-side data source control to automatically manage the rows returned by a Recordset. Basically, the ADO Data control works very much like the RemoteData control in that you must specify enough of the properties for ADO to figure out what to do. Yes, several of these properties overlap, which reflects ADO's flexibility. For example, you can specify a ConnectionString, DSN, *and* provider even though the provider can be contained in or implied by the ConnectionString (as can the DSN). I don't expect you'll have any trouble figuring out the ADO Data control's properties. Once you set up the ADO Data control, you can add as many form-based controls as needed and connect them to the control.

NOTE No, you don't have to use the ADO Data control to act as your data source. You can use the Data Environment Commands as well. We'll talk about this in the chapter on the Data Environment (Chapter 37).

An ADO data source exposes a new level of granularity—the DataMember, which lets you create (as in write your own if needed) a data source that exposes more than one dataset. A data provider can have multiple sets of data that a data consumer can choose to connect to, each identified by specific DataMember objects. The DataMembers collection manages these strings.

When you create a User Control configured as a data source (by setting the DataSourceBehavior to vbDataSource), you should add the names of each Recordset to the DataMembers collection in the Initialize event. When you set the DataSource property to the user control and click DataMembers on the Properties window, the members of the DataMembers collection appear in the drop-down list.

Using the GetRows Method

GetRows does indeed suck the data out of a Recordset faster than your spouse can clean out your wallet while you're dozing. In Visual Basic 5.0 the ugly part of GetRows is that once you had it, there wasn't much you could do with it. Before you ran GetRows, the data was in a Recordset object. And although some of the data was cached in RAM and more was still on the server, you could easily get to an individual row, sort it, search it, or change its data through ADO methods and properties. Now that you've run GetRows, the data is all in a lump—in a single multidimensional Variant array. Swell. You can pass it to another program, but if you try to use it yourself, you have to write looping code to unravel the rows and columns. That is unless you use the new Visual Basic 6.0 functions that convert arrays to delimited strings. You can then take one of these strings and pass it to the Clip property of the MSFlexGrid control.

TIP I've also had considerable problems with ADO's version of GetRows. It seems to balk at BLOB columns and some other distasteful data types. This reluctance might be fixed by the time you get your code. I expect the ADO team is working to fix bugs that are more important. Refer to Chapter 29 for details on how to code the GetRows method.

Using the GetString Method

The GetString method was added to ADO after a number of discussions I had with the team when I noticed that an equivalent of RDO's GetClipString was missing in ADO. They argued that ADO has a number of new ways to address the problem that GetClipString solves: quickly populating controls from a result set. It's true, ADO is especially adept at handling bound controls and really makes the need for this method moot. I suggested that it would still be easier to convert code if we had a similar method—so they relented. (See Chapter 29 for details on how to code the GetString method.) The real advantage to the Get(Clip)String method is the ability to pass the resultant Recordset (in the form of a string) to a control's Clip property. Actually, in order to use the Clip property with a grid, you have to set up the "paste" region first. This setup code can take more time than building a BindingCollection and dropping in some bound controls. Not only that, but the Clip technique doesn't let you create a bound control. You have to do all the update work yourself. Take a look at this code:

```
FGrid1.Rows = 51
FGrid1.Row = 1
FGrid1.Col = 0
FGrid1.RowSel = FGrid1.Rows - 1
FGrid1.ColSel = FGrid1.Cols - 1
FGrid1.Clip = rs1.GetClipString(50, , , "-")
```

This example uses the MSFlex grid control that ships with Visual Basic. Once you have the grid filled, now what? You have to intercept the click and scroll events and do all the other work to bind this control to the data if you choose to use the grid to update the data. Gee, it seems to me that binding is a lot easier.

Filtering, Finding, and Sorting ADO Recordset Data

Wait a minute. Client-side filtering, finding, and sorting? Isn't that something that just the Jet database engine could do? Not anymore. Now ADO and its data providers are capable of providing these and a throng of other services—thanks to technology developed over the years by the Microsoft FoxPro team. It works like this. First you build an "original," or unfiltered, Recordset using whatever technique you care to use. Next you set the Filter property to a valid criteria string. When you start fetching rows from the Recordset, ADO uses the Filter property on the rows—if they qualify, your code can see them; if not, they remain in the Recordset, but hidden from view. If you set the Filter property to a null string or adFilterNone, the filter is turned off and you see all the rows. It's that simple.

Nope, it isn't always wise to do these kinds of operations on large result sets, but it makes abundant sense to leverage the client's ability to process data—assuming the client system has the horsepower to do so. And yes, these services consume more client resources; but if the overall effect can be smoother performance and less load on the wires, using them could make sense and mean more scalability.

Generally, you can let SQL Server fetch the data and provide you with an original sort/filter result set. That is, this original result set is *already* "filtered" and sorted. No, you do *not* want to simply open a table or a query that returns all the rows from a set of tables and start to filter or sort. Sure, you can do this for a tiny database or with an application that you don't expect to scale, but if you're creating a serious application that has to scale, keep the size of the Recordsets small.

Once the original result set is in place and displayed, if your users want another sequence or want to modify the selection criteria on the fly, let them. This technology can improve productivity on client applications working over a slow link or the Internet because it requires *no* further trips back to the server to run the query. You might even consider dropping the connection while the user ponders the rows. Of course, the longer you wait, the staler the data becomes, so you might build in a refresh strategy for more volatile data.

> **NOTE** Volatile data is the kind that doesn't keep well when left out of the refrigerator on a warm summer afternoon—you know, like your spouse's potato salad. Airline reservation data can be this volatile. It's what makes you sick when you fly.

Filtering Your ADO Recordsets

You'll also find that the Filter property is quite talented. You can use it to find just those rows that have changed in a Recordset—right in the middle of a batch update operation. For example, after your UpdateBatch method returns, ADO presents you with a Recordset whose status bits are set to show which rows survived the update—and which didn't. You can also use the Filter property to expose rows that have been deleted but not yet posted to the database. Yes, this property is very handy. But don't fall prey to the cursor sirens calling from that alluring island.

> **TIP** Before you run out and try the Filter property, keep in mind that you have to set the CursorLocation to adUseClient—unless you have an OLE DB provider that supports filtering on its own.

I wrote a little sample to illustrate how the Filter property works and how to compose valid filter strings on the fly. You have to use a very small font to get that much code written on the back of an insect, but it can be done. Basically, this application opens a Recordset against the Titles table in the *Biblio* database. The WHERE clause is gated with a year range that you can change with a TextBox control on the form. You press the Run button to get the query to execute. Once the Recordset is built, I used the Fields collection to populate the list of valid columns and to populate a ComboBox control with this list. The operator list is in Combo2, and this list is populated in the Form_Load event procedure. I let you fill in an operator (such as = or <), and based on the Type property of the Field chosen, I add quotes—but only if you forgot to. Figure 31-2 shows how the sample looks.

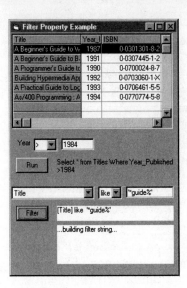

Figure 31-2 *Sample that uses the Filter property to filter ADO Recordsets*

When you press the Filter button, I build up a filter criterion and apply it to the Filter property. I then test the Recordset.EOF property to see whether any rows are left after the filter was applied. If any rows are left over, I repopulate the grid. Notice that you get to use *both* the * and % LIKE operators, and you can use more than one of these in your LIKE expression—in any combination. As shown in Figure 31-2, I used '*guide%' to return any row that had the word *guide* in the Title column. Sure, you can also build up more complex criteria to filter on more than one column or with more than one test. Remember to frame dates in the # character instead of quotes like you do for SQL Server. This requirement is because ADO and the data provider are finding the rows—not SQL Server. There's also the matter of the underscore character. I experimented with it and found that it worked in some cases—but not always as I expected. I would have thought this operator would mark a single "any" character in a Like expression as it does in the Jet Find methods. I submitted a bug on this, so it might be working better by the time Visual Basic 6.0 ships.

NOTE If you need to include the single quote character in your filter, simply double it up ('): for example, "Fred''s new hair". Be sure to check out the Replace function if you want Visual Basic to replace single quotes with two single quotes (as shown here).

The following code gets the connection open and populates the ComboBox controls with all of the valid operators.

```
Dim rs As New Recordset
Dim cnn As New Connection
Dim ADOEr As ADODB.Error
Dim i As Integer
```

```
Private Sub Form_Load()
cnn.CursorLocation = adUseClient
cnn.Open "dsn=biblio"
For i = 1 To 7
    Combo2.AddItem Choose(i, "like ", "=", "<", ">", "<=", _
        ">=", "<>")
Next i
Combo2.ListIndex = 0
For i = 1 To 6
    Combo3.AddItem Choose(i, "=", "<", ">", "<=", ">=", "<>")
Next i
Combo3.ListIndex = 2
End Sub
```

OK, the connection is open and the form is set up and ready to go. The RunButton routine runs the query based on a value in the YearRange TextBox. If any rows come back from the server, show them in the grid. The cursor is limited to 50 rows.

```
Private Sub RunButton_Click()
On Error GoTo EH
RunButton.Enabled = False
If rs.State = adStateOpen Then Set rs = Nothing
rs.MaxRecords = 50
rs.Open "Select * from Titles Where Year_Published " & _
    Combo3 & YearRange, cnn
SQL = rs.ActiveCommand.CommandText
If rs.EOF Then Else RAutoGrid1.ShowADOData rs
FilterButton.Default = True
RunButton.Enabled = True
Exit Sub
```

NOTE This sample also uses my RDO/ADO "instant" grid control (RDOADOGrid) to dump the contents of a random Resultset or Recordset to the MSFlex grid—titles and all. Copies of this sample and the control are on the companion CD.

When the user first touches the list of valid columns (Combo1), I populate it with the Recordset field names:

```
Private Sub Combo1_GotFocus()
If Combo1.ListCount > 0 Then Exit Sub
If rs.State = adStateOpen Then
    Dim fld As Field
    For Each fld In rs.Fields
        Combo1.AddItem fld.Name
    Next
    Combo1.AddItem "<No Filter>"
    Combo1.ListIndex = 0
End If
End Sub
```

CAUTION
Because of limitations in OLE DB, you aren't permitted to submit a filter that implies that the search string "starts with" a value. For example, "*aughn" is unacceptable, but "*aughn*" and "Vaughn*" are both OK. Go figure.

We have a Recordset, so let's give the user a chance to narrow the focus of the search using the Filter property. Notice that we have to add quotes (single quotes) to the Like expression string and any character types if they are chosen for the test column. I also frame the column chosen with brackets to deal with multiword columns. Of course, SQL Server doesn't support these... but just in case.

```
Private Sub FilterButton_Click()
Dim ft As String
On Error GoTo EH
ErrorText = "...building filter string..."
If Combo1 = "<No Filter>" Then
    rs.Filter = adFilterNone
Else
    Select Case rs.Fields((Combo1))).Type
        Case adVarChar, adChar: If Left(Operand, 1) <> "'" Then _
            Operand = "'" & Operand & "'"
        Case adDate, adDBDate: If Left(Operand, 1) <> "#" Then _
            Operand = "#" & Operand & "#"
    End Select
    FilterText = "[" & Combo1 & "] " & Combo2 & " " & Operand
    ft = FilterText      ' to force string type (bug?)
    rs.Filter = ft
End If
SQL = rs.ActiveCommand.CommandText
If rs.EOF Then
    MsgBox "The filtered recordset is empty..."
Else
    RAutoGrid1.ShowADOData rs
End If
Exit Sub
EH:
    ErrorText = Err.Description
    Debug.Print Err
    For Each ADOEr In cnn.Errors
        Debug.Print ADOEr.Description
    Next
    Resume Next
End Sub
```

Finding Stuff in Your ADO Recordset Data

Remember how you used to be able to find specific rows in a Recordset using DAO and the Jet engine? Well, in ADO, you pretty much use the same—but not completely identical—process. (The processes are similar because the FoxPro team develops much of the code that ADO's data providers use.) Before we discuss the many similarities in any more detail, however, let's take a look at the differences:

- In DAO, you had the FindFirst, FindNext, FindPrevious, FindLast, and FindANewJob methods, but in ADO, you have just the one Find method. It has a SearchDirection argument that sets the direction.

(Remember that we went over the syntax details in Chapter 29, so refer there for any nitty-gritty details.)

- Keep in mind that if ADO doesn't locate a match based on your Find criteria, you need to be prepared to be repositioned to EOF. Nope, you won't be left at the previously current row. Sure, you can save the current row's bookmark (if the Recordset supports this) and position back to it later.

- If ADO finds a match, the EOF property is set to False and your Recordset object's current-row pointer is positioned to the located row. There is no NoMatch property as in DAO—not unless you implement it.

- ADO lets you start searching at the current row or skip over it. You do this by specifying a value in the SkipRecords argument. You can make changes to an entire result set and restart your search to include your changes. You can also skip "backward" by using a negative number. (Note that the SkipRecords argument has changed since ADO 1.5—it used to be a Boolean.)

- You can provide a bookmark as a starting point, by using the Start argument.

- The Criteria argument passes a criteria string to ADO and the data provider. You construct this string as you would the WHERE clause in a SQL statement but without the word WHERE. Is that like saying it's a cat but without pointy ears, fur, and a tail? Check out Chapter 29 for more details.

- Unlike the Filter property, you can't reference more than one column in your criteria. You also can't use a negative value in your criteria. In other words, you can't do a find for a row that does not match a value. (Well, duh!)

- Just like the Filter property, you have to frame your strings in single quotes (" ' ") and your dates in pound cakes ("#")—surely you have some left over from the holidays.

Sorting Your ADO Recordset Data

You can get SQL Server to sort your data six ways from Detroit before it arrives at your client, and that versatility is still a good idea. However, given the way clients like to resort everything, it is often necessary to resort the data yet again. Well, in ADO, you can resort to your heart's content—using the same technology we used for the Filter and Find techniques. In this case, you can use the Recordset object's Sort property to set the order of the rows presented. Nope, the rows are *not* physically reordered while you wait, but a new temporary index is created against the Recordset in local memory—if ADO can't find one it can use. However, you have to set the CursorLocation property to adUseClient for this to work. Setting the Sort property to an empty string resets the rows to their original order and deletes temporary indexes. Existing indexes are *not* deleted.

When it comes time to display your rows, ADO and the data provider walk this new index(es) to fetch the Recordset rows for you. And no, this doesn't necessarily mean that any more fetches are made to the server to get the live data—except when the chosen cursor requires that. This kind of operation is done best with static cursors—to prevent overtaxing the network and your user's patience.

Setting up the sort is easy. Simply build a string with the column (Field) to sort followed by an optional DESCENDING keyword (ascending is assumed). ADO seems to prefer DESC and ASC, but this might be a bug. Try the short version if the long version doesn't work. Shown below is a routine I added to the Filter sample to sort the grid, first using the ascending sequence and then the descending. The code picks up the column to sort on based on the clicked-on column in the grid.

```
Private Sub RAutoGrid1_Click()
Dim fld As String, sfld As String
If rs.EOF Then rs.MoveFirst
fld = rs.Fields(RAutoGrid1.Col).Name
On Error GoTo Eh
sfld = rs.Sort
If Left(sfld, Len(fld)) = fld Then
    If Right(sfld, 4) = "DESC" Then
        rs.Sort = fld & " ASC"
    Else
        rs.Sort = fld & " DESC"
    End If
Else
    rs.Sort = fld
End If
SortField = rs.Sort
If rs.EOF Then Else RAutoGrid1.ShowADOData rs
Exit Sub
Eh:
    Debug.Print Err.Description
    Resume Next
End Sub
```

32

Working with ADO Events and Asynchronous Operations

ADO Event Types

Enabling Event Handlers

Examining Event Handler Arguments

Two Event Examples

Working with Will and Complete Event Handlers

Managing Asynchronous Operations

ActiveX Data Objects (ADO) 2.0 has finally caught up with the innovation that Remote Data Objects (RDO) introduced when it added event handlers and asynchronous operations to its repertoire. Of course, these are nothing new for RDO developers—they've been using them for some time. What is new with ADO events is the number and scope of them—ADO 2.0 has lots more than RDO. Events are simply programmatic notifications that tell you when certain data access operations are about to occur, are occurring, or have already occurred. Do you need to be running in asynchronous mode to have events fire? Nope. Events work independently of asynchronous execution, but they sure make asynchronous operations easier to use by eliminating the need to poll for completion. Asynchronous operations let your code continue to run while ADO (or RDO) keeps working on the last-assigned operation. If you enable events, when the operation is done, ADO (or RDO) signals completion by setting properties and firing "completed" events.

Events can play an integral role in the design of your application—with or without asynchronous operations. When you add asynchronous functionality, however, you really leverage ADO's ability to minimize application wait time and make your user happier and more productive. Without events and good event handlers, you're stuck with a single-threaded conversation with the server. You tell the system to do something, and you wait until it's done—at least done to the point at which ADO, its data providers, and Microsoft SQL Server are ready to return. Working with a synchronous connection is like working with a gardener who has to be told what to do chore by chore—one chore at a time. You have to stand there and wait while he hoes. With an event model, you can start an operation and go back to do other work of your own. Your own processing thread isn't consumed waiting for the roses to be pruned by someone else. Perhaps you'll have enough cycles to get another door opened in Riven.

ADO Event Types

In ADO, events are exposed only on the Connection and Recordset objects. This makes things simpler—even though there are more events than ever for you to keep track of. No, you don't have to trap them all—just deal with the ones you need, and the rest will take care of themselves.

Events are classified into three types, based on when and why they fire:

- **Will events**   Fire before an operation. For example, the WillConnect event is a Will event.

- **During events**   Fire during an operation. For example, the InfoMessage event is a during event.

- **Complete events**   Fire when the operation is done. For example, the ConnectComplete event is a Complete event.

Let's look at each type of event in a bit more detail.

Will Events

Will event handlers are called before the operation starts. They offer you the opportunity to examine or modify the operation parameters and then either cancel the operation or allow it to complete. It might be easier to think of Will events as operations in progress, but generally, the operation in question hasn't really begun. One of the most useful Will events is the WillChangeRecordset event, which can be used to intercept update operations, substitute other operations, and disconnect ADO from its normal update operation.

During Events

During event handlers are invoked while the operation is taking place. There are only a few during events, including InfoMessage, EndOfRecordset, Disconnect, and FetchProgress. These events inform you of the progress of an operation or simply provide extra information about what's going on.

Complete Events

Complete event handlers are called after an operation finishes. They notify your application that an asynchronous operation has concluded. Complete event handlers are also called when a pending operation is cancelled by a Will event handler. Complete events indicate that the Open method has finished connecting to a server (or that it failed to do so) or that the Execute method finished running a query (even if it returned no rows or got a syntax error). Events go off whether or not you have activated asynchronous operations. We saw this when we studied the Recordset events. For example, the ExecuteComplete event is fired whether or not you executed the method to build your Recordset using the asynchronous option.

Enabling Event Handlers

All ADO events are processed by event handler routines that are exposed *only* if you declare the Connection and Recordset objects correctly. If you don't provide event handler code for these events, nothing happens—just as nothing happens unless you write event handlers for the Form object or TextBox control events. For example, you have to declare the ADO Connection object using the WithEvents keyword to build the right kind of infrastructure to fire events. The following code shows a sample:

```
Dim WithEvents MyCn as Connection
Set MyCn = New Connection
```

This pair of statements is required if you expect ADO (or RDO for that matter) to fire events on your Connection object. When your application starts, the events fire when the right circumstances call for them. If you've provided code to handle these events, that code is executed when the event fires.

TIP When you're in interactive debug mode, some events might not get fired because the interactive nature of Microsoft Visual Basic sometimes prevents them from going off. Visual Basic 6.0 seems to do a better job at this, but don't be surprised if events don't seem to go off when you're in debug mode. Consider that events are simply messages placed on the Windows message loop by low-level drivers such as the keyboard, mouse, or ADO data access libraries. This mechanism has a limited capacity, so some events might be dropped in situations where your event handler doesn't get a chance to process the event in time.

Typically, you pair Will events with Complete events. However, after the first event notification, you can request that an event handler not receive any more notifications. Therefore, you can choose to receive only Will events or Complete events.

Examining Event Handler Arguments

Each event handler is called with more or less the same set of handler arguments that tell you vital information about the operation in question. These arguments can tell you whether the completed operation succeeded or failed and why, and which object caused the event. Each event handler is called with a status parameter to indicate success or failure—and to short-circuit the operation in progress. Most Complete events have an error parameter to provide additional error information about the operation causing the event. The arguments also return an object parameter to identify the ADO object to which the operation applied. Will events are also passed the parameters to be used in the pending operation. This gives you the opportunity to examine or modify the parameters and determine whether or not the operation should complete. Let's take a closer look at some of these arguments.

Status Argument

When the event handler routine is called, the status argument tells you if the completed operation succeeded and if you can interrupt a Will event operation. The status argument is set to one of the values listed in Table 32-1.

Table 32-1
Status Argument Values

Constant	Description
adStatusOK	The operation that caused the event occurred successfully.
adStatusErrorsOccurred	The operation that caused the event occurred unsuccessfully, or a Will event cancelled the operation. Check the pError parameter for more details. If a Will event cancelled the operation, the Error object Number property will be adErrOperationCancelled.
adStatusCantDeny	A Will event can't request that the operation about to occur be cancelled. If this bit is set, you can't cancel the operation.

Status argument return values

Before the event handler routine returns, you can leave the adStatus argument unchanged, set it to continue processing, cancel the Will operation, or tell ADO not to fire this event again—at least not until further notice. You can set the return status to any of the values listed in Table 32-2. No, this doesn't mean passing an argument back via the "function" return status. All you have to do is exit the handler after having changed the adStatus parameter to one of the values in the table.

Table 32-2
Status Argument Return Values

Constant	Description
adStatusOK	Status parameter is unchanged.
adStatusUnwantedEvent	Requests that this event handler receive no further notifications.
adStatusCancel	Requests that the operation about to occur be cancelled. In other words, you don't want the update or other operation to continue. You use this option when you have performed the operation yourself.

Depending on the event type, the status argument can have one of the values listed in Table 32-3 when the event handler is called.

Table 32-3
Status Argument Values When Event Handler Is Called

Event Type	Constant
Will	adStatusOK, adStatusCantDeny
Complete	adStatusOK, adStatusErrorsOccurred

Depending on the event type, the status argument can have one of the values listed in Table 32-4 when the event handler returns.

Table 32-4
Status Parameters Value When Event Handler Returns

Event Type	Constant
Will	adStatusOK, adStatusCancel, adStatusUnwantedEvent
Complete	adStatusOK, adStatusUnwantedEvent

Error Argument

The event's Error argument is a reference to an ADO Error object containing details about why the operation failed if the status argument equals adStatus-ErrorsOccurred.

Object Argument

The Object argument is a reference to the ADO object involved in the operation just completed or about to be executed. For example, you could have several Connection objects open at one time and only one Disconnect event handler. If any one connection closes, the Disconnect event handler is called with the Object argument set to the Connection object that closed. You can create as many Connection objects as you require. Although this option is expensive, each Connection object can have its own event handler.

Reason Argument

When an event fails, one of the EventReasonEnum values is passed to the event handler via the adReason argument. The list of EventReasonEnum values appears in the Object Browser but seems to be missing from all of the documentation I have at my disposal, so Table 32-5 is a summary of what these event codes mean. Basically, these events expose low-level OLE DB notification reasons. Unfortunately, the OLE DB SDK 1.1 documentation gives very little supplementary information about these reason codes, and most of the information (again) is written for OLE DB provider developers.

Table 32-5
EventReasonEnum Constants

Constant	Reason: An Operation Attempted to:
adRsnAddNew	Execute the AddNew method
adRsnClose	Execute the Close method
adRsnDelete	Execute the Delete method
adRsnFirstChange	Change the object (a Field or Recordset)
adRsnMove	Move the current-row pointer
adRsnMoveFirst	Move the current-row pointer to the first row
adRsnMoveLast	Move the current-row pointer to the last row
adRsnMoveNext	Move the current-row pointer to the next row
adRsnMovePrevious	Move the current-row pointer to the previous row
adRsnRequery	Execute the Requery method
adRsnResynch	Execute the Resync method
adRsnUndoAddNew	Execute the CancelUpdate method with an AddNew pending
adRsnUndoDelete	Execute the CancelUpdate method with a Delete pending
adRsnUndoUpdate	Execute the CancelUpdate method with an Update pending
adRsnUpdate	Execute the Update method

Two Event Examples

This section contains two simple examples that utilize ADO events. The first example shows events triggered when opening a connection. The second example shows events triggered when connecting, executing a query, and populating a Recordset.

Connect Example

The following example shows how I coded a simple set of event handlers to manage opening a connection when a form loads. The user can choose to abort the open operation and continue processing—assuming the connection would be opened later or the user simply wants to work off line.

First an instance of the Connection object that has been declared to have the additional event handler hooks is created. Next a connection in asynchronous mode is opened. Nope, I didn't have to use the adAsyncExecute option—the events fire in either case.

```
Dim WithEvents cnn As Connection

Private Sub Form_Load()
Set cnn = New Connection
cnn.Open "dsn=pubs",options:=adAsyncConnect
End Sub
```

The first event to fire is the WillConnect event. This event tells which object (the *cnn* Connection object in this case) and UserID and Password are specified. I could have prevented the connection from completing simply by changing the adStatus argument to adStatusCancel. Instead I chose to ask the user to decide whether this connection should be opened. Yep, this situation is somewhat contrived, but you get the idea. You really should test the adStatus parameter first to see whether it's possible to derail this particular operation.

```
Private Sub cnn_WillConnect(ConnectionString As String, _
UserID As String, Password As String, Options As Long, _
adStatus As ADODB.EventStatusEnum, _
ByVal pConnection As ADODB.Connection)
Dim i As Integer
i = MsgBox("About to connect to " & ConnectionString, vbOKCancel)
If i <> vbOK Then
    If adStatus <> adStatusCantDeny Then adStatus = adStatusCancel
    MsgBox "Connection cancelled."
End If
End Sub
```

The ConnectComplete event fires when the user decides that the connection can be opened. It indicates the Connection object involved and whether ADO could establish the connection. If no connection could be established, the pError.Description property tells what went wrong.

```
Private Sub cnn_ConnectComplete(ByVal pError As ADODB.Error, _
adStatus As ADODB.EventStatusEnum, _
ByVal pConnection As ADODB.Connection)
If adStatus = adStatusOK Then
    MsgBox "Connection complete to " & pConnection.DefaultDatabase
Else
    MsgBox "Connection failed. " & pError.Description
End If
End Sub
```

The InfoMessage event provides interesting feedback—perhaps more than you would expect. All the PRINT messages come from this handler. So if your stored procedures return information in PRINT or RAISERROR messages, you had better have this event handler coded.

```
Private Sub cnn_InfoMessage(ByVal pError As ADODB.Error, _
adStatus As ADODB.EventStatusEnum, _
ByVal pConnection As ADODB.Connection)
Debug.Print pError.Description
End Sub
```

Query Example

As I've said before, you don't have to use asynchronous operations to get events
to fire in ADO. Just as in RDO, when you declare your Connection and Recordset variables using the WithEvents syntax, ADO exposes a cornucopia of events.
All these events are listed in Chapter 29, so I won't repeat them here; but let's
go over a typical query and population to see what happens.

I created this small sample that uses the Recordset.Open method to retrieve all the rows from the Publishers table in the *Pubs* database:

```
Option Explicit
Dim WithEvents rst As Recordset
Dim WithEvents cnn As Connection

Private Sub Form_Load()
Dim fld As Field
Dim prm As Parameter
Dim SQL As String
Set cnn = New Connection
Set rst = New Recordset
cnn.Open "dsn=pubs"
cnn.CursorLocation = adUseClient
SQL = "Select * from Publishers"
rst.Open SQL, cnn, adOpenKeyset, adLockOptimistic
For Each fld In rst.Fields
    Debug.Print fld.Name,
Next fld
Debug.Print
Do Until rst.EOF
    For Each fld In rst.Fields
        Debug.Print fld.Value,
    Next fld
    Debug.Print
    rst.MoveNext
Loop
End Sub
```

I coded a message for each event on the Recordset and Connection objects and got these results:

```
WillConnect event fired. adStatus=1
ConnectComplete event fired. adStatus=1
InfoMessage event fired. adStatus=1
WillExecute event fired. adStatus=1
```

(continued)

```
WillMove event fired. adStatus=3 adReason=10
MoveComplete event fired. adStatus=1 adReason=10
ExecuteComplete event fired. adStatus=1
pub_id       pub_name              city        state        country
WillMove event fired. adStatus=1 adReason=10
MoveComplete event fired. adStatus=1 adReason=10
0736         New Moon Books        Boston      MA           USA
WillMove event fired. adStatus=1 adReason=13
MoveComplete event fired. adStatus=1 adReason=13
0877         Binnet & Hardley      Washington  DC           USA

    ... (remaining rows processed)

WillMove event fired. adStatus=1 adReason=13
MoveComplete event fired. adStatus=1 adReason=13
9999         Lucerne Publishing  Paris         Null         France
WillMove event fired. adStatus=1 adReason=13
EndOfRecordset event fired. adStatus=1
MoveComplete event fired. adStatus=1 adReason=13
```

Notice there was no Recordset event to tell me that the Open succeeded—as I would have expected (I used the Recordset Open method). However, the Connection WillConnect and ConnectComplete events fired before and after the connection was made. To get this to happen, I referenced the predefined Connection object in the Open method. If you have the Recordset.Open method create the Connection for you, you won't see these events.

After that, the WillExecute event fired to tell me that ADO was about to run the query, and the WillMove and MoveComplete events fired to tell me that ADO was moving the current-row pointer to populate the first row. After the first row arrived, the ExecuteComplete event fired to tell me that the query was complete. When I executed the MoveNext method, the WillMove and MoveComplete events fired to tell me that the current row was changing. When I finally hit EOF, the EndOfRecordset event fired.

NOTE   While processing some events, ADO will be in a nonreentrant state for certain methods. Your code can trip a run-time error if, while handling an event, you make a method call that would compromise the integrity of the action being fired. For example, it is illegal to close a Recordset while in the WillChangeRecord and RecordChangeComplete event handler code.

Preventing operations—or running your own

Will events let you interrupt and optionally terminate the intended operation. This means that when a Will event is fired, you can substitute your own code in the event handler to run a stored procedure (or anything else within reason). If necessary, you can cancel the operation by changing the status parameter (the adStatus argument of the event handler) to adStatusCancel. The adStatusCancel argument indicates that the operation about to be executed should not continue, but does not prevent the Complete event of the operation from firing. Cancelling an operation does trip a trappable error, "The change was canceled during notification; no columns are changed" -2147217842 (0x80040E4E), which you should be prepared to catch in code. No, don't show this message to an unsuspecting user. Be aware that you can't use adStatusCancel if the status parameter is set to adStatusCantDeny. The adStatusCantDeny argument indicates that the pending operation can't be cancelled.

A WillChangeRecord or RecordChangeComplete event can fire as a result of the following Recordset operations: Update, Delete, CancelUpdate, AddNew, UpdateBatch, and CancelBatch. During the WillChangeRecord event, the Recordset Filter property is set to adFilterAffectedRecords. It is illegal to change this property while processing the event.

Working with Will and Complete Event Handlers

You can use Will and Complete event handlers in pairs or separately. First let's examine what happens when a Will event succeeds. Imagine paired WillChangeField and FieldChangeComplete events for a Recordset object. In your application, you start to change the value of a field. The WillChangeField event handler is called, and it returns an indication that it's all right to change the field. The operation completes, and a FieldChangeComplete event notifies your application that the operation has ended. The event handler pError argument reports the success of the operation.

Suppose you change another field. This fires the WillChangeField event handler. You set the adStatus argument to adStatusCancel to indicate that it's *not* all right to change the field. The operation changing the field doesn't complete, and the FieldChangeComplete event notifies your application that the operation has ended. The event handler adStatus argument is set to adStatusErrorsOccurred; the pError argument refers to an Error object; and the Error object Number property is set to adErrOperationCancelled.

TIP My testing didn't show the right return code when I tried this. I expected adErrOperationCancelled (3712), but I got -2147217842 (0x80040E4E). A bug? Probably.

More than one Will and Complete event handler can be called for the same operation. Let's examine what happens when multiple Will events succeed. Consider that the WillChangeField, FieldChangeComplete, WillChangeRecord, and RecordChangeComplete events are a matched set of events for a Recordset object. Once you start to change the value of a field, several things can happen.

- The WillChangeRecord event handler is called, and it indicates that the operation should complete.

- The WillChangeField event handler is called, and it returns an indication that it's all right to change the field. (In general, all the Will event handlers pertaining to a particular instance of an ADO object will be called, though not in any particular order.)

- When the operation completes, the FieldChangeComplete and Record-ChangeComplete event handlers are called.

More than one Will and Complete event handler can be called for the same operation, but a Will event might cancel the pending operation. Let's examine what happens when the first of a series of Will events cancels an operation. Once again, imagine paired WillChangeField and FieldChangeComplete events and WillChangeRecord and RecordChangeComplete events.

- You start to change the value of a field.

- The WillChangeRecord event handler is called. Perhaps your code determines that the field change is all right in itself but will create an error in the record as a whole. The handler returns adStatusCancel to indicate that it's not all right to change the field.

- The operation does not complete because the WillChangeRecord event handler cancelled it.

- The RecordChangeComplete event handler is called with the adStatus argument set to adStatusErrorsOccurred.

- The WillChangeField (and thus the FieldChangeComplete) event handler is not called, however, because the first Will event cancelled the operation. In general, if a Will event cancels an operation, no remaining Will event handlers will be called.

Let's examine what happens when the last of a series of multiple Will events cancels an operation. Once again, imagine the same set of paired event handlers as before.

- You start to change the value of a field.

- The WillChangeRecord event handler is called. Your code does nothing in this case.

- The WillChangeField event handler is called, and it returns adStatus-Cancel to indicate that it's not all right to change the field.

- The operation does not complete.

- The FieldChangeComplete event notifies your application that the operation has ended with the status and error parameters set appropriately.

- The RecordChangeComplete event handler is also called with the status and error parameters set appropriately.

Unpaired Event Handlers

You can turn off event notifications for any event by returning adStatusUn-wantedEvent in the status parameter. For example, when your first Complete event handler is called, return adStatusUnwantedEvent and you will subsequently receive only Will events. Single Will event handlers can be useful when you want to examine the parameters that will be used in an operation. You can modify those operation parameters, or as mentioned earlier, cancel the operation.

Alternatively, you can leave the Complete event notification turned on, and when your first Will event handler is called, return adStatusUnwanted-Event. You will subsequently receive only Complete events. Single Complete event handlers can be useful for managing asynchronous operations. Each asynchronous operation has an appropriate Complete event. For example, it can take a long time to populate a very large Recordset object. If your application is appropriately written, you can start a Recordset.Open(…,adAsyncExecute) operation and continue with other processing. An ExecuteComplete event will eventually notify your application when the Recordset is populated.

Multiple Event Handlers and Single Operations

It's possible, though less useful, to associate one ADO object and its operations to multiple sets of event handlers. For example, you could create multiple WillChangeField event handlers and have each perform a particular field validation edit. If a field were about to change, one Will event could validate some aspect of the field value, then another Will event could validate a different aspect.

The reason I don't consider this technique as very useful is that you could simply perform or call all your edits from a single event handler. Of course, if you're being paid by the hour or like to decorate your applications with lots of impressive-looking code, go for it. However, I mention this technique to show you how flexible ADO events can be—add a little TLC and they'll bend over backward for you.

Managing Asynchronous Operations

All multitasking operating systems such as Microsoft Windows (and this includes both Windows 95/98 *and* Microsoft Windows NT) permit applications to create isolated streams of execution that are designed to run independently of other code. Each of these *threads* of execution can be thought of as a separate subroutine that has an existence of its own. A thread must stop execution or *block* when it has to wait for another resource or thread before continuing. Windows can block a thread when resources are not available or mark the thread as *dispatchable* (ready to run) when resources are available. Windows manages a whole set of resources, including CPU time, memory, disk space, input-output channels, screen resources, and much, much more. It does not, however, have much control over your users' most precious resource—their time. That's your job.

How well an application is accepted is often a function of how often it blocks or waits while waiting for resources. Applications that lock up frequently frustrate users and waste their time—a resource your application should focus on conserving. It is very easy to block out your user if you don't effectively manage the threads allocated to your application. No, Visual Basic still won't let you get into the inner-workings of the threads, so you're pretty much at the mercy of the Windows thread dispatcher and how it allocates CPU time to your application. However, you do have a number of chances to break ADO's grip on your application while it works on a query or simply populates a cursor. Yes, ADO does a lot of background work for you, and these operations often run on separate threads. But you can also use both the asynchronous options and the event interface in ADO 2.0 to run your code more smoothly.

Using the Asynchronous Options

The key to enabling asynchronous operations is the adAsyncExecute and adAsyncFetch options. These tell ADO to return control to your application immediately after launching the operation—at least after the first 50 rows are cached (assuming that you're using client-side cursors). This means that the Recordset object ADO is building for you won't be ready to use, but you can continue with other work until it is. ADO works differently than RDO when it comes to enabling asynchronous operations. In RDO, individual methods must have the asynchronous bit flag set (rdAsyncEnable); in ADO, the asynchronous options apply more broadly. In other words, when you create a Recordset with the adAsyncFetch bit option set, *all* fetch operations on the Recordset are done asynchronously. For example, when you execute the MoveLast method on an asynchronous-enabled Recordset, control returns to your application immediately (after the first 50 rows are fetched) and ADO performs the Recordset population in the background on another thread. Table 32-6 lists ADO's asynchronous methods.

Table 32-6
ADO Asynchronous Methods

Methods	Asynchronous Options
Execute	adAsyncExecute, adAsyncFetch
Open	adAsyncConnect
Requery	adAsyncFetch

How do you know when the asynchronous operation is done? Simple, right? *Just* check the object's State property for adStateConnecting or adStateExecuting? Wrong—but thanks for playing. It's tougher than that. Sure, in RDO, testing for query completion was fairly easy:

```
Do While rs.StillExecuting
    DoEvents
Loop
```

In ADO, we have a "better" way to test for completion of events. We now get to test a bit flag—one of several State property flags. Aren't we *lucky*! Our ADO code to test for a completed query now looks like this:

```
Do While (cnn.State AND adStateExecuting) = adStateExecuting
    DoEvents
Loop
```

This ANDing is required because the cnn.State property is a set of bits and more than one bit can be set at a time. In the case of the Connection object, the adStateOpen bit (1) is on when you're ready to test for the completion of a query (adStateExecuting (4)). So while the cnn.State property = adStateOpen + adStateExecuting, the query is still running. When the cnn.State changes to just adStateOpen, the toast is done and you can use the Recordset—but not before.

Another approach to testing for completion of an asynchronous operation is to use the Command object and test its State property bits. However, I would draw the line at testing the Connection object's State property—which, theoretically, is supposed to expose the adStateExecuting bit. OK, so if this bit is set, which Command or Recordset is still executing? Sure, test the Connection.State property for adStateConnecting since only one object can be running at any one time. Better yet, trap the ExecuteComplete event fired when the operation finishes. But you know that. We just talked about it. We also discussed event and asynchronous operations in Part IV, on RDO. Much of what we talked about there applies here too.

Some Nuances of Asynchronous Operations

Consider the following tidbits as extra hints that will help you when you're working in asynchronous mode:

- ADO no longer supports asynchronous operations on the Move methods. The RDO asynchronous MoveLast was put in to alleviate the delay one gets when opening a large result set and then immediately calling MoveLast to fetch the pipe clean. The async fetch (or background fetch) option added to the ADO cursor engine is the replacement for this. Once the ADO cursor engine has the data, the MoveLast is (more or less) immediate and therefore doesn't require any asynchronous ability.

  Moving to the last row on a server-side cursor is also immediate—this is actually one of the advantages of server-side cursors. Although there is the delay imposed by going back to the server, the processing on the server is just as immediate as it is in the client cursor engine. Microsoft didn't add asynchronous ability to MoveNext in RDO because it gets way too hard to program when you're just moving around and have to wait for events to fire to know when the move was actually done (and most of the time it was instantaneous).

- When you request the next result set of a multiple result set in ADO, you block until it is available—even when you fetched the first result set in asynchronous mode.

33

Taking ADO Off Road

Building Custom ADO Command Objects

Managing Complex (Stored) Procedures

Performing Optimistic Client-Batch Operations

Working with Page-Based Data

Handling Special Cases

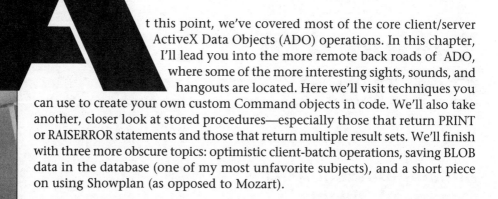

t this point, we've covered most of the core client/server ActiveX Data Objects (ADO) operations. In this chapter, I'll lead you into the more remote back roads of ADO, where some of the more interesting sights, sounds, and hangouts are located. Here we'll visit techniques you can use to create your own custom Command objects in code. We'll also take another, closer look at stored procedures—especially those that return PRINT or RAISERROR statements and those that return multiple result sets. We'll finish with three more obscure topics: optimistic client-batch operations, saving BLOB data in the database (one of my most unfavorite subjects), and a short piece on using Showplan (as opposed to Mozart).

> **TIP** Before you actually write some of your own code, you might want to try out the new Data Environment designer—which will (eventually) replace the UserConnection designer. I talk about the Data Environment and some of the other new Microsoft Visual Basic 6.0 tools in Part VI of this guide. However, the Data Environment isn't going to be a way to completely replace solid ADO code—so don't worry about job security.

Building Custom ADO Command Objects

A "custom" ADO Command object is really another name for a SQL procedure exposed as a method on the Connection object. In this section, we're going to go deeper into the details of how to create these custom commands and how ADO can execute queries that you haven't predefined.

As we discussed in previous chapters, the Command object represents a specific command that you intend to execute against the data source—usually more than once. In many ways, the Command object in ADO is very similar to the rdoQuery object in Remote Data Objects (RDO) 2.0. You can also use the Execute method against the Command object or the Connection object to create a Recordset object, but this is simply a shortcut for executing one-time commands that don't require output parameters or preparation.

In any case, the Command object either creates a Recordset object or executes an action (non-row-returning) query. In the process, ADO and the OLE DB provider instruct Microsoft SQL Server 6.*x* to build a temporary stored procedure in the TempDB database. If something goes wrong and ADO doesn't have a chance to tell SQL Server to drop this procedure, the procedure is orphaned on the server. Sure, ODBC, RDO, ADO, and even DAO/Jet know how to build and discard these procedures. However, a user will invariably turn off his or her system, or something else will happen that prevents the cleanup code from running. I suggest you plan to have a procedure-cleaning party every few days for just such contingencies.

That is unless you're running SQL Server 7.0. This new version of SQL Server eliminates the problem by eliminating the need to create temporary stored procedures anywhere. Because SQL Server 7.0 knows how to share procedures in memory across users, you no longer need to build and save these procedures in TempDB.

Another important technique, first exposed in RDO, is the ability to execute procedures as methods of the Connection object. In ADO, *all* the Command objects you define appear as methods on the Connection object. In addition, ADO even attempts to run commands you don't formally define as Command objects. Let's look at how ADO does this.

Commands as Connection Methods

In RDO 2.0, you can define an rdoQuery object so that it is exposed as a method on the rdoConnection object. Query results return via the LastQueryResults property on the rdoConnection object. In ADO, any Command object associated with a connection also exposes a dynamic method associated with the Connection object. This method takes all the parameters associated with the original command, along with one additional parameter (tacked on the end) that references the Recordset object. You can use this Recordset reference to preset properties and customize the resulting Recordset. Yes, that means it's both a gazinta and a gazouta.

When no Recordsets are returned from the query, all parameters are filled with the values returned from the data source—as when your query specifies output parameters and return values. If any Recordsets are returned, the Recordset parameter at the end of the command references the resulting rows.

The following code is an example of calling a named procedure as a method of the Connection object. Notice that you have the option of resetting the properties initialized by the Refresh method.

```
Dim cnn As New Connection
Dim cmd As New Command
Dim rst As New Recordset
Dim fld As Field
```

(continued)

```
cnn.Open "dsn=pubs"
cnn.CursorLocation = adUseClient
cmd.CommandText = "{call testout(?,?)}"
cmd.Name = "Test"
Set cmd.ActiveConnection = cnn
cmd.Parameters.Refresh
cmd.Parameters(1).Direction = adParamOutput
cnn.Test "USA", rst      ' Here we use our "Test" method.
Debug.Print rst(0)
' We are ready to look at our OUTPUT parameter.
' The stored procedure calls this "@TotalHits".
Debug.Print "Total Hits="; cmd.Parameters("@TotalHits")
```

> **NOTE** In this case, ADO didn't get the Direction property right for the output parameter. It thought it was an input/output parameter. I don't know if this is a bug or a "feature"—seriously, ADO might default output parameters to input/output to let you supply the value at run time.

To get at the rows returned, you simply need to reference the Recordset object returned into the *rst* variable passed as the last argument. No, ADO has no LastQueryResults.

ADO 2.0 also introduced a "shortcut method" of calling a stored procedure on the server. The following code illustrates the syntax:

```
cnn.<myprocname> param, param, param, ...
```

For example, I suppose you might try to call SP_WHO by calling

```
cnn.sp_who
```

If ADO doesn't recognize <myprocname> as one of its own Command objects, it hands the command and parameters to the data source to see whether it can handle the syntax. Because no parameter type definitions are specified, ADO makes its best guess with some help from the data definition language (DDL) calls to SQL Server.

Actually, at first I thought this new feature was pretty lame. Take the example in question: SP_WHO. It returns a result set, so it didn't seem to make much sense to execute it like this. Where is the result set returned? Well, I coded this up to try it, and I discovered that if I passed a Recordset as a final argument, ADO figured out that I wanted to return the result set in that Recordset. So, to *really* execute SP_WHO and capture the result set, use this code:

```
cnn.sp_who Myrs      ' where Myrs is a Recordset
```

What about trying to execute some command like *Use Master* to switch to another database or *Set RowCount, 50*? These commands don't return a result set. Unfortunately, it seems that ADO can't figure out what Master is supposed to be because it's trying to use the Call syntax intended for stored procedures. USE and SET aren't stored procedures, so you can't EXECUTE them. Therefore, this shortcut works for some commands but not all. It works for most stored procedures.

Managing Complex (Stored) Procedures

In this section, we'll walk through the use of ADO to deal with more complex problems. Here we'll discuss the ADO peculiarities of multiple result sets, how to handle output parameters, and some of the other more difficult aspects of stored procedures.

Managing Multiple Result Sets

Many developers unfamiliar with SQL Server are unaware that it really works better if you can give it several tasks to do at once. For example, using SQL Server can be compared to a "Dilbert" manager delegating projects. The manager sends notes—one at a time throughout the day—requesting his staff to complete projects. Mr. Adams and I (and I expect you too) would agree that it would be more efficient if the manager sent a single memo to his staff outlining the projects for the entire day. Sure, you do have to follow a set of rules when you're submitting batches and scripts to SQL Server. We went over these rules earlier in this guide, and the SQL Server documentation outlines what's possible with a batch or script. Basically, all you have to do is separate your queries and commands with white space (or a semicolon if that makes you happier). What about putting *GO* between the statements as ISQL/w does? Ah, no. This convention is something that only the interactive batch processors such as ISQL/w, SQL Enterprise Manager, or Visual InterDev understand. Sure, these batch separators are important. They usually separate parts of a script that can't be executed together with other Transact-SQL (TSQL) code. If you're using

CAUTION
No, you can't execute a multiple result set stored procedure using the "disjoint" ADO or Remote Data Services (RDS) tools. TheNextRecordset method simply won't work.

one of these scripts as a model, keep in mind that you probably can't submit more than one set of code between the GO separators. That is, each section has to be executed as a unit.

OK, so what happens when SQL Server gets this load of work to do? Well, it runs a quick syntax check on the whole string, and if the string passes this test, SQL Server puts the script in your connection's server-side "IN" box and starts to work on each query, one by one. Each query returns from one to any number of result sets. Each result set can contain zero or more sets of rows—result sets. You have to process each result set in turn—one at a time. If you don't want the data returned, you must cancel the current command or cancel the whole batch. Cancelling is dangerous, however, and you should avoid it—but we'll get to that later. And, no, it doesn't look like you can cancel the individual commands in a batch the way you can in VBSQL.

TIP Remember that SQL Server's server-side cursors can't handle complex stored procedures. You must use the client-side cursor libraries to handle this type of cursor—or simply use firehose cursors.

When we worked with DB-Library, we had much finer control over whether and how individual queries in a script were executed. In ADO, it seems that the provider's zeal has taken much of that control away from us. In VBSQL, we had to walk through the result sets one by one—as we must do in ADO. However, at any time, we could issue a cancel command that would cancel the current operation and go on to the next task, or cancel the remaining tasks in the batch and prepare for the next script. ADO seems to be processing these result sets in the background. This robs us of the opportunity to stop in the middle of a script to make a decision about what to do because one of the queries did or didn't work as intended.

What if you want to execute action queries instead of row-returning queries? In this case, you can still use the same batch techniques. Although action queries do not return data rows, they do return result sets. Each result set also carries with it a "rows affected" value and (possibly) a rowset. Using this value, you can see how many rows your action query inserted, deleted, or updated. Yes, even the NextRecordset method returns a valid RecordsAffected argument.

The following sample illustrates how to deal with several typical script problems. First, I had to create a test table. I created this table in SQL Enterprise Manager and saved the script. Yes, I could have created it in the new Data View window as it also creates a script for you. The script included two GO statements separating parts of the script that couldn't be executed together. In this case, you can't create or drop a table and reference it in the same batch (at least not in SQL Server 6.5—maybe you can do it in SQL Server 7.0). So I then had to break up these two parts of the script into individual commands, which I ran with the Execute method.

```
Dim cnn As Connection
Dim cmd As New Command
Dim rs As Recordset
Dim SQL As String, Title As String
Dim er As Error

Private Sub Form_Load()
Set cnn = New Connection
cnn.Open "dsn=biblio"
End Sub

Private Sub BuildButton_Click()
SQL = "if exists (select * from sysobjects where id = " & _
    "object_id('dbo.TestTable') and sysstat & 0xf = 3) " & _
    "drop table dbo.TestTable"
cnn.Execute SQL
SQL = "CREATE TABLE dbo.TestTable ( ID int IDENTITY (1, 1) " & _
    "NOT NULL , Title varchar (255) NOT NULL , " & _
    "ISBN varchar (255) NULL , PubID int NULL , " & _
    "CONSTRAINT PK___1__12 PRIMARY KEY  CLUSTERED (ID))"
cnn.Execute SQL
For Each er In cnn.Errors
    Debug.Print er.Description
Next
MsgBox "Table created"
End Sub
```

For the next part of the sample, I fetched rows from the Titles table in the *Biblio* database and used the MaxRecords property to limit the number to 51. I used 50 rows of this data to build INSERT statements against the TestTable table. I concatenated all these statements to be executed as a script. I then doubled the test rows by concatenating the SQL string to itself. To the end of this script, I added a DELETE statement to drop all rows in TestTable meeting a certain condition. I then added a final query to the script to count up all the rows in TestTable.

```
Private Sub InsertButton_Click()
Dim i As Integer
Dim Records As Integer
Set rs = New Recordset
rs.MaxRecords = 51
cnn.Execute "Truncate table TestTable"
SQL = ""
rs.Open "SELECT Title, ISBN, PubID from Titles", cnn
For i = 1 To 50
    Title = FixQuotes(rs(0))
    SQL = SQL & "INSERT TestTable values ('" & Title & "', '" & _
        rs(1) & "'," & rs(2) & ") "
    rs.MoveNext
Next i
SQL = SQL & SQL      'Double the number of test rows
```

(continued)

```
SQL = SQL & "DELETE TestTable where Title like '%e%' "
SQL = SQL & "SELECT Count(*) as TestRows from TestTable "
rs.Close
```

The next part of the sample runs the script using a Command object. This technique eliminates the unnecessary step of creating a temporary stored procedure to run the script.

```
cmd.CommandText = SQL
cmd.CommandType = adCmdText
cmd.ActiveConnection = cnn
Set rs = cmd.Execute(Records)
```

Once the script is executed, I start working through the result sets, as shown in the following code. I test the State property to see whether the Recordset returned has any rowsets. If it does, I dump them to the form and go to the next Recordset. I also dump the number of rows affected to see how the queries worked. The INSERT queries all returned a RecordsAffected value of 1. The SELECT returned a –1, and the DELETE returned 94 (or the number of rows in the TestTable). Why 94 and not 50? Well, even though the Max-Records property was set at 51, ADO sent a SET ROWCOUNT 0 to the server when the Recordset was closed. DumpRS is simply my routine for displaying a Recordset to the form.

```
Debug.Print Records
i = 0
While Not rs Is Nothing
    If rs.State = adStateOpen Then DumpRS
    Debug.Print i, "State:"; rs.State;
    Set rs = rs.NextRecordset(Records)
    Debug.Print "Records Affected:"; Records
    i = i + 1
Wend
Print i; " rows inserted"
End Sub
```

I used the FixQuotes routine to find any single quotes and "double" them before sending the string to the server. I needed to do this because many of the titles contain apostrophes. Without this routine, I would have gotten syntax errors because SQL Server can't parse a query with loose apostrophes. Actually, this code is only for those of you still using Visual Basic 5.0 and earlier.

```
Function FixQuotes(A As String)
Dim i As Integer
i = InStr(A, "'")
Do While i > 0
    A = Left(A, i) & Mid(A, i)
    i = InStr(i + 2, A, "'")
Loop
FixQuotes = A
End Function
```

The Visual Basic 6.0 version is a little simpler—and a lot faster.

```
Function FixQuotes(A As String)
FixQuotes = Replace (A, "'", "''")
End Function
```

NOTE In the middle of writing the last sample, I tripped over an old nemesis—embedded quotes in strings. When I got the following error, I knew that I'd found a new manifestation of this age-old problem: "Error: The name 'Classification Algorithms' is illegal in this context. Only constants, constant expression, or variables allowed here. Column names are illegal." You might also get a syntax error or another confusing message. What happened? Well, ADO had sent "SET Quoted_Identifier ON" to SQL Server in my behalf. Yes, you can turn off this option in the data source name (DSN). There's also a Quoted Identifier Sensitivity property that you might be able to set to change this on the fly. But when this option is enabled, SQL Server doesn't let you pass strings framed with double quotes—it thinks most of these are object names—thus the reference to the Column name. To get around this, you must use single quotes (') to frame your strings, and you must make sure the string itself either has no single quotes or has doubled ('') quotes where they are required. We talked about using the new Visual Basic 6.0 Replace function, but in case you're still working with an older version of Visual Basic, the previously discussed routine does the same thing (only slower).

SQL Server doesn't start working on the subsequent tasks in your "IN" basket until you (or your OLE DB provider) have completed processing the result set from the current task. It seems that ADO does this processing for you by attempting to populate your Recordset in the background, so it might not be clear that you've done anything to complete work on a part of your script. If you get an error message about "unprocessed pending results," you haven't finished processing a task SQL Server is working on.

TIP No, you can't submit another query or script until you and ADO are done processing the current set of tasks. But you can tell SQL Server to dump your "IN" box into the bit-bucket by using the Close or Cancel methods on the Recordset object.

When multiple result sets are generated, it is important to fetch one result set at a time until no more are available. The NextRecordset method of the Recordset object allows you to fetch each subsequent query result set. If no more result sets are available, the returned Recordset object's State property is set to adStateClosed. If the current Recordset contains a rowset (even one that has no rows), the Recordset.State property is set to adStateOpen. If there are rows, the Recordset.EOF property is False. No, you can't test the EOF property on a closed Recordset. And no, the RecordCount property won't tell you much until you (or the OLE DB provider) populate the Recordset.

When you build a script, you can reduce by a great deal the network traffic that would ordinarily be required to process each of the commands one at a time. However, you also have to take into account some other considerations:

- The cursor you describe when creating the initial Recordset is used for all result sets and rowsets generated by the script. If you use the defaults, a cursorless result set is generated. It's fast, but it's read-only.

- You can pick off one of the Recordsets and clone it to be bound to a set of controls on your form—but finding the right result set in the script might be problematic.

- There is an upper limit on the size of a script. In some versions of SQL Server, this maximum is around 128 KB. SQL Server 7.0 puts it around 64 KB times the network packet size. However, a practical limit might be much smaller once you take into account transaction log management and other factors. Over the years, I've found that using about 50 INSERT statements yields the highest rows-inserted-per-second performance. Your mileage may vary as you start to run up against SQL Server resource limits.

- You can bind together stored procedures in your batch. This binding opens up a whole new dimension to the situation, however. Because stored procedures can call procedures that can call other procedures, you'll have to write your code to deal with *n* levels of result sets.

- You'll invariably discover that you can't execute a script using the server-side library. If you try to create a cursor-based Recordset to manage your script rowsets and you forget to switch the CursorLocation to adUseClient or adUseClientBatch, you get a trappable error complaining about queries that have more than a single SELECT statement. But wait! The preceding example didn't do this—so what happened? Well, I didn't try to create a cursor. The default settings in ADO don't create a cursor.

- I generally run scripts using the adRunAsync option because scripts tend to tie up the application for long periods of time. You can use the Connection.ExecuteComplete event to process the result sets, but you'll need more logic to figure out which command is being executed. The entire script gets executed and handled as a single operation. Check out the following ExecuteComplete event handler. It looks for the script command containing the Insert statement and works through the result sets once it finds that statement.

```
Private Sub cnn_ExecuteComplete( _
    ByVal RecordsAffected As Long, _
    ByVal pError As ADODB.Error, _
    adStatus As ADODB.EventStatusEnum, _
    ByVal pCommand As ADODB.Command, _
    ByVal pRecordset As ADODB.Recordset, _
    ByVal pConnection As ADODB.Connection)
If adStatus = adStatusOK Then
```

```
    If InStr(pCommand.CommandText, "Insert") Then
        Debug.Print Records
        i = 0
        While Not rs Is Nothing
            If rs.State = adStateOpen Then DumpRS
            Debug.Print i, "State:"; rs.State;
            Set rs = rs.NextRecordset(Records)
            Debug.Print "Records Affected:"; Records
            i = i + 1
        Wend
        Print i; " rows inserted"
    End If
Else
    MsgBox "Query failed. " & pError.Description
End If
End Sub
```

Managing Output and Return Value Parameters

ADO implements output and return value parameters differently than RDO does. How do I know? Well, during a somewhat heated debate with the ADO developers, I discovered that they seem to think the output parameters and the return status from a stored procedure or ordinary query should remain locked within OLE DB (and ADO) until the Recordset pipe is closed. They tell me that one accomplishes this by:

- Closing the Recordset

- Using the NextRecordset method on the Recordset

- Setting the Recordset to Nothing

No, the developers say you don't have to take all of these actions—just one will do. Or so I was told. However, I didn't have to do any of these to retrieve the OUTPUT parameters using fairly vanilla code as shown below. The test procedure is coded as follows:

```
Create Procedure TestOut @Country Varchar(30), @TotalHits Int OUTPUT
as
    select * From Publishers where Country = @Country
    select @totalhits=@@rowcount

return (@@rowcount)
```

Here is the Visual Basic 6.0 code to call this stored procedure and get back the OUTPUT parameter:

```
Private Sub Form_Load()
Dim cnn As New Connection
Dim cmd As New Command
Dim rs As New Recordset
```

(continued)

```
Dim fld As Field
Dim prm As Parameter

cnn.Open "dsn=pubs"
cnn.CursorLocation = adUseClient
cmd.CommandText = "TestOut"
cmd.CommandType = adCmdStoredProc
cmd.Name = "Test"
Set prm = cmd.CreateParameter("Country", adVarChar, adParamInput, 20)
cmd.Parameters.Append prm
Set prm = cmd.CreateParameter("TotalHits", adInteger, adParamOutput, 4)
cmd.Parameters.Append prm
Set cmd.ActiveConnection = cnn
cnn.Test "USA", rs
Debug.Print Now, "Total Hits="; cmd.Parameters("TotalHits")
For Each fld In rs.Fields
    Debug.Print fld.Name,
Next fld
Debug.Print
Do Until rs.EOF
    For Each fld In rs.Fields
        Debug.Print fld.Value,
    Next fld
    Debug.Print
    rs.MoveNext
Loop
End Sub
```

I tried this stored procedure with and without a result set. Without a set of rows coming back, the code fails when it tries to access the rs.EOF statement. As I expected, you can't reference a closed Recordset.

Note that I didn't include a parameter for the @@RowCount return value. If you want this value back, you have to append another Parameter object to the collection. But hold on—there's a trick to this. You have to append the return value to the Parameters collection *first*. It *has* to be cmd.Parameters(0) for reasons known only to the ADO developers. Just add these two lines to the code right after the line cmd.Name ="Test":

```
Set prm = cmd.CreateParameter("RV", adInteger, adParamReturnValue)
cmd.Parameters.Append prm
```

After this addition, you can reference the value your TSQL statement sends back via RETURN by:

```
RetValue = cmd.Parameters("RV")
```

This brings up another point. The order in which you build the Parameters collection *is* significant. No, ADO doesn't try to match up the members of the collection with the named parameters being passed to SQL Server. And no, you still can't reference named parameters in SQL statements.

Let's look at another variation. This time we'll use the Command object's Refresh method. Using this method will save us several lines of code, but it's going to cost us at run time. I looked at SQL Trace (which in SQL Server 7.0 has been updated and renamed SQL Server Profiler) and saw that ADO had to ask SQL Server for details on the TestOut stored procedure. SQL Server created a cursor to return the status and this cursor returned four rows (one for each parameter) with the intimate details about the stored procedure.

```
sp_ddopen 25, "sp_sproc_columns", 8, 1, 1, "testout", NULL, NULL, NULL
sp_cursorfetch 29891376, 2, 1, 1
sp_cursorfetch 29891376, 2, 1, 1
sp_cursorfetch 29891376, 2, 1, 1
sp_cursorfetch 29891376, 2, 1, 1
sp_cursorclose 29891376
```

This is a one-time initialization hit, however, so it's not going to knock the moon out of its orbit—performance wise. I also modified the stored procedure somewhat to pass back a meaningful return value.

```
Create Procedure TestOut @Country Varchar(30), @TotalHits Int OUTPUT
as
declare @rc integer
    select * From Publishers where Country = @Country
    select @rc = @@rowcount
    select @totalhits=@rc
return (@rc)
```

The Visual Basic code to extract the rowset and the parameters is shown below. Notice that we can call the Refresh method before or after the connection is turned on, but we can't reference the Parameters collection until after the ActiveConnection is pointing to a good connection. We also have to address the Parameter objects by the names assigned by ADO (and our stored procedure). All the Parameter objects were set up correctly except the OUTPUT parameter, which was set to Input/Output. This caused ADO to try to execute the stored procedure with an extra parameter. To circumvent this problem, I forced the Direction property of the OUTPUT parameter (@TotalHits) to adParamOutput:

NOTE Early versions of ADO required that you close the Recordset before the OUTPUT parameters were made available. Although it doesn't appear that ADO 2.0 works this way, ADO might be "fixed" to force this change in your approach.

```
Private Sub Form_Load()
Dim cnn As New Connection
Dim cmd As New Command
Dim rs As New Recordset
Dim fld As Field
Dim prm As Parameter
```

(continued)

```
cnn.Open "dsn=pubs"
cnn.CursorLocation = adUseClient
cmd.CommandText = "TestOut"
cmd.CommandType = adCmdStoredProc
cmd.Name = "Test"
Set cmd.ActiveConnection = cnn
cmd.Parameters.Refresh
cmd.Parameters("@TotalHits").Direction = adParamOutput
cnn.Test "USA", rs
Debug.Print Now, "Total Hits="; cmd.Parameters("@TotalHits"), _
    cmd.Parameters("RETURN_VALUE")
    ...
End Sub
```

NOTE   I performed the preceding tests with the OLE DB provider for
ODBC. When using different OLE DB providers, your results might vary.

To test this stored procedure with ISQL/w, I wrote the following batch.
You can use it to test your development stored procedures to make sure that
they are returning what's expected.

TIP   If you run action queries via stored procedures, you lose control
over the individual queries—the INSERTs and UPDATEs.

```
declare @hits integer
declare @return_value integer
exec @return_value = testout 'USA', @hits output
select Hits=@hits, RV=@return_value
```

Using the Data Environment
to Manage Stored Procedures

Of course, this entire exercise is really unnecessary. You can eliminate virtually all of it by creating a Data Environment Command to handle the whole
deal—input, output, return value—the works. The following three lines of code
use a Data Environment that points to the *Biblio* database, opens the connection asynchronously, and runs a parameter-based stored procedure Command
object associated with the Data Environment. The result set is passed back in
its own Recordset object named after the Command object. The Data Environment uniquely names this output Recordset object by prefixing *rs* to the Command object's name.

```
de.Biblio.Open
de.GetCoverByTitle (TitleWanted.Text)
Set rs = de.rsGetCoverByTitle
```

Because all of the setup is done at design time, this approach is much
more economical to code and maintain—and it runs faster too since there are

fewer lines of Visual Basic code to run. I devote an entire chapter to the Data Environment, so look at Chapter 37 for more details.

Using the Data Object Wizard to Work with Stored Procedures

One of the chores you usually end up doing when you're working with stored-procedure–based designs is the four-headed business object. That is, you create one (or more) stored procedures to fetch rows based on a key, and one (usually three) more to do the insert, update, and delete tasks. The Data Object Wizard is designed to identify each of these stored procedures and the key values associated with each one and then build a custom Data class component to handle the whole operation. Be sure to check out Chapter 38, which focuses on this new tool.

Performing Optimistic Client-Batch Operations

Batch updates are called "optimistic" because they assume that the rows being updated won't encounter collisions when changes are made. This assumption is certainly erroneous when you're designing an airline reservation system, for example. However, in many other cases, you can "check out" rows to a chosen user, who can be assured that others won't disturb the rows until they are "checked in." The material in this section will help you design error handlers to deal with the errors you *might* encounter when using batch operations.

Many of the examples I use are fairly simple. They don't, by any means, reflect the complexity of true-to-life production stored procedures. Unfortunately, I'm hearing a number of reports that tell me ADO is, in some cases, not up to dealing with these stored procedures. It often has problems deciding what kind of result set will be constructed by the stored procedure. For these reasons, ADO 2.0 still doesn't seem able to handle the rigors of some production situations—at least not on its own. Given a little additional help in code, you might be able to get over these issues.

> **NOTE** This section is excerpted from a set of training materials graciously contributed by David Sceppa—one of those clever engineers you get to talk to on the phone when you have a problem.

As a developer, you are responsible for specifying what types of conflicts ADO should report, asking ADO to retrieve information about conflicts, interpreting that information, and determining how to handle the conflicts. It would be nice if ADO automatically determined which conflicts it should report, retrieved all pertinent information, interpreted it, and handled the conflicts. David would also like to see ADO pay off his college loans for him—but he's not holding his breath.

Let's consider a couple of typical (although somewhat unoptimistic) examples. If one user retrieves information about a particular customer and attempts to change the phone number for that customer, but another user has changed the billing address in the meantime, do you want ADO to report this as a conflict? Keep in mind that just because ADO reports a conflict it doesn't mean that you can't perform the update. If you want to make a number of changes to a table (or a series of tables) and conflicts occur, do you want to keep the changes that succeeded or do you want the operation to be all or nothing?

How do you want to handle a simple conflict such as when another user has modified the field in the row that a user wanted to change? If the field is Balance Due, the important information might be how each user wanted to change the field rather than the value each one wanted to set it to. For example, the Balance Due field has an original value of $100. Alberta tries to set it to $150, but Carl has since set it to $175. In this situation, you might want your code to handle the conflict and change the Balance Due to $225. In other cases, you might want to retrieve the original value of the field, the value the user wanted to place in the field, and the value currently in the database. Confused? Well, ADO can't automatically handle the conflicts the way you want. It's up to you to tell it how to do that.

Conflict Management

No, this is not another one of those interpersonal effectiveness classes that a lot of us were forced to attend in the 1970s. These conflicts are the ones caused when ADO can't finish the update you asked it to perform. When you use the UpdateBatch method, the ADO client cursor engine executes a series of individual action queries to update the database according to the changes made to the Recordset. These action queries have WHERE clauses to locate the row to modify. The information in the WHERE clauses can also be used to ensure that changes made by other users are not automatically overwritten.

Controlling your updates with the Update Criteria property

ADO allows you to control the way the client engine creates the queries to update your back-end database with the Update Criteria property. Ah, excuse me? Isn't that a typo? How can a property have an embedded space? Well, as you'll soon discover, using this property is not very straightforward.

When ADO's client cursor engine performs updates, it creates action queries like this one:

```
UPDATE MyTable SET SomeField = 'SomeValue' WHERE IDField = n
```

The Update Criteria property allows you to control how ADO creates the WHERE clauses in the query. For example, you might want to take one of the following actions:

- Use only the primary key columns in the WHERE clause and force your changes through, regardless of whether or not the information in that row has changed since you first retrieved it.

- Use all the fields in the Recordset in the WHERE clause to make sure that if any of the information in the row has changed since you retrieved it that your update fails (and ADO marks this attempt as a conflict).

- Use only the fields you're modifying in the WHERE clause if you're concerned only about the fields you'll update in your query.

- Base the query on a timestamp field.

OK, you want to use the Update Criteria property, but you can't find it in the Object Browser. So, where is it? I don't see it as an available property. In fact, it's not. The Update Criteria property is an entry in the Recordset's Properties collection—but only *after* you set the CursorLocation property to adUseClient. That's because only the client cursor library supports batch updates. Makes sense?

Now it's there but it's read-only! Yes, once you open the Recordset, this property is marked read-only, so you have to set the property *before* you open the Recordset. Here's some code that sets the Update Criteria property:

```
With rsUpdate
    .CursorLocation = adUseClient
    .Properties("Update Criteria") = adCriteriaKey
    .Open Source:=strSQL, ActiveConnection:=cnTest, _
        CursorType:=adOpenStatic, _
        LockType:=adLockBatchOptimistic
End With
```

Table 33-1 lists the valid Update Criteria values.

Table 33-1
Update Criteria Values

Constant	Purpose
adCriteriaKey	Base the WHERE clause on the primary key
adCriteriaAllCols	Test all columns to see whether values have changed
adCriteriaUpdCols (Default)	Test just the columns specifically updated
adCriteriaTimeStamp	Test based on a TIMESTAMP column

ADO determines whether or not the action query succeeded by asking how many rows were affected by the action query. Affecting one row implies success. If more than one row is affected, however, you probably have a primary key problem. Affecting zero rows implies that the contents of the row have changed and one of the WHERE clauses prevented the update from occurring. ADO considers this last case to be a conflict.

Five types of conflicts can arise from attempting to perform the batch update:

- Modify a field that has since been modified
- Modify a field where another field in that row has since been modified
- Modify a row that has since been deleted
- Delete a row that has since been modified
- Delete a row that has since been deleted

Depending on your choice of value for the Update Criteria property, certain types of conflicts might not occur. For example, if you use the default value of adCriteriaUpdCols, the second and fourth scenarios will succeed without causing a conflict.

Causing Conflicts

If you're designing an application that uses batch updating, you should have a good idea about what possible conflicts can and should occur. The best way to be sure that your code handles the conflicts correctly is to test your code by causing the conflicts you expect. You can do this by changing the data in another instance of your application, in the Data View window, or even in the same application you're building.

I prefer to create a separate application that creates and populates the table on the server, retrieves the Recordset, ensures conflicts by executing a number of action queries on the connection, attempts to update the Recordset (causing the conflicts), and then reports the conflicts. This way, I know what my code should be doing. I know exactly which updates should succeed and which should be marked as conflicts. I know how my code should interpret the conflicts and how I want it to handle them. Once my code handles the conflicts the way I want it to, I use that code in my real application. Before deploying an application that needs to handle batch conflicts, you should cause the types of conflicts you expect to occur in case these values have changed or don't apply to the database you've chosen.

Recognizing Conflicts

Once you have determined which types of conflicts you expect and have written code to cause those conflicts, you need to understand how to figure out which attempted updates caused conflicts and understand why those conflicts occurred.

When you call UpdateBatch, ADO 2.0 behaves in a slightly different way than previous versions did when conflicts occurred. In ADO 2.0, if conflicts occur, ADO raises an error when UpdateBatch is called. Currently, this error is the rather generic "Errors occurred" error message. I check for an error on the next line, and if one exists, I assume that there were conflicts.

Setting the Recordset object's filter to adFilterConflictingRecords lets you view the rows that didn't update because of conflicts. If you want to make sure the error was due to conflicts, you could use this filter and then check the RecordCount property to make sure it's positive. If it's zero, the error wasn't caused by UpdateBatch conflicts.

For each conflicting row, the row's Status property contains information about what type of change was made to the row in the Recordset object:

- Failed modifications result in a Status of 2050 (adRecConcurrencyViolation + adRecModified)

- Failed deletions have a Status of 2052 (adRecConcurrencyViolation + adRecDeleted)

- An insertion that fails because of a primary key constraint returned a Status of 131073 (adRecSchemaViolation + adRecNew)

NOTE Keep in mind that I found these results at the time of the March 1998 PreRelease against SQL Server 6.5 with the SQL Server ODBC driver and the SQL Server OLE DB provider—hopefully your results won't vary. And here's another important Beta note: previous versions of ADO, including Beta drops of ADO 2.0, marked deleted rows with a Status of adRecDBDeleted rather than adRecDeleted.

Resync Method

To determine what type of modification ADO wanted to perform on the row (update, delete, or insert), you can start with the Status property—but you have more work to do. You also need to determine *why* that attempted modification resulted in a conflict. The Recordset object has a Resync method that retrieves the latest information for that row based on its primary key value for that row.

The Resync method has two optional parameters:

- AffectRecords controls which rows you want to resynchronize: just the current row (adAffectCurrent), all rows currently visible (adAffectGroup), or all rows in the Recordset (adAffectAllChapters, the default). Poor use of this method could cause significant performance problems. (Did you want information only on a particular conflict or on all 10,000 rows you updated?)

- ResyncValues controls where the information on the row's current state in the database is stored. ADO can place this information in the Field object's Value property or its UnderlyingValue property. The default (adResyncAllValues) behavior places this information in the Value property, overwriting any changes you had previously made to this row. If you need to examine the original value in the field, the value you tried to place in the database, and the value that currently resides in the database, you should make sure you use adResyncUnderlyingValues as the value for this parameter.

TIP If the row has been deleted from the database, you'll receive error number -2147217885—"A given HROW referred to a hard- or soft-deleted row" when you try to check the value of a field after calling Resync. If there's a chance that the row might have been deleted, it is very important that you test for this case.

Once you've called the Resync method, subsequent attempts to update that row use the newly retrieved information about the current state of the row in the WHERE clauses of the action query when calling UpdateBatch. However, this doesn't mean that the subsequent call to UpdateBatch won't encounter conflicts. It is possible that between the call to Resync and the call to Update-Batch, someone *else* might change that data. If that occurs, conflicts will occur and you need to go directly to jail without passing Go.

Transactions and Conflicts

If you wrap your batch updates in a transaction, you can undo all your changes by aborting the transaction. Another major benefit to performing batch updates in a transaction is that it simplifies the process of resolving conflicts. You can be sure that the data in the database won't change between when you call Resync and when you handle the conflict.

Working with Page-Based Data

Anyone who knows me and my writing very well knows that I don't approve, endorse, or recommend putting Binary Large Object (BLOB) data in a SQL Server database. I've explained the reasons for my bias earlier in the book (Chapter 25), so I won't bore you with the details here. However, I realize that you should know how to use BLOBs so that in the event that someone holds your kids hostage, you'll be able to get the job done quickly. I include a sample application that works out all of the code details on the CD.

BLOB data types include SQL server TEXT and IMAGE data types. Although some refer to TEXT data types as Character Large Object (CLOB) data types, I'll refer to this class of data simply as "BLOBs." Sometimes, this data can fit into memory. In most cases, however, BLOB data is so huge that it can't be retrieved in a single operation or fit into memory at all. Fortunately, if the BLOB data can all fit into memory, you can use the Value property of the Field object to retrieve or write all the data in one operation. If this is the case, you got off lucky and you get to go home early. If the long data is too big to fit into memory, however, the data must be retrieved or written in *chunks*—go back three squares.

No, even though you might feel like spewing chunks when you find out how "challenged" this technique is, the "chunks" I'm talking about here aren't some sort of gelatinous stomach contents. Chunks are simply variable-length blocks of data that you send to and from SQL Server to break up monstrously large BLOB (or CLOB) data fields. Because each chunk operation requires a round-trip to the server, I'm in favor of making these chunks fairly large—say, 32 KB or so. Using chunks this size eliminates about 31 extra round-trips to SQL Server when compared to using 1-KB chunks, as some examples suggest. It also sidesteps the 64-KB barriers you might experience with Visual Basic. Of course, if your BLOB is smaller than about 64 KB, it might be (far) easier just to work with the Value property.

You can manipulate the long data in chunks in two ways: through the Field object and through the Parameter object. Both these objects expose the AppendChunk method to write BLOB data, and the Field object exposes the GetChunk method to read BLOB data.

The Field object allows you to write and read BLOB data through the Recordset object. The AppendChunk method of the Field object appends data at the end of the current data when the query has already been executed. The GetChunk method reads the data in chunks.

The Parameter object handles BLOB data in a similar way. There is no GetChunk method for the Parameter object, and there is no Recordset object when you're dealing with BLOB data at run time. With the Parameter object, BLOB data is bound at run time and executed with the Command object. This means you can (try to) pass BLOB data as parameters to procedures.

The OLE DB provider for ODBC imposes some restrictions when accessing BLOB data. (We talked about these restrictions when we discussed the RDO chunk methods in Chapter 25.) For example, if you don't use a server-side cursor, all the BLOB columns must be to the right of all non-BLOB columns. If you have multiple long columns, you must access the BLOB columns in order (from left to right).

When a BLOB column is included in a query result set, ADO has to make a couple of decisions about how and when to fetch it. If the column data is too large, your client's system will slow to a crawl if ADO brings over every BLOB field in every row as you navigate through the result set. However, most interfaces defer accessing the BLOB data until you actually reference the specific field. Then and only then does ADO submit a separate fetch to retrieve the BLOB information. This saves lots of time and network capacity. But it also means that if you need to build a cursor and disconnect from the server, the rows had better be fully populated (including the BLOB columns) before you disconnect.

The following example shows reading and writing data using the AppendChunk and GetChunk methods. To keep from screwing up an existing table, let's create one of our own to test with:

```
DROP TABLE myBLOB
go
CREATE TABLE myBLOB( id int unique, info text)
go
INSERT INTO myBLOB values(1, 'test')
go
```

I've included this program on the CD with a routine that creates the table and adds a single row built from the Cover1.BMP file. The ADO code is:

```
Dim Cn As New Connection
Dim rsRead As New Recordset
Dim rsWrite As New Recordset
Dim strChunk As String
Dim Offset As Long
```

(continued)

```
Dim Totalsize As Long
Dim Remainder As Long
Dim Chunks As Long
Const ChunkSize As Long = 8192
Const TempFile As String = "C:\tempfile.tmp"

Private Sub Form_Load()
Cn.Open "biblio"     ' Assumes a DSN setup to point to biblio (any) db.
End Sub

Private Sub MakeTableButton_Click()
On Error GoTo MtEh
Cn.Execute "Drop table Myblob"
Cn.Execute "Create table Myblob (id int unique, info TEXT)"
FileCopy "c:\Cover1.bmp", TempFile
WriteButton_Click
quitMT:
On Error GoTo 0
Exit Sub
MtEh:
    ' The table does not exist
    If Err = -2147217865 Then Resume Next
    MsgBox "Could not create table"
    Resume quitMT
End Sub

Private Sub ReadButton_Click()
Image1.Picture = Nothing
Open TempFile For Binary Access Write As #1
rsRead.CursorType = adOpenStatic
rsRead.Open "SELECT * FROM Myblob", Cn
Totalsize = rsRead("info").ActualSize
Chunks = Totalsize \ ChunkSize       ' Integer divide
Remainder = Totalsize Mod ChunkSize
strChunk = rsRead("info").GetChunk(Remainder)
Put #1, , strChunk
Offset = Remainder
Do While Offset < Totalsize
    strChunk = rsRead("info").GetChunk(ChunkSize)
    Offset = Offset + ChunkSize
    Put #1, , strChunk
Loop
rsRead.Close
Close #1
Image1.Picture = LoadPicture(TempFile)
End Sub

Private Sub WriteButton_Click()
Dim t() As Byte
Open TempFile For Binary Access Read As #1
rsWrite.CursorType = adOpenKeyset
rsWrite.LockType = adLockOptimistic
```

```
rsWrite.Open "SELECT * FROM MyBlob", Cn
If rsWrite.EOF Then rsWrite.AddNew
Totalsize = FileLen(TempFile)
Chunks = Totalsize \ ChunkSize
Remainder = Totalsize Mod ChunkSize
ReDim t(Remainder)
Get #1, , t()
Offset = Remainder
rsWrite("info").AppendChunk t()
ReDim t(ChunkSize)
Do While Offset < Totalsize
    Get #1, , t()
    Offset = Offset + ChunkSize
    rsWrite("info").AppendChunk t()
Loop
rsWrite.Update
rsWrite.Close
Close #1
End Sub
```

The example is shown in three parts: the procedure that creates the working table, the procedure that writes the file to the database using Append-Chunk, and the procedure that opens an ADO Recordset against the table and uses GetChunk to read in the bits from the TEXT column. Yes, I used a TEXT type column here because when I tried the exact same application with an IMAGE data type, ADO failed to record the information correctly. And yes, I submitted a bug on this.

Notice that both the AppendChunk and GetChunk procedures start from the size of the BLOB as returned by the ActualSize property. Next, the code computes the number of chunks to process and the size of any remainder. I usually deal with the remainder first (using AppendChunk and GetChunk) and then simply loop on the remaining chunks. In this case, I had considerable difficulty getting Visual Basic to handle the chunk data correctly. Visual Basic and ADO insisted on addressing the data in 16-bits/character (DBCS) form, which doubles the size of the temporary file. After the rsRead and rsWrite Recordsets are created, the size of the BLOB data is stored in the *Totalsize* variable. In the WHILE loop, BLOB data is inserted in chunks of 8192 (8 KB) bytes. Yes, this could be larger, but I had problems as the chunk size approached 16 KB. After the insertion is completed, the Update method is used to commit the data. Yes, you can use adLockBatchOptimistic and UpdateBatch to defer the actual operations until you are ready.

Unfortunately, this kind of test masks a whole set of issues. I tried to create a more sophisticated test for one of my presentations that showed the real differences between file-based and chunk-based BLOB I/O. This code brought out a multitude of issues (which we'll go over here) that have colored my opinion about handling BLOBs.

To make things clearer, let me paste in an excerpt from the Blob Comparison demo application that should clear up some of the thornier issues. First, here are the declares that apply to the chunk operations:

```
Dim Fl As Long
Const ChunkSize As Long = 8196
Const TempFile As String = "PicTemp.bmp"
```

Next, let's examine the routine to find a book by a selected filename. We pick the filename out of a ComboBox control filled in the Biblio_Connect-Complete event procedure. Notice the absence of any chunk code here. That's right folks, no bitslicing, dicing, or BLOB-O-MATIC code required.

```
Private Sub FindBookByFile_Click()
ButtonFrame.Enabled = False
STime = Timer
Status1.Status = StatusY
de.dbo_GetCoverFileNameByTitle TitleWanted
Set rs = de.rsdbo_GetCoverFilenameByTitle
If rs.State = adStateClosed Then Status1.Status = StatusY: Beep
CPicture(1) = LoadPicture(rs!FileName)
ShowTime1 = Format((Timer - STime), "####.##")
DoEvents
rs.Close
Status1.Status = StatusG
ButtonFrame.Enabled = True
End Sub
```

OK, now let's examine the routine to find a book by a selected ISBN. This routine calls a Data Environment Command to fetch the cover BLOB from the database. Here's where some of the magic is. After a long struggle, I found out that you *must* return the BLOB as the last column of your result set and you must include a key in the query so that ADO can refetch the data. I also passed back the binary length of the cover BLOB by including a DATALENGTH expression in my fetch procedure.

```
Private Sub FindBookWithBLOB_Click()
Dim sTemp As String, Fl As Long
Dim Chunks As Long, Fragment As Long, Chunk() As Byte
Dim SQL As String

On Error GoTo GetBlobEH
ButtonFrame.Enabled = False
STime = Timer
Status1.Status = StatusY
```

```
de.GetCoverByISBN (ISBNList(TitleWanted.ListIndex))
Set rs = de.rsGetCoverByISBN
If rs.State = adStateClosed Then
    Status1.Status = StatusY
    Beep
    Exit Sub
End If
```

Once we have the Recordset row containing the BLOB column, we can use the length provided by SQL Server to compute how to chop up the image. We have to do this binary data chopping because of limitations of the available memory, packet size, and other constraints. We save the image to a binary file so that the Picture control can read it in later. We use a Byte array to store the data as it arrives to sidestep the problem of having to work with DBCS (16-bit) character strings. When we're done, we have a binary file identical to the one we used to create the database image in the first place.

```
Fl = rs("CoverLength")
Chunks = Fl \ ChunkSize
Fragment = Fl Mod ChunkSize
ReDim Chunk(Fragment)
Chunk() = rs("Cover").GetChunk(Fragment)
Open TempFile For Binary Access Write As #1
Put #1, , Chunk()
ReDim Chunk(ChunkSize)
    For i = 1 To Chunks
    Chunk() = rs("cover").GetChunk(ChunkSize)
    Put #1, , Chunk()
Next i
Close #1
ReDim Chunk(0)


    . . .
```

If you run this sample application from the CD, you'll discover how much faster the bitmaps can be read from files. In this case, the files are stored locally on your local hard disk. Yes, you'll need to copy the Cover Pictures directory over to your C drive—or better yet, change the sample to point to your CD. However, if you do this, you'll have to change the path arriving from the database to reference your CD drive instead of C:\Cover Pictures.

TIP In SQL Server 7.0, you can store up to 8000 bytes (no, not 8 KB) in a VarChar or VarBinary column. This might preclude the need to store BLOB data in TEXT or IMAGE columns.

Handling Special Cases

In this section, I've included some odd cases that don't really fit anywhere else. These are mostly tips and tricks that other writers have passed on to me or that I've gleaned from the news groups.

Processing PRINT and RAISERROR

When I first started working with ADO 2.0 many months ago, I encountered a number of issues with TSQL PRINT statements. After having completed a few sample applications, I was pleasantly surprised to find that most of these issues had been resolved. Getting at the PRINT message text is now almost as easy as it was in VBSQL—and there it was fall-off-a-slippery-log easy. You do have to set up the ADO Connection object using the WithEvents syntax to enable the InfoMessage event, but after that, it's pretty intuitive. Check out the following code. Notice that I declare the ADO Connection variable With-Events, and simply trap the InfoMessage event. Here I dump the Connection.Errors collection. The first TSQL PRINT statement returned from the procedure is addressed by pError, but all the PRINT statements (including the first) are visible in the Errors collection:

```
Dim WithEvents cn As Connection

Private Sub Form_Load()
Dim cmd As New Command
Dim rs As New Recordset
Set cn = New Connection
cn.Open "dsn=pubs"
cmd.CommandText = "PrintSample"
cmd.CommandType = adCmdStoredProc
cmd.Parameters.Refresh
cmd.ActiveConnection = cn
cn.PrintSample
End Sub

Private Sub cn_InfoMessage(ByVal pError As ADODB.Error, _
    adStatus As ADODB.EventStatusEnum, _
    ByVal pConnection As ADODB.Connection)
Dim er As ADODB.Error
Debug.Print "pError:"; pError.Description
For Each er In cn.Errors
    Debug.Print "cn.Error:"; er.Description
Next
cn.Errors.Clear
End Sub
```

Here is the code for the PrintSample stored procedure:

```
Create Procedure PrintSample
as
declare @cnt integer
declare @msg varchar(50)
```

```
Select @cnt = 5
While @cnt > 0
begin
    select @msg = 'This is test ' + convert(char(1), @cnt)
    print @msg
    select @cnt = @cnt - 1
end
```

The PRINT messages themselves are not exactly as "sent" by the stored procedure. Each has the traditional [Microsoft][ODBC SQL Server Driver][SQL Server] prefix tacked on to make your life tougher. I added a little prefix myself so that I could see where the messages were coming from. Here's what was printed in the Immediate debug window:

```
pError:[Microsoft][ODBC SQL Server Driver][SQL Server]This is a test 5
cn.Error:[Microsoft][ODBC SQL Server Driver][SQL Server]This is a test 5
cn.Error:[Microsoft][ODBC SQL Server Driver][SQL Server]This is a test 4
cn.Error:[Microsoft][ODBC SQL Server Driver][SQL Server]This is a test 3
cn.Error:[Microsoft][ODBC SQL Server Driver][SQL Server]This is a test 2
cn.Error:[Microsoft][ODBC SQL Server Driver][SQL Server]This is a test 1
```

OK, that was easy. But what about the other kind of PRINT statement, the RAISERROR statement? How do RAISERROR statements appear? Do they derail the procedure being executed? When we wrote VBSQL programs, we used these statements for a variety of purposes. For example, we used PRINT statements to produce simple reports or to trace our progress through a complex procedure. We also used RAISERROR statements to signal the state of things going on within the procedure. For example, we could pass out a message with a numeric code to tell the application that we had reached a chosen stocking level. Let's try a procedure like that and see what happens with ADO.

We'll start our test with a stored procedure to illustrate how ADO manages the errors and messages. In this case, we mix two row-returning result sets with a set of logic that tests an integer value and issues one or more RAISERROR statements based on this value. Notice how TSQL supports the C-language PRINTF syntax to insert values into the string. This approach is a lot more efficient and more flexible than trying to concatenate strings passed to a PRINT or RAISERROR statement.

```
Create Procedure TestRaisError AS
declare @rc int
    select * from authors
    Select @rc=count(*) from authors
    if @rc >= 1 and @rc < 5
RAISERROR('Count=%d. between 1 and 4',1,2, @rc) WITH SETERROR
    if @rc > 4 and @rc < 9
    select * from Publishers
    Select @rc=count(*) from publishers
    if @rc >= 1 and @rc < 5
RAISERROR('Count=%d. between 1 and 4',1,2, @rc) WITH SETERROR
    if @rc > 4 and @rc < 9
    ...
RAISERROR('Count=%d. between 1 and 50',1,2, @rc) WITH SETERROR
return (@rc)
```

I used the code we just discussed for the PRINT statements for this test with a few minor modifications to deal with the new stored procedure and the multiple result sets. I expected the RAISERROR messages to appear in the Errors collection and let me know they arrived through the InfoMessage event. However, they didn't appear at all. I raised this issue with the ADO team—and it should be fixed eventually. It seems we'll have to wait for yet another version before this is working, however.

```
Dim WithEvents cn As Connection
Dim cmd As New Command
Dim rs As New Recordset

Private Sub Command1_Click()
cn.TestRaisError rs
RAutoGrid1.ShowADOData rs
MsgBox "Authors"              ' Pause between result sets
Set rs = rs.NextRecordset    ' Get the second result set
RAutoGrid1.ShowADOData rs
End Sub

Private Sub Form_Load()
Set cn = New Connection
cn.Open "dsn=pubs"
cmd.CommandText = "TestRaisError"
cmd.CommandType = adCmdStoredProc
cmd.ActiveConnection = cn
End Sub

Private Sub cn_InfoMessage(ByVal pError As ADODB.Error, _
    adStatus As ADODB.EventStatusEnum, _
    ByVal pConnection As ADODB.Connection)
Dim er As ADODB.Error
Debug.Print "pError:"; pError.Description
For Each er In cn.Errors
    Debug.Print "cn.Error:"; er.Description
Next
cn.Errors.Clear
End Sub
```

Handling COMPUTE Clauses

The next interesting challenge is how ADO handles the unusual structures returned by the TSQL COMPUTE clauses. You use a COMPUTE clause with row aggregate functions (SUM, AVG, MIN, MAX, and COUNT) in a SELECT statement to generate control-break summary values. The summary values appear as additional rows in the query results, allowing you to see detail rows and summary rows within one result set. You can calculate summary values for subgroups, and you can calculate more than one aggregate function for the same group. You can also use the COMPUTE keyword without BY to generate grand totals, grand counts, and so on. The ORDER BY clause is optional only if you use the COMPUTE keyword without BY.

The COMPUTE BY clause variation indicates that values for row aggregate functions are to be calculated for subgroups. Whenever the value of BY changes, row aggregate function values are generated. If you use BY, you must also use an ORDER BY clause. Listing more than one item after BY breaks a group into subgroups and applies a function at each level of grouping. The columns listed after the COMPUTE clause must be identical to or a subset of those listed after the ORDER BY clause, and they must be in the same left-to-right order, start with the same expression, and not skip any expression.

For example, if the ORDER BY clause is

```
ORDER BY a, b, c
```

the COMPUTE clause can be any (or all) of these:

```
COMPUTE BY a, b, c
COMPUTE BY a, b
COMPUTE BY a
```

For more information on how to code and build COMPUTE clauses into your TSQL procedures, consult SQL Server Books Online.

Now that we understand the basic semantics of the COMPUTE statement, let's see what a typical call returns. Here's a procedure right out of the old Transact-SQL User's Guide that used to ship with SQL Server before they went to online docs:

```
Create Procedure TestCompute @TypeWanted VarChar(20) = '%Cook'
As
Select type, price from titles where type like @TypeWanted
Order by type, price
COMPUTE sum(price) by type
return (@@rowcount)
```

Seems simple enough. In VBSQL, you have to jump through quite a few hoops to get this to return anything intelligent—but you can do it. If you run this query in Visual Database Tools or ISQL/w, you'll get output that looks something like this:

```
Running Stored Procedure dbo.TestCompute ( @TypeWanted = %Cook ).
type          price
-----------   ---------------------
mod_cook      2.9900
mod_cook      19.9900
(2 row(s) affected)

sum
--------------------
22.9800
(1 row(s) affected)

type          price
-----------   ---------------------
trad_cook     11.9500
```

(continued)

```
trad_cook      14.9900
trad_cook      20.9500
(3 row(s) affected)

sum
--------------------
47.8900
(1 row(s) affected)
Finished running dbo.TestCompute.
RETURN_VALUE = 7
```

As you can see, this procedure can be very handy when you need some roll-up totals. ADO deals with COMPUTE clauses by passing back *n* sets of result sets—one for each group SQL Server found after running the query. This means that you don't have to do anything special—except deal with all the result sets generated. Here's the code that shows how to provide some roll-up totals:

```
Dim WithEvents cn As Connection
Dim cmd As New Command
Dim rs As New Recordset

Private Sub cn_InfoMessage(ByVal pError As ADODB.Error, _
    adStatus As ADODB.EventStatusEnum, _
    ByVal pConnection As ADODB.Connection)
Dim er As ADODB.Error
Debug.Print "pError:"; pError.Description
For Each er In cn.Errors
    Debug.Print "cn.Error:"; er.Description
Next
cn.Errors.Clear
End Sub

Private Sub Command1_Click()
Dim fld As Field
Form1.Cls
' This is an another way to pass the parameter
cmd("@TypeWanted") = Text1.Text
cn.TestCompute Text1.Text, rs
Do
    For Each fld In rs.Fields
        Print fld.Name,
    Next fld
    Print
    Do Until rs.EOF
        For Each fld In rs.Fields
            Print fld.Value,
        Next fld
        Print
        rs.MoveNext
    Loop
    Set rs = rs.NextRecordset
Loop Until rs.State = adStateClosed
End Sub
```

```
Private Sub Form_Load()
Set cn = New Connection
cn.Open "dsn=pubs"
cmd.CommandText = "TestCompute"
cmd.CommandType = adCmdStoredProc
cmd.Parameters.Refresh
cmd.ActiveConnection = cn
End Sub
```

I left in the InfoMessage event because it returns a "No more results" message when the last of the Recordset objects is returned. This produces output very similar to that from Visual Database Tools or ISQL/w—but without the horizontal lines. Still want the lines? Add them in yourself.

Handling NULLs

One of the problems that seems to be coming up a lot is how to handle NULLs. Apparently, the new ANSI SQL-92 behavior won't allow a statement like this:

```
SELECT * FROM Employee WHERE age = null
```

ISQL takes this statement because of the TSQL extension that supports it. However, because we have to use ODBC (or OLE DB and ADO) to get to SQL Server, we have to behave ourselves. To solve this little dilemma, we must use this statement instead:

```
SELECT * FROM Employee WHERE age IS NULL
```

TIP Want to compute the size of a Recordset? To tell how much data is being transferred over the wire when you send back a disjoint Recordset, save it to disk using the Save method and check out the size.

Debugging with Showplan

I had someone ask me how to get the messages generated when you turn on the Showplan option. No, if you aren't familiar with this option, it has nothing to do with the nineteenth-century Polish composer; it is a way to see the steps SQL Server is taking to run your query. Ken Nilsen (one of the original inventors of RDO) tipped me off that these messages are returned to RDO in the rdoErrors collection, and he sent me some code to prove it. I tested this code and left a version of it on the CD. However, I tried the same thing in ADO, and it seems to work very differently. Although this difference might be a bug, it might also be a feature. In the ADO program, it seems that the SET SHOW-PLAN ON statement doesn't "stick," which means that you have to submit it *with* the statement to be examined, as shown here:

```
Set Showplan on  Select * from Authors
```

If you have to take this course, make sure you submit a NextRecordset method to pick off the result set rows from the second result set. If you turn on the events for your connection, the Errors collection will contain the Showplan messages. These messages can be very informative when you're trying to figure out why the heck SQL Server is taking so long to run your query. The ADO version of this program is also on the CD.

Building the Recordset and the DataReport with the Data Environment

Visual Basic 6.0 allows you to create simple hierarchical data reports. For example, as a simple scenario, you can create a report listing the orders for each customer. In this section, I'll show you how to bind a DataReport to an ADO Recordset. The simplest and fastest way to build the hierarchical Recordset and the DataReport, which will display its contents, is to use the Data Environment designer.

Building the hierarchical Recordset with the Data Environment

Let's use the Data Environment to connect to our database and build our hierarchical query. For this lesson, we'll use the standard Northwind database. You might need to change the connect string information slightly to connect to your copy of the database.

First create a hierarchical Recordset where the parent Recordset contains information from the Customers table and the child Recordset is the set of orders for that customer. To create the child Recordset, create a query on the Orders table and set the relation to be based on the CustomerID field.

Then create a report that has one grouping. Drag the desired fields from the customer query into the header for the group. Drag the desired fields from the orders query into the details section. You might want to set the Data Environment so that it doesn't automatically include a label that acts as a caption for the field you're including.

Binding the DataReport to the DataEnvironment Command object

The simplest way to ensure that the results of the DataEnvironment Command object's queries appear in the DataReport is to bind the DataReport to the DataEnvironment Command object at design time. This involves setting the DataSource property of the DataReport to the DataEnvironment Command object you've created.

You also need to set the DataMember property of the DataReport to the query that refers to the top level of the report. In this case, the customer information is the top level of the report, so you should set the DataMember property of the DataReport to the name of the customer query in the Data Environment. Once you set the DataSource property of the DataReport object at design time, you should see that selecting the DataMember property makes a drop-down combo box available that lists the possible choices for the property.

Now the only task left is to show the report. You can display the report in one of two ways:

- Set the project's Startup Object in the Project Properties sheet to the report.

- Call the Show method on the Report object.

Binding the DataReport object to the DataEnvironment Command object at run time

To bind the DataReport object to the DataEnvironment Command object at run time, you do the same thing that we did in the preceding section programmatically:

```
With rptCustomerOrders
    Set .DataSource = deCustomerOrders
    .DataMember = "Customers"
    .Show
End With
```

Binding the DataReport object to a Recordset object

In some cases, the data that the customer wants to display in a report won't come directly from a Data Environment. The Recordset might come from a Data Environment in a middle-tier business object, or perhaps from an ADO Recordset created from code. In this case, the DataMember property of the DataReport object becomes an issue.

DataMember is a very helpful property for a Data Environment because the Data Environment can contain many Recordsets, and this property allows us to specify which Recordset we want. When setting the DataReport object's DataSource property to a particular Recordset rather than to a DataEnvironment object at run time, the DataMember property for the DataReport object is irrelevant. Although the DataMember property is still important for the fields in the DataReport, you should set the DataMember property for the report itself to an empty string.

Once you've set the DataSource property of the DataReport object and cleared its DataMember property, you still have one more counterintuitive obstacle to overcome. The DataMember property of each of the bound controls on the DataReport was set automatically when the control was placed onto the DataReport when you dragged it from the Data Environment. This information is extremely helpful for the child Recordset objects. The DataReport needs to know that the OrderID field is in the orders Recordset, which is a child Recordset contained within the customers Recordset.

When binding directly to a Recordset, you must also clear the DataMember property for the bound controls for the top-level Recordset. You do this in a way similar to how you clear the DataMember property on the DataReport itself. You can do it at design time or at run time—if you know the name of the section on the report that contains those controls.

Below is a code example of binding a DataReport directly to a Recordset, clearing the DataMember property for both the report itself and for the top-level bound controls. The TypeOf function allows us to determine whether or not the control has a DataMember property to clear—in the case of RptTextBox or RptFunction.

```
With rptCustomerOrders
    Set .DataSource = rsCustomerOrders
    .DataMember = ""
    With .Sections("Section2").Controls
        For intCtrl = 1 To .Count
            If TypeOf .Item(intCtrl) Is RptTextBox Or _
                TypeOf .Item(intCtrl) Is RptFunction Then
                .Item(intCtrl).DataMember = ""
            End If
        Next intCtrl
    End With
    .Show
End With
```

34

Migrating from RDO to ADO

ADO from an RDO Perspective

To ADO or Not to ADO

**Using RDO to Solve Basic
Data Access Problems**

**Using RDO to Access
More Complex Data**

**Using ADO to Solve Basic
Data Access Problems**

**Using ADO to Access
More Complex Data**

Conversion Tips and Techniques

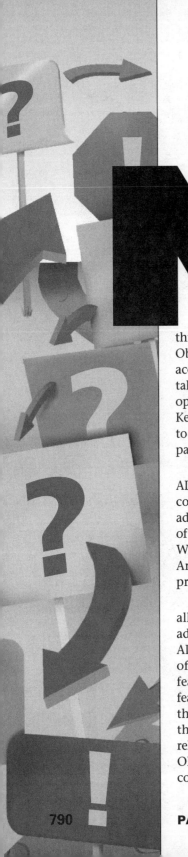

o consultant worth his or her salt will tell you to fix something that isn't broken. This chapter isn't about "fixing" existing data access applications that use Remote Data Objects (RDO)—not as long as they are doing the job they were designed to do. On the surface, this chapter is about how to migrate an application from RDO to ActiveX Data Objects (ADO). Actually, it's more about how to approach basic ADO data access problems from an RDO point of view. To illustrate this perspective, we'll take a working RDO application that performs a number of basic data access operations and examine how these same operations are carried out using ADO. Keep in mind that even though ADO 2.0 has arrived, it still doesn't make sense to dump working applications in favor of this new technology—unless you get paid by the hour.

Yes, ADO does add a number of new choices for accessing data. Specifically, ADO is designed to better address the special needs of Internet and middle-tier component developers and those needing to access special types of data in addition to traditional relational sources, and in the process, permit the creation of faster, smaller (well, in some cases), and more efficient applications. Question: Will developers have to rewrite their RDO code now that ADO 2.0 is here? Answer: No—not unless ADO's expanded features offer real solutions to problems that RDO can't solve.

In this chapter, I'll also explain why Microsoft has chosen to create a new all-encompassing data access interface and how your applications can take advantage of its new features. Does ADO replace RDO? No, as I've said before, ADO is implemented *alongside* RDO and Data Access Objects (DAO)—both of these established data interfaces are still supported. Virtually all of RDO's features (except size and performance) are supported in ADO 2.0. Yes, some features were left behind to accommodate a more "generic" interface. Remember the adaptations we had to make when we moved from VBSQL to ODBC? In that case, we moved from a SQL Server–specific interface to a more generic relational interface. As we migrate to ADO, we're moving from that fairly generic ODBC interface to a more generic OLE DB platform. Will RDO 2.0 code easily convert to ADO 2.0? Well, while the problems RDO solves can also be solved in ADO, ADO approaches these problems in a somewhat different way. Functionally, you should be able to convert—but it won't simply be a matter of running a wizard. You'll have to rethink some of your approaches—to connecting, security management, query processing, and result set processing.

ADO from an RDO Perspective

As I've mentioned in earlier chapters, the ADO object model is flatter (has fewer objects) but has more properties, methods, and method arguments than RDO. For example, ADO has no equivalent to the rdoEngine or rdoEnvironment object. (These objects expose the ODBC Driver Manager and *hEnv* interfaces.) This means that the underlying ODBC *hStmt* and *hEnv* handles are no longer available and that you can't create ODBC data sources from ADO—despite the fact that your interface might be through the OLE DB provider for ODBC. As we work through the rest of the ADO interface, we'll find other dissimilarities. Some of these differences are covered by new approaches to the problem (and are addressed), some were left behind for one good reason or another, and some have yet to be implemented.

TIP   Remember some years ago when I told you to stay away from the ODBC APIs? Remember when I said they would be tough to convert someday? Well, since you took my advice, I don't get to say "I told you so...." Or do I?

Remember that ADO also implements something new for developers using Microsoft Visual Basic. Sure, you're probably very familiar with variables containing values passed *into* a method as an argument (gazintas)—but ADO also supports methods that return values passed *back* to variables (gazoutas). For example, when you code a query as a method off of the Connection object, you pass the variable declared as a New Recordset to the method as its final argument. The Recordset that results from the method is returned into this variable.

To ADO or Not to ADO

The marketing people here at Microsoft (including myself) have been telling you that with the introduction of ADO, developers can create applications that perform all of the fundamental and advanced data access operations that all client/server and multitier applications require. This includes virtually all the features that RDO 2.0 supports. No, you won't have to dump your existing applications. Some of you are still working with DAO or RDO and this kind of change and the trauma it promises seems to be much ADO about nothing. You might be right.

While Visual Basic (and this guide) make it easy to run your existing Visual Basic applications in Visual Basic 6.0, it doesn't mean that the code you've been writing in RDO and DAO will automatically morph over to equivalent ADO code when the time comes to convert. However, it does mean that the problems you've solved with these older object models will also be solvable with ADO—and more. ADO implements a number of new data access strategies never before available to address your data access problems.

When deciding whether to migrate to ADO, you have to decide whether ADO's additional capabilities are enough to justify converting existing software. Another consideration is how your existing developers can leverage their existing RDO development skills. Although RDO will be available indefinitely, it's a good idea to consider ADO for applications currently under design.

Let's look at a few features that both ADO and RDO support to make it clear which parts of your design will remain unchanged and which parts will have to go under the knife. Both ADO 2.0 and RDO now support asynchronous operations and events. Although ADO supports many more events than RDO does, it uses similar code techniques to enable them. For example, polling to determine the completion state of ADO events is done differently because ADO exposes a State property whose bitmask indicates the running status of an operation. In addition, ADO also reports on the fetch status of an operation by firing a FetchProgress event periodically during the course of populating a cursor. (But I haven't seen this working so far.)

Both ADO and RDO support "queries as methods." Although this approach might execute slightly slower in ADO (because of "late" binding), these queries are far easier to code than traditional techniques and can dramatically reduce the number of lines of code you have to write, test, and support. This technique sets up each of the queries to be executed as a separate rdoQuery or ADO Command object—all of which are exposed on the rdoConnection or ADO Connection object they are (currently) assigned to. Yes, this approach has its advantages and disadvantages. For instance, you can't run a query as a method asynchronously. If you have to change the other default settings (such as CacheSize), you have to do so using indirect references through the ADO Connection object. Both ADO and RDO also support the use of a central results handler—at least for most operations. This is another feature that will eliminate a lot of duplicate code. Although this routine is more complex (it has to handle several different types of result sets), it is easier to maintain because all completed queries on the connection use it.

In the remainder of the chapter, you'll find out how to solve some basic data access problems by using RDO 2.0 and then by using equivalent ADO 2.0 code. Each of these "problems" addresses a SQL Server database—a variation of the *Biblio* database installed with Visual Basic 5.0 and 6.0.

Using RDO to Solve Basic Data Access Problems

In the RDO sections that follow, we'll walk through code used to build an application that uses RDO to access SQL Server. To set up this application, we'll build a form that has six command buttons to test each operation. We'll also reference a custom control used to dump result sets to a grid control. The source for this control and the sample applications is available on the CD.

This application illustrates executing parameter-based SELECT statements and stored procedures as well as multiple result set, OUTPUT parameter, and action queries. It also displays the query about to be executed and the SQL actually run in the TextBox at the bottom of the form. The parameter query draws one of its parameters from the TextBox containing "1947" on the form. Figure 34-1 shows a sample of this application in action.

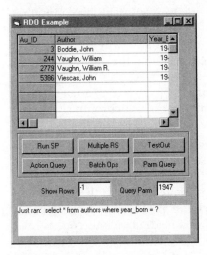

Figure 34-1 *Sample application that uses RDO to access SQL Server*

RDO: Coding Global Variables

The application manages its rdoConnection objects with two global variables. The second connection is used to manage the optimistic batch update example. We'll also build five separate rdoQuery objects to manage the application-generated queries. This technique illustrates the use of queries as methods on the rdoConnection object, but more important, it emphasizes that application-generated queries should be generated only once—not repeatedly throughout the application. The following code shows how the global variables are declared. Notice that the *Cn* variable is built to support events.

```
Option Explicit
Dim WithEvents Cn As rdoConnection
Dim CnB As New rdoConnection
Dim Rs As rdoResultset
Dim Qy As New rdoQuery, Qy1 As rdoQuery, Qy2 As rdoQuery, _
    Qy3 As rdoQuery, Qy4 As rdoQuery
Dim SQL As String
Dim i As Integer, j As Integer
Dim Changes As Integer
Dim bms() As Variant
Dim Batchflag As Boolean
Const ConnectString = "uid=;pwd=;driver={SQL Server};" & _
    "Server=betav1;Trusted_Connection=Yes;database=biblio;dsn=''"
```

This connect string constant accesses a specific SQL Server and permits ODBC to open a "DSN-less" connection. Notice that this is a typical ODBC connect string with all the standard arguments plus the new ODBC 3.*x* "Trusted_Connection=Yes" argument.

RDO: Establishing a Connection

As we've discussed before, all data sources require that you establish a connection to the information source you want to access. Getting a connection open requires a connect string containing the "who," "what," "where," and "how" information needed to identify the user, the server, and the default database. Note that a connection is *not* required by RDO to create an rdoQuery object but *is* required to initially create an rdoResultset object—which is *not* required in ADO. In this example, we'll open the connection asynchronously so that the Form_Load event handler can complete quickly and paint the form.

The following code establishes a connection specifying the type of cursor driver and login timeout. By default, RDO uses rdUseIfNeeded, which invokes server-side cursors on SQL Server—we must include code to override this type of cursor in our example. We also choose to generate an error if the user ID and password don't match. The second connection performs the client-batch updates. Notice that the connect string defined in the previous code is used in both connection.

```
Private Sub Form_Load()
Set Cn = New rdoConnection
On Error GoTo EH
With Cn
    .Connect = ConnectString
    .LoginTimeout = 5
    .CursorDriver = rdUseNone
    .EstablishConnection rdDriverNoPrompt, Options:=rdAsyncEnable
End With
With CnB
    .Connect = ConnectString
    .CursorDriver = rdUseClientBatch
    .EstablishConnection
End With
```

The following code handles any (well, most) errors that prevent the connection operation from starting. Other errors are handled by the Connect event, which fires when the connection operation is completed. This way, we can test to see whether the connection operation succeeded and enable any buttons that rely on an open connection.

```
exitfl:
Exit Sub
EH:
    Select Case Err
        Case 40002: MsgBox "Could not connect... " & Error
        Resume exitfl
    End Select
End Sub
```

RDO: When the Connection Operation Completes

The Connect event fires when the operation started by the EstablishConnection method completes—whether or not it succeeded. RDO returns a single Boolean flag to indicate success or failure. You have to dig into the rdoErrors collection to see which specific errors occurred. The following code shows the start of the Connect event handler.

```
Private Sub Cn_Connect(ByVal ErrorOccurred As Boolean)
If ErrorOccurred Then
    MsgBox "Could not open connection", vbCritical
    Unload Me
    End
Else
```

Once we know that the connection opened, we can set up each of the application-managed queries as shown in the code below. Yes, we must create each of these objects individually because RDO maintains them in the rdoQueries collection so that they can be exposed as methods on the rdoConnection object. For the more sophisticated stored procedure calls, we have to alter the rdoParameters collection to indicate direction—input, output, or return status. Once all the queries are set up, we enable the frame containing all the buttons on the loaded form. This prevents users from pressing buttons to run queries if the connection isn't established.

```
    ' Set up each of the queries to be executed as methods
    ' on the connection
    Set Qy1 = Cn.CreateQuery("TestOut", _
        "{? = Call TestOut (?,?)}")
    Qy1.rdoParameters(0).Direction = rdParamReturnValue
    Qy1.rdoParameters(1).Direction = rdParamInput
    Qy1.rdoParameters(2).Direction = rdParamOutput
    Set Qy2 = Cn.CreateQuery("AuthorsSP", _
        "{? = Call AuthorByYearBorn (?,?)}")
    Qy2.rdoParameters(0).Direction = rdParamReturnValue
    SQL = "Select * from Authors Where year_born is not null; " _
        & "Select * from Authors where year_born is null"
    Set Qy3 = Cn.CreateQuery("Multiple", SQL)
    Set Qy4 = Cn.CreateQuery("AuthorsByYearBorn", _
        " select * from authors where year_born = ?")
    RunOKFrame.Enabled = True
    Batchflag = False
End If
End Sub
```

RDO: Running a Basic Query

At this point, we're ready to run our first example query. The following code shows a parameter being passed to the AuthorByYearBorn query, which is subsequently executed. In this case, we simply refer to the RDO query as a method on the rdoConnection object. We pick up a parameter from a TextBox control on the form. This query returns an rdoResultset that can be referenced through the

LastQueryResults property, but we leave the task of displaying the result set to the common QueryComplete event handler. The QueryComplete event handler is fired whenever a query is finished.

```
Private Sub ParmQueryButton_Click()
Cn.AuthorByYearBorn (QueryParam.Text)
End Sub
```

RDO: Using the WillExecute Event

Before the query is executed, the WillExecute event fires. This gives us an opportunity to view or modify the command about to be executed. It also provides a very useful way to debug applications still under development. As shown in the following WillExecute event handler code, once we get an indication that we're about to execute a query, we disable the button frame to prevent more than one operation at a time. We'll reenable the frame once the query is done.

```
Private Sub cn_WillExecute(ByVal Query As RDO.rdoQuery, _
    Cancel As Boolean)
QuerySQL.Text = "About to execute: " & Query.SQL
QuerySQL.Refresh
RunOKFrame.Enabled = False
Screen.MousePointer = vbHourglass
End Sub
```

RDO: Managing the Result Sets

We use the QueryComplete event handler, as shown in the following code, to manage all result sets generated by the primary connection (Cn). Using this event handler reduces the amount of code we need in the application but makes the job of handling result sets more complex because we have to handle all possible types of result sets that our application generates. If an error occurs, we throw up a message box to tell the user:

```
Private Sub cn_QueryComplete(ByVal Query As RDO.rdoQuery, _
    ByVal ErrorOccurred As Boolean)
On Error GoTo QCEh
If ErrorOccurred Then
    MsgBox "Query failed... tried to run " & Query.SQL
Else
```

If the query works, however, we can capture the LastQueryResults property and save it in a global variable so the calling method's procedure can see it. Once we touch LastQueryResults, it can't be seen or touched again. The QueryComplete handler also has to deal with the possibility that the query returns more than one set of results. RDO's MoreResults property returns a Boolean if there are more result sets to manage. We stop between result sets to let the user examine the results one at a time.

```
    QuerySQL.Text = "Just ran:" & Query.SQL
    ' So the calling routine can see it too...
    Set Rs = Cn.LastQueryResults
    If Rs Is Nothing Then
```

```
        Else
            RAutoGrid1.ShowRDOData Rs
            ShowRows = Rs.RowCount
            Rs.Cancel
            i = Rs.MoreResults
            Do While i = True
                j = MsgBox("Ready to continue?", vbYesNo)
                If j = vbYes Then
                    RAutoGrid1.ShowRDOData Rs
                    ShowRows = Rs.RowCount
                    Rs.Cancel
                End If
                i = Rs.MoreResults
            Loop
        End If
End If
ExitQH:
RunOKFrame.Enabled = True
Screen.MousePointer = vbDefault
Exit Sub
QCEh:
    Debug.Print Err, Error$
    Resume ExitQH
End Sub
```

RDO: Displaying a Result Set in an MSFlexGrid

The following routine is the ShowRDOData method of a custom ActiveX control
used to display data from a result set in an MSFlexGrid. The code sets up the
grid based on the rdoColumns property titles and initializes the grid, making
it ready for the data. Notice the use of the OrdinalPosition property to index
the result set rdoColumns property.

```
Public Function ShowRDOData(Rsl As rdoResultset) As Variant
Dim cl As rdoColumn
Dim MaxL As Integer
Dim Rows As Variant
On Error GoTo ShowDataEH
    FGrid1.Rows = 51
    FGrid1.Cols = Rsl.rdoColumns.Count
    FGrid1.Row = 0
    For Each cl In Rsl.rdoColumns
        FGrid1.Col = cl.OrdinalPosition - 1
        FGrid1 = cl.Name
        If Rsl.rdoColumns(cl.OrdinalPosition - 1).ChunkRequired _
            Then
            MaxL = 1
        Else
            MaxL = Rsl.rdoColumns(cl.OrdinalPosition - 1).Size _
                + 4

        End If
```

(continued)

```
            If MaxL > 20 Then MaxL = 20
            FGrid1.ColWidth(FGrid1.Col) = _
                TextWidth(String(MaxL, "N"))
        Next cl
        GridSetup = True

        FGrid1.Rows = 1        'Clear Grid of data (except titles)
        FGrid1.Rows = 51
        FGrid1.Row = 1
        FGrid1.Col = 0
        FGrid1.RowSel = FGrid1.Rows - 1
        FGrid1.ColSel = FGrid1.Cols - 1
        FGrid1.Clip = Rs1.GetClipString(50, , , "<Null>")
ExitShowData:
        FGrid1.RowSel = 1
        FGrid1.ColSel = 0
End Function
```

NOTE This is a condensed version of the RDOADOGrid control code that illustrates just the salient points. The fully functional version is on the companion CD.

Using RDO to Access More Complex Data

In this section, we'll execute a parameter-driven stored procedure (without the benefit of the UserConnection designer) and execute an optimistic batch update operation. If you recall how I did this in the white paper on RDO and ADO 1.5 conversion I published last year, however, you'll notice that we've been able to simplify the approach this time—both for RDO and ADO. The goal of that earlier paper was to create RDO code that could be easily converted to ADO. I didn't want to make ADO 1.5 look *too* bad.

NOTE This discussion doesn't include treatment of the RDO User-Connection designer (UCD). The UCD is clearly an easier way to set up queries—especially those executing stored procedures. (See Chapter 22 for more complete information on using the RDO UCD.) Yes, the UCD morphs fairly easily over to ADO with the Data Environment designer.

RDO: Executing More Complex Procedures

Because many client/server applications depend heavily on stored procedures, any data access interface worth the blood, sweat, and tears to write must be able to execute them quickly and efficiently. Stored procedures pose a number of complex issues to the developer. In some cases, stored procedures require management of OUTPUT and return status values and other, more conventional arguments. In addition, a stored procedure can return several complex result sets, including PRINT or RAISERROR statement return values. So does it make sense to make your stored procedures this complex? Well, sometimes, but not always. It might be easier to keep stored procedures simpler and more modular and use Visual Basic application code to tie them together. This "modular" architecture also might better lend itself to Microsoft Transaction Server–managed components—but that's meat for another meal.

The code samples below show how RDO approaches these problems. To start, we'll execute a simple parameter-based stored procedure and show the results in a grid control. We'll be using the same connections we established previously. Ideally, using the UCD is the most efficient way to execute a parameter-driven stored procedure. Programs that use UserConnection objects can be converted fairly painlessly to using DataEnvironment objects.

NOTE Our code requires us to include a correct ODBC "call" statement. Again, this statement isn't necessary in the UserConnection designer, but it's essential here in the RDO code-based approach. We do use the stand-alone rdoQuery object and assign the already open Connection to it. This object can then be used in subsequent calls to handle a parameter query—that's the next set of code. In addition, the code doesn't attempt to reference the return status argument. This value isn't available until the result set is fully populated—only then does SQL Server return this value.

To execute stored procedures that require parameters, we must use a CALL statement. In the following example, we execute that code in the Connect event handler in which we set up an rdoQuery object to handle the operation:

```
Set Qy2 = Cn.CreateQuery("AuthorsSP", _
    "{? = Call AuthorByYearBorn (?,?)}")
Qy2.rdoParameters(0).Direction = rdParamReturnValue
```

When we're ready to run this query, we use the OpenResultset method (in asynchronous mode) after having set the two input parameters, as shown in the following code. Consider that this is only one of about four different ways to execute queries in RDO.

```
Private Sub RunSPButton_Click()
Set Qy = Cn.rdoQueries!AuthorsSP
Qy(1) = "1947"
Qy(2) = "1948"
Set Rs = Qy.OpenResultset(Options:=rdAsyncEnable)
End Sub
```

RDO: Executing Stored Procedures That Return OUTPUT Values

We can also set up stored procedures that return OUTPUT arguments in a similar fashion, but this time we have to pass RDO a few more tips on how to manage the parameters. The code on the next page shows an example.

```
Set Qy1 = Cn.CreateQuery("TestOut", "{? = Call TestOut (?,?)}")
Qy1.rdoParameters(0).Direction = rdParamReturnValue
Qy1.rdoParameters(1).Direction = rdParamInput
Qy1.rdoParameters(2).Direction = rdParamOutput
```

Once the query is set up, we execute it as a method on the rdoConnection object. The following code shows an example. Notice how we pass in the stored procedure's parameter as a method argument.

```
Private Sub TestOutButton_Click()
Set Qy = Cn.rdoQueries!TestOut
Qy(1) = "CA"
' Execute to get OUTPUT value
Qy.Execute
MsgBox "OUTPUT value returned: " & Qy(2)
' Execute query again to get result set
Cn.TestOut "CA"
End Sub
```

In the previous code you will notice that the query is executed two times. First with the Execute method and second with the TestOut method on the rdoConnection object. I executed the query twice so that I could get both the OUTPUT value and the result set. When I used a single query, I could get the OUTPUT value or the result set, but not both. Should it work this way? Nope.

RDO: Executing a Multiple-Result-Set Stored Procedure

Our next challenge is to execute a query that returns more than one result set. It isn't unusual for a stored procedure to return more than a single set of rows or a result set that contains results from an action query—as a matter of fact, it's quite common. Your code must deal with each of the result sets individually, unless you want to toss out the entire product of your query. In RDO, it's fairly simple to fetch the next result set—you simply use the MoreResults method to step through the result sets one at a time. Each call to MoreResults closes the current result set and moves to the next (if there is one).

Our multiple-result-set query executes two simple SELECT statements back to back, as shown in the following code. As in earlier examples, we create an rdoQuery to manage this query for us.

```
SQL = "Select * from Authors Where year_born is not null; " _
    & "Select * from Authors where year_born is null"
Set Qy3 = Cn.CreateQuery("Multiple", SQL)
```

Once the query is set up, execution is no more complex than before, as you can see in the following code. However, the code to manage the result sets has to include code to handle each result set in turn. In this case, our QueryComplete event includes the MoreResults property.

```
Private Sub MultipleRSButton_Click()
Cn.Multiple
End Sub
```

RDO: Executing Action Queries

No, queries don't necessarily have to return rows—they can be action queries as well. With action queries, we forgo the setup of an rdoQuery object and execute the hard-coded SQL statement directly. If your application needs to manipulate tables directly or simply perform a maintenance operation (such as SQL Server's DBCC functions), you can use the Execute method to run the query directly. In this case, we don't need ODBC (or SQL Server) to create a temporary stored procedure to run the query because we won't be running the query again. Of course, if this were a regular (multiple occurrence) operation, creating a stored procedure to do it would make sense. The following code shows a sample of executing an action query. Notice that the RowsAffected property is used to pick up the rows affected by this query.

```
Private Sub ExecuteButton_Click()
SQL = "Begin Transaction " _
    & "Update Authors " _
    & "set Year_Born = 1900 where year_born is null " _
    & "rollback transaction"
Cn.Execute SQL, rdExecDirect
ShowRows = Cn.RowsAffected
End Sub
```

RDO: Executing Optimistic Batch Queries

In this section, we'll execute a query that can be used to drive a subsequent optimistic batch update operation. We'll fetch a result set using the Client Batch cursor library and save the bookmarks for each row fetched, as shown in the following code:

```
Private Sub BatchOpsButton_Click()
SQL = "Select * from Authors where year_born is null"
CnB.QueryTimeout = 45
QuerySQL.Text = "About to execute: " & SQL
QuerySQL.Refresh
Screen.MousePointer = vbHourglass
Set Rs = CnB.OpenResultset(SQL, rdOpenKeyset, rdConcurBatch)
Rs.MoveLast: Rs.MoveFirst
ReDim bms(Rs.RowCount + 1) As Variant
i = 1
Do Until Rs.EOF
    bms(i) = Rs.Bookmark
    i = i + 1
    Rs.MoveNext
Loop
Rs.MoveFirst
RAutoGrid1.ShowRDOData Rs
ShowRows = Rs.RowCount
Screen.MousePointer = vbDefault
QuerySQL.Text = "Just ran: " & SQL
Batchflag = True
End Sub
```

Once the grid is filled with the rows that meet the criteria in the WHERE clause executed above, we can trap the grid control's Click event to set up an update to modify one or more rows of the grid, as shown in the code below. In this case, we choose to use the Update method to indicate that we aren't ready to post the changes to the database and the BatchUpdate method to post all pending changes to the tables.

```
Private Sub RAutoGrid1_Click()
If Batchflag Then
Dim NewValue
NewValue = InputBox("Enter new year born -- 1900 to 1997", _
    "Year_Born", "1947")
If NewValue <> "" Then
    Rs.Bookmark = bms(RAutoGrid1.Row)
    RAutoGrid1.Col = 1
    Debug.Print "Recordset:" & Rs!Author & " Grid:" & _
        RAutoGrid1.Text
    Rs.Edit
    Rs!Year_Born = NewValue
    Rs.Update
    Changes = Changes + 1
    i = MsgBox("Commit all (" & Changes & ") changes?", _
        vbYesNoCancel)
    Select Case i
        Case vbYes
            Rs.BatchUpdate
            Changes = 0
        Case vbNo
            Exit Sub
        Case vbCancel
            Changes = 0
            i = MsgBox("Cancel just this change (Yes) or all " _
                & Changes & " made so far (No)?", vbYesNo)
            If i = vbYes Then
                Rs.CancelBatch (True)
            Else
                Rs.CancelBatch
            End If
    End Select
End If
End If
End Sub
```

When the user chooses a row in the grid (where the rows are displayed), we'll ask the user to provide a new value and post that value to the result set. The trick is that these changes aren't made against the data until we finally decide to run the BatchUpdate method.

Using ADO to Solve Basic Data Access Problems

Now we'll shift our focus from RDO to ADO. We'll walk through the code used to perform the same basic operations in ADO that we just examined using RDO. Initially, we'll create a set of stand-alone ADO objects referenced off of the ADODB object. We'll flesh out these objects later in the code, when we set specific properties to open connections and execute result sets. In many ways, the ADO code is very similar to the RDO equivalent—I tried to follow the RDO development tactics whenever possible. In most cases, this was fairly easy; however, I did think about how the ADO application would have to be written as I coded the RDO application—so I cheated (at least a little). Figure 34-2 shows a sample of this ADO application in action.

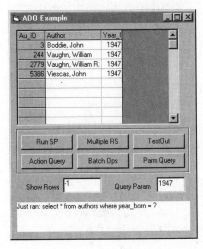

Figure 34-2   *Sample application that uses ADO to access SQL Server*

TIP   ADO objects can be prefixed with the ADODB qualifier if your code includes DAO references. Otherwise, the prefix isn't necessary. ADO and RDO object names don't ever collide.

ADO: Coding Global Variables

As in the RDO code, the ADO application manages its Connection objects with two global variables. The second connection is used to manage the optimistic batch update example. We'll also build four separate Command objects to manage the application-generated queries. This technique illustrates the use of queries as methods on the ADO Connection object, but more important, it emphasizes that application-generated queries should be generated only once—not repeatedly throughout the application. The following code shows how the global variables are declared. Notice that we build the *Cn* variable to support events.

```
Option Explicit
Dim WithEvents Cn As Connection
Dim CnB As New Connection
Dim rs As New Recordset
Dim rsB As New Recordset
Dim cmd1 As New Command, cmd2 As New Command, _
    cmd3 As New Command, cmd4 As New Command
Dim bms() As Variant
Dim SQL As String
Dim i As Integer, j As Integer
Dim Changes As Integer
Dim Batchflag as Boolean
Const ConnectString = "Provider=sqloledb;Data Source=betav1;" & _
    "Initial Catalog=biblio;User Id=;Password=;" & _
    "Integrated Security=SSPI;Persist Security Info=False;"
```

Here we use a connect string constant different from the one used in the RDO example. Here the native OLE DB provider to access SQL Server is used. You could use the exact same connect string used in the RDO example, but I found that I had fewer coding problems when using the native OLE DB provider. You'll find that ADO supports a wide variety of ways to get your work done without having to formally establish a Connection object.

ADO: Establishing a Connection

In the Form_Load event handler, shown in the code below, we start the connection operation—but don't wait for it to complete. The default cursor in ADO actually isn't a cursor at all but a forward-only, read-only, single-row (Cache-Size=1) result set—a firehose cursor. Because of this, ADO doesn't build a complex cursor. Building a firehose cursor by default also means that we don't have to set the CursorLocation property prior to running the query.

> **TIP** When you start working with ADO code, don't be fooled by the familiarity of the enumerated constants used to select the options. Although these constants might look like their RDO cousins, they don't always work the same way.

You'll see that we have to use the ADO Properties collection to deal with the desired prompt behavior—but ADO defaults to "no prompt," which makes more sense anyway, so you shouldn't have to specify the prompting behavior. In RDO, we could simply set the behavior using the Prompt argument of the rdoEnvironment OpenConnection method or set the Prompt argument of the rdoConnection EstablishConnection method. In ADO, we have to set the Properties ("Prompt") property.

```
Private Sub Form_Load()
Set Cn = New Connection
On Error GoTo EH
With Cn
    .ConnectionTimeout = 5
```

```
    .Open ConnectString, Options:=adAsyncConnect
End With
With CnB
    .CursorLocation = adUseClient
    .Open ConnectString
End With
exitfl:
Exit Sub
EH:
    Select Case Err
        Case 40002: MsgBox "Could not connect... " & Error
        Resume exitfl
        Case Else
            Debug.Print Err, Error
        Resume exitfl
    End Select
End Sub
```

ADO: When the
Connection Operation Completes

Now that ADO 2.0 supports events, we can leverage our RDO event handler code. However, in ADO, we don't get a simple Boolean ErrorOccurred to test for—we have to see whether the Error object returned has been instantiated. Notice that we need fewer lines of code to perform the same operation we coded in RDO.

The ADO equivalent to RDO's Connect event is the ConnectComplete event, which fires when the operation started by the Open method completes—whether or not it succeeded. ADO returns an Error object to indicate success or failure; if this object is set to Nothing, no errors occurred. As with RDO, you have to dig into the Errors collection to see what specific errors occurred. However, ADO also returns more informative information—the Connection object and a status flag. In the ADO version, we set up four of our queries ahead of time as ADO Command objects. As with RDO, the queries are stored internally—but this time there is no queries collection to manage them. This makes the object model simpler. In RDO we could use the CreateQuery method to build our rdoQuery objects, but ADO has no equivalent, so we have to build the Command objects property by property, one at a time. We also opt to build the ADO Parameter objects one at a time—but here we can use the CreateParameter method to expedite the process. For the first time, we can also specify the size and precision of these parameters—an important new feature in ADO 2.0. The following code shows the ConnectComplete event handler:

```
Private Sub Cn_ConnectComplete(ByVal pError As ADODB.Error, _
    adStatus As ADODB.EventStatusEnum, _
    ByVal pConnection As ADODB.Connection)
If pError Is Nothing Then
    ' Set up Commands
    cmd1.CommandText = "{?=call TestOut (?,?)}"
    cmd1.CommandType = adCmdText
```

(continued)

```
        cmd1.Name = "TestOut"
        cmd1.Parameters.Append _
        cmd1.CreateParameter("RV", adInteger, adParamReturnValue)
        cmd1.Parameters.Append _
            cmd1.CreateParameter("StateWanted", adVarChar, _
            adParamInput, 2)
        cmd1.Parameters.Append _
            cmd1.CreateParameter("Found", adInteger, adParamOutput)
        Set cmd1.ActiveConnection = Cn
        cmd2.CommandText = "AuthorByYearBorn"
        cmd2.CommandType = adCmdStoredProc
        cmd2.Name = "AuthorsSP"
        Set cmd2.ActiveConnection = Cn
        cmd3.CommandText = "Select * from Authors Where " & _
            "year_born is not null; Select * from Authors where " & _
            "year_born is null"
        cmd3.CommandType = adCmdText
        cmd3.Name = "MultipleQy"
        Set cmd3.ActiveConnection = Cn
        cmd4.CommandText = "select * from authors where year_born = ?"
        cmd4.CommandType = adCmdText
        cmd4.Name = "AuthorsQy"
        cmd4.Parameters.Append _
            cmd4.CreateParameter("YB", adInteger, adParamInput)
            ' Force correct parameter type (bug?)
        Set cmd4.ActiveConnection = Cn
        Batchflag = False
        RunOKFrame.Enabled = True
    Else
        MsgBox "Could not open connection", vbCritical
    End If
End Sub
```

ADO: Running a Basic Query

Once the connection is open, we can proceed to run a query. The following code shows a sample. This code is very similar to the code we just executed with RDO. Yes, you have lots of other options in ADO, and I'll show you a couple of these before we're done. And yes, you can choose to code the ADO query using asynchronous operations, just as you can in RDO 2.0. As with RDO, we reference the query (our ADO Command object) by name against the ADO Connection object. The code passes in the current Text property of the TextBox control.

```
Private Sub ParmQueryButton_Click()
Cn.authorsQY (QueryParam.Text), rs
End Sub
```

ADO: Using the WillExecute Event

Just as with RDO, we can trap an execute event that gives us the option of viewing or altering the SQL statement about to be executed. Whereas RDO passes only two arguments to the WillExecute event, ADO passes eight. These additional arguments support a lot more flexibility in your approach and reduce the code needed to reference these objects at run time.

The following WillExecute event handler executes the query and disables the button frame to prevent overlapping operations.

```
Private Sub Cn_WillExecute(Source As String, _
    CursorType As ADODB.CursorTypeEnum, _
    LockType As ADODB.LockTypeEnum, Options As Long, _
    adStatus As ADODB.EventStatusEnum, _
    ByVal pCommand As ADODB.Command, _
    ByVal pRecordset As ADODB.Recordset, _
    ByVal pConnection As ADODB.Connection)
QuerySQL.Text = "About to execute: " & Source
QuerySQL.Refresh
RunOKFrame.Enabled = False
Screen.MousePointer = vbHourglass
End Sub
```

ADO: Managing the Result Sets

Following the RDO model, we use the equivalent of RDO's QueryComplete event handler to manage all result sets generated by the primary connection (*Cn*). In ADO, this event is exposed as the Connection object's ExecuteComplete event. Using this event handler reduces the amount of code in the application but makes the job of handling result sets more complex because we have to handle all possible types of result sets that our application generates.

As with the other ADO events we've seen so far, the ExecuteComplete event returns a bevy of arguments to make our coding easier. One important difference here is that ADO has no equivalent for RDO's LastQueryResults property. However, the ExecuteComplete event returns the Recordset that you can use instead.

No, we didn't have to change much here to convert from RDO—the logic is very similar to the RDO model. But notice that the technique to manage multiple result sets has changed. In ADO, there is no MoreResults property. Instead, you'll find a NextRecordset method that serves a similar purpose. In this case, ADO returns either the next Recordset in the series or a "closed" Recordset.

In addition, we often have to test whether the ADO Recordset is closed by testing the State property. No, this isn't a Boolean—it's a bitmask. This means you shouldn't use the "=" operator with it. You need to test individual bits of the mask with the And operator, as shown here:

```
Private Sub Cn_ExecuteComplete(ByVal RecordsAffected As Long, _
    ByVal pError As ADODB.Error, _
    adStatus As ADODB.EventStatusEnum, _
    ByVal pCommand As ADODB.Command, _
    ByVal pRecordset As ADODB.Recordset, _
    ByVal pConnection As ADODB.Connection)
On Error GoTo QCEh
If pError Is Nothing Then
    QuerySQL.Text = "Just ran: " & pCommand.CommandText
```

(continued)

```
            If pRecordset Is Nothing Then
            Else
                Set rs = pRecordset
                RAutoGrid1.ShowADOData rs
                ShowRows = rs.RecordCount
                rs.Cancel
                If rs.State And adStateOpen Then
                    Set rs = rs.NextRecordset
                    While rs.State And adStateOpen
                        j = MsgBox("Ready to continue?", vbYesNo)
                        If j = vbYes Then
                            RAutoGrid1.ShowADOData rs
                            ShowRows = rs.RecordCount
                            Set rs = rs.NextRecordset
                            rs.Cancel
                        Else
                            rs.Close
                        End If
                    Wend
                End If
            End If
    Else
        MsgBox "Query failed... tried to run " & _
            pCommand.CommandText & vbCrLf & pError.Description
        Dim er As Error
        For Each er In Cn.Errors
            Debug.Print er.Description
        Next
    End If
ExitQH:
RunOKFrame.Enabled = True
Screen.MousePointer = vbDefault
Exit Sub
QCEh:
    Debug.Print Err, Error$
    Resume ExitQH
End Sub
```

ADO: Displaying a Result Set in an MSFlexGrid

The code on page 809 implements the ShowADOData method of a custom
ActiveX control adapted from the MSFlexGrid control. This is a new routine for
this control since ADO 2.0 now supports an equivalent to RDO's GetClipString
method. ADO's GetString method performs the same operation—but with more
options (which is why the call was changed slightly). In the first place, you have
to add an argument to specify the conversion style. Although ADO 2.0's Get-
String method supports only a single format, future versions promise to support
others. You can also tell the GetString method to pass back all of the rows generated, but in this code this operation is limited to the first 50.

RDO's OrdinalPosition property can no longer be used as an index on the
Fields collection to pull out the column titles. To deal with this change, we
substitute a new integer counter to address the column being worked on.

```
Public Function ShowADOData(Resultset As Recordset) As Variant
Dim cl As Field
Dim MaxL As Integer
Dim Op As Integer
Dim Rsl As Recordset
Dim Rows As Variant
Dim MaxRows As Integer

On Error GoTo ShowADODataEH
    Set Rsl = Resultset
    FGrid1.Rows = 51
    FGrid1.Cols = Rsl.Fields.Count
    FGrid1.Row = 0
    Op = 0
    For Each cl In Rsl.Fields
        FGrid1.Col = Op
        FGrid1 = cl.Name
        If Rsl.Fields(Op).DefinedSize > 255 Then
            MaxL = 1
        Else
            MaxL = Rsl.Fields(Op).ActualSize + 4
        End If
        If MaxL > 20 Then MaxL = 20
        FGrid1.ColWidth(FGrid1.Col) = TextWidth(String(MaxL, "n"))
        Op = Op + 1
    Next cl
    GridSetup = True
    FGrid1.Rows = 1        'Clear Grid of data (except titles)
    FGrid1.Rows = 51
    FGrid1.Row = 1
    FGrid1.Col = 0
    FGrid1.RowSel = FGrid1.Rows - 1
    FGrid1.ColSel = FGrid1.Cols - 1
    FGrid1.Clip = Rsl.GetString(adClipString, 50, , , "<Null>")

ExitADOShowData:
    FGrid1.RowSel = 1
    If FGrid1.ColSel > 0 Then FGrid1.ColSel = 0
Exit Function
ShowADODataEH:
    Debug.Print Err, Err.Description
    Select Case Err
        Case 40022, 3021:
            FGrid1.Clear
            Resume ExitADOShowData
        Case 13, Is < 0
            Rows(j, i) = "< >"
            Resume Next
        Case Else
            MsgBox "Could not display data: " & _
                Err & vbCrLf & Error$
            Resume ExitADOShowData
    End Select
End Function
```

Using ADO to Access More Complex Data

Using the preceding code as a base, our next task will be to perform several more demanding operations with ADO. In some cases, as in the first example below, the migration from RDO to ADO is fairly significant. Yes, I expect that some of the code might not be absolutely necessary; after all, the properties being set would work with their default settings. However, I included what I did because I wanted to boost performance in some cases—by avoiding unneeded calls to the database management system (DBMS) for more information.

ADO: Executing a Parameter Query

ADO gives you a lot of flexibility when it comes to executing a parameter query—in most cases, more than RDO. By telling ADO everything it needs to know about a query, you'll prevent ADO from having to execute informational queries against the DBMS to get missing information. This means your queries will usually run faster—the first time and every time—and will run the way you want them to. The downside to this approach is that it makes your code more complex. But if you play your cards right, this query setup code is run only once, when your application first starts, so its negative impact can be minimal.

We don't *have* to build the ADO Parameters collection in code—it's created for us, as it is when we use RDO. It is possible to build this collection in code, and doing so can improve performance—but of course your application will be more complex to write. You'll have to weigh the benefits of additional coding effort versus enhanced performance when deciding whether you want to build the ADO Parameters collection in code. If you do try to roll the Parameters collection yourself, just make sure that the Command object is associated with an open connection so that ADO can query the OLE DB provider (and the server) for the description of the parameters.

ADO: Executing a Parameter-Driven Stored Procedure

ADO has a lot of flexibility when it comes to executing stored procedures. This flexibility comes with a price tag, however: taking full advantage of ADO's versatility will require more code. As with the previous example, you still should build up your own ADODB Parameters collection to improve performance. Actually, using the Data Environment designer to build your Command objects would probably make more sense. It would certainly take less time than the techniques shown here.

In the following code, we're executing a simple two-argument stored procedure, AuthorsByYearBorn, that returns a small result set. One trick you can try is to get ADO to populate the Parameters collection for you using the Refresh method and then replace these values with code-driven settings.

```
cmd2.CommandText = "AuthorByYearBorn"
cmd2.CommandType = adCmdStoredProc
cmd2.Name = "AuthorsSP"
Set cmd2.ActiveConnection = Cn
```

When you're ready to execute this stored procedure, you can use a number of techniques, including the same query-as-method syntax we used in the similar RDO example. In the following code, we pass in the two input arguments (hard-coded for our example) and a variable to hold the returned Recordset that results from the query. The ExecuteComplete event handler deals with the rows that return.

```
Private Sub RunSPButton_Click()
Cn.authorsSP 1947, 1948, rs
End Sub
```

ADO: Executing Stored Procedures That Return OUTPUT Values

ADO also supports the ability to handle complex stored procedures—even those that return OUTPUT or return status values. The following code shows one technique for setting up an ADO Command object to handle one or more OUTPUT arguments or Return status values. In this case, we use the CALL syntax to mark each of the input, output, and return value parameters. Next we build our own ADO Parameter objects using the CreateParameter method—appending to the ADO Parameters collection as we go. Each parameter is named, typed, and sized where needed. After naming these parameters, we can reference them by name. No, ADO doesn't support referencing stored procedure parameters by their Transact-SQL (TSQL) name—but then neither does RDO.

```
cmd1.CommandText = "{?=call TestOut (?,?)}"
cmd1.CommandType = adCmdText
cmd1.Name = "TestOut"
cmd1.Parameters.Append _
    cmd1.CreateParameter("RV", adInteger, adParamReturnValue)
cmd1.Parameters.Append _
    cmd1.CreateParameter("StateWanted", adVarChar, adParamInput, 2)
cmd1.Parameters.Append _
    cmd1.CreateParameter("Found", adInteger, adParamOutput)
Set cmd1.ActiveConnection = Cn
```

Executing the query is just as easy as running any other query, as shown here:

```
Private Sub TestOutButton_Click()
Cn.TestOut "CA", rs
MsgBox "OUTPUT value returned: " & cmd1("Found")
End Sub
```

ADO: Executing a Multiple-Result-Set Stored Procedure

Our next challenge is the more complex multiple-result-set stored procedure. As I've said before, this practice is fairly common, so you probably won't be able to get by without knowing how to deal with this type of stored procedure. The ADO approach is very unlike the RDO approach. ADO uses the NextRecordset method, which lets you assign the next Recordset in the batch to an ADO Recordset object. Because you might not know how many result sets will be generated by your query, you must test the Recordset State property to see whether it's still open—you no longer have a Boolean return value to test, as you do in RDO.

I used a Command object to set up the query, and it is defined in the following way:

```
cmd3.CommandText = _
    "Select * from Authors Where year_born is not null; " & _
    "Select * from Authors where year_born is null"
cmd3.CommandType = adCmdText
cmd3.Name = "MultipleQy"
Set cmd3.ActiveConnection = Cn
```

The following code shows how to execute the multiple result set query. The ExecuteComplete event handler uses the NextRecordset method to display the results.

```
Private Sub MultipleRSButton_Click()

Cn.MultipleQy rs
End Sub
```

ADO: Executing Action Queries

Action queries don't return rowsets, but they do perform a specific set of operations on the data—such as INSERT, UPDATE, and DELETE statements. When you need to execute an action query, you can take advantage of the Execute method in ADO to do the job, as shown in this code:

```
Private Sub ExecuteButton_Click()
Dim rowsAffect
SQL = "Begin Transaction " _
    & "Update Authors " _
    & "set Year_Born = 1900 where year_born is null " _
    & "rollback transaction"
Cn.Execute SQL, rowsAffect, adExecuteNoRecords
ShowRows = rowsAffect
End Sub
```

ADO: Executing Optimistic Batch Queries

Our final ADO example implements a batch operation. The ADO coverage of this functionality is very comprehensive—mainly because it was based on the RDO programming model. The following code used to perform the batch update is pretty much the same as the code we used in the RDO sample. Notice that the routine used to change the chosen row in the read/write result set didn't require starting an "Edit" session. Simply changing the contents of a Field and using the Update or UpdateBatch method was enough to make the changes to the database.

We don't set up a global ADO Command object this time because we want to use the Open method against the ADO Recordset object. The Open method accepts the SQL statement, Connection information (object or connect string), and arguments to choose the type of cursor handling required.

As a general rule of thumb, if you want the default cursor behavior (forward-only, read-only, cache-size=1, server-side cursorless result set), use the Execute method. If this method isn't what your application calls for, use the Open method. The following code shows a sample of the Open method being used in this context:

```
Private Sub BatchOpsButton_Click()
If rsB.State And adStateOpen Then rsB.Close
SQL = "Select * from Authors where year_born is null"
QuerySQL.Text = "About to execute: " & SQL
QuerySQL.Refresh
Screen.MousePointer = vbHourglass
rsB.Open SQL, CnB, adOpenKeyset, adLockBatchOptimistic
rsB.MoveLast: rsB.MoveFirst
ReDim bms(rsB.RecordCount + 1) As Variant
i = 1
Do Until rsB.EOF
    bms(i) = rsB.Bookmark
    i = i + 1
    rsB.MoveNext
Loop
rsB.MoveFirst
RAutoGrid1.ShowADOData rsB
ShowRows = rsB.RecordCount
Screen.MousePointer = vbDefault
QuerySQL.Text = "Just ran: " & SQL
Batchflag = True
End Sub
```

Once the grid is filled and the array of bookmarks is created, the grid's Click event handler is used to allow modification of the Year_Born values.

```
Private Sub RAutoGrid1_Click()
If Batchflag Then
Dim NewValue
NewValue = InputBox("Enter year born -- 1900 to 1997", _
    "Year_Born", "1947")
If NewValue <> "" Then
    rsB.Bookmark = bms(RAutoGrid1.Row)
    RAutoGrid1.Col = 1: Debug.Print "RS Name:" & rsB!Author & _
        "Grid name:" & RAutoGrid1.Text     ' Should match
    rsB!Year_Born = NewValue
```

(continued)

```
        rsB.Update
        Changes = Changes + 1
        i = MsgBox("Commit all (" & Changes & ") changes?", _
            vbYesNoCancel)
        Select Case i
            Case vbYes
                rsB.UpdateBatch
                Changes = 0
            Case vbNo
                Exit Sub
            Case vbCancel
                Changes = 0
                i = MsgBox("Cancel just this change (Yes) or all " _
                    & Changes & " made so far (No)?", vbYesNo)
                If i = vbYes Then
                    rsB.CancelBatch (True)
                Else
                    rsB.CancelBatch
                End If
        End Select
    End If
    End If
    End Sub
```

Conversion Tips and Techniques

In this final section, I'll be your tour guide as we take a leisurely look at many of the conversion issues you'll face if you decide to migrate from RDO to ADO. Throughout, I'll suggest ways to convert your existing applications or designs to ADO 2.0's way of thinking.

- ADO morphed many of the property names from RDO, so Rows are now Records, Columns are now Fields, and so forth. This renaming means that we now have a RecordCount property instead of a RowCount property, and a MaxRecords property instead of a MaxRows property.

- ADO's object model doesn't implement as many collections as RDO's does, so there is no equivalent in ADO for the rdoConnections, rdoQueries, or rdoResultsets collections. As a result, ADO doesn't seem to leave as many orphaned objects lying around.

- RDO's events are almost universally supported in ADO, but with different names. While you'll have most of the same events, you have a lot more flexibility to deal with more complex operations. You'll also have a better idea of what object fired the event and why, because of additional arguments.

- In RDO, you use rdoQuery objects and the rdoQueries collection to manage application-generated queries. These can be executed individually by name or as methods on the rdoConnection object. ADO supports this query-as-method syntax, but not with a collection of Command objects.

- When you specify a Command object in ADO and name it, the name must be unique—even though ADO doesn't build a formal collection of these Command objects.

- In RDO, the ODBC prompt behavior is set by a parameter on the EstablishConnection method or by the Prompt property. In ADO, this is set via the ADO Properties collection.

- In RDO, you have five different CursorDriver options. In ADO, you have only two: server-side and client-side.

- In RDO, the default cursor used a RowsetSize property of 100, which disabled firehose cursors. In ADO, the CacheSize property defaults to 1, which enables firehose cursors.

- In RDO, you had to test an object for existence to determine its state. In ADO, you can examine the bitmask State property.

- In RDO, there is no way to specify the size of an rdoParameter object's rdoColumn. It is figured for you automatically—in a take-it-or-leave-it manner. In ADO, you can specify the size of the Field property as well as the Precision property and other properties.

- In RDO, you couldn't create your rdoParameters collection manually— you could create it only by polling the server. For the most part, you had to take what was returned. In ADO, you can have ADO build the Parameters collection for you, or you can build it yourself in code.

- In RDO, you use the EstablishConnection or OpenConnection method to open a connection. In ADO, you use the Open method, or you have ADO open the connection by indirect reference.

- In RDO, you have a single asynchronous option: rdAsyncEnable. In ADO, you have several asynchronous options that apply to opening connections, running queries, fetching, and more.

- In RDO, to poll for completion of an asynchronous connection or OpenResultset operation, you test the StillConnecting and StillExecuting properties. In ADO, you test the bitmask State property for adStateConnecting or adStateExecuting bits.

- In RDO, you test the ErrorOccurred Boolean value in event handlers to see whether the operation succeeded. In ADO, you test the Error object returned for Nothing—if it is instantiated, the operation failed.

- In RDO, after having executed a query as an rdoConnection method, you can examine the LastQueryResults property (once) to get the result set. In ADO, the query as method returns the Recordset into the last variable passed to the method.

- In RDO, you can access the LastQueryResults on the rdoConnection object. ADO has no equivalent property on the Connection object but does expose the Recordset in the ExecuteComplete event as well as in most other pertinent events in which you might need access to the global result set.

- In RDO, you have no way to tell ODBC what kind of query is being executed. RDO has to ask the ODBC driver and the back end to figure it out. In ADO, you can set the CommandType property to specifically reference a command style.

- Be sure to choose the correct ADO CommandType property. If you don't choose correctly, ADO might not parse your command as desired. For example, it might think a named-object reference refers to a stored procedure.

- RDO's GetClipString is now supported, but as GetString in ADO. It also takes an additional argument that specifies the type of conversion.

- In RDO, you can test the EOF property on closed rdoResultset objects. In ADO, this isn't permitted. You must verify that the State property is set to adStateOpen before testing the EOF property—it simply isn't available on a "closed" ADO Recordset.

- In RDO, you test for additional result sets by using the MoreResults property. In ADO, you must assign a Recordset variable with the NextRecordset method. This returns a closed Recordset if no more result sets are available.

- In RDO, you can access the ODBC hEnv and hStmt handles. These are not available in ADO, so you'll have to come up with other strategies that replace this low-level ODBC functionality. I think you'll find that the absence of these handles might pose a problem that's kinda tough to solve. I would be sure to check out the copious ADO properties before I gave up though.

- In RDO, you have to use the Edit method before writing to an updateable rdoResultset. In ADO, the Edit method is neither needed nor supported. Simply accessing the Recordset object's Fields collection enables the EditMode.

- In RDO, you have to pass back data from a middle-tier component by using a Variant array or a delimited string. In ADO, you can also pass back a disjoint Recordset—or stick with the Variant array or string.

- In RDO, you can build a disjoint rdoResultset, but only by executing a query on a database. In ADO, you can build a Recordset object without using a database, and you can save this Recordset (or any Recordset) to a file to be retrieved later.

- In RDO, you have to specify the number of rows to fetch with GetRows or GetClipString. In ADO, you can tell ADO to fetch all remaining rows. Actually, in RDO, you can simply use a very large value as the number of rows to fetch. The problem with this approach is that it allocates memory based on this value.

Still want to migrate? Many of you won't. You'll decide that your existing code works fine and that you don't need what ADO has to offer. You know that with the new features come new headaches or at least a lot of hacking through uncharted territory. And yes, some of you will venture forth into the swamp lusting for a few milliseconds of performance or a few dozen lines of code that won't have to be written. My advice? Keep your eyes open and watch out for those long snakes.

PART VI

Using the New Tools

35

Using the Transact-SQL Debugger

Setting Up SQL Server and Visual Basic

Invoking the TSQL Debugger Interactively

Invoking the TSQL Debugger from Code

Debugging the TSQL Debugger

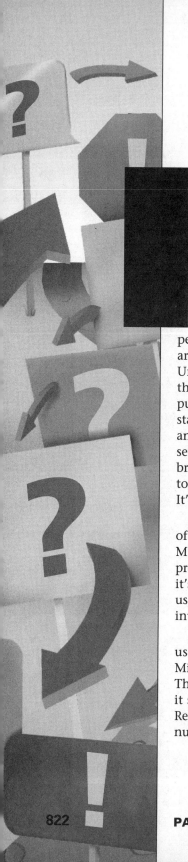

ave you noticed that I keep encouraging you to move more and more of your query logic to the server? For many of you front-line developers, that has meant creating stored procedures—often by the hundreds. Some servers manage an avalanche of stored procedures developed by people long since departed. Some of these procedures could have been lying around since I first started lecturing on Microsoft SQL Server seven years ago. Until Microsoft Visual Basic 5.0 introduced Transact-SQL (TSQL) debugging, the writing, tuning, and fixing of these procedures was expensive. It meant putting extra code into the procedures to dump the time; exposing variable states and logic flow; building stored procedures up in small, testable pieces; and using a host of other tricks of the trade that remain the closely guarded secrets of the stored-procedure development teams. When a stored procedure breaks, you have to deal with the logic very much in the way we used to have to deal with COBOL programs run off 80-column cards in the IBM 360 days. It's a real PIA.

SQL Server 6.5 added support for a feedback mechanism to help take some of this burden off your shoulders. After talking with some friends over in our MIS department, I think that the TSQL Debugger in SQL Server will help these professional stored-procedure developers to some extent, though I don't think it's a complete solution. However, it *will* go a long way toward helping all of us learn to use stored procedures more efficiently and get a feel for how they interact with the front-end applications we write.

Initially, the grand plan showed that SQL Server 6.5 and later were to use the SDI.DLL and Remote Automation (Microsoft Windows 95/98 and Microsoft Windows NT 3.51), and DCOM was to be used in Windows NT 4.0. These protocols set up a back link to the applications being tested. However, it seems that all versions of the Windows operating system still depend on Remote Automation. Basically, the back link routines pass back the current line number and other essential information so that the TSQL Debugger can display the stored-procedure text and current line number. The TSQL Debugger opens an additional connection to fetch SQL system tables, SQL stored-procedure text, and global variables. This extra connection shouldn't affect your maximum user count, but it will impact how much performance you can expect out of your server. Turning on the TSQL Debugger is like tying a Chevy Nova to your horse's tail just before yelling "giddyap!" Although the SDI DLL might not bring the system to its knees, it will likely influence overall system performance. It will *certainly* impact the performance of a running stored procedure while it is being watched.

TIP Most of the problems I've had setting up and running TSQL debugging have been caused by balky Remote Automation connections and problems with setting up the correct accounts to manage these intersystem connections. Pay close attention to these setup details. One piece of advice that might get you through a number of these problems is to run SQL Server 6.5 in "console" mode by using the *-e* option to start it. However, we do this only when we demo TSQL debugging on the same system running the server. No, this doesn't appear to work with SQL Server 7.0.

The TSQL Debugger works interactively as a stand-alone program, or you can launch it from Visual Basic when you're debugging your own code since your code launches a stored procedure via RDO or ADO. Visual Basic also invokes the TSQL Debugger to walk through your triggers if you perform an action query that causes a trigger to fire on the server. The TSQL Debugger also supports the following features:

- **Displaying the TSQL call stack, global variables, local variables, and parameters for the SQL stored procedure** When a procedure calls a procedure, as when a trigger calls a procedure, you'll be able to tell how you got into the current pothole. You'll also be able to examine any of the selected global variables or the parameters for the stored procedure being executed.

- **Setting and managing breakpoints in stored procedure code** You can stop execution at a chosen point to examine the stored procedure state.

- **Viewing and manipulating local variables** You can also examine the variables declared within the stored procedure and change their values as needed.

- **Creating your own stored procedures interactively, using an edit window** I don't use this feature much now that Visual Database Tools is incorporated into Visual Basic. It has its own stored procedure editor.

This chapter is a little far afield from my usual focus on the programming aspects of client/server development, and the documentation on the TSQL Debugger is OK. So why am I including this chapter? I thought it would help you get a better feel for the application and perhaps encourage you to try it. The application is also tricky to set up; I hope the tips here can help.

Setting Up SQL Server and Visual Basic

Depending on the version of Visual Basic you're using and the version of SQL Server and Windows NT you're running, TSQL Debugger setup can be fairly complicated or it can be an even more complex multistep manual process. The setup process has been improved lately and integrated into the Visual Basic and Visual Studio setup scripts.

Client-Side Setup

To activate the TSQL Debugger, you need to make a few adjustments on the client side—on your development workstation. In Visual Basic 5.0, Enterprise Edition, design mode, go to the Add-Ins menu and choose Add-In Manager. Next check the VB T-SQL Debugger add-in, and click OK. After an initialization dialog box is displayed, you can then use the TSQL Debugger interactively or you can have it launched automatically as you execute stored procedures. If the VB T-SQL Debugger add-in isn't listed in the Add-In Manager dialog box, run the Visual Basic Setup, choose Add/Remove, and make sure the SQL Debugging option (under the Enterprise Features option) is installed.

In Visual Basic 6.0, Enterprise Edition, you also need to select the Add-In Manager from the Add-Ins menu to enable and load the TSQL debugging add-in. In the Add-In Manager dialog box, scroll down in the list presented to VB T-SQL Debugger and in the Load Behavior frame, check Loaded/Unloaded. If you want the debugger to come up each time (you probably don't), also check Load on Startup. After clicking OK, an initialization dialog box is displayed and your Tools menu will show a T-SQL Debugging Options item. Click on this item to change the TSQL Debugger settings. If the VB T-SQL Debugger add-in isn't listed in the Add-In Manager dialog box, run the Visual Basic Setup, choose Add/Remove, and make sure the Visual Basic Enterprise Components option (under the Enterprise Features and Tools option) is installed.

TIP Unless you're logging in as system administrator, you need to grant execute permissions on sp_sdidebug to permit other login IDs to use TSQL debugging—assuming you want them to.

Server-Side Setup

You *must* install a few DLLs on the server to get TSQL debugging to work. I've included instructions for both Visual Basic 5.0 and Visual Basic 6.0 here in case you haven't yet migrated to Visual Basic 6.0.

Server-side setup when using Visual Basic 5.0

For Visual Basic 5.0, the TSQL debugger code and interface libraries are located in the TOOLS\TSQL directory on the Visual Basic 5.0, Enterprise Edition, CD. No, this code is not included with the Learning or Professional editions. You'll find two directories in the TOOLS\TSQL directory: the SQL65.SP2 directory that contains the SQL Server 6.5 service pack 2 (SP2) and the SRVSETUP directory that contains additional code especially for Windows NT 3.51 systems. Nope, Windows NT 4.0 doesn't come with some of this stuff already installed. If you haven't yet installed SQL 6.5, skip to the next chapter and come back here when you upgrade.

TIP Find and follow the late-breaking instructions found in the README.TXT file supplied with the TSQL Debugger code in the Visual Basic 5.0 \TOOLS\TSQL\SRVSETUP directory. The TSQL debugging code for the server does *not* get installed automatically on your hard disk when you install Visual Basic—it doesn't need to be.

You must follow these steps to install TSQL debugging on your server:

1. Install the SQL Server 6.5 SP1 or SP2 code, unless you're already on SP2 or higher. The SQL Server service packs include support for the new debugging interface.

2. Check the MSSQLServer service in the Services Control Panel to make sure that SQL Server is configured so that it doesn't start up with a System Account. Specify a Windows NT user account with sufficient permission to access the SDI automation interface. The account you specify could be a separate account that doesn't expire—or at least one that doesn't get tired too quickly.

3. Using the Services Control Panel, make sure that the start-up type for the Remote Procedure Call (RPC) Locator and the Remote Procedure Call (RPC) Service are set to Automatic so that they start when the system boots.

4. Finally, you must install and register the SQL Debugging interface and Remote Automation components. This setup for Windows NT 4.0 is described in the following text.

If you're using Windows NT 4.0, the setup process for the SQL Debugging interface and Remote Automation components is handled by the SDI_NT4.EXE program as supplied in the \TOOLS\TSQL\SRVSETUP directory. When this application runs, it guesses the location of your SQL Server installation directory, prompts you with this guess (as shown in Figure 35-1), and asks for verification. This directory is usually C:\MSSQL. Just type *MSSQL*, and the setup program knows to copy the files to the \BINN directory.

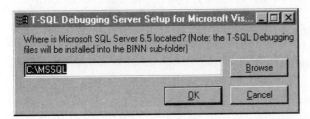

Figure 35-1 *Server Setup dialog box displayed when SDI_NT4.EXE is executed*

If this process doesn't seem to work you might check the Windows NT event log, because any errors encountered will be logged by Windows NT. If you're still having problems, fall back 10 yards and punt—or try the Windows NT 3.51 manual setup instructions.

Server-side setup when using Visual Basic 6.0

The server-side SQL debugging setup has been integrated with the Visual Basic and Visual Studio 6.0 setup process. During the installation of Visual Basic 6.0, a Server Setups screen is displayed, as shown in Figure 35-2.

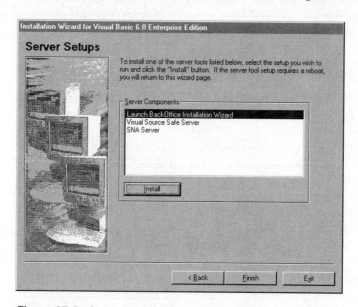

Figure 35-2 Server Setups screen displayed during the setup of Visual Basic 6.0, Enterprise Edition

If you select the Launch BackOffice Installation Wizard item from the Server Components list and click Install, a BackOffice wizard is started. If you perform a custom install, you're given the option of installing the SQL Server Debugging components, as shown in Figure 35-3.

I won't get into the unbelievably complex issue of BackOffice setup, but let's just suffice it to say that you could use this tool to set up SQL debugging—Microsoft Internet Explorer 4.0 and all. Sigh.

I did, however, find an SQDB_SS directory on both the Visual Basic and Visual Studio Enterprise CDs. In this directory, you'll find a SETUP.EXE for the Microsoft SQL Debugging Server Setup, which installs the SQL debugging and Remote Automation components. The minimum requirements for this setup include Windows NT 4.0 with SP3 (or Windows NT 3.51 with SP5) and SQL Server 6.5 with SP3. You must follow these steps to get TSQL debugging installed on your server:

1. Install the SQL Server 6.5 SP3 or SP4 code. There is a SQL directory on the Visual Basic Enterprise and Visual Studio Enterprise CDs that contains the SQL Server 6.5 SP4 code.

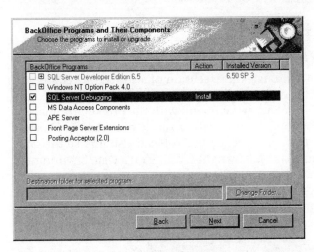

Figure 35-3 SQL Server Debugging option selected in the BackOffice installation wizard

2. Check the MSSQLServer service in the Services Control Panel to make sure that SQL Server is configured so that it doesn't start up with a System Account. Specify a Windows NT user account with sufficient permission to access the SDI automation interface. You can configure the system account by creating a separate account that doesn't expire.

3. Using the Services Control Panel, make sure that the startup type for the Remote Procedure Call (RPC) Locator and the Remote Procedure Call (RPC) Service are set to Automatic so that they start when the system boots.

4. Finally, you must install the SQL Debugging interface and the Remote Automation components by running SETUP.EXE in the SQDBG_SS directory. I tested the setup with SQL Server 7.0 Beta 3. Figure 35-4 shows a dialog box displayed during the setup.

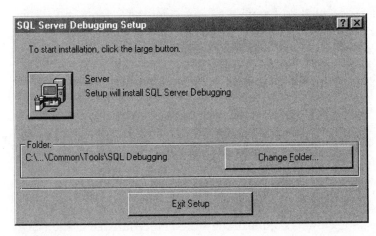

Figure 35-4 SQL Server Setup dialog box displayed when SQDBG_SS\SETUP.EXE is executed

Invoking the TSQL Debugger Interactively

If you simply want to walk through the execution of a stored procedure, you can launch the TSQL Debugger via Visual Basic at design time. From the Add-Ins menu, select the T-SQL Debugger command with the little lightning bolt. If you don't see the T-SQL Debugger entry here, go back to the Add-In Manager and make sure VB T-SQL Debugger is checked. You can also invoke the same interactive session in Visual Basic 6.0 by right-clicking on a Data Environment Command object and choosing Debug.

If everything is installed correctly, you should get the virgin Batch T-SQL Debugger window shown in Figure 35-5.

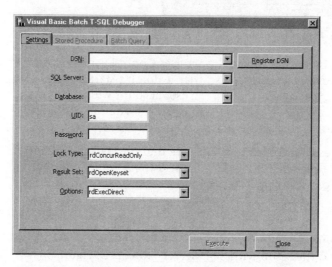

Figure 35-5 *Virgin Visual Basic Batch T-SQL Debugger window*

Notice that the Stored Procedure and Batch Query tabs aren't active. They won't be until you choose a data source name (DSN). Let's do that now. Because we're running interactively, the TSQL Debugger needs to connect to your server before it can pull down the list of available stored procedures. You can click the Register DSN button to launch the ODBC dialog boxes used to build and register new DSNs. Once the connection is open, you can click the Stored Procedure tab and choose a stored procedure from the drop-down list. You can enter the name of a stored procedure, but if your server can't find it, you won't be able to continue.

If you configure the T-SQL Debugger to reference the SQL Server Master database, you can select sp_helpdb (which is a fairly harmless stored procedure) from the Procedure Name drop-down list. It accepts a single parameter (the database name to display). Type *Pubs* in the Value text box, and click Execute. Figure 35-6 shows a sample of the Stored Procedure tab of the T-SQL Debugger window.

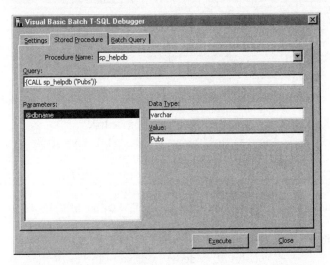

Figure 35-6 *The Stored Procedure tab of the Visual Basic Batch T-SQL Debugger window with the sp_helpdb stored procedure selected*

After you click the Execute button and the TSQL Debugger establishes a connection and launches the stored procedure, you see a window containing the stored-procedure code ready to be stepped into. You can press F8 at this point to step through the stored procedure. Figure 35-7 shows the T-SQL Debugger window.

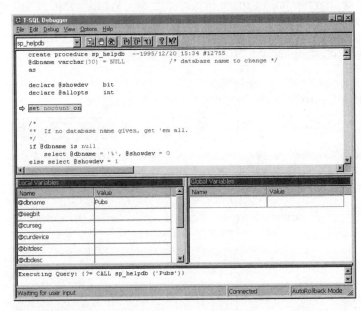

Figure 35-7 *The T-SQL Debugger window containing the sp_helpdb stored procedure code after the F8 key has been pressed*

Try this yourself and step through the whole procedure. Notice how the local variables change as you go. You can choose from a number of options on the toolbar and from the menus. These options are listed in Table 35-1.

Table 35-1
TSQL Debugger Options

Option	What It Does
Go	Same as the Run button or the F5 key in Visual Basic. Runs until the next breakpoint or the end of the stored procedure.
Set and clear breakpoints	Same as the F9 key. Toggles a breakpoint on the current line.
Step	Same as the F8 key. Executes the current line and break.
Step into subexpression	Same as the F8 key, but follows execution into procedure.
Step over subexpression	Does not follow trace into procedure.
Run to cursor	Executes all code without stopping until the trace reaches the selected line.
Stop debugging	Continues execution to the end of the procedure.
Restart	Starts the procedure from the beginning.

If you want to take a peek at the global variables, click under the Name column heading in the Global Variables window and type in one of the valid global variables. Remember, all of these begin with @@. While some global variables apply to the system as a whole, some are connection-specific because their contents apply only to the current connection. Table 35-2 lists a number of interesting connection-specific global variables.

Table 35-2
Some Connection-Specific Global Variables

Global Variable	What It Does
@@CURSOR_ROWS	Specifies the number of qualifying rows in the last-opened cursor. @@CURSOR_ROWS returns the following:
	-m If the cursor is being populated asynchronously. The value returned (-m) refers to the number of rows currently in the keyset.
	n If the cursor is fully populated. The value returned (n) refers to the number of rows.
	0 If no cursors have been opened or the last opened cursor has been closed or deallocated.
@@ERROR	Specifies the last error number generated by the system for the user connection. The @@ERROR global variable is commonly used to check the error status (success or failure) of the most recently executed statement. It contains 0 if the last state-

Global Variable	What It Does
	ment succeeded. Using @@ERROR with control-of-flow statements is advantageous for handling errors. The statement IF @@ERROR <> 0 RETURN exits if an error is returned.
@@IDENTITY	Saves the last-inserted IDENTITY value. The @@IDENTITY variable is updated specifically for each user when an INSERT or SELECT INTO statement or a bulk copy insertion into a table occurs.
@@NESTLEVEL	Specifies the nesting level of the current execution (initially 0). Each time a stored procedure calls another stored procedure, the nesting level is incremented. If the maximum of 16 is exceeded, the transaction is terminated.
@@ROWCOUNT	Specifies the number of rows affected by the last statement. This variable is set to 0 by any statement that doesn't return rows, such as an IF statement.
@@TRANCOUNT	Specifies the number of currently active transactions for the current user.

Invoking the TSQL Debugger from Code

Now that you have a feel for how a stored procedure can be debugged interactively, let's try to do the same thing from Visual Basic RDO or ADO code. (This doesn't work from ODBCDirect code.) The TSQL Debugger is tightly integrated with the UserConnection and the Data Environment designers. This means that you don't really have to do anything special besides setting the TSQL Debugger option that says to step into your stored procedures as they are encountered in code. If you loaded the TSQL Debugger using the Add-In Manager, you should have a T-SQL Debugging Options item on the Tools menu. When you select T-SQL Debugging Options from the Tools menu, the T-SQL Debugging Options dialog box shown in Figure 35-8 on the following page is displayed.

This dialog box informs Visual Basic to watch out for stored procedure invocations so that if your code happens to trip a stored procedure, even when executing an Update method that invokes a trigger, the next screen you see (after a 10-second to 30-second wait) is the TSQL Debugger window, waiting for you to step through the code. You can also set the Safe Mode option that makes sure the operations you perform in the stored procedure are rolled back when you exit. There is also a cap to limit the number of rows sent back by the procedure and a cap on the time that the TSQL Debugger waits while trying to get SQL Server to wake up and return status information. In this dialog box, the timeout limit is 10,000. However, 10,000 seconds seems like a *very* long time—that's about 2.8 hours, if the unit of measure is indeed seconds. (Actually, it's *milli*seconds, which puts the delay time at 10 seconds. Either delay should be long enough.)

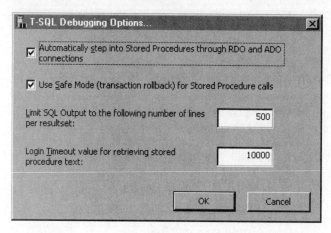

Figure 35-8 *The T-SQL Debugger Options dialog box*

Once you've selected the Automatically Step Into Stored Procedures Through RDO And ADO Connections check box, and if you step into (F8) a line of code that executes an RDO or ADO method that invokes a stored procedure, the debugger starts automatically. You can then step through the stored procedure and continue debugging your Visual Basic code. You can also debug a stored procedure from within a Visual Basic UserConnection or Data Environment Command object if the need presents itself—just right-click on the object and select Debug Stored Procedure or Debug from the pop-up menu to start a debug session for the stored procedure in that query.

NOTE SQL Server will return from a stored procedure before the stored procedure has finished executing once the stored procedure has returned enough data to fill its buffers. However, the stored procedure might not be complete at this point. If this happens, both the T-SQL Debugger and the Visual Basic debugger will be active at the same time. Your Visual Basic code must fetch the results from RDO or ADO before the stored procedure will complete its execution. You can make sure your code reads the result sets by placing Visual Basic in run mode (F5) and by setting breakpoints where you would like to stop execution. You can toggle back and forth between Visual Basic and the T-SQL Debugger by using the taskbar or by using the Alt-Tab key sequence.

Debugging the TSQL Debugger

When something goes wrong with the TSQL Debugger, the fault can often be found on the server end of the wire. Check the SQL Server and Windows NT event log. If SDI gets into trouble, it records its woes in the log in the application section. Use the Event Viewer to examine the log. You might also find reports from the Remote Automation components there because COM or DCOM might log events that can tell you what went wrong. Watch out for a few more hazards:

- If you're using TCP/IP, make sure that the two machines are on speaking terms. You can use the Ping application to test this interface. Just type this:

  Ping *servername*

  If this fails, there is no way that the TSQL Debugger can work.

- Make sure the file SDI.DLL resides in the same directory as SQLSERVR.EXE. This will be in the BINN subdirectory under the main SQL Server directory. The default is C:\MSSQL\BINN.

- Ensure that the Remote Procedure Call (RPC) services are started on your SQL server. You do this by opening the Control Panel on the Windows NT server, starting the Services application, and checking to be sure the Remote Procedure Call (RPC) Service and Remote Procedure Call Locator are running and set to start automatically. These services should have been set up when the TSQL Debugger was installed, but sometimes they are turned off by those not familiar with what's needed and what's extra baggage.

- Ensure that SQL Server isn't set to log on using the system account. You do this by opening the Services Control Panel applet and double-clicking on the MSSQLServer service. If the service is set to run using the system account, change this so the server will log on to a specific account that is valid to the domain that you're in. If debugging still fails, make sure the SQL Server account has sufficient rights to launch an Automation server on the client machine. (If you don't have access to a domain controller, you might have to run the SQL server in console mode.)

- If you see COM error 80080005 in the event log, make sure that you didn't start Remote Automation (AUTMGR32) from the command prompt. AUTMGR32.EXE should be running only in the account on which SQL Server logged in. If AUTMGR32.EXE is running in another account, other computers won't have sufficient permissions to perform global operations. Therefore, if AUTMGR32.EXE isn't running in the SQL Server account, close down AUTMGR32.EXE via the Task Manager and let SDI.DLL and AUTPRX32.DLL load AUTMGR32 via COM.

- Make sure Remote Automation is successfully installed on the server and the client machine if neither the client nor the server have DCOM installed and loaded.

- If your client is running Windows NT 4.0 or later, run DCOMCNFG and make sure that everyone has launch and access permission for VBSDICLI.EXE.

CAUTION

The TSQL Debugger has been one of the balkiest mules in the Visual Basic team. It has embarrassed me a dozen times from the podium when it sat on its butt and refused to move. I sometimes feel like dealing with this beast the way Patton dealt with those mules on the bridge in Sicily. I sure hope this version is in better shape. I can't say that it is at this writing. But there's still time. I would hate to pull out my ivory-handled .45 and put it out of its misery.

36

Using the Data View Window and Query Builder

The Data View Window

Using the Visual Database Tools to Manage Your SQL Server Database

Creating Queries with Query Builder

Using Query Builder with SQL Server

ne of the chapters that didn't make it into the last edition of the *Hitchhiker's Guide* was about the Microsoft Visual Database Tools. These tools have revolutionized the way developers work with Microsoft SQL Server database tables and stored procedures. They have also relieved the need to depend on Microsoft Access to build queries. The Visual Database Tools used to be hard to find because they weren't installed when you installed Microsoft Visual Basic—and since they came only with the Enterprise Edition, many developers never really got a chance to use them.

Well, the Visual Database Tools have been reborn. Instead of being installed and run as a separate application, they're now integrated into Visual Basic's user interface as the Data View window. The Visual Database Tools also appear in one form or another in SQL Server 7.0, Visual InterDev, and most of the other Visual Studio languages. In this chapter, we'll tour the Data View and you'll see how you can work with existing tables, views, stored procedures, and database schemas on SQL Server or on any back-end database you choose. The Data View window also exposes the Query Designer, which can really make it easy to generate your basic queries.

TIP   The MSDN documentation still appears to be calling these tools the Visual Database Tools rather than the Data View window or other related window names. Therefore, you might want to search for the term "Visual Database Tools" when you're looking for online help related to database access with Visual Basic 6.0.

The Data View Window

The Data View window is easy to access. It has a permanent icon on the Visual Basic "standard" toolbar. You can click this icon or choose Data View Window from the View menu. This window is one of those "dockable" critters that seems to attach itself to any nearby neighbor. This can be a real pain when you're hurting for screen real estate or you want to see the form underneath the "undocked" window.

> **TIP** Right-click on the Data View window and turn off the Dockable button. This prevents the Data View window from lying around on top of the stack and docking to the closest available window.

No, the Visual Basic 6.0 Query Designer really doesn't deal particularly well with complex procedures, and it doesn't let you graphically create stored procedures or multiple-result-set stored procedures. To make things worse, it also doesn't let you enter and test your own queries if they are more than fairly simple SELECT statements.

Once the Data View window is open, the currently registered Data Links are listed in an explorer-style list. Figure 36-1 shows a Data Link I created using the default name (not advisable), DataLink1.

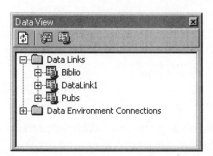

Figure 36-1   *Data Links displayed in the Data View window*

Data Links are merely ways to record an OLE DB ConnectionString in a standard location. You can install these files as part of your application's installation setup regimen. They are very much like file-based data source names (DSNs) but are a lot more flexible now that the OLE DB interface supports many more parameters in the ConnectionString.

Adding Data Links

In Chapter 30, I introduced you to Data Links and we talked about some of their characteristics. Here we're going to briefly review how you add them to your Visual Basic integrated development environment (IDE). No, Data Links are not saved with your application or component. They provide a list of data sources to make it easy to do database maintenance or build new application Connection objects or Command objects through the Data Environment designer.

Basically, to add a new Data Link, you have to touch the third icon from the left on the Data View window—Add A New Data Link—or right-click the Data Links folder and choose Add A Data Link. Either of these choices opens the Data Link Properties dialog box shown in Figure 36-2. (Recall that we already discussed this dialog box in Chapter 30; you can refer to that chapter if you want more details.) It's in this dialog box that you specify the OLE DB (or ODBC) provider and all the other parameters needed to identify the server, the database, and yourself to SQL Server.

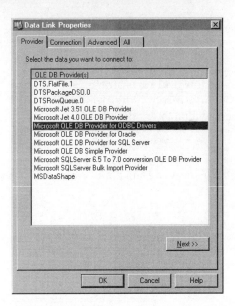

Figure 36-2 *The Data Link Properties dialog box*

When you finish providing the parameters to the Data Link Properties dialog box, control returns to the Data Link and the name is selected, so you can change it. I recommend that you do change it to make it easy to tell what you're linking to. For example, two of the Data Links shown in Figure 36-1 point to the *Biblio* and *Pubs* databases.

Once the new Data Link is installed, you can right-click on its icon and choose either Properties (to see a static list of properties, as shown in Figure 36-3), or Modify (to change the properties), which displays the Data Link Properties dialog box. Yes, this is very strange. I guess they were sleepy when they designed this.

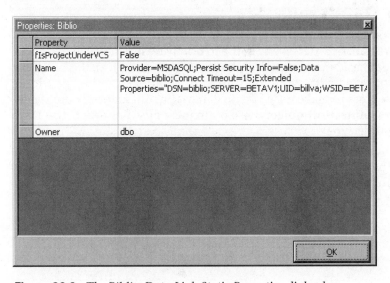

Figure 36-3 *The* Biblio *Data Link Static Properties dialog box*

Adding DataEnvironment Connections

We've also talked about adding, changing, and leveraging DataEnvironment Connection objects. The Data View window shows all the DataEnvironment Connections you have set up in your application. As you activate (by filling in the properties), add, or subtract Connections, these are automatically exposed in the Data View window. You can use an existing Data Link to create a new DataEnvironment Connection object or Command object simply by dragging the Data Link to the DataEnvironment window. Be sure to double-check the connection properties after you do so to make sure the connection information is still valid.

Exploring Your SQL Server Database

One of the benefits of the Data View window is that it exposes SQL Server's data interfaces. Once you click the + next to a Data Link or the Data Environment folder in the Data View window, Visual Basic (and ADO) opens the connection and queries for all the data definition language (DDL) structures in the database. This exposes all the database designs, tables, views, and stored procedures that are visible to your login ID. Yes, the database schema designs you and the rest of your team have created are all stored in the database, where everyone can see them. As I've said before, if you don't have permission to see parts of the database, those restricted portions won't appear in the list—you won't even get connected unless you have permission to log in. Using the appropriate folder icons, go ahead and explode the lists one by one. I clicked on the Biblio folder. If you do, too, you should see something like Figure 36-4. Notice that I also (single) clicked on the Authors table and exploded the column names.

WARNING!
The Data View window is a "live" interface. If you press Delete, your table will be deleted! This could be bad. Only providence and a foreign key relationship (that my wife doesn't know about) saved me when I did this by accident.

Figure 36-4 *Viewing the Biblio tables with a Data Link in the Data View window*

You can explode the column views on any of the objects by single-clicking on them. Double-clicking opens the object in "run" mode and lets you see the data in the database table view. However, double-clicking a stored procedure opens it in edit mode (for some reason that eludes me). We won't change the data yet, but this exercise will give you a feel for how it's done.

Double-click on the Authors icon in the *Biblio* database. (You have a backup copy of this database on the CD, so if you screw up you can easily restore it.) You should see a new window with a simple grid containing the rows from the table, as shown in Figure 36-5.

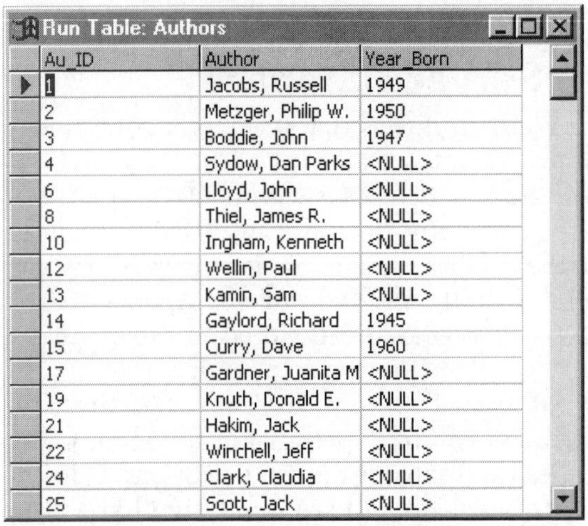

Au_ID	Author	Year_Born
1	Jacobs, Russell	1949
2	Metzger, Philip W.	1950
3	Boddie, John	1947
4	Sydow, Dan Parks	<NULL>
6	Lloyd, John	<NULL>
8	Thiel, James R.	<NULL>
10	Ingham, Kenneth	<NULL>
12	Wellin, Paul	<NULL>
13	Kamin, Sam	<NULL>
14	Gaylord, Richard	1945
15	Curry, Dave	1960
17	Gardner, Juanita M	<NULL>
19	Knuth, Donald E.	<NULL>
21	Hakim, Jack	<NULL>
22	Winchell, Jeff	<NULL>
24	Clark, Claudia	<NULL>
25	Scott, Jack	<NULL>

Run Table: Authors

Figure 36-5 *The Authors table in the* Biblio *database opened from the Data View window*

As tempting as it is to access the tables, remember our discussions earlier in the book about basing your designs around stored procedures. Yes, this data is live, so you can make changes—assuming you have permission to do so. Unfortunately, there is no mechanism to restrict the number of rows retrieved, so you might inadvertently impose a table lock on the database table if you aren't careful. On the other hand, the Data View window will time out after about a minute and close the query that created the table grid—whether or not you respond to the dialog box. Sure, you can choose to keep it open if you want to—but trust me, you don't.

If you right-click on the Authors table folder in the Data View window, another list of functions is exposed. From the pop-up menu, you can choose among the following options:

- **New Table** Exposes a dialog box that walks you through the process of creating a new table from scratch.

- **Open** Provides another way to enter "run" mode and see the data in the table.

- **Design**   Opens a dialog box used to modify an existing table.

- **New Trigger**   Helps you create one or more stored procedures to act as a trigger for your table.

- **Delete**   Lets you delete the selected object. Yes, if you choose this option, the table, view, stored procedure, or database diagram will be gone forever.

- **Rename**   Runs the required SQL commands to rename the object in question. This option appears when the Data View window can rename the object in question.

- **Refresh**   Instructs ADO and Visual Basic to requery the database for new or changed objects, such as newly added tables or stored procedures.

- **Dockable**   Tells Visual Basic if this window is dockable.

- **Hide**   Tells Visual Basic to hide this window.

- **Properties**   Shows detailed information about the structure and settings assigned to the chosen object.

Using the Visual Database Tools to Manage Your SQL Server Database

You can set up your database almost completely from the Data View window. No, the tools can't create a new database unless you want to run the right Disk Init, Create Database, and other sundry Transact-SQL (TSQL) commands. And no, you don't really want to do this—unless you have a lot of time to spend. SQL Enterprise Manager makes setting up a database very easy. Its dialog boxes are adequate and fairly intuitive. So go into SQL Server and create your database using its tools. And yes, SQL Server 7.0 also uses the same Visual Database Tools and a few more to make this process easy—and familiar to Visual Basic developers.

Creating Tables

OK, you're ready to create a new table. Far be it from me to tell you how to create a table. At least five chapters in this book cover that subject—and if you've gotten this far, you should already know how to create tables. But if you know what you want your table to look like, the Data View window is the way to create it. Right-click on the Tables folder in the Data View window, and choose New Table. You're immediately confronted with your first decision: What are you going to name the table? Let's call our new table *AuthorInfo* because we want to store more information on the author than is available for most authors. The dialog box in which we'll specify our table's name is shown in Figure 36-6.

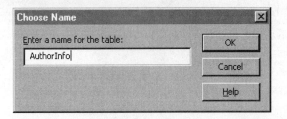

Figure 36-6   *The Choose Name dialog box displayed when creating a new table using the Data View window*

We'll put the author's picture here (or at least a path to that author's photo file) and other ancillary information that needn't clog up the regular Authors table. After you click OK to accept the new table's name, the New Table window appears.

Notice that this window lets you specify the name, the data type (from a drop-down list), and all the other attributes for each column. Specify the three columns (AU_ID, Photo, and Year_Died), as shown in Figure 36-7.

Column Name	Datatype	Length	Precision	Scale	Allow Nulls	Default Value	Identity	Identity Seed	Identity Increment
AU_ID	int	4	10	0			✓	1	1
Photo	varchar	255	0	0	✓				
Year_Died	smallint	2	5	0	✓				

Figure 36-7   *The New Table window with the columns for the AuthorInfo table specified*

If you choose Save Change Script from the File menu, the Data View Window prompts you with the SQL script it is about to execute to build the new table. A sample SQL script is shown in Figure 36-8.

You can save this script for your files to make database maintenance easier or to show to your administrator as a template of what you want him or her to change for you. If you examine this script, you'll notice that something is missing. Visual Database Tools knows nothing about *setting* permissions—that is, unless the permissions are already in place. This means that you can modify a table with permissions and the Visual Database Tools will restore these permissions for you when the script is run. Click Yes to save the script.

You can save the table definition by choosing Save Table from the File menu. If the Automatically Generate Change Script On Every Save checkbox is checked in the Save Change Script dialog box, the Save Change Script dialog box will be displayed again. Once the AuthorInfo table is saved, you can close the New Table window.

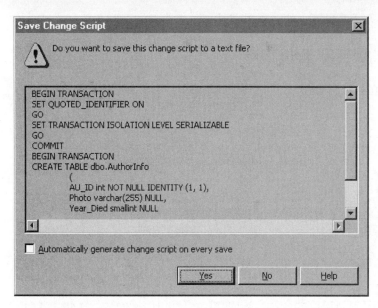

Figure 36-8 *SQL script generated to create the AuthorInfo table*

Modifying Tables

Changing existing tables is just as easy as creating new ones. You can right-click on any table (or view) and edit its structure using a similar window. We're going to modify our new table, but before we do, go over to SQL Enterprise Manager and assign permissions to the table. Here you'll see what permissions are granted by default; and when you get back, you'll see how the script reflects your changes. When you get to Enterprise Manager, remember to click Refresh on the Tables list to make sure your new table shows up. In SQL Server 6.5, simply right-click on the AuthorInfo table and select Permissions. This exposes the Object Permissions dialog box to set the column-by-column permissions. Click the Grant All button, and then click Set. Click Close and come back to your Visual Database Tools session.

Right-click on the AuthorInfo table, and choose Design. Add a new column named Year_Married that has the same column attributes used for the Year_Died column. You also need to change the Photo data type length from VarChar 255 to VarChar 200. Of course, this means that the whole table will have to be rebuilt—data and all. And yes, you can do this kind of edit on a pop-ulated table. The Data View window knows how to do this without your help.

Let's take a look at the script generated by all of these edits before we commit them to the database. Choose Save Change Script from the File menu. We'll save the script to a file and take a look at what's about to be changed. Unfortunately, this version of Visual Database Tools doesn't let us choose where the script is saved, so we have to dig into the directories to find it. My script was saved at C:\Program Files\Microsoft Visual Studio\VB98\DbDgm1.sql. The contents of DbDgm1.sql are shown on the following page.

```
BEGIN TRANSACTION
SET QUOTED_IDENTIFIER ON
GO
SET TRANSACTION ISOLATION LEVEL SERIALIZABLE
GO
COMMIT
BEGIN TRANSACTION
CREATE TABLE dbo.Tmp_AuthorInfo
    (
    AU_ID int NOT NULL IDENTITY (1, 1),
    Photo varchar(200) NULL,
    Year_Died smallint NULL,
    Year_Married smallint NULL
    ) ON "default"
GO
SET IDENTITY_INSERT dbo.Tmp_AuthorInfo ON
GO
IF EXISTS(SELECT * FROM dbo.AuthorInfo)
    EXEC('INSERT INTO dbo.Tmp_AuthorInfo(AU_ID, Photo, Year_Died)
        SELECT AU_ID, CONVERT(varchar(200), Photo),
        Year_Died FROM dbo.AuthorInfo TABLOCKX')
GO
SET IDENTITY_INSERT dbo.Tmp_AuthorInfo OFF
GO
DROP TABLE dbo.AuthorInfo
GO
EXECUTE sp_rename 'dbo.Tmp_AuthorInfo', 'AuthorInfo'
GO
GRANT REFERENCES ON dbo.AuthorInfo TO public
GRANT SELECT ON dbo.AuthorInfo TO public
    ... many permission commands removed for brevity.
GRANT UPDATE ON dbo.AuthorInfo TO SQL$Server$Users
COMMIT
```

Notice that the Visual Database Tools remembered to do a number of things you might have forgotten to do if you were to write this script by hand. The script provides blow-by-blow documentation of what changes were made. The script was also executed in a transaction batch to make sure that the whole operation completes or rolls back as an atomic unit. Notice that the old data was extracted and inserted into the new table through an INSERT TSQL statement driven from data in the old table. I couldn't have done it better myself.

Creating Indexes

Once you create a table, it's important to create indexes where it makes sense. If you expect to create updateable cursors on the tables, you have to create a unique key—the primary key using one or more columns of the table. Yes, the Visual Database Tools know how to do this too. In the Table window, select the column you want to designate as containing the primary key. I chose the AU_ID column as the primary key. If there is more than one column in the key, use the Ctrl-click technique to choose as many columns as makes sense. Next, right-click on the selected column set, and you'll get a pop-up menu of commands that includes Set Primary Key. Click on this command, and the Data View window creates the appropriate script to create the index. Keep in mind that a primary key can't be created on a column that allows null values. When you choose Save AuthorInfo (the name of our new table) from the File menu, Visual Database Tools executes the script to create the index. In this case, the script contains the table definition and a clause to create a constraint that defines the primary key.

Creating Relationships

Another, perhaps even easier way to designate the primary key is by using the Database Diagram window. Next you need to decide how the new table will "relate" to the original set of tables. This relationship is referred to in relational-speak as establishing a primary-key-to-foreign-key relationship. For example, for a new row in the AuthorInfo table to be valid, its AU_ID column value must match an existing Au_ID value in a row in the Authors table.

To establish this relationship, we need to start from a new or existing database diagram. In the Data View window, right-click the Database Diagrams folder and select New Diagram, or right-click one of the existing Database Diagrams and select Open. In the Database Diagram window, drag in the appropriate tables from the list of valid tables in the Data View window (or create a new table). I dragged in the Authors table and the AuthorInfo table. Right-drag the proposed key column (the Au_ID) from the Authors table to the AuthorInfo table. You'll be presented with the Create Relationship dialog box, shown in Figure 36-9, which asks how you want SQL Server to manage the table relationship and asks you to confirm your choice of column(s) that will participate in the relationship.

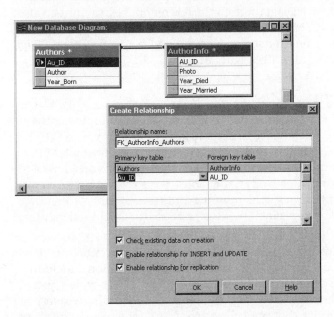

Figure 36-9 *The Create Relationship dialog box displayed when creating a relationship between the Authors table and the AuthorInfo table*

It's tough to make a mistake here because the Data View window checks to make sure that the data types match and that you didn't make any other mistakes when defining the table or relationship. Notice that I didn't name the AuthorInfo AU_ID column the same as the Authors Au_ID column—yes, just the capitalization on the *u* is different. Although SQL Server maintains case on the columns and other objects you create, this capitalization difference is *not* significant unless you install your server in case-sensitive mode. Unless you're really into abuse, I wouldn't do this—the case-insensitive default is far easier to work with.

Once the relationship is defined, whenever you hover over the lines connecting the tables in the Database Diagram window, the Data View window shows a ToolTip that describes it. You can also permanently turn on the relationship labels (by right-clicking the Data Diagram window and choosing it from the menu) to document what you're doing—as well as to add text annotations to the diagram. The connecting line between the two tables is also informative. It shows a one (the end with the little key)–to–many (the end with the infinity symbol) relationship. Remember that the diagram is stored in the database and viewable by anyone on your team using the Visual Database Tools—from any Visual Studio language.

Creating Database Schemas

You've already started to create a database diagram. The two-table relationship we just plotted is the beginning of our diagram. To flesh out the diagram, drag the remaining tables from the *Biblio* database to the diagram. The Visual Database Tools fills in the relationships it knows about. You can fill in whatever documentation you feel is appropriate or even pass on tips or warnings to other developers to keep their hands off your private tables. To save your database schema diagram, select Save Diagram from the File menu. Yes, saving can also generate a script because Visual Database Tools might need to make changes to the database tables or relationships. A completed diagram for the *Biblio* database could look something like Figure 36-10.

Creating Views

A SQL View is a logical representation of your data. A View is implemented as a SELECT statement that references one or more tables—usually with a WHERE clause. It can't include an ORDER BY clause, but it can have considerable "filter" logic in the WHERE clause. We can assign separate permissions on Views and henceforth use them anywhere we can use tables, with very few restrictions. This means you can expose selected columns and rows of tables to enforce security or simply make query generation easier. See SQL Server Books Online for more information on TSQL Views.

To use Data View window to create a View, simply right-click on the Views folder in the Data View window. This exposes a menu of options, including New View. When you choose New View, you expose a four-pane "query" window—because a View is created like and looks like an ordinary query in most ways. However, notice that there is no way to ask for a sort. A sample of the View window is shown in Figure 36-11.

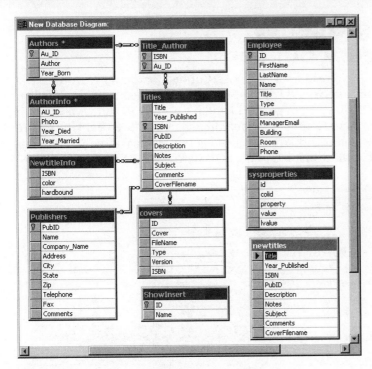

Figure 36-10 *Possible* Biblio *database diagram*

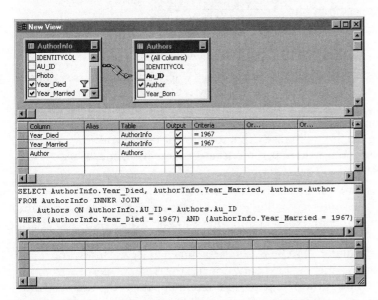

Figure 36-11 *The View window being used to create a View*

Creating Queries with Query Builder

Remember when you read about the UserConnection designer in the RDO chapters and when I said don't push the Build button when creating your own SQL statement? Well, you can go ahead and push the SQL Builder button on the Data Environment Command Properties dialog box (General tab). Figure 36-12 shows the Command Properties dialog box. To make the SQL Builder button active, you must first select the SQL Statement option.

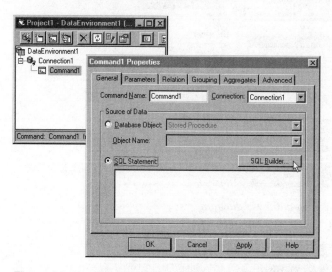

Figure 36-12 *The SQL Builder button in the Command Properties dialog box*

This launches the Visual Database Tools Query Builder and is similar to the window used to create Views. This puppy is the neatest part of the Visual Database Tools. It's designed to provide you with a four-pane view on your query. Check out MSDN Help for more detailed information on this tool, but come back here when you're ready to know how it really works. Apparently, the documentation was written before Visual Basic 6.0 was done, so it describes a few features that aren't quite there.

First add a new Data Environment if you don't already have one. Configure the Connection to point to the *Biblio* database and create a new Command in the Data Environment. No, you don't have to point the Command at any particular table just yet. Go to the property page of your new Command, and launch the Query Builder. The Query Builder is shown in Figure 36-13. The upper pane is the Diagram pane, the next pane down is the Grid or Query By Example (QBE) pane, the third is the SQL pane, and the final pane is the Results pane.

The easiest way to use the Query Builder is with the Data View window open alongside it, as shown in Figure 36-13. This arrangement is best because the Query Builder wants to get table references from the list of tables exposed with your DataEnvironment Connection. No, you can't drag tables from the Data Links list in the Data View window. This query needs to be built from the DataEnvironment Connections list of tables in the Data View window.

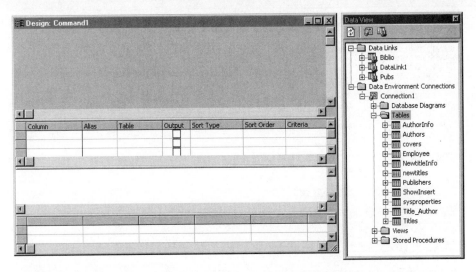

Figure 36-13 *The Query Builder window and the DataEnvironment Connections list of tables in the Data View window*

OK, start by dragging the Authors table from the Data View window tables list under your new Command to the top Diagram pane. This automatically starts a SQL query that is written to the SQL pane.

Of course, you could have just typed *Select * From authors* in the SQL pane and the same thing would have happened—only in reverse. The Data View window would have built a graphical representation of your table in the Diagram pane. You can drag over as many tables or views as you want to. You can even drag over diagrams from the Database Diagrams list. You can't drag over stored procedures, however. Once you change the SQL pane (and change focus), the Query Builder updates the other panes to reflect your changes (if it can). You can verify your SQL syntax by choosing Verify SQL Syntax from the Query menu or right-clicking in the SQL pane and choosing the Verify SQL Syntax option.

As you drag tables, views or diagrams over to the Diagram pane, Visual Database Tools converts the table relationships to SQL joins. You can right-click on the join graphics to make whatever changes are appropriate for your particular query. Just keep in mind that if you get it wrong, the right SQL syntax will be created—but the wrong rows might result from your query. On the other hand, if you type in the SQL statement yourself, the wrong SQL syntax might be generated—but then again, the wrong rows might still result. Dem's the breaks.

Once the tables are in place, choose the columns to include in the query by clicking on the check box(es) associated with each table column. In this case, I chose the Author and Year_Born columns from the Authors table. When you make these column selections, the middle QBE pane appears, displaying the selections, as shown in Figure 36-14.

Frankly, I find this somewhat difficult to fathom. The Data View tables are associated with persisted data sources, not ADO Connections. When you change the properties of a DataEnvironment Command, it is associated with an ADO Command object that might have different properties than the Data View data source. In any case, ADO and the Data Environment designer figure all of this out for you.

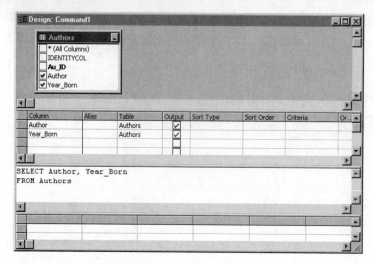

Figure 36-14 *Using the Query Builder to create a SQL query for a Data Environment Command*

This Microsoft Access–like interface lets you choose the columns to display or simply include in the query and any criteria or sort information. This interface is intuitive enough for most of you, and it has few surprises. Notice that when you select a column to sort, the Diagram pane table graphic changes to show that the chosen column is being sorted.

Of course, what we just created was a SELECT query. If you right-click on the Query Designer or choose Change Type from the Query menu, you can choose either a Select, Insert, Insert Values, Update, Delete, or Make Table query. Visual Database Tools does its best to make sure you enter the right arguments at the right time. Yes, you can execute any of these queries from a Command object.

When your query is done, simply press the close button on the form (upper-right X). If all you want to do is save your work, choose Save Command1 (the name of the Command you're working on) from the File menu.

Testing Your Query

If you feel brave, you can test your query. But wait, before you do, consider that you might be running against live data. Is this really what you want to do? Consider that your query doesn't have a WHERE clause (unless you added one), and if it's an action query (such as UPDATE, DELETE, or INSERT), it might make irreversible changes to the database. Like the Visual Basic 5.0 version, this version of Visual Database Tools doesn't support row limits, so your queries will return data until Thursday unless you tell SQL Server to do otherwise. Yes, you can set row limits on your Command object, but these won't be used until you run the Command. Here we're just running the SQL statement on its own to see if it compiles and runs without throwing a rod.

To test your query, right-click on the Query window and select Run. Any rows that return appear in the bottom Results pane. This pane is editable, so you can change the data if SQL Server and ADO can figure out how to do so. It's not always possible, so don't get your hopes up. You should see something like Figure 36-15.

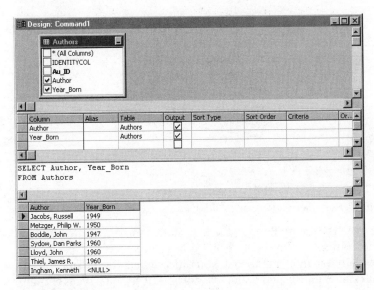

Figure 36-15   *The results of executing a risky query*

> **TIP**   If you don't close this Results pane in a few minutes, Visual Database Tools closes it for you to free the countless locks you created by running an unbounded SELECT statement (with no WHERE clause).

Creating Parameter Queries

OK, we're ready to go to the next level in your tour of the Visual Database Tools. Since most of your serious queries are going to call for parameters, you'll need to know how to build parameter queries with the Query Designer. Actually, you can do this in a variety of ways—but I'll lead you down the easiest path.

For some reason, the Query Builder hasn't figured out that we're talking to SQL Server (it *should* know), so we have to tell it that SQL Server uses the @ character to delineate stored procedure parameters. Right-click on the Query window (anywhere), and choose Properties. Next choose the Parameters tab. In the Prefix Characters field, enter @ (just the "at" sign) and close the window. We're now ready to modify our query to accept a parameter. Add the following SQL code to the SQL pane (at the bottom of the query):

```
WHERE Author Like @AuthorWanted
```

Run your query again. Notice how the Query Builder exposes a dialog box to capture the parameter(s), as shown in Figure 36-16. Enter appropriate values, and click OK. The query will be run with this value, and if any rows qualify, they are shown in the Results pane.

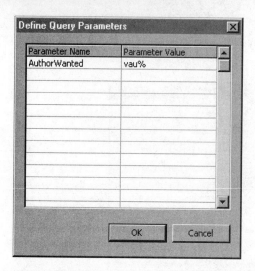

Figure 36-16 *The Define Query Parameters dialog box*

When you close the Query Builder, the SQL statement you created will be posted back to the Command object you're building—parameters and all (assuming your query contains parameter markers). You can switch to the Parameters tab and supply default values for the parameters as well as tune the data types chosen.

Creating Stored Procedures

The next step is to build a stored procedure. This is a critical step in most serious SQL Server implementations, so I expect you'll spend quite a bit of time on it. Building stored procedures involves two fairly easy steps:

1. Create the SQL statement for the procedure as well as for any parameters—including input, output, input/output, or return value.

2. Create the stored procedure using the query.

We'll use the Query Builder to create the stored procedure SQL. We could also use Data View window to either build a new stored procedure or edit an existing TSQL procedure.

To begin, create a Command object, and start the Query Builder as before. Create the stored procedure code if possible. The Query Builder won't understand your query if it is anything except a common query. You will likely get the dialog box shown in Figure 36-17, which informs you that the Query Builder can't keep the Diagram, Grid, and SQL panes in sync. This means that although you can use the Query Builder to create simple queries, you can't use it for the remaining logic. You'll have to deal with this on your own in the Stored Procedure Editor.

OK, let's assume you have a prototype query built with the Query Builder. Select the query using Ctrl-A, and press Ctrl-C to copy it to the clipboard. We'll paste it into the stored procedure editor window in a minute.

Right-click on the Stored Procedures folder in your Data View window, and choose New Stored Procedure. This launches the Stored Procedure Editor with a template stored procedure already filled in—in full color. (See Figure 36-18.)

This is really disappointing. I fully expected that the Data View window and Visual Database Tools incorporated in the other languages and tools would have done a better job dealing with the intricacies of stored procedures. Perhaps some other version will catch up.

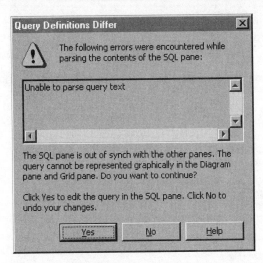

Figure 36-17   *The Query Definitions Differ dialog box, indicating the SQL pane is out of sync with other panes*

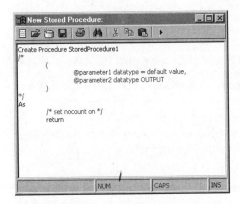

Figure 36-18   *The Stored Procedure Editor*

You need to fill in a few values to get your stored procedure to work:

● **The stored procedure name**   After the Create Procedure keywords, fill in the name of your stored procedure using standard SQL Server naming conventions. No, the name doesn't have to be particularly meaningful—you just won't be able to find it later if it isn't. I'll name my procedure AuthorByName.

● **The input parameters**   Notice the open parenthesis "(" and @parameter1 datatype entry in green? This is a commented-out line to remind you of the syntax. Remove the comments if your procedure has a parameter and fill in the name of the parameter and its datatype and default value (if any). I'll use *@AuthorWanted VarChar(30)* for my parameter name and data type. If your parameter is an OUTPUT parameter, add the keyword OUTPUT to the end of the Parameter declaration line.

- **The SQL needed to perform the operation** After the As keyword, paste in the SQL we just built, or type in your own. I just pasted in the SELECT statement from the previous example. The parameter in the query has to match the input parameter provided above.

When you're done, you should have something that looks like Figure 36-19.

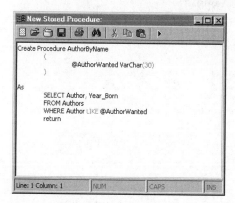

Figure 36-19 *The AuthorByName stored procedure in the Stored Procedure Editor*

If you're happy with the stored procedure code, you can run it through the TSQL Debugger by right-clicking on the procedure and choosing Debug. To save your procedure to the database, use the right-click Save To Database option or click on the database icon at the top of the editor window. This does all of the required TSQL operations to remove existing stored procedures of the same name and installs your new version. It's that easy.

Certainly, creating stored procedures can be more complex than this. But you get the idea.

Using Query Builder with SQL Server

The following guidelines highlight the differences you'll notice in the Visual Database Tools' Query Designer when you work with SQL Server. They will also provide you with information about SQL Server–specific features you can leverage.

SQL Server Version

The Query Designer is designed to support versions 6.5 and 7.0 of SQL Server but is fully compatible with earlier versions as well. If you're using a version of SQL Server earlier than 6.0, the Query Designer won't recognize SQL Server–specific features (such as syntax elements or functions). Instead, the Query Designer will recognize only standard ODBC syntax.

SQL Syntax

When the Query Designer builds a statement in the SQL pane, it uses syntax specific to SQL Server whenever possible. For example, database objects such as tables and views are qualified using SQL Server owner names. You can also enter your own SQL Server–specific syntax in the SQL pane. In some cases when you verify a query, the Query Designer converts server-specific syntax to ANSI standard syntax. However, the changed query should return the same results.

Identifying Database Objects

When you enter the names of database objects (tables, views, and columns) in the SQL pane, you must provide sufficient information for SQL Server to identify the object you want. Database objects are identified with unique names that consist of up to three parts (for tables and views) or four parts (for columns):

- database.owner.table
- database.owner.table.column

In general, you need to provide only enough qualifiers to uniquely identify the object you want to work with. For example, if you're working with a column named "price" in the titles table in the current database, you can simply reference the column by name, as in this SQL statement:

```
SELECT price
FROM titles
```

However, if you're working with two tables, say, orders and products, and each has a column named "price," you must qualify references to the column with the appropriate table name, as in this example:

```
SELECT products.prod_id, orders.price
FROM orders INNER JOIN products ON
 orders.prod_id = products.prod_id
```

When you use the Data View window Query Designer's Diagram and Grid panes to work with tables in the current database, the Query Designer automatically adds owner and table qualifiers for you. If you're not the owner of a table that you're working with, the owner's name will appear in the table names. For example, if you work in the *Pubs* database, the owner name *dbo* will appear in front of table names. If you're working with multiple tables, the Query Designer adds table name qualifiers to column names.

For compatibility with other databases, you can bracket ([ ]) identifier names in the SQL pane. When the SQL statement is reformatted, the brackets are replaced with double quotation marks ("), which are used to mark database identifiers.

Using Quotation Marks

The standard delimiters for literal strings in SQL are single quotation marks ('). By default, SQL Server reserves double quotation marks (") as delimiters for database objects. The SQL Server ODBC driver supports a Quoted Identifiers setting for the session or connection. If this setting is on, the driver interprets double quotation marks as delimiters for identifiers. If you turn off this setting, however, the driver interprets double quotation marks as delimiters for literal strings.

To avoid ambiguity, the Query Designer always sets Quoted Identifiers on so that double quotation marks are always interpreted as database object delimiters. If you have previously turned off Quoted Identifiers, the Query Designer overrides your setting. Therefore, in the Query Designer, always use single quotation marks to enclose string literals. Use double quotation marks only as needed for database objects delimiters.

Case Sensitivity

Text information in a SQL Server database can be stored in uppercase letters, lowercase letters, or a combination of both. For example, a last name can appear as SMITH, Smith, or smith. Depending on how you installed SQL Server, databases can be case-sensitive or case-insensitive. If a database is case-sensitive, when you search for text data, you must construct your search conditions using the exact combination of uppercase and lowercase letters. For example, if you're looking for the name "Smith," you can't use the search conditions "=smith" or "=SMITH." In addition, if the server was installed as case-sensitive, you must provide database, owner, table, and column names using the correct combination of uppercase and lowercase characters. If the case of the name you provide doesn't match exactly, SQL Server returns an error reporting an "invalid object name."

When you create queries using the Diagram and Grid panes, the Query Designer will always accurately reflect the case sensitivity of your server. If you enter queries in the SQL pane, however, you must be careful to match names to the way the server will interpret them.

If the server was installed with a case-insensitive option, you can enter database object identifiers and search conditions using any combination of uppercase and lowercase characters. However, the server doesn't discriminate between database values having different cases. For example, SMITH, Smith, smith, and SmITh are all considered identical values.

TIP   To determine the case sensitivity of a server, execute the stored procedure sp_server_info and then examine the contents of row 18. If the server has been installed with the case-insensitive setting, the option for sort_order will be set to nocase.

Creating Aliases

In the SQL pane, you can use the = operator to specify an alias, as in this example:

```
SELECT tax = price * .1
FROM table
```

When you change panes or execute the query, the SQL statement is reformatted and the = is replaced with AS.

Using Operators in Expressions

SQL Server supports all standard operators for expressions, including % for modulus. In addition, you can use the bitwise operators shown below in expressions.

Operator	Meaning
&	BITAND
|	BITOR
^	BITXOR
~	BITNOT

Entering Keywords in the Grid and SQL Panes

The Visual Database Tools' Query Designer supports the use of certain SQL Server constants, variables, and reserved column names in the Grid and SQL panes. Generally, you can enter these values by typing them in, but the Grid pane won't display them in drop-down lists. Examples of supported names include these:

- **IDENTITYCOL**   If you enter this name in the Grid or SQL pane, SQL Server will recognize it as a reference to an auto-incrementing column.

- **Predefined global values**   You can enter values such as @@CONNECTIONS and @@CURSOR_ROW into the Grid and SQL panes.

- **Constants (niladic functions)**   You can enter constant values such as CURRENT_TIMESTAMP and CURRENT_USER in either pane.

- **NULL**   If you enter NULL in the Grid or SQL panes, it is treated as a literal value, not a constant.

Entering Currency Values

In the Grid pane, to specify that you want data interpreted as money, precede the value with $ or $- (for negative values). Do not include a comma or other delimiter to indicate thousands. Formatting values this way alerts the Query Designer that you are entering values to be treated as or compared to data in money or smallmoney type columns. Values are rounded to the nearest hundredth of a unit.

You can use $ no matter what currency you're working with. When a query displays values from money columns in the Results pane, it doesn't include the $ prefix. Depending on the setting in the Windows Regional Settings dialog box, currency data might or might not include a comma or other delimiter for thousands.

Using DISTINCT

If you're working with SQL Server 6.5 or earlier, using the DISTINCT keyword creates a query that can't be updated in the Results pane.

Creating Outer Joins

In the SQL pane, you can use the SQL Server–specific *= and =* operators to specify an outer join. When you change panes or execute the query, the Query Designer reformats your SQL statement and replaces *= with LEFT OUTER JOIN and =* with RIGHT OUTER JOIN.

Entering Blanks

In SQL Server, two single quotation marks are treated as a single space (as far as Visual Database Tools is concerned). For example, you can use quotation marks in the following expression: 'abc' + '' + 'def'. The resulting value will be 'abd def'.

Including Optimizer Hint Comments

If you're entering a query directly in the SQL pane, you can add optimizer hints to specify the use of specific indexes, locking methods, and so on. However, when reformatting the contents of the SQL pane, the Query Designer might not maintain these comments. Optimizer comments are not represented graphically. For more details about optimizer hints, refer to the SQL Server documentation.

ANSI to OEM Character Conversion

Data containing extended characters—that is, characters outside the ASCII range 32 (space) to 126 (~), including international characters such as ä, ç, é, ñ, and ß—can require special handling when you're working with SQL Server.

The representation of extended characters in a result set depends on the code page in use. A *code page* is a character set that a computer uses to interpret and display data properly. Code pages usually correspond to different platforms and languages and are used in international applications. For example, the ASCII value 174 might appear as the symbol ® in one code page but as a chevron character in another code page.

In general, code pages are divided into ANSI code pages and OEM code pages. ANSI code pages, in which high-numbered ASCII values represent international characters, are used in Microsoft Windows. OEM code pages, in which high-numbered ASCII values represent line-drawing and punctuation characters, were designed for MS-DOS.

When data is entered into a SQL Server database, ODBC settings on the local (client) computer specify whether the data is stored in ANSI or OEM format. The option is specified using the Convert OEM To ANSI Characters option in the ODBC SQL Server Setup dialog box.

By default, this option is not selected for the SQL Server ODBC driver, a choice which causes the data to be stored in ANSI format. However, if this option has been selected, the ODBC driver converts high-numbered ASCII characters to OEM characters. For example, if the OEM conversion option is set and you enter the name "Günther" in a column and then save the row, the character "ü" will be converted to another character before the row is stored in the database.

The results of queries that you create in the Query Designer are affected by the format in which extended-character data is stored in combination with the setting of the OEM conversion option in the ODBC SQL Server Setup dialog box. Depending on these variables, you might be faced with the following situations:

- You might not be able to search for data that includes high-order ASCII characters.

- Your query results might appear in the Results pane with incorrect characters substituted for high-order ASCII characters.

In general, if data is stored in OEM format, you should set the OEM conversion option so that the data will display properly and so that you can search it. If data is stored in ANSI format (that is, it wasn't converted to OEM format) but you've set the OEM conversion option, the data won't display properly and you won't be able to search for it.

To determine whether data was stored in OEM format, you can use a query to display the contents of the table or tables you're working with. If extended characters appear incorrect, the OEM conversion setting is probably wrong. Close the query and the project, change the setting in the ODBC SQL Server Setup dialog box, and open the project and query again.

Unsupported and Partially Supported Query Types

Some types of legal SQL Server queries can't be represented graphically in the Query Designer. You can still enter them in the SQL pane, and they will execute correctly. However, the Query Designer will display the Query Definitions Differ dialog box and report an error when you execute your query or change panes.

The following types of SQL Server queries are not supported graphically:

- Queries using INTERSECT

- Queries using MINUS

- Queries using UNION [ALL]

- Queries using CASE

- Any DDL query, including CREATE TABLE, ALTER TABLE, CREATE PROCEDURE, ALTER PROCEDURE, and so on. CREATE VIEW and ALTER VIEW queries are not supported graphically, but you can use the View Designer to create and edit views.

- Update and Delete queries that include an extra FROM clause (FROM table FROM table) that specifies the list of rows to update or delete.

The following types of queries can't be represented graphically, so you must enter them in the SQL pane. They don't result in errors when you execute them or change panes.

- Queries using the FOR BROWSE clause

- Queries that include TSEQUAL and UPDATE as a search condition

- Queries that include CURRENT OF

37

Taking the Data Environment Designer Out for a Spin

Getting Started with the Data Environment Designer

Working with Stored Procedures from the Data Environment

Working with Hierarchical Result Sets and Other Children

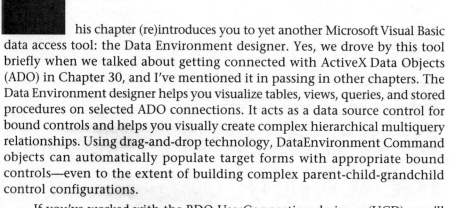

This chapter (re)introduces you to yet another Microsoft Visual Basic data access tool: the Data Environment designer. Yes, we drove by this tool briefly when we talked about getting connected with ActiveX Data Objects (ADO) in Chapter 30, and I've mentioned it in passing in other chapters. The Data Environment designer helps you visualize tables, views, queries, and stored procedures on selected ADO connections. It acts as a data source control for bound controls and helps you visually create complex hierarchical multiquery relationships. Using drag-and-drop technology, DataEnvironment Command objects can automatically populate target forms with appropriate bound controls—even to the extent of building complex parent-child-grandchild control configurations.

If you've worked with the RDO UserConnection designer (UCD), you'll easily understand the first few pages of this material. (Reread Chapter 22 if you need a quick refresher on the UCD.) You'll quickly find that the Data Environment designer is far more ambitious than the UCD—especially when it comes to acting as a data source control. Keep in mind that the Data Environment designer is based on ADO instead of RDO. That's good because you can use it with ADO, but bad because it works only with relational data sources—those that expose their data in terms of tables accessed via SQL statements. Many other OLE DB providers aren't exposed using the Data Environment designer—including Microsoft Index Server and others. But all of your ODBC data sources will work, and you're just interested in Microsoft SQL Server, right? And yes, you can use the DataEnvironment objects from code, pretty much like you use the UCD. Well, sort of—you'll have to watch out for several new potholes.

As with the Data control and the UCD, you can create virtually codeless applications with the Data Environment designer. (And yes, those "code-free" days were rough too.) Remember how Visual Basic 3.0 was initially demonstrated by dragging the Data control to a form followed by a handful of TextBox and Picture controls? Remember how easy all of this looked and how poorly it performed and scaled when used with client/server systems? In many ways, you can think of the DataEnvironment object as a type of Data control—because it's another "data source" interface. No, there is no "control" associated with the DataEnvironment object, as there is for the Data control, so you'll have to expose your own navigation buttons if they're called for. And no, even though Microsoft Visual InterDev includes a neat Data Navigator control, Visual Basic 6.0 doesn't include an equivalent function—but sure, you can write your own fairly easily. Data-aware controls such as the TextBox, ListBox, Grid, and all the other "bound" controls recognize the DataEnvironment object as a valid source of data. That's because Visual Basic 6.0 redefines the way data binding works. And that's good—it's about time. You can hook up the DataEnvironment object to a table (if you have rocks in your head), to a view, with a query you write, or with a stored procedure. The DataEnvironment object can also link several queries together in a hierarchy, so you can leverage the ADO SQL SHAPE syntax to create hierarchical Recordset objects. But I'm getting ahead of myself.

So let's take the step-at-a-time tour of the Data Environment designer, solving little problems along the way and working up to a more complex solution. This tour should save you a couple of days at least (days I already spent figuring this out). Some of the things going on are pretty intuitive, but not all (by far). Keep in mind that despite the rough edges, the Data Environment designer can save you time (and money) even if you don't choose to drag a single DataEnvironment Command object over to a form to get instant binding. If you think of the Data Environment designer as an ADO-based UCD, you'll be a lot happier with what it can accomplish for you.

Like the UCD, the Data Environment designer builds objects that encapsulate design-time-captured properties and settings used at run time to establish a connection and execute predefined queries. Unlike the UserConnection object, which mapped to a single connection, a single DataEnvironment object can have as many Data Environment "connections" as you need. These connections are exposed as ADO Connection objects. Under each, you can add as many Commands as needed to define the query, table, view, stored procedures, and any parameters required.

The Data Environment designer provides a design-time interface to the ADO Connection and Command objects that the Visual Basic development system builds for you behind the scenes. A DataEnvironment object also exposes itself at run time so that the individual Command objects and result sets can all be accessed through typical Component Object Model (COM) interfaces. You can have as many DataEnvironment objects as you like. No, that's not really true. Consider that each DataEnvironment object consumes at least one connection—one for each Connection object you create. So, practically, you're limited by the sanity of scalability and resource sharing. No, these connections aren't *all* opened when the application starts. That is, unless you bind a Command to a control—then Visual Basic tries to open each referenced connection and build the Recordset before Form load—just like the Data control. And yes, there are ways to get around this. Just stay tuned.

As I said earlier, the Data Environment designer is an ambitious feature. When first described in the Visual Basic 6.0 spec some time ago, it seemed that it would solve many of the nagging problems developers were having when binding complex result sets—especially with stored procedures. However, what was implemented fell considerably short of the mark. In its defense, it was under a great deal of pressure from a variety of "client" applications, such as Microsoft Visual Studio, Microsoft Office, and SQL Server 7.0. Each of these organizations had its own agenda, and although each wanted the best experience for its customers, these goals were often contradictory—or so it seemed. The result is a feature that seems to work fine on the surface, with simple queries and simple table access (as long as the tables are small), but when pressed by more complex result sets, the paradigm often breaks down.

Getting Started with the Data Environment Designer

To get started, you need to load a Visual Basic 6.0–based application using either the Standard or new Data Project template. We'll be using the *Biblio* database for this tour. (Appendix A contains information about how to set up *Biblio*.) So get your SQL Server fired up. Sure, all of this works with SQL Server 6.0 and 6.5 as well as 7.0 (and Oracle too).

Here's what you do when starting from a clean-slate form. First choose Add Data Environment from the Project menu or the Add Data Environment icon in the Data View window. This launches the DataEnvironment window—no, it doesn't launch into a designer as the UCD does. Hover over each of the toolbar buttons and the ToolTip will tell you what each does:

- **Add Connection**   Sets up a new Connection object. You'll have to fill in the properties yourself.

- **Add Command**   Sets up a new Command on a chosen Connection.

- **Insert Stored Procedures**   Launches a finder dialog box to show all stored procedures on the DataEnvironment Connection object.

- **Add Child Command**   Adds a child Command object to your current command hierarchy.

- **Delete, Refresh**   Performs the typical functions.

- **Design**   Launches the Query designer when the selected Command has a SQL statement or text command source.

- **Properties**   Lets you modify the properties of the selected object.

- **View Code**   Opens the code pane for the selected Command, Connection, or Data Environment.

- **Options**   Lets you change the behavior of the Data Environment designer. I like to change the Show Properties… to checked—that way when you create a new Connection or Command the properties window pops up automatically. This button is also how you change the Field Mapping.

- **Arrange By**   Connections/Arrange By Objects Changes the sort order of the Data Environment objects.

Now that you've added a Data Environment, name the Connection after the server or the database (if there's only one database). We'll name this Connection object *Biblio*—you'll have to right-click on the Connection icon to rename it. You'll use this name in code to refer to the connection.

You'll need to set one or more additional Connection properties. There are two locations where we set Connection properties, which are very different. First right-click on the Data Environment Connection (you named it Biblio) and choose Properties. This brings up our old pal the Data Link Properties dialog box. Go ahead and fill in the blanks to establish the connection and click OK to close the properties dialog box.

You can set additional Connection properties via the Visual Basic 6.0 Properties window. You can set both design-time and run-time behaviors for your Connection in this window. Be sure that Biblio DEConnection appears in the Properties window list box. Set the DesignPromptBehavior and the RunPromptBehavior to 4 - adPromptNever. You might also want to set the CursorLocation property to 2 - adUseServer if you need to build a keyset or dynamic cursor—otherwise, leave it alone.

OK, you're ready to create your first DataEnvironment Command object. Right-click on the Connection (Biblio) you just created and choose Add Command, or click on the Add Command toolbar button in the DataEnvironment window. If you had wanted to reference a stored procedure at this point (and you will eventually want to do this), you could have chosen Insert Stored Procedures—but we're not ready for that quite yet.

TIP Yes, you can drag a selected table, view, or stored procedure from a Data Link in the Data View window to the DataEnvironment window. This creates a whole new DataEnvironment Connection object and one or more Command objects—one for each object or group of objects you select to drag. This might be a viable approach when you want to quickly set up a DataEnvironment Connection object and a set of related Commands. If you drag the Tables or Stored Procedures folder from a Data Link in the Data View window, bring your lunch. It could take a while.

We want to rename this Command object because it will be exposed as a method on the DataEnvironment object (on our Connection object Biblio). And because this command will reference the Authors table, we'll simply call it Authors. It's a good idea to name your commands to describe their functionality. For example, AuthorByYearBorn, GetCoverByISBN, or TitlesByAuthor are names that make it clear what the command does. Anyone accessing the Data Environment later can easily understand the purpose of the connections and methods. Yes, these names have to conform to the Visual Basic naming conventions—so no embedded spaces. The DataEnvironment window should now look like Figure 37-1.

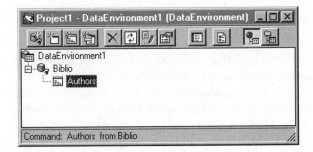

Figure 37-1 *The DataEnvironment window with a Connection set to the Biblio database and a Command named Authors*

TIP No, not all of these DataEnvironment objects are stored on the SQL Server. Just the database schema diagrams are persisted on the server. This way, other developers can't see them—not unless you pass them around your development team by sharing the DSR file. That's up to you. Check out the Visual Component Manager. It can help you keep track of these components using the repository.

If you right-click on the new Authors Command and choose the Properties option, you should be staring at the Authors Properties dialog box wondering what to do. Next tell the Authors Properties dialog box that you'll be referencing a table. You're right, this isn't the best way to do things—but for purposes of this exercise and for simplicity's sake we'll stick with a table for now. Select Table in the Database Object drop-down list. Choose the Authors table in the Object Name drop-down list. Figure 37-2 shows the completed Authors Properties dialog box. Click the OK button—we're done with this dialog box for now. We'll be back when we're ready to be more adventurous.

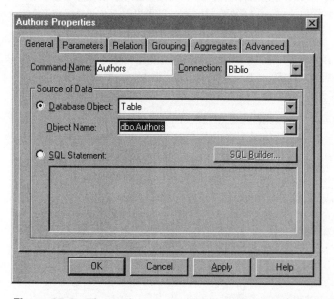

Figure 37-2 *The Authors Properties dialog box with the selections made for the Authors Command*

Now for the fun part. Left-click on the Authors Command icon and drag it to the form. This tells Visual Basic to create a bound control for each of the columns returned by the query (in this case, SELECT * FROM Authors). Yes, Visual Basic makes some intelligent choices about what kind of bound control is used, and you can select alternatives if you want to. I'll show you how to do that later.

Once you drag the Authors icon over to the Visual Basic form, you should see something like Figure 37-3.

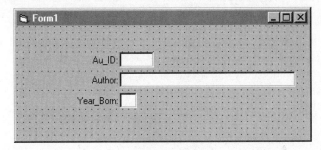

Figure 37-3 *A Visual Basic form after the Authors icon in the DataEnvironment window was dragged over it*

We're now ready to try our little application. Yes, I know, we didn't add any code. Is that all right with you? You can stick some in to make it look like you coded something if you want to. We don't need it (yet), but if it makes you feel better go ahead—we don't want people thinking this is *too* easy.

Figure 37-4 shows what the application will look like. When you run your application, you might notice something interesting if you look closely. Notice that the Au_ID TextBox and Year_Born TextBox are not the right size—the Au_ID TextBox is too large and the Year_Born TextBox is too small. Actually, we don't even need the Au_ID to show up at all—but we'll deal with that in a minute. The reason behind this seemingly callous disregard for the size of the actual data is the way the columns were defined in the database. Oops, it's something silly I did earlier. If you check, you'll discover that Au_ID is defined as an Integer and Year_Born is defined as a SmallInteger.

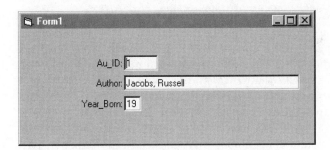

Figure 37-4 *Running the Authors application*

Visual Basic and the Data Environment designer choose and set up an appropriate control on the form based on these data types. If you feel a need to change these settings, you can right-click on the individual fields exposed under the Authors Command in the DataEnvironment window and choose Properties. This exposes yet another dialog box, which lets you see and set some of the properties. No, you can't change the data type, size, scale, or precision here—you have to do that in the database. To change the width of the bound controls, switch back to the form and make the changes there.

Mapping Controls to Your Fields

Check out the Options button on the DataEnvironment window. Click this button to launch yet another dialog box—this one will let you walk down the list of recognized data types (based on the fact that you're connected to SQL Server) and choose an appropriate bound control for each. Figure 37-5 shows the Field Mapping tab of the Options dialog box.

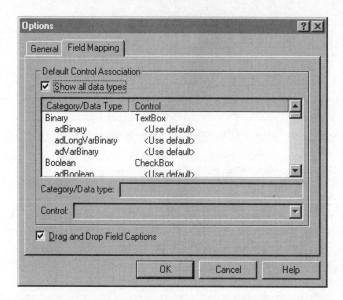

Figure 37-5 *The Field Mapping tab of the Options dialog box*

The Options dialog box lets you change the control that Visual Basic and the Data Environment choose for each column of the result set and set the caption assigned. You might have a better control in mind. For example, you might want to choose a MaskedEdit or a simple Label control instead of a TextBox. You might also want to build and choose your own custom control. In addition, you can change the assigned caption. The data type, size, scale, and precision settings for the column as defined in the database are also exposed. Sure, it would be nice if your control choice was persisted in the database. That might come later—but not in Visual Basic 6.0. What you can do is change the "default" control Visual Basic chooses for each of the data types. This way, if you write your own control or buy one at Kmart, you can tell the Data Environment how and when to choose it. This mapping information *is* persisted in the Registry, so you won't have to make these changes again.

Something else of interest has been done for us here. Behind the scenes, Visual Basic has pointed the bound controls at our DataEnvironment object— we know that happened, but did you notice that the bound control's DataMember property has been set to the Command (Authors)? This is how Visual Basic manages DataEnvironment objects that contain more than one Command object. So you can have this connection manage more than one result set. Each result set (each Command object) is considered a separate data member to be bound and managed independently from all others.

If you look back at Figure 37-4, you'll notice that once the form is loaded, our little application displays the first row of the Authors table. This means that several things happened when we clicked Run:

1. Visual Basic passed ADO the property settings you supplied to the dialog boxes. These settings include the ConnectionString, the Prompt, and CursorLocation as well as the user ID and password.

2. The WillConnect event fired to (theoretically) give you a chance to change the Connection properties.

3. The connect string you modified in the WillConnect event handler was then used to establish a (single) connection to SQL Server—before the Form_Load event handler was called.

4. The WillExecute event fired to (theoretically) give you the chance to change query parameters.

5. The Form_Load procedure was executed. The connection had already been made and the query had already populated the first row *before* the Form_Load event was run, so it's too late to do much—and you had to wait while all of this was taking place. No, there is no asynchronous option on this operation, so your application is blocked while it runs.

This process works very much like the Data control. This similarity means that your error handling is complicated by the fact that your first form isn't loaded when this startup code is run—so none of your error handlers are hot yet and the user still hasn't seen the first form. This also means that if you have several Command objects defined in a DataEnvironment object, ADO will open individual connections for each and every one of them on demand. That is, if the connection is bound to a control on the form, it's opened automatically when the form is loaded. Isn't that *special*. I thought we had already been there, done that, and decided it wasn't a good idea. In addition, if you reference one of the DataEnvironment object's Commands, ADO opens the Connection automatically. Yes, you can avoid this and open the Connection yourself after making changes to the underlying properties.

NOTE When you're working with the DataEnvironment object in design mode, Visual Basic holds a connection open for you in anticipation of some activity that would require a data definition language (DDL) query. Just keep this in mind when you're working with limited-resource systems. Some evidence suggests that this connection might eventually get dropped on one end or the other if it isn't kept active.

You're going to want to keep this kind of connection behavior from happening in your application or use another paradigm. (Don't worry, there are lots of other ways to set up your connections.) You don't want the application to just charge off and start making connections and running queries—not until you're ready for it to do so. If you *do* let this happen, your application will grab a set of connections and immediately begin executing queries designed to populate the bound controls. No, this isn't good. It can mean that your application takes considerable time to load and might be running queries long before your user is ready. The operations are based on hard-coded application logon parameters, which might not be appropriate for this user.

Unfortunately, there's no clean way to disarm this behavior. I asked for one, but it was never implemented. The one thing we *can* do to avoid part of these problems is *not load the form*. In other words, don't put any bound controls on the *initial* form (usually Form1). This way, you can tell Visual Basic to load the form containing the bound controls when and only when (or if) you need this functionality. No, you still don't have much error handling over this code running in your behalf, but you don't have to have the user stare at the desktop while it loads—wondering whether or not to give up and load Riven. Let's keep moving through this swamp. I hear that drier ground is just around the next bend.

Using the Data View Window to Add Data Environment Objects

A neat trick with Visual Basic 6.0 is the ability to drag objects from the Data View window right to the DataEnvironment window—automatically creating new Command objects based on a table, view, or stored procedure. Dragging and dropping is far easier than filling in all those dialog boxes. You can still go back and fill in the properties later if you want to.

When you start Visual Basic 6.0, one of the first new windows you'll notice is the Data View window. I devoted Chapter 36 to this puppy, but let's take a quick look to see where it fits when you're using the Data Environment designer.

First, the Data View window can be used to expose Data Environment Connections as well as registered Data Links. Once you create a Data Environment connection, it appears in the Data View window. You can also expand the Data Environment Connections to see the following items:

- **Database Diagrams** These hold schema diagrams for your SQL Server database. These are stored in the database, so all developers get to see these detailed relationship schema diagrams.

- **Tables** This folder exposes the tables and provides a way to modify the root database tables—or create new ones.

- **Views Again** This shows a list of known views and a way to create new ones.

- **Stored Procedures** This shows a list of all stored procedures visible to your login ID and a way to create new stored procedures on the server.

TIP You can also create queries using some neat (OK, Microsoft Access–like) tools developed for Visual InterDev. These queries are persisted in Data Environment Command objects and can also be shared by your whole team—just by sharing the DSR file.

Working with Stored Procedures from the Data Environment

For our next exercise, we're going to add another Command object to our Biblio DataEnvironment object. This time we're going to reference a new stored procedure I just wrote, named JustHitch. It is simply a SQL statement:

```
SELECT * FROM Titles WHERE Title LIKE '%hitch%'
```

This example will show you what differences you'll have to deal with when accessing stored procedures from the Data Environment.

You can add Command objects based on stored procedures using the Data Environment designer in at least three ways. You can access the first two techniques by right-clicking on a Data Environment Connection (Biblio); the last one uses drag-and-drop from the Data View window.

- You can choose Insert Stored Procedures after right-clicking on a Data Environment Connection. This launches the Insert Stored Procedures dialog box, shown in Figure 37-6, that exposes all of the stored procedures visible to your connection and your user ID. This dialog box is a little different than the UCD equivalent. It seems to move stored procedures from the left pane (a list of all visible stored procedures) right to the Data Environment. This movement happens behind the dialog box, so you might not see it. Just don't be worried if the list on the right (the selected stored procedures) empties out.

- You can click the Add Command button in the DataEnvironment window, right-click on the new command and choose Properties, and then use the Properties dialog box to set the type of command (Stored Procedure) and its name—and yes, you can choose from a list.

- You can drag a stored procedure from the Data View window to the DataEnvironment window. This creates not only a new Connection but also a new Command. You might have to verify the Connection settings because this feature wasn't working at this writing. No, there is no way to choose which Connection to "drop" the stored procedure on. And no, you can't drag a Command from one Connection to another.

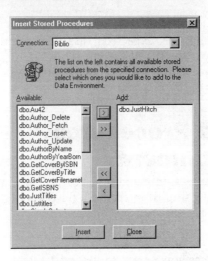

Figure 37-6 *The Insert Stored Procedures dialog box with the JustHitch stored procedure selected to be added to the Data Environment*

In the process of adding the stored procedure, you can set up the parameters and other details, but let's keep it simple for now. Just add the JustHitch stored procedure to your Biblio Data Environment. If you don't have this stored procedure, you'll have to create it. I'll wait here while you get it installed. Ready to go again? OK, once you've added the new stored procedure, you'll be able to see the columns it returns in the DataEnvironment window, as shown in Figure 37-7.

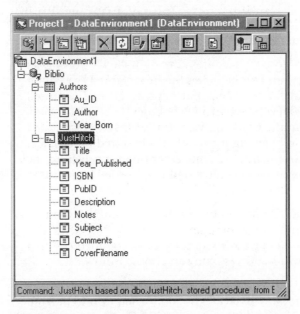

Figure 37-7 *The DataEnvironment window after the JustHitch stored procedure has been added*

If your stored procedure returns rows, however, you (might) need to go over to the Advanced tab of the Properties dialog box (as shown in Figure 37-8) and double-check the Recordset Returning option. If this option isn't set, you won't see the Recordset rows when you run the procedure. This dialog box is also handy if you need to change the command timeout, cursor location (server-side or client-side), or the lock type. Although it is possible to change the Call Syntax, I wouldn't advise it. It's probably right just as it is. No, you don't need to check the Prepare Before Execution option—there's no need to do this with a stored procedure.

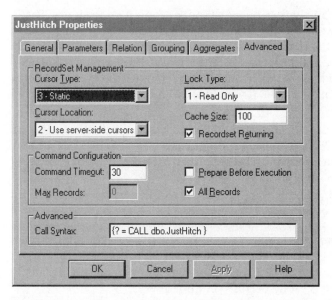

Figure 37-8   *The Advanced tab of the Properties dialog box for the JustHitch stored procedure*

NOTE   If you create a new stored procedure, be sure to grant yourself and your intended user permission to access it. Otherwise, all of this work is for naught. If the stored procedure you created doesn't appear in the list of stored procedures, you probably haven't done it right. If your favorite stored procedure is missing, you might also call 911 and file a "missing procedure" report—but it hasn't always helped me.

Once the stored procedure is installed as a Data Environment Command, you can drag the JustHitch Command icon from the DataEnvironment window over to the form—assuming you want to use it with bound controls. Please don't, though, because this time, let's approach the problem of running the Data Environment Command from a different point of view—a more pragmatic one. This time we're going to see how Command objects are exposed in *code*. You just need to follow some very simple steps.

First double-click on Form1 to get into the Form_Load event handler. Then use the following code to declare the Data Environment object and a place to put the Recordset that it's going to create:

```
Dim de As New DataEnvironment1
Dim rs As New Recordset
```

Next you reference the Command object as a method against the Data Environment object—just as we did with the UCD.

```
de.JustHitch
```

Notice that we don't have to open the connection—it's done for us. That's a mixed blessing, however: although not as much code is required, the default behavior set up with the Data Link properties isn't correct. If you have bound controls on the form, don't bother opening the Data Environment object—it's already open. You need to write your code to reference the existing objects and not create more of your own. If you do create more objects, you'll simply get more connections.

The ADO Recordset object created is exposed a little differently. Instead of being exposed as a property off of the Data Environment object (such as LastQueryResults), each Command object gets its own uniquely named Property—in this case *rsJustHitch*—as shown here:

```
Set rs = de.rsJustHitch
```

NOTE This Recordset object won't show up if you (or the Data Environment designer) forget to specify that this query returns rows. Use the Advanced tab on the Command Properties dialog box to do this. Yes, in some cases this flag is set by default—but not always.

Once you have the ADO Recordset, you're free to do as you choose. It doesn't get much simpler than that.

Accessing Parameterized Stored Procedures

OK, let's say you want to execute something a little more sophisticated—a stored procedure that requires input parameters. For this exercise, we're going to use my old standby stored procedure AuthorByYearBorn. The SQL looks like this:

```
SELECT Authors.Author, Authors.Year_Born, Titles.Title,
    Publishers.Name
FROM Authors INNER JOIN Title_Author
    ON Authors.Au_ID = Title_Author.Au_ID
    INNER JOIN Titles ON Title_Author.ISBN = Titles.ISBN
    INNER JOIN Publishers ON Titles.PubID = Publishers.PubID
WHERE (Authors.Year_Born BETWEEN @YearLow AND @yearhigh)
return (@@rowcount)
```

This fairly simple query returns a number of columns from the *Biblio* database based on a range of years. It also returns the total number of rows that satisfied the WHERE clause as a Return Status value. If you've seen me demo this procedure in one of my VBits sessions, you'll know how I built it—with Visual Database Tools.

To be able to execute this parameter-based stored procedure, we have to set up a DataEnvironment object that includes it as a Command object—so let's do it. You can use the Data View window to drag over the AuthorByYearBorn stored procedure if you want to, or follow along as we build a Data Environment Command with the dialog boxes.

Start from a clean slate and set up the Data Environment pointing to the *Biblio* database. Then right-click on the *Biblio* DataEnvironment object, and select Insert Stored Procedures. A list of stored procedures visible to you (based on how you logged into the database) is exposed.

NOTE   Remember, if you aren't logged in as the user on SQL Server, you won't be able to tell if the run-time permissions you're using will expose the stored procedure or other objects being referenced. That means that your application might work now, but might *not* work when deployed.

Next choose AuthorByYearBorn from the list. Open the Command Properties dialog box. We need to check out the Parameters tab that map the stored procedure parameters. These should already be set up for us. That's because when we pointed to the stored procedure, Visual Basic and the Data Environment ran a couple of (hopefully) harmless system stored procedures to figure out what the stored procedure looks like and what kind of parameters it expects. Figure 37-9 shows the Parameters tab of the Properties dialog box.

CAUTION
The Parameters collection created by the Data-Environment object is base 1 when you use the View Locals window. That is, the Return Value parameter is "Item 1," the first parameter is "Item 2," and so forth. I expected this collection to be 0-based. Well, it is when you refer to parameters in code. The return value is still ordinal 0. Confused? Thank the Microsoft Office people. They like it this way.

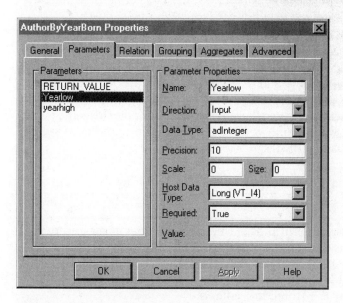

Figure 37-9   *The Parameters tab of the Properties dialog box for the AuthorByYearBorn stored procedure*

As you can see, ADO and the Data Environment found the gazintas (the input parameters) and the gazoutas (the return status parameters). Yes, if necessary, you can tweak the data type, precision, scale, and size—but at your own peril. In RDO, you can make minor tweaks (to the data type), but little else. ADO exposes everything you need, including the initial parameter value.

> **TIP** ADO seems to have difficulty figuring out what a stored procedure's result set is going to look like. In some cases, it simply can't map the returning columns to the Fields collection, so your application might not be able to "automatically" bind to some stored procedures. If you don't install SQL Server 6.5 Service Pack 4 (SP4), it won't have a chance. SP4 will eventually be available with Visual Basic 6.0, Enterprise Edition—no it won't be included until the Windows NT folks get it done. It installs several enhancements to better report the underlying DDL of stored procedures. It also adds support for middle-tier debugging needed by Microsoft Transaction Server.

Once the AuthorByYearBorn stored procedure is all set up, you can run it in code (as explained below) or do the drag-the-command-to-the-form thing. On the surface, the problem with the drag technique is that the system has no obvious mechanism to capture the input parameters from your code. *Before* you start filling in the Value property, however, you need to consider several issues. If you do provide the parameter values in the Properties dialog box (as shown in Figure 37-9), these values will *always* be used to automatically bind to your controls whenever Visual Basic runs the stored procedure. If you don't want Visual Basic always to use the same parameters, you had better leave the Value setting empty in the Parameters tab of the Properties dialog box.

So how *do* you pass in parameters? Well, you have a couple of choices. Because you want the bound controls to contain proper Recordset values when the form is first loaded, you need to supply the parameters *before* the query is executed. This is where the DataEnvironment object's WillExecute event handler comes in. In this procedure, you simply set the parameter values in the ADO Command being executed. Because the event handler (usually) passes in the Command as pCommand, your code in the event handler to set the parameters would look like this:

```
pCommand("YearLow") = Form1.Text1
pCommand("YearHigh") = Form1.Text2
```

> **TIP** If you set a breakpoint in the event handler, you *might* find that the event handler is called more than once. You can also verify this with SQL Trace (or the SQL Server Profiler in SQL Server 7.0). This repeated call to the event handler can be caused by ADO attempting to reverify the schema returned by the stored procedure.

You have another choice when it comes to passing parameters—but this time, you do the passing after the form is loaded. In this case, you can simply reexecute the Command, passing in the procedure parameters as method arguments or directly addressing the Parameters collection of the Command object. You'll have to close the Command object's Recordset before you execute it again—and no, you can't use the Requery method with this technique. Here's the code for this technique:

```
DataEnvironment1.rsAuthorByYearBorn.Close
DataEnvironment1.AuthorByYearBorn Text1, Text2
```

Once the Recordset object is rebuilt, you still have work to do. If you're using "simple" bound controls, you have to tell them (each of them) that the DataSource has changed. This requires a little more code:

```
RebindControls Me, "TextBox", "AuthorByYearBorn", DataEnvironment1
```

No, this isn't a built-in Visual Basic function. It's a routine written by one of the clever testers across campus. It looks like this close up:

```
Sub RebindControls(FormName, ControlType As String, _
    CommandName, DE)
Dim ctl As Control
For Each ctl In FormName.Controls
    If InStr(ControlType & ",", TypeName(ctl) & ",") Then
        If ctl.DataMember = CommandName Then
            Set ctl.DataSource = DE
        End If
    End If
Next
End Sub
```

This procedure walks the form's Controls collection looking for any TextBox controls bound to the specified ADO Command. If the procedure finds one, it sets the control's DataSource property to the DataEnvironment object passed in as an argument. Sure, you could have simply reset the DataSource property in each of your controls manually, but this routine is a more elegant.

Once the bound controls are populated with data, you can use any of the current-row repositioning methods, such as Move, MoveNext, and so on to change the current row and repopulate the bound control(s) from the new current row. The trick is to use the Recordset created by the Data Environment. This Recordset is named after the (stored) procedure Command you executed. For example, in this case the AuthorByYearBorn stored procedure. This means that the Recordset is named rsAuthorByYearBorn. To reposition the current-row pointer to another row, simply use the Recordset object's Move methods. The rules here are pretty much the same as those you follow when working with any data source control (such as the Data, RemoteData, or ADO Data control). The code to move to the next row of your bound Recordset is easy:

```
DataEnvironment1.rsAuthorByYearBorn.MoveNext
```

You have to reference the existing Recordset that belongs to the current DataEnvironment object that's already bound to the data-aware controls. Visual Basic takes care of repopulating the bound controls.

WARNING!

In some cases (not usually with SQL Server), ADO and the Data Environment designer actually run the stored procedure to do the DDL snooping. This is necessary when the provider doesn't support sufficient functions to let ADO map the result set. This has never been a problem before because ODBC supported API calls that passed back all the needed information—without running the query. In these cases, I would be very, very careful before using this feature. In many cases, you won't want to run stored procedures just to figure out what columns they return. It's kinda like using a match to check whether a fuel drum is empty. In any case, ADO prompts you before the stored procedure is run. Try choosing "No" and see whether the Data Environment set up for you works anyway—it might. This is especially true when working with action queries that don't return result sets.

OK, so you don't want to use the bound controls. Here's the code to run a parameter-driven stored procedure and put its Recordset into an unbound grid—using my custom RDOADOGrid control (which you can find on the companion CD).

```
Dim de As New DataEnvironment1

Private Sub Form_Load()
de.AuthorByYearBorn YearLow.Text, YearHigh.Text
RAutoGrid1.ShowADOData de.rsAuthorByYearBorn
End Sub
```

Looks familiar? Well, if you've been using RDO and the UCD, it should look very familiar. Notice that we no longer have to open the connection explicitly—that's done automatically by ADO when you reference the Command. And instead of LastQueryResults, we have a custom Recordset object created for the Command being executed.

TIP   Want to avoid this rebinding silliness? It's easy—when you drag the Command from the Data Environment explorer, use the Right button to do so. When you release the right mouse button while hovering over the form, you get a choice of Data Grid, Hierarchical Flex Grid, and Bound Controls. Visual Basic defaults to bound controls, as we discussed above. If you choose either of the grid controls, the binding is done for you automatically.

Working with Hierarchical Result Sets and Other Children

One of the new gizmos we get to scoot around on the carpet this time is the new Hierarchical MSFlexGrid. This shiny new truck is designed to display (just display—not update) data from parent-child–style result sets. You've been writing these for years to display master-detail results. For example, when you work with a parts database, you open customer invoices to log one or more orders for one or more parts. Parts can also be made up of more parts (parts have parts). And this can be recursive, so parts can have parts that have parts ad nauseam. Often you want to display a customer, a selected invoice, and perhaps the list of items on that invoice.

Visual Basic 6.0, the Data Environment designer, and the Hierarchical MSFlexGrid are designed to work as a team to make displaying these result sets painless. (Or at least you won't feel like you were just hit by a milk truck pulling out of the dairy.) While I won't go into the gory details in this guide, I will walk you through the process of setting up a parent-child-child result set and get it displayed in the MSFlexGrid. Keep in mind, however, that this technique is another one of those "bound" jobs that might not work in your scenario—especially if you're using stored procedures.

The intelligence behind all of this technology is something added to ADO 2.0: the *Shape Language*. This Shape Language is implemented by extending SQL to include SHAPE statements, which are interpreted by the Microsoft Data Shape Provider (on the client). A Shape Language command is executed just like any other ADO SQL command; however, its result is a *hierarchical* Recordset. You can use the Shape commands to create these special Recordset objects in two ways:

- Append a child Recordset to a parent Recordset, as we're about to do in the example below.

- Compute an aggregate operation on a child Recordset that generates a parent Recordset. We'll do that in a minute, too.

Again, this isn't the place to get into the nitty-gritty details of how these are written—I'll leave that up to other authors. I will say that Visual Basic (and Visual Studio) tools offer a number of ways to automatically generate the right Shape commands.

In the following example, we're going to create a parent-child hierarchy between the Authors and Titles tables. This hierarchy will show all titles for a selected author. Of course, there is no relationship between these two tables—we'll need the Title_Author table for that, so we'll be creating a three-level hierarchy. The example uses the Hierarchical MSFlexGrid and a Data Environment that we're about to build. The completed sample is in the Chap37 directory on the companion CD. You should start with a Data Environment named Biblio and a Command object named Authors built against the Authors table. No, don't do any dragging yet. The next step is to add a child Command object by right-clicking on the Authors Command icon and selecting Add Child Command. (If only it were that easy for real parents.) The child command will appear under the Authors table in the DataEnvironment window.

Now right-click the newly added child command, and select Properties. You should see a Properties dialog box for the new Command. Fill in the Command name Title_Author, and point it at the Title_Author table. Don't click OK—we're not done yet.

Click on the Relation tab. (No, this isn't where you get to delete your mother-in-law. You wouldn't want to do that anyway—she's so sweet.) This is where we'll choose the columns (ADO fields) in each table that form the parent-child relationship. In this case, we want to link the parent field in the Authors table (dbo.Authors.Au_ID) with the corresponding child field in the Title_Author table (dbo.Title_Author.Au_ID). To set up this relation, select the parent field and child field from the relation drop-down lists and click the Add button. This tells ADO (and SQL Server) how to fetch rows from the child once a parent row is selected. Under the covers, this operation sets up a specially constructed SQL statement that includes the Shape Language to tell ADO how to fetch the rows you need. Figure 37-10 shows the completed relation settings.

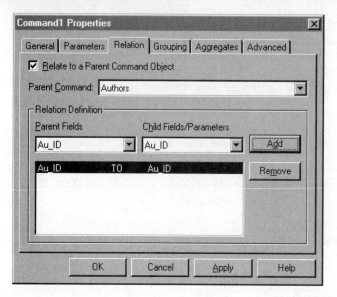

Figure 37-10 *A parent-child relationship defined between Author.Au_ID and Title_Author.Au_ID*

Now let's add the last child in our hierarchy so we can see what kind of SQL code was generated for us. Click OK in the Properties dialog box to save the relation settings and return back to the DataEnvironment window. Right-click on the Title_Author Command, and choose Add Child Command again. Right-click on the new Command and choose Properties. This time, name the Command Titles, point it to the Titles table, and set up a relation between the dbo.Title_Author.ISBN and the dbo.Titles.ISBN columns. When you're done, your hierarchy should look like Figure 37-11.

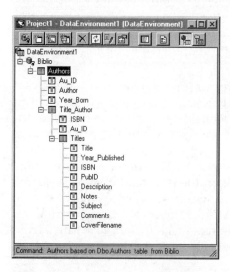

Figure 37-11 *The hierarchy between the Authors, Title_Author, and Titles tables*

Once we've built the hierarchy between the Authors, Title_Author, and Titles tables, we can examine the entire Shape Language statement the Data Environment designer created for us. No, this isn't TSQL. This is ADO SQL understood and parsed behind the scenes by the ADO Microsoft Data Shape Provider. First right-click on the Authors Command object—the parent object in this hierarchy—and choose Hierarchy Info. This displays the Hierarchy Information dialog box shown in Figure 37-12. Yes, you can also choose to view the ADO hierarchy, but that just shows the tables involved in the hierarchy—not very interesting.

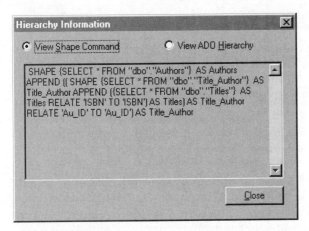

Figure 37-12 *The Hierarchy Information dialog box showing the Shape Language statement*

Building Bound Interfaces to the Hierarchy

OK, now we're ready to tell Visual Basic how to display and manage this query. Actually, this part is very easy. Click on the Parent object (Authors, remember?), and drag it to the form. Notice that we've ended up with three TextBox controls—one for each column in the Authors table, and an MSHFlexGrid control for the children. When you press run (and wait awhile), you should get something that looks like Figure 37-13.

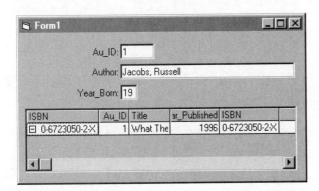

Figure 37-13 *A basic hierarchical form where a relationship exists between the two Au_IDs and the two ISBNs*

No, this isn't particularly useful. First, it took a full 20 seconds for my server to drag it up. Part of the problem is that the queries executed simply did SELECT * with no WHERE clause—a really bad idea. We'll need to fix that. To top that off, we don't have any navigation buttons to move to the next author—we'll have to add those ourselves along with a few text boxes to capture the input parameters. We also have a couple of redundant fields here in the grid, and the Year_Born TextBox is still too small. To clean this up, let's build a more reasonable query by deleting unnecessary information.

Cleaning Up the Grid

To tune up the MSHFlexGrid, right-click on the grid and select Retrieve Structure. This obtains the field format from the query and posts the column names to the grid column headings. After that, it's easy to get into the grid property page to make the grid more efficient:

Drop any redundant columns. For example, we don't need to see Au_ID in the grid, and we need to see ISBN only once. As it is, these both appear twice. I also selected a few of the other columns to delete as well. No, this doesn't make the query run any faster, but it does make the grid populate sooner and consume less real estate. How did I delete the grid columns? Easy—just click on the Bands tab in the grid property page, and choose the band that corresponds with the parent or one of the children. Uncheck any column you don't want to show up on the form. You can also set other font and formatting here. Figure 37-14 shows the Bands tab of the MSHFlexGrid Property Pages dialog box.

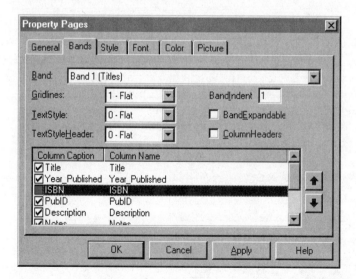

Figure 37-14 *Setting displayed column headings from the Bands tab of the MSHFlexGrid Property Pages dialog box*

38

Test Driving the Data Object Wizard

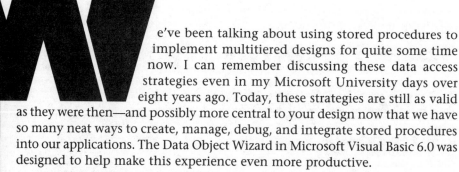

e've been talking about using stored procedures to implement multitiered designs for quite some time now. I can remember discussing these data access strategies even in my Microsoft University days over eight years ago. Today, these strategies are still as valid as they were then—and possibly more central to your design now that we have so many neat ways to create, manage, debug, and integrate stored procedures into our applications. The Data Object Wizard in Microsoft Visual Basic 6.0 was designed to help make this experience even more productive.

The Data Object Wizard (DOW, pronounced "Dough!" in some circles, as Homer Simpson would say) takes a different approach from most of the tools we've discussed so far. To start with, it's the first "code generator" we've come across. Although Visual Basic 6.0 sports other code generators, such as the Data Form Wizard, the Visual Modeler, and others, the DOW seems especially suited to two-tier and three-tier Microsoft SQL Server designs. When you point the DOW at a set of stored procedures or ADO Commands, it simply creates a set of Visual Basic classes and procedures to manage the result set. As a result, you write less code, but your application doesn't get any smaller, as it does with the Data Environment designer or the UserConnection designer. Another important difference between the DOW and other tools is that the DOW is designed specifically for ADO Commands that access procedures—especially SQL Server *stored* procedures. Sure, the DOW works with that other vendor's stored procedures and simpler ADO Commands. In essence, the DOW is used to create data Class modules and user controls that can be used to expose data (resulting from running selected stored procedures).

Getting Started with the Data Object Wizard

OK, before you get started, you need to figure out how you're going to get the data out of the database. Sure, this extraction can be fairly painless; and while I recommend using stored procedures to do it, all you really need is a Data Environment Command object. You'll also need at least one more Data Environment Commands to post changes to the database—perhaps as many as three: one to update, one to delete, and one to add new rows. And yes, you have to use the Data Environment designer to create these Command objects. Once we get into the DOW, you might want to expose one or more Commands to do foreign-key lookup operations as well.

The Data class the DOW creates can be bound to ADO data consumers, or you can use manual techniques to extract and manipulate the data from the class. The DOW can help you build a UserControl based on a DataGrid, ComboBox, or ListBox control; or simply create a single-record interface to expose and manipulate data from your DOW-generated Data class.

Yes, you could (and probably have tried to) create procedure-based interfaces to your SQL Server data on your own. However, the DOW makes this process easier by dealing with several complex design considerations—some of which you might not discover until something goes wrong. And since the DOW creates code that can be easily modified, you aren't stuck with an interface that runs like a black box—such as the Data Environment designer or the UserConnection designer—over which you have very little control.

DOW Design Issues

When you build your DOW-based application, you're given a couple of options that help you implement common user interface scenarios. For example, you can create the "instant-gratification" scenario that lets a user enter data and click a Save button to post changes to the database. You can also choose to implement a "batch" operation that saves up changes to be posted later using sets of SQL commands—all routed through your designated Data Environment (really ADO) Command objects.

Whenever we work with foreign-key relationships, we often like to intelligently populate lookup tables so that the user doesn't have to type anything. As you know, most system errors are user-induced and any time a user (especially marketing types) enters data, it's likely to be "almost" correct. The chances of an error are greatly reduced if you force (or at least encourage) the user to choose an entry from a list. That's where the DOW's lookup capabilities come in. In some cases, you'll also want to substitute a coded value for a plain-language value. For example, your procedure might expect you to pass in a state code. Instead of making the user memorize these codes, the DOW will help you expose a list of state names and, once one is selected, substitute the correct code for that entry. We'll see how this works later.

To identify a specific row in the result set, we use one or more columns of the table as a primary key. As we've discussed before, there are a litany of ways to create primary keys—each with its advantages and disadvantages. It would be pretty tough for the DOW to try to figure out how your primary key was created (or spawned), so it assumes your Insert Command will deal with the issue or at least let the user (heaven forbid) enter the correct value.

The DOW expects your Insert Command to return the primary key it generated (or SQL Server generated) so the key can be fed back into the system to coordinate the data. This allows immediate update or deletion of the new record.

The DOW also helps you deal with NULL values. Since the user needs to be able to recognize that some fields have "unknown" values, as opposed to empty strings or incomplete (or incorrect) entries, the DOW converts these entries to a string of your choosing—such as "None," "Nada," or "BHOM."

Virtually all stored procedures and serious ADO Commands accept input parameters, and the DOW is prepared to handle these intelligently. It deals with these parameters by creating a DataClass property for each DOW Select and Lookup Command. You'll have a chance to set these properties either on the DOW UserControl Property Sheet at design time or manually in code at run time.

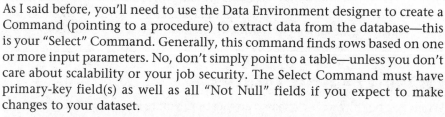

Setting Up DOW Commands

As I said before, you'll need to use the Data Environment designer to create a Command (pointing to a procedure) to extract data from the database—this is your "Select" Command. Generally, this command finds rows based on one or more input parameters. No, don't simply point to a table—unless you don't care about scalability or your job security. The Select Command must have primary-key field(s) as well as all "Not Null" fields if you expect to make changes to your dataset.

WARNING!

When you create your Select query, be sure to construct it such that the final column returned is *not* used as a foreign-key "lookup" value. Even if you simply pass a holding character, you won't have much luck trying to use the final field in the SELECT statement to reference foreign-key values. We'll get into this a little later. Incidentally, this will probably be one of the first things fixed in a subsequent release of Visual Basic 6.0.

Next, you might want to create one or more Data Environment Commands to perform the Insert, Update, and Delete operations—again using parameters that identify the specific row to add, change, or drop. If you need to provide a more sophisticated foreign-key lookup operation, you'll need one or more Lookup Commands as well. The rows retrieved from the Lookup Commands are displayed in a DOW-generated UserCommand ComboBox. The DOW automatically maps selected fields in the Select Command to primary-key fields in the Lookup Command(s).

Assuming you want to be able to add new rows to your database, you'll need to set up at least one Insert Command using the Data Environment. Again, you'll need parameters for each Not Null column defined by the Select Command to provide values for the new row. Of course, you might be able to set up default values that take care of this for you—which is not a bad idea. Again, the DOW helps you map the fields returned by the Select Command to the parameters of the Insert Command. Keep in mind that if the Insert Command depends on system-generated primary-key values (as when you use an Identity column), and these are returned via Output parameters to the Insert Command, the DOW-generated code will persist these values and supply them to the newly inserted row. This facilitates immediate Updates and Deletes using these values to identify the target row.

To be able to change the data retrieved, you'll need to create an Update Command with the Data Environment designer. This Command also needs to identify the primary key so SQL Server knows which row to change. The DOW helps you map the fields of the Select Command to the parameters of the Update Command. Sure, you can use the same Data Environment Command for both Insert and Update if the procedure being executed can play this dual role.

To delete selected rows from the dataset, you'll need to create a Delete Command. As with the other commands, the DOW helps you map these Primary Key fields of the Select Command to the parameters of the Delete Command.

Let's take one last high-level look at these Data Environment Commands you're about to leverage with the DOW:

- The Select command must have a Primary Key field if Update and Delete operations are to be performed with DOW-generated objects.

- A Lookup command typically consists of one or more Primary Key fields and a Description field. The Lookup command can be based on a single table, or it might be a join of several parent tables, with the Description field being concatenated from description fields in the parent tables.

- One Lookup (Foreign Key) field must be in the Select command for each Primary Key field in the Lookup command. These field names don't need to be the same; the DOW foreign-key Mapping screens will allow you to map fields that have different names.

- If the system is generating primary-key values for Inserted records, create Input/Output command parameters for these primary keys. Have the Insert command set these parameters with the system-generated values. The DOW data Class will retrieve these values so that immediate Updates and Inserts can be performed on newly Inserted records.

A Simple DOW Example

Just after I finished my first crack at this chapter on the DOW, I started to work on my VBits presentation that will go over the mechanics of its use in detail. Unfortunately, I discovered that despite having just written a chapter on the subject, I was still puzzled about a number of details. So I decided to create a simple sample that uses the *Biblio* database.

TIP   The original author of the Data Object Wizard (O'Farrell Consulting) was kind enough to provide me (and you) with a comprehensive sample application that illustrates the DOW. This sample shows how each of the UserControl types can be used. The Chap38 directory on the companion CD has all of the code for this sample. Also, for a visual demonstration of the DOW, be sure to check out the AVI file I have included in the Data Object Wizard AVI directory on the companion CD.

First I made some changes to the *Biblio* database to illustrate the use of the DOW a little more clearly. I also wanted to have a Lookup field associated with the Publishers table that would illustrate the use of the DOW's lookup feature. Ideally, this should be a one-to-many relationship such as a list of valid states for publishers. To accomplish this, I created a new table, named ValidStates, and added 60 rows to it that contained the state code (the two-letter identifier) and the full state name. The plan is to have a grid that lists the publishers and shows a drop-down list of valid state names instead of the two-letter state code.

Let's walk through the steps needed to generate a simple grid-based application. We'll focus on a practical exercise that has all the potholes marked or filled in.

1. Using ISQL/w, the Query Analyzer, or your tool of choice, run the MakeValidStatesTable.SQL script against the *Biblio* database to add the new ValidStates table and fill in the data values. (This script is on the companion CD.)

2. Run the PublisherSPs.SQL script against the *Biblio* database to create the new Publisher table stored procedures. (This script is on the companion CD.)

3. Create a new Data Project in Visual Basic 6.0; remove the report designer.

4. Open the Data View window, and open your Data Link to *Biblio*.

5. Right-click on the Biblio icon and choose Refresh to ensure that the new ValidStates table and the new Publisher stored procedures are displayed.

6. Double-click on the DataEnvironment1 icon in the project window.

7. Delete Connection1—we want the Data View window to create a new Connection1 object.

8. Drag the following stored procedures over to the DataEnvironment window: Publisher_Delete, Publisher_Insert, and Publisher_Update. No, don't let ADO "run" these procedures as they're being installed into the Data Environment. Just click No when prompted to run them.

9. Drag the Publisher_Fetch stored procedure to the DataEnvironment window.

10. Drag the ValidStates table to the Data Environment under Connection1.

When finished, your Data Environment window should look like the one in Figure 38-1.

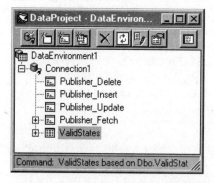

Figure 38-1 *The Data Environment window after the Publisher stored procedures and ValidStates table have been added*

Using the DOW to Create a Data Class

Once you have all of your DataEnvironment Commands set up, you can proceed to the next step. From the Add-Ins menu, choose Add-In Manager. In the Add-In Manager dialog box that appears, select VB 6 Data Object Wizard. In the Load Behavior frame, check the Loaded/Unloaded checkbox and click OK. This will load the DOW Add-In and add it to the Add-Ins menu. To start the DOW, select VB 6 Data Object Wizard from the Add-Ins menu.

After you click Next in the Introduction dialog box, the Create Object dialog box is displayed, as shown in Figure 38-2. You use this dialog box to specify the type of object you want to create. Select the A Class To Which Other Objects Can Bind Data option, and click Next.

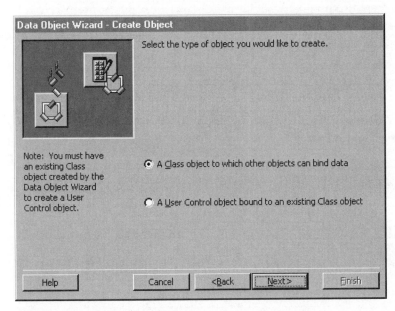

Figure 38-2 *Data Object Wizard Create Object dialog box*

In the next dialog box, the DOW will search your Data Environment and display all available Commands, as shown in Figure 38-3. In this dialog box choose the Data Environment Command that will serve as your Select Command—the one that returns rows from your dataset. In this case, select Publisher_Fetch as your primary source of data.

Next you'll be prompted to indicate the field(s) returned from the Select Command that compose the primary key, and which are nullable ADO can usually figure out these settings, but sometimes it's not possible, so you'll have to fill in the missing information. If a field is a Primary Key, it isn't necessarily a Not Null field from the DOW's perspective. An example of this is a Select command that provides system-generated primary-key values through input/output parameter(s). In this case, set the PubID field as the Primary Key. The Define Class Field Information dialog box is shown in Figure 38-4.

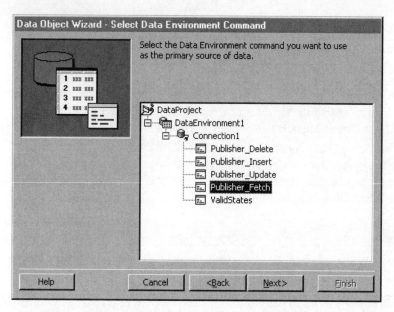

Figure 38-3   *Select Data Environment Command dialog box*

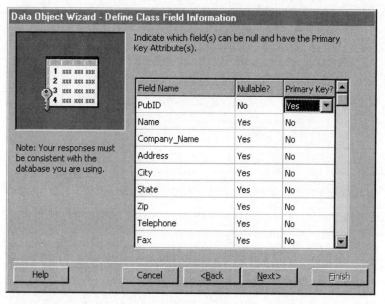

Figure 38-4   *The Define Class Field Information dialog box*

Now we can define any lookup table(s) by specifying relationships for the Select Command. Each lookup relationship has one or more foreign-key fields in the Select Command. And no, none of this lookup stuff is required, but no, your Select Command should *not* return a lookup foreign key as the *last* field—at least not until they fix an "issue" that makes the DOW ignore the final field returned. To hike around this sinkhole, simply rearrange the fields returned in the SELECT or pass a placeholder instead of a field. The Define Lookup Table Information dialog box is shown in Figure 38-5.

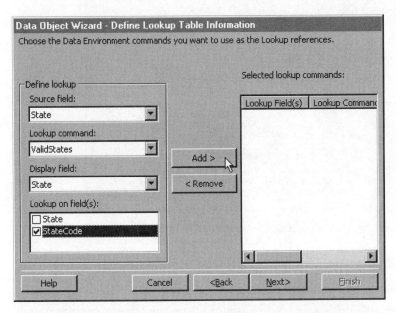

Figure 38-5 *The Define Lookup Table Information dialog box*

This dialog box prompts you to specify a "Source" (Select) field, a specific Lookup Command, the lookup field to display, and the Primary Key fields in the Lookup command. Choose State as your Source Field, ValidStates as your Lookup Command, and State as your Display Field. Check StateCode as your Lookup On Field(s). Once you provide all this relationship information, click the Add button to include the relationship in the Selected Lookup Commands.

Next we need to tell the DOW how to map the Lookup Fields for each relationship. Because each lookup relationship can have more than one field, each relationship has its own Map Lookup Fields screen. The DOW automatically attempts to match Select Command field names with Lookup Command field names, displaying these matches in a grid. If the mapping is incorrect or other mapping rows need to be added, click on the appropriate cell and choose the correct Select field name from the Source Command Fields ComboBox and the correct Lookup field name from the Lookup Command Fields ComboBox. If a mapping row exists that shouldn't be there, choose "(None)" from the ComboBox for both the Select and Lookup field names.

In our example, change the Lookup Command Fields to statecode, as shown in Figure 38-6. This tells the DOW to create code to update or insert rows containing the selected valid state code into the updated or new row. If you skip over this option, the Lookup Description field is passed to the server as the field contents.

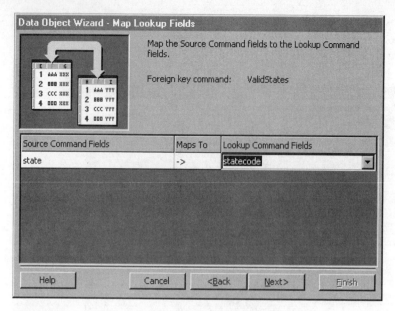

Figure 38-6 *The Map Lookup Fields dialog box*

Define and Map Insert Data Command

Are you still with me? We're now ready to set up the Insert Command used to add rows to the dataset. Once you identify the Data Environment Command designated as your Insert Command, the DOW will attempt to map its Fields to parameters with the same names.

This Define And Map Insert Data Command dialog box that's shown in Figure 38-7 is functionally similar to the dialog box used to map the Lookup fields. If the default mapping isn't correct, you can change it by clicking on the incorrect cell and selecting the correct values from the ComboBoxes. Choose Publisher_Insert as the Insert Data Command.

Define and Map Update Data Command

The Define And Map Update Data Command dialog box shown in Figure 38-8 is similar to the Define And Map Insert Data Command dialog box, except that if you're using the same command, you can just check Use Insert Command For Update. The DOW figures out what to do from there. Choose Publisher_Update as the Update Data Command.

Define and Map Delete Data Command

As with the other Commands, the Define And Map Delete Data Command dialog box (shown in Figure 38-9 on page 894) identifies the Command you plan to use to delete rows from your dataset. If the DOW has figured out the correct field mapping, just click Next. Otherwise, you'll need to choose the appropriate primary-key field to identify the row to drop. Choose Publisher_Delete as the Delete Command.

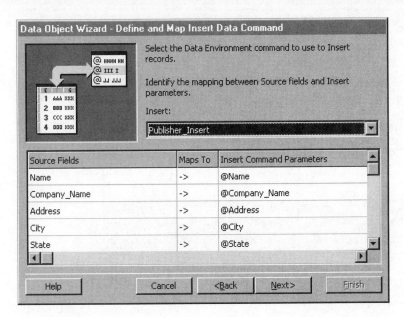

Figure 38-7   *The Define And Map Insert Data Command dialog box*

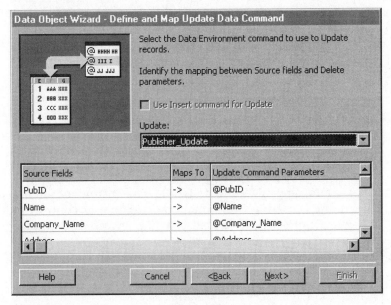

Figure 38-8   *The Define And Map Update Data Command dialog box*

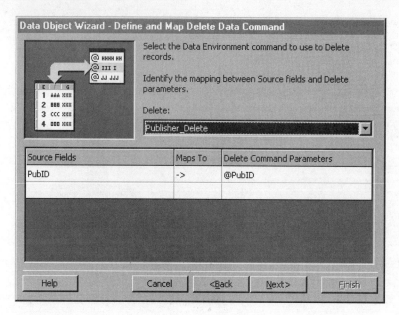

Figure 38-9 *The Define And Map Delete Data Command dialog box*

The last step of the process asks you to name your new data Class, as shown in Figure 38-10. Nope, you can't use the name of an existing class unless you want to drop it and start over again. This means that all existing work on the existing data Class is lost—both the code created by the DOW and the code you might have added later. Enter the name *Publishers* for your control, and click Finish.

Using the DOW to Create a Data-Bound UserControl

To make it easy to display and update the data in your new DOW-generated Data class, the DOW is also capable of setting up custom UserControls to match the new data Class. Again, all you need to do is follow the instructions in the wizard. You can choose DataGrid, ComboBox, or ListBox user controls to display and manage multiple rows, or you create a "simple record" to display just a single row of data. The DOW uses a ComboBox to display selected lookup items. A little later in this chapter, we'll go over the properties, methods, and events of these UserControls.

DataGrid

Let's walk through the process of creating a DataGrid using the DOW's UserControl option and I'll point out several tips and tricks along the way. Start the DOW again, but this time choose A User Control Object Bound To An Existing Class Object, as shown in Figure 38-11, so that we can build a control to expose and manipulate the new Publishers data Class.

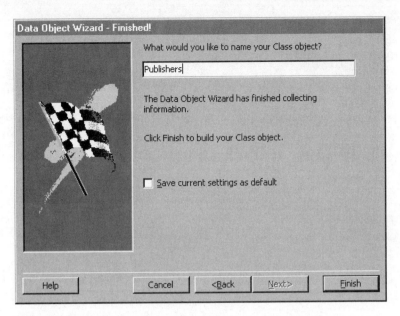

Figure 38-10 *The last dialog box of the Data Object Wizard*

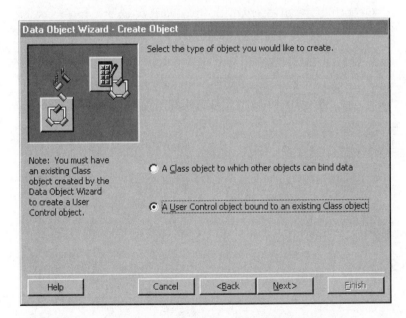

Figure 38-11 *Data Object Wizard Create Object dialog box*

In the next dialog box, choose rsclsPublishers as the Data class to use as the Data Source for your User Control object. Figure 38-12 shows the Data classes that can be used.

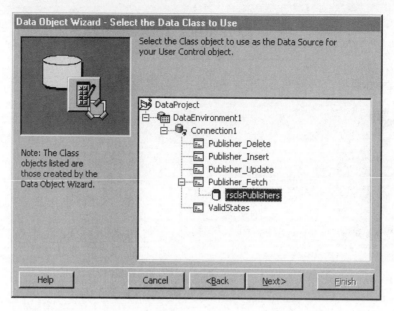

Figure 38-12 *The Select The Data Class To Use dialog box*

Next we select the type of User control we want to create. In this case, we're creating a DataGrid. Figure 38-13 shows this dialog box. (Folks, it doesn't get much easier than this.)

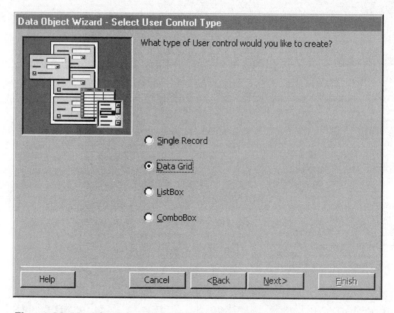

Figure 38-13 *The Select User Control Type dialog box*

Now we can map each field to a chosen control. Here are our options:

- **(None)**   Don't show the field in the UserControl.

- **ComboBox**   If the field is a Lookup field in the Select command, we can choose to show the "display" field of the Lookup command in this field instead of the actual Lookup fields.

- **TextBox**   This shows the value of the field as it exists in the Select command field.

If the field is a Primary Key, the DOW defaults to (None), assuming that in most applications, primary-key values are system-generated and not supplied by the user. If the field is a Lookup field, a ComboBox is shown by default. ComboBox controls are intended only for Lookup fields and are therefore ignored if the field is a non-Lookup field, in which case a TextBox is displayed. Figure 38-14 shows this dialog box. Click Next, because the controls chosen are fine as is.

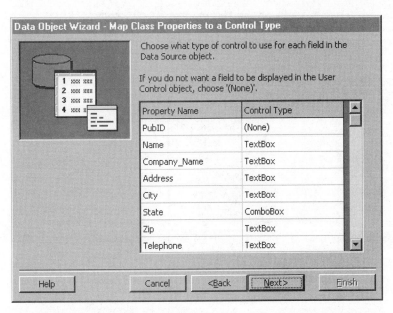

Figure 38-14   *The Map Class Properties To A Control Type dialog box*

Once you've selected a control to map to each field (or taken the defaults), you must name your new DOW-generated UserControl. The DOW will notify you if the UserControl already exists, in which case you can choose a new name or overwrite the existing UserControl. Accept the default of Publishers shown in Figure 38-15, and click Finish to create the control. Figure 38-16 shows the DOW-generated DataGrid UserControl.

WARNING!
You will lose any unsaved work on an existing UserControl if you choose to overwrite it.

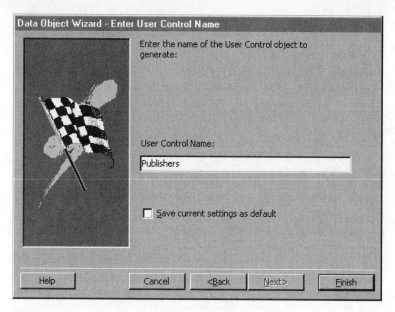

Figure 38-15 *The Enter User Control Name dialog box*

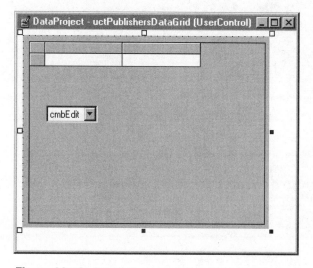

Figure 38-16 *DOW-Generated DataGrid UserControl*

Finishing the Simple Example

To wind up our example, just follow these steps:

1. Click the Close (X) button to close the UserControl window. It should now appear in the Visual Basic 6.0 toolbox.

2. From the Project window, open your frmDataEnv. Double-click the new uctPublishersDataGrid UserControl in the toolbox to place the new control on your form. Size the control to an appropriate size. The table has a lot of fields, so make it pretty big.

3. With the uctPublishersDataGrid1 control placed on the form, change the following properties:

- GridEditable set to True
- ManualInitialize set to True

4. Drop a TextBox and CommandButton control on your form to hold the StateWanted values and to give you a way to select other states. Name the TextBox *StateWanted* and set the Text property to *NY*. Name the CommandButton *FetchButton*.

5. Add the following code to the FetchButton_Click event procedure:

```
Me.uctPublishersDataGrid1.Publisher_FetchStateWanted = _
    StateWanted.Text
Me.uctPublishersDataGrid1.InitPublishers
```

6. Add the following code to your Form_Load procedure:

```
FetchButton_Click
```

That's it. I encourage you to try this simple example and examine the code it generates. You can modify the DOW-generated Data class code to deal with special situations as you see fit. Figure 38-17 shows this example in action.

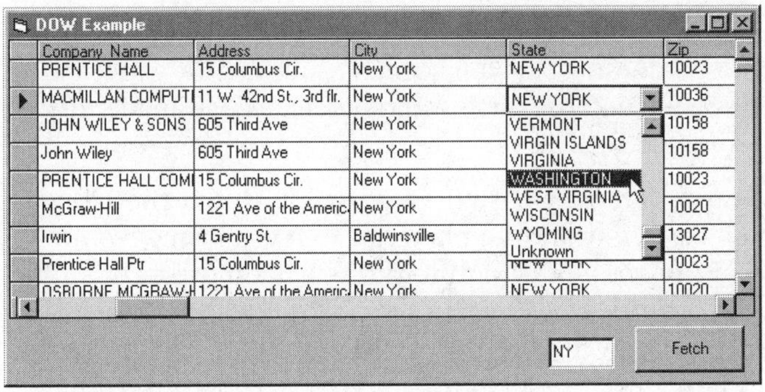

Figure 38-17 Running the simple DOW example

DOW Tips

The following tips should help you find your way when you're working with this new wizard. They are in no particular order.

- When you're working with stored procedures—as I know you will be—you can use SQL Enterprise Manager to create them a little easier than you can in Visual Basic. You can also right-click on the stored procedures in SQL Enterprise Manager and generate a script to document them as well. That feature is there in Visual Basic 6.0 too, but you can't generate more than one script at a time.

- Whenever you change a procedure on the server (no matter which tool you use), you *must* refresh the DataEnvironment Commands that call them so that ADO can figure out how the parameters work and what columns will be returning. It's not enough to refresh the Data Links. You'll also discover that even after you refresh a DataEnvironment Command, it still doesn't reflect the correct parameter or output columns as required or returned by the stored procedure. In this case, it's easier simply to drop the DataEnvironment Command and re-add it.

- If you make any changes to the underlying stored procedures, you *must* rerun the DOW to recreate the data Class and UserControl. The DOW makes lots of assumptions based on the layout of the stored procedures. Before you rerun the DOW, it's a good idea to drop the DOW-generated UserControls from the Project window and your forms. This will help the DOW create new versions without getting confused.

- Be sure to use SQL Trace (or SQL Server Profiler in SQL Server 7.0) to "watch" what's going on with the procedures and table lookups. You'll notice that the DOW code you generated does the table lookup en masse each time you hit the drop-down. This can be *very* expensive, so use this feature with caution.

- The FetchPublishers stored procedure takes a parameter, so you'll have to figure out how to pass that value to the stored procedure if you expect to get any rows populated in the grid. Actually, I showed you how to do that in the preceding discussion.

- The Insert_Publishers doesn't take a parameter, nor does it expect to have the PubID passed in because the row ID is generated via an identity column in the table and SQL Server generates the unique number.

- You'll have to watch out how Visual Basic breaks down the User-Control. For some reason, it drops a reference to it each time it's run at design time. This means you'll want to right-click on the form and click Update UserControls. Just keep in mind that updating controls resets all properties that haven't been persisted in the control—like the ManualInitialize and stored procedure parameter properties. Hopefully, this will be fixed eventually.

- Set the GridEditable to True if you want the drop-down list to appear.

- The Data Grid is smart enough to hold all of your changes until the user changes focus to another row or control. Then and only then is the Update or Insert stored procedure executed. To delete a row, simply highlight the whole row and press delete. This fires the Delete-Publishers stored procedures using the current PubID as the key.

- Remember, this wizard creates code. You can do anything you want with the generated code to make it better—I encourage you to do just that.

Using DOW Objects in an Application

Let's take a closer look at some considerations when using DOW objects. Later, I will list the DOW-generated properties, methods, and events for the data Class and UserControl.

Other Control Variations

If you choose to create a SingleRecord UserControl, the operation of the DOW is nearly the same as when you create the DataGrid. The ComboBox and ListBox options are basically the same, but all Lookup, Insert, Update, and Delete command information in the data Class is ignored since Lookup and data manipulation operations don't apply to these two UserControls. The field displayed in the Combo/ListBox controls is the first field in the Select command that is displayed with a TextBox. If you'd rather have a different field displayed in the ComboBox, see the comments in the "Public Function Init..." in the generated Combo/ListBox code.

Data Class Events

Certain methods raise the ClassError event. The DataGrid and SingleRecord UserControls both sink this event and display the error description from this event. The rsMoveComplete event is useful in a DataGrid/SingleRecord Master/ Detail scenario. When the user changes record focus in the DataGrid, the SingleRecord can refresh its data based on that record by sinking this event. The DeleteRecordComplete event notifies the UserControl that the record has been successfully completed. The rsUpdateEvent fires when the method rsUpdate is complete.

Data Binding

There are two kinds of binding: simple bound and complex bound. Simple binding can be applied to controls that are not "binding aware." Simple binding requires the BindingCollection object. Simple binding is really a "property setter"—that is, it sets a property of another control to a value of a field in a Recordset. For example, you can set the Text Property of a TextBox to the value of a particular field in a Recordset. The TextBoxes and CheckBoxes of the DOW SingleRecord UserControl use simple binding.

Complex binding refers to data controls that are "binding aware." These controls functionality similar to the BindingCollection built into the control. The DOW DataGrid is "complex" bound to the Select Recordset in the data Class.

Recordsets

Lookup command display fields do not exist in the Select command. For them to be shown in a bound DataGrid, these fields must be added to the Select command Recordset. Therefore, for any Select command that has Lookup relationships, a new Recordset is created that includes a Lookup display field for each relationship. Select commands without Lookup relationships use the Data Environment designer Select command directly.

The Select Recordset is disconnected from its data source either because it is a locally created Recordset or the Data Environment designer Select command DataSource is set to Nothing. This allows substituting other Data Environment designer commands for Update, Insert, and Delete operations.

Init... Methods

The Init... methods return the data Class object and have an optional parameter that is a data Class object. Because of this, the same instance of the data Class can be used by more than one UserControl. An example of this is a Master Detail Form, where the Master could be a DataGrid that contains a few fields of a Recordset. The Detail could be a SingleRecord UserControl that contains all the fields of the same Recordset. In this case, the DataGrid UserControl would instantiate the data Class (returned from the Init... method), then pass it as a parameter of the SingleRecord Init method).

System-Generated Primary-Key Values

If your Insert command generates primary-key values from the system and has parameters for each of these primary keys, these values are returned to the data Class. This allows immediate Updates or Deletes following an Insert.

In this case, set the "nullability" of the Primary Key fields to "Yes" so that the DOW-generated data class doesn't require value(s) for Primary Key fields.

UserControl Initialization

Auto initializing allows the generated UserControls to run and be filled with data by two easy steps: placing the UserControl on a Form and setting its Select command parameter properties.

By default, the property ManualInitialize is False. If your Select command has parameters, they appear on the Property Sheet (for the UserControl on the form). For example, if you have a parameter named YearBorn and a data class named Author, the property page will expose a property named Author_YearBorn. If you fill in the parameter properties at design time, the UserControl will load with data on initialization. If the parameter Property values are missing or of the wrong data type, for example, the form will load but the UserControl will have no data.

Manual initializing is the normal mode of initialization in most applications. If ManualInitialize = True, the values for the parameter Properties are set in code, usually in the form that contains the UserControl. The Init... method is run (generally from the form) to initialize the UserControl and load data.

TIP The ManualInitialize property is very skittish. Sometimes when you set or reset it, it clears the parameter properties.

DOW-Generated Data Class Code

In this section, I lay out the DOW-created data Class—its properties, methods, and events. I'll leave you to add the code to manipulate them.

clsDow

When a DOW Data Class is generated, if a class clsDow is not in the VB Project, it is added. clsDow contains the definition for EnumSaveMode.

rscls...

The rscls... class contains the DOW-generated properties, methods, and events listed in the following three tables.

DOW-Generated Data Class Properties

Property	Purpose
Select Command Field Properties	Each field in the Select command has corresponding Property Lets and Gets that allow reading and writing to the current Select command record. These properties have the same name as the field in the Select command.
Select Command Parameter Properties	Each parameter in the Select command has corresponding properties that allow setting the Select command parameter values. These properties have names that are the concatenation of the Select command name and the Select parameter name.
Lookup Commands Parameter Properties	Each parameter in each Lookup command has corresponding properties that allow setting the Lookup command parameter values. These Properties have names that are the concatenation of the Lookup command name and the Lookup parameter name.
Lookup Commands Recordset Properties	Each Lookup command has a corresponding Public Recordset Property. These Recordsets are named with the Lookup command name preceded by *rs*.
AbsolutePosition As Long	Returns the Select Recordset.AbsolutePosition.
BOF As Boolean	Returns the Select Recordset.BOF value.
EOF As Boolean	Returns the Select Recordset.EOF value.
SaveMode As EnumSaveMode	AdImmediate sets LockType to Optimistic and automatically saves when moving to a new current record in the Recordset. AdBatch sets LockType to BatchOptimistic and saves the current record manually with the Update method. It saves all dirty records manually with the UpdateBatch method.

DOW-Generated Data Class Methods

Method	Purpose
Sub AddRecord()	Adds a blank record to the Select Recordset.
Sub Delete()	Deletes the current Select Recordset record and runs the DED Delete command.
Sub Move(lRows As Long)	The record lRows from the current Select record becomes the current record.
Sub MoveFirst()	The first record in the Select Recordset becomes the current record.
Sub MoveLast()	The last record in the Select Recordset becomes the current record.
Sub MoveNext()	The next record in the Select Recordset becomes the current record.
Sub MovePrevious()	The previous record in the Select Recordset becomes the current record.
Sub rsUpdate(vFieldName)	Updates the field vFieldName with the correct display Lookup command field value for the Select command Lookup fields.
Sub Update()	Saves all the dirty records (SaveMode = adBatch), running the DED Update command.
Sub UpdateBatch()	Saves the current record (SaveMode = adBatch), running the DED update command.
Function ValidateData() As Boolean	Validates the data values in the current record.

DOW-Generated Data Class Events

Event	Purpose
ClassError(sProcedureName As String, oErr As ErrObject)	Occurs for certain application errors. Returns the Procedure name, sProcedureName, and the Err object.
DeleteRecordComplete()	Occurs after a record has been deleted from the Select Recordset.
rsMoveComplete()	Occurs after the Select Recordset has completed a move to a new current record.
rsUpdateEvent(vFieldName)	Occurs after the Lookup display fields have been updated for field vFieldName.

DOW-Generated UserControl Code

In the remainder of this chapter, I lay out the DOW-created UserControl—its properties, methods, and events for the SingleRecord, the DataGrid, and the ListBox/ComboBox UserControl types.

SingleRecord UserControl Type

DOW-Generated SingleRecord UserControl Properties

Property	Purpose
Select Command Parameter Properties	Each parameter in the Select command has corresponding properties that allow setting the data Class Select command parameter values. These properties have names that are the concatenation of the Select command name and the Select parameter name.
Lookup Commands Parameter Properties	Each parameter in each Lookup command has corresponding properties that allow setting the data Class Lookup command parameter values. These properties have names that are the concatenation of the Lookup command name and the Lookup parameter name.
ManualInitialize As Boolean	Set to False to enable filling the SingleRecord UserControl with data when the UserControl is initialized. This allows the control to be fully operational after the SingleRecord UserControl is generated, after any Command parameter property values are entered on the Property Sheet, and after the UserControl is placed on a form.
	When set to True, parameter values are not read from the PropertySheet. Select and Lookup command parameter property values are set from code in the form containing the UserControl.
SaveMode As EnumSaveMode	AdImmediate sets data Class LockType to Optimistic and automatically saves when moving to a new current record in the Recordset.
	AdBatch sets data Class LockType to BatchOptimistic and saves the current record manually with Update method. It saves all dirty records manually with the UpdateBatch method.

DOW-Generated SingleRecord UserControl Methods

Method	Purpose
AddRecord()	Runs the data Class AddRecord method.
Delete()	Runs the data Class Delete method.
Function Init({DataClass}) As Object	Initializes the SingleRecord UserControl by setting command parameters, setting the DataSource of the UserControl to the data Class, hiding Lookup fields, and so on. DataClass is an optional parameter. If passed, this instance of the data Class is used as the UserControl's DataSource; otherwise, a new instance of the data Class is created. The object returned is the data Class used as the SingleRecord DataSource.
Sub MoveFirst()	Runs the data Class MoveFirst method. The first record in the Select Recordset becomes the current record.
Sub MoveLast()	Runs the data Class MoveLast method. The last record in the Select Recordset becomes the current record.
Sub MoveNext()	Runs the data Class MoveNext method. The next record in the Select Recordset becomes the current record.
Sub MovePrevious()	Runs the data Class MovePrevious method. The previous record in the Select Recordset becomes the current record.
Update()	Runs data Class method, Update, saving all the dirty records (SaveMode = adBatch), using the DED Update command.
UpdateBatch()	Runs the data Class method, UpdateBatch, saving the current record (SaveMode = adBatch), using the DED update command.

DOW-Generated SingleRecord UserControl Event

Event	Purpose
MoveComplete(oDataSource As Object)	Sinks the data Class rsMove_Complete event. Returns the SingleRecord data Class.

DataGrid UserControl Type

DOW-Generated DataGrid UserControl Properties

Property	Purpose
Select Command Parameter Properties	Each parameter in the Select command has corresponding Properties that allow setting the data Class Select command parameter values. These properties have names that are the concatenation of the Select command name and the Select parameter name.
Lookup Commands Parameter Properties	Each parameter in each Lookup command has corresponding properties that allow setting the data Class Lookup command parameter values. These properties have names that are the concatenation of the Lookup command name and the Lookup parameter name.
GridEditable As Boolean	Set to True to enable data modifications to the DataGrid and to enable the Lookup command ComboBoxes on the Lookup display fields.
ManualInitialize As Boolean	Set to False to enable filling the DataGrid with data when the UserControl is initialized. This allows the control to be fully operational after the DataGrid UserControl is generated, after any Command property parameter values are entered on the Property Sheet, and after the UserControl is placed on a form. When set to True, parameter values are not read from the PropertySheet. Select and Lookup command parameter property values are set from code in the form containing the UserControl.
SaveMode As EnumSaveMode	AdImmediatesets data Class LockType to Optimistic and automatically saves when moving to a new current record in the Recordset. AdBatch sets data Class LockType to BatchOptimistic and saves the current record manually with the Update method. It saves all dirty records manually with the UpdateBatch method.

DOW-Generated DataGrid UserControl Methods

Method	Purpose
Function(s) UpdateFK{FKCommand} (nSurrogateKey As Integer)	For each Lookup command, sets the Lookup fields for the current {FKCommand} record to the Lookup Recordset record fields having a Surrogate Key of nSurrogateKey.
Function Init({DataClass}) As Object	Initializes the DataGrid by setting command parameters, setting the DataSource of the DataGrid to the data Class, setting data updatability according to GridEditable, hiding Lookup fields, and so on. DataClass is an optional parameter. If passed, this instance of the data Class is used as the DataGrid DataSource; otherwise, a new instance of the data Class is created. The Object returned is the data Class used as the DataGrid DataSource.
Update()	Runs the data Class method, Update, saving all the dirty records (SaveMode = adBatch), using the DED Update command.
UpdateBatch()	Runs the data Class method, UpdateBatch, saving the current record (SaveMode = adBatch), using the DED Update command.

DOW-Generated DataGrid UserControl Event

Event	Purpose
MoveComplete(oDataSource As Object)	Sinks the data Class rsMove_Complete event. Returns the DataSource data Class.

ListBox/ComboBox UserControl Type

DOW-Generated ListBox/ComboBox UserControl Properties

Property	Purpose
Select Command Parameter Properties	Each parameter in the Select command has corresponding Properties that allow setting the data Class Select command parameter values. These properties have names that are the concatenation of the Select command name and the Select parameter name.
ManualInitialize As Boolean	Set to False to enable filling the Combo/ListBox UserControl with data when the UserControl is initialized. This allows the control to be fully operational after the Combo/ListBox UserControl is generated, after any Command parameter property values are entered on the Property Sheet, and after the UserControl is placed on a form.
	When set to True, parameter values are not read from the PropertySheet. Select and Lookup command parameter property values are set from code in the form containing the UserControl.
NoneFirst As Boolean	If True, loads "(None)" in the first row of the Combo/ListBox. Used in relationships that allow nulls in the foreign-key side of the relationship.

DOW-Generated ListBox/ComboBox UserControl Methods

Method	Purpose
Function Init({DataClass}) As Object	Initializes the Combo/ListBox UserControl by setting command parameters, setting the DataSource of the UserControl to the data Class, and so on.
	DataClass is an optional parameter. If passed, this instance of the data Class is used as the UserControl's DataSource, otherwise a new instance of the data Class is created.
	The Object returned is the data Class used as the Combo/ListBox DataSource.

DOW-Generated ListBox/ComboBox UserControl Event

Event	Purpose
Combo/ListBoxClick(PKVal1, ...,PKValN)	Occurs when a user clicks on a Combo/ListBox row. This event supplies primary-key values PKVal1 through PkValN for the record.

A

Setting Up the Test Databases

Installing the *Biblio* Database

Creating a DSN

Adding Stored Procedures

The Attach.MDB Database

Setting Up the Sample Applications

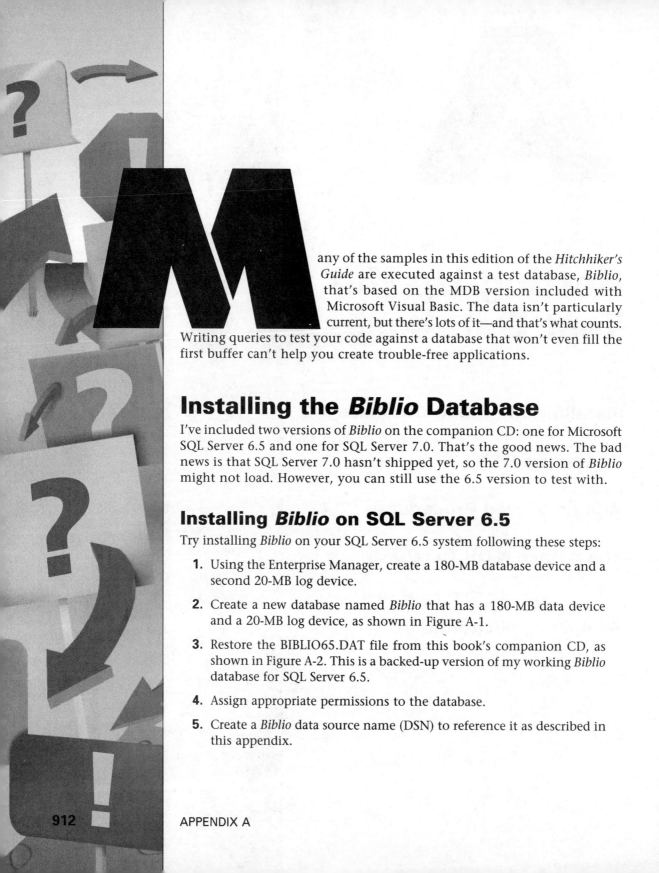

any of the samples in this edition of the *Hitchhiker's Guide* are executed against a test database, *Biblio*, that's based on the MDB version included with Microsoft Visual Basic. The data isn't particularly current, but there's lots of it—and that's what counts. Writing queries to test your code against a database that won't even fill the first buffer can't help you create trouble-free applications.

Installing the *Biblio* Database

I've included two versions of *Biblio* on the companion CD: one for Microsoft SQL Server 6.5 and one for SQL Server 7.0. That's the good news. The bad news is that SQL Server 7.0 hasn't shipped yet, so the 7.0 version of *Biblio* might not load. However, you can still use the 6.5 version to test with.

Installing *Biblio* on SQL Server 6.5

Try installing *Biblio* on your SQL Server 6.5 system following these steps:

1. Using the Enterprise Manager, create a 180-MB database device and a second 20-MB log device.

2. Create a new database named *Biblio* that has a 180-MB data device and a 20-MB log device, as shown in Figure A-1.

3. Restore the BIBLIO65.DAT file from this book's companion CD, as shown in Figure A-2. This is a backed-up version of my working *Biblio* database for SQL Server 6.5.

4. Assign appropriate permissions to the database.

5. Create a *Biblio* data source name (DSN) to reference it as described in this appendix.

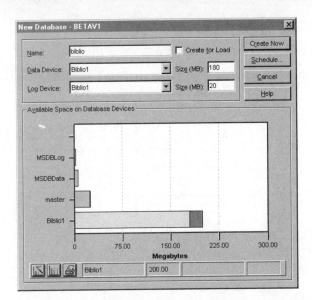

Figure A-1 *Creating a new Biblio database with SQL Server 6.5*

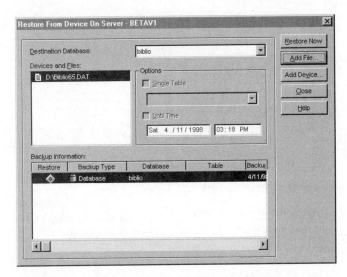

Figure A-2 *Restoring the Biblio database in SQL Server 6.5*

TIP If you plan to sort anything, create cursors, or use complex result sets, it would be a good idea to increase the size of your TempDB database. If you're overflowing it during testing, you sure as death and taxes are going to fill it up when a bunch of users are logged on using your new application.

Installing *Biblio* on SQL Server 7.0

Try installing *Biblio* on your SQL Server 7.0 system following these steps:

1. Using the Enterprise Manager, create a new database named *Biblio* that has an initial size of 90 MB and a transaction log with an initial size of 10 MB, as shown in Figure A-3.

NOTE The SQL Server 7.0 version of *Biblio* on the companion CD is based on Beta 3 of SQL Server 7.0, so it might or might not work with your SQL Server 7.0 system.

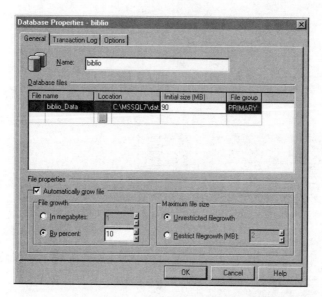

Figure A-3 *Creating a new* Biblio *database with SQL Server 7.0 Beta 3*

2. Restore the BIBLIO70.DAT file from this book's companion CD, as shown in Figure A-4. This is a backed-up version of my working *Biblio* database for SQL Server 7.0.

NOTE You might need to select the Force Restore Over Existing Database check box on the Options tab of the Restore Database dialog box.

---

3. Assign appropriate permissions to the database.

4. Create a *Biblio* DSN to reference it as described in this appendix.

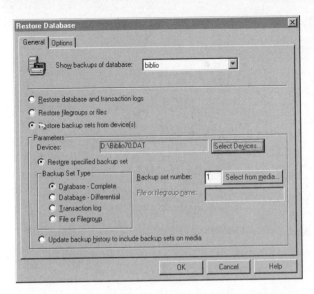

Figure A-4 *Restoring the* Biblio *database in SQL Server 7.0 Beta 3*

Creating a DSN

Many of the samples in this guide require that you register a DSN. A DSN contains parameters from the connect string and other information provided by the developer when it is installed. Once registered, the DSN includes the name of the data source, the name of the server, the type of driver, and other data about the network interface and security settings. In 32-bit systems, all this information is kept in the Microsoft Windows Registry, so it can be somewhat costly to retrieve.

You can set up DSNs in a variety of ways, including using the ODBC control panel applet, using programmatic API calls, and simply copying files. Some connection techniques don't use DSNs at all. In fact, ADO and OLE DB doesn't usually need DSNs because this interface uses several new connection strategies.

For the purposes of most samples in this guide, you can create a User DSN or a System DSN, but I don't think you can get away with a file-based DSN. To create a DSN, open the ODBC applet in the Windows Control Panel. This starts the ODBC Data Source Administrator. On the User DSN or System DSN tab, you have the options of adding, removing, or configuring an ODBC DSN. Click the Add button to create a new DSN that points to the *Biblio* (or *Pubs)* database. Select *SQL Server* as the driver name, as shown in Figure A-5. If you don't see *SQL Server* in the list of available drivers, either you didn't check it in the Visual Basic Setup dialog boxes or it's been misplaced. Go back and reinstall it now—without this driver, you won't get anywhere.

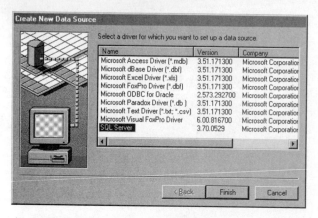

Figure A-5 *Creating a new User DSN by using the ODBC control panel applet*

Clicking the Finish button starts a wizard to create a SQL Server DSN, as shown in Figure A-6. In this first screen, enter the following information:

- **The name of your data source** This doesn't have to be any particular name, but it should be something that identifies where the SQL Server data is coming from. I usually name my data sources after the database, not the server.

- **An optional description of the data source** Again, you have free rein; enter anything that helps identify this data source. This information shows up in the ODBC dialog boxes.

- **The network name of the server that is running SQL Server** Nope, don't add \\ to the name. For Microsoft Windows NT or OS/2 servers, simply give the server name.

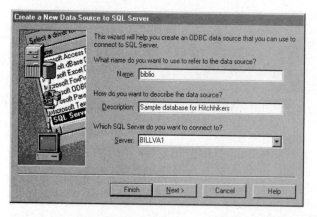

Figure A-6 *The first screen of the data source wizard, which you use to create a new data source to SQL Server*

Click Next. This takes you to the security screen shown in Figure A-7, in which you describe how ODBC should try to get through the network and SQL Server security. Although you might have to supply a login ID and a password at this time, these values are not stored in the DSN. If you plan to provide a SQL Server login ID and password, choose the With SQL Server Authentication... option and enter the login ID and password in the boxes provided. If you don't know your login ID and password, you need to get them from your system administrator. If you plan to pass your current Windows user ID to SQL Server and let it use Windows NT authentication, simply click Next to go to the next dialog box.

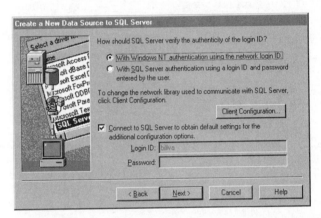

Figure A-7 *The second screen of the data source wizard, which allows you to specify authentication and configuration information to connect to SQL Server*

When you press Next on the security dialog box, ODBC attempts to make a connection to your SQL Server. Yes, it must be running and it must recognize the ID and password provided. If it doesn't, you'll hang for 60 seconds or so while ODBC waits for some server somewhere to respond. If you do get in, however, you'll see the screen shown in Figure A-8.

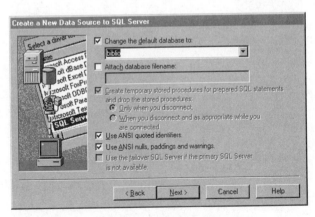

Figure A-8 *The third screen of the data source wizard, which allows you to specify the name of the default SQL Server database*

NOTE Visual Basic 6.0 includes the new ODBC 3.6 ODBC Driver Manager and support code that has a (mostly) new set of interactive ODBC DSN dialog boxes. Although these might not be familiar to old ODBC hands, they are pretty intuitive and offer far more flexibility than previous versions.

You are now connected to SQL Server. To choose the default database from the list of available databases, check the Change The Default Database To checkbox and choose *Biblio* or *Pubs* from the drop-down list. Don't worry about the other options at this time—the default options are fine.

Depending on your version of ODBC, you'll typically have two more screens that you can ignore for now, so simply press Next until you get to the last screen.

When you press the Finish button on the last screen, the dialog box shown in Figure A-9 is displayed. This dialog box lists the configuration information.

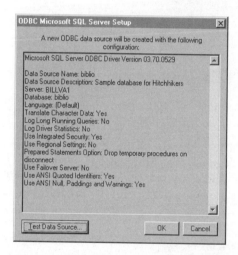

Figure A-9 *Dialog box that shows selected data source configuration information*

Here's where you get to verify the settings you just made. Click the Test Data Source button to test the data source—if this doesn't work, go back and make whatever changes the error dialog boxes call for. When you connect successfully, press OK and your DSN will be registered for you.

Adding Stored Procedures

Some of the samples require certain stored procedures to be installed in the *Biblio* or *Pubs* database. I've included SQL script files with the samples on the companion CD that require these procedures. Use the ISQL/w or the Query Analyzer to install them on your database. Figure A-10 shows a SQL script opened in ISQL/w.

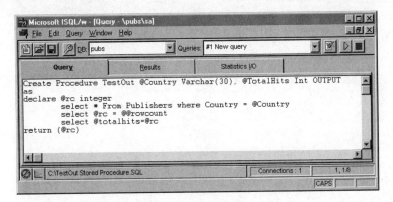

```
Microsoft ISQL/w - [Query - \pubs\sa]
 File  Edit  Query  Window  Help

        DB: pubs              Queries: #1 New query

    Query          Results          Statistics I/O

Create Procedure TestOut @Country Varchar(30), @TotalHits Int OUTPUT
as
declare @rc integer
        select * From Publishers where Country = @Country
        select @rc = @@rowcount
        select @totalhits=@rc
return (@rc)


  C:\TestOut Stored Procedure.SQL              Connections : 1      1, 1/8
                                                            CAPS
```

Figure A-10 *A SQL script opened in ISQL/w*

The Attach.MDB Database

A couple of the samples use the Attach.MDB database. This database is simple
enough; it has attached tables that point to the *Biblio* SQL Server database.
There are copies in the appropriate directories on the companion CD, but you'll
have to rebuild the attachments because they point to my server—unless you
can figure out how to link to my server, in which case at least give me a call
so that I can turn on the server.

Setting Up the Sample Applications

Don't try to run these from the companion CD. You'll have better luck if you
copy the code samples to your hard drive. You can also run the Setup program
in the Code Samples directory to copy the code samples to your hard drive.
This Setup program also clears the read-only flag on the files. Many of the
chapter code samples include Readme files that explain how to run the sample.
If you have trouble getting a chapter code sample to run, be sure to check out
the Readme file.

B

SQL Server Error Codes Decoded

The first of the three tables in this appendix lists errors that any front end to Microsoft SQL Server might encounter. In the Microsoft Jet, ADO, and RDO models, they appear in the Errors collection. In the ODBC API, they're exposed by the SQLError function. In VBSQL, they're trapped by DB-Library and returned in the Error and Message event handlers. (For the exact text of error messages generated by the server, see the *SysMessages* table of the *Master* database, where the messages are enumerated and documented.) The second table lists cursor function errors. No manifest constants or error codes are defined in the VBSQL documentation for the cursor functions. The third table lists the meanings of error severity codes.

Errors SQL Server Might Encounter

Manifest Constant	Value	Severity Level	Error Message	Context/Notes
SQLEMEM	10000	8	*Unable to allocate sufficient memory*	Raised by any function that allocates memory (opens, reads, and so forth)
SQLENULL	10001	7	*Asqlconn identifier with a value of 0 was encountered*	Raised by any function requiring the connection token returned from SQLOpen (Connection has died or integer holding the token returned from SQLOpen was altered.)

Manifest Constant	Value	Severity Level	Error Message	Context/Notes
SQLENLOG	10002	11	A loginrec with a value of 0 was encountered	Raised by SQLOpen or any of the SQLSetL... functions (SQLLogin not executed before SQLSetLUser, SQLSetLPwd, SQLSetLHost, SQLSetLApp, or SQLOpen)
SQLEPWD	10003	2	Login incorrect	Raised by SQLOpen, when logon name isn't a valid user on the SQL server (password used in LoginRec structure or in SQLOpenConnection is incorrect for user name provided)
SQLECONN	10004	9	Unable to connect: SQL Server is unavailable or does not exist	Raised by SQLOpen (Server LAN down or LAN permissions or resources won't allow connection; too many LAN users on server; too many LAN resources in use on workstation)
SQLEDDNE	10005	1	SQL Server connection is dead	Raised by any function requiring the connection token returned from SQLOpen (bad connection token)
SQLENULLO	10006	11	Attempt to log in with a LoginRec value of 0	C error code (not listed in VBSQL.BI); see SQLNULLO
SQLNULLO	10006	11	Attempt to log in with a LoginRec value of 0	Raised by SQLOpen; see SQLENLOG
SQLESMSG	10007	5	General SQL Server error has occurred: Check message from SQL Server	Usually after opening, during row processing; fairly common (check messages from the SQL server)
SQLEBTOK	10008	9	Bad token from SQL Server: data stream out of sync	Rarely encountered (suspect network error or alteration of the Tabular Data Stream data)
SQLENSPE	10009	7	Nonspecific general error	Rarely encountered (not described in Visual Basic programmer's reference)
SQLEREAD	10010	9	Read from SQL Server failed	Usually after opening, during row processing (suspect LAN protocol error)
SQLECNOR	10011	7	Column number out of range	When SQLData column reference doesn't match SQL query
SQLETSIT	10012	1	Attempt to call SQLTsPut with an invalid TimeStamp	Raised by SQLTsPut (error in VBSQL documentation)
SQLEPARM	10013	11	Invalid parameter in DB-Library function reference	Raised by any function call
SQLEAUTN	10014	7	Attempt to update the TimeStamp of a table that has no TimeStamp column	Raised by SQLExec, SQLSend (invalid query)

(continued)

Manifest Constant	Value	Severity Level	Error Message	Context/Notes
SQLECOFL	10015	4	*Data conversion resulted in overflow*	Unlikely; no conversion in DB-Library for Visual Basic applications (data conversion errors done via TSQL CONVERT verb reported via SQL Server error messages; possibly applicable to Visual Basic)
SQLERDCN	10016	4	*Requested data conversion does not exist*	Unlikely; no conversion in DBLIB for Visual Basic applications (data conversion errors done via TSQL CONVERT verb reported via SQL Server error messages; possibly applicable to Visual Basic)
SQLEICN	10017	7	*Invalid ComputeID or computer column number*	Raised by SQLAData or any of the Compute columns (*ComputeID* passed back from DB-Library by SQLNextRow)
SQLECLOS	10018	9	*Error in closing network connection*	Rarely encountered
SQLENTXT	10019	7	*Attempt to get a Text identifier or Text TimeStamp from a non-Text column*	Raised by SQLTxPtr, SQLTxTimeStamp, SQLTxTsNewVal, SQLTsNewVal
SQLEDNTI	10020	7	*Attempt to use SQLTxTsPut to put a new Text TimeStamp into a column whose data type is neither Text nor Image*	Raised by SQLTxTsPut
SQLETMTD	10021	7	*Attempt to send too much Text data by using SQLMoreText*	Raised by SQLMoreText
SQLEASEC	10022	7	*Attempt to send an empty command buffer to SQL Server*	Raised by SQLExec, SQLSend (execute SQLCmd before executing SQLExec; SQLSendCmd has no query)
SQLENTLL	10023	2	*Name too long for LoginRec*	Raised by SQLSetL... functions
SQLETIME	10024	6	*SQL Server connection timed out*	Raised by any query after SQLExec or SQLSend
SQLEWRIT	10025	9	*Write to SQL Server failed*	When network has problems or libraries are out of sync (error number might be unused)
SQLEMODE	10026	9	*Network connection not in correct mode; invalid SQL Server connection*	Rarely encountered
SQLEOOB	10027	9	*Error in sending out-of-band data to SQL Server*	Rarely encountered
SQLEITIM	10028	7	*Illegal timeout value specified*	Raised by SQLSetTime, SQLSetLoginTime

Manifest Constant	Value	Severity Level	Error Message	Context/Notes
SQLEDBPS	10029	8	*Invalid or out-of-range parameter to a Visual Basic option*	Raised by SQLOpen (memory constraints limit number of possible connections on workstation; use SQLMaxProcs to allocate more)
SQLEIOPT	10030	7	*Attempt to use invalid Visual Basic option*	Rarely encountered (unknown severity level)
SQLEASNL	10031	7	*Attempt to set fields in a login record with LoginRecvalue of 0*	Raised by SQLSetL... functions (call SQLLogin before setting any LoginRec fields)
SQLEASUL	10032	7	*Attempt to set unknown LoginRec field*	Raised by SQLSetL... functions; rarely encountered
SQLENPRM	10033	7	*This Visual Basic option cannot have a parameter that is an empty string*	
SQLEDBOP	10034	7	*Invalid or out-of-range parameter to a Visual Basic option*	
SQLENSIP	10035	7	*Negative starting index passed to SQLStrCpy*	Raised by SQLStrCpy
SQLECNULL	10036	7	*You have used 0 as an identifier for a Text TimeStamp*	
SQLESEOF	10037	9	*Unexpected EOF from SQL server*	At SQLOpen time (named-pipe connection to the SQL server closed unexpectedly; SQL server might be down or network might have closed your pipe connection; suspect no more connections available; later, suspect network failure)
SQLERPND	10038	7	*Attempt to initiate a new SQL Server operation with results pending*	Raised by SQLExec, SQLSendCmd, SQLSend (results pending)
SQLECSYN	10039	4	*Attempt to convert data stopped by syntax error in source field*	Unlikely; no conversion in DB-Library for Visual Basic applications
SQLENONET	10040	9	*DB-Library network communications layer not loaded*	SQLInit (usually required DLLs not in place)
SQLEBTYP	10041	7	*Unknown bind type passed to DB-Library function*	

(continued)

Manifest Constant	Value	Severity Level	Error Message	Context/Notes
SQLEABNC	10042	7	*Attempt to bind to a nonexistent column*	
SQLEABMT	10043	7	*User attempted a dbbind with mismatched column and variable types*	
SQLEABNP	10044	7	*Attempt to bind using NULL pointers*	
SQLEBNCR	10045	7	*Attempt to bind user variable to a non-existent compute row*	
SQLEAAMT	10046[1]	7	*User attempted a dbaltbind with mismatched column and variable types*	
SQLENXID	10047	3	*The server did not grant a distributed-transaction ID*	Not applicable to Visual Basic (used only in two-phase commit)
SQLEIFNB	10048[2]	7	*Illegal field number passed to BCP_control*	Possibly with SQLBCPControl (not listed as valid VBSQL error)
SQLEKBCO	10049	1	*1000 rows successfully copied to host file*	Raised by bulk copy operations
SQLEBBCI	10050	1	*Batch successfully copied to SQL Server*	Raised by bulk copy operations
SQLEKBCI	10051	1	*1000 rows sent to SQL Server*	Raised by bulk copy operations
SQLEBCWE	10052	3	*I/O error while writing a BCP data file*	Raised by bulk copy operations
SQLEBCNN	10053	2	*Attempt to copy a Null value into a SQL Server column that does not accept Null values*	Raised by bulk copy operations
SQLEBCOR	10054	11	*Attempt to bulk copy an oversized row to SQL Server*	Raised by bulk copy operations
SQLEBCPI	10055	7	*Call SQLInit$ before any other BCP routines*	Raised by bulk copy operations (error in VBSQL documentation)
SQLEBCPN	10056	7	*Use bcp_bind, bcp_collen, and bcp_colptr only after calling bcp_init with the copy direction set to DB_IN*	

Manifest Constant	Value	Severity Level	Error Message	Context/Notes
SQLEBCPB	10057	7	Do not use bcp_bind after bcp_init has been passed a non-Null data file name	
SQLEVDPT	10058	2	For bulk copy, all variable-length data must have either a length-prefix or a terminator specified	Raised by bulk copy operations (for bulk copy, all variable-length data must have a specified-length prefix or terminator)
SQLEBIVI	10059	7	Use SQLBCPColumns and SQLBCPColfmt only after SQLInit$ has been passed a valid data file	Raised by SQLBCPColumns, SQLBCPColfmt (error in VBSQL documentation)
SQLEBCBC	10060	7	Call SQLBCPColumns before SQLBCPColfmt	Raised by SQLBCPColfmt
SQLEBCFO	10061	2	Host files must contain at least one column: BCP	Raised by bulk copy operations
SQLEBCVH	10062	7	Call SQLBCPExec only after SQLBCPInit has been passed a valid host file	Raised by SQLBCPExec
SQLEBCUO	10063	8	Unable to open host data file: BCP	Raised by bulk copy operations
SQLEBUOE	10064	8	Unable to open error file: BCP	Raised by bulk copy operations
SQLEBWEF	10065	3	I/O error writing BCP error file	Raised by bulk copy operations
SQLEBTMT	10066	7	Attempt to send too much data with BCP_moretext	Raised by bulk copy operations (error in VBSQL documentation)
SQLEBEOF	10067	3	Unexpected end of file encountered in BCP data file	Raised by bulk copy operations (data file might not be structured as described; suspect comma-delimited files not properly converted)
SQLEBCSI	10068	11	Host file columns may be skipped only when copying to the SQL server	Not listed as VBSQL error
SQLEPNUL	10069	11	Null program pointer encountered	Not listed as VBSQL error
SQLEBSKERR	10070	11	Cannot seek in data file	Not listed as VBSQL error
SQLEBDIO	10071	7	Bad bulk-copy direction	Raised by bulk copy operations

(continued)

Manifest Constant	Value	Severity Level	Error Message	Context/Notes
SQLEBCNT	10072	2	*Attempt to use bulk copy with non-existent server table*	With bulk copy operations
SQLEMDBP	10073	7	*Attempt to set maximum number of DBPROCESSes lower than 1*	
SQLINIT[3]	10074	?		Not listed in VBSQL or C documentation; unknown severity level

1. Error codes 10041–10046 not applicable to VBSQL; pertain to errors in binding that are possible only with C interface.
2. Error codes 10048–10110 not defined in SQL.BI; functions not supported in VBSQL interface.
3. Same spelling as SQLInit$() function.

Cursor Function Errors

Manifest Constant	Value	Severity Level	Error Message	Context/Notes
SQLCRSINV	10075	7	*Invalid cursor statement*	Raised by cursor operations
SQLCRSCMD	10076	7	*Attempt to call cursor function when there are commands waiting to be executed*	Raised by cursor operations
SQLCRSNOIND	10077	1	*One of the tables involved in the cursor statement does not have a unique index*	Raised by cursor operations
SQLCRSDIS	10078	7	*Cursor statement contains one of the disallowed phrases COMPUTER, UNION, FOR BROWSE, or SELECT INTO*	Raised by cursor operations
SQLCRSAGR	10079	7	*Aggregate functions are not allowed in a cursor statement*	Raised by cursor operations
SQLCRSORD	10080	7	*Only fully keyset-driven cursors can have ORDER BY, GROUP BY, or HAVING phrases*	Raised by cursor operations
SQLCRSMEM	10081	7	*Keyset or window scroll size exceeds the memory limitations of this computer*	Raised by cursor operations
SQLCRSBSKEY	10082	7	*Keyset cannot be scrolled backward in mixed cursors with a previous fetch type*	
SQLCRSNORES	10083	1	*Cursor statement generated no results*	

Manifest Constant	Value	Severity Level	Error Message	Context/Notes
SQLCRSVIEW	10084	7	A view cannot be joined with another table or a view in a cursor statement	
SQLCRSBUFR	10085	7	Row buffering should not be turned on when using cursor functions	
SQLCRSFROWN	10086	1	Row number to be fetched is outside valid range	
SQLCRSBROL	10087	7	Backward scrolling cannot be used in a forward-scrolling cursor	
SQLCRSFRAND	10088	7	Fetch types RANDOM and RELATIVE can be used only within the keyset of keyset-driven cursors	
SQLCRSFLAST	10089	7	Fetch type LAST requires fully keyset-driven cursors	
SQLCRSRO	10090	7	Data locking or modifications cannot be made in a read-only cursor	
SQLCRSTAB	10091	7	Table name must be determined in operations involving data locking or modifications	
SQLCRSUPDTAB	10092	7	Update or insert operations using bind variables require single-table cursors	
SQLCRSUPDNB	10093	7	Update or insert operations cannot use bind variables when binding type is NOBIND	
SQLCRSVIIND	10094	7	The view used in the cursor statement does not include all the unique index columns of the underlying tables	
SQLCRSNOUPD	10095	1	Update or delete operation did not affect any rows	
SQLCRSOS2	10096	7	Cursors are not supported for this server	Cursors aren't supported on Sybase SQL Servers?
SQLEBCSA	10097		The BCP hostfile %s contains only %ld rows; skipping all of these rows is not allowed	
SQLCRSRO	10098		Data locking or modifications cannot be made in a read-only cursor	
SQLEBCNE	10099		The table %s contains only %ld rows; copying up to row %ld is not possible	

(continued)

Manifest Constant	Value	Severity Level	Error Message	Context/Notes
SQLEBCSK	10100		*The table %s contains only %ld rows. Skipping all of these rows is not allowed.*	
SQLEUVBF	10101		*Attempt to read unknown version of bcp format file.*	
SQLEBIHC	10102		*Incorrect host-column number found in bcp format file.*	
SQLEBWFF	10103		*I/O error while reading bcp format file.*	
SQLNUMVAL	10104		*The data stored in the DBNUMERIC/DBDECIMAL structure is invalid.*	
SQLEOLDVR	10105		*The SQL Server's TDS is obsolete with this version of DB-Library.*	
SQLEBCPS	10106		*The row length exceeds SQL Server's maximum allowable size.*	
SQLEDTC	10107		*Microsoft Distributed Transaction Coordinator call failed.*	
SQLENOTIMPL	10108		*This function is not supported on this platform at this time.*	
SQLENONFLOAT	10109		*Float conversion attempt failed. The source is invalid.*	
SQLECONNFB	10110		*Unable to connect: DB Server is unavailable or does not exist—will attempt a fallback connection.*	

Error Severity Codes

Severity Level Constant	Severity Level Number	Description
EXINFO	1	Informational, nonerror
EXUSER	2	User error
EXNONFATAL	3	Nonfatal error
EXCONVERSION	4	Error in VBSQL data conversion
EXSERVER	5	Server returned an error flag
EXTIME	6	Timeout period exceeded while user waits for response from server; *SQLConn* still alive
EXPROGRAM	7	Coding error in user program
EXRESOURCE	8	Resources running low; *SQLConn* possibly dead
EXCOMM	9	Failure in communication with server; *SQLConn* dead
EXFATAL	10	Fatal error; *SQLConn* dead
EXCONSISTENCY	11	Internal software error; need to notify Microsoft Technical Support

C

SQL Server
Tips and Tricks

Tips on the Bulk Copy Program

Tips on Stored Procedures

General Tips on Transact-SQL

Tips for Enhancing Performance

Tips for Efficient Designs

**Accessing Visual Basic
Components from SQL Server**

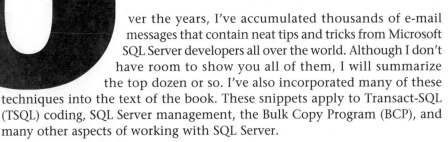

O ver the years, I've accumulated thousands of e-mail messages that contain neat tips and tricks from Microsoft SQL Server developers all over the world. Although I don't have room to show you all of them, I will summarize the top dozen or so. I've also incorporated many of these techniques into the text of the book. These snippets apply to Transact-SQL (TSQL) coding, SQL Server management, the Bulk Copy Program (BCP), and many other aspects of working with SQL Server.

First, a tip on finding more tips. The Microsoft Knowledge Base and MSDN are great places to find current information. Unfortunately, these sources include so much information that you might find the prospect of pawing through all that hay to find the single needle of valuable information daunting. To streamline your search, try searching on *OpenConnection* to find all articles containing code on RDO, or search on *ADODB.* to find all the ADO-based articles with examples.

Tips on the Bulk Copy Program

- When you refer to SQL Server in the BCP command line, don't include the \\. BCP only needs the name of the SQL Server passed as an argument.

- A number of developers have reported having difficulty working with BCP. One developer, Troy King (*katravax@soonernet.com*), provides examples of using BCP, sample BCP in/out batch files, 1000 rows of sample data, and the format files in a ZIP file. His examples are for comma-separated, tab-separated, and fixed-width file transfers. His Web site, which has a link to a BCP tutorial, is at *http://www.soonernet.com/~katravax*. Be sure to contact Troy with your comments and suggestions.

Here are some generic BCP tips (most of which you probably already know, but here they are anyway):

- Remember that the command line is case-sensitive.

- Unless you're using native mode, use SQLCHAR as the data type for all fields. This can be tricky if you follow the prompts rather than build your FMT file by hand because NATIVE data types, not SQLCHAR data types, are the default.

- In fixed-width files, use "" as the delimiter (to show that there isn't one), as shown here:

```
/***For Comma-Separated:***/
bcp demo.dbo.datacsv in DBFILE.CSV.csv /e datacsv.err /
b 1000 /c /t , /r \n
/U sa /P deletedpw /S rhiannon
/***For sample data:***/
1,Fred,Hill,4023 Sixth Blvd.,Brusly,IA,33457,4/16/
93,35369.2594
/***I don't use a Format file with CSV files.***/

/***For Tab-Separated***/
bcp demo.dbo.datatab in DBFILE.TSV /
f Database(tab)format.fmt /e datatab.err
/b 1000 /c /U sa /P deletedpw /S rhiannon
/***For sample data: ***/
1 Fred Hill 4023 Sixth Blvd. Brusly IA 33457 4/16/
93 35369.2594
/***And the Format File (we could also get away without a
format file in this case, but what the heck:***/
6.0
9
1 SQLCHAR 0 5 "\t" 1 ID
2 SQLCHAR 0 10 "\t" 2 First
3 SQLCHAR 0 15 "\t" 3 Last
4 SQLCHAR 0 30 "\t" 4 Address
5 SQLCHAR 0 15 "\t" 5 City
6 SQLCHAR 0 2 "\t" 6 State
7 SQLCHAR 0 8 "\t" 7 Salary
8 SQLCHAR 0 8 "\t" 8 Date_Hired
9 SQLCHAR 0 15 "\r\n" 9 Value

/***For Fixed-Width:***/
bcp demo.dbo.dataspace in DBFILE.SPC /f FIXEDWITH.FMT /
e dataspace.err /b
1000 /U sa /P deletedpw /S rhiannon
/***For sample data:***/
1Fred    Hill      4023 Sixth Blvd.          Brusly      IA
33457   4/16/9335369.259
/***and the format file***/
6.0
9
1 SQLCHAR 0 8      ""       1 ID
2 SQLCHAR 0 9 ""      2 First
3 SQLCHAR 0 11 ""      3 Last
```

(continued)

```
4 SQLCHAR 0 29 ""        4 Address
5 SQLCHAR 0 14   ""      5 City
6 SQLCHAR 0 2    ""      6 State
7 SQLCHAR 0 10   ""      7 Salary
8 SQLCHAR 0 9 ""       8 Date_Hired
9 SQLCHAR 0 9 "\r\n" 9 Value
```

- You can also run BCP from a stored procedure using the following TSQL command:

```
Master.xp_cmdshell 'CMD /C BCP biblio..authors out
\\mydir\test.out -c -Usa -P -Shs_lein'
```

Tips on Stored Procedures

- In some cases, your application or the data access interface might not be smart enough to deal with OUTPUT parameters. If this is the case, add a little extra logic to the stored procedure that returns the OUTPUT value as a rowset. You can enable this extra SELECT statement in the stored procedure by using an extra input parameter, like this:

```
CREATE PROCEDURE DualOutput
    @YearWanted smallint=1947,
    @ReturnOutput bit=0,
    @OutputValue char(80) OUTPUT
AS

Declare @MyOutValue char(80)
Print 'Create output value'
select @MyOutValue=login_Time
    From master..sysprocesses s where s.spid = @@spid
Print 'Create select rowset'
Select * from Authors where Year_born = @YearWanted
if @ReturnOutput = 1
begin
    Print 'Create output rowset'
    select @MyOutValue OutputValue
end
return (0)
```

- If you need to pass a NULL to a stored procedure, remember that NULL is not a data type but a data "unvalue." That is, it has neither a type nor a value. Simply pass the keyword *null* to the stored procedure as the argument:

```
Sp_MyProc '111', 'xxx', null
```

However, you can't set a parameter to NULL in the SQL-92 standard because it's a TSQL extension. Because ODBC calls for SQL-92 behavior, the SQL Server ODBC driver automatically turns on several ANSI options, including ANSI_NULLS.

General Tips on Transact-SQL

- If you get an error from SQL Server telling you that a perfectly good table name is an "Invalid object," the name might not be fully qualified. Even if you connect as the database owner (DBO), if some other user owns the table you might not be able to access it without providing the user name, as shown here:

```
MyDB.MyOwnerName.TableName
```

- A developer from Great Britain needed to return the current time in dd/mm/ccyy HH:MM:SQL Server (24-hour) format. We suggested that he use the CONVERT function as follows:

```
SELECT CONVERT(char(20), GETDATE( ), 113)
```

- To extract the current user's Windows NT login identity, you can reference the NT_UserName column in master.sysprocesses.

- When you add rows to a table that contains an identity whose value is automatically generated, insert TSQL code in your add procedure to return the @@IDENTITY as an OUTPUT parameter or the Return Status.

- To select 50 rows (or so) at a time, try these steps:

  1. Get the primary key of the row you want.

  2. Set ROWCOUNT to 50.

  3. Get the first 50 rows by selecting for the rows >= the primary key.

  4. Go back by selecting a descending set of rows < the primary key.

  5. Be sure to set ROWCOUNT (or MaxRows/MaxRecords) back to 0.

- When you create #Temp tables, be sure to explicitly specify the nullability of each column. This prevents a number of problems related to accessing these tables with Visual Basic.

- To access TIMESTAMP values from your stored procedure, such as when you want to inspect the value, type the value as BINARY(8).

- If the stored procedure returns a date/time value (which is different from the SQL Server idea of "timestamp," which really isn't a date/time value at all), ADO returns a date/time variant. When you print out the date, Visual Basic might use a format such as the short date format of the system, but the time part is still there. To force a particular format of the data, use the Visual Basic for Applications (VBA) Format function. For example, try this stored procedure:

```
create proc GetDateTime as
select GetDate()
```

Here is the corresponding Visual Basic code:

```
Sub Main()
Dim cn As New Connection
Dim rs As New Recordset
cn.Open "Pubs"
rs.Open "{call GetDateTime}", cn
Debug.Print "Type is " & rs(0).Type
Debug.Print "Value is " & rs(0).Value
End Sub
```

You'll notice that the value is printed with the date and time:

```
Type is 135
Value is 8/13/98 1:00:24 PM
```

The debug window's print routine prints in the long date/time format. Putting the value into certain controls might force a different format; if you need to use a particular format, use the Format function.

TIP Be *sure* to think about year-2000 issues when you work with dates!

- If you need to convert a Microsoft Access database to SQL Server, check out the SQL Server Developer's Resource Kit, which is on this book's companion CD. You can also download it from *http://backoffice.microsoft.com/downtrial/moreinfo/sqldrk.asp*. It's designed for SQL Server 6.5 and ADO 1.5, but it has lots of good articles—even one on converting Oracle databases.

- To determine the last day of the month, try this simple function:

```
Public Function LastDayofMonth(dvWhen As Date) As Date
Dim NextMonth As Date
NextMonth = DateAdd("m", 1, dvWhen)
LastDayofMonth = DateAdd("d", -1, _
    CDate(DatePart("m", NextMonth) & "/01/" & _
    DatePart("yyyy", NextMonth)))
End Function
```

Tips for Enhancing Performance

How much RAM is enough? One developer asked the list server mentors how to make his database queries run faster. He had 128 MB of RAM on the server and had assigned 40 MB to SQL Server and 15 MB to TempDB (in RAM). Performance Monitor usually showed 100 to 115 MB of memory on the average, even after the machine had been running for weeks without a reboot. Despite this, some queries used up to 80 percent of his CPU on both Pentium Pro 150s in his machine. "Is this a processor or a RAID issue?" he asked. "At what point is RAM no longer a factor?"

NOTE Several of the following suggestions were provided by Bill Wunder, who can be reached at *bwunder@cocis.com* and at his Web site: *http://www.nyx.net/~bwunder*.

One list server mentor suggested that he look in at least four areas to find the answers to his questions:

- SQL Server configuration
- Performance Monitor benchmark and analyses
- Query performance
- SQL Server release level

The mentor continued to explain that there's no order of importance among these four areas because you must look at *all* indicators to form a comprehensive solution. If your server seems to enjoy intense processing at times but doesn't seem to be process bound, the problem might be compounded by coincidental processing in competition with SQL Server. Does a memory problem exist when a system spikes to 80 percent CPU? Is the developer trying to fix a noticeable (perhaps only perceived) slowness in the application?

If he configured SQL Server for 55 MB of RAM (40 for SQL Server plus 15 MB for TempDB) and correctly expressed this in 2-KB pages, the most SQL Server and TempDB will use is 55 MB. The rest of the use must be attributed to Windows NT and other resident processes. He should consider what other tasks he's assigning to the system and how much of the use goes toward processes that compete with SQL Server. The configuration might be inconsistent with published guidelines. The Knowledge Base article "Recommended SQL Server for NT Memory Configurations" at *http://premium.microsoft.com/support/kb/articles/q110/9/83.asp* can provide more information.

It makes sense to benchmark at the *recommended* configuration before you determine that a value of about half the guideline is adequate and thus deduce a processor or RAID problem or justify a need for more memory. The SMP configuration value can further compound any interpretation of performance issues. DBCC MEMUSAGE and DBCC SQLPERF(...) show how SQL Server–allotted memory is used.

Here are some additional questions he should ask: What else shows up in ongoing Performance Monitor evaluations of the system? What does the Page Faults/Sec counter look like in the Perfmon Memory object? If he's getting increased page faults during the CPU spikes, he might be experiencing some incipient thrashing as a result of the small SQL Server image space. He should also evaluate the impact of such a small TempDB on the paging counter. A TempDB of this size might need more space to build temp tables, cursors, and so forth when a poorly tuned query is executed or the space required for the temporary object(s) is large. At any rate, paging might reveal that SQL Server needs more memory space, and an investigation of Performance Monitor counters can help with correctly configuring and diagnosing the system.

He should also look at the Statistics I/O information that SQL Server provides in these costly identified queries. He can easily tune a query that produces generous physical I/O if there's a bottleneck. There doesn't seem to be a correct memory or hardware configuration for a bad query.

A possible final area of investigation is this: Perceived slowness also implicates client-side and network issues. Based on the configuration the developer described, he probably has enough memory to speed up his queries. He can increase the amount of memory allocated to SQL Server to fully use the existing RAM space. He can decrease the memory SQL Server uses through additional query tuning. He can move competing processes off SQL Server or move TempDB to disk and/or make it bigger.

NOTE   These memory management tuning tips really apply only to SQL Server 6.5. Memory management in SQL Server 7.0 is far more dynamic because the system self-tunes for best performance—that is, if you cough up the bucks for the extra RAM.

Tips for Efficient Designs

Last year at one of the VBits conferences, I stood at the back of a popular session on client/server application development. The speaker (who shall remain nameless) was extolling the virtues of his sample application code when I noticed that the segment of code he was showing looked something like this:

```
Function MyGetData(IDWanted as Integer) as Variant
Dim rs as rdoResultset
Dim rowsfound as Integer
Dim SQL as string
SQL = "Select Count(*) From MyTable Where ID = " & IDWanted
Set rs = db.OpenResultset(SQL, rdOpenForwardOnly, rdConcurReadOnly)
rowsfound = rs(0)             'The count of rows where ID =
SQL = "Select * From MyTable Where ID = " & IDWanted
Set rs = db.OpenResultset(SQL, rdOpenForwardOnly, rdConcurReadOnly)
MyGetData = GetRows(rowsfound)
Exit Function
```

I gulped and left the room, knowing that I'd have to do some damage control when I got back. When I talked with the speaker, a well-known consultant, he said that this approach was a well-accepted way of dealing with the problem of not knowing how many rows would result from a query. I disagreed, and we agreed to disagree and leave it at that. Let's take a closer look at the problem—which we could also call the "counting your rows before they're laid, or why COUNT(*) doesn't always work" problem—and how various approaches deal or don't deal with the issues.

First, lets assume that you're building a query that returns an unknown but finite number of rows. You know from experience that the number of hits will be in the range of, say, 0 to 50 rows. This upper limit might be much higher, but you know what I think about large result sets, so your WHERE clause limits this number to a fairly small number of rows. You want to get these rows out of the result set quickly, and you've learned that GetRows does a neat job of this with a single command—not to mention that it's also dramatically faster than looping through the rows.

The problem is that you don't know *exactly* how many rows will result from your query. You want to know because it makes coding GetRows easier. If you knew, you could "get" just that many rows and you wouldn't have to add code to check for more (or fewer) rows. However, you need to consider the problem that the query processor has to deal with. For example, imagine the farmer's daughter going into the hen house to collect eggs for the first time. She wants to know how many eggs are there so she can bring the right number of egg cartons. Because she has no experience with egg gathering, she goes in and counts the eggs first. With this knowledge, she returns from the house with the exact number of cartons, only to discover that she has more eggs than the cartons will hold. She returns with more cartons and starts to fetch again, only to discover that she now has far more cartons than needed. What she doesn't know is that the family dachshund has an affinity for eggs (and chickens) and visited the hen house between her visits. You can have the same experience with fetching rows; leaving out data rows that are there but unfetched can leave egg on your face.

Looking more closely at the code, we discover that SELECT COUNT(*) doesn't return the number of rows that you might get in subsequent queries. Sure, COUNT(*) indicates how many rows *would* have been returned if the operation had been performed at the instant the first query was executed. But a multiuser database management system (DBMS) doesn't work that way any more than chickens lay eggs on demand. What if a number of rows were added to the database between the time the first and second queries were executed? This situation isn't so unlikely because the data we work on is often the data that other users are also working on.

The other problem with the consultant's example is performance—especially since it was offered as a way to boost performance. In fact, his approach cuts performance nearly in half. That is, both queries must do the following:

- Be compiled. (They were submitted as SQL statements and not stored procedures or even rdoQuery objects.)

- Be executed. (The query engine must fetch all of the rows that qualify into RAM and count them up the first time, and then return all of the rows the next time.)

- Return a result set. (The ODBC and RDO layers must deal with building the rdoResultset object.)

- Make at least one round-trip each (and more likely several round-trips) to the server to set up and deal with the queries.

Once the first query is executed, the data pages that hold the rows are probably in the cache. But that doesn't mean that the query processor can skip this step—it still has to redetermine which rows qualified and at least make sure these pages have been loaded. If the system is busy or the data is scattered over a dozen pages, the chance that they're still in RAM gets even slimmer. Sure, no data-IO is needed if the page is in memory, and this can save time. However, if this is a complex query, the chances of the results being the same are slimmer yet—because the number of potentially inclusive operations is greater.

A more reasonable approach—one that I like to call "Do it right the first time"—is to code GetRows so that it fetches one of the following:

- A number of rows greater than the expected rows. This way, you can be reasonably certain that you'll get all rows. It's like taking a few more egg cartons to the hen house based on yesterday's egg production. No one ever broke eggs by dropping empty cartons.

- A manageable number of rows to be processed by the user with the option of returning for additional rows as needed.

In either case, you should check the result set EOF property to ensure that all rows are fetched—even if you choose to ignore my advice and use COUNT(*).

Accessing Visual Basic Components from SQL Server

Leo is a Visual Basic developer who's trying to build a system that accesses Visual Basic code from SQL Server. In a sense, this approach might seem backward from the traditional approach of accessing SQL Server from Visual Basic, but it makes abundant sense in many situations. Microsoft Transaction Server (MTS) is designed to execute Visual Basic code directly, but this requires an evolutionary redesign from traditional two-tiered designs. Leo's approach uses existing stored procedure technology to access business logic, utility functions, or validation routines—all written in Visual Basic. These stored procedures can be executed as triggers or simply called from the client, but they're accessible to all applications with access to the database.

Understanding the Architecture

In the past, we didn't consider Visual Basic to be a particularly good way to build "headless" components because Visual Basic applications usually had a user interface of some kind—even if it was an unattended dialog box—and building native-code DLLs with Visual Basic simply wasn't possible. However, with the Visual Basic 5.0 native code compiler, the number of low-level operations we can expect Visual Basic to perform grew considerably. On the other hand, stored procedures don't really support any type of user interface—especially not an interactive one. Transact-SQL is certainly capable of handling many sophisticated functions. However, TSQL falls short when you need to show the user anything besides simple text values—and then SQL Server depends on the front end to display these values. It seems natural to use Visual Basic or other "Visual" tools to provide a user interface and enhanced functionality to SQL Server stored procedures.

Consider that stored procedures and centralized code have been an integral part of DBMS designs since their introduction—soon after SQL Server's initial release. This body of TSQL code manages many of the referential integrity, data integrity, and business rules that are too sophisticated for simple TSQL "rule" logic. Developers are always looking for ways to extend this fairly simple language to deal with more complex and extra-system operations. This architecture permits easier development of larger DBMS systems by centralizing much of the code that's needed to keep the system working on an even keel. It's similar to the more sophisticated MTS designs because it exposes stored procedures as business interfaces that perform specific data-related operations—at least to a limited extent. As developers who work in teams have discovered, centralized code has a number of distinct advantages. This technology simply expands that functionality by exposing interfaces to other tools and compatible applications.

Examining Typical Scenarios

This leads us back to development tools and applications that can deal with the data retrieved by SQL Server. Many scenarios are beyond the capability of TSQL stored procedures but are easily handled by Visual Basic or other stand-alone applications. Consider the following scenarios—I'm sure one will fit if you use the right shoehorn:

- **Access a Microsoft Jet or other external database, another SQL Server or ODBC data source, or simply a flat file** This permits manageable coordination or replication between disparate database formats. Should you reference back into the same SQL Server database? I'd probably leave that up to the stored procedure itself.

- **Leverage an existing business object written in Visual Basic** For example, a stored procedure exposed to a developer can simply be an interface to a Customer object with its own properties and methods. Individual stored procedures can invoke the Customer.Add method to add a new customer or simply access the individual customer properties. This technique relegates low-level data management to Visual Basic code. The Visual Basic code might not establish an additional connection to perform the actual update action query—but then again, it might. More realistically, the update operation can probably be done in the stored procedure itself and simply use the Customer object to build or filter the Insert statement.

- **Graphically display the current status of your server or database** This is something that TSQL is simply incapable of dealing with. First, SQL Server assumes that no one is there to see the server's monitor, so it doesn't bother to provide a way to display data other than character data. Getting the results of a query into a graph would be fairly simple if you connected a stored procedure batch to Microsoft Excel or to a Visual Basic application that knew what to do with the data. The real difference here is that no user would be required because Visual Basic would act as the "server"—a graphics server. The data to be displayed would be "pushed" to Visual Basic.

- **Send mail or create a report, a spreadsheet, or a chart** If you extend this concept to other applications, creating mail (with Microsoft Outlook), a report (with Microsoft Access), or a chart or spreadsheet (with Microsoft Excel) is fairly easy. Since all of these applications (and many others) have adopted the Component Object Model (COM) interface, getting them to perform their specific functions is as easy as setting properties and calling methods.

- **Perform a complex data manipulation operation such as encryption or a compression routine** This is another interesting scenario. Consider a situation in which your data column is encrypted or simply compressed. When a client application wants to extract this data, it must handle the complex (and possibly confidential) process of decryption/encryption or decompression/compression. In some cases, it makes sense to handle compression at the server end and decompression at the client end. This is especially applicable when server-side logic must deal with encrypted or compressed data structures to make logic decisions.

Another basic benefit is the ability to call this Visual Basic code while still in P-code form so that you can interactively debug it. Although a simple interactive TSQL stored procedure debugger is available in Visual Studio and in the Visual Basic Enterprise editions, it's a far cry from Visual Basic when it comes to edit-and-continue and many other features. Can you step from stored procedure debugging right back into Visual Basic debugging? Well, it's possible if you're running the Visual Basic component in interactive mode—on the server.

In the bigger picture, this technique isn't applicable to the majority of designs in which developers move logic to middle tiers managed by MTS. However, it does build a bridge to that technology—so the process of building discrete components isn't wasted. You can leverage these same components from MTS when your design evolves to this more sophisticated multi-tiered model.

Trying to Use Extended Stored Procedures

Leo thought that the promise of using Visual Basic code from SQL Server stored procedures was too good an opportunity to pass up. Apparently, he had tried to execute a Visual Basic–developed DLL from SQL Server using an Extended Stored Procedure (ESP). This works just fine when you create a C-based DLL. So it seemed reasonable to him that Visual Basic would do the same—at least after he used the new native code compiler to build his DLL. I thought so too, until I got the same error he did.

To try this, I performed the following steps:

- Compiled a simple Visual Basic DLL that puts up a message box when the XP_Hello entry point is called.

- Copied the DLL into the Windows NT path and registered it using Regsvr32.

- Told SQL Server to add the new DLL as a stored procedure by using the following:

```
sp_addextendedproc 'XP_Hello', 'Hello.DLL'
```

- Verified that the XP was seen by using the following command:

```
sp_helpextendedproc xp_Hello
```

The extended stored procedure and its DLL were displayed, indicating that SQL Server had found the DLL and knew that it was supposed to look for the XP_Hello entry point. However, when I executed the SQL Server code, I got the same error message that Leo did:

```
Cannot find the function 'xp_helloworld' in the library
    'helloworld.exe'.
Reason: '127(The specified procedure could not be found.)'
```

This error message means that SQL Server could reference the DLL but didn't find the specified entry point. Now I was just as puzzled as Leo and started sending mail to Dave Stearns and some of my other mentors in the development group. I got several useful responses that boiled down to the simple fact that Visual Basic does *not* compile DLLs that have "ordinary" entry points—it only compiles COM interfaces. It was these ordinary "C-style" entry points that SQL Server was looking for. Because Visual Basic was moving away from raw DLL calls and toward COM, the development team had little interest in reengineering these DLLs to be backward compatible with the old technology.

Accessing COM Objects from Stored Procedures

I had hit a dead-end, but I didn't give up because a couple of the developers said that there was another, better way—and Leo kept writing. Considering that COM was the interface du jour, it made sense to try to access our Visual Basic code using the exposed COM interfaces. When they built version 6.5, the SQL Server people also thought that this was a good idea. And there it was—right there in the Books Online documentation under "What's New in SQL Server 6.5," Section 5: "What's New for OLE Automation Stored Procedures."

SQL Server 6.5 includes OLE Automation stored procedures. The documentation doesn't use the "ActiveX" terminology to describe these, but it's basically the same thing. The following table lists these stored procedures.

OLE Automation Stored Procedures

Stored Procedure	Function
sp_OACreate	Creates a reference to a specified COM object
sp_OADestroy	Drops the reference
sp_OAGetErrorInfo	Acquires error information based on the last operation
sp_OAGetProperty	Gets the value from a component property
sp_OAMethod	Executes a component method
sp_OASetProperty	Sets the value of a component property
sp_OAStop	Stops the OLE Automation engine (server-wide)

The OLE Automation stored procedures allow you to use standard OLE Automation (ActiveX) objects within a TSQL statement batch. Because these OLE objects reside and run on the SQL Server computer, they behave like OLE extended stored procedures. However, each stored procedure is a separate instance, so there's no persistence between invocations of the stored procedure. This means that component references created in one invocation don't affect other stored procedures that are running or that will be run later. All created OLE objects are destroyed automatically at the end of every statement batch, so all operations must be done in a single stored procedure "batch."

This also means that you must write multiuser Visual Basic code. For example, if you open or access a file, the file-access technique must assume that others will try to open and access the same file at the same time. The code you write must also be "stateless." That is, it can't be expected to maintain internal variables from instance to instance.

This technology leverages Visual Basic's ability to create COM-compatible components. You can use existing COM components, such as the SQL Distributed Management Objects (SQL-DMO) or ActiveX DLLs. You can even use Microsoft C++, Microsoft J++, Microsoft FoxPro, or any other COM-capable development tool to build these components.

SQL Server OLE Stored Procedures

You can use the following ActiveX (OLE Automation) stored procedures to create and use our Visual Basic components on the SQL Server system:

- Call sp_OACreate to create an instance of the object. This stored procedure takes either the GUID or the object name as a string and returns an integer (the object ID), which is used to reference the object in subsequent OLE Automation calls. Once the object ID integer is created, you can use it to get and set component properties, invoke methods, and get error status if something goes wrong.

- Call sp_OAGetProperty to get a property value.

- Call sp_OASetProperty to set a property to a new value.

- Call sp_OAMethod to call a method.

- Call sp_OAGetErrorInfo to get the most recent error information.

- Call sp_OADestroy to destroy the object when you're done. (No, you don't really have to do this because the object is released automatically when the stored procedure ends.)

At first glance, this interface looked somewhat intimidating, but I decided that it was worthwhile to give this technology a try. Let's walk through the process of creating a sample Visual Basic application that can be called, debugged, and executed right from a SQL Server stored procedure.

Building a Visual Basic Component

First we need to start a Visual Basic project. We can do this on a client, but we should debug it on the Windows NT server to make the process of finding the ActiveX COM component easier when we're ready to test it. We'll use our sample project to save a status message passed as a string to a log file. Since we're using a common file, the code must deal with several separate procedures accessing the file at the same time. Take the following steps:

1. Start Visual Basic (at least version 5.0). When prompted, choose ActiveX DLL as the project type. This builds a prototype application with no forms and an empty Class module.

2. Start the Class Builder Utility (a Visual Basic add-in) to create and manage the Class module we'll be building. This will simplify the process of setting up the properties and methods and ensure that we do it right the first time.

3. Set the Properties of the default class to a name that better describes what the component will do. I used *Bridge* as the class name because the component is a bridge between Visual Basic and SQL Server. I also set the Instancing property to Global Multi Use.

4. Create a set of new properties and methods to control the component. Set as many of the ancillary properties (such as the description) as you want. Some of these might seem redundant or simply unnecessary, but they do serve to illustrate accessing properties and methods from stored procedures.

5. When your code is ready, go ahead and run the application from interactive design mode. There's no need to compile just yet. Just be sure to specify "Start with full compile." This compiles the P-code and registers the application so SQL Server can see it. It's OK to set break-points at strategic locations. When SQL Server calls your code, you can trap the code and see what's going on. Keep in mind that the first thing called is the Class_Initialize event. This is invoked when SQL Server builds an instance of your class.

The following table lists the properties and methods I used in this project.

Bridge Properties and Methods

Name	Data Type	Type	Function
bfSuccess	Boolean	Property	Shows the success or failure of the operation
bfFileName	String	Property	Shows name of the file opened
bfError	String	Property	Shows error message from last operation
bfOpen	Integer	Method	Opens the specified file
bfWrite	Integer	Method	Saves the specified data array
bfClose	Integer	Method	Closes the file

Here's the source code for the Bridge application:

```
Bridge.CLS:
VERSION 1.0 CLASS

BEGIN

  MultiUse = -1  'True

END
Attribute VB_Name = "Bridge"
Attribute VB_GlobalNameSpace = False
Attribute VB_Creatable = True
Attribute VB_PredeclaredId = False
Attribute VB_Exposed = True
Attribute VB_Ext_KEY = "SavedWithClassBuilder" ,"Yes"
Attribute VB_Ext_KEY = "Top_Level" ,"Yes"
Option Explicit
'local variable(s) to hold property value(s)
Private mvarSuccess As Integer 'local copy
Public bfFileName As String
Attribute bfFileName.VB_VarDescription = "Filename opened"
Public bfErrorMessage As String
Attribute bfErrorMessage.VB_VarDescription = _
    "Returns last error message"

Public Function bfOpen(ByVal FileName As String) As Integer
    If FileName = "" Then
        FileName = "C:\Default.txt"
    Else
        On Error GoTo bfOpenEH
        Open FileName For Append As #1 Len = 2048
        mvarSuccess = True
    End If
    bfFileName = FileName
ExitbfOpen:
    bfOpen = mvarSuccess
Exit Function
bfOpenEH:
    Select Case Err
        Case 55: Resume Next
        Case Else
        mvarSuccess = False
        Debug.Print Err, Error$
        bfErrorMessage = Error$
        Resume ExitbfOpen
    End Select
End Function

Public Function bfWrite(ByVal DataValue As String) As Integer
On Error GoTo bfWriteEH
    Print #1, Now, Timer, DataValue
    mvarSuccess = True
```

```
ExitbfWrite:
    bfWrite = mvarSuccess
Exit Function
bfWriteEH:
    bfErrorMessage = Error$
    mvarSuccess = False
    Resume ' ExitbfWrite
End Function


Public Function bfClose() As Integer
On Error GoTo bfCloseEH
    Print #1, "<<Close request. " & Now & ">>"
    Close #1
mvarSuccess = True
ExitbfClose:
    bfClose = mvarSuccess
Exit Function
bfCloseEH:
    bfErrorMessage = Error$
    mvarSuccess = False
    Resume ExitbfClose
End Function


Public Property Get bfSuccess() As Integer
Attribute bfSuccess.VB_Description = _
    "Indicate success -1 or Failure 0 of last operation"
' Used when retrieving value of a property, on the right side of
' an assignment.
'Syntax: Debug.Print X.Success
bfSuccess = mvarSuccess
End Property


Private Sub Class_Initialize()
mvarSuccess = -2          ' initialize variables
bfErrorMessage = "No errors..."
bfFileName = "C:\TestClass.txt"
End Sub
```

Examining the Server-Side OLE Automation Stored Procedures Batch

At this point, we need to see how these Visual Basic properties and methods were accessed from SQL Server. The following listing shows how these stored procedures were set up and called:

```
-- Establish the local variables.
DECLARE @object int
DECLARE @hr int
DECLARE @property varchar(255)
DECLARE @return varchar(255)
DECLARE @Status varchar(255)
```

We'll create a string to show what activity has taken place so far. This string is built from SQL Server global variables:

```
-- Snapshot status
set nocount ON
Select @Status = 'Errors:' + convert(varchar(255), @@Total_Errors)
    + ', Reads: ' + convert(varchar(255), @@Total_Read)
    + ', Writes:' + convert(varchar(255), @@Total_Write)
    + ', Connections: ' + convert(varchar(255), @@Connections)
```

Now we'll get SQL Server to locate and build an instance of our Visual Basic component and reference the class we created. This stored procedure expects us to pass the Project name and class name (pBridge.Bridge). If Visual Basic isn't running and you haven't left a copy of the DLL where SQL Server can find it, you'll get an immediate error. However, if you're trying this in interactive mode and SQL Server isn't running in "console mode," the stored procedure will hang for over a minute while it waits for Windows NT to locate the component. Then you'll get an error in the stored procedure. Note that this stored procedure routine uses the sp_DisplayOAError stored procedure, which was created and installed separately. The code is shown here:

```
-- Create an object
EXEC @hr = sp_OACreate 'pBridge.Bridge', @object OUT
IF @hr <> 0
BEGIN
    EXEC sp_displayoaerrorinfo @object, @hr
    RETURN
END
```

Once the object reference is created, an integer handle to the new instance is passed back to SQL Server and your stored procedure. This handle is used in all subsequent OLE Automation stored procedures to reference this component. You can invoke more than one component, but be sure to keep the handles straight. This snippet of code invokes one of our Bridge component's methods. In this case, we ask for the bfOpen method by name, provide an OUTPUT parameter to receive the return code, and pass in the name of the file to open as a string. You don't have a lot of options when you pass data to and from these stored procedures, but we'll discuss that later. If something goes wrong with the open, we'll examine the component's bfErrorMessage property to see what happened. In this case, we expect the local variable @property to be passed the error message string.

```
-- Call a method with a parameter that returns a value
-- Open the data file
EXEC @hr = sp_OAMethod @object, 'bfOpen', @return OUT,
    @Filename='C:\Bridge.Txt'
-- If an error occurred, get the error property and display it
IF @hr <> 0
BEGIN
    EXEC sp_displayoaerrorinfo @object, @hr
    EXEC @hr = sp_OAGetProperty @object, 'bfErrorMessage',
        @property OUT
    PRINT @property
    RETURN
END
```

The file is open, so we're ready to pass the string over to Visual Basic to record to the log file. This method is coded just like the bfOpen method:

```
-- Call a method with a parameter that returns a value
-- Write the status info to the data file
EXEC @hr = sp_OAMethod @object, 'bfWrite', @return OUT,
    @DataValue=@Status
-- If an error occurred, get the error property and display it
IF @hr <> 0
BEGIN
    EXEC sp_displayoaerrorinfo @object, @hr
    EXEC @hr = sp_OAGetProperty @object, 'bfErrorMessage',
        @property OUT
    PRINT @property
    RETURN
END
```

For the sake of formality, we'll destroy (release) the instance of the Visual Basic object we created earlier. This is actually unnecessary because the components are released automatically when the stored procedure ends.

```
-- Destroy the object
EXEC @hr = sp_OADestroy @object
IF @hr <> 0
BEGIN
    EXEC sp_displayoaerrorinfo @object, @hr
    RETURN
END
```

Data Type Conversions

Because SQL Server uses TSQL data types and ActiveX (OLE Automation) uses Visual Basic data types, the OLE Automation stored procedures must convert the data that passes between them. The following table shows the conversion from SQL Server to Visual Basic data types.

Converting from SQL Server to Visual Basic Data Types

SQL Server Data Type	Visual Basic Data Type
char, varchar, text, decimal, numeric	String
Bit	Boolean
binary, varbinary, image	One-dimensional Byte() array
Integer	Long
Smallint	Integer
Tinyint	Byte
Float	Double
Real	Single
money, smallmoney	Currency
datetime, smalldatetime	Date
anything set to NULL	Variant set to Null

All SQL Server values are converted to a Visual Basic value, with the exception of binary, varbinary, and image values. These values are converted to a one-dimensional Byte() array in Visual Basic. This array has a range of Byte(0 To length-1), where length is the number of bytes in the SQL Server binary, varbinary, or image values.

The following table shows the conversion of Visual Basic data types to SQL Server data types. That is, data passed back from Visual Basic properties is converted to the indicated SQL Server data type.

Converting from Visual Basic to SQL Server Data Types

Visual Basic Data Type	SQL Server Data Type
Long, Integer, Byte, Boolean, Object	Integer
Double, Single	Float
Currency	money
Date	datetime
String with 255 characters or less	varchar
String with more than 255 characters	text
One-dimensional Byte() array with 255 bytes or less	varbinary
One-dimensional Byte() array with more than 255 bytes	image

Examining the OLE Automation Stored Procedure Error Handlers

This listing shows the error and message handlers for the OLE Automation stored procedures. This code is included in the SQL Server Books Online documentation.

NOTE These procedures return an integer return code. The return code is 0 when successful; it is a nonzero HRESULT when an error occurs. An HRESULT is an OLE error code of the hexadecimal form 0x800nnnnn, but when it is returned as an integer value, it has the form –214nnnnnn.

For example, passing an invalid object name (such as SQLOLE.Xyzzy) to sp_OACreate causes it to return an integer HRESULT of –2147221005, which is 0x800401f3 in hexadecimal.

You can use CONVERT(binary(4), @hresult) to convert an integer HRESULT to a binary value. However, using CONVERT(char(10), CONVERT(binary(4), @hresult)) results in an unreadable string because each byte of the HRESULT is converted to a single ASCII character. You can also use the following sample stored procedure sp_hexadecimal to convert an integer HRESULT to a char value that contains a readable hexadecimal string. In any case, you must install these two stored procedures on your SQL server before the example OLE Automation stored procedure code will compile.

```
CREATE PROCEDURE sp_hexadecimal
    @binvalue varbinary(255),
    @hexvalue varchar(255) OUTPUT
AS
DECLARE @charvalue varchar(255)
DECLARE @i int
DECLARE @length int
DECLARE @hexstring char(16)
SELECT @charvalue = '0x'
SELECT @i = 1
SELECT @length = DATALENGTH(@binvalue)
SELECT @hexstring = '0123456789abcdef'
WHILE (@i <= @length)
BEGIN
    DECLARE @tempint int
    DECLARE @firstint int
    DECLARE @secondint int
    SELECT @tempint = CONVERT(int, SUBSTRING(@binvalue,@i,1))
    SELECT @firstint = FLOOR(@tempint/16)
    SELECT @secondint = @tempint - (@firstint*16)
    SELECT @charvalue = @charvalue +
        SUBSTRING(@hexstring, @firstint+1, 1) +
        SUBSTRING(@hexstring, @secondint+1, 1)
    SELECT @i = @i + 1
END
SELECT @hexvalue = @charvalue
```

You can use the following sample stored procedure to display OLE Automation error information when one of these procedures returns a nonzero HRESULT return code. This stored procedure uses the sp_hexadecimal sample stored procedure—so you have to create it first.

```
CREATE PROCEDURE sp_displayoaerrorinfo
    @object int,
    @hresult int
AS
DECLARE @output varchar(255)
DECLARE @hrhex char(10)
DECLARE @hr int
DECLARE @source varchar(255)
DECLARE @description varchar(255)
PRINT 'OLE Automation Error Information'
EXEC sp_hexadecimal @hresult, @hrhex OUT
SELECT @output = '  HRESULT: ' + @hrhex
PRINT @output
EXEC @hr = sp_OAGetErrorInfo @object, @source OUT, @description OUT
IF @hr = 0
```

(continued)

```
BEGIN
    SELECT @output = '  Source: ' + @source
    PRINT @output
    SELECT @output = '  Description: ' + @description
    PRINT @output
END
ELSE
BEGIN
    PRINT "  sp_OAGetErrorInfo failed."
    RETURN
END
```

Although executing COM from SQL Server stored procedures is a little verbose and not quite as flexible as some other techniques, it's a powerful and useful way to leverage existing COM components. Considering that you can also access Excel, Microsoft Word, Access, or any other COM-accessible application, this interface is even more interesting. I suspect that it's possible to build or simply launch Access reports from SQL Server. You can also directly generate Word form letters or Excel-based charts and graphs in the same way. All of this is possible because of the role that COM plays in all of Microsoft's applications and systems software products.

INDEX

Page numbers in italic refer to figures or tables.

development tools and technologies, *continued*
  new and unproven, 74
  Query Builder (*see* Query Builder)
  SQL Server 7.0, 7 (*see also* Microsoft SQL Server)
  Transact-SQL Debugger (*see* Transact-SQL Debugger)
  Visual Basic, 7–8, 10 (*see also* Microsoft Visual Basic)
  Visual Database Tools (*see* Microsoft Visual Database Tools)
diagrams. *See* schemas, database
dialog boxes, avoiding login, 145–46, *146, 147. See also* prompting behavior
Direction property, 505–6, 660, 758
direct links, 222–24
directories, support library, 153–54
DisableAsync setting, ODBC, 244
Disconnect event, 408
dissociating rdoResultsets, 450, 455, *456,* 480–81
DISTINCT keyword
  ADO support, 728
  Jet engine support, 328
  Query Builder support, 857
Distributed COM (DCOM), 561
distributed component architecture, 79, 86–90
distributed engine architecture
  accessing centralized engine with, 109–10
  client/server vs., 106–9
  cost per user, 104, *105*
  database size, 106–7
  data page management, 108
  hypothetical configuration, 101–6
  index management, 108
  input/output ratio, 107–8
  LAN performance, 101–3
  lock management, 108
  overview, 78, 84–86
  performance, 105–6
  periodic maintenance, 109
  recovery, 108
  typical configurations, 103–4
DLLs. *See* libraries
domain-managed security, 39–40, 82, 143, 690
drivers
  cursor, 389–90, 435–36, *445–47*
  ODBC, 25, 32 (*see also* Microsoft ODBC driver)
  OLE DB Provider for ODBC, 27, 60, 560–61, 672

DSNs (data source names). *See also* security management
  connection parameters, *406*
  connect strings and, 144 (*see also* connect strings)
  creating, for sample applications, 31–34
  creating, for test databases, 915–18
  errors, 260
  file, 403–4
  getting valid, 144–45
  RDO connections and, 398–400
  saving file, 404–7
During events, ADO, 741
dynamic cursors, 122, 440
dynamic properties, ADO, 577, 661
dynaset cursors, 121–22
dynaset-type Recordset objects, 202, 265, 270–71

edit masks, 135
efficiency tips, 940–42
English Query, 174–75
Enterprise Manager. *See* Microsoft SQL Enterprise Manager
enumerated constants, 804
EOFAction property, 282
EOF property, 282, *630,* 641
equal asterisk (=*), 858
equal sign (=), 856
error codes, SQL Server, *922–31*
  cursor function errors, *929–30*
  error severity codes, *931*
  errors SQL Server might encounter, *922–28*
Error event, 550
error management. *See also* debugging; error codes, SQL Server
  ADO decimal parameters, 713
  ADO event handler, 748
  client/server, 81, 83
  connection (*see* connection error management)
  DAO/Jet data retrieval, 291, *292*
  DAO/Jet SQL pass-through query, 309–12
  DAO/ODBCDirect, 350–51
  design mistakes, 126–29
  OLE Automation stored procedure, 952–54
  optimistic batch update, 484
  query messages, 179

William R. VAUGHN

(Bill to his friends) was born in Washington, D.C., and was raised as an Army brat. He traveled with his family all over the world, to Germany, Thailand, and throughout the United States. He attended International School, in Bangkok, Thailand; Augustana College, in Sioux Falls, South Dakota; the University of Kansas at Lawrence; Mary Hardin-Baylor College, in Killeen, Texas; and the University of Texas at Dallas. As a result of this diverse schooling, Bill earned his pilot's wings from the Army, an associate's degree in systems analysis, a bachelor's degree in computer science, and a master's degree in interdisciplinary studies.

In the early 1970s, Bill started working in Austin, Texas, as a mainframe programmer for the Texas Department of Public Safety, where he developed a statewide database management system that is still in use today (but might come to an abrupt halt on 1/1/2000). Bill might still be there today if Electronic Data Systems hadn't moved him to Dallas. After several years of bulldogging mainframe health-care systems, he began working as a microsystems consultant to Ross Perot and developed an accounting system on the IBM 5110 (IBM's first attempt at the PC).

Bill spent about a decade in the Dallas area, working for Mostek, Challenge Systems (you never heard of it), Digital Research, and CPT Corporation. He wore many hats at those companies, learning about hardware systems as well as writing, designing, marketing, supporting, and implementing a number of Z80 and PC-based systems, but he kept his focus on micro-computers.

In 1986, Microsoft moved Bill to Redmond, Washington, to work in the Windows development liaison group. Bill went on to spend more than five years at Microsoft University, developing and teaching courses on DB-Library, Transact-SQL, OS/2, and Visual Basic. After some time off to write the first edition of the *Hitchhiker's Guide*, he joined the Visual Basic team. Bill spent five years there as a senior technical writer in the User Education unit, with responsibility for much of the Visual Basic data access documentation, especially that related to client/server systems and front ends. In addition to writing the Visual Basic 3.0 data access guide, he wrote the back half of the Visual Basic 4.0–specific *Building Client/Server Applications with Visual Basic* and about a bazillion Help topics for Visual Basic 3.0 through 5.0. In September 1996, Bill was promoted to Visual Basic Enterprise Product Manager. In this role, he gets to listen to customers and tell them (and the press) what Visual Basic is capable of doing. Today, Bill is still with the Visual Basic marketing team. He now spends much of his time lecturing and writing about Visual Basic and has been rated as the top speaker at VBits and other conferences—when he's not offending someone with his impersonations of Ross Perot or Robin Williams.

Bill married in 1968 while at flight school—just before he went to Vietnam. His wife Marilyn earned her bachelor's degree in mathematics and taught for many years before she got her master's degree in math and environ-mental studies. She retired from teaching when their first daughter was born, when she took up full-time daughter raising, homemaking, gardening, soccer management, Girl Scout troop leading, and backseat driving. She is quite accomplished at all of these endeavors. She has accompanied Bill on several domestic and European lecture tours—just to keep him out of trouble.

Bill's younger daughter, Christina (a.k.a. Fred), is attending Whitman College, where she is working on a degree in English and classics. When she's not being serenaded by one or more of the fraternities, she stays in shape by playing soccer. Last season she played as a starting forward and was voted "best" (or was it "most"?) offensive player.

Bill's older daughter, Victoria (a.k.a. George), graduated this year from the University of Washington with a master's degree in environmental engineering. (Bill had to send her back to the Civil Engineering school at the University of Washington because her chemical engineering degree left her far from "civil.") She made the Dean's List and will make a dynamite engineer. Last summer, Victoria married Michael Ballard, who plans a career in the Air Force. Now that she's married, her initials are "V.B." (of course).

The manuscript for this book was prepared and submitted to Microsoft Press in electronic form. Text files were prepared using Microsoft Word 97. Pages were composed by Microsoft Press using Adobe PageMaker 6.52 for Windows, with text in Stone Serif and display type in UniversBlack. Composed pages were delivered to the printer as electronic prepress files.

Cover Designer
Tim Girvin Design, Inc.

Cover Illustrator
Glenn Mitsui

Interior Graphic Artist
Michael Victor

Principal Desktop Publisher
Steven Hopster

Indexer
Shane-Armstrong
Information Systems

The Comprehensive
Official Resource
for Microsoft
Visual Basic 6.0.

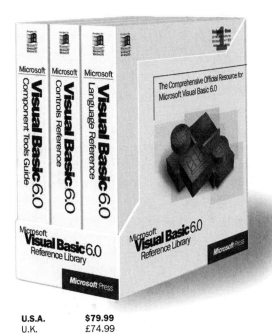

U.S.A.	**$79.99**
U.K.	£74.99
Canada	$115.99
ISBN	1-57231-864-3

The three-volume MICROSOFT® VISUAL BASIC® 6.0 REFERENCE LIBRARY is the official print documentation for version 6.0 of Visual Basic—one of the world's most popular and prolific programming languages. This portable, easy-reference library includes *Microsoft Visual Basic 6.0 Language Reference*, an A–Z compilation of Visual Basic objects, functions, statements, methods, properties, and events; *Microsoft Visual Basic 6.0 Controls Reference*, a complete alphabetic listing of the ActiveX® controls within Visual Basic, along with relevant properties, events, and methods; and *Microsoft Visual Basic 6.0 Component Tools Guide*, covering every tool from add-ins and Dynamic Link Libraries (DLLs) to ActiveX components. Must-have tools for the Visual Basic programmer!

Microsoft *Press*

Advance *your mastery* of *32-bit Windows* **programming.**

U.S.A.	**$49.99**
U.K.	£46.99 [V.A.T. included]
Canada	$71.99
ISBN	1-57231-883-X

What's new in Visual Basic® 6.0? Plenty—and these innovations can give you a tremendous edge in Windows® 98 and Windows NT® development. In the MICROSOFT® VISUAL BASIC 6.0 DEVELOPER'S WORKSHOP, Fifth Edition, you'll find a concise introduction to version 6.0 right up front—learning how these new capabilities can power up projects with greater efficiency and functionality. You'll also discover smart solutions to a wide range of specific, *How do I do that?* questions, along with a toolbox full of ready-to-use source code, projects, forms, and files on CD-ROM. If you've already demonstrated some fluency in Visual Basic, you'll get a major skills upgrade with the MICROSOFT VISUAL BASIC 6.0 DEVELOPER'S WORKSHOP.

Microsoft® Press

Get the *inside story* from the *(and practical advice)* *ultimate insider.*

U.S.A. **$49.99**
U.K. £46.99 [V.A.T. included]
Canada $69.99
ISBN 1-57231-331-5

This comprehensive guide, written by Microsoft insider and SQL guru Ron Soukup, provides an authoritative conceptual and architectural overview along with advice on installation, administration, and programming with SQL and Transact-SQL. The author also provides examples and candid answers to frequently asked questions gleaned from his years of service as general manager of the SQL Server™ development group at Microsoft. This book is for MIS professionals in large companies, vertical applications developers, custom solution providers, and anyone else working with mid-level to high-end relational databases. In fact, it's a must-read for all those who want to understand Microsoft® SQL Server from the inside out.

Microsoft®*Press*

MICROSOFT LICENSE AGREEMENT
(Hitchhiker's Guide to Visual Basic and SQL Server, Sixth Edition - Book Companion CD)

IMPORTANT—READ CAREFULLY: This Microsoft End-User License Agreement ("EULA") is a legal agreement between you (either an individual or an entity) and Microsoft Corporation for the Microsoft product identified above, which includes computer software and may include associated media, printed materials, and "on-line" or electronic documentation ("SOFTWARE PRODUCT"). Any component included within the SOFTWARE PRODUCT that is accompanied by a separate End-User License Agreement shall be governed by such agreement and not the terms set forth below. By installing, copying, or otherwise using the SOFTWARE PRODUCT, you agree to be bound by the terms of this EULA. If you do not agree to the terms of this EULA, you are not authorized to install, copy, or otherwise use the SOFTWARE PRODUCT; you may, however, return the SOFTWARE PRODUCT, along with all printed materials and other items that form a part of the Microsoft product that includes the SOFTWARE PRODUCT, to the place you obtained them for a full refund.

SOFTWARE PRODUCT LICENSE

The SOFTWARE PRODUCT is protected by United States copyright laws and international copyright treaties, as well as other intellectual property laws and treaties. The SOFTWARE PRODUCT is licensed, not sold.

1. **GRANT OF LICENSE.** This EULA grants you the following rights:
   a. **Software Product.** You may install and use one copy of the SOFTWARE PRODUCT on a single computer. The primary user of the computer on which the SOFTWARE PRODUCT is installed may make a second copy for his or her exclusive use on a portable computer.
   b. **Storage/Network Use.** You may also store or install a copy of the SOFTWARE PRODUCT on a storage device, such as a network server, used only to install or run the SOFTWARE PRODUCT on your other computers over an internal network; however, you must acquire and dedicate a license for each separate computer on which the SOFTWARE PRODUCT is installed or run from the storage device. A license for the SOFTWARE PRODUCT may not be shared or used concurrently on different computers.
   c. **License Pak.** If you have acquired this EULA in a Microsoft License Pak, you may make the number of additional copies of the computer software portion of the SOFTWARE PRODUCT authorized on the printed copy of this EULA, and you may use each copy in the manner specified above. You are also entitled to make a corresponding number of secondary copies for portable computer use as specified above.
   d. **Sample Code.** Solely with respect to portions, if any, of the SOFTWARE PRODUCT that are identified within the SOFTWARE PRODUCT as sample code (the "SAMPLE CODE"):
      i. **Use and Modification.** Microsoft grants you the right to use and modify the source code version of the SAMPLE CODE, *provided* you comply with subsection (d)(iii) below. You may not distribute the SAMPLE CODE, or any modified version of the SAMPLE CODE, in source code form.
      ii. **Redistributable Files.** Provided you comply with subsection (d)(iii) below, Microsoft grants you a nonexclusive, royalty-free right to reproduce and distribute the object code version of the SAMPLE CODE and of any modified SAMPLE CODE, other than SAMPLE CODE (or any modified version thereof) designated as not redistributable in the Readme file that forms a part of the SOFTWARE PRODUCT (the "Non-Redistributable Sample Code"). All SAMPLE CODE other than the Non-Redistributable Sample Code is collectively referred to as the "REDISTRIBUTABLES."
      iii. **Redistribution Requirements.** If you redistribute the REDISTRIBUTABLES, you agree to: (i) distribute the REDISTRIBUTABLES in object code form only in conjunction with and as a part of your software application product; (ii) not use Microsoft's name, logo, or trademarks to market your software application product; (iii) include a valid copyright notice on your software application product; (iv) indemnify, hold harmless, and defend Microsoft from and against any claims or lawsuits, including attorney's fees, that arise or result from the use or distribution of your software application product; and (v) not permit further distribution of the REDISTRIBUTABLES by your end user. Contact Microsoft for the applicable royalties due and other licensing terms for all other uses and/or distribution of the REDISTRIBUTABLES.

2. **DESCRIPTION OF OTHER RIGHTS AND LIMITATIONS.**
   - **Limitations on Reverse Engineering, Decompilation, and Disassembly.** You may not reverse engineer, decompile, or disassemble the SOFTWARE PRODUCT, except and only to the extent that such activity is expressly permitted by applicable law notwithstanding this limitation.
   - **Separation of Components.** The SOFTWARE PRODUCT is licensed as a single product. Its component parts may not be separated for use on more than one computer.
   - **Rental.** You may not rent, lease, or lend the SOFTWARE PRODUCT.
   - **Support Services.** Microsoft may, but is not obligated to, provide you with support services related to the SOFTWARE PRODUCT ("Support Services"). Use of Support Services is governed by the Microsoft policies and programs described in the user manual, in "on-line" documentation, and/or in other Microsoft-provided materials. Any supplemental software code provided to you as part of the Support Services shall be considered part of the SOFTWARE PRODUCT and subject to the terms and conditions of this EULA. With respect to technical information you provide to Microsoft as part of the Support Services, Microsoft may use such information for its business purposes, including for product support and development. Microsoft will not utilize such technical information in a form that personally identifies you.

- **Software Transfer.** You may permanently transfer all of your rights under this EULA, provided you retain no copies, you transfer all of the SOFTWARE PRODUCT (including all component parts, the media and printed materials, any upgrades, this EULA, and, if applicable, the Certificate of Authenticity), **and** the recipient agrees to the terms of this EULA.
- **Termination.** Without prejudice to any other rights, Microsoft may terminate this EULA if you fail to comply with the terms and conditions of this EULA. In such event, you must destroy all copies of the SOFTWARE PRODUCT and all of its component parts.

3. **COPYRIGHT.** All title and copyrights in and to the SOFTWARE PRODUCT (including but not limited to any images, photographs, animations, video, audio, music, text, SAMPLE CODE, REDISTRIBUTABLES, and "applets" incorporated into the SOFTWARE PRODUCT) and any copies of the SOFTWARE PRODUCT are owned by Microsoft or its suppliers. The SOFTWARE PRODUCT is protected by copyright laws and international treaty provisions. Therefore, you must treat the SOFTWARE PRODUCT like any other copyrighted material **except** that you may install the SOFTWARE PRODUCT on a single computer provided you keep the original solely for backup or archival purposes. You may not copy the printed materials accompanying the SOFTWARE PRODUCT.

4. **U.S. GOVERNMENT RESTRICTED RIGHTS.** The SOFTWARE PRODUCT and documentation are provided with RESTRICTED RIGHTS. Use, duplication, or disclosure by the Government is subject to restrictions as set forth in subparagraph (c)(1)(ii) of the Rights in Technical Data and Computer Software clause at DFARS 252.227-7013 or subparagraphs (c)(1) and (2) of the Commercial Computer Software—Restricted Rights at 48 CFR 52.227-19, as applicable. Manufacturer is Microsoft Corporation/One Microsoft Way/Redmond, WA 98052-6399.

5. **EXPORT RESTRICTIONS.** You agree that you will not export or re-export the SOFTWARE PRODUCT, any part thereof, or any process or service that is the direct product of the SOFTWARE PRODUCT (the foregoing collectively referred to as the "Restricted Components"), to any country, person, entity, or end user subject to U.S. export restrictions. You specifically agree not to export or re-export any of the Restricted Components (i) to any country to which the U.S. has embargoed or restricted the export of goods or services, which currently include, but are not necessarily limited to, Cuba, Iran, Iraq, Libya, North Korea, Sudan, and Syria, or to any national of any such country, wherever located, who intends to transmit or transport the Restricted Components back to such country; (ii) to any end user who you know or have reason to know will utilize the Restricted Components in the design, development, or production of nuclear, chemical, or biological weapons; or (iii) to any end user who has been prohibited from participating in U.S. export transactions by any federal agency of the U.S. government. You warrant and represent that neither the BXA nor any other U.S. federal agency has suspended, revoked, or denied your export privileges.

6. **NOTE ON JAVA SUPPORT.** THE SOFTWARE PRODUCT MAY CONTAIN SUPPORT FOR PROGRAMS WRITTEN IN JAVA. JAVA TECHNOLOGY IS NOT FAULT TOLERANT AND IS NOT DESIGNED, MANUFACTURED, OR INTENDED FOR USE OR RESALE AS ON-LINE CONTROL EQUIPMENT IN HAZARDOUS ENVIRONMENTS REQUIRING FAIL-SAFE PERFORMANCE, SUCH AS IN THE OPERATION OF NUCLEAR FACILITIES, AIRCRAFT NAVIGATION OR COMMUNICATION SYSTEMS, AIR TRAFFIC CONTROL, DIRECT LIFE SUPPORT MACHINES, OR WEAPONS SYSTEMS, IN WHICH THE FAILURE OF JAVA TECHNOLOGY COULD LEAD DIRECTLY TO DEATH, PERSONAL INJURY, OR SEVERE PHYSICAL OR ENVIRONMENTAL DAMAGE.

DISCLAIMER OF WARRANTY

NO WARRANTIES OR CONDITIONS. MICROSOFT EXPRESSLY DISCLAIMS ANY WARRANTY OR CONDITION FOR THE SOFTWARE PRODUCT. THE SOFTWARE PRODUCT AND ANY RELATED DOCUMENTATION IS PROVIDED "AS IS" WITHOUT WARRANTY OR CONDITION OF ANY KIND, EITHER EXPRESS OR IMPLIED, INCLUDING, WITHOUT LIMITATION, THE IMPLIED WARRANTIES OF MERCHANTABILITY, FITNESS FOR A PARTICULAR PURPOSE, OR NONINFRINGEMENT. THE ENTIRE RISK ARISING OUT OF USE OR PERFORMANCE OF THE SOFTWARE PRODUCT REMAINS WITH YOU.

LIMITATION OF LIABILITY. TO THE MAXIMUM EXTENT PERMITTED BY APPLICABLE LAW, IN NO EVENT SHALL MICROSOFT OR ITS SUPPLIERS BE LIABLE FOR ANY SPECIAL, INCIDENTAL, INDIRECT, OR CONSEQUENTIAL DAMAGES WHATSOEVER (INCLUDING, WITHOUT LIMITATION, DAMAGES FOR LOSS OF BUSINESS PROFITS, BUSINESS INTERRUPTION, LOSS OF BUSINESS INFORMATION, OR ANY OTHER PECUNIARY LOSS) ARISING OUT OF THE USE OF OR INABILITY TO USE THE SOFTWARE PRODUCT OR THE PROVISION OF OR FAILURE TO PROVIDE SUPPORT SERVICES, EVEN IF MICROSOFT HAS BEEN ADVISED OF THE POSSIBILITY OF SUCH DAMAGES. IN ANY CASE, MICROSOFT'S ENTIRE LIABILITY UNDER ANY PROVISION OF THIS EULA SHALL BE LIMITED TO THE GREATER OF THE AMOUNT ACTUALLY PAID BY YOU FOR THE SOFTWARE PRODUCT OR US$5.00; PROVIDED, HOWEVER, IF YOU HAVE ENTERED INTO A MICROSOFT SUPPORT SERVICES AGREEMENT, MICROSOFT'S ENTIRE LIABILITY REGARDING SUPPORT SERVICES SHALL BE GOVERNED BY THE TERMS OF THAT AGREEMENT. BECAUSE SOME STATES AND JURISDICTIONS DO NOT ALLOW THE EXCLUSION OR LIMITATION OF LIABILITY, THE ABOVE LIMITATION MAY NOT APPLY TO YOU.

MISCELLANEOUS

This EULA is governed by the laws of the State of Washington USA, except and only to the extent that applicable law mandates governing law of a different jurisdiction.

Should you have any questions concerning this EULA, or if you desire to contact Microsoft for any reason, please contact the Microsoft subsidiary serving your country, or write: Microsoft Sales Information Center/One Microsoft Way/Redmond, WA 98052-6399.

Register Today!

Return this
*Hitchhiker's Guide to Visual Basic®
and SQL Server™, Sixth Edition*
registration card today

Microsoft®Press

mspress.microsoft.com

1-57231-848-1

HITCHHIKER'S GUIDE TO VISUAL BASIC®
AND SQL SERVER™, SIXTH EDITION

FIRST NAME	MIDDLE INITIAL	LAST NAME

INSTITUTION OR COMPANY NAME

ADDRESS

CITY	STATE	ZIP

( )

E-MAIL ADDRESS	PHONE NUMBER

U.S. and Canada addresses only. Fill in information above and mail postage-free.
Please mail only the bottom half of this page.

start faster
go
farther

For information about Microsoft Press® products, visit our Web site at **mspress.microsoft.com**

Microsoft Press

BUSINESS REPLY MAIL
FIRST-CLASS MAIL   PERMIT NO. 108   REDMOND WA

POSTAGE WILL BE PAID BY ADDRESSEE

MICROSOFT PRESS
PO BOX 97017
REDMOND, WA 98073-9830

NO POSTAGE
NECESSARY
IF MAILED
IN THE
UNITED STATES